America's
TEST KITCHEN

Also by the Editors at America's Test Kitchen

The Cook's Illustrated Baking Book

The Science of Good Cooking

The Cook's Illustrated Cookbook

The America's Test Kitchen Menu Cookbook

The America's Test Kitchen Quick Family Cookbook

The America's Test Kitchen Healthy Family Cookbook

The America's Test Kitchen Family Baking Book

The America's Test Kitchen Family Cookbook

The America's Test Kitchen Library series:

Slow Cooker Revolution Volume 2: The Easy-Prep Edition

The 6-Ingredient Solution

Comfort Food Makeovers

The America's Test Kitchen D.I.Y. Cookbook

Pasta Revolution

Simple Weeknight Favorites

Slow Cooker Revolution

The Best Simple Recipes

The TV Companion series:

The Complete Cook's Country TV Show Cookbook

The Complete America's Test Kitchen TV Show Cookbook 2001–2014

America's Test Kitchen: The TV Companion Cookbook (2009 and 2011–2014 Editions)

Behind the Scenes with America's Test Kitchen

Test Kitchen Favorites

Cooking at Home with America's Test Kitchen

America's Test Kitchen Live!

Inside America's Test Kitchen

Here in America's Test Kitchen

The America's Test Kitchen Cookbook

America's Test Kitchen annuals:

The Best of America's Test Kitchen (2007–2014 Editions)

Cooking for Two (2010–2013 Editions)

Light & Healthy (2010–2012 Editions)

The Cook's Country series:

From Our Grandmothers' Kitchens

Cook's Country Blue Ribbon Desserts

Cook's Country Best Potluck Recipes

Cook's Country Best Lost Suppers

Cook's Country Best Grilling Recipes

The Cook's Country Cookbook

America's Best Lost Recipes

The Best Recipe series:

The New Best Recipe

More Best Recipes

The Best One-Dish Suppers

Soups, Stews & Chilis

The Best Skillet Recipes

The Best Slow & Easy Recipes

The Best Chicken Recipes

The Best International Recipe

The Best Make-Ahead Recipe

The Best 30-Minute Recipe

The Best Light Recipe

The Cook's Illustrated Guide to Grilling and Barbecue

Best American Side Dishes

Cover & Bake

Steaks, Chops, Roasts & Ribs

Baking Illustrated

Italian Classics

American Classics

For a Full Listing of All Our Books or to Order Titles:

CooksIllustrated.com

AmericasTestKitchen.com

or call 800-611-0759

Praise for other America's Test Kitchen Titles

"Ideal as a reference for the bookshelf . . . , this volume will be turned to time and again for definitive instruction on just about any food-related matter."
PUBLISHERS WEEKLY ON *THE SCIENCE OF GOOD COOKING*

"The perfect kitchen home companion. The practical side of things is very much on display. . . . cook-friendly and kitchen-oriented, illuminating the process of preparing food instead of mystifying it."
THE WALL STREET JOURNAL ON *THE COOK'S ILLUSTRATED COOKBOOK*

"This nearly 900-page volume lands with an authoritative wallop. . . . Everything is here. Everything. What's more, the why and how of recipes are explained in a way that sets the home cook up with the confidence to wade right in, no matter the dish."
THE CHICAGO TRIBUNE ON *THE COOK'S ILLUSTRATED COOKBOOK*

"If this were the only cookbook you owned, you would cook well, be everyone's favorite host, have a well-run kitchen, and eat happily every day."
THECITYCOOK.COM ON *THE AMERICA'S TEST KITCHEN MENU COOKBOOK*

"There are pasta books . . . and then there's this pasta book. Flip your carbohydrate dreams upside down and strain them through this sieve of revolutionary, creative, and also traditional recipes."
SAN FRANCISCO BOOK REVIEW ON *PASTA REVOLUTION*

"This book upgrades slow cooking for discriminating, 21st-century palates—that is indeed revolutionary."
THE DALLAS MORNING NEWS ON *SLOW COOKER REVOLUTION*

"Forget about marketing hype, designer labels, and pretentious entrées: This is an unblinking, unbedazzled guide to the Beardian good-cooking ideal."
THE WALL STREET JOURNAL ON *THE BEST OF AMERICA'S TEST KITCHEN 2009*

"The best instructional book on baking this reviewer has seen."
THE LIBRARY JOURNAL (STARRED REVIEW) ON *BAKING ILLUSTRATED*

"Expert bakers and novices scared of baking's requisite exactitude can all learn something from this hefty, all-purpose home baking volume."
PUBLISHERS WEEKLY ON *THE AMERICA'S TEST KITCHEN FAMILY BAKING BOOK*

"Scrupulously tested regional and heirloom recipes."
THE NEW YORK TIMES ON *THE COOK'S COUNTRY COOKBOOK*

"If you're hankering for old-fashioned pleasures, look no further."
PEOPLE MAGAZINE ON *AMERICA'S BEST LOST RECIPES*

"This tome definitely raises the bar for all-in-one, basic, must-have cookbooks. . . . Kimball and his company have scored another hit."
THE OREGONIAN ON *THE AMERICA'S TEST KITCHEN FAMILY COOKBOOK*

"A foolproof, go-to resource for everyday cooking."
PUBLISHERS WEEKLY ON *THE AMERICA'S TEST KITCHEN FAMILY COOKBOOK*

"The strength of the Best Recipe series lies in the sheer thoughtfulness and details of the recipes."
PUBLISHERS WEEKLY ON *THE BEST RECIPE SERIES*

"These dishes taste as luxurious as their full-fat siblings. Even desserts are terrific."
PUBLISHERS WEEKLY ON *THE BEST LIGHT RECIPE*

"Further proof that practice makes perfect, if not transcendent. . . . If an intermediate cook follows the directions exactly, the results will be better than takeout or Mom's."
THE NEW YORK TIMES ON *THE NEW BEST RECIPE*

"Like a mini–cooking school, the detailed instructions and illustrations ensure that even the most inexperienced cook can follow these recipes with success."
PUBLISHERS WEEKLY ON *BEST AMERICAN SIDE DISHES*

THE AMERICA'S TEST KITCHEN

Cooking School COOKBOOK

EVERYTHING YOU NEED TO KNOW TO BECOME A GREAT COOK

BY THE EDITORS AT
America's Test Kitchen

PHOTOGRAPHY BY
Daniel J. van Ackere and Anthony Tieuli

America's Test Kitchen
17 Station Street, Brookline, MA 02445

Library of Congress Cataloging-in-Publication Data

The America's test kitchen cooking school cookbook : everything you need to know to become a great cook / by the editors at America's Test Kitchen ; photography by Daniel J. van Ackere and Anthony Tieuli.
      pages cm
  Includes index.
  ISBN 978-1-936493-52-4
  1. Cooking. I. America's Test Kitchen (Firm)
  TX651.A53 2013
  641.5--dc23
                              2013018559

Manufactured in the United States of America
10 9 8 7 6 5 4 3 2

HARDCOVER: $45 US

Distributed by America's Test Kitchen
17 Station Street, Brookline, MA 02445

EDITORIAL DIRECTOR: Jack Bishop

PROJECT EDITOR: Louise Emerick

CONTRIBUTING EDITORS: Elizabeth Carduff and Bridget Lancaster

ASSOCIATE EDITOR: Alyssa King

DESIGN DIRECTOR: Amy Klee

ART DIRECTOR: Greg Galvan

DESIGNER: Taylor Argenzio

STAFF PHOTOGRAPHER: Daniel J. van Ackere

PHOTOGRAPHY: Anthony Tieuli

ADDITIONAL PHOTOGRAPHY: Stephen Klise and Carl Tremblay

PHOTO EDITOR: Stephen Klise

FOOD STYLING: Catrine Kelty and Marie Piraino

PHOTOSHOOT KITCHEN TEAM:

   ASSOCIATE EDITOR: Chris O'Connor

   TEST COOKS: Daniel Cellucci and Sara Mayer

   ASSISTANT TEST COOK: Cecelia Jenkins

ILLUSTRATIONS: Jay Layman

PRODUCTION DIRECTOR: Guy Rochford

SENIOR PRODUCTION MANAGER: Jessica Quirk

SENIOR PROJECT MANAGER: Alice Carpenter

PRODUCTION AND TRAFFIC COORDINATOR: Brittany Allen

WORKFLOW AND DIGITAL ASSET MANAGER: Andrew Mannone

SENIOR COLOR AND IMAGING SPECIALIST: Lauren Pettapiece

PRODUCTION AND IMAGING SPECIALISTS: Heather Dube and Lauren Robbins

COPY EDITOR: Jeff Schier

PROOFREADER: Jane Tunks Demel

INDEXER: Elizabeth Parson

Contents

Preface

In Vermont, nobody ever tells you what to do—they show you. When I kneaded bread improperly, Marie Briggs, the town baker, appeared next to me and kneaded *her* dough the right way. Not a word said. Or, when I chainsawed a fallen maple from the top down (the chain binds if the trunk is lying on the ground), Harley Smith came over, sawed from the bottom up, and left. This all reminds me of the oft-told story of the city kid up for a Vermont summer. When he pokes a toad with a stick, a local boy tells him to cut it out and the city kid says, "Well, he's my toad, ain't he?" The Vermonter shoots back, "Nope . . . in Vermont he's his own toad." That pretty much sums up everything you need to know about Vermonters and why locals are unlikely to tell you what to do.

When it comes to learning how to cook, even if you are lucky enough to have a parent, a grandparent, other relative, or a friend to help teach you the basics, our test kitchen just outside of Boston offers one huge advantage. We have taken the trial-and-error approach to cooking to a whole new level by scientifically testing almost every possible way of cooking just about every recipe in the American repertoire. We boiled 1,000 eggs to find the best method. We cooked 130 old-fashioned chocolate cakes to get just the right balance of fat to flour. We have roasted, over the past 20-some years, thousands of chickens to arrive at the very best methods. This book, therefore, offers more than just one cook's perspective—you are getting tens of thousands of test-cook hours, all organized clearly and simply so you can have instant access to the fruits of our labor, whether that is the best way to sharpen a knife, roast salmon (preheat the baking sheet and score the skin), make a pound cake (melt the butter, don't cream it, and use a food processor for mixing), make easy-to-roll, flaky pie dough (use half vodka and half water), or whip heavy cream (add the sugar at the outset so it dissolves properly).

To some extent, good cooking is about familiarity and predictability. We find that when one understands the WHYs of cooking, one is much more likely to use the proper techniques. Once the home cook understands why some mashed potatoes turn out bland, why roast chicken often produces flabby skin, and why cakes don't rise properly, then he or she will take the time to do it right. That is the essence of this volume—to explain why we do things the way we do. We know the answers to these questions because *we have actually tested the other methods,* so we can speak from experience. Sometimes a high oven is best, sometimes low. Some dough has to be kneaded a lot, while other recipes are best if the dough is barely kneaded but left in the refrigerator overnight. Great teachers have a lifetime of hands-on experience, *and this cookbook offers many, many lifetimes of experience*: 45 test cooks working 5 days per week over 20 years. The result is an unimpeachable source of solid cooking information that you simply cannot find elsewhere. (We know that the best way to learn is through our mistakes and, believe me, we have made thousands of them!)

All of this, one hopes, leads to confidence. A good cook is a confident cook, able to make midcourse corrections, adjust for the ingredients on hand, even turn a culinary disaster into a satisfying dinner. You can arrive at self-confidence through long years of personal experience, or you can get a helping hand, a jump start on what works and what doesn't. You will still need to preheat the oven, cook the meat, sauté the onions, and bake the biscuits, but you can start with the best cooking school in the world, *The America's Test Kitchen Cooking School Cookbook*. It's all here—just about everything we know—on paper, in color, and fully illustrated.

As my Vermont neighbor once replied when I said "nice day" late one August afternoon, this doesn't mean that our test kitchen work is done. (He considered my remark for a bit and then intoned, "Well, so far.") Nobody ever finishes learning how to cook, but we think that this volume will be "useful," as they say in the Green Mountains. Enjoy the book and enjoy your time well spent in the kitchen.

Cordially,

CHRISTOPHER KIMBALL
Founder, America's Test Kitchen

Welcome to America's Test Kitchen

This book has been tested, written, and edited by the folks at America's Test Kitchen, a very real 2,500-square-foot kitchen located just outside of Boston. It is the home of *Cook's Illustrated* magazine and *Cook's Country* magazine and is the Monday-through-Friday destination for more than three dozen test cooks, editors, food scientists, tasters, and cookware specialists. Our mission is to test recipes over and over again until we understand how and why they work and until we arrive at the "best" version.

We start the process of testing a recipe with a complete lack of conviction, which means that we accept no claim, no theory, no technique, and no recipe at face value. We simply assemble as many variations as possible, test a half-dozen of the most promising, and taste the results blind. We then construct our own hybrid recipe and continue to test it, varying ingredients, techniques, and cooking times until we reach a consensus. The result, we hope, is the best version of a particular recipe, but we realize that only you can be the final judge of our success (or failure). As we like to say in the test kitchen, "We make the mistakes, so you don't have to."

All of this would not be possible without a belief that good cooking, much like good music, is indeed based on a foundation of objective technique. Some people like spicy foods and others don't, but there is a right way to sauté, there is a best way to cook a pot roast, and there are measurable scientific principles involved in producing perfectly beaten, stable egg whites. This is our ultimate goal: to investigate the fundamental principles of cooking so that you become a better cook. It is as simple as that.

You can watch us work (in our actual test kitchen) by tuning in to *America's Test Kitchen* (AmericasTestKitchen.com) or *Cook's Country from America's Test Kitchen* (CooksCountryTV.com) on public television, or by subscribing to *Cook's Illustrated* magazine (CooksIllustrated.com) or *Cook's Country* magazine (CooksCountry.com), which are each published every other month. We welcome you into our kitchen, where you can stand by our side as we test our way to the best recipes in America.

Inside This Chapter

CHAPTER 1

Cooking Basics

Cooking isn't complicated, but it is complex. Small variables can have a significant effect on the quality of the finished dish. This chapter will teach you the basics, from how to sharpen a knife and how to measure properly to the best pots and pans and pantry items you should stock. There's a lot of information here, but it can be boiled down to a single bit of advice: Think before you cook.

12 Tips That Will Make You a Better Cook

Cooking is a skill that can take a lifetime to perfect, and even the best of cooks can produce disappointing results. However, there are some basic rules you can follow that will help you use recipes—successfully—in your kitchen.

1. Read the Recipe Carefully Almost everyone has embarked upon preparing a recipe only to realize midway through that the dish needed hours of chilling before it could even be served. By reading the recipe completely through before you start to cook, you will avoid any surprises along the way, including not having that special, essential ingredient.

2. Follow Directions, at Least the First Time Cooking is a science, but it is also an art. Our advice is simple: Make the recipe as directed the first time. Once you understand the recipe, you can improvise and make it your own the next time you prepare it.

3. Be Prepared Set out and organize all of the equipment you will need for a recipe and prep all of the ingredients for it before you start to cook. In cooking school, this is referred to as *mise en place*. A recipe is a lot simpler to make when all the components and tools for it are at your fingertips. We can't tell you the number of pounds of pasta that we've over-cooked while looking for a colander at the last minute.

4. Start with Good Ingredients Don't expect to turn old eggs into a nicely risen soufflé. Likewise, low-quality meats will yield low-quality results. Freshness matters. When it comes to pantry items, follow our recommendations (pages 32 through 44) when possible. A can of sweet, lively tomatoes will make a far better sauce than a can of bitter, stringy tomatoes.

5. Prepare Ingredients as Directed Be sure to prepare food as instructed in the ingredient list. Food that is uniformly and properly cut will not only cook at the same rate but will also be more visually appealing.

6. Keep Substitutions to a Minimum There are certain sub-stitutions that we have found acceptable in a pinch. But, in general, it is best if you use the ingredients called for in the recipe; this is especially true in baking, where even the slight-est change can spell disaster. See page 45 for our test kitch-en's list of emergency substitutions.

7. Use the Appropriately Sized Equipment Make sure to use the cookware and bakeware noted in the recipe. If you pour cake batter into a 9-inch pan when the recipe says 8 inch, you will end up with thinner cake layers that cook more quickly. If you try to cook four chicken cutlets in a 10-inch skillet, rather than in the 12-inch skillet called for in the recipe, the chicken will steam because the pan is too crowded.

8. Preheat Your Oven Most ovens need at least 15 minutes to preheat fully. Plan accordingly. If you don't preheat your oven fully prior to baking or roasting, then your food will spend more time in the oven and, as a result, will likely be dry and overcooked (and baked goods may suffer even more dire consequences). Also, position the racks in the oven as directed. Pie crusts that brown properly on the lower rack emerge pale when baked on the middle rack.

9. Monitor the Dish as It Cooks The cooking times in our recipes are meant as guidelines only. Because ingredients and equipment inevitably vary, it is important to follow the visual clues provided in the recipe. And don't wait until the prescribed time has elapsed to check the doneness of a particular recipe: It is good practice to start checking 5 to 10 minutes before the designated time.

10. Taste the Dish Before Serving Most recipes end by instructing the cook to adjust the seasonings. You must taste the food in order to adjust the seasonings successfully. We generally season food lightly throughout the cooking process and then add more salt as needed. Foods that will be served chilled, such as gazpacho, should be tasted again before serv-ing. The cold mutes the effect of the seasoning, and, in the case of gazpacho, you might need to add a bit more salt, pepper, or vinegar before serving.

11. Learn from Your Mistakes Even the experienced cooks in our test kitchen often turn out less-than-perfect food. A good cook is able to analyze failure, pinpoint the cause, and then avoid that pitfall the next time. Repetition is key to any learn-ing process, and cooking is no different. Don't make a new recipe every night of the year. Make a dish at least once or twice a month until you master it.

12. Enjoy Yourself The successful cook is someone who enjoys cooking. Take pride in accomplishments. If you enjoy cooking, you will get in the kitchen more often—and practice really does make perfect.

Cooking Terminology

The first step to the successful completion of a recipe is understanding what the recipe is telling you to do. Some recipes are precise blueprints, specifying particular sizes, shapes, quantities, and cooking times. Other recipes are rough sketches that leave the cook to fill in the blanks.

In addition to the level of detail supplied by the recipe writer, the level of knowledge the cook brings to the process varies tremendously. Unfamiliar language and terminology are a particular problem, especially for novice cooks trying to work their way through a recipe. These are some often-used recipe terms you should know.

Barbecue To cook large, tough cuts of meat like beef brisket and pork shoulder using the indirect, low, and gentle heat from an outdoor fire. Barbecued foods derive their "barbecued" flavor from wood chips or chunks.

Boil To heat liquid until large bubbles energetically break the surface at a rapid and constant rate.

Braise To cook foods by cooking and then gently simmering them in a flavorful liquid in a covered pot.

Cook en Papillote To cook food by enclosing it in a parchment paper packet. The food steams in its own juices so that the flavors are pure and clean. Although parchment is the traditional choice in this classic French cooking method, aluminum foil can be used.

Deep-Fry To cook in hot oil deep enough to fully surround the food.

Deglaze To use liquid (usually wine or broth) to loosen the flavorful browned bits (called fond) that develop and stick to a pan during the sautéing or searing process. A wooden spoon is often used to help loosen the fond, which dissolves into the deglazing liquid.

Grill To cook relatively small, individually sized, and quick-cooking foods such as steaks, chops, and skewers directly over an outdoor fire. Grilled foods derive their "grilled" flavor from the dripping juices and fat that hit the heat source and create smoke that subtly seasons the exterior of the food.

Grill-Roast To cook large, tender cuts of meat, such as a butterflied whole chicken, prime rib roast, and beef tenderloin, using indirect and moderate heat from an outdoor fire.

Poach To cook food in hot water or other liquid that is held below the simmering point.

Puree To grind raw or cooked ingredients to a uniform consistency, often in a food processor or blender.

Reduce To partially evaporate liquids, especially sauces, during cooking, to concentrate flavors and thicken consistency. If a recipe says to simmer a sauce or liquid until reduced by half. You can gauge the volume by noting the level of the liquid in the pan before simmering and monitoring the level as it simmers and evaporates. However, a more precise way is to measure the liquid before simmering and to remeasure when the halfway level seems near.

Roast To cook foods in a pan in a hot oven. High oven temperatures promote more browning; low oven temperatures ensure even cooking and minimize moisture loss.

Sauté To cook food in a small amount of fat over moderately high heat, usually with the goal of browning the food. The word *sauté* comes from the French verb *sauter,* meaning "to jump," since traditionally, food is tossed about by jerking the pan back and forth. Stirring food accomplishes the same thing and prevents scorching.

Sear To cook food over high or very high heat, usually with the goal of creating a deeply browned crust. While sautéing involves frequent stirring, seared foods are best left alone so that a crust can develop. A single turn is sufficient.

Shallow-Fry (Pan-Fry) To cook in hot oil deep enough to partially surround the food. Foods are generally halfway submerged in hot fat as they cook and must be turned once to ensure even cooking.

Simmer To heat liquid until small bubbles gently break the surface at a variable and infrequent rate.

Skim To remove the fat that floats to the surface of pan drippings or braising liquids after roasting or braising fatty cuts of beef, pork, or poultry. To remove small amounts, tilt the pan and use a wide, shallow soupspoon to skim off the fat. A fat separator is the best way to remove large amounts of fat. If you are cooking in advance, overnight refrigeration will cause the fat to congeal on the surface; the fat can then be removed easily.

Steam To cook foods using the steam released from boiling liquid. Steamed foods should be placed in a basket above the liquid, and the cooking environment should be closed (usually with a lid) to trap the steam.

Sweat To cook over gentle heat in a small amount of fat in a covered pot. Vegetables are often sweated.

Toast To cook or brown food by dry heat, and without adding fat, using an oven or skillet. This technique is frequently used to bring out the flavors of nuts, spices, and seeds.

Basic Knife Skills

Knives are the most important tools in your kitchen; using them properly is essential. Here are three key points to remember:

Good Technique = Less Risk

If you use proper techniques, you are less likely to injure yourself with the knife. It is crucial to keep knives sharp so that they cut through food with less slippage. It is also important to grip the knife and know how to position your noncutting hand.

Good Technique = Faster Results

If you use proper techniques, you will be able to prepare food faster. This one is pretty simple. Would you rather take two minutes or five minutes to chop an onion? It may not seem like a big difference, but in a recipe with a lot of vegetable or protein prep, all those extra minutes can really add up.

Good Technique = Better Results

If you use proper techniques, you will produce food that is evenly cut and therefore will cook at an even rate. Cooks with poor knife skills end up with unevenly diced carrots or minced garlic with large hunks. Poorly cut food will not cook properly. For instance, those large hunks of garlic will burn and impart a harsh flavor to your food.

THE THREE KNIVES YOU REALLY NEED, PLUS ONE MORE

Although there are hundreds of gadgets for sale that claim they can help you prep ingredients more quickly, we've found that very few of them actually work. So instead of wasting your money (and your counter space) on these products, just invest in three good knives: a chef's knife, a paring knife, and a serrated knife (or bread knife). If you cook a lot of roasts, we suggest buying a slicing knife as well. See page 18 for details on each of these knives.

Chef's Knife   **Paring Knife**   **Serrated Knife**   **+**   **Slicing Knife**

Setting Up Your Cutting Station

In our test kitchen, "setting up your board" means setting up your cooking station before you begin to prep and cook. Setting up your board at home is just as important, so that you're organized and efficient.

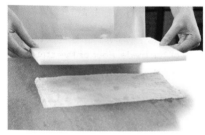

Anchor Your Board

A cutting board that slides all over the counter is not only annoying, it is unsafe. If your cutting board doesn't have nonslip grips on the bottom, place either a square of wet paper towel or a small piece of shelf liner between the counter and the cutting board.

Organize Your Prep

Organizing your prepped ingredients into little bowls isn't just for TV chefs—it's a great idea for home cooks too. This setup makes it easy to grab an ingredient and add it to a hot pan at just the right moment.

Keep It Tidy

Don't push vegetable trimmings to one side of the cutting board. This reduces the usable work area on your board, and those trimmings always have a way of getting back under your knife. Designate a small bowl or plastic grocery bag for trimmings.

Caring for Your Knives

A sharp knife is a fast knife, and a dull knife is an accident waiting to happen. Dull knives are dangerous because a dull blade requires more force to do the job and so has a higher chance of slipping and missing the mark. Even the best knives will dull over time with regular use.

Is It Sharp?

To determine if your knife needs sharpening, put it to the paper test. Hold a folded, but not creased, sheet of newspaper by one end. Lay the blade against the top edge at an angle and slice outward. If the knife fails to slice cleanly, try steeling it (see below). If it still fails, it needs sharpening.

When to Use a Knife Sharpener

If your knife is quite dull, you'll need to reshape its edge. This requires removing a fair amount of metal—more than you could ever remove with a steel. To restore a very dull knife, you have three choices: You can send it out; you can use a whetstone (tricky for anyone but a professional); or—the most convenient option—you can use an electric or manual sharpener.

WHEN TO USE A SHARPENING STEEL

A so-called sharpening steel, the metal rod sold with most knife sets, doesn't really sharpen a knife, but rather it hones the edge of a slightly dulled blade. Sweeping the blade along the steel realigns the edge. Throughout this motion, make sure to maintain a 20-degree angle between the blade and the steel.

1. To safely use a steel, hold it vertically with the tip firmly planted on the counter. Place the heel of the blade against the tip of the steel and point the knife tip slightly upward. Hold the blade at a 20-degree angle away from the steel.

2. Maintaining light pressure and a 20-degree angle between the blade and the steel, slide the blade down the length of the steel in a sweeping motion, pulling the knife toward your body so that the middle of the blade is in contact with the middle of the steel.

3. Finish the motion by passing the tip of the blade over the bottom of the steel. Repeat this motion on the other side of the blade. Four or five strokes on each side of the blade (a total of eight to ten alternating passes) should realign the edge.

Holding a Knife

Much as how someone holds a baseball bat, how you hold a knife makes a difference in terms of control and force. And don't forget about the other hand—the one that holds the food securely in place while you cut. How you hold the food steady makes a difference in terms of fingertip safety.

Control Grip
For more control, choke up on the handle and actually grip the blade of the knife between your thumb and forefinger.

Force Grip
Holding the knife on the handle allows you to use more force and is helpful when cutting through hard foods or bone.

Protect Your Fingertips
Use the "bear claw" grip to hold food in place and minimize danger. Tuck your fingertips in, away from the knife, and rest your knuckles against the blade. During the upward motion of slicing, reposition your guiding hand for the next cut.

Basic Cutting Motions

Depending on the food being prepared, you will use different parts of the knife blade and different motions. Here are four basic motions used.

SMALL ITEMS: Keep Tip Down
To cut small items, such as celery, push the blade forward and down, using the blade's curve to guide the middle of the knife through smooth strokes. The tip of the blade should touch the board at all times when cutting small food.

LARGE ITEMS: Lift Blade Up
To cut large items, such as eggplant, lift the entire blade off the board to help make smooth strokes.

MINCING: Use Both Hands
To mince herbs and garlic, grip the handle with one hand and rest the fingers of the other hand lightly on the knife tip. This grip facilitates the up-and-down rocking motion needed for mincing. To make sure the food is evenly minced, pivot the knife as you work through the pile of food.

TOUGH ITEMS: Use the Heel
To cut tough foods like winter squash or bone-in chicken parts, use the heel of the knife. Use one hand to grip the handle, and place the flat palm of your other hand on top of the blade. Cut straight down into the item, pushing the blade gently. Be careful and make sure your hand and the knife are dry to prevent slippage.

Food Prep Terminology

Your knife is sharp and your work area is ready. It's time to start preparing ingredients. But what exactly does it mean when we call for an ingredient to be "minced" or "chopped fine" or "chopped medium"? Here's an overview of key cutting terms.

Minced
To cut into ⅛-inch pieces or smaller

Chopped Fine
To cut into ⅛- to ¼-inch pieces

Chopped Medium
To cut into ¼- to ½-inch pieces

Chopped Coarse
To cut into ½- to ¾-inch pieces

Cut Into Chunks
To cut into ¾-inch pieces or larger

Sliced
To cut into pieces with two flat edges (the thickness of the slices will depend on the recipe)

Diced
To cut into uniform cubes (the size of the dice will depend on the recipe)

Cut on the Bias or Diagonal
To cut across the food with the knife held at a 45-degree angle to the food (used for longer, slender items)

Cut Lengthwise
To cut with the length of the food, or from end to end

Cut Crosswise or Widthwise
To cut across the food, perpendicular to its length

Cut into Chiffonade
To cut into very thin strips (such as basil leaves)

Julienned (or Cut into Matchsticks)
To cut into matchstick-size pieces, usually about 2 inches long and ⅛ inch thick

Basic Measuring Skills

Measuring matters. In fact, accurate measuring is often the difference between success and failure in the kitchen. Let's examine the tools we use to measure when cooking, then explore how best to use them.

Measuring Tools

You'll need a set of dry measuring cups, liquid measuring cups, and measuring spoons, to measure wet and dry ingredients accurately. We also highly recommend a digital scale and kitchen ruler. Let's review when to use these tools and why they're needed.

DRY MEASURING CUPS

Why You Need Them: These straight-sided cups typically have flat tops that make leveling dry ingredients easy. Dry ingredients like flour and sugar should always be measured in a dry measuring cup; in a wet measuring cup, it is impossible to level the surface of the contents to obtain an exact measurement.

- **Buy sturdy cups.** Look for either heavy, well-constructed stainless steel models or sturdy plastic cups that are comfortable and solid. Stay away from flimsy plastic cups that can warp in the dishwasher or melt easily.
- **Get a complete set.** Buy a set of measuring cups that also includes in-between sizes, like ¾ cup and ⅔ cup, and you'll never have to do grade-school math (common denominator, anyone?) or eyeball it and gauge ⅓ cup of flour in a ½-cup measure.
- **Look for a long, solid handle.** An extra-long 4-inch handle makes dipping into a bin of flour a clean endeavor. A short, awkward handle can make dipping difficult, and a shoddy, thin handle will bend under the slightest pressure, landing your cup of sugar on the counter, not in the mixing bowl. Also, avoid handle-heavy cups that tilt when set down.

LIQUID MEASURING CUPS

Why You Need Them: These cups are designed to make pouring easy and measuring liquids accurate and mess-free.

- **Look for easy-to-read markings.** They should be clear, easily readable (even when the cup is full), and cover a range of gradations.
- **Shop for sturdy, clear cups.** Clear cups are our preference. The transparent surface makes it simple to gauge how much ingredient is in the cup because the meniscus line is easily discernible.
- **Keep your kitchen supplied with a variety of sizes.** The most useful are 2- and 4-cup measures, but a 1-cup measure is worth having on hand, too, when you're working with smaller amounts.

MEASURING SPOONS

Why You Need Them: Because simply eyeballing an amount won't cut it—especially when you're baking. These spoons are vital for measuring everything from granular ingredients like salt, pepper, and spices to small amounts of liquids like lemon juice and water.

- **Look for a flat top.** As with dry measuring cups, measuring spoons should have a handle that is flush with the rim of the bowl so that dry ingredients can be easily leveled.
- **Oval-shaped spoons and deep bowls make scooping easy.** The oval shape can reach into tall, narrow jars exceptionally well, while deep (not shallow) bowls keep the ingredient in the spoon, not on the counter.

KITCHEN RULER

Why You Need It: One often-overlooked but useful tool is the kitchen ruler. In fact, we think it is indispensable and we reach for it constantly, whether we are cutting up beef for a stew, prepping vegetables, or making pastry.

- **Stainless steel, not wood.** Stainless steel is easy to clean and dishwasher-safe.
- **18 inches is best.** Don't get caught short with a 12-inch ruler, and forget about longer ones better suited to carpentry. An 18-inch ruler will handle all kitchen tasks and will fit in a kitchen drawer.

DIGITAL SCALE

Why You Need It: When you're baking, weighing your ingredients is the most accurate method of measurement. Once you buy a scale, however, you'll find it useful in many other applications, from portioning out specific amounts of ground meat to figuring out how many apples or potatoes you'll need from the big bag you've bought. Given the choice between electronic and mechanical kitchen scales, we'll take electronic any day for their easy readability and incredible precision.

- **Readability is key.** Look for an easy-to-read display that isn't obscured when a big bowl (or anything else) is placed on the weighing platform.

- **Choose by weight range.** The larger the weight range (we like scales that measure from ¼ ounce up to 10 pounds at least), the more versatile your scale is and the more you'll turn to it in the kitchen.

- **Make sure you can "zero" in.** If your scale can be zeroed, you can automatically subtract the weight of the weighing vessel (and anything already in it) to measure only the ingredients being added—helpful when you need to make incremental additions to your mixing bowl.

How to Measure

Even though weight is a more accurate way to measure than volume, we know that most cooks will rely on measuring cups and spoons, not scales. That's fine, but there are ways to increase your accuracy when using volume measures. One note about liquid and dry measuring cups: Don't use them interchangeably—if you do, your ingredient amounts may be significantly off. Also see Conversions and Equivalencies on page 784.

Read the Meniscus
For an accurate reading in a liquid measuring cup, set the cup on a level surface and bend down to read the bottom of the concave arc at the liquid's surface, known as the meniscus line, at eye level.

Dip and Sweep Dry Ingredients
For accuracy, nothing beats weighing dry ingredients, but the dip-and-sweep method is also reliable. Dip the measuring cup into the ingredient, like flour or sugar, and sweep away the excess with a straight-edged object, like the back of a knife.

Pack Brown Sugar
Brown sugar is so moist and clumpy that it must be packed into a measuring cup to get an accurate reading. To do this, use your fingers or the bottom of a smaller cup to tap and press the sugar into the measuring cup.

WHEN TO MEASURE

It addition to how you measure, it matters when you measure an ingredient. For instance, "1 cup walnuts, chopped" is not the same thing as "1 cup chopped walnuts." In the first example, "1 cup walnuts, chopped," the cook should measure, then chop the walnuts. In the second example, "1 cup chopped walnuts," the cook should chop, then measure.

Because the volume of ingredients is different when chopped, this really matters. One cup of unchopped walnuts weighs 4 ounces, while one cup of chopped walnuts weighs 4.8 ounces—that's 20 percent more nuts.

Apply this principle to other ingredients (such as "sifted flour" versus "flour, sifted") and you can see how this makes a significant difference in the final outcome of a recipe.

Using a Thermometer

Thermometers take the guesswork out of knowing when foods are done. They are vital for ensuring success in the kitchen. A well-stocked kitchen will contain the three types of thermometers listed below; in addition to these three, a refrigerator/freezer thermometer is also a good idea.

INSTANT-READ THERMOMETER

Why You Need It: An instant-read thermometer, coupled with knowledge of how temperatures relate to doneness, will ensure success in the kitchen. And an instant-read thermometer is vital when cooking steaks or beef roasts to a specific doneness (rare, medium-rare, etc.), or for ensuring a perfectly cooked chicken or pork.

- **Buy a digital model.** These models (as opposed to dial-face models) are easier to use because you can take a quick look and immediately know the temperature of your food.
- **Look for a long stem.** A long stem is key for measuring the temperature in the thickest part of a large cut of meat or an entire bird. It also comes in handy for checking when large baked goods, like long loaves of bread, are done.
- **A quick response is vital.** You don't want to keep your hand in the oven or over the grill any longer than necessary, so a thermometer that takes more than 5 or 10 seconds to warm up and respond isn't very helpful.
- **Water-resistant is good.** Kitchen mishaps do occur from time to time. If your thermometer is water-resistant, it won't be down for the count if you accidentally drop it in water.

CANDY THERMOMETER

Why You Need It: Candy thermometers are designed for stovetop recipes where close monitoring of temperature is key. Unless you have a high-end instant-read thermometer with a range that reaches up to 400 degrees, you won't be able to monitor the temperature of very hot oil or other liquids, such as caramel sauce, without a candy/deep-fry thermometer.

- **Readability is key.** Because these thermometers are used around hot liquids that are often bubbling or sputtering, the console has to be easy to read without you needing to lean in to decipher the temperature.
- **Get one that attaches.** Your candy thermometer should mount easily to the pan, so you don't have to hold it in place while you stir.

OVEN THERMOMETER

Why You Need It: Since it is fairly common for ovens to run either hot or cold, the most reliable way to know the exact temperature of your oven is to use an oven thermometer. Since oven thermometers are so cheap and easy to use, there is no reason not to rely on one to keep tabs on your oven and adjust accordingly if necessary.

- **Look for a clear display with large numbers.** For an oven thermometer to be useful, it should be easy to read. You can't exactly get up close to read something that's hooked onto a 350-degree oven rack.
- **It should attach securely.** Look for a stable base or hook so the thermometer is easy to place and doesn't fall over or get knocked around the oven, especially when sliding racks in and out.

Calibrating an Instant-Read Thermometer

You should check your instant-read thermometer's accuracy when you first buy it and then again periodically. Here's how.

Make an Icy Slush
Put a mixture of ice and cold tap water in a glass or bowl; allow this mixture to sit for several minutes to let the temperature stabilize. Put the probe in the slush, being careful not to touch the sides or bottom of the glass or bowl. On a digital thermometer, press the "calibrate" button to 32 degrees; on a dial-face thermometer, turn the dial to 32 degrees (the method differs from model to model; you may need pliers to turn a small knob on the back).

Knowing When Food Is Done

Whether cooking a burger or roasting a beef tenderloin, you should always take the temperature of the area of the meat that will be the last to finish cooking, which is the thickest part or, in some cases, the center. Bones conduct heat, so if the meat you are cooking contains bone, make sure that the thermometer is not touching it. For especially large roasts, take more than one reading to confirm you're at the right point of doneness. Also see Doneness Temperatures for Meat, Poultry, and Fish, page 783.

Steaks, Chops, and Small Roasts

When taking the temperature of thin steaks or pork chops, it's easy to insert the thermometer too far or not far enough. To avoid this, use tongs to hold the meat, then insert the thermometer sideways into the center, taking care not to hit any bones. You can also use this technique for pork tenderloin or rack of lamb; just lift the meat with a pair of tongs and insert the thermometer into the end, parallel to the meat.

Burgers

Leave the burger in the pan (or on the grill), slide the tip of the thermometer into the burger at the top edge, and push it toward the center, making sure to avoid hitting the pan (or grill) with the probe. This technique keeps the burger in the pan (rather than requiring you pick it up with tongs) and prevents it from falling apart.

Poultry

Because breast meat cooks faster than thigh meat, you should take the temperature of both when cooking poultry. When doing so, try to avoid hitting bones, cavities, or the surface of the pan, as this will result in an inaccurate reading. When temping a whole chicken, use the following methods:

A. For thigh meat: Insert the thermometer at an angle into the area between the drumstick and the breast, taking care not to hit the bone. It should register 175 degrees.

B. For breast meat: Insert the thermometer from the neck end, holding the thermometer parallel to the bird. It should register 160 degrees.

If cooking chicken or turkey pieces, use the same technique described above, while lifting the piece with tongs and inserting the thermometer sideways into the thickest part of the meat, taking care to avoid bones.

Bread

A thermometer is useful when baking bread. First, you can use it to check the temperature of the liquid, which is crucial in many recipes. And you can use it to be sure your bread is done. Rustic breads are generally done at 200 to 210 degrees, while rich, buttery yeast breads are done when they reach 190 to 200 degrees.

A. For free-form loaves: Insert the probe through the side or bottom of the loaf, making sure the probe reaches the center.

B. For loaves baked in a pan: To avoid a hole in the top crust, insert the thermometer from the side, just above the edge of the pan, directing it downward toward the center of the loaf.

How to Make Food Taste Better

Sometimes it's the small touches that make the biggest difference. These simple tricks for prepping, cooking, and seasoning are designed to boost flavor in everyday cooking.

Prep Tips

Don't Prepare Garlic and Onions in Advance
Chopping garlic and onions releases sharp odors and strong flavors that become overpowering with time, so it's best to cut them at the last minute. Soaking sliced or chopped onions in a solution of baking soda and water (1 tablespoon per cup of water) tames their pungency for raw applications; just be sure to rinse them thoroughly before using.

Trim Green Shoots from Garlic
It seems fussy, but those little green shoots are quite bitter. Always make sure to trim and discard them before preparing garlic.

Don't Seed Tomatoes
The seeds and surrounding "jelly" contain most of the flavor, so don't seed tomatoes unless called for in a recipe where excess moisture will ruin a dish.

Score Meat Before Marinating It
Prick meat all over with a fork to help marinades penetrate quickly. And forget about acidic marinades—salty ones work better.

Flip or Stir Meat While Marinating
Place meat in a zipper-lock bag or use a large baking dish covered with plastic wrap. Flip the bag or stir the meat halfway through the soaking time to ensure that all of the meat gets equal exposure to the marinade.

Trim Beef Stew Meat; Leave Fat on Pork
Remove all hard fat and connective tissue from the exterior of beef stew meat before cooking; its intramuscular marbling will keep it plenty moist and tender during cooking. But a thick layer (⅛ inch) of fat left on pork will baste and flavor the leaner meat.

Keep Fats Tasting Fresh
The fats in butter, oils, and nuts can go rancid and impart off-flavors to your cooking. Minimize their exposure to oxygen and light to slow down this process. Store butter and nuts in the freezer, keep nut oils in the fridge, and store vegetable oils in a dark pantry.

Cooking Tips

Strike Only When the Pan Is Hot
The temperature of the cooking surface will drop the minute food is added, so don't rush the preheating step at the start of most sautés. Wait for the oil to shimmer when cooking vegetables. When cooking proteins, wait until you see the first wisps of smoke rise from the oil.

Season with Sugar, Too
Browned food tastes better, and the best way to accelerate this process is with a pinch of sugar sprinkled on lean proteins (chicken and seafood) or vegetables.

Save Your Parmesan Rinds
Parmesan rinds add savory notes to soups, sauces, and stews. Once the cheese has been grated, store the rind in the freezer. Let the rind simmer away in almost any long-cooked dish. Do fish out and discard the rind before serving.

Never Discard the Fond
Those caramelized browned bits that stick to the bottom of the pan after cooking are packed with savory flavor. Deglaze the hot pan with liquid (wine, broth, or juice) and scrape the bits free with a wooden spoon to incorporate the fond into sauces, soups, or stews.

Save Those Meat Juices
As meat rests, it releases flavorful juices that can be added back to the skillet when making a pan sauce. If the juices are plentiful enough to thin the sauce, allow it to simmer an additional minute or two to restore its proper consistency.

Always Toast Nuts
Toasting nuts brings out their aromatic oils, contributing to a stronger, more complex flavor and aroma. When using more than 1 cup, oven-toast nuts on a roomy baking sheet. The oven offers not only more space than a skillet, but also more even heat than a stove, and there's less need for stirring.

Bloom Spices and Dried Herbs in Fat
To intensify the flavor of ground spices and dried herbs, cook them for a minute or two in a little butter or oil before adding liquid to the pan. If the recipe calls for sautéing aromatics (like onions), add the spices to the fat in the pan when the vegetables are nearly cooked.

Brown Breads, Pies, and Pastries
Browning equals flavor, so don't take breads, pies, or even cakes out of the oven until the exterior is deep golden brown. We bake all pies in a glass plate so we can track color development. When working with puff pastry or other flaky dough on a baking sheet, we lift up the bottom of individual pieces and look for even browning.

Underbake Chocolate Desserts
The flavor compounds in chocolate are extremely volatile, so the longer you cook brownies or cookies the more flavor is lost. Err on the side of underbaking and remember that residual heat will continue to cook baked goods as they cool.

Seasoning Tips

Add Acid Before Serving

As mentioned earlier, never serve anything without first tasting it. Adjust seasonings, adding salt and pepper as needed. Just as important, many soups, stews, and sauces benefit from a last-minute addition of lemon juice or vinegar. As little as ⅛ teaspoon will brighten other flavors in the dish.

Use Kosher Salt for Seasoning Before Cooking

The large grains of kosher salt distribute more evenly than fine table salt, making kosher salt the best choice for seasoning proteins before cooking. Use ⅛ teaspoon kosher salt per portion.

Pep Up—or Tone Down—Your Pepper

When exactly you apply black pepper to meat—before or after searing—will affect the strength of its bite. If you want assertive pepper flavor, season meat after searing since keeping the pepper away from the heat will preserve its volatile compounds. Alternatively, seasoning before cooking will tame pepper's punch.

Season Cold Food Aggressively

Chilling foods dulls flavors and aromas, so it's important to compensate by seasoning cold soups and chilled dishes like potato salad generously—but judiciously. To keep from overdoing it, season with a normal amount of salt before chilling and then taste and add more salt (as well as fresh herbs and acidic ingredients like vinegar) just before serving.

Incorporate Fresh Herbs at the Right Time

Add hardy herbs like thyme, rosemary, oregano, sage, and marjoram to dishes early in the cooking process; this way, they release maximum flavor while ensuring that their texture will be less intrusive. Save delicate herbs like parsley, cilantro, tarragon, chives, and basil for the last minute, or they will lose their fresh flavor and bright color.

Add a Little Umami or Savoriness

Soy sauce and anchovies contain high levels of glutamates, which give dishes a savory, meaty boost. Add a teaspoon or two of soy sauce to chili, or cook a few minced anchovies along with the vegetables in a soup or stew.

When Seasonings Go Awry

If you've added too much salt, sugar, or spice to a dish, the damage is usually done. In mild cases, it can sometimes be masked by the addition of another seasoning from the opposite end of the flavor spectrum. Remember to account for the reduction of liquids when seasoning a dish—a perfectly seasoned stew will likely taste too salty after several hours of simmering. Your best bet: Season with a light hand during the cooking process, then adjust the seasoning just before serving. Note: Despite popular lore, a few slices of potato cannot fix an overseasoned soup or stew. Yes, the potatoes might absorb some of the salty liquid, but the remaining liquid will still be too salty.

IF YOUR FOOD IS	ADD	SUCH AS
Too Salty	an acid or sweetener	vinegar, lemon or lime juice, or canned, unsalted tomatoes; sugar, honey, or maple syrup
Too Sweet	an acid or seasonings	vinegar or citrus juice; chopped fresh herbs, dash of cayenne, or, for sweet dishes, a bit of liqueur or espresso powder
Too Spicy or Acidic	a fat or sweetener	butter, cream, sour cream, cheese, or olive oil; sugar, honey, or maple syrup

How to Fix Common Mistakes

Even the best cooks make mistakes despite reading a recipe correctly and using common sense. Ever wish there were an emergency hotline you could call for advice when a recipe takes a turn for the worse? These tips and guidelines are the next-best thing to a 24-hour food emergency operator.

Troubleshooting at the Stovetop

When certain things burn there is no going back, and the successful cook learns to recognize the point of no return. Scorched oil and garlic, for example, will contribute a burnt, bitter flavor to the finished dish. In this case, it's best to wipe the pan clean and start over. But such problems can typically be avoided from the start by choosing the proper pan, cooking fat, and burner setting for the job. That said, here's what to do if . . .

The Food Won't Simmer Slowly

If it's hard to get your stovetop burners to maintain a very low flame (necessary when trying to cook soups or stews at a bare simmer) and you don't have a flame tamer, improvise and make one out of a thick ring of aluminum foil. Set the foil ring on the burner, then place the pot on top.

The Pan Gets Too Dark

Searing meat in a pan produces fond, which can add great flavor to soups, stews, and sauces. But when those brown bits turn black, that's a problem. Areas between pieces of meat are often the first to blacken. To guard against this, position the meat over the darker spots. The juices released will help to deglaze the pan. When searing meat in batches, you may need to deglaze the pan between batches.

Melting Butter Starts to Burn

Blackened butter will impart a bitter flavor to a finished dish and should be thrown away. However, slightly browned butter is no problem—in fact, it has a pleasantly nutty flavor. If you are worried about browned butter becoming burnt, you can add a small amount of vegetable oil to the pan. With its higher smoke point, vegetable oil is more resistant to burning and will help keep the butter from blackening.

Food Sticks to the Pan

Food that initially sticks to the pan usually releases on its own after a crust begins to form. As long as the food is not burning, wait a minute or two and then try again. For stubbornly stuck-on pieces of meat or fish, dip a thin, flexible spatula into cold water and slide the inverted spatula blade underneath the food.

Meat Is Undercooked

The meat has rested and been sliced, and it's underdone in the center. Simply putting the slices in the oven to finish cooking is not a good idea—they will dry out and quickly turn gray. Boston chef Gordon Hamersley has the solution: Place sliced meat on a wire rack set over a rimmed baking sheet, then cover the meat with lettuce leaves and put it under the broiler. The meat will gently steam under the lettuce.

WHAT IF A FIRE BREAKS OUT?

Probably the most unfortunate recipe mishap you could have is a kitchen fire. Do you have a kitchen fire plan? You should. According to authorities, most home fires are started in the kitchen. If you feel a fire is quickly growing out of control, your first instinct should be to get out of your house and alert the fire department. However, many small stovetop fires can be safely smothered by placing a lid over the burning pan and turning off the burner. Salt or baking soda, if handy, will also put out the flames. Most important, never use water to douse a grease fire. The safest course is to keep a portable ABC-type fire extinguisher within easy reach of your stove.

Basic Food Safety

Basic sanitation practices can dramatically reduce the risk of food-borne illness. Here's what you need to know.

Keep It Clean

Depending on factors such as moisture, temperature, and surface porosity microbes can live as long as 60 hours. But you don't need anything special to clean a kitchen—for the most part, we rely on old-fashioned soap and hot water or a bleach solution.

Wash Your Hands
Washing your hands is one of the best ways to stop the spread of food-borne pathogens. Wash before and during cooking, especially after touching raw meat and poultry. The U.S. Food and Drug Administration (FDA) recommends at least 20 seconds in warm, soapy water. How long is that? Try singing "Happy Birthday."

Sanitize Your Sink
Studies have found that the kitchen sink is crawling with even more bacteria than the garbage bin. The faucet handle, which can reintroduce bacteria to your hands after you've washed them, is a close second. Though we've found that hot, soapy water is amazingly effective at eliminating bacteria, for added insurance, clean these areas frequently with a solution of 1 tablespoon bleach per quart of water.

Clean Your Sponges
A wet sponge is an ideal host for bacteria; whenever possible, use a paper towel or dishcloth instead. If you do use a sponge, disinfect it. We tested myriad methods, including microwaving, freezing, bleaching, and boiling, and lab results showed that microwaving and boiling were most effective. Since sponges have been known to catch fire in high-powered microwaves, we prefer to boil them for five minutes.

Clean Your Cutting Boards
While bamboo boards do have natural antimicrobial properties that help kill off bacteria, we have found that cutting boards of all materials will come perfectly clean when scrubbed thoroughly with hot, soapy water. Some boards are dishwasher-safe, but wooden boards should never go through the dishwasher. See page 19 for tips on removing odors and stains from your cutting boards.

Avoid the Danger Zone

Within the "danger zone" of 40 to 140 degrees, bacteria double about every 20 minutes. As a general rule, food shouldn't stay in this zone for more than two hours (one hour if the room temperature is over 90 degrees).

Defrost in the Fridge
Defrosting should always be done in the refrigerator, not on the counter, where the temperature is higher and bacteria can multiply rapidly. Always place food on a plate or in a bowl while defrosting to prevent any liquid it releases from coming in contact with other foods. Most food will take 24 hours to thaw fully. (Larger items, like whole turkeys, can take far longer. Count on about five hours per pound.)

Cool on the Counter, Not in the Fridge
Don't put hot foods in the fridge right after cooking. This will cause the temperature in the refrigerator to rise, potentially making it hospitable to the spread of bacteria. The FDA recommends cooling foods to 70 degrees within the first two hours after cooking, and to 40 degrees within another four hours. We cool food on the counter for about an hour, until it reaches 80 to 90 degrees, then put it in the fridge.

Reheat Rapidly
When food is reheated, it should be brought through the danger zone as rapidly as possible—don't let it come slowly to a simmer. Bring leftover sauces, soups, and gravies to a boil and make sure casseroles reach at least 165 degrees, using an instant-read thermometer to determine when they're at the proper temperature.

Handle Foods Carefully

Raw meat, poultry, and eggs may carry harmful bacteria like salmonella, listeria, or E. coli. Cooking kills off these bacteria—ensuring the food is perfectly safe to eat—but it's critical to be careful about how you handle raw foods in the kitchen in order to avoid cross-contamination.

Separate Raw and Cooked Foods

Keep raw and cooked foods separate to prevent the spread of bacteria. Never place cooked food on a plate or cutting board that has come into contact with raw food (meat or not), and wash any utensil (including a thermometer) that comes in contact with raw food before reusing it.

Put Up Barriers

Items that come in contact with both raw and cooked food, like scales and platters, should be covered with aluminum foil or plastic wrap to create a protective barrier. Once the item has been used, the protective layer should be discarded—taking any bacteria with it. Similarly, wrapping your cutting board with plastic wrap before pounding meat and poultry on it will limit the spread of bacteria.

Don't Rinse Raw Meat and Poultry

Avoid rinsing raw meat and poultry, as doing so is likely to spread contaminants around your sink. The only exception is brined food, which needs to be rinsed before cooking. In this case, once the brined food is rinsed, make sure to clean and sanitize the sink and surrounding areas. Cooking food to a safe internal temperature will kill surface bacteria more effectively than rinsing.

Season Safely

Though most bacteria can't live for more than a few minutes in direct contact with salt, it can live on the edges of a box or shaker. To avoid contamination, we grind pepper into a clean small bowl and then mix it with salt (using a ratio of 1 part pepper to 4 parts kosher salt or 2 parts table salt). We reach into the bowl for seasoning without having to wash our hands every time. Then the bowl goes in the dishwasher.

Don't Recycle Used Marinades

It may seem economical to reuse marinades, but used marinade is contaminated with raw meat juice and is therefore unsafe to consume. If you want a sauce to serve with cooked meat, make a little extra marinade and set it aside before adding the rest to the raw meat.

KEEP YOUR FRIDGE COOL

A refrigerator thermometer will tell you if your fridge and freezer are working properly. Check the temperature of your refrigerator regularly to ensure that it is between 35 and 40 degrees; your freezer should be below zero degrees.

At right are the recommended storage temperatures for specific foods. Keep in mind that the back of a refrigerator is the coldest while the door is the least cold. Make sure that raw meat is stored well wrapped and never on shelves that are above other food.

Fish and Shellfish: 30 to 34 degrees
Meat and Poultry: 32 to 36 degrees
Dairy Products: 36 to 40 degrees
Eggs: 38 to 40 degrees
Produce: 40 to 45 degrees

COOK MEAT THOROUGHLY

The doneness temperatures in the charts on page 783 represent the test kitchen's best assessment of palatability weighed against safety. In most cases, those concerns align. Rare chicken isn't very tasty, or very safe. There are a few notable exceptions, especially in regards to ground meat. If safety is your primary concern, you don't want to eat rare burgers.

The USDA has issued a complex set of rules regarding the cooking of meat and poultry. Here are the basics:

Whole Cuts: Cook whole cuts of meat, including pork, to an internal temperature of at least 145 degrees and let rest at least three minutes.
Ground Meat: Cook all ground meats to an internal temperature of at least 160 degrees.
Poultry: Cook all poultry, including ground poultry, to an internal temperature of at least 165 degrees.

How to Equip Your Kitchen

Despite the marketing hype, you don't need a lot of equipment in order to cook well. Your grandmother likely made do with beat-up cookware, a temperamental oven, and a minimum of gadgets. In the following pages, we cover the absolute basics—knives and cutting boards, cookware, small appliances, bakeware, and gadgets. Also make sure to review the material on key measuring tools (pages 8 and 9) and thermometers (page 10) discussed earlier in this chapter. Items that have a more limited, specialized use can be found in the Getting Started section in each of the recipe chapters in the book. (For instance, you will find information about tart pans in the Getting Started section of the Pies and Tarts chapter.)

Essential Knives and Cutting Boards

Knives are probably the most useful tools a cook owns; think of them as extensions of your hands. When shopping for knives, be sure to select ones that are made from high-carbon stainless steel, a hard metal that, once sharpened, tends to stay that way. Some purists prefer carbon steel knives, which may take a sharper edge initially but won't retain it for as long. Expensive ceramic blades are ultrasharp but very fragile. When it comes to handles, we prefer molded plastic over wood (which can collect grease and dirt) or metal (which can get slippery), a simple shape (no "ergonomic" bumps), and a smooth texture rather than a pebbled finish. When shopping for a knife, always make sure that it feels comfortable in your hand—otherwise, even the smallest amount of knife work will become a daunting task.

CHEF'S KNIFE

Why You Need It: We use this knife for everything from chopping onions to mincing herbs to butchering a chicken. This one knife, with its pointed tip and slightly curved blade, will handle 90 percent of your kitchen cutting work.

- **Look for an 8-inch blade.** This length provides plenty of power without being unwieldy. The blade of a good chef's knife should have a long, gently sloping curve suited to the rocking motion of mincing and chopping.
- **The knife should be substantial, but lightweight.** The knife should have enough heft to get the job done but not be so heavy that it becomes tiring to use. Keep in mind that forged blades—meaning the blade is molded from hot steel—are weightier than stamped blades, which are punched out of a sheet of steel. (Both styles perform equally well.) Also, the handle should help to balance the blade's weight.
- **Look for a comfortable grip.** When purchasing a knife, pick it up and hold it before making your choice; a good handle should be comfortable and virtually disappear in your grip. The handle should resist slipping, even when your hand is wet or greasy.

PARING KNIFE

Why You Need It: The small blade of a paring knife allows you more dexterity and precision than a chef's knife can provide. We reach for a paring knife for jobs that require a bit more accuracy and exactitude, such as coring apples, deveining shrimp, cutting citrus segments, and peeling garlic. Its small, pointed tip is also great for testing the tenderness of meat or vegetables.

- **Look for a 3- to 3½-inch blade.** This size is just right for a variety of cutlery tasks.
- **Choose a blade with agility.** A sharp, agile blade, which can fit into tight corners and can handle tight curves when peeling and paring, is much more important than weight and balance. The blade of a paring knife should be somewhat flexible for easy maneuvering into tight spots (such as tomato cores) and for handling curves when peeling and paring.
- **Look for a comfortable grip.** The handle should allow you to perform a variety of tasks nimbly.

SERRATED KNIFE (BREAD KNIFE)

Why You Need It: This knife features pointed serrations that allow it to glide through crusty breads, bagels, tomato skins, and more to produce neat slices.

- **Look for a 10- to 12-inch blade.** Knives shorter than 10 inches tend to catch their tips on larger loaves. Also, the blade should be slightly flexible for better maneuverability yet firm enough to allow for proper control.
- **A curved blade makes cutting easier.** A slightly curved blade facilitates a rocking motion to keep knuckles from scraping the cutting board.
- **Go for pointed, not wavy, serrations.** Pointed serrations give the blade a good grip on the food right away, while wavy serrations slide around.

SLICING KNIFE (CARVING KNIFE)

Why You Need It: This knife is specially designed to cut neatly through meat's muscle fibers and connective tissues. No other knife can cut through meat with such precision in a single stroke. Our holiday birds and roasts would be torn to shambles—hardly presentable—without this knife.

- **Look for a 12-inch blade with a rounded tip.** A blade about 12 inches long and 1½ inches wide allows for a single stroke to cut through even large cuts of meat. For easy slicing, a round tip is vital because it won't get caught on meat the way a pointed tip would when cutting downward.
- **Get a granton-edged knife.** These knives have oval scallops carved into both sides of the blade, making a thinner edge on the blade possible without sacrificing the heft or rigidity carried by the top of the blade—perfect for producing thinner slices with little effort.
- **Tapering is important.** The thickness of the blade should taper significantly from the handle to the tip. Thinness near the tip helps to control the knife, while the thicker base contributes the heft needed to cut cleanly through large pieces of meat.
- **Look for a comfortable grip.** Make sure the handle is comfortable because you will often need to put pressure on it when facing resistance (like when you are slicing a huge roast).

KNIFE SHARPENER

Why You Need It: Dull knives are much less useful—and more dangerous—than sharp knives, so keeping your knives' edges in tune is key. While a steel is fine for a light touch-up (see page 5 for information on using a steel), it can't sharpen a really dull knife.

- **Electric is easiest.** If you have the money, buy an electric sharpener, which can rework even the dullest knife blade. A manual sharpener is cheaper, but don't expect it to rescue really dull blades.

CUTTING BOARDS

Why You Need Them: Any well-stocked kitchen needs several good cutting boards. Having a solid base upon which to cut makes food preparation easier and prevents kitchen mishaps.

- **The board should be sturdy but not too hard.** The ideal surface should be soft enough to keep your knife in good shape but sturdy enough to absorb significant abuse.
- **Look for a midweight (5 pounds or less) board.** A cutting board shouldn't be so heavy that you hesitate to pull it out; on the flip side, a lightweight cutting board could be too flimsy to withstand much cutting.
- **Wooden and plastic boards must be cleaned differently.** Keep in mind that wooden and bamboo boards require hand-washing and occasional maintenance, while a plastic board can be cleaned in the dishwasher.

Cleaning and Caring for Your Cutting Boards

Depending on the type of board, you will need to clean and care for it differently. Here are some basic tips.

Scrub Your Board

Routine cleaning is essential; scrub your board thoroughly in hot, soapy water (or put it through the dishwasher if it's dishwasher-safe) to kill harmful bacteria, then rinse it well and dry it completely. For stubborn odors, scrub the cutting board with a paste of 1 tablespoon of baking soda and 1 teaspoon of water, then wash with hot, soapy water.

Soak It in Bleach and Water

To remove stubborn stains from plastic boards, mix a solution of 1 tablespoon of bleach per quart of water in the sink and immerse the board, dirty side up. When the board rises to the surface, drape a kitchen towel or two over its surface and sprinkle the towel with about ¼ cup bleach solution. Let it sit overnight, then wash it with hot, soapy water.

Apply Oil

If using a wood or bamboo board, maintain it by applying a food-grade mineral oil every few weeks when the board is new, and a few times a year thereafter. The oil soaks into the fibers, creating a barrier to excess moisture. (Don't use olive or vegetable oil, which can become rancid.) Avoid leaving wood or bamboo boards resting in water, or they will eventually split.

Essential Cookware

Cookware is made from a variety of metals, each with its own pros and cons. The ability of the metal to withstand and conduct heat will determine how well you can brown food, how easily food can burn, and how evenly the heat is distributed. Weight matters too—buy a lightweight stainless steel pan and your stew meat will stick to the pot. Ease of cleaning varies as well. Here's what you need to know about the most commonly available materials on the market.

Aluminum is second to copper (which we don't think is worth the expense) in conductivity among the metals used for cookware, but it is also light and inexpensive and retains heat well when sufficiently thick; however, the soft metal dents and scratches easily. Anodized aluminum cookware has a harder and less reactive outer surface, but its dark color can make it tricky to monitor the development of fond.

The bottom line: Unless anodized, aluminum is best used in combination with other metals.

Cast iron heats up slowly but retains heat well. Cast-iron cookware is also inexpensive and lasts a lifetime, but it is heavy, reactive, and must be seasoned before use unless you buy preseasoned cast-iron cookware (which we recommend).

The bottom line: Cast iron is great for skillets, but we like enameled cast iron for Dutch ovens since the enamel coating prevents the iron from rusting and from reacting with foods.

Clad cookware is what we recommend most of the time. The "cladding" label means that it is made from layers of metal that have been bonded under intense pressure and heat. These layers often form a sandwich, with a "filling" made of aluminum and the other layers made of stainless steel.

The bottom line: We rely on clad cookware in the test kitchen—it heats evenly and quickly, and is easy to care for.

Stainless steel is a poor heat conductor. Inexpensive cookware made entirely of thin-gauge stainless steel is prone to hot spots and warping. Stainless steel is, however, nonreactive, durable, and attractive, making it an excellent choice for coating, or "cladding," aluminum or copper cookware.

The bottom line: Don't buy cookware made from stainless steel alone—it should be combined with other metals.

SAUCEPANS

Why You Need Them: We use these multitaskers to make rice, sauces, vegetables, gravy, pastry cream, pudding, and poached fruit, to name just a few. They are easy to maneuver and stay out of your way on a crowded stovetop.

- **Buy at least two.** Every kitchen should be equipped with two saucepans: one with a capacity of 3 to 4 quarts, and a second 2-quart nonstick saucepan. Each excels at different cooking tasks. A larger saucepan is great for sauces and vegetables, while a smaller saucepan can be used for cooking foods that stick easily, like oatmeal and rice pudding, and for reheating leftovers.
- **Handles should be comfortable and stay cool.** A comfortable, stay-cool handle is a must given that you need to hold the pot to incorporate ingredients fully and also to scrape them out. In addition, the handle should be long enough for two-handed carrying when the pan is full.
- **Make sure they have tight-fitting lids.** There is nothing worse than trying to make rice or steam vegetables with a leaky lid. It pays to buy saucepans with lids engineered to fit snugly.

RIMMED BAKING SHEETS

Why You Need Them: We use rimmed aluminum baking sheets for everything from roasting vegetables and baking cookies to cooking meat and baking the occasional sheet cake. Fitted with the right-size wire cooling rack, this versatile pan can stand in for a roasting pan.

- **Keep it light and thick.** A light-colored surface will heat and brown evenly, making for perfectly cooked meat, vegetables, or cookies. A pan that isn't thick enough can buckle and transfer heat too intensely, burning the food.
- **Have an extra on hand.** Be sure to buy at least two baking sheets. They have so many different uses that having more than one available is a good plan.
- **Buy the right size.** We prefer baking sheets that are 18 by 13 inches with a 1-inch rim all around. Parchment paper and standard cooling racks won't fit if you buy a pan with different dimensions.

ROASTING PAN

Why You Need It: This holiday staple is also incredibly useful year-round. Besides roasting our Thanksgiving turkey, this pan shows up whenever we want to roast large cuts of meat. Its low sides and open design provide roasts with maximum exposure to the oven's hot air for even browning.

- **Bigger is better.** A roaster should be heavy enough to handle large birds and roasts without buckling, but not so heavy as to be backbreaking.
- **Take measurements.** Be sure to measure your oven before shopping for a roasting pan; it should fit with about 2 inches of clearance on all sides. Most of the large roasters we tested were between 16 and 18 inches long and would hold a turkey weighing up to 25 pounds.
- **Upright, riveted handles are key.** Maneuvering a big bird in and out of the oven is tricky, and the right handles make the job easier. They should be sturdy, upright, and large enough to accommodate thick oven mitts.
- **Look for a light-colored interior.** When you're monitoring the progress of a large turkey or roast, it's helpful to be able to see what's happening on the pan bottom. A pan with a nonstick finish makes this task especially difficult.
- **Make sure it's flameproof.** A roasting pan often ends up on the stovetop when making gravy or jus, so if it's not flameproof—forget it.
- **Buy a V-rack too.** Some pans come with a V-shaped rack for holding meat as it roasts; if yours doesn't, buy one. A V-rack lifts meat off the bottom of the pan so heat can circulate evenly around it.

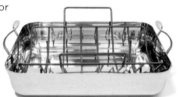

DUTCH OVEN

Why You Need It: The best choice for soups and stews, a Dutch oven is also ideal for frying, braising, steaming, and boiling. Built for both oven and stovetop use, a Dutch oven is generally wider and shallower than a conventional stockpot—it's easier to reach into and provides a wider surface area for browning. Its heft translates into plenty of heat retention—perfect for keeping frying oil hot or maintaining a low simmer.

- **Buy big and wide.** We find the most useful size to be 6 to 8 quarts. Also, our favorite pots measure more than 9 inches across—any less and you'll be stuck browning meat in batches.
- **Look for wide handles.** Looping handles should be extremely sturdy and wide enough to grab with thick oven mitts. Tiny handles make it awkward to hold and move the pot.
- **Check out the lid.** Lids should be tight fitting and heavy enough not to clatter when the pot contents are simmering below.

STOCKPOT

Why You Need It: This big pot is useful for handling a variety of big jobs, from steaming lobsters and cooking pasta and bushels of corn to canning and making huge batches of chili or homemade stock.

- **Wide beats tall and narrow.** Greater width allows you to see and manipulate food better and makes for much easier cleaning and storage.
- **Extending handles matter.** The best handles extend from the pot at least 1¾ inches and are either flat or thick and round for easy gripping, even with potholders and a potful of steaming chili.
- **Heavier pots perform better.** Lighter pots do a fine job cooking corn and pasta—in fact, they heat up faster than heavier pots. But for cooking applications where sticking and scorching are risks (such as chili), a heavier pot, especially one with a thick bottom, is a must.

SAUTÉ PAN

Why You Need It: Sauté pans aren't an absolute must-have for every kitchen—the other cookware listed here will get most jobs done. That said, these midheight, midweight, lidded vessels are ideal for cooking down a batch of collard greens, and their straight sides—high enough to corral splatters but low enough to easily reach into with tongs—are great for shallow frying. It's also a good pan to use for braising recipes that require browning and then adding liquid.

- **Opt for aluminum core with layers of stainless steel.** Aluminum is an excellent heat conductor but highly reactive with acidic foods, while nonreactive, less-conductive stainless steel modulates heat distribution. Skip the nonstick and anodized pans.
- **Look for hefty but well balanced.** Heft translates to steady heating and even browning, but a heavy pan must be well proportioned so picking it up to transfer it from stovetop to oven isn't problematic.
- **Straight sides and a 10-inch diameter is best.** These pans are made either tall and narrow, or wide and shallow. You want one that isn't so narrow that you have to brown meat in batches, but you don't want it so wide that cooking oil spreads too thinly across the pan. Wider models also brown unevenly. We have found that 9½ to 10 inches in diameter is the sweet spot. Straight walls prevent spills as you stir, pour off oil, or transfer the pan from stove to oven.
- **A tight-fitting lid is key.** You want a lid that will tightly lock in all the moisture (and flavor) during cooking. Tempered glass tops aren't as handy as they seem; if they steam up, they obscure any view of the cooking progress.

TRADITIONAL SKILLET

Why You Need It: This multiuse pan is key when we want to pan-sear meat or pan-roast chicken parts. The finish (not non-stick) helps develop fond—the crusty browned bits that are used to make pan sauces. The flared, shallow sides encourage rapid evaporation of moisture, so foods sear and brown, rather than steam, and pan sauces reduce quickly.

- **12 inches is a must.** Although there are times when you might need a smaller skillet, a skillet with a 12-inch diameter (measured across the rim) is the best all-around choice, capable of fitting four large chops or a whole cut-up chicken.
- **Heavy, clad construction performs best.** For the best conduction of heat, the pan should be clad, meaning the entire pan is made of three or more metal layers and does not have a disk bottom (an attached disk of metal). A heavy clad base will distribute heat evenly. (See page 20 for more about pan materials.)
- **Look for a comfortable, ovensafe handle.** A comfy handle will help you lift and hold on to the pan, and ovensafe means no worries when sliding it into the oven or under the broiler.

NONSTICK SKILLET

Why You Need It: We use this pan to cook or sauté delicate items that tend to stick or break apart during cooking, like fish, stir-fries, pancakes, and egg dishes. Flared sides allow for the quick redistribution of food (think omelet) by jerking and sliding the pan. Plus, cleanup is a snap.

- **12 inches is a must.** A 12-inch nonstick skillet is the most versatile choice to handle fish fillets or a stir-fry serving four. Smaller nonstick skillets (8 inches or 10 inches) are a good choice if you frequently cook fewer or smaller servings.

- **Look for a comfortable, ovensafe handle.** The handle should feel comfortable and sturdy, and stay cool during cooking. Look for a handle that can go into the oven since many recipes start on the stovetop and finish in the oven.

CAST-IRON SKILLET

Why You Need It: Cast iron is just the thing for searing or blackening food quickly over very high heat. It heats evenly to high temperatures and stays hot, and, if well seasoned, releases food just as well as a nonstick surface. Also, cast iron helps oil stay hot, so this skillet is great for shallow frying. When we're after a really dark, even crust on steaks or chops, or even cornbread, there's nothing better than cast iron. Plus it's dirt cheap.

- **Heavier is better.** The heavier the pan, the more heat it will retain, and the better the crust that will develop on your food.
- **Look for a large cooking surface.** If the pan is too small, the crowded food will steam. An 11- or 12-inch pan is best.
- **Buy a preseasoned pan.** We prefer factory-preseasoned pans because they perform better than unseasoned pans, which must be seasoned in the oven before use (a messy process that creates fumes). Both preseasoned and unseasoned cast-iron skillets should be oiled to help keep them in good working order and prevent rust.

SKILLET BASICS

Skillets can have various names, depending on the manufacturer. A skillet may be called everything from an omelet pan to a fry pan, so make sure you're buying the right equipment. Here's what you need to know.

Design Skillets come in various sizes and finishes, but they all have sloped sides, which facilitate quick evaporation of moisture and prevent food from stewing in its own released juices. This is what makes a skillet perfect for getting a nice brown crust on meat or for making a pan sauce. (When you do want food to cook in its own juices, as with shallow braising, you would need a straight-sided sauté pan.)

Ovensafe Look for traditional and nonstick skillets that are ovensafe. An ovensafe skillet (handle and all) is required when you want to brown food on the stovetop and then move it to the oven to finish cooking.

Using Your Cookware

Apart from choosing the right pan for the right job, there are a few techniques that will make you more successful in the kitchen and allow you to turn out perfectly browned chicken breasts and tender pan-seared scallops each and every time.

Use the Right Size
Follow the recipe and use the skillet size called for in the recipe. If the pan is too small, the food will be crowded and will steam, not brown. To determine the size of your skillet, measure it from outer lip to outer lip. Also make sure to use a burner similar in size to the pan.

Heat Oil Until Shimmering
If your skillet isn't hot enough, food won't develop a crust and will stick to the pan. If it's too hot, food will char and burn. When the oil starts to shimmer, it's the right temperature to sauté vegetables that don't need to be browned and would burn at a higher temperature.

Heat Oil Until Smoking
When cooking meat, chicken, and other foods that require a good crust, more heat is necessary. When the oil starts letting off wisps of smoke, the pan is ready.

Don't Crowd the Pan
Allowing space between each piece of food in the pan will keep it from steaming. Four chicken cutlets fit perfectly into a 12-inch skillet with room to spare, but jam a fifth or sixth cutlet into the same pan and the chicken will steam, not brown.

Don't Fuss with Food
Turn food just once. If you move or flip food a lot as it's cooking, it will never be in contact with the hot pan long enough to brown and form a flavorful crust. Also, if you flip meat before a crust has formed, it may stick. Flip beef, pork, and chicken just once to brown the second side.

Cook in a Circle
To keep track of small food, like shrimp or scallops, position the items in a circular pattern and work your way around the pan. When it's time to flip or remove them, start again at the same place so all the food is in the pan for the same amount of time. Tongs come in handy for this.

Rescue Stuck-On Food
If your meat or fish fuses to the skillet, there's an easy way to break the seal. Simply dip a flexible spatula into cold water and slide the spatula blade, inverted, underneath the sticking food. The cool spatula will break the bond between food and pan.

Wrap the Handle
To avoid burning your hands on a hot skillet that's been in the oven, wrap a dry dish towel or oven mitt around the handle to move it. Leave the towel or mitt on the handle while the skillet is on the stovetop so that you don't forget it's still hot.

Tame the Mess
Don't forget the splatter screen. Hot oil can make for one heck of a greasy, sticky mess on your stovetop. To minimize the mess, we use a splatter screen to cover the skillet when searing or sautéing food.

Cleaning Your Cookware: The Basics

We've created our share of messes in the test kitchen and have had a few cooking snafus that required tons of cleanup. Along the way, we've learned a few tricks to get those dirty, greasy pans shining like new again.

CLEANING EVERYDAY MESSES

1. Boil Water To clean a dirty traditional skillet (this usually isn't necessary for non-stick pans), fill it halfway with tap water and put the pan on the stovetop, uncovered. Bring to a boil and boil briskly for two or three minutes. Turn off the burner.

2. Scrape Off Residue Then scrape the pan with a wooden spatula, pour off the water, and let the pan sit briefly. Residue will start to flake off as the pan dries. Wash the skillet with hot water and dishwashing liquid, and dry.

CLEANING STUBBORN MESSES

1. Sprinkle Cleanser on Top To clean stuck-on gunk, we use powdered cleansers, like Cameo (for stainless steel, anodized aluminum, or nonstick surfaces) and Bar Keepers Friend (for stainless steel or nonstick surfaces). Moisten the pan with water, then shake some cleanser on top.

2. Scrub the Pan Using a copper scrubber for stainless steel skillets and a nylon scrubber for nonstick or anodized aluminum skillets, scrub the pan with circular motions. Finish by washing the pan with hot water and dishwashing liquid, then dry.

CLEANING BURNT AND BLACKENED MESSES

1. Apply Oven Cleaner For stainless steel pans (not nonstick or anodized aluminum) with burnt-on messes, we recommend oven cleaner as a last resort, to be used only on the exterior of the pan. Place the pan upside down on newspapers (preferably in a shady spot outdoors) and, wearing rubber gloves, apply an even layer of cleaner. Let the pan sit for 20 minutes (or the time recommended on the oven cleaner can).

2. Wipe It Off and Rinse Wipe off the oven cleaner and discard the newspapers. Rinse the pan thoroughly in the sink under warm running water. Then wash it with hot water and dishwashing liquid, rinse thoroughly, and dry.

Cleaning and Caring for Your Cookware: The Finer Points

Certain pans require special treatment, specifically nonstick and cast-iron skillets. Nonstick skillets have a more delicate surface, while cast-iron pans have seasoning that you want to maintain (and build up) and are also prone to rusting.

CLEANING CAST-IRON PANS

If you buy a preseasoned pan (and you should), you can use the pan with little fuss. For regular, everyday cleaning, rinse it with hot water but do not use soap or leave it in the sink to soak. Rinse and dry the pan thoroughly and then put it on a burner on low heat until no traces of moisture remain. Add a few drops of oil to the pan and use paper towels to lightly coat the pan's surface. The oil builds up a protective layer, seasoning the pan and preventing it from rusting.

If your pan is unseasoned or looks dull, patchy, and dry, you can season it with oil. Heat the pan until a drop of water evaporates, then wipe it with a wad of paper towels dipped in oil. Wipe out the excess and repeat until the pan is slick and black.

To clean extra-cruddy cast-iron skillets, here's what we suggest.

1. Loosen the Dirt and Rust Start by rubbing the cast-iron pan's surface with fine steel wool to loosen dirt and rust, then wipe the dirt away with a cloth. Repeat until the rust is gone.

2. Heat the Pan and Scrub Then heat the pan on a burner over medium heat and add vegetable oil to coat the pan bottom heavily. After five minutes, turn off the heat and add salt to form a paste. Holding the handle of the pan with a potholder or dish towel, wear a rubber glove on your other hand and scrub the pan with a thick wad of paper towels. Repeat these steps until the pan is slick and black. Rinse the pan thoroughly in hot water, wipe dry, and coat with a thin film of vegetable oil, wiping off any excess.

CARING FOR NONSTICK PANS

Nearly all nonstick pans rely on a top coat of polytetrafluoroethylene (PTFE) that keeps the surface slick and prevents food from sticking. Cooking over high heat, using abrasive pads, or washing the pan in the dishwasher will all cause this polymer to wear away. To prolong the nonstick coating's life, wash nonstick pans gently with a nonabrasive pad, and once they are dry, we recommend storing them using one of the following two methods.

A. Separate and Stack The surface of a nonstick skillet can chip or scratch easily, especially if you stack it with other pans. To protect the nonstick surface, place a double sheet of paper towels, bubble wrap, or a cheap paper plate between each pan as you stack them.

B. Seal and Stack Alternatively, before stacking smaller nonstick pans, slide them into large zipper-lock bags (2-gallon size for 10-inch pans and 1-gallon size for 8-inch pans). The plastic will protect the nonstick surface. Note that a 12-inch skillet will not fit in a zipper-lock bag.

Essential Bakeware

Avid bakers will likely own a lot of stuff—everything from pizza peels and baking stones to springform pans and tart pans. Consider the list that follows the absolute essentials. See the Getting Started pages in each of the baking chapters in this book for information on these specialty items.

GLASS BAKING DISH

Why You Need It: This versatile dish is ideal for casseroles and large crisps and cobblers. It's also the perfect dish to grab when marinating a large steak or transporting piles of loaded skewers out to the grill.

- **Pick Pyrex.** It's sturdy and dishwasher-safe, and the thick tempered glass retains plenty of heat to ensure deep, even browning. Also, because it's glass, it is naturally scratch-resistant, which means you can cut and serve straight from the pan with sharp knives and metal spatulas. Plus, the clear glass lets you see exactly how brown (or burnt) the food is on the bottom.
- **A 13 by 9-inch dish is the best all-around option.** While we don't use these to bake cakes (we rely on a metal pan for that), we do use them to cook a full tray of baked ziti or a huge cobbler for a summer picnic.
- **Handles are essential.** Make sure there are handles on either side of the dish for easy maneuvering in and out of the oven.

METAL BAKING PANS

Why You Need Them: We use these versatile pans to bake snack cakes, brownies, and bar cookies. Also, they work well for baking casseroles, both small and large. For rectangular and square cakes and bar cookies, these pans can't be beat. Their nonstick surface releases food easily—unlike a glass pan—so there's nothing left behind in the pan.

- **A nonstick finish is the only way to go.** Nonstick pans release evenly and produce cakes that are nicely browned.
- **Buy several.** You need two sizes of square pans; it's useful to have both an 8- and a 9-inch square pan. Also get a 13 by 9-inch pan for baking sheet cakes and bar cookies.
- **Handles are helpful.** While you won't find them on smaller baking pans, handles are a nice feature on a larger pan. Instead of flailing around the oven with potholders, trying to coax the cake pan out, you can simply grab the handles and pull out your finished cake.

ROUND CAKE PANS

Why You Need Them: We use our cake pans to—surprise—bake cakes, but we've also encountered a few hidden uses, like using a cake pan as a shallow dish when rolling cookies in sugar, for small baking tasks like toasting a few nuts in the oven, or even to help press peppercorns into steaks when making Steak au Poivre.

- **Look for pans with high, straight sides.** Pans with short sides have a hard time accommodating tall cakes, such as an upside-down cake, and flared sides produce cakes with uneven sides.
- **Choose cake pans with a dark, nonstick finish.** Dark-colored pans produce nicely browned cakes that release easily, while light-colored tinned or stainless steel pans actually prevent the cake from browning and often release the cake in pieces.
- **Buy several.** You need multiple round cake pans (it's good to have two 8-inch and two 9-inch) on your shelf for different recipes.

TUBE PAN

Why You Need It: Essential for cooking angel food cake, a 16-cup tube pan is also a good choice for baking pound cake (when you want it in cake rather than loaf form). The tube isn't just for looks; it helps cakes bake faster and more evenly by providing more surface area in which to heat a thick batter quickly.

- **A heavy removable bottom is a must.** A removable bottom ensures success when removing delicate angel food cake from the pan. Avoid pans with lighter removable bottoms, which aren't heavy enough to create a leak-free seal. Pans that are heavier overall retain heat better, resulting in more even browning.
- **Dark pans are better than light.** Darker pans absorb heat rather than reflect it, a trait that also encourages even browning.
- **Feet are nice.** We find pans with feet on the top rim handy for elevating an upturned pan during cooling.

BUNDT PAN

Why You Need It: This pan, modeled on a classic German pan called the *kugelhopf*, ushered in a revolution in home baking. The decorative pan produces a cake that looks impressive; all it needs is a dusting of confectioners' sugar or drizzle with a simple glaze and the cake is ready to serve.

- **Make sure it's heavy and nonstick.** The nooks and crannies mean that sticking is a threat with this pan, even more so if it is lightweight.
- **Look for defined ridges.** A pan that has clearly defined ridges will deliver a cake that not only has neat lines but is also less likely to stick.
- **Handles are helpful.** Given its weight and somewhat awkward shape, handles will make removing a hot Bundt pan from the oven, and flipping the pan to remove the cake, easier.
- **A 12- or 15-cup capacity is fine.** Standard recipes call for a 12-cup pan, although we have found that most recipes will work fine when baked in a 15-cup model.

SPRINGFORM PAN

Why You Need It: This two-piece pan allows you to make sticky cakes like cheesecakes and skip inverting the cake to remove it from the pan.

- **Look for a tight seal.** A good springform pan will have a tight seal that minimizes leaking.
- **It needs to be nonstick.** A nonstick surface will help the sides of the pan pull away from the cake with minimal damage.
- **Handles are helpful.** Most cheesecake recipes require putting the pan in a water bath for gentle, even cooking. Handles make it easy to move the pan in and out of the bath.

LOAF PAN

Why You Need It: A loaf pan makes great quick breads or yeast breads. It's also a good vehicle for making a soufflé or even a mini-casserole for two.

- **Select a loaf pan with a light gold or dark nonstick surface.** This surface will ensure that your breads will brown nicely and release easily.
- **Buy two sizes.** Loaf pans exist in a dizzying number of sizes and styles and, contrary to what many think, not all are 9 by 5 inches. Be sure to pay attention to the size specified in the recipe—baking with the wrong-size pan will result in squat loaves or loaves that overflow the pan. We recommend buying both 8½ by 4½-inch and 9 by 5-inch loaf pans for maximum versatility.
- **Double up.** Many recipes yield two loaves, so you should own two of each size.

PIE PLATE

Why You Need It: A pie plate is the obvious thing to grab when making a pie or quiche, but it's usefulness doesn't end there. We use these small, shallow dishes all the time for simple tasks such as breading chicken cutlets and baking off just one or two chicken breasts, and as a holding dish in which to set aside freshly browned meat when building a soup or stew.

- **Glass is good.** Pyrex promotes even browning and is scratch-resistant, so you can cut and serve right from the dish. The best part about using a Pyrex pie plate is that it allows you to monitor the bottom crust during baking.
- **Lots of lip is essential.** Pretty pies with a decorated or fluted edge need a roomy lip around the pie plate for support. Also, when the crust edge rests on the pie plate lip, the lip helps prevent it from slipping down during baking.
- **Look for shallow, angled sides.** Sides at a steep angle will cause your crust to slump.
- **It's nice to have two.** When the holidays roll around, you are probably going to want more than one pie plate, plus with so many uses, it's good to have more than one at the ready.

MUFFIN TIN

Why You Need It: For cupcakes and muffins, a muffin tin is a necessity. It's also handy for making individually portioned recipes, from desserts (cheesecakes) to egg dishes (frittatas).

- **Buy nonstick.** A dark, nonstick coating promotes even browning and ensures every muffin or cupcake will come out in one piece without the need for prodding and poking.
- **Look for handles or extended rims.** When pulling a hot muffin tin out of the oven, you want to have a grip on either side that is big enough to hold comfortably while using an oven mitt or potholder.
- **Go with the standard size.** While mini muffins are cute, a standard 12-cup tin with ½-cup wells is most useful.

WIRE RACKS

Why You Need Them: You can cool cookies, cakes, and bread on a wire rack, but we also set them inside a rimmed baking sheet for roasting meats and poultry.

- **Woven grid is best.** Don't buy a rack with bars that run in just one direction. A woven grid, with bars running perpendicularly, supports both delicate and heavy foods better.
- **Bigger is better.** Buy racks that fit snugly inside a standard 18 by 13-inch rimmed baking sheet. A rack that measures 17 by 12 inches is perfect.
- **Dishwasher-safe is a plus.** Cleaning the crannies of a wire rack is a pain; a dishwasher-safe rack will save you time and frustration.

Essential Small Appliances

The average kitchen will contain nearly a dozen small appliances, everything from a coffee maker to a toaster. Here we focus on the tools that are used most heavily in the preparation of recipes.

In a nutshell, every cook should own a good blender and a good food processor. As for electric mixers, you have a choice between a hand-held mixer and a stand mixer. Hand-held mixers are less expensive and smaller (thus easier to store), but they are also less powerful and for most tasks take a few minutes longer than the stand mixer. That said, a hand-held mixer can accomplish many of the same tasks as a stand mixer, with one exception: kneading bread dough. A stand mixer also keeps your hands free to do something else.

BLENDER

Why You Need It: It's the only tool that can blend all manner of liquid-y foods (whether hot or cold) to a smooth texture. Blenders are great for making smoothies, milkshakes, and frozen drinks and for pureeing soups and sauces until they are silky smooth.

- **Look for a tapered jar.** A tapered jar funnels the liquid down around the spinning blades for the smoothest possible texture. Jars with straight or flared sides allow some food to miss the blades completely, producing less smooth purees. (And don't be impressed with any advertised "extra" blades, especially if the jar isn't tapered.)
- **Heavy plastic or glass beats thin plastic.** Cheap plastic jars are prone to scratching and retaining the color and odor of foods over years of use.
- **Wattage doesn't matter, but pulse does.** High speed, at which nearly all blending takes place, is essentially the same for all blenders. The pulse feature, however, is useful; it gets food moving and breaks it down.

FOOD PROCESSOR

Why You Need It: A food processor is great for prepping everything you probably don't like to do by hand, like chopping messy things such as canned tomatoes, grinding delicate foods like fresh bread into fine crumbs, slicing vegetables, and shredding cheese without straining an arm muscle.

- **Don't cheap out.** Less expensive food processors (less than $150 or so) just aren't worth the money, as they can't perform even the most basic tasks very well. The better, pricier models have motors with more weight, run more quietly, and don't slow down under a heavy load of bread dough.
- **Blades should be sharp and sturdy.** If the blades aren't sharp, they will mangle the food rather than cut through it, leaving you with a pile of wasted ingredients and a clogged machine.
- **A large feed tube is key.** The feed tube is used mainly for shredding and slicing, so it should be large enough to fit potatoes, hunks of cheese, and other big foods. But the tube shouldn't be too big or food will fall out of position for the blade.

HAND-HELD MIXER

Why You Need It: The hand-held mixer's light weight and ease of use make it an essential tool for anyone who wants to bake, even if only occasionally. It's great for most baking tasks, like whipping cream or egg whites, creaming butter and sugar, or making cake batter; the only thing it can't handle is kneading dough, especially wet or heavy bread doughs. It's also easy to store (compared with a stand mixer).

- **Look for a lightweight mixer.** The weight of a mixer can affect how fatiguing it is to use. Look for a mixer that is comfortable to hold and easy to maneuver around a workbowl. Also, an angled handle helps because it allows you to relax your elbow at your side when mixing.
- **Slim wire beaters work best.** We prefer simple, slim beaters to traditional beaters with flat metal strips around a center post, since this post tends to be a good spot for batter to collect.

STAND MIXER

Why You Need It: If you are a serious cook or baker, a stand mixer is simply something you need within reach on your counter. If you bake only occasionally, a hand-held mixer is fine.

- **Planetary action is vital.** Mixers with a stationary bowl and a single mixing arm that uses planetary action work much better than those with a rotating bowl and two stationary beaters because they are much less likely to get clogged up when mixing stiff doughs and batters.
- **Look for a slightly squat bowl that holds at least 4½ quarts.** If the bowl is too large, small batches of batter don't get mixed properly, and scraping down the sides of the bowl will be impossible to do without getting your sleeves dirty.
- **Operation should be easy and intuitive.** Some stand mixers require brute force just to lock the mixer arm into place. Other mixers have beater-ejector buttons that are hard to locate. A good stand mixer should be easy to operate and have intuitive controls.

Tips for Using Mixers

Blenders and electric mixers are supposed to make you a better and more efficient cook. But ask any experienced chef, and he or she will tell you that these pieces of machinery can just as easily make a mess of your kitchen if you're not paying attention or are in a rush. Here are some of our favorite tricks and tips to keep in mind when using these machines.

USING A BLENDER

Prevent a Mess To prevent getting sprayed or burned by an exploding blender top, fill it only two-thirds full (or less), hold the lid in place with a folded dish towel, and pulse the blender a couple of times before blending continuously.

Clean It with Soapy Water After you're done using your blender, clean it by "blend-ing" a warm soapy water mixture until the blades and jar are mostly clean, then rinse out the blender.

USING A HAND-HELD MIXER

Stabilize the Bowl To free up a hand when using a hand-held mixer, nest the bowl inside a coiled damp dish towel to prevent it from moving.

USING A STAND MIXER

Pick the Right Attachment Use the whisk to whip cream and beat egg whites. The paddle creams butter and mixes batters; the dough hook kneads dough.

When Adding Dry Ingredients To keep dry ingredients from flying out of the mixer, pile them in the center of a piece of parchment paper, then fold the two sides up to make a channel through which the ingredients easily slide.

When Adding Wet Ingredients To avoid splattering or prevent ingredients from sticking to the bowl, pour the liquids slowly into the batter, aiming halfway between the edge of the beaters and the side of the bowl.

13 Most Essential Gadgets

The accomplished cook will likely accumulate dozens of gadgets over time. Here are the thirteen tools we think are most essential. These tools divide neatly into the following categories: tools for cutting; tools for straining and/or cleaning; and tools for stirring and/or turning.

VEGETABLE PEELER

Why You Need It: Most people have some kind of peeler that does an OK job on carrots and potatoes. But for other peeling jobs—say, the thick peel of a winter squash or the delicate skin of a pear—you need better than OK. We rely on vegetable peelers that have maneuverable blades. Serrated blades are good for peeling more delicate foods; a classic model will handle all the other usual tasks.

- **Look for a rubberized handle.** Given that our hands are constantly wet in the kitchen, we like a rubberized handle that's easy to grip.
- **Get a metal blade.** Ceramic blades dull easily so always choose a peeler with a metal blade.
- **The shape doesn't really matter.** We've found that Y-shaped peelers and straight peelers function similarly.

COARSE GRATER

Why You Need It: A sharp grater is indispensable for many tasks, from uniformly grating blocks of cheddar cheese to shredding potatoes. We like a flat grater because it gets the job done and is easy to store.

- **Razor-sharp teeth are a must.** If you want to grate quickly and efficiently, sharp teeth are the only choice.
- **It should be a decent size, and inflexible.** A solid, rigid frame with a larger surface area enables continuous grating, rather than short bursts.
- **Bent legs with rubber feet are a big plus.** Rubber-bottomed feet ensure the grater will stay put when held at any angle. Bent legs can hook around the lip of large and medium bowls.

RASP-STYLE GRATER

Why You Need It: A finely textured rasp-style grater (so-called because it's modeled after the woodworker's filelike tool) is portable, allowing you to grate or zest at the stove or table.

- **Razor-sharp teeth are a must.** If you want to grate hard Parmesan in a flash, you need sharp teeth.

GARLIC PRESS

Why You Need It: We press hundreds of garlic cloves each month. In numerous tests, we've found that a garlic press does a better job of mincing than one can do by hand, producing a fuller, less acrid flavor that is more evenly distributed throughout a dish. It keeps the garlic off your fingers, too.

- **A sturdy construction is key.** Many garlic presses are poorly made. The handle and hopper should be sturdy and durable. The hopper should be large enough to hold two cloves of garlic.
- **A long handle is best.** A long handle is more comfortable and reduces the effort necessary to squeeze the garlic through the holes in the hopper.

PEPPER MILL

Why You Need It: The preground stuff sold in the spice aisle is insipid when compared with freshly ground, and just about every savory recipe calls for (at the very least) seasoning with ground pepper before serving.

- **It should offer a wide range of grinds.** The best mills can grind pepper from very coarse to very fine.
- **Look for a big hopper.** A large hopper (with a large opening) means less refilling.
- **Faster is easier.** A slow grinder makes grinding fresh pepper a chore.

KITCHEN SHEARS

Why You Need Them: Our favorite tool for cutting up and trimming chicken, kitchen shears are also ideal for trimming pie dough, snipping herbs, and cutting parchment paper rounds. Try severing twine without them.

- **Slip-resistant handles are key.** When butchering chicken, your hands get very greasy, so the handles should be secure in your hand.
- **Take-apart blades are easy to clean.** No bits of food can hide between the blades when they come apart.

FINE-MESH STRAINER

Why You Need It: Essential for tasks like dusting a tart with confectioners' sugar, removing bits of curdled egg from a pudding, or turning cooked raspberries into a seedless sauce, a fine-mesh strainer also makes an excellent stand-in for a sifter.

- **Look for a sturdy, deep bowl.** Bigger is better, and make sure to pick a strainer that won't bend or twist over time.
- **An ergonomic handle is best.** An uncomfortable handle makes slow jobs (like straining pudding) a chore.

COLANDER

Why You Need It: How else are you going to drain pasta and vegetables?

- **5 quarts is good.** A large capacity means you can cook a lot of veggies or pasta and not worry about the food spilling into the sink.
- **Meshlike perforations work fast.** Minute perforations actually drain water faster than large holes.

SALAD SPINNER

Why You Need It: Wet greens can't be dressed properly, and they result in a soggy salad. We also use a salad spinner to wash and dry herbs.

- **A pump is best.** Rather than a crank, we prefer models with a top-mounted pump, which requires very little effort to use.
- **A nonskid bottom is nice.** Forget slipping and sliding in the sink.
- **Get a leakproof bowl.** Don't wash greens in the sink. Instead, choose a model with a solid bowl so you can wash greens right in the spinner.

HEAT-RESISTANT RUBBER SPATULA

Why You Need It: Nothing is better suited to a multitude of tasks, be it reaching into the corners of bowls and pots, stirring batters, icing cakes, or folding egg whites than a rubber spatula. With the introduction of heat-resistant models, the tool is even more indispensable.

- **Look for a stiff but flexible blade.** A wide, firm blade should be rigid enough to mix the stiffest batter yet flexible enough to reach into tight spaces.
- **A stain- and odor-resistant blade is a must.** A silicone spatula shouldn't pick up stains (even from tomato sauce or chili) or odors.

SPATULA/TURNER

Why You Need It: No other tool can flip pancakes, crab cakes, burgers, and more.

- **A thin edge and a big head are key.** A thin front edge will glide under food without tearing it, while a large head (ideally 3 inches wide and 5 inches long) will hold even big items.
- **Slots are nice.** Long vertical slots let excess grease drip away.
- **Buy two.** A metal spatula is durable and works best in traditional pans, but a nonstick spatula is a good idea when dealing with eggs and fish in a nonstick pan.

TONGS

Why You Need Them: Acting like an extension of the hand, tongs can lift, flip, turn, and rotate most any type of food, from small shrimp to a 5-pound rib roast—all while avoiding burning your fingers.

- **Rubber grips are easy to hold.** We like stainless steel tongs with rubber grips that enable us to old the tongs comfortably and securely.
- **Some spring is good.** Tongs should have enough spring to pick up small items but should open easily enough to hold large roasts.
- **Buy two.** In addition to stainless steel tongs, buy a pair with nylon tips for use in nonstick skillets.

WHISK

Why You Need It: Useful not only for whipping cream and egg whites, a whisk can also mix batters and make pan sauces and gravies. Judging from all the shapes and sizes of whisks that are out there, you might think you need a different one for every task. Not so.

- **Long and narrow is best.** A 12-inch whisk can reach into deep pots and bowls, and a tight radius (rather than a balloon design) can reach more easily into tight corners.
- **Tines should be flexible but should not twist.** Make sure the tines, while flexible, are sturdy and won't bend too much or twist over time.

How to Stock Your Pantry and Refrigerator

The ingredients on the following pages are used over and over again in countless recipes. Here's what you need to know about buying, storing, and using these key ingredients. See pages 48–49 for more information on eggs. See page 44 for information about Ingredient Assumptions We Make in Our Recipes. Also, refer to the Emergency Substitutions chart on page 45.

Salt

While gourmet shops and high-end supermarkets carry a staggering array of salts from all corners of the globe these days, there are really just three main types of salt.

TABLE SALT

Table salt can be used in any application. It dissolves quickly and easily, making it especially great for baking or for using in a brine.

KOSHER SALT

Kosher salt crystals are larger than those of table salt, making them easier to sprinkle over foods before cooking. We also like to use kosher salt as part of a rub for barbecued foods.

SEA SALT

Sea salt can be purchased as fine grains, crystals, or flakes. There are tiny differences in flavor from brand to brand, and some have a welcome briny taste from the sea. Crystal size and "crunch" can also vary. For this reason, we suggest using sea salt as an at-table condiment.

SUBSTITUTING SALTS

Types of salt are almost always interchangeable by adjusting the amount, but note that because of varying crystal sizes, you must make adjustments when substituting one brand or type of salt for another. See the Emergency Substitutions chart on page 45.

Pepper

Once the shell of the peppercorn is cracked, its aroma immediately starts to fade, and most of its scent and flavor disappears within a half-hour. We don't recommend buying ground pepper. Replacing your pepper shaker with a good pepper mill is one of the simplest ways to enhance your cooking.

BLACK PEPPER

This is the classic choice when cooking. Until recently, supermarket brands never specified origin or variety of peppercorns; suppliers bought the cheapest they could get. But specialty retailers offering exotically named varieties like Sarawak, Lampong, and Tellicherry have raised awareness. When we tested eight varieties, we could detect differences—some are floral, others more spicy—but it was hard to make value judgments. Personal preferences really come into play.

WHITE PEPPER

The pepper berries used to make white pepper are the same as those used to make black pepper, but they are harvested at a riper stage. The hulls are then removed, and with them goes the heat that is characteristic of black pepper. What's left is more floral and aromatic than spicy. We use white pepper in dishes where black specks might be unwelcome (such as a white sauce) or where its floral flavor works well with other ingredients. We especially like white pepper in Thai dishes with citrus, lemon grass, and chiles.

GREEN PEPPER

Green peppercorns are peppercorns picked before they ripen. They are available in dried form, which adds a fresh, clean flavor to dishes, or you can buy them preserved in brine or vinegar. The latter are often used in sauces to add a little heat and tang.

PINK PEPPER

This floral, pungent spice is not related to black peppercorns; it comes from a different plant. We rarely use pink peppercorns in the test kitchen.

Herbs

We use fresh herbs (with the exception of bay leaf) in most savory recipes. However, dried herbs play an important role in many long-cooked dishes, such as soups and stews (see Guidelines for Using Dried Herbs on opposite page). For information on chives, see page 36.

BASIL

Sometimes labeled Genoa basil, this slightly acidic herb balances licorice and citrus notes. Because basil bruises easily when it's chopped, we like to stack several leaves, roll them tightly, then slice the basil into thin strips (called chiffonade), or we simply shred or chop the leaves just before using. Use basil raw or add it at the end of cooking since heat kills its flavor. Basil doesn't keep for more than a few days. To prolong its life, store the bunch in a glass of water on your counter (like flowers) and change the water every day.

BAY LEAF

Bay leaves are a standard addition to soups, stews, and bean dishes. We prefer dried bay leaves to fresh; they work just as well in long-cooked recipes, are cheaper, and will keep for months in the freezer. We prefer Turkish bay leaves to those from California. The California bay leaf has a medicinal and potent flavor, like something you'd put in a cough drop. The Turkish bay leaf has a mild, green, and slightly clovelike flavor.

CILANTRO (CHINESE PARSLEY)

Cilantro, the fresh leaves and stems of the coriander plant, is a love-it-or-loathe-it herb. It's beloved in Southeast Asian and Latin cuisines, where it's a core ingredient. The flavorful stems can be chopped and used along with the leaves. Because cooking attenuates the flavor, we almost always add cilantro after we take dishes off the heat. Store it like basil, with its stems in water, or wrap it in damp paper towels and store it in a plastic bag in the crisper drawer of your refrigerator.

DILL

Dill's feathery fronds are slightly bitter, with a refreshing, lemony quality and an aroma akin to caraway seeds. Dill matches perfectly with cucumbers (both pickled and raw); its summery freshness also works well for seafood, potatoes, and eggs. It's best used as a finishing herb.

MARJORAM

A member of the mint family, fresh marjoram is often mistaken for oregano. Its flavor is sweet, with a delicate, fleeting spiciness. Marjoram is often paired with poultry, lamb, or vegetables and is best used as a finishing herb.

MINT

Although there are more than 2,000 varieties of mint, spearmint is the most common. The flavor of mint can be described as smooth and bright, with a eucalyptus quality. Mint is often bruised or muddled to release its flavor. It's best used as a finishing herb.

OREGANO

This hardy perennial shrub has fuzzy, spade-shaped leaves and tough vinyl stems. Another member of the mint family, it has a potent flavor that can be described as earthy and musty, with a spicy-hot bite. Add the minced leaves at the outset of cooking. Oregano is great in tomato sauces, chili, and Mexican and Latin dishes, and sprinkled on pizza. Note: Dried oregano does not have the same sharp bite as fresh, but it does have a distinct and recognizable floral element.

PARSLEY

In the test kitchen, we prefer flat-leaf (or Italian) parsley, which is more assertive than the curly-leaf parsley that once made its living as a ubiquitous restaurant garnish. Parsley stems have a lot of flavor; save them for stocks and soups. Store parsley either with its stems in water or wrapped in damp paper towels and refrigerated. Parsley freezes well (with some discoloration that doesn't affect flavor) in an airtight container for up to four months.

ROSEMARY

This evergreen-like herb has an obvious pine aroma. When it's used in moderation its taste is clean, sweet, and floral, but if overused it can be like Vicks VapoRub. Strip the leaves off the stems and mince, or add whole sprigs during the last 30 minutes of cooking and remove before serving. Rosemary works well in long-cooked dishes (especially those with Italian flavors) like soups, stews, and braises. Note: Too much dried rosemary can turn a dish bitter, so use sparingly.

SAGE

Perhaps best known as the main herb in poultry seasonings, sage flavors a range of foods, from breakfast sausages to Thanksgiving stuffing. Its taste is earthy and floral, with a musky bite. Because of its cottony texture when raw, sage should be cooked. Note: In its dried form, we prefer rubbed (or finely crumbled) sage to the ground and chopped kinds.

TARRAGON

In France, this slender-leafed herb is called "little dragon" because of its fiery quality. Its flavor is very assertive, with a mouth-numbing, anesthetic quality and a sweet orange-anise aroma. Tarragon can be used in fish, egg, and chicken dishes.

THYME

Thyme is good in long-cooked soups and stews and with roasted meats and poultry; it pairs well with mustard and lemon flavors. Its flavor mellows with cooking, so we often add extra at the end of a recipe. To remove leaves, run your thumb and forefinger down the length of the stem, pinching the stem and removing the leaves as you go. If the stems are young and tender, chop them and use with the leaves. If they're woody, add whole sprigs to soups and stews and remove before serving. Store thyme in a plastic bag in the refrigerator.

GUIDELINES FOR USING DRIED HERBS

Dried herbs are more convenient to use than fresh because they require no more prep than a twist of a lid. But they can add a dusty quality to recipes, especially when used to finish dishes. Here are some recommendations based on extensive testing in our kitchen.

Long-Cooked Recipes Only some dried herbs are passable, mainly in recipes involving fairly long cooking times (20 minutes plus) and a good amount of moisture. Chili stands out as one dish that is better made with a dried herb (oregano) than with a fresh one. Dried rosemary, sage, and thyme also fare reasonably well in certain applications.

Avoid Some Dried Herbs Those herbs that we consider delicate (basil, chives, and parsley) lose most of their flavor when dried; we prefer fresh forms of these herbs. Two herbs, tarragon and dill, fall into a middle category: They do add flavor in their dried form, but that flavor is more muted than that provided by other dried herbs.

Use Less than Fresh Use one-third as much dried herbs as fresh, and add them early in the cooking process so they have time to soften.

Replace Frequently Dried herbs lose their potency 6 to 12 months after opening; you can test dried herbs for freshness by rubbing them between your fingers—if they don't smell bright, throw them away and buy a new jar.

Spices

A key element in many recipes, spices lend depth and complexity to everything from rice and bean dishes to barbecue recipes. Here are the spices we use most often in the test kitchen, which you should consider stocking in your pantry.

ALLSPICE

Allspice tastes like a combination of cinnamon, clove, and nutmeg, hence its name. Ground allspice is used in sweets such as mincemeat pie and gingerbread, and it's a hallmark of Caribbean cooking and jerk seasoning. In the test kitchen, to bring out the flavor of the spice we sometimes cook (or "bloom") ground allspice in butter and then add the spiced butter to a dough or batter.

CARDAMOM

Fragrant cardamom comes in pods, either green or black, each holding many tiny seeds. Seeds from the more common green pods are used in many Scandinavian baked goods, Indian sweets, and chai tea. Although the whole pods can be toasted and ground or steeped, most of the highly aromatic flavors live in the seeds. The flavor doesn't stick around, so buy whole pods and then remove and grind the seeds as needed.

CINNAMON

Americans love cinnamon and use it freely in favorites like apple crisp, sticky buns, and pumpkin pie. Most cinnamon sold in this country is actually cassia, not true Ceylon cinnamon (also known as canela). Both are the dried bark of tropical evergreen trees, but the bolder, spicier cassia is cheaper to process. In the test kitchen, we use ground cinnamon that is cassia.

CLOVES

Pungent, peppery cloves are the dried, unopened buds of an Indonesian tree. They resemble nails (the word "clove" comes from the Latin word for nail, *clavus*). Ground cloves are potent, so the test kitchen uses them sparingly. Add whole cloves to the poaching liquid for fruit or, on the savory side, employ them to flavor stocks and to stud holiday hams.

CORIANDER

This light-brown spherical seed is the dried fruit of the herb cilantro, a member of the parsley family. Coriander possesses a sweet, almost fruity flavor with just a hint of the soapy-metallic character of mature cilantro.

CUMIN

Like coriander, these tiny, elongated seeds belong to a plant in the parsley family. Their flavor is earthy and warm, but it's their pungent, almost musty aroma that sets them apart from other warm spices.

FENNEL SEED

Fennel seeds come from a bulbless variety of the fennel plant. They exhibit a heavy anise flavor reminiscent of black jelly beans and have an earthy, butterscotch-like aroma.

GINGER

Yes, ground ginger comes from the dried fresh root, but don't substitute one for the other. They taste quite different, as fresh is more floral while dried is spicier. They also work differently in baking; fresh is moister and less potent. We do, however, sometimes reinforce ground ginger with grated fresh ginger in the test kitchen (to make gingerbread, for instance).

GUIDELINES FOR USING GROUND SPICES

Purchasing whole spices and grinding them yourself is ideal. Whole spices have a longer shelf life than ground spices (which lose their punch after a year), and fresh-ground spices have a superior flavor. If you want to grind your own spices, invest in a small coffee grinder and reserve it for just this purpose. However, the reality is that most cooks, including those who work in our test kitchen, typically rely on the convenience of ground spices. Here are a few things you can do to ensure the best results when using ground spices.

Clean Out Your Pantry Regularly If you have spices that you moved from your last house or apartment, they need to be retired. Ground spices will lose their punch after a year. We recommend using stick-on dots to label each jar with a purchase date and then regularly purge your pantry of spices that are more than 12 months old. Don't buy spices in bulk.

Keep Them Cool and in the Dark Heat and sunlight will rob spices of their potency. Keep them in a cool, dark pantry to prolong their freshness. Don't store spice jars on the counter or near the stove.

Bloom for Big Flavor Heating changes the flavor of spices, making them taste richer and more complex. Ground spices that are used in barbecue rubs will see plenty of heat on the grill. (In effect, the spices are toasted as the food cooks.) Spices that are used in dishes with liquids (such as chili, curry, or soup) should be bloomed in oil before the liquid is added to the pot. You can cook the spices in a little butter or oil for a minute or two and then add the mixture to the recipe. Or, simpler still, add the spices once the aromatics (such as onions) are cooked and before the tomatoes, broth, wine, or other liquid is added. We often add ground spices with the garlic—they both require a minute or so to develop their flavors.

MUSTARD

These acrid seeds are typically yellow, brown, or black. The brown and black varieties are prized for their stronger flavor. Mustard seeds have almost no aroma, but their flavor is earthy and sharp, with a strong peppery kick.

NUTMEG

Heady and powerful, nutmeg is a hard, brown seed from a tropical tree. It's often used in dairy-based savory dishes, like quiche and creamed spinach, or for sweets such as spice cake. We compared fresh with preground and found that in dishes in which nutmeg is the sole spice, grinding it yourself (we like to use a rasp-style grater) is important. But in foods with lots of spices, preground nutmeg is fine.

SAFFRON

Pound for pound the most expensive spice in the world, saffron is the stigma from a variety of crocus flower. Just the slightest pinch lends a raisinlike flavor and a vibrant orange hue to a dish. When buying saffron, look for dark red threads devoid of yellow or orange.

STAR ANISE

As the name suggests, these pods are star-shaped and they taste like anise. The warm, licorice-like flavor of star anise works well in both sweet and savory foods (Asian marinades, custards). It's an essential element of five-spice powder. Try flavoring sugar syrup with whole pods and drizzling the syrup over citrus fruits.

Garlic

Garlic (along with onions) is the base for many savory dishes. When shopping for garlic, choose unpackaged, loose garlic heads so you can examine them closely. Pick heads without spots, mold, or sprouting. Squeeze them to make sure they are not rubbery, have no soft spots, and aren't missing cloves. The garlic shouldn't have much of a scent; if it does, you're risking spoilage. Here are the types of garlic you will find at the market.

SOFTNECK GARLIC

Of the two main garlic varieties, your best bet at the supermarket is softneck, since it stores well and is heat-tolerant. This variety features a circle of large cloves surrounding a small cluster at the center.

HARDNECK GARLIC

Distinguished by a stiff center staff surrounded by large, uniform cloves, hardneck garlic has a more intense, complex flavor. But since it's easily damaged and doesn't store as well as softneck garlic, wait to buy it at the farmers' market.

ELEPHANT GARLIC

The huge individual cloves of so-called elephant garlic—which is actually a member of the leek family—are often sold alongside regular garlic. We find it far milder than regular garlic and don't recommend it for recipes.

STORING GARLIC

With proper storage, whole heads of garlic should last at least a few weeks. Store heads in a cool, dark place with plenty of air circulation to prevent spoiling and sprouting. (A small basket in the pantry is ideal.) Store cut garlic in oil in the refrigerator for no more than four days. The bacteria that cause botulism grow in exactly this kind of oxygen-free environment, so it's actually a health hazard.

PREPARING GARLIC

Keep these two rules in mind when preparing garlic.

Fine Mince = Strong Flavor Garlic's pungency emerges only after its cell walls are ruptured, triggering the creation of a compound called allicin. The more a clove is broken down, the more allicin—and more flavor (and aroma)—is produced. Thus you can control the amount of bite garlic contributes to a recipe by how finely (or coarsely) you cut it.

Don't Chop Garlic in Advance In tests, we've found that since garlic flavor comes from the compound allicin, which is released and starts to build only when the cloves are ruptured, the longer cut garlic sits, the harsher its flavor.

COOKING GARLIC

Garlic is sharpest when raw. When it is heated above 150 degrees, its enzymes are destroyed and no new flavor is produced; only flavor created up to the inactivation temperature remains. This is why toasted or roasted garlic has a mellow, slightly sweet flavor. Alternatively, garlic browned (or overbrowned) at very high temperatures (300 to 350 degrees) results in a bitter flavor. (Garlic chips are the exception, since they are mellowed first, then crisped, which creates a sweet flavor with only hints of bitterness.) Here are some tips for cooking garlic.

Wait to Add Garlic Wait to add garlic to the pan until other aromatics or ingredients have softened (push these to the perimeter) to avoid browning and the creation of bitter compounds.

Cook Only Until Fragrant Don't cook garlic over high heat for much longer than 30 seconds; you want to cook it only until it turns fragrant. And make sure to stir constantly.

Add to Cold Pan Do add garlic to a cold pan when it is the only flavoring, and cook it over low to medium heat to give it time to release its flavors and keep it from burning.

Onions

Many supermarkets stock a half-dozen types of onions. They don't all look the same or taste the same. Here are the onions and their close relatives that you will find in most markets.

YELLOW ONIONS
These strong-flavored onions maintain their potency when cooked, making them our first choice for cooking.

WHITE ONIONS
These pungent onions are similar to yellow onions but lack some of their complexity.

RED ONIONS
These crisp onions lose their sweet, peppery flavor when cooked and are often used raw in salads and for pickling.

SWEET ONIONS
Vidalia, Maui, and Walla Wallas are three common sweet varieties. Their texture can become stringy when cooked, so these sugary onions are best used raw.

PEARL ONIONS
These crunchy, small onions are generally used in soups, stews, and side dishes. Peeling them is a chore, so we recommend buying frozen pearl onions that are already peeled.

SHALLOTS
Shallots have a complex, subtly sweet flavor. When cooked, they become very soft and almost melt away, making them the perfect choice for sauces.

SCALLIONS
Scallions have an earthy flavor and delicate crunch that work well in dishes that involve little or no cooking, like stir-fries.

CHIVES
The smallest member of the onion family, chives look like long, hollow blades of grass. They have a very mild flavor and are sold near the herbs in supermarket produce sections.

LEEKS
Because of their fibrous texture, leeks are usually cooked, which makes them tender and sweet. Both the white and the light green parts are used in most recipes (save dark green parts for stock). Leeks are very sandy; wash them thoroughly.

STORING ONIONS

All varieties of onions and shallots should be stored in the same way: at cool room temperature, away from light. Don't store onions in the refrigerator, where their odors can permeate other foods. Delicate scallions, chives, and leeks do belong in the refrigerator, stored in loosely closed plastic bags.

Potatoes

When shopping for potatoes, make sure they are firm and free of green spots, sprouts, and cracks. Buy loose potatoes rather than those sold in plastic bags, which can act like greenhouses and cause potatoes to sprout, soften, and rot. Potato varieties can be divided into three major categories based on texture, which is determined by its starch content.

DRY, FLOURY POTATOES
Also known as "baking" potatoes, this group contains more total starch (20 to 22 percent) than other categories, giving these varieties a dry, mealy texture. These potatoes are the best choice when baking and frying. In our opinion, they are also the best potatoes for mashing because they can drink up butter and cream. They are also good when you want to thicken a stew or soup, but not when you want distinct chunks of potatoes. Common varieties: Russet, Russet Burbank, Idaho.

"IN BETWEEN" POTATOES
These potatoes contain less total starch (18 to 20 percent) than dry, floury potatoes but more total starch than firm, waxy potatoes. Although they are considered "in between" potatoes, their texture is more mealy than that of waxy potatoes, putting them closer to dry, floury potatoes. In between potatoes can be mashed or baked but won't be as fluffy as dry, floury potatoes. They can be used in salads and soups but won't be quite as firm as waxy potatoes. Common varieties: Yukon Gold, Yellow Finn, Purple Peruvian, Kennebec, Katahdin.

FIRM, WAXY POTATOES
Also know as "boiling" potatoes, these contain a relatively low amount of total starch (16 to 18 percent), which means they have a firm, smooth, and waxy texture. Often they are called "new" potatoes because they are less mature potatoes harvested in the late spring and summer. They are less starchy than "old" potatoes because they haven't had time to convert their sugar to starch (they also have thinner skins). Firm, waxy potatoes are perfect when you want the potatoes to hold their shape, as with potato salad. They are also a good choice when roasting or boiling. Common varieties: Red Bliss, French Fingerling, Red Creamer, White Rose.

STORING POTATOES

If stored under unsuitable heat and light circumstances, potatoes will germinate and grow. To avoid this, keep them in a cool, dark place. Although some experts warn that refrigerating potatoes can dramatically increase the sugar level, we've never encountered this problem in the test kitchen. Store potatoes in a paper (not plastic) bag and keep them away from onions, which give off gases that will hasten sprouting. Most varieties should keep for several months. The exception is new potatoes—because of their thinner skins, they will keep for no more than one month.

Canned Tomatoes

Since canned tomatoes are processed at the height of freshness, they deliver better flavor than off-season fresh tomatoes. But with all the options lining supermarket shelves, it's not always clear what you should buy. We tested the most common varieties of canned tomato products to determine the best uses for each, and our favorite brand of each.

WHOLE TOMATOES

Whole tomatoes are peeled tomatoes packed in their own juice or puree. They are best used in recipes where fresh tomato flavor is a must. Whole tomatoes are quite soft and break down quickly when cooked. We have found that those packed in juice rather than in puree have a livelier, fresher flavor. Our top-rated brand is Progresso Italian-Style Whole Peeled Tomatoes with Basil. (Progresso sells whole tomatoes packed both in juice and in puree, so be sure to read the label.)

DICED TOMATOES

Diced tomatoes are peeled whole tomatoes that have been machine-diced and packed in their own juice or puree. Many brands contain calcium chloride, a firming agent that helps the chunks maintain their shape. Diced tomatoes are best for rustic tomato sauces with a chunky texture and in long-cooked stews and soups where you want the tomatoes to hold their shape. We favor diced tomatoes packed in juice because they have a fresher flavor than those packed in puree. Our preferred brand is Hunt's Diced Tomatoes, which has a fresh flavor and a good balance of sweet and tart notes.

CRUSHED TOMATOES

Crushed tomatoes are whole tomatoes ground very finely, then enriched with tomato puree. They work well in smoother sauces, and their thicker consistency makes them ideal when you want to make a sauce quickly. Texture varies dramatically among brands; some are thick as puree while others are watery. We prefer chunky, fresh-tasting Tuttorosso Crushed Tomatoes in Thick Puree with Basil (not to be confused with Tuttorosso's New World Style Crushed Tomatoes, which we don't recommend). Muir Glen Organic Crushed Tomatoes with Basil came in a close second. If you can't find either recommended brand, crush your own using canned diced tomatoes and a food processor.

TOMATO PUREE

Tomato puree is made from cooked tomatoes that have been strained to remove their seeds and skins. Tomato puree works well in long-simmered, smooth, thick sauces with a deep, hearty flavor. We found Hunt's Tomato Puree, with its thick consistency and tomatoey flavor, to be the best, though most supermarket brands will work just fine.

TOMATO PASTE

Tomato paste is tomato puree that has been cooked to remove almost all moisture. Tomato paste lends a deeper, rounded tomato flavor and color to many slow-simmered pasta sauces as well as to Italian soups and stews. Our preferred brand is Goya Tomato Paste, for its fresh, full tomato flavor.

Cooking Oils

In the test kitchen, we use different cooking oils to suit the flavor and cooking temperature requirements of the recipe at hand. The following are the oils we commonly use.

VEGETABLE OIL

Loosely speaking, a vegetable oil is made from any number of "vegetable" sources, including nuts, grains, beans, seeds, and olives. In the narrow confines of recipe writing, it usually refers to one of the more popular brands of cooking oil labeled "vegetable oil"; on inspection of the ingredient label, you'll usually find that these generic vegetable oils consist of soybean oil. These oils, and canola oil (a vegetable oil prepared from rapeseed), have high smoke points and almost no flavor; we use them for shallow frying, sautéing, stir-frying, and in dressings with strong flavors. With the exception of canola oil (which can give food an off-flavor when the oil is heated for a long time), these oils are also fine for deep frying.

OLIVE OIL

Also called "pure" olive oil, this product adds some—but not too much—fruity flavor to foods. Unlike extra-virgin olive oil, basic olive oil has been refined so it has a higher smoke point. We use it to brown meats, to start soups and stews, and in sauces and dressings with strong flavors. We especially like to use olive oil for dishes with Mediterranean flavors.

EXTRA-VIRGIN OLIVE OIL

Although extra-virgin olive oil's strong flavors dissipate when exposed to high heat, we use it in dishes that are cooked quickly. We also use it to dress vegetables and to drizzle over soups and grilled foods; it's our choice in most vinaigrettes. It will lose freshness, even unopened, rather quickly. After 12 months, you can taste the difference, and after 18 months the oil should be replaced. Depending on the region, the harvest occurs between September and December, so a bottle labeled "2011" will be past its prime in 2013.

TOASTED SESAME OIL

The potent flavor of toasted sesame oil (sometimes labeled Asian sesame oil) fades quickly when exposed to heat, so we add this oil in the final moments of cooking. We use toasted sesame oil in Asian-inspired dishes, dressings, sauces, and marinades. It is highly perishable, so store it in the refrigerator.

PEANUT OIL

Refined peanut oil, such as Planters, is our first choice for deep frying. It has a neutral flavor and high smoke point, and it doesn't break down and impart off-flavors, even with prolonged heat (a problem we've had with other oils). Unrefined peanut oil, which has a nutty flavor that we like in stir-fries, is sold in small bottles for a hefty price.

STORING OILS

Aside from nut oils, which belong in the refrigerator, keep cooking oils in a cool, dark pantry to prevent rancidity.

Vinegars

Of course we use vinegars in salad dressings, but we also use them to perk up sauces, stews, soups, and bean dishes. Here are the vinegars you should stock at home.

DISTILLED WHITE VINEGAR

Made from grain alcohol, white vinegar has no added flavor and is therefore the harshest—and yet most pure—vinegar. We use it most often to make pickles and, diluted with water, as a cleaning agent for kitchen surfaces and hard-skinned fruits and vegetables.

CIDER VINEGAR

This vinegar has a tangy bite and a fruity sweetness that work perfectly in bread-and-butter pickles, barbecue sauce, and coleslaw. Unfiltered varieties of cider vinegar typically have the most apple flavor.

RED WINE VINEGAR

Use this slightly sweet, sharp vinegar for bold vinaigrettes and rich sauces—it works particularly well with potent flavors. We prefer red wine vinegars made from a blend of wine grapes and Concord grapes (typically used in grape juice) because the latter add a welcome hint of sweetness.

WHITE WINE VINEGAR

This vinegar's refined, fruity bite makes it the perfect complement to light vinaigrettes and buttery sauces. We use white wine vinegar in dishes like potato salad and hollandaise sauce, where the color of red wine vinegar would detract from the presentation.

RICE VINEGAR

Also referred to as rice wine vinegar, this vinegar is made from steamed rice. Since rice vinegar has lower acidity than other vinegars, we use it to add gentle balance to Asian-influenced marinades and dressings. Avoid cooking with seasoned rice vinegar, as it can taste overly sweet.

BALSAMIC VINEGAR

While expensive Italian balsamic vinegars are highly concentrated and aged for years, less-expensive commercial balsamic vinegars are often simply young wine vinegars with sugar and coloring added. We use this vinegar in vinaigrettes and glazes and to finish soups and sauces.

Wine

Over the years, the test kitchen has developed hundreds of recipes with wine. We've learned that you should not cook with anything you would not drink. This includes "cooking wines" sold in many supermarkets. They taste horrible and include a lot of sodium, so if the wine is cooked down it can make your recipe unappetizingly salty. That said, there's no need to spend a fortune on wine destined for sauces or stews. We've tested good $10 bottles versus better-tasting $30 wines. While we can tell a difference in the glass, we can't tell a difference in a cooked application.

RED WINE

The best red wines for cooking are medium-bodied, unoaked varieties that aren't terribly tannic. Go with blended (nonvarietal) American or Australian wines, or a French Côtes du Rhône. Heavy Cabernets are generally not the best choice for cooking.

WHITE WINE

The best white wines for cooking are medium-bodied, unoaked varieties that aren't terribly sweet. We prefer clean, crisp, dry Sauvignon Blancs to sweet Rieslings or heavily oaked Chardonnays, which can dominate subtle flavors.

VERMOUTH

Dry vermouth, with a shelf life of several months, makes a good substitute for white wine in many sauces and other savory recipes. Vermouth adds herbaceous notes to any dish and is a bit more alcoholic than white wine. Replace white wine with an equal amount of vermouth.

NONALCOHOLIC SUBSTITUTIONS FOR WINES

Broth can work as an equal replacement in sauces and stews that call for small amounts of wine. The dish won't taste exactly the same, but at least the recipe will work. For every ½ cup broth used, you should also stir in ½ teaspoon red or white wine vinegar or lemon juice before serving, which will mimic some of the acidity otherwise provided by the wine.

Broth

We prefer chicken broth to beef broth and vegetable broth, though all have their place in our recipes and we often use them in combination. When shopping for broths, you want to be careful to choose a low-sodium option in recipes where the broth is reduced to a fraction of its original volume (a sauce or risotto)—most of the liquid might be cooked off but all the salt is still there.

CHICKEN BROTH

When buying chicken broth, look for a sodium content between 400 and 700 milligrams per serving—some is critical for flavor, but too much will be overwhelming when the broth is reduced. Our favorite, Swanson Chicken Stock, achieves it's rich, meaty flavor the old fashioned way: with a relatively high percentage of meat-based protein (it contains 4 grams of protein per serving). Our Best Buy and runner-up, Better than Bouillon Chicken Base, produces a savory broth that our tasters likewise approved. Plus, as a concentrate it's an economical choice since you can use just what you need and it has a long shelf life.

BEEF BROTH

Historically, we've found beef broth to be light on beefy flavor, but that said, sometimes it adds a much-needed kick. Our top two beef broths deliver on rich, beefy flavor yet use very

COOKING WITH HOMEMADE STOCK

Yes, homemade stock tastes better than packaged broth, but the reality is that the majority of us rely on supermarket broth for most recipes. So when should you make the effort to use homemade stock? Here are some general guidelines.

When Homemade Stock Is a Must Homemade stock makes a big difference in brothy soups with simple flavorings, such as chicken noodle soup, beef noodle soup, matzo ball soup, wonton soup, and egg drop soup. The stock is the main element in all of these soups, which are all very lightly flavored (sometimes with nothing more than salt), so you can really appreciate the flavor and gelatinous consistency of the stock. We wouldn't make these soups with packaged broths.

When Homemade Stock Is Optional Soups with bold flavors, such as Mexican tortilla soup or Thai coconut chicken soup, can be made with either homemade stock or packaged broth. The flavor of the broth is still important, but it's really

in the background and you don't actually taste the stock by itself. All of these soups will taste better with homemade stock, but supermarket broth makes a fine substitute—just use a light hand with added salt since packaged broths already contain so much sodium.

When Homemade Stock Won't Make a Big Difference It's a waste to use homemade stock in dairy-rich pureed soups, such as cream of broccoli or cream of tomato soup. Also, it will be hard to appreciate homemade stock in a soup thick with beans (such as black bean soup) or a soup with lots of canned tomatoes. Packaged broth will also work just fine in all stews.

---

different ingredients. The winning brand, Rachael Ray Stock in-a-Box All-Natural Beef Flavored Stock, has a comparatively short ingredient list that starts with concentrated beef stock, giving it more fresh, real meat than other brands. The runner-up, College Inn, relies on beef, beef derivatives, and glutamate-rich additives (such as yeast extract and tomato paste) for flavor, and other additives for body.

VEGETABLE BROTH

We turn to vegetable broth for vegetarian dishes and for lighter soups or vegetable dishes that might be overwhelmed by the flavor of chicken broth. Often we use a mix of chicken and vegetable broths since vegetable broth can be too sweet when used alone. The top brands have a hefty amount of salt, along with the presence of enough actual vegetable content to be listed on the ingredient list. Swanson Vegetarian Vegetable Broth is our favorite.

Butter

When shopping for butter, you can buy salted or unsalted. In many markets, you can also buy cultured butter, which has been lightly fermented. Here's what you need to know.

SALTED BUTTER

Avoid buying salted butter for use in recipes. The amount of salt varies from brand to brand (although ⅜ teaspoon per stick is the average). In some recipes, that level of salt will ruin the dish. (A buttercream made with several sticks of salted butter will contain a teaspoon or more of salt!) In addition, salt masks the flavor nuances in butter—you taste salt, not cream. Finally, salted butter often contains more water than the amount in unsalted butter, and the excess water can interfere with the development of gluten when baking.

UNSALTED BUTTER

We use regular unsalted butter when cooking or baking. We don't think premium, high-fat butters are worth the extra money, at least for cooking; Land O'Lakes has received top ratings in test kitchen taste tests. The USDA requires that all butter must consist of at least 80 percent milk fat. (The rest is mostly water, with some milk solids, too.) Because fat costs money, regular supermarket butter rarely contains more than 80 percent. Premium butters, many of which are imported from Europe, have a slightly higher fat level; up to 86 percent. Our tasting of leading butters, both regular and premium, indicated that fat level doesn't really make much difference.

CULTURED BUTTER

Culturing, or fermenting cream before churning it into butter, is standard practice in Europe and builds tangy, complex flavors. Our tasters found it fairly easy to detect cultured butter's nuances when spread on toast, though in baking and cooking the differences are quite slight. It also tends to be more expensive, and as such, we recommend buying cultured butter for eating rather than cooking or baking.

STORING BUTTER

Butter can pick up off-flavors and turn rancid when kept in the refrigerator for longer than a month. If you don't use it much, store butter in the freezer for up to four months in a zipper-lock bag and thaw sticks as needed.

Milk, Cream, and Other Dairy Products

Fresh and cultured dairy products are common ingredients in baked goods as well as in many savory dishes. Here's what you need to know about the six most important dairy products. Refer to the Emergency Substitutions chart on page 45 for tips on replacing one type of liquid dairy with another.

MILK

Milk is a basic ingredient in many baked goods and desserts as well as some sauces. In general, we use whole milk (which is 3.5 percent fat) in the test kitchen. We have found that low-fat milk (either 2 percent or 1 percent) will work in most baking recipes, but avoid skim milk in straightforward recipes like yellow layer cake—the results will be less rich and more wan-tasting. One dish where whole milk makes a real difference is pudding, because the milk (plus half-and-half or cream typically) is responsible for the texture of the dish. Using low-fat or skim milk in these cases will cause the texture to suffer.

CREAM

Old-fashioned cream was simply the fatty liquid that floated to the top of fresh milk. Today, cream is made by removing much of the water from milk to produce a thick, rich liquid. Most cream is ultra-pasteurized—that is, heated to a very high temperature to kill bacteria, thus extending its shelf life. By law, heavy cream must consist of at least 36 percent milk fat. With this much fat, the cream can be whipped to soft peaks. Whipping cream, or light whipping cream, contains at least 30 percent fat, but despite the name it is not the best choice for whipping. We find it lighter and more airy than heavy cream when whipped, and it's not as stable, becoming watery after a few hours in the refrigerator. Either heavy cream or whipping cream will work well in savory recipes, lending creaminess and richness to soups and sauces. Unlike other forms of dairy, cream won't break when heated, so it's the best choice for casseroles or other recipes that require significant oven time.

HALF-AND-HALF

As the name suggests, half-and-half is a mixture of milk and cream. According to the USDA, half-and-half must contain 10.5 to 18 percent fat. In baked goods that call for half-and-half, you can probably get away with using whole milk (with 3.5 percent fat), but in dishes where you're looking for creaminess (not just fat and flavor), the differences will be noticeable although generally not unacceptable. Some richer pudding recipes call for half-and-half; they won't be the same when made with just milk.

BUTTERMILK

Buttermilk is a decidedly misleading word. Many assume the product is infused with butter and high in fat, when the truth is quite the opposite. The name refers to the watery end product of butter making—the "milk" left behind after the solid fat has been removed by churning cream into butter. Like most things modern, however, buttermilk is no longer the simple liquid just described.

Today buttermilk is a fermented product made by culturing whole, low-fat, or nonfat (skim) milk. Lactic acid–producing bacteria are added to milk, the milk is heated to 72 degrees, and the harmless bacteria convert lactose (milk sugar) to lactic acid, which gives the final product a slightly thickened, rich texture, and tangy, somewhat salty flavor.

Buttermilk is essential in pancakes, muffins, and many cakes. It keeps for several weeks in the refrigerator. You can also freeze it, but the emulsion will break, so blend it after thawing to re-emulsify it for salad dressings or dip. (Thawed buttermilk is fine as is in recipes for baked goods.)

YOGURT

Add bacteria to whole, low-fat, or nonfat milk and you get yogurt. We add whole-milk yogurt to sauces, soups, and dressings, and use both whole-milk and low-fat yogurt to make especially moist cakes. We don't recommend cooking with nonfat yogurt.

Greek yogurt (which also can be made with milks of varying fat levels) is thicker, drier, and tangier than ordinary yogurt. It is made by allowing the watery whey to drain from yogurt, giving it a smooth, thick texture. American-style yogurt still contains whey, so it has more moisture and a thinner, runnier consistency.

SOUR CREAM

Sour cream is made from cultured light cream (approximately 18 to 20 percent butterfat). It is pasteurized and then treated with lactic acid–producing bacteria. The bacterial action thickens the cream to a semisolid and gives the sour cream its recognizably piquant flavor. Sour cream has a markedly wet texture (the whey often floats on top) and a light, fleeting sensation when eaten. Quite versatile, it may serve as a base for dips, a topping for potatoes, or a garnish for soups, and it is also used to moisten cakes and other baked goods. When we're stirring sour cream into stews or sauces, we always do so off the heat to keep it from separating.

Cheeses

We use dozens of cheeses in the test kitchen. Here's what you need to know about the more commonly used types.

ASIAGO

This cow's-milk cheese is sold at various ages. Fresh Asiago is firm like cheddar or Havarti, and the flavor is fairly mild. Aged Asiago is drier, almost like Parmesan, and has a much sharper, saltier flavor.

BOURSIN

Boursin is a fresh cow's-milk cheese from France that is flavored with garlic and herbs (and sometimes black pepper) and has a rich, creamy character. Serve it on crackers or spread it on sandwiches and vegetables.

BRIE

Brie is a popular soft cow's-milk cheese from France that is creamy with a slight mushroom flavor, subtle nuttiness, and a white, edible rind. It is a classic choice for serving on a cheese tray. With the rind removed, it's a good melting cheese.

CAMEMBERT

Camembert is a soft cow's-milk cheese from France with an edible rind. Similar to Brie in texture, Camembert is more pungent, with a stronger flavor.

CHEDDAR

This cow's-milk cheese is made predominantly in Great Britain and the United States. The American versions are usually softer in texture, with a tangy sharpness, whereas British cheddars are drier—even crumbly—with a nutty sharpness. Older farmhouse cheddar is best eaten by itself. Young cheddar is the quintessential melting cheese. Cheddar can also be found smoked. It is made in both white and orange forms (the color comes from the addition of annatto), but we've found the flavor difference between the two is nearly imperceptible.

COLBY

Colby is a semisoft cow's-milk cheese from the United States that is very mild in flavor. One of only a few cheeses that have true American roots, Colby is a wonderful melting cheese.

EMMENTALER

This semifirm cow's-milk cheese from Switzerland and France is made into wheels sometimes as large as 200 pounds and measuring up to 3½ feet in diameter. A classic Swiss-style cheese, it has a fruity flavor with a sweet, buttery nuttiness.

FETA

A fresh cheese made from cow's, goat's, or sheep's milk (or a combination thereof), feta is a staple in many Mediterranean countries. It can be made in a variety of styles, from dry and crumbly to soft and creamy; flavors range from mild to tangy and salty. It is often crumbled over salads and eaten with fresh vegetables.

FONTINA

Known more formally as Fontina Val d'Aosta, true fontina is a semisoft cow's-milk cheese from Italy with an earthy and delicately herbaceous flavor. The domestic variety (with its bright red coating) is buttery and melts well but lacks the complex flavor of the Italian original.

GOAT CHEESE

Produced in many countries in numerous forms, goat cheeses range from creamy fresh cheeses with a mild tanginess to aged cheeses that are firm, dry, and pungent. French goat cheeses (called *chèvres*) are typically more complex in flavor than most of their American counterparts.

GORGONZOLA

Gorgonzola can be aged and quite crumbly or fairly young and creamy. Aged Gorgonzola has a much more potent blue cheese flavor, similar to Roquefort. In general, we like young Gorgonzola; its flavor is less overwhelming, and the cheese yields a luxurious, creamy sauce when melted. When shopping, look for Gorgonzola dolce (sweet Gorgonzola), or simply shop by texture. If the cheese looks creamy enough to spread on bread, it should have a pleasant but not overpowering blue cheese flavor.

GOUDA

Gouda is a semifirm to firm cow's-milk cheese from Denmark. Semisoft gouda is mild and slightly sweet, whereas aged gouda is dry and crumbly, with deep caramel flavors and a sharp zing.

GRUYÈRE

Gruyère is a semifirm cow's-milk cheese from France and Switzerland that is strong, fruity, and earthy in flavor, with a hint of honey-flavored sweetness.

JACK CHEESE

There are two types of Jack cheese, both from California and both made from cow's milk: Monterey Jack and Dry Jack. Monterey Jack is semisoft, tangy, and great for melting, whereas Dry Jack, which is aged for 7 to 10 months, is crumbly and nutty in flavor, with a flavor that's similar to a good Parmesan.

MANCHEGO

Manchego is a semifirm to firm sheep's-milk cheese from Spain that is nutty, salty, and acidic. Serve it with fresh fruit and crackers.

MASCARPONE

This creamy Italian cheese has a consistency similar to cream cheese beaten with a little heavy cream. Generally sold in tubs, American versions of mascarpone are now reasonably easy to find. Unlike American cream cheese, mascarpone is not tangy, but rather it has a buttery, creamy flavor. Although there is no substitute for authentic Italian mascarpone, we find that American versions of this highly perishable cheese are admirable and work as well as Italian mascarpone in recipes.

MOZZARELLA

The two types of mozzarella do not taste alike, and they perform quite differently in the kitchen. Shrink-wrapped mozzarella is fine for pizzas. It melts beautifully, and no one notices how bland this cheese is when covered with pepperoni and tomato sauce. However, in simple salads, we prefer fresh mozzarella packed in water. This type of mozzarella has a milky, sometimes floral flavor and a moist, appealing texture. We generally prefer the richer flavor of whole-milk mozzarella, although part-skim mozzarella can be used successfully in most recipes.

PARMESAN

When it comes to buying Parmesan, there are a wide range of options, from the whitish powder in green-topped containers to imported wedges. Parmesan is classified as a grana-type cheese, a hard, grainy cheese made from cow's milk. We recommend authentic Italian Parmigiano-Reggiano, which has a depth and complexity of flavor and a smooth, melting texture that none of the others can match. Most of the other Parmesan-type cheeses are too salty and one-dimensional; we suggest spending the money on the real deal. When shopping, make sure the words "Parmigiano-Reggiano" are stenciled on the golden rind.

PECORINO ROMANO

Pecorino Romano is a bone-white cheese with an intense peppery flavor and a strong sheepy quality. Like Parmesan, Pecorino Romano is designed for grating, but it has a much saltier and more pungent flavor. It works best in dishes with assertive ingredients like capers, olives, or red pepper flakes. It is traditionally made entirely from sheep's milk, although some manufacturers add some cow's milk to reduce the pungency and/or save money. In Italy, pecorino is often sold fresh or lightly aged and served as an eating cheese. These young pecorinos are not widely known elsewhere; most of the pecorino that is exported has been aged much longer.

PROVOLONE

Provolone, a cow's-milk cheese from Italy, is made in two styles. The semifirm mild version is widely available and is usually sold sliced. There is also a firm, aged style that is salty, nutty, and spicy, with a light caramel sweetness. The latter makes a nice addition to any cheese platter.

RICOTTA

Good ricotta is creamy and thick, not watery and curdish like so many supermarket brands sold in plastic containers. In Italy, local cheesemakers produce fresh ricotta with a dry, firm consistency that's similar to goat cheese, and its flavor is sweet and milky. This cheese is so perishable that it is rarely exported. In the United States, however, locally made fresh ricotta is available in and near urban centers with large Italian-American populations. This cheese shares many qualities with the Italian version. You can use supermarket ricotta cheese, but it tastes bland by comparison.

RICOTTA SALATA

Fresh ricotta cheese is salted and pressed to make this firm but crumbly cheese with a texture that is similar to feta but with a flavor that is milder and far less salty. Ricotta salata is pleasingly piquant, although it is milder than pecorino. Ricotta salata is generally shredded and used like mozzarella in baked pasta dishes, or tossed with hot pasta when a sharper, saltier cheese flavor is desired.

ROQUEFORT

Roquefort is a blue-veined sheep's-milk cheese from France. Aged in specially designated caves, it's probably the oldest cheese known. Roquefort's flavor is bold but not overpowering, salty with a slight mineral tinge.

STORING CHEESES

For long-term storage in the refrigerator, we find that cheeses are best wrapped in parchment paper and then in aluminum foil. The paper allows the cheese to breathe a bit, while the foil keeps out off-flavors from the refrigerator and prevents the cheese from drying out. Simply placing the cheese in a plastic bag, pressing out all the air, and then sealing the bag tightly is our second choice. We find that pressing plastic wrap directly against the surface of most cheeses will cause a slight sour flavor to develop over time, and we do not recommend this storage method.

PREPARING CHEESES

We prefer the rasp-style grater when handling hard "grating" cheeses like Parmesan or Pecorino Romano, although you can certainly grate these cheeses on the fine holes of a coarse grater. For shredded semisoft cheeses, like mozzarella or fontina, we recommend using the large holes of a coarse grater. Although you can shred semisoft cheeses with the shredding disk of a food processor, the metal blade of a food processor does a poor job of grating hard cheese, so we don't recommend using this otherwise versatile appliance for this purpose.

Flour

There are many types of flour, not to mention brands, and each has its place and special use. The main difference between types of flour is the amount of protein they contain, which varies depending on what type of wheat is used.

ALL-PURPOSE FLOUR

All-purpose flour has a moderate protein level (9 to 12 percent). We prefer unbleached flour over bleached because we've found that bleached flour sometimes carries off-flavors that can be detected in simple recipes like bread and biscuits. In the test kitchen, we develop recipes with widely available Pillsbury unbleached (10.5 percent protein). Gold Medal unbleached (also 10.5 percent protein) offers comparable results. If you use a higher protein all-purpose flour (such as King Arthur, with 11.7 percent protein) in our recipes, the results may be slightly drier and chewier. You can lower the protein content of higher protein all-purpose flour by replacing 1 tablespoon of flour per cup with 1 tablespoon of cornstarch.

BREAD FLOUR

Bread flour has a high protein level (12 percent or above) and is often labeled "made for bread machines." The high protein content ensures strong gluten development and a sturdy dough, which translates to good flavor, chewy texture, and a crisp crust. Not all breads and pizzas require bread flour, so be sure to check the recipe before shopping.

CAKE FLOUR

Cake flour has a low protein level (6 to 8 percent) and delivers delicate, fine-crumbed cakes and light, airy biscuits. Not all cakes require cake flour, and we call for it only in a few recipes, like angel food cake, where we feel it delivers decidedly better results than all-purpose flour. You can also approximate cake flour by mixing cornstarch with all-purpose flour. For each cup of cake flour, use $7/8$ cup all-purpose flour mixed with 2 tablespoons cornstarch. Cake flour is rarely used in pizza or bread recipes.

WHOLE-WHEAT FLOUR

Whole-wheat flour has a high protein level (about 13 percent) and a distinctive flavor and texture because it is made from the entire wheat berry. A wheat berry has three elements: the outer bran layer, the germ, and the endosperm (white flours are ground solely from the endosperm). Whole-wheat flour behaves very differently than white flour. That said, you can often replace up to one-third of the all-purpose or bread flour in a recipe with an equal amount of whole-wheat flour and still obtain good results.

STORING FLOUR

To make measuring neat and easy, we recommend storing flour in a large widemouthed airtight container. Whole-wheat flour contains more fat than refined flours like all-purpose and can turn rancid quickly at room temperature. For this reason, we recommend storing all whole-grain flours in the freezer. We keep refined flours in the pantry away from light and heat. Of course, refined flours certainly can go into the freezer, too. However, make sure to bring all flours kept in the freezer back to room temperature before using them. (Cold flour can inhibit rise in bread and yield dense loaves.)

Sugar and Other Sweeteners

Sugar and its variants are commonly produced from either sugarcane or sugar beets. Here's what you need to stock at home. Refer to the Emergency Substitutions chart on page 45 for tips on replacing one type of sweetener with another.

GRANULATED SUGAR

Granulated sugar is, of course, widely available and is the sugar most commonly used in cooking.

SUPERFINE SUGAR

Superfine sugar is finely processed granulated sugar that dissolves more readily than conventional granulated sugar; it is sometimes used in baking, especially in items that have a delicate texture.

CONFECTIONERS' SUGAR

Confectioners', or powdered, sugar is finely milled sugar that has been mixed with cornstarch to prevent clumping. Confectioners' sugar is used for dusting cakes and cookies and in making quick glazes and icings.

BROWN SUGAR

Light and dark brown sugar are granulated sugars that have been flavored with molasses. Light brown sugar contains about 3 percent molasses; dark brown sugar has twice that. If light or brown is not specified in a recipe, you can use them interchangeably.

MOLASSES

Molasses is a dark, thick syrup that is the by-product of sugarcane refining. Molasses comes in three types: light or mild, dark or robust, and blackstrap. We prefer either light or dark molasses in baking and generally avoid using bitter blackstrap molasses.

STORING SWEETENERS

Most sugars do best in an airtight container away from heat and moisture, but follow these additional tips for specific sweeteners.

Brown Sugar When brown sugar comes into contact with air, the moisture in the sugar evaporates, and the sugar turns rock-hard. Store brown sugar in a sealed container with a terra-cotta Brown Sugar Bear, which gets a brief soak in water before being added to the sugar. If brown sugar becomes hard, it can be revived: Place the hardened sugar in a bowl with a slice of sandwich bread, cover the bowl, and microwave for 10 to 20 seconds.

Molasses and Honey Keep molasses and honey in the pantry (in the fridge, molasses temporarily turns into a thick, unpourable sludge, and honey crystallizes). If honey crystallizes, put the opened jar in a saucepan filled with 1 inch of water, and heat the honey until it reaches 160 degrees (make sure the container is heatproof).

Maple Syrup Because of its high moisture level and lack of preservatives, maple syrup is susceptible to the growth of yeasts, molds, and bacteria. Refrigeration not only helps it retain flavor but also prevents microorganisms from growing. Once opened, it will keep six months to a year in the refrigerator. For long-term storage, maple syrup can be kept in the freezer without suffering any flavor degradation. It will never freeze solid because of the high sugar concentration. At most, the syrup will become thick, viscous, or crystallized during freezing, but a quick zap in the microwave will restore it.

Leaveners

Baked goods generally rely on a chemical leavener (baking soda and/or baking powder) or yeast for lift. Without some sort of leavener, most baked goods would be very dense and/or very flat. When shopping for yeast, keep in mind that there are a few different types sold in markets.

CAKE YEAST

Cake yeast, aka fresh yeast or compressed yeast, is stocked in the refrigerator section of the store. This type of yeast, sold as little cubes, is reliably active, but very perishable, which is why cake yeast is used more often in commercial bakeries than in the home kitchen.

ACTIVE DRY YEAST

Active dry yeast sold in packets or jars is probably called for the most in bread recipes. (However, we prefer instant yeast; see below.) To produce active dry yeast, yeast is given heat treatment that kills the outermost cells. Therefore, in order to use active dry yeast, the granules must first be proofed, or dissolved in liquid, with some sugar to speed up the process. Proofing sloughs off the dead cells and renders the yeast active. To substitute active dry for instant yeast, use 25 percent more active dry. For example, if the recipe calls for 1 teaspoon of instant yeast, use 1¼ teaspoons of active dry. And don't forget to proof the yeast—that is, dissolve it in a portion of the water called for in the recipe, heated to 105 degrees.

INSTANT (RAPID-RISE) YEAST

Instant, or rapid-rise, yeast is much like active dry yeast, but it has undergone a gentler drying process that has not destroyed the outer cells. Instant yeast does not require proofing and can be added directly to the dry ingredients when making bread—hence the name "instant." Our recipes call for instant yeast because it's easier to use. We have also found that when making basic breads, such as baguettes, that contain just flour, salt, water, and yeast, instant yeast yields a cleaner, purer flavor than active dry yeast because it doesn't contain any dead yeast cells. However, in breads that contain butter, sugar, and other flavorings, we find virtually no difference in flavor between instant and active dry yeasts. If you have a recipe that calls for active dry yeast, you can use instant as long as you reduce the amount of yeast by 25 percent. For example if the recipe calls for 1 packet, or 2¼ teaspoons, of active dry yeast, use 1¾ teaspoons of instant yeast. You don't need to proof the yeast; just add it to the dry ingredients.

BAKING SODA

Baking soda is a leavener that provides lift to cakes, muffins, biscuits, and other baked goods. When baking soda, which is alkaline, encounters an acidic ingredient (such as sour cream, buttermilk, or brown sugar), carbon and oxygen combine to form carbon dioxide. The tiny bubbles of carbon dioxide then lift up the dough. Baking soda also promotes browning.

BAKING POWDER

Baking powder also creates carbon dioxide to provide lift to a wide range of baked goods. The active ingredients in baking powder are baking soda and an acidic element, such as cream of tartar. It also contains cornstarch to absorb moisture and keep the powder dry. Cooks use baking powder rather than baking soda when there is no natural acidity in the batter.

There are two kinds of baking powder. A single-acting baking powder has only one acid combined with the baking soda: a quick-acting acid that begins to work when liquid is added to the batter. A double-acting baking powder (like most supermarket brands) has two acids added to the baking soda: The second acid (often sodium aluminum sulfate) begins to work only when the dish is put in the oven, after the temperature has climbed above 120 degrees.

We recommend using double-acting baking powder in all recipes—baked goods rise higher since most of the rise with baking powder occurs at oven temperatures. Double-acting baking powder also provides sufficient lift in the oven to allow you to bake frozen dough. Also, we have found that single-acting baking powder doesn't provide sufficient leavening for doughs with little liquid, such as scones or muffins.

STORING YEAST AND CHEMICAL LEAVENERS

Keep baking powder and baking soda in the pantry. Despite most manufacturer claims of one year, our tests have proven baking powder loses its potency after six months. Put yeast in the refrigerator or freezer to slow deterioration. And because yeast is a living organism, the expiration date on the package should be observed.

INGREDIENT ASSUMPTIONS WE MAKE IN OUR RECIPES

Unless a recipe in this book specifically states otherwise, you should assume the following ingredients rules are being observed.

Flour: Unbleached, all-purpose
Sugar: Granulated
Salt: Table
Kosher Salt: Diamond Crystal (see Emergency Substitutions chart, Table Salt, opposite, if using Morton)
Pepper: Freshly ground black
Spices: Ground

Herbs: Fresh
Broths: Low-sodium
Butter: Unsalted
Eggs: Large
Dairy: Whole milk, or full-fat (although low-fat will generally work; skim won't)

Emergency Substitutions

No one wants to run out to the market for just one ingredient. Perhaps something you've got on hand will do the trick. We tested scores of widely published ingredient substitutions to figure out which ones work under what circumstances and which ones simply don't work. Below is a list of ingredients commonly called for in recipes and the items you are likely to have on hand that will work as substitutions.

TO REPLACE	AMOUNT	SUBSTITUTE				
Whole Milk	1 cup	⅝ cup skim milk + ⅜ cup half-and-half ⅔ cup 1 percent low-fat milk + ⅓ cup half-and-half ¾ cup 2 percent low-fat milk + ¼ cup half-and-half ⅞ cup skim milk + ⅛ cup heavy cream				
Half-and-Half	1 cup	¾ cup whole milk + ¼ cup heavy cream ⅔ cup skim or low-fat milk + ⅓ cup heavy cream				
Heavy Cream	1 cup	1 cup evaporated milk *Not suitable for whipping or baking, but fine for soups and sauces.*				
Eggs	LARGE	JUMBO	EXTRA-LARGE	MEDIUM	*For half of an egg,*	
	1	1	1	1	*whisk the yolk and*	
	2	1½	2	2	*white together and*	
	3	2½	2½	3½	*use half of the liquid.*	
	4	3	3½	4½		
	5	4	4	6		
	6	5	5	7		
Buttermilk	1 cup	¾ cup plain whole-milk or low-fat yogurt + ¼ cup whole milk 1 cup whole milk + 1 tablespoon lemon juice or distilled white vinegar *Not suitable for raw applications, such as a buttermilk dressing.*				
Sour Cream	1 cup	1 cup plain whole-milk yogurt *Nonfat and low-fat yogurts are too lean to replace sour cream.*				
Plain Yogurt	1 cup	1 cup sour cream				
Cake Flour	1 cup	⅞ cup all-purpose flour + 2 tablespoons cornstarch				
Bread Flour	1 cup	1 cup all-purpose flour *Bread and pizza crusts may bake up with slightly less chew.*				
Baking Powder	1 teaspoon	¼ teaspoon baking soda + ½ teaspoon cream of tartar (use right away)				
Light Brown Sugar	1 cup	1 cup granulated sugar + 1 tablespoon molasses	*Pulse the molasses in a food processor*			
Dark Brown Sugar	1 cup	1 cup granulated sugar + 2 tablespoons molasses	*along with the sugar or simply add it along with the other wet ingredients.*			
Confectioners' Sugar	1 cup	1 cup granulated sugar + 1 teaspoon cornstarch, ground in a blender (not a food processor) *Works well for dusting over cakes, less so in frostings and glazes.*				
Table Salt	1 teaspoon	1½ teaspoons Morton Kosher Salt or fleur de sel 2 teaspoons Diamond Crystal Kosher Salt or Maldon Sea Salt *Not recommended for use in baking recipes.*				
Fresh Herbs	1 tablespoon	1 teaspoon dried herbs				
Wine	½ cup	½ cup broth + 1 teaspoon wine vinegar (added just before serving) ½ cup broth + 1 teaspoon lemon juice (added just before serving) *Vermouth makes an acceptable substitute for white wine.*				
Unsweetened Chocolate	1 ounce	3 tablespoons cocoa powder + 1 tablespoon vegetable oil 1½ ounces bittersweet or semisweet chocolate (remove 1 tablespoon sugar from the recipe)				
Bittersweet or Semisweet Chocolate	1 ounce	⅔ ounce unsweetened chocolate + 2 teaspoons sugar *Works well with fudgy brownies. Do not use in a custard or cake.*				

Inside This Chapter

CHAPTER 2

How to Cook Eggs

As an ingredient, eggs are indispensable in the kitchen. They can bind, thicken, emulsify, clarify, and even leaven. They are also versatile on their own and can be prepared in a number of ways: fried, scrambled, poached, hard-cooked, or made into omelets and frittatas. In general, you want to cook eggs until they are set. But with continued cooking eggs quickly turn rubbery and tough. The difference between perfection and failure is generally a minute or less, so good cooking technique really matters. Also see chapter 18 (page 755) for information on making custards.

Getting Started

How to Buy Eggs

FRESHNESS

Egg cartons are marked with both a sell-by date and a pack date. The pack date is the day the eggs were graded and packed, which is generally a week within being laid but, legally, may be within as much as 30 days. The pack date is printed on egg cartons as a three-digit code just below the sell-by date, and it runs consecutively from 001 (January 1) to 365 (December 31).

The sell-by date, which is the legal limit set by the USDA, is within 30 days of the pack date. In short, a carton of eggs may be up to two months old by the end of the sell-by date. Even so, according to the U.S. Department of Agriculture (USDA), eggs are still fit for consumption for an additional three to five weeks past the sell-by date.

In the test kitchen, we tasted two- and three-month-old eggs and found them perfectly palatable. At four months, the white was very loose and the yolk tasted faintly of the refrigerator, though it was still edible. Our advice is to use your discretion. If the eggs smell odd or display discoloration, pitch them. Older eggs also lack the structure-lending properties of fresh eggs, so beware when baking.

COLOR

The shell's hue depends on the breed of the chicken. The run-of-the-mill leghorn chicken produces the typical white egg. Brown-feathered birds, such as Rhode Island Reds, produce ecru- to coffee-colored eggs. Despite marketing hype extolling the virtues of nonwhite eggs, our tests proved that shell color has no effect on flavor.

FARM-FRESH AND ORGANIC

In our taste tests, farm-fresh eggs were standouts. The large yolks were shockingly orange and sat very high above the comparatively small whites, and the flavor of these eggs was exceptionally rich and complex. The organic eggs followed in second place, with eggs from hens raised on a vegetarian diet in third, and the standard supermarket eggs last. Differences were easily detected in egg-based dishes like an omelet or a frittata but not in cakes or cookies.

EGGS AND OMEGA-3

Several companies are marketing eggs with a high level of omega-3 fatty acids, the healthful unsaturated fats also found in some fish. We set up a blind tasting of eggs containing various levels of omega-3. Our finding: More omega-3s translates into a richer egg flavor and a deeper yolk color. Why? Commercially raised chickens usually peck on corn and soy, while chickens on an omega-3-enriched diet have supplements of greens, flaxseeds, and algae, which also add flavor, complexity, and color. When shopping for a good egg, buyer beware: Brands may claim a high level of omega-3s, but the fine print sometimes reveals that the number refers to the level present in two eggs, not one. Look for brands that guarantee at least 200 milligrams per egg.

EGG SIZES

Eggs vary in size, which will make a difference in recipes, especially those that call for several eggs. We use large eggs in our recipes. If you do the math, you can substitute one size for another. For instance, four jumbo eggs are equivalent to five large eggs (both weigh 10 ounces).

APPROXIMATE WEIGHTS OF EGG SIZES	
Medium	1.75 ounces
Large	2.00 ounces
Extra-Large	2.25 ounces
Jumbo	2.50 ounces

EGG SUBSTITUTES

Egg substitutes are made with egg whites (some brands contain up to 99 percent egg whites) along with a mixture of vegetable gums, dairy products, vitamins and other nutrients, water, and coloring agents. We tasted both refrigerated and frozen egg substitutes against whole eggs in a basic scrambled egg recipe. Not surprisingly, the real eggs were the runaway winners. Only one brand, refrigerated Egg Beaters Original (not to be confused with frozen or flavored Egg Beaters), could ever be considered an alternative; despite an unnaturally bright yellow color and a slightly spongy texture, the scrambled eggs made with this product had decent flavor that our tasters found acceptable. Scrambled eggs made with the other products tasted disturbingly artificial or had a texture akin to watery cottage cheese.

The egg substitutes fare much better in baking tests. Our tasters couldn't distinguish between cakes, cookies, and brownies made with real eggs and those made with substitutes. Feel free to use egg substitutes in any baked good, replacing each whole egg in a recipe with ¼ cup of egg substitute.

LIQUID EGG WHITES

Chances are good that you're tossing egg yolks down the drain when making recipes that call for egg whites only. A better option might be liquid egg whites. We tested three brands of liquid egg whites alongside hand-separated whites in our recipes for egg white omelets, meringue cookies, and angel food cake. They all made acceptable substitutes in omelets; in baked goods, however, they came up a bit short—literally. The USDA requires that liquid egg whites be pasteurized, and this process compromises the whites' structure. As a result they can't achieve the same volume when whipped as fresh whites. Our top-ranked Eggology 100% Egg Whites are a good substitute for fresh whites in omelets, scrambles, and frittatas, and they make satisfactory baked goods.

Storing Tips

REFRIGERATOR

Eggs suffer more from improper storage than age. If your refrigerator has an egg tray in the door, don't use it—eggs should be stored on the shelf, where the temperature is below 40 degrees (average refrigerator door temperature in our kitchen is closer to 45 degrees). Eggs are best stored in their cardboard carton, which protects them from absorbing flavors from other foods. The carton also helps maintain humidity, which slows down evaporation of the eggs' contents.

FREEZER

Extra whites can be frozen for later use, but we have found their rising properties compromised (angel food cake didn't rise quite as well). Frozen whites are best in recipes that call for small amounts (an egg wash) or don't depend on whipping (an omelet). Yolks can't be frozen as is, but adding sugar syrup (2 parts sugar to 1 part water) to the yolks allows them to be frozen. Stir a scant ¼ teaspoon sugar syrup per yolk into the yolks before freezing. Defrosted yolks treated this way will behave just like fresh yolks in custards and other recipes.

Cold vs. Room Temperature

Unless otherwise directed, you should keep eggs in the refrigerator until needed. However, some baking recipes call for room-temperature eggs. So when are room-temperature eggs essential?

In the test kitchen, we compared yellow cakes made with cold eggs against cakes made with room-temperature eggs and found both acceptable. Yes, the cake made with room-temperature eggs had a slightly finer, more even crumb, but the cake made with cold eggs was similar (although it did take an extra 5 minutes to bake). Cold eggs did cause a problem when we tested finickier recipes, such as pound cake and chiffon cake. These recipes rely on air beaten into the eggs as a primary means of leavening. Cold eggs didn't whip as well as room-temperature eggs, and the resulting cakes baked up quite dense.

In sum, if a recipe says to use room-temperature eggs, there's probably a good reason. You can let eggs sit out on the counter for an hour, or you can speed up the process by placing the eggs in a bowl of warm water for about 5 minutes.

Safety Tips

The Egg Safety Center estimates that one in 20,000 eggs is contaminated by salmonella bacteria. Salmonella, if present, can be on the outside of the eggshell or inside the egg if the hen that laid it was infected.

COOKING

Salmonella is destroyed at 160 degrees. Eggs that have just barely set or are still runny will not reach this temperature. Eggs that are fully set and dry, as they are when hard-cooked or used in a frittata, will reach this temperature.

SHOPPING

Pasteurized eggs have been put through a washing process that kills bacteria. For the most part, we found that they performed on par with standard eggs in applications (such as mayonnaise) in which pasteurized eggs might be beneficial; we had less success using them in cakes and cookies.

Essential Equipment

While a handful of recipes, like quiche and soufflé, require particular baking dishes, for most egg-based recipes you only need a few pieces of equipment, which you probably already have on hand.

NONSTICK SKILLET

Most egg recipes are best prepared in a nonstick skillet. Yes, for many centuries cooks scrambled and fried eggs in conventional skillets, but they used more fat and still had problems with eggs sticking. Pay close attention to the size of the skillet called for in the recipe. In many cases, we crowd eggs into a relatively small skillet to keep them from drying out. For more details on what to look for, see page 22.

HEAT-RESISTANT RUBBER SPATULA

Nonstick skillets demand nonstick tools, and a rubber spatula is key, whether you're making scrambled eggs or a frittata. Our favorite model has a wide, stiff blade and thin, flexible edges. For more details on what to look for, see page 31.

WHISK

A whisk is essential for dishes like frittatas and quiches, when you must whip whole eggs until yolks and whites are thoroughly combined. Choose a whisk that is long and narrow, with tines that are flexible but sturdy. For more details on what to look for, see page 31.

How to Crack and Separate Eggs

ESSENTIAL EQUIPMENT

• small glass bowls

Everyone can crack an egg but not everyone can perform this task cleanly, without getting bits of shell mixed in when separating the yolk and white. Separated eggs are often called for; a dish may require lift from whipped whites, more richness from yolks, or moisture or structure from additional whites. There are several gadgets that assist in separating the yolk from the white; however, we think it's just as easy to use either the broken shell or your hand.

We strongly recommend that you separate eggs when they are cold. Yolks are more taut and less apt to break into the whites when cold. Since even a speck of yolk in the whites can prevent them from whipping properly, separating eggs when cold is especially important in dishes like soufflés that rely on whipped whites for volume. If a recipe calls for separated eggs at room temperature, separate the eggs while cold, cover both bowls with plastic wrap (make sure the wrap touches the surface of the eggs to keep them from drying out), and let sit on the counter.

1. CRACK ON COUNTER
Crack side of egg against flat surface of counter or cutting board.
WHY? Cracking the egg on a flat surface, rather than the edge of the counter or a mixing bowl, results in the cleanest break, and you should always aim to crack an egg cleanly. A clean break not only eliminates those annoying bits of shell that can wind up in a batter, it makes using the shell to separate whites from yolks easier, too.

2A. SEPARATE WITH SHELL
Holding broken shell halves over bowl, gently transfer egg yolk back and forth between them, letting egg white fall between shells and into bowl.
WHY? As long as the shell splits neatly into two pieces, this method is easy and your hands stay relatively clean.

2B. SEPARATE BY HAND
Cup your hand over bowl, then open cracked egg into palm. Slowly unclench fingers to allow white to slide through and into bowl, leaving yolk intact in palm.
WHY? This method is a good option if the shell has not split neatly into two halves. If using your hands, make sure they are very clean, especially if you plan on whipping the whites.

3. USE THREE BOWLS
Separate each egg over first bowl and let white fall in. Transfer yolk to second bowl and pour white into third bowl.
WHY? When you're separating eggs for whipping the whites, the merest amount of yolk will prevent whites from whipping. By using this method, if you happen to get yolk into the white when separating an egg, you can simply throw out that one egg (or use it in another recipe that calls for whole eggs)—much better than separating a dozen eggs only to drop some yolk from the last egg into a big bowl of clean whites.

How to Whip Egg Whites

Whipped egg whites provide lift and structure to cakes (think angel food), soufflés, and countless other dishes. Perfectly whipped egg whites begin with a scrupulously clean bowl—fat inhibits egg whites from whipping properly.

Choosing the right bowl is essential too. Bowls made from plastic, a petroleum product with a porous surface, retain an oily film even when washed carefully and should not be used for whipping egg whites. Glass and ceramic should be avoided as well, as their slippery surfaces make it harder for whites to billow up. The two best choices are stainless steel and, for those who have it, copper. Wash the bowl in soapy, hot-as-you-can-stand-it water, rinse with more hot water, and dry with paper towels. A dish towel may have traces of oil within its fibers that could be transferred to the bowl. Also see How to Crack and Separate Eggs (opposite page).

ESSENTIAL EQUIPMENT

- stand mixer, or hand-held mixer and large stainless steel or copper bowl

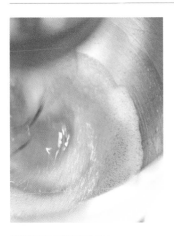

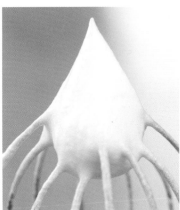

1. START LOW

Whip egg whites and pinch cream of tartar (with whisk attachment if using stand mixer) on medium-low speed until foamy, about 1 minute.
WHY? Starting slowly breaks up the whites and ensures that the cream of tartar is evenly distributed. Whites that are gradually beaten to the desired texture will be more stable. Cream of tartar is a white powder sold in the spice aisle. This dry acid helps egg whites whip to a large and more stable volume.

2. INCREASE SPEED (AND ADD SUGAR)

Increase mixer speed to medium-high, adding sugar if called for. Continue to whip whites until soft and billowy.
WHY? Once the eggs are foamy, you can increase the mixer speed. We find that it's best to get some air into the eggs before adding the sugar. If the sugar is added sooner, the foam can be less stable; if it's added later, it won't dissolve.

3A–3B. SLOW DOWN AND ASSESS

Turn off mixer and lift tip of whisk from whites. Soft peaks (left) will droop slightly downward. Stiff peaks (right) will stand tall.
WHY? Overbeaten eggs can ruin a recipe, so it's best to reduce the mixer speed when you think you're getting close. We often detach the whisk and use it to gently finish the job by hand. With the whisk attachment in your hand, it's also easy to assess the progress of the whites.

4. AVOID OVERBEATING

Overbeaten whites will look curdled and separated.
WHY? The beating action turns liquid egg whites into a voluminous foam. More beating will yield a more voluminous, more stable foam, but only to a point. If you stretch the egg white proteins too much, the network that supports the foam will rupture, squeezing out the liquid contained in the whites. The result is a curdled mess, and you must start over with fresh whites.

How to Hard-Cook Eggs

Hard-cooked eggs can be eaten on their own or used in myriad recipes, from egg salad to deviled eggs. You might think it's the easiest way to cook an egg, but all too often boiling produces eggs with a greenish-colored yolk and a sulfurous odor. The boiling is the problem, which is why we think the process is best called "hard-cooking" rather than "hard-boiling." The classic method—cooking the eggs in a pot of boiling water for a precise period of time—doesn't account for variations in heat output of stoves or conductivity of pans. And because the water is boiling, the margin for error is quite small. Since you can't tell when the eggs are done, this method is unreliable.

After countless tests, we found that we got the best results when we covered the eggs with an inch of water, brought it to a boil, covered the pan, and removed it from the heat. After 10 minutes, we drained the eggs and cooled them in ice water. The residual heat perfectly cooked the eggs, and since the pot is off the heat there's no chance of overcooking.

ESSENTIAL EQUIPMENT

- medium saucepan with lid
- large bowl
- liquid measuring cup
- slotted spoon

1. ADD EGGS FIRST
Place eggs in medium saucepan in single layer and cover with 1 inch of tap water.
WHY? With each egg resting on the bottom of the pan, they will cook evenly. If you're cooking more than six eggs, you might want to switch to a Dutch oven. The timing will be the same as long as the eggs are kept in a single layer.

2. BRING TO BOIL
Turn heat to high and bring water to boil.
WHY? Since this recipe relies on residual heat to cook the eggs, it's important that the water comes to a boil. Look for large, rolling bubbles on the surface.

3. TAKE POT OFF HEAT
Once water is boiling, remove pot from heat, cover with lid, and set timer for 10 minutes.
WHY? A tight-fitting lid traps heat and ensures that the water doesn't cool off too quickly. If you want slightly undercooked eggs with creamy yolks (perfect for egg salad; see recipe on page 80), then set the timer for 8 minutes.

4. MAKE ICE BATH
While eggs cook off heat, fill large bowl with 4 cups cold water and 4 cups ice cubes.
WHY? The ice bath will stop the eggs from cooking further. If you skip this step, residual heat trapped inside the egg will turn a perfectly cooked egg into an overcooked egg.

5. POUR OFF WATER, CRACK EGGS
When timer goes off, immediately pour off water from saucepan and gently shake pan back and forth to crack egg shells.
WHY? A perfectly cooked egg isn't much good if you can't remove the shell. Cracking the shells at this point allows water in the ice bath to get under the shells, and this helps to loosen them. The cracked eggs also cool off more quickly.

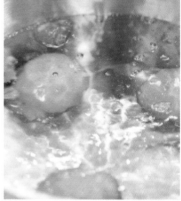

6. TRANSFER EGGS TO WATER BATH

Use slotted spoon to transfer eggs to ice bath and let sit for 5 minutes.

WHY? Once the shells are cracked, get them into the ice bath to cool. The draining, cracking, and transferring process should take less than 1 minute.

7. PEEL IN ONE STRIP

Starting at wider end of each egg, peel away shell in one strip.

WHY? If you try to remove the peel bit by bit, you will end up sticking your fingernail into the white and making unattractive gouges. The wider end of the egg actually contains an air pocket, so you can tear this part of the shell away without harming the white. With some of the shell in your hand, the rest should come off quite easily.

8. RINSE OFF STRAY BITS

If necessary, dunk egg back into ice bath to remove any remaining bits of shell.

WHY? It's easy to shake loose tiny bits of shell when the peeled egg is submerged; this way you don't risk any gouges.

Troubleshooting Hard-Cooked Eggs

PROBLEM	SOLUTION
I want perfectly centered yolks.	For attractive deviled eggs, it helps if the yolks are perfectly centered. (If they are not, you can tear the white when removing the yolk.) Fresh eggs are the best choice for this kind of recipe. (If you're dicing eggs for egg salad, it doesn't matter.) That's because the cordlike strands that center the yolk weaken with age. If in doubt, place the carton of eggs on its side in the refrigerator the day before the eggs are to be cooked. This moves the yolk away from the large end of the egg—which is where the yolk generally settles after packaging—and toward the center.
I want to hard-cook eggs in advance.	Hard-cooked eggs can be refrigerated for up to 3 days. If they have been shelled, make sure to store them in an airtight container so they don't pick up odors in your fridge. You can also refrigerate the eggs without peeling them, but if you do, skip the cracking step and simply transfer the cooked eggs to the ice bath. It will be more difficult to peel the eggs once they have been in the refrigerator for a few days.

How to Fry Eggs

ESSENTIAL EQUIPMENT

Anyone can make fried eggs, but few and far between are the cooks who can make them perfectly every time. Eggs can stick, yolks can break, and over- or undercooking is the norm.

The first thing to do when about to fry an egg is to reach for a nonstick skillet. The initial heat setting is also important: A five-minute preheating of the skillet over very low heat puts it at just the right temperature. Cover the skillet as soon as the eggs are added and cook 2 to 3 minutes. Since burners vary, it may take cooking an egg or two to determine the ideal heat setting for your stovetop. Follow visual cues and increase or lower the heat if necessary (if the butter melts and browns in less than a minute, it's too hot). You can use bacon grease in place of the butter for really tasty fried eggs. Unlike butter, however, bacon grease will not go through visual changes that you can use to gauge the skillet's heat. Exact amounts for each ingredient and skillet size depends on the number of servings; see chart on opposite page.

- 10- or 12-inch nonstick skillet with lid
- small bowls or teacups
- thin, wide nonstick spatula

1. HEAT EMPTY SKILLET

Heat nonstick skillet over low heat for 5 minutes. **WHY?** If the skillet is even slightly too hot, the whites will toughen before the yolks are set. And if the skillet is very hot, there's little chance of producing runny yolks. Heating the skillet over low heat ensures that it is evenly heated (no cold spots) but not searing hot. A heavy-bottomed skillet will heat more evenly than one that is lightweight and is preferred in this recipe.

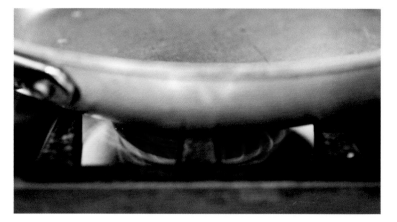

2. CRACK EGGS INTO BOWLS

While skillet heats, crack egg(s) into small bowls or teacups.
WHY? Cracking the eggs right into the skillet means that the first egg will get a head start and possibly overcook. The bowls ensure that all the eggs start at the same time. Also, if you crack the eggs into the skillet you risk cooking bits of shell with the eggs. If you crack the eggs into bowls, you can fish out any shell before cooking. The bowls make it easier to get the eggs into the skillet without breaking the yolks. That's because you can place the lip of the bowl very close to the skillet surface and basically slide the eggs out. This process is much gentler than dropping the cracked eggs directly into the skillet.

3. SWIRL BUTTER IN HOT SKILLET

Add unsalted butter to skillet. Let butter melt and foam. When foam subsides, swirl skillet to distribute fat evenly.
WHY? Butter makes fried eggs taste great. If you heat the butter when preheating the skillet, the butter will burn. Adding the butter to the hot skillet is a great way to check the pan's temperature. This entire process should take about 1 minute; if the butter melts and browns in less than a minute, the skillet is too hot and you'll want to take it off the heat and start over.

4. ADD EGGS SIMULTANEOUSLY

Working quickly, position bowls on either side of skillet and add eggs simultaneously.

WHY? Eggs that start at the same time will finish at the same time. Adding the eggs from opposite sides of the skillet ensures that each egg has plenty of room to cook.

5. SEASON EGGS AND COVER

Season eggs with salt and pepper and cover skillet immediately.

WHY? The eggs need seasonings, but don't dawdle. The cold eggs will lower the temperature of the skillet, and if you don't get the lid on quickly, the timing will be off.

6. CHECK EARLY

Set timer for 2 minutes for runny yolks, 2½ minutes for soft but set yolks, and 3 minutes for firmly set yolks. After allotted time, remove lid and check eggs. If necessary, cover and continue cooking to desired doneness. Transfer eggs to plate and serve.

WHY? If the eggs are slightly undercooked, you can always put the cover back in place and continue cooking them. Once a fried egg is overcooked, there's no going back.

Formula for Fried Eggs

The trick to fried eggs is using two bowls to add the eggs to the skillet. (Put two eggs in each bowl if cooking four eggs.) Make sure to use a nonstick skillet.

EGGS	BUTTER	SEASONINGS	SKILLET SIZE	COOKING TIME (OVER LOW HEAT)
2	1½ teaspoons	pinch salt, pinch pepper	10 inches	2 minutes for runny yolks, 2½ minutes for soft but set yolks, 3 minutes for firmly set yolks
4	1 tablespoon	pinch salt, pinch pepper	12 inches	2 minutes for runny yolks, 2½ minutes for soft but set yolks, 3 minutes for firmly set yolks

How to Scramble Eggs

For many cooks, scrambled eggs is the first dish they learn that requires cooking. If you can crack an egg and if you can stir, you can make scrambled eggs—at least in theory. But good scrambled eggs do require some finesse. The goal is to produce tender, fluffy curds. Heat is what puffs up the eggs into large, moist curds, but heat will also make eggs rubbery and tough. Here are the key steps to perfect scrambled eggs. Exact amounts for each ingredient and skillet size depends on the number of servings; see chart on page 58.

ESSENTIAL EQUIPMENT

- mixing bowl
- fork
- measuring spoons
- 8- or 10-inch nonstick skillet
- heat-resistant rubber spatula

1. ADD EXTRA YOLKS

Crack eggs into bowl and add the extra yolk(s).
WHY? The extra yolks give the finished dish a rich flavor and better texture. That's because the flavorful yolks contain most of the fat and emulsifiers in the egg and raise the coagulation temperature, thus helping to prevent overcooking of the eggs. The yolks also mask the dairy flavor.

2. SEASON BEFORE COOKING

Add salt and pepper to bowl with eggs.
WHY? Adding the salt to raw (rather than cooked) eggs will make scrambled eggs more tender. That's because the salt tenderizes the protein network in the eggs so that they don't bond as tightly. Salting before cooking also ensures more even cooking.

3. ADD DAIRY

Add half-and-half to bowl with eggs.
WHY? Dairy helps eggs cook up light and tender, and half-and-half yields soft eggs that won't weep. The water in half-and-half turns to steam and helps the eggs puff up. The extra fat (versus milk) raises the coagulation temperature of the egg proteins by keeping them from bonding together as tightly.

4. BEAT LIGHTLY

Beat eggs, half-and-half, salt, and pepper in bowl with fork just until eggs are thoroughly combined, bubbles have formed, and color is pure yellow.
WHY? Overbeating causes premature coagulation and can yield tough results. A fork is gentler on the eggs than a whisk or egg beater. Once the eggs are uniform and large bubbles have formed, stop beating.

5. HEAT BUTTER IN NONSTICK SKILLET

Heat unsalted butter in nonstick skillet over medium-high heat until foaming subsides, swirling to coat skillet (butter should not brown).

WHY? Using butter makes tasty eggs, and the hot skillet jump-starts the cooking process, quickly turning water in the egg mixture to steam. The nonstick surface means you don't have to use a lot of butter, and crowding the eggs into a relatively small skillet traps steam and ensures tender, fluffy eggs (steam dissipates more quickly in a larger skillet, causing eggs to dry out faster).

6. COOK AND SCRAPE

Add egg mixture and, using heat-resistant rubber spatula, constantly and firmly scrape along bottom and sides of skillet until eggs begin to clump and spatula leaves trail on bottom of skillet, 30 seconds to 2½ minutes, depending on number of eggs in skillet.

WHY? Stirring with a spatula ensures that the eggs coagulate into large clumps and don't over-brown. Once the spatula leaves a trail through the eggs, it's your sign that they are nearly done.

7. LOWER HEAT

Reduce heat to low and gently but constantly fold eggs until clumped and slightly wet, 30 to 60 seconds. Immediately transfer eggs to warmed plates and season with salt to taste. Serve immediately.

WHY? Once the eggs are nearly done, reducing the burner heat to low reduces the chance of overcooking. If using an electric stove, move the skillet to a second burner preheated on low.

Formula for Scrambled Eggs

Half-and-half adds liquid that turns to steam when eggs are cooked, thus helping them cook into soft, fluffy mounds. You need 1 tablespoon of half-and-half for each serving of eggs. In addition to varying the half-and-half to match the number of eggs, you will need to vary the seasonings, pan size, and cooking time. Here's how to do that.

SERVINGS	EGGS	HALF-AND-HALF	SEASONINGS	BUTTER	SKILLET SIZE	COOKING TIME
1	2 large, plus 1 yolk	1 tablespoon	pinch salt pinch pepper	¼ tablespoon	8 inches	30-60 seconds over medium-high, 30-60 seconds over low
2	4 large, plus 1 yolk	2 tablespoons	⅛ teaspoon salt ⅛ teaspoon pepper	½ tablespoon	8 inches	45-75 seconds over medium-high, 30-60 seconds over low
3	6 large, plus 1 yolk	3 tablespoons	¼ teaspoon salt ⅛ teaspoon pepper	¾ tablespoon	10 inches	1-2 minutes over medium-high, 30-60 seconds over low
4	8 large, plus 2 yolks	¼ cup	¼ teaspoon salt ¼ teaspoon pepper	1 tablespoon	10 inches	1½–2½ minutes over medium-high, 30 to 60 seconds over low

Troubleshooting Scrambled Eggs

PROBLEM	SOLUTION
I don't have large eggs.	See the Approximate Weights of Egg Sizes chart on page 48 if using extra-large or jumbo eggs.
I don't have half-and-half.	You can replace the half-and-half with 2 parts whole milk and 1 part heavy cream. For instance, if making eggs to serve 3 people, replace 3 tablespoons half-and-half with 2 tablespoons whole milk and 1 tablespoon heavy cream.
I'm working on a slow-to-respond electric stove.	On a gas stovetop, turning the heat from medium-high to low will widen the window of doneness. On an electric stove, adjusting the burner won't have the same effect. Instead, heat a second burner to low before you start cooking. Once the spatula leaves a trail in the eggs, move the skillet to the cooler burner to bring down the heat under the skillet and let the eggs finish cooking a bit more gently.

How to Poach Eggs

Eggs can be cracked open and slid into a pan of simmering water—a technique known as poaching because the water is below the boil. When poaching is done right, the egg white coagulates and protects the yolk. The challenge is to keep the white from fraying and to make sure that the yolk flows when the diner cuts into it. Our method reinvents the process from start to finish and takes the guesswork out of poaching eggs. This technique can be used to poach 2 eggs, or 12 eggs, although timing will change based on the number of eggs added to the pan. The times in the chart on page 61 will yield set whites and slightly runny yolks. For firmer yolks, let the eggs cook an additional 30 to 60 seconds. Note that all times are for large eggs.

ESSENTIAL EQUIPMENT

- 12-inch nonstick skillet with tight-fitting lid
- teacups with handles
- slotted spoon
- large plate
- paper towels

1. FILL SKILLET WITH WATER

Fill 12-inch nonstick skillet nearly to rim with water.

WHY? Traditional recipes poach eggs in a saucepan. Yes, the eggs are surrounded by water in a saucepan too, but it's challenging to get the eggs in and out of a tall, narrow pan. A skillet makes it easy to slide eggs into the water and then remove them with a slotted spoon once they're cooked. A nonstick skillet eliminates the risk of the eggs sticking although this is unlikely to happen in a traditional skillet, which is another option. Fill the skillet nearly to the rim so there's enough water to surround the eggs.

2. ADD SALT AND VINEGAR

Add 1 teaspoon salt and 2 tablespoons distilled white vinegar to water.

WHY? The salt and vinegar season the eggs as they cook, and the vinegar also helps the proteins in the whites to set more quickly, which reduces the risk of fraying. You can use other types of vinegar (white wine, rice, and cider are fine options) but avoid dark vinegars like balsamic that might give the eggs an unattractive hue.

3. HEAT WATER

Bring to boil over high heat.

WHY? The eggs will be poached using residual heat, but you need to start by bringing the water to a good rolling boil. Don't shortcut this process. If the water is merely simmering, there won't be sufficient heat to cook the eggs properly.

HOW TO COOK EGGS

4. CRACK EGGS INTO TEACUPS

Crack 2 eggs into teacup. Repeat with more eggs and up to 4 teacups, as desired.

WHY? If you crack the eggs directly into the water (as most recipes direct), the first egg into the skillet will cook faster than the last egg, and it's very difficult to monitor which egg was in the skillet first. Cracking the eggs into teacups allows you to add as many as eight eggs (using four cups) at once, and you know they all will be done at the same time. For a dozen eggs, crack three eggs into each cup (you can't really hold more than two teacups in each hand at one time).

5. ADD EGGS

Simultaneously lower lips of cups into water and tip eggs into water.

WHY? This is another reason why we love teacups—it's easy to lower their rims into the water and gently slide the eggs out. If using more than one teacup, hold the cups in each hand and lower the eggs into the pan from opposite sides. This method gives the eggs plenty of room to spread out in the skillet.

6. COOK COVERED OFF HEAT

Cover skillet, slide off heat, and poach eggs until whites are cooked but yolks are still runny in center, 3½ to 6 minutes, depending on number of eggs being cooked.

WHY? Bubbles will cause the eggs to fray and blow apart so we move the skillet off the heat and let the residual heat cook the eggs through gently. Before moving the skillet, cover it with a lid. The lid traps heat and ensures that the eggs will cook properly. If you don't cover the skillet, the water will cool off too quickly.

7. REMOVE EGGS

Using slotted spoon, quickly and carefully remove eggs, one at a time, letting water drain back into skillet, and transfer to large paper towel–lined plate. Season eggs with salt and pepper to taste and serve immediately.

WHY? A slotted spoon is easy to slide under each egg and lets excess water fall back into the skillet. Letting the eggs drain on paper towels removes any last traces of water.

Troubleshooting Poached Eggs

PROBLEM	SOLUTION
I got some shell mixed in with the cracked eggs.	Use a thin skewer or chopstick to lift out the piece of shell. Be very careful not to break the yolk or you risk mixing it with the white.
I want to poach extra-large or jumbo eggs.	If poaching extra-large eggs, add 30 to 60 seconds to the cooking time as shown in the chart below. For jumbo eggs, add 60 to 90 seconds to the cooking time.
I don't have teacups with handles.	A liquid measuring cup can work in a pinch, especially if you are poaching just a few eggs. However, to get a lot of eggs into the water at once, you really need small teacups. In theory, you can also use small bowls, but the lack of handles means your fingers will be close to the boiling water; bowls are also more likely to slip in your hands.
I don't have distilled white vinegar.	The vinegar isn't flavoring the eggs; it's added to lower the pH of the water and help set the egg whites faster. You can use any light-colored vinegar, including rice vinegar or cider vinegar. Even lemon juice will work. Don't use red wine or balsamic vinegar, which will tint the whites slightly.
I don't have a slotted spoon.	A plastic pancake turner (with slots) can be used in place of the spoon.
I won't be serving the poached eggs right away.	Some poached-egg recipes call for shocking the eggs in ice water after poaching to halt the cooking so that the eggs can be held before serving. We generally don't do that because we prefer poached eggs to be warm when they go to the table. However, if you're using poached eggs in a recipe with other components, and those components are not done, you can slide the poached eggs into a bowl of ice water. The eggs won't be hot, but at least the yolks won't continue to cook and firm up.
Can I use a traditional skillet?	We use a nonstick skillet because it eliminates the risk of the eggs sticking, but a traditional skillet can also be used. If you find an egg has become stuck to the bottom of the skillet during cooking, nudge it gently with the slotted spoon to loosen, trying to avoid hitting the tender yolk.
I don't have a lid for my skillet.	This recipe relies on trapping residual heat in the skillet to gently cook the eggs through, so not just a lid but one that is tight-fitting is essential to consistent, successful results. If you have another lid that fits loosely over the skillet, you can give it a try, but you will likely have to tinker with the cooking times, and the eggs probably won't cook evenly.

Cooking Times for Poached Eggs

NUMBER OF EGGS	COOKING TIME
2 large	3½ minutes
4 large	4 minutes
8 large	5 minutes
12 large	6 minutes

How to Make a Fluffy Omelet

ESSENTIAL EQUIPMENT

- hand-held mixer or stand mixer
- mixing bowls
- heat-resistant rubber spatula
- coarse grater
- 10-inch ovensafe nonstick skillet with lid
- cutting board

How do you turn several eggs into a towering diner-style omelet? Beating the eggs with an electric mixer to incorporate air is a good start. You also need help from a surprise ingredient—whipped cream. In order to make a big, thick omelet we use five eggs, so the skillet is very full, and overcooking is a real danger. So how do you get the omelet cooked through without overcooking the bottom and making it tough and rubbery?

We start the omelet in a skillet on the stovetop over medium-low heat, and once the edges are barely set—after no more than 3 minutes of cooking—we move the omelet to a hot oven so the interior can cook through. Since the heat isn't attacking the bottom of the omelet (as it does on the stovetop), there's no risk of a rubbery omelet. A hand-held mixer makes quick work of whipping the cream, but a stand mixer fitted with the whisk attachment would work fine. For filling recipes, see page 86.

1. PREHEAT OVEN
Adjust oven rack to middle position and heat oven to 400 degrees.
WHY? Ordinary omelets cook entirely on the stovetop, but we use a combination of the stovetop and oven to ensure even cooking and a fluffy—not rubbery—texture.

2. WHIP CREAM
Whip 3 tablespoons cold heavy cream in medium bowl at medium-low speed until foamy, about 1 minute. Increase speed to high and whip until soft peaks form, 1 to 3 minutes.
WHY? Whipped cream ensures that the eggs will have a light, fluffy texture. Cold cream will achieve maximum volume.

3. BEAT EGGS
Beat 5 large room-temperature eggs and ¼ teaspoon salt in large bowl on high speed until frothy and eggs have at least doubled in volume, about 2 minutes.
WHY? Eggs whip best at room temperature. Take the eggs out of the fridge an hour in advance or let them warm up in a bowl of warm water for 5 minutes. Make sure the volume of eggs doubles during the beating process.

4. FOLD CREAM INTO EGGS
Using rubber spatula, gently fold whipped cream into beaten eggs.
WHY? Gentle folding is a must—you don't want to deflate the eggs or cream.

5. HEAT BUTTER, ADD EGGS
Melt 2 tablespoons unsalted butter in 10-inch nonstick ovensafe skillet over medium-low heat, swirling skillet to coat bottom and sides. Add egg mixture and cook until edges are nearly set, 2 to 3 minutes.
WHY? A nonstick skillet is a must, and don't use a 12-inch skillet (the eggs will spread out too much). Medium-low heat ensures that the bottom of the omelet will cook gently.

6. ADD HALF OF CHEESE

Sprinkle with ¼ cup shredded cheese (and half of any filling, if using).

WHY? Don't add all the cheese and filling at this point—if you do, they will weigh down the omelet and prevent it from properly puffing in the oven. But adding some of the cheese now ensures that it melts in the oven.

7. BAKE UNTIL SET

Place skillet in preheated oven and bake until eggs are set and edges being to brown, 6 to 8 minutes.

WHY? The even heat of the oven ensures even cooking. Once the eggs are set, it's time to take the omelet out of the oven.

8. ADD MORE CHEESE

Remove skillet from oven and sprinkle with another ¼ cup shredded cheese.

WHY? If all the cheese is added before baking, the interior of the omelet takes too long to set. Adding half up front ensures that the eggs cook through. More cheese added at this point ensures enough cheese flavor in the finished omelet.

9. COVER AND WAIT

Cover with lid and let sit until cheese melts, about 1 minute.

WHY? The lid traps just enough heat to finish setting up the omelet and melt the cheese.

10. SLIDE HALF OF OMELET ONTO CUTTING BOARD

Tilt skillet and, using heat-resistant rubber spatula, nudge half of omelet onto cutting board.

WHY? Sliding just half of the omelet out of the skillet is the first step to producing the classic half-moon shape. A big omelet needs support to come out of the skillet intact, so make sure to use a spatula.

11. FOLD OVER

Tilt skillet so that omelet folds over itself to form half-moon shape. Cut omelet in half to create two portions, and serve.

WHY? Let the skillet do the work of flipping the omelet and thus reduce the risk of tearing. However, if you are using a filling (beyond the cheese), slide the entire omelet onto the cutting board and sprinkle half of the omelet with the remaining filling. Then use a spatula to fold the omelet closed.

How to Make a Frittata

A frittata is Italy's version of an omelet—the difference being that the ingredients are cooked into the eggs rather than added to the eggs once they're cooked. Although eggs make a great base for holding fillings (we use asparagus, ham, and cheese here), it can be very tricky to cook the eggs so that the interior of the frittata is moist and tender and the exterior is brown but not scorched. For a perfectly cooked frittata, we start the eggs over moderate heat on the stovetop, and once they're mostly set we put them (still in the skillet) under the broiler for a few minutes to finish cooking and to achieve a golden surface. We also rely on a small measure of half-and-half to provide fat and moisture that help keep the eggs creamy and rich. We add asparagus, ham, and Gruyère here. See our variation on page 87, and of course experiment with whatever combination of add-ins sounds appealing.

ESSENTIAL EQUIPMENT

- whisk
- mixing bowl
- 12-inch ovensafe nonstick skillet
- heat-resistant rubber spatula
- paring knife
- chef's knife
- cutting board

1. SET UP BROILER

Adjust oven rack 5 inches from broiler element and heat broiler.

WHY? On the stovetop, the bottom of the frittata will set up nicely but the top will remain runny. The broiler finishes the job. To keep the frittata from scorching, make sure the skillet won't be too close to the broiler element.

2. WHISK EGGS AND HALF-AND-HALF

Whisk 12 large eggs, 3 tablespoons half-and-half, ½ teaspoon salt, and ¼ teaspoon pepper in bowl until just combined, about 30 seconds.

WHY? If milk is used in place of half-and-half, the lower fat content can mean the difference between a perfectly rich and moist frittata and one that's slightly dry.

3. COOK VEGETABLES AND/OR MEAT

Cook vegetables and/or meat add-ins in 12-inch ovensafe nonstick skillet over medium heat until tender and lightly browned.

WHY? Water from vegetables can ruin a frittata, so cook them in a little oil before adding them to the eggs. Cook fatty meats, like bacon or sausage, first, then spoon off excess fat (using the rest to cook any vegetables, if desired). Lean meats like ham just need to be warmed through.

4. ADD CHEESE TO EGGS, POUR INTO SKILLET

Stir 3 ounces of any cheese, cut into ¼-inch cubes, into eggs, then pour egg mixture into skillet with vegetables and/or meat.

WHY? We like gooey bits of Gruyère, cheddar, or goat cheese in frittata, so we cut (or crumble) the cheese into small cubes instead of shredding it. You should have about ¾ cup. Make sure the heat is set at medium; at higher temperatures the bottom of the frittata can scorch.

5. STIR AND SCRAPE

Cook, using heat-resistant rubber spatula to stir and scrape bottom of skillet, until large curds form and spatula begins to leave trail but eggs are still very wet, about 2 minutes.

WHY? Some recipes just pour the eggs into the skillet and wait. But for a thick frittata made with a dozen eggs, we found some stirring at the outset ensures that the eggs set evenly.

6. LET EGGS SET

Shake skillet to distribute eggs evenly, using spatula to even out top of frittata. Cook without stirring for 30 seconds to let bottom set.

WHY? Once the eggs form large curds, you want to shape and compact them slightly. Otherwise, you end up with scrambled eggs, not a frittata. Let the cohesive frittata cook for 30 seconds to help set the bottom.

7. BROIL

Slide skillet under preheated broiler.

WHY? The bottom of the frittata is probably almost done, but the top is still moist and runny. More heating on the stovetop isn't going to solve that problem.

8. CHECK FOR DONENESS

Broil until frittata has risen and surface is puffed and spotty brown, 3 to 4 minutes. Cut into frittata with paring knife; eggs should be slightly wet and runny.

WHY? Broilers vary tremendously in heat output, so watch for the visual clues. Once the top is spotty brown, peek into the frittata. It should be almost cooked through. If your broiler runs hot, check the frittata sooner and be prepared to rotate the skillet if you notice that the surface is not browning evenly.

9. USE RESIDUAL HEAT

Remove skillet from oven and let stand 5 minutes to finish cooking.

WHY? The residual heat in the skillet can finish setting the interior of the frittata without exposing it to further heat that might make the top leathery and tough.

10. SLIDE AND CUT

Use rubber spatula to loosen frittata. Slide frittata onto cutting board, cut into wedges with chef's knife, and serve.

WHY? The frittata should release easily from a nonstick skillet, but it doesn't hurt to run a spatula around the edges of the skillet and under the frittata to ensure it doesn't tear.

How to Make a Quiche

Eggs (and pastry) are the star ingredients in a quiche. The eggs are enriched with dairy to create a velvety custard that sets up in the heat of the oven. We tested various combinations of dairy and eggs and hit upon a formula that is rich, but not overly so, and perfectly smooth when baked. To ensure a flaky crust, it's important to parbake the pie shell before adding the custard to the warm shell and baking the quiche. Refer to How to Bake a Single-Crust Pie Shell (page 720) for tips on blind-baking the pie shell. Also see How to Make Pie Dough (page 716) and How to Roll Out Pie Dough (page 719). For variations on this recipe, see page 88.

ESSENTIAL EQUIPMENT

- 9-inch glass pie plate
- aluminum foil
- plastic wrap
- pie weights
- whisk
- mixing bowl
- wire rack
- rimmed baking sheet
- large liquid measuring cup
- butter or paring knife

1. MAKE PIE SHELL

Make pie dough, fit dough into pie plate, flute edges, line with plastic, and place in freezer until firm, about 30 minutes.

WHY? Good quiche starts with a flaky, buttery crust. Make our Foolproof Single-Crust Pie Dough and fit it into a 9-inch glass pie plate as directed on pages 719–720. Freezing the pie shell reduces the risk of shrinking in the oven and allows the crust to hold all of the filling.

2. BLIND-BAKE PIE SHELL

Remove plastic wrap, line chilled pie shell with foil, fill with weights, and partially bake in 375-degree oven on lower-middle rack until set and very lightly colored, 25 to 30 minutes.

WHY? There is only one way to keep a quiche crust from turning soggy, and that is to parbake it before adding the custard. To prevent the crust from shrinking as it parbakes, we use pie weights; a sheet of foil makes it easy to remove the weights when the crust is done.

3. MAKE CUSTARD

In large bowl, whisk together 5 large eggs, 2 cups half-and-half, and ¼ teaspoon each salt and pepper.

WHY? The trick to making the custard is to get the ingredients well combined with no streaks of eggs. Since the custard should be added to the pie shell as soon as it has finished parbaking, start making the custard immediately after the pie shell goes into the oven.

4. ADD CHEESE AND OTHER INGREDIENTS

Whisk in cheese, herbs, vegetables, and meats.

WHY? We find that 1 cup of shredded or crumbled cheese is ideal. Don't bother with dried herbs, but fresh herbs (especially chives) are a nice addition. If using vegetables, cook them first to remove moisture that otherwise could make the filling watery. (Frozen spinach can simply be wrung dry.) If using bacon or another fatty meat, cook it first to render excess grease.

5. FILL WARM SHELL IN OVEN

Transfer parbaked pie shell to wire rack and use foil to remove pie weights. Place rimmed baking sheet in oven and decrease oven temperature to 350 degrees. Place pie plate on sheet and fill with custard just until it reaches about ½ inch below top edge of crust.

WHY? To prevent the quiche from expanding over the edges of the crust, it is important to add the custard just until it reaches just below the top edge of the crust; you might not use all of the custard, especially if the pie shell has shrunk slightly. Since it can be tricky to put a full quiche into the oven without spilling the contents, it's best to transfer the custard to a 4-cup liquid measuring cup and then pour the custard into the shell after placing the pie plate on a baking sheet in the oven. The sheet will catch any drips and will also conduct heat and help crisp up the bottom of the pie shell.

6. DON'T OVERBAKE

Bake until top of quiche is lightly browned, center is set but soft, and knife inserted 1 inch from edge comes out clean, 40 to 50 minutes.

WHY? If you overbake a quiche, the eggs can curdle and the filling will be grainy and dry. Pull the quiche out of the oven before it is completely done, as it will continue to cook and set up as it cools. When the quiche is ready to come out of the oven, the center will still jiggle loosely.

7. WAIT TO SLICE

Transfer baked quiche to wire rack and cool for at least 1 hour or up to 3 hours.

WHY? It's important to let the filling set up before slicing into it, or you will have a mess on your hands. This will take at least an hour, perhaps a bit longer in a warm kitchen. The quiche can be kept at room temperature for up to 3 hours.

Troubleshooting Quiche

PROBLEM	SOLUTION
I want to make the quiche early in the day and reheat it.	The quiche can spend up to 3 hours cooling on a wire rack. After that, it will keep in the refrigerator for another 6 hours, although the crust might suffer a bit. Serve the quiche chilled, at room temperature, or warmed. If you want to warm the quiche, take it straight out of the fridge and place it in a 350-degree oven for 10 to 15 minutes. Don't heat the quiche too long, or it will dry out.
I want to make the quiche a day in advance.	The crust will become soggy if the quiche is made in advance. Make (but don't pre-bake) the pie shell a day or two ahead; keep it covered in the refrigerator. You can precook add-ins and refrigerate them for a day. Make the custard at the last minute.

Eggs Benedict

Recipe Stats

TOTAL TIME **40 minutes**
PREPARATION TIME **15 minutes**
ACTIVE COOKING TIME **25 minutes**
YIELD **6 servings**
MAKE AHEAD **Hollandaise can be refrigerated
for up to 3 days; English muffins can be toasted and
bacon can be warmed up to 20 minutes ahead**
DIFFICULTY **Intermediate**

Tools

- teakettle
- medium saucepan
- rimmed baking sheet
- 12-inch nonstick skillet with
  tight-fitting lid
- liquid measuring cup
- measuring spoons
- citrus juicer
- heat-resistant rubber
  spatula

- instant-read thermometer *
- large heatproof bowl
- large plate
- slotted spoon
- soupspoon
- teacups with handles (4)
- whisk
- paper towels
- plastic wrap

* Don't attempt this recipe without an instant-read thermometer; it's nearly impossible to judge the doneness of the sauce
on appearance alone.

Ingredients

FOOLPROOF HOLLANDAISE
- **12   tablespoons unsalted butter, softened**
- **6   large egg yolks**
- **½   cup boiling water**
- **2   teaspoons lemon juice**
- **⅛   teaspoon cayenne pepper**
      Salt

POACHED EGGS
- **2   tablespoons distilled white vinegar**
- **1   teaspoon salt**
- **12   large eggs**

- **6   English muffins, split**
- **12   slices Canadian bacon**

Overview

Eggs Benedict relies on two tricky egg-based components—
poached eggs and hollandaise sauce. If you follow our method
for poaching eggs (see How to Poach Eggs on page 59), the
first part is easy. Adding vinegar to the water helps to set the
whites and prevents feathery whites. Cracking the eggs into
teacups and gently and simultaneously sliding the eggs into
the salted, acidulated water ensures they all begin cooking at
the same time—and means that they will also be done at the
same time. Water temperature is key when poaching eggs.
We bring the water to a boil, add the eggs, then quickly cover
the skillet, and remove it from the heat. The gentle residual
heat produces restaurant-worthy poached eggs, with soft,
runny yolks and perfectly formed, round whites.

As for the hollandaise, many newer recipes call for making it in a blender or food processor to ensure an emulsified
sauce without the tedious whisking. These methods work,
but only if the sauce is served immediately. We developed
an unconventional technique that requires whisking softened (rather than the usually melted) butter and egg yolks
together on the stovetop in a double boiler. We use a lot of
water in this sauce and add the lemon juice off the heat. The
sauce is foamier than a classic hollandaise, but it holds well,
without breaking, until the other components are ready. It can
also be refrigerated for up to three days and reheated in the
microwave for 1 minute at 50 percent power, stirring every
10 seconds, without breaking.

If you like, you can toast the English muffins and warm
the Canadian bacon 20 minutes in advance. Reheat them in a
200-degree oven just before serving.

What Can Go Wrong

Here's a list of common mistakes cooks make when preparing this recipe.

COMMON MISTAKE	BAD OUTCOMES	WHAT YOU SHOULD DO
Overcooking Hollandaise	• **The sauce breaks.** • **The eggs curdle.**	Use an instant-read thermometer when preparing the hollandaise sauce. Once the sauce reaches 160 degrees, the eggs will have thickened the sauce to the proper consistency, and it's time to remove the sauce from the heat. Whisk in the lemon juice to start the cooling down process. Also, make sure the bowl containing the sauce is suspended over—not in—the simmering water. If the bowl is touching the water, the risk of overheating the sauce is very high.
Omitting Vinegar	• **The whites are feathery.**	Turning off the heat helps the eggs cook up with a nice rounded shape, but the whites can still feather. That's where the vinegar helps. The vinegar lowers the pH of the water, which helps the egg whites to stay intact. (The vinegar also flavors the eggs and helps balance the richness of the sauce.)
Adding Eggs One at a Time	• **The yolks are too runny.** • **The yolks are too firm.**	This recipe depends on getting all the eggs into the skillet at the same time and then setting the timer. If you crack the eggs individually into the water, it will take at least 2 minutes to get a dozen eggs into the skillet, and there's no way to ensure that all the eggs are cooked to the same degree. Cracking the eggs into four teacups allows all 12 eggs to start cooking at precisely the same moment. With the skillet off the heat, the timing is pretty basic—6 minutes for yolks that are set but still slightly runny.
Poaching Eggs in Simmering Water	• **The eggs are misshapen.** • **The eggs are blown apart.**	Many recipes suggest poaching eggs in simmering water, but it's all too easy for the water to overheat (while you're working on another component in the recipe) and jostle the eggs. We prefer a more reliable method. Once the water comes to a rolling boil, add the eggs (quickly), put the lid in place, and move the skillet off the heat. Residual heat cooks the eggs, but since the water isn't moving the eggs hold their shape better.
Timing Components Poorly	• **The English muffins are cold.** • **The Canadian bacon is cold.** • **The hollandaise is cold.** • **The eggs are cold, and the yolks are firm.**	Eggs Benedict has four components, and each must be well executed for this dish to work. Many cooks don't strategize properly, and one component or more ends up stone cold. The hollandaise is easy. Make the sauce first, pour it into a liquid measuring cup, and then reheat it when needed in the microwave. (And because the sauce is in a measuring cup, it will be easy to portion.) The muffins and bacon should go under the broiler right after you put the eggs in the water to poach. If the eggs are not quite done when the bacon has finished broiling, simply turn off the broiler and move the muffins and bacon to the bottom rack, where they will stay warm but won't continue to cook. Finally, once the eggs are out of the poaching liquid, don't delay. Not only will the eggs get cold rather quickly, but the yolk will continue to set up. Another option is to toast the muffins and heat the bacon a little earlier—up to 20 minutes in advance of serving—and then simply reheat them in a 200-degree oven.

1. PREPARE HOLLANDAISE: Bring water to boil in kettle.

2. Fill medium saucepan with about ½ inch of water and bring to bare simmer.

3. Place 12 tablespoons softened unsalted butter and 6 large egg yolks in large heatproof bowl.

4. Set bowl over barely simmering water (don't let bowl touch water).

5. Whisk eggs and butter together.

6. Pour ½ cup boiling water from kettle into liquid measuring cup.

7. Whisk ½ cup boiling water into bowl with butter and eggs.

8. Cook, whisking constantly, until thickened and sauce registers 160 degrees, 7 to 10 minutes.

9. Carefully remove bowl from saucepan. Stir in 2 teaspoons lemon juice and ⅛ teaspoon cayenne pepper. Season sauce with salt to taste.

10. Transfer sauce to liquid measuring cup and cover with plastic wrap. (Sauce can be held at room temperature for up to 1 hour.)

11. Adjust oven rack 8 inches from broiler element and heat broiler.

12. POACH EGGS: Fill 12-inch nonstick skillet nearly to rim with water. Add 2 tablespoons white vinegar and 1 teaspoon salt and bring to boil over high heat.

13. Crack 3 large eggs each into 4 teacups (12 eggs total).

14. All at once, lower lips of cups into boiling water and tip eggs into water.

15. Cover skillet and poach eggs off heat until whites are set but yolks are still slightly runny, about 6 minutes.

16. Using slotted spoon, remove eggs one at a time, letting water drain back into skillet, and transfer to large paper towel–lined plate.

17. BROIL MUFFINS AND BACON: While eggs poach, arrange 6 split English muffins, split side up, on rimmed baking sheet.

18. Broil English muffins until golden brown, 2 to 4 minutes.

19. Place 1 slice Canadian bacon (12 slices total) on each English muffin half and broil until beginning to brown, about 1 minute.

20. Turn off broiler and transfer baking sheet to lower rack to keep warm until eggs are done, if necessary.

21. ASSEMBLE AND SERVE: Place 2 English muffin halves each on 6 serving plates. Arrange 1 poached egg on top of each English muffin half.

22. If necessary, reheat hollandaise in microwave on 50 percent power, stirring every 10 seconds, until heated through, about 1 minute.

23. Spoon 1 to 2 tablespoons hollandaise over each egg. Serve, passing remaining hollandaise separately.

French Omelets

Overview

Fluffy American omelets (see page 62) are as much about the fillings than they are the eggs. French-style omelets are all about the eggs, and almost not at all about the fillings. The folded half-moon shape of a typical American omelet provides plenty of room for a generous filling of meat, vegetables, and/or cheese. A French omelet is rolled so the filling is generally nothing more than a few tablespoons of cheese.

With the emphasis on the eggs, a French omelet requires precise cooking technique. This recipe takes all the guesswork out of the equation and delivers rich, flavorful, elegant rolled omelets, accented only with cheese and fresh chives.

An extra yolk is added to whole eggs to boost richness, the eggs are lightly beaten, and a dual heat setting is used starting over low heat and finishing over medium-high. You can make only one omelet at a time (the recipe calls for enough ingredients to make two), so consider your first omelet a rehearsal and the second one showtime.

These omelets can be served for breakfast, lunch, or dinner. A green salad is a perfect accompaniment.

Recipe Stats

TOTAL TIME **30 minutes**
PREPARATION TIME **10 minutes**
ACTIVE COOKING TIME **20 minutes**
YIELD **2 servings**
MAKE AHEAD **Serve immediately**
DIFFICULTY **Intermediate**

Tools

- 8-inch nonstick skillet with tight-fitting lid
- chef's knife
- cutting board
- measuring spoons
- chopsticks or wooden skewers *
- coarse grater
- fork
- heat-resistant rubber spatula
- mixing bowls
- whisk
- paper towels

* The chopsticks or skewers are used for scrambling the eggs. Chopsticks that are not varnished (such as those that come with takeout) are best. If you don't have chopsticks or skewers, use the handle of a wooden spoon.

Ingredients

2 tablespoons unsalted butter, cut into 2 pieces
½ teaspoon vegetable oil
6 large eggs, cold
¼ teaspoon salt
**   Pepper**
2 tablespoons shredded Gruyère cheese *
4 teaspoons minced fresh chives **

* Gruyère is our favorite cheese for these omelets, but if you prefer, you can substitute a different type of cheese. Just make sure that it is a good melting cheese, such as cheddar or Monterey Jack, and that it has decent flavor; do not use a hard grating cheese such as Parmesan.
** Fresh chives are an absolute must in this recipe; do not substitute dried.

What Can Go Wrong

Here's a list of common mistakes cooks make when preparing this recipe.

COMMON MISTAKE	BAD OUTCOMES	WHAT YOU SHOULD DO
Overbeating Eggs	• **The omelet is dense.** • **The omelet is tough.**	Beat the eggs with a fork just until the yolks and whites are combined, and no longer. The eggs for this omelet should not be overbeaten. Overbeating unfolds the proteins, which sets them up to bind together tightly when cooked, and the result is a dense, tough omelet.
Not Heating Skillet Long Enough	• **The omelet cooks unevenly.**	A properly preheated skillet is important for a perfectly cooked omelet. Because the oil won't give any visual clues as to when the skillet is fully heated, the best thing to do is to set a timer for 10 minutes after the skillet, with oil, has been set over low heat. This way, you won't have to take any guesses at how long the skillet has been heating.
Not Adding Butter to Uncooked Eggs	• **The omelet is dry.**	Freezing the butter before adding it to the eggs boosts the creaminess, but it's easy to forget about the butter once it's in the freezer. But the butter is essential for a rich, moist omelet, so don't forget to add it to the eggs.
Keeping Heat Too Low	• **The eggs do not puff up.**	After adding the eggs to the skillet, make sure to increase the burner setting to medium-high. Medium-high heat helps the eggs form light, puffy curds; if they are cooked over low heat, the egg curds will take much longer to cook and the omelet will wind up dense and heavy. If using an electric stovetop, preheat a second burner to medium-high and move skillet to this burner at the appropriate time.
Not Stirring Eggs Properly	• **The egg curds are too large.**	Although it may seem awkward—maybe even counterintuitive—to stir the eggs with chopsticks or wooden skewers, the utensil has a big impact on the texture of the omelet, so don't reach for a rubber spatula for this step. Stir the eggs with chopsticks or skewers until the eggs are almost cooked, but still quite moist and runny, 45 to 90 seconds.
Not Finishing Eggs Off Heat	• **The omelet is too wet.** • **The omelet will not roll.**	After sprinkling the eggs with the cheese and chives, cover the skillet and allow the eggs to stand for 1 to 2 minutes. This off-heat covered cooking time is essential for getting the eggs to set into a lightly cohesive mass that can be rolled into an omelet. If the eggs are not allowed to stand, they will be too wet and loose, more like scrambled eggs than an omelet.

1. Cut 2 tablespoons unsalted butter into 2 pieces.

2. Cut 1 piece butter in half again; set aside.

3. Cut second piece butter into small dice and transfer to small bowl. Freeze diced butter for at least 10 minutes.

4. Meanwhile, place ½ teaspoon vegetable oil in 8-inch nonstick skillet. Heat over low heat for 10 minutes.

5. Crack 2 cold eggs into medium bowl. Separate third egg; reserve white for another use and add yolk to bowl.

6. Add ⅛ teaspoon salt and pinch pepper.

7. Break yolks with fork, then beat eggs at moderate pace, about 80 strokes, until yolks and whites are well combined.

8. Stir in half of frozen butter cubes.

9. When skillet is fully heated, use paper towels to wipe out oil, leaving thin film on bottom and sides of skillet.

10. Add ½ tablespoon reserved butter to skillet.

11. Heat until foaming subsides, 45 to 90 seconds. Swirl butter to coat skillet.

12. Add egg mixture and increase heat to medium-high. (Move skillet to burner preheated to medium-high if using electric stovetop.)

13. Using 2 chopsticks, scramble eggs with quick circular motion, moving around skillet and scraping cooked egg from sides as you go.

14. Continue scrambling motion until eggs are almost cooked but still slightly runny, 45 to 90 seconds.

15. Turn off heat. (Remove skillet from heat if using electric burner.)

16. Smooth eggs into even layer using heat-resistant rubber spatula.

17. Sprinkle omelet with 1 tablespoon grated Gruyère cheese and 2 teaspoons minced fresh chives.

18. Cover skillet with tight-fitting lid. Let sit 1 minute for runnier omelet or 2 minutes for firmer omelet.

19. Heat skillet over low heat for 20 seconds.

20. Uncover and, using rubber spatula, loosen edges of omelet from skillet.

21. Place folded square of paper towel onto warmed plate.

22. Slide omelet out of skillet onto paper towel so that omelet lies flat and hangs about 1 inch off paper towel.

23. Using paper towel to lift omelet, roll it into neat cylinder and set aside.

24. Return skillet to low heat and heat for 2 minutes. Repeat from step 5 to make second omelet. Serve.

Cheese Soufflé

Overview

Soufflés have a reputation for being difficult to prepare and temperamental in the oven. But in reality a soufflé is quite simple to execute. Many recipes are fragile because they contain more whites than yolks. Yes, these formulas might produce a soufflé with a dizzying height, but the failure rate can be high as well. To stabilize the soufflé, we use an equal number of yolks and whites. And to make the whites more stable, we add a little cream of tartar when whipping them.

A classic cheese soufflé begins with a béchamel sauce (flour and butter cooked to form a roux and then thinned out with milk). We start by sautéing a shallot in the butter to add flavor. Once the béchamel is finished, we stir in a generous amount of Gruyère along with a little dry mustard, nutmeg, salt, and pepper to boost the flavor of the cheese. The egg yolks are added to this base, while the whites are whipped and then folded into the base.

For an extra shot of cheese, sprinkle the greased soufflé dish as well as the top of the soufflé with a little grated Parmesan. Also, after pouring the batter into the dish, trace a circle in the batter with your finger, about ½ inch from the edge of the dish. We found this breaks the surface tension and helps the soufflé achieve a high, even rise.

Don't open the oven door during the first 15 minutes of baking time; as the soufflé nears the end of its baking, you can check its progress by opening the oven door slightly. A soufflé is done when the top is deep golden brown and the center jiggles slightly. The interior should be moist but not soupy, and creamy but not dry.

Before you begin, see How to Crack and Separate Eggs on page 50 and How to Whip Egg Whites on page 51. For variations on this recipe, see page 89.

Recipe Stats

TOTAL TIME **55 minutes**
PREPARATION TIME **15 minutes**
ACTIVE COOKING TIME **15 minutes**
YIELD **3 to 4 servings**
MAKE AHEAD **Serve immediately**
DIFFICULTY **Intermediate**

Tools

- medium saucepan
- 1½-quart soufflé dish *
- stand mixer **
- liquid measuring cup
- measuring spoons
- coarse grater
- heat-resistant rubber spatula
- mixing bowls
- rasp-style grater ***
- whisk
- paper towels

* This recipe can be prepared in an 8½ by 4½-inch glass loaf pan if you don't have a soufflé dish.
** A stand mixer makes it easy to switch gears from preparing the base to whipping the whites, but whip the whites with a hand-held mixer if you prefer.
*** We like to grate Parmesan on a rasp-style grater, but you can also use the small holes of a box grater.

Ingredients

3   **large eggs, separated, room temperature** *
¼   **cup grated Parmesan cheese**
3   **tablespoons unsalted butter**
1   **shallot, minced**
3   **tablespoons all-purpose flour**
1   **cup whole milk**
4   **ounces Gruyère cheese, shredded (1 cup)** **
½   **teaspoon salt**
¼   **teaspoon dry mustard**
¼   **teaspoon pepper**
   Pinch ground nutmeg
¼   **teaspoon cream of tartar**

* Separate the eggs straight from the refrigerator but allow the whites to come to room temperature before whipping them.
** Any cheese that melts well, including cheddar, Swiss, or gouda, can be substituted for the Gruyère.

What Can Go Wrong

Here's a list of common mistakes cooks make when preparing this recipe.

COMMON MISTAKE	BAD OUTCOMES	WHAT YOU SHOULD DO
Not Cleanly Separating Eggs	• **The soufflé doesn't rise enough.**	A soufflé depends on whipped egg whites for proper height. If bits of yolk end up contaminating the whites, the whites won't whip up properly. Separate the eggs straight from the fridge (when chilled, the yolks are taut and less likely to break), but let the whites warm up a bit before beating them. See How to Crack and Separate Eggs on page 50.
Letting Base Cool Off	• **The soufflé doesn't rise enough.**	Timing is key in this recipe. Begin beating the egg whites as soon as you finish making the soufflé base. If the base cools off too much, the soufflé won't rise properly.
Folding Excessively	• **The soufflé is dense and heavy.**	If you are too aggressive when folding the whites into the soufflé base, you will knock all the air out of the whites and the soufflé will bake up heavy and dense. The problem is that the soufflé base is quite thick, so it's not all that easy to mix in the billowy whites. That's why we fold the whipped egg whites into the soufflé base in two batches. A small portion of the whites is used to lighten the consistency of the base. Fold this first batch of egg whites into the base until almost no streaks of whites remain. With the base lightened up, you can now proceed to fold in the remaining whites until just incorporated. You should leave a few streaks of whites visible.
Opening Oven Door	• **The soufflé collapses.**	If you open the oven door early in the baking process, you can disturb the airflow in the oven, and this will cause the soufflé to collapse. (And if you then slam the oven door shut, you will almost certainly cause this to happen.) Resist the temptation to peek into the oven until the soufflé has baked for at least 15 minutes. As the soufflé nears the end of its baking time, you can check its progress by opening the oven door slightly.
Overbaking Soufflé	• **The soufflé is dry.** • **The soufflé is bland.**	Many novice cooks overbake soufflés, thinking that more time will equal greater rise. However, during the final 10 minutes in the oven the soufflé isn't really rising as much as it is cooking through. Overbaking not only compromises the texture of the soufflé but also dulls the flavors. Unfortunately, it can be tricky to determine when the center of the soufflé is perfectly cooked—that is, creamy and moist but not runny. Use the "jiggle" test to determine when the soufflé is done. Very gently move the soufflé dish and watch how the center behaves. It should jiggle slightly when shaken. If in doubt, use two soupspoons to pull open a small crack in the top to judge the consistency. Remember that the soufflé will continue to set up a bit as you get everyone to the table.

1. Separate 3 large cold eggs and let yolks and whites come to room temperature.

2. Adjust oven rack to middle position and heat oven to 350 degrees.

3. Spray 1½-quart soufflé dish with vegetable oil spray.

4. Sprinkle 2 tablespoons Parmesan into dish and shake to coat evenly; tap out any excess.

5. Melt 3 tablespoons unsalted butter in medium saucepan over medium heat.

6. Add 1 minced shallot and cook until softened, about 2 minutes.

7. Stir in 3 tablespoons flour and cook until golden, about 1 minute.

8. Slowly whisk in 1 cup whole milk.

9. Bring to simmer and cook, whisking constantly, until thickened and smooth, about 1 minute.

10. Off heat, whisk in 1 cup shredded Gruyère, ½ teaspoon salt, ¼ teaspoon dry mustard, ¼ teaspoon pepper, and pinch nutmeg.

11. Scrape mixture into medium bowl.

12. Whisk in egg yolks until incorporated.

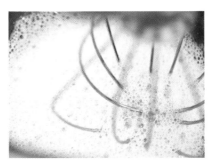

13. Using stand mixer fitted with whisk, whip egg whites and ¼ teaspoon cream of tartar on medium-low speed until foamy, about 1 minute.

14. Increase speed to medium-high and continue to whip until whites are glossy and form stiff peaks, 3 to 4 minutes.

15. Using rubber spatula, fold one-quarter of whipped egg whites into warm soufflé base until almost no white streaks remain.

16. Fold in remaining egg whites until just incorporated.

17. Gently pour mixture into prepared dish, wiping any batter from rim with wet paper towel.

18. Trace circle in batter with your finger, about ½ inch from edge of dish (this will help soufflé rise nicely).

19. Sprinkle top of soufflé with 2 tablespoons Parmesan.

20. Bake soufflé until surface is deep brown and it has risen 2 to 2½ inches above rim of dish, 22 to 27 minutes.

21. When soufflé is done, center should jiggle slightly when shaken. Serve immediately.

Recipe Library

Hard-Cooked Eggs

✓ **WHY THIS RECIPE WORKS:** Hard-cooking an egg can be a crapshoot. There's no way to watch it cook inside its shell, and you certainly can't poke it with an instant-read thermometer. We finally got our foolproof recipe by tinkering with a technique recommended by the American Egg Board. We started the eggs in cold water, brought the water to a boil, then removed the pan from the heat and let the eggs steep for 10 minutes. This method consistently turned out perfect hard-cooked eggs with moist and creamy yolks, firm yet tender whites, and no trace of a green ring.

Hard-Cooked Eggs

MAKES 4

You can double or triple this recipe as long as you use a pot large enough to hold the eggs in a single layer, covered by an inch of water. See Core Technique on page 52 for more details on this recipe.

- **4 large eggs**

Place eggs in medium saucepan, cover with 1 inch water, and bring to boil over high heat. Remove pot from heat, cover, and let sit for 10 minutes. Meanwhile, fill medium bowl with 4 cups cold water and 4 cups ice cubes. Transfer eggs to ice bath with slotted spoon; let sit for 5 minutes. Peel eggs.

Classic Egg Salad

✓ **WHY THIS RECIPE WORKS:** For creamy, flavorful egg salad with perfectly cooked eggs and just the right amount of crunch, we followed a few simple steps. First, we relied on our recipe for Hard-Cooked Eggs, which yielded eggs with perfectly creamy yolks, tender whites, and no green ring. We diced the eggs to keep the salad from turning pasty. Then we combined them with mayonnaise (our tasters dismissed ingredients such as cottage cheese, sour cream, and cream cheese as extraneous), lemon juice, mustard, red onion, celery, and parsley.

Classic Egg Salad

MAKES 2½ CUPS, ENOUGH FOR 4 SANDWICHES

Be sure to use red onion; yellow onion is too harsh.

- **6 Hard-Cooked Eggs, peeled and diced medium**
- **¼ cup mayonnaise**
- **2 tablespoons finely chopped red onion**
- **1 tablespoon minced fresh parsley**
- **½ celery rib, minced**
- **2 teaspoons Dijon mustard**
- **2 teaspoons lemon juice**
- **¼ teaspoon salt**
- **Pepper**

Mix all ingredients together in medium bowl, including pepper to taste. Serve. (Egg salad can be refrigerated in an airtight container for up to 1 day.)

Egg Salad with Radish, Scallions, and Dill

Substitute 1 thinly sliced scallion for red onion, 1 tablespoon minced fresh dill for parsley, and add 3 minced radishes.

Curried Egg Salad

Substitute 1 tablespoon minced fresh cilantro for parsley and add 1½ teaspoons curry powder. Omit salt.

Creamy Egg Salad with Capers and Anchovies

Add 1 minced small garlic clove, 2 tablespoons chopped capers, and 1 minced anchovy fillet. Omit salt.

Creamy Egg Salad with Bacon, Shallots, and Watercress

In 10-inch skillet over medium heat, cook 4 slices bacon, cut into ¼-inch pieces, until crisp, 5 to 7 minutes. Transfer bacon with slotted spoon to paper towel–lined plate; pour off all but 1 tablespoon of fat from skillet. Add 2 chopped large shallots and cook until softened and browned, about 5 minutes. Omit celery and salt, substitute cooked shallots for red onion, and add bacon and ¼ cup watercress leaves, chopped coarse.

Classic Deviled Eggs

✓ **WHY THIS RECIPE WORKS:** Deviled eggs often fall to the extremes, with fillings that are either smooth, pasty, and monotonous or reminiscent of chunky egg salad. We had in mind the deviled eggs of our childhood: perfectly cooked nests of egg whites cradling a creamy filling made with simple ingredients and quickly whipped together. Naturally, it was key to start with perfectly hard-cooked eggs. We combined the yolks with mayonnaise, whole-grain mustard, cider vinegar, and Worcestershire sauce, which gave us a full-flavored, but balanced, filling. We like to use a pastry bag for filling the eggs, but a zipper-lock bag with the corner snipped off also works well.

Classic Deviled Eggs

MAKES 1 DOZEN

During testing we found it usual for a couple of the cooked whites to rip at least slightly, which worked out well because it meant the remaining whites were very well stuffed. If all of your egg white halves are in perfect shape, discard two. If you have a pastry bag, use it to fill the eggs with a large open-star tip or a large plain tip. Alternatively, a plastic bag can be used to fill the eggs. Fill the eggs as close to serving as possible for fresh, bright flavor.

7 large eggs
3 tablespoons mayonnaise
1½ teaspoons cider vinegar (or vinegar of your choice)
¾ teaspoon whole-grain mustard
¼ teaspoon Worcestershire sauce
Salt and pepper

1. Place eggs in medium saucepan, cover with 1 inch of water, and bring to boil over high heat. Remove pot from heat, cover, and let sit for 10 minutes. Meanwhile, fill large bowl with 4 cups cold water and 4 cups ice cubes. Transfer eggs to ice bath with slotted spoon; let sit 5 minutes.

2. Peel eggs and slice each in half lengthwise with paring knife. Remove yolks to small bowl. Arrange whites on serving platter, discarding 2 worst-looking halves. Mash yolks with fork until no large lumps remain. Add mayonnaise, vinegar, mustard, Worcestershire, and salt and pepper to taste. Mix with rubber spatula, mashing mixture against side of bowl until smooth.

3. Fit pastry bag with large open-star or plain tip. Fill bag with yolk mixture, twisting top of pastry bag to help push mixture toward tip of bag. Pipe yolk mixture into egg white halves, mounding filling about ½ inch above flat surface of whites. Serve at room temperature.

TO MAKE AHEAD: Follow recipe through step 2. Wrap peeled egg-white halves tightly with double layer of plastic wrap and place filling in zipper-lock plastic bag, squeezing out all the air. Refrigerate for up to 2 days, then fill and serve as directed in step 3.

Classic Deviled Eggs with Anchovy and Basil

Rinse, dry, and mince 8 anchovy fillets. Mince 2 tablespoons fresh basil. Mix anchovy fillets and 2 teaspoons minced basil into mashed yolks along with mayonnaise, vinegar, mustard, Worcestershire, and salt and pepper. Sprinkle filled eggs with remaining 4 teaspoons shredded basil.

Classic Deviled Eggs with Tuna, Capers, and Chives

Drain and finely chop 2 ounces canned tuna (you should have about ½ cup). Rinse and drain 1 tablespoon capers; chop 1 tablespoon fresh chives. Mix tuna, capers, and 2 teaspoons chives into mashed yolks along with mayonnaise, vinegar, mustard, and salt and pepper. Omit Worcestershire. Sprinkle filled eggs with remaining 1 teaspoon chives.

Soft-Cooked Eggs

✔ **WHY THIS RECIPE WORKS:** We wanted a soft-cooked eggs recipe that delivered a set white and fluid yolk every time. Calling for fridge-cold eggs and boiling water reduced temperature variables and provided the steepest temperature gradient, ensuring that the yolk at the center stayed fluid while the white cooked through. Using only ½ inch of boiling water to cook the eggs meant the recipe took less time and energy. And because of the eggs' curved shape, they have very little contact with the water so they do not lower the temperature when they go into the saucepan. This means the same timing for anywhere from one to six eggs works without altering the finished product.

Soft-Cooked Eggs
MAKES 4

Be sure to use large eggs that have no cracks and are cold from the refrigerator. Because precise timing is vital to the success of this recipe, we strongly recommend using a digital timer. You can use this method for one to six large, extra-large, or jumbo eggs without altering the timing. If you have one, a steamer basket does make lowering the eggs into the boiling water easier. We recommend serving these eggs in eggcups and with buttered toast for dipping, or you may simply use the dull side of a butter knife to crack the egg along the equator, break the egg in half, and scoop out the insides with a teaspoon.

4 large eggs, cold
Salt and pepper

1. Bring ½ inch water to boil in medium saucepan over medium-high heat. Using tongs, gently place eggs in boiling water (eggs will not be submerged). Cover saucepan and cook eggs for 6½ minutes.

2. Remove cover, transfer saucepan to sink, and place under cold running water for 30 seconds. Remove eggs from pan and serve, seasoning with salt and pepper to taste.

Soft-Cooked Eggs with Sautéed Mushrooms
SERVES 2

Heat 2 tablespoons olive oil in large skillet over medium-high heat until shimmering. Add 12 ounces sliced white or cremini mushrooms and pinch salt and cook, stirring occasionally, until liquid has evaporated and mushrooms are lightly browned, 5 to 6 minutes. Stir in 2 teaspoons chopped fresh herbs (chives, tarragon, parsley, or combination). Season with salt and pepper to taste, and divide between 2 plates. Top each serving with 2 peeled Soft-Cooked Eggs (above), split crosswise to release yolks, and season with salt and pepper to taste.

Soft-Cooked Eggs with Steamed Asparagus
SERVES 2

Steam 12 ounces asparagus (spears about ½ inch in diameter, trimmed) over medium heat until crisp-tender, 4 to 5 minutes. Divide between 2 plates. Drizzle each serving with 1 tablespoon extra-virgin olive oil and sprinkle each serving with 1 tablespoon grated Parmesan. Season with salt and pepper to taste. Top each serving with 2 peeled Soft-Cooked Eggs (above), split crosswise to release yolks, and season with salt and pepper to taste.

Soft-Cooked Eggs with Salad
SERVES 2

Combine 3 tablespoons olive oil, 1 tablespoon balsamic vinegar, 1 teaspoon Dijon mustard, and 1 teaspoon minced shallot in jar, seal lid, and shake vigorously until emulsified, 20 to 30 seconds. Toss with 5 cups assertively flavored salad greens (arugula, radicchio, watercress, or frisée). Season with salt and pepper to taste, and divide between 2 plates. Top each serving with 2 peeled Soft-Cooked Eggs (above), split crosswise to release yolks, and season with salt and pepper to taste.

Fried Eggs

✔ WHY THIS RECIPE WORKS: Anyone can make fried eggs, but few and far between are the cooks who can make them perfectly every time. Eggs can stick to the skillet, yolks can break, and over- or undercooked eggs seem to be the norm. We decided to eliminate the guesswork and figure out the best and easiest way to fry the perfect egg every time. For us, this meant a firm white and a yolk that was thick yet still runny. A nonstick skillet proved key. The initial heat setting was also important. Preheating the skillet over very low heat put it at just the right temperature to receive the eggs, which were added all at once with the help of teacups. Covering the skillet as soon as the eggs were added and cooking them just two or three minutes delivered perfect fried eggs every time.

Fried Eggs
SERVES 4

Since burners vary, it may take an egg or two before you determine the ideal heat setting for frying eggs on your stovetop. It's important to follow visual cues, as skillet thickness will have an effect on cooking times. See Core Technique on page 54 for more details on this recipe.

- **4 large eggs**
- **1 tablespoon unsalted butter, chilled**
  Salt and pepper

1. Heat 12-inch nonstick skillet over low heat for 5 minutes. Meanwhile, crack open 2 eggs into teacup or small bowl; crack remaining 2 eggs into second teacup or small bowl. Add butter to skillet, let melt, and swirl to coat skillet.

2. Working quickly, pour 2 eggs into skillet on one side and remaining 2 eggs on opposite side. Season eggs with salt and pepper, cover, and cook about 2 minutes for runny yolks, 2½ minutes for soft but set yolks, or 3 minutes for firmly set yolks. Remove lid and check eggs; if necessary, cover and continue to cook to desired doneness. Slide eggs onto plate; serve.

Spaghetti with Fried Eggs and Bread Crumbs

✔ WHY THIS RECIPE WORKS: This rustic Italian specialty of garlicky spaghetti topped with fried eggs and crunchy bread crumbs shows how spectacular a simple meal can be if done well. The key is adding the eggs to the skillet all at once, rather than cracking them in one by one, to ensure that they finish cooking at the same time. Covering the skillet during cooking helped the surface of the eggs set so that we didn't have to flip them. But our perfectly fried eggs couldn't wait for the pasta—if they sat around for even a minute, the yolks firmed up, so we made sure to prepare the bread crumbs, garlic, and pasta before tackling the eggs.

Spaghetti with Fried Eggs and Bread Crumbs
SERVES 4

- **2 slices hearty white sandwich bread, torn into quarters**
- **½ cup plus 2 tablespoons extra-virgin olive oil**
  Salt and pepper
- **4 garlic cloves, minced**
- **1 pound spaghetti**
- **1 ounce Parmesan cheese, grated (½ cup), plus extra for serving**
- **4 large eggs**

1. Adjust oven rack to middle position and heat oven to 375 degrees. Pulse bread in food processor to coarse crumbs, about 10 pulses. Toss crumbs with 2 tablespoons oil, season with salt and pepper, and spread over rimmed baking sheet. Bake, stirring often, until golden, 8 to 10 minutes.

2. Cook 3 tablespoons oil, garlic, and ¼ teaspoon salt in 12-inch nonstick skillet over low heat, stirring often, until garlic foams and is sticky and straw-colored, 8 to 10 minutes; transfer to bowl.

3. Meanwhile, bring 4 quarts water to boil in large pot. Add pasta and 1 tablespoon salt and cook, stirring often, until al dente. Reserve 1 cup cooking water, then drain pasta and return it to pot. Add garlic mixture, 3 tablespoons oil, Parmesan, and ½ cup reserved cooking water and toss to combine; cover and set aside while cooking eggs.

4. About 5 minutes before pasta is ready, wipe now-empty skillet clean with paper towels and place over low heat for 5 minutes. Meanwhile, crack open 2 eggs into 1 teacup or small bowl; crack remaining 2 eggs into second teacup or small bowl. Add remaining 2 tablespoons oil to skillet and swirl to coat. Working quickly, pour 2 eggs into skillet on one side and remaining 2 eggs on opposite side. Season eggs with salt and pepper, cover, and cook until whites are set but yolks are still runny, about 2 minutes.

5. Season pasta with salt and pepper to taste and add reserved cooking water as needed to adjust consistency. Top individual portions with bread crumbs and fried egg and serve with extra Parmesan.

Best Scrambled Eggs

✔ WHY THIS RECIPE WORKS: Scrambled eggs often end up as tough, dry slabs or pebbly, runny curds. We wanted foolproof scrambled eggs with fluffy, moist curds that were creamy and light. The first step was to add salt to the uncooked eggs; salt dissolves some of the egg proteins so they are unable to bond when cooked, creating more tender curds. Beating the eggs gently with a fork until thoroughly combined ensured our scramble didn't turn tough. Half-and-half was preferred over milk, producing clean-tasting curds that were both fluffy and stable. To replicate the richer flavor of farm-fresh eggs, we added extra yolks. We started the eggs on medium-high heat to create puffy curds, then finished them over low heat to ensure that they wouldn't overcook.

Best Scrambled Eggs

SERVES 4

It's important to follow visual cues, as skillet thickness will have an effect on cooking times. If you don't have half-and-half, you can substitute 2 tablespoons plus 2 teaspoons whole milk and 4 teaspoons heavy cream. To dress up the eggs, add 2 tablespoons minced fresh parsley, chives, basil, or cilantro or 1 tablespoon minced fresh dill or tarragon after reducing the heat to low. See Core Technique on page 56 for more details on this recipe.

- **8 large eggs plus 2 large yolks**
- **¼ cup half-and-half**
  Salt
- **¼ teaspoon pepper**
- **1 tablespoon unsalted butter, chilled**

1. Beat eggs and yolks, half-and-half, ¼ teaspoon salt, and pepper with fork until thoroughly combined and mixture is pure yellow; do not overbeat.

2. Melt butter in 10-inch nonstick skillet over medium-high heat until foaming just subsides, swirling to coat skillet (butter should not brown). Add egg mixture and, using heat-resistant rubber spatula, constantly and firmly scrape along bottom and sides of skillet until eggs begin to clump and spatula leaves trail on bottom of skillet, 1½ to 2½ minutes. Reduce heat to low and gently but constantly fold eggs until clumped and slightly wet, 30 to 60 seconds. Immediately transfer eggs to warmed plates and season with salt to taste. Serve immediately.

Best Scrambled Eggs for Two

Reduce eggs to 4, egg yolks to 1, half-and-half to 2 tablespoons, salt and pepper to ⅛ teaspoon each, and butter to ½ tablespoon. Cook eggs in 8-inch skillet for 45 to 75 seconds over medium-high heat and then 30 to 60 seconds over low heat.

Best Scrambled Eggs for One

Reduce eggs to 2, egg yolks to 1, half-and-half to 1 tablespoon, salt and pepper to pinch each, and butter to ¼ tablespoon. Cook eggs in 8-inch skillet for 30 to 60 seconds over medium-high heat and then 30 to 60 seconds over low heat.

Smoked Salmon Scrambled Eggs with Chive Butter

☑ **WHY THIS RECIPE WORKS:** Scrambled eggs may seem straightforward, but we tested a variety of methods for making them and had dramatically different results with each. First, we learned that adding a couple of extra yolks enriched the flavor, and the extra fat and emulsifiers raised the coagulation temperature, which helped eliminate the issue of overcooking. A hot skillet and a unique folding method yielded the creamiest, softest scrambled eggs. Pushing the eggs gently to and fro with a spatula instead of constantly stirring them produced large, airy curds and fluffy scrambled eggs. We also used a dual-heat method, starting the eggs over medium-high heat for puffy curds and then turning the heat down to gently finish.

Smoked Salmon Scrambled Eggs with Chive Butter

SERVES 4 TO 6

You can substitute ¼ cup whole milk mixed with 2 tablespoons heavy cream for the half-and-half if necessary. It's important to follow the visual cues when cooking the eggs, as skillet thickness will affect cooking times. Most electric burners do not react quickly enough for the change in heat level (from medium-high to low) as directed in step 3; instead, preheat a second burner on low, and slide the skillet onto it as you begin step 3. If desired, garnish with extra chives.

- **10 large eggs plus 2 large yolks**
- **6 tablespoons half-and-half**
- **¾ teaspoon salt**
- **¼ teaspoon pepper**
- **4 tablespoons unsalted butter, softened**
- **¼ cup minced fresh chives**
- **6 (1-inch-thick) slices rustic white bread, toasted**
- **4 ounces smoked salmon**

1. Beat eggs and yolks, half-and-half, salt, and pepper with fork until thoroughly combined and mixture is pure yellow; do not overbeat. In separate bowl, mash butter and chives together. Spread 3 tablespoons chive butter over toast; set aside.

2. Melt remaining 1 tablespoon chive butter in 12-inch nonstick skillet over medium-high heat until foaming just subsides, swirling to coat skillet (butter should not brown). Add egg mixture and, using heat-resistant rubber spatula, constantly and firmly scrape along bottom and sides of skillet until eggs begin to clump and spatula leaves trail on bottom of skillet, 1½ to 2½ minutes.

3. Reduce heat to low and gently but constantly fold eggs until clumped and slightly wet, 30 to 60 seconds. Immediately spoon eggs on top of buttered toast, top with salmon, and serve.

Poached Eggs

☑ **WHY THIS RECIPE WORKS:** A poached egg should be tender and evenly cooked, with a white like baked custard and a yolk that runs just a little. But a poached egg is very delicate; it can be hard to get it in and out of the water without breaking it, and the boiling water or the bottom of the pot can damage it as well. There's also the problem of those unappealing wandering strands of egg white. To address these difficulties, we traded in the usual saucepan for a shallow nonstick skillet, which gives the cook much easier access to the eggs. The addition of vinegar to the cooking water helped to set the eggs quickly, and salting the water seasoned the eggs nicely. Removing the skillet from the heat limited the eggs' exposure to rapidly boiling water, which can cause them to disintegrate. These simple tricks gave us perfectly cooked eggs with no feathering of whites.

Poached Eggs

SERVES 2

You will need a 12-inch nonstick skillet with a tight-fitting lid. See Core Technique on page 59 for more details on this recipe.

Salt and pepper
2 tablespoons distilled white vinegar
4 large eggs

1. Fill 12-inch nonstick skillet nearly to rim with water, add 1 teaspoon salt and vinegar, and bring to boil over high heat. Crack 2 eggs each into 2 teacups with handles.

2. Lower lips of cups into water and tip eggs into skillet. Cover, remove from heat, and let sit until whites are set, about 4 minutes (yolks will be slightly runny; for firmer yolks, cook an additional 30 to 60 seconds).

3. Using slotted spoon, carefully remove each egg, letting water drain back into skillet, and transfer to large paper towel–lined plate. Season with salt and pepper to taste and serve immediately.

Eggs Benedict

✔ **WHY THIS RECIPE WORKS:** Seasoning the water with both salt and white vinegar was an essential first step for our Eggs Benedict. Not only did they flavor the eggs, the vinegar also helped to set the whites as they cooked and prevented uneven, feathery whites. We cracked the eggs into teacups and then gently slid the eggs into the hot water all at once; this technique enabled us to achieve even cooking and ensured the eggs remained intact. We covered the skillet and removed it from the heat because rapidly boiling water can cause the eggs to disintegrate. We let the eggs sit in the skillet so that they could cook gently in the residual heat, ensuring the whites were tender and whole. This method produces restaurant-worthy poached eggs, with soft, runny yolks and perfectly formed, round whites.

Eggs Benedict

SERVES 6

The test kitchen's favorite Canadian bacon is Applegate Farms. If you like, you can toast the English muffins and warm the bacon up to 20 minutes in advance of cooking the eggs. Reheat them in a 200-degree oven just before serving. You will need a 12-inch nonstick skillet with a tight-fitting lid for this recipe. See Recipe Tutorial on page 68 for more details on this recipe.

2 tablespoons distilled white vinegar
1 teaspoon salt
12 large eggs
6 English muffins, split
12 slices Canadian bacon
1 recipe Foolproof Hollandaise (recipe follows)

1. Adjust oven rack 8 inches from broiler element and heat broiler. Fill 12-inch nonstick skillet nearly to rim with water. Add vinegar and salt and bring to boil over high heat. Crack 3 eggs each into 4 teacups with handles.

2. Lower lips of teacups into water and tip eggs into skillet. Cover, remove from heat, and let sit until whites are set, about 6 minutes (yolks will be slightly runny; for firmer yolks, cook an additional 30 to 60 seconds). Using slotted spoon, carefully remove each egg, letting water drain back into skillet, and transfer to large paper towel–lined plate.

3. While eggs are poaching, arrange English muffins, split side up, on rimmed baking sheet and broil until golden brown, 2 to 4 minutes. Place 1 slice Canadian bacon on each English muffin and broil until beginning to brown, about 1 minute. (If eggs aren't done, turn off broiler and transfer sheet to lower rack to keep warm.)

4. Arrange 1 poached egg on top of each English muffin half. Spoon 1 to 2 tablespoons hollandaise over each egg. Serve, passing remaining hollandaise separately.

Foolproof Hollandaise

✔ **WHY THIS RECIPE WORKS:** Many newer recipes call for making hollandaise in a blender or food processor to ensure an emulsified sauce. These methods work, but only if the sauce is served immediately. Our unconventional technique began with whisking softened butter and egg yolks together on the stovetop in a double boiler, then adding a lot of water, followed by lemon juice off the heat. It was foamier than a classic hollandaise, but it held without breaking until the other components were ready.

Foolproof Hollandaise

MAKES ABOUT 2 CUPS

For an accurate measurement of boiling water, bring a full kettle of water to a boil, then measure out the desired amount. You will need an instant-read thermometer to make this recipe.

12 tablespoons unsalted butter, softened
6 large egg yolks
½ cup boiling water
2 teaspoons lemon juice
⅛ teaspoon cayenne pepper
Salt

Whisk butter and egg yolks together in large heatproof bowl set over medium saucepan filled with ½ inch of barely simmering water (don't let bowl touch water). Slowly add boiling water and cook, whisking constantly, until thickened and sauce registers 160 degrees, 7 to 10 minutes. Off heat, stir in lemon juice and cayenne. Season with salt to taste. Serve.

TO MAKE AHEAD: Hollandaise can be held at room temperature for up to 1 hour or refrigerated in an airtight container for up to 3 days. To warm before serving, microwave on 50 percent power, stirring every 10 seconds, until heated through, about 1 minute.

Eggs Florentine

☑ **WHY THIS RECIPE WORKS:** This healthy take on eggs Benedict swaps in spinach, tomato, and a spread of goat cheese for the bacon and hollandaise, but like the original, it relies on perfectly poached eggs. Cracking the eggs into teacups allowed up to slip them into the water simultaneously, and cooking them covered off the heat, with a little vinegar in the water, ensured perfectly cooked eggs. After sautéing the spinach, we squeezed out the excess water to keep the muffins from becoming soggy.

Eggs Florentine

SERVES 4

You will need a 12-inch nonstick skillet with a tight-fitting lid for this recipe.

- 2 **ounces goat cheese, crumbled (½ cup)**
- ½ **teaspoon lemon juice**
   Salt and pepper
- 2 **English muffins, split, toasted, and still warm**
- 1 **tomato, cored, seeded, and sliced thin (about 8 slices)**
- 2 **teaspoons olive oil**
- 1 **shallot, minced**
- 1 **garlic clove, minced**
- 4 **ounces (4 cups) baby spinach**
- 2 **tablespoons distilled white vinegar**
- 4 **large eggs**

1. Adjust oven rack to middle position and heat oven to 300 degrees. Combine goat cheese, lemon juice, and ⅛ teaspoon pepper in bowl until smooth. Spread goat cheese mixture evenly over English muffin halves, top with tomato, and arrange on baking sheet; keep warm in oven.

2. Heat oil in 12-inch nonstick skillet over medium heat until shimmering. Add shallot and cook until softened, about 2 minutes. Stir in garlic and cook until fragrant, about 30 seconds. Stir in spinach and ⅛ teaspoon salt and cook until wilted, about 1 minute. Using tongs, squeeze out any excess moisture from spinach and divide evenly among English muffins.

3. Wipe out now-empty skillet with paper towels and fill it nearly to rim with water. Add vinegar and 1 teaspoon salt and bring to boil over high heat. Crack 2 eggs each into 2 teacups with handles. Lower lips of teacups into water and tip eggs into skillet. Cover, remove from heat, and let sit until whites are set, about 4 minutes (yolks will be slightly runny; for firmer yolks, cook an additional 30 to 60 seconds).

4. Using slotted spoon, carefully remove each egg, letting water drain back into skillet, and transfer to large paper towel–lined plate. Arrange 1 poached egg on top of each spinach-topped muffin half. Season with salt and pepper to taste and serve.

Fluffy Diner-Style Cheese Omelet

☑ **WHY THIS RECIPE WORKS:** For a tall, fluffy, omelet, we ditched the whisk for an electric mixer, which helped us incorporate air into the eggs. Cream added richness, but when we added it to the whipped eggs, the omelet lost its fluffiness. Combining the cream and eggs before whipping didn't work either; the fat in the cream made it impossible to whip air into the eggs. So we whipped the dairy first, then folded it into the whipped eggs. After letting the bottom of the omelet set on the stovetop, we popped the skillet into the oven, and 6 minutes later we had a perfectly puffy, fluffy omelet.

Fluffy Diner-Style Cheese Omelet

SERVES 2

A hand-held mixer makes quick work of whipping such a small amount of cream, but you can also use a stand mixer fitted with the whisk attachment. To make two omelets, double this recipe and cook the omelets simultaneously in two skillets. If you have only one skillet, prepare a double batch of ingredients and set half aside for the second omelet. Be sure to wipe out the skillet before making the second omelet. See Core Technique on page 62 for more details on this recipe.

- 3 **tablespoons heavy cream, chilled**
- 5 **large eggs, room temperature**
- ¼ **teaspoon salt**
- 2 **tablespoons unsalted butter**
- 2 **ounces sharp cheddar cheese, shredded (½ cup)**
- 1 **recipe omelet filling (optional) (recipes follow)**

1. Adjust oven rack to middle position and heat oven to 400 degrees. Using hand-held mixer, whip cream on medium-low speed until foamy, about 1 minute. Increase speed to high and whip until soft peaks form, 1 to 3 minutes. Set whipped cream aside. Using dry, clean whisk attachment, whip eggs and salt in large bowl on high speed until frothy and eggs have at least doubled in volume, about 2 minutes. Using rubber spatula, gently fold whipped cream into eggs.

2. Melt butter in 10-inch nonstick ovensafe skillet over medium-low heat, swirling skillet to coat bottom and sides. Add egg mixture and cook until edges are nearly set, 2 to 3 minutes. Sprinkle with ¼ cup cheddar and half of omelet filling, if using, and transfer to oven. Bake until eggs are set and edges are beginning to brown, 6 to 8 minutes.

3. Carefully remove skillet from oven (handle will be hot), sprinkle eggs with remaining ¼ cup cheddar. Let sit, covered, until cheese melts, about 1 minute. Tilt skillet and, using rubber spatula, push half of omelet onto cutting board, then fold omelet over itself on cutting board to form half-moon shape (or, if filling omelet, after cheese melts, slide entire omelet onto cutting board, sprinkle half of omelet with remaining filling, then fold closed). Cut omelet in half and serve.

Sausage and Pepper Filling
MAKES ENOUGH FOR 1 RECIPE FLUFFY
DINER-STYLE CHEESE OMELET

- 4 ounces hot or sweet Italian sausage, casings removed
- 1 tablespoon unsalted butter
- 1 small onion, chopped
- ½ red bell pepper, chopped
   Salt and pepper

Cook sausage in 10-inch nonstick skillet over medium heat, breaking up clumps with wooden spoon, until browned, about 6 minutes. Transfer to paper towel–lined plate. Add butter, onion, and bell pepper to now-empty skillet and cook until softened, about 10 minutes. Stir in sausage and season with salt and pepper to taste.

Loaded Baked Potato Filling
MAKES ENOUGH FOR 1 RECIPE FLUFFY
DINER-STYLE CHEESE OMELET

- 1 large Yukon Gold potato, peeled and cut into ½-inch pieces
- 4 slices bacon, chopped
- 2 scallions, sliced thin
   Salt and pepper

Microwave potato, covered, in large bowl until just tender, 2 to 5 minutes. Cook bacon in 10-inch nonstick skillet over medium heat until crisp, about 8 minutes. Transfer bacon to paper towel–lined plate; pour off all but 1 tablespoon bacon fat. Add potato to skillet and cook until golden brown, about 6 minutes. Transfer potato to bowl, add cooked bacon, and stir in scallions. Season with salt and pepper to taste.

Perfect French Omelets

✔ **WHY THIS RECIPE WORKS:** In contrast to half-moon, diner-style omelets stuffed to the seams, the French omelet is a pristine rolled affair. The temperature of the skillet must be just right, the eggs beaten just so, and hand movements must be as swift as the ability to gauge the exact second the omelet is done. Even a few extra seconds can spell disaster. A French omelet should boast an ultracreamy texture, rolled over minimal filling. We replaced the classic omelet skillet and fork with a simple nonstick skillet and wooden chopsticks. We preheated the skillet slowly over low heat to eliminate hot spots. Exact timing gives the omelet its creaminess, but we wanted to cheat with creamy ingredients; cold butter worked perfectly. Beating the eggs correctly is the key to lightness so we found the perfect number of strokes. We needed at least medium-high heat to puff up the

eggs with steam, but the omelet cooked too quickly to judge when it was done. We turned off the heat when the eggs were still runny, letting residual heat do the rest of the cooking, giving us a flawless, creamy French omelet.

Perfect French Omelets
SERVES 2

Because making omelets is such a quick process, make sure to have all your ingredients and equipment at the ready. If you don't have chopsticks or skewers to stir the eggs in step 3, use the handle of a wooden spoon. Warm the plates in a 200-degree oven. See Recipe Tutorial on page 72 for more details on this recipe.

- 2 tablespoons unsalted butter, cut into 2 pieces
- ½ teaspoon vegetable oil
- 6 large eggs, cold
- ¼ teaspoon salt
   Pepper
- 2 tablespoons shredded Gruyère cheese
- 4 teaspoons minced fresh chives

1. Cut 1 tablespoon butter in half. Cut remaining 1 tablespoon butter into small pieces, transfer to small bowl, and place in freezer while preparing eggs and skillet, at least 10 minutes. Meanwhile, heat oil in 8-inch nonstick skillet over low heat for 10 minutes.

2. Crack 2 eggs into medium bowl and separate third egg; reserve egg white for another use and add egg yolk to bowl. Add ⅛ teaspoon salt and pinch pepper. Break egg yolks with fork, then beat eggs at moderate pace, about 80 strokes, until yolks and whites are well combined. Stir in half of frozen butter cubes.

3. When skillet is fully heated, use paper towels to wipe out oil, leaving thin film on bottom and sides of skillet. Add ½ tablespoon reserved butter to skillet and heat until melted. Swirl butter to coat skillet, add egg mixture, and increase heat to medium-high. Using 2 chopsticks or wooden skewers, scramble eggs with quick circular motion, moving around skillet and scraping cooked egg from side of skillet as you go, until eggs are almost cooked but still slightly runny, 45 to 90 seconds. Turn off heat (remove skillet from heat if using electric burner) and smooth eggs into even layer using heat-resistant rubber spatula. Sprinkle omelet with 1 tablespoon Gruyère and 2 teaspoons chives. Cover skillet with tight-fitting lid and let sit for 1 minute for runnier omelet or 2 minutes for firmer omelet.

4. Heat skillet over low heat for 20 seconds, uncover, and, using rubber spatula, loosen edges of omelet from skillet. Place folded square of paper towel onto warmed plate and slide omelet out of skillet onto paper towel so that omelet lies flat on plate and hangs about 1 inch off paper towel. Using paper towel to lift omelet, roll omelet into neat cylinder and set aside. Return skillet to low heat and heat for 2 minutes before repeating instructions for second omelet starting with step 2. Serve.

Hearty Frittata

WHY THIS RECIPE WORKS: More challenging to cook properly than a classic frittata, a thick frittata loaded with meat and vegetables often ends up dry, overstuffed, and overcooked. We wanted a frittata big enough to make a substantial meal for six to eight people. For the cheese, Gruyère, cheddar, goat cheese, and fontina worked well. We found that vegetables and meats must be cut into small pieces and precooked to drive off excess moisture and fat. A little half-and-half added a touch of creaminess. Given the large number of eggs, we started the eggs on medium heat and stirred them so they could cook quickly yet evenly. Then we slid the skillet under the broiler until the top had puffed and browned, removing it just before the frittata was cooked through, allowing the residual heat to finish cooking the center.

Hearty Frittata with Asparagus, Ham, and Gruyère

SERVES 6 TO 8

A 12-inch ovensafe nonstick skillet is a must for this recipe. Because broilers vary so much in intensity, watch the frittata carefully as it cooks. See Core Technique on page 64 for more details on this recipe.

- 12 **large eggs**
- 3 **tablespoons half-and-half**
- ½ **teaspoon salt**
- ¼ **teaspoon pepper**
- 2 **teaspoons olive oil**
- 8 **ounces asparagus, trimmed and cut on bias into ¼-inch pieces**
- 4 **ounces ¼-inch-thick deli ham, cut into ¼-inch cubes**
- 1 **shallot, minced**
- 3 **ounces Gruyère cheese, cut into ¼-inch cubes (¾ cup)**

1. Adjust oven rack 5 inches from broiler element and heat broiler. Whisk eggs, half-and-half, salt, and pepper in medium bowl until well combined, about 30 seconds; set aside.

2. Heat oil in 12-inch ovensafe nonstick skillet over medium heat until shimmering; add asparagus and cook, stirring occasionally, until lightly browned and almost tender, about 3 minutes. Add ham and shallot; cook until shallot begins to soften, about 2 minutes. Stir Gruyère into eggs. Add egg mixture to skillet and cook, using heat-resistant rubber spatula to stir and scrape bottom of skillet, until large curds form and spatula begins to leave trail but eggs are still very wet, about 2 minutes. Shake skillet to distribute eggs evenly, using spatula to even out top of frittata. Cook without stirring for 30 seconds to let bottom set.

3. Broil until frittata has risen and surface is puffed and spotty brown, 3 to 4 minutes; when cut into with paring knife, eggs should be slightly wet and runny. Remove skillet from oven; let sit for 5 minutes. Using spatula, loosen frittata from skillet and slide onto serving platter or cutting board. Cut into wedges and serve.

Hearty Frittata with Leek, Prosciutto, and Goat Cheese

SERVES 6 TO 8

A 12-inch ovensafe nonstick skillet is a must for this recipe. Because broilers vary so much in intensity, watch the frittata carefully as it cooks. See Core Technique on page 64 for more details on this recipe.

- 12 **large eggs**
- 3 **tablespoons half-and-half**
- ¾ **teaspoon salt**
- ¼ **teaspoon pepper**
- 2 **tablespoons unsalted butter**
- 2 **small leeks, white and light green parts only, halved lengthwise, sliced thin, and washed thoroughly**
- 4 **ounces goat cheese, crumbled (1 cup)**
- 3 **ounces thinly sliced prosciutto, cut into ½-inch strips**
- ¼ **cup chopped fresh basil**

1. Adjust oven rack 5 inches from broiler element and heat broiler. Whisk eggs, half-and-half, ½ teaspoon salt, and pepper in medium bowl until well combined, about 30 seconds; set aside.

2. Melt butter in 12-inch ovensafe nonstick skillet over medium heat. Add leeks and remaining ¼ teaspoon salt; reduce heat to low and cook covered, stirring occasionally, until softened, 8 to 10 minutes. Stir half of goat cheese, then prosciutto, and basil into eggs; add egg mixture to skillet and cook, using heat-resistant rubber spatula to stir and scrape bottom of skillet, until large curds form and spatula begins to leave trail but eggs are still very wet, about 2 minutes. Shake skillet to distribute eggs evenly, using spatula to even out top of frittata. Cook without stirring for 30 seconds to let bottom set.

3. Sprinkle remaining goat cheese evenly over frittata. Broil until frittata has risen and surface is puffed and spotty brown, 3 to 4 minutes; when cut into with paring knife, eggs should be slightly wet and runny. Remove skillet from oven; let sit for 5 minutes. Using spatula, loosen frittata from skillet and slide onto serving platter or cutting board. Cut into wedges and serve.

Simple Cheese Quiche

WHY THIS RECIPE WORKS: Our ideal quiche should have a tender, buttery pastry case embracing a velvety smooth custard that is neither too rich nor too lean. We tested numerous combinations of dairy and eggs to find the perfect combination. The baking temperature was equally important; 350 degrees was low enough to set the custard gently and hot enough to brown the top before the filling became dried out and rubbery. To keep the crust from becoming soggy, we parbaked it before adding the filling. To avoid spilling the custard, we set the parbaked crust on the baking sheet and poured the custard directly into the pastry shell. For perfectly baked quiche every time, we pulled it out of the oven when it was still slightly soft and allowed it to set up as it cooled.

Simple Cheese Quiche

SERVES 6 TO 8

Be sure to add the custard to the pie shell while it is still warm so the quiche will bake evenly. You can substitute other fresh herbs for the chives, like thyme, parsley, or marjoram. See Core Technique on page 66 for more details on this recipe and page 744 for more details on making our Foolproof Pie Dough.

    5 large eggs
    2 cups half-and-half
    ¼ teaspoon salt
    ¼ teaspoon pepper
    4 ounces cheddar cheese, shredded (1 cup)
    1 tablespoon minced fresh chives
    1 recipe Foolproof Single-Crust Pie Dough (page 744), partially baked and still warm

1. Adjust oven rack to lower-middle position and heat oven to 350 degrees. Whisk eggs, half-and-half, salt, and pepper together in large bowl. Stir in cheddar and chives until well combined. Transfer filling to 4-cup liquid measuring cup.

2. Place warm pie shell on rimmed baking sheet and place in oven. Carefully pour egg mixture into warm shell until it reaches about ½ inch from top edge of crust (you may have extra egg mixture).

3. Bake quiche until top is lightly browned, center is set but soft, and knife inserted about 1 inch from edge comes out clean, 40 to 50 minutes. Let quiche cool for at least 1 hour or up to 3 hours. Serve slightly warm or at room temperature.

TO MAKE AHEAD: Let quiche cool completely, then cover with plastic wrap and refrigerate for up to 6 hours. (Crust of refrigerated quiche will be less crisp.) Quiche can be served slightly chilled, at room temperature, or warm; to serve warm, reheat in 350-degree oven for 10 to 15 minutes.

Quiche Lorraine

Fry 4 slices finely chopped bacon in 10-inch skillet over medium heat until crisp, 5 to 7 minutes. Transfer bacon to paper towel–lined plate and discard all but 2 teaspoons bacon fat from skillet. Add 1 small minced onion to skillet and cook over medium heat until lightly browned, about 5 minutes. Substitute 1 cup shredded Gruyère for cheddar, and stir bacon and onion into egg mixture with cheese in step 1.

Leek and Goat Cheese Quiche

Melt 2 tablespoons unsalted butter in 10-inch skillet over medium-high heat. Add 2 finely chopped leeks, white and light green parts only, and cook until softened, about 6 minutes. Substitute 1 cup crumbled goat cheese for cheddar, and stir cooked leeks into egg mixture with cheese in step 1.

Spinach and Feta Quiche

Removing the excess moisture from the spinach is crucial here. Omit chives and substitute 1 cup crumbled feta cheese for cheddar. Stir 1 (10-ounce) package frozen chopped spinach, thawed and squeezed dry, into egg mixture with cheese in step 1.

Asparagus and Gruyère Quiche

Do not substitute precooked or frozen asparagus here. Substitute 1 cup shredded Gruyère for cheddar, and stir 1 bunch asparagus, trimmed and sliced on bias into ¼-inch-thick pieces, into egg mixture with cheese in step 1.

Broccoli and Cheddar Quiche

Do not substitute frozen broccoli here. Bring 4 cups chopped broccoli florets, ½ cup water, and ¼ teaspoon salt to boil in covered 12-inch skillet and cook until broccoli is bright green, about 3 minutes. Uncover and continue to cook until broccoli is tender and water has evaporated, about 3 minutes. Pat broccoli dry with paper towels, then sprinkle over warm pie shell before adding egg mixture in step 2.

Cheese Soufflé

✔ **WHY THIS RECIPE WORKS:** A classic cheese soufflé begins with a béchamel sauce (flour and butter cooked to form a roux and then thinned out with milk). We started by sautéing a shallot in the butter to add flavor. Once the béchamel was finished, we stirred in a generous amount of Gruyère along with a little dry mustard, nutmeg, salt, and pepper to boost the flavor of the cheese. We then added the egg yolks to this base before whipping the whites (with a little cream of tartar for stability) and folding them in last. For an extra shot of cheese, sprinkle the greased soufflé dish as well as the top of the soufflé with a little grated Parmesan. Also, after pouring the batter into the dish, trace a circle in the batter with your finger, about ½ inch from the edge of the dish. We found this breaks the surface tension and helps the soufflé achieve a high, even rise.

Cheese Soufflé

SERVES 3 TO 4 AS A MAIN DISH

Cheddar, Swiss, or gouda can be substituted for the Gruyère. Begin beating the egg whites as soon as you finish making the soufflé base—don't let the base cool too much. Do not open the oven door during the first 15 minutes of baking time; as the soufflé nears the end of its baking, you can check its progress by opening the oven door slightly. This recipe can be prepared in an 8½ by 4½-inch glass loaf pan if you don't have a soufflé dish. See Recipe Tutorial on page 76 for more details on this recipe.

    ¼ cup grated Parmesan cheese
    3 tablespoons unsalted butter
    1 shallot, minced
    3 tablespoons all-purpose flour
    1 cup whole milk
    4 ounces Gruyère cheese, shredded (1 cup)
    ½ teaspoon salt
    ¼ teaspoon dry mustard
    ¼ teaspoon pepper
       Pinch ground nutmeg
    3 large eggs, separated, room temperature
    ¼ teaspoon cream of tartar

1. Adjust oven rack to middle position and heat oven to 350 degrees. Spray 1½-quart soufflé dish with vegetable oil spray, then sprinkle 2 tablespoons Parmesan into dish and shake to coat evenly; tap out any excess.

2. Melt butter in medium saucepan over medium heat. Add shallot and cook until softened, about 2 minutes. Stir in flour and cook until golden, about 1 minute. Slowly whisk in milk. Bring to simmer; cook, whisking constantly, until thickened and smooth, about 1 minute. Off heat, whisk in Gruyère, salt, mustard, pepper, and nutmeg. Scrape mixture into medium bowl. Whisk in egg yolks until incorporated (this is soufflé base).

3. Using stand mixer fitted with whisk, whip egg whites and cream of tartar on medium-low speed until foamy, about 1 minute. Increase speed to medium-high and continue to whip until stiff peaks form, 3 to 4 minutes.

4. Using rubber spatula, fold one-quarter of whipped egg whites into warm soufflé base until almost no white streaks remain. Fold in remaining egg whites until just incorporated. Gently pour mixture into prepared dish, wiping any batter from rim with wet paper towel. Trace circle in batter with your finger, about ½ inch from edge of dish (this will help soufflé rise nicely). Sprinkle with remaining 2 tablespoons Parmesan.

5. Bake soufflé until surface is deep brown, center jiggles slightly when shaken, and soufflé has risen 2 to 2½ inches above rim of dish, 22 to 27 minutes. Serve immediately.

Cheese Soufflé with Fines Herbes

Stir 1 tablespoon minced fresh chives, 1 tablespoon minced fresh parsley, and 1½ teaspoons minced fresh tarragon into soufflé base with egg yolks in step 2.

Cheese Soufflé with Spinach

Stir 4 ounces chopped frozen spinach, thawed and squeezed dry, and ½ teaspoon minced fresh thyme into soufflé base with egg yolks in step 2.

Chocolate Soufflé

☑ **WHY THIS RECIPE WORKS:** The texture of a perfect soufflé should graduate from crusty exterior to airy but substantial outer layer to rich, soft center. For a chocolate soufflé, the chocolate notes should be deep and strong. We began with a béchamel base (a classic French sauce made with equal amounts of butter and flour and whisked with milk over heat) and eggs, but the milk muted the chocolate. Removing the milk and the flour, upping the chocolate, and reducing the butter improved the chocolate flavor. For the eggs, we separated them and beat the yolks with sugar until thick. Whipping the whites, plus two additional whites, delivered a soufflé with lift and superior texture.

Chocolate Soufflé
SERVES 6 TO 8

To melt the chocolate using a microwave, heat it at 50 percent power for 2 minutes; stir the chocolate, add the butter, and continue heating until melted, stirring once every additional minute. A soufflé waits for no one, so be ready to serve it immediately.

- **4 tablespoons unsalted butter, cut into ½-inch pieces, plus 1 tablespoon, softened**
- **⅓ cup (2⅓ ounces) plus 1 tablespoon sugar**
- **8 ounces bittersweet or semisweet chocolate, chopped coarse**
- **1 tablespoon orange-flavored liqueur, such as Grand Marnier**
- **½ teaspoon vanilla extract**
- **⅛ teaspoon salt**
- **6 large eggs, separated, plus 2 large whites**
- **¼ teaspoon cream of tartar**

1. Adjust oven rack to lower-middle position and heat oven to 375 degrees. Grease 2-quart soufflé dish with 1 tablespoon softened butter, then coat dish evenly with 1 tablespoon sugar; refrigerate until ready to use.

2. Melt chocolate and remaining 4 tablespoons butter in medium heatproof bowl set over saucepan of barely simmering water, stirring occasionally, until smooth. Stir in liqueur, vanilla, and salt; set aside.

3. Using stand mixer fitted with paddle, beat egg yolks and remaining ⅓ cup sugar on medium speed until thick and pale yellow, about 3 minutes. Fold into chocolate mixture.

4. Using dry, clean bowl and whisk attachment, whip egg whites and cream of tartar on medium-low speed until foamy, about 1 minute. Increase speed to medium-high and whip until stiff peaks form, 3 to 4 minutes.

5. Using rubber spatula, vigorously stir one-quarter of whipped whites into chocolate mixture. Gently fold in remaining whites until just incorporated. Gently pour mixture into prepared dish, wiping any batter from rim with wet paper towel. Trace circle in batter with your finger, about ½ inch from edge of dish (this will help soufflé rise nicely). Bake until fragrant, fully risen, and exterior is set but interior is still a bit loose and creamy, about 25 minutes. (Use 2 large spoons to pull open top and peek inside.) Serve immediately.

Mocha Soufflé

Add 1 tablespoon instant espresso powder dissolved in 1 tablespoon hot water when adding vanilla to chocolate mixture in step 2.

Individual Chocolate Soufflés

Omit 2-quart soufflé dish. Grease eight 8-ounce ramekins with butter and sugar and refrigerate as directed. In step 5, transfer soufflé mixture to ramekins, making sure to completely fill each ramekin and wipe each rim with wet paper towel. Reduce baking time to 16 to 18 minutes.

Make-Ahead Individual Chocolate Soufflés

Omit 2-quart soufflé dish. Grease eight 8-ounce ramekins with butter and sugar and refrigerate as directed. In step 3, bring sugar and 2 tablespoons water to boil in small saucepan, then reduce heat and simmer until sugar dissolves. With mixer running, slowly add sugar syrup to egg yolks and beat until mixture triples in volume, about 3 minutes. Whip egg whites as directed, beating in 2 tablespoons confectioners' sugar. Stir and fold into chocolate base as directed. Fill each chilled ramekin almost to rim, wiping each rim clean with wet paper towel. Cover each ramekin tightly with plastic wrap and freeze until firm, at least 3 hours or up to 1 month. (Do not thaw before baking.) To serve, heat oven to 400 degrees and reduce baking time to 16 to 18 minutes.

Inside This Chapter

CHAPTER 3

How to Cook Vegetables

Turning out perfectly cooked, flavorful vegetable dishes requires some finesse. In this chapter, we start with demystifying the art of picking out the freshest vegetables at the market, share the best ways to store them, and illustrate how to prepare them for cooking. There are numerous ways you can cook vegetables, and each method has its own tricks. Here we cover everything from properly boiling and steaming to roasting, frying, grilling, to mashing. Casseroles that make vegetables the star are also included.

Getting Started

Vegetables A to Z

Over the years, we've developed some different preferences in the test kitchen when it comes to sizes and varieties of vegetables you should buy. We've summarized this advice in the entries that follow. We also describe any unusual techniques that we've developed to prolong freshness, along with general cooking information for vegetables that can often cause confusion. Also see salad greens on pages 472–473.

ARTICHOKES
- Buy small or medium artichokes; large artichokes can be tough and fibrous. Look for artichokes that are compact, unblemished, and bright green. Avoid those with shriveled brown stems or leaves. If you tug at a leaf, it should snap off cleanly.
- It is important to submerge artichokes in acidulated water (water with a small amount of vinegar, or lemon or lime juice) as soon as they are cut to prevent browning.
- It is best to steam medium artichokes and serve with a lemony vinaigrette. Small or baby artichokes are best roasted.
- Artichokes will keep for up to five days if sprinkled lightly with water and stored in a zipper-lock bag.

ASPARAGUS
- Medium-thick asparagus (about ⅝ inch) work best in most recipes, since larger spears must be peeled and pencil-thin specimens overcook easily.
- White asparagus has no color because it is grown without light. It costs more than traditional asparagus, and its delicate flavor doesn't survive long-distance shipping. Buy white asparagus only if very fresh.
- To perk up slightly limp asparagus, trim ends and stand spears up in a glass or jar filled with 1 inch of water; refrigerate overnight. In fact, we like to store asparagus this way, covered with plastic wrap.

AVOCADOS
- Buy small, rough-skinned Hass variety rather than larger, smooth-skinned Fuerte; Hass are creamier and less watery.
- Don't use an avocado until it is ripe; it should yield slightly to a gentle squeeze. If in doubt, try to remove the small stem; it should flick off easily and reveal green underneath.
- Halved and pitted avocados can be stored cut side down on a plate drizzled with olive oil.
- Avocados have a small window of ripeness. Underripe avocados will ripen in about two days if left on the counter, but they will do so unevenly; it's better to ripen them in the refrigerator, though this will take about four days. Putting avocados in a paper bag won't accelerate ripening. Ripe avocados stored in the refrigerator can last up to five days.

BEETS
- Healthy leaves are an easy-to-recognize sign of freshness when buying beets with stems and leaves attached. If buying roots only, make sure they are firm and the skin is smooth.
- Beets are best steamed or roasted (wrapped in foil). Do not peel the skin or slice off the tops prior to cooking to minimize bleeding.
- It's easiest to peel whole beets after cooking. To minimize mess, simply use a paper towel to wipe the skin off.
- To remove beet stains from a cutting board, scrub the board with salt.
- Beets with greens attached can be stored in the refrigerator in a loosely sealed plastic bag for several days. If you remove the greens, beets will keep for one week.

BELL PEPPERS
- Choose sweeter red, yellow, and orange bell peppers over green peppers, which taste bitter. Look for brightly colored peppers that are glossy and firm to the touch. If you are stuffing peppers, choose those with a well-rounded shape and even bottoms.
- Roasted bell peppers have many applications and are easy to make (see page 108). Bell peppers are also great in salads and stir-fries.
- You can store peppers in a loosely sealed plastic bag in the refrigerator for up to one week.

BOK CHOY
- Buy bok choy with leaves that are bright green and crisp; wilted leaves are a sign of age. Stalks should be bright white and not be covered with any brown spots.
- Bok choy is best stir-fried or braised; tough stalks need a head start and should go into the pan before the leaves.
- Store bok choy in the refrigerator in a loosely sealed plastic bag for up to three days. Don't wash bok choy until you are ready to cook it.

BROCCOLI

- Buy whole broccoli, not just the crowns or florets, as the stalks are quite flavorful. Avoid broccoli with stalks that have dry cracks or that bend easily, or with florets that are yellow or brown. The cut ends of the stalks should look fresh, not dry and brown.
- Broccoli is best steamed, stir-fried, pan-roasted, or roasted. Note that for all methods other than steaming, the tougher stems must be cooked before the florets.
- To revive limp broccoli, trim the stalk, stand it in 1 inch of water, and refrigerate it overnight.
- Store broccoli unrinsed in an open plastic bag in the crisper drawer. It will keep for about one week.

BROCCOLI RABE

- Buy broccoli rabe with fresh leaves and an abundance of small green florets.
- Store broccoli rabe unrinsed in an open plastic bag in the crisper drawer, where it will keep for several days.
- It is best to blanch and then sauté broccoli rabe; blanching tames its bitterness.

BROCCOLINI

- Buy broccolini that is bright green with firm stems.
- Store broccolini unrinsed in an open plastic bag in the crisper drawer, where it will keep for several days.
- It is best to steam-cook broccolini in a small amount of water and add seasonings after all the water has evaporated.

BRUSSELS SPROUTS

- For the best flavor, buy Brussels sprouts with small, tight heads, no more than 1½ inches in diameter, although larger sprouts can often be trimmed of loose leaves along the stem and still be quite good. Look for sprouts that are bright green and have no black spots or yellowing.
- The best way to cook Brussels sprouts is to braise or roast them. Braising produces tender, nutty-flavored, and bright-green sprouts. Roasting produces Brussels sprouts that are well caramelized on the outside and tender on the inside. Larger sprouts cook best when cut in half.
- Store Brussels sprouts in a vented container in the refrigerator for no longer than five days. Don't wash the sprouts until you are ready to cook them. If you have bought them on the stem, remove them from the stem for storage.

CABBAGES

- When buying red or green cabbage, look for smaller, looser heads covered with thin outer leaves.
- Red and green cabbage are best braised or salted and used to make coleslaw. Napa cabbage is perfect for stir-frying and salads.
- Store cabbage loosely wrapped in plastic in the refrigerator for about four days. Remove the tough outer leaves before using.

CARROTS

- Buy fresh carrots with greens attached for the best flavor. If buying bagged carrots, check that they are evenly sized and firm (they shouldn't bend). Don't buy extra-large carrots, which are often woody and bitter.
- The most flavorful ways to cook carrots are roasting and braising.
- To prevent shriveling, store carrots in the crisper drawer in a partially open zipper-lock bag or in their original plastic bag. Before storing green-topped carrots, remove and discard the greens or the carrots will become limp. Both bagged and fresh carrots will keep for several weeks.

CAULIFLOWER

- Buy heads of cauliflower with tight, firm florets without any discoloration.
- When cooking cauliflower, the key is not to cook it in a lot of liquid since it is a very porous vegetable. It is best to steam or roast cauliflower.
- Cauliflower wrapped in plastic can be stored in the refrigerator for several days.

CELERY

- Buy loose celery heads, not bagged celery heads (with clipped leaves) or bagged celery hearts. Loose celery heads tend to be fuller and fresher. Look for glossy green stalks without brown edges or yellowing leaves.
- Revive limp celery stalks by cutting off about 1 inch from both ends and submerging the stalks in a bowl of ice water for 30 minutes.
- The best way to store celery is to wrap it in foil and store it in the refrigerator. It will keep for several weeks.

CELERY ROOT

- Buy celery root that feels heavy for its size and has a hard and firm exterior.
- Store celery root in the refrigerator wrapped tightly in plastic wrap for up to two weeks. If you buy celery root with stalks and leaves attached, remove these before storing.

CORN

- Corn loses it sweetness soon after it is harvested, so buy the freshest corn you can find. Look for plump ears with green husks and golden silk extending from the tops (the more silk the better since it is an indicator of the number of kernels). Peel back the husk to check for brown spots and to make sure the kernels are firm.
- If you must store corn, wrap it, husk and all, in a wet paper bag and then in a plastic bag and place it in the refrigerator for up to 24 hours.

CUCUMBERS

- Buy regular American cucumbers that are dark green, firm, and without shriveled ends. Seedless English cucumbers have a weak cellular structure that turns them mushy when cut and salted (which we do for salads), and they have less flavor.
- We use cucumbers primarily to make cucumber salads or relishes. Cucumbers must be salted and weighted to ensure a crunchy, not soggy, salad.
- Cucumbers can be stored in the crisper drawer as is; the waxed coating most wholesalers apply will keep cucumbers fresh for at least one week. Unwaxed cucumbers can be stored in a loosely sealed plastic bag for up to one week.

EGGPLANTS

- Buy globe eggplants unless a recipe specifies a specific type of eggplant. Look for eggplant that is firm, deep purple, glossy, and without blemishes. A ripe eggplant will feel heavy in your hand. Larger eggplants tend to be more bitter and have more seeds.
- We cook globe eggplants in many ways, including roasting, baking, sautéing, stewing, and stir-frying. In most applications, the eggplant must be salted first to draw out excess water.
- Store eggplants at room temperature away from direct sunlight.

ENDIVES

- Choose endives with crisp, unblemished outer leaves. The leaves should be compact and tightly closed, and the stem should be firm and white.
- Endive is great braised, roasted, or grilled. We also like it thinly sliced in salads.
- Store endive in a partially open zipper-lock bag; it will stay fresh for several days.

FENNEL

- Buy fennel bulbs that are creamy white and firm with little or no discoloration. Stems should be crisp and the feathery fronds bright green.
- Fennel bulbs are great sautéed, grilled, or roasted, all of which concentrate its anise flavor. Braising is another good cooking method. Use the fronds as a garnish.
- Store fennel in the refrigerator in a zipper-lock bag for up to three days.

GARLIC

- Buy heads of garlic with firm, tightly bound cloves. Do not buy garlic with green sprouts emerging from the cloves (the sprouts taste bitter). For information on various types of garlic, see page 35.
- Store garlic at room temperature in an open basket that allows for air circulation. Do not remove the papery outer skin until you are ready to use the cloves.

GREEN BEANS

- Buy green beans that are brightly colored and fresh-looking. Thinner beans are generally sweeter and more tender.
- The best ways to cook green beans are boiling, braising, and roasting.
- Store green beans in the refrigerator in a loosely sealed plastic bag.

HEARTY (WINTER) GREENS

- Buy kale, Swiss chard, or collard greens with leaves that are dark green and crisp. with no signs of wilting or yellowing. We recommend cleaning these greens in a sink full of water, where there is ample room to swish the leaves.
- These assertive greens are best blanched and then sautéed or braised. They also work well in soups and stews.
- You can store greens in the refrigerator in an open plastic bag for several days. Blot up any excess moisture on leaves before storing. Do not clean the greens until you are ready to cook them.

LEEKS

- Buy leeks that have not been trimmed (some markets remove the tops when leeks start to wilt) and that appear to have most of their green leaves intact. Look for leeks that are firm with crisp, dark green leaves.
- Leeks are best braised or steamed.
- Store leeks in the crisper drawer wrapped tightly in plastic; they will stay fresh for up to one week.

MUSHROOMS

- There are many varieties of fresh mushrooms available at the supermarket now: the humble white button mushroom, as well as cremini, shiitake, oyster, and portobello mushrooms, for starters. We find cremini mushrooms to be firmer and more flavorful than white button mushrooms; the two are interchangeable in any recipe.
- Buy mushrooms loose if possible so that you can inspect their quality. When buying button or cremini mushrooms, look for mushrooms with whole, intact caps; avoid those with discoloration or dry, shriveled patches. Pick mushrooms with large caps and minimal stems.
- When you are ready to cook mushrooms, they can be rinsed under cold running water. If you are planning to serve them raw, do not rinse them but rather brush them clean with a pastry brush or soft cloth.
- You can store loose mushrooms in the crisper drawer in a partially open zipper-lock bag for several days. Store packaged mushrooms in their original containers, as these are designed to "breathe," maximizing the life of the mushrooms. After removing the amount of the mushrooms called for in a recipe, simply rewrap the box with plastic wrap.

ONIONS

- Choose onions with dry, papery skins. They should be rock-hard, with no soft spots or powdery mold on the skin. Avoid onions with green sprouts. Everyday yellow onions have the richest flavor, but milder, sweeter red onions are great grilled or minced raw for a salad or salsa. For more on various types of onions and their uses, see page 36.
- Store onions in a cool, well-ventilated spot away from light. Do not store onions in the refrigerator, where their odors can permeate other foods.

PARSNIPS

- Look for parsnips that are on the smaller side (about 4 ounces) because they are sweeter. Large parsnips (8 ounces and larger) have a core that must be cut out. Look for hard parsnips without any soft spots.
- Parsnips can be prepared and cooked in the same way as carrots and are particularly well suited to braising and roasting.
- You can store parsnips in the refrigerator in a partially sealed zipper-lock bag for at least one week.

PEAS

- When buying snow peas or sugar snap peas, look for those that are crisp and bright green without obvious blemishes or dry spots. If buying shelling peas, look for pods that are filled out. (Note that shelling peas are hard to find and require a lot of work, so we use frozen peas in many applications. They are frozen right after being shucked and are often sweeter and fresher-tasting than shelling peas.)
- Snow peas are best stir-fried. Sugar snap peas should be blanched and then sautéed or stir-fried. Shelling peas are best boiled and buttered or braised, or used in soups and stews.
- Store peas in the refrigerator in a partially sealed zipper-lock bag. Fresh shelling peas are very perishable and should be used right away. Snow and sugar snap peas will keep for several days.

POTATOES

- Since potatoes have varying textures (determined by starch level), you can't just reach for any potato and expect great results. Potatoes fall into three main categories (baking, boiling, or all-purpose) depending on texture. For more details on how to match types of potatoes and cooking methods, see page 36.
- Buy potatoes that show no signs of sprouting. Potatoes with a greenish tinge beneath the skin have had too much exposure to light and should also be avoided.
- Try to buy loose potatoes since bagged potatoes can hasten deterioration and sprouting. Store potatoes in a paper bag in a cool, dry place and away from onions, which give off gases that hasten sprouting. New potatoes should be used within one month, but other potato varieties will hold for several months.

RADISHES

- Try to buy radishes with their greens attached; if the greens are healthy and crisp, it is a good sign that the radishes are fresh. If the radishes are sold without their greens, make sure they are firm and the skin is smooth and not cracked. Avoid very large radishes, which can be woody.
- Radishes can be braised, roasted, or eaten raw in salads.
- You can store radishes in a partially sealed zipper-lock bag for up to one week. If you buy radishes with greens attached, remove the greens before storing them.

RUTABAGAS

- Most rutabagas are quite large (1 to 2 pounds) and usually waxed to prolong their shelf life. Buy small, unwaxed rutabagas if you can. Avoid those that have cracks or look shriveled.
- Rutabagas are best when mashed or roasted.
- Store rutabagas in the crisper drawer; they will stay fresh for several weeks.

SPINACH

- Flat-leaf spinach is available in bunches, baby spinach is sold either loose or in bags, and curly-leaf spinach is bagged. Look for spinach that is a deep green in color (never yellow), with smooth leaves and crisp stems.
- Curly-leaf and baby spinach (if bought bagged) should be stored in their original packaging, which is designed to keep the spinach fresh. Flat-leaf spinach should be stored in a dry, open zipper-lock bag.

SWEET POTATOES

- Choose firm sweet potatoes with skins that are taut, not wrinkled.
- Many varieties are available, and they can range quite a bit in color, texture, and flavor. Beauregard (usually sold as a conventional sweet potato) and Jewel are sweet and moist, and have the familiar sweet-potato flavor. Red Garnet is more savory and has a looser texture. Nontraditional varieties that are lighter in color, like the Japanese White, White Sweet, Batata, and purple potatoes, tend to be starchier and drier.
- Store sweet potatoes in a dark, well-ventilated spot (do not store them in a plastic bag); they will keep for about one week.

TOMATOES

- Choose locally grown tomatoes if at all possible, as this is the best way to ensure a flavorful tomato. Heirloom tomatoes are some of the best local tomatoes you can find. When selecting local tomatoes, looks aren't everything. Choose tomatoes that smell fruity and feel heavy.

- If supermarket tomatoes are your only option, look for tomatoes sold on the vine. Although this does not mean that they were fully ripened on the vine, they are better than regular supermarket tomatoes, which are picked when still green and blasted with ethylene gas to develop texture and color.

- Never refrigerate tomatoes; the cold damages enzymes that produce flavor compounds, and it ruins their texture. Even cut tomatoes should be kept at room temperature (wrap them tightly in plastic wrap).

- If the vine is still attached, leave it on and store the tomatoes stem end up. Tomatoes off the vine should be stored stem side down at room temperature. We have found that this prevents moisture from escaping and bacteria from entering, and thus prolongs shelf life.

- To quickly ripen hard, unripened tomatoes, store them in a paper bag with a banana or apple, both of which emit ethylene gas, which hastens ripening.

WINTER SQUASH

- Whether acorn, butternut, delicata, or another variety, squash should feel hard; soft spots are an indication that the squash has been mishandled. Squash should also feel heavy for its size, a sign that the flesh is moist and soft.

- Most supermarkets sell butternut squash that has been completely or partially prepped. Whole squash you peel yourself has the best flavor and texture, but if you are looking to save a few minutes of prep, we have found the peeled and halved squash is fine. We don't like the butternut squash sold in chunks; while it's a timesaver, the flavor is wan and the texture stringy.

- You can store winter squash in a cool, well-ventilated spot for several weeks.

ZUCCHINI AND SUMMER SQUASH

- Choose zucchini and summer squash that are firm and without soft spots. Smaller squash are more flavorful and less watery than larger specimens; they also have fewer seeds. Look for zucchini and summer squash no heavier than 8 ounces, and preferably just 6 ounces.

- Unless grilling or shredding zucchini or summer squash, salting is often necessary to eliminate excess water.

- You can store the squash in the refrigerator in a partially sealed zipper-lock bag for several days.

Essential Equipment

Prepping vegetables generally doesn't require an arsenal of tools, just a few items in the cutlery and peeling categories. And when it's time to cook, a baking sheet, Dutch oven, and nonstick skillet will cover most bases. The only other task that will come up time and again when cooking vegetables is mashing—not just potatoes but also butternut squash, parsnips, and turnips—and you have a few options for what to use.

CHEF'S KNIFE

When it comes to vegetable prep, a good chef's knife is absolutely essential. This knife can handle myriad tasks large and small, from chopping onions and splitting butternut squash through the center to trimming asparagus. Look for a chef's knife that is 8 inches long and that has a pointed tip, a comfortable grip, and a curved edge, which helps when rhythmically rocking the blade to chop a pile of carrots or dice an onion. A good chef's knife will be substantial but lightweight. Look for one made from high-carbon stainless steel, a hard metal that, once sharpened, tends to stay that way. For more details on what to look for, see page 18. Also see page 5 for details on caring for your knives.

PARING KNIFE

For detail work, like peeling a hot, cooked potato or julienning small vegetables, we turn to a paring knife. Its smaller, more maneuverable, and slightly curved blade makes precision tasks faster and easier. Although paring knives come in a range of shapes, we prefer the versatility of the classic style, which resembles a mini chef's knife with its slightly curved blade and pointed tip. Blades of 3 to 3½ inches are best, as this size is just right for a variety of cutlery tasks. For more details on what to look for, see page 18. Also see page 5 for details on caring for your knives.

PEELERS

Dull and inefficient, a subpar peeler makes a mountain of tiresome work out of a simple task. A good peeler should be fast and smooth—no clogging up with peels, jamming on bumps, or making you go over and over a spot to remove all of the peel. It should make thin peels, not waste a lot of good food. It shouldn't hurt or tire your hands, and it should stay sharp. In the test kitchen, we keep two peelers: a classic model that handles the usual tasks, and a second model with a serrated blade designed to remove peels from delicate foods like peaches and tomatoes. We found that straight peelers, with blades that extend directly out from the handle, and Y peelers, with a blade running perpendicular to the handle (resembling a wishbone), function similarly. Ceramic blades will dull very quickly and become discolored; stick with metal blades. For more details on what to look for, see page 30.

CUTTING BOARDS

When you're prepping a pile of vegetables, a good cutting board is absolutely essential. You want plenty of work space (think about the vegetable prep for ratatouille, a gratin, or a curry or stir-fry): We recommend buying a board with at least 15 or 20 inches of space. We prefer wood and bamboo boards to plastic, glass, or acrylic because their soft, subtly textured surfaces offer just enough give and "grip" for the knife to stick lightly with each stroke while nimbly dicing vegetables. Knives can slip on plastic boards, while glass and acrylic boards are so hard they dull knives more quickly than the others. For more details on what to look for and on care and cleaning, see page 19.

STEAMER BASKET

Inexpensive collapsible stainless steel baskets perform the simplest of vegetable cookery—steaming—flawlessly. While they aren't practical for steaming large quantities of vegetables, they can steam enough of most vegetables to serve four. Look for one with an adjustable center rod that makes for easier lifting from the pot and unscrews for storage.

POTATO MASHER

The disk-style potato masher with small holes is the tool just about everyone has for mashing potatoes. Our preference for a ricer notwithstanding, if you plan to buy a masher, there are a few things to look for. We like oval-shaped mashers because their rounded edges snuggle right into the curves of a saucepan. We also like mashers with a rounded handle, which makes it easy to grip. Don't bother with the wire-looped models; we found that they just didn't perform all that well.

POTATO RICER

For smooth and fluffy mashed potatoes, a potato ricer is the best tool. Potato ricers look and work just like giant garlic presses: You put the cooked potatoes in a hopper and squeeze the handles to force the spuds through a perforated disk. The idea is simple, but some are simpler to use and clean—and deliver better results—than others. A hopper with more holes on the bottom makes the job much easier (but be aware that perforations on the sides aren't a bonus; they actually make the process messier). The plunger's angle of approach is also important: The plunger should stay steady and hit the potato head-on, to ensure efficient ricing and easier squeezing, and to prevent spuds from spurting up and out of the hopper. Look for a ricer that is easy and intuitive to dismantle, clean, and reassemble.

FOOD MILL

A food mill will turn out silky-smooth mashed potatoes, but it's a bit harder to use (and clean) than a ricer (see above). However, if you also puree foods, like butternut squash and tomatoes, a food mill is a tool you should own since it purees food and strains it at the same time. Food is placed in the hopper, and a hand-crank mechanism turns a conical blade in the hopper against a perforated disk, forcing the food through the disk. Most food mills have three interchangeable disks with various-size holes. A food mill can thus not only make mashed potatoes but make them from unpeeled potatoes, forcing the flesh through the holes in the disk while holding back the skins. A food mill will also puree butternut squash while holding back the skin, seeds, and stringy pith, and it's ideal when making fresh tomato sauce since it will strain out the skin for you.

MANDOLINE

Even if you have the knife skills of a professional chef, slicing a pile of potatoes (or any other vegetable) razor thin with the help of only a chef's knife is a trying task. Fortunately, the mandoline is a device that makes the job easy and precise. This countertop specialty tool resembles a horizontal grater. It has two working surfaces: a razor-sharp blade and an adjustable platform that creates a downward cutting angle. Once the desired thickness is set, slicing requires nothing more than running a piece of food against the blade. Look for a mandoline with a handguard to shield your fingers, gripper tongs to grasp food, and a measurement-marked dial for precision cuts.

How to Prepare Vegetables A to Z

Whether you are simply steaming a vegetable or using it as one component of a more involved recipe, usually some basic vegetable prep is required. True, you might cook a vegetable any number of ways—for example, a potato could be fried, mashed, or roasted—but generally there are some standard prep steps required first. After years of peeling, seeding, and chopping vegetables in the test kitchen, we've found the following methods are the easiest and most efficient ways to prepare a number of vegetables for myriad uses. Also see How to Wash and Dry Salad Greens (page 477).

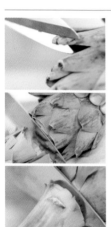

ARTICHOKE: PREPARING

1. Grasp artichoke by stem and hold horizontal to counter. Use kitchen shears to trim pin-sharp thorns from tips of leaves, skipping top two rows.
2. Rest artichoke on cutting board. Holding stem in one hand, cut off top two rows of leaf tips with chef's knife.
3. Cut stem flush with base of bulb. To prevent browning, drop trimmed artichoke into bowl of water mixed with juice of 1 lemon until ready to steam.

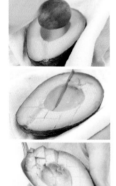

ASPARAGUS: TRIMMING

1. Remove one stalk of asparagus from bunch and bend it at thicker end until it snaps.
2. With broken asparagus as guide, trim tough ends from remaining asparagus bunch, using chef's knife.

AVOCADO: CUTTING UP

1. After slicing avocado in half around pit with chef's knife, lodge edge of knife blade into pit and twist to remove.
2. Use dish towel to hold avocado steady. Make ½-inch crosshatch incisions in flesh of each avocado half with knife, cutting down to, but not through, skin.
3. Insert soupspoon between skin and flesh and gently scoop out avocado cubes.

BEET: PEELING COOKED

To avoid stained dish towels or messy hands, cradle cooked beets in paper towel and gently rub off skin.

BELL PEPPER: CUTTING UP

1. Slice off top and bottom of pepper and remove seeds and stem.
2. Slice down through side of pepper.
3. Lay pepper flat, trim away remaining ribs and seeds, then cut into pieces or strips as desired.

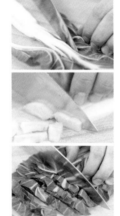

BOK CHOY: PREPARING

1. Trim bottom 1 inch from head of bok choy. Wash and pat leaves and stalks dry. Cut leafy green portion away from either side of white stalk.
2. Cut each white stalk in half lengthwise, then crosswise into thin strips.
3. Stack leafy greens and slice crosswise into thin strips. Keep sliced stalks and leaves separate.

BROCCOLI: PREPARING

1. Place head of broccoli upside down on cutting board and use chef's knife to trim off florets very close to heads. Cut florets into 1-inch pieces.
2. After cutting away tough outer peel of stalk, square off stalk, then slice stalk into ¼-inch thick pieces.

BROCCOLI RABE: TRIMMING

Trim off and discard thick stalk ends (usually bottom 2 inches of each stalk).

BROCCOLINI: PREPARING

For any stems ½ inch or thicker, use paring knife to trim bottom 2 inches from stems.

BRUSSELS SPROUT: PREPARING

Peel off any loose or discolored leaves and use paring knife to slice off bottom of stem end, leaving leaves attached.

CABBAGE: SHREDDING

1. Cut cabbage into quarters, then trim and discard hard core.
2. Separate cabbage into small stacks of leaves that flatten when pressed.
3. Use chef's knife to cut each stack of leaves into thin shreds (you can also use slicing disk of food processor to do this).

CARROT: CUTTING ON BIAS AND INTO MATCHSTICKS

1. Slice carrot on bias into 2-inch-long, oval-shaped pieces.
2. For matchsticks, lay ovals flat on cutting board, then slice into 2-inch-long matchsticks, about ¼ inch thick.

CAULIFLOWER: PREPARING FOR STEAMING OR BRAISING

1. Pull off any leaves, then cut out core of cauliflower using paring knife.
2. Separate florets from inner stem using tip of paring knife.
3. Cut larger florets into smaller pieces by slicing through stem.

CELERY: CHOPPING QUICKLY

Using chef's knife, trim leaves from top of celery bunch. Then chop across bunch until you have desired amount.

CELERY ROOT: PREPARING

1. Using chef's knife, cut ½ inch from both root end and opposite end.
2. To peel, cut from top to bottom, rotating celery root while removing wide strips of skin.

CORN: CUTTING KERNELS OFF THE COB

After removing husk and silk, stand ear upright in large bowl and use paring knife to slice kernels off of cob.

CORN: PREPARING FOR THE GRILL

1. Remove all but innermost layer of husk from each ear of corn.
2. Use scissors to snip off tassel.

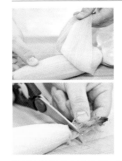

CUCUMBER: SEEDING

Halve peeled cucumber lengthwise. Run small spoon inside each cucumber half to scoop out seeds and surrounding liquid.

ENDIVE: PREPARING FOR BRAISING

1. Trim off discolored end of endive (cut thinnest slice possible so leaves remain intact).
2. Cut endive in half lengthwise through core end.

FENNEL: PREPARING

1. Cut off stems and feathery fronds. Trim thin slice from base and remove any tough or blemished outer layers from bulb.

2A. For braising or grilling, slice bulb vertically through base into ½-inch-thick slices, making sure to leave core intact.

2B. For sautéing, roasting, or salads, cut bulb in half through base, then use paring knife to remove pyramid-shaped core. Slice each half into thin strips, cutting from base to stem end.

GARLIC: MASHING TO A PASTE

Sprinkle minced garlic with salt, then scrape blade of knife back and forth over garlic until it forms sticky paste.

GARLIC: MINCING

1. Trim off root end of garlic clove, then crush clove gently between side of chef's knife and cutting board to loosen papery skin (it will fall away from garlic).

2. Using two-handed chopping motion, run knife over garlic repeatedly to mince it.

GREEN BEANS: TRIMMING

Line beans up on cutting board and trim ends with one slice.

HEARTY (WINTER) GREENS:
PREPARING SWISS CHARD, KALE, OR COLLARD GREENS

1. Cut away leafy portion from stalk or stem using chef's knife.

2. Stack several leaves and either slice crosswise or chop into pieces according to recipe.

3. If using chard stems in recipe, cut into pieces as directed after separating from leafy portion. (Discard collard and kale stems.)

LEEK: PREPARING

1. Trim and discard root and dark green leaves.

2. Cut trimmed leek in half lengthwise, then slice crosswise into ½-inch-thick pieces.

3. Rinse cut leeks thoroughly to remove dirt and sand using salad spinner or bowl of water.

ONION: CHOPPING

1. Halve onion through root end, then peel onion and trim top. Make several horizontal cuts from one end of onion to other but don't cut through root end.

2. Make several vertical cuts. Be sure to cut up to but not through root end.

3. Rotate onion so root end is in back; slice onion thinly across previous cuts. As you slice, onion will fall apart into chopped pieces.

PEA: TRIMMING SNOW AND SNAP PEAS

Use paring knife and thumb to snip off tip of pod and pull along flat side to remove string at same time.

POTATO: CUTTING INTO EVENLY SIZED PIECES

1. Using chef's knife, cut 1 thin sliver from one side of potato. Set potato on cut side, and slice potato crosswise into even planks.

2. Stack several planks and cut crosswise, then rotate 90 degrees and cut crosswise again to create evenly sized pieces as directed in recipe.

POTATO: CUTTING FOR OVEN FRIES

Quarter potato lengthwise, then carefully slice each quarter into two or three wedges.

SHALLOT: MINCING

1. Make closely spaced horizontal cuts through peeled shallot, leaving root end intact.

2. Next, make several vertical cuts through shallot.

3. Finally, thinly slice shallot crosswise, creating fine mince.

TOMATO: CORING AND DICING

1. Remove core of tomato using paring knife.

2. Slice tomato crosswise.

3. Stack several slices of tomato, then slice both crosswise and widthwise into pieces as desired.

TOMATO: PEELING

1. Score X at each tomato's base using paring knife. Using slotted spoon, lower tomatoes, a few at a time, into large pot of boiling water and boil for 30 to 60 seconds, just until skin at X begins to loosen.

2. Using slotted spoon, quickly transfer tomatoes to prepared ice bath and let cool for 1 minute.

3. Starting at X, use paring knife to remove loosened peel in strips.

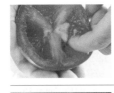

TOMATO: SEEDING

Halve tomato through equator, then use your finger to pull out seeds and surrounding gel.

WINTER SQUASH: SEEDING SAFELY

1. Set squash on damp dish towel to hold it in place. Position cleaver on skin of squash. Strike back of cleaver with mallet to drive cleaver deep into squash. Continue to hit cleaver with mallet until cleaver cuts completely through squash.

2. Using soupspoon, scoop out and discard seeds.

WINTER SQUASH: CUTTING UP BUTTERNUT SQUASH

1. After peeling squash, use chef's knife to trim off top and bottom and then cut squash in half where narrow neck and wide curved bottom meet.

2. Cut neck of squash into evenly sized planks according to recipe.

3. Cut planks into evenly sized pieces according to recipe.

4. Cut base in half lengthwise and scoop out and discard seeds and fibers. Slice each base half into evenly sized lengths according to recipe.

5. Cut lengths into evenly sized pieces according to recipe.

ZUCCHINI: SEEDING

Halve zucchini lengthwise. Run small spoon inside each zucchini half to scoop out seeds.

How to Boil and Steam Vegetables

ESSENTIAL EQUIPMENT

• large pot
• steaming rack or pasta insert
• colander

When you want to cook vegetables with a minimum of work, boiling and steaming will get the job done. Each method has its own pros and cons. Boiling allows you to season vegetables with salt as they cook, but more flavor is washed away. Steaming leaves vegetables crisper than boiling but you can steam only smaller batches (1 pound or less). Whichever method you use, it is important to prep the vegetables properly and monitor the cooking time closely. Once cooked, serve them simply with salt, pepper, and a squeeze of lemon. Or you can dress them a number of ways, from tossing with a compound butter, pesto, or vinaigrette to sprinkling with a fruity extra-virgin olive oil plus grated Parmesan, fresh herbs, or red pepper flakes. Tossing with a browned butter and topping with toasted nuts is another option. The equipment needed will depend on the method you are using.

1. TO BOIL (OR BLANCH) VEGETABLES

Bring 4 quarts water and 1 tablespoon salt to boil in large pot over high heat. Cook vegetables until tender. Drain well and toss with flavorings if desired before serving.

WHY? For even cooking, make sure to use plenty of water when boiling vegetables. Boiling washes away some of the vegetables' flavor, but adding a full tablespoon of salt to the cooking water gives them a boost. For crudités and other occasions when you want to lose a vegetable's raw edge but retain its texture, flavor, and color, we blanch it. Blanching is also a good way to remove the bitter edge from some greens, such as broccoli rabe, or to loosen the skins of tomatoes (or peaches) for easier peeling. Cook the vegetable in the boiling water only until its color turns bright and its texture is crisp-tender, just a minute or two depending on the vegetable. Then drain the vegetable and immediately plunge it into an ice bath to stop the cooking.

2A–2B. TO STEAM VEGETABLES

Place steaming rack or pasta insert in large pot and add water until it touches bottom of rack. Bring to boil over high heat. Lay vegetables in steaming rack, cover, and steam until tender. Check pot periodically to make sure water has not boiled dry, adding more water as needed. Toss with flavorings if desired before serving.

WHY? There is nothing worse than a pot that scorches badly because all the water evaporates during steaming and you don't realize it in time. For vegetables that take awhile to cook through, make sure to check the pot periodically. Placing a few glass marbles in the pot along with the water is a good trick in these cases; when the water level starts to get too low, the marbles will rattle around. You can also avoid the need to add more water by placing three crumpled balls of aluminum foil in the pot and setting the steamer basket on top of the foil. The foil elevates the steamer basket, creating room for extra water.

How to Grill Vegetables

Not only does grilling vegetables give you side dishes with bright, intense flavors, but it's also quick and easy to do. We tested many vegetables to find the best grilling methods for each. We discovered a handful of common problems: They burned, they cooked unevenly, they fell through the cooking grate. Fortunately, these problems are easily overcome. Vegetables are best cooked over a medium-hot single-level fire (see page 392), so adjust the grill as necessary. If using a charcoal grill, spread the hot coals in an even layer and, if necessary, add more briquettes to increase the heat of the fire. Vegetables can be served hot off the grill or at room temperature. The equipment needed will depend on the method you are using; you will need only metal skewers for certain vegetables. Also see recipes for Mexican-Style Grilled Corn (page 432) and Grilled Potatoes with Garlic and Rosemary (page 433) in the How to Grill chapter.

ESSENTIAL EQUIPMENT

- chef's knife
- metal skewers
- rimmed baking sheet
- basting brush
- tongs

1A–1B. MAKE THE RIGHT CUT

Cut vegetables exactly as directed and slide onto skewers if required.

WHY? There are two goals when preparing vegetables for the grill: maximizing surface area to increase flavorful browning, and cutting them in a way that keeps pieces from falling apart or slipping through the cooking grate. Flattening a bell pepper into a single strip, cutting an eggplant into rounds, and cutting fennel into planks all maximize surface area for browning and ensure even cooking. Some vegetables, like potatoes, mushrooms, and onions, have to be skewered before grilling so they do not fall through the grate and are easy to flip.

2. BRUSH WITH OIL

Place vegetables on baking sheet and, using basting brush, thoroughly brush with extra-virgin olive oil and season well with salt and pepper.

WHY? Applying a thin layer of extra-virgin olive oil to vegetables (except corn) before grilling encourages even browning and helps prevent them from sticking to the cooking grate.

3. GRILL OVER MEDIUM-HOT FIRE

Remove meat or fish from grill, if cooking, then, if using charcoal, spread coals in single layer. Make sure fire is medium-hot; add more coals if necessary. Place vegetables on cooking grate and turn frequently; remove when tender and streaked with grill marks.

WHY? When grilling vegetables to accompany meat, we cook the meat first, while the fire is at its hottest. By the time the meat is done, the heat has subsided a bit and the vegetables can cook at a more moderate temperature. (For a gas grill, simply adjust as needed for a medium-hot fire.) To test the temperature of the grill, place your hand 5 inches above the cooking grate. You should be able to hold it there comfortably for 3 to 4 seconds. Tender vegetables will need 5 to 7 minutes to cook through. Tougher vegetables will take 8 to 12 minutes.

How to Mash Potatoes

ESSENTIAL
EQUIPMENT

Mashed potatoes are a deceptively simple dish, which is no doubt why many cooks feel they don't need to consult a recipe. The truth, however, is that the details matter if you want fluffy and spectacularly smooth mashed potatoes that are sturdy enough to stand up to gravy or sauce. First, choose the right potatoes, because while you can mash just about any potato, the variety you choose makes a significant difference in the end result. High-starch (and low-moisture) potatoes (russets) will maintain their integrity when mashed, and their low water content allows them to absorb dairy without becoming gummy. Following our simple method will ensure perfect results every time. The steps below show how to make enough mashed potatoes to serve four people. You can scale up this recipe but you will need to use a Dutch oven or stockpot to cook the potatoes. The mashed potatoes are easy to dress up; for variations on this recipe, see page 127. For more information on tools for mashing vegetables, see page 97.

- large saucepan
- colander
- potholder or dish towel
- paring knife
- ricer or potato masher
- whisk
- liquid measuring cup

1. USE WHOLE RUSSETS

Put 2 pounds russet potatoes in large saucepan, cover with 1 inch cold water, and bring to boil over high heat.

WHY? Russet potatoes are high in starch and low in moisture, which translates to a fluffy, full texture in mashed potatoes and a nice ability to absorb dairy without becoming gummy. Cooking the potatoes with their skins on protects the starch granules and thus reduces gumminess in the final dish. We also cook them whole and peel them later because some of the potato flavor gets washed away when peeled-and-cut potatoes are boiled. Mashed potatoes made by boiling unpeeled potatoes taste rich, earthy, and sweet.

2. SIMMER POTATOES

After bringing water to boil, lower heat and simmer potatoes until just tender (paring knife can be slipped in and out of potatoes with little resistance), 20 to 30 minutes. Drain.

WHY? It is important to avoid overcooking the potatoes because the starch cells will begin to break down and create a sticky rather than fluffy mash. Drain the potatoes well because again, excess water combining with starch creates gumminess.

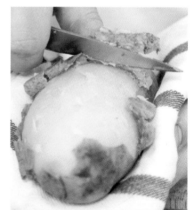

3. PEEL POTATOES

Using potholder or folded dish towel to hold potatoes, peel just-boiled potatoes with paring knife.

WHY? Peeling just-boiled potatoes is a lot easier if you hold the hot potato with a potholder or clean dish towel in your hand to protect against the heat.

4. MASH POTATOES

Working in batches, cut peeled potatoes into large chunks and press or mill into saucepan.

WHY? We like using a ricer, which turns potatoes into fine, thin threads for the smoothest texture, though you can also use a food mill or potato masher.

5. ADD BUTTER

Stir in 8 tablespoons melted unsalted butter until incorporated.

WHY? When water interacts with the starch molecules in potatoes, the result is gummy mashed potatoes. We add the melted butter before the dairy so that the fat can coat the starch molecules, creating a protective barrier that keeps the starch from interacting with the water in the half-and-half, which gets added next. The result: silky, rather than gummy, mashed potatoes.

6. ADD HALF-AND-HALF

Gently whisk in 1 cup warm half-and-half, 1½ teaspoons salt, and pepper to taste.

WHY? We use warm half-and-half simply to keep the potatoes up to temperature. And we prefer half-and-half to milk for the richness it adds.

Troubleshooting Mashed Potatoes

PROBLEM	SOLUTION
Can I make mashed potatoes ahead of time?	Sure. Follow the recipe as directed, then place the mashed potatoes in a large bowl, cover with aluminum foil, and keep in a warm in a 200-degree oven for up to 1 hour. Before serving, adjust the consistency as needed with additional melted butter or warm half-and-half. If you have a slow cooker, you can also put mashed potatoes in the insert, cover, and keep on the low setting for up to 2 hours.
My mashed potatoes are too thin.	If you let the potatoes sit in the pot for a few minutes, they will thicken up. Warm over low heat if necessary.
My mashed potatoes are dry.	Make sure to boil the potatoes until they are tender. If you mash undercooked potatoes, they will absorb more liquid than properly cooked potatoes and come out dry.
My mashed potatoes taste bland.	You probably overcooked the potatoes. Cooking them for too long causes them to absorb excess water, which leads to a washed-out flavor, plus they can't absorb all of the liquid ingredients that add flavor.

How to Fry Potatoes

Homemade French fries—with their crisp exteriors, airy interiors, and earthy, sweet flavor—are a revelation. When you start with fresh potatoes and cook them in peanut oil, the results are hard to beat. When making fries, every detail matters, from the size of the fries to the temperature of the oil. Our foolproof method requires two rounds of frying. The first stage, or par-fry, helps the interior of the fries cook through and is done at a lower temperature than the second-stage frying, which browns and crisps the exteriors of the fries. And the secret ingredient? Cornstarch. It is the key to a shatteringly crisp crust. Be sure to use russet potatoes. Their high starch and low moisture content mean they fry up with crisp exteriors and light, fluffy interiors. Yukon Golds, Red Bliss, and all-purpose potatoes, all lower in starch and higher in moisture than russets, make French fries that are dense, waxy, and soft. Also see How to Fry (page 301).

ESSENTIAL EQUIPMENT

- chef's knife
- large bowl
- dish towels
- wire rack
- rimmed baking sheet
- candy/deep-fry thermometer
- large Dutch oven
- paper towels
- spider skimmer

1. PREPARE POTATOES

Trim thin slice from each side of 2½ pounds russet potatoes to square them off, then slice each squared potato lengthwise into ¼-inch-thick planks. Cut each plank into ¼-inch fries.

WHY? It is important to cut the potatoes evenly so that all of the fries are the same size. This method makes it easy to cut the potatoes into evenly sized fries.

2. RINSE AND SOAK POTATOES

Rinse cut potatoes in large bowl under cold running water until water turns clear. Cover with cold water and refrigerate for 30 minutes or up to 12 hours.

WHY? Russet potatoes are starchy, so it is important to rinse the starch off the surface after cutting them. We refrigerate the potatoes in cold water because this allows for the slow, thorough cooking of the potato interiors. Otherwise, the potatoes brown before the interiors are fully cooked.

3. COAT POTATOES WITH CORNSTARCH

Drain potatoes, then spread potatoes out on clean dish towels and dry thoroughly. Transfer potatoes to large bowl and toss with 2 tablespoons cornstarch until evenly coated.

WHY? The cornstarch forms a protective sheath around each fry, helping create the ideal crispy crust.

4. LET POTATOES REST ON WIRE RACK

Transfer potatoes to wire rack set in rimmed baking sheet. Let rest until fine white coating forms, about 20 minutes.

WHY? You will get crisper results if you let the cornstarch-coated potatoes air-dry for a bit before frying. This rest gives the cornstarch enough time to absorb some of the surface moisture on the potatoes and create a gel-like coating around each fry that fries up perfectly crisp.

5. HEAT OIL

Clip candy/deep-fry thermometer onto side of large, heavy-bottomed Dutch oven with at least a 6-quart capacity. Heat 3 quarts peanut or vegetable oil in Dutch oven over medium heat to 325 degrees.

WHY? A moderate oil temperature works best for the initial fry to cook the potatoes through. The heat is high enough to turn the water in the potatoes to steam and dry out the edges, and to release the potatoes' flavor without burning their exterior. If the temperature goes over, remove the pot from the heat; let the temperature drop to 325 degrees before adding the potatoes.

6. PAR-FRY POTATOES

Add half of potatoes, a handful at a time, to hot oil and increase heat to high. Fry, stirring with spider skimmer or large-hole slotted spoon, until potatoes start to turn from white to blond, 4 to 5 minutes. (Oil temperature will drop about 75 degrees.) Transfer fries to paper towels or thick paper bag. Return oil to 325 degrees and repeat with remaining potatoes. Let fries cool, at least 10 minutes or up to 2 hours.

WHY? Cooking in batches minimizes the drop in oil temperature that occurs when the potatoes are added. Cooking in batches, adding by the handful, and stirring help keep the fries from sticking to each other.

7. FINISH FRYING

When ready to finish frying, increase heat to medium-high and heat oil to 375 degrees. Add half of fries, a handful at a time, and fry until golden brown and puffed, 2 to 3 minutes. Transfer to paper towels. Return oil to 375 degrees and repeat with remaining fries. Season fries with salt and serve immediately.

WHY? Because the fries have been parcooked, they just need to finish frying in hotter oil until golden and crisp. Seasoning the fries right after they come out of the oil is key because the hot fat will help the salt granules adhere.

Troubleshooting French Fries

PROBLEM	SOLUTION
The fries are undercooked or overcooked.	Make sure to cut the fries to the right size; use a ruler if necessary (or a mandoline). If your prepped potatoes are discoloring, place the cut ones in a bowl of cold water.
The fries are greasy and do not brown properly.	Use a thermometer to monitor the oil's temperature, and don't add the potatoes until the oil reaches 325 degrees for the par-fry and 375 degrees for the second-stage cooking. If, after 10 or 15 minutes, the oil refuses to come up to temperature, turn up the burner a bit. If the potatoes are added before the oil is ready, the fries will be greasy and won't brown or crisp properly. Also, make sure the end of the thermometer is not touching the bottom of the pot, which will give you a false temperature reading.

How to Roast Red Bell Peppers

Red bell peppers become sweet and smoky when roasted and have myriad uses: They make great dips, pesto, and sauces, and of course are essential for antipasto platters. Our method for roasting peppers is easier than most because we flatten the peppers and roast them on a baking sheet close to the broiler element instead of roasting them over a gas burner and then laboriously removing the skin. Also see page 98 for steps on cutting up a bell pepper.

ESSENTIAL EQUIPMENT

- chef's knife
- rimmed baking sheet
- aluminum foil
- mixing bowl

1. PREPARE PEPPERS

Slice ¼ inch from top and bottom of each of 4 peppers and gently remove stem from top lobe. Pull stem and seeds out of peppers. Make slit down one side of each pepper and lie flat, skin side down, in long strip. Slide knife along inside of peppers to remove ribs and remaining seeds.
WHY? It is much easier to roast bell peppers that lie flat, and this method is the easiest way to achieve that. (We have found that this is generally the best method to use when you want to cut up bell peppers for any recipe.)

2. ARRANGE PEPPERS ON BAKING SHEET

Arrange strips of pepper and top and bottom lobes, skin side up, on aluminum foil-lined rimmed baking sheet. Flatten strips with palm of your hand.
WHY? If you have cut the peppers properly, simply pressing on them with your hands will flatten them, which allows the entire surface area of the skin to broil efficiently.

3. BROIL PEPPERS

Broil peppers 2½ to 3½ inches from broiler element until skin is charred but flesh is still firm, 8 to 10 minutes, rotating baking sheet halfway through cooking.
WHY? For effective roasting and to char the skin, the peppers need to be very close to the broiler element. If necessary, set an upside-down rimmed baking sheet on the oven rack to elevate the pan. The goal here is to char the peppers (they will be spotty brown and puffed up) but keep the flesh firm, not mushy. Rotating the sheet ensures even cooking.

4. TRANSFER PEPPERS TO BOWL

Transfer peppers to bowl, cover with foil, and let steam until skin peels off easily, 10 to 15 minutes.
WHY? By covering the bowl of still hot peppers, the steam does most of the work for you, making it super-easy to remove the skin without tearing the peppers or leaving bits of skin behind.

How to Braise Winter Greens

Meaty and assertively flavored hearty greens like collards and kale lose their appeal and personality if simply boiled for hours along with a ham hock. We wanted a technique that would preserve their earthy, almost mineral flavor, hearty texture, and deep color—one that wouldn't take hours. After trying various methods including blanching and then sautéing, we found a reliable one-pot method that delivered on all fronts. The key is to use plenty of liquid, add the greens in two batches (we cook 2 pounds of greens to serve four people), and use plenty of aromatics. Also see page 100 for steps on removing stems from winter greens. You can season greens simply, with salt, pepper, and lemon juice, or make heartier versions with additions like bacon or chorizo (see recipes on page 124).

ESSENTIAL EQUIPMENT

- Dutch oven
- wooden spoon
- liquid measuring cup

1. CREATE FLAVOR BASE

Heat 2 tablespoons olive oil in Dutch oven over medium heat until shimmering. Add 1 finely chopped onion and cook, stirring frequently, until softened and beginning to brown, about 5 minutes. Add 5 minced garlic cloves and ⅛ teaspoon red pepper flakes and cook until garlic is fragrant, about 1 minute.

WHY? Hearty greens need to be infused with flavor so that they don't taste bland.

2. WILT HALF OF GREENS

Add 1 pound kale or collard greens, stemmed and leaves chopped into 3-inch pieces. Stir until beginning to wilt, about 1 minute.

WHY? It doesn't work to add 2 pounds of greens to the pot at once. The pot would be too full and the greens on the bottom would scorch. So we add half our greens and let them wilt.

3. ADD REMAINING GREENS AND LIQUID

Add remaining greens, 1 cup chicken broth, 1 cup water, and ¼ teaspoon salt. Cover and reduce heat to medium-low. Cook, stirring occasionally, until greens are tender, 25 to 35 minutes for kale and 35 to 45 minutes for collards.

WHY? The greens require a liberal amount of liquid to cook through. Covering the pot allows the greens to cook through more quickly and evenly.

4. UNCOVER AND INCREASE HEAT

Remove lid and increase heat to medium-high. Cook, stirring occasionally, until most of liquid has evaporated, 8 to 12 minutes.

WHY? To avoid soupy greens, it is necessary to evaporate some of the liquid by cooking the greens with the lid off once they are tender.

5. SEASON

Off heat, stir in 2 teaspoons lemon juice and 1 tablespoon more oil. Season with salt, pepper, and lemon juice to taste and serve.

WHY? Seasoning the greens simply allows their earthy flavor to shine.

How to Sauté Mushrooms

If you are lucky enough to have access to expensive wild mushrooms, this recipe is not for you, as all they need beyond a hot pan is some butter and garlic to have a company-worthy side of mushrooms. But the same cannot be said for supermarket white mushrooms, whose absorbent texture and high water content make them tricky to cook to perfection. However, with the right technique, these affordable mushrooms can take center stage instead of being simply a gratuitous addition to a salad or pizza. We developed a simple method for transforming these lowly mushrooms into a flavorful side that brings out the deep, rich, earthy flavors for which their tonier cousins are so highly prized. The steps below demonstrate our method and include some basic flavorings. You can replace the shallot with scallion or ginger and the thyme with another herb. You can also glaze the mushrooms with other potent liquid ingredients, such as soy sauce or port.

1. PREPARE MUSHROOMS
Clean 1½ pounds white mushrooms, trim stems, and quarter if medium-sized or halve if small.
WHY? Thin slices of mushrooms are likely to dry out; this is much less likely to happen with larger pieces, plus their final texture will be meatier and more substantial.

2. COOK MUSHROOMS
Heat 1 tablespoon vegetable oil in 12-inch skillet over medium-high heat until shimmering. Add mushrooms and cook, stirring occasionally, until mushrooms release liquid, about 5 minutes. Increase heat to high and cook, stirring occasionally, until liquid has completely evaporated, about 8 minutes.
WHY? We start with the mushrooms over medium-high heat so they can begin cooking and release their liquid. Then we crank up the heat so the moisture can evaporate and the mushrooms can start to brown. Without this two-step process, the mushrooms would just steam in the released liquid.

3. ADD BUTTER
Add 1 tablespoon unsalted butter, reduce heat to medium, and continue to cook, stirring once every minute, until mushrooms are dark brown, about 8 minutes.
WHY? Adding additional fat in the form of butter partway through cooking keeps the mushrooms from burning, adds flavor, and improves browning.

4. ADD AROMATICS AND WINE
Add 1 minced shallot, 1 tablespoon minced fresh thyme, and ¼ cup dry Marsala and cook until liquid has evaporated, about 2 minutes. Season with salt and pepper to taste and serve.
WHY? Just a few aromatics plus potent Marsala are all the finishing touches needed to transform basic white mushrooms into a richly flavored side dish.

Scalloped Potatoes

Overview

Traditionally reserved for holidays and special events because they are so over-the-top rich not to mention time-consuming to make, scalloped potatoes feature thinly sliced potatoes layered with a flour-thickened cream sauce (plus cheese). The whole thing is then baked for well over an hour. This recipe, while plenty rich, offers a lighter option and speeds up the whole process by parcooking the potatoes on the stovetop and then finishing them in a casserole dish in a hot oven. Instead of using copious amounts of heavy cream, we found equal amounts of heavy cream and chicken broth deliver a casserole that is more balanced and lighter but still flavorful.

Russet potatoes, with their tender bite and earthy flavor, are key to this recipe; they also form the cohesive layers that are the hallmark of this dish because of their high starch content. This is a weeknight-worthy version of scalloped potatoes that suits the holiday table as well, yet it's faster and easier to make and requires no fussy layering.

To make this casserole ahead, once the potatoes have been pressed into an even layer in the casserole dish, refrigerate for up to one day. When ready to bake, add the cheese, cover with aluminum foil, and bake in a 400-degree oven until the mixture is hot and bubbling, about 45 minutes. Remove the foil and cook until the cheese begins to brown, about 30 minutes longer. For variations on this recipe, see page 128.

Recipe Stats

TOTAL TIME **1 hour**
PREPARATION TIME **20 minutes**
ACTIVE COOKING TIME **20 minutes**
YIELD **4 to 6 servings**
MAKE AHEAD **Refrigerate unbaked casserole for up to 1 day**
DIFFICULTY **Intermediate**

Tools

- Dutch oven
- 8-inch square baking dish
- food processor or mandoline *
- chef's knife
- cutting board
- paring knife
- dry measuring cups
- liquid measuring cup
- measuring spoons
- coarse grater
- kitchen ruler
- rubber spatula
- vegetable peeler

* A food processor fitted with the ⅛-inch slicing blade is the quickest, most convenient way to slice the potatoes, but a mandoline will also work.

Ingredients

- **2 tablespoons unsalted butter**
- **1 onion, chopped fine**
- **1 tablespoon minced fresh thyme**
- **2 garlic cloves, minced**
- **1¼ teaspoons salt**
- **¼ teaspoon pepper**
- **2½ pounds russet potatoes, peeled and sliced ⅛ inch thick**
- **1 cup chicken broth**
- **1 cup heavy cream ***
- **2 bay leaves**
- **4 ounces cheddar cheese, shredded (1 cup) ****

* Do not substitute half-and-half or milk, or this casserole will not taste rich enough.
** You can substitute Parmesan or Gruyère cheese if desired.

What Can Go Wrong

Here's a list of common mistakes cooks make when preparing this recipe.

COMMON MISTAKE	BAD OUTCOMES	WHAT YOU SHOULD DO
Using Wrong Potato Variety	• **The potatoes taste waxy.** • **The potato layers are not cohesive.**	Russet potatoes have a high starch content, so they form tight, cohesive layers, which is what you want when making this recipe. They also have a tender bite and earthy flavor that is ideal here. While you can make scalloped potatoes with Yukon Gold potatoes, they taste a bit waxy and aren't our first choice for this casserole. Don't try to make this recipe with red potatoes; they don't have enough starch to form a cohesive casserole.
Cutting Potatoes Too Thick or Too Thin	• **The potatoes slide apart when served.** • **The potato layers melt together, producing a mashed potato-like texture.**	It is important to slice the potatoes into ⅛-inch-thick slices. If they are cut thicker, they won't form tidy, cohesive layers and will not hold together when served. If sliced too thinly, they melt together entirely so you lose the structure of a properly made scalloped potato casserole. While you can cut the potatoes by hand, it is far easier to achieve consistent results when using a food processor or mandoline. Check the first few slices with a kitchen ruler, and then once you've hit the mark just make sure all the slices are the same thickness.
Potato Slices Discolor as They Sit	• **The casserole looks unattractive.**	Potatoes will become discolored after slicing if they sit exposed to the air long enough because enzymes they contain react with the air and cause oxidation. You can keep the potato slices from discoloring if you put them in a bowl and cover them with the cream and the chicken broth.
Cooking Potatoes Too Long on Stovetop	• **The potatoes break into pieces when transferred to the baking dish.**	The key is to parcook the potatoes on the stovetop until almost tender (a paring knife can be slipped in and out of potato slices with some resistance). If you cook them beyond this point—until they are totally soft and tender—they will break into pieces when you move them to the baking dish, and you will not have the beautiful layers of potatoes that are the hallmark of this dish.
Using Preshredded Cheese	• **The cheese doesn't melt properly.**	Preshredded cheese is treated with a coating that helps extend its shelf life. This coating also keeps it from melting properly. For the right gooey texture, buy a block of cheddar cheese and shred it yourself.
Not Cooling Before Serving	• **The potatoes don't come out in attractive pieces.**	If you slice the casserole right when it comes out of the oven, the cheese will be molten and will ooze. Cooling the casserole for 10 minutes after it comes out of the oven gives it time to set up, ensuring you get attractive slices (and it will still be plenty hot).

1. Adjust oven rack to middle position and heat oven to 425 degrees.

2. Peel 2½ pounds russet potatoes.

3. Slice potatoes ⅛ inch thick using food processor or mandoline.

4. Melt 2 tablespoons unsalted butter in Dutch oven over medium-high heat.

5. Add 1 finely chopped onion and cook, stirring occasionally, until soft and lightly browned, about 4 minutes.

6. Add 1 tablespoon minced fresh thyme, 2 minced garlic cloves, 1¼ teaspoons salt, and ¼ teaspoon pepper and cook until fragrant.

7. Add potatoes, 1 cup chicken broth, 1 cup heavy cream, and 2 bay leaves and bring to simmer.

8. Cover, reduce heat to medium-low, and simmer until potatoes are almost tender, about 10 minutes. Discard bay leaves.

9. Transfer mixture to 8-inch square baking dish and press into even layer.

10. Sprinkle evenly with 1 cup shredded cheddar cheese.

11. Bake until top is golden brown, about 15 minutes.

12. Cool on wire rack for 10 minutes before serving.

Eggplant Parmesan

Overview

Making eggplant Parmesan at home is such a major undertaking, involving salting, breading, frying, simmering, and, finally, baking, that ordering it at a restaurant sounds like a pretty good alternative. Yet it's one of those dishes that is almost guaranteed to disappoint when ordered out.

Our recipe not only renders the dish doable in just a couple of hours, but it also delivers spectacular results. Gone are the soggy, slick eggplant slices and heavy, lifeless flavors—we bake our breaded eggplant slices, make a quick-cooked tomato sauce, and assemble with care to make the easiest and best-tasting Eggplant Parmesan. This recipe requires salting eggplant slices, and although it takes some time, it's a simple step that has a big impact on the finished dish.

Recipe Stats

TOTAL TIME **2 hours**
PREPARATION TIME **20 minutes**
ACTIVE COOKING TIME **1 hour**
YIELD **6 to 8 servings**
MAKE AHEAD **Serve immediately**
DIFFICULTY **Intermediate**

Tools

- large saucepan
- pie plates (2)
- rimmed baking sheets (3) *
- 13 by 9-inch baking dish
- food processor
- chef's knife
- cutting board
- dry measuring cups
- measuring spoons
- can opener
- coarse grater
- colander
- garlic press
- metal spatula
- mixing bowls
- rasp-style grater
- rubber spatula
- wire rack
- wooden spoon
- large zipper-lock bag
- paper towels

* Two of the three baking sheets are used to oven-fry the breaded eggplant slices. (The third is used to hold the breaded slices before baking.) For best results, use heavy-gauge baking sheets that won't warp and that conduct heat evenly so that the eggplant slices will brown well and uniformly.

Ingredients

- 2   **pounds eggplants, sliced into ¼-inch-thick rounds**
     Kosher salt and pepper *
- 8   **slices hearty white sandwich bread, torn into quarters ****
- 3   **ounces Parmesan cheese, grated (1½ cups)**
- 1   **cup all-purpose flour**
- 4   **large eggs**
- 6   **tablespoons vegetable oil**
- 3   **(14.5-ounce) cans diced tomatoes**
- 2   **tablespoons extra-virgin olive oil**
- 4   **garlic cloves, minced**
- ¼   **teaspoon red pepper flakes**
- ½   **cup chopped fresh basil, plus 10 extra leaves for garnish**
- 8   **ounces whole-milk or part-skim mozzarella cheese, shredded (2 cups) *****

* Use kosher salt when salting the eggplant. Because these coarse grains don't dissolve as readily as the fine grains of regular table salt, any excess can be easily wiped away. And we continue to use kosher salt throughout the recipe to keep it simple.

** The bread is used to make fresh bread crumbs for coating the eggplant. Choose a sandwich bread with a hearty, sturdy crumb; avoid loaves that have a soft, squishy texture.

*** For this recipe, be sure to use low-moisture mozzarella cheese, not fresh mozzarella, which is usually sold packed in water.

What Can Go Wrong

Here's a list of common mistakes cooks make when preparing this recipe.

COMMON MISTAKE	BAD OUTCOMES	WHAT YOU SHOULD DO
Not Salting Eggplant	• **The breading doesn't crisp properly.** • **The cooked eggplant has a spongy, underdone texture.**	Don't skip the salting step. Salting draws out some of the eggplant's moisture, and also begins to break down the eggplant's structure. If the eggplant slices are not salted, the moisture will prevent the breading from crisping properly, and the eggplant will not fully soften with cooking.
Not Wiping Salt Off Eggplant	• **The eggplant is too salty.**	When salting is complete, make sure to wipe any undissolved salt off of the eggplant slices. If the salt is left on, the final dish will taste extremely salty.
Using Wrong Bread Crumbs	• **The breading is thin.** • **The breading is not crisp.** • **The breading tastes stale.**	Don't try to take a shortcut by using store-bought bread crumbs instead of making your own fresh bread crumbs. Commercial bread crumbs are so fine that they're dusty, and they have a stale off-flavor that doesn't do any dish any favors. Fresh homemade bread crumbs are quick and easy to make in a food processor and have a flavor and texture that are superior to store-bought bread crumbs.
Not Preheating Baking Sheets	• **The breaded eggplant does not brown on the bottom.** • **The breaded eggplant does not crisp on the bottom.**	Put the baking sheets in the oven before turning on the oven. This will allow the baking sheets to heat up thoroughly so that when the eggplant slices are placed on them, they will immediately begin to brown and crisp.
Processing All Three Cans of Tomatoes	• **The tomato sauce lacks texture.**	When preparing the tomatoes for the tomato sauce, pulse only two of the three cans of diced tomatoes in the food processor. Pulsing breaks down the tomato bits into a more saucelike consistency, but using the tomatoes straight from the third can gives the sauce just the right amount of tomato chunks and textural interest.
Not Simmering Tomato Sauce Long Enough	• **The tomato sauce is watery.** • **The eggplant turns soggy.**	Make sure to simmer the tomato sauce until it is slightly thickened and the juices don't form large, watery pools. If the sauce is too thin, its flavor will be a little weak and the breading on the eggplant will turn very soft and soggy.
Oversaucing Top Eggplant Layer	• **The eggplant does not have any crisped areas.**	When adding the final layer of sauce, do not completely cover the eggplant slices. Leaving some areas free of sauce will allow those areas to remain crisp, which lends nice textural contrast to the finished dish.

1. PREPARE EGGPLANT: Toss 1 pound eggplant, cut into ¼-inch-thick rounds, with 1½ teaspoons kosher salt in bowl until combined.

2. Transfer to colander set over bowl. Repeat with 1 pound more eggplant. Let sit until about 2 tablespoons liquid is released, 30 to 45 minutes.

3. Arrange eggplant in single layer on triple layer of paper towels and cover with another triple layer. Press to remove excess liquid. Wipe off salt.

4. Adjust oven racks to upper-middle and lower-middle positions. Place 1 rimmed baking sheet on each rack and heat oven to 425 degrees.

5. PREPARE BREAD CRUMBS: Tear 8 slices sandwich bread into quarters and add to food processor. Pulse bread to fine, even crumbs, about 15 pulses.

6. Transfer crumbs to pie plate and stir in 1 cup grated Parmesan, ¼ teaspoon salt, and ½ teaspoon pepper.

7. Remove blade, wipe out food processor bowl (do not wash), and replace blade.

8. MAKE SAUCE: Process 2 (14.5-ounce) cans diced tomatoes and their juice in food processor until almost smooth, about 5 seconds.

9. Cook 2 tablespoons olive oil, 4 minced garlic cloves, and ¼ teaspoon pepper flakes over medium-high heat until garlic is golden, 2 minutes.

10. Stir in processed tomatoes and additional 14.5-ounce can diced tomatoes. Bring sauce to boil, then reduce heat to simmer.

11. Simmer sauce, stirring occasionally, until slightly thickened, about 15 minutes. Stir in ½ cup chopped basil. Season with salt and pepper.

12. COOK EGGPLANT: After wiping salt off eggplant, combine 1 cup flour and 1 teaspoon pepper in large zipper-lock bag and shake to combine.

13. Beat 4 large eggs in second pie plate.

14. Place 8 to 10 eggplant slices in bag with flour mixture. Seal bag and shake to coat eggplant. Remove eggplant slices, shaking off excess flour.

15. Dip eggplant slices in eggs and let excess egg run off. Coat slices evenly with bread-crumb mixture.

16. Set breaded slices on wire rack set over baking sheet. Repeat with remaining eggplant, overlapping slices as necessary.

17. Remove preheated sheets from oven. Add 3 tablespoons vegetable oil to each sheet. Arrange breaded eggplant rounds on sheets in single layer.

18. Bake eggplant 10 minutes. Switch and rotate baking sheets. Continue to bake 10 minutes longer.

19. Flip eggplant slices. Bake until eggplant is well browned and crisp, about 10 minutes longer. Remove eggplant from oven. Do not turn off oven.

20. ASSEMBLE AND BAKE: Spread 1 cup tomato sauce in bottom of 13 by 9-inch baking dish. Layer in half of eggplant slices, overlapping slices to fit.

21. Distribute 1 cup sauce over eggplant. Sprinkle with 1 cup shredded mozzarella.

22. Layer in remaining eggplant and dot with 1 cup sauce, leaving majority of eggplant exposed so it will remain crisp.

23. Sprinkle with ½ cup grated Parmesan and 1 cup shredded mozzarella. Bake until cheese is browned, 13 to 15 minutes. Cool 10 minutes.

24. FINISH AND SERVE: Tear 10 basil leaves into small pieces and scatter over top of casserole. Serve, passing remaining tomato sauce separately.

HOW TO COOK VEGETABLES

Vegetable Curry

Recipe Stats

TOTAL TIME **50 minutes**
PREPARATION TIME **15 minutes**
ACTIVE COOKING TIME **35 minutes**
YIELD **4 to 6 servings**
MAKE AHEAD **Serve immediately**
DIFFICULTY **Intermediate**

Tools

- Dutch oven
- small skillet
- food processor
- chef's knife
- cutting board
- liquid measuring cup
- measuring spoons
- can opener
- garlic press
- rasp-style grater
- rubber spatula
- wooden spoon

Ingredients

- 2 **tablespoons sweet or mild curry powder**
- 1½ **teaspoons garam masala** *
- 1 **(14.5-ounce) can diced tomatoes**
- ¼ **cup vegetable oil**
- 2 **onions, chopped fine**
- 12 **ounces red potatoes, unpeeled, cut into ½-inch pieces**
- 3 **garlic cloves, minced**
- 1 **tablespoon grated fresh ginger**
- 1–1½ **serrano chiles, minced** **
- 1 **tablespoon tomato paste**
- ½ **head cauliflower (1 pound), cored and cut into 1-inch florets**
- 1 **(14-ounce) can chickpeas, rinsed**
- 1¼ **cups water**
  Salt
- 1½ **cups frozen peas**
- ½ **cup heavy cream or canned coconut milk**

* If you can't find garam masala, substitute 2 teaspoons ground coriander, ½ teaspoon pepper, ¼ teaspoon ground cardamom, and ¼ teaspoon ground cinnamon.

** For a milder curry, remove the seeds and ribs. For a hotter curry, remove the stem and then mince the chile and seeds.

Overview

A complex and flavorful curry with vegetables front and center requires a few tricks—the bar is definitely higher here compared with a meat-based curry, where deeper, more complex flavor is inherently easier to achieve. We developed this bold curry for vegetable lovers unwilling to make compromises on flavor but also reluctant to spend hours in the kitchen. This recipe, which is more streamlined than most, uses supermarket staples and store-bought curry powder and garam masala, which we toast in a dry skillet to ramp up their flavor. With chickpeas, potatoes, cauliflower, and peas, it offers an interesting and appealing combination of textures and flavors.

Building flavor carefully was key, and we found you couldn't just build a sauce and cook the vegetables in it or you risked a bland curry at best. To start, we created a fond (flavorful browned bits) in the Dutch oven by browning onions and also the potatoes; this gave us a good foundation upon which to layer the flavors, and, as a bonus, the potatoes took on more flavor than if added raw. Following an Indian cooking method known as *bhuna,* we cleared the center of the pot and added a fragrant mixture of oil, tomato paste, garlic, ginger, chiles, and finally, the spices that had been toasted and set aside. Adding the remaining vegetables in stages, along with the pureed canned tomatoes and water, meant that they all cooked through properly, and the simmering sauce infused them with deep flavor. With all the complex flavor, no one will even miss the meat.

Serve this curry with Basmati Rice Pilaf (page 204) and Cilantro-Mint Chutney (page 131).

What Can Go Wrong

Here's a list of common mistakes cooks make when preparing this recipe.

COMMON MISTAKE	BAD OUTCOMES	WHAT YOU SHOULD DO
Not Toasting Curry Powder and Garam Masala	• **The curry tastes harsh.** • **The curry is not fully flavored.**	Toasting the spices is incredibly beneficial to the flavor of this dish. When spices are added to a simmering sauce, they can be heated only to 212 degrees. But in a dry skillet, temperatures can exceed 500 degrees, causing the flavors to hit a whole new level. Also, since we didn't want to go to the trouble of replicating curry powder or garam masala ourselves, we turned to store-bought spices instead. Although these spices tend to be less flavorful, toasting them narrowed the difference between a curry made with store-bought versus homemade spice blends.
Not Browning Potatoes	• **The potatoes taste lackluster.**	While browning the potatoes adds an extra step to making this curry and is rather unconventional, we found that browning them along with the onions substantially boosted the flavor of the potatoes.
Using Wrong Type of Canned Tomatoes	• **The flavors of the vegetables and spices are masked.**	We found that a can of diced tomatoes, pulsed in the food processor until just small pieces remained, provided the best base for the sauce. We mixed the tomatoes with just enough water to provide the perfect amount of liquid in which to simmer the vegetables and allow the spices to infuse the sauce. If you use crushed or whole tomatoes, the consistency of the sauce will not be the same and the tomato flavor will overwhelm the curry.
Shortcutting Cooking Time for Aromatics and Spices	• **The flavors are flat.** • **The spices taste raw.**	It's critical to cook the tomato paste, ginger, serrano, and garlic for 30 seconds in the oil, then add the toasted spices and cook for another full minute. This deepens the flavor of each of these components, and it also removes the raw edge of the spices, whose flavors mellow and deepen when cooked in oil.

1. Toast 2 tablespoons curry powder and 1½ teaspoons garam masala in small skillet over medium-high heat until fragrant, about 1 minute. Set aside.

2. Pulse 1 (14.5-ounce) can diced tomatoes and their juice in food processor until coarsely chopped, 3 or 4 pulses.

3. Heat 3 tablespoons vegetable oil in Dutch oven over medium-high heat until shimmering.

4. Add 2 finely chopped onions and 12 ounces red potatoes, cut into ½-inch pieces. Cook until onions and potatoes are golden brown, about 10 minutes.

5. Reduce heat to medium. Clear center of pot and add 1 tablespoon vegetable oil.

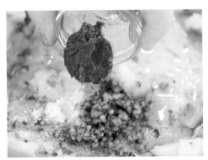

6. Add 3 minced garlic cloves, 1 tablespoon grated ginger, 1–1½ minced serrano chiles, and 1 tablespoon tomato paste. Cook for 30 seconds.

7. Add reserved toasted spices and cook, stirring constantly, for 1 minute.

8. Add ½ head cauliflower, cut into 1-inch florets, and cook, stirring constantly, until spices coat florets, about 2 minutes.

9. Add tomatoes, 1 (14-ounce) can rinsed chickpeas, 1¼ cups water, and 1 teaspoon salt.

10. Increase heat to medium-high and bring mixture to boil, scraping pan bottom to loosen browned bits.

11. Cover, reduce heat to medium, and simmer briskly, stirring occasionally, until vegetables are tender, 10 to 15 minutes.

12. Stir in 1½ cups frozen peas and ¼ cup heavy cream and cook until heated through, about 2 minutes. Adjust seasonings and serve.

Recipe Library

Pan-Roasted Asparagus

✓ **WHY THIS RECIPE WORKS:** Pan roasting is a simple stovetop cooking method that delivers crisp, evenly browned spears without the fuss of having to rotate each spear individually. We started with thicker spears (thin ones overcooked before browning) and arranged them in the pan with half pointed in one direction and half in the other. To help the asparagus release moisture, which would encourage caramelization and better flavor, we parcooked it, covered, with butter and oil before browning it. The water evaporating from the butter helped to steam the asparagus, producing bright green, crisp-tender spears. At this point, we removed the lid and cranked up the heat until the spears were evenly browned on the bottom. We found there was no need to brown the asparagus all over; tasters preferred the flavor of spears browned on only one side and, as a bonus, the half-browned spears never had a chance to go limp. We then came up with a few variations that included accent ingredients like cherry tomatoes, olives, sautéed red peppers, and goat cheese. We simply cooked any garnish ingredients first, then set them aside while we prepared the asparagus.

Pan-Roasted Asparagus
SERVES 4 TO 6

This recipe works best with asparagus that is at least ½ inch thick near the base. If using thinner spears, reduce the covered cooking time to 3 minutes and the uncovered cooking time to 5 minutes. Do not use pencil-thin asparagus; it cannot withstand the heat and overcooks too easily.

- 1 **tablespoon olive oil**
- 1 **tablespoon unsalted butter**
- 2 **pounds thick asparagus, trimmed**
  Salt and pepper
- ½ **lemon (optional)**

1. Heat oil and butter in 12-inch skillet over medium-high heat. When butter has melted, add half of asparagus to skillet with tips pointed in one direction; add remaining spears with tips pointed in opposite direction. Using tongs, distribute spears evenly (spears will not quite fit into single layer); cover and cook until asparagus is bright green and still crisp, about 5 minutes.

2. Uncover and increase heat to high; season asparagus with salt and pepper to taste. Cook until spears are tender and well browned along one side, 5 to 7 minutes, using tongs to occasionally move spears from center of pan to edge of pan to ensure all are browned. Transfer asparagus to serving dish, adjust seasonings with salt and pepper, and, if desired, squeeze lemon half over spears. Serve immediately.

Pan-Roasted Asparagus with Toasted Garlic and Parmesan

Heat 2 tablespoons olive oil and 3 garlic cloves, sliced thin, in 12-inch skillet over medium heat. Cook, stirring occasionally, until garlic is crisp and golden but not dark brown, about 5 minutes. Using slotted spoon, transfer garlic to paper towel–lined plate. Follow recipe for Pan-Roasted Asparagus, adding butter to oil already in skillet. After transferring asparagus to serving dish, sprinkle with 2 tablespoons grated Parmesan and toasted garlic. Season with lemon juice, salt, and pepper to taste and serve immediately.

Roasted Red Bell Peppers

✓ **WHY THIS RECIPE WORKS:** Sweet red bell peppers take on a whole new layer of complex, smoky flavor when roasted. We wanted a method for roasting them that was more efficient than the common technique of roasting each pepper over a gas burner, letting it steam in a covered bowl, then laboriously removing the skin bit by bit. We discovered the broiler offered an easy, consistent, and more hands-off option than the burner (roasting in either a hot or low oven yielded soggy, overcooked peppers). To get around the issue of whole peppers hitting the broiler element, we cut the peppers into pieces that lay flat on a baking sheet. After 8 to 10 minutes, the peppers were done and we could easily peel off the blistered skin.

Roasted Red Bell Peppers
MAKES 4 ROASTED PEPPERS

Cooking times vary, depending on the broiler, so watch the peppers carefully as they roast. You can substitute yellow or orange bell peppers here, but note that they roast faster than red ones, so decrease their cooking time by 2 to 4 minutes. See Core Technique on page 108 for more details on this recipe.

- 4 **red bell peppers, stemmed, seeded, ribs removed, and cut to lie flat**

1. Adjust oven rack 2½ to 3½ inches from broiler element and heat broiler. If necessary, set upside-down rimmed baking sheet on oven rack to elevate peppers to proper height. Line baking sheet with aluminum foil.

2. Spread peppers out over prepared baking sheet and broil until skin is charred and puffed but flesh is still firm, 8 to 10 minutes, rotating baking sheet halfway through cooking.

3. Transfer peppers to medium bowl, cover with foil, and let steam until skin peels off easily, 10 to 15 minutes. Peel and discard skin.

Roasted Broccoli

✔ **WHY THIS RECIPE WORKS:** Roasting is a great way to deepen the flavor of vegetables, but broccoli can be tricky to roast given its awkward shape, dense, woody stalks, and shrubby florets. We wanted a roasted broccoli recipe that would give us evenly cooked broccoli—stalks and florets—and add concentrated flavor and dappled browning. The way we prepared the broccoli was the key. We cut each crown into uniform wedges. We cut the stalks into rectangular pieces slightly smaller than the more delicate wedges. This promoted even cooking and great browning by maximizing the vegetable's contact with the baking sheet. Tossing a scant ½ teaspoon of sugar over the broccoli along with salt, pepper, and a few tablespoons of olive oil gave us blistered, bubbled, and browned stalks that were sweet and full flavored, along with crisp-tipped florets.

Roasted Broccoli

SERVES 4

Make sure to trim away the outer peel from the broccoli stalks as directed; otherwise, it will turn tough when cooked.

1¾ **pounds broccoli**
3 **tablespoons extra-virgin olive oil**
½ **teaspoon salt**
½ **teaspoon sugar**
Pepper
Lemon wedges

1. Adjust oven rack to lowest position, place large rimmed baking sheet on rack, and heat oven to 500 degrees. Cut broccoli at juncture of florets and stalks; remove outer peel from stalk. Cut stalk into 2- to 3-inch lengths and each length into ½-inch-thick pieces. Cut crowns into 4 wedges if 3 to 4 inches in diameter or 6 wedges if 4 to 5 inches in diameter. Place broccoli in large bowl; drizzle with oil and toss well until evenly coated. Sprinkle with salt, sugar, and pepper to taste and toss to combine.

2. Working quickly, remove baking sheet from oven. Carefully transfer broccoli to baking sheet and spread into even layer, placing flat sides of broccoli pieces down. Return baking sheet to oven and roast until stalks are well browned and tender and florets are lightly browned, 9 to 11 minutes. Transfer to platter and serve immediately with lemon wedges.

Roasted Broccoli with Shallots, Fennel Seeds, and Parmesan

While broccoli roasts, heat 1 tablespoon extra-virgin oil in 8-inch skillet over medium heat until shimmering. Add 3 thinly sliced shallots and cook, stirring frequently, until soft and beginning to turn light golden brown, 5 to 6 minutes. Add 1 teaspoon coarsely chopped fennel seeds and continue to cook until shallots are golden brown, 1 to 2 minutes longer. Off heat, toss roasted broccoli with shallots, sprinkle with 1 ounce shaved Parmesan, and serve immediately.

Roasted Broccoli with Garlic

Stir 3 cloves minced garlic into olive oil before drizzling it over prepared broccoli in step 1.

Roasted Broccoli with Olives, Garlic, Oregano, and Lemon

Omit pepper when seasoning broccoli in step 1. While broccoli roasts, heat 2 tablespoons extra-virgin olive oil, 5 thinly sliced garlic cloves and ½ teaspoon red pepper flakes in 8-inch skillet over medium-low heat. Cook, stirring frequently, until garlic is soft and beginning to turn light golden brown, 5 to 7 minutes. Remove from heat and stir in 2 tablespoons finely chopped pitted black olives, 1 teaspoon minced fresh oregano, and 2 teaspoons lemon juice. Toss roasted broccoli with olive mixture and serve immediately.

Glazed Carrots

✔ **WHY THIS RECIPE WORKS:** For well-seasoned carrots with a glossy, clingy, yet modest glaze, we started by slicing the carrots on the bias, which lent visual appeal without requiring much work. Most glazed carrot recipes start by steaming, parboiling, or blanching the carrots prior to glazing. To make glazed carrots a one-pot operation, we steamed them directly in the skillet, and we used chicken broth rather than water (along with some salt and sugar) for fuller flavor. When the carrots were almost tender, we removed the lid and turned up the heat to reduce the cooking liquid. Then we added butter and a bit more sugar, and finally finished with a sprinkling of fresh lemon juice and a bit of black pepper to give the dish sparkle.

Glazed Carrots

SERVES 4

Glazed carrots are a good accompaniment to roasts of any kind—beef, pork, lamb, or poultry. A nonstick skillet is easier to clean, but this recipe can be prepared in any 12-inch skillet with a cover.

1 **pound carrots, peeled and sliced ¼ inch thick on bias**
½ **cup chicken broth**
3 **tablespoons sugar**
½ **teaspoon salt**
1 **tablespoon unsalted butter, cut into 4 pieces**
2 **teaspoons lemon juice**
Pepper

1. Bring carrots, broth, 1 tablespoon sugar, and salt to boil, covered, in 12-inch nonstick skillet over medium-high heat. Reduce heat to medium and simmer, stirring occasionally, until carrots are almost tender when poked with paring knife, about 5 minutes. Uncover, increase heat to high, and simmer rapidly, stirring occasionally, until liquid is reduced to about 2 tablespoons, 1 to 2 minutes.

2. Add butter and remaining 2 tablespoons sugar to skillet, toss carrots to coat, and cook, stirring frequently, until carrots are completely tender and glaze is light gold, about 3 minutes. Off heat, add lemon juice and toss to coat. Transfer carrots to serving dish, scraping glaze from pan. Season with pepper to taste and serve immediately.

Glazed Carrots with Ginger and Rosemary

Add one 1-inch piece ginger, peeled and sliced into ¼-inch-thick rounds, to skillet along with carrots and 1 teaspoon minced fresh rosemary along with butter. Discard ginger pieces before serving.

Honey-Glazed Carrots with Lemon and Thyme

Substitute 3 tablespoons honey for sugar and add ½ teaspoon minced fresh thyme and ½ teaspoon grated lemon zest along with butter.

Glazed Curried Carrots with Currants and Almonds

Toast ¼ cup sliced almonds in 12-inch nonstick skillet over medium heat until fragrant and lightly browned, about 5 minutes; transfer to small bowl and set aside. Off heat, sprinkle 1½ teaspoons curry powder in skillet; stir until fragrant, about 2 seconds. Add carrots, broth, 1 tablespoon sugar, and salt to skillet along with curry powder. Add ¼ cup currants along with butter and remaining 2 tablespoons sugar; add toasted almonds along with lemon juice.

Roasted Cauliflower

✓ **WHY THIS RECIPE WORKS:** We wanted to add flavor to cauliflower without drowning it in a heavy blanket of cheese sauce, so we developed a roasted cauliflower recipe that gave us cauliflower with a golden, nutty exterior and sweet interior. We discovered that steaming (in a covered baking sheet) followed by roasting produced nicely caramelized cauliflower with a creamy texture. Though the cauliflower is excellent on its own, we also developed some simple sauces to dress it up.

Roasted Cauliflower

SERVES 4 TO 6

This dish stands well on its own, drizzled with extra-virgin olive oil, but it can also be prepared with a sauce (recipes follow). We prefer kosher salt here but table salt will also work fine.

- 1 head cauliflower (2 pounds)
- ¼ cup olive oil
  Kosher salt and pepper

1. Adjust oven rack to lowest position and heat oven to 475 degrees. Trim outer leaves off cauliflower and cut stem flush with bottom. Cut head into 8 equal wedges. Place wedges cut side down on aluminum foil– or parchment-lined rimmed baking sheet. Drizzle with 2 tablespoons oil and season with salt and pepper to taste. Gently rub seasonings and oil into cauliflower. Gently flip cauliflower and repeat on second cut side with remaining 2 tablespoons oil, salt, and pepper.

2. Cover baking sheet tightly with foil and cook for 10 minutes. Remove foil and continue to roast until bottoms of cauliflower pieces are golden, 8 to 12 minutes. Remove baking sheet from oven, and, using spatula, carefully flip wedges. Return baking sheet to oven and continue to roast until cauliflower is golden all over, 8 to 12 minutes longer. Season with salt and pepper to taste and serve immediately.

Spicy Roasted Cauliflower

Stir 2 teaspoons curry powder or chili powder into the oil before seasoning the cauliflower in step 1.

Curry-Yogurt Sauce with Cilantro

MAKES ENOUGH FOR 1 RECIPE ROASTED CAULIFLOWER

If using this sauce, use vegetable oil to roast the cauliflower instead of olive oil.

- 1 tablespoon vegetable oil
- 1 shallot, minced
- 2 teaspoons curry powder
- ¼ teaspoon red pepper flakes
- ⅓ cup water
- ¼ cup plain whole-milk yogurt
- 2 tablespoons minced fresh cilantro
- 1 teaspoon lime juice
  Salt and pepper

Heat oil in small skillet over medium-high heat until shimmering. Add shallot and cook until softened, about 2 minutes. Stir in curry powder and pepper flakes; cook until fragrant, about 1 minute. Off heat, whisk in water, yogurt, cilantro, lime juice, and salt and pepper to taste. Drizzle sauce over roasted cauliflower before serving.

Soy-Ginger Sauce with Scallion

MAKES ENOUGH FOR 1 RECIPE ROASTED CAULIFLOWER

If using this sauce, use vegetable oil to roast the cauliflower instead of olive oil.

- 2 teaspoons vegetable oil
- 1 tablespoon grated fresh ginger
- 2 garlic cloves, minced
- ¼ cup water
- 2 tablespoons soy sauce
- 2 tablespoons mirin
- 1 tablespoon rice vinegar
- 1 teaspoon toasted sesame oil
- 1 scallion, sliced thin

Heat oil in 8-inch skillet over medium-high heat until shimmering. Add ginger and garlic and cook until fragrant, about 1 minute. Reduce heat to medium-low and add water, soy sauce, mirin, and vinegar. Simmer until slightly syrupy, 4 to 6 minutes. Drizzle sauce and sesame oil over roasted cauliflower and garnish with scallion before serving.

Braised Winter Greens

✔ **WHY THIS RECIPE WORKS:** We wanted a one-pot approach to turning winter greens like kale and collards tender, without spending hours or leaving them awash in liquid. We sautéed half of the greens before adding the rest with a little bit of liquid and covered the pot. When the greens almost had the texture we wanted, we removed the lid to allow the liquid to cook off. With the texture right where we wanted it, all we had to do was come up with a few flavorful ingredients to add to the pot.

Braised Winter Greens
SERVES 4

For the best results, be sure the greens are fully cooked and tender in step 1 before moving on to step 2. For more information on preparing kale and collard greens, see page 100. See Core Technique on page 109 for more details on this recipe.

- 3 **tablespoons olive oil**
- 1 **onion, chopped fine**
- 5 **garlic cloves, minced**
- ⅛ **teaspoon red pepper flakes**
- 2 **pounds kale or collard greens, stemmed and leaves chopped into 3-inch pieces**
- 1 **cup chicken broth**
- 1 **cup water**
-   **Salt and pepper**
- 2-3 **teaspoons lemon juice**

1. Heat 2 tablespoons oil in Dutch oven over medium heat until shimmering. Add onion and cook, stirring frequently, until softened and beginning to brown, 4 to 5 minutes. Add garlic and pepper flakes and cook until garlic is fragrant, about 1 minute. Add half of greens and stir until beginning to wilt, about 1 minute. Add remaining greens, broth, water, and ¼ teaspoon salt. Quickly cover pot and reduce heat to medium-low. Cook, stirring occasionally, until greens are tender, 25 to 35 minutes for kale and 35 to 45 minutes for collards.

2. Remove lid and increase heat to medium-high. Cook, stirring occasionally, until most of liquid has evaporated (bottom of pot will be almost dry and greens will begin to sizzle), 8 to 12 minutes. Off heat, stir in 2 teaspoons lemon juice and remaining 1 tablespoon oil. Season with salt, pepper, and lemon juice to taste and serve.

Braised Winter Greens with Bacon and Onion

Cook 6 slices bacon, cut into ¼-inch pieces, over medium heat until crisp, 5 to 7 minutes. Transfer bacon to paper towel–lined plate and pour off all but 2 tablespoons fat. Substitute rendered fat for 2 tablespoons olive oil; 1 red onion, halved and cut into ¼-inch slices, for minced onion; and 3 to 4 teaspoons cider vinegar for lemon juice. Stir reserved bacon into greens before serving.

Braised Winter Greens with Coconut and Curry

Substitute 2 teaspoons grated fresh ginger and 1 teaspoon curry powder for red pepper flakes and 1 (14-ounce) can coconut milk for water. Substitute 2 to 3 teaspoons lime juice for lemon juice and sprinkle greens with ⅓ cup toasted cashews before serving.

Braised Winter Greens with Chorizo

Heat oil as directed in step 1, then add 8 ounces Spanish chorizo sausage, cut into ¼-inch-thick half-moons, and cook until lightly browned, 4 to 6 minutes. Transfer chorizo to paper towel–lined plate. Proceed with recipe, cooking onion and garlic in remaining oil and substituting 1½ teaspoons ground cumin for red pepper flakes. Stir in reserved chorizo before serving.

Sautéed Green Beans

✔ **WHY THIS RECIPE WORKS:** For tender, lightly browned, fresh-tasting beans using just one pan, we turned to sautéing. But simply sautéing raw beans in oil resulted in blackened exteriors and undercooked interiors. Cooking the beans in water in a covered pan, then removing the lid to evaporate the liquid and brown the beans was better, but not foolproof. For the best results, we sautéed the beans until spotty brown, then added water to the pan and covered it so the beans could cook through. Once the beans were soft, we lifted the lid to vaporize whatever water remained in the pan and promote additional browning. A little softened butter added to the pan at this stage lent richness and promoted even more browning. A few additional ingredients, such as garlic and herbs, added flavor without overcomplicating our recipe.

Sautéed Green Beans with Garlic and Herbs
SERVES 4

This recipe yields crisp-tender beans. If you prefer a slightly more tender texture (or you are using large, tough beans), increase the water by 1 tablespoon and increase the covered cooking time by 1 minute.

- 1 **tablespoon unsalted butter, softened**
- 3 **garlic cloves, minced**
- 1 **teaspoon chopped fresh thyme**
- 1 **teaspoon olive oil**
- 1 **pound green beans, trimmed and cut into 2-inch lengths**
-   **Salt and pepper**
- 1 **tablespoon chopped fresh parsley**
- 2 **teaspoons lemon juice**

1. Combine butter, garlic, and thyme in small bowl; set aside. Heat oil in 12-inch nonstick skillet over medium heat until just smoking. Add beans, ¼ teaspoon salt, and ⅛ teaspoon pepper; cook, stirring occasionally, until spotty brown, 4 to 6 minutes. Add ¼ cup water, cover, and cook until beans are bright green and still crisp, about 2 minutes. Uncover, increase heat to high, and cook until water evaporates, 30 to 60 seconds.

2. Add butter mixture to skillet and continue to cook, stirring frequently, until beans are crisp-tender, lightly browned, and beginning to wrinkle, 1 to 3 minutes longer. Transfer beans to serving bowl and toss with parsley and lemon juice. Season with salt and pepper to taste and serve immediately.

Sautéed Mushrooms

✓ **WHY THIS RECIPE WORKS:** Supermarket mushrooms shrink and shrivel when sautéed. We wanted to develop a quick sauté method that delivered enough white mushrooms to make a delicious, ample side dish. To get more flavor and less shriveling, we discovered that overloading the skillet and extending the cooking time allowed the mushrooms to give up just enough liquid to eventually fit in a single layer without shrinking to nothing. They browned nicely after we added a little oil or butter, and from there it was easy to enhance the mushrooms with shallot, thyme, and Marsala.

Sautéed Mushrooms with Shallots and Thyme
SERVES 4

Marsala is a classic choice for complementing the earthy flavor of mushrooms. See Core Technique on page 110 for more details on this recipe and additional flavoring suggestions.

- 1 tablespoon vegetable oil
- 1½ pounds white mushrooms, trimmed and halved if small or quartered if large
- 1 tablespoon unsalted butter
- 1 shallot, minced
- 1 tablespoon minced fresh thyme
- ¼ cup dry Marsala
  Salt and pepper

1. Heat oil in 12-inch skillet over medium-high heat until shimmering. Add mushrooms and cook, stirring occasionally, until mushrooms release liquid, about 5 minutes. Increase heat to high and cook, stirring occasionally, until liquid has completely evaporated, about 8 minutes longer. Add butter, reduce heat to medium, and continue to cook, stirring once every minute, until mushrooms are dark brown, about 8 minutes longer.

2. Add shallot and thyme and cook until softened, about 3 minutes. Add Marsala and cook until liquid has evaporated, about 2 minutes. Season with salt and pepper to taste and serve.

Roasted Red Potatoes

✓ **WHY THIS RECIPE WORKS:** We found that the most crucial characteristic for roasted potatoes was texture. High-starch, low-moisture potatoes, such as russets, didn't brown well and cooked up mealy. Medium-starch, all-purpose potatoes, such as Yukon Golds, browned nicely but were too dry. Low-starch, high-moisture potatoes, such as Red Bliss, offered a crisp yet delicate crust and a moist, dense interior. As for the cooking method, many recipes call for partially boiling the potatoes before roasting them. Although this technique works well, it is tedious. Instead, we covered the potatoes with foil for the first 20 minutes of cooking so that they would steam in their own moisture. From here, we removed the foil and roasted the potatoes until they became crusty and golden on the outside and creamy on the interior. These potatoes were great served simply as is, or varied with simple additions of aromatics, fresh herbs, and even cheese and olives.

Roasted Red Potatoes
SERVES 4

We use medium red potatoes, measuring 2 to 3 inches in diameter; however, it's most important that your potatoes are of similar size to ensure even cooking. If using very small potatoes, cut them in half instead of into wedges.

- 2 pounds red potatoes, unpeeled, cut into ¾-inch wedges
- 2 tablespoons olive oil
  Salt and pepper

1. Adjust oven rack to middle position and heat oven to 425 degrees. Toss potatoes with oil, ½ teaspoon salt, and ¼ teaspoon pepper. Arrange potatoes, 1 cut side down, in single layer on rimmed baking sheet and cover tightly with aluminum foil. Roast for 20 minutes.

2. Remove foil and continue to roast until bottoms of potatoes are crusty and golden, about 15 minutes. Flip potatoes and continue to roast until crusty and golden brown on both sides, about 8 minutes longer. Season with salt and pepper to taste and serve.

Roasted Red Potatoes with Garlic and Rosemary

Sprinkle 2 tablespoons minced fresh rosemary over potatoes during final 3 minutes of roasting. Toss roasted potatoes with 1 garlic clove, mashed to paste, before serving.

Roasted Red Potatoes with Garlic, Shallot, Lemon, and Thyme

Sprinkle 1 teaspoon minced fresh thyme over potatoes during final 3 minutes of roasting. Toss roasted potatoes with 1 garlic clove, mashed to paste, 1 minced shallot, ½ teaspoon grated lemon zest, and 1 teaspoon lemon juice before serving.

Roasted Red Potatoes with Garlic, Feta, Olives, and Oregano

Sprinkle 1 tablespoon minced fresh oregano over potatoes during final 3 minutes of roasting. Toss roasted potatoes with 1 garlic clove, mashed to paste, ½ cup crumbled feta, ¼ cup pitted and chopped kalamata olives, and 1 tablespoon lemon juice before serving.

French Fries

✓ **WHY THIS RECIPE WORKS:** We wanted to find a recipe and method for making French fries that would rival restaurant versions. For us, the ideal fry would be long and crisp, with right-angle sides, a nice crunch on the outside, and an earthy potato taste. Waxy potatoes were too watery and fried up with hollow cavities that simply filled with oil. Russet potatoes turned out to be the best choice, but because they are starchy, we found it was important to rinse the starch off the surface after cutting the potatoes. Refrigerating the potatoes for at least 30 minutes in water made lighter, crispier fries and improved their browning. Coating the fries in a little cornstarch prior to cooking absorbed some of the surface moisture on the potatoes and created a protective sheath that turned into a shatteringly crisp crust once fried. We preferred our fries cooked in peanut oil but vegetable oil was a good second choice. We fried the potatoes twice: The first fry was at a relatively low temperature to secure a soft and rich-tasting interior; the quick second fry was at a higher temperature to crisp and color the exterior.

French Fries

SERVES 4

You will need a Dutch oven with at least a 6-quart capacity and a candy thermometer or another thermometer that registers high temperatures for this recipe. See Core Technique on page 106 for more details on this recipe.

2½ **pounds russet potatoes, unpeeled, sides squared, and cut lengthwise into ¼-inch-thick fries**
2   **tablespoons cornstarch**
3   **quarts peanut or vegetable oil**
     Salt

1. Rinse cut potatoes in large bowl under cold running water until water turns clear. Cover with cold water and refrigerate for 30 minutes or up to 12 hours.

2. Pour off water, spread potatoes onto clean dish towels, and dry thoroughly. Transfer potatoes to large bowl and toss with cornstarch until evenly coated. Transfer potatoes to wire rack set in rimmed baking sheet and let rest until fine white coating forms, about 20 minutes.

3. Meanwhile, heat oil in large Dutch oven over medium heat to 325 degrees.

4. Add half of potatoes, a handful at a time, to hot oil and increase heat to high. Fry, stirring with mesh spider or large-hole slotted spoon, until potatoes start to turn from white to blond, 4 to 5 minutes. (Oil temperature will drop about 75 degrees during frying.) Transfer fries to thick paper bag or paper towels. Return oil to 325 degrees and repeat with remaining potatoes. Let fries cool, at least 10 minutes or up to 2 hours.

5. When ready to finish frying, increase heat to medium-high and heat oil to 375 degrees. Add half of fries, a handful at a time, and fry until golden brown and puffed, 2 to 3 minutes. Transfer to thick paper bag or paper towels. Return oil to 375 degrees and repeat with remaining fries. Season fries with salt and serve immediately.

Oven Fries

✔ **WHY THIS RECIPE WORKS:** The ease and neatness of oven frying is such an engaging proposition that we decided to try to make oven fries worth eating on their own terms. We were after fries with a golden, crisp crust and a creamy interior. We soaked wedges of peeled russets in hot water for 10 minutes to remove excess starch. To prevent the potatoes from sticking, we poured oil on the baking sheet, then sprinkled it with salt and pepper, which elevated them just enough. We covered the potatoes with aluminum foil to steam them for the first 5 minutes of cooking, then uncovered them and continued to bake until they were golden and crisp. See page 101 for information on cutting potatoes for oven fries.

Oven Fries

SERVES 3 TO 4

Take care to cut the potatoes into evenly sized wedges so that all of the pieces will cook at about the same rate. Although it isn't required, a nonstick baking sheet works particularly well for this recipe. It not only keeps the fries from sticking to the pan but, because of its dark color, it also encourages deep and even browning. Whether you choose a nonstick baking sheet or a regular baking sheet, make sure that it is heavy duty. The intense heat of the oven may cause lighter pans to warp.

2¼ **pounds russet potatoes, peeled and cut lengthwise into 10 to 12 even wedges**
5   **tablespoons peanut or vegetable oil**
     Salt and pepper

1. Adjust oven rack to lowest position and heat oven to 475 degrees. Place potatoes in large bowl, cover with hot tap water, and soak for 10 minutes. Meanwhile, coat 18 by 12-inch heavy-duty rimmed baking sheet with 4 tablespoons oil and sprinkle evenly with ¾ teaspoon salt and ¼ teaspoon pepper; set aside. Line second baking sheet with triple layer of paper towels and set aside.

2. Drain potatoes. Spread potatoes out on paper towel–lined baking sheet, then thoroughly pat dry with additional paper towels. Rinse and wipe out now-empty bowl. Return potatoes to bowl and toss with remaining 1 tablespoon oil. Arrange potatoes in single layer on oiled baking sheet, cover tightly with aluminum foil, and bake 5 minutes. Remove foil and continue to bake until bottoms of potatoes are spotty golden brown, 15 to 20 minutes, rotating baking sheet after 10 minutes. Using metal spatula and tongs, scrape to loosen potatoes from pan, then flip each wedge, keeping potatoes in single layer. Continue baking until fries are golden and crisp, 5 to 15 minutes longer, rotating pan as needed if fries are browning unevenly.

3. While fries bake, line baking sheet with triple layer of paper towels. Transfer baked fries to prepared baking sheet to drain. Season with salt and pepper to taste and serve.

Mashed Potatoes

✔ **WHY THIS RECIPE WORKS:** Many people would never consider consulting a recipe when making mashed potatoes, instead adding chunks of butter and spurts of cream until their conscience tells them to stop. Little wonder then that mashed potatoes made this way are consistent only in their mediocrity. We wanted mashed potatoes that were perfectly smooth and creamy, with great potato flavor and plenty of buttery richness. We began by selecting russets for their high starch content. Boiling them whole and unpeeled yielded mashed potatoes that were rich, earthy, and sweet. A food mill or ricer delivered the smoothest texture (a potato masher could be used if you prefer your potatoes a little chunky). We added melted butter first and then half-and-half. Melting, rather than merely softening, the butter enabled it to coat the starch molecules quickly and easily, so the potatoes turned out creamy and light. From there, it was easy to come up with a number of flavorful variations.

Classic Mashed Potatoes

SERVES 4

Russet potatoes make fluffier mashed potatoes, but Yukon Golds have an appealing buttery flavor and can be used. See Core Technique on page 104 for more details on this recipe.

> 2 **pounds russet potatoes, unpeeled**
> 8 **tablespoons unsalted butter, melted**
> 1 **cup warm half-and-half**
> 1½ **teaspoons salt**
> **Pepper**

1. Place potatoes in large saucepan and cover with 1 inch cold water. Bring to boil over high heat, reduce heat to medium-low, and simmer until potatoes are just tender (paring knife can be slipped in and out of potatoes with little resistance), 20 to 30 minutes. Drain.

2. Set ricer or food mill over now-empty saucepan. Using potholder or folded dish towel (to hold potatoes) and paring knife, peel skins from potatoes. Working in batches, cut peeled potatoes into large chunks and press or mill into saucepan.

3. Stir in butter until incorporated. Gently whisk in half-and-half, add salt, and season with pepper to taste. Serve.

Garlic Mashed Potatoes

Avoid using unusually large garlic cloves, which will not soften adequately during toasting. For chunky mashed potatoes, use a potato masher, decrease the half-and-half to ¾ cup, and mash the garlic to a paste before you add it to the potatoes.

Toast 22 unpeeled garlic cloves (about 3 ounces, or ⅔ cup), covered, in 8-inch skillet over low heat, shaking pan frequently, until cloves are dark spotty brown and slightly softened, about 22 minutes. Off heat, let sit, covered, until fully softened, 15 to 20 minutes. Peel cloves and, with paring knife, cut off woody root end; set aside. Press or mill garlic along with potatoes in step 2.

Garlic Mashed Potatoes with Smoked Gouda and Chives

Reduce salt in Garlic Mashed Potatoes to 1¼ teaspoons and stir in 1 cup grated smoked Gouda along with half-and-half; set pot over low heat and stir until cheese is melted and incorporated. Stir in 3 tablespoons chopped fresh chives.

Mashed Potatoes with Scallions and Horseradish

You can substitute 2 tablespoons prepared horseradish for the grated fresh horseradish root.

After stirring butter into potatoes in step 3, season with 1½ teaspoons salt and ½ teaspoon pepper. Whisk 2 tablespoons prepared horseradish, ¼ cup grated fresh horseradish root, and 3 minced scallions, green parts only, into warm half-and-half. Add mixture to potatoes and stir until just combined. Serve immediately.

Mashed Potatoes with Smoked Cheddar and Grainy Mustard

After stirring butter into potatoes in step 3, season with 1¼ teaspoons salt and ½ teaspoon pepper. Add 2 tablespoons whole-grain mustard and ¾ cup shredded smoked cheddar with half-and-half, and stir until just combined. Serve immediately.

Mashed Potatoes with Smoked Paprika and Toasted Garlic

The extra steps in this variation are worth the trouble.

While potatoes are simmering, toast 1 teaspoon smoked paprika in 8-inch skillet over medium heat, stirring frequently, until fragrant, about 2 minutes. Transfer to small bowl; set aside. Melt 8 tablespoons butter in small saucepan over medium-low heat. Add 3 minced garlic cloves, reduce heat to low, and cook, stirring frequently, until garlic begins to brown, 12 to 14 minutes. Remove saucepan from heat immediately and set aside for 5 minutes (garlic will continue to brown). Pour butter-garlic mixture through fine-mesh strainer; reserve butter and set toasted garlic aside. Rice or mill potatoes as directed, then stir butter into potatoes until just incorporated. Season potatoes with toasted paprika, 1½ teaspoons salt, and ½ teaspoon pepper. Add warm half-and-half and stir until just combined. Serve immediately, sprinkling with reserved toasted garlic.

Scalloped Potatoes

✓ **WHY THIS RECIPE WORKS:** Rich and creamy scalloped potatoes are a holiday favorite and typically require labor-intensive preparation. We wanted a lighter, quicker version that we could make for weeknight dinners. We used traditional russet potatoes to form tight, cohesive layers, and equal parts canned chicken broth and heavy cream to offset the typical heaviness of the dish. We parboiled the sliced potatoes in the broth-cream mixture on top of the stove, then poured the whole mixture into a casserole dish and finished it in the oven.

Scalloped Potatoes

SERVES 4 TO 6

The quickest way to slice the potatoes is in a food processor fitted with an ⅛-inch slicing blade. If the potatoes are too long to fit into the feed tube, halve them crosswise and put them in the feed tube cut side down so that they sit on a flat surface. If the potato slices discolor as they sit, put them in a bowl and cover with the cream and chicken broth. You can substitute Parmesan for the cheddar if desired. See Recipe Tutorial on page 111 for more details on this recipe.

> 2 **tablespoons unsalted butter**
> 1 **onion, chopped fine**
> 1 **tablespoon minced fresh thyme**
> 2 **garlic cloves, minced**
> 1¼ **teaspoons salt**
> ¼ **teaspoon pepper**
> 2½ **pounds russet potatoes, peeled and sliced ⅛ inch thick**
> 1 **cup chicken broth**
> 1 **cup heavy cream**
> 2 **bay leaves**
> 4 **ounces cheddar cheese, shredded (1 cup)**

1. Adjust oven rack to middle position and heat oven to 425 degrees.

2. Melt butter in Dutch oven over medium-high heat. Add onion and cook, stirring occasionally, until soft and lightly browned, about 4 minutes. Add thyme, garlic, salt, and pepper and cook until fragrant, about 30 seconds. Add potatoes, chicken broth, cream, and bay leaves and bring to simmer. Cover, reduce heat to medium-low, and simmer until potatoes are almost tender (paring knife can be slipped in and out of potato slice with some resistance), about 10 minutes. Remove and discard bay leaves.

3. Transfer mixture to 8-inch square baking dish (or other 1½-quart gratin dish), press into an even layer, and sprinkle evenly with cheese. Bake until cream is bubbling around edges and top is golden brown, about 15 minutes. Cool 10 minutes before serving.

TO MAKE AHEAD: Once potatoes have been pressed into an even layer in step 3, refrigerate for up to 1 day. When ready to bake, add cheese, cover with aluminum foil, and bake in 400-degree oven until mixture is hot and bubbling, about 45 minutes. Remove foil and cook until cheese begins to brown, about 30 minutes longer. Cool for 10 minutes before serving.

Scalloped Potatoes with Chipotle Chile and Smoked Cheddar Cheese

Add 2 teaspoons minced canned chipotle chile in adobo sauce along with thyme, garlic, salt, and pepper in step 2, and substitute smoked cheddar for cheddar.

Scalloped Potatoes with Wild Mushrooms

Add 8 ounces cremini mushrooms, trimmed and sliced ¼ inch thick, and 4 ounces shiitake mushrooms, stemmed and sliced ¼ inch thick, to butter along with onion in step 2; cook until moisture released by mushrooms has evaporated, about 5 minutes.

Mashed Sweet Potatoes

WHY THIS RECIPE WORKS: We wanted a method for making mashed sweet potatoes that would push their deep, earthy sweetness to the fore and produce a silky puree with enough body to hold its shape on a fork. We braised sliced sweet potatoes in a mixture of butter and heavy cream to impart a smooth richness. Adding salt brought out the potatoes' delicate flavor, and just a teaspoon of sugar bolstered their sweetness. Once the potatoes were tender, we mashed them in the saucepan with a potato masher. We skipped the typical pumpkin pie seasoning and instead let the simple sweet potato flavor shine through.

Mashed Sweet Potatoes
SERVES 4

Cutting the sweet potatoes into slices of even thickness is important in getting them to cook at the same rate.

2 **pounds sweet potatoes, peeled, quartered lengthwise, and cut crosswise into ¼-inch-thick slices**
4 **tablespoons unsalted butter, cut into 4 pieces**

2 **tablespoons heavy cream**
1 **teaspoon sugar**
½ **teaspoon salt**
   Pinch pepper

1. Combine sweet potatoes, butter, cream, sugar, and salt in large saucepan and cook, covered, over low heat, stirring occasionally, until potatoes fall apart when poked with fork, 35 to 45 minutes.

2. Off heat, mash sweet potatoes in saucepan with potato masher. Stir in pepper; serve immediately.

Maple-Orange Mashed Sweet Potatoes
Stir in 2 tablespoons maple syrup and ½ teaspoon grated orange zest along with pepper just before serving.

Acorn Squash with Brown Sugar

WHY THIS RECIPE WORKS: After what seems like eons in the oven, acorn squash often lands on the table with little flavor and a dry, grainy texture. We wanted perfectly cooked squash with a sweet, nutty flavor and moist flesh—without taking hours. Microwaving turned out to be the winning cooking method, resulting in squash that was tender and silky, with nary a trace of dryness or stringiness. We found it was best to halve and seed the squash before cooking; whole pierced squash cooked unevenly. Equal portions of butter and dark brown sugar gave the squash ample but not excessive sweetness. Briefly broiling the squash gave it a welcome roasted texture and a perfectly glazed surface.

Acorn Squash with Brown Sugar
SERVES 4

Squash smaller than 1½ pounds will likely cook faster, so begin checking for doneness a few minutes early. Conversely, larger squash will take slightly longer. However, keep in mind that the cooking time is largely dependent on the microwave. If microwaving the squash in Pyrex, the manufacturer recommends adding water to the dish (or bowl) prior to cooking. If you are cooking the squash in a bowl, you will need one that holds about 4 quarts. See page 101 for information on seeding winter squash safely.

2 **acorn squash (1½ pounds each), halved pole to pole and seeded**
   Salt
3 **tablespoons unsalted butter**
3 **tablespoons packed dark brown sugar**

1. Sprinkle squash halves with salt and place, cut sides down, in 13 by 9-inch baking dish or arrange halves in large bowl so that cut sides face out. If using Pyrex, add ¼ cup water to dish or bowl. Cover and microwave until squash is very tender and offers no resistance when poked with paring knife, 15 to 25 minutes. Remove baking dish or bowl from microwave and set on clean, dry surface (avoid damp or cold surfaces).

2. While squash is cooking, adjust oven rack 6 inches from broiler element and heat broiler. Melt butter, brown sugar, and ⅛ teaspoon salt in small saucepan over low heat, whisking occasionally, until combined.

3. Using tongs, transfer cooked squash, cut side up, to rimmed baking sheet. Spoon portion of butter mixture onto each squash half. Broil until brown and caramelized, 5 to 8 minutes, rotating baking sheet as necessary and removing squash halves as they are done. Serve immediately.

Roasted Root Vegetables

WHY THIS RECIPE WORKS: When properly roasted, root vegetables develop wonderfully complex and intense flavors. We started with sweet carrots and parsnips, whose flavors are concentrated and caramelized in the heat of the oven. By properly preparing each vegetable, we can simply roast them all together in one batch. To speed up the cooking process, the vegetables are microwaved and then to jump-start the browning, we place them on a preheated baking sheet.

Roasted Root Vegetables
SERVES 6
Use turnips that are roughly 2 to 3 inches in diameter.

- 1 celery root (14 ounces), peeled
- 4 carrots, peeled and cut into 2½-inch lengths, halved or quartered lengthwise if necessary to create pieces ½ to 1 inch in diameter
- 12 ounces parsnips, peeled and sliced 1 inch thick on bias
- 5 ounces small shallots, peeled
    Kosher salt and pepper
- 12 ounces turnips, peeled, halved horizontally, and each half quartered
- 3 tablespoons vegetable oil
- 2 tablespoons chopped fresh parsley

1. Adjust oven rack to middle position, place rimmed baking sheet on rack, and heat oven to 425 degrees. Cut celery root into ¾-inch-thick rounds. Cut each round into ¾-inch-thick batons about 2½ inches in length.

2. Toss celery root, carrots, parsnips, and shallots with 1 teaspoon salt and pepper to taste in large microwave-safe bowl. Microwave, covered, until small pieces of carrot are just pliable enough to bend, 8 to 10 minutes, stirring once halfway through microwaving. Drain vegetables well. Return vegetables to bowl, add turnips and oil, and toss to coat.

3. Working quickly, remove baking sheet from oven and carefully transfer vegetables to baking sheet; spread into even layer. Roast for 25 minutes.

4. Using thin metal spatula, stir vegetables and spread into even layer. Rotate pan and continue to roast until vegetables are golden brown and celery root is tender when pierced with tip of paring knife, 15 to 25 minutes longer. Transfer to platter, sprinkle with parsley, and serve.

Sautéed Spinach with Garlic and Lemon

WHY THIS RECIPE WORKS: Overcooked spinach, burnt garlic, and pallid lemon flavor are all too often the hallmarks of this side dish. We were after tender sautéed spinach seasoned with a perfect balance of garlic and lemon. We started with bunched flat-leaf spinach and cooked it in fruity extra-virgin olive oil with slivered garlic (lightly browned in the pan before the spinach was added). Squeezing the spinach in a colander got rid of excess moisture. A combination of lemon juice and zest gave it the right lemony flavor, and red pepper flakes lent some good heat.

Sautéed Spinach with Garlic and Lemon
SERVES 4
The amount of spinach may seem excessive, but the spinach wilts considerably with cooking. We like to use a salad spinner to wash and dry the spinach. If you have kosher or coarsely ground sea salt on hand, use it for the final sprinkling just before serving. This spinach dish makes an excellent accompaniment to almost any main course, from chicken and fish to steak and pork.

- 2 tablespoons plus 1 teaspoon extra-virgin olive oil
- 4 garlic cloves, sliced very thin
- 30 ounces curly-leaf spinach, stemmed
- ½ teaspoon grated lemon zest plus 2 teaspoons juice
    Salt
    Pinch red pepper flakes

1. Heat 2 tablespoons oil and garlic in Dutch oven over medium-high heat and cook until garlic is light golden brown, shaking pan back and forth when garlic begins to sizzle, about 3 minutes (stirring with a spoon will cause the garlic to clump). Add spinach by the handful, using tongs to stir and coat spinach with oil.

2. Once all spinach is added, sprinkle with lemon zest, ¼ teaspoon salt, and pepper flakes and continue stirring with tongs until spinach is uniformly wilted and glossy green, about 2 minutes. Using tongs, transfer spinach to colander and gently squeeze with tongs to release excess liquid. Return spinach to Dutch oven, sprinkle with lemon juice, and stir to coat. Drizzle with remaining 1 teaspoon oil and season with additional salt to taste. Serve immediately.

Sautéed Zucchini with Lemon and Herbs

WHY THIS RECIPE WORKS: For the best sautéed zucchini recipe, we picked smaller zucchini, which are more flavorful and less watery than the larger ones. We removed excess moisture by either tossing slices with salt and letting them sit for 30 minutes or grating zucchini and wrapping it in several layers of paper towels or a large dish towel and squeezing. Even in a blazing-hot pan, the zucchini would soon start to steam in its own juices if not salted or shredded and squeezed.

Sautéed Zucchini with Lemon and Herbs

SERVES 4

Salt causes zucchini rounds to release excess water. This important extra step helps the zucchini to sauté rather than stew in its own juices. Quarter-inch slices are the perfect thickness; thinner slices fall apart during cooking, while thicker slices require a longer salting time. If you want to use more intense herbs such as oregano, thyme, and rosemary, halve the amount of herbs indicated in the recipe. If you do not have kosher salt on hand, use 1 teaspoon of table salt.

- 1⅓ pounds zucchini, sliced crosswise into ¼-inch-thick rounds
  Kosher salt
- 3 tablespoons olive oil
- 1 small onion, chopped fine, or 2 large shallots, minced
- 1 teaspoon grated lemon zest plus 1 tablespoon juice
- 1–2 tablespoons minced fresh herbs
  Pepper

1. Place zucchini slices in colander set over bowl and sprinkle with 2 teaspoons salt. Let sit until about ⅓ cup water drains from zucchini, about 30 minutes. Rinse and thoroughly dry zucchini.

2. Heat oil in large skillet over medium heat. Add onion and cook until nearly softened, about 3 minutes. Increase heat to medium-high; add zucchini and lemon zest and cook until zucchini is golden brown, about 10 minutes.

3. Stir in lemon juice and herbs, and season with pepper to taste. Adjust seasonings and serve immediately.

Eggplant Parmesan

WHY THIS RECIPE WORKS: Frying the eggplant for this classic Italian dish is not only time-consuming but can also make the dish heavy and dull. We opted to cook the breaded eggplant in the oven after salting and draining the slices (which removed bitterness and improved texture). Baking the eggplant on preheated and oiled baking sheets resulted in crisp, golden slices, and a traditional bound breading of flour, egg, and fresh bread crumbs worked best for giving the eggplant a crisp coating. While the eggplant was salting and draining, we made a quick tomato sauce. We layered the sauce, baked eggplant slices, and mozzarella in a baking dish. Leaving the top layer of eggplant mostly unsauced ensured it would crisp up nicely in the oven.

Eggplant Parmesan

SERVES 6 TO 8

Use kosher salt when salting the eggplant. The coarse grains don't dissolve as readily as the fine grains of table salt, so any excess can be easily wiped away. See Recipe Tutorial on page 114 for more details on this recipe.

EGGPLANT

- 2 pounds eggplant, sliced into ¼-inch-thick rounds
  Kosher salt and pepper
- 8 slices hearty white sandwich bread, torn into quarters

- 2 ounces Parmesan cheese, grated (1 cup)
- 1 cup all-purpose flour
- 4 large eggs
- 6 tablespoons vegetable oil

SAUCE

- 3 (14.5-ounce) cans diced tomatoes
- 2 tablespoons extra-virgin olive oil
- 4 garlic cloves, minced
- ¼ teaspoon red pepper flakes
- ½ cup chopped fresh basil
  Kosher salt and pepper

- 8 ounces whole-milk or part-skim mozzarella, shredded (2 cups)
- 1 ounce Parmesan cheese, grated (½ cup)
- 10 fresh basil leaves, roughly torn

1. FOR THE EGGPLANT: Line baking sheet with triple layer of paper towels and set aside. Toss half of eggplant and 1½ teaspoons salt together in bowl, then transfer to colander. Repeat with remaining eggplant and 1½ teaspoons more salt. Let sit until eggplant releases about 2 tablespoons liquid, 30 to 45 minutes. Wipe excess salt from eggplant, then arrange on prepared baking sheet. Cover with another triple layer of paper towels and firmly press each slice to remove as much liquid as possible.

2. While eggplant is draining, adjust oven racks to upper-middle and lower-middle positions, place rimmed baking sheet on each rack, and heat oven to 425 degrees. Pulse bread in food processor to fine, even crumbs, about 15 pulses (you should have about 4 cups). Transfer crumbs to pie plate or shallow dish and stir in Parmesan, ¼ teaspoon salt, and ½ teaspoon pepper; set aside. Wipe out food processor bowl (do not wash) and set aside.

3. Combine flour and 1 teaspoon pepper in large zipper-lock bag and shake to combine. Beat eggs in second pie plate or shallow dish. Place 8 to 10 eggplant slices in bag with flour, seal bag, and shake to coat eggplant. Remove eggplant slices, shaking off excess flour, then dip in eggs, letting excess egg run off. Then coat evenly with bread-crumb mixture. Set breaded slices on wire rack set in rimmed baking sheet. Repeat with remaining eggplant.

4. Remove preheated baking sheets from oven. Add 3 tablespoons oil to each sheet, tilting to coat evenly with oil. Place half of breaded eggplant on each baking sheet in single layer; bake until eggplant is well browned and crisp, about 30 minutes, switching and rotating baking sheets after 10 minutes, and flipping eggplant slices with wide spatula after 20 minutes. (Do not turn off oven.)

5. FOR THE SAUCE: While eggplant bakes, process 2 cans diced tomatoes and their juice in food processor until almost smooth, about 5 seconds. Heat olive oil, garlic, and pepper flakes in large saucepan over medium-high heat, stirring occasionally, until fragrant and garlic is light golden, about 2 minutes. Stir in processed tomatoes and remaining can diced tomatoes. Bring sauce to boil, then reduce heat to medium-low and simmer, stirring occasionally, until slightly thickened and reduced, about 15 minutes (you should have about 4 cups). Stir in basil and season with salt and pepper to taste.

6. TO ASSEMBLE: Spread 1 cup tomato sauce over bottom of 13 by 9-inch baking dish. Layer in half of eggplant slices, overlapping slices to fit. Distribute 1 cup sauce over eggplant, then sprinkle with 1 cup mozzarella. Layer in remaining eggplant, then dot with 1 cup sauce, leaving majority of eggplant exposed so it will remain crisp. Sprinkle with Parmesan and remaining 1 cup mozzarella. Bake until bubbling and cheese is browned, 13 to 15 minutes. Cool 10 minutes, scatter basil over top, and serve, passing remaining tomato sauce separately.

Indian-Style Vegetable Curry

✓ **WHY THIS RECIPE WORKS:** Vegetable curries can be complicated affairs, with lengthy ingredient lists and fussy techniques meant to compensate for the lack of meat. We wanted a curry we could make on a weeknight in less than an hour without sacrificing flavor or overloading the dish with spices. Toasting curry powder in a skillet turned it into a flavor powerhouse and adding a few pinches of garam masala lent even more spice flavor. To build the rest of our flavor base we started with a generous amount of sautéed onion, garlic, ginger, fresh chile, and tomato paste for sweetness. When we chose our vegetables (chickpeas and potatoes for heartiness and cauliflower and peas for texture and color), we found that sautéing the spices and main ingredients together enhanced and melded the flavors. Finally, we rounded out our sauce with a combination of water, canned diced tomatoes, and a splash of cream or coconut milk.

Indian Curry with Potatoes, Cauliflower, Peas, and Chickpeas

SERVES 4 TO 6

This curry is moderately spicy when made with one chile. For more heat, use an additional half chile. For a mild curry, remove the chile's ribs and seeds before mincing. The onions can be pulsed in a food processor. You can substitute 2 teaspoons ground coriander, ½ teaspoon ground pepper, ¼ teaspoon ground cardamom, and ¼ teaspoon ground cinnamon for the garam masala. Serve with Basmati Rice Pilaf (page 204) and plain whole-milk yogurt. See Recipe Tutorial on page 118 for more details on this recipe.

  2 **tablespoons sweet or mild curry powder**
1½ **teaspoons garam masala**
  1 **(14.5-ounce) can diced tomatoes**
  ¼ **cup vegetable oil**
  2 **onions, chopped fine**
 12 **ounces red potatoes, unpeeled, cut into ½-inch pieces**
  3 **garlic cloves, minced**
  1 **tablespoon grated fresh ginger**
1–1½ **serrano chiles, minced**
  1 **tablespoon tomato paste**
  ½ **head cauliflower (1 pound), cored and cut into 1-inch florets**

  1 **(14-ounce) can chickpeas, rinsed**
1¼ **cups water**
     Salt
1½ **cups frozen peas**
  ¼ **cup heavy cream or coconut milk**
     Cilantro-Mint Chutney (recipe follows)

1. Toast curry powder and garam masala in small skillet over medium-high heat, stirring constantly, until spices darken slightly and become fragrant, about 1 minute. Transfer to small bowl and set aside. Pulse tomatoes in food processor until coarsely chopped, 3 or 4 pulses.

2. Heat 3 tablespoons oil in large Dutch oven over medium-high heat until shimmering. Add onions and potatoes and cook, stirring occasionally, until onions are caramelized and potatoes are golden brown on edges, about 10 minutes. (Reduce heat to medium if onions darken too quickly.)

3. Reduce heat to medium. Clear center of pot and add remaining 1 tablespoon oil, garlic, ginger, serrano, and tomato paste and cook, stirring constantly, until fragrant, about 30 seconds. Add reserved toasted spices and cook, stirring constantly, about 1 minute. Add cauliflower and cook, stirring constantly, until spices coat florets, about 2 minutes longer.

4. Add tomatoes and their juice, chickpeas, water, and 1 teaspoon salt. Increase heat to medium-high and bring mixture to boil, scraping bottom of pot with wooden spoon to loosen browned bits. Cover and reduce heat to medium. Simmer briskly, stirring occasionally, until vegetables are tender, 10 to 15 minutes.

5. Stir in peas and cream and continue to cook until heated through, about 2 minutes. Season with salt to taste and serve immediately, passing Cilantro-Mint Chutney separately.

Indian-Style Curry with Sweet Potatoes, Eggplant, Green Beans, and Chickpeas

Substitute 12 ounces sweet potatoes, peeled and cut into ½-inch dice, for red potatoes. Substitute 1½ cups green beans, trimmed and cut into 1-inch pieces, and 1 eggplant, cut into ½-inch pieces (3 cups), for cauliflower. Omit peas.

Cilantro-Mint Chutney

MAKES ABOUT 1 CUP

  2 **cups fresh cilantro leaves**
  1 **cup fresh mint leaves**
  ⅓ **cup plain whole-milk yogurt**
  ¼ **cup finely chopped onion**
  1 **tablespoon lime juice**
1½ **teaspoons sugar**
  ½ **teaspoon ground cumin**
  ¼ **teaspoon salt**

Process all ingredients in food processor until smooth, about 20 seconds, scraping down sides of bowl halfway through. (Chutney can be refrigerated for up to 1 day.)

Inside This Chapter

CHAPTER 4

How to Cook Pasta

It's easy to understand the popularity of pasta. It's inexpensive, quick to prepare, and easy to vary. In this chapter we cover basics, from the must-have tools to choosing the right canned tomatoes to matching pasta shapes and sauces. We explain how to cook dried pasta perfectly and make the sauces and classic pasta dishes that have been favorites for generations. And since pasta made from scratch is a must for some recipes, we also show you how to make your own fresh pasta.

Getting Started

Essential Ingredients

Pasta is perhaps Italy's greatest contribution to cooking around the world. For most Americans (as well as Italians), pasta means dried pasta made from durum wheat. Most Italian pasta recipes call for cheese and/or canned tomatoes. Here are the basics of buying these ingredients.

DRIED PASTA

To make dried pasta, semolina (coarsely ground durum wheat) is mixed with water, kneaded into a dough, and pressed through the holes of a die (either bronze or Teflon) to make specific shapes. Then the pasta is dried in drying rooms or special high-temperature ovens. The finished product is shelf-stable for years. Just boil and serve.

Classic Dried Pasta

The spaghetti, penne, and ziti we typically buy and use in our recipes is made from semolina that has been refined during processing to remove the bran and germ. (It's the equivalent of white flour.) In addition to refined durum wheat flour, classic dried pasta contains just water and salt. In our taste tests of various shapes and brands, we have found minimal differences. Yes, some brands have stronger wheaty, buttery, or nutty notes. But once the sauce is added, those flavor differences are very hard to detect. Some brands seem to cook up firmer, but again differences are quite small. In general, we have found both Italian and American brands that we like.

Whole-Wheat Pasta

In our testing of these pastas, we found that some were puzzlingly similar to white pasta while others were heavy, dense, and rough. It turns out that several were made entirely of whole durum wheat, but many so-called whole-wheat pastas in fact contain a minimal amount of whole-grain flour that is mixed with refined white flour. So unless the pasta you reach for says "100 percent whole wheat" it may be far from it. Most of the 100 percent whole-wheat and whole-grain pastas we tasted confirmed what we expected: pasta with mushy and doughy textures, and, in many cases, with a sour and fishy taste. But we can recommend one brand, Italian-produced Bionaturae Organic 100% Whole-Wheat Spaghetti, made entirely of whole wheat but with an appealingly chewy and firm texture like the pastas with little or no whole grains. The manufacturer's secret? Custom milling (which ensures good flavor), extrusion through a bronze, not Teflon, die (which helps build gluten in the dough), and a slower drying process at low temperatures (which yields sturdier pasta).

No-Boil Lasagna Noodles

Over the past few years, no-boil (also called oven-ready) lasagna noodles have become a permanent fixture on supermarket shelves. These noodles are made with the same ingredients as classic dried pasta: semolina and water. Much like instant rice, no-boil noodles are precooked at the factory and then dried. During baking, the moisture from the sauce softens, or rehydrates, the noodles, especially when the pan is covered as the lasagna bakes. Three of these rectangular noodles make a single layer in a conventional 13 by 9-inch lasagna pan when they swell in the oven. Our favorite oven-ready lasagna noodles are made by Barilla. These delicate, flat noodles closely resemble fresh pasta in texture.

CHEESE

Dozens of cheeses appear in pasta recipes but these four cheeses are the most common choices. Also see page 40 for more information on buying cheeses.

Mozzarella

Most supermarkets stock two main varieties: fresh (usually packed in brine) and low-moisture (sold either as a block or preshredded). We prefer the sweet richness and tenderness of the fresh for snacking, sandwiches, and Caprese salad but don't use it often in cooked applications, since heat can destroy its delicate flavor and texture. For most baked dishes, we turn to the low-moisture kind (preferably whole-milk but part-skim works fine): It offers mellow flavor and melts nicely.

Parmesan

Parmesan is classified as a grana-type cheese: a hard, grainy cheese made from cow's milk. We recommend authentic Parmigiano-Reggiano, which has a depth and complexity of flavor and a smooth, melting texture that none of the others can match. Most of the other Parmesan-type cheeses are too salty and one-dimensional. When shopping, make sure some portion of the words "Parmigiano-Reggiano" are stenciled on the golden rind. To ensure that you're buying a properly aged cheese, examine the condition of the rind. It should be a few shades darker than the straw-colored interior and penetrate about a ½ inch deep (younger or improperly aged cheeses will have a paler, thinner rind). And closely scrutinize the center of the cheese. Those small white spots found on many samples are actually good things—they signify the presence of calcium phosphate crystals, which are formed only after the cheese has been aged for the proper amount of time.

Pecorino Romano

Pecorino Romano is a bone-white cheese with an intense peppery flavor and a strong sheepy quality. It is best in dishes with assertive ingredients like capers, olives, or red pepper flakes. It is traditionally made from sheep's milk, although some manufacturers add some cow's milk to reduce the pungency and/or save money. Most of the Pecorino that is exported has been aged. Like Parmesan, it is best for grating, but Pecorino has a much saltier flavor.

Ricotta

Originally crafted from the whey by-product that forms during the making of Pecorino Romano cheese, ricotta cheese has garnered fame on its own as a white, cushiony filling for baked pasta dishes. As ricotta has gained global popularity, however, preservation methods used by many large-scale manufacturers have turned these once fluffy, buttery, sweet curds into chalky, sour spreads. We are not big fans of most supermarket ricottas, as they are packed with gums and other stabilizers to guarantee a shelf life of weeks. Our favorite brand is Calabro, whose curds are fresh drawn from nothing other than Vermont farm whole milk, skim milk, a starter, and a sprinkle of salt. Granted, its shelf life spans only a matter of days, but one spoonful should be enough to guarantee its quick disappearance from your fridge. If you can't find this particular brand, check labels and look for another fresh ricotta without gums or preservatives. We prefer whole-milk ricotta but part-skim ricotta is fine. Do not try to use nonfat ricotta, as it is very dry and flavorless.

CANNED TOMATOES

Since good-quality fresh tomatoes are available only a few months of the year, our pasta sauces rely mostly on canned tomatoes. For detailed information on various canned tomato products, see page 37. Here's a quick rundown.

Whole Tomatoes

Whole tomatoes are best reserved for recipes with a short simmering time, such as our Marinara Sauce (page 167). We found that whole tomatoes packed in juice rather than in puree had a livelier, fresher flavor.

Crushed Tomatoes

Crushed tomatoes work well in smoother sauces, such as our Quick Tomato Sauce (page 167), offering both great flavor and body. We also employ crushed tomatoes in casseroles where we want long-simmered flavor without having to cook the sauce separately for a long time.

Diced Tomatoes

Diced tomatoes are best for rustic tomato sauces with a chunky texture, such as our Spaghetti Puttanesca (page 168). Diced tomatoes may also be processed with their juice in a food processor and used in place of crushed tomatoes when called for in a recipe. They are available packed both in juice and in puree; we favor diced tomatoes packed in juice because they have a fresher flavor.

Tomato Puree and Tomato Sauce

Tomato puree and tomato sauce are both cooked and strained to remove the tomato seeds, making them much smoother and thicker than other canned tomato products. We found that tomato puree works well when we need a thick sauce, as in our Simple Lasagna with Hearty Meat Sauce (page 174). We prefer tomato sauce when we need a slightly thinner sauce but still want the same smooth texture and long-simmered tomato flavor, as in our Baked Ziti (page 173).

Tomato Paste

Because it's naturally full of glutamates, which stimulate taste buds, tomato paste brings out subtle depths and savory notes. We use it in a variety of recipes, including both long-simmered sauces and quicker-cooking dishes, to lend a deeper, well-rounded tomato flavor and color.

Essential Equipment

There are plenty of pots, utensils, and gadgets that are supposed to make cooking and serving pasta easier and neater. We tried out a variety—from $269 pasta pots to $14 pasta tongs—to see which, if any, are worth the expense and the space they take up in the cabinet or drawer. In the end, we recommend skipping the pasta accessories and sticking with the basics.

DUTCH OVEN

Though it doesn't really matter what kind of pot you use for boiling pasta, we prefer a Dutch oven, which is more compact and easier to maneuver than a big stockpot—especially when it's full of boiling water and a pound of pasta. In addition to cooking pasta in it, we also use this pot to make some pasta sauces. Look for one that's midweight—if it is too heavy, it'll be a pain to move when you need to drain your pasta, and if it's too light, it will heat too quickly and could result in burnt sauce. Look for a pot with a capacity of at least 6 quarts. For more details on what to look for, see page 21.

SKILLETS

The wide, flat surface of the skillet encourages evaporation, so pasta sauces reduce and thicken quickly. We think every kitchen should be stocked with two kinds—traditional and nonstick. A traditional skillet lets you build pasta sauces with rich, deep, long-simmered flavor because it allows for the formation of fond—browned bits left behind after cooking aromatics and vegetables or browning meats—which contribute flavor. For recipes such as our Skillet Meaty Lasagna (page 175), where the pasta cooks right in the sauce, we like to use a nonstick skillet. For more details on what to look for, see page 22.

COLANDER

A sturdy colander is crucial when you are wrestling with a huge pot of boiling water and pasta. Look for a 5-quart stainless steel colander that has a metal ring on the bottom (so it won't tip over) and that has a lot of perforations for quick draining. For more details on what to look for, see page 31.

LADLE

A ladle is the easiest way to sauce your pasta without making a huge mess. We prefer a stainless steel model; plastic can stain easily and melt on the stovetop. Look for a ladle with a deep bowl to hold a good amount of sauce, and a spill prevention rim for tidy transport from pot to pasta bowl.

WOODEN AND SLOTTED SPOONS

To stir aromatics, sauces, and pasta, you need a good solid wooden spoon. Big spoons with hulking handles will make extended stirring tiresome, while spoons that are too light can snap or break easily. Aim for a midweight model with a broad bowl, which can cover a lot of surface area, and thin edges, which scrape more effectively than thick edges. A slotted spoon with a deep bowl is useful for testing pasta for doneness.

HEAT-RESISTANT RUBBER SPATULA

Heat-resistant spatulas are useful for any number of pasta-related applications, from scraping up stuck-on bits from a pan's surface to folding delicate vegetables into a pot of pasta.

Look for one that has a long, comfortable handle as well as a wide, stiff blade with a thin, flexible edge so that you can easily get into the corners of a pan. For more details on what to look for, see page 31.

GARLIC PRESS

If you're cooking a pasta dish, chances are good that you'll need to mince garlic, and using a garlic press is the easiest and fastest way to do that. We prefer presses that have a large chamber to hold multiple cloves of garlic. For more details on what to look for, see page 30.

GRATERS

When a recipe calls for grated Parmesan (or other hard cheese), we reach for our rasp-style grater. With its super-sharp teeth, it can turn a hunk of hard cheese into ultra-fine shreds quickly. A coarse grater is essential when you need to blast through a big block of mozzarella for a casserole. We like a flat grater with sharp teeth; it gets the job done and is easy to store. Look for one with a rigid frame and rubber-bottomed legs. For more details on what to look for, see page 30.

TONGS

We like to use tongs for handling and portioning strand pasta. Tongs can also be used to stir pasta as it cooks, and they come in handy when tossing pasta and sauce. For more details on what to look for, see page 31.

MEASURING LESS THAN A POUND OF PASTA

It's easy enough to measure out a pound of pasta, as most packages are sold in this quantity. But when a recipe calls for less it's good to have the cup measurements below for shaped pasta. When it comes to strand pasta, determining the diameter works well as a guideline.

PASTA TYPE*	8 OUNCES	12 OUNCES
Elbow Macaroni and Small Shells	2 cups	3 cups
Orecchiette	2¼ cups	3⅓ cups
Penne, Ziti, and Campanelle	2½ cups	3¾ cups
Rigatoni, Fusilli, Medium Shells, Wagon Wheels, Wide Egg Noodles	3 cups	4½ cups
Farfalle	3¼ cups	4¾ cups

* These amounts do not apply to whole-wheat pasta.

When 8 ounces of uncooked strand pasta are bunched together into a tight circle, the diameter measures about 1¼ inches. When 12 ounces of uncooked strand pasta are bunched together, the diameter measures about 1¾ inches.

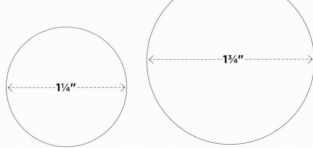

Matching Pasta Shapes and Sauces

In classic Italian cooking, matching pasta shapes to the sauce is an art form. In our simplified, pragmatic approach, the texture of the sauce is the most important consideration. Here is the rule we follow: Thick, chunky sauces go with short pastas, and thin, smooth, or light sauces with strand pasta. We've organized dried pasta shapes into two groups: short and strand. For each shape, we've listed the literal translation of the Italian name (often quite funny).

SHORT PASTAS

Short tubular or molded pasta shapes do an excellent job of trapping and holding on to chunky sauces. Sauces with very large chunks are best with rigatoni or other large tubes. Sauces with small chunks make more sense with fusilli or penne.

FARFALLE
butterflies, bow ties

FUSILLI
little springs

PENNE
pens, quills

ORECCHIETTE
little ears

CONCHIGLIE
conch shells

GEMELLI
twins

MACARONI
elbows

ZITI
bridegrooms

RIGATONI
fluted tubes

CAMPANELLE
bellflowers

STRAND PASTAS

Long strands are best with smooth sauces or sauces with very small chunks. In general, wider noodles such as pappardelle and fettuccine can support slightly chunkier sauces like Bolognese (see page 160).

VERMICELLI
little worms

**SPAGHETTINI OR
THIN SPAGHETTI**
little spaghetti

SPAGHETTI
little strings

BUCATINI
little holes

LINGUINE
little tongues

FETTUCCINE
little ribbons

PAPPARDELLE
gulp down

How to Cook Dried Pasta

ESSENTIAL EQUIPMENT

• Dutch oven
• tongs or pasta fork
• liquid measuring cup
• colander
• ladle

Cooking dried pasta seems simple enough. Bring water to a boil, add pasta, and cook until done, right? Well, not exactly. Pasta is one of those things that is easy to cook, but hard to cook just right. For perfect pasta, you must pay attention to everything from the water-to-pasta ratio to the time between draining and saucing. We've been cooking pasta for a long time and have come up with a few simple steps that deliver perfectly cooked al dente pasta every time. We don't think many specialty pasta tools are that useful, but we do think a pasta fork is handy when stirring strand pasta and testing it for doneness. It also doubles as a serving spoon, which simplifies tasks. However, it is a specialty tool and not a must; a pair of tongs will work. If you do buy a pasta fork, look for one that features a long handle, small drainage holes, and a gently angled head, making it comfortable and easy to maneuver.

1. USE PLENTY OF WATER

To cook 1 pound pasta, bring 4 quarts water to rolling boil in Dutch oven or large pot.

WHY? Pasta leaches starch as it cooks; without plenty of water to dilute the starch, it will coat the noodles and they will stick together. Use a pot with at least a 6-quart capacity, and fill it with cold tap water; warm water can pick up off-flavors from your water heater. Make sure to bring the water to a rolling boil over high heat. If you're using a large enough pot, boilovers should not be a concern and pasta cooks best (and fastest) in boiling, rather than simmering, water.

2. SALT THE WATER, DON'T OIL IT

Add 1 tablespoon salt to boiling water.

WHY? Salt is crucial because it adds flavor to the pasta (most of the salt will go down the drain with the cooking water). Adding oil to the cooking water just creates a slick on the surface of the water, doing nothing for the pasta. Oil also prevents the sauce from adhering to the pasta.

3. ADD PASTA AND STIR

Add pasta to boiling salted water and stir constantly for 1 to 2 minutes.

WHY? Stirring the pasta when you first add it to the water, and occasionally as it cooks, will prevent it from sticking together and to the pot.

4. CHECK OFTEN FOR DONENESS

Several minutes before pasta should be done, begin tasting it. When pasta is almost al dente, remove pot from heat.

WHY? Tasting for doneness is really the only way to know when to stop cooking pasta. The timing instructions given on the box are almost always too long and will result in mushy, overcooked pasta. And because the pasta continues to cook after it is drained, you need to compensate by draining when it is a little underdone.

5. RESERVE COOKING WATER, THEN DRAIN

Reserve ½ cup cooking water (amount can vary based on recipe), then drain pasta in colander. Shake drained pasta once or twice to remove excess liquid.

WHY? The cooking water is flavorful and can also help loosen a thick sauce, so it's smart to reserve some prior to draining. Once you've drained the pasta in the colander, don't rinse it or shake the colander too vigorously. And never shake pasta bone-dry; the small amount of cooking water that remains on the pasta helps to spread the sauce and is especially useful when tossing pasta with relatively dry, oil-based sauces.

6. SAUCE IN POT

Return drained pasta to now-empty pot, add sauce, and toss using tongs or pasta fork. Add pasta cooking water as needed until sauce reaches proper consistency.

WHY? You can never coat the pasta properly or evenly with sauce if you serve up the cooked pasta and then top it with sauce. Saucing pasta in the pot ensures evenly coated, hot pasta (and a more attractive dish). You usually need 3 to 4 cups of sauce per pound of pasta.

Troubleshooting Dried Pasta

PROBLEM	SOLUTION
I am cooking 2 pounds of pasta; how much water is sufficient?	Pasta needs to cook in a fair amount of water, although not as much as many cookbooks specify. We recommend 2 quarts of water for up to ½ pound of pasta, 4 quarts for ½ to 1 pound of pasta, and 6 quarts for 1 to 2 pounds. If you are cooking more than 2 pounds of pasta, use two pots. If cooked in too little water, pasta has a tendency to stick together because the starch released by the pasta grows too concentrated and turns the water into a sticky slurry.
My pasta dishes don't stay hot long enough.	Be sure that you sauce your pasta in the hot pot in which it was cooked. You may even want to put the pot over low heat as you toss the pasta to ensure it is piping hot. Another key to properly served (and hot) pasta is to warm your serving plates or bowls. If your bowls are ovensafe, you can warm them in a low oven. You can also use the drying cycle of the dishwasher to warm them up. Another option is to bring a little extra water to boil for cooking the pasta and then ladle some of the boiling water into bowls and let them warm up as you cook the pasta.

How to Make Pesto Sauce

ESSENTIAL EQUIPMENT

- 8-inch skillet
- wooden spoon
- chef's knife
- zipper-lock bag
- meat pounder or rolling pin
- food processor
- rubber spatula
- rasp-style grater
- spoon

The best pesto sauce is silky in texture and infused with bright basil flavor and undertones of mellowed, not harsh, garlic. And while it might seem that making pesto is a simple matter of throwing a handful of ingredients—nuts, cheese, basil, oil, and garlic—into a food processor, the truth is that turning out a good pesto requires some finesse and technique. And once you master the basics, it's easy to vary the herbs, nuts, and other ingredients for simple, pungent sauces that not only dress up pasta but add flavor to soups, sandwiches, vegetables, and more. Our pesto recipe makes enough to sauce 1 pound of pasta.

1. TOAST UNPEELED GARLIC CLOVES

Toast 3 unpeeled garlic cloves in 8-inch skillet over medium heat, shaking pan occasionally until softened and spotty brown, about 8 minutes. Set garlic aside to cool.

WHY? Toasting the garlic mellows its flavor; if the garlic is added raw to the pesto it will give it a sharp, acrid taste that is not at all appealing. By leaving the cloves whole and unpeeled, we can toast them longer without fear of burning the garlic.

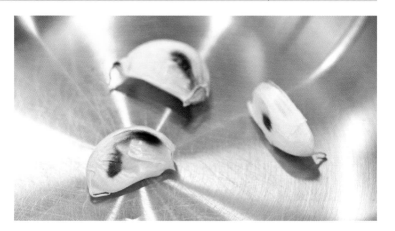

2. TOAST NUTS

While garlic cools, toast ¼ cup pine nuts in now-empty skillet over medium heat, stirring often, until golden and fragrant, 2 to 4 minutes.

WHY? Toasting the nuts releases their essential oils, giving them a more intense flavor. We prefer using pine nuts because they become very creamy when processed, yielding pesto with a smooth, luxurious texture.

3. PEEL AND CHOP GARLIC

Peel cooled garlic cloves and chop coarsely.

WHY? We like to chop the garlic before adding it to the food processor, otherwise the pieces never become fine enough in the finished sauce.

4. BRUISE HERBS

Place 2 cups fresh basil leaves and 2 tablespoons fresh parsley leaves in 1-gallon zipper-lock bag. Pound bag with flat side of meat pounder or with rolling pin until all leaves are bruised.

WHY? Bruising the basil releases its flavorful oils, making the pesto substantially more fragrant. We add parsley leaves to the mix because basil tends to turn dark, unlike the parsley, which boosts the green color a little.

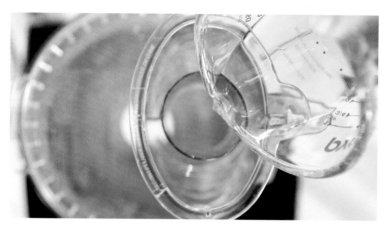

5. PROCESS UNTIL SMOOTH

Process garlic, nuts, basil, parsley, and ½ teaspoon salt in food processor until smooth, about 1 minute, scraping down bowl as needed. With processor running, add 7 tablespoons extra-virgin olive oil.

WHY? The food processer makes quick work of these ingredients with the help of a hefty amount of olive oil, which enables them to blend smoothly. To ensure that all the ingredients are properly chopped, it is necessary to stop and scrape down the bowl at least once prior to adding the olive oil. Be sure to use a good extra-virgin olive oil, as you will really be able to taste it in the sauce.

6. ADD CHEESE

Transfer mixture to small bowl, stir in ¼ cup finely grated Parmesan cheese, and season with salt and pepper to taste.

WHY? We add the cheese at the end because we like the texture the cheese adds to the sauce.

Troubleshooting Pesto

PROBLEM	SOLUTION
Can I substitute any other nuts for the pine nuts?	You can use an equal amount of toasted chopped almonds or walnuts, but the flavor and texture of the pesto will be different. Almonds are relatively sweet but are fairly hard, so they give the pesto a coarse, granular texture. Walnuts are softer but still fairly meaty in texture and flavor.
I don't have Parmesan; is there another cheese I can use?	You can replace the Parmesan with an equal amount of finely grated Pecorino Romano, which will give the pesto a sharper flavor.
My pesto turns army green when stored.	The best way to store pesto and preserve its green color is to drizzle a little olive oil over the top and press a sheet of plastic wrap flush to the surface before refrigerating it. Stored this way, pesto can be made up to three days ahead. It can also be frozen for up to three months.
I'm having trouble combining the cooked pasta evenly with the pesto sauce.	First, if you have refrigerated your pesto, bring it to room temperature prior to using. Second, reserve at least 1 cup of the pasta cooking water; you will need a good portion of it to thin out your sauce so it coats the pasta evenly. Add ½ cup of the pasta cooking water directly to the sauce before tossing the drained pasta with the sauce. Add the remaining ½ cup cooking water as needed.

How to Make Tomato Sauce

ESSENTIAL EQUIPMENT

• garlic press
• medium saucepan
• wooden spoon
• can opener
• chef's knife

Making tomato sauce from scratch is a simple proposition and a recipe everyone should know by heart. When made properly, it tastes worlds better than any jarred sauce you can buy at the supermarket. And contrary to what many people think, it needn't take hours. In fact, we found that if you simmer a simple sauce much longer than 20 minutes, you actually cook out the flavor. One batch makes 4 cups, the perfect amount to sauce a pound of pasta. See chart on opposite page for ways to customize this sauce. Make sure to buy good-quality canned tomatoes; see pages 37 and 135. Our top-rated brands of crushed tomatoes are Tuttorosso, Muir Glen, and Hunt's; the latter two companies make our favorites diced tomatoes as well.

1. COOK GARLIC SLOWLY

Add 3 minced garlic cloves and 3 tablespoons extra-virgin olive oil to medium saucepan, turn heat to medium, and cook, stirring often, until fragrant but not browned, about 2 minutes.

WHY? Many recipes suggest heating the oil and then adding the garlic, but we find this method often results in overcooked garlic. The goal of this step is to cook the garlic until straw-colored and sweet, not browned and bitter. Heating the oil and garlic together allows the process to unfold more slowly. A good extra-virgin olive oil adds richness to this simple sauce. Make sure to monitor the garlic as it cooks and be ready to add the tomatoes as soon as the garlic is fragrant.

2. ADD TWO TYPES OF CANNED TOMATOES

Stir in 1 (28-ounce) can crushed tomatoes and 1 (14.5-ounce) can diced tomatoes and their juice as soon as garlic smells fragrant.

WHY? We have found that canned tomatoes consistently taste better than flavorless out-of-season tomatoes from the supermarket. Diced tomatoes add good chunky texture, while the crushed tomatoes provide a nice smooth foundation.

3. SIMMER

After adding tomatoes, bring sauce to simmer and cook until slightly thickened, 15 to 20 minutes.

WHY? Simmering thickens the tomato juices, softens the diced tomatoes, and allows the sauce to mellow and develop good flavor. If you cook this sauce any longer, it will overreduce and lose its delicate flavor.

4. ADD FRESH BASIL AND SUGAR

Once sauce has thickened slightly, add 3 tablespoons chopped fresh basil and ¼ teaspoon sugar. Season with salt and pepper to taste.

WHY? The fresh basil gives the sauce a needed burst of fresh herbal flavor. Dried basil has very little flavor and is not appropriate in this recipe (better to use another fresh herb). And just a little sugar mellows the acidity of the sauce. Finally, season with salt and pepper to taste.

Customizing Simple Tomato Sauce

This basic sauce is easy to dress up; use the ideas below singly or in combination.

TO INCORPORATE	DO THIS
Red Pepper Flakes	Cook 1 teaspoon with garlic and oil
Parsley	Replace basil with ¼ cup minced fresh
Heavy Cream	Add ¾ cup to finished sauce and simmer until thickened, about 3 minutes
Anchovies	Cook 8 minced fillets with garlic and oil
Olives	Add ½ cup pitted and chopped with basil
Capers	Add 3 tablespoons rinsed with basil

Troubleshooting Tomato Sauce

PROBLEM	SOLUTION
I don't have crushed tomatoes; what else can I use?	You can substitute a 28-ounce can of whole or diced tomatoes; just process them and their juice in a food processor until smooth.
My garlic browned; should I start over?	If the garlic has browned, it will add a bitter taste to the sauce, so you do need to start over with fresh garlic and oil. Do not heat the oil first but rather heat the oil and garlic together just until the garlic is straw-colored.
Can I double this recipe?	Yes, this recipe can be easily doubled, but you will need to simmer the sauce an additional 10 minutes. Replace the medium saucepan with a large saucepan or Dutch oven.

How to Make Lasagna

ESSENTIAL EQUIPMENT

• 13 by 9-inch baking dish
• rubber spatula
• mixing bowls
• soupspoon
• aluminum foil

It is easy to understand the enduring appeal of lasagna. This dish is endlessly variable and can be simple or fancy, but even the most basic lasagna tastes rich and is satisfying. Sure, it requires a few steps and some prep work, but it is certainly not hard, especially if you use no-boil noodles and make a quick homemade sauce. A simple-to-follow layering process and a baking method in which the lasagna is baked first covered and then uncovered yield a bubbling lasagna with a crowning layer of beautifully browned cheese. We use our Simple Cheese Lasagna here to demonstrate the assembly process; see the recipe, as well as additional lasagna recipes, on pages 173–176.

1. ADD SAUCE TO BAKING DISH
Spread ¼ cup tomato sauce over bottom of 13 by 9-inch baking dish.
WHY? Adding a little sauce to the bottom of the pan keeps the noodles from sticking to the pan. Also, the moisture from the sauce helps to hydrate the noodles on the bottom layer. There's no need to grease the baking dish.

2. START LAYERING
Arrange 3 no-boil lasagna noodles crosswise in baking dish on top of sauce, leaving space between noodles.
WHY? The noodles should not be touching when you put them in the baking dish. They will appear to have a lot of space around them, but they will expand during the baking time.

3. DISTRIBUTE FILLING EVENLY
Spoon filling onto each noodle and, steadying each noodle, spread to even thickness, if necessary.
WHY? For a basic cheese lasagna, we like to use a simple ricotta filling enriched with an egg, grated Parmesan cheese, basil, salt, and pepper. It makes it easier to spread the ricotta if you hold the edge of each noodle, and portioning the ricotta carefully ensures a well-balanced lasagna. Looser fillings can simply be spooned evenly over the noodles.

4. ADD MOZZARELLA AND SAUCE
Sprinkle evenly with 1 cup shredded mozzarella cheese, then pour 1½ cups tomato sauce evenly over mozzarella. Repeat layering process two more times (noodles, filling, mozzarella, sauce) before assembling final layer.
WHY? Careful layering and precise portioning of cheese and sauce ensure a well-constructed lasagna.

5. MAKE FINAL LAYER

Place 3 noodles on top. Spread remaining 1¼ cups sauce over noodles. Sprinkle with 1 cup mozzarella and ¼ cup Parmesan.

WHY? Finishing with sauce and two types of cheese makes for a browned and appealingly cheesy casserole. Just a little grated Parmesan adds a hit of flavor to the top of the lasagna.

6. COVER DISH AND START BAKING

Spray large sheet of aluminum foil lightly with vegetable oil spray and cover lasagna. Bake on middle rack in 375-degree oven for 15 minutes.

WHY? Covering the lasagna helps it cook through without drying out and facilitates a moist environment in which the no-boil noodles can soften and expand. We spray the foil with oil to keep it from sticking to the cheesy top.

7. FINISH BAKING UNCOVERED

Remove foil and continue to bake until cheese is browned and sauce is bubbling, about 25 minutes longer. Let cool 10 minutes before serving.

WHY? Baking the lasagna uncovered for the last 25 minutes allows excess moisture to cook off and gives the top of the lasagna a chance to brown attractively. It is important to let the lasagna sit for at least 10 minutes before serving; it needs to firm up a little before you cut it.

Troubleshooting Lasagna

PROBLEM	SOLUTION
Can I use part-skim ricotta?	We prefer whole-milk ricotta, but part-skim will work fine. But don't use nonfat ricotta, which is bland and extremely gummy. The same thing holds true for the mozzarella—either whole-milk or part-skim cheese is fine but avoid nonfat mozzarella.
Can I make this lasagna ahead of time?	Yes. The assembled, unbaked lasagna, covered tightly in plastic wrap, can be held in the refrigerator for up to 1 day. Allow the lasagna to sit at room temperature for 1 hour before baking. You can also additionally cover the lasagna with aluminum foil and freeze it for up to 2 months. Defrost the lasagna in the refrigerator for 1 day, then allow it to sit at room temperature for 1 hour before baking.
I don't have no-boil noodles; can I use traditional lasagna noodles?	We have tried—and failed—in the past to substitute regular boiled lasagna noodles in recipes designed for no-boil noodles. Recipes using no-boil noodles need more liquid, so if you use traditional noodles instead, the lasagna will be too watery.

How to Make Meatballs

Making tender, flavorful meatballs is a time-consuming endeavor, one that is often disappointing in the end. The test kitchen's method eliminates the need to brown the meatballs in a skillet, turning to the oven instead. Most meatball recipes call for equal amounts of pork and beef, but ours has much more beef than pork. This drier, leaner mixture holds its shape well and is helped by a sturdy panade, a mixture of bread mashed with milk, which binds the meatballs and adds moisture and richness. The meatballs and marinara sauce can be served as is, used to make meatball subs, or tossed with 2 pounds of pasta. The cooked meatballs and sauce can be refrigerated for up to one day or frozen for up to one month.

1. COOK ONIONS AND AROMATICS

Cook 1½ pounds finely chopped onions and ¼ cup olive oil in Dutch oven over medium-high heat until golden brown, 10 to 15 minutes. Add 8 minced garlic cloves, 1 tablespoon dried oregano, and ¾ teaspoon red pepper flakes and cook until fragrant, about 30 seconds. Transfer half of mixture to large bowl and reserve for meatballs.
WHY? The fond from the browned onions will add depth to the sauce and meatballs. Cooking, or "blooming," the aromatics draws out their flavor. It also saves time to cook just one large batch of onions and aromatics and use it for both the sauce and the meatballs.

2. ADD TOMATO PASTE AND WINE

Add 1 (6-ounce) can tomato paste to remaining onions in pot and cook 1 minute, then add 1 cup dry red wine and cook 2 minutes.
WHY? Cooking the tomato paste brings out its flavor. The wine needs to reduce and cook out some of the alcohol.

3. STIR IN TOMATOES AND WATER

Reduce heat to low and add 4 (28-ounce) cans crushed tomatoes and 1 cup water and simmer over low heat until thickened, 45 to 60 minutes. Stir in ½ cup grated Parmesan and 2 tablespoons chopped fresh basil. Season with salt and sugar to taste.
WHY? The sauce needs to cook for at least 45 minutes to develop flavor—without the water, it would overreduce and be too thick. The cheese adds flavor, the basil brings freshness, and sugar helps balance the acidity of the tomatoes. Depending on the brand of tomatoes, you might need as much as 2 teaspoons of sugar.

4. MAKE PANADE

Use fork to mash 4 slices hearty white sandwich bread and ¾ cup milk into reserved onion mixture until thoroughly combined.
WHY? The paste, which is called a panade, binds the meatballs and adds moisture and richness.

5. ADD SAUSAGE AND FLAVORINGS

Remove ½ pound sweet Italian sausage from casings and crumble into bowl with onion mixture. Add 1 cup grated Parmesan, ½ cup chopped fresh parsley, 2 large eggs, 2 minced garlic cloves, and 1½ teaspoons salt and mash with fork to combine.

WHY? These ingredients season and help bind the meatballs, so it's important that they're thoroughly incorporated.

6. ADD GROUND CHUCK LAST

Using hands, gently work 2½ pounds 80 percent lean ground chuck into mixture.

WHY? Overworked ground beef makes for dense, rubbery meatballs. Adding it last helps prevent overkneading.

7. FORM INTO BALLS

Gently roll mixture into sixteen 2½-inch meatballs and place on rimmed baking sheet.

WHY? Even sizing means even cooking—this recipe makes big meatballs. Use a kitchen ruler to measure the first meatball, which will serve as your guide as you form the rest of the meatballs.

8. BROWN MEATBALLS IN OVEN

Bake meatballs on upper-middle rack in 475-degree oven until well browned, about 20 minutes.

WHY? The hot oven will give the meatballs a tasty seared crust, and baking is easier and neater than browning on the stovetop.

9. FINISH MEATBALLS IN SAUCE

Transfer browned meatballs to pot with marinara and simmer for 15 minutes.

WHY? The meatballs will finish cooking evenly in the sauce (and flavor the sauce in the process).

Classic Macaroni and Cheese

Overview

In the world of macaroni and cheese, there's a broad spectrum of possibilities. Versions that are geared for adults tend to be decadent, often packed with exotic cheeses—and too much of them—and flavored with indulgences like black truffles, prosciutto, and even lobster. On the other hand, kid-friendly recipes tend to go too easy on the cheese—and on the flavor. We developed a recipe that hits the middle ground: It's rich and undeniably cheesy, but with sharp cheddar and Monterey Jack as the cheeses, it's a classic version, one that the whole family can agree on. The crowning glory is a sprinkling of buttery homemade bread crumbs to add textural contrast.

Recipe Stats

TOTAL TIME **1 hour**
PREPARATION TIME **10 minutes**
ACTIVE COOKING TIME **50 minutes**
YIELD **6 to 8 servings**
MAKE AHEAD **Serve immediately**
DIFFICULTY **Easy**

Tools

- Dutch oven or large pot
- 13 by 9-inch broiler-safe baking dish *
- food processor
- chef's knife
- cutting board
- liquid measuring cup
- measuring spoons
- coarse grater
- colander
- soupspoon
- whisk
- wooden spoon

* Glass Pyrex baking dishes are standard in most home kitchens, but they are not made to withstand the intense heat of a broiler. A porcelain baking dish, which is broiler-safe, is required to make this recipe.

Ingredients

   5 **slices hearty white sandwich bread, torn into quarters**
   8 **tablespoons unsalted butter**
   1 **pound elbow macaroni**
      Salt
   6 **tablespoons all-purpose flour**
1½ **teaspoons dry mustard**
   ¼ **teaspoon cayenne pepper (optional)**
   5 **cups milk ***
   8 **ounces Monterey Jack cheese, shredded (2 cups) ****
   8 **ounces sharp cheddar cheese, shredded (2 cups) *****

* Whole, 1- and 2-percent, and skim milk all work well in this recipe.
** Monterey Jack doesn't have much flavor, but it ensures that the sauce is creamy rather than curdled. Don't replace the Monterey Jack with more cheddar cheese.
*** For best flavor, use a good-quality yellow or white sharp cheddar; mild cheddar simply doesn't pack enough punch. Well-aged extra-sharp cheddars don't melt very well and can result in a grainy sauce.

What Can Go Wrong

Here's a list of common mistakes cooks make when preparing this recipe.

COMMON MISTAKE	BAD OUTCOMES	WHAT YOU SHOULD DO
Using Store-Bought Bread Crumbs	• **The topping lacks crispness and crunch.** • **The topping tastes stale.**	Don't try to take a shortcut by using store-bought bread crumbs instead of making your own fresh bread crumbs. Commercial bread crumbs are so fine that they're dusty, and they have a stale off-flavor that doesn't do any dish any favors. Fresh homemade bread crumbs are quick and easy to make in a food processor and have a flavor and texture that's superior to store-bought.
Boiling Pasta Until Just al Dente	• **The cheese sauce is overly starchy.**	Pasta is usually cooked until al dente, but for this recipe the macaroni should be boiled until it is past al dente and just tender. Al dente pasta will release starch into the cheese sauce, causing it to be too thick and starchy.
Overcooking Pasta	• **The pasta does not absorb any cheese sauce during baking.**	While the pasta should be cooked until it is past al dente, it shouldn't be boiled so long that it becomes soft and soggy. Not only will overcooked pasta be lifeless in the casserole, it won't absorb any of the cheese sauce during baking, so the consistency will be too saucy and loose.
Using Wrong Cheeses	• **Cheese doesn't melt properly or smoothly.** • **Flavor is bland.**	For a velvety-smooth cheese sauce with deep cheese flavor, we found that two cheeses are better than one. Sharp cheddar gives this dish good cheese flavor, while Monterey Jack, because of its higher moisture content, looks creamier when melted and ensures that the sauce does not curdle. Do not use preshredded cheese as it is not as flavorful as freshly grated cheese and doesn't melt as well due to the added coatings to keep it fresh longer.
Adding Cheese Too Early	• **The sauce does not thicken properly.** • **The sauce has a raw-starch flavor.**	The flour-thickened sauce should simmer for at least 5 minutes before the cheese is added. This cooking time allows the raw flour taste to cook out of the sauce and ensures that the flour has thickened the sauce sufficiently.
Not Cooking Pasta and Sauce on Stovetop	• **The casserole is not heated through.** • **The sauce is soupy.**	After adding the cooked pasta to the cheese sauce in the pot, cook the mixture until it is heated through, about 6 minutes. Once in the baking dish, the mac and cheese spends just a few short minutes under the broiler to crisp the bread crumbs—not enough time to heat the baking dish's contents, so the pasta and cheese sauce must be hot before they go into the oven. The stovetop cooking time also allows the pasta to absorb some of the sauce so that the components meld and the sauce attains the proper thickness.

1. Tear 5 slices hearty white sandwich bread into quarters.

2. Cut 3 tablespoons cold unsalted butter into 6 pieces.

3. Pulse cut butter pieces and bread in food processor to coarse crumbs (should be no larger than ⅛ inch), 10 to 15 pulses.

4. Adjust oven rack to lower-middle position and heat broiler.

5. Bring 4 quarts water to boil in Dutch oven or large pot over high heat.

6. Add 1 pound elbow macaroni and 1 tablespoon salt.

7. Cook, stirring often, until pasta is tender. (Pasta should be a little past al dente.)

8. Drain pasta and set aside in colander.

9. In now-empty pot, melt 5 tablespoons unsalted butter over medium-high heat.

10. Add 6 tablespoons all-purpose flour, 1½ teaspoons dry mustard, 1 teaspoon salt, and ¼ teaspoon cayenne, if using, and whisk to combine.

11. Continue whisking until mixture becomes fragrant and deepens in color, about 1 minute.

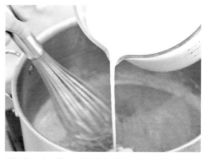

12. Gradually whisk in 5 cups milk.

13. Bring mixture to boil, whisking constantly (mixture must reach full boil to fully thicken).

14. Reduce heat to medium and simmer, whisking occasionally, until thickened to consistency of heavy cream, about 5 minutes.

15. Off heat, whisk in 2 cups shredded Monterey Jack cheese and 2 cups shredded sharp cheddar cheese until fully melted.

16. Add pasta and cook over medium-low heat, stirring constantly, until mixture is steaming and heated through, about 6 minutes.

17. Transfer pasta mixture to 13 by 9-inch broiler-safe baking dish.

18. Sprinkle evenly with bread-crumb mixture.

19. Broil until crumbs are deep golden brown, 3 to 5 minutes, rotating pan if necessary for even browning.

20. Let cool 5 minutes, then serve.

Baked Manicotti

Overview

If you've ever tried making baked manicotti, you know how much work it can be, from precooking the pasta tubes to the fussy task of stuffing each tube (and trying to avoid tearing them). Our streamlined version cuts down on the work dramatically while delivering an elegant and company-worthy dish that tastes every bit as good, if not better, than the original. The trick here is to use no-boil lasagna noodles instead of dried pasta tubes; we soak them briefly in a casserole dish filled with boiling water until they become a little soft and pliable. These noodles can then be spread with a rich ricotta filling and easily rolled into attractive tube shapes, topped with a flavorful homemade sauce, covered (so that the noodles soften properly), and baked. The addition of additional Parmesan cheese at the end and a quick run under the broiler deliver an attractively browned casserole. We think the more delicate no-boil noodles, which closely mimic sheets of fresh pasta, are actually an improvement over dried pasta and allow the flavors of the sauce and the filling to stand out.

Manicotti can be assembled and sauced, covered with a sheet of parchment paper, wrapped in aluminum foil, and refrigerated for up to three days or frozen for up to one month. (If frozen, thaw the manicotti in the refrigerator for one to two days before baking.) In either case, to bake, remove parchment, replace foil, and increase the baking time to 1 to 1¼ hours.

Recipe Stats

TOTAL TIME **1½ hours**
PREPARATION TIME **15 minutes**
ACTIVE COOKING TIME **45 minutes**
YIELD **6 to 8 servings**
MAKE AHEAD **Refrigerate assembled unbaked casserole for up to 3 days or freeze for up to 1 month**
DIFFICULTY **Intermediate**

Tools

- large saucepan
- 13 by 9-inch broiler-safe baking dish *
- chef's knife
- cutting board
- dry measuring cups
- measuring spoons
- can opener
- coarse grater
- dish towels
- mixing bowls
- rasp-style grater
- rubber spatula
- wooden spoon
- aluminum foil
- paper towels

* Glass Pyrex baking dishes are standard in most home kitchens, but they are not made to withstand the intense heat of a broiler. A porcelain baking dish, which is broiler-safe, is required to make this recipe.

Ingredients

SAUCE
- **4 tablespoons unsalted butter**
- **½ cup grated onion**
- **½ teaspoon dried oregano**
  Salt and pepper
- **4 garlic cloves, minced**
- **2 (28-ounce) cans crushed tomatoes**
- **½ teaspoon sugar**
- **¼ cup chopped fresh basil**
- **2 tablespoons extra-virgin olive oil**

CHEESE FILLING
- **24 ounces (3 cups) part-skim ricotta cheese**
- **8 ounces mozzarella cheese, shredded (2 cups) ***
- **4 ounces Parmesan cheese, grated (2 cups)**
- **2 large eggs, lightly beaten**
- **2 tablespoons minced fresh parsley**
- **2 tablespoons chopped fresh basil**
- **¾ teaspoon salt**
- **½ teaspoon pepper**

- **16 no-boil lasagna noodles ****

* Use low-moisture mozzarella, not fresh mozzarella, which doesn't melt as well and can make the dish watery.
** We prefer Barilla no-boil lasagna noodles. Pasta DeFino and Ronzoni brands contain 12 no-boil noodles per package.

What Can Go Wrong

Here's a list of common mistakes cooks make when preparing this recipe.

COMMON MISTAKE	BAD OUTCOMES	WHAT YOU SHOULD DO
Chopping Onion	• **The onion is too crunchy.** • **The sauce tastes a bit flat.**	Be sure to grate the onion rather than chop or mince it; use the large holes on a coarse grater. Grated, the onion will soften and caramelize quickly so that it won't add a crunchy, uncooked texture to the sauce, but instead will help round out the sauce by inserting sweet-savory flavor.
Overcooking Garlic	• **The sauce tastes like toasted garlic.** • **The sauce tastes like bitter, burnt garlic.**	After adding the garlic to the pot, stir constantly and be quite vigilant. The garlic should be cooked only until it is fragrant, not until browned—this will take only about 30 seconds, and no longer than 1 minute. Browned garlic has a toasty flavor profile that is very different than what is desirable for the sauce; if cooked even just a few seconds too long, it takes on a bitterness that will permeate the sauce.
Using Poor-Quality Tomatoes	• **The sauce tastes dull.** • **The sauce lacks fresh tomato flavor.**	The quality of canned crushed tomatoes varies greatly from brand to brand because the product is not regulated by industry standards. For best results, seek out one of the two winners of our canned crushed tomato tasting: Tuttorosso and Muir Glen.
Stacking Noodles During Soaking	• **The noodles stick together.** • **The noodles do not soften evenly.**	Adding the noodles one at a time to the soaking water ensures that each one is moistened on all sides and softens fully and evenly. If the noodles are added as stacks to the water, the layers are likely to stick together, and the ones at the center may remain quite firm.
Forgetting to Sauce Baking Dish	• **The noodles stick to the baking dish.** • **The noodles do not soften on the bottom.**	Be sure to sauce the bottom of the baking dish before setting the filled pasta inside. The sauce on the bottom not only helps prevent the pasta from sticking to the baking dish, it provides moisture that helps the bottoms of the manicotti tubes become tender.
Saucing Top Unevenly	• **The unsauced areas of noodles do not soften.** • **The unsauced areas of noodles dry out.**	Just as sauce in the bottom of the dish is important for the manicotti tubes to become tender on the bottom, saucing the surface of the manicotti helps the tops to become tender. Take care to sauce the surface evenly so that all areas are coated. Patches that are not coated will remain chewy after baking because they lack the sauce's moisture to soften properly, and they are liable to toughen and dry out when the dish is broiled. Also, it's imperative to cover the baking dish with foil; the foil traps steam and helps soften the noodles.

1. PREPARE SAUCE: Peel 1 onion and coarsely grate to yield ½ cup.

2. Coarsely chop basil leaves to yield 6 tablespoons. Reserve ¼ cup for sauce and 2 tablespoons for cheese filling.

3. Heat 4 tablespoons unsalted butter in large saucepan over medium heat until melted.

4. Add grated onion, ½ teaspoon dried oregano, and 1 teaspoon salt.

5. Cook, stirring occasionally, until liquid has evaporated and onion is golden brown, 7 to 10 minutes.

6. Add 4 minced garlic cloves and cook until fragrant, about 30 seconds.

7. Stir in 2 (28-ounce) cans crushed tomatoes and ½ teaspoon sugar. Increase heat to high and bring to simmer.

8. Lower heat to medium-low and simmer until thickened slightly, 15 to 20 minutes.

9. Off heat, stir in ¼ cup chopped basil and 2 tablespoons extra-virgin olive oil into tomato sauce and season with salt and pepper to taste.

10. PREPARE CHEESE FILLING: While sauce is simmering, grate 2 cups mozzarella cheese and 2 cups Parmesan cheese.

11. Chop 2 tablespoons each basil and parsley, then lightly beat 2 large eggs in small bowl.

12. Combine 3 cups ricotta, 2 cups mozzarella, 1 cup Parmesan, eggs, basil and parsley, ¾ teaspoon salt and ¼ teaspoon pepper.

13. ASSEMBLE MANICOTTI: Adjust oven rack to middle position and heat oven to 375 degrees.

14. Pour 1 inch boiling water into 13 by 9-inch broiler-safe baking dish. Add 16 no-boil lasagna noodles, 1 at a time.

15. Let noodles soak until pliable, about 5 minutes, separating noodles with tip of sharp knife to prevent sticking.

16. Remove noodles from water and place in single layer on clean dish towels.

17. Discard water in baking dish and dry with paper towels.

18. Spread bottom of baking dish evenly with 1½ cups sauce.

19. Spread ¼ cup cheese filling mixture onto bottom three-quarters of each noodle (with short side facing you), leaving top quarter of noodle exposed.

20. Roll into tube shape and arrange in baking dish seam side down.

21. Top evenly with remaining sauce, making certain that pasta is completely covered.

22. Cover manicotti with aluminum foil. Bake until bubbling, about 40 minutes, then remove baking dish from oven.

23. Adjust oven rack 6 inches from broiler element and heat broiler. Remove foil cover and sprinkle manicotti with 1 cup Parmesan.

24. Broil until cheese is spotty brown, 4 to 6 minutes. Cool 15 minutes and serve.

HOW TO COOK PASTA

Fresh Egg Pasta

Recipe Stats

TOTAL TIME **45 minutes**
PREPARATION TIME **0 minutes**
ACTIVE TIME **30 minutes**
YIELD **1 pound fresh pasta**
MAKE AHEAD **Keep uncooked noodles at room temperature for up to 4 hours**
DIFFICULTY **Intermediate**

Tools

- rimmed baking sheet
- food processor
- pasta machine
- bench scraper *
- dry measuring cups
- measuring spoons
- dish towels
- plastic wrap

* A bench scraper is a handy tool for slicing the dough but a chef's knife can be used instead.

Ingredients

2 cups all-purpose flour *
3 large eggs **

* Don't attempt to use semolina flour to make fresh pasta; this flour has a very high protein content and requires industrial machines to make the dough.
** With just two ingredients, the size of the eggs is crucial. If you use extra-large or jumbo eggs, the dough will be too moist.

Overview

Fresh pasta is delicate, with a soft, not mushy, texture, and the wheat is complemented by a strong egg flavor. Since fresh pasta tends to absorb sauces—unlike dried pasta, where the sauces cling to the pasta—it is the best choice for cream-based sauces like Alfredo. And although it has a reputation for being difficult to make, it is actually surprisingly easy. Yes, you will need a hand-cranked pasta machine, but the ingredient list could not be shorter (just eggs and flour), and the results are much better than anything you can buy.

We make the dough in the food processor, because this technique is easier and more foolproof than mixing the dough by hand. Keep in mind that while pasta dough is easy to make, it is not very forgiving. Too dry and the dough won't roll out easily; too wet and the dough is a sticky mess. The difference between a dough that is too wet and one that is too dry can be just a tablespoon or two of liquid. But it is easy enough to add more flour or water to make adjustments as needed.

This recipe yields 1 pound of Fresh Egg Pasta. You can cut the pasta into fettuccine for use in recipes like Fettuccine Alfredo (page 176) and Classic Pasta Bolognese (page 170). You can also use sheets of fresh pasta to make ravioli (see Squash Ravioli with Sage and Hazelnut Browned Butter Sauce on page 177). While we suggest using a pasta machine to cut fettuccine, you can cut fresh sheets of pasta by hand. Simply fold each sheet crosswise into thirds or quarters. Use a sharp chef's knife and cut perpendicular to folds to form noodles of desired width. This technique comes in handy when you want to make wider shapes, like pappardelle or tagliatelle. Pappardelle should be cut ¾ to 1 inch wide; tagliatelle should be cut ¼ to ⅜ inch wide. If cutting fettuccine by hand, ⅛ to ¼ inch is ideal.

What Can Go Wrong

Here's a list of common mistakes cooks make when preparing this recipe.

COMMON MISTAKE	BAD OUTCOMES	WHAT YOU SHOULD DO
Using Too Much Flour	• **The dough is crumbly.** • **The dough falls apart when rolled.**	If the dough seems very dry and resembles small pebbles, add water, ½ teaspoon at a time, to the food processor and continue processing until the dough forms a rough ball. (It's fine if there are a few small pebbles; you can incorporate them into the dough by hand.) Make sure to process the water into the dough before adding another ½ teaspoon.
Using Too Little Flour	• **The dough is very sticky.** • **The dough sticks to the pasta machine when rolled.**	If the dough sticks to the sides of the food processor bowl, it's too wet. Add flour, 1 tablespoon at time, and continue processing until the dough forms a rough ball around the blade. As you're rolling out the pasta sheets, don't hesitate to dust the pasta with more flour if it starts to stick. That said, it's so much easier to work with pasta dough that has the right amount of flour added at the outset, when the dough is still in the food processor.
Not Resting the Dough	• **The dough is very hard to roll out.** • **The sheets of dough never get thin enough.**	Once the dough comes out of the food processor, knead it briefly to form a smooth ball, cover the dough with plastic wrap, and set it aside for at least 15 minutes. The gluten in the dough needs time to relax, and if you try to roll the dough now it will snap back. Don't forget the plastic wrap, which prevents the pasta from drying out. If the pasta does dry out, it will be very difficult to roll out.
Not Rolling Dough Thin Enough	• **The pasta is doughy and chewy.** • **The edges of filled pastas are dry and tough.**	It's important to roll pasta quite thin. On most machines you shouldn't stop until you reach the last or next-to-last setting. When you place your hand under the pasta sheet and can see the outline of your fingers, you know you've got the pasta thin enough. Sheets of pasta that are a bit thick will make OK fettuccine. However, if you try to make filled pasta with thick pasta sheets the results will be inferior. That's because the doubled edges of the ravioli will cook up dry and tough.
Not Separating Strands of Pasta	• **The pasta sticks together.**	Once you cut the pasta into strands, place those strands on a baking sheet lined with a clean dish towel and separate the stands by hand. If you skip this step, the noodles can fuse together as they dry.
Cooking Fresh Pasta Too Long	• **The pasta is mushy and soft.**	You won't be cooking the fresh pasta in this tutorial but we can't stress enough the importance of treating fresh pasta differently than dried. It will cook in a fraction of the time so taste early and often.

1. Pulse 2 cups all-purpose flour in food processor to aerate and break up clumps so that flour evenly absorbs eggs.

2. Add 3 large eggs and process until dough forms rough ball, about 30 seconds.

3. If dough resembles small pebbles, dough is too dry; add water, ½ teaspoon at a time, and process until dough forms rough ball.

4. If dough sticks to sides of bowl, dough is too wet; add flour, 1 tablespoon at a time, and process until dough forms rough ball.

5. Turn dough ball and small bits out onto dry counter.

6. Knead by hand until dough is smooth, elastic, and homogenous, 1 to 2 minutes.

7. Cover dough with plastic wrap and set aside for at least 15 minutes or up to 2 hours to allow gluten to relax so that dough rolls out easily.

8. Cut about one-fifth of dough from ball and flatten into disk.

9. Re-cover remaining dough with plastic wrap to prevent it from drying out.

10. Run disk through rollers of pasta machine set to widest position.

11. Bring ends of dough toward middle and press down to seal.

12. Feed open side of pasta through rollers.

13. Fold and roll dough once more.

14. If dough is at all sticky, lightly dust with flour.

15. Without folding again, run pasta through widest setting twice or until dough is smooth.

16. Roll pasta thinner by putting it through machine repeatedly, narrowing setting each time. Roll until dough is thin and satiny.

17. After dough is rolled through narrowest setting, you should be able to see outline of your hand through pasta.

18. Lay sheet of pasta on clean dish towel and cover it with damp dish towel to keep it from drying out.

19. Repeat with other pieces of dough.

20. To cut pasta sheets into fettuccine, affix cutting attachment.

21. Run each sheet through pasta machine.

22. Spread strands out on rimmed baking sheet lined with dish towels, separating individual strands as best as you can.

23. Cover with slightly damp dish towel to prevent pasta from drying out.

HOW TO COOK PASTA

Classic Pasta Bolognese

Overview

Bolognese sauce, called *ragù* in Italian, is a meat sauce that hails from the city of Bologna in the Emilia-Romagna region of northern Italy. Bolognese sauce is not a tomato-based meat sauce like the type that is common in America—it is a richly complex, silky-textured, and wonderfully elegant sauce that is traditionally paired with wide, flat pasta strands such as fettuccine. It is also used in the classic lasagna alla Bolognese.

Although the cooking time for Bolognese sauce is long, the hands-on prep time is very brief. Technique and time are important to success here, so don't be tempted to take shortcuts to speed up the process. This recipe is best when prepared with fresh pasta—either homemade (see recipe tutorial on page 156) or store-bought—although dried pasta will work.

Recipe Stats

TOTAL TIME **5 hours**
PREPARATION TIME **10 minutes**
ACTIVE COOKING TIME **1½ hours**
YIELD **4 to 6 servings**
MAKE AHEAD **Sauce can be refrigerated for up to 2 days or frozen for up to 1 month**
DIFFICULTY **Easy**

Tools

- Dutch oven (2) *
- food processor
- chef's knife
- cutting board
- dry measuring cups
- liquid measuring cup
- measuring spoons
- can opener
- colander
- flame tamer **
- large spoon
- rasp-style grater
- tongs
- wooden spoon

* A heavy-bottomed Dutch oven conducts heat evenly and steadily, which is important for a slow-simmered sauce like Bolognese, and the wide width and relatively shallow depth of a Dutch oven facilitates evaporation of liquids so that the sauce achieves the proper texture. You will need a second pot for cooking the pasta (a Dutch oven or other large pot will work).

** If your stove burner runs hot and it is difficult to keep liquids at the barest simmer, you may need a flame tamer (heat diffuser)—a metal disk that fits over the burner (electric or gas) and tempers the heat transfer. If you don't own a flame tamer and you have a gas stove, you can fashion a flame tamer from aluminum foil. Take a long sheet of foil and shape it into a 1-inch thick ring that will fit on the burner. Make sure that the ring is of an even thickness so that a pot will sit level on it.

Ingredients

- **5 tablespoons unsalted butter**
- **¼ cup finely chopped onion**
- **¼ cup minced carrot**
- **¼ cup minced celery**
- **Salt**
- **1 pound meatloaf mix ***
- **1½ cups whole milk ****
- **1½ cups dry white wine**
- **3 (14.5-ounce) cans diced tomatoes**
- **1 pound fresh or dried fettuccine**
- **Grated Parmesan cheese**

* Meatloaf mix is a combination of equal parts ground chuck, veal, and pork. If your store doesn't sell it, opt for ⅓ pound each type of ground meat.

** The richness of whole milk is important to the flavor balance of the sauce. Do not substitute low-fat or skim milk. Do not use heavy cream, which will make the sauce taste overly heavy.

What Can Go Wrong

Here's a list of common mistakes cooks make when preparing this recipe.

COMMON MISTAKE	BAD OUTCOMES	WHAT YOU SHOULD DO
Using All Ground Beef	• **The sauce tastes one-dimensional.** • **The meat is not meltingly tender.**	For the best-tasting and best-textured sauce, use meatloaf mix or ⅓ pound each of 80 percent lean ground beef, veal, and pork. The beef gives the sauce meatiness; the veal adds a soft, velvety texture; and the pork lends a mild sweetness. It's not uncommon for Bolognese sauce to be made only with beef, but we find an all-beef sauce to taste rather one-dimensional and the texture to be not quite as yielding and velvety.
Not Using Whole Milk	• **The sauce tastes lean.** • **The sauce lacks richness.**	Although many of us keep low-fat or skim milk in the refrigerator, whole milk is key to the richness of the Bolognese sauce. Lower-fat types of milk used in place of whole milk will result in a sauce that tastes lean and weak.
Using Wrong Type of Tomatoes	• **The sauce is too thick.** • **The sauce is prone to scorching on the bottom during simmering.**	Canned crushed tomatoes are a thick, viscous, coarse purée; canned diced tomatoes are chunks of tomatoes packed in a thin, watery juice. Tempting though it may be to use crushed tomatoes instead of diced tomatoes (which must be broken down a bit in a food processor before they are added to the pot), crushed tomatoes have a tendency to scorch during the long simmering time. Crushed tomatoes will also make the sauce too tomatoey in both appearance and flavor.
Letting Meat Brown	• **The meat will be tough.** • **The sauce will not thicken properly.**	The key to a silky Bolognese is to add the milk just when the meat loses its raw color. This way the milk penetrates the meat more easily, tenderizing it and making it especially sweet. If the meat browns before you add the milk, it will not become tender nor will it absorb the milk properly.
Simmering Sauce Too Vigorously	• **The sauce scorches on the bottom before the meat is fully tender.** • **The sauce is dry and doesn't coat the pasta.**	Be sure to use a heavy-bottomed Dutch oven so that the sauce can be kept at the barest simmer during the long cooking time. If the sauce is simmered too vigorously, the meat will not become meltingly tender. In addition, at a full simmer, the moisture evaporates too quickly, and the sauce risks scorching on the bottom of the pot.
Undercooking Sauce	• **The meat is not fully tender.** • **The sauce is too soupy.**	Unfortunately, to make an authentic Bolognese sauce, there is no way to shortcut the 3- to 3½-hour simmering time. It takes that long for the meat to become meltingly tender and the sauce to take on a thick, velvety texture. If the sauce is taken off the heat before it's ready, the meat may still have some bite, the consistency may be too soupy, and the flavors may not be sufficiently concentrated.

1. Peel 1 small onion and finely chop to yield ¼ cup.

2. Peel 1 small carrot and mince to yield ¼ cup.

3. Mince 1 small celery rib to yield ¼ cup.

4. Drain 3 (14.5-ounce) cans diced tomatoes, reserving 1½ cups juice.

5. Pulse drained tomatoes in food processor until slightly chunky, about 8 pulses.

6. Melt 3 tablespoons unsalted butter in Dutch oven over medium heat.

7. Add onion, carrot, celery, and 1 teaspoon salt and cook until softened, 6 to 8 minutes.

8. Stir in 1 pound meatloaf mix and cook, breaking up meat with a wooden spoon, until no longer pink, about 3 minutes.

9. Stir in 1½ cups whole milk and bring to a simmer.

10. Cook until milk has evaporated and only clear fat remains, about 25 minutes.

11. Stir in 1½ cups dry white wine and bring to simmer.

12. Cook until wine has evaporated, about 25 minutes.

13. Add tomatoes and reserved juice to pot and bring to bare simmer.

14. Cook gently over low heat until liquid has evaporated, 3 to 3½ hours. If using meatloaf mix, skim off fat that rises to surface using large spoon.

15. Season with salt to taste.

16. When sauce is almost ready, bring 4 quarts water to boil in Dutch oven or large pot.

17. Add 1 pound pasta and 1 tablespoon salt and cook, stirring often, until al dente.

18. Reserve ½ cup cooking water.

19. Drain pasta.

20. Return pasta to pot, and add sauce and 2 tablespoons unsalted butter.

21. Toss to combine, adding cooking water as needed so that sauce coats the pasta.

22. Serve, passing Parmesan separately.

HOW TO COOK PASTA

Fettuccine Alfredo

Recipe Stats

TOTAL TIME **35 minutes**
PREPARATION TIME **5 minutes**
ACTIVE COOKING TIME **30 minutes**
YIELD **4 to 6 servings**
MAKE AHEAD **Serve immediately**
DIFFICULTY **Easy**

Tools

- Dutch oven or large pot
- large sauté pan *
- dry measuring cups
- liquid measuring cup
- measuring spoons
- colander
- ladle
- rasp-style grater
- serving bowls
- tongs

* The sauté pan is used for heating the cream and butter that form the Alfredo sauce. Later, the cooked and drained pasta is added to the pan for saucing and to finish cooking, so make sure to use a sauté pan that is large enough to hold all of the pasta comfortably; a 3-quart pan will work well.

Overview

Since its creation in Rome in the early twentieth century, fettuccine Alfredo has morphed into what it often is today: a not-too-tempting dish of pasta cloaked in a gloppy, gluey, remarkably bland white cheese sauce. Our recipe returns fettuccine Alfredo to its original splendor, with finely finessed tastes and textures.

The simplicity of a proper fettuccine Alfredo like this one allows diners to fully appreciate the elegance of fresh pasta. The dish is a perfect—and very easy—way to showcase your homemade fresh egg pasta (see recipe tutorial on page 156). However, if you can find freshly made store-bought pasta, that also will work; do not used dried pasta.

The richness of fettuccine Alfredo is best enjoyed in small portions, either as a starter or as a pasta course in a multi-course meal; it is simply too heavy as a main dish. Be sure to warm the bowls for serving—fettuccine Alfredo is always at its best when hot.

Ingredients

1⅔ cups heavy cream, preferably not ultrapasteurized *
5   tablespoons unsalted butter
    Salt and pepper
1   pound fresh fettuccine **
2   ounces Parmesan cheese, grated (1 cup)
    Pinch ground nutmeg

* For the best tasting fettuccine Alfredo, try to find cream that has been only pasteurized, not ultrapasteurized.

** Homemade pasta (see Recipe Tutorial on page 156) is the best choice here, although if you have access to good-quality store-bought fresh fettuccine, it can certainly be used.

What Can Go Wrong

Here's a list of common mistakes cooks make when preparing this recipe.

COMMON MISTAKE	BAD OUTCOMES	WHAT YOU SHOULD DO
Using Ultrapasteurized Cream	• The sauce tastes "cooked." • The sauce tastes flat.	Ultrapasteurized cream has been heated to a high temperature that extends its shelf life; this treatment results in cream that tastes rather dull and cooked. Pasteurized cream has been heated to kill bacteria, but it has not been subjected to the same temperatures used for ultra-pasteurized cream. Its flavor, by comparison, is fresher, sweeter, and purer—the difference can be tasted in a dish like fettuccine Alfredo, where the cream plays a lead role. Ultra-pasteurized cream won't ruin this dish, but pasteurized cream will make it better.
Overcooking the Cream and Butter	• The sauce is too thick. • The sauce is gluey.	Heat the cream and butter mixture gently, over low heat, just until the butter has melted and the cream has attained a bare simmer. If the mixture is allowed to reach a full simmer or to simmer vigorously, too much of the moisture will evaporate and the sauce will be thick and unctuous instead of silky and creamy.
Substituting Dried Fettuccine	• The sauce does not adhere to the pasta.	The success of fettuccine Alfredo is dependent on fresh pasta. If you are not starting this recipe with homemade fresh pasta, opt for good-quality store-bought fresh egg pasta instead, but do not substitute dried fettuccine. Dried pasta lacks the porosity of fresh, so the sauce does not cling to the strands and instead winds up in the bottom of the bowl.
Boiling Pasta Until al Dente	• The pasta is mushy by the time it is served.	Drain the pasta before it is al dente. After draining, the pasta is briefly cooked in the sauce so that it has an opportunity to absorb some of the flavors. During this process, the pasta continues to soften. If the pasta is drained when it is fully al dente, it will become too soft after cooking some more in the sauce. Remember that fresh pasta cooks much faster than dried pasta and might be done in as little as 2 or 3 minutes if rolled very thin.
Using Poor-Quality Parmesan	• The sauce lacks cheese flavor. • The sauce is chalky and grainy.	Use real Parmesan cheese, aka Parmigiano-Reggiano. Fettuccine Alfredo is not the place to use anything less than genuine Italian-made Parmesan cheese. True Parmesan has a nutty, deeply complex flavor that is the raison d'être of Alfredo sauce. It also possesses melting properties that facsimiles do not. Low-quality Parmesan will make this dish salty and gritty; don't attempt this dish without the real thing.
Using Cold Serving Bowls	• The sauce congeals very quickly.	Warmed bowls are a must for this recipe. Bring a little extra water to boil for cooking the pasta and then ladle some of the boiling water into bowls. Alternatively, if your bowls are ovensafe, you can warm them in a very low oven. The reason for warmed bowls is simple: The texture of the sauce changes dramatically as it cools, becoming thick and congealed. Warmed bowls keep the sauce fluid long enough for you to finish eating the pasta before this happens.

1. Bring 4½ quarts water to rolling boil in Dutch oven or large pot.

2. Combine 1⅓ cups heavy cream and 5 tablespoons unsalted butter in large sauté pan.

3. Heat over low heat until butter is melted and cream comes to bare simmer.

4. Remove pan from heat and set aside.

5. Using ladle or heatproof measuring cup, fill each individual serving bowl with about ½ cup boiling water.

6. Add 1 tablespoon salt and 1 pound fresh pasta to pot of boiling water.

7. Cook, stirring often, until almost al dente.

8. Reserve ½ cup pasta cooking water.

9. Drain pasta and add to sauté pan with cream mixture.

10. Add ⅓ cup cream, 1 cup grated Parmesan cheese, ½ teaspoon salt, pepper to taste, and pinch nutmeg.

11. Cook over very low heat, tossing to combine, until sauce is slightly thickened, 1 to 2 minutes, adding reserved cooking water as needed.

12. Working quickly, empty water from serving bowls and divide pasta among warmed bowls. Serve immediately.

Recipe Library

Quick Tomato Sauce

✓ **WHY THIS RECIPE WORKS:** It needn't take hours to make a terrific homemade tomato sauce. In fact, we found that if you simmer a simple tomato sauce (one without meat) for much longer than 20 minutes, you actually cook out the flavor. We also found that canned tomatoes consistently taste better than those flavorless, out-of-season supermarket tomatoes. After testing every option for canned tomatoes and tomato products on the market—tomato paste and whole, diced, crushed, and pureed tomatoes among them—we found that a combination of diced and crushed tomatoes works the best. The diced tomatoes add good chunky texture, while the crushed tomatoes provide a nice smooth foundation. We learned it was easy to scorch the garlic when cooking it in the olive oil; as soon as it smelled fragrant, we added the tomatoes to the pot. As for additional seasoning, we kept it simple with basil and a touch of sugar for balancing sweetness.

Quick Tomato Sauce

MAKES 4 CUPS; ENOUGH FOR 1 POUND OF PASTA

This recipe can be easily doubled, but you will need to simmer the sauce an additional 10 minutes. Quick Tomato Sauce works well with any type or shape of pasta. When tossing sauce with pasta, add some of the pasta cooking water as needed to loosen the consistency of the sauce as desired. See Core Technique on page 142 for more details on this recipe.

- 3 **tablespoons extra-virgin olive oil**
- 3 **garlic cloves, minced**
- 1 **(28-ounce) can crushed tomatoes**
- 1 **(14.5-ounce) can diced tomatoes**
- 3 **tablespoons chopped fresh basil**
- ¼ **teaspoon sugar**
  Salt

1. Cook oil and garlic in medium saucepan over medium heat, stirring often, until fragrant but not browned, about 2 minutes. Stir in crushed and diced tomatoes and their juice. Bring to simmer and cook until slightly thickened, 15 to 20 minutes.

2. Stir in basil and sugar and season with salt to taste.

Marinara Sauce

✓ **WHY THIS RECIPE WORKS:** For a multidimensional marinara sauce that would take less than an hour to prepare, we chose canned whole tomatoes for their flavor and texture, hand-crushing them and removing the hard core and stray bits of skin at the same time. A finely chopped onion lent our sauce sweet flavor. We boosted tomato flavor by sautéing the tomatoes until they glazed the bottom of the pan, after which we added their liquid. We also shortened the simmering time by using a skillet instead of a saucepan (the greater surface area of a skillet encourages faster evaporation and flavor concentration). Red wine added depth and complexity and uncooked tomatoes, basil, and olive oil added just before serving, gave our sauce a bright, fresh finish.

Marinara Sauce

MAKES 4 CUPS; ENOUGH FOR 1 POUND OF PASTA

Chianti or Merlot work well for the dry red wine. We like a smoother marinara, but if you prefer a chunkier sauce, give it just three or four pulses in the food processor in step 4.

- 2 **(28-ounce) cans whole peeled tomatoes**
- 3 **tablespoons extra-virgin olive oil**
- 1 **onion, chopped fine**
- 2 **garlic cloves, minced**
- 2 **teaspoons minced fresh oregano or**
  ½ **teaspoon dried**
- ⅓ **cup dry red wine**
- 3 **tablespoons chopped fresh basil**
  Salt and pepper
  Sugar

1. Pour tomatoes and their juice into strainer set over large bowl. Open tomatoes with hands and remove and discard seeds and fibrous cores; let tomatoes drain excess liquid, about 5 minutes. Remove ¾ cup tomatoes from strainer and set aside. Reserve 2½ cups tomato juice and discard remainder.

2. Heat 2 tablespoons oil in 12-inch skillet over medium heat until shimmering. Add onion and cook until softened and lightly browned, 5 to 7 minutes. Stir in garlic and oregano and cook until fragrant, about 30 seconds.

3. Stir in strained tomatoes and increase heat to medium-high. Cook, stirring often, until liquid has evaporated, tomatoes begin to stick to bottom of pan, and brown fond forms around pan edges, 10 to 12 minutes. Stir in wine and cook until thick and syrupy, about 1 minute. Stir in reserved tomato juice, scraping up any browned bits. Bring to simmer and cook, stirring occasionally, until sauce is thick, 8 to 10 minutes.

4. Transfer sauce and reserved tomatoes to food processor and pulse until slightly chunky, about 8 pulses. Return sauce to now-empty skillet, stir in basil and remaining 1 tablespoon oil, and season with salt, pepper, and sugar to taste.

Pasta with Tomato, Bacon, and Onion

✓ **WHY THIS RECIPE WORKS:** Like most Roman cooking, pasta alla Amatriciana is bold and brash. We wanted to create a recipe that would do this classic sauce justice, using ingredients found locally. To start, we used pancetta, if available (and substituted bacon if not). Diced tomatoes, onion, and red pepper flakes gave our sauce lively flavor. And adding the cooked pancetta at the end kept it crisp.

Pasta with Tomato, Bacon, and Onion (Pasta alla Amatriciana)

SERVES 4

This dish is traditionally made with bucatini, also called perciatelli, which appear to be thick, round strands but are actually thin, extra-long tubes. Linguine works fine, too. When buying pancetta, ask the butcher to slice it ¼ inch thick; if using bacon, buy slab bacon and cut it into ¼-inch-thick slices yourself. If the pancetta that you're using is very lean, it's unlikely that you will need to drain off any fat before adding the onion.

- 2 tablespoons extra-virgin olive oil
- 6 ounces pancetta or bacon, sliced ¼ inch thick and cut into strips about 1 inch long and ¼ inch wide
- 1 onion, chopped fine
- ½ teaspoon red pepper flakes, or to taste
- 1 (28-ounce) can diced tomatoes
- 1 pound bucatini, perciatelli, or linguine
  Salt
- 1½ ounces Pecorino Romano cheese, grated (¾ cup)

1. Heat oil in 12-inch skillet over medium heat until shimmering. Add pancetta and cook, stirring occasionally, until crisp, 5 to 7 minutes. Remove pancetta with slotted spoon and transfer to paper towel–lined plate. Pour off all but 2 tablespoons fat from skillet, add onion, and cook over medium heat until softened, about 5 minutes. Stir in pepper flakes and cook until fragrant, about 30 seconds. Stir in tomatoes and their juice, bring to simmer, and cook until slightly thickened, about 10 minutes.

2. Meanwhile, bring 4 quarts water to boil in large pot. Add pasta and 1 tablespoon salt and cook, stirring often, until al dente. Reserve ½ cup cooking water, then drain pasta and return it to pot.

3. Stir crisp pancetta into sauce and season with salt to taste. Add sauce and Pecorino to pasta and toss to combine. Add reserved cooking water as needed to adjust consistency. Serve.

Spaghetti Puttanesca

✔ **WHY THIS RECIPE WORKS:** Many recipes for puttanesca produce a dish that is too fishy, too garlicky, too briny, or just plain too salty and acidic. Others are timidly flavored and dull. We wanted to bring out as much flavor as we could from each of the ingredients in our version, while not letting any one preside over the others. We bloomed the garlic, anchovies, and red pepper flakes in hot olive oil to develop and blend their flavors. Then we added tomatoes and simmered for only 8 minutes to preserve their sweetness and meaty texture. A drizzle of olive oil over individual portions adds moisture and richness.

Spaghetti Puttanesca

SERVES 4

The pasta and sauce cook in just about the same amount of time, so begin the sauce just after you add the pasta to the boiling water in step 1.

- 1 pound spaghetti
  Salt
- 1 (28-ounce) can diced tomatoes, drained with ½ cup juice reserved
- 2 tablespoons olive oil, plus extra for drizzling
- 8 anchovy fillets, rinsed, patted dry, and minced
- 4 garlic cloves, minced
- 1 teaspoon red pepper flakes
- ½ cup pitted kalamata olives, chopped coarse
- ¼ cup minced fresh parsley
- 3 tablespoons capers, rinsed

1. Bring 4 quarts water to boil in large pot. Add pasta and 1 tablespoon salt and cook, stirring often, until al dente. Reserve ½ cup cooking water, then drain pasta and return it to pot. Add ¼ cup reserved tomato juice and toss to combine.

2. Meanwhile, heat oil, anchovies, garlic, and pepper flakes in 12-inch skillet over medium heat. Cook, stirring often, until garlic turns golden but not brown, about 3 minutes. Stir in tomatoes and cook until slightly thickened, about 8 minutes.

3. Stir olives, parsley, and capers into sauce. Add sauce to pasta and toss to combine. Add remaining ¼ cup reserved tomato juice or reserved cooking water as needed to adjust consistency. Season with salt to taste. Drizzle additional olive oil over individual portions and serve immediately.

Spaghetti alla Carbonara

✔ **WHY THIS RECIPE WORKS:** Standard carbonara is often a lackluster spaghetti dish—either covered in a leaden sauce or riddled with dry bits of cheese. To add to the problems, if the dish gets to the table a few minutes too late, the sauce congeals and the pasta turns rubbery. We wanted a method for producing al dente spaghetti with a velvety sauce punctuated by bits of bacon and a trace of garlic. We determined that three whole eggs gave our carbonara superior texture and richness. Combining Pecorino Romano and Parmesan cheese gave us creaminess with a little bit of bite. Domestic bacon contributed the perfect crunch and smoky flavor. Combining the hot pasta with the sauce in a warm serving bowl produces a silky, not clumpy, sauce.

Spaghetti alla Carbonara

SERVES 4 TO 6

Although we call for spaghetti in this recipe, you can substitute linguine or fettuccine.

- ¼ cup extra-virgin olive oil
- 8 slices bacon, halved lengthwise and cut into ¼-inch pieces
- ½ cup dry white wine
- 3 large eggs
- 1½ ounces Parmesan cheese, grated (¾ cup)
- ¼ cup finely grated Pecorino Romano cheese
- 2 garlic cloves, minced
- 1 pound spaghetti
  Salt and pepper

1. Adjust oven rack to lower-middle position, set large heat-proof serving bowl on rack, and heat oven to 200 degrees.

2. Heat oil in 12-inch skillet over medium heat until shimmering. Add bacon and cook until crisp, about 8 minutes. Stir in wine, bring to simmer, and cook until alcohol aroma has cooked off and wine is slightly reduced, 6 to 8 minutes. Remove from heat and cover to keep warm. Beat eggs, Parmesan, Pecorino, and garlic together with fork in bowl; set aside.

3. Meanwhile, bring 4 quarts water to boil in large pot. Add pasta and 1 tablespoon salt and cook, stirring often, until al dente. Reserve ½ cup cooking water, then drain pasta and transfer it to warmed serving bowl. Immediately pour bacon and egg mixture over hot pasta and toss to combine. Add reserved cooking water as needed to adjust consistency. Season with salt and pepper to taste and serve immediately.

Penne alla Vodka

✓ WHY THIS RECIPE WORKS: Splashes of vodka and cream can turn run-of-the-mill tomato sauce into luxurious restaurant fare or a boozy mistake. To achieve a sauce with the right balance of sweet, tangy, spicy, and creamy, we pureed half the tomatoes (which helped the sauce cling nicely to the pasta) and cut the rest into chunks. For sweetness, we added sautéed onion. We found that we needed a liberal amount of vodka to cut through the richness and add zing to the sauce, but we had to add it to the tomatoes early on to allow the alcohol to mostly (but not completely) cook off and prevent a harsh alcohol flavor. Adding a little heavy cream to the sauce gave it a nice consistency, and we finished cooking the penne in the sauce to encourage cohesiveness.

Penne alla Vodka

SERVES 4 TO 6

So that the sauce and pasta finish cooking at the same time, drop the pasta into boiling water just after adding the vodka to the sauce. Use the smaller amount of red pepper flakes for a milder sauce.

- 1 (28-ounce) can whole tomatoes, drained with juice reserved
- 2 tablespoons olive oil
- ¼ cup finely chopped onion
- 1 tablespoon tomato paste
- 2 garlic cloves, minced
- ¼–½ teaspoon red pepper flakes
  Salt
- ⅓ cup vodka
- ½ cup heavy cream
- 1 pound penne
- 2 tablespoons chopped fresh basil
  Grated Parmesan cheese

1. Pulse half of tomatoes in food processor until smooth, about 12 pulses. Cut remaining tomatoes into ½-inch pieces, discarding cores. Combine pureed and chopped tomatoes in liquid measuring cup (you should have about 1⅔ cups). Add reserved juice to equal 2 cups; discard remaining juice.

2. Heat oil in large saucepan over medium heat until shimmering. Add onion and tomato paste and cook, stirring occasionally, until onion is softened and lightly browned, 5 to 7 minutes. Add garlic and pepper flakes and cook until fragrant, about 30 seconds.

3. Stir in tomato mixture and ½ teaspoon salt. Remove saucepan from heat and add vodka. Return saucepan to medium-high heat and simmer briskly, stirring often, until alcohol flavor is cooked off, 8 to 10 minutes, reducing heat if simmering becomes too vigorous. Stir in cream and cook until hot, about 1 minute.

4. Meanwhile, bring 4 quarts water to boil in large pot. Add pasta and 1 tablespoon salt and cook, stirring often, until al dente. Reserve ½ cup cooking water, then drain pasta and return it to pot. Add sauce to pasta and cook over medium heat, tossing to combine, until pasta absorbs some of sauce, 1 to 2 minutes. Add reserved cooking water as needed to adjust consistency. Stir in basil and season with salt to taste. Serve immediately, passing Parmesan separately.

Classic Basil Pesto

✓ WHY THIS RECIPE WORKS: Our goal in developing our pesto was to heighten the basil and subdue the garlic flavors so that each major element balanced the other. We started with plenty of fresh basil and pounded to bruise it and release flavorful oils. Basil usually darkens in homemade pesto, so we boost the green color a little by adding parsley. To tame the raw garlic edge, we toasted it, toasting the nuts as well to give them more intense flavor. And we used a food processor to combine the ingredients in our pesto quickly and easily.

Classic Basil Pesto

MAKES ABOUT ¾ CUP; ENOUGH FOR 1 POUND OF PASTA

When adding pesto to cooked pasta, reserve 1 cup pasta cooking water before draining. Add ½ cup of the cooking water directly to the sauce, tablespoon by tablespoon, then toss the sauce with the drained pasta. Add the remaining ½ cup cooking water as needed. See Core Technique on page 140 for more details on this recipe.

- 3 garlic cloves, unpeeled
- ¼ cup pine nuts
- 2 cups fresh basil leaves
- 2 tablespoons fresh parsley leaves
  Salt and pepper
- 7 tablespoons extra-virgin olive oil
- ¼ cup finely grated Parmesan cheese

1. Toast garlic in 8-inch skillet over medium heat, shaking pan occasionally, until softened and spotty brown, about 8 minutes; when cool enough to handle, remove and discard skins and chop coarsely.

2. While garlic cools, toast nuts in now-empty skillet over medium heat, stirring often, until golden and fragrant, 2 to 4 minutes.

3. Place basil and parsley in 1 gallon zipper-lock bag. Pound bag with flat side of meat pounder or rolling pin until all leaves are bruised.

4. Process garlic, nuts, basil, parsley, and ½ teaspoon salt in food processor until smooth, about 1 minute, scraping down bowl as needed. With processor running, slowly add oil and process until combined. Transfer mixture to small bowl, stir in Parmesan, and season with salt and pepper to taste. (Pesto can be refrigerated for up to 3 days or frozen for up to 3 months in bowl with plastic wrap or thin layer of oil covering surface.)

Meatballs and Marinara

✔ **WHY THIS RECIPE WORKS:** Most meatball recipes call for equal amounts of pork and beef, but ours has more beef than pork—the drier, leaner mixture held its shape well. For extra flavor, we chose sweet Italian sausage for the pork portion of the mix. Browning the meatballs in the oven was easier than cooking them on the stovetop, and finishing them in the tomato sauce flavored both components.

Meatballs and Marinara

SERVES 8

The meatballs and sauce use the same onion mixture. Sausage adds extra seasoning to the meatballs; use hot sausage instead of mild if you like. This recipe makes enough to sauce 2 pounds of pasta. See Core Technique on page 146 for more details on this recipe.

ONION MIXTURE
¼ cup olive oil
1½ pounds onions, chopped fine
8 garlic cloves, minced
1 tablespoon dried oregano
¾ teaspoon red pepper flakes

EASY MARINARA
1 (6-ounce) can tomato paste
1 cup dry red wine
4 (28-ounce) cans crushed tomatoes
1 cup water
1 ounce Parmesan cheese, grated (½ cup)
2 tablespoons chopped fresh basil
Salt
1–2 teaspoons sugar, as needed

MEATBALLS
4 slices hearty white sandwich bread
¾ cup milk
½ pound sweet Italian sausage, casings removed
2 ounces Parmesan cheese, grated (1 cup)
½ cup chopped fresh parsley
2 large eggs
2 garlic cloves, minced
1½ teaspoons salt
2½ pounds 80 percent lean ground chuck

1. FOR THE ONION MIXTURE: Heat oil in Dutch oven over medium-high heat until shimmering. Add onions and cook until golden brown, 10 to 15 minutes. Add garlic, oregano, and pepper flakes and cook until fragrant, about 30 seconds. Transfer half of onion mixture to large bowl and set aside.

2. FOR THE EASY MARINARA: Add tomato paste to onion mixture remaining in pot and cook until fragrant, about 1 minute. Add wine and cook until slightly thickened, about 2 minutes. Stir in crushed tomatoes and water and simmer over low heat until sauce has thickened, 45 to 60 minutes. Stir in Parmesan and basil. Season with salt and sugar to taste.

3. FOR THE MEATBALLS: Meanwhile, adjust oven rack to upper-middle position and heat oven to 475 degrees. Use fork to mash bread and milk together in bowl with reserved onion mixture until thoroughly combined. Add sausage, Parmesan, parsley, eggs, garlic, and salt, and mash to combine. Add beef and gently knead with hands until combined (do not overwork). Form mixture into sixteen 2½-inch meatballs, place on rimmed baking sheet, and bake until well browned, about 20 minutes.

4. Transfer meatballs to pot with thickened sauce and simmer for 15 minutes. Serve over pasta. (Meatballs and marinara can be frozen for up to 1 month.)

Classic Pasta Bolognese

✔ **WHY THIS RECIPE WORKS:** A good Bolognese sauce should be thick and smooth with rich, complex flavor. We built our Bolognese in layers, starting with onions, carrots, and celery, sautéed in butter before adding meatloaf mix. For dairy, we used milk, which complemented the meat flavor without adding too much richness. Once the milk was reduced, we added white wine to the pot for a more robust sauce, followed by diced tomatoes. A long, slow simmer produced a luxuriously rich sauce with layers of flavor and tender meat.

Classic Pasta Bolognese

SERVES 4 TO 6

If you would like to double this recipe, increase the simmering times for the milk and the wine to 30 minutes each, and the simmering time once the tomatoes are added to 4 hours. You can substitute equal amounts of 80 percent lean ground beef, ground veal, and ground pork for the meatloaf mix (the total amount of meat should be 1 pound). Just about any pasta shape complements this meaty sauce, but fettucine is the test kitchen favorite. This is a great recipe for showing off homemade pasta (see Recipe Tutorial on page 156 and recipe page 176). See Recipe Tutorial on page 160 for more details on this recipe.

5 tablespoons unsalted butter
¼ cup finely chopped onion
¼ cup minced carrot
¼ cup minced celery
Salt
1 pound meatloaf mix
1½ cups whole milk
1½ cups dry white wine

3 **(14.5-ounce) cans diced tomatoes, drained,
1½ cups juice reserved**
1 **pound fresh or dried fettuccine
Grated Parmesan cheese**

1. Melt 3 tablespoons butter in Dutch oven over medium heat. Add onion, carrot, celery, and 1 teaspoon salt and cook until vegetables are softened, 6 to 8 minutes. Stir in meatloaf mix and cook, breaking up meat with a wooden spoon, until no longer pink, about 3 minutes.

2. Stir in milk, bring to simmer, and cook until milk has evaporated and only clear fat remains, about 25 minutes. Stir in wine, bring to simmer, and cook until wine has evaporated, about 25 minutes.

3. Meanwhile, pulse tomatoes in food processor until slightly chunky, about 8 pulses. Add tomatoes and reserved juice to pot and bring to bare simmer. Cook sauce gently over low heat until liquid has evaporated, 3 to 3½ hours, skimming fat from surface using large spoon as needed. Season with salt to taste.

4. When sauce is almost ready, bring 4 quarts water to boil in large pot. Add pasta and 1 tablespoon salt and cook, stirring often, until al dente. Reserve ½ cup pasta cooking water, then drain pasta and return it to pot. Add sauce and remaining 2 tablespoons butter and toss to combine. Before serving, add reserved cooking water as needed to adjust consistency. Serve, passing Parmesan separately. (Sauce can be refrigerated for up to 2 days or frozen for up to 1 month.)

Spring Vegetable Pasta

✔ **WHY THIS RECIPE WORKS:** In pasta primavera, the vegetables and pasta are tossed together in a heavy cream sauce. We love this classic, but sometimes we want a lighter, brighter version—one with a creamy sauce, but without the cream. As for the vegetables, we wanted true spring vegetables. To start, we chose asparagus and green peas, adding chives for bite and garlic and leeks for depth and sweetness. For a deeply flavored sauce that would unify the pasta and vegetables, we borrowed a technique from risotto, lightly toasting the pasta in olive oil before cooking it in broth and white wine. The sauce flavored the pasta as it cooked while the pasta added starch to the sauce, thickening it without the need for heavy cream. This nontraditional approach gave us a light but creamy sauce with sweet, grassy flavors that paired perfectly with the vegetables for a dish that truly tasted like spring.

Spring Vegetable Pasta
SERVES 4 TO 6
Campanelle is our pasta of choice in this dish, but farfalle and penne are acceptable substitutes.

1½ **pounds leeks, white and light green parts halved lengthwise, sliced ½ inch thick, and washed thoroughly; 3 cups coarsely chopped dark green parts, washed thoroughly**
1 **pound asparagus, tough ends trimmed, chopped coarse, and reserved; spears cut on bias into ½-inch lengths**

2 **cups frozen peas, thawed**
4 **garlic cloves, minced**
4 **cups vegetable broth**
1 **cup water**
2 **tablespoons minced fresh mint**
2 **tablespoons minced fresh chives**
½ **teaspoon grated lemon zest plus 2 tablespoons juice**
6 **tablespoons extra-virgin olive oil
Salt and pepper**
¼ **teaspoon red pepper flakes**
1 **pound campanelle**
1 **cup dry white wine**
1 **ounce Parmesan cheese, grated (½ cup), plus extra for serving**

1. Bring leek greens, asparagus trimmings, 1 cup peas, half of garlic, broth, and water to simmer in large saucepan. Reduce heat to medium-low and simmer gently for 10 minutes. While broth simmers, combine mint, chives, and lemon zest in bowl; set aside.

2. Strain broth through fine-mesh strainer into large liquid measuring cup, pressing on solids to extract as much liquid as possible (you should have 5 cups broth; add water as needed to measure 5 cups). Discard solids and return broth to saucepan. Cover and keep warm.

3. Heat 2 tablespoons oil in Dutch oven over medium heat until shimmering. Add leeks and pinch salt and cook, covered, stirring occasionally, until leeks begin to brown, about 5 minutes. Add asparagus and cook until asparagus is crisp-tender, 4 to 6 minutes. Add remaining garlic and pepper flakes and cook until fragrant, about 30 seconds. Add remaining 1 cup peas and continue to cook 1 minute longer. Transfer vegetables to plate and set aside. Wipe out pot.

4. Heat remaining ¼ cup oil in now-empty pot over medium heat until shimmering. Add pasta and cook, stirring often, until just beginning to brown, about 5 minutes. Add wine and cook, stirring constantly, until absorbed, about 2 minutes.

5. When wine is fully absorbed, add warm broth and bring to boil. Cook, stirring frequently, until most of liquid is absorbed and pasta is al dente, 8 to 10 minutes. Off heat, stir in half of herb mixture, vegetables, lemon juice, and Parmesan. Season with salt and pepper to taste and serve immediately, passing additional Parmesan and remaining herb mixture separately.

Classic Macaroni and Cheese

✔ **WHY THIS RECIPE WORKS:** This family favorite should boast tender pasta in a smooth, creamy sauce with great cheese flavor. Too often, the dish, which is baked in the oven, dries out or curdles. We aimed to create a foolproof version. We cooked the pasta until just past al dente and then combined it with a béchamel-based cheese sauce. For the best flavor and a creamy texture, we used a combination of sharp cheddar and Monterey Jack. We combined the cooked pasta with the sauce and heated it through on the stovetop, rather than in the oven. This step helped ensure the dish didn't dry out, but remained smooth and creamy. And to give the dish a browned topping, we sprinkled it with buttery bread crumbs and ran it briefly under the broiler.

Classic Macaroni and Cheese

SERVES 6 TO 8

It's crucial to cook the pasta until tender—that is, just past the al dente stage. Whole, low-fat, and skim milk all work well in this recipe. The recipe may be halved and baked in an 8-inch square broiler-safe baking pan. If desired, offer celery salt or hot sauce for sprinkling at the table. See Recipe Tutorial on page 148 for more details on this recipe.

  5 **slices hearty white sandwich bread, torn into quarters**
  8 **tablespoons unsalted butter, 3 tablespoons cut into 6 pieces and chilled**
  1 **pound elbow macaroni**
     Salt
  6 **tablespoons all-purpose flour**
1½ **teaspoons dry mustard**
 ¼ **teaspoon cayenne pepper (optional)**
  5 **cups milk**
  8 **ounces Monterey Jack cheese, shredded (2 cups)**
  8 **ounces sharp cheddar cheese, shredded (2 cups)**

1. Pulse bread and 3 tablespoons chilled butter in food processor to coarse crumbs, 10 to 15 pulses; set aside.

2. Adjust oven rack to lower-middle position and heat broiler. Bring 4 quarts water to boil in large pot. Add pasta and 1 tablespoon salt and cook, stirring often, until tender; drain pasta.

3. Melt remaining 5 tablespoons butter in now-empty pot over medium-high heat. Add flour, mustard, 1 teaspoon salt, and cayenne, if using, and cook, whisking constantly, until mixture becomes fragrant and deepens in color, about 1 minute. Gradually whisk in milk; bring mixture to boil, whisking constantly. Reduce heat to medium and simmer, whisking occasionally, until thickened, about 5 minutes. Off heat, slowly whisk in Monterey Jack and cheddar until completely melted. Add pasta to sauce and cook over medium-low heat, stirring constantly, until mixture is steaming and heated through, about 6 minutes.

4. Transfer mixture to 13 by 9-inch broiler-safe baking dish and sprinkle with bread-crumb mixture. Broil until topping is deep golden brown, 3 to 5 minutes, rotating pan halfway through cooking. Cool casserole for 5 minutes before serving.

Baked Manicotti

 WHY THIS RECIPE WORKS: Despite being composed of a straightforward collection of ingredients, manicotti is surprisingly fussy to prepare. Blanching, shocking, draining, and stuffing slippery pasta tubes require a lot of patience and time. We wanted an easier recipe that still produced great-tasting manicotti. Our biggest challenge was filling the slippery manicotti tubes. We solved the problem by discarding the tubes completely and spreading the filling onto softened lasagna noodles, which we then rolled up. No-boil lasagna noodles were ideal. We soaked the noodles in boiling water for 5 minutes until pliable, using the tip of a knife to separate them and prevent sticking. For the cheese filling, part-skim ricotta had an ideal level of richness). Eggs, Parmesan, and an ample amount of mozzarella

added richness, flavor, and structure to the ricotta filling. For a quick but brightly flavored tomato sauce, grated onion cooked in butter, plus sugar, garlic, oregano, and basil enhanced the flavor of canned crushed tomatoes with minimal work.

Baked Manicotti

SERVES 6 TO 8

Note that some pasta brands contain only 12 no-boil noodles per package; this recipe requires 16 noodles. If your baking dish is not broiler-safe, brown the manicotti at 500 degrees for about 10 minutes. See Recipe Tutorial on page 152 for more details on this recipe.

TOMATO SAUCE

  4 **tablespoons unsalted butter**
 ½ **cup grated onion**
 ½ **teaspoon dried oregano**
     Salt and pepper
  4 **garlic cloves, minced**
  2 **(28-ounce) cans crushed tomatoes**
 ½ **teaspoon sugar**
 ¼ **cup chopped fresh basil**
  2 **tablespoons extra-virgin olive oil**

CHEESE FILLING

24 **ounces (3 cups) part-skim ricotta cheese**
  8 **ounces mozzarella cheese, shredded (2 cups)**
  4 **ounces Parmesan cheese, grated (2 cups)**
  2 **large eggs, lightly beaten**
  2 **tablespoons minced fresh parsley**
  2 **tablespoons chopped fresh basil**
 ¾ **teaspoon salt**
 ½ **teaspoon pepper**

16 **no-boil lasagna noodles**

1. FOR THE SAUCE: Melt butter in large saucepan over medium heat. Add onion, oregano, and 1 teaspoon salt and cook, stirring occasionally, until onion is softened and lightly browned, 7 to 10 minutes. Stir in garlic and cook until fragrant, about 30 seconds. Stir in tomatoes and sugar and bring to simmer. Lower heat to medium-low and simmer until slightly thickened, 15 to 20 minutes. Off heat, stir in basil and oil and season with salt and pepper to taste.

2. FOR THE CHEESE FILLING: Combine ricotta, mozzarella, 1 cup Parmesan, eggs, parsley, basil, salt, and pepper in bowl.

3. Adjust oven rack to middle position and heat oven to 375 degrees. Pour 1 inch boiling water into 13 by 9-inch broiler-safe baking dish. Slip noodles into water, 1 at a time, and soak until pliable, about 5 minutes, separating noodles with tip of sharp knife to prevent sticking. Remove noodles from water and place in single layer on clean dish towels; discard water and dry dish with paper towels.

4. Spread 1½ cups sauce evenly over bottom of dish. Using spoon, spread ¼ cup cheese mixture evenly onto bottom three-quarters of each noodle (with short side facing you), leaving top quarter of noodle exposed. Roll into tube shape and arrange in dish seam side down. Top evenly with remaining sauce, making certain that pasta is completely covered.

5. Cover dish tightly with aluminum foil and bake until bubbling, about 40 minutes. Remove dish from oven and remove foil. Adjust oven rack 6 inches from broiler element and heat broiler. Sprinkle manicotti evenly with remaining 1 cup Parmesan. Broil until cheese is spotty brown, 4 to 6 minutes. Cool manicotti for 15 minutes before serving.(Assembled manicotti can be covered with sheet of parchment paper, wrapped in foil, and refrigerated for up to 3 days or frozen for up to 1 month. If frozen, thaw manicotti in refrigerator for 1 to 2 days. To bake, remove parchment, replace foil, and increase baking time to 1 to 1¼ hours.)

Baked Ziti

✓ **WHY THIS RECIPE WORKS:** For a sauce that's big on flavor and light on prep, we cooked sautéed garlic with canned diced tomatoes and tomato sauce. Rather than using traditional ricotta, we turned to cottage cheese—its curds have a texture similar to ricotta, but are creamier and tangier. For more flavor, we combined the cottage cheese with eggs, Parmesan, and heavy cream thickened with cornstarch. As for the pasta, we undercooked it and then baked it with a generous amount of sauce for perfectly al dente pasta and plenty of sauce left to keep our baked ziti moist. We cut the mozzarella into small cubes instead of shredding it, which dotted the finished casserole with gooey bits of cheese.

Baked Ziti

SERVES 8 TO 10

We prefer baked ziti made with heavy cream, but whole milk can be substituted by increasing the amount of cornstarch to 2 teaspoons and increasing the cooking time in step 3 by 1 to 2 minutes. Part-skim mozzarella can also be used.

1	**pound ziti, penne, or other short, tubular pasta**
	Salt and pepper
1	**pound (2 cups) whole-milk or 1-percent cottage cheese**
2	**large eggs**
3	**ounces Parmesan cheese, grated (1½ cups)**
2	**tablespoons extra-virgin olive oil**
5	**garlic cloves, minced**
1	**(28-ounce) can tomato sauce**
1	**(14.5-ounce) can diced tomatoes**
1	**teaspoon dried oregano**
½	**cup plus 2 tablespoons chopped fresh basil**
1	**teaspoon sugar**
¾	**teaspoon cornstarch**
1	**cup heavy cream**
8	**ounces whole-milk mozzarella cheese, cut into ¼-inch pieces (1½ cups)**

1. Adjust oven rack to middle position and heat oven to 350 degrees. Bring 4 quarts water to boil in large pot. Add pasta and 1 tablespoon salt and cook, stirring often, until pasta begins to soften but is not yet cooked through, 5 to 7 minutes. Drain pasta and leave in colander (do not wash pot).

2. Meanwhile, whisk cottage cheese, eggs, and 1 cup Parmesan together in medium bowl; set aside. Heat oil and garlic in 12-inch skillet over medium heat. Cook, stirring often, until garlic turns golden but not brown, about 3 minutes. Stir in tomato sauce, diced tomatoes, and oregano, bring to simmer, and cook until thickened, about 10 minutes. Off heat, stir in ½ cup basil and sugar and season with salt and pepper to taste.

3. Stir cornstarch and heavy cream together in small bowl; transfer mixture to now-empty pot set over medium heat. Bring to simmer and cook until thickened, 3 to 4 minutes. Off heat, stir in cottage cheese mixture, 1 cup of tomato sauce, and ¾ cup of mozzarella. Add pasta to sauce and toss to combine.

4. Transfer pasta to 13 by 9-inch baking dish and spread remaining tomato sauce evenly over top. Sprinkle with remaining ¾ cup mozzarella and remaining ½ cup Parmesan. Cover dish tightly with aluminum foil that has been sprayed with vegetable oil spray. Bake for 30 minutes, then remove foil and continue to bake until cheese is bubbling and beginning to brown, about 30 minutes longer. Cool casserole for 20 minutes, then sprinkle with remaining 2 tablespoons basil and serve.

Simple Cheese Lasagna

✓ **WHY THIS RECIPE WORKS:** Lasagna is the ultimate in Italian comfort food, and while you could spend hours in the kitchen making the noodles and sauce, a simple cheese lasagna can be made in a fraction of the time using no-boil noodles and a homemade sauce that takes just 25 minutes. A simple-to-follow layering process and a baking method where the lasagna is baked first covered and then uncovered yield a bubbling lasagna with a crowning layer of beautifully browned cheese.

Simple Cheese Lasagna

SERVES 6 TO 8

See Core Technique on page 144 for more details on this recipe.

CHUNKY TOMATO SAUCE

1	**tablespoon olive oil**
1	**onion, chopped fine**
	Salt and pepper
6	**garlic cloves, minced**
1	**(28-ounce) can crushed tomatoes**
1	**(28-ounce) can diced tomatoes**
¼	**teaspoon dried oregano**
⅛	**teaspoon red pepper flakes**

CHEESE FILLING

16	**ounces (2 cups) whole-milk ricotta cheese**
2½	**ounces Parmesan cheese, grated (1¼ cups)**
½	**cup chopped fresh basil**
1	**large egg, lightly beaten**
½	**teaspoon salt**
½	**teaspoon pepper**

12	**no-boil lasagna noodles**
1	**pound whole-milk mozzarella, shredded (4 cups)**

1. FOR THE SAUCE: Heat oil in large saucepan over medium heat until shimmering. Add onion and 1 teaspoon salt and cook until softened, about 5 minutes. Add garlic and cook until fragrant, about 30 seconds. Stir in tomatoes and their juice, oregano, and pepper flakes. Simmer until sauce is slightly thickened, about 15 minutes. Season with salt and pepper to taste.

2. FOR THE FILLING: Adjust oven rack to middle position and heat oven to 375 degrees. Mix ricotta, 1 cup Parmesan, basil, egg, salt, and pepper together in bowl until well combined.

3. Spread ¼ cup sauce over bottom of 13 by 9-inch baking dish. Place 3 noodles on top of sauce, then dollop 3 tablespoons of ricotta mixture down center of each noodle and spread to even thickness. Sprinkle evenly with 1 cup mozzarella. Spoon 1½ cups sauce evenly over mozzarella. Repeat layering of noodles, ricotta mixture, mozzarella, and sauce two more times.

4. For final layer, place 3 remaining noodles on top. Spread remaining 1¼ cups sauce over noodles. Sprinkle with remaining 1 cup mozzarella, then remaining ¼ cup Parmesan.

5. Spray large sheet of aluminum foil lightly with vegetable oil spray and cover lasagna. Bake for 15 minutes. Remove foil and continue to bake until cheese is browned and sauce is bubbling, about 25 minutes longer. Let cool for 10 minutes before serving.

TO MAKE AHEAD: Assembled, unbaked lasagna can be refrigerated, wrapped tightly in plastic wrap, for up to 24 hours. Allow lasagna to sit at room temperature for 1 hour before baking. It can also be frozen, covered with plastic and then aluminum foil, for up to 2 months. To bake, defrost in refrigerator for 24 hours, then allow lasagna to sit at room temperature for 1 hour before baking.

Simple Lasagna with Hearty Tomato-Meat Sauce

WHY THIS RECIPE WORKS: Determined to formulate a really good 90-minute meat lasagna recipe, we came up with several shortcuts: We made a 12-minute tomato-meat sauce by cooking onions, garlic, and meatloaf mixture (ground beef, pork, and veal) and then adding cream and tomatoes. We chose no-boil lasagna noodles to eliminate the process of boiling and draining. We created a classic cheese layer quickly with ricotta, mozzarella, Parmesan, fresh basil, and an egg to help thicken and bind the mixture. Covering the lasagna with aluminum foil before baking helped soften the noodles; removing the foil during the last 25 minutes of baking allowed the cheeses to brown properly.

Simple Lasagna with Hearty Tomato-Meat Sauce

SERVES 8 TO 10

You can substitute equal amounts of 85 percent lean ground beef, ground veal, and ground pork for the meatloaf mix (the total amount of meat should be 1 pound).

TOMATO-MEAT SAUCE
- 1 tablespoon olive oil
- 1 onion, chopped fine
- 6 garlic cloves, minced
- 1 pound meatloaf mix
- ½ teaspoon salt
- ½ teaspoon pepper
- ¼ cup heavy cream
- 1 (28-ounce) can tomato puree
- 1 (28-ounce) can diced tomatoes, drained

CHEESE FILLING
- 14 ounces (1¾ cups) whole-milk or part-skim ricotta cheese
- 2½ ounces Parmesan cheese, grated (1¼ cups)
- ½ cup chopped fresh basil
- 1 large egg, lightly beaten
- ½ teaspoon salt
- ½ teaspoon pepper
- 1 pound whole-milk mozzarella, shredded (4 cups)
- 12 no-boil lasagna noodles

1. FOR THE SAUCE: Heat oil in Dutch oven over medium heat until shimmering. Add onion and cook, stirring occasionally, until softened, about 5 minutes. Stir in garlic and cook until fragrant, about 30 seconds. Stir in meatloaf mix, salt, and pepper, increase heat to medium-high, and cook, breaking up any large pieces with wooden spoon, until no longer pink, about 3 minutes. Add cream, bring to simmer, and cook, stirring occasionally, until liquid evaporates and only rendered fat remains, about 4 minutes. Stir in tomato puree and diced tomatoes, bring to simmer, and cook until flavors meld, about 3 minutes. Set aside. (Sauce can be cooled and refrigerated for up to 2 days; reheat before assembling lasagna.)

2. FOR THE CHEESE FILLING: Adjust oven rack to middle position and heat oven to 375 degrees. Combine ricotta, 1 cup Parmesan, basil, egg, salt, and pepper in bowl.

3. Spread ¼ cup sauce evenly over bottom of 13 by 9-inch baking dish (avoiding large chunks of meat). Arrange 3 noodles in single layer on top of sauce. Spread each noodle evenly with 3 tablespoons of ricotta mixture and sprinkle entire layer with 1 cup mozzarella. Spoon 1½ cups sauce over top. Repeat layering of noodles, ricotta mixture, mozzarella, and sauce 2 more times. For final layer, arrange remaining 3 noodles on top and cover completely with remaining sauce. Sprinkle with remaining 1 cup mozzarella, then sprinkle with remaining ¼ cup Parmesan.

4. Cover dish tightly with aluminum foil that has been sprayed with vegetable oil spray. Bake for 15 minutes, then remove foil, and continue to bake until cheese is spotty brown and edges are just bubbling, about 25 minutes longer. Cool lasagna for 15 minutes before serving.

TO MAKE AHEAD: Assembled, unbaked lasagna can be refrigerated, wrapped tightly in plastic wrap, for up to 24 hours. Allow lasagna to sit at room temperature for 1 hour before baking. It can also be frozen, covered with plastic and then aluminum foil, for up to 2 months. To bake, defrost in refrigerator for 24 hours, then allow lasagna to sit at room temperature for 1 hour before baking.

Hearty Vegetable Lasagna

✓ **WHY THIS RECIPE WORKS:** For a complex vegetable lasagna with bold flavor, we started with a summery mix of zucchini, yellow squash, and eggplant, salting and microwaving the eggplant and sautéing the vegetables to cut down on excess moisture and deepen their flavor. Garlic and spinach and olives added textural contrast and flavor without much work. We dialed up the usual cheese filling by switching mild-mannered ricotta for tangy cottage cheese mixed with heavy cream for richness and Parmesan and garlic for flavor.

Hearty Vegetable Lasagna

SERVES 8 TO 10

Part-skim mozzarella can also be used in this recipe, but avoid preshredded cheese, as it does not melt well. We prefer kosher salt because it clings best to the eggplant. If using table salt, reduce salt amounts by half. To make assembly easier, the roasted vegetable filling can be made and stored in the refrigerator for up to 1 day.

TOMATO SAUCE

- 1 (28-ounce) can crushed tomatoes
- ¼ cup chopped fresh basil
- 2 tablespoons extra-virgin olive oil
- 2 garlic cloves, minced
- 1 teaspoon kosher salt
- ¼ teaspoon red pepper flakes

CREAM SAUCE

- 8 ounces (1 cup) whole-milk cottage cheese
- 1 cup heavy cream
- 4 ounces Parmesan cheese, grated (2 cups)
- 2 garlic cloves, minced
- 1 teaspoon cornstarch
- ½ teaspoon kosher salt
- ½ teaspoon pepper

VEGETABLE FILLING

- 1½ pounds eggplant, peeled and cut into ½-inch pieces
  Kosher salt and pepper
- 1 pound zucchini, cut into ½-inch pieces
- 1 pound yellow summer squash, cut into ½-inch pieces
- 5 tablespoons plus 1 teaspoon extra-virgin olive oil
- 4 garlic cloves, minced
- 1 tablespoon minced fresh thyme
- 12 ounces baby spinach (12 cups)
- ½ cup pitted kalamata olives, minced
- 12 ounces whole-milk mozzarella cheese, shredded (3 cups)
- 12 no-boil lasagna noodles
- 2 tablespoons chopped fresh basil

1. FOR THE TOMATO SAUCE: Whisk all ingredients together in bowl; set aside.

2. FOR THE CREAM SAUCE: Whisk all ingredients together in separate bowl; set aside.

3. FOR THE VEGETABLE FILLING: Adjust oven rack to middle position and heat oven to 375 degrees. Toss eggplant with 1 teaspoon salt in large bowl. Line surface of large plate with double layer of coffee filters and lightly spray with vegetable oil spray. Spread eggplant in even layer over coffee filters; wipe out and reserve bowl. Microwave eggplant, uncovered, until dry to touch and slightly shriveled, about 10 minutes, tossing halfway through cooking. Cool slightly. Return eggplant to bowl and toss with zucchini and yellow summer squash.

4. Combine 1 tablespoon oil, garlic, and thyme in small bowl. Heat 2 tablespoons oil in 12-inch nonstick skillet over medium-high heat until shimmering. Add half of eggplant mixture, ¼ teaspoon salt, and ¼ teaspoon pepper and cook, stirring occasionally, until vegetables are lightly browned, about 7 minutes. Clear center of skillet, add half of garlic mixture, and cook, mashing with spatula, until fragrant, about 30 seconds. Stir garlic mixture into vegetables and transfer to medium bowl. Repeat with remaining eggplant mixture, 2 tablespoons oil, and remaining garlic mixture; transfer to bowl.

5. Heat remaining 1 teaspoon oil in now-empty skillet over medium-high heat until shimmering. Add spinach and cook, stirring frequently, until wilted, about 3 minutes. Transfer spinach to paper towel–lined plate and drain for 2 minutes. Stir into eggplant mixture.

6. Grease 13 by 9-inch baking dish. Spread 1 cup tomato sauce evenly over bottom of dish. Arrange 4 noodles on top of sauce (noodles will overlap). Spread half of vegetable mixture over noodles, followed by half of olives. Spoon half of cream sauce over top and sprinkle with 1 cup mozzarella. Repeat layering with 4 noodles, 1 cup tomato sauce, remaining vegetables, remaining olives, remaining cream sauce and 1 cup mozzarella. For final layer, arrange remaining 4 noodles on top and cover completely with remaining tomato sauce. Sprinkle with remaining 1 cup mozzarella.

7. Cover dish tightly with aluminum foil that has been sprayed with oil spray and bake until edges are just bubbling, about 35 minutes, rotating dish halfway through baking. Cool lasagna for 25 minutes, then sprinkle with basil and serve.

Skillet Meaty Lasagna

✓ **WHY THIS RECIPE WORKS:** Lasagna is one of our favorite casseroles here in the test kitchen. That's why we decided to come up with a streamlined skillet version. To start, we created a richly flavored, yet quickly simmered, tomato sauce with canned whole tomatoes, which we pulsed in the food processor. Meatloaf mix, which we browned first, contributed deep, meaty flavor but kept our shopping list short (it's a mix of ground beef, pork, and veal). To fit the lasagna noodles in the pan, we broke them into short lengths. Finally, for the cheesy layer, we not only stirred in some shredded mozzarella, but we also sprinkled more mozzarella and dropped big dollops of ricotta on top; covering the pan briefly provided enough residual heat to melt them into a creamy topping.

Skillet Meaty Lasagna

SERVES 4

Do not substitute no-boil lasagna noodles for the traditional curly-edged lasagna noodles. Meatloaf mix is sold prepackaged in many supermarkets; if unavailable, use 8 ounces each ground pork and 85 percent lean ground beef. You can substitute part-skim ricotta if desired, but do not use nonfat ricotta, which has a very dry texture and bland flavor.

 3 (14.5-ounce) cans whole peeled tomatoes
 1 tablespoon olive oil
 1 onion, chopped fine
    Salt and pepper
 3 garlic cloves, minced
 ⅛ teaspoon red pepper flakes
 1 pound meatloaf mix
10 curly-edged lasagna noodles, broken into 1½- to 2-inch lengths
 2 ounces mozzarella cheese, shredded (½ cup)
 ¼ cup grated Parmesan cheese
 6 ounces (¾ cup) whole-milk ricotta cheese
 3 tablespoons chopped fresh basil

1. Pulse tomatoes in food processor until coarsely ground and no large pieces remain, about 12 pulses.

2. Heat oil in 12-inch nonstick skillet over medium heat until shimmering. Add onion and ½ teaspoon salt and cook, stirring often, until softened, 5 to 7 minutes. Stir in garlic and pepper flakes and cook until fragrant, about 30 seconds. Add meatloaf mix and cook, breaking up meat with wooden spoon, until no longer pink, 3 to 5 minutes.

3. Scatter pasta in skillet, then pour processed tomatoes over top. Cover, increase heat to medium-high, and cook at vigorous simmer, stirring often, until pasta is tender, about 20 minutes.

4. Off heat, stir in half of mozzarella and half of Parmesan. Season with salt and pepper to taste. Dot heaping tablespoons of ricotta over noodles, then sprinkle with remaining mozzarella and Parmesan. Cover and let stand off heat until cheese melts, 2 to 4 minutes. Sprinkle with basil and serve.

Fresh Egg Pasta

✔ WHY THIS RECIPE WORKS: Some sauces, such as Alfredo sauce, are best paired with fresh pasta, and some filled pasta, like ravioli, also require fresh pasta. We wanted a foolproof, easy-to-knead recipe for fresh pasta. We found that the food processor effectively kneaded our dough almost to perfection. Kneading the dough by hand for an additional minute or two made our pasta dough silky and smooth. Running the dough, in pieces, through a manual pasta machine until it was translucent gave us the delicate pasta we were after.

Fresh Egg Pasta

MAKES ABOUT 1 POUND

Although the food processor does most of the work, finish kneading this dough by hand. See Recipe Tutorial on page 156 for more details on this recipe.

 2 cups all-purpose flour
 3 large eggs

1. Pulse flour in food processor to aerate. Add eggs and process until dough forms rough ball, about 30 seconds. (If dough resembles small pebbles, add water, ½ teaspoon at a time, or if dough sticks to side of bowl, add flour, 1 tablespoon at a time, and process until dough forms rough ball.)

2. Turn out dough ball and any small bits onto counter and knead by hand until dough is smooth, 1 to 2 minutes. Cover with plastic wrap and set aside to relax for at least 15 minutes or up to 2 hours.

3. Cut dough into 5 even pieces and, using manual pasta machine, roll out dough into sheets. Leave pasta in sheets for filled and hand-shaped pastas, or cut into long strands.

Fresh Herb Pasta

Add ⅓ cup minced fresh herbs (parsley, basil, mint, or any combination) to flour along with eggs.

Fresh Spinach Pasta

Decrease eggs to 2. Add 3 ounces frozen chopped spinach, thawed and squeezed very dry, with eggs.

Fettuccine Alfredo

✔ WHY THIS RECIPE WORKS: Balancing two of the richer ingredients was key to success: 1 cup Parmigiano-Reggiano and 5 tablespoons butter lent distinctive flavor and the richness this dish is known for. Our real challenge was managing the heavy cream, which is usually reduced by half, making the sauce unpalatably thick. Instead, we brought most, but not all, of our cream to a simmer with the butter. Once the pasta was cooked, we added it to the pan along with the remaining cream, Parmesan, and seasoning. It took only a minute or two from there for our sauce to reach the perfect consistency.

Fettuccine Alfredo

SERVES 4 TO 6

Try to find cream that has been only pasteurized, not ultrapasteurized. Ultrapasteurized cream has been heated to a high temperature to extend its shelf life, and it tastes flat. Genuine Parmigiano-Reggiano is absolutely essential here. Warmed bowls are a must as well since the sauce will become thick and congealed once cooled. We bring a little extra water to boil for cooking the pasta and then ladle some of the boiling water into bowls. Dried noodles do not work well in this recipe. Use fresh homemade fettucine (see Recipe Tutorial on page 156) or store-bought fettuccine. See Recipe Tutorial on page 164 for more details on this recipe.

1⅔ cups heavy cream, preferably not ultra-pasteurized
 5 tablespoons unsalted butter
    Salt and pepper
 1 pound fresh fettuccine
 2 ounces Parmesan cheese, grated (1 cup)
    Pinch ground nutmeg

1. Bring 4½ quarts water to boil in large pot. While water comes to boil, heat 1⅓ cups cream and butter in large sauté pan over low heat until butter is melted and cream comes to bare simmer. Remove from heat; set aside.

2. When water comes to boil, fill individual serving bowls with about ½ cup boiling water each using ladle or heatproof measuring cup; set aside. Add 1 tablespoon salt and pasta to pot. Cook, stirring often, until pasta is just shy of al dente. Reserve ½ cup cooking water, then drain pasta.

3. Transfer drained pasta to sauté pan with cream and butter. Add remaining ⅓ cup cream, Parmesan, ½ teaspoon salt, and nutmeg. Season with pepper to taste.

4. Cook over very low heat, tossing to combine, until sauce is slightly thickened, 1 to 2 minutes, adding reserved cooking water as needed to adjust consistency. Working quickly, empty water from serving bowls, divide pasta among warmed bowls, and serve immediately.

Squash Ravioli with Sage and Hazelnut Browned Butter Sauce

WHY THIS RECIPE WORKS: For our winter squash filling, butternut provided the sweetest, most concentrated flavor and creamiest texture. Microwaving the squash was easy and every bit as good as squash prepared by more complicated methods. The food processor transformed it into a smooth paste, while nutmeg, brown sugar, butter, and Parmesan gave it the right flavor profile. We found it was key to roll our homemade fresh pasta very thin to avoid edges that turned out too thick and chewy, and a generous teaspoon of filling per ravioli was plenty and helped keep ravioli from exploding in the cooking water. While most recipes recommend brushing the dough edges with water or egg for a tight seal, this made the dough sticky and hard to handle. We had more success simply rolling out and filling one sheet of dough at a time to ensure it stayed as moist and fresh as possible. Tossed with a little sage brown butter and hazelnuts, these ravioli tasted far better than anything we could have bought.

Squash Ravioli with Sage and Hazelnut Browned Butter Sauce

MAKES ABOUT 45 RAVIOLI; SERVES 6 TO 8

Do not use frozen squash here; its flavor is bland and will be disappointing. Sliced or slivered almonds can be substituted for the hazelnuts.

RAVIOLI
- **1 pound butternut squash, peeled, seeded, and cut into 1-inch chunks (3½ cups)**
- **4 tablespoons unsalted butter**
- **1 tablespoon packed brown sugar**
  Salt
  Pinch ground nutmeg
- **2 ounces Parmesan cheese, grated (1 cup)**
- **⅛ teaspoon pepper**
  All-purpose flour, for dusting
- **1 recipe Fresh Egg Pasta (page 176)**

SAUCE
- **8 tablespoons unsalted butter, cut into 4 pieces**
- **¼ cup hazelnuts, toasted, skinned, and chopped coarse**
- **2 tablespoons minced fresh sage**
- **¼ teaspoon salt**
- **2 teaspoons lemon juice**
- **1 ounce Parmesan cheese, shaved**

1. FOR THE RAVIOLI: Place squash in microwave-safe bowl, cover tightly with plastic wrap, and microwave until tender and easily pierced with fork, 10 to 15 minutes.

2. Remove plastic (watch for steam), drain squash, and transfer to food processor. Add butter, sugar, ¼ teaspoon salt, and nutmeg and process until mixture is smooth, 15 to 20 seconds, stopping to scrape down sides of bowl as needed. Transfer to bowl, stir in Parmesan and pepper, and refrigerate until no longer warm, 15 to 25 minutes.

3. Dust 2 large rimmed baking sheets liberally with flour; set aside. Divide pasta dough into 5 even pieces and wrap with plastic. Unwrap 1 piece of dough, flatten into disk, and run disk through pasta machine rollers set to widest position. Bring ends of dough toward middle and press down to seal edges together. Position open side of dough in rollers and roll to flatten folds. Repeat folding and rolling process. Without folding, run dough through widest setting twice or until dough is smooth. If dough is sticky, dust with flour. Roll dough through machine repeatedly, narrowing setting each time, until thin and satiny. Lay sheet of pasta on clean dish towel and cover with damp dish towel to keep from drying out. Repeat rolling process with 4 remaining pieces of dough.

4. Use pizza wheel or sharp knife to cut 1 pasta sheet at a time into long rectangles measuring 4 inches across. Place teaspoon-size balls of filling 1 inch from bottom of sheet. Leave 1¼ inches between each ball. Fold pasta over filling. Press dough together around filling, sealing open sides with your finger. (If edges of dough seem dry, dab with water.) After trimming edges, run pastry wheel between balls of filling to cut out ravioli. Transfer finished ravioli to floured baking sheet, cover with damp dish towel, and set aside. Repeat shaping process with remaining pasta sheets and filling. (Towel-covered baking sheets of ravioli can be wrapped tightly in plastic and refrigerated for up to 4 hours.)

5. FOR THE SAUCE: Before cooking ravioli, combine butter, hazelnuts, sage, and salt in 10-inch skillet over medium-high heat and cook, swirling skillet constantly, until butter is melted and has golden-brown color and nutty aroma, about 3 minutes. Off heat, stir in lemon juice; set aside.

6. Bring 4 quarts water to boil in large pot. Add 1 tablespoon salt and half of ravioli. Cook, stirring often and lowering heat if necessary to keep water at gentle boil, until ravioli are tender, about 2 minutes. Using slotted spoon or spider skimmer, transfer cooked ravioli to warm serving platter, spoon some butter sauce over top, and cover with aluminum foil to keep warm. Return water to boil, cook remaining ravioli, and transfer to platter. Swirl 2 tablespoons ravioli cooking water into remaining butter sauce, then pour sauce over ravioli, top with shaved Parmesan, and serve immediately.

Inside This Chapter

CHAPTER 5

How to Cook Rice, Grains, and Beans

Rice, grains, and beans are inexpensive and nutritious, and because they are shelf-stable, they are central to any well-stocked pantry. Grains (a category that technically includes rice) and beans are both small, hard, dry seeds. In this chapter, we will explore two methods for preparing white rice, a foolproof method for cooking brown rice, a novel technique for cooking creamy polenta, as well as general approaches to cooking dried beans and the most popular grains.

Getting Started

Rice 101

All rice (except wild) starts out as brown rice. A grain of rice is made up of endosperm, germ, bran, and hull or husk. Brown rice is simply husked and cleaned. White rice has the germ and bran removed. This makes the rice cook up faster and softer, and it's more shelf-stable, but this process also removes much of the fiber, protein, and other nutrients, as well as flavor.

LONG-GRAIN WHITE RICE

This broad category includes generic long-grain rice as well as aromatic varieties such as basmati (see below), Texmati, and jasmine. The grains are slender and elongated and measure four to five times longer than they are wide. It cooks up light and fluffy with firm, distinct grains, making it good for pilafs and salads. Avoid converted rice, which is parboiled during processing. This tan-colored rice cooks up too separate in our opinion, and the flavor seems a bit off.

MEDIUM-GRAIN WHITE RICE

This category includes a wide variety of specialty rices used to make risotto (Arborio) and paella (Valencia), as well as many Japanese and Chinese brands. The grains are fat and measure two to three times longer than they are wide. It cooks up a bit sticky (the starch is what makes risotto so creamy), and when simmered, the grains clump together, making this rice a common choice in Chinese restaurants.

SHORT-GRAIN WHITE RICE

With the exception of sushi, we don't eat much short-grain rice in this country. The grains are almost round, and the texture is quite sticky and soft when cooked.

BROWN RICE

As with white rice, brown rice comes in a variety of grain sizes: short, medium, and long. Long-grain brown rice, the best choice for pilafs, cooks up fluffy with separate grains. Medium-grain brown rice is a bit more sticky, perfect for risotto, paella, and similar dishes. Short-grain brown rice is the most sticky, ideal for sushi and other Asian dishes where getting the grains to clump together is desired.

BASMATI RICE

Prized for its nutty flavor and sweet aroma, basmati rice is eaten in pilafs and biryanis and with curries. Indian basmati is aged for a minimum of one year, though often much longer, before being packaged. Aging dehydrates the rice, which translates into grains that, once cooked, expand greatly. We don't recommend American-grown basmati.

WILD RICE

Wild rice is technically not in the same family as other rices; it's actually an aquatic grass. Wild rice is North America's only native grain. It grows naturally in lakes and is cultivated in man-made paddies in Minnesota, California, and Canada. We prefer brands that parboil the grains during processing.

Beans 101

Beans and lentils (and split peas) are generally classified as legumes. These tiny fruits or seeds are nutrient-dense and versatile. Look for specimens that are uniform in size and that have a smooth exterior. Avoid batches with many broken bits.

DRIED BEANS

Dried beans come in a range of colors, shapes, and sizes, with flavors from earthy to nutty. Cooking times vary greatly, depending on the type of bean and its age. Buy them at a store with good turnover; very old beans can refuse to soften. Note that beans can have trouble softening when cooked in mineral-rich tap water (hard water). If you are in a hard-water area, cook dried beans in bottled water.

CANNED BEANS

We use convenient canned beans in many soups and salads. Buy brands with some added salt for flavor, and rinse them thoroughly before use. Because of the way they cook and absorb moisture, it's hard to replace dried beans in a recipe

with canned. On some occasions (such as for a salad or quick pasta dish), a recipe might call for dried beans to be cooked, drained, and then added. In these instances, you can substitute canned beans. A general rule is that 1 pound of dried beans equals 58 ounces of canned beans.

LENTILS

Lentils come in dozens of sizes and colors. Although lentils are not traditionally soaked, we find that brining them in warm salt water for an hour improves their texture. French green lentils, or *lentilles du Puy,* are our preferred choice for most recipes, but supermarket brown lentils are fine for salads and soups. Red and yellow lentils disintegrate completely when cooked and are best used in Indian recipes, such as dal.

Grains 101

There are more than a dozen grains sold in your typical natural foods store, and almost as many at the supermarket. The following are our favorites. This list includes cornmeal and couscous, which are not seeds, and therefore technically not grains, but we include them here since they are prepared and served like grains. To prevent oxidation, whole grains are best stored in the freezer. You can store grains in the pantry—just make sure they are in an airtight container, and use them within six months.

BARLEY

Best known in this country as a staple used in soups, this high-fiber grain has a nutty, subtly sweet flavor that makes it an ideal accompaniment to meat, chicken, and fish. Both hulled and pearl barley (the most widely available varieties) are stripped of their tough outer covering, but we prefer quicker-cooking pearl barley, which has been polished to remove the bran layer as well. For a hearty alternative to risotto, substitute pearl barley for the Arborio rice typically used. Like rice, the barley will release starches when stirred, creating a creamy consistency. Be sure to add extra liquid since barley takes a bit longer to cook.

BULGUR

Bulgur is made from wheat berries that have been steamed or boiled and then ground into fine, medium, coarse, or very coarse grain. Don't confuse it with cracked wheat, which is not parcooked. Instead of simmering it in water, we often reconstitute fine- or medium-grain bulgur by soaking it in water flavored with lemon, lime, or tomato juice.

FARRO

A favorite ingredient in Tuscan cuisine, these hulled whole-wheat kernels boast a sweet, nutty flavor and chewy bite. In Italy, the grain is available in three sizes, but the midsize (*farro medio*) type is most common in the United States. When cooked, the grains are tender with a slight chew, similar to al dente pasta. Farro takes best to the pasta cooking method because abundant water cooks the grains evenly.

MILLET

The mellow corn flavor and fine texture of these tiny seeds make them extremely versatile in both savory and sweet applications, including flatbreads, polenta-like puddings, and pan-fried cakes. We particularly like them in pilafs or even just mixed with a pat of butter. Millet cooks up quite soft. Slightly overcooking millet causes the seeds to burst and release starch, creating a creamy consistency that makes this grain ideal for breakfast porridge.

QUINOA

Quinoa is often referred to as a "super-grain" because it's a nutritionally complete protein. We love the pinhead-size seeds (which can be white, red, black, or purple) for their faint crunch and mineral taste. When cooked, the grains will unfurl and expand to about three times their size. Toast quinoa in a dry (no oil or butter) pot before adding water; we've found that toasting it in fat gives the grain a slightly bitter flavor.

WHEAT BERRIES

These are not berries at all but whole husked wheat kernels that have a rich, earthy flavor and firm chew. Because they're unprocessed, they remain firm (though softened), smooth, and distinct when cooked, which makes them great for salads. We toast wheat berries in oil before adding them to the water, because it brings out their nutty flavor.

CORNMEAL/POLENTA

Cornmeal can be labeled anything from yellow grits to corn semolina. Forget the names. When shopping for the right product to make polenta, there are three things to consider: "instant" or "quick-cooking" versus the traditional style; degerminated or full-grain meal; and grind size. Avoid instant and quick-cooking, which are parcooked and comparatively bland. Though we love the full-corn flavor of whole-grain cornmeal, it remains slightly gritty no matter how long you cook it. We prefer degerminated cornmeal, in which the hard hull and germ are removed from each kernel (check the back label or ingredient list to see if cornmeal is degerminated; if it's not labeled as such, you can assume it's whole grain). As for grind, we found coarser grains are best for polenta. Finer grinds are fine for baking muffins or cornbread. Grind coarseness can vary dramatically from brand to brand, and labels aren't very helpful; look for grains about the size of couscous.

COUSCOUS

Couscous is a starch made from durum semolina, the high-protein wheat flour that is also used to make Italian pasta. Traditional Moroccan couscous is made by rubbing coarse-ground durum semolina and water between the hands to form small granules. The couscous is then dried and cooked over a simmering stew in a steamer called a couscoussier. About the size of bread crumbs, the boxed couscous found in most supermarkets is a precooked version that needs only a few minutes of steeping in hot liquid in order to be fully cooked. Israeli couscous, also known as pearl couscous, is larger than traditional couscous (about the size of a caper) and is not precooked. It has a unique, nutty flavor.

Essential Equipment

Cooking rice, grains, and beans requires very few pieces of equipment. A large saucepan, Dutch oven, colander, and fine-mesh strainer are most often used and items you likely already have on hand. Additionally, a nonstick saucepan is good for making rice pilaf. See pages 20, 21, and 31 for more details on these items.

How to Make Rice Pilaf

Rice pilaf should be fragrant, fluffy, and tender. Recipes abound but none seem to agree on the best method for guaranteeing these results. Many espouse rinsing the rice and soaking it overnight; while we found that rinsing removes excess surface starch on the grains (and thus promotes a fluffy texture), overnight soaking made the pilaf soggy. We found that most recipes use too much water to avoid scorching, and the resulting pilaf is sticky and soft. Our recipe uses far less water and relies on very low heat and a nonstick saucepan to reduce the risk of scorching. The recipe here will serve six people; you can double it to serve 10 to 12. Use 4½ cups water and 3 cups rice, and switch to a Dutch oven. To make rice pilaf in advance, once the rice has been fluffed, transfer it to a microwave-safe bowl, cover tightly, and refrigerate for up to two days. To reheat, microwave until the rice is hot, 12 to 14 minutes, fluff with a fork, and season to taste. For variations on this recipe, see page 204.

ESSENTIAL EQUIPMENT

- fine-mesh strainer
- large saucepan, preferably nonstick, with lid
- chef's knife
- heat-resistant rubber spatula
- liquid measuring cup
- dish towel
- fork

1. RINSE RICE

Place 1½ cups long-grain white, basmati, jasmine, or Texmati rice in fine-mesh strainer and rinse under cold running water until water runs clear, occasionally stirring rice lightly with your hand. Set strainer over bowl to drain.

WHY? Rinsing washes away excess starch that otherwise will make pilaf sticky and gummy. You can make pilaf with any long-grain white rice. Basmati makes a particularly fluffy and fragrant rice pilaf, but regular long-grain white rice works well, too.

2. COOK ONION

Heat 1 tablespoon olive oil or unsalted butter in large saucepan, preferably nonstick, over medium heat until shimmering. Add 1 small finely chopped onion and ¼ teaspoon salt and cook, stirring occasionally, until onion is softened, about 5 minutes.

WHY? The sautéed onion provides depth to this simple dish. The salt helps the onion release its juices and soften more quickly. If you want plain pilaf, you can omit the onion and add the salt with the water. If you tend to season foods more aggressively, increase the amount of salt to ½ teaspoon.

3. TOAST RICE

Stir in rice and cook, stirring often, until edges of grains begin to turn translucent, about 3 minutes.

WHY? Toasting the rice highlights its nutty flavor and helps it to cook up fluffy and light. Make sure the rice is not scorching, and be prepared to adjust the heat if necessary. The rice should smell fragrant but shouldn't change color.

4. USE LESS WATER

Stir in 2¼ cups water and bring to simmer. Reduce heat to low, cover, and continue to simmer until rice is tender and water is absorbed, 16 to 18 minutes.

WHY? Most rice recipes call for too much water, and the end result is soggy rice. We have found that a ratio of 3 parts water to 2 parts rice yields fluffier results. Make sure to bring the water to a simmer before turning down the heat. Once the lid is in place, don't stir the rice. The gentle heat (adjust the heat setting as low as possible) will prevent scorching. And don't peek—you don't want to let steam or heat escape.

5. STEAM OFF HEAT

Remove pot from heat and lay folded dish towel underneath lid. Let sit for 10 minutes.

WHY? To ensure that all the grains are evenly cooked, we let the rice rest, off the heat, for 10 minutes. Heat trapped in the pot will ensure that all grains, even those at the top of the pot, will be tender. A dish towel placed under the lid while the rice rests absorbs any excess moisture in the pot and keeps the rice from becoming gummy.

6. FLUFF AND SERVE

Fluff rice with fork, season with salt and pepper to taste, and serve immediately.

WHY? A fork (rather than a spoon or a spatula) will do the best job of separating the individual grains and producing a light, fluffy pilaf. Don't stir the rice too much, or you can break up the grains and make the pilaf starchy. It's best to sprinkle salt and pepper over the rice as you fluff it—this will distribute the seasonings evenly.

Troubleshooting Rice Pilaf

PROBLEM	SOLUTION
My pilaf has a tannish color and doesn't seem as flavorful as I expected.	If you use converted long-grain rice, this can be problem. This product, designed to cook up with separate grains, is made by steaming the grains still in the husk (hence the tannish color). We think the process affects flavor negatively, and the appearance is a bit off-putting. We prefer regular long-grain or basmati rice.
Basmati rice from India is pricey. Can I use cheaper domestic brands?	The quality of domestic basmati doesn't compare to authentic Indian basmati. In our tests, American basmati weren't nearly as aromatic as Indian, and the cooked grains were soft and stubby. If you want to save money, use regular long-grain white rice.

How to Cook Brown Rice

ESSENTIAL EQUIPMENT

- Dutch oven with tight-fitting lid
- chef's knife
- wooden spoon
- fork
- dish towel

Brown rice is considered a whole grain and a good source of fiber since each grain has the bran, a nutrient-rich coating, still attached. However, the bran makes cooking brown rice more of a challenge than cooking white rice. The tough coating makes it difficult for liquid to penetrate into the grain, which can lead to uneven cooking and extended cooking times. To avoid the pitfalls of burnt rice and undercooked grains, we found the oven to be the perfect solution. Although baking the rice in the oven doesn't save time, it provides more precise temperature control than the stovetop does, and the steady, even heat eliminates the risk of scorching (especially on the bottom of the pot, which invariably happens on the stovetop). This foolproof method produces light, fluffy grains every time. We like long-grain brown rice, but short-grain or medium-grain brown rice can be used in this recipe—they will cook up a bit more sticky but the formula is the same. There's no need to rinse brown rice before cooking since there's no surface starch to wash away. For variations on this recipe, see page 205.

1. COOK ONION

Heat 1 tablespoon olive oil in Dutch oven over medium heat until shimmering. Add 1 small finely chopped onion and ¼ teaspoon salt and cook, stirring occasionally, until browned, 12 to 14 minutes.

WHY? Browned onion provides sweetness that contrasts nicely with the slightly bitter, earthy flavor of the brown rice. Adding a little salt draws moisture out of the onion and ensures even cooking without scorching. A Dutch oven, with its heavy bottom and tight-fitting lid, is essential in this recipe—both to ensure even browning of the onion and for the oven portion of the recipe.

2. ADD WATER AND BROTH, THEN RICE

Add 2¼ cups water and 1 cup chicken broth, cover, and bring to boil. Off heat, stir in 1½ cups long-grain brown rice.

WHY? A little chicken broth adds savory notes to this dish, although you can use all water if you prefer. (Replacing the chicken broth with vegetable broth also works well.) Don't replace the entire amount of water with broth—the rice would taste too chicken-y.

3. BAKE UNTIL TENDER

Cover pot and place on middle rack in 375-degree oven. Bake until rice is tender, 65 to 70 minutes.

WHY? A tight-fitting lid is essential. If the lid rattles, too much steam is escaping and the rice might not cook fully. If in doubt, cover the pot first with a piece of heavy-duty aluminum foil, crimping the edges tightly around the rim of the pot, then with the lid. Don't stir the rice or open the pot as it cooks—this will just slow down the cooking time.

4. FLUFF WITH FORK

Remove pot from oven, uncover, and fluff rice with fork, scraping up any rice stuck to bottom. **WHY?** A fork does a nice job of separating the individual grains.

5. STEAM OFF HEAT

Lay clean folded dish towel underneath lid. Let sit for 10 minutes. Season with salt and pepper to taste and serve.

WHY? Letting the rice rest off the heat for 10 minutes ensures that all of the grains are tender. The towel absorbs excess moisture that otherwise might make the rice soggy and heavy.

Finishing with Flavor

You can certainly build flavor into brown rice from the outset by sautéing vegetables or adding other spices. (See the recipes on page 205 for some ideas.) But it's just as easy to finish with a burst of flavor. Simply stir in any of these ingredients (or a combination of these ingredients) when fluffing the rice.

INGREDIENT	AMOUNT
Fresh herbs, minced	¼ cup parsley, basil, mint, or cilantro
Lemon, lime, or orange zest	½ to 1 teaspoon grated
Lemon, lime, or orange juice	½ to 1 teaspoon
Parmesan cheese, grated	¼ to ½ cup
Feta cheese, crumbled	½ cup
Frozen peas, thawed	1 cup
Jarred roasted red peppers	¾ cup finely chopped

Troubleshooting Brown Rice

PROBLEM	SOLUTION
The rice isn't cooked through in the specified amount of time.	It's important to bring the liquid to a boil before adding the rice. If you skip this step, the rice will need more time in the oven; this is likely the result if the rice isn't done and there's still liquid in the pot. If the rice isn't done but the pot is dry, it may be that the lid on your Dutch oven is too loose, and a lot of water, in the form of steam, has escaped into the oven. You can add a bit more water and return the pot to the oven. Next time, first cover the top with heavy-duty aluminum foil, then the lid.
The rice seems heavy and starchy.	For the fluffiest results, use long-grain brown rice rather than starchier medium-grain or short-grain brown rice. That said, don't ever expect brown rice to be as light and fluffy as long-grain white rice. When properly cooked, the grains should separate from each other, but they will never really be "light."
The rice has a funky taste.	Brown rice becomes rancid much more quickly than refined white rice. The natural oils in the bran and germ are the culprit. Buy brown rice from a store that has a good turnover and use it up within a few months. (Don't buy a 5-pound bag at a wholesale club unless you make brown rice several times a month.) To prolong freshness, store brown rice (like other whole grains) in a zipper-lock bag in the freezer.

How to Make Chinese-Style Rice

ESSENTIAL EQUIPMENT

• fine-mesh strainer
• large saucepan with lid

When making rice pilaf (page 182), the goal is to produce a dish with separate grains. The texture should be light and fluffy and the grains of rice relatively firm and dry. Chinese-style rice is quite different, in part because of the way it's served (with saucy stir-fries) and eaten (with chopsticks). Chinese-style rice should be soft (to soak up sauces) and sticky (so it clumps on the ends of chopsticks). Changing the ratio of the water to rice, as some recipes suggest, just makes the rice soggy or crunchy. Instead, you need to change the cooking method. While pilaf is about minimizing starch development, Chinese-style rice is cooked in such a way to bring out just the right amount of starch, without compromising the integrity of the individual grains. The following makes enough rice to serve four to six with a stir-fry. You can use a nonstick saucepan to prepare this recipe, but it is not required.

1. RINSE RICE

Place 2 cups long-grain white rice in fine-mesh strainer. Rinse under cold running water, swishing with hands until water runs clear.

WHY? There's a lot of starch on the outside of white rice grains. If you don't rinse the rice, the finished dish will be gluey rather than sticky. The water will run cloudy at first (that's the starch). Once the water runs clear, you're done.

2. BOIL VIGOROUSLY

Bring rice, 3 cups water, and ½ teaspoon salt to boil in large saucepan over medium-high heat. Cook, uncovered, until water level drops below surface of rice and small holes form, about 5 minutes.

WHY? The boiling water agitates the rice just enough to cause the release of starch. Do not stir the rice—we found that stirring is too rough because it causes the individual grains to break up. Once the water level drops below the surface of the rice, tiny holes will emerge. Once you see those holes, it's a sign that enough starch has been released and it's time to turn down the heat.

3. COVER AND COOK GENTLY

Reduce heat to low, cover, and cook until rice is tender and water is fully absorbed, about 15 minutes. Serve.

WHY? Once the water level drops below the surface of the rice, you must lower the heat (otherwise you risk scorching the rice). The cover ensures even cooking of all the grains in the pot. There's no need to fluff or let the rice steam off the heat since the grains are supposed to clump together. That said, if you're still working on the main course, the finished rice can stand off the heat, covered, for up to 15 minutes.

How to Make Creamy Polenta

ESSENTIAL EQUIPMENT

- large saucepan, with heavy bottom and tight-fitting lid
- wooden spoon or rubber spatula
- whisk
- rasp-style grater

Polenta is traditionally a labor of love. Classic recipes call for stirring cornmeal into a pot of salted water and then cooking—and stirring—for nearly an hour. Although the cornmeal appears to absorb the water quickly, it actually takes a long time for the granules to soften fully and lose their gritty texture. And the constant stirring is necessary to ensure even cooking. Our method alleviates the need for constant stirring with super-low heat and a covered pot. The cover traps steam, which helps distribute heat evenly in the pot without stirring. And the low heat (and a heavy-bottomed pan) means no scorching. The polenta should do little more than release wisps of steam as it cooks. Coarse-ground cornmeal, with grains the size of couscous, works best. We like degerminated cornmeal, which cooks up creamier and is less likely to become rancid than whole-grain cornmeal. Avoid instant and quick-cooking products. Polenta is a flexible staple: Serve it as is as a side dish or turn into an entrée by topping it with sautéed vegetables and beans, a saucy tomato-based ragu, or sausage.

1. SPIKE WATER WITH BAKING SODA

Bring 7½ cups water to boil in heavy-bottomed large saucepan over medium-high heat. Stir in 1½ teaspoons salt and pinch baking soda.

WHY? Because water is better able to penetrate cornmeal in an alkaline environment, a pinch of baking soda shaves 30 minutes from the cooking time and makes the polenta creamier. Don't use more than a pinch, or it will impart a soapy flavor.

2. ADD CORNMEAL SLOWLY, THEN COVER AND COOK ON LOW

Slowly pour in 1½ cups coarse-ground degerminated cornmeal in steady stream while stirring with wooden spoon or rubber spatula. Bring mixture to boil, stirring constantly, about 1 minute. Reduce heat to lowest setting. Cover.

WHY? If the cornmeal is poured in all at once and without stirring, it will form stubborn clumps that cannot simply be whisked out. Low heat prevents scorching and is absolutely essential to success, as is a tight-fitting lid.

3. WHISK, THEN WALK AWAY

After 5 minutes, whisk polenta to smooth out any lumps, about 15 seconds. Scrape down sides and bottom of pan. Cover and continue to cook, without stirring, until grains are tender but slightly al dente, about 25 minutes longer.

WHY? If the polenta bubbles or sputters even slightly after the first 10 minutes, the heat is too high. You may need a flame tamer—a metal disk that sits over the burner and tempers the heat. On a gas stove, you can shape aluminum foil into a 1-inch-thick ring that will fit on the burner.

4. ENRICH, REST, AND SERVE

Remove polenta from heat, stir in 2 cups grated Parmesan, 2 tablespoons unsalted butter, and season with pepper to taste. Let stand, covered, for 5 minutes.

WHY? The butter gives the polenta a glossy finish; the cheese adds flavor. Omit the cheese (but not the butter) if you prefer a simple side dish.

How to Cook Grains

There are two basic ways to cook grains—either with a measured amount of water or in abundant water. The latter method (called the pasta method) is best for larger grains that take a long time to cook. Simply boil them in a big pot of salted water and drain when tender. With so much water in the pot, there's no risk of the pot running dry. and all that water ensures even, thorough cooking. For smaller grains, we treat them like rice and cook them in a covered pot over low heat, using either the absorption or the pilaf method. Once all the water has been absorbed, the grains are done—assuming you have started with the right amount of water. In general, we prefer the pilaf method because it adds a nutty, toasted flavor. However, the absorption method can work well in dishes where the grains will be seasoned aggressively once they are cooked. While we cook coarse bulgur using the absorption method, you can reconstitute fine- or medium-grain bulgur by soaking it in water flavored with lemon, lime, or tomato juice for 60 to 90 minutes. The exact amounts of water and grain needed, and the cooking time, will depend on the grain you are using; see chart on opposite page.

ESSENTIAL EQUIPMENT

- fine-mesh strainer
- rimmed baking sheet
- dish towel
- mixing bowl
- liquid measuring cup
- medium saucepan or Dutch oven
- heat-resistant rubber spatula

1. RINSE WELL

Rinse grains in fine-mesh strainer under cold running water until water runs clear. Drain briefly. **WHY?** Most grains should be rinsed before cooking to remove surface starch, detritus, or bitter coatings, Note that some quinoa is sold "prewashed," but if you're unsure rinse it anyway to be sure to remove its saponin coating, which is mildly toxic.

2. DRY ON TOWEL

Spread grains on rimmed baking sheet lined with clean dish towel. Let dry for 15 minutes. To remove grains from towel, pick up towel by corners and gently shake grains into mixing bowl. **WHY?** Soggy grains can throw off the water-to-grain ratio. Also, soggy grains are hard to toast. There's no need to dry grains if cooking them via the pasta method.

3A. COOK VIA ABSORPTION METHOD

Combine 1 cup rinsed and dried grains, water, and ½ teaspoon salt in medium saucepan. Bring mixture to simmer, then reduce heat to low, cover, and simmer until grains are tender and liquid is absorbed. Off heat, let sit, covered, for 10 minutes. Fluff with fork and serve. **WHY?** This is the simplest way to prepare small grains, including bulgur, millet, and quinoa. It's ideal when using these grains in salads or other dishes. If you want fluffy rather than sticky grains, place a clean folded dish towel between the pot and lid during the resting step to absorb excess moisture.

3B. COOK VIA PILAF METHOD

Heat 1 tablespoon unsalted butter or oil in medium saucepan over medium-high heat until melted or shimmering, according to recipe. Add 1 cup rinsed and dried grains and toast until lightly golden and fragrant, about 3 minutes. Add ½ teaspoon salt and water. Bring mixture to simmer, then reduce heat to low, cover, and simmer until grains are tender and liquid is absorbed. Off heat, let sit, covered, for 10 minutes. Fluff with fork and serve.

WHY? Toasting the grains in fat develops nutty flavor (however, we toast quinoa in a dry pan since toasting in fat makes the grain taste slightly bitter). You can also sauté spices and aromatics before adding grains; swap in chicken broth for some of the water; and stir in fresh herbs before serving. If you want fluffy rather than sticky grains, place a clean folded dish towel under the lid during the resting step to absorb moisture.

3C. COOK VIA PASTA METHOD

Bring 4 quarts water to boil in Dutch oven. Stir in 1 cup rinsed grains and 1 tablespoon salt (for wheat berries, only add ¼ teaspoon salt). Return to boil, reduce heat to low, and simmer until grains are tender. Drain in strainer in sink. Let sit in strainer for 5 minutes before using (or pat dry with paper towels) to remove excess moisture.

WHY? This method cooks grains in abundant water and is well suited to larger grains (like barley, farro, and wheat berries) that might not cook evenly in the small amount of water used in the absorption and pilaf methods. In some cases (barley, wheat berries), toasting the grains before adding the water lends a flavor boost. Grains cooked this way are ready to use in salads and soups. To quickly cool boiled grains for a salad, rinse them with cold running water after draining.

Cooking Various Grains

Use this chart to determine the amount of water and the cooking time needed to prepare 1 cup of grains. Most grains should be rinsed first. If using the absorption or pilaf methods, they should be rinsed and dried well. You can cook 2 or 3 cups of raw grains listed below using the pasta method with no changes to the water or cook time. You can cook 2 cups of grains using the absorption or pilaf method by doubling the amount of water and salt; the cooking time might require a few extra minutes.

GRAIN	METHOD(S)	WATER	TIME	YIELD
Barley	Pasta	4 quarts	20–25 minutes	3½–4 cups
Bulgur, coarse-grind	Absorption	1 cup	13–18 minutes	2¼ cups
Farro	Pasta	4 quarts	15–20 minutes	3 cups
Millet	Absorption or Pilaf	2¼ cups	25–30 minutes	2¼ cups
Quinoa	Absorption or Pilaf	1 cup	16–18 minutes	2¾ cups
Wheat Berries	Pasta	4 quarts	1 hour	3 cups

How to Cook Dried Beans

Dried beans—everything from chickpeas to black beans—have a far superior texture and better flavor than canned beans. It's not hard to cook dried beans, but it does require some planning. Ideally, you will soak beans the day before you cook them. (However, we do have a quick-soak method that requires just 1 hour.) Once beans have been cooked, they can be used in salads, soups, stews, or chili. Note that some recipes—including Cuban Black Beans and Rice on page 196—call for reserving some of the bean cooking liquid; it's actually quite flavorful and can be used to cook rice or grains, to puree beans for dips or refried beans, or as a "broth" to build a flavorful soup or stew. If cooking dried beans as part of another dish, follow the first few steps to rinse, pick through, and soak the beans. And make sure to hold back on adding acidic ingredients until the beans are nearly done. For an example of how we cook soaked beans as part of another recipe, see the Recipe Tutorial for Hearty Tuscan Bean Stew on page 200.

ESSENTIAL EQUIPMENT

- colander or fine-mesh strainer
- large bowl or container
- Dutch oven
- wooden spoon

1. RINSE AND PICK THROUGH
Place 1 pound dried beans in colander or fine-mesh strainer and rinse well, picking through to remove any stones as well as beans that are broken or shriveled.

WHY? Rinsing the beans washes away any traces of soil. Beans often contain little pebbles; make sure to comb through the beans with your fingers to find and remove all foreign matter. Finally, discard any broken or shriveled beans.

2A. SALT-SOAK, OVERNIGHT METHOD
Pour 4 quarts cold water into large bowl or container. Add 2 tablespoons salt and stir to dissolve. Add beans and soak at room temperature for at least 8 hours or up to 24 hours.

WHY? Soaking shortens the cooking time and results in creamier beans with fewer burst or starchy samples. Soaking beans in salt water is more effective than soaking them in plain water; the sodium and calcium ions in the salt weaken the structure of the beans' skin, allowing water to penetrate more easily. The result is a creamy bean with a softer skin.

2B. SALT-SOAK, QUICK METHOD
Bring 2 quarts water to boil in Dutch oven. Slide pot off heat. Add 3 tablespoons salt and stir to dissolve. Add beans and soak, off heat, for 1 hour.

WHY? The overnight soak is more effective than this quick-soak method, but a quick soak is certainly better than no soak.

3. DRAIN AND RINSE
Drain beans, discarding soaking liquid, and rinse well before cooking.

WHY? Don't try to use the soaking liquid for cooking the beans—it's too salty. In addition, the soaking liquid contains some of the complex carbohydrates in beans that many people have trouble digesting. Soaking beans (and discarding this liquid) can reduce this discomfort. Once the beans are drained, rinse them to wash away any traces of salt.

4. SIMMER GENTLY

Bring 4 quarts water, soaked beans, and 1 teaspoon salt to boil in Dutch oven. Reduce heat to gentle simmer and cook, stirring occasionally, until beans are tender, 40 to 60 minutes.

WHY? Once the beans have been soaked and rinsed, they are ready to be cooked. The key is to use gentle heat. (If the beans are boiled, the violent churning of the water will blow them apart.) So as soon as the water has come to a boil, reduce the heat to a gentle simmer. Also, make sure to add some salt to the water—it will season the beans. The timing will depend on the freshness of the beans and variety. If most of the beans are perfectly cooked but a few are lagging behind, cover the pot and set it aside for a few minutes to let gentle residual heat soften the remaining beans without overcooking the others.

5. DRAIN

Drain beans in colander, reserving cooking liquid as needed for recipes.

WHY? Once the beans are cooked, they should be drained and used in salads, soups, stews, and other recipes. In certain recipes, you might be instructed to reserve some of the cooking water (for soups and stews, for instance).

Troubleshooting Beans

PROBLEM	SOLUTION
Can I soak beans longer than 24 hours?	Soaking beans for more than a day isn't a good idea because the beans will lose flavor and develop a mealy texture. If you aren't ready to cook beans when they are done soaking, you can transfer the soaked and drained beans to an airtight container and refrigerate them for up to 4 days before cooking them.
My beans aren't softening, despite prolonged cooking.	If your beans are extremely old (which can be hard to tell), they might take a very long time to cook. Another possible culprit is hard water. A pinch of baking soda (no more than ¼ teaspoon) can help combat the effect of the hard water. Another option is to use bottled water when cooking the beans. Finally, don't add acidic ingredients (like canned tomatoes or vinegar) to the pot until the beans are nearly cooked.
Can I flavor the soaking liquid?	Yes, but you need to use ingredients with big flavors, such as garlic, onion, and fresh herbs. We found that pureeing the garlic and herbs helped release their flavor, and potent herbs (such as oregano) add more flavor to beans than milder herbs (like parsley). When soaking a batch of beans, try four pureed garlic cloves, a sliced onion, or ⅓ cup minced fresh herb. That said, it's probably easier to flavor beans as they cook.

Almost Hands-Free Risotto with Chicken

Recipe Stats

TOTAL TIME **1½ hours**
PREPARATION TIME **15 minutes**
ACTIVE COOKING TIME **1 hour**
YIELD **6 servings**
MAKE AHEAD **Serve immediately**
DIFFICULTY **Easy**

Tools

- Dutch oven *
- large saucepan
- chef's knife
- cutting board
- dry measuring cups
- liquid measuring cup
- measuring spoons
- citrus juicer
- instant-read thermometer
- kitchen shears
- kitchen timer **
- ladle
- large plate
- rasp-style grater
- tongs
- wooden spoon
- paper towels

* A heavy-bottomed Dutch oven conducts heat evenly and steadily, which is important for evenly cooked risotto, and a tight-fitting lid traps heat and moisture inside the pot.
** This unconventional cooking method for risotto leaves you free to do other tasks in the kitchen as the rice cooks, but it does require careful timing. We recommend that you use a timer when simmering the rice to ensure that the rice does not wind up soft and overcooked.

Overview

Risotto is a classic rice dish from northern Italy. It's well loved for its lush, velvety texture and al dente rice grains; the medium-grain Italian rice that's used to make risotto releases its plentiful starch during cooking and gives the appearance of being bathed in a creamy sauce.

The traditional cooking method for risotto tethers the cook to the stove for at least 30 minutes of focused cooking and constant stirring. In the test kitchen, we devised an easier, almost no-stir technique that yields great-tasting results.

First, we swap out the saucepan for a Dutch oven, which has a thick, heavy bottom, deep sides, and a tight-fitting lid—perfect for trapping and distributing heat as evenly as possible. Classic recipes call for adding the broth in small increments (and stirring constantly after each addition), but we add most of the broth at once and cover the pan, allowing the rice to simmer until almost all of the broth is absorbed (stirring just twice). After adding the second and final addition of broth, we stir the pot to ensure the bottom doesn't cook more quickly than the top and turn off the heat. Without sitting over a direct flame, the sauce turns out perfectly creamy, and the rice is thickened, velvety, and just barely chewy.

Italians typically serve risotto as a first course or as an accompaniment to stews or braises, but since Americans often opt for risotto as a main dish, we've added shredded chicken to this recipe so that it's hearty enough to be the focal point of the meal. For a simple version with just Parmesan and herbs, see the recipe on page 207.

Ingredients

- 5 **cups chicken broth ***
- 2 **cups water**
- 1 **tablespoon olive oil**
- 2 **(12-ounce) bone-in split chicken breasts, trimmed and cut in half crosswise**
- 4 **tablespoons unsalted butter**
- 1 **large onion, chopped fine**
  Salt and pepper
- 1 **garlic clove, minced**
- 2 **cups Arborio rice**
- 1 **cup dry white wine**
- 2 **ounces Parmesan cheese, grated (1 cup) ****
- 2 **tablespoons chopped fresh parsley**
- 2 **tablespoons chopped fresh chives**
- 1 **teaspoon lemon juice**

* Homemade Chicken Stock (see recipe page 459) will yield the best-tasting risotto, but store-bought broth will work. Be sure to use a broth with a sodium content between 400 and 700 milligrams per serving, which allows you to control the saltiness of the stew. See page 38 for more information about broth.
** For best results, make sure to use genuine Italian Parmigiano-Reggiano, not domestically made Parmesan cheeses.

What Can Go Wrong

Here's a list of common mistakes cooks make when preparing this recipe.

COMMON MISTAKE	BAD OUTCOMES	WHAT YOU SHOULD DO
Using Wrong Rice	• The rice is mushy. • The risotto isn't creamy.	Don't attempt to make risotto unless you're using the right rice. There are several Italian varieties of rice, including Carnaroli and Vialone Nano, that can be used to make risotto. Our preference, however, is to stick with the classic choice, Arborio rice. It cooks up creamy and with a pleasantly al dente texture. Long-grain rice will be very mushy and not terribly creamy if you use it in this recipe.
Using Boneless, Skinless Chicken Breasts	• The broth isn't very chicken-y. • The chicken meat dries out.	We use bone-in, skin-on split chicken breasts in this recipe because the chicken meat cooks up moister and more flavorful on the bone. Since the chicken cooks in the broth that will later be used in the risotto, the bones impart additional flavor to this broth—and the finished dish. If you use boneless, skinless chicken breasts, the chicken won't add much flavor to the broth and the cooking time will be off, resulting in overcooked chicken meat.
Using Lightweight Pot	• The rice cooks unevenly. • The rice scorches on the bottom.	Use a heavy-bottomed Dutch oven for cooking the risotto. This unconventional cooking technique relies upon the even heat transfer of a pot with heft to help produce perfectly cooked grains of rice. In a flimsy, lightweight pot, the risotto will be prone to scorching on the bottom because of hot spots, and the grains near the surface may not cook through evenly.
Using All Chicken Broth, No Water	• The risotto tastes too chicken-y. • The risotto is too salty.	Make sure to dilute the chicken broth with water as the recipe instructs, and use store-bought chicken broth with a sodium content of 400 to 700 milligrams per serving if you're not using homemade. Chicken broth used full-strength yields risotto that tastes overwhelmingly of chicken; cutting the broth with water allows the other flavors in the dish to come through. Chicken broth with a moderate sodium content allows you to control the saltiness of the risotto—a sodium content any higher can result in risotto that tastes too salty, especially for salt-sensitive palates (remember, too, that Parmesan cheese contains a fair amount of sodium).
Not Stirring Rice During Simmering	• The rice grains near the surface are not cooked through. • The rice cooks unevenly.	Remember to stir the rice twice during cooking; set the timer as a reminder, if you're forgetful. Stirring redistributes the rice and liquid throughout the pot so that all the grains cook through evenly. It's especially important to mix the grains that were near the surface into the lower reaches of the pot, where the heat and moisture are more concentrated.
Not Stirring After Simmering	• The risotto is not very creamy. • The risotto is unevenly cooked.	The 3-minute stir at the end of simmering, after the final ¾ cup of hot liquid is added, jostles the rice grains so that they release their starch, which creates a rich, creamy consistency. At this point, the risotto is already quite thick, so stirring also redistributes the rice grains in the pot to ensure that every grain is as tender as the next.

1. Bring 5 cups chicken broth and 2 cups water to boil in large saucepan over high heat.

2. Reduce heat to medium-low to maintain gentle simmer.

3. Using chef's knife, cut 2 (12-ounce) bone-in, skin-on chicken breast halves in half crosswise.

4. Heat 1 tablespoon olive oil in large Dutch oven over medium heat until just starting to smoke.

5. Pat chicken dry with paper towels. Add chicken, skin side down, and cook without moving until golden brown, 4 to 6 minutes.

6. Flip chicken and cook second side until lightly browned, about 2 minutes.

7. Transfer chicken to saucepan of simmering broth. (Do not wash Dutch oven.) Cook until chicken registers 165 degrees, 10 to 15 minutes.

8. Transfer chicken to large plate.

9. Add 2 tablespoons unsalted butter to Dutch oven set over medium heat.

10. When butter has melted, add 1 large finely chopped onion and ¾ teaspoon salt.

11. Cook, stirring frequently, until onion is softened but not browned, 4 to 5 minutes.

12. Add 1 minced garlic clove and stir until fragrant, about 30 seconds.

13. Add 2 cups Arborio rice and cook, stirring frequently, until grains are translucent around edges, about 3 minutes.

14. Add 1 cup dry white wine and cook, stirring constantly, until fully absorbed, 2 to 3 minutes.

15. Stir 5 cups hot broth mixture into rice.

16. Reduce heat to medium-low, cover, and simmer until almost all liquid is absorbed and rice is just al dente, 16 to 18 minutes. Stir twice during cooking.

17. Add ¾ cup hot broth mixture to risotto and stir gently and constantly until risotto becomes creamy, about 3 minutes.

18. Stir in 1 cup grated Parmesan cheese.

19. Remove pot from heat, cover, and let stand for 5 minutes.

20. Meanwhile, remove and discard skin and bones from chicken, and shred meat into bite-size pieces.

21. Gently stir chicken, 2 tablespoons unsalted butter, 2 tablespoons each chopped parsley and chives, and 1 teaspoon lemon juice into risotto.

22. If desired, add up to ½ cup additional broth mixture to loosen texture of risotto.

23. Season with salt and pepper to taste. Serve immediately.

Cuban Black Beans and Rice

Recipe Stats

TOTAL TIME **10½ hours**
PREPARATION TIME **20 minutes**
ACTIVE COOKING TIME **1 hour**
YIELD **6 to 8 servings**
MAKE AHEAD **Serve immediately**
DIFFICULTY **Intermediate**

Tools

- Dutch oven *
- food processor
- chef's knife
- cutting board
- dry measuring cups
- liquid measuring cup
- measuring spoons

- colander
- fine-mesh strainer
- fork
- garlic press
- mixing bowls
- tongs
- wooden spoon

* Make sure to a use a large, heavy Dutch oven with a capacity of at least 6 quarts for this recipe.

Overview

Beans and rice—a humble comfort food—sounds like a simple proposition, but more often than not the dish ends up soggy, mushy, and completely bland, and there's not much comforting about it. We found that we couldn't just throw beans and rice into a pot and expect them to cook into a satisfying, toothsome mix, so we had to make some recipe refinements.

This recipe for Cuban-style beans and rice employs several core techniques discussed earlier in this chapter. First, the beans are salt-soaked. After being salt-soaked, they're simmered—not boiled, which would cause them to blow out—on the stovetop with aromatic vegetables until the beans are just tender. Long-grain rice is rinsed and then cooked using a variation on the pilaf technique (the rice here is stirred into sautéed aromatic vegetables but is not truly toasted as it would be for a proper pilaf). Finally, the precooked beans are simmered with the rice in a low oven—not on the stovetop—where the steady, gentle heat keeps the pot's contents from cooking too vigorously (and precludes the need for constant burner adjustments). The result is perfectly tender beans and fluffy rice.

Lean salt pork, aromatic vegetables (onion, green bell pepper, and garlic—known as *sofrito* in Cuban and Latin American cooking), and a good dose of ground cumin provide the flavor backbone for our Cuban Black Beans and Rice. It's a great accompaniment to just about any kind of meat, poultry, or fish preparation, or it can be served as a main course along with a simple salad. For a vegetarian variation on this recipe, see page 213.

Ingredients

      Salt
- 1   **cup dried black beans, picked over and rinsed**
- 2   **cups chicken broth ***
- 2   **cups water**
- 2   **large green bell peppers, halved, stemmed, and seeded**
- 1   **large onion, halved at equator and peeled, root end left intact ****
- 1   **head garlic, 5 cloves minced, rest of head halved at equator with skin left intact**
- 2   **bay leaves**
- 1½   **cups long-grain white rice**
- 2   **tablespoons olive oil**
- 6   **ounces lean salt pork, cut into ¼-inch dice ****
- 4   **teaspoons ground cumin**
- 1   **tablespoon minced fresh oregano**
- 2   **tablespoons red wine vinegar**
- 2   **scallions, sliced thin**
      Lime wedges

* For a vegetarian version of this recipe, use water instead of chicken broth, omit the salt pork, cook 1 tablespoon of tomato paste with the vegetables, and increase the salt added along with the precooked beans and vinegar to 1½ teaspoons.

** This preparation makes it easier to discard the spent onion at the end of the cooking process.

*** It's important to use lean—not fatty—salt pork. If you can't find it, substitute 6 slices of bacon. Bacon browns and renders more quickly than salt pork, so decrease the cooking time before adding the sofrito—the chopped aromatic vegetables—to 8 minutes from the 15 or 20 minutes that salt pork requires.

What Can Go Wrong

Here's a list of common mistakes cooks make when preparing this recipe.

COMMON MISTAKE	BAD OUTCOMES	WHAT YOU SHOULD DO
Shortening Soaking Time	• **The beans take longer to cook than indicated.** • **The beans cook up with an uneven texture.** • **The skins are tough.**	Plan ahead and allow the beans at least 8 hours of soaking time, or up to 24 hours. If the soaking time is cut short, the beans will not hydrate thoroughly, which means they'll take longer to cook and they may cook up unevenly. The salt may also not take full effect on the bean skins, so the skins may remain a bit tough even though the bean interiors may be tender. If you're short on time, use the quick-soak method: Place the rinsed beans in a large heat-resistant bowl. Bring 2 quarts of water and 1½ tablespoons salt to a boil, combine with the beans in a large bowl or container, and let the beans soak for 1 hour. Drain and rinse the beans and use them in place of the long-soaked beans.
Simmering Beans Too Vigorously	• **The beans explode.** • **The beans partially disintegrate.**	Simmer the beans very gently over low heat so that they don't burst or explode, and then disintegrate into the liquid. Don't be tempted to turn up the temperature in an attempt to get the beans to cook more quickly.
Using Salt Pork That Is Too Fatty	• **The rice and beans are greasy.** • **The salt pork is unpleasant to eat.**	At the grocery store, look for pieces of salt pork that contain large meaty streaks. If you can't find any such pieces, use 6 slices of bacon instead. The pork or bacon is used for flavoring, but should also be lean enough that the pieces are not unpleasant to eat.
Not Rinsing Rice	• **The rice is gluey.** • **The rice clumps together.**	This recipe calls for long-grain white rice, which should be rinsed before cooking to remove surface starch so that the grains cook up loose and fluffy. After rinsing, be sure to drain the rice well so that excess water clinging to the grains doesn't make it into the pot.
Cooking Rice and Beans on Stovetop	• **The rice cooks unevenly.** • **The rice sticks to bottom of pot.**	It may be tempting to keep the entire cooking action on the stovetop. Unfortunately, with so much food in the pot the rice will cook very unevenly on the stovetop. The grains on the bottom of the pot are likely to overcook (or stick) while the grains at the top of the pot will remain crunchy. Cooking the rice and beans in the even heat of the oven ensures perfect results.

1. Rinse 1 cup dried black beans and pick out any blemished beans and stones.

2. Dissolve 1½ tablespoons salt in 2 quarts cold water in large container. Add beans and soak at room temperature at least 8 hours or up to 24 hours.

3. Drain beans and rinse well.

4. Halve, stem, and seed 2 large green bell peppers.

5. Halve 1 large onion through root end. Peel halves.

6. Remove 5 cloves from 1 head garlic. Peel and mince. Keep skins on head and halve at equator.

7. Combine beans, 2 cups broth, 2 cups water, 1 bell pepper half, 1 onion half, halved garlic head, 2 bay leaves, and 1 teaspoon salt in Dutch oven.

8. Bring to simmer over medium-high heat. Cover and reduce heat to low. Cook until beans are just soft, 30 to 40 minutes.

9. Using tongs, remove and discard bell pepper, onion, garlic, and bay leaves.

10. Drain beans in colander set over large bowl, reserving 2½ cups cooking liquid. (Add water to equal 2½ cups if necessary.)

11. Set Dutch oven aside (do not wash it). Adjust oven rack to middle position and heat oven to 350 degrees.

12. Place 1½ cups long-grain white rice in large fine-mesh strainer and rinse under cold running water until water runs clear, about 1½ minutes.

13. Shake strainer vigorously to remove all excess water. Set rice aside.

14. Cut remaining 3 bell pepper halves and remaining onion half into 2-inch pieces.

15. Pulse bell pepper and onion in food processor until broken into rough ¼-inch pieces, about 8 pulses, scraping down sides of bowl as necessary.

16. In now-empty Dutch oven, heat 1 tablespoon olive oil and 6 ounces salt pork, cut into ¼-inch dice, over medium-low heat.

17. Cook, stirring frequently, until lightly browned and fat has rendered, 15 to 20 minutes.

18. Add remaining 1 tablespoon oil, chopped bell peppers and onion, 4 teaspoons ground cumin, and 1 tablespoon minced fresh oregano.

19. Increase heat to medium and continue to cook, stirring frequently, until vegetables are softened and beginning to brown, 10 to 15 minutes longer.

20. Add 5 minced garlic cloves and cook, stirring constantly, until fragrant, about 1 minute.

21. Add rice and stir to coat, about 30 seconds. Stir in beans, reserved bean cooking liquid, 2 tablespoons red wine vinegar, and ½ teaspoon salt.

22. Increase heat to medium-high and bring to simmer. Cover and transfer to oven. Bake until liquid is absorbed and rice is tender, about 30 minutes.

23. Fluff with fork and let rest, uncovered, 5 minutes.

24. Serve beans and rice, passing 2 thinly sliced scallions and lime wedges separately.

Hearty Tuscan Bean Stew

Recipe Stats

TOTAL TIME **10 hours**
PREPARATION TIME **15 minutes**
ACTIVE COOKING TIME **45 minutes**
YIELD **8 servings**
MAKE AHEAD **Serve immediately**
DIFFICULTY **Easy**

Tools

- Dutch oven *
- chef's knife
- cutting board
- paring knife
- dry measuring cups
- liquid measuring cup
- measuring spoons
- can opener
- colander
- dish towels
- fine-mesh strainer
- large container
- soupspoon
- vegetable peeler
- wooden spoon

* A heavy-bottomed Dutch oven conducts heat evenly and steadily, which is important for evenly cooked beans, and a tight-fitting lid traps heat and moisture inside the pot.

Overview

This simple, hearty bean stew hails from Tuscany and show-cases one of the region's favorite ingredients: cannellini beans. We've fortified this version of the dish with pancetta, aromatic vegetables, and hearty greens to make a meal in a bowl.

So that the beans cook up plump, whole, and tender-skinned, we soak them for at least 8 hours, or up to 24 hours, in salt water before cooking and cook the stew in a low oven. We discovered that gently cooking the beans in a 250-degree oven was the key to producing perfectly cooked beans that stayed intact. We added the tomatoes toward the end of cooking since their acid kept the beans from softening prop-erly. To complete our stew, we chose other traditional Tuscan flavors, including kale, lots of garlic, and a sprig of rosemary.

For an even more substantial dish, toast 1¼-inch slices of rustic bread under the broiler until golden on both sides and rub the cut sides with a crushed garlic clove. Set one piece of bread in the bottom of each serving bowl and ladle over the stew. Drizzle bowls of stew with good olive oil.

Ingredients

  Salt and pepper
1 **pound dried cannellini beans (2½ cups), picked over and rinsed**
1 **tablespoon extra-virgin olive oil, plus extra for drizzling**
6 **ounces pancetta, cut into ¼-inch pieces ***
1 **large onion, chopped**
2 **carrots, peeled and cut into ½-inch pieces**
2 **celery ribs, cut into ½-inch pieces**
8 **garlic cloves, lightly crushed and peeled**
4 **cups chicken broth ****
3 **cups water**
2 **bay leaves**
1 **pound kale or collard greens, stemmed and chopped into 1-inch pieces (about 8 cups loosely packed)**
1 **(14.5-ounce) can diced tomatoes, drained**
1 **sprig fresh rosemary**

* Pancetta is Italian unsmoked bacon. If it is unavailable, substitute 4 ounces of regular bacon (about 4 slices).
** Homemade Chicken Stock (see recipe page 459) will yield the best-tasting bean stew, but store-bought broth will work well, too. Be sure to use a broth with a sodium content between 400 and 700 milligrams per serving, which allows you to control the saltiness of the stew. See page 38 for more information about broth.

What Can Go Wrong

Here's a list of common mistakes cooks make when preparing this recipe.

COMMON MISTAKE	BAD OUTCOMES	WHAT YOU SHOULD DO
Shortening Soaking Time	• **The beans take longer to cook than indicated.** • **The beans cook up with an uneven texture.** • **The skins are tough.**	Plan ahead and allow the beans at least 8 hours of soaking time, or up to 24 hours. If the soaking time is cut short, the beans will not hydrate thoroughly, which means they'll take longer to cook, and they may cook up unevenly. The salt may also not take full effect on the bean skins, so the skins may remain a bit tough even though the bean interiors may be tender. If you're short on time, use the quick-soak method: Place the rinsed beans in a large heat-resistant bowl. Bring 2 quarts of water and 3 tablespoons salt to a boil, combine with the beans in a large bowl or container, and let the beans soak for 1 hour. Drain and rinse the beans and use them in place of the long-soaked beans.
Adding Salt to Stew Too Early	• **The beans have a mealy texture.**	For many cooks, seasoning with salt is almost a reflexive action. In this recipe, do not salt the stew until late in the cooking process, after the beans have softened. Salt interferes with the gelatinization of the bean starch; if seasoned early on, the beans will have a mealy, gritty texture and will not fully soften. Salt doesn't have this effect during the salt-soaking process, where its effect is limited to the skins.
Simmering Beans Too Vigorously	• **The beans partially disintegrate.**	Cook the beans in a 250-degree oven. A low oven temperature keeps the beans at the barest simmer so that they don't burst or explode, and then disintegrate into the stew. Don't be tempted to hike up the temperature so that the beans cook more quickly. If you find that the beans are bubbling away at 250 degrees, turn down the oven to try to maintain a near simmer, and use an oven thermometer to test the accuracy of your oven thermostat.
Adding Tomatoes Too Early	• **The beans are tough.** • **The beans are mealy.**	The acidity in the tomatoes can slow down the cooking time for the beans. We add the tomatoes (drained of excess liquid) once the beans are nearly tender. (The greens go into the pot at the same time; added earlier, they will overcook.) The pot of beans goes back into the oven so the greens can soften and the flavors can meld.
Adding Rosemary Too Early	• **The rosemary flavor is overpowering.** • **The broth is bitter.** • **The broth has a medicinal flavor.**	Rosemary is strong stuff and can easily overpower most ingredients. Rather than mincing the rosemary and adding it at the outset, we leave it whole and add the sprig once the dish is done. After steeping in the stew for 15 minutes, we remove and discard the rosemary sprig. The stew will have a touch of rosemary's woodsy, piney flavor but none of the bitter, medicinal notes that rosemary can impart to delicate dishes like this one.

1. Rinse 1 pound dried cannellini beans and pick out any blemished beans and stones.

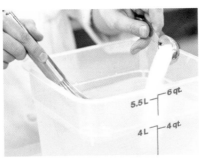

2. Dissolve 3 tablespoons salt in 4 quarts cold water in large bowl or container.

3. Add beans and soak at room temperature for at least 8 hours or up to 24 hours.

4. Drain beans and rinse well.

5. Trim stems from 1 pound kale or collard greens. Chop leaves into 1-inch pieces. You should have about 8 cups loosely packed.

6. Drain 1 (14.5-ounce) can diced tomatoes.

7. Adjust oven rack to lower-middle position and heat oven to 250 degrees.

8. Heat 1 tablespoon olive oil and 6 ounces pancetta, cut into ¼-inch pieces, in large Dutch oven over medium heat.

9. Cook, stirring occasionally, until pancetta is lightly browned and fat has rendered, 6 to 10 minutes.

10. Add 1 large chopped onion, 2 carrots, peeled and cut into ½-inch pieces, and 2 celery ribs, cut into ½-inch pieces.

11. Cook, stirring occasionally, until vegetables are softened and lightly browned, 10 to 16 minutes.

12. Stir in 8 lightly crushed and peeled garlic cloves and cook until fragrant, about 1 minute.

13. Stir in 4 cups chicken broth, 3 cups water, 2 bay leaves, and soaked beans.

14. Increase heat to high and bring to simmer.

15. Cover pot and transfer to oven.

16. Cook until beans are almost tender (very center of beans will still be firm), 45 minutes to 1 hour.

17. Remove pot from oven and stir in chopped greens and drained tomatoes.

18. Cover pot and return to oven. Continue to cook until beans and greens are fully tender, 30 to 40 minutes longer.

19. Remove pot from oven and submerge 1 sprig fresh rosemary in stew.

20. Cover and let stand 15 minutes.

21. Discard bay leaves and rosemary sprig and season stew with salt and pepper to taste.

22. If desired, use back of spoon to press some beans against side of pot to thicken stew.

23. Drizzle individual portions with olive oil and serve.

Recipe Library

Simple White Rice

✓ **WHY THIS RECIPE WORKS:** White rice seems like an easy enough dish to make, but it can be deceptively temperamental, quickly dissolving into unpleasant, gummy grains. For really great long-grain rice with distinct, separate grains that didn't clump together, we rinsed the rice of excess starch first. Then, to add a rich dimension, we sautéed the grains in butter, before covering them with water. After simmering the rice until all of the liquid was absorbed, we placed a dish towel between the lid and pot to absorb excess moisture and ensure dry, fluffy grains.

Simple White Rice

SERVES 6

You will need a saucepan with a tight-fitting lid for this recipe.

    2 cups long-grain white rice
    1 tablespoon unsalted butter or vegetable oil
    3 cups water
    1 teaspoon salt

1. Place rice in colander or fine-mesh strainer and rinse under cold running water until water runs clear. Place strainer over bowl and set aside.

2. Melt butter in large saucepan over medium heat. Add rice and cook, stirring constantly, until grains become chalky and opaque, 1 to 3 minutes. Add water and salt, increase heat to high, and bring to boil, swirling pot to blend ingredients. Reduce heat to low, cover, and simmer until all liquid is absorbed, 18 to 20 minutes. Off heat, remove lid and place dish towel folded in half over saucepan; replace lid. Let stand for 10 to 15 minutes. Fluff rice with fork and serve.

Basmati Rice Pilaf

✓ **WHY THIS RECIPE WORKS:** Many rice pilaf recipes call for an overnight soak, but we found this wasn't necessary; rinsing the rice before cooking removed excess starch and ensured the fluffy, rather than clumpy, grains that we were after. We sautéed onion in our pan first for an easy flavor boost, then we added the rice. Toasting the rice for a few minutes in the pan deepened its flavor. When it came to the liquid, instead of following the traditional ratio of 1:2 for rice and water, we found using a little less delivered better results. Placing a dish towel under the lid while the rice finished steaming off the heat absorbed excess moisture in the pan and guaranteed our rice was perfectly fluffy.

Basmati Rice Pilaf

SERVES 6

Long-grain white, jasmine, or Texmati rice can be substituted for the basmati. A nonstick saucepan works best here, although a traditional saucepan will also work. See Core Technique on page 182 for more details on this recipe.

    1½ cups basmati rice
    1   tablespoon olive oil
    1   small onion, chopped fine
        Salt and pepper
    2¼ cups water

1. Place rice in colander or fine-mesh strainer and rinse under cold running water until water runs clear. Heat oil in large saucepan over medium heat until shimmering. Add onion and ¼ teaspoon salt and cook, stirring occasionally, until onion is softened, about 5 minutes.

2. Stir in rice and cook, stirring often, until grain edges begin to turn translucent, about 3 minutes. Stir in water and bring to simmer. Reduce heat to low, cover, and continue to simmer until rice is tender and water is absorbed, 16 to 18 minutes.

3. Remove pot from heat and lay clean folded dish towel underneath lid. Let sit for 10 minutes. Fluff rice with fork, season with salt and pepper to taste, and serve.

Herbed Basmati Rice Pilaf

Add 2 minced garlic cloves and 1 teaspoon minced fresh thyme to pot with rice. Before covering rice with dish towel in step 3, sprinkle ¼ cup minced fresh parsley and 2 tablespoons minced fresh chives over top.

Basmati Rice Pilaf with Peas, Scallions, and Lemon

Add 2 minced garlic cloves, 1 teaspoon grated lemon zest, and ⅛ teaspoon red pepper flakes to pot with rice. Before covering rice with dish towel in step 3, sprinkle ½ cup thawed frozen peas over top. When fluffing rice, stir in 2 thinly sliced scallions and 1 tablespoon lemon juice.

Basmati Rice Pilaf with Currants and Toasted Almonds

Add 2 minced garlic cloves, ½ teaspoon turmeric, and ¼ teaspoon ground cinnamon to pot with rice. Before covering rice with dish towel in step 3, sprinkle ¼ cup currants over top. When fluffing rice, stir in ¼ cup toasted sliced almonds.

Mexican Rice

✓ **WHY THIS RECIPE WORKS:** Rice cooked the Mexican way is a flavorful pilaf-style dish, but we've had our share of soupy or greasy versions. We wanted tender rice infused with fresh flavor. To keep the grains distinct, we rinsed the rice before cooking it. Sautéing the rice in vegetable oil before adding the liquid produced superior grains. We found that equal parts chicken broth and fresh tomatoes (combined in a 2:1 ratio with the rice) were ideal for a flavorful base. For flavor, color, and texture, we added a little tomato paste and stirred the rice midway through cooking to reincorporate the tomato mixture. Baking the rice ensured even cooking. Cilantro, jalapeño, and lime juice complemented the richer tones of the cooked tomatoes, garlic, and onion.

Mexican Rice

SERVES 6 TO 8

Because the spiciness of jalapeños varies from chile to chile, we try to control the heat by removing the ribs and seeds from those chiles that are cooked in the rice. It is important to use an ovensafe pot about 12 inches in diameter so that the rice cooks evenly and in the time indicated. The pot's depth is less important than its diameter; we've successfully used both a straight-sided sauté pan and a Dutch oven. Whichever type of pot you use, it should have a tight-fitting, ovensafe lid. Vegetable broth can be substituted for the chicken broth.

2	tomatoes, cored and quartered
1	white onion, quartered
3	jalapeño chiles
2	cups long-grain white rice
⅓	cup vegetable oil
4	garlic cloves, minced
2	cups chicken broth
1	tablespoon tomato paste
1½	teaspoons salt
½	cup minced fresh cilantro
	Lime wedges

1. Adjust oven rack to middle position and heat oven to 350 degrees. Process tomatoes and onion in food processor until smooth, about 15 seconds, scraping down bowl if necessary. Transfer mixture to liquid measuring cup; you should have 2 cups (if necessary, spoon off excess so that volume equals 2 cups). Remove ribs and seeds from 2 jalapeños and discard; mince flesh and set aside. Mince remaining jalapeño, including ribs and seeds; set aside.

2. Place rice in fine-mesh strainer and rinse under cold running water until water runs clear. Shake rice vigorously in strainer to remove excess water.

3. Heat oil in ovensafe 12-inch straight-sided sauté pan or Dutch oven over medium-high heat for 1 to 2 minutes. Drop 3 or 4 grains rice in oil; if grains sizzle, oil is ready. Add rice and cook, stirring frequently, until rice is light golden and translucent, 6 to 8 minutes. Reduce heat to medium, add garlic and seeded minced jalapeños, and cook, stirring constantly, until fragrant, about 1½ minutes. Stir in pureed tomatoes and onions, chicken broth, tomato paste, and salt, increase heat to medium-high, and bring to boil. Cover pan and transfer to oven; bake until liquid is absorbed and rice is tender, 30 to 35 minutes, stirring well halfway through cooking.

4. Stir in cilantro and reserved minced jalapeño with seeds to taste. Serve immediately, passing lime wedges separately.

Easy Baked Brown Rice

✔ **WHY THIS RECIPE WORKS:** Brown rice should be ultimately satisfying, with a nutty, gutsy flavor and more textural personality—slightly sticky and just a bit chewy—than white rice. We found moving the recipe to the oven ensured more even cooking and guarded against scorching. For evenly cooked grains, we had to tweak the liquid-to-rice ratio established in our Simple White Rice (page 204), settling on 3¼ cups liquid to 1½ cups

brown rice. Rice made with only chicken broth was too salty, so we used a combination of water and broth. Unlike our white rice method, we cooked the rice in the oven to approximate the controlled, indirect heat of a rice cooker. This steady, even heat eliminated the risk of scorching and produced light and fluffy grains every time.

Easy Baked Brown Rice

SERVES 5

Short-grain brown rice can be substituted for the long-grain rice. A Dutch oven with a tight-fitting lid is essential for this recipe. If in doubt, first cover the pot with heavy-duty aluminum foil after adding the rice, crimping the edges to seal, before placing the lid on top and transferring the pot to the oven. See Core Technique on page 184 for more details on this recipe.

1	tablespoon olive oil
1	small onion, chopped fine
	Salt and pepper
2¼	cups water
1	cup chicken broth
1½	cups long-grain brown rice

1. Adjust oven rack to middle position and heat oven to 375 degrees. Heat oil in Dutch oven over medium heat until shimmering. Add onion and ¼ teaspoon salt and cook, stirring occasionally, until well browned, 12 to 14 minutes.

2. Add water and broth, cover, and bring to boil. Off heat, stir in rice. Cover, transfer pot to oven, and bake rice until tender, 65 to 70 minutes.

3. Remove pot from oven and uncover. Fluff rice with fork, scraping up any rice that has stuck to bottom. Lay clean folded dish towel underneath lid. Let sit for 10 minutes. Season with salt and pepper to taste and serve.

Baked Brown Rice with Parmesan, Lemon, and Herbs

When fluffing rice in step 3, stir in ½ cup grated Parmesan, ¼ cup minced fresh parsley, ¼ cup chopped fresh basil, 1 teaspoon grated lemon zest, and ½ teaspoon lemon juice.

Baked Brown Rice with Peas, Feta, and Mint

When fluffing rice in step 3, stir in 1 cup thawed frozen peas, ¼ cup minced fresh mint, and ½ teaspoon grated lemon zest. Sprinkle with ½ cup crumbled feta cheese before serving.

Hearty Baked Brown Rice

✔ **WHY THIS RECIPE WORKS:** We set out to make our Easy Baked Brown Rice a heartier dish, with aromatics and vegetables added to complement the flavor and texture of the rice. Onions and bell peppers could go into the pot with the uncooked rice, but we caramelized them first for deeper flavor. Other ingredients, like jarred roasted red peppers, peas, and beans, did best with just a gentle warming by stirring them into the rice after it was removed from the oven. Just before serving, fresh herbs and a squeeze of citrus brightened the flavors.

Hearty Baked Brown Rice with Onions and Roasted Red Peppers

SERVES 4 TO 6

Short-grain brown rice can also be used.

4	teaspoons olive oil
2	onions, chopped fine
2¼	cups water
1	cup chicken broth
1½	cups long-grain brown rice
1	teaspoon salt
¾	cup chopped jarred roasted red peppers
½	cup minced fresh parsley
¼	teaspoon pepper
1	ounce Parmesan cheese, grated (½ cup)
	Lemon wedges

1. Adjust oven rack to middle position and heat oven to 375 degrees. Heat oil in Dutch oven over medium heat until shimmering. Add onions and cook, stirring occasionally, until well browned, 12 to 14 minutes.

2. Add water and broth, cover, and bring to boil. Off heat, stir in rice and salt. Cover, transfer pot to oven, and bake rice until tender, 65 to 70 minutes.

3. Remove pot from oven and uncover. Fluff rice with fork, stir in red peppers, and replace lid; let sit for 5 minutes. Stir in parsley and pepper. Serve, passing Parmesan and lemon wedges separately.

Hearty Baked Brown Rice with Black Beans and Cilantro

Substitute 1 finely chopped green bell pepper for 1 onion. Once vegetables are well browned in step 1, stir in 3 minced garlic cloves and cook until fragrant, about 30 seconds. Substitute one 15-ounce can black beans for roasted red peppers and ¼ cup minced fresh cilantro for parsley. Omit Parmesan and substitute lime wedges for lemon wedges.

Hearty Baked Brown Rice with Peas, Feta, and Mint

Reduce amount of olive oil to 1 tablespoon and omit 1 onion. Substitute 1 cup thawed frozen peas for roasted red peppers, ¼ cup minced fresh mint for parsley, ½ teaspoon grated lemon zest for pepper, and ½ cup crumbled feta for Parmesan.

Hearty Baked Brown Rice with Andouille, Corn, and Red Peppers

If you cannot find andouille sausage, substitute chorizo, linguiça, or kielbasa.

Reduce amount of olive oil to 1 tablespoon and omit 1 onion. Heat olive oil in Dutch oven over medium heat until shimmering. Add 6 ounces andouille sausage, cut into ½-inch pieces, to pot and cook until lightly browned, 4 to 6 minutes. Using slotted spoon, transfer sausage to paper towel–lined plate; set aside. Add onion and 1 finely chopped red bell pepper to fat left in pot and cook, stirring occasionally, until well browned, 12 to 14 minutes; add 3 minced garlic cloves and cook until fragrant, about 30 seconds, before adding water and broth. Substitute ½ cup thawed frozen corn for roasted red peppers; add reserved sausage with corn. Substitute ¼ cup chopped fresh basil for parsley and omit Parmesan.

Chinese-Style Sticky Rice

✔ **WHY THIS RECIPE WORKS:** Chinese-style sticky rice should be just soft enough to soak up sauces in dishes like General Tso's Chicken and just sticky enough to be easily eaten with chopsticks. We found rinsing the rice prior to cooking was a must to ensure sticky, not gummy, rice. We started by cooking the rice in boiling water to agitate the grains, which helped to release its starch and thus encouraged stickiness. When the escaping steam formed holes in the rice's surface, we knew that the water level had dropped as low as we could permit. We covered the pot and let the rice finish over low heat to prevent scorching and allow for more even cooking. After 15 minutes, the rice was done, no fluffing necessary since we were after sticky grains.

Chinese-Style Sticky Rice

SERVES 4 TO 6

Do not stir the rice as it cooks. The finished rice can stand off the heat, covered, for up to 15 minutes. See Core Technique on page 186 for more details on this recipe.

2	cups long-grain white rice
3	cups water
½	teaspoon salt

1. Place rice in colander or fine-mesh strainer and rinse under cold running water until water runs clear.

2. Bring rice, water, and salt to boil in large saucepan over medium-high heat. Cook, uncovered, until water level drops below surface of rice and small holes form, about 5 minutes.

3. Reduce heat to low, cover, and cook until rice is tender and water is fully absorbed, about 15 minutes. Serve.

Wild Rice Pilaf with Pecans and Dried Cranberries

✔ **WHY THIS RECIPE WORKS:** Sometimes wild rice turns out undercooked and difficult to chew, other times the rice is overcooked and gluey. We wanted to figure out how to turn out properly cooked wild rice every time. Through trial and error, we learned to simmer the rice slowly in plenty of liquid, checking it for doneness every couple of minutes past the 35-minute mark. For the simmering liquid, we combined water and chicken broth—the broth's mild yet rich profile tempered the rice's muddy flavor to a pleasant earthiness and affirmed its subdued nuttiness. To further tame the strong flavor of the wild rice, we added some white rice to the mixture, then added onion, carrot, dried cranberries, and toasted pecans for a winning pilaf.

Wild Rice Pilaf with Pecans and Dried Cranberries

SERVES 6 TO 8

Wild rice goes quickly from tough to pasty, so begin testing the rice at the 35-minute mark and drain the rice as soon as it is tender.

1¾   cups chicken broth
2½   cups water
 2   bay leaves
 8   sprigs fresh thyme, divided into 2 bundles, each tied together with kitchen twine
 1   cup wild rice, picked over and rinsed
1½   cups long-grain white rice
 3   tablespoons unsalted butter
 1   onion, chopped fine
 1   large carrot, peeled and chopped fine
     Salt and pepper
 ¾   cup dried cranberries
 ¾   cup pecans, toasted and chopped coarse
4½   teaspoons minced fresh parsley

1. Bring broth, ¼ cup water, bay leaves, and 1 bundle thyme to boil in medium saucepan over medium-high heat. Add wild rice, cover, and reduce heat to low; simmer until rice is plump and tender and has absorbed most of liquid, 35 to 45 minutes. Drain rice in fine-mesh strainer to remove excess liquid. Remove bay leaves and thyme sprigs. Return wild rice to now-empty saucepan, cover, and set aside.

2. While wild rice is cooking, place white rice in medium bowl and add enough water to cover by 2 inches; using hands, gently swish grains to release excess starch. Carefully pour off water, leaving rice in bowl. Repeat 4 to 5 times, until water runs almost clear. Drain rice in fine-mesh strainer.

3. Melt butter in medium saucepan over medium-high heat. Add onion, carrot, and 1 teaspoon salt and cook, stirring frequently, until vegetables are softened but not browned, about 4 minutes. Add rinsed white rice and stir to coat grains with butter; cook, stirring frequently, until grains begin to turn translucent, about 3 minutes. Meanwhile, bring remaining 2¼ cups water to boil in small saucepan or in microwave. Add boiling water and second thyme bundle to white rice and return to boil. Reduce heat to low, sprinkle cranberries evenly over white rice, and cover. Simmer until all liquid is absorbed, 16 to 18 minutes. Off heat, remove thyme springs and fluff rice with fork.

4. Combine wild rice, white rice mixture, pecans, and parsley in large bowl and toss with rubber spatula. Season with salt and pepper to taste; serve immediately.

Almost Hands-Free Risotto

✔ **WHY THIS RECIPE WORKS:** Classic risotto can demand half an hour of stovetop tedium for the best creamy results. Our goal was 5 minutes of stirring, tops. First, we swapped out the saucepan for a Dutch oven, which has a thick, heavy bottom, deep sides, and tight-fitting lid—perfect for trapping and distributing heat as evenly as possible. Typical recipes dictate adding the broth in small increments after the wine has been absorbed (and stirring constantly after each addition), but we added most of the broth at once and covered the pan, allowing the rice to simmer until almost all the broth had been absorbed (stirring just twice). After adding the second and final addition of broth, we stirred the pot to ensure the bottom didn't cook more quickly than the top and turned off the heat. Without sitting over a direct flame, the sauce turned out perfectly creamy and the rice was thickened, velvety, and just barely chewy. To finish, we simply stirred in butter, herbs, and a squeeze of lemon juice to brighten the flavors.

Almost Hands-Free Risotto with Parmesan and Herbs

SERVES 6

This more hands-off method requires precise timing, so we strongly recommend using a timer.

 5   cups chicken broth
1½   cups water
 4   tablespoons unsalted butter
 1   large onion, chopped fine
     Salt and pepper
 1   garlic clove, minced
 2   cups Arborio rice
 1   cup dry white wine
 2   ounces Parmesan cheese, grated (1 cup)
 2   tablespoons chopped fresh parsley
 2   tablespoons chopped fresh chives
 1   teaspoon lemon juice

1. Bring broth and water to boil in large saucepan over high heat. Reduce heat to medium-low to maintain gentle simmer.

2. Melt 2 tablespoons butter in Dutch oven over medium heat. Add onion and ¾ teaspoon salt and cook, stirring frequently, until onion is softened, 4 to 5 minutes. Add garlic and stir until fragrant, about 30 seconds. Add rice and cook, stirring frequently, until grains are translucent around edges, about 3 minutes.

3. Add wine and cook, stirring constantly, until fully absorbed, 2 to 3 minutes. Stir 5 cups hot broth mixture into rice; reduce heat to medium-low, cover, and simmer until almost all liquid has been absorbed and rice is just al dente, 18 to 19 minutes, stirring twice during cooking.

4. Add ¾ cup hot broth mixture and stir gently and constantly until risotto becomes creamy, about 3 minutes. Stir in Parmesan. Remove pot from heat, cover, and let stand for 5 minutes. Stir in remaining 2 tablespoons butter, parsley, chives, and lemon juice. To loosen texture of risotto, add up to ½ cup remaining broth mixture to taste. Season with salt and pepper to taste and serve immediately.

Almost Hands-Free Risotto with Chicken and Herbs

SERVES 6

This more hands-off method requires precise timing, so we strongly recommend using a timer. Be aware that the thinner ends of the chicken breasts may be fully cooked by the time the broth is added to the rice, with the thicker ends finishing about 5 minutes later. See Recipe Tutorial on page 192 for more details on this recipe.

- 5 cups chicken broth
- 2 cups water
- 1 tablespoon olive oil
- 2 (12-ounce) bone-in split chicken breasts, trimmed and cut in half crosswise
- 4 tablespoons unsalted butter
- 1 large onion, chopped fine
  Salt and pepper
- 1 garlic clove, minced
- 2 cups Arborio rice
- 1 cup dry white wine
- 2 ounces Parmesan cheese, grated (1 cup)
- 2 tablespoons chopped fresh parsley
- 2 tablespoons chopped fresh chives
- 1 teaspoon lemon juice

1. Bring broth and water to boil in large saucepan over high heat. Reduce heat to medium-low to maintain gentle simmer.

2. Heat oil in Dutch oven over medium heat until just starting to smoke. Add chicken, skin side down, and cook without moving until golden brown, 4 to 6 minutes. Flip chicken and cook second side until lightly browned, about 2 minutes. Transfer chicken to saucepan of simmering broth and cook until chicken registers 165 degrees, 10 to 15 minutes. Transfer to large plate.

3. Melt 2 tablespoons butter in now-empty Dutch oven over medium heat. Add onion and ¾ teaspoon salt and cook, stirring frequently, until onion is softened, 4 to 5 minutes. Add garlic and stir until fragrant, about 30 seconds. Add rice and cook, stirring frequently, until grains are translucent around edges, about 3 minutes.

4. Add wine and cook, stirring constantly, until fully absorbed, 2 to 3 minutes. Stir 5 cups hot broth mixture into rice; reduce heat to medium-low, cover, and simmer until almost all liquid has been absorbed and rice is just al dente, 16 to 18 minutes, stirring twice during cooking.

5. Add ¾ cup hot broth mixture to risotto and stir gently and constantly until risotto becomes creamy, about 3 minutes. Stir in Parmesan. Remove pot from heat, cover, and let stand for 5 minutes.

6. Meanwhile, remove and discard skin and bones from chicken and shred meat into bite-size pieces. Gently stir shredded chicken, remaining 2 tablespoons butter, parsley, chives, and lemon juice into risotto. To loosen texture of risotto, add up to ½ cup remaining broth mixture to taste. Season with salt and pepper to taste and serve immediately.

Spring Vegetable Risotto

✔ **WHY THIS RECIPE WORKS:** Bland flavor and mushy vegetables can ruin this Italian classic. We wanted a risotto primavera with fresh yet complex flavors and vegetables that retained some bite. We started with the classic combination of asparagus and leeks. The leeks melted down beautifully as their delicate flavor infused the rice. The asparagus had to be handled separately; sautéing the trimmed spears and stirring them into the rice right before serving kept them from turning into mush. For a third vegetable, we added frozen peas. For a stronger backbone of flavor, we simmered the leek greens and tough stems of the asparagus in the chicken broth we used for cooking the rice. To round out and brighten the dish, we topped it with a gremolata of parsley, mint, and lemon zest.

Spring Vegetable Risotto

SERVES 4

To make this dish vegetarian, replace the chicken broth with vegetable broth. Onions can be substituted for the leeks. If substituting onions, use 1 roughly chopped onion in the broth and 2 finely chopped onions in the risotto.

GREMOLATA

- 2 tablespoons minced fresh parsley, stems reserved
- 2 tablespoons minced fresh mint, stems reserved
- ½ teaspoon grated lemon zest

RISOTTO

- 1 pound asparagus, tough ends chopped coarse, spears cut on bias into ½-inch lengths
- 1 pound leeks, white and light green parts halved lengthwise, sliced thin, and washed thoroughly; dark green parts chopped coarse and washed thoroughly
- 4 cups chicken broth
- 3 cups water
- 5 tablespoons unsalted butter
  Salt and pepper
- ½ cup frozen peas
- 2 garlic cloves, minced
- 1½ cups Arborio rice
- 1 cup dry white wine
- 1½ ounces Parmesan cheese grated (¾ cup), plus extra for serving
- 2 teaspoons lemon juice

1. FOR THE GREMOLATA: Combine all ingredients in small bowl and set aside.

2. FOR THE RISOTTO: Bring chopped asparagus ends, chopped dark green leek parts, reserved parsley and mint stems, broth, and water to boil in large saucepan over high heat. Reduce heat to medium-low, partially cover, and simmer 20 minutes. Strain broth through fine-mesh strainer into medium bowl, pressing on solids to extract as much liquid as possible. Return strained broth to saucepan, cover, and set over low heat to keep broth warm.

3. Melt 1 tablespoon butter in Dutch oven over medium heat. Add asparagus spears, pinch salt, and pinch pepper. Cook, stirring occasionally, until asparagus is crisp-tender,

4 to 6 minutes. Add peas and continue to cook for 1 minute. Transfer vegetables to plate and set aside.

4. Melt 3 tablespoons butter in now-empty Dutch oven over medium heat. Add white and light green leek parts, garlic, ½ teaspoon salt, and ½ teaspoon pepper. Cook, stirring occasionally, until leeks are softened, 5 to 7 minutes. Add rice and cook, stirring frequently, until grains are translucent around edges, about 3 minutes.

5. Add wine and cook, stirring frequently, until fully absorbed, 2 to 3 minutes. Add 3 cups hot broth mixture to rice. Simmer, stirring every 3 to 4 minutes, until liquid is absorbed and bottom of pan is almost dry, about 12 minutes.

6. Stir in about ½ cup hot broth mixture and cook, stirring constantly, until absorbed, about 3 minutes; repeat with additional broth mixture 3 or 4 times until rice is al dente. Off heat, stir in remaining 1 tablespoon butter, Parmesan, and lemon juice. Gently fold in asparagus and peas. To loosen texture of risotto, add up to ½ cup remaining broth mixture to taste. Serve immediately, sprinkling each serving with gremolata and passing Parmesan separately.

Spring Vegetable Risotto with Carrots and Watercress

Substitute 3 carrots, peeled and cut into ½-inch pieces, peels and trimmings chopped coarse, for asparagus; boil chopped carrot peels and trimmings with dark green leek parts. Cook carrots in step 3 until crisp-tender, 8 to 10 minutes; transfer to plate and set aside. Substitute 4 cups watercress for peas; once rice is al dente in step 6, stir in watercress, cover pot, and let stand for 1 minute. After stirring in butter, Parmesan, and lemon juice, gently fold in carrots.

Spring Vegetable Risotto with Fennel and Spinach

Substitute 1 large bulb fennel, trimmed of stalks, bulb halved, cored, and cut into ½-inch pieces, stalks and core chopped coarse, for asparagus; boil chopped fennel stalks and core with dark green leek parts. Cook fennel in step 3 until crisp-tender, 8 to 10 minutes; transfer to plate and set aside. Substitute 6 cups baby spinach for peas; once rice is al dente in step 6, stir in spinach, cover pot, and let stand for 1 minute. After stirring in butter, Parmesan, and lemon juice, gently fold in fennel.

Barley Risotto with Roasted Butternut Squash

✓ **WHY THIS RECIPE WORKS:** We used pearl barley in our barley risotto recipe for two reasons—it is widely available in supermarkets and, because the bran has been removed from the outside of the grain, the starchy interior is exposed, which helps to create a supple, velvety sauce when simmered. We used our well-tested risotto cooking method with one minor change: We added more liquid to our barley risotto recipe because barley takes a bit longer to cook.

Barley Risotto with Roasted Butternut Squash
SERVES 4

Serve this dish with extra grated Parmesan cheese if desired.

- **2 pounds butternut squash, peeled, seeded, and cut into ½-inch cubes (3½ cups)**
- **1 tablespoon olive oil**
- **Salt and pepper**
- **4 cups chicken broth**
- **4 cups water**
- **1 onion, chopped fine**
- **2 garlic cloves, minced**
- **1½ cups pearl barley, rinsed and drained**
- **1 cup dry white wine**
- **1½ ounces grated Parmesan cheese (¾ cup)**
- **1 tablespoon unsalted butter**
- **1 teaspoon minced fresh sage**
- **⅛ teaspoon ground nutmeg**

1. Adjust oven rack to upper-middle position and heat oven to 450 degrees. Line rimmed baking sheet with parchment paper. Toss squash with 2 teaspoons oil, ¼ teaspoon salt, and ⅛ teaspoon pepper and spread out over prepared baking sheet. Roast squash until tender and golden brown, about 30 minutes; set aside until needed.

2. Meanwhile, bring broth and water to simmer in medium saucepan. Reduce heat to lowest possible setting and cover to keep warm.

3. Combine remaining 1 teaspoon oil and onion in large saucepan. Cover and cook over medium-low heat, stirring occasionally, until onion is softened, 8 to 10 minutes. Stir in garlic and cook until fragrant, about 30 seconds.

4. Stir in barley, increase heat to medium, and cook, stirring often, until lightly toasted and aromatic, about 4 minutes. Stir in wine and continue to cook, stirring often, until wine has been completely absorbed, about 2 minutes.

5. Stir in 3 cups warm broth and half of roasted squash. Simmer, stirring occasionally, until liquid is absorbed and bottom of pan is dry, 22 to 25 minutes. Stir in 2 cups more warm broth and continue to simmer, stirring occasionally, until liquid is absorbed and bottom of pan is dry, 15 to 18 minutes longer.

6. Continue to cook risotto, stirring often and adding additional broth, ½ cup at a time as needed, to keep pan bottom from becoming dry (about every 4 minutes), until barley is cooked through but still somewhat firm in center, 15 to 20 minutes longer. Off heat, stir in remaining roasted squash, Parmesan, butter, sage, and nutmeg. Season with salt and pepper to taste and serve.

Creamy Parmesan Polenta

WHY THIS RECIPE WORKS: If you don't stir polenta almost constantly, it forms intractable lumps. Is there a way to get creamy, smooth polenta with rich corn flavor, but without the fussy process? From the outset, we knew that the right type of cornmeal was essential. Coarse-ground degerminated cornmeal gave us the soft but hearty texture and nutty flavor we were looking for. Taking a clue from dried bean recipes, which use baking soda to help break down the tough bean skins and accelerate cooking, we added a pinch to our polenta. The baking soda helped soften the cornmeal's endosperm, which cut the cooking time in half and eliminated the need for stirring. Parmesan cheese and butter, stirred in at the last minute, ensured a satisfying, rich dish.

Creamy Parmesan Polenta
SERVES 4

Coarse-ground degerminated cornmeal such as yellow grits (with grains the size of couscous) works best in this recipe. Avoid instant and quick-cooking products, as well as whole-grain, stone-ground, and regular cornmeal. Do not omit the baking soda—it reduces the cooking time and makes for a creamier polenta. If the polenta bubbles or sputters even slightly after the first 10 minutes, the heat is too high and you may need a flame tamer. For a main course, serve the polenta with a wedge of rich cheese (like Gorgonzola) or a meat sauce. See Core Technique on page 187 for more details on this recipe.

 7½ **cups water**
 1½ **teaspoons salt**
      Pinch baking soda
 1½ **cups coarse-ground cornmeal**
  4 **ounces Parmesan cheese, grated (2 cups), plus extra for serving**
  2 **tablespoons unsalted butter**
      Pepper

1. Bring water to boil in large, heavy-bottomed saucepan over medium-high heat. Stir in salt and baking soda. Slowly pour cornmeal into water in steady stream, while stirring back and forth with wooden spoon or rubber spatula. Bring mixture to boil, stirring constantly, about 1 minute. Reduce heat to lowest setting and cover.

2. After 5 minutes, whisk polenta to smooth out any lumps that may have formed, about 15 seconds. (Make sure to scrape down sides and bottom of pan.) Cover and continue to cook, without stirring, until grains of polenta are tender but slightly al dente, about 25 minutes longer. (Polenta should be loose and barely hold its shape but will continue to thicken as it cools.)

3. Remove from heat, stir in Parmesan and butter, and season with pepper to taste. Let stand, covered, for 5 minutes. Serve, passing extra Parmesan separately.

Bulgur with Red Grapes and Feta

WHY THIS RECIPE WORKS: Since bulgur is made from wheat berries that have been steamed or boiled and then ground into fine, medium, coarse, or very coarse grains, we knew a gentle cooking method would work best. While it was a candidate for the straightforward absorption cooking method, we found that if we used fine- or medium-grind grains, we could reconstitute it by soaking it for an hour and thus ensure grains that stayed intact—ideal for a salad application. Adding a little lemon juice to the soaking water boosted the flavor, as did a straightforward dressing spiked with cayenne and cumin. Grapes, feta, and almonds gave the salad a Mediterranean profile, while scallions and mint lent a touch of freshness and color.

Bulgur with Red Grapes and Feta
SERVES 4

Do not use coarse-grind bulgur in this recipe.

 1½ **cups fine- or medium-grind bulgur, rinsed**
  ¾ **cup water**
  ¼ **cup plus 1 tablespoon lemon juice**
      Salt
  ¼ **cup extra-virgin olive oil**
  ¼ **teaspoon ground cumin**
      Pinch cayenne pepper
  6 **ounces seedless red grapes, quartered (1 cup)**
  ½ **cup slivered almonds, toasted**
  2 **ounces feta cheese, crumbled (½ cup)**
  2 **scallions, sliced thin**
  ¼ **cup chopped fresh mint**

1. Combine bulgur, water, ¼ cup lemon juice, and ¼ teaspoon salt in bowl. Let stand until grains are softened, about 1 hour.

2. Whisk oil, remaining 1 tablespoon lemon juice, cumin, ¼ teaspoon salt, and cayenne together in large bowl. Add soaked bulgur, grapes, ⅓ cup almonds, ⅓ cup feta, scallions, and mint; toss to combine and season with salt to taste. Sprinkle with remaining almonds and feta before serving.

Farro with Mushrooms and Thyme

WHY THIS RECIPE WORKS: Although we usually turn to the absorption method for quicker-cooking grains, a few tests proved that farro takes better to the pasta method because the abundance of water cooks the grains more evenly. Since farro is a popular ingredient in Tuscan cuisine, we decided to give this dish a simple and fresh Italian profile. Mushrooms sautéed with shallot and thyme lent the dish some meatiness, and using sherry to deglaze the pan after the mushrooms browned was a natural complement and added some complexity to the dish. Finishing with sherry vinegar and a couple tablespoons of fresh parsley added brightness and freshness that balanced the hearty, savory flavors.

Farro with Mushrooms and Thyme

SERVES 4

White mushrooms can be substituted for the cremini.

- 1 **cup farro, rinsed**
  Salt and pepper
- 2 **tablespoons vegetable oil**
- 8 **ounces cremini mushrooms, trimmed and chopped coarse**
- 1 **shallot, minced**
- 1 **teaspoon minced fresh thyme**
- 2 **tablespoons dry sherry**
- 2 **tablespoons minced fresh parsley**
- 1 **teaspoon sherry vinegar**

1. Bring 4 quarts water to boil in Dutch oven. Stir in farro and 1 tablespoon salt. Return to boil, reduce heat, and simmer until tender, 15 to 20 minutes. Drain well and set aside.

2. Heat oil in 12-inch skillet over medium-high heat until shimmering. Add mushrooms, shallot, thyme, and ¼ teaspoon salt; cook, stirring frequently, until moisture has evaporated and vegetables start to brown, 5 to 8 minutes. Add sherry and cook, scraping up any browned bits, until pan is almost dry, 1 to 2 minutes. Add farro and cook, stirring constantly, until heated through, about 1 minute. Remove pan from heat, stir in parsley and vinegar, and season with salt and pepper to taste. Serve.

Millet Porridge with Maple Syrup

✔ **WHY THIS RECIPE WORKS:** The mellow corn flavor and fine texture of tiny millet seeds make them extremely versatile in both savory and sweet applications. During our testing, we discovered that slightly overcooking millet causes the seeds to burst and release starch, creating a creamy consistency that makes a great breakfast porridge. We cooked the millet in water until it was almost tender, then added milk to the pan to finish cooking it through and add richness. Simple flavorings of maple syrup and cinnamon were all it needed.

Millet Porridge with Maple Syrup

SERVES 4

We prefer this porridge made with whole milk, but 1- or 2-percent or skim milk can be substituted.

- 3 **cups water**
- 1 **cup millet, rinsed**
- ⅛ **teaspoon ground cinnamon**
- ⅛ **teaspoon salt**
- 1 **cup whole milk**
- 3 **tablespoons maple syrup**

1. Bring water, millet, cinnamon, and salt to boil in medium saucepan over high heat. Reduce heat to low, cover, and cook until millet has absorbed all water and is almost tender, about 20 minutes.

2. Increase heat to medium, add milk, and simmer, stirring frequently, until millet is fully tender and mixture is thickened, about 10 minutes. Stir in maple syrup and serve.

Quinoa Salad with Red Bell Pepper and Cilantro

✔ **WHY THIS RECIPE WORKS:** Though it's technically a seed, we typically treat quinoa as we would a grain, serving it as a side dish or lunchtime salad. We rinsed the grains to remove the bitter protective layer, then toasted them to bring out flavor before adding liquid to the pan. Spreading the cooked quinoa over a rimmed baking sheet to cool produced the fluffiest grains. We found we needed a little more liquid than our usual 1:1 quinoa-to-water ratio because we were serving this quinoa at room temperature. The extra cooking liquid ensured the grains stayed fluffy and separate as they cooled on the baking sheet. Given its South American origins, jalapeño, red onion, cilantro, and bell pepper made sense as add-ins. A bright dressing with lime juice, garlic, and cumin brought it all together.

Quinoa Salad with Red Bell Pepper and Cilantro

SERVES 4

Do not add oil or butter to the pot when toasting the quinoa, as it will make the grains taste slightly bitter. To make this dish spicier, add the chile seeds. After 12 minutes of cooking, there will still be a little bit of water in the pan, but this will evaporate as the quinoa cools.

- 1 **cup quinoa, rinsed and dried on dish towel**
- 1½ **cups water**
  Salt and pepper
- ½ **red bell pepper, chopped fine**
- ½ **jalapeño chile, minced**
- 2 **tablespoons finely chopped red onion**
- 1 **tablespoon minced fresh cilantro**
- 2 **tablespoons lime juice**
- 1 **tablespoon extra-virgin olive oil**
- 2 **teaspoons Dijon mustard**
- 1 **small garlic clove, minced**
- ½ **teaspoon ground cumin**

1. Toast quinoa in large saucepan over medium heat, stirring often, until quinoa is lightly toasted and aromatic, about 5 minutes. Stir in water and ¼ teaspoon salt and bring to simmer. Reduce heat to low, cover, and continue to simmer until water is mostly absorbed and quinoa is nearly tender, about 12 minutes. Spread quinoa out over rimmed baking sheet and set aside until tender and cool, about 20 minutes.

2. Transfer cooled quinoa to large bowl. Stir in bell pepper, jalapeño, onion, and cilantro. In separate bowl, whisk lime juice, oil, mustard, garlic, and cumin together, then pour over quinoa mixture and toss to coat. Season with salt and pepper to taste and serve. (Quinoa salad can be refrigerated for up to 2 days; season with additional salt, pepper, and lime juice to taste before serving.)

Wheat Berry Salad with Orange and Scallions

✓ **WHY THIS RECIPE WORKS:** Since wheat berries remain firm, smooth, and distinct when cooked, they lend themselves to a salad nicely. We found it easiest to cook the kernels like pasta, simply simmering the wheat berries in a large amount of water. After an hour of simmering, they had good texture, but we were disappointed to find that the flavor had been somewhat diluted by the water. Just ¼ teaspoon of salt boosted the flavor of the grains; any more salt and the salinity of the water prevented the wheat berries from absorbing the water, making the grains hard and crunchy. Their rich, earthy flavor paired well with a citrusy dressing sweetened with a touch of honey, while shredded carrots and minced scallions lent color and fresh flavor.

Wheat Berry Salad with Orange and Scallions
SERVES 4

If the water level gets low as the wheat berries simmer in step 1, add more boiling water to prevent the pan from drying out.

- 1 **cup wheat berries**
- **Salt and pepper**
- 1 **carrot, peeled and shredded**
- 2 **scallions, minced**
- 1 **tablespoon minced fresh parsley**
- 2 **tablespoons red wine vinegar**
- 2 **tablespoons orange juice**
- 1 **tablespoon extra-virgin olive oil**
- 1 **tablespoon Dijon mustard**
- 1 **small shallot, minced**
- 1 **garlic clove, minced**
- 1 **teaspoon honey**

1. Toast wheat berries in large saucepan over medium heat, stirring often, until wheat berries are fragrant and beginning to darken, about 5 minutes. Stir in 4 quarts water and ¼ teaspoon salt and bring to simmer. Reduce heat to low, partially cover, and continue to simmer, stirring often, until tender (wheat berries should remain slightly chewy), about 1 hour.

2. Drain wheat berries, spread out over rimmed baking sheet, and let cool to room temperature, about 30 minutes.

3. Transfer cooled wheat berries to large bowl. Stir in carrot, scallions, and parsley. In separate bowl, whisk vinegar, orange juice, oil, mustard, shallot, garlic, and honey together, then pour over wheat berry mixture and toss to coat. Season with salt and pepper to taste and serve. (Wheat berry salad can be refrigerated for up to 2 days; season with additional salt, pepper, orange juice, and vinegar to taste before serving.)

Couscous

✓ **WHY THIS RECIPE WORKS:** Couscous, granules of semolina, traditionally serves as a sauce absorber under stews and braises, but it can also be a quick and flavorful side dish for a variety of foods. We wanted to develop a classic version for saucy dishes as well as a handful of flavor-packed versions, as convenient as the box kind, but much fresher-tasting. Toasting the couscous grains in butter deepened their flavor and helped them cook up fluffy and separate. And to bump up the flavor even further, we replaced half of the cooking liquid with chicken broth. For our enriched variations, dried fruit, nuts, and citrus juice added textural interest and sweet, bright notes.

Classic Couscous
SERVES 4 TO 6

- 2 **tablespoons unsalted butter**
- 2 **cups couscous**
- 1 **cup water**
- 1 **cup chicken broth**
- 1 **teaspoon salt**
- **Pepper**

Melt butter in medium saucepan over medium-high heat. Add couscous and cook, stirring frequently, until grains are just beginning to brown, about 5 minutes. Add water, broth, and salt and stir briefly to combine. Cover and remove pan from heat. Let stand until grains are tender, about 7 minutes. Uncover and fluff grains with fork. Season with pepper to taste and serve.

Couscous with Dates and Pistachios
Increase butter to 3 tablespoons and add ½ cup chopped pitted dates, 1 tablespoon grated fresh ginger, and ½ teaspoon ground cardamom to saucepan with couscous. Increase water to 1¼ cups. Stir ¾ cup coarsely chopped toasted pistachios, 3 tablespoons minced fresh cilantro, and 2 teaspoons lemon juice into couscous before serving.

Couscous with Carrots, Raisins, and Pine Nuts
Increase butter to 3 tablespoons and add 2 grated carrots and ½ teaspoon ground cinnamon; cook, stirring frequently, until carrot softens, about 2 minutes. Add ½ cup raisins to saucepan with couscous and increase water to 1¼ cups. Stir ¾ cup toasted pine nuts, 3 tablespoons minced fresh cilantro, ½ teaspoon grated orange zest, and 1 tablespoon orange juice into couscous before serving.

Couscous with Shallots, Garlic, and Almonds
Increase butter to 3 tablespoons and add 3 thinly sliced shallots; cook, stirring frequently, until softened and lightly browned, about 5 minutes. Add 1 minced garlic clove and cook until fragrant, about 30 seconds. Stir ¾ cup toasted sliced almonds, ¾ cup minced fresh parsley, ½ teaspoon grated lemon zest, and 2 teaspoons lemon juice into couscous before serving.

Cuban Black Beans and Rice

✓ **WHY THIS RECIPE WORKS:** Beans and rice is a familiar combination the world over, but Cuban black beans and rice is unique in that the rice is cooked in the inky concentrated liquid left over from cooking the beans, which renders the grains just as flavorful. For our own superlative version, we reserved a portion of the *sofrito* (the traditional combination of garlic, bell pepper, and onion) and simmered it with our beans to infuse them with flavor. Instead of just draining off and throwing away the flavorful bean cooking liquid, we used it again to cook our rice and beans together. Lightly browning the remaining sofrito vegetables and spices with rendered salt pork added complex, meaty flavor, and baking the dish in the oven eliminated the crusty bottom that can form when the dish is cooked on the stove.

Cuban Black Beans and Rice

SERVES 6 TO 8

It is important to use lean—not fatty—salt pork. If you can't find it, substitute 6 slices of bacon. If using bacon, decrease the cooking time in step 4 to 8 minutes. You will need a Dutch oven with a tight-fitting lid for this recipe. See Recipe Tutorial on page 196 for more details on this recipe.

>   Salt
> 1   **cup dried black beans, picked over and rinsed**
> 2   **cups chicken broth**
> 2   **cups water**
> 2   **large green bell peppers, halved, stemmed, and seeded**
> 1   **large onion, halved at equator and peeled, root end left intact**
> 1   **garlic head, 5 cloves minced, rest of head halved at equator with skin left intact**
> 2   **bay leaves**
> 1½ **cups long-grain white rice**
> 2   **tablespoons olive oil**
> 6   **ounces lean salt pork, cut into ¼-inch dice**
> 4   **teaspoons ground cumin**
> 1   **tablespoon minced fresh oregano**
> 2   **tablespoons red wine vinegar**
> 2   **scallions, sliced thin**
>   **Lime wedges**

1. Dissolve 1½ tablespoons salt in 2 quarts cold water in large bowl or container. Add beans and soak at room temperature for at least 8 hours or up to 24 hours. Drain and rinse well.

2. In Dutch oven, stir together drained beans, broth, water, 1 bell pepper half, 1 onion half (with root end), halved garlic head, bay leaves, and 1 teaspoon salt. Bring to simmer over medium-high heat, cover, and reduce heat to low. Cook until beans are just soft, 30 to 40 minutes. Using tongs, remove and discard bell pepper, onion, garlic, and bay leaves. Drain beans in colander set over large bowl, reserving 2½ cups bean cooking liquid. (If you don't have enough bean cooking liquid, add water to equal 2½ cups.) Do not wash out Dutch oven.

3. Adjust oven rack to middle position and heat oven to 350 degrees. Place rice in large fine-mesh strainer and rinse under cold running water until water runs clear, about 1½ minutes. Shake strainer vigorously to remove all excess water; set rice aside. Cut remaining bell peppers and onion into 2-inch pieces and process in food processor until broken into rough ¼-inch pieces, about 8 pulses, scraping down bowl as necessary; set vegetables aside.

4. In now-empty Dutch oven, heat 1 tablespoon oil and salt pork over medium-low heat and cook, stirring frequently, until lightly browned and rendered, 15 to 20 minutes. Add remaining 1 tablespoon oil, chopped bell peppers and onion, cumin, and oregano. Increase heat to medium and continue to cook, stirring frequently, until vegetables are softened and beginning to brown, 10 to 15 minutes longer. Add minced garlic and cook, stirring constantly, until fragrant, about 1 minute. Add rice and stir to coat, about 30 seconds.

5. Stir in beans, reserved bean cooking liquid, vinegar, and ½ teaspoon salt. Increase heat to medium-high and bring to simmer. Cover and transfer to oven. Cook until liquid is absorbed and rice is tender, about 30 minutes. Fluff with fork and let rest, uncovered, 5 minutes. Serve, passing scallions and lime wedges separately.

Vegetarian Cuban Black Beans and Rice

Substitute water for chicken broth and omit salt pork. Add 1 tablespoon tomato paste with vegetables in step 4 and increase amount of salt in step 5 to 1½ teaspoons.

Boston Baked Beans

✓ **WHY THIS RECIPE WORKS:** To create a recipe for Boston baked beans packed with multiple levels of intense flavor, yet traditional enough to make a New Englander proud, we started with a combination of salt pork and bacon and browned them in a Dutch oven before adding dried white beans. Using the oven, not the stovetop, ensured the beans cooked through gently and evenly. Cider vinegar gave our sauce tanginess while mustard and molasses boosted its flavor. We removed the lid for the last hour of cooking to reduce the sauce to a syrupy, intensified state.

Boston Baked Beans

SERVES 4 TO 6

Be sure to use mild molasses in this recipe; dark molasses will taste too strong.

> 4   **ounces salt pork, rind removed, cut into ½-inch pieces**
> 2   **slices bacon, cut into ¼-inch pieces**
> 1   **onion, chopped fine**
> 9   **cups water**
> 1   **pound (2½ cups) dried small white beans, picked over and rinsed**
> ½   **cup plus 1 tablespoon molasses**
> 1½ **tablespoons brown mustard**
>   **Salt and pepper**
> 1   **teaspoon cider vinegar**

1. Adjust oven rack to lower-middle position and heat oven to 300 degrees. Cook salt pork and bacon in Dutch oven over medium heat, stirring occasionally, until lightly browned and most of fat is rendered, about 7 minutes. Add onion and continue to cook, stirring occasionally, until onion is softened, 5 to 7 minutes. Add water, beans, ½ cup molasses, mustard, and 1¼ teaspoons salt, increase heat to medium-high, and bring to boil. Cover pot and transfer to oven. Bake until beans are tender, about 4 hours, stirring halfway through cooking.

2. Carefully remove lid and continue to bake until liquid has thickened to syrupy consistency, 1 to 1½ hours longer. Remove beans from oven. Stir in remaining 1 tablespoon molasses and vinegar and season with salt and pepper to taste. Serve. (Baked beans can be cooled and refrigerated for up to 4 days.)

Hearty Tuscan Bean Stew

✔ **WHY THIS RECIPE WORKS:** We wanted to convert rustic Tuscan bean soup into a hearty stew. To avoid tough, exploded beans, we soaked the beans overnight in salted water, which softened the skins. Then we experimented with cooking times and temperatures, discovering that gently cooking the beans in a 250-degree oven produced perfectly cooked beans that stayed intact. We added tomatoes toward the end of cooking, since their acid kept the beans from becoming too soft. To complete our stew, we chose other traditional Tuscan flavors, including pancetta, kale, lots of garlic, and a sprig of rosemary.

Hearty Tuscan Bean Stew
SERVES 8

We prefer the creamier texture of beans soaked overnight for this recipe. If you're short on time, you can quick-soak them (see page 190) before proceeding with step 2. If pancetta is unavailable, substitute 4 slices of bacon. See Recipe Tutorial on page 200 for more details on this recipe.

> Salt and pepper
> 1 pound dried cannellini beans (2½ cups), picked over and rinsed
> 1 tablespoon extra-virgin olive oil, plus extra for drizzling
> 6 ounces pancetta, cut into ¼-inch pieces
> 1 large onion, chopped
> 2 carrots, peeled and cut into ½-inch pieces
> 2 celery ribs, cut into ½-inch pieces
> 8 garlic cloves, lightly crushed and peeled
> 4 cups chicken broth
> 3 cups water
> 2 bay leaves
> 1 pound kale or collard greens, stemmed and chopped into 1-inch pieces
> 1 (14.5-ounce) can diced tomatoes, drained
> 1 sprig fresh rosemary
> 8 slices rustic white bread, 1¼ inch thick, broiled until golden brown on both sides and rubbed with crushed garlic clove (optional)

1. Dissolve 3 tablespoons salt in 4 quarts cold water in large bowl or container. Add beans and soak at room temperature for at least 8 hours or up to 24 hours. Drain and rinse well.

2. Adjust oven rack to lower-middle position and heat oven to 250 degrees. Heat oil and pancetta in Dutch oven over medium heat. Cook, stirring occasionally, until pancetta is lightly browned and fat has rendered, 6 to 10 minutes. Add onion, carrots, and celery and cook, stirring occasionally, until vegetables are softened and lightly browned, 10 to 16 minutes. Stir in garlic and cook until fragrant, about 1 minute. Stir in broth, water, bay leaves, and soaked beans. Increase heat to high and bring to simmer. Cover pot, transfer to oven, and cook until beans are almost tender (very center of beans will still be firm), 45 minutes to 1 hour.

3. Remove pot from oven and stir in kale and tomatoes. Cover pot, return to oven, and continue to cook until beans and greens are fully tender, 30 to 40 minutes longer.

4. Remove pot from oven and submerge rosemary in stew. Cover and let stand 15 minutes. Discard bay leaves and rosemary and season stew with salt and pepper to taste. If desired, use back of spoon to press some beans against side of pot to thicken stew. Serve over toasted bread, if desired, and drizzle with olive oil.

Lentil Salad With Olives, Mint, and Feta

✔ **WHY THIS RECIPE WORKS:** The most important step in making a lentil salad is perfecting the cooking of the lentils so they maintain their shape and firm-tender bite. There turns out to be two key steps. The first is to salt-soak the lentils in warm salt water. With salt-soaking, the lentil's skin softens, which leads to fewer blowouts. The second step is to cook the lentils in the oven, which heats them gently and uniformly. Once we had perfectly cooked lentils, all we had left to do was to pair the earthy beans with a tart vinaigrette and boldly flavored mix-ins.

Lentil Salad With Olives, Mint, And Feta
SERVES 4 TO 6

French green lentils, or *lentilles du Puy,* are our preferred choice for this recipe, but it works with any type of lentil except red or yellow. Salt-soaking helps keep the lentils intact, but if you don't have time, they'll still taste good. The salad can be served warm or at room temperature.

> 1 cup lentils, picked over and rinsed
>   Salt and pepper
> 6 cups water
> 2 cups chicken broth
> 5 garlic cloves, lightly crushed and peeled
> 1 bay leaf
> 5 tablespoons extra-virgin olive oil
> 3 tablespoons white wine vinegar
> ½ cup coarsely chopped pitted kalamata olives
> ½ cup fresh mint leaves, chopped
> 1 large shallot, minced
> 1 ounce feta cheese, crumbled (¼ cup)

1. Place lentils and 1 teaspoon salt in bowl. Cover with 4 cups warm water (about 110 degrees) and soak for 1 hour. Drain well. (Drained lentils can be refrigerated for up to 2 days before cooking.)

2. Adjust oven rack to middle position and heat oven to 325 degrees. Place drained lentils, 2 cups water, broth, garlic, bay leaf, and ½ teaspoon salt in medium saucepan. Cover and bake until lentils are tender but remain intact, 40 to 60 minutes. Meanwhile, whisk oil and vinegar together in large bowl.

3. Drain lentils well; remove and discard garlic and bay leaf. Add drained lentils, olives, mint, and shallot to dressing and toss to combine. Season with salt and pepper to taste. Transfer to serving dish, sprinkle with feta, and serve.

Lentil Salad with Spinach, Walnuts, and Parmesan Cheese

Substitute sherry vinegar for white wine vinegar. Place 4 cups baby spinach and 2 tablespoons water in bowl. Cover and microwave until spinach is wilted and volume is halved, 3 to 4 minutes. Remove bowl from microwave and keep covered for 1 minute. Transfer spinach to colander; gently press to release liquid. Transfer spinach to cutting board and roughly chop. Return to colander and press again. Substitute chopped spinach for olives and mint and ¾ cup coarsely grated Parmesan cheese for feta. Sprinkle with ⅓ cup coarsely chopped toasted walnuts before serving.

Lentil Salad with Hazelnuts and Goat Cheese

Substitute red wine vinegar for white wine vinegar and add 2 teaspoons Dijon mustard to dressing in step 2. Omit olives and substitute ¼ cup chopped parsley for mint. Substitute ½ cup crumbled goat cheese for feta and sprinkle with ⅓ cup coarsely chopped toasted hazelnuts before serving.

Lentil Salad with Carrots and Cilantro

Substitute lemon juice for white wine vinegar. Toss 2 carrots, peeled and cut into 2-inch-long matchsticks, with 1 teaspoon ground cumin, ½ teaspoon ground cinnamon, and ⅛ teaspoon cayenne pepper in bowl. Cover and microwave until carrots are tender but still crisp, 2 to 4 minutes. Substitute carrots for olives and ¼ cup chopped cilantro for mint. Omit shallot and feta.

Best Vegetarian Chili

✓ **WHY THIS RECIPE WORKS:** Vegetarian chilis are often little more than a mishmash of beans and vegetables. In order to create a chili—not a bean and vegetable stew—we've found replacements for the different ways in which meat adds depth and flavor to chili. Walnuts, soy sauce, dried shiitake mushrooms and tomatoes add hearty savoriness. Bulgur fills out the chili, giving it a substantial texture. The added oil and nuts lend a richness to the chili, for full, lingering flavor.

Best Vegetarian Chili
SERVES 6 TO 8

We prefer to make this chili with whole dried chiles, but it can be prepared with jarred chili powder. If using chili powder, grind the shiitakes and oregano and add them to the pot with ¼ cup of chili powder in step 4. We also recommend a mix of at least two types of beans, one creamy (such as cannellini or navy) and one earthy (such as pinto, black, or red kidney). Serve with lime wedges, sour cream, diced avocado, chopped red onion, and shredded Monterey Jack or cheddar cheese, if desired.

    Salt
1 **pound (2½ cups) dried beans, picked over and rinsed**
2 **dried ancho chiles**
2 **dried New Mexican chiles**
½ **ounce dried shiitake mushrooms, rinsed and chopped coarse**
4 **teaspoons dried oregano**
½ **cup walnuts, toasted**
1 **(28-ounce) can diced tomatoes, drained with juice reserved**
3 **tablespoons tomato paste**
1–2 **jalapeño chiles, stemmed and coarsely chopped**
6 **garlic cloves, minced**
3 **tablespoons soy sauce**
¼ **cup vegetable oil**
2 **pounds onions, chopped fine**
1 **tablespoon ground cumin**
7 **cups water**
⅔ **cup medium-grind bulgur, rinsed**
¼ **cup chopped fresh cilantro**

1. Bring 4 quarts water, 3 tablespoons salt, and beans to boil in large Dutch oven over high heat. Remove pot from heat, cover, and let stand for 1 hour. Drain beans and rinse well. Wipe out pot.

2. Adjust oven rack to middle position and heat oven to 300 degrees. Arrange anchos and New Mexican chiles on rimmed baking sheet and toast until fragrant and puffed, about 8 minutes. Transfer to plate and let cool, about 5 minutes. Stem and seed anchos and New Mexican chiles. Working in batches, grind toasted chiles, mushrooms, and oregano in spice grinder or with mortar and pestle until finely ground.

3. Process walnuts in food processor until finely ground, about 30 seconds. Transfer to bowl. Process drained tomatoes, tomato paste, jalapeños, garlic, and soy sauce in food processor until tomatoes are finely chopped, about 45 seconds, scraping down bowl as needed.

4. Heat oil in now-empty Dutch oven over medium-high heat until shimmering. Add onions and 1¼ teaspoons salt; cook, stirring occasionally, until onions begin to brown, 8 to 10 minutes. Reduce heat to medium and add ground chile mixture and cumin; cook, stirring constantly, until fragrant, about 1 minute. Add rinsed beans and water and bring to boil. Cover pot, transfer to oven, and cook for 45 minutes.

5. Remove pot from oven. Stir in bulgur, ground walnuts, tomato mixture, and reserved tomato juice. Cover pot and return to oven. Cook until beans are fully tender, about 2 hours.

6. Remove pot from oven, stir chili well, and let stand, uncovered, for 20 minutes. Stir in cilantro and serve. (Chili can be refrigerated for up to 3 days.)

Inside This Chapter

CHAPTER 6

How to Cook Meat

Many cooks grade their overall skill level in the kitchen by their success rate at preparing meat. Because meat is often the focal point of the meal (and because it's so expensive), proper cooking is key. This chapter focuses on beef and pork, although it also offers some information on lamb. More meat recipes appear in chapter 9 (page 387), which is devoted to grilling. In this chapter, we focus on indoor methods, including pan-searing, stir-frying, roasting, braising, and stewing.

Getting Started

How to Buy Meat

There are dozens of beef cuts and just as many pork cuts, and the naming conventions vary from market to market (and region to region). Some markets sell multiple grades of meat, and then there's the issue of provenance (whether to buy organic meat, grass-fed beef, or imported lamb). Which should you buy? In this section, we help you answer that question. Let's start with some broad strategies for successful meat buying. It's simple: Just ask yourself these four questions.

DO YOU WANT A STEAK, CHOP, OR ROAST?

The terms "steak" and "chop" refer to any relatively thin cut, with or without a bone. Most steaks and chops are tender and need only a quick sear in a hot pan or a brief sizzle on the grill. (Exceptions to this rule include fattier chops, such as lamb shoulder chops or pork blade chops, which can be braised.) Most steaks and chops are sold in individual portions.

In contrast, a roast is suitable for longer cooking. Tender roasts, generally from the loin section of the animal, are best roasted or grilled to desired doneness (we think medium-rare is best for most beef and lamb roasts, and medium-well is best for most pork roasts). This category includes everything from beef tenderloin and pork loin to rack of lamb and butterflied leg of lamb. Naturally tough roasts, such as beef brisket or pork shoulder, are generally cooked by low-heat cooking methods such as braising and barbecuing.

DO YOU WANT BONES OR NO BONES?

The answer to this question is not always clear. Sure, if you're making a stew you want boneless meat. And flank steak will always be boneless. But many cuts are sold with and without the bone. Prime rib, a roast cut from the cow's rib section, contains a large muscle and several bones. If this roast is cut between the bones into individual steaks, you have rib steaks, which have a single bone running along one side. If the meat is removed from the bone, you have rib-eye steaks. All three cuts are cut from the same part of the cow. When it makes sense for the dish, we often prefer bone-in cuts because bones help retain moisture and add flavor.

HOW MANY PEOPLE ARE YOU SERVING?

If you're serving a cut that should be served whole (chops or small steaks), buy meat by the piece: four chops to feed four people. If you plan to slice the meat before serving (roasts), buy between 6 and 8 ounces of meat per serving, which will yield a slightly smaller serving once the meat has been cooked. If you're buying a bone-in or fatty cut, you will want to compensate and buy a bit more per person.

HOW DO YOU WANT TO COOK THE MEAT?

It's imperative to match the cut with the cooking method. A chuck-eye roast is our favorite cut of beef for pot-roasting because braising turns all the fat and connective tissue into gelatin, and the result is flavorful and tender. Take that same cut and try roasting it, and the results are fatty and tough.

Tough cuts, which generally come from the heavily exercised parts of the animal, such as the shoulder or rump, respond best to slow-cooking methods, such as pot-roasting, stewing, or barbecuing. The primary goal of slow cooking is to melt collagen in the connective tissue, thereby transforming a tough piece of meat into a tender one. These cuts are always served well done.

Tender cuts with little connective tissue generally come from parts of the animal that receive little exercise (like the loin, the area along the back of the cow or pig). These cuts respond best to quicker, dry-heat cooking methods, such as grilling or roasting. These cuts are cooked to a specific doneness. Prolonged cooking increases moisture loss and can turn these tender cuts tough.

How to Buy Beef

Before you pick a particular cut of beef, it's helpful to understand some basic information as well as the primal cuts from which the retail cuts are butchered.

GRAIN- VS. GRASS-FED

Most U.S. beef is raised on grain, but grass-fed beef is becoming increasingly popular. Grain-fed beef is generally considered to be richer and fattier, while grass-fed is leaner, chewier, and gamier—or at least that's the conventional wisdom. In our taste tests, we pitted grain-fed and grass-fed rib-eye steaks and strip steaks against each other. We found differences between the strip steaks to be small. Grain-fed rib-eyes had a milder flavor compared with the nutty, complex flavor of the grass-fed rib-eyes, but our tasters' preferences were evenly split. The texture of all samples was similar.

ORGANIC VS. NATURAL

The government regulates the use of the term "organic" on beef labels, but producers set their own guidelines when it comes to the term "natural." If you want to ensure that you're buying meat raised without antibiotics or hormones and fed an organic diet (and no mammalian or aviary products), then look for the U.S. Department of Agriculture organic seal.

GRADING

Most meat available to consumers is confined to three of the quality grades assigned by the USDA: prime, choice, and select. Grading is voluntary on the part of the meat-packer. If meat is graded, it should bear a USDA stamp indicating the grade, though it may not be visible to the consumer. To grade meat, inspectors evaluate color, grain, surface texture, and fat content and distribution.

Prime meat is heavily marbled with intramuscular fat, which makes for a tender, flavorful steak. About 2 percent of graded beef is considered prime. Prime meats are most often served in restaurants or sold in high-end butcher shops. The majority of graded beef is choice. While the levels of marbling in choice beef can vary, it is generally moderately marbled with intramuscular fat. Select beef has little marbling.

Our blind tasting of all three grades of rib-eye steaks produced predictable results: Prime ranked first for its tender, buttery texture and rich flavor. Next came choice, with good meaty flavor and more chew. The tough and stringy select steak followed, with flavor that was barely acceptable. Our advice: When you're willing to splurge, go for prime steak, but a choice steak that exhibits a moderate amount of marbling is a fine, affordable option. Just stay clear of select-grade steak.

GROUND BEEF

Supermarkets label ground beef either by fat content (for example, "90 percent lean" or "80 percent lean") or by cut (for example, "ground chuck"). Ideally, we like to buy meat that is labeled both ways, but you may not always have that option.

Shopping by cut: Ground chuck generally has quite a lot of fat, which translates to rich flavor and tender texture—it's the best choice for burgers. Ground sirloin has good flavor but is a bit less tender (because it's leaner). Ground sirloin is great in meatloaf and Bolognese sauce but can be a bit dry in burgers. Ground round is often gristly and lacking in beef flavor; we don't recommend it.

Shopping by fat: For burgers, we recommend buying beef labeled 80 percent lean (or 85 percent lean). Ideally, the label will indicate that the meat is from the chuck, but round can have a similar content. For recipes with additional sources of fat and moisture (such as meatloaf), 85 percent lean or even 90 percent lean ground beef is best. Ground sirloin usually is 90 percent to 93 percent lean and is a good choice here.

Primal Cuts of Beef

Eight different cuts of beef are sold at the wholesale level. From this first series of cuts, known in the trade as primal cuts, a butcher will make the retail cuts that you bring home from the market.

CHUCK/SHOULDER

The chuck (or shoulder) runs from the neck down to the fifth rib. There are four major muscles in this region. Meat from the chuck tends to be flavorful and fairly fatty, which is why ground chuck makes the best hamburgers. Chuck also contains a fair amount of connective tissue, so when the meat is not ground it generally requires a long cooking time.

RIB

The rib section extends along the back of the animal from the sixth to the twelfth rib. Prime rib and rib-eye steaks come from this area. Rib cuts have great beefy flavor and are tender.

SHORT LOIN

The short loin (also called the loin) extends from the last rib back through the midsection of the animal to the hip area. It contains two major muscles: the tenderloin and the shell. The tenderloin is extremely tender (it is positioned right under the spine) and has a quite mild flavor. The shell is a much larger muscle and has a more robust beef flavor as well as more fat.

SIRLOIN

The sirloin contains relatively inexpensive cuts that are sold as both steaks and roasts. We find that sirloin cuts are fairly lean and tough. In general, we prefer other parts of the animal, although top sirloin makes a decent roast.

ROUND

Roasts and steaks cut from the back of the cow, called the round, are usually sold boneless; they are quite lean and can be tough. Again, we generally prefer cuts from other parts of the cow, although we have found that top round can be roasted with some success.

BRISKET, PLATE, AND FLANK

Moderately thick boneless cuts are removed from the three primal cuts that run along the underside of the animal. The brisket is rather tough and contains a lot of connective tissue. The plate is rarely sold at the retail level (it is used to make pastrami). The flank is a leaner cut that makes an excellent steak when grilled.

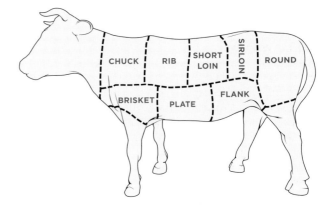

Our Favorite Beef Steaks

These 10 steaks are our top picks. We've rated each steak on a scale from 1 to 4 stars for both tenderness and flavor. We've also listed the primal cut from which the steak is cut.

TOP BLADE STEAK (CHUCK/SHOULDER)

Top blade (or simply blade) steak is a small shoulder cut. It is an all-purpose steak. While it is very tender and richly flavored, a line of gristle that runs through the center of the meat makes it a poor option for serving whole. Remove the gristle and slice the steak thinly for stir-fries, or cut into cubes for kebabs or stews.

Tenderness: ★★★
Flavor: ★★★

SHOULDER STEAK (CHUCK/SHOULDER)

Sometimes labeled as London broil or chuck steak, this 1½- to 2-pound boneless steak is a great value for cost-conscious cooks. Although cut from the shoulder, it is relatively lean, with a moderately beefy flavor. Since this steak can be a bit tough, it should be sliced thinly on the bias after cooking. Grill or pan-roast.

Tenderness: ★★
Flavor: ★★

RIB-EYE STEAK (RIB)

Cut from the rib area just behind the shoulder, a rib-eye steak is essentially a boneless piece of prime rib. This pricey, fat-streaked steak is tender and juicy, with a pronounced beefiness. In the West, rib-eyes are sometimes labeled Spencer steaks; in the East, they may be called Delmonico steaks. Grill, pan-sear, or broil.

Tenderness: ★★★
Flavor: ★★★★

STRIP STEAK (SHORT LOIN)

Available both boneless and bone-in, this moderately expensive steak is also called top loin, shell, sirloin strip, Kansas City strip, or New York strip. Cut from the shell muscle that runs along the middle of the steer's back, strip steaks are well marbled, with a tight grain, pleasantly chewy texture, and big, beefy flavor. Grill, pan-sear, or broil.

Tenderness: ★★★
Flavor: ★★★★

TENDERLOIN STEAK (SHORT LOIN)

Cut from the center of the back, the tenderloin is the most tender (and most expensive) cut of the cow. Depending on their thickness, tenderloin steaks may be labeled (from thickest to thinnest) Châteaubriand, filet mignon, or tournedo. Tenderloin steaks are buttery smooth and very tender, but have little flavor. Grill, pan-sear, or broil.

Tenderness: ★★★★
Flavor: ★

T-BONE STEAK (SHORT LOIN)

A classic grilling steak, this cut is named for the T-shaped bone that runs through the meat. This bone separates two muscles, the flavorful strip (or shell, top of photo) and the buttery tenderloin (bottom of photo). Because the tenderloin is small and will cook more quickly than the strip, this steak should be positioned over the cooler side of the fire when grilling. Grill.

Tenderness: ★★★
Flavor: ★★★★

PORTERHOUSE STEAK (SHORT LOIN)

The porterhouse is really just a huge T-bone steak with a larger tenderloin section, which accounts for its higher price. It is cut farther back on the animal than the T-bone. Like the T-bone steak, the porterhouse steak, with both strip and tenderloin sections, has well-balanced flavor and texture. Most porterhouse steaks are big enough to serve two. Grill.

Tenderness: ★★★
Flavor: ★★★★

TOP SIRLOIN STEAK (SIRLOIN)

Cut from the hip, this steak (along with its bone-in version, round-bone steak) is sometimes called New York sirloin steak or sirloin butt. Top sirloin steak is a large, inexpensive steak with decent tenderness and flavor, but do not confuse it with the superior strip steak. Slice thinly against the grain after cooking. Grill or pan-sear.

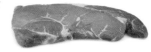

Tenderness: ★★
Flavor: ★★

FLAP MEAT SIRLOIN STEAK (SIRLOIN)

Cut from the area just before the hip, this large (upward of 2½ pounds), rectangular steak is most often sold in strips or cubes. To ensure that you are buying the real thing, buy the whole steak and cut it yourself. Though not particularly tender, flap meat has a distinct grain and a robust beefiness. Slice thinly against the grain after cooking. Grill, pan-roast (whole), or pan-sear (strips).

Tenderness: ★★
Flavor: ★★★

FLANK STEAK (FLANK)

Flank steak, aka jiffy steak, is a large, flat cut from the underside of the cow, with a distinct longitudinal grain. Flank steak is thin and cooks quickly, making it ideal for the grill. Although very flavorful, flank is slightly chewy. It should not be cooked past medium and should always be sliced thinly across the grain. Grill, pan-sear, or slice thinly and stir-fry.

Tenderness: ★★
Flavor: ★★★

Our Favorite Beef Roasts

These eight roasts are our top picks. We've rated each roast on a scale from 1 to 4 stars for flavor. Given that even the toughest cut can make a great roast if cooked properly, we don't rate these cuts for tenderness. We've also listed the primal cut from which each roast is cut.

CHUCK-EYE ROAST (CHUCK/SHOULDER)

This boneless roast is cut from the center of the first five ribs (the term "eye" refers to any center-cut piece of meat). It is very tender and juicy but also contains an excessive amount of fat. This cut should be trussed using kitchen twine, so if the butcher has not done it for you, do it yourself. It is also called boneless chuck roll and boneless chuck fillet. We like the chuck-eye roast for its compact, uniform shape, deep flavor, and tenderness in pot roast. This is our top choice for stewing and braising.

Flavor: ★★★

TOP BLADE ROAST (CHUCK/SHOULDER)

This broad, flat cut is quite flavorful, and because it is boneless it's the best substitute for a chuck-eye roast. Even after cooking, this cut retains a distinctive strip of connective tissue, which is not unpleasant to eat. This roast is sometimes labeled as blade roast or top chuck roast.

Flavor: ★★★

RIB ROAST, FIRST CUT (RIB)

Butchers tend to cut a rib roast, which consists of ribs 6 through 12 if left whole, into two distinct cuts. The more desirable of the two cuts consists of ribs 10 through 12. Since this portion of the roast is closer to the loin end, it is sometimes called the "loin end." Other butchers call it the "small end" or the "first cut." Whatever it is called, it is more desirable because it contains the large, single rib-eye muscle and is less fatty.

Flavor: ★★★★

RIB ROAST, SECOND CUT (RIB)

A less desirable cut, but still an excellent roast, it consists of ribs 6 to 9, closer to the chuck end, and is sometimes called the second cut. The closer to the chuck, the more multimuscled the roast becomes, and since muscles are surrounded by fat, this means a fattier roast. While some cooks may prefer this cut because the fat adds flavor, the more tender and more regularly formed loin end is considered the best.

Flavor: ★★★★

TENDERLOIN ROAST (SHORT LOIN)

The tenderloin (also called the whole filet) is the most tender piece of beef you can buy. Its flavor is pleasantly mild, almost nonbeefy. Unpeeled tenderloins come with an incredibly thick layer of exterior fat still attached, which should be removed. Peeled roasts have scattered patches of fat that need not be removed. This roast can be cut into individual steaks to make filets mignons.

Flavor: ★

TOP SIRLOIN ROAST (SIRLOIN)

This cut from the hip area tastes incredibly meaty and has plenty of marbling, which makes for a succulent roast. Aside from the vein of gristle that runs through it, which we found slightly unpleasant to eat, the roast was tender and juicy, with big, beefy flavor. Other parts of the sirloin are lean and tough, but top sirloin roast is one of our favorite inexpensive roasts.

Flavor: ★★★

EYE-ROUND ROAST (ROUND)

This boneless roast is quite inexpensive but not nearly as flavorful as the top cuts. However, it does have a nice shape that slices neatly, making it a better choice than other round or rump roasts. In order to make this lean cut as tender as possible, roast it in a very low oven.

Flavor: ★★

BRISKET (BRISKET)

This large, rectangular cut weights 13 pounds, so it is often divided into two subcuts, the flat cut (pictured here) and the point cut. The flat cut is leaner, thinner, and more widely available. When shopping for flat-cut brisket, look for a roast with a decent fat cap on top. The point cut is well marbled and thicker; if you can find it, you can use it in place of the flat-cut brisket in most recipes; however, the cooking time might need to be extended slightly.

Flavor: ★★★

How to Buy Pork

Before you pick a particular cut of pork, it's helpful to understand some basic information as well as the primal cuts from which the retail cuts are butchered.

THE OTHER WHITE MEAT

The majority of pork sold in today's supermarkets bears little resemblance to the pork our grandparents consumed. New breeding techniques and feeding systems have slimmed down the modern pig, which contains a third less fat than it did 30 years ago. As you might imagine, leaner pork is not as flavorful and is prone to drying out as it cooks. We find that lean cuts of pork should be cooked to an internal temperature of 140 to 145 degrees. By the time the meat rests, the internal temperature will rise to 150 degrees. The pork will have a slight tinge of pink, and it will be juicy. If you cook lean pork just 10 degrees higher (as recommended in many older books), the meat will be tough and dry.

HERITAGE BREEDS

After years of advertising pork as "the other white meat," some pork producers have started to change their tune. Nowadays, fat, flavor, and even deeper color are making a comeback, with chefs and consumers paying top dollar for specialty breeds touted as being fattier, juicier, and far more flavorful.

When we tasted 100 percent Berkshire pork against standard supermarket pork, we found the differences to be astounding. The Berkshire meat had a rich crimson color and smoky, intensely pork flavor. It was also very tender and juicy. The pale supermarket pork was bland and chewy in comparison. Other heritage breeds (including Duroc) failed to impress our tasters, but if you can find Berkshire pork we recommend buying it.

ENHANCED OR NOT?

Because modern pork is so lean and therefore somewhat bland and prone to dryness if overcooked, many producers now inject their fresh pork products with a sodium solution. So-called enhanced pork is now the only option at many supermarkets, especially when buying lean cuts like the tenderloin. (To be sure, read the label; if the pork has been enhanced it will have an ingredient label.)

Enhanced pork is injected with a solution of water, salt, sodium phosphates, sodium lactate, potassium lactate, sodium diacetate, and varying flavor agents, generally adding 7 to 15 percent extra weight. While enhanced pork does cook up juicier (it has been pumped full of water!), we find the texture almost spongy, and the flavor is often unpleasantly salty. We prefer the genuine pork flavor of natural pork and brine lean cuts to keep them juicy (see page 226 for information on brining). Note that enhanced pork loses six times more moisture when frozen and thawed compared to natural pork—yet another reason to avoid enhanced pork.

CURED PORK

Various cured pork products appear in recipes throughout this book, including bacon, pancetta, salt pork, and fatback. The location on the pig and processing methods define these pork products, which are commonly used as flavoring ingredients. Pancetta, American bacon, and salt pork all come from the belly, while fatback comes, as its name implies, from the back of the pig. Pancetta, bacon, and salt pork are all cured (pancetta's cure includes salt and spices; the others just salt), but bacon is also smoked. Fatback, on the other hand, is not cured, salted, or smoked; it's simply fresh pork fat.

NITRITES VS. NITRATES

Cured pork products, such as bacon, often contain nitrites and/or nitrates. Nitrites have been shown to form carcinogenic compounds called nitrosamines when heated in the presence of proteins, like those in pork. While nitrites and nitrates are virtually identical, only nitrites have been shown to form potentially harmful nitrosamines.

So should you buy "nitrate-free" or "nitrite-free" bacon? These products are generally brined with salt, a bacterial lactic-acid starter culture, and celery juice (which is sometimes listed as "natural flavor"). The problem is that celery juice contains a high level of nitrate, which is converted to the problematic nitrite by the bacteria in the starter culture. While technically these products can be labeled "no nitrates or nitrites added," the compounds are naturally formed during production.

When we analyzed various brands of bacon, we found that regular bacon actually contained lower levels of nitrites and nitrates than some brands labeled "no nitrites or nitrates added." All bacons tested fell well within federal standards for these compounds, but if you want to avoid nitrites and nitrates you need to avoid bacon and other processed pork products altogether.

Primal Cuts of Pork

Five different cuts of pork are sold at the wholesale level. From this first series of cuts, known in the trade as primal cuts, a butcher (usually at a meatpacking plant in the Midwest but sometimes on-site at your market) will make the retail cuts that you bring home from the market.

BLADE SHOULDER

Cuts from the upper portion of the shoulder are well marbled with fat and contain a lot of connective tissue, making them ideal candidates for slow-cooking methods like braising, stewing, or barbecuing.

ARM SHOULDER

Cuts from the arm, or picnic shoulder, are a bit more economical than those from the blade area but are otherwise quite similar.

LOIN

The area between the shoulder and back legs is the leanest, most tender part of the animal. Rib and loin chops are cut from this area, as are pork loin roasts and tenderloin roasts. These cuts will be dry if overcooked.

LEG

The rear legs are often referred to as "ham." This primal cut is sold as large roasts and is available fresh or cured.

SIDE

The underside is the fattiest part of the animal and is home to bacon and spareribs.

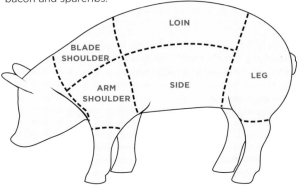

Our Favorite Pork Cuts

These 13 cuts are our top picks. We've rated each cut on a scale from 1 to 4 stars for flavor. (Given that even the toughest cut can make a great dish if cooked properly, we haven't rated these cuts for tenderness.). We've also listed the relevant primal cut.

PORK BUTT (BLADE SHOULDER)

This large, flavorful cut (often labeled Boston butt or pork shoulder at markets) can weigh as much as 8 pounds when sold with the bone in. Many markets take out the bone and sell this cut in smaller chunks, often wrapped in netting to hold the roast together. This cut is ideal for slow roasting, barbecuing, stewing, or braising. Use it for pulled pork and other shredded pork dishes, like carnitas.
Flavor: ★★★★

SHOULDER ARM PICNIC (ARM SHOULDER)

This affordable cut (often labeled "picnic roast" at markets) can be sold bone-in or boneless. It is rich in fat and connective tissue. Use it like pork butt for barbecuing, braising, or other slow-cooking methods.
Flavor: ★★★★

BONELESS BLADE-END ROAST (LOIN)

This is our favorite boneless roast for roasting. It is cut from the shoulder end of the loin and has more fat (and flavor) than the boneless center-cut loin roast. Unfortunately, this cut can be hard to find in many markets. This roast is also sold with the bone in, although this cut is even harder to locate.
Flavor: ★★★

CENTER-CUT LOIN ROAST (LOIN)

This boneless roast is widely available and a good choice for roasting. We prefer the more flavorful boneless blade roast, but the two cuts can be used interchangeably. Make sure to buy a center-cut roast with a decent fat cap on top.
Flavor: ★★

CENTER RIB ROAST (LOIN)

Often referred to as the pork equivalent of prime rib or rack of lamb, this mild, fairly lean roast consists of a single muscle with a protective fat cap. It may be cut with anywhere from five to eight ribs. Because the bones (and nearby fat) are still attached, we find this roast a better option than the center-cut loin roast, which is cut from the same muscle but is minus the bones and fat.

Flavor: ★★★

TENDERLOIN ROAST (LOIN)

This lean, delicate, boneless roast cooks very quickly because it's so small, usually weighing just about 1 pound. Since there is very little marbling, this roast (which is equivalent to beef tenderloin) cannot be overcooked without ruining its texture. Tenderloins are often sold two to a package. Many tenderloins sold in the supermarket are enhanced; look for one that has no ingredients other than pork on the label.

Flavor: ★

BLADE CHOP (LOIN)

Cut from the shoulder end of the loin, these chops can be difficult to find at the market. They are fatty and tough, despite good flavor and juiciness. These chops are best suited to low-and-slow cooking methods that break down their connective tissue, such as braising or barbecuing.

Flavor: ★★★

RIB CHOP (LOIN)

Cut from the rib section of the loin, these chops have a relatively high fat content, rendering them flavorful and unlikely to dry out during cooking. They are a favorite in the test kitchen. These chops are easily identified by the bone that runs along one side and the one large eye of loin muscle. These tender chops are a good choice for grilling and pansearing.

Flavor: ★★★

CENTER-CUT CHOP (LOIN)

These chops can be identified by the bone that divides the loin meat from the tenderloin muscle. The lean tenderloin section cooks more quickly than the loin section, making these chops a challenge. They have good flavor, but since they contain less fat than the rib chops, they are not quite as moist. Because the loin and tenderloin muscles in these chops are bisected by bulky bone or cartilage, they don't lie flat, making these chops a poor choice for pan searing. Save them for the grill, but position the ultralean tenderloin away from the fire to keep it from drying out.

Flavor: ★★

BABY BACK RIBS (LOIN)

Baby back ribs (also referred to as loin back ribs) are cut from the section of the rib cage closest to the backbone. Loin center-cut roasts and chops come from the same part of the pig, which explains why baby back ribs can be expensive. This location also explains why baby back ribs are much leaner than spareribs—and why they need special attention to keep from drying out on the grill.

Flavor: ★★★

ST. LOUIS SPARERIBS (SIDE)

Regular spareribs are cut close to the belly of the pig (which is also where bacon comes from). Because whole spareribs contain the brisket bone and surrounding meat, each rack can weigh upward of 5 pounds. Some racks of spareribs are so big they barely fit on the grill. We prefer this more manageable cut because the brisket bone and surrounding meat are trimmed off to produce a narrower, rectangular rack that usually weighs in at a relatively svelte 3 pounds.

Flavor: ★★★★

COUNTRY-STYLE RIBS (LOIN)

These meaty, tender, boneless ribs are cut from the upper side of the rib cage from the fatty blade end of the loin. Butchers usually cut them into individual ribs and package several ribs together. These ribs can be braised and shredded for pasta sauce, or pounded flat and grilled or pan-seared as cutlets.

Flavor: ★★★

FRESH HAM, SHANK END (LEG)

The leg is divided into two cuts—the tapered shank end and the more rounded sirloin end. The sirloin end has a lot of bones that make carving tricky. We prefer the shank end. This cut is usually covered in a thick layer of fat and skin, which should be scored before roasting. This cut is not as fatty as you might think and benefits from brining.

Flavor: ★★★

How to Buy Lamb

Americans don't buy much lamb, so there aren't that many choices when shopping. Most markets contain just a few of our favorite cuts, and you may need to special-order lamb. While almost all of the beef and pork sold in American markets are raised domestically, you can purchase imported as well as domestic lamb. Domestic lamb is distinguished by its larger size and milder flavor, while lamb imported from Australia and New Zealand features a far gamier taste. The reason for this difference in taste boils down to diet and the chemistry of lamb fat. Imported lamb is pasture-fed on mixed grasses, while lamb raised in the United States begins on a diet of grass but finishes with grain. The switch to grain has a direct impact on the composition of the animal's fat, reducing the concentration of the medium-length branched fatty-acid chains that give any lamb its characteristic "lamby" flavor—and ultimately leading to sweeter-tasting meat.

Our Favorite Lamb Cuts

These six cuts are the ones we cook most often in the test kitchen.

SHOULDER CHOP

If you think all lamb chops are expensive, think again. Lamb rib chops and loin chops are indeed pricey (about $13 and $10 per pound, respectively); they're also relatively lean and best cooked to medium-rare. But inexpensive shoulder chops (about $5 per pound) are an excellent value. Cooked slow and low in order to break down their connective tissue, the chops become moist, flavorful, and tender. Stews may also benefit from the bones, which add both body and deep meaty savor. Some markets sell blade shoulder chops (more rectangular in shape and a bit fattier), while others sell round-bone chops (more oval in shape, with a cross section of arm bone at one end). Either type of shoulder chops can be used in our recipes.

RIB CHOP

This is the best (and most expensive) lamb chop you can buy—it's basically the rack of lamb cut into individual chops. The bone runs along one side of the chop, and the meat is a single muscle that is well marbled with fat. You can trim exterior fat scrupulously and try to cook these indoors, but we think rib chops are best grilled. Don't overcook rib chops; they are best served rare or medium-rare.

LOIN CHOP

This chop looks like a tiny T-bone steak, with the bone running down the center and meat on either side. The protruding bone makes it very difficult to pan-sear these chops—they are best grilled. The small piece of meat is very easy to overcook, so position these chops with this part facing away from the heat.

RACK OF LAMB

The equivalent to prime rib on a cow, this cut is extremely flavorful and tender—and very expensive. This roast usually contains either eight or nine rib bones and will feed two to three people. Although you can roast this cut in the oven (browning it first on the stovetop), it's easier to cook it on the grill. Don't overcook this roast, as it will become tough and dry; it is best enjoyed when cooked to medium-rare.

LEG OF LAMB

The whole leg generally weighs 6 to 10 pounds (although smaller legs are available from younger lambs, especially imported ones). Ask the butcher to remove the hip bone and aitchbone to make carving easier. We think it's easier to cook a boneless leg of lamb, plus you can buy smaller cuts better suited to today's smaller dinner parties and holiday gatherings.

BONELESS LEG OF LAMB

A leg of lamb is so big and so tricky to cook that we generally opt for a boneless leg, which is usually butterflied into a single piece of varying thickness. This cut can be grilled as is (the thicker parts will provide rare or medium-rare meat for those who like it) or stuffed, rolled, and tied. An entire leg of lamb consists of three main parts: Up near the hip is the butt end (which includes the sirloin, or hip meat); below that is the shank end, with the shank (or ankle) at the very bottom. We prefer the shank end, which is easier to work with and yields more meat.

Preparing Meat Before Cooking

Buying the right cut is the first step. There are several steps in between purchasing meat and cooking meat, and they can have a significant effect on the final dish.

FREEZING MEAT

In general, meat tastes best when it hasn't been frozen. The slow process of freezing that occurs in a home freezer (as compared with a commercial freezer) causes large ice crystals to form. The crystals rupture the cell walls of the meat, permitting the release of juices during cooking. If you're going to freeze meat, wrap it well in plastic and then place the meat in a zipper-lock bag and squeeze out excess air. Label the bag and use the meat within a few months. Thaw all frozen meats on a plate or rimmed baking sheet in the refrigerator—not on the counter, where bacteria will rapidly multiply.

According to the USDA, frozen food that is properly thawed in the refrigerator is safe to refreeze in its raw state. However, a second freeze-thaw cycle aggravates the moisture loss problem and is not recommended.

RINSING MEAT

Don't rinse raw meat (or poultry). Rinsing is more likely to spread contaminants around the sink. Since brined meats need to be rinsed before cooking, thoroughly clean the sink and surrounding areas after rinsing. Do blot meat dry with paper towels before cooking to ensure good browning.

SEASONING MEAT

No matter how well cooked the meat is, if it's not properly seasoned it won't taste very good. Meat should be seasoned with salt and pepper before cooking. You will also want to taste meat before serving to adjust the seasonings. Heat tames the punch of pepper, so use it sparingly after cooking.

As for salt, you can season the meat right before cooking for flavor, but you can also use salt (and time) in advance of cooking to improve the texture of many cuts. There are two ways to do this: salting or brining. Salting is more convenient (no need to cram a large container of salt water in the fridge), and it won't thwart the goal of crispy skin on poultry or a well-browned crust on steak, chops, and roasts since no moisture is added to their exteriors. However, salting is a slow process and takes more time than brining.

When salt is applied to raw meat, juices inside the meat are drawn to the surface. The salt then dissolves in the exuded liquid, forming a brine that is eventually reabsorbed by the meat. The salt changes the structure of the muscle proteins, allowing them to hold on to more of their own natural juices. Salting is the best choice for meats that are already relatively juicy and/or well marbled.

We prefer to use kosher salt for salting because it's easier to distribute the salt evenly. The chart lists the meat items that we typically salt, along with notes on timing and method. If using Morton Kosher Salt, reduce the amounts listed by 33 percent. See page 288 for details on salting poultry.

Brining works pretty much the same way as salting. Salt in the brine seasons the meat and promotes a change in its protein structure, reducing its overall toughness and creating gaps that fill up with water and keep the meat juicy and flavorful. Brining works faster than salting and can also result in juicier lean cuts—such as pork tenderloin—since it adds, versus merely retains, moisture. Note that brining inhibits browning, and it requires fitting a brining container in fridge.

We prefer to use table salt for brining since it dissolves quickly in the water. The chart lists the meat items that we typically brine, along with notes on timing and the amount of water needed. See page 288 for details on brining poultry.

Salting Meat

CUTS	TIME	KOSHER SALT	METHOD
Steaks, Lamb Chops, Pork Chops	1 hour	¾ teaspoon per 8-ounce chop or steak	Apply salt evenly over surface and let rest at room temperature, uncovered, on wire rack set in rimmed baking sheet.
Beef, Lamb, and Pork Roasts	At least 6 hours and up to 24 hours	1 teaspoon per pound	Apply salt evenly over surface, wrap tightly with plastic wrap, and let rest in refrigerator.

Brining Meat

CUT	TIME	COLD WATER	TABLE SALT
4 (12-ounce) bone-in pork rib chops, 1½ inches thick	1 hour	1½ quarts	3 tablespoons
1 (3- to 6-pound) pork roast	1½ to 2 hours	2 quarts	¼ cup

Three Principles of Meat Cookery

Meat can be prepared by numerous cooking methods—everything from roasting to grilling. However, there are three basic principles that apply to the vast majority of these recipes, as well as to most poultry recipes.

BROWN IS GOOD
Browning creates a tremendous amount of flavor and is a key step when cooking meat. This happens through a process called the Maillard reaction, named after the French chemist who first described it in the early 1900s. The Maillard reaction occurs when the amino acids and sugars in the food are subjected to heat, which causes them to combine. In turn, hundreds of different flavor compounds are created. These compounds break down to form yet more new flavor compounds, and so on, and so on. It's kind of like rabbits multiplying.

When browning meat, you want a deep brown sear and a discernibly thick crust on all sides—best obtained by quick cooking over high heat. To ensure that meat browns properly, first make sure the meat is dry before it goes into the pan; pat it thoroughly with paper towels. This is especially important with previously frozen meat, which often releases a great deal of water. Second, make sure the pan is hot by preheating it over high heat until fat added to the pan is shimmering or almost smoking. Finally, make sure not to overcrowd the pan; there should be at least ¼ inch of space between the pieces of meat. If there isn't, the meat is likely to steam instead of brown. If need be, cook the meat in two or three batches.

LOW HEAT PRESERVES MOISTURE
For large cuts of meat or poultry, we often advocate a low-and-slow cooking method. We find that this approach allows the center to come up to the desired internal temperature with less risk of overcooking the outer layers.

An experiment we recently conducted proves that even cooking isn't the only benefit of slow roasting: It also helps minimize the loss of flavorful juices (and fat). We took two 6-pound rib roasts and roasted one at 450 degrees and the other at 250 degrees until each was medium-rare. We then weighed the cooked roasts. The slow-cooked roast had lost about 9.25 percent of its starting weight, while the high-temperature roast had lost nearly 25 percent of its original weight. Why the difference? Proteins shrink less and express less moisture and fat when cooked at moderate temperatures than when roasted at high heat.

LET IT REST
A final but very important step when cooking all red meat and pork (as well as poultry) is a resting period after the meat comes off the heat. As the proteins heat up during cooking they coagulate, which basically means they uncoil and then reconnect in a different configuration. When the proteins coagulate, they squeeze out part of the liquid that was trapped in their coiled structures and in the spaces between the individual molecules. The heat from the cooking source drives these freed liquids toward the center of the meat.

This process of coagulation explains why experienced chefs can determine the doneness of a piece of meat by pushing on it and judging the amount of resistance; the firmer the meat, the more done it is. But the coagulation process is apparently at least partly reversible, so as you allow the meat to rest and return to a lower temperature after cooking, some of the liquid is reabsorbed by the protein molecules as their capacity to hold moisture increases. As a result, if given a chance to rest, the meat will lose less juice when you cut into it, which in turn makes for much juicier and more tender meat.

A thin steak or chop should rest for 5 to 10 minutes, while a thicker roast requires 15 to 20 minutes. When cooking a huge turkey, the bird should rest for 30 minutes before it is carved. To keep meat warm while it rests, tent it loosely with foil. But don't crimp the foil around the edges of the pan or plate; this can trap steam and soften the crust or skin.

Essential Equipment

The cookware you need to cook meat will vary based on the cooking method, but there are a few basics you'll want to make sure you own.

INSTANT-READ THERMOMETER
Given the importance of cooking meat to a target temperature to achieve your desired doneness, having a good instant-read thermometer is a priority. For details on what to look for in an instant-read thermometer, see page 10.

KITCHEN TWINE
Kitchen twine is key when cooking roasts, as tying ensures even cooking. We find linen twine easier to tie, and it pulls away from cooked meat easily. That said, cotton twine works nearly as well as linen and is a more economical choice. A commonly suggested alternative is unwaxed dental floss, but we wouldn't recommend it. It is so thin that it often cuts through meat, and after cooking, it is almost translucent, so it can be difficult to remove.

CARVING BOARD
When you are dealing with larger cuts, you want a carving board. Look for a heavy, sturdy board with a deep, wide trench around the perimeter to catch juices. A central well that keeps meat in place as you carve is helpful. If you are using a carving board, you likely will need a slicing knife; for more details on what to look for when buying a slicing knife, see page 19.

How to Pan-Sear Steaks and Chops

ESSENTIAL EQUIPMENT

- paring knife
- cutting board
- paper towels
- 12-inch skillet
- tongs
- measuring spoons
- instant-read thermometer
- large plate
- aluminum foil

Cooking a steak or chop in a skillet is a basic technique that should be in every cook's repertoire. When the steak or chop is thicker than 1 or 1¼ inches you need to use a combination method that starts in the oven and finishes in the skillet (see page 230). But for your average supermarket steaks or chops, the operation can take place entirely on top of the stove. We prefer to use this method with boneless steaks and chops since the bone can make it difficult to get a good sear. Strip steaks and rib-eye steaks are our favorite beef cuts for this technique; boneless pork chops as well as thinner bone-in pork rib chops are our favorite pork cuts. To determine doneness, refer to the chart on page 783. While the steaks or chops rest, make a quick pan sauce (see page 232).

1. TRIM FAT

Use sharp paring knife to trim hard, white fat from perimeter of 4 steaks and chops. Leave no more than ⅛ inch fat.

WHY? When searing meat on the stovetop, keep the splattering to a minimum by trimming excess fat. You can also place a splatter screen over the skillet as the meat cooks.

2. PAT DRY

Blot meat surfaces dry with paper towels.

WHY? Browning equal flavors, and browning occurs only once all surface moisture has evaporated. If you skip this step, the meat will steam.

3. SEASON LIBERALLY

Sprinkle meat with kosher salt and ground pepper. Make sure to coat both sides.

WHY? Seasoning before cooking is imperative. We prefer the large crystals of kosher salt because they are easier to distribute. For individual steaks and chops, use ½ teaspoon kosher salt. Freshly ground pepper is a must; use as much as you like (a 4:1 salt-to-pepper ratio generally works well). To avoid contaminating the pepper grinder or salt box, we often premeasure the salt and pepper into a ramekin.

4. GET PAN HOT

Heat 1 tablespoon vegetable oil in large skillet over medium-high heat until just smoking.

WHY? Many cooks fail to get the pan hot enough. As a result, browning is poor and the meat can stick to the cold pan. We use the temperature of the oil to gauge the temperature of the pan. When vegetable oil begins to smoke, the pan is about 450 degrees, the perfect temperature for searing. A traditional skillet is key for maximum browning. Do not attempt to sear meat in a non-stick skillet, especially if you want to make a pan sauce. Those browned bits (called fond) that stick to a traditional surface are packed with flavor and will be the backbone of any pan sauce.

5. GIVE THEM ROOM

Lay steaks or chops in pan, making sure to leave room between them.

WHY? Make sure to use a pan large enough to accommodate the steaks or chops in a single layer, with about ¼ inch between each piece. If the meat is crowded into the pan, it will steam instead of brown. A 12-inch skillet is the right size to cook four small steaks or chops. A heavy skillet conducts and holds heat better than a light-weight pan and is essential when searing meat.

6. LEAVE THEM ALONE

Wait 3 or 4 minutes, leaving meat undisturbed, then lift edge of steak or chop to check for browning. If color looks good, use tongs to flip meat.

WHY? Leaving the meat in place helps build a better crust. Also, meat will tend to stick when first added to the pan. If you leave it alone, a crust will form and the meat will free itself naturally from the pan. Don't turn steaks and chops with a fork—you end up piercing the meat and causing the loss of precious juices—tongs are the tool for the job.

7. TAKE THEIR TEMPERATURE

Let steaks or chops cook another 3 to 5 minutes and then test for doneness. Use tongs to lift meat out of pan and slide instant-read thermometer through side of steak or chop. Make sure to test center of meat, avoiding any bones.

WHY? Don't attempt to gauge doneness by cutting into the meat. Use a good thermometer and you will never overcook another steak or chop. See page 783 for doneness temperatures for meat.

8. REST BEFORE SERVING

Transfer meat to large plate, loosely cover with aluminum foil, and let rest 5 to 10 minutes.

WHY? A short rest allows the muscle fibers in the meat to relax and reabsorb their natural juices. Use this time to make a quick sauce in the pan, turning those browned bits into a potent flavor source.

How to Pan-Sear Thick Cuts

If you attempt to cook thicker steaks and chops (1½ to 1¾ inches thick) entirely on the stovetop, you end up with a burnt exterior and a raw center. Even if you can manage to avoid burning the exterior, the meat around the perimeter is way overcooked by the time the center comes up to temperature. The secret to getting a great crust on extra-thick chops and steaks without making them tough is to cook them in a very low oven, then quickly sear them. The gentle oven heat minimizes moisture loss and promotes a natural enzymatic reaction that breaks down connective tissue in the meat and makes it especially tender. The stint in the oven also dries the surface of the meat. The steaks and chops brown in record time, and since the meat is in the pan for just a few minutes, there isn't time for it to lose much moisture. When the steaks and chops are done, make a quick pan sauce (see page 232) or a compound butter.

ESSENTIAL EQUIPMENT

- wire rack
- rimmed baking sheet
- instant-read thermometer
- 12-inch skillet
- measuring spoons
- tongs
- plate
- aluminum foil

1. PLACE SEASONED MEAT ON RACK

Pat 4 (1½-inch-thick) chops or (1½- to 1¾-inch-thick) steaks dry with paper towels. Season meat with kosher salt and pepper. Place meat on wire rack set in rimmed baking sheet.

WHY? This recipe starts like traditional recipes—by drying and seasoning the meat. However, since these chops are going into the oven, they need to be set on a wire rack nestled into a rimmed baking sheet. The rack is essential since it allows the gentle heat of the oven to circulate evenly around the meat. Note that if you're cooking pork chops, cut two slits about 2 inches apart through the outer layer of fat and connective tissue; this will keep the chops from buckling when they are seared.

2. PLACE IN LOW-TEMPERATURE OVEN

Transfer baking sheet to middle rack in 275-degree oven.

WHY? The low oven temperature accomplishes two things—it ensures that the exterior part of the steaks and chops doesn't race ahead of the interior. Also, it prolongs the period during which a natural enzymatic reaction in the meat breaks down muscle fibers. Steaks and chops cooked this way are more tender because this gentle heat gives more time for natural enzymes in the meat to work their magic.

3. BAKE UNTIL NEARLY DONE

Cook chops until instant-read thermometer inserted into centers (and away from bones) registers 120 to 125 degrees, 30 to 45 minutes. Cook steaks until instant-read thermometer inserted into centers registers 90 to 95 degrees (for rare to medium-rare), 20 to 25 minutes, or 100 to 105 degrees (for medium), 25 to 30 minutes.

WHY? Since these chops or steaks are going to be seared just before serving, you don't want to overcook them in the oven. Once the internal temperature is 25 to 30 degrees shy of the desired final internal temperature, it's time to take the meat out of the oven.

4. GET SKILLET HOT

Heat 1 tablespoon vegetable oil in 12-inch skillet over high heat until just smoking.

WHY? The searing part of this process should happen quickly. Get the pan very hot so you can put a crust on the meat swiftly. If you slow down this process, the meat can overcook.

5. SEAR FIRST SIDE

Place chops or steaks in skillet and sear until well browned, 1½ to 3 minutes, lifting once halfway through to redistribute fat under each piece of meat.

WHY? Other than lifting the chops once to let the fat redistribute itself under the meat, leave the meat alone so that a crust can form. If cooking large chops, you will want to sear them in batches, putting just 2 chops in the pan at a time. You should be able to fit 4 steaks into the pan in a single batch.

6. SEAR SECOND SIDE, TRANSFER TO PLATE

Use tongs to turn meat and cook until well browned on second side, 2 to 3 minutes. Transfer meat to plate or wire rack set over baking sheet and reduce heat to medium.

WHY? Once the second side is browned, it's time to brown the edges of the chops or steaks. You want to do this in batches, with the heat turned down to prevent the fond from burning, so transfer them to a plate first.

7. SEAR THE SIDES

Use tongs to stand 2 chops or steaks on their sides in hot skillet. Sear until edges (except bone) are well browned, about 1½ minutes. Return chops or steaks to plate or wire rack and repeat browning sides of remaining 2 chops or steaks. When second batch is browned, set them aside with first batch, tent with aluminum foil, and let rest for 10 minutes.

WHY? The edges on a thick steak or chop are so tall that it seems like a mistake not to brown them as well. Once the flat sides are browned, we brown the sides, two at a time, in the pan. Don't worry about getting a perfect crust here—the idea is to put some color on the sides and boost overall flavor.

8. MAKE PAN SAUCE

While meat rests, prepare pan sauce in empty skillet. Spoon prepared sauce over meat and serve immediately.

WHY? Thick chops or steaks should rest for 10 minutes before serving so the meat fibers have time to reabsorb their juices. That skillet is filled with flavorful fond, and you might as well turn it into a quick sauce.

HOW TO COOK MEAT

How to Make a Pan Sauce

ESSENTIAL EQUIPMENT

- large plate
- 12-inch skillet
- small bowl
- chef's knife
- cutting board
- wooden spoon
- liquid measuring cup
- whisk
- wide, shallow spoon

Pan sauces are the easiest way to dress up pan-seared steaks or chops. These sauces start in the empty pan used to cook the steaks or chops. (The technique is also sometimes used with roasts as well as with boneless, skinless chicken breasts and chicken parts.) There are browned bits (called fond) sticking to that pan from the searing process, and that fond is packed with flavor. The goal is to build on that flavor, then loosen and dissolve the fond to create a simple sauce. (The process of loosening and dissolving fond with liquid is called deglazing.) Although the ingredients and amounts change depending on the sauce, the steps are the same—sauté aromatics, add liquid and scrape the pan, simmer to reduce and concentrate flavors, then finish with butter. The basic steps for any pan sauce are the same; in the following steps we make a Red Wine Pan Sauce (see recipe on page 266). See the recipe library at the end of this chapter, as well as the libraries at the end of the Poultry and Seafood chapters, for a number of pan sauce recipes.

1. POUR OFF EXCESS FAT

Once meat is cooked, transfer to large plate to rest. Pour off all but 2 teaspoons fat from skillet. **WHY?** Don't wash that skillet—it's packed with flavorful fond. If there's more than 2 teaspoons of fat in the pan, you want to pour off the excess—otherwise the sauce will be greasy. If there's very little fat in the pan, add a little vegetable oil (up to 2 teaspoons) as needed.

2. ADD AROMATICS

Add minced shallot, garlic, onion, or leek and cook over medium or medium-high heat, stirring frequently, until softened, 1 to 3 minutes. **WHY?** Don't go overboard here—you're making about ½ cup of sauce, so a single shallot, a garlic clove or two, a small onion, or a single leek will be sufficient. Don't let the aromatics burn—garlic will cook very quickly, while onions and leeks will require a bit more time.

3. DEGLAZE THE PAN

Add liquid (1 to 1¼ cups is sufficient) and use wooden spoon to scrape up browned bits on pan bottom. **WHY?** Choose potent liquids (wine, brandy, vermouth, broth, cider, orange juice), and use them in combination for more complexity. With liquid in the pan, you can now loosen the fond on the pan bottom. It will dissolve as the liquid simmers, enriching the sauce with meaty flavors.

4. SIMMER AND MEASURE

Simmer until liquid is reduced to about ⅓ cup, about 5 minutes. **WHY?** Once the liquid is in the pan, it should simmer briskly. (If necessary, raise the burner temperature.) You want to reduce the liquid to both concentrate flavors and change its consistency. If in doubt, pour off the liquid into a measuring cup to check your progress. Don't shortcut this process, or your sauce will be too watery.

5. STIR IN MEAT JUICES

Stir in any meat juices that have accumulated on plate.

WHY? These juices are potent and shouldn't go to waste. If you end up adding more than 1 tablespoon of juices, continue to simmer until the liquid reduces again to ⅓ cup.

6. WHISK IN BUTTER

Remove pan from heat. Whisk in 3 tablespoons of chilled unsalted butter, 1 tablespoon at a time.

WHY? Chilled butter will emulsify the sauce and make it thick and glossy. We generally add two or three pieces, each about 1 tablespoon, to a pan sauce.

7. FINISH AND SERVE

Add any fresh herbs or potent ingredients and season with salt and pepper to taste. Spoon sauce over meat and serve immediately.

WHY? Wait to add fresh herbs and other potent ingredients (mustard, horseradish, vinegar, lemon juice) until the end to preserve their flavor. Make sure to adjust the seasonings with salt and pepper.

Troubleshooting Pan Sauces

PROBLEM	SOLUTION
My sauce tastes burnt and has flecks of black floating in it.	Fond is the secret to a great-tasting sauce, but if the fond burned while the meat was cooking, it can ruin a pan sauce. It's fine if the fond is richly colored. However, if it's blackened or burnt, you need to wash the pan and cook the aromatics with some vegetable oil in the clean pan. Yes, your sauce won't taste as meaty as one made with good fond, but at least it won't taste burnt. Do remember to add back any juices that accumulate as the meat rests. And, of course, pay attention while the meat is cooking; if the fond starts to burn, lower the heat. Also, if you find that you're always burning the fond, you need a heavier skillet.
My sauce is too salty.	The meat and sauce are seasoned at several points, so make sure to season lightly at each step. Overseasoning the meat before cooking will make the fond too salty. One teaspoon of kosher salt per pound of meat is sufficient. Also, make sure to use broth with a moderate amount of sodium (400 to 700 milligrams per serving; see page 38 for more detail on buying broth) and unsalted butter. Taste the final sauce and add salt (and pepper) as needed.
The shallot/garlic/onion/leek in my sauce tastes burnt.	If you work quickly, the pan can still be quite hot by the time you go to add the aromatics. If so, slide the pan off the heat and let the aromatics cook via residual heat in the pan. Also, be prepared to add a little liquid to the pan to keep the aromatics from burning. As soon as the aromatics are softened and fragrant, add the liquid base for the sauce to protect them from further browning.
My sauce took a long time to reduce.	It sounds like your stovetop isn't the greatest. Once the liquid is in the pan, crank up the heat so that it is boiling quite rapidly. Don't turn up the heat earlier—you don't want to burn the aromatics.

How to Stir-Fry

ESSENTIAL EQUIPMENT

- chef's knife
- cutting board
- mixing bowls
- 12-inch nonstick skillet
- nonstick tongs
- wooden spoon or heatproof plastic spoon
- whisk

Stir-frying is a great way to turn meat (or other protein) and vegetables into a complete dinner. However, the classic restaurant method doesn't work at home. Conical woks rest in cutouts in the stovetop, and intense flames heat the entire pan. At home, on a flat burner, the results are usually underwhelming, with poor browning and not nearly enough evaporation and concentration of flavors.

Our advice is to skip a wok in favor of a large nonstick skillet. The diameter of a large skillet provides a wide, broad cooking surface that promotes good browning, which translates to great flavor. We like a nonstick pan (to reduce the amount of oil needed). It is essential to use a skillet that heats evenly and quickly recovers heat each time food is added to the pan.

These following steps outline the basic method for preparing any stir-fry with meat or other protein. To create your own stir-fry to serve four people, follow this procedure using 1 pound of protein and 1½ pounds of vegetables of your choice, both prepared according to the charts on pages 236 and 237, with one of the sauces on pages 270–271. Serve with Chinese-Style Sticky Rice (page 206).

1. FREEZE MEAT, THEN SLICE THIN

Place meat in freezer until just firm, about 20 minutes. With very sharp knife, cut meat across grain into thin pieces, ⅛ to ¼ inch thick.
WHY? Slicing the meat thin is key to ensuring maximum surface and thus maximum browning. A sharp knife is essential. We find it helpful to freeze the meat briefly to make it firmer for slicing. Make sure the final cut is against the grain of the meat. If you look closely at a piece of meat, you'll notice little bundles of closely packed muscle fibers that run parallel to one another. This pattern of fibers is known as the grain. Recipes recommend slicing across the grain—perpendicular to the fibers—to shorten them and thereby make the meat easier to chew. Plan on about 1 pound of meat for a main-course stir-fry to feed four.

2. MARINATE MEAT

Toss sliced meat with soy sauce and marinate for at least 10 minutes but not longer than 1 hour.
WHY? A quick marinade that includes salt or a salty ingredient such as soy sauce guarantees that the meat will taste well seasoned. A marinade can act as a brine so that the meat takes in liquid to help keep it moist during cooking. Be sure to drain off any moisture from the marinade before stir-frying so that the meat will brown in the skillet.

3. CUT VEGETABLES TO RIGHT SIZE

Cut vegetables into uniform pieces.
WHY? Cutting the vegetables to the right size will help ensure that they cook evenly. If the pieces are cut too small, you risk overcooking, and the added volume may require you to cook an additional batch. If cut too large, the food may not cook through and the quantity may appear scant. Plan on about 1½ pounds of vegetables to make a main-course stir-fry that feeds four.

4. PREPARE SAUCE, THEN SET UP TO COOK

For a classic stir-fry sauce, whisk together ½ cup chicken broth, ¼ cup Chinese rice wine, 3 tablespoons hoisin sauce, 1 tablespoon soy sauce, 2 teaspoons cornstarch, and 1 teaspoon toasted sesame oil in small bowl. Arrange bowls of sauce, vegetables, aromatics, and meat next to stove.

WHY? Stir-fry sauce recipes often call for too much cornstarch, resulting in gloppy sauces. We use just enough to thicken the sauce so that it lightly coats the ingredients. With the sauce prepared, you should have all of the components in bowls ready to go. In professional kitchens, this is referred to as *mise en place* (French for "put in place"), and it means measuring and laying out all the items you'll need to execute a recipe. With stir-frying, it's imperative because cooking occurs so quickly.

5. USE HIGH HEAT (MOST OF THE TIME)

Heat 1½ teaspoons vegetable oil in 12-inch nonstick skillet over high heat until just smoking. **WHY?** In most cases, high heat is best for stir-frying. It helps with browning, and the pan will quickly regain its temperature once food is added so that moisture cooks off and the food sears nicely. The exception is shrimp, which are best cooked over medium-low heat.

6. COOK IN BATCHES, MINIMIZE STIRRING

Drain excess marinade from meat. Add half of meat to skillet, break up clumps with tongs, and cook without stirring until pieces are browned on both sides, turning once. Transfer to plate or bowl and repeat with remaining meat.

WHY? Meat and vegetables usually cook at different rates, so it's key to stir-fry them separately and bring them together at the end. Cook protein in batches, with space between pieces so that they brown well. If a pound of thinly sliced meat is crowded into a skillet, the meat turns unappealingly gray and steams. And despite the name of this technique, don't stir the food as it cooks; leave it alone so it can brown.

7. COOK VEGETABLES, THEN ADD AROMATICS

Add 1 tablespoon oil to skillet and cook vegetables. When vegetables are nearly done, clear center of skillet and add aromatics. Cook, mashing into pan, until fragrant, 15 to 30 seconds.

WHY? Many stir-fry recipes add aromatics early in the process. We add them near the end so that they don't scorch. Mashing the aromatics into the skillet ensures they cook through and won't taste harsh or raw in the finished stir-fry—before integrating it into the vegetables.

8. REWHISK SAUCE, ADD TO PAN, AND COOK TO THICKEN

Stir aromatics into vegetables. Rewhisk sauce, add to pan along with browned protein, and cook until everything is sizzling and sauce is slightly thickened, 30 to 60 seconds.

WHY? Before adding the sauce mixture to the pan, remember to stir it until smooth to recombine the ingredients (the cornstarch will settle to the bottom).

Troubleshooting Stir-Fries

PROBLEM	SOLUTION
I didn't get much browning on the meat.	Make sure to drain the excess marinade and cook the meat in batches. And get the pan very hot. If the output on your stovetop isn't the greatest, you might consider cooking the meat in three batches, rather than two.
Can I use toasted sesame oil instead of vegetable oil?	No. Toasted sesame oil has a great flavor, but it has a very low smoke point and isn't a good choice for any recipe that involves high-heat cooking, including stir-frying or sautéing. Use vegetable oil or refined peanut oil instead. If you like the flavor of toasted sesame oil, add a little to the sauce.
I don't really like garlic. Can I leave it out?	Aromatics are a key ingredient in any stir-fry. In most stir-fries, you will want to add 3 tablespoons of minced aromatics. The classic formula is equal parts minced garlic, minced ginger, minced scallion whites (the sliced greens are usually added just before serving). You can certainly alter the formula, increasing or eliminating any of these ingredients. Minced fresh chiles (choose something mild) or red pepper flakes can also be added.

Best Proteins For Stir-Frying

Good protein choices for stir-fries are cuts that are tender to start—more or less the same ones that do well cooked on a grill or seared in a hot pan on the stovetop—because stir-frying happens so quickly that it doesn't give tough muscles a chance to become tender. Here are our favorite choices. Note that tofu should be cooked in several tablespoons of oil for the best results.

INGREDIENT	PREPARATION
Blade steak	Freeze 20 minutes, cut in half lengthwise along line of gristle, trim gristle, slice both pieces crosswise into ¼-inch-thick pieces
Flank steak	Cut lengthwise with grain into 2-inch-wide strips, freeze 20 minutes, cut crosswise against grain into ⅛-inch-thick slices
Pork tenderloin	Freeze 30 minutes, cut crosswise into ¼-inch-thick slices, then cut into ¼-inch-wide strips
Boneless, skinless chicken breasts	Freeze 20 minutes, slice crosswise into ¼-inch-thick pieces; cut tenderloin and tapered ends into 1-inch squares about ¼ inch thick
Tofu, extra-firm	Cut into 1-inch cubes, then lightly dust with cornstarch
Shrimp, extra-large	Peel and devein

Best Vegetables for Stir-Frying

Choose relatively sturdy vegetables that can withstand high heat but that cook quickly. Remember that they'll cook best if the pieces are uniform in size and that a crisp-tender or al dente texture is desirable. Here are our favorites. Cooking times depend greatly on the quantity of ingredients in the pan; cook in batches if the pan will be too crowded.

VEGETABLE	PREPARATION	STIR-FRY TIME
Asparagus (medium thickness)	Trim or snap off tough bottoms, then cut spears on bias into 2-inch lengths	3 minutes
Bell peppers	Stem, seed, and cut into ½-inch dice or strips ¼ to ½ inch wide	2 minutes
Bok choy	Cut greens into ½- to 1-inch-wide ribbons; cut stalks crosswise into ¼- to 1-inch-wide pieces	1 to 3 minutes (stalks); 30 seconds (greens)
Broccoli	Cut florets into ¾- to 1-inch pieces; peel stalks and cut into ⅛- to ¼-inch-thick slices	30 seconds, then add ⅓ cup water, cover, and steam for 2 minutes
Carrots	Peel and cut into matchsticks or ¼-inch-thick slices on bias	2 minutes
Cauliflower	Cut into ¾- to 1-inch florets	3 to 4 minutes
Celery	Cut on bias about ½ inch thick	1 to 2 minutes
Eggplant	Cut into ¾-inch cubes	5 to 7 minutes
Green beans	Trim and cut on bias into 1- to 2-inch lengths	4 to 5 minutes
Onions	Peel and cut into ¼- to ½-inch wedges or ½- to ¾-inch dice	2 minutes
Shiitake mushrooms	Remove stems; slice caps ⅛ to ½ inch wide	3 minutes
Snap peas	Remove strings	1 to 3 minutes
Snow peas	Remove strings; cut extra-large peas in half on bias	1 minute
Zucchini	Cut into ¾-inch dice	2 to 4 minutes

How to Stew and Braise Meat

ESSENTIAL EQUIPMENT

- cutting board
- chef's knife
- paper towels
- Dutch oven
- tongs
- mixing bowl
- wooden spoon
- paring knife

Stewing and braising (also known as pot-roasting) are moist-heat cooking methods that transform tough, sinewy cuts into tender, yielding meat in a rich sauce. Braising is the umbrella term used to describe the combination cooking method that involves browning food and then gently simmering it in liquid. Stewing is a subset of braising, and the term applies to dishes with small chunks of boneless meat. The steps that follow demonstrate stewing, but the technique for braising a large cut is similar.

Skip prepackaged stew meat and choose a cut from the shoulder and cut the beef into 1½-inch pieces. Meat from the shoulder is full of beefy flavor and contains a good amount of fat that will keep the meat moist throughout the long, slow cooking process. The best beef cuts for trimming into stew meat are chuck-eye roast and blade steak. For pork stew, Boston butt and picnic shoulder are the two top choices. Lamb shoulder roasts are not easy to find; thickly cut shoulder chops are a fine alternative, but chops contain bone, so they will require some extra knife work.

1. START WITH BIG ROAST

Pull apart roast at its major seams (delineated by lines of fat). Cut away all exposed fat.

WHY? Packaged stew meat sold in most supermarkets is cut much too small, so it overcooks and becomes tough. And who knows what cut you're getting. For the best results, buy a roast (a 3½-pound roast is enough for a batch of stew that feeds six to eight people) and cut it yourself. Start by pulling the roast apart and trimming away the big pieces of fat.

2. CUT INTO BIG CHUNKS

Cut meat into 1½-inch chunks, trimming additional fat.

WHY? We think bigger chunks make a better stew. They are less likely to overcook, and they give the dish heft. (Chili is an exception; in this case, we like small pieces of meat that can really absorb the intense flavor of the sauce.)

3. BROWN IN BATCHES

Pat meat dry with paper towels and season with salt and pepper according to recipe. Heat 1 tablespoon of vegetable oil in Dutch oven over high heat until just smoking, then add first batch of beef. Cook meat turning pieces several times, until well browned all over. Transfer to bowl and repeat with remaining batches.

WHY? Make sure to dry the stew meat with paper towels so it can brown, and season it lightly with salt and pepper. (Remember, there are a lot of salty ingredients to come, so go lightly. In our beef stew recipe, we skip seasoning at this point altogether.) In a large Dutch oven, you will be able to brown all the meat in two batches; if using a smaller Dutch oven, divide the meat into three batches, making sure to leave room between each piece. Don't let the fond at the bottom of the pot burn. If you notice the fond starting to get dark between batches, add a little water or broth to the pot, scrape up the fond, and then add this liquid to the bowl with the browned beef.

4. SAUTÉ AROMATICS

Once meat has been browned and reserved in bowl, heat more oil in empty pot and cook aromatic vegetables until well browned.

WHY? The pot should be covered with fond. The goal is to build more flavor with sautéed aromatics (such as onion, carrot, celery, leek, and garlic). Chop the aromatics quite fine so they melt into the sauce. (The vegetables added in step 7 should be much larger.) We often add flavor-boosting ingredients like tomato paste at this point. If flour is being used to thicken the stew or braise, it should be stirred into the sautéed aromatic vegetables before the liquid is added. The flour mixed with the fat already in the pot creates what is known as a roux in classic French cooking, a fat-and-flour paste for thickening sauces.

5. ADD LIQUID AND SCRAPE UP FOND

Add wine, broth, or other liquids as directed in recipe, using wooden spoon to scrape and loosen fond on bottom of pot.

WHY? Before the meat and vegetables go into the pot, loosen the fond so it can dissolve into the liquid ingredients. Use wine good enough to drink and avoid so-called cooking wine, which is way too salty. Also, use broths with a moderate sodium content of 400 to 700 milligrams per serving—the liquid will be reducing and can become very salty if the broth is salty.

6. SIMMER IN OVEN

Bring liquid to boil, return meat to pot, cover, transfer pot to lower-middle rack in 300-degree oven, and cook until meat is tender, 2½ to 3 hours.

WHY? Most stew recipes stay on the stovetop, but this means you have to stir often. By moving the action to the oven, you eliminate the risk of scorching the bottom of the pot and you get much more even cooking—the food at the top of the pot is cooking at the same rate as the food at the bottom of the pot. A low oven temperature is essential. Long, slow simmering allows the connective tissue in meat to break down into gelatin, which makes meat tender and silky.

7. STAGGER ADDITION OF VEGETABLES

Add vegetables, cut into uniform pieces as directed, to pot in batches based on vegetable's cooking time.

WHY? Many old-fashioned stew recipes add the vegetables way too early, and the result is a mushy mess. We generally add slow-cooking vegetables, like potatoes, at the midway point in the cooking time. More delicate vegetables, like leafy greens and peas go in at the last minute.

HOW TO COOK MEAT

How to Roast Meat

ESSENTIAL EQUIPMENT

- kitchen twine
- paper towels
- 12-inch skillet
- tongs
- wire rack or V-rack
- rimmed baking sheet or roasting pan

As you will see in the roast recipes at the end of this chapter, the oven temperature can vary considerably. In general, tender cuts, such as beef tenderloin and pork loin, can be roasted in a moderately hot oven: 300 to 375 degrees. Tougher cuts benefit from long, slow cooking, with oven temperatures below 300 degrees. For beef, this applies to chuck roasts and round roasts. For pork, Boston butt, picnic shoulder, and fresh hams are the best cuts for slow roasting, as is leg of lamb.

While we generally brown before roasting, there are recipes where we roast first and brown last. (This method works especially with beef tenderloin roast; see recipe on page 271.) The important thing is to brown the meat at some point in the process. Make sure to refer to the doneness chart on page 783—it's a shame to ruin an expensive cut of meat by overcooking it. See the recipes at the end this chapter for specific oven temperatures and cooking times. And don't forget to let all roasts rest for at least 15 minutes before slicing; during this time the meat fibers will relax and reabsorb juices so that they end up in the meat, not on the carving board.

1A–1B. TIE ROAST

For long roasts, wrap piece of kitchen twine around roast and fasten with double knot, repeating along length of roast, spacing each tie about 1½ inches apart. For squat roasts, wrap piece of twine around roast about 1 inch from bottom and tie with double knot. Repeat with second piece of twine, wrapping it about 1 inch from top. Knots should be snug but not tight.

WHY? Most roasts are unevenly shaped, which leads to uneven cooking. For cylindrical cuts, such as beef tenderloin or pork loin, we even out thickness with a series of ties down the length. You can also fold the thin end under the roast and tie it in place. For squat roasts such as the eye-round, wrap longer pieces of twine around the perimeter to cinch in the sides and give the roast a neater shape.

2. BROWN IN SKILLET

Blot roast dry with paper towels and season with salt and pepper. Heat 1 tablespoon vegetable oil in 12-inch skillet over medium-high heat until just smoking. Add roast and brown on all sides.

WHY? The sloped sides allow for quick evaporation of moisture, and the traditional finish encourages the development of a flavorful crust.

3. ELEVATE ON RACK, THEN ROAST SLOWLY

Transfer roast to rack set in rimmed baking sheet or V-rack set in roasting pan. Place on middle rack in preheated oven. Cook to desired doneness.

WHY? The rack ensures even heating and means you don't have to turn the roast. Also, elevating the roast keeps the bottom crust intact. For most cuts of beef, we roast low and slow to keep the internal temperature of the meat below 122 degrees. This allows the enzymes in the meat to break down the muscle fibers, effectively tenderizing the meat. Low heat also reduces the temperature differential between the exterior and the interior of the meat, so you end up with a roast that is cooked more uniformly.

RECIPE TUTORIAL

GETTING STARTED
CORE TECHNIQUES
MEAT | RECIPE TUTORIALS
RECIPE LIBRARY

241

Slow-Roasted Beef

Overview

Roast beef is a familiar recipe most cooks get wrong. Most recipes rely on a hot oven, and the result is a tough, dry roast. In the test kitchen, we've developed a unique method that can turn a chewy, tough cut of cheap beef into a succulent and tender centerpiece for the dinner table.

Our recipe is very simple and straightforward, and mostly hands-off. The technique requires a very low oven (225 degrees) to promote the enzymatic breakdown of the muscle fibers within the beef. That breakdown will happen only when the internal temperature of the beef is below 122 degrees. To extend the maximum amount of tenderizing time, we allow the meat to sit in a turned-off oven while it comes up to the desired serving temperature.

Once you master this recipe, you'll find that other cuts of beef, from top sirloin to the ubiquitous holiday prime rib, also benefit from slow-roasting. Serve with Horseradish Cream Sauce (page 273).

Recipe Stats

TOTAL TIME **36 hours**
PREPARATION TIME **15 minutes**
ACTIVE COOKING TIME **20 minutes**
YIELD **6 to 8 servings**
MAKE AHEAD **Serve immediately**
DIFFICULTY **Easy**

Tools

- rimmed baking sheet
- 12-inch skillet
- carving board
- slicing knife
- measuring spoons
- meat-probe or instant-read thermometer *
- tongs
- wire rack
- paper towels
- plastic wrap

* A thermometer is essential for this recipe. While an instant-read thermometer is adequate, this recipe is perfect for a meat-probe thermometer, which is inserted into the roast before it goes into the oven and connects to a display that sits on the counter. This setup allows the cook to monitor the progress of food as it cooks without opening the oven door.

Ingredients

1 **(3½- to 4½-pound) boneless eye-round roast, trimmed ***
4 **teaspoons kosher salt ****
2 **teaspoons plus 1 tablespoon vegetable oil**
2 **teaspoons pepper**

* If you're able to locate only a larger (4½- to 6-pound) roast, cut it in half crosswise (creating two smaller roasts) for this recipe; there's no need to use more salt and pepper. However, for a smaller (2½- to 3½-pound) roast, reduce the amount of kosher salt to 1 tablespoon and pepper to 1½ teaspoons.
** We prefer kosher salt for sprinkling over meat because it's easier to distribute the larger crystals evenly, but table salt can be substituted. To convert the amount of kosher salt to table salt, see page 45.

What Can Go Wrong

Here's a list of common mistakes cooks make when preparing this recipe.

COMMON MISTAKE	BAD OUTCOMES	WHAT YOU SHOULD DO
Skipping Overnight Salting	• **The meat is bland.** • **The meat is tough.**	Don't skip this step! A long, slow salting is essential to ensuring that the salt has time to work its way into the very center of the roast. In addition to seasoning this large cut of meat evenly, the salt needs time to break down proteins and help tenderize the meat.
Not Getting Skillet Hot Enough	• **The exterior is spotty brown.** • **The roast is bland.**	Really heat the skillet well when searing the meat. Because the roast is going into such a cool oven, little browning occurs during the roasting process. Since browning adds so much flavor, take the time to get the pan really hot and turn the roast so that it browns on all sides.
Oven Is Too Hot	• **The meat is tough.**	You started with a pretty tough cut of meat. In order for the enzymes in the meat to break down the tough connective tissue, the internal temperature of the meat needs to stay below 122 degrees. After searing the beef, we roast it in a low, 225-degree oven to help this enzymatic breakdown occur. If your oven runs even 25 degrees too hot, the meat will reach the final serving temperature too quickly—before the enzymes have been able to break down tough connective tissue. It's worth investing in an oven thermometer if you are not sure.
Oven Is Too Cool	• **The roast is underdone.** • **The roast takes longer to get done.**	Low-temperature roasting requires that you exercise some patience—and not open the oven door too often as the meat cooks. A meat-probe thermometer that you can snake through the oven door is ideal. If you're using a regular instant-read thermometer (and you better be using something), just be patient and don't take the temperature of the roast too often—it climbs very slowly in such a cool oven. Also, make sure your oven is properly calibrated. (Check this with an oven thermometer.) If your oven runs 25 degrees too cool, the roast will take much longer to cook.
Forgetting to Turn Oven Off	• **The meat is tough.**	The enzymatic breakdown of the connective tissue cannot continue to happen if the meat continues to roast in a 225-degree oven; the internal temperature of the beef will rise above 122 degrees before the maximum tenderizing can occur. So to continue tenderizing the beef, while slowly allowing it to come to the desired internal temperature, we turn the oven off and let the beef sit inside for another 30 minutes. Sounds crazy, but it works.

1. Sprinkle 1 (3½- to 4½-pound) trimmed boneless eye-round roast with 4 teaspoons kosher salt. Wrap with plastic wrap and refrigerate 18 to 24 hours.

2. Adjust oven rack to middle position and heat oven to 225 degrees. Pat roast dry with paper towels.

3. Rub roast with 2 teaspoons vegetable oil. Sprinkle all sides evenly with 2 teaspoons pepper.

4. Heat 1 tablespoon oil in 12-inch skillet over medium-high heat until starting to smoke.

5. Sear roast until browned on all sides, 3 to 4 minutes per side.

6. Transfer roast to wire rack set in rimmed baking sheet.

7. Roast until meat registers 115 degrees for medium-rare, 1¼ to 1¾ hours, or 125 degrees for medium, 1¾ to 2¼ hours.

8. Turn oven off.

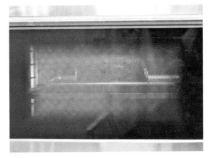

9. Leave roast in oven until center of roast registers 130 degrees for medium-rare or 140 degrees for medium, 30 to 50 minutes longer.

10. If roast does not reach desired temperature after 50 minutes, heat oven to 225 degrees for 5 minutes, shut it off, and cook until roast is done.

11. Transfer roast to carving board. Let rest 15 minutes.

12. Slice meat crosswise as thinly as possible and serve.

HOW TO COOK MEAT

Pepper-Crusted Filets Mignons

Recipe Stats

TOTAL TIME **2 hours**
PREPARATION TIME **15 minutes**
ACTIVE COOKING TIME **30 minutes**
YIELD **4 servings**
MAKE AHEAD **Serve immediately**
DIFFICULTY **Intermediate**

Tools

- 8-inch skillet
- rimmed baking sheets (2) *
- small saucepan
- 12-inch skillet
- cutting board
- paring knife
- measuring spoons
- fork
- instant-read thermometer
- large plate
- mixing bowls
- rubber spatula
- soupspoon
- tongs
- wire rack
- aluminum foil
- plastic wrap

* Ideally, you will have two baking sheets for this recipe; one for use in the oven and one for use after the steaks come out of the oven. If you have only one baking sheet, set the rack with the resting steaks on a cutting board instead of inside a baking sheet.

Ingredients

- **5 tablespoons black peppercorns, crushed ***
- **5 tablespoons plus 2 teaspoons olive oil**
- **1½ teaspoons plus ⅛ teaspoon salt**
- **4 (7- to 8-ounce) center-cut filets mignons, 1½ to 2 inches thick, trimmed ****
- **1½ ounces mild blue cheese, room temperature *****
- **3 tablespoons unsalted butter, softened**
- **2 tablespoons minced fresh chives**

* Don't even think about using ground pepper is this recipe. You must start with peppercorns and crack them yourself with the back of a heavy skillet.

** Make sure to buy center-cut filets that are at least 1½ inches thick. They should also have a uniform thickness to ensure even cooking. If you can't find nicely butchered filet mignon, buy a 2-pound center-cut beef tenderloin roast (called Châteaubriand) and cut the roast into four steaks at home.

*** While we generally prefer sharper blue cheese, such as Stilton or Gorgonzola, for eating, we find that a milder, creamier blue cheese, such as Stella Blue from Wisconsin, works best with the pepper crust in this recipe.

Overview

Filet mignon is ultratender, but it has only mild, beefy flavor. Chefs often compensate by wrapping the delicate meat in bacon or puff pastry, serving it with rich wine sauces or flavored butter, or giving it a crust of cracked black peppercorns. We decided to pursue the peppercorn approach and found several problems to solve: The peppercorns tend to fall off in the pan, interfere with the meat's browning, and—when used in sufficient quantity to create a real crust—deliver punishing pungency.

Our first step was to mellow the peppercorns' heat by gently simmering them in olive oil. We then created a well-browned and attractive pepper crust using a two-step process: First, we rubbed the raw steaks with a paste of the cooked cracked peppercorns, salt, and oil, then we pressed the paste into each steak through a sheet of plastic wrap. We let the steaks sit, covered, for an hour before cooking. The paste not only added flavor to the meat but drew out the meat's own beefy flavor. While the steaks sat wrapped and covered in paste, we had plenty of time to make a compound butter.

Your average steak can be seared entirely on the stovetop. When brown on both sides, it's likely done. Thick filets require a variation on the classic stovetop technique for pan searing, because the exterior will start to burn before the interior comes up to temperature. The solution is simple: Move the browned steaks to a preheated baking sheet in the oven. After just a few minutes in a hot oven, the interior temperature of the steaks will rise and the steaks will be ready to rest and serve. You can also serve these steaks with a Port-Cherry Reduction (see page 267) instead of the Blue Cheese–Chive Butter.

What Can Go Wrong

Here's a list of common mistakes cooks make when preparing this recipe.

COMMON MISTAKE	BAD OUTCOMES	WHAT YOU SHOULD DO
Buying Filets That Are Too Thin	• **The steaks are overcooked.** • **The peppercorn crust is overpowering.**	It should be no surprise that if you buy thinner steaks they will overcook, unless you reduce the cooking time. However, even if you take this step, you will find that the peppercorn crust overpowers the beef. That's because you've changed the ratio of meat to peppercorns. If your supermarket doesn't sell thick filets (at least 1½ inches thick, and preferably closer to 2 inches), buy a small center-cut beef tenderloin roast and cut the steaks yourself.
Not Crushing Peppercorns	• **The peppercorns are too crunchy and hard to eat.** • **The peppercorns are too overpowering.**	A proper peppercorn crust is made with crushed, not ground, pepper—so don't even think of trying to grind the pepper in your mill. Instead, you want to crush the peppercorns using the "heel" of a heavy skillet. This is hard work—you will need to apply considerable pressure. The goal is to break each individual peppercorn into several pieces. If you're having trouble with this task, you can try using a spice grinder (in the test kitchen, we set aside a coffee grinder for just this purpose). Pulse two or three times—no more or you risk grinding the pepper too finely.
Not Using Enough Heat	• **The steaks aren't well browned.**	Because these steaks are finished in the oven, there's no danger that they won't be cooked to your liking (provided that you use an instant-read thermometer). However, if you don't use enough heat on the stovetop, the exterior of the steaks will be pale and bland. Filet mignon is a very lean cut with a mild flavor. It really needs the flavor boost provided by a thick, dark brown crust. Crank up the heat and make sure the steaks are really browned before they go into the oven to finish cooking through.
Using a Lightweight Pan	• **The peppercorn crust scorches.**	A lightweight pan will overheat, which will cause the peppercorn crust to scorch. Pay close attention to the steaks as they cook. If the crust is getting too dark, be prepared to lower the heat and/or move the steaks to the oven. Better yet, prevent this problem by using a heavy-bottomed skillet. A good 12-inch skillet should weigh about 3 pounds.
Not Using an Instant-Read Thermometer	• **The steaks are undercooked and bloody.** • **The steaks are overcooked and gray.**	Don't try to guess if the steaks are done. You spent a lot of money on filet and there's nothing worse than overcooking (or undercooking) this pricey cut. Check the progress of the steaks with an instant-read thermometer inserted through the sides of the steaks. It's a good idea to let steaks rest for 5 minutes before serving them—they will do a better job of holding on to their juices. During the resting time, residual heat will continue to cook the steaks. For example, if you want rare steaks, take them out of the oven when the internal temperature reaches 115 to 120 degrees. The temperature will climb 5 degrees during the resting period—reaching the perfect temperature (120 to 125 degrees) for rare beef.

1. Place 3 tablespoons unsalted butter in bowl. Add 1½ ounces blue cheese and bring to room temperature, at least 30 minutes.

2. Spread 2½ tablespoons black peppercorns on cutting board. Place 8-inch skillet on top and press down firmly with both hands.

3. Use rocking motion to crush peppercorns, redistributing them as needed. Repeat with another 2½ tablespoons peppercorns.

4. Trim fat and silverskin from 4 center-cut filets mignons, each measuring 1½ to 2 inches thick and weighing 7 to 8 ounces.

5. Heat crushed peppercorns and 5 tablespoons olive oil in small saucepan over low heat until faint bubbles appear.

6. Continue to cook at bare simmer, swirling pan occasionally, until pepper is fragrant, 7 to 10 minutes.

7. Remove from heat and set aside to cool.

8. When mixture is room temperature, add 1½ teaspoons salt and stir to combine.

9. Rub steaks with oil and pepper mixture, thoroughly coating top and bottom of each steak with peppercorns.

10. Cover steaks with plastic wrap and press gently to make sure peppercorns adhere; let stand at room temperature for 1 hour.

11. Meanwhile, add ⅛ teaspoon salt to bowl with softened butter and cheese and mix with stiff rubber spatula until smooth.

12. Fold in 2 tablespoons minced fresh chives.

13. Adjust oven rack to middle position, place rimmed baking sheet on oven rack, and heat oven to 450 degrees.

14. Heat 2 teaspoons olive oil in 12-inch heavy-bottomed skillet over medium-high heat until faint smoke appears.

15. Place steaks in skillet.

16. Cook, without moving steaks, until dark brown crust has formed, 3 to 4 minutes.

17. Using tongs, turn steaks.

18. Cook until well browned on second side, about 3 minutes.

19. Remove pan from heat.

20. Transfer steaks to hot baking sheet.

21. Roast 3 to 5 minutes for rare (115 to 120 degrees on instant-read thermometer), 5 to 7 minutes for medium-rare to medium (120 to 135 degrees).

22. Transfer steaks to wire rack set in second rimmed baking sheet.

23. Spoon 1 to 2 tablespoons compound butter over each steak.

24. Let rest, tented loosely with foil, for 5 minutes before serving.

HOW TO COOK MEAT

Stir-Fried Beef and Broccoli

Overview

This recipe is standard Chinese takeout fare. Most versions fall very flat, and that's why we've come to think of beef and broccoli as uninteresting, one-dimensional, and utterly uninspired. The beef is usually gray and tasteless, and the broccoli's not much better. And the sauce? It's little more than a thick, brown soy sauce–spiked gravy. This recipe revives the old standard, turning it into a delicious dish with rich-tasting beef, crisp-tender broccoli, and a salty-sweet sauce full of depth and complexity.

Broccoli requires steaming to cook through, so you'll put into practice a skillet steaming technique for hardy vegetables that doesn't require any additional pots or pans, or any precooking. Before you begin, see How to Stir-Fry on page 234. Don't forget to complete your *mise en place* before you begin cooking! Serve the stir-fry with Chinese-Style Sticky Rice (page 206).

Recipe Stats

TOTAL TIME **1 hour**
PREPARATION TIME **45 minutes**
ACTIVE COOKING TIME **15 minutes**
YIELD **4 servings**
MAKE AHEAD **Serve immediately**
DIFFICULTY **Easy**

Tools

- 12-inch nonstick skillet with lid *
- chef's knife
- cutting board
- liquid measuring cup
- measuring spoons
- fine-mesh strainer
- garlic press
- large plate
- mixing bowls
- nonstick tongs **
- serving platter
- whisk
- wooden or heatproof plastic spoon
- paper towels
- plastic wrap

* We prefer to stir-fry in a nonstick skillet rather than a wok. A lid is essential for steaming the broccoli.
** Nylon-tipped tongs won't scratch your nonstick pan. If you don't have nonstick tongs, use a wooden spoon instead.

Ingredients

SAUCE

- **5 tablespoons oyster sauce ***
- **2 tablespoons chicken broth**
- **1 tablespoon dry sherry**
- **1 tablespoon packed light brown sugar**
- **1 teaspoon toasted sesame oil**
- **1 teaspoon cornstarch**

BEEF STIR-FRY

- **1 (1-pound) flank steak, trimmed and sliced thin against grain on slight bias**
- **3 tablespoons soy sauce**
- **6 garlic cloves, minced (about 2 tablespoons)**
- **1 tablespoon grated fresh ginger**
- **3 tablespoons peanut or vegetable oil**
- **1¼ pounds broccoli, florets cut into bite-size pieces, stalks peeled and cut ⅛ inch thick on bias**
- **⅓ cup water**
- **1 small red bell pepper, stemmed, seeded, and cut into ¼-inch pieces**
- **3 scallions, sliced ½ inch thick on bias**

* Oyster sauce, a thick, salty-sweet, and very assertive brown sauce, is a rich, concentrated mixture of oyster extractives, soy sauce, and seasonings. It is used to enhance the flavor of many Asian dishes and stir-fries. It's sold in most well-stocked supermarkets in the Asian food aisle.

What Can Go Wrong

Here's a list of common mistakes cooks make when preparing this recipe.

COMMON MISTAKE	BAD OUTCOMES	WHAT YOU SHOULD DO
Cutting Broccoli Poorly	• **The broccoli cooks unevenly.**	Cut the broccoli into ¾- to 1-inch florets and cut the peeled stalks into ⅛-inch-thick slices. If cut too large, the broccoli will be crunchy and undercooked; if cut too small, it will be soft and overdone. In addition, try to make sure that all the broccoli florets and stem pieces are uniformly prepped to the correct size so that you don't end up with a mixture of overcooked and undercooked pieces.
Slicing Meat Too Thickly	• **The meat is tough.** • **The meat is chewy.**	Freeze the meat for 20 to 30 minutes before slicing so that it firms up and is easier to cut into ¼-inch-thick slices. If the meat is cut too thickly, it will have an extremely tough, chewy texture. Also, be sure to cut the meat against the grain. A sharp chef's knife is essential.
Not Mincing or Grating Garlic and Ginger Finely Enough	• **Some bites are too pungent with garlic and/or ginger.**	When prepping the garlic and ginger, take the time to mince or grate them finely. If you prefer, use a garlic press to ensure that the garlic has a uniformly even, almost pureed texture.
Not Draining Meat After Marinating	• **The meat does not brown well.** • **The marinade burns in the skillet.**	Drain the meat of its marinade before cooking. Although the marinade consists of only 3 tablespoons soy sauce and is seemingly innocuous, any excess moisture that finds its way into the pan will inhibit browning on the meat. Excess soy sauce also runs the risk of scorching in the skillet, forcing you to wash out the skillet after cooking each batch of meat.
Insufficiently Heating Skillet	• **The meat and vegetables do not brown.** • **The flavors are underdeveloped.**	Add the oil to the skillet and heat them together. Give the skillet a minute or two to heat and keep a watch on the oil—as it heats, it will begin to shimmer and will eventually release wisps of smoke. When it begins to smoke, you'll know that the pan is sufficiently hot; do not add food any sooner, as it will cause the pan's temperature to plummet and the food won't brown well. Without good browning, the flavor of the stir-fry will be underdeveloped.
Cooking Meat in One Batch	• **The meat does not brown.** • **The meat tastes steamed and bland.**	Even though all the meat can fit in the skillet in a single batch, cook it in two batches. If all the meat is added at once, the pieces will be crowded and the pan's temperature will drop, causing the meat to steam instead of sear.
Stirring Meat Constantly	• **The meat does not brown.**	After placing the meat in the skillet, let it cook undisturbed for a minute before checking for browning or turning the pieces. If the meat is moved about too often, it will not attain a deep sear, which will adversely affect flavor development.

1. PREPARE BROCCOLI AND MEAT: Cut florets from 1¼ pounds broccoli into ¾- to 1-inch pieces.

2. Trim and peel broccoli stalks.

3. Cut trimmed stalks on diagonal into ⅛-inch-thick slices.

4. Cut 1 pound flank steak with grain into 2-inch-wide strips. Freeze steak for about 20 minutes to make it easier to slice.

5. Cut each strip of meat against grain into ⅛-inch-thick slices.

6. Combine beef and 3 tablespoons soy sauce in medium bowl. Cover with plastic wrap and refrigerate at least 10 minutes or up to 1 hour, stirring once.

7. PREPARE SAUCE AND AROMATICS: Whisk together 5 tablespoons oyster sauce, 2 tablespoons chicken broth, and 1 tablespoon dry sherry.

8. Whisk in 1 tablespoon packed light brown sugar, 1 teaspoon toasted sesame oil, and 1 teaspoon cornstarch.

9. Combine 6 minced garlic cloves, 1 tablespoon grated fresh ginger, and 1½ teaspoons peanut or vegetable oil in small bowl.

10. COOK STIR-FRY: Drain beef in fine-mesh strainer and discard liquid.

11. Heat 1½ teaspoons peanut or vegetable oil in 12-inch nonstick skillet over high heat until smoking. Add half of beef to skillet and break up clumps.

12. Cook, without stirring, for 1 minute, then turn pieces and cook until beef is browned on both sides, about 30 seconds. Transfer beef to medium bowl.

13. Heat 1½ teaspoons peanut or vegetable oil in skillet and repeat with remaining beef.

14. Add 1 tablespoon peanut or vegetable oil to now-empty skillet and heat until just smoking. Add broccoli and cook 30 seconds.

15. Add ⅓ cup water. Cover pan and lower heat to medium.

16. Steam broccoli until crisp-tender, about 2 minutes. Transfer broccoli to paper towel–lined plate.

17. Add 1½ teaspoons peanut oil to skillet. Increase heat to high and heat until just smoking.

18. Add 1 small red bell pepper, stemmed, seeded, and cut into ¼-inch pieces, and cook, stirring frequently, until spotty brown, about 1½ minutes.

19. Push bell pepper to sides of skillet to clear center.

20. Add garlic and ginger mixture to clearing and cook, mashing into pan, until fragrant, 15 to 20 seconds, then stir mixture into peppers.

21. Return beef and broccoli to skillet.

22. Whisk sauce to recombine, then add to skillet and toss with beef and broccoli to combine.

23. Cook, tossing constantly, until sauce is thickened and evenly distributed, about 30 seconds.

24. Transfer to serving platter, sprinkle with 3 scallions, sliced ½ inch thick on bias, and serve.

Modern Beef Burgundy

Overview

This hearty stew is arguably one of the most defining dishes in French cuisine. By gently simmering large chunks of well-marbled beef in stock and plenty of red wine, you get fork-tender meat and a braising liquid that's transformed into a silky, full-bodied sauce. The problem is that preparation of all the components (browning the bacon lardons, searing the beef, sautéing the mushroom and pearl onion garnish) typically happens in the same Dutch oven on the stovetop. The process requires hours and hours of attention.

We transferred practically the entire operation to the oven. We start by roasting salt pork and beef trimmings in a roasting pan until deeply browned. At the same time, we roast the mushroom and onion garnish until lightly glazed.

Once the salt pork and beef scraps are browned, we whisk in flour to form a roux to thicken the dish. Beef broth and several cups of good red Burgundy or Pinot Noir go into the pan, along with gelatin to boost the sauce's body. We add tomato paste, anchovy paste, dried porcini mushrooms, and aromatic vegetables. With so much flavor, we found we could skip the tedious batch-searing of the meat—we simply place the raw salted chunks of beef on top of the ingredients in the roasting pan. After 3 to 3½ hours, we strain the sauce, add the glazed vegetables and wine, and finish the dish on the stovetop.

Recipe Stats

TOTAL TIME **5½ hours**
PREPARATION TIME **30 minutes**
ACTIVE COOKING TIME **1 hour**
YIELD **6 to 8 servings**
MAKE AHEAD **Refrigerate for up to 3 days**
DIFFICULTY **Intermediate**

Tools

- Dutch oven
- rimmed baking sheet
- roasting pan *
- chef's knife
- cutting board
- dry measuring cups
- liquid measuring cup
- measuring spoons
- fork
- fine-mesh strainer **
- fork
- mixing bowls
- rubber spatula
- slotted spoon
- vegetable peeler
- wide, shallow spoon
- wooden spoon
- whisk
- plastic wrap

* A heavy-duty roasting pan—at least 15 inches by 11 inches, if not larger—is essential in this recipe. A pan with sturdy handles will make it easier to transfer the heavy pan, which is filled with many ingredients and a fair amount of liquid.
** Rinse the dried porcini in the strainer, which is also used to strain out the solid ingredients from the braising liquid. You will want a heavy-duty strainer, one that can withstand some force as you press on the solid ingredients.

Ingredients

1 **(4-pound) boneless beef chuck-eye roast, trimmed and cut into 1½- to 2-inch pieces, scraps reserved * Salt and pepper**
6 **ounces salt pork, cut into ¼-inch pieces**
3 **tablespoons unsalted butter**
1 **pound cremini mushrooms, trimmed and halved ****
1½ **cups frozen pearl onions, thawed *****
1 **tablespoon sugar**
⅓ **cup all-purpose flour**
4 **cups beef broth**
1 **(750-ml) bottle red Burgundy or Pinot Noir**
5 **teaspoons unflavored gelatin**
1 **tablespoon tomato paste**
1 **teaspoon anchovy paste ******
2 **onions, chopped coarse**
2 **carrots, peeled and cut into 2-inch lengths**
1 **garlic head, cloves separated, unpeeled, and crushed**
2 **bay leaves**
½ **teaspoon black peppercorns**
½ **ounce dried porcini mushrooms, rinsed**
10 **sprigs fresh parsley, plus 3 tablespoons minced**
6 **sprigs fresh thyme**

* Make sure to reserve the scraps from trimming the beef; they are roasted along with the salt pork to create a meaty flavor base for this stew.
** If your mushrooms are large, cut them into quarters.
*** If the pearl onions have a papery outer coating, remove it by rinsing them in warm water and gently squeezing individual onions between your fingertips.
**** Two minced anchovy fillets can be used in place of the anchovy paste.

What Can Go Wrong

Here's a list of common mistakes cooks make when preparing this recipe.

COMMON MISTAKE	BAD OUTCOMES	WHAT YOU SHOULD DO
Cutting Beef Chunks Too Small	• **The meat doesn't have enough presence in the final stew.** • **The meat overcooks and is dry.**	This dish demands large chunks of beef, at least 1½ inches if not 2 inches on all sides. The big chunks can withstand the long cooking time needed to transform all the ingredients in the sauce—including an entire bottle of wine—into a harmonious dish.
Submerging Beef in Liquid	• **The stew is bland.**	This recipe begins by roasting the diced salt pork and beef scraps in a large roasting pan. When they are well browned, other ingredients are added (flour, broth, wine) along with the aromatic vegetables (chopped onions, carrots chunks, and whole garlic cloves). At this point, you add the raw beef to the pan. Make sure to spread the solid ingredients (the browned meat and the raw vegetables) evenly into the roasting pan so that they support the beef pieces, which should bob above the surface. The portion of the meat that is above the liquid will brown, adding depth to the meat itself as well as to the sauce.
Adding Entire Bottle of Wine at Outset	• **The sauce doesn't have enough wine flavor.** • **The stew seems heavy and dull.**	After more than 3 hours in the oven, the flavor of the wine will mellow considerably. To punch up the wine flavor, we reserve a portion of the bottle of the wine and add it back to the final sauce as it simmers on the stovetop. This simple technique produces a noticeably bright flavor in the final dish.
Not Extracting Flavor from Solids in Braising Liquid	• **The sauce is bland.**	Once the beef is tender, you should remove it from the roasting pan with a slotted spoon (it can go into the bowl with the roasted mushrooms and onions). At this point, the rest of the contents in the roasting pan (the salt pork, the meat scraps, the aromatic vegetables, and all that liquid) should be poured into a fine-mesh strainer set over a large bowl. Make sure to use a wooden spoon or rubber spatula to press down on the solids to extract every bit of their flavor. Skip this step and you will end up throwing out a lot of flavor.
Not Allowing Braising Liquid to Settle	• **The sauce is very greasy.**	Once the liquid has been strained, it must settle. After about 10 minutes, the fat in the sauce (and there will be quite a lot) will rise to the surface. Use a wide, shallow spoon to skim off the fat. If you hurry up this process, the finished sauce (and the stew) will be quite greasy.
Not Reducing Braising Liquid	• **The stew is watery.** • **The stew is bland.**	Once the braising liquid has been strained and defatted, it must be simmered in a Dutch oven on the stovetop. Don't shortcut this process. The more the sauce reduces, the better it tastes. Once the sauce has the consistency of heavy cream you can add back the meat and the glazed mushrooms and onions. Don't worry if the sauce seems a bit thick before this point; the meat and vegetables will shed some liquid and thin the sauce out a bit.

1. Trim 1 (4-pound) boneless beef chuck-eye roast and reserve scraps. Cut roast into 1½- to 2-inch pieces.

2. Toss beef and 1½ teaspoons salt together in bowl and let stand at room temperature for 30 minutes.

3. Trim and halve 1 pound cremini mushrooms, and thaw 1½ cups frozen pearl onions.

4. Coarsely chop 2 onions, and peel and cut 2 carrots into 2-inch lengths.

5. Remove garlic cloves from 1 head garlic (do not peel cloves) and crush cloves.

6. Adjust oven racks to lower-middle and lowest positions and heat oven to 500 degrees.

7. Place 6 ounces salt pork, cut into ¼-inch pieces, beef scraps, and 2 tablespoons unsalted butter in roasting pan.

8. Roast on lower-middle rack until well browned and fat has rendered, 15 to 20 minutes.

9. Toss halved mushrooms and thawed pearl onions with 1 tablespoon butter and 1 tablespoon sugar on rimmed baking sheet.

10. Roast on lowest rack, stirring occasionally, until moisture released by mushrooms evaporates and vegetables are lightly glazed, 15 to 20 minutes.

11. Transfer cremini mushrooms and pearl onions to large bowl, cover, and refrigerate.

12. Remove roasting pan from oven and reduce temperature to 325 degrees.

13. Sprinkle ⅓ cup all-purpose flour over rendered fat in roasting pan and whisk until no dry flour remains.

14. Whisk in 4 cups beef broth, 2 cups red Burgundy, 5 teaspoons unflavored gelatin, 1 tablespoon tomato paste, and 1 teaspoon anchovy paste.

15. Add onions, carrots, garlic cloves, 2 bay leaves, ½ teaspoon black peppercorns, ½ ounce rinsed dried porcini, 10 sprigs parsley, and 6 sprigs thyme.

16. Arrange beef in single layer on top of vegetables. Add water as needed to come three-quarters up side of beef (beef should not be submerged).

17. Return pan to oven and cook until meat is tender, 3 to 3½ hours, stirring after 90 minutes and adding water to keep meat at least half-submerged.

18. Using slotted spoon, transfer beef to bowl with cremini mushrooms and pearl onions; cover and set aside.

19. Strain braising liquid through fine-mesh strainer set over another large bowl, pressing on solids to extract as much liquid as possible; discard solids.

20. Stir in remaining wine (you should have almost 1¼ cups left in bottle), and let cooking liquid settle, 10 minutes.

21. Using wide, shallow spoon, skim fat off surface and discard. Transfer liquid to Dutch oven.

22. Bring mixture to boil over medium-high heat. Simmer briskly, stirring, until thickened to consistency of heavy cream, 15 to 20 minutes.

23. Reduce heat to medium-low, stir in beef and mushroom-onion garnish, cover, and heat through, 5 to 8 minutes. Season to taste, and stir in 3 tablespoons minced parsley.

Classic Pot Roast

Overview

There is no shortage of ways to cook a pot roast, but the simple approach is our favorite. Our recipe starts with a chuck-eye roast, a well-marbled roast particularly suited to braising. We first dealt with the globs of interior fat that refuse to render during cooking. We opened our roast along its natural seam and trimmed away excess fat. Leaving the two lobes as separate roasts shaved about an hour off the cooking time, and all that exposed surface area meant that the salt we applied to it before cooking would penetrate even further.

We determined that the initial sear most recipes called for wasn't necessary. We found that the part of the meat that stays above the braising liquid browns, even without searing.

To beef up the gravy, we used a combination of beef broth and red wine for the braising liquid. We also added tomato paste (to enhance meaty flavor), plus garlic, herbs, and the *mirepoix* trio of onions, carrots, and celery, sautéed in butter. At the end of cooking, the vegetables had broken down and started to thicken the gravy. To eke out more flavor, we blended them with the defatted cooking liquid and extra beef broth. Just before serving, we stirred in a spoonful of balsamic vinegar and a bit more wine for brightness.

Chilling the cooked pot roast overnight improves its flavor and makes it more moist and easier to slice. Transfer the cooked roasts to a large bowl. Strain and defat the liquid, and add beef broth to bring the liquid amount to 3 cups; transfer the liquid and vegetables to the bowl with the roasts, let cool for 1 hour, cover with plastic wrap, cut vents in the plastic, and refrigerate for up to 2 days. One hour before serving, adjust an oven rack to the middle position and heat the oven to 325 degrees. Slice the roasts as directed, place in a 13 by 9-inch baking dish, cover tightly with aluminum foil, and bake until heated through, about 45 minutes. Blend the liquid and vegetables, bring the gravy to a simmer, and finish as directed.

Recipe Stats

TOTAL TIME **5 hours**
PREPARATION TIME **15 minutes**
ACTIVE COOKING TIME **30 minutes**
YIELD **6 to 8 servings**
MAKE AHEAD **Refrigerate for up to 2 days**
DIFFICULTY **Easy**

Tools

- Dutch oven
- medium saucepan
- rimmed baking sheet
- blender
- boning knife *
- chef's knife
- carving board
- cutting board
- slicing knife
- liquid measuring cup
- measuring spoons
- fine-mesh strainer
- fork
- garlic press
- serving platter
- tongs
- vegetable peeler
- wide, shallow spoon
- wire rack
- wooden spoon
- aluminum foil **
- kitchen twine
- paper towels

* We use a boning knife to trim the roast, but a chef's knife will also work.

** The small amount of liquid in the pot means the meat can brown during the long cooking time. The pot is covered with foil to ensure a tight seal and that the pot doesn't run dry.

Ingredients

1 **(3½- to 4-pound) boneless beef chuck-eye roast, pulled apart at natural seams and trimmed**
  Kosher salt and pepper *
2 **tablespoons unsalted butter**
2 **onions, halved and sliced thin ***
1 **large carrot, peeled and chopped**
1 **celery rib, chopped**
2 **garlic cloves, minced**
2–3 **cups beef broth ****
¾ **cup dry red wine**
1 **tablespoon tomato paste**
1 **bay leaf**
1 **sprig fresh thyme, plus ¼ teaspoon chopped**
1 **tablespoon balsamic vinegar**

* We prefer the coarse crystals in kosher salt for salting. If you're using table salt, use just 1½ teaspoons.

** This recipe calls for pureeing the vegetables with the liquid to make a thick gravy. If you want to serve large chunks of vegetables, see Classic Pot Roast with Root Vegetables on page 276.

*** Part of the broth goes into the pot with the meat, but most is reserved to make the gravy. The amount needed will vary depending on how much liquid is left in the pot.

What Can Go Wrong

Here's a list of common mistakes cooks make when preparing this recipe.

COMMON MISTAKE	BAD OUTCOMES	WHAT YOU SHOULD DO
Buying Wrong Roast	• **The meat is dry.** • **The meat is chalky.** • **The meat is bland.**	Don't pay attention to stickers added by the butcher, including those that say "great for pot roast." Some markets slap these stickers on lean roasts from the round. These cuts will be very tough and very dry if cooked by this method. Pot-roasting demands a well-marbled cut from the chuck. A boneless chuck-eye roast is our favorite cut. However, other roasts from the chuck, including the top blade roast, can be used, although the cooking time will vary.
Not Halving Roast	• **The meat is fatty.** • **The meat is not cooked in allotted time.** • **The gravy is greasy.**	There are two kinds of fat in any cut of meat—the internal marbling (fine white lines that run throughout the meat) and the exterior fat (hard white knobs or bands of fat between various muscles). On a steak, it's easy enough to trim away excess exterior fat. On a chuck roast, there are several muscles, and some of the exterior fat is actually inside the roast. Pulling apart the roast at its natural seam gives you better access to these large knobs of fat. Also, separating the meat into two smaller, well-trimmed roasts cuts the cooking time by about 1 hour.
Not Salting Roast	• **The meat is a bit bland.**	Salting the roast for an hour draws moisture out of the meat, forming a shallow brine, that over time migrates back into the meat to season it throughout rather than just on the exterior. In addition to improving overall seasoning, the salt enhances the beefy flavor of this cut.
Adding All Broth at Outset	• **The meat doesn't brown.** • **The meat tastes bland.**	In most braises, you add all the liquid before the roast goes into the oven. In this recipe, we reserve most of the beef broth and some of the wine for finishing the gravy. That's because we want most of the meat to sit above the liquid in the pot. This way, the roast will brown during the 3½- to 4-hour cooking time. Why is this important? We found that with so little liquid in the pot, we got enough browning during the pot-roasting phase that we could skip the traditional searing of the meat—a messy process that no one likes.
Not Defatting Braising Liquid	• **The gravy is greasy.**	Once the meat has been removed from the pot, the braising liquid is strained into a 4-cup liquid measuring cup. The solids go into the blender, and the liquid is defatted. This process is simple—just wait 5 minutes and the fat will rise to the surface, where it can be easily removed with a wide, shallow spoon.
Not Pureeing Gravy in Blender	• **The gravy is too thin.** • **The gravy is bland.**	The aromatic vegetables and garlic are pureed with braising liquid in a blender to create a naturally thickened gravy for our pot roast. If you skip this step, the braising liquid will be quite thin and won't coat the sliced roast nicely. More important, pureeing the vegetables ekes out the last bit of their flavor.

1. Pull apart 1 (3½- to 4-pound) boneless beef chuck-eye roast at its major seam (delineated by lines of fat) to yield 2 smaller roasts.

2. Cut away all large knobs of fat from each piece of meat.

3. Season meat with 1 tablespoon kosher salt, place on wire rack set in rimmed baking sheet, and let stand at room temperature for 1 hour.

4. Adjust oven rack to lower-middle position and heat oven to 300 degrees.

5. Melt 2 tablespoons unsalted butter in Dutch oven over medium heat.

6. Add 2 onions, halved and sliced thin, and cook, stirring occasionally, until softened and beginning to brown, 8 to 10 minutes.

7. Add 1 large carrot, peeled and chopped, and 1 chopped celery rib. Continue to cook, stirring occasionally, for 5 minutes.

8. Add 2 minced garlic cloves and cook until fragrant, about 30 seconds.

9. Stir in 1 cup beef broth, ½ cup dry red wine, 1 tablespoon tomato paste, 1 bay leaf, and 1 sprig fresh thyme. Bring to simmer.

10. Pat beef dry with paper towels and season with pepper.

11. Tie 3 pieces of kitchen twine around each piece of meat to form even shape.

12. Nestle meat on top of vegetables.

13. Cover pot tightly with large piece of aluminum foil and cover with lid; transfer pot to oven.

14. Cook beef until fully tender and fork slips easily in and out of meat, 3½ to 4 hours, turning meat halfway through cooking.

15. Transfer roasts to carving board and tent loosely with foil.

16. Strain liquid through fine-mesh strainer into 4-cup liquid measuring cup. Discard bay leaf and thyme sprig.

17. Transfer vegetables to blender.

18. Let liquid settle for 5 minutes, then skim fat.

19. Add 1–2 cups beef broth to bring liquid amount to 3 cups.

20. Add liquid to blender and blend until smooth, about 2 minutes.

21. Transfer sauce to medium saucepan and bring to simmer over medium heat.

22. Meanwhile, remove twine from roasts and slice against grain into ½-inch-thick slices. Transfer meat to serving platter.

23. Stir ¼ cup dry red wine, ¼ teaspoon chopped fresh thyme, and 1 tablespoon balsamic vinegar into gravy and season with salt and pepper to taste.

24. Spoon half of gravy over meat; pass remaining gravy separately.

HOW TO COOK MEAT

Maple-Glazed Pork Roast

Overview

Today's pork is at least 30 percent leaner than the pork sold in supermarkets a few decades go. Old-fashioned methods for preparing pork yield tough, dry roasts. Modern loin roasts require gentle handling.

Searing the roast creates a nice browned crust, and then sliding the roast—still in the skillet—into the oven allows the interior to come up to temperature with a minimum of moisture loss. This method also allows a glaze or sauce to be prepared in the skillet. The roast cooks right in the glaze, adding flavor and moisture to this lean cut.

This method works for both pork loin and pork tenderloin, and the sauce or glaze ingredients can be varied. The one rule about the sauce or glaze: It should be thick enough to cling to the pork. For variations on this recipe, see page 273.

Recipe Stats

TOTAL TIME **1½ hours**
PREPARATION TIME **10 minutes**
ACTIVE COOKING TIME **20 minutes**
YIELD **4 to 6 servings**
MAKE AHEAD **Serve immediately**
DIFFICULTY **Intermediate**

Tools

- 12-inch ovensafe skillet *
- chef's knife
- carving board
- cutting board
- slicing knife **
- liquid measuring cup
- measuring spoons
- instant-read thermometer ***
- kitchen shears
- large plate
- potholder
- tongs
- wooden spoon
- kitchen twine ****
- paper towels

* Yes, a nonstick pan will be easier to clean, but because this recipe can be tough on delicate nonstick surfaces, we prefer to use a traditional skillet. To remove the sticky glaze, let the pan cool completely and then bring a cup or two of water to a boil in the pan. The boiling water will loosen the glaze and make cleaning a snap. Also, make sure to use a 12-inch skillet for this recipe; a smaller pan cannot accommodate a pork loin.

** We use a slicing knife when serving the roast, but a chef's knife will also work.

*** Loin roasts are fairly lean and will be dry if overcooked. Use an instant-read thermometer to determine when the roast is ready to come out of the oven and you will be guaranteed to serve a juicy, tender roast.

**** Straight from the supermarket packaging, most pork loin roasts will lie flat in the pan and cook unevenly. Tying the roast not only yields more attractive slices, but also ensures that the roast will have the same thickness from end to end so that it cooks evenly. We like cotton or linen twine sold in most supermarkets, usually near the disposable baking pans.

Ingredients

½ **cup maple syrup, preferably grade B**
⅛ **teaspoon ground cinnamon**
  Pinch ground cloves
  Pinch cayenne pepper
1 **(2½-pound) boneless blade-end pork loin roast, tied at even intervals along length with 5 pieces kitchen twine ***
1½ **teaspoons kosher salt**
½ **teaspoon pepper**
2 **teaspoons vegetable oil**

* You can buy several roasts from the loin. The blade-end roast has the most fat and flavor so it's our first choice. However, the center-cut roast will also work in this recipe. In either case, look for a roast with a thin fat cap (about ¼ inch thick). Also, pay attention to the weight and size of the roast. Large roasts (more than 3 pounds) may not fit in your skillet, and a shorter, fatter roast is a better choice than a longer, thinner roast (which also may not fit in the pan).

What Can Go Wrong

Here's a list of common mistakes cooks make when preparing this recipe.

COMMON MISTAKE	BAD OUTCOMES	WHAT YOU SHOULD DO
Buying Wrong Roast	• **The roast is tough.** • **The roast is dry.** • **The roast is bland.**	The blade-end roast is the best choice for this recipe. It's lean but not too lean. A center-cut roast is a second choice because it can cook up drier and tougher. It also has less flavor than the blade-end roast.
Shortcutting Browning	• **The roast is not browned all over.** • **The flavor of the glaze is not fully developed.**	While steaks and chops can be flipped just once to brown the majority of the exterior, a roast requires more attention. We use tongs to turn the roast three times as it browns in the skillet. A one-quarter turn each time ensures that a flavorful browned crust covers the entire roast.
Not Using Instant-Read Thermometer	• **The roast is overcooked and gray.** • **The roast is dry and chalky.**	Don't try to guess if the roast is done. Check the progress of the roast with an instant-read thermometer inserted into the center. It's a good idea to let the roast rest for 20 minutes before serving—it will do a better job of holding on to its juices. During the resting time, residual heat will continue to cook the meat. So, while 140 to 145 degrees might seem a little low, the final serving temperature of the roast will actually be 150 degrees—juicy with just a hint of rosy color.
Not Using Pure Maple Syrup	• **The meat is too sweet.** • **The glaze is one-dimensional.**	Don't even consider making this roast with pancake syrup—it's much too sweet and bland for this dish. You must use pure maple syrup. We like the robust flavor of grade B syrup—this syrup comes from the end of the sap run and boasts a darker color and more intense flavor. Lighter grade A syrups are better reserved for pancakes and waffles—dishes where you can appreciate their subtle nuances—however, they will certainly work in this recipe.
Glaze Is Too Thin	• **The glaze won't stick to the roast.**	If the glaze is too thin, it will run right off the roast. This can happen if you used very thin syrup or if you purchased an enhanced roast injected with a salt solution. In the latter instance, the liquid leaches out of the meat in the oven and dilutes the glaze. Before serving, check the consistency of the glaze and simmer it briefly (minding the very hot handle) if necessary.
Forgetting Skillet Handle Is Very Hot	• **You badly burn your hand.** • **You drop the pan.**	Not only do you need a potholder or dish towel to remove the skillet from the oven, but you will also need to protect your hand when pouring the thickened glaze over the roast. Leave a potholder on the handle to remind yourself not to touch the bare metal.

1. Combine ½ cup maple syrup, ⅛ tea-spoon ground cinnamon, pinch ground cloves, and pinch cayenne. Heat oven to 325 degrees.

2. Tie 2½-pound boneless blade-end pork loin roast at even intervals with 5 pieces of kitchen twine.

3. Pat roast dry with paper towels, then sprinkle evenly with 1½ teaspoons kosher salt and ½ teaspoon pepper.

4. Heat 2 teaspoons vegetable oil in 12-inch ovensafe skillet over medium-high heat until just beginning to smoke, about 3 minutes.

5. Place roast fat side down in skillet and cook until well browned on all sides, 7 to 10 minutes, using tongs to rotate roast one-quarter turns.

6. Transfer roast to large plate. Reduce heat to medium and pour off fat from skillet.

7. Add maple syrup mixture and cook, stirring constantly, until fragrant, about 30 seconds (syrup will bubble immediately).

8. Off heat, return roast to skillet. Using tongs, roll to coat roast with glaze on all sides and place skillet in preheated oven on middle rack.

9. Roast until center registers 140 to 145 degrees on instant-read thermo-meter, 35 to 55 minutes, turning roast to coat with glaze halfway through.

10. Using potholder or dish towel, remove skillet from oven. Transfer roast to carving board. Set skillet aside to cool slightly to thicken glaze, about 5 minutes.

11. Being careful of hot handle, pour glaze over roast. Let rest 10 to 15 min-utes longer.

12. Remove twine from roast. Cut into ½-inch-thick slices and serve immediately.

Slow-Roasted Pork Shoulder

Tools

- rimmed baking sheet
- roasting pan with V-rack *
- small saucepan
- carving board
- chef's knife
- cutting board
- paring knife **
- slicing knife
- dry measuring cups
- liquid measuring cup
- measuring spoons
- baster
- dish towel
- fat separator
- instant-read thermometer
- mixing bowl
- tongs
- aluminum foil
- paper towels
- plastic wrap

* A V-rack is essential for elevating the roast above the roasting pan and the juices in the pan. The V-rack ensures that a crisp crust develops and permits the roast to cook evenly.

** To start the carving process, use a paring knife to cut around the bone in the roast, and then pull out the bone with your hands. Once the bone is removed, switch to a slicing knife to carve the roast.

Overview

Low-temperature roasting is a great way to prepare very fatty roasts, such as a pork shoulder. The effect is akin to barbecue, minus the smoke. Pork shoulder is an incredibly flavorful cut. It's also very cheap. This cut is the traditional choice for pulled pork.

We found that roasting this big cut at 325 degrees for 5 to 6 hours gave plenty of time for fat to melt and the connective tissue to break down. The result is a succulent roast.

We made a few refinements along the way. As with a cheap cut of beef, we found pork shoulder benefited from an overnight salt rub. Adding brown sugar to the mix helped create a roast with a crackling crisp crust. (And a little sweetness works well with pork.) We found it best to elevate the roast in a V-rack so it cooked evenly. Some water in the pan prevented the pan drippings from burning during the very long roasting time.

We use the pan drippings to make a quick sauce with peaches, sugar, wine, rice vinegar, grainy mustard, and thyme. If you prefer, you could make a sauce made with cherries, red wine, and ruby port (see recipe on page 274).

Ingredients

PORK ROAST
- 1 (6- to 8-pound) bone-in pork butt roast *
- ⅓ cup kosher salt **
- ⅓ cup packed light brown sugar **
- Pepper

PEACH SAUCE
- 10 ounces frozen peaches, cut into 1-inch chunks ***
- 2 cups dry white wine
- ½ cup granulated sugar
- ¼ cup plus 1 tablespoon rice vinegar
- 2 sprigs fresh thyme
- 1 tablespoon whole-grain mustard

* We prefer natural to enhanced pork (pork that has been injected with a salt solution to increase moistness and flavor), though both will work in this recipe. Pork butt is a shoulder roast and is sometimes labeled Boston butt.

** Kosher salt is much easier to spread over the roast than table salt. The salt seasons the meat nicely, while the brown sugar helps with browning. For the salt and sugar to do their work, the roast must be refrigerated overnight.

*** Since the peaches are cooked for a half-hour, frozen are the better option, unless you have really good fresh peaches on hand—use 2 fresh peaches, peeled, pitted, and cut into ½-inch wedges, if desired.

Recipe Stats

TOTAL TIME **36 hours**
PREPARATION TIME **15 minutes**
ACTIVE COOKING TIME **1 hour**
YIELD **8 to 12 servings**
MAKE AHEAD **Serve immediately**
DIFFICULTY **Easy**

What Can Go Wrong

Here's a list of common mistakes cooks make when preparing this recipe.

COMMON MISTAKE	BAD OUTCOMES	WHAT YOU SHOULD DO
Buying Wrong Cut	• **The meat is tough.** • **The meat is dry.**	Not many cuts can withstand 6 hours in the oven. A bone-in pork butt (or pork shoulder) has a ton of fat and connective tissue, so it is best cooked to an internal temperature of 190 degrees. Try this method with a lean cut, such as pork loin, and the texture will be like jerky.
Not Salting Roast Overnight	• **The roast is bland.** • **The roast is dry.**	The overnight salting accomplishes two things. As you might imagine, the salt has time to penetrate deep into the meat, so this large cut is well seasoned, right down to the bone. In addition, the salt changes the structure of the muscle fibers and keeps this cut from drying out during its long stint in the oven.
Letting Pan Run Dry	• **The sauce tastes scorched.** • **The sauce isn't very meaty tasting.**	The water in the roasting pan keeps the flavorful drippings from scorching. That's important because those drippings are used to create a simple sauce. Put 1 quart (yes, 4 cups) of water into the roasting pan at the outset, but make sure to check the pan a few times, especially during those last hours in the oven. If the pan is looking dry, add another cup or so of water.
Shortchanging Resting Period	• **The roast is dry.** • **The roast shreds when sliced.**	All roasts must rest before you slice into them. The muscle fibers need time to relax and grab hold of the meat's natural juices. If you hurry up this process (this cut needs 60 minutes), those juices will end up on the cutting board, not in the meat. Even worse, if you don't rest this roast, it will shred when sliced. This is a big risk whenever you cook meat to 190 degrees (think brisket). Giving the roast a full hour to rest gives you a good shot at carving neat slices.
Not Defatting Jus	• **The sauce is greasy.**	The liquid at the bottom of the roasting pan is a key component in the sauce served with this roast. However, the liquid must be defatted in a fat separator. (If you don't have a fat separator, let the liquid settle in a measuring cup and pour off the fat that rises to the top.) Whatever you do, don't add all of the jus to the sauce. The liquid is very intense, and it can make the sauce both too salty and too sweet if you add more than ¼ cup defatted jus.

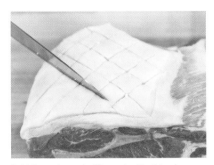

1. Using sharp knife, cut slits 1 inch apart in crosshatch pattern in fat cap of 6- to 8-pound bone-in pork butt, being careful not to cut into meat.

2. Combine ⅓ cup kosher salt and ⅓ cup packed light brown sugar in medium bowl. Rub salt mixture over entire pork shoulder and into slits.

3. Wrap roast tightly in double layer of plastic wrap, place on rimmed baking sheet, and refrigerate at least 12 hours and up to 24 hours.

4. Adjust oven rack to lowest position and heat oven to 325 degrees. Unwrap roast, brush excess salt mixture from surface, and season with pepper.

5. Spray V-rack with vegetable oil spray and set rack inside large roasting pan. Transfer roast to rack.

6. Add 1 quart water to roasting pan. (Monitor roasting pan during final hours of cooking; if it runs dry, add another cup or so of water.)

7. Cook roast, basting twice, until meat is very tender and thermometer inserted near but not touching bone registers 190 degrees, 5 to 6 hours.

8. Transfer roast to carving board and let rest, tented loosely with aluminum foil, 1 hour.

9. Transfer liquid in roasting pan to fat separator. Let sit 5 minutes. Pour off ¼ cup jus and transfer to small saucepan; discard fat and remaining jus.

10. Add 10 ounces frozen peaches, cut into 1-inch chunks, 2 cups white wine, ½ cup granulated sugar, ¼ cup rice vinegar, and 2 sprigs thyme to saucepan.

11. Simmer until reduced to 2 cups, about 30 minutes. Stir in 1 tablespoon rice vinegar and 1 tablespoon whole-grain mustard. Remove thyme.

12. Cut around inverted T-shaped bone until it can be pulled free from roast using clean dish towel. Slice roast. Serve, passing sauce separately.

Recipe Library

Pan-Seared Steaks with Red Wine Pan Sauce

✔ **WHY THIS RECIPE WORKS:** A well-caramelized exterior is the key to a great steak. But developing this flavorful crust indoors can be difficult. We found there were a few keys to success. The most important step was to get the pan really hot; we waited until the oil was smoking before adding the steaks. Cooking steaks in a pan that wasn't properly preheated led to steaks that overcooked before they could develop a good crust. Also, we patted the steaks dry before searing and, other than turning them once, did not move them after putting them in the skillet. Finally, we made sure to use the right piece of cookware. A 12-inch traditional skillet ensured that the steaks had enough room to sear and encouraged the development of browned bits, the key to a flavorful sauce. Once the steaks were done, we made a simple red wine pan sauce while the steaks rested.

Pan-Seared Steaks with Red Wine Pan Sauce
SERVES 4

To ensure that the steaks remain juicy after cooking, let them rest for 5 minutes even if you're not making the pan sauce. Strip steaks and rib-eye steaks are our favorite choices for this method, but it works for any of the boneless steaks on page 220 as long as they are the proper weight and thickness. If using a large steak, such as round bone or shoulder, however, only one steak will fit in the pan at a time, so plan accordingly. We cook these steaks to rare or medium-rare; to cook to a different degree of doneness see chart on page 783. If there is very little fat left in the skillet after cooking the steaks, add up to 2 teaspoons vegetable oil before adding the shallot. See Core Techniques on page 228 and 232 for more details on this recipe.

STEAKS
- 4 (8-ounce) boneless beef steaks, 1 to 1¼ inches thick, trimmed
  Kosher salt and pepper
- 1 tablespoon vegetable oil

RED WINE PAN SAUCE
- 1 shallot, minced
- ¾ cup chicken broth
- ½ cup dry red wine
- 2 teaspoons packed brown sugar
- 3 tablespoons unsalted butter, cut into 3 pieces and chilled
- 1 teaspoon minced fresh thyme
  Salt and pepper

1. FOR THE STEAKS: Pat steaks dry with paper towels, then season with salt and pepper. Heat oil in 12-inch skillet over medium-high heat until just smoking. Add steaks and cook until browned on first side, 3 to 4 minutes.

2. Flip steaks over and continue to cook until meat registers 115 to 120 degrees (for rare) or 120 to 125 degrees (for medium-rare), 3 to 5 minutes. Transfer steaks to large plate, tent with aluminum foil, and let rest for 5 to 10 minutes.

3. FOR THE SAUCE: Pour off all but 2 teaspoons fat from skillet. Add shallot and cook over medium-high heat until softened, about 2 minutes. Stir in broth, wine, and brown sugar, scraping up any browned bits, and simmer until sauce is thickened and reduced to ⅓ cup, about 5 minutes.

4. Stir in any accumulated meat juices. Off heat, whisk in butter, one piece at a time. Stir in thyme and season with salt and pepper to taste. Spoon sauce over steaks and serve.

Pan-Seared Thick-Cut Strip Steaks

✔ **WHY THIS RECIPE WORKS:** Pan-searing thick-cut steaks poses one main problem—by the time a good crust has developed and the very center is a rosy medium-rare, the rest of the meat is dry and gray. We needed to find a way to quickly sear the exterior while slowly cooking the interior to allow for more even heat distribution. We tried flipping the steaks every 15 seconds and also pan-roasting them (searing them on the stovetop then moving the skillet to a hot oven), but neither approach was practical or worked very well. The key turned out to be starting the steaks in a warm oven and then quickly searing them to keep the meat directly under the crust from turning gray. Cooked this way, the steaks developed a beautiful brown crust, while the rest of the meat stayed pink, juicy, and tender.

Pan-Seared Thick-Cut Strip Steaks
SERVES 4

Rib eye or filet mignon of similar thickness can be substituted for the strip steaks. If using filet mignon, buying a 2-pound center-cut tenderloin roast and portioning it into four 8-ounce steaks yourself will produce more consistent results than individual store-cut steaks. If using filet mignon, increase the oven time by about 5 minutes. When cooking lean strip steaks (without an external fat cap) or filet mignon, add an extra tablespoon of oil to the pan. Serve with Red Wine Pan Sauce or Port-Cherry Reduction (page 267). Another option is to spoon a compound butter (see recipes pages 267 and 271) onto the steaks as they rest. See Core Technique on page 230 for more details on this recipe.

- 2 (1-pound) boneless strip steaks, 1½ to 1¾ inches thick
  Salt and pepper
- 1 tablespoon vegetable oil

1. Adjust oven rack to middle position and heat oven to 275 degrees. Pat steaks dry with paper towels. Cut each steak in half vertically to create four 8-ounce steaks. Season steaks with salt and pepper; gently press sides of steaks until uniform 1½ inches thick. Place steaks on wire rack set in rimmed baking sheet. Transfer to oven and cook until meat registers 90 to 95 degrees (for rare to medium-rare), 20 to 25 minutes, or 100 to 105 degrees (for medium), 25 to 30 minutes.

2. Heat oil in 12-inch skillet over high heat until just smoking. Place steaks in skillet and sear until well browned and crusty, about 1½ to 3 minutes, lifting once halfway through cooking to redistribute fat underneath each steak. (Reduce heat if fond begins to burn.) Using tongs, turn steaks and cook until well browned on second side, 2 to 3 minutes. Transfer all steaks to plate and reduce heat to medium. Use tongs to stand 2 steaks on their sides. Holding steaks together, return to skillet and sear on all sides until browned, about 1½ minutes. Repeat with remaining 2 steaks.

3. Transfer steaks to wire rack and let rest, tented loosely with aluminum foil, for 10 minutes. Arrange steaks on individual plates and serve.

Pepper-Crusted Filets Mignons

✔ **WHY THIS RECIPE WORKS:** Black peppercorns can give mild-tasting filet mignon a welcome flavor boost. But they can also create a punishing blast of heat. For a pepper-crusted filet mignon with a crust that wouldn't overwhelm the meat, we mellowed the peppercorns' heat by gently simmering them in olive oil. We then used a two-step process to create a well-browned and attractive pepper crust: First, we rubbed the raw steaks with a paste of the cooked cracked peppercorns, oil, and salt; then we pressed the paste into each steak using a sheet of plastic wrap to ensure it stayed put. The paste not only added flavor to the meat but also drew out the meat's own beefy flavor.

Pepper-Crusted Filets Mignons

SERVES 4

To crush the peppercorns, spread half of them on a cutting board, place a skillet on top, and, pressing down firmly with both hands, use a rocking motion to crush the peppercorns beneath the "heel" of the skillet. Repeat with the remaining peppercorns. While heating the peppercorns in oil tempers much of their pungent heat, this recipe is still pretty spicy. If you prefer a very mild pepper flavor, drain the cooled peppercorns in a fine-mesh strainer in step 1, toss them with 5 tablespoons of fresh oil, add the salt, and proceed. Serve with either Blue Cheese–Chive Butter or Port-Cherry Reduction (recipes follow). See Recipe Tutorial on page 244 for more details on this recipe.

- 5 **tablespoons black peppercorns, crushed**
- 5 **tablespoons plus 2 teaspoons olive oil**
- 1½ **teaspoons salt**
- 4 **(7- to 8-ounce) center-cut filets mignons, 1½ to 2 inches thick, trimmed**

1. Heat peppercorns and 5 tablespoons oil in small saucepan over low heat until faint bubbles appear. Continue to cook at bare simmer, swirling pan occasionally, until pepper is fragrant, 7 to 10 minutes. Remove from heat and set aside to cool. When mixture is room temperature, add salt and stir to combine. Rub steaks with oil and pepper mixture, thoroughly coating top and bottom of each steak with peppercorns. Cover steaks with plastic wrap and press gently to make sure peppercorns adhere; let stand at room temperature for 1 hour.

2. Meanwhile, adjust oven rack to middle position, place baking sheet on oven rack, and heat oven to 450 degrees. When oven reaches 450 degrees, heat remaining 2 teaspoons oil in 12-inch heavy-bottomed skillet over medium-high heat until just smoking. Place steaks in skillet and cook, without moving, until dark brown crust has formed, 3 to 4 minutes. Using tongs, turn steaks and cook until well browned on second side, about 3 minutes. Off heat, transfer steaks to hot baking sheet in oven. Roast until meat registers 115 to 120 degrees (for rare), 120 to 125 degrees (for medium-rare), or 130 to 135 degrees (for medium), 3 to 7 minutes. Transfer steaks to wire rack set in rimmed baking sheet and let rest, tented loosely with aluminum foil, for 5 minutes before serving.

Blue Cheese–Chive Butter

MAKES ABOUT ½ CUP, ENOUGH FOR 1 RECIPE PEPPER-CRUSTED FILETS MIGNONS

While we generally prefer sharper blue cheese, such as Stilton or Gorgonzola, for eating, when cooking we find that a milder, creamier blue cheese, such as Stella Blue from Wisconsin, works best with the pepper crust in the accompanying recipe.

- 1½ **ounces mild blue cheese, room temperature**
- 3 **tablespoons unsalted butter, softened**
- ⅛ **teaspoon salt**
- 2 **tablespoons minced fresh chives**

Combine blue cheese, butter, and salt in medium bowl and mix with stiff rubber spatula until smooth. Fold in chives. While steaks are resting, spoon 1 to 2 tablespoons butter onto each one.

Port-Cherry Reduction

MAKES ABOUT 1 CUP, ENOUGH FOR 1 RECIPE PEPPER-CRUSTED FILETS MIGNONS

Any decent ruby port will work here.

- 1½ **cups ruby port**
- ½ **cup balsamic vinegar**
- ½ **cup dried tart cherries**
- 1 **shallot, minced**
- 2 **sprigs fresh thyme**
- 1 **tablespoon unsalted butter**
  Salt

1. Combine port, vinegar, cherries, shallot, and thyme in medium saucepan; simmer over medium-low heat until liquid has reduced to about ⅓ cup, about 30 minutes. Set aside, covered.

2. While steaks are resting, reheat sauce. Off heat, remove thyme sprigs, then whisk in butter until melted. Season with salt to taste; spoon over steak and serve.

Glazed Pork Chops

✓ **WHY THIS RECIPE WORKS:** Thin boneless chops often cook up dry and bland, but their convenience is enticing. For moist chops with a pronounced sear and moist, juicy interior, we determined that pan searing was the best method. For flavor, we decided to add a glaze. To prevent the chops from drying out, we seared them on just one side until they were well browned, added the glaze mixture, then gently "poached" the chops in the glaze. This approach helped the chops retain moisture and reduced the glaze to the right consistency.

Glazed Pork Chops

SERVES 4

If your chops are on the thinner side, check their internal temperature after the initial sear. If they are already at the 145-degree mark, remove them from the skillet and allow them to rest, tented loosely with aluminum foil, for 5 minutes, then add the pork juices and glaze ingredients to the skillet and proceed with step 3. If your chops are closer to 1 inch thick, you may need to increase the simmering time in step 2.

- ½ cup distilled white vinegar or cider vinegar
- ⅓ cup packed light brown sugar
- ⅓ cup apple cider or apple juice
- 2 tablespoons Dijon mustard
- 1 tablespoon soy sauce
  Pinch cayenne pepper
- 4 (5- to 7-ounce) boneless pork chops, ½ to ¾ inch thick, trimmed
  Salt and pepper
- 1 tablespoon vegetable oil

1. Combine vinegar, sugar, cider, mustard, soy sauce, and cayenne in bowl; mix thoroughly and set aside. Pat chops dry with paper towels. Cut 2 slits, about 2 inches apart, through outer layer of fat and silverskin on each chop. Season chops with salt and pepper.

2. Heat oil in 12-inch skillet over medium-high heat until just smoking. Add chops to skillet and cook until well browned, 4 to 6 minutes. Turn chops and cook 1 minute longer; transfer chops to plate and pour off any oil in skillet. Return chops to skillet, browned side up, and add glaze mixture; cook over medium heat until chops register 145 degrees, 5 to 8 minutes. Transfer chops to clean platter, tent loosely with foil, and let rest for 5 minutes.

3. When chops have rested, add any accumulated juices to skillet and set over medium heat. Simmer, whisking constantly, until glaze is thick and color of dark caramel (heat-resistant rubber spatula should leave wide trail when dragged through glaze), 2 to 6 minutes. Return chops to skillet; turn to coat both sides with glaze. Transfer chops back to platter, browned side up, and spread remaining glaze over chops. Serve.

Glazed Pork Chops with Asian Flavors

Toast 1 teaspoon sesame seeds in small dry skillet over medium heat, stirring frequently, until lightly browned and fragrant, 3 to 5 minutes; set aside in bowl. Substitute ½ cup rice vinegar for white vinegar, omit cider, and add 3 tablespoons each orange juice and mirin and 1 teaspoon grated fresh ginger to glaze ingredients. In step 3, stir another 2 teaspoons rice vinegar into glaze before returning chops to skillet. Before serving, garnish chops with reserved sesame seeds and 1 teaspoon toasted sesame oil.

Glazed Pork Chops with German Flavors

Toast ¾ teaspoon caraway seeds in small dry skillet over medium heat, stirring frequently, until fragrant, 3 to 5 minutes. Chop seeds coarse and set aside. Substitute ⅓ cup beer for cider, reduce soy sauce to 2 teaspoons, and add 3 tablespoons whole-grain mustard (along with Dijon mustard), 1 tablespoon minced fresh thyme, and reserved caraway seeds to glaze ingredients. Omit cayenne.

Pan-Seared Thick-Cut Pork Chops

✓ **WHY THIS RECIPE WORKS:** Thick pork chops typically boast a juicy interior or a nicely caramelized exterior—but rarely both. We wanted it all, in one recipe. To start, we turned the conventional cooking method upside down, first cooking salted chops in a low oven, then searing them in a super-hot pan. Slowly cooking the meat allowed enzymes to break down protein, tenderizing the chops. The salted surface gently dried out in the oven and became beautifully caramelized in the pan. The result was pan-seared pork chops that were perfect inside and out.

Pan-Seared Thick-Cut Pork Chops

SERVES 4

Buy chops of similar thickness so that they cook at the same rate. If the pork is enhanced (injected with a salt solution), do not salt in step 1, and season with salt in step 2. Serve the chops with a pan sauce (recipes follow) or with applesauce. See Core Techniques on page 230 and 232 for more details on this recipe.

- 4 (12-ounce) bone-in pork rib chops, 1½ inches thick, trimmed
  Kosher salt and pepper
- 1–2 tablespoons vegetable oil
- 1 recipe pan sauce (recipes follow)

1. Adjust oven rack to middle position and heat oven to 275 degrees. Pat chops dry with paper towels. Cut 2 slits, about 2 inches apart, through outer layer of fat and silverskin on each chop. Sprinkle each chop with 1 teaspoon salt. Place chops on wire rack set in rimmed baking sheet and let stand at room temperature for 45 minutes.

2. Season chops with pepper; transfer baking sheet to oven. Cook until chops register 120 to 125 degrees, 30 to 45 minutes.

3. Heat 1 tablespoon oil in 12-inch skillet over high heat until just smoking. Place 2 chops in skillet and sear until well browned and crusty, 1½ to 3 minutes, lifting once halfway through to redistribute fat underneath each chop. (Reduce heat if browned bits in pan start to burn.) Using tongs, turn chops and cook until well browned on second side, 2 to 3 minutes. Transfer chops to plate and repeat with remaining 2 chops, adding extra 1 tablespoon oil if pan is dry.

4. Reduce heat to medium. Use tongs to stand 2 pork chops on their sides. Holding chops together with tongs, return to skillet and sear sides of chops (with exception of bone side) until browned and chops register 145 degrees, about 1½ minutes. Repeat with remaining 2 chops. Let chops rest, tented loosely with aluminum foil, for 10 minutes while preparing sauce.

Cilantro and Coconut Pan Sauce

MAKES ½ CUP, ENOUGH FOR 1 RECIPE PAN-SEARED THICK-CUT
PORK CHOPS

- 1 large shallot, minced
- 1 tablespoon grated fresh ginger
- 2 garlic cloves, minced
- ¾ cup canned coconut milk
- ¼ cup chicken broth
- 1 teaspoon sugar
- ¼ cup chopped fresh cilantro
- 2 teaspoons lime juice
- 1 tablespoon unsalted butter
  Salt and pepper

Pour off all but 1 teaspoon fat from pan used to cook chops and return pan to medium heat. Add shallot, ginger, and garlic and cook, stirring constantly, until softened, about 1 minute. Add coconut milk, broth, and sugar, scraping bottom of pan with wooden spoon to loosen any browned bits. Simmer until reduced to ½ cup, 6 to 7 minutes. Off heat, stir in cilantro and lime juice, then whisk in butter. Season with salt and pepper to taste and serve with chops.

Garlic and Thyme Pan Sauce

MAKES ½ CUP, ENOUGH FOR 1 RECIPE PAN-SEARED THICK-CUT
PORK CHOPS

- 1 large shallot, minced
- 2 garlic cloves, minced
- ¾ cup chicken broth
- ½ cup dry white wine
- 1 teaspoon minced fresh thyme
- ¼ teaspoon white wine vinegar
- 3 tablespoons unsalted butter, cut into 3 pieces and chilled

Pour off all but 1 teaspoon fat from pan used to cook chops and return pan to medium heat. Add shallot and garlic and cook, stirring constantly, until softened, about 1 minute. Add broth and wine, scraping bottom of pan with wooden spoon to loosen any browned bits. Simmer until reduced to ½ cup, 6 to 7 minutes. Off heat, stir in thyme and vinegar, then whisk in butter, 1 piece at a time. Season with salt and pepper to taste and serve with chops.

Stir-Fried Beef and Broccoli with Oyster Sauce

✔ **WHY THIS RECIPE WORKS:** Order beef and broccoli in most Chinese restaurants, and you are served a pile of tough meat with overcooked army-issue broccoli all drenched in a thick-as-pudding brown sauce. We set out to rescue beef and broccoli. For the meat, we found that flank steak offered the biggest beefy taste and slicing it thin made it tender. We cooked the beef in two batches over high heat to make sure it browned and didn't steam. Then we cooked the broccoli until crisp-tender using a combination of methods—sautéing and steaming—and added some red bell pepper for sweetness and color. For the sauce, oyster sauce, chicken broth, dry sherry, brown sugar, and sesame oil, lightly thickened with cornstarch made a sauce that clung to the beef and vegetables without being gloppy.

Stir-Fried Beef and Broccoli with Oyster Sauce

SERVES 4

To make slicing the flank steak easier, freeze it for 15 minutes. Serve with Chinese-Style Sticky Rice (page 206). See Recipe Tutorial on page 248 for more details on this recipe.

SAUCE
- 5 tablespoons oyster sauce
- 2 tablespoons chicken broth
- 1 tablespoon dry sherry
- 1 tablespoon packed light brown sugar
- 1 teaspoon toasted sesame oil
- 1 teaspoon cornstarch

BEEF STIR-FRY
- 1 (1-pound) flank steak, trimmed and sliced thin against grain on slight bias
- 3 tablespoons soy sauce
- 6 garlic cloves, minced
- 1 tablespoon grated fresh ginger
- 3 tablespoons peanut or vegetable oil
- 1¼ pounds broccoli, florets cut into bite-size pieces, stalks peeled and cut ⅛ inch thick on bias
- ⅓ cup water
- 1 small red bell pepper, stemmed, seeded, and cut into ¼-inch pieces
- 3 scallions, sliced ½ inch thick on bias

1. FOR THE SAUCE: Whisk all ingredients together in small bowl and set aside.

2. FOR THE STIR-FRY: Combine beef and soy sauce in medium bowl and toss to coat. Cover with plastic wrap and let marinate at least 10 minutes or up to 1 hour, stirring once. Meanwhile, combine garlic, ginger, and 1½ teaspoons oil in small bowl.

3. Drain beef and discard liquid. Heat 1½ teaspoons oil in 12-inch nonstick skillet over high heat until just smoking. Add half of beef in single layer, break up clumps, and cook, without stirring, for 1 minute. Stir beef and continue to cook until beef is browned, about 30 seconds. Transfer beef to medium bowl. Repeat with 1½ teaspoons oil and remaining beef.

4. Add 1 tablespoon oil to skillet and heat until just smoking. Add broccoli and cook for 30 seconds. Add water to pan, cover, and lower heat to medium. Steam broccoli until crisp-tender, about 2 minutes, then transfer to paper towel–lined plate. Add remaining 1½ teaspoons oil to skillet, increase heat to high and heat until just smoking. Add bell pepper and cook, stirring frequently, until spotty brown, about 1½ minutes. Clear center of skillet, add garlic mixture, and cook, mashing mixture into pan, until fragrant, 15 to 20 seconds, then stir mixture into bell pepper.

5. Return beef and broccoli to skillet and toss to combine. Whisk sauce to recombine, then add to skillet and cook, stirring constantly, until sauce is thickened and evenly distributed, about 30 seconds. Transfer to platter, sprinkle with scallions, and serve.

Stir-Fried Pork with Oyster Sauce

✓ **WHY THIS RECIPE WORKS:** Marinating pork tenderloin in a soy-sherry mixture and cooking it quickly in batches over high heat ensured the meat was flavorful, juicy, and perfectly cooked. Because different vegetables cook at different rates, we batch-cooked the vegetables and added aromatics (like ginger and garlic) at the end so they cooked long enough to develop their flavors without burning. Chicken broth gave the sauce some backbone, and cornstarch helped ensure the sauce lightly coated the meat and vegetables.

Stir-Fried Pork, Green Beans, and Red Bell Pepper with Gingery Oyster Sauce

SERVES 4

To make slicing the pork easier, freeze it for 15 minutes. Serve with Chinese-Style Sticky Rice (page 206). See Core Technique on page 234 for more details on how to stir-fry.

SAUCE

- ⅓ **cup chicken broth**
- 2½ **tablespoons oyster sauce**
- 1 **tablespoon dry sherry**
- 2 **teaspoons toasted sesame oil**
- 1 **teaspoon rice vinegar**
- 1 **teaspoon cornstarch**
- ¼ **teaspoon white pepper**

PORK STIR-FRY

- 1 **(12-ounce) pork tenderloin, trimmed and cut into thin strips**
- 2 **teaspoons soy sauce**
- 2 **teaspoons dry sherry**
- 2 **tablespoons grated fresh ginger**
- 2 **garlic cloves, minced**
- 3 **tablespoons vegetable oil**
- 12 **ounces green beans, trimmed and cut on bias into 2-inch lengths**
- 1 **large red bell pepper, stemmed, seeded, and cut into ¾-inch squares**
- 3 **scallions, sliced thin on bias**

1. FOR THE SAUCE: Whisk all ingredients together in small bowl and set aside.

2. FOR THE STIR-FRY: Combine pork, soy sauce, and sherry in small bowl and toss to coat. Cover with plastic wrap and refrigerate for at least 20 minutes or up to 1 hour. Meanwhile, combine ginger, garlic, and 1½ teaspoons oil in small bowl.

3. Drain pork and discard liquid. Heat 1½ teaspoons oil in 12-inch nonstick skillet over high heat until just smoking. Add half of pork in single layer, break up clumps, and cook without stirring for 1 minute. Stir and continue to cook until well browned, about 1 minute. Transfer pork to medium bowl. Repeat with 1½ teaspoons oil and remaining pork.

4. Add 1 tablespoon oil to skillet. Add green beans and cook, stirring occasionally, until spotty brown and crisp-tender, about 5 minutes. Transfer to bowl with pork. Add remaining 1½ teaspoons oil to skillet, add bell pepper, and cook, stirring frequently, until spotty brown, about 2 minutes.

5. Clear center of skillet, add ginger mixture, and cook, mashing mixture into pan, until fragrant, 15 to 20 seconds, then stir mixture into bell pepper.

6. Return pork and green beans to skillet and toss to combine. Whisk sauce to recombine, then add to skillet and cook, stirring constantly, until sauce is thickened and evenly distributed, about 30 seconds. Transfer to platter, sprinkle with scallions, and serve.

Stir-Fry Sauces

✓ **WHY THIS RECIPE WORKS:** After creating a basic stir-fry procedure for cooking proteins and vegetables (see page 234), all we needed were a handful of sauce options. Chicken broth (or tangerine or orange juice, a good choice for shrimp stir-fries in particular) made the best base since the flavor was not overpowering. Soy, hoisin, oyster, and black bean sauces, as well as toasted sesame oil, all proved excellent flavor enhancers. Adding a little cornstarch ensured the sauce could cling to the protein and vegetables, but we were careful not to go overboard to avoid creating a gloppy sauce. We made sure to whisk together our sauce before we started cooking, and after stir-frying the protein, vegetables, and aromatics, we added our sauce to the pan and gave it just a little time to thicken up and coat the ingredients before our stir-fry was ready to serve.

Classic Stir-Fry Sauce

MAKES ENOUGH FOR 1 POUND PROTEIN PLUS 1½ POUNDS VEGETABLES

This quintessential stir-fry sauce pairs well with any combination of protein and vegetables. See How to Stir-Fry on page 234 for details on how to combine this sauce with your choice of protein and vegetables to create your own stir-fry.

- ½ **cup chicken broth**
- ¼ **cup Chinese rice wine or dry sherry**
- 3 **tablespoons hoisin sauce or oyster sauce**
- 1 **tablespoon soy sauce**
- 2 **teaspoons cornstarch**
- 1 **teaspoon toasted sesame oil**

Whisk all ingredients together in bowl and use as directed.

Tangerine Stir-Fry Sauce

MAKES ENOUGH FOR 1 POUND PROTEIN PLUS 1½ POUNDS VEGETABLES

Orange juice can be used in place of the tangerine juice. See How to Stir-Fry on page 234 for details on how to combine this sauce with your choice of protein and vegetables to create your own stir-fry.

- 2 (2-inch) strips tangerine zest plus ¾ cup juice (3 or 4 tangerines)
- 2 tablespoons soy sauce
- 2 tablespoons black bean garlic sauce
- 1 tablespoon sugar
- 1 teaspoon cornstarch
- 1 teaspoon toasted sesame oil
- ¼ teaspoon red pepper flakes

Whisk all ingredients together in bowl and use as directed.

Sesame Stir-Fry Sauce

MAKES ENOUGH FOR 1 POUND PROTEIN PLUS 1½ POUNDS VEGETABLES

For a vegetarian stir-fry, substitute vegetable broth for the chicken broth. See How to Stir-Fry on page 234 for details on how to combine this sauce with your choice of protein and vegetables to create your own stir-fry.

- ¾ cup chicken broth
- ¼ cup soy sauce
- 2 tablespoons Chinese rice wine or dry sherry
- 1 tablespoon cornstarch
- 1 tablespoon sugar
- 1 tablespoon sesame seeds, toasted
- 2 teaspoons toasted sesame oil
- 1 teaspoon Sriracha sauce

Whisk all ingredients together in bowl and use as directed.

Roast Beef Tenderloin

✓ **WHY THIS RECIPE WORKS:** Most roast beef tenderloins have one of two problems: either the meat is evenly cooked but lacks a caramelized crust, or the beef has optimal flavor and an appealing crust but is marred by a gray band of overdone meat. We wanted perfectly cooked, deeply flavored meat, ideally without much fuss. We decided to use a Châteaubriand; this center-cut roast has an even shape and smaller size, making it easier to cook evenly. We reversed the usual cooking process for tenderloin, roasting first and then searing, to eliminate the ring of overdone meat and give the roast a ruby coloring from edge to edge. Salting the meat and rubbing it with softened butter helped it hold on to its juices and gave it richness.

Roast Beef Tenderloin

SERVES 4 TO 6

Ask your butcher to prepare a trimmed center-cut Châteaubriand from the whole tenderloin, as this cut is not usually available without special ordering. If you are cooking for a crowd, this recipe can be doubled to make two roasts. Sear the roasts one after the other, wiping out the pan and adding new oil after searing the first roast. Both pieces of meat can be roasted on the same rack.

- 1 (2-pound) center-cut beef tenderloin Châteaubriand, trimmed
- 2 teaspoons kosher salt
- 1 teaspoon coarsely ground pepper
- 2 tablespoons unsalted butter, softened
- 1 tablespoon vegetable oil
- 1 recipe flavored butter (recipes follow)

1. Using 12-inch lengths of kitchen twine, tie roast crosswise at 1½-inch intervals. Sprinkle roast evenly with salt, cover loosely with plastic wrap, and let stand at room temperature for 1 hour. Meanwhile, adjust oven rack to middle position and heat oven to 300 degrees.

2. Pat roast dry with paper towels. Sprinkle roast evenly with pepper and spread unsalted butter evenly over surface. Transfer roast to wire rack set in rimmed baking sheet. Roast until meat registers 125 degrees (for medium-rare), 40 to 55 minutes, or 135 degrees (for medium), 55 to 70 minutes, flipping roast halfway through cooking.

3. Heat oil in 12-inch skillet over medium-high heat until just smoking. Place roast in skillet and sear until well browned on all sides, 4 to 8 minutes. Transfer roast to carving board and spread 2 tablespoons flavored butter evenly over top of roast; let rest 15 minutes. Remove twine and cut meat crosswise into ½-inch-thick slices. Serve, passing remaining flavored butter separately.

Shallot-Parsley Butter

MAKES ABOUT ½ CUP, ENOUGH FOR 1 RECIPE ROAST BEEF TENDERLOIN

- 4 tablespoons unsalted butter, softened
- 1 small shallot, minced
- 1 tablespoon minced fresh parsley
- 1 garlic clove, minced
- ¼ teaspoon salt
- ¼ teaspoon pepper

Combine all ingredients in bowl.

Chipotle and Garlic Butter with Lime and Cilantro

MAKES ABOUT ½ CUP, ENOUGH FOR 1 RECIPE ROAST BEEF TENDERLOIN

- 5 tablespoons unsalted butter, softened
- 1 tablespoon minced canned chipotle chile in adobo sauce, with 1 teaspoon adobo sauce
- 1 tablespoon minced fresh cilantro
- 1 garlic clove, minced
- 1 teaspoon honey
- 1 teaspoon grated lime zest
- ½ teaspoon salt

Combine all ingredients in bowl.

Best Prime Rib

✓ **WHY THIS RECIPE WORKS:** The perfect prime rib should have a deep-colored, substantial crust encasing a tender, juicy, rosy-pink center. To achieve this perfect roast, we started by salting the roast overnight. The salt enhanced the beefy flavor while dissolving some of the proteins, yielding a buttery-tender roast. To further enhance tenderness, we cooked the roast at a very low temperature, which allowed the meat's enzymes to act as natural tenderizers, breaking down its tough connective tissue. A brief stint under the broiler before serving ensured a crisp, flavorful crust.

Best Prime Rib

SERVES 6 TO 8

Look for a roast with an untrimmed fat cap (ideally ½ inch thick). We prefer the flavor and texture of prime-grade beef, but choice grade will work as well. To remove the bones from the roast, use a sharp knife and run it down the length of the bones, following the contours as closely as possible until the meat is separated. Monitoring the roast with a meat-probe thermometer is best. If you use an instant-read thermometer, open the oven door as little as possible and remove the roast from the oven while taking its temperature. If the roast has not reached the correct temperature in the time range specified in step 3, heat the oven to 200 degrees, wait for 5 minutes, then shut it off and continue to cook the roast until it reaches the desired temperature.

1 **(7-pound) first-cut beef standing rib roast (3 bones), meat removed from bones, bones reserved**
  Kosher salt and pepper
2 **teaspoons vegetable oil**

1. Using sharp knife, cut slits in surface layer of fat, spaced 1 inch apart, in crosshatch pattern, being careful to cut down to, but not into, meat. Rub 2 tablespoons salt over entire roast and into slits. Place meat back on bones (to save space in refrigerator), transfer to large plate, and refrigerate, uncovered, at least 1 day and up to 4 days.

2. Adjust oven rack to middle position and heat oven to 200 degrees. Heat oil in 12-inch skillet over high heat until just smoking. Sear sides and top of roast (reserving bone) until browned, 6 to 8 minutes total (do not sear side where roast was cut from bone). Place meat back on ribs so bones fit where cut, and let cool for 10 minutes; tie meat to bones between ribs with 2 lengths of kitchen twine. Transfer roast, fat side up, to wire rack set in rimmed baking sheet and season with pepper. Roast until meat registers 110 degrees, 3 to 4 hours.

3. Turn off oven; leave roast in oven, opening door as little as possible, until meat registers 120 degrees (for rare) or 125 degrees (for medium-rare), 30 to 75 minutes longer.

4. Remove roast from oven (leave roast on baking sheet), tent loosely with aluminum foil, and let rest for at least 30 minutes and up to 75 minutes.

5. Adjust oven rack 8 inches from broiler element and heat broiler. Remove foil from roast, form into 3-inch ball, and place under ribs to elevate fat cap. Broil until top of roast is well browned and crisp, 2 to 8 minutes.

6. Transfer roast to carving board; cut twine and remove ribs from roast. Slice meat into ¾-inch-thick slices. Season with salt to taste, and serve.

Slow-Roasted Beef

✓ **WHY THIS RECIPE WORKS:** Roasting inexpensive beef usually yields tough meat best suited for sandwiches. We wanted to transform a bargain cut into a tender, juicy roast that could stand on its own at dinner. The eye-round roast has good flavor and relative tenderness, and it also has a uniform shape that guarantees even cooking. Searing the meat before roasting as well as salting it a full 24 hours before roasting vastly improved flavor. But the big surprise was the method that produced remarkably tender and juicy beef—roasting the meat at a very low 225 degrees and then turning off the oven toward the end of cooking. This approach allowed the meat's enzymes to act as natural tenderizers, breaking down its tough connective tissue.

Slow-Roasted Beef

SERVES 6 TO 8

We don't recommend cooking this roast past medium. Open the oven door as little as possible and remove the roast from the oven while taking its temperature. If the roast has not reached the desired temperature in the time specified in step 3, heat the oven to 225 degrees for 5 minutes, shut it off, and continue to cook the roast to the desired temperature. For a smaller (2½- to 3½-pound) roast, reduce the amount of kosher salt to 1 tablespoon and pepper to 1½ teaspoons. For a 4½- to 6-pound roast, cut in half crosswise before cooking to create two smaller roasts. Slice the roast as thinly as possible and serve with Horseradish Cream Sauce (recipe follows), if desired. See Recipe Tutorial on page 241 for more details on this recipe.

1 **(3½- to 4½-pound) boneless eye-round roast, trimmed**
4 **teaspoons kosher salt**
2 **teaspoons plus 1 tablespoon vegetable oil**
2 **teaspoons pepper**

1. Season all sides of roast evenly with salt. Wrap with plastic wrap and refrigerate 18 to 24 hours.

2. Adjust oven rack to middle position and heat oven to 225 degrees. Pat roast dry with paper towels; rub with 2 teaspoons oil and season all sides evenly with pepper. Heat remaining 1 tablespoon oil in 12-inch skillet over medium-high heat until just smoking. Sear roast until browned on all sides, about 12 to 16 minutes. Transfer roast to wire rack set in rimmed baking sheet. Roast until meat registers 115 degrees (for medium-rare), 1¼ to 1¾ hours, or 125 degrees (for medium), 1¾ to 2¼ hours.

3. Turn oven off; leave roast in oven, without opening door, until meat registers 130 degrees (for medium-rare) or 140 degrees (for medium), 30 to 50 minutes longer. Transfer roast to carving board and let rest for 15 minutes. Slice meat crosswise as thinly as possible and serve.

Horseradish Cream Sauce

MAKES ABOUT 1 CUP, ENOUGH FOR 1 RECIPE SLOW-ROASTED BEEF

Make sure to buy refrigerated prepared horseradish, not the shelf-stable kind, which contains preservatives and additives.

½ **cup heavy cream**
½ **cup prepared horseradish**
1 **teaspoon salt**
⅛ **teaspoon pepper**

Whisk cream in bowl until thickened but not yet holding soft peaks, 1 to 2 minutes. Gently fold in horseradish, salt, and pepper. Transfer to serving bowl and refrigerate at least 30 minutes or up to 1 hour before serving.

Maple-Glazed Pork Roast

✔ **WHY THIS RECIPE WORKS:** Sweet maple syrup, with its delicate flavor notes of smoke, caramel, and vanilla, makes an ideal foil for pork, and maple-glazed pork roast is a New England classic. But this dish often fall short of its savory-sweet promise; dry pork is a problem, yes, but the real issue is the glaze, which is usually either too thin or overly sweet. We found that searing the roast (tasters preferred a blade-end loin roast) first on the stovetop ensured a crisp, caramelized crust before reducing the maple syrup in the skillet used to sear the pork. Roasting the pork in that same skillet was the best way to get a beautifully glazed roast.

Maple-Glazed Pork Roast

SERVES 4 TO 6

The blade-end roast has the most fat and flavor so it's our first choice. However, the center-cut roast will also work in this recipe. In either case, look for a roast with a thin fat cap (about ¼ inch thick) and don't trim this thin layer of fat. The flavor of grade B maple syrup (sometimes called "cooking maple") is stronger and richer than grade A, but grade A syrup will work well, too. This dish is unapologetically sweet, so we recommend side dishes that take well to the sweetness. Garlicky sautéed greens, braised cabbage, and soft polenta are good choices. See Recipe Tutorial on page 260 for more details on this recipe.

½ **cup maple syrup**
⅛ **teaspoon ground cinnamon**
   Pinch ground cloves
   Pinch cayenne pepper
1 **(2½-pound) boneless blade-end pork loin roast, tied at even intervals along length with 5 pieces kitchen twine**
1½ **teaspoons kosher salt**
½ **teaspoon pepper**
2 **teaspoons vegetable oil**

1. Adjust oven rack to middle position and heat oven to 325 degrees. Stir maple syrup, cinnamon, cloves, and cayenne together in measuring cup or bowl; set aside. Pat roast dry with paper towels, then season with salt and pepper.

2. Heat oil in 12-inch ovensafe skillet over medium-high heat until just smoking, about 3 minutes. Place roast fat side down in skillet and cook until well browned, about 3 minutes. Using tongs, rotate roast one-quarter turn and cook until well browned, about 2½ minutes; repeat until roast is well browned on all sides. Transfer roast to large plate. Reduce heat to medium and pour off fat from skillet; add maple syrup mixture and cook, stirring constantly, until fragrant, about 30 seconds (syrup will bubble immediately). Off heat, return roast to skillet; using tongs, roll to coat roast with glaze on all sides. Place skillet in oven and roast until meat registers 140 to 145 degrees, 35 to 55 minutes, using tongs to roll and spin roast to coat with glaze halfway through roasting time (skillet handle will be hot). Transfer roast to carving board; set skillet aside to cool slightly to thicken glaze, about 5 minutes. Pour glaze over roast and let rest 10 to 15 minutes longer. Snip twine off roast, cut into ½-inch-thick slices, and serve.

Maple-Glazed Pork Roast with Rosemary

Substitute 2 teaspoons minced fresh rosemary for cinnamon, cloves, and cayenne.

Maple-Glazed Pork Roast with Orange Essence

Add 1 tablespoon grated orange zest to maple syrup along with spices.

Maple-Glazed Pork Roast with Star Anise

Add 4 star anise pods to maple syrup along with spices.

Maple-Glazed Pork Roast with Smoked Paprika

Add 2 teaspoons hot smoked paprika to maple syrup along with spices.

Slow-Roasted Pork Shoulder

✔ **WHY THIS RECIPE WORKS:** When we think of a pork roast, the first thing that comes to mind these days is pork loin. It may be lean, but it typically needs a serious flavor boost. We wanted to explore the glories of old-fashioned, more flavorful (read: less lean) pork. One such cut is the shoulder roast. It may take longer to cook, but it's also inexpensive, loaded with flavorful intramuscular fat, and boasts a thick fat cap that renders to a bronze, baconlike crust. We started by rubbing the roast's exterior with brown sugar and salt, then left it to rest overnight. The sugar dried out the exterior and boosted browning. Elevating the pork shoulder on a V-rack and pouring water in the roasting pan kept the pork's drippings from burning as it roasted. It also created a significant jus. Finally, a fruity sauce with sweet and sour elements cut the pork shoulder's richness.

Slow-Roasted Pork Shoulder with Peach Sauce

SERVES 8 TO 12

Pork butt roast is often labeled Boston butt in the supermarket. Add more water to the roasting pan as necessary during the last hours of cooking to prevent the fond from burning. Serve the pork with the accompanying peach sauce or with cherry sauce (recipe follows). See Recipe Tutorial on page 263 for more details on this recipe.

PORK ROAST

- 1 **(6- to 8-pound) bone-in pork butt roast**
- ⅓ **cup kosher salt**
- ⅓ **cup packed light brown sugar**
     Pepper

PEACH SAUCE

- 10 **ounces frozen peaches, cut into 1-inch chunks, or 2 fresh peaches, peeled, pitted, and cut into ½-inch wedges**
- 2 **cups dry white wine**
- ½ **cup granulated sugar**
- ¼ **cup plus 1 tablespoon rice vinegar**
- 2 **sprigs fresh thyme**
- 1 **tablespoon whole-grain mustard**

1. FOR THE PORK ROAST: Using sharp knife, cut slits 1 inch apart in crosshatch pattern in fat cap of roast, being careful not to cut into meat. Combine salt and brown sugar in bowl. Rub salt mixture over entire pork shoulder and into slits. Wrap roast tightly in double layer of plastic wrap, place on rimmed baking sheet, and refrigerate for 12 to 24 hours.

2. Adjust oven rack to lowest position and heat oven to 325 degrees. Unwrap roast and brush any excess salt mixture from surface. Season roast with pepper. Spray V-rack with vegetable oil spray, set rack in large roasting pan, and place roast on rack. Add 1 quart water to roasting pan.

3. Cook roast, basting twice during cooking, until meat is extremely tender and roast near (but not touching) bone registers 190 degrees, 5 to 6 hours. Transfer roast to carving board and let rest, tented loosely with aluminum foil, for 1 hour. Transfer liquid in roasting pan to fat separator and let sit for 5 minutes. Pour off ¼ cup jus and set aside for sauce; discard fat and remaining jus.

4. FOR THE SAUCE: Bring peaches, wine, sugar, ¼ cup vinegar, ¼ cup defatted jus, and thyme sprigs to simmer in small saucepan; cook, stirring occasionally, until reduced to 2 cups, about 30 minutes. Stir in remaining 1 tablespoon vinegar and mustard. Remove thyme sprigs, cover, and keep warm.

5. Using sharp paring knife, cut around inverted T-shaped bone until it can be pulled free from roast (use clean dish towel to grasp bone). Using slicing knife, slice roast. Serve, passing sauce separately.

Slow-Roasted Pork Shoulder with Cherry Sauce

Substitute 10 ounces fresh or frozen pitted cherries for peaches, red wine for white wine, and red wine vinegar for rice vinegar, and add ¼ cup ruby port along with defatted jus. Increase granulated sugar to ¾ cup, omit thyme sprigs and mustard, and reduce mixture to 1½ cups.

Glazed Spiral-Sliced Ham

✓ **WHY THIS RECIPE WORKS:** Glazed ham is appealingly simple but often comes out dry and jerkylike. We wanted a top-notch glazed ham that is always moist and tender, with a glaze that complements but doesn't overwhelm the meat. Bone-in hams that have been spiral-sliced offered the best flavor with the least amount of carving necessary. We found it important to avoid labels that read "ham with water added" as these hams simply didn't taste as good. Heating the ham to an internal temperature of no higher than 120 degrees was enough to take the chill off without drying it out. Soaking the ham in warm water before heating it and placing it in an oven bag kept it moist and also reduced cooking time. Finally, we determined that it was best to apply the glaze toward the end of cooking and then again once it came out of the oven.

Glazed Spiral-Sliced Ham
SERVES 12 TO 14, WITH LEFTOVERS

You can bypass the 90-minute soaking time, but the heating time will increase to 18 to 20 minutes per pound for a cold ham. If there is a tear or hole in the ham's inner covering, wrap it in several layers of plastic wrap before soaking it in hot water. Instead of using the plastic oven bag, the ham may be placed cut side down in the roasting pan and covered tightly with foil, but you will need to add 3 to 4 minutes per pound to the heating time. If using an oven bag, be sure to cut slits in the bag so it does not burst. We've included three optional glazes.

- 1 **(7- to 10-pound) spiral-sliced bone-in half ham**
- 1 **large plastic oven bag**
- 1 **recipe glaze (recipes follow)**

1. Leaving ham's inner plastic or foil covering intact, place ham in large container and cover with hot tap water; set aside for 45 minutes. Drain and cover again with hot tap water; set aside for another 45 minutes.

2. Adjust oven rack to lowest position and heat oven to 250 degrees. Unwrap ham; remove and discard plastic disk covering bone. Place ham in oven bag. Gather top of bag tightly so bag fits snugly around ham, tie bag, and trim excess plastic. Set ham cut side down in large roasting pan and cut 4 slits in top of bag with paring knife.

3. Bake ham until center registers 100 degrees, 1 to 1½ hours (about 10 minutes per pound).

4. Remove ham from oven and increase oven temperature to 350 degrees. Cut open oven bag and roll back sides to expose ham. Brush ham with one-third of glaze and return to oven until glaze becomes sticky, about 10 minutes (if glaze is too thick to brush, return to heat to loosen).

5. Remove ham from oven, transfer to carving board, and brush entire ham with one-third of glaze. Let ham rest, tented loosely with aluminum foil, for 15 minutes. While ham rests, heat remaining one-third of glaze with 4 to 6 tablespoons of ham juices until it forms thick but fluid sauce. Carve and serve ham, passing sauce at table.

Cherry-Port Glaze

MAKES 1 CUP, ENOUGH FOR 1 RECIPE GLAZED SPIRAL-SLICED HAM

- ½ cup ruby port
- 1 cup packed dark brown sugar
- ½ cup cherry preserves
- 1 teaspoon pepper

Simmer port in small saucepan over medium heat until reduced to 2 tablespoons, about 5 minutes. Add remaining ingredients and cook, stirring occasionally, until sugar dissolves and mixture is thick, syrupy, and reduced to 1 cup, 5 to 10 minutes; set aside.

Maple-Orange Glaze

MAKES 1 CUP, ENOUGH FOR 1 RECIPE GLAZED SPIRAL-SLICED HAM

- ¾ cup maple syrup
- ½ cup orange marmalade
- 2 tablespoons unsalted butter
- 1 tablespoon Dijon mustard
- 1 teaspoon pepper
- ¼ teaspoon ground cinnamon

Combine all ingredients in small saucepan. Cook over medium heat, stirring occasionally, until mixture is thick, syrupy, and reduced to 1 cup, 5 to 10 minutes; set aside.

Apple-Ginger Glaze

MAKES 1½ CUPS, ENOUGH FOR 1 RECIPE GLAZED SPIRAL-SLICED HAM

- 1 cup packed dark brown sugar
- ¾ cup apple jelly
- 3 tablespoons apple butter
- 1 tablespoon grated fresh ginger
  Pinch ground cloves

Combine all ingredients in small saucepan. Cook over medium heat, stirring occasionally, until sugar dissolves and mixture is thick, syrupy, and reduced to 1½ cups, 5 to 10 minutes; set aside.

Roast Butterflied Leg of Lamb

✔ **WHY THIS RECIPE WORKS:** Swapping in a butterflied leg of lamb for the usual bone-in or boned, rolled, and tied leg options provided us with a number of benefits: thorough seasoning, a great ratio of crust to meat, and faster, more even cooking. By first roasting the lamb in a 250-degree oven, we were able to keep the meat juicy, while a final blast under the broiler was all it took to crisp and brown the exterior. We ditched the usual spice rub (which had a tendency to scorch under the broiler) in favor of a slow-cooked spice-infused oil that both seasoned the lamb during cooking and provided the basis for a quick sauce.

Roast Butterflied Leg of Lamb with Coriander, Cumin, and Mustard Seeds

SERVES 8 TO 10

We prefer the subtler flavor and larger size of lamb labeled "domestic" or "American" for this recipe. The amount of salt (2 tablespoons) in step 1 is for a 6-pound leg. If using a larger leg (7 to 8 pounds), add an additional teaspoon of salt for every pound.

LAMB

- 1 (6- to 8-pound) butterflied leg of lamb
  Kosher salt
- ⅓ cup vegetable oil
- 3 shallots, sliced thin
- 4 garlic cloves, peeled and smashed
- 1 (1-inch) piece ginger, peeled, sliced into ½-inch-thick rounds and smashed
- 1 tablespoon coriander seeds
- 1 tablespoon cumin seeds
- 1 tablespoon mustard seeds
- 3 bay leaves
- 2 (2-inch) strips lemon zest

SAUCE

- ⅓ cup minced fresh mint
- ⅓ cup minced fresh cilantro
- 1 shallot, minced
- 2 tablespoons lemon juice
  Salt and pepper

1. FOR THE LAMB: Place lamb on cutting board with fat cap facing down. Using sharp knife, trim any pockets of fat and connective tissue from underside of lamb. Flip lamb over, trim fat cap to be between ⅛ and ¼ inch thick, and pound roast to even 1-inch thickness. Cut slits, spaced ½ inch apart, in fat cap in crosshatch pattern, being careful to cut down to but not into meat. Rub 2 tablespoons kosher salt over entire roast and into slits. Let stand, uncovered, at room temperature for 1 hour.

2. Meanwhile, adjust oven racks 4 to 5 inches from broiler element and to lower-middle position and heat oven to 250 degrees. Stir together oil, shallots, garlic, ginger, coriander seeds, cumin seeds, mustard seeds, bay leaves, and lemon zest on rimmed baking sheet and bake on lower-middle rack until spices are softened and fragrant and shallots and garlic turn golden, about 1 hour. Remove sheet from oven and discard bay leaves.

3. Thoroughly pat lamb dry with paper towels and transfer, fat side up, to sheet (directly on top of spices). Roast on lower-middle rack until lamb registers 120 degrees, 30 to 40 minutes. Remove sheet from oven and heat broiler. Broil lamb on upper rack until surface is well browned and charred in spots and lamb registers 125 degrees, 3 to 8 minutes for medium-rare.

4. Remove sheet from oven and, using 2 pairs of tongs, transfer lamb to carving board (some spices will cling to bottom of roast); tent loosely with aluminum foil and let rest for 20 minutes.

5. FOR THE SAUCE: Meanwhile, carefully pour pan juices through fine-mesh strainer into medium bowl, pressing on solids to extract as much liquid as possible; discard solids. Stir in mint, cilantro, shallot, and lemon juice. Add any accumulated lamb juices to sauce and season with salt and pepper to taste.

6. With long side facing you, slice lamb with grain into 3 equal pieces. Turn each piece and slice against grain into ¼-inch-thick slices. Serve with sauce. (Briefly warm sauce in microwave if it has cooled and thickened.)

Roast Butterflied Leg of Lamb with Coriander, Rosemary, and Red Pepper

Omit cumin and mustard seeds. Toss 6 sprigs fresh rosemary and ½ teaspoon red pepper flakes with oil mixture in step 2. Substitute parsley for cilantro in sauce.

Classic Pot Roast

WHY THIS RECIPE WORKS: We started our pot roast by selecting a well-marbled chuck-eye roast. Splitting the roast along its natural seams meant we could trim off excess fat that would have made the finished dish greasy. Working with two smaller roasts instead of one large one also allowed us to cut back on cooking time. To beef up the gravy, we used a combination of water, beef broth, and red wine for the braising liquid. We also added a bit of glutamate-rich tomato paste. In the interest of streamlining, we determined that the initial sear called for in most pot roast recipes wasn't necessary—we found that the "dry" part of the meat that stays above the braising liquid eventually browns, even without searing. Blending the cooked vegetables with the defatted cooking liquid and extra beef broth gave us a full-bodied gravy, which we finished with a spoonful of balsamic vinegar and a bit more wine for brightness.

Classic Pot Roast

SERVES 6 TO 8

Chilling the whole cooked pot roast overnight improves its flavor and makes it moister and easier to slice. See Recipe Tutorial on page 256 for more details on this recipe.

  1   (3½- to 4-pound) boneless beef chuck-eye roast, pulled into 2 pieces at natural seam and trimmed of large knobs of fat
       Kosher salt and pepper
  2   tablespoons unsalted butter
  2   onions, halved and sliced thin
  1   large carrot, peeled and chopped
  1   celery rib, chopped
  2   garlic cloves, minced
2–3   cups beef broth
  ¾   cup dry red wine
  1   tablespoon tomato paste
  1   bay leaf
  1   sprig fresh thyme, plus ¼ teaspoon chopped
  1   tablespoon balsamic vinegar

1. Season pieces of meat with 1 tablespoon salt, place on wire rack set in rimmed baking sheet, and let stand at room temperature for 1 hour.

2. Adjust oven rack to lower-middle position and heat oven to 300 degrees. Melt butter in Dutch oven over medium heat. Add onions and cook, stirring occasionally, until softened and beginning to brown, 8 to 10 minutes. Add carrot and celery; continue to cook, stirring occasionally, about 5 minutes. Add garlic and cook until fragrant, about 30 seconds. Stir in 1 cup broth, ½ cup wine, tomato paste, bay leaf, and thyme sprig; bring to simmer.

3. Pat beef dry with paper towels and season with pepper. Tie 3 pieces of kitchen twine around each piece of meat to form even shape.

4. Nestle meat on top of vegetables. Cover pot tightly with large piece of aluminum foil and cover with lid; transfer pot to oven. Cook beef until fully tender and fork slips easily in and out of meat, 3½ to 4 hours, turning meat halfway through cooking.

5. Transfer roasts to carving board and tent loosely with foil. Strain liquid through fine-mesh strainer into 4-cup liquid measuring cup. Discard bay leaf and thyme sprig. Transfer vegetables to blender. Let liquid settle for 5 minutes, then skim fat; add 1 to 2 cups beef broth to bring liquid amount to 3 cups. Add liquid to blender and blend until smooth, about 2 minutes. Transfer sauce to medium saucepan and bring to simmer over medium heat.

6. Meanwhile, remove twine from roasts and slice against grain into ½-inch-thick slices. Transfer meat to serving platter. Stir remaining ¼ cup wine, chopped thyme, and vinegar into gravy and season with salt and pepper to taste. Spoon half of gravy over meat; pass remaining gravy separately.

TO MAKE AHEAD: Pot roast can be made up to 2 days ahead. Follow recipe through step 4, then transfer cooked roasts to large bowl. Strain and defat liquid and add beef broth to bring liquid amount to 3 cups; transfer liquid and vegetables to bowl with roasts, let cool for 1 hour, cover with plastic wrap, cut vents in plastic, and refrigerate overnight or up to 48 hours. One hour before serving, adjust oven rack to middle position and heat oven to 325 degrees. Slice roasts as directed, place in 13 by 9-inch baking dish, cover tightly with foil, and bake until heated through, about 45 minutes. Blend liquid and vegetables, bring gravy to simmer, and finish as directed.

Classic Pot Roast with Root Vegetables

Add 1 pound carrots, peeled and cut into 2-inch pieces, 1 pound parsnips, peeled and cut into 2-inch pieces, and 1½ pounds russet potatoes, peeled and halved lengthwise, each half quartered, to pot after cooking beef for 3 hours. Continue to cook until beef is fully tender, 30 minutes to 1 hour longer. Transfer large pieces of carrot, parsnip, and potato to serving platter using slotted spoon, cover tightly with aluminum foil, and proceed with recipe as directed.

Classic Pot Roast with Mushroom and Prune Gravy

Substitute ½ cup dark beer (porter or stout) for red wine. Add 1 ounce dried porcini mushrooms, rinsed, soaked for 1 hour, and drained, and ½ cup pitted prunes with broth and beer. While roast is resting, sauté 1 pound thinly sliced cremini mushrooms in 2 tablespoons butter until softened and lightly browned and add to finished gravy, along with ¼ cup dark beer instead of balsamic vinegar.

French-Style Pot Roast

🔪 **WHY THIS RECIPE WORKS:** To update *boeuf à la mode* while maintaining its status as an elegant dish that takes the simple pot roast to a new level, we eliminated the fussy step of larding the beef, which involves inserting strips of fat into the meat. Instead we salted the meat and browned it in bacon drippings to add a little smoky flavor. Reducing the wine before adding it to the braising liquid maximized its complex fruit flavors and minimized sourness and astringency. This step also eliminated the need for a marinade. Since the braising liquid is used for the final sauce, we balanced the wine flavor by adding sautéed onion and garlic and large chunks of carrots. Our final challenge in updating the French-style pot roast was to achieve the proper consistency, which we managed to do not with pork trotters and split calves' feet, as is tradition, but by adding gelatin after the sauce had finished reducing.

French-Style Pot Roast
SERVES 6 TO 8

A medium-bodied, fruity red wine, such as a Côtes du Rhône or Pinot Noir, is best for this recipe. The gelatin lends richness and body to the finished sauce; don't omit it. Serve this dish with boiled potatoes, buttered noodles, or steamed rice.

- 1 **(4- to 5-pound) boneless beef chuck-eye roast, pulled into 2 pieces at natural seam and trimmed of large knobs of fat**
  Kosher salt and pepper
- 1 **(750-ml) bottle red wine**
- 10 **sprigs fresh parsley, plus 2 tablespoons minced**
- 2 **sprigs fresh thyme**
- 2 **bay leaves**
- 3 **slices thick-cut bacon, cut into ¼-inch pieces**
- 1 **onion, chopped fine**
- 3 **garlic cloves, minced**
- 1 **tablespoon all-purpose flour**
- 2 **cups beef broth**
- 4 **carrots, peeled and sliced 1½ inches thick on bias**
- 2 **cups frozen pearl onions, thawed**
- 3 **tablespoons unsalted butter**
- 2 **teaspoons sugar**
- ¾ **cup water**
- 10 **ounces white mushrooms, trimmed, halved if small or quartered if large**
- 1 **tablespoon unflavored gelatin**

1. Season pieces of meat with 2 teaspoons salt, place on wire rack set in rimmed baking sheet, and let stand at room temperature for 1 hour.

2. Meanwhile, bring wine to simmer in large saucepan over medium-high heat. Cook until reduced to 2 cups, about 15 minutes. Using kitchen twine, tie parsley sprigs, thyme sprigs, and bay leaves into bundle.

3. Pat beef dry with paper towels and season generously with pepper. Tie 3 pieces of kitchen twine around each piece of meat to keep it from falling apart.

4. Adjust oven rack to lower-middle position and heat oven to 300 degrees. Cook bacon in Dutch oven over medium-high heat, stirring occasionally, until crisp, 6 to 8 minutes. Using slotted spoon, transfer bacon to paper towel–lined plate and reserve. Pour off all but 2 tablespoons fat; return Dutch oven to medium-high heat and heat until fat begins to smoke. Add beef to pot and brown on all sides, 8 to 10 minutes total. Transfer beef to large plate and set aside.

5. Reduce heat to medium; add onion and cook, stirring occasionally, until beginning to soften, 2 to 4 minutes. Add garlic, flour, and reserved bacon; cook, stirring constantly, until fragrant, about 30 seconds. Add reduced wine, broth, and herb bundle, scraping bottom of pot to loosen browned bits. Return roast and any accumulated juices to pot; increase heat to high and bring liquid to simmer, then place large piece of aluminum foil over pot and cover tightly with lid. Set pot in oven and cook, using tongs to turn beef every hour, until fork slips easily in and out of meat, 2½ to 3 hours, adding carrots to pot after 2 hours.

6. While meat cooks, bring pearl onions, butter, sugar, and ½ cup water to boil in 12-inch skillet over medium-high heat. Reduce heat to medium, cover, and cook until onions are tender, 5 to 8 minutes. Uncover, increase heat to medium-high, and cook until all liquid evaporates, 3 to 4 minutes. Add mushrooms and ¼ teaspoon salt; cook, stirring occasionally, until vegetables are browned and glazed, 8 to 12 minutes. Remove from heat and set aside. Place remaining ¼ cup water in small bowl and sprinkle gelatin on top.

7. Transfer beef to carving board; tent with foil to keep warm. Let braising liquid settle, about 5 minutes; using large spoon, skim fat from surface. Remove herb bundle and stir in onion-mushroom mixture. Bring liquid to simmer over medium-high heat and cook until mixture is slightly thickened and reduced to 3¼ cups, 20 to 30 minutes. Season sauce with salt and pepper to taste. Add softened gelatin and stir until completely dissolved.

8. Remove twine from roasts and discard. Slice meat against grain into ½-inch-thick slices. Divide meat among warmed bowls or transfer to platter; arrange vegetables around meat, pour sauce over top, and sprinkle with minced parsley. Serve immediately.

TO MAKE AHEAD: Follow recipe through step 7, skipping step of softening and adding gelatin. Place meat back in pot, cool to room temperature, cover, and refrigerate for up to 2 days. To serve, slice beef and arrange in 13 by 9-inch baking dish. Bring sauce to simmer and stir in gelatin until completely dissolved. Pour warm sauce over meat, cover with foil, and bake in 350-degree oven until heated through, about 30 minutes.

Modern Beef Burgundy

✔ **WHY THIS RECIPE WORKS:** We wanted our *boeuf bourguignon* recipe to have tender braised beef napped in a silky, rich sauce with bold red wine flavor but without all the work that the classic recipe requires. We cook the stew in the oven, uncovered in a roasting pan, so that the exposed surfaces of the meat brown as it braises, allowing us to eliminate the time-consuming step of searing it beforehand. Similarly, we used the oven, rather than the stovetop, to render the salt pork and to prepare the traditional mushroom and pearl onion garnish.

Modern Beef Burgundy

SERVES 6 TO 8

If the pearl onions have a papery outer coating, remove it by rinsing them in warm water and gently squeezing individual onions between your fingertips. Two minced anchovy fillets can be used in place of the anchovy paste. To save time, salt the meat and let it stand while you prep the remaining ingredients. Serve with mashed potatoes or buttered noodles. See Recipe Tutorial on page 252 for more details on this recipe.

- 1 **(4-pound) boneless beef chuck-eye roast, trimmed and cut into 1½- to 2-inch pieces, scraps reserved Salt and pepper**
- 6 **ounces salt pork, cut into ¼-inch pieces**
- 3 **tablespoons unsalted butter**
- 1 **pound cremini mushrooms, trimmed, halved if medium or quartered if large**
- 1½ **cups frozen pearl onions, thawed**
- 1 **tablespoon sugar**
- ⅓ **cup all-purpose flour**
- 4 **cups beef broth**
- 1 **(750-ml) bottle red Burgundy or Pinot Noir**
- 5 **teaspoons unflavored gelatin**
- 1 **tablespoon tomato paste**
- 1 **teaspoon anchovy paste**
- 2 **onions, chopped coarse**
- 2 **carrots, peeled and cut into 2-inch lengths**
- 1 **garlic head, cloves separated, unpeeled, and crushed**
- 2 **bay leaves**
- ½ **teaspoon black peppercorns**
- ½ **ounce dried porcini mushrooms, rinsed**
- 10 **sprigs fresh parsley, plus 3 tablespoons minced**
- 6 **sprigs fresh thyme**

1. Toss beef and 1½ teaspoons salt together in bowl and let stand at room temperature for 30 minutes.

2. Adjust oven racks to lower-middle and lowest positions and heat oven to 500 degrees. Place salt pork, beef scraps, and 2 tablespoons butter in large roasting pan. Roast on lower-middle rack until well browned and fat has rendered, 15 to 20 minutes.

3. While salt pork and beef scraps roast, toss cremini mushrooms, pearl onions, remaining 1 tablespoon butter, and sugar together on rimmed baking sheet. Roast on lowest rack, stirring occasionally, until moisture released by mushrooms evaporates and vegetables are lightly glazed, 15 to 20 minutes. Transfer vegetables to large bowl, cover, and refrigerate.

4. Remove roasting pan from oven and reduce temperature to 325 degrees. Sprinkle flour over rendered fat and whisk until no dry flour remains. Whisk in broth, 2 cups wine, gelatin, tomato paste, and anchovy paste until combined. Add onions, carrots, garlic, bay leaves, peppercorns, porcini mushrooms, parsley sprigs, and thyme sprigs to pan. Arrange beef in single layer on top of vegetables. Add water as needed to come three-quarters up side of beef (beef should not be submerged). Return roasting pan to oven and cook until meat is tender, 3 to 3½ hours, stirring after 90 minutes and adding water to keep meat at least half-submerged.

5. Using slotted spoon, transfer beef to bowl with cremini mushrooms and pearl onions; cover and set aside. Strain braising liquid through fine-mesh strainer set over large bowl, pressing on solids to extract as much liquid as possible; discard solids. Stir in remaining wine and let cooking liquid settle, 10 minutes. Using wide, shallow spoon, skim fat off surface and discard.

6. Transfer liquid to Dutch oven and bring mixture to boil over medium-high heat. Simmer briskly, stirring occasionally, until sauce is thickened to consistency of heavy cream, 15 to 20 minutes. Reduce heat to medium-low, stir in beef and mushroom-onion garnish, cover, and cook until just heated through, 5 to 8 minutes. Season with salt and pepper to taste. Stir in minced parsley and serve. (Stew can be refrigerated for up to 3 days.)

Ultimate Beef Chili

✔ **WHY THIS RECIPE WORKS:** Our goal in creating an "ultimate" beef chili was to determine which of the "secret ingredients" recommended by chili experts were spot-on, and which were expendable. Most recipes call for ground beef, but we preferred blade steaks, which don't require much trimming and stayed in big chunks. We traded in commercial chili powder in favor of ground dried ancho and de árbol chiles; for a grassy heat, we added fresh jalapeños. Dried beans, brined before cooking, stayed creamy for the duration. Beer and chicken broth outperformed red wine, coffee, and beef broth as the liquid component. To balance the sweetness, light molasses beat out other offbeat ingredients (including prunes and Coca-Cola). For the right level of thickness, flour and peanut butter didn't perform as promised; instead, a small amount of cornmeal sealed the deal.

Ultimate Beef Chili

SERVES 6 TO 8

A 4-pound chuck-eye roast, well trimmed of fat, can be substituted for the blade steak. Because much of the chili flavor is held in the fat of this dish, refrain from skimming fat from the surface. Dried New Mexican or guajillo chiles make a good substitute for the anchos; each dried de árbol may be replaced with ⅛ teaspoon cayenne pepper. If you prefer not to work with any whole dried chiles, the anchos and de árbols can be replaced with ½ cup commercial chili powder and ¼ to ½ teaspoon cayenne pepper, though the texture of the chili will be slightly compromised. Good choices for condiments include diced avocado, finely chopped red onion, chopped fresh cilantro, lime wedges, sour cream, and shredded Monterey Jack or cheddar cheese.

Salt

8 ounces (1¼ cups) dried pinto beans, picked over and rinsed

6 dried ancho chiles, stemmed, seeded, and torn into 1-inch pieces

2–4 dried de árbol chiles, stemmed, seeded, and split in 2 pieces

3 tablespoons cornmeal

2 teaspoons dried oregano

2 teaspoons ground cumin

2 teaspoons unsweetened cocoa powder

2½ cups chicken broth

2 onions, cut into ¾-inch pieces

3 small jalapeño chiles, stemmed, seeded, and cut into ½-inch pieces

3 tablespoons vegetable oil

4 garlic cloves, minced

1 (14.5-ounce) can diced tomatoes

2 teaspoons molasses

3½ pounds blade steak, ¾ inch thick, trimmed and cut into ¾-inch pieces

1 (12-ounce) bottle mild lager, such as Budweiser

1. Combine 3 tablespoons salt, 4 quarts water, and beans in Dutch oven and bring to boil over high heat. Remove pot from heat, cover, and let stand 1 hour. Drain and rinse well.

2. Adjust oven rack to lower-middle position and heat oven to 300 degrees. Place ancho chiles in 12-inch skillet set over medium-high heat; toast, stirring frequently, until flesh is fragrant, 4 to 6 minutes, reducing heat if chiles begin to smoke. Transfer to food processor and cool. Do not wash out skillet.

3. Add de árbol chiles, cornmeal, oregano, cumin, cocoa, and ½ teaspoon salt to food processor with toasted ancho chiles; process until finely ground, about 2 minutes. With processor running, slowly add ½ cup broth until smooth paste forms, about 45 seconds, scraping down sides of bowl as necessary. Transfer paste to small bowl. Place onions in now-empty processor and pulse until roughly chopped, about 4 pulses. Add jalapeños and pulse until consistency of chunky salsa, about 4 pulses, scraping down bowl as necessary.

4. Heat 1 tablespoon oil in Dutch oven over medium-high heat. Add onion mixture and cook, stirring occasionally, until moisture has evaporated and vegetables are softened, 7 to 9 minutes. Add garlic and cook until fragrant, about 1 minute. Add chile paste, tomatoes and their juice, and molasses; stir until chile paste is thoroughly combined. Add remaining 2 cups broth and drained beans; bring to boil, then reduce heat to simmer.

5. Meanwhile, heat 1 tablespoon oil in 12-inch skillet over medium-high heat until shimmering. Pat beef dry with paper towels and sprinkle with 1 teaspoon salt. Add half of beef and cook until browned on all sides, about 10 minutes. Transfer meat to Dutch oven. Add half of beer to skillet, scraping up browned bits from bottom of pan, and bring to simmer. Transfer beer to Dutch oven. Repeat with remaining 1 tablespoon oil, remaining steak, and remaining beer. Stir to combine and return mixture to simmer.

6. Cover pot and transfer to oven. Cook until meat and beans are fully tender, 1½ to 2 hours. Let chili stand, uncovered, for 10 minutes. Stir well, season with salt to taste, and serve. (Chili can be refrigerated up to 3 days.)

Modern Beef Stew

✔ **WHY THIS RECIPE WORKS:** We wanted a rich-tasting but approachable beef stew with tender meat, flavorful vegetables, and a rich brown gravy. We planned to take a no-holds-barred attitude toward the ingredient list. To begin, we chose a tasty cut of beef, chuck, and browned it properly, taking care not to crowd the meat in the pan. Along with traditional stew components like onion, carrots, garlic, red wine, and chicken broth, we added glutamate-rich ingredients like tomato paste, salt pork, and anchovies. Glutamates are compounds that give meat its savory taste and they contribute considerable flavor to the dish. To mimic the luxurious, mouth-coating texture of beef stews made with homemade stock (provided by the collagen in bones that is transformed into gelatin when simmered), we included powdered gelatin and flour. Potatoes, pearl onions, and peas rounded out our rich-tasting, yet updated, take on beef stew.

Modern Beef Stew

SERVES 6 TO 8

Use a good-quality, medium-bodied wine, such as a Côtes du Rhône or Pinot Noir, for this stew. Try to find beef that is well marbled with white veins of fat. Meat that is too lean will come out slightly dry. You can use 4 pounds of blade steaks, trimmed, instead of the chuck-eye roast. While the blade steak will yield slightly thinner pieces after trimming, it should still be cut into 1½-inch pieces. Look for salt pork that is roughly 75 percent lean.

2 garlic cloves, minced

4 anchovy fillets, rinsed and minced

1 tablespoon tomato paste

1 (4-pound) boneless beef chuck-eye roast, pulled apart at seams, trimmed, and cut into 1½-inch pieces

2 tablespoons vegetable oil

1 large onion, halved and sliced ⅛ inch thick

4 carrots, peeled and cut into 1-inch pieces

¼ cup all-purpose flour

2 cups red wine

2 cups chicken broth

4 ounces salt pork, rinsed

2 bay leaves

4 sprigs fresh thyme

1 pound Yukon Gold potatoes, unpeeled, cut into 1-inch pieces

1½ cups frozen pearl onions, thawed

2 teaspoons unflavored gelatin

½ cup water

1 cup frozen peas, thawed

Salt and pepper

1. Adjust oven rack to lower-middle position and heat oven to 300 degrees. Combine garlic and anchovies in small bowl; press with back of fork to form paste. Stir in tomato paste and set aside.

2. Pat meat dry with paper towels. Do not season. Heat 1 tablespoon oil in Dutch oven over high heat until just starting to smoke. Add half of beef and cook until well browned on all sides, about 8 minutes. Transfer beef to large plate. Repeat with remaining beef and remaining 1 tablespoon oil, leaving second batch of meat in pot after browning.

3. Reduce heat to medium and return first batch of beef to pot. Stir in onion and carrots and cook, scraping bottom of pan to loosen browned bits, until onion is softened, 1 to 2 minutes. Add garlic mixture and cook, stirring constantly, until fragrant, about 30 seconds. Add flour and cook, stirring constantly, until no dry flour remains, about 30 seconds.

4. Slowly add wine, scraping bottom of pan to loosen browned bits. Increase heat to high and simmer until wine is thickened and slightly reduced, about 2 minutes. Stir in broth, pork, bay leaves, and thyme sprigs. Bring to simmer, cover, transfer to oven, and cook for 1½ hours.

5. Remove pot from oven; discard bay leaves and salt pork. Stir in potatoes, cover, return to oven, and cook until potatoes are almost tender, about 45 minutes.

6. Using large spoon, skim excess fat from surface of stew. Stir in pearl onions; cook over medium heat until potatoes and onions are cooked through and fork slips easily in and out of beef (meat should not be falling apart), about 15 minutes. Meanwhile, sprinkle gelatin over water in small bowl and allow to soften for 5 minutes.

7. Increase heat to high, stir in softened gelatin mixture and peas; simmer until gelatin is fully dissolved and stew is thickened, about 3 minutes. Season with salt and pepper to taste; serve. (Stew can be refrigerated for up to 2 days.)

Smothered Pork Chops

⚫ **WHY THIS RECIPE WORKS:** Smothered pork chops is a homey dish of chops braised in deeply flavored onion gravy—that is, if dry pork and near tasteless, gelatinous gravy don't ruin it. We determined that bone-in pork rib chops were the most juicy and flavorful. Further, we found that thin, ½-inch chops picked up more flavor than thick chops and didn't overwhelm the gravy. The best cooking method was to sear the chops in bacon fat, then braise them in an onion gravy thickened with a bacon fat and flour roux; the sweet, salty, smoky flavor of the roux underscored and deepened all of the other flavors.

Smothered Pork Chops
SERVES 4

Serve these smothered chops with a starch to soak up the rich gravy. Simple egg noodles are our favorite, but rice or mashed potatoes also taste great.

- 3 **slices bacon, cut into ¼-inch pieces**
- 2 **tablespoons all-purpose flour**
- 1¾ **cups chicken broth**
- 4 **(6- to 8-ounce) bone-in pork rib chops, ½ to ¾ inch thick, trimmed**
  Salt and pepper
- 2 **tablespoons vegetable oil, plus extra as needed**
- 2 **onions, halved and sliced thin**
- 2 **tablespoons water**
- 2 **garlic cloves, minced**
- 1 **teaspoon minced fresh thyme**
- 2 **bay leaves**
- 1 **tablespoon minced fresh parsley**

1. Fry bacon in small saucepan over medium heat, stirring occasionally, until lightly browned, 8 to 10 minutes. Using slotted spoon, transfer bacon to paper towel–lined plate, leaving fat in saucepan (you should have 2 tablespoons bacon fat; if not, supplement with vegetable oil). Reduce heat to medium-low and gradually whisk flour into fat until smooth. Cook, whisking frequently, until mixture is light brown, about the color of peanut butter, about 5 minutes. Whisk in broth in slow, steady stream; increase heat to medium-high and bring to boil, stirring occasionally; cover and set aside off heat.

2. Pat pork chops dry with paper towels and season with ½ teaspoon pepper. Heat 1 tablespoon oil in 12-inch skillet over high heat until just smoking. Brown chops in single layer until deep golden brown on first side, about 3 minutes. Flip chops and cook until browned on second side, about 3 minutes longer. Transfer chops to large plate and set aside.

3. Reduce heat to medium and add remaining 1 tablespoon oil, onions, ¼ teaspoon salt, and water to now-empty skillet. Scrape bottom of skillet with wooden spoon to loosen any browned bits and cook, stirring frequently, until onions are softened and browned around the edges, about 5 minutes. Stir in garlic and thyme and cook until fragrant, about 30 seconds. Return chops to skillet in single layer, covering chops with onions. Pour in warm sauce and any accumulated juices from pork; add bay leaves. Cover, reduce heat to low, and simmer until pork is tender and paring knife inserted in chops meets very little resistance, about 30 minutes.

4. Transfer chops to warmed serving platter and tent loosely with aluminum foil. Increase heat to medium-high and simmer sauce rapidly, stirring frequently, until thickened to gravylike consistency, about 5 minutes. Discard bay leaves, stir in parsley, and season with salt and pepper to taste. Spoon sauce over chops, sprinkle with reserved bacon, and serve.

Smothered Pork Chops with Cider and Apples
Substitute apple cider for chicken broth and 1 large Granny Smith apple, peeled, cored, and cut into ⅜-inch wedges, for one of the onions, and increase salt added to onions to ½ teaspoon.

Smothered Pork Chops with Spicy Collard Greens
Increase oil in step 3 to 2 tablespoons, omit 1 onion, and increase garlic to 4 cloves. Just before returning browned chops to pan in step 3, add 4 cups stemmed and thinly sliced collard greens and ½ teaspoon red pepper flakes.

Pork Schnitzel

⚫ **WHY THIS RECIPE WORKS:** Pork schnitzel is often a soggy, greasy affair. But when done right, it features an irresistible combination of light, puffy bread-crumb coating and tender juicy meat. For tender texture and mild flavor, we used pounded medallions of pork tenderloin. Homemade bread crumbs were superior to store-bought, and a quick spin in the microwave produced dry crumbs that cooked up extra-crisp. To achieve the wrinkled, puffy exterior that is schnitzel's signature, it was essential to use an ample amount of oil and to shake the pan, gently and continuously, while the cutlets cooked.

Pork Schnitzel

SERVES 4

The 2 cups of oil called for in this recipe may seem like a lot, but this amount is necessary to achieve a wrinkled texture on the finished cutlets. When properly cooked, the cutlets absorb very little oil. To ensure ample cooking space, a large Dutch oven is essential. Cutting the tenderloin at about a 20-degree angle yields pounded cutlets that easily fit in the pot. In lieu of an instant-read thermometer to gauge the oil's temperature, place a fresh (not dry) bread cube in the oil and start heating; when the bread is deep golden brown, the oil is ready.

PORK

- **7 slices hearty white sandwich bread, crusts removed, cut into ¾-inch cubes**
- **½ cup all-purpose flour**
- **2 large eggs**
- **1 tablespoon plus 2 cups vegetable oil**
- **1 (1¼-pound) pork tenderloin, trimmed and cut on angle into 4 equal pieces**
  Salt and pepper

GARNISHES

- **Lemon wedges**
- **2 tablespoons chopped fresh parsley**
- **2 tablespoons capers, rinsed**
- **1 large hard-cooked egg, yolk and white separated and passed separately through fine-mesh strainer (optional)**

1. Place bread cubes on large plate. Microwave on 100 percent power for 4 minutes, stirring well halfway through cooking. Microwave on 50 percent power until bread is dry and few pieces start to lightly brown, 3 to 5 minutes longer, stirring every minute. Process dry bread in food processor to very fine crumbs, about 45 seconds. Transfer bread crumbs to shallow dish (you should have about 1¼ cups crumbs). Spread flour in second shallow dish. Beat eggs with 1 tablespoon oil in third shallow dish.

2. Working with 1 piece at a time, place pork, with 1 cut side down, between 2 sheets of parchment paper or plastic wrap and pound to even thickness between ⅛ and ¼ inch. Pat cutlets dry with paper towels and season with salt and pepper. Working with 1 cutlet at a time, dredge cutlets thoroughly in flour, shaking off excess, then coat with egg mixture, allowing excess to drip back into dish to ensure very thin coating, and coat evenly with bread crumbs, pressing on crumbs to adhere. Place breaded cutlets in single layer on wire rack set over baking sheet; let coating dry for 5 minutes.

3. Heat remaining 2 cups oil in Dutch oven over medium-high heat until it registers 375 degrees. Lay 2 cutlets, without overlapping, in pot and cook, shaking pan continuously and gently, until cutlets are wrinkled and light golden brown on both sides, 1 to 2 minutes per side. Transfer cutlets to paper towel–lined plate and flip cutlets several times to blot excess oil. Repeat with remaining cutlets. Serve with garnishes.

Mexican Pulled Pork

 WHY THIS RECIPE WORKS: Like the best barbecue, *carnitas*, Mexico's version of pulled pork, offers fall-apart hunks of crisp meat. The flavor of the pork, subtly accented by oregano and orange, takes center stage. Rather than deep-frying the meat in lard, we were able to replicate the taste and texture by first braising the pork in a small amount of liquid, then reducing the liquid to a syrupy consistency and incorporating it back into the dish. Then we broiled the glazed meat on a rack to crisp the exterior and allow the excess fat to drip off. Refining the cooking liquid's flavors with lime and orange juices, bay leaves, and oregano was the finishing touch.

Mexican Pulled Pork (Carnitas)

SERVES 6

We like serving carnitas spooned into small corn tortillas, taco-style, but you can also use it as a filling for tamales, enchiladas, and burritos. Pork butt roast is often labeled Boston butt in the supermarket.

PORK

- **1 (3½- to 4-pound) boneless pork butt roast, fat cap trimmed to ⅛ inch thick and cut into 2-inch chunks**
- **2 cups water**
- **1 onion, halved**
- **2 tablespoons lime juice**
- **1 teaspoon dried oregano**
- **1 teaspoon ground cumin**
- **2 bay leaves**
  Salt and pepper
- **1 orange, halved**

TORTILLAS AND GARNISHES

- **18 (6-inch) corn tortillas, warmed**
  Lime wedges
  Minced white or red onion
  Fresh cilantro leaves
  Thinly sliced radishes
  Sour cream

1. Adjust oven rack to lower-middle position and heat oven to 300 degrees. Combine pork, water, onion, lime juice, oregano, cumin, bay leaves, 1 teaspoon salt, and ½ teaspoon pepper in Dutch oven (liquid should just barely cover meat). Juice orange into bowl and remove any seeds (you should have about ⅓ cup juice). Add juice and spent orange halves to pot. Bring mixture to simmer over medium-high heat, stirring occasionally. Cover pot and transfer to oven; cook until meat is soft and falls apart when prodded with fork, about 2 hours, flipping pieces of meat once during cooking.

2. Remove pot from oven and turn oven to broil. Using slotted spoon, transfer pork to bowl; remove orange halves, onion, and bay leaves from cooking liquid and discard (do not skim fat from liquid). Place pot over high heat (use caution, as handles will be very hot) and simmer liquid, stirring frequently, until thick and syrupy (heat-resistant spatula should leave wide trail when dragged through glaze), 8 to 12 minutes. You should have about 1 cup reduced liquid.

3. Using 2 forks, pull each piece of pork in half. Fold in reduced liquid; season with salt and pepper to taste. Spread pork in even layer on wire rack set in rimmed baking sheet or on broiler pan (meat should cover almost entire surface of rack or broiler pan). Place baking sheet on lower-middle rack and broil until top of meat is well browned (but not charred) and edges are slightly crisp, 5 to 8 minutes. Using wide metal spatula, flip pieces of meat and continue to broil until top is well browned and edges are slightly crisp, 5 to 8 minutes longer. Serve with warm tortillas and garnishes.

Glazed All-Beef Meatloaf

✔ **WHY THIS RECIPE WORKS:** For a tender, moist, and light meatloaf, using a combination of ground beef, pork, and veal (known as meatloaf mix) is usually the way to go. But sometimes we can't find meatloaf mix or don't have it on hand for a quick, last-minute dinner. For an all-beef loaf that's just as good as one made with meatloaf mix, we used equal parts ground chuck and sirloin, which provided just the right balance of juicy, tender meat and assertive beefy flavor. Chicken broth was a surprisingly successful add-in; it transformed the loaf from liver-y to savory. To replace the gelatin that was lost with the ground veal in the meatloaf mix, we used a mere half teaspoon of powdered gelatin to give the texture of our glazed meatloaf a luxurious smoothness.

Glazed All-Beef Meatloaf
SERVES 6 TO 8

If you can't find chuck and/or sirloin, substitute any 85 percent lean ground beef. Handle the meat gently; it should be thoroughly combined but not pastelike. To avoid using the broiler, glaze the loaf in a 500-degree oven; increase cooking time for each interval by 2 to 3 minutes.

MEATLOAF
- 3 ounces Monterey Jack cheese, shredded (¾ cup)
- 1 tablespoon unsalted butter
- 1 onion, chopped fine
- 1 celery rib, chopped fine
- 2 teaspoons minced fresh thyme
- 1 garlic clove, minced
- 1 teaspoon paprika
- ¼ cup tomato juice
- ½ cup chicken broth
- 2 large eggs
- ½ teaspoon unflavored gelatin
- ⅔ cup crushed saltines (about 16)
- 2 tablespoons minced fresh parsley
- 1 tablespoon soy sauce
- 1 teaspoon Dijon mustard
- ¾ teaspoon salt
- ½ teaspoon pepper
- 1 pound ground sirloin
- 1 pound ground beef chuck

GLAZE
- ½ cup ketchup
- 1 teaspoon hot sauce
- ½ teaspoon ground coriander
- ¼ cup cider vinegar
- 3 tablespoons packed light brown sugar

1. FOR THE MEATLOAF: Adjust oven rack to middle position; heat oven to 375 degrees. Spread cheese on plate and place in freezer until ready to use. Fold piece of heavy-duty aluminum foil to form 10 by 6-inch rectangle. Center foil on wire rack and place rack in rimmed baking sheet. Poke holes in foil with skewer about ½ inch apart. Spray foil with vegetable oil spray and set aside.

2. Melt butter in 10-inch skillet over medium-high heat; add onion and celery and cook, stirring occasionally, until beginning to brown, 6 to 8 minutes. Add thyme, garlic, and paprika and cook, stirring constantly, until fragrant, about 1 minute. Reduce heat to low and add tomato juice. Cook, scraping bottom of skillet with wooden spoon to loosen any browned bits, until thickened, about 1 minute. Transfer mixture to bowl and set aside to cool.

3. Whisk broth and eggs in large bowl until combined. Sprinkle gelatin over liquid and let stand for 5 minutes. Stir in saltines, parsley, soy sauce, mustard, salt, pepper, and onion mixture. Crumble frozen cheese into coarse powder and sprinkle over mixture. Add ground beef; mix gently with hands until thoroughly combined, about 1 minute. Transfer meat to aluminum foil rectangle and shape into 10 by 6-inch oval about 2 inches high. Smooth top and edges of meatloaf with moistened spatula. Bake until meatloaf registers 135 to 140 degrees, 55 to 65 minutes. Remove meatloaf from oven and turn on broiler.

4. FOR THE GLAZE: While meatloaf cooks, combine glaze ingredients in small saucepan; bring to simmer over medium heat and cook, stirring, until thick and syrupy, about 5 minutes. Spread half of glaze evenly over cooked meatloaf with rubber spatula; place under broiler and cook until glaze bubbles and begins to brown at edges, about 5 minutes. Remove meatloaf from oven and spread evenly with remaining glaze; place back under broiler and cook until glaze is again bubbling and beginning to brown, about 5 minutes more. Cool meatloaf about 20 minutes before slicing.

Juicy Pub-Style Burgers

✔ **WHY THIS RECIPE WORKS:** Few things are as satisfying as a thick, juicy pub-style burger. But avoiding the usual gray band of overcooked meat is a challenge. We wanted a patty that was well seared, juicy, and evenly rosy from center to edge. Grinding our own meat in the food processor was a must, and sirloin steak tips were the right cut for the job. Cutting the meat into small ½-inch chunks before grinding and lightly packing the meat to form patties gave the burgers just enough structure to hold their shape in the skillet. A little melted butter improved their flavor and juiciness, but our biggest discovery came when we transferred the burgers from the stovetop to the oven to finish cooking—the stovetop provided intense heat for searing, while the oven's gentle ambient heat allowed for even cooking, thus eliminating the overcooked gray zone.

Juicy Pub-Style Burgers

SERVES 4

Sirloin steak tips are also sold as flap meat. When stirring the butter and pepper into the ground meat and shaping the patties, take care not to overwork the meat or the burgers will become dense. For the best flavor, season the burgers aggressively just before cooking. The burgers can be topped as desired or with one of the test kitchen's favorite combinations (recipes follow).

- 2 **pounds sirloin steak tips or boneless beef short ribs, trimmed and cut into ½-inch chunks**
- 4 **tablespoons unsalted butter, melted and cooled**
  Salt and pepper
- 1 **teaspoon vegetable oil**
- 4 **large hamburger buns, toasted and buttered**

1. Place beef chunks on baking sheet in single layer. Freeze meat until very firm and starting to harden around edges but still pliable, 15 to 25 minutes.

2. Place one-quarter of meat in food processor and pulse until finely ground into $1/16$-inch pieces, about 35 pulses, stopping and redistributing meat around bowl as necessary to ensure beef is evenly ground. Transfer meat to baking sheet, overturning workbowl and without directly touching meat. Repeat grinding with remaining 3 batches of meat. Spread meat over baking sheet and inspect carefully, discarding any long strands of gristle or large chunks of hard meat or fat.

3. Adjust oven rack to middle position and heat oven to 300 degrees. Drizzle melted butter over ground meat and add 1 teaspoon pepper. Gently toss with fork to combine. Divide meat into 4 lightly packed balls. Gently flatten into patties ¾ inch thick and about 4½ inches in diameter. Refrigerate patties until ready to cook. (Patties can be refrigerated for up to 1 day.)

4. Season 1 side of patties with salt and pepper. Using spatula, flip patties and season other side. Heat oil in 12-inch skillet over high heat until just smoking. Using spatula, transfer burgers to skillet and cook without moving for 2 minutes. Using spatula, flip burgers over and cook for 2 minutes longer. Transfer patties to rimmed baking sheet and bake until burgers register 125 degrees (for medium-rare), 3 to 5 minutes.

5. Transfer burgers to plate and let rest for 5 minutes. Transfer to buns and serve.

Pub-Style Burger Sauce

MAKES ABOUT 1 CUP, ENOUGH FOR 1 RECIPE JUICY PUB-STYLE BURGERS

- ¾ **cup mayonnaise**
- 2 **tablespoons soy sauce**
- 1 **tablespoon packed dark brown sugar**
- 1 **tablespoon Worcestershire sauce**
- 1 **tablespoon minced chives**
- 1 **garlic clove, minced**
- ¾ **teaspoon pepper**

Whisk all ingredients together in bowl.

Juicy Pub-Style Burgers with Crispy Shallots and Blue Cheese

Heat ½ cup vegetable oil and 3 thinly sliced shallots in medium saucepan over high heat; cook, stirring frequently, until shallots are golden, about 8 minutes. Using slotted spoon, transfer shallots to paper towel–lined plate, season with salt, and let drain until crisp, about 5 minutes. (Cooled shallots can be stored at room temperature for up to 3 days.) Top each burger with ¼ cup crumbled blue cheese before transferring to oven. Top with crispy shallots just before serving.

Juicy Pub-Style Burgers with Sautéed Onions and Smoked Cheddar

Heat 2 tablespoons vegetable oil in 12-inch skillet over medium-high heat until just smoking. Add 1 thinly sliced onion and ¼ teaspoon salt; cook, stirring frequently, until softened and lightly browned, 5 to 7 minutes. Top each burger with ¼ cup grated smoked cheddar cheese before transferring to oven. Top with onions just before serving.

Juicy Pub-Style Burgers with Peppered Bacon and Aged Cheddar

Adjust oven rack to middle position and heat oven to 375 degrees. Arrange 6 bacon slices on rimmed baking sheet and sprinkle with 2 teaspoons coarsely ground pepper. Place second rimmed baking sheet on top of bacon and bake until bacon is crisp, 15 to 20 minutes. Transfer bacon to paper towel–lined plate and cool. Cut bacon in half crosswise. Top each burger with ¼ cup grated aged cheddar cheese before transferring to oven. Top with bacon just before serving.

Juicy Pub-Style Burgers with Mushrooms and Gruyère

Heat 2 tablespoons vegetable oil in 12-inch skillet over medium-high heat until just smoking. Add 10 ounces thinly sliced cremini mushrooms, ¼ teaspoon salt, and ¼ teaspoon pepper; cook, stirring frequently, until browned, 5 to 7 minutes. Add 1 minced shallot and 2 teaspoons minced thyme and cook until fragrant. Remove skillet from heat and stir in 2 tablespoons dry sherry. Top each burger with ¼ cup grated Gruyère cheese before transferring to oven. Top with mushrooms just before serving.

Inside This Chapter

CHAPTER 7

How to Cook Poultry

Because of its affordability, versatility, and low fat content, chicken is a staple in most kitchens, but along with turkey and Cornish game hens, it requires some know-how to cook properly. Delicate breast meat can easily overcook, and while fattier dark meat offers more leeway, the fact that it has to cook to a different temperature than the white meat complicates things when cooking mixed parts. In this chapter, we show you how to successfully pan-roast, braise, sauté, fry, and roast poultry. Also see the How to Grill chapter on page 387 and How to Stir-Fry on page 234.

Getting Started

How to Buy Chicken

The U.S. poultry industry (the largest in the world) each year processes upward of eight billion chickens destined for the dinner table. Today, Americans consume about 84 pounds of chicken per person annually. These birds, once a protein so luxurious that the 1928 presidential election campaign promise to put one in "every pot" seemed unreachable, have become a cheap supermarket staple. But the ability to pick up a chicken at any local market doesn't make shopping easy.

There's a lot of labeling terminology that doesn't (necessarily) mean much. Companies can exploit plenty of loopholes to qualify for "Natural/All-Natural," "Hormone-Free," and "Vegetarian Diet/Fed" labeling. "USDA Organic," however, isn't all hype: The poultry must eat organic feed that doesn't contain animal by-products, be raised without antibiotics, and have access to the outdoors. Alternative growing and processing methods may not directly affect the flavor of the chickens, but they may keep the birds, and us, healthier down the road, which makes us feel better about buying them.

WHOLE: BROILERS, FRYERS, AND ROASTERS

Whole chickens come in various sizes. Broilers and fryers are chickens that have been slaughtered when they were younger and weigh 2½ to 4½ pounds. A roaster (or "oven-stuffer roaster") is an older chicken and usually clocks in between 5 and 7 pounds. Stewing chickens, which are older laying hens, are best used for stews since the meat is tougher and more stringy. A 3- to 4½-pound bird will feed 3 to 4 people.

It pays to inspect the packaging. Our tasting and research proved processing is the major player in texture and flavor. We found specimens that are "water-chilled" (soaked in a water bath in which they absorb up to 14 percent of their weight in water, which you pay for since chicken is sold by the pound) or "enhanced" (injected with broth and flavoring) are unnaturally spongy and are best avoided. Labeling law says water gain must be shown on the product label, so these should be easily identifiable. When buying a whole bird, look for those that are labeled "air-chilled." Without the excess water weight, we found these chickens to be less spongy in texture (but still plenty juicy) and to taste more chicken-y.

BONE-IN PARTS

You can buy a whole cut-up chicken or chicken parts at your supermarket, but sometimes it's hard to tell by looking at the package if it's been properly butchered. If you have a few minutes of extra time, consider buying a whole chicken and butchering it yourself (see page 290 for more detail).

BONELESS, SKINLESS BREASTS AND CUTLETS

If you're buying boneless, skinless breasts, you should be aware that breasts of different sizes are often packaged together, which is a problem since they won't cook through at the same rate. Try to pick a package with breasts of similar size, and pound them to an even thickness.

You can buy cutlets ready to go at the grocery store, but we don't recommend it. These cutlets are usually ragged and of various sizes; it's better to cut your own cutlets from breasts. See How to Make Chicken Cutlets on page 294 for more details.

GROUND

Ground chicken is typically sold one of two ways: prepackaged or ground to order. The prepackaged variety is made from either dark or white meat. Higher-end markets and specialty markets grind their chicken to order, and therefore the choice of meat is yours. When it comes to flavor, however, our tasters were unanimous—dark meat is far superior. In most of our testing, we found ground white meat chicken to be exceedingly dry and almost void of flavor. The dark meat was more flavorful and juicy due to its higher fat content. Make sure not to buy ground breast meat (also labeled 99 percent fat free).

How to Buy Turkey

Most of us purchase a whole turkey just a few times a year, but typically it's for a special occasion so its key to shop wisely. There are also turkey breasts and ground meat to consider.

WHOLE

Modern commercial turkeys don't contain much fat, yet, as we all know, fat is what provides meat with juiciness and flavor. To make up for it, some birds are "prebasted" (injected with a solution), but our tasters found that these birds can have a "wet" texture. Pasture-raised, organic turkeys promise a flavor improvement because of their diverse diet, but we didn't find that to be the case, plus the meat was slightly stringier and tougher (you will need to brine these birds if you buy them). Heritage turkeys are directly descended from wild turkeys, and they nearly disappeared in the mid-20th century as commercial Broad-Breasted Whites were bred by the poultry industry. We have certainly found favor with the heritage turkeys that we've tried over the years, but given the range of taster opinion about flavor, from "outstanding" to "funky," we aren't sure the high price tag and effort it takes to track one down are worth it.

We like turkeys that have been koshered (covered in kosher salt, then rinsed multiple times). Koshering works to season the meat, improve its texture, and help it retain moisture—if you buy a kosher turkey there's no need to brine or salt it. However, kosher turkeys aren't always easy to find, so we typically call for "all-natural" turkeys. These turkeys have been fed a vegetarian diet and are free to roam. These turkeys tend to contain less fat, which translates to a drier bird, so we always recommend brining these turkeys.

BONE-IN BREASTS

Most supermarkets regularly offer two slightly different styles of whole bone-in turkey breast: regular (aka true cut) and hotel (aka country-style). Regular-cut turkey breast includes the whole bone-in breast with ribs, a portion of the wing meat, and a portion of the back and neck skin. The hotel-cut turkey breast is essentially the same cut, though it comes with its wings, neck, and giblets, all important material if you intend to make a gravy or sauce to accompany the cooked meat. These tend to cost a little more and are almost always sold fresh, not frozen.

Whichever style you find and purchase, try to avoid turkey breasts that have been injected with a saline solution (a brine of sorts)—these are often called "self-basters." We found the solution masks the natural flavor of the turkey. (If the only bird you can find is a self-baster, do not brine it, as the meat will already be quite salty.) Also, ignore the pop-up timer that comes with some turkey breasts; the meat will be long overcooked before the popper pops. If your turkey has a pop-up timer, leave it in and gauge doneness according to an instant-read thermometer. Don't remove the timer until the meat is done; otherwise it will leave a gaping hole from which juices will flow.

GROUND

The guidelines for buying ground turkey are the same as those for buying ground chicken. Ground dark meat has more flavor than white, so make sure you buy ground turkey that is a mix of the two; do not buy ground turkey breast (also labeled 99 percent fat free).

Four Principles of Poultry Cookery

A number of cooking methods work well when preparing poultry. But whether you are roasting a whole turkey, grilling chicken parts, or sautéing cutlets, there are a few basic cooking principles that you should always keep in mind.

BRINE OR SALT TO INCREASE JUICINESS

In the same way that you prepare to cook beef or pork, brining poultry in a saltwater solution boosts the flavor and juiciness of the meat. However, there's a drawback to brining skin-on poultry: Because it's soaking up liquid, achieving perfectly crisp skin is more difficult. In these cases, make sure to pat the skin as dry as possible prior to cooking. Alternatively, for some cuts you might opt to salt the poultry. See page 226 for more general information about how brining and salting works; for details on salting and brining specific cuts of poultry, see page 288.

COOK WHITE MEAT LESS THAN DARK MEAT

Dark meat (thighs and drumsticks) cooks more slowly than white breast meat. This is mainly a result of the fact that dark meat is denser because it has more fat and proteins. To account for this difference when cooking a whole bird we've found it best to shield the breast meat to protect it from the heat by starting the bird either breast side down or with the breast to the side, then finishing breast side up. When cooking chicken pieces, things are a little bit easier because you can remove pieces as they are done, if necessary. White meat should be cooked only to an internal temperature of 160 degrees, while dark meat should be cooked to 175 degrees. Having a good instant-read thermometer is essential.

CRISP THE SKIN OR LOSE THE SKIN

For many of us, crisp skin on a piece of chicken or turkey is the best part. And on the flip side, flabby chicken or turkey skin isn't something anyone wants to eat (nor is it visually appealing). So either make sure the skin is crispy or remove it. The key to crisp skin is rendering all the fat that is between the skin and the meat. When cooking skin-on chicken pieces, we typically will brown the skin in a hot skillet, then finish cooking the chicken over a lower temperature or in the even heat of the oven (this has the added benefit of creating flavorful browned bits—fond—in the skillet, great for making a pan sauce). When roasting a whole bird, if you don't want to serve the skin you can still keep it on while roasting to protect the delicate breast meat from the heat, but discard it before serving. For stews and braises, if you don't crisp the skin and render the fat, you should typically discard the skin before cooking. If you don't, the fat will render into the stew or sauce, which will wind up being overly greasy.

LET IT REST

As poultry cooks, the juices are driven toward the center of the cut, so a resting period after cooking is essential to allow those juices time to redistribute evenly throughout. Logically, the larger the piece of poultry, the longer the resting time required. A big turkey needs 30 minutes, a whole chicken 10 to 20 minutes, and chicken parts 5 to 10 minutes. For more general information about resting, see page 227.

Salting Poultry

Salting poultry in advance is one way to season the meat and keep it juicy. When salt is applied to raw poultry, juices inside are drawn to the surface. The salt then dissolves in the exuded liquid, forming a brine that is eventually reabsorbed by the poultry. The salt changes the structure of the muscle proteins, allowing them to hold on to more of their own natural juices. Salting requires time, but it won't thwart the goal of crispy skin. We prefer to use kosher salt for salting because it's easier to distribute the salt evenly. The chart below lists the poultry items that we typically salt, along with notes on timing and method. We use Diamond Crystal Kosher Salt; If using Morton Kosher Salt, reduce the amounts listed by 33 percent (e.g. use ⅔ teaspoon Morton Kosher Salt or 1 teaspoon Diamond Crystal).

CUTS	TIME	KOSHER SALT	METHOD
Whole Chicken	At least 6 hours and up to 24 hours	1 teaspoon per pound	Apply salt evenly inside cavity and under skin of breasts and legs and let rest in refrigerator on wire rack set in rimmed baking sheet. (Wrap with plastic wrap if salting for longer than 12 hours.)
Bone-In Chicken Pieces; Boneless or Bone-In Turkey Breast	At least 6 hours and up to 24 hours	¾ teaspoon per pound	If poultry is skin-on, apply salt evenly between skin and meat, leaving skin attached, and let rest in refrigerator on wire rack set in rimmed baking sheet. (Wrap with plastic wrap if salting for longer than 12 hours.)
Whole Turkey	24 to 48 hours	1 teaspoon per pound	Apply salt evenly inside cavity and under skin of breasts and legs, wrap tightly with plastic wrap, and let rest in refrigerator.

Brining Poultry

Brining works in much the same way as salting. Salt in the brine seasons the poultry and promotes a change in its protein structure, reducing its overall toughness and creating gaps that fill up with water and keep the meat juicy and flavorful. Brining works faster than salting and can also result in juicier lean cuts since it adds, versus merely retains, moisture. But note that brining inhibits browning, and it requires fitting a brining container in the fridge. We prefer to use table salt for brining since it dissolves quickly in the water. The chart below lists the poultry items that we typically brine, along with notes on timing and the amount of water needed.

CHICKEN	TIME	COLD WATER	TABLE SALT
1 whole chicken (3½ to 4 pounds)	½ to 1 hour	2 quarts	½ cup
2 whole chickens (3½ to 4 pounds each)	½ to 1 hour	3 quarts	¾ cup
4 pounds bone-in chicken pieces (whole breasts, split breasts, leg quarters, thighs, and/or drumsticks)	½ to 1 hour	2 quarts	½ cup
4 boneless, skinless chicken breasts	½ to 1 hour	2 quarts	¼ cup
TURKEY			
1 whole turkey (12 to 17 pounds)	6 to 12 hours	2 gallons	1 cup
1 whole turkey (18 to 24 pounds)	6 to 12 hours	3 gallons	1½ cups
1 bone-in turkey breast (6 to 8 pounds)	3 to 6 hours	1 gallon	½ cup

Storing and Safety

Bacteria, including E. coli, salmonella, and listeria, can be found on raw poultry, and while cooking will kill any pathogens, the increasing number of headlines announcing food-borne illness outbreaks is a reminder of how important it is to follow some basic safety procedures to keep your kitchen clean and safe.

REFRIGERATING
Keep poultry refrigerated until just before cooking. Bacteria thrive at temperatures between 40 and 140 degrees. This means leftovers should also be promptly refrigerated.

FREEZING AND THAWING
Poultry can be frozen in its original packaging or after repackaging. If you are freezing it for longer than two months, rewrap (or wrap over packaging) with foil or plastic wrap, or place inside a zipper-lock freezer bag. You can keep poultry frozen for several months, but after two months the texture and flavor will suffer. Don't thaw frozen poultry on the counter; this puts it at risk of growing bacteria. Thaw it in its packaging in the refrigerator overnight (in a container to catch its juices), or in the sink under cold running water. Count on 1 day of defrosting in the refrigerator for every 4 pounds of bird.

RINSING
The U.S. Department of Agriculture advises against washing poultry. Rinsing poultry will not remove or kill much bacteria, and the splashing of water around the sink can spread the bacteria found in raw chicken.

HANDLING RAW POULTRY
When handling raw poultry, make sure to wash hands, knives, cutting boards, and counters (and anything else that has come into contact with the raw bird, its juices, or your hands) with hot, soapy water. Be especially careful not to let the poultry, its juices, or your unwashed hands touch foods (like salad ingredients) that will be eaten raw.

When seasoning raw poultry, touching the saltshaker or pepper mill once you've handled the bird can lead to cross-contamination. To avoid this, mix the necessary salt and pepper in a ramekin before handling the chicken.

COOKING AND LEFTOVERS
Breasts should be cooked to an internal temperature of 160 degrees, and thighs/drumsticks to 175 degrees, to ensure any bacteria has been killed. Leftover cooked poultry should be refrigerated and consumed within 3 days.

Essential Equipment

You can cook chicken any number of ways, so the cookware you need will vary based on the method you choose. However, there are a few basics you'll want to make sure you own.

INSTANT-READ THERMOMETER
Given the importance of cooking white and dark meat to the proper target temperatures, having a good instant-read thermometer is a priority. You want one that can take a reading quickly, especially when you are opening the oven door to check the temperature of a whole bird. For more details on what to look for, see page 10.

KITCHEN SHEARS
You'll use them for a lot of kitchen tasks; they are our favorite tool for cutting up and trimming chicken. Look for slip-resistant handles; you'll be glad you did when you are butchering a slippery chicken. And when the job is done and it's time for cleanup, take-apart blades are nice since they're easy to clean. For more details on what to look for, see page 30.

CARVING BOARD
Whether you're cooking chicken breasts or a whole bird, the cooked meat will release some juices as it rests and when you are carving it. A good carving board isn't really a must for smaller cuts—a cutting board could get the job done—but when you are dealing with a whole bird, a turkey breast, or Cornish hens for a crowd, you will want a carving board. Look for a heavy, sturdy board with a deep, wide trench around the perimeter to catch juices. A central well is also really helpful, as it will hold large cuts snugly and keep them in place as you carve.

How to Cut Up a Whole Chicken

ESSENTIAL EQUIPMENT

• cutting board
• chef's knife
• kitchen shears

Cutting up a whole chicken may seem like an intimidating process, but it's a handy technique to learn. For one thing, cutting up a chicken yourself is economical since you aren't paying for the labor to have someone cut up the chicken for you. If a recipe calls for four split breasts, you can simply butcher two whole chickens and save the thighs, wings, and drumsticks for another recipe. Second, butchering your own chicken ensures the parts are the right size and properly butchered—not always the case with the prepackaged pieces you buy at the supermarket. You'll find cutting up a whole chicken comes in handy for a number of recipes; see How to Pan-Roast Chicken Pieces on page 296 and our recipe tutorial for Extra-Crunchy Fried Chicken on page 316.

1. REMOVE EACH LEG QUARTER

Remove chicken giblets and discard. Using chef's knife, cut off legs, one at a time, by severing joint between leg and body.

WHY? Cutting off the somewhat awkward leg quarters first makes it easier to butcher the rest of the chicken properly. Start cutting where the leg attaches to the breast. After this initial cut, you can pop the leg joint out of its socket with your hands, then continue cutting through to detach the leg from the body.

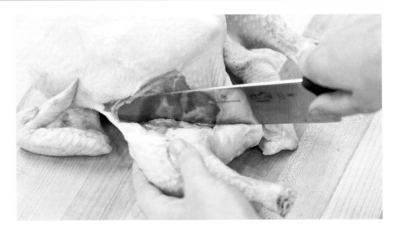

2. HALVE EACH LEG QUARTER

Cut each leg into 2 pieces—drumstick and thigh—by slicing through joint, marked by thin line of fat.

WHY? A few recipes out there call for whole leg quarters, but most often you'll want to separate drumsticks and thighs.

3. REMOVE WINGS

Flip chicken over and remove wings by slicing through each wing joint. Then cut through cartilage around wingtip to remove and discard.

WHY? Most recipes calling for a whole butchered chicken don't utilize the wings since they're far smaller and less meaty than the other pieces, but you shouldn't throw them away. Freeze them and use them for making stock (see page 438) or, of course, cut them into sections to make a batch of game-day chicken wings.

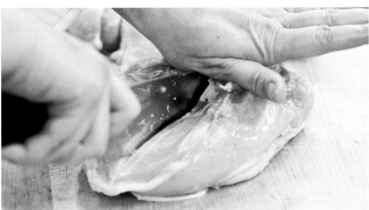

4. REMOVE BACKBONE

Turn chicken on its side and, using kitchen shears, remove back.

WHY? The back of a chicken has almost no meat, and the bone only gets in the way of butchering the breast. However, the backbone, like the wings, is good to use when making stock.

5. SPLIT BREAST

Flip breast skin side down and, using chef's knife, cut in half through breast plate, which is marked by thin white line of cartilage.

WHY? Split breasts are perhaps the most common cut of chicken; rarely will you see a recipe calling for a single whole breast. Using a good chef's knife is key for this step.

6. CUT BREAST INTO QUARTERS

Flip each breast piece over and cut in half crosswise.

WHY? Whole split breasts are fairly large, so cutting each split breast in half crosswise speeds up the cooking time. You'll need to do this for recipes that call for a whole chicken cut into eight pieces (like fried chicken): After reserving the wings for another recipe, you will have two drumsticks, two thighs, and four breast pieces.

Troubleshooting Cutting Up a Whole Chicken

PROBLEM	SOLUTION
The chicken keeps slipping around while I cut.	Straight out of the packaging, the chicken will be fairly slippery, which will make it more difficult for you to get a good grip on it. It helps to pat it dry with paper towels before you start.
I'm having a hard time cutting through to remove the leg quarter.	Sometimes you'll hit cartilage that is harder to cut through, but make sure you are actually at the joint, not trying to cut through bone. After you've made the initial cut where the breast and leg quarter meet, remember to stop and pop the joint out of its socket with your hands, applying pressure up and away from the breast. If you aren't sure you're in the right spot, feel for the ball-and-socket joint.

How to Butterfly a Whole Chicken

ESSENTIAL EQUIPMENT

• cutting board
• kitchen shears

Butterflying a chicken is called for in some grilling recipes (like our Italian-Style Grilled Chicken on page 421) and some roasting recipes. It involves removing the backbone, then opening and flattening the bird. Butterflying offers two advantages. First, it allows for more even cooking by giving the thighs greater exposure to the heat so that they cook at the same rate as the more delicate white breast meat. Second, butterflying allows you to cook a whole chicken in less time. And because the backbone has been removed, it's easy to add flavor under the skin with a spice rub or compound butter. If you are grilling or roasting, it's wise to brine the chicken prior to butterflying it to help protect the meat from drying out during cooking (see the brining chart on page 288). You can use this same method to butterfly a turkey. Because of a turkey's larger size, using the handle of a wooden spoon to gently loosen the skin works well. And, of course, you'll need more compound butter or spice rub to cover a turkey than you would for a chicken.

1. REMOVE BACKBONE
Place chicken on cutting board breast side down and cut along each side of backbone to remove it.
WHY? Removing the backbone is what will allow you to flatten the chicken. This isn't a job you want to do with a knife; using shears makes the task fast, simple, and safe.

2. FLATTEN CHICKEN
Flip chicken breast side up, then use heel of your hand to flatten chicken.
WHY? The chicken will easily flatten with just a little pressure applied with the heel of your hand. You will actually hear a crack when you've done it correctly. Some recipes may also call for pounding the chicken with a mallet or meat pounder once you've flattened it by hand to ensure an even thickness.

3. TUCK WINGS
Tuck wings behind back of chicken.
WHY? The thin, small wingtips easily burn, so it's best to protect them by hiding them away under the back of the chicken. This is particularly important when roasting them in the oven.

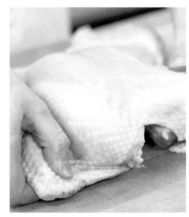

4. LOOSEN SKIN
Slip your fingers between skin and breast, loosening membrane.
WHY? The skin is attached to the meat with a thin membrane. It takes only a little force with your fingers to loosen it. The skin should stretch easily to allow you to season the chicken. Work carefully so you don't poke a hole in the skin. You can spread a compound butter or spice rub under the skin, or simply use salt and pepper. A little oil on the skin will help it crisp nicely. From here, it's ready for the oven or the grill.

How to Split and Trim Breasts

ESSENTIAL EQUIPMENT

- cutting board
- chef's knife
- kitchen shears

We typically buy breasts already split, but more than once we've gotten back to the kitchen only to discover that they aren't similar in size. That leads to uneven cooking and uneven portions. Buying one whole breast from the butcher and splitting it yourself offers an advantage: You are guaranteed evenly sized pieces. If you plan to buy chicken breasts that have already been split, inspect the package and make sure they are of similar size.

Whether you buy them split or split your own, you should always trim off the rib section from each split breast prior to cooking. This allows you to fit more chicken breasts in the pan or pot and ensures even cooking. We also trim excess fat and skin to prevent greasiness.

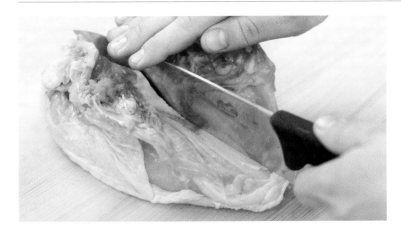

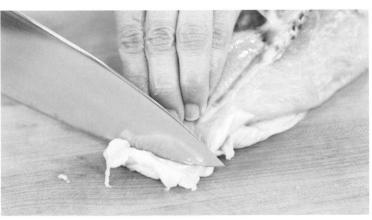

1. CUT WHOLE BREAST IN HALF

With whole breast skin side down on cutting board, center knife on breastbone, then apply pressure to cut through and separate breast into two halves.

WHY? To cut the whole breast in half, it's easiest to see where to cut if it's skin side down. You'll see a thin white line of cartilage where you should cut. It's critical to have a good chef's knife for this step.

2. TRIM RIB SECTION

Using kitchen shears, trim off rib section from each breast, following vertical line of fat from tapered end of breast up to socket where wing was attached.

WHY? There isn't a lot of meat on the rib section anyway, so we always trim it off to allow more room in the pan for the chicken breasts. Removing it also allows for more even cooking since the breasts can lay flat in the pot or skillet. Even if you buy breasts that have already been split, take the time to perform this step as well as the next one.

3. TRIM FAT AND EXCESS SKIN

Using chef's knife or kitchen shears, trim excess fat and skin from chicken breasts prior to cooking.

WHY? To avoid a final dish that is greasy, we often trim excess fat and skin from the chicken before adding it to the pot or skillet.

How to Make Chicken Cutlets

ESSENTIAL EQUIPMENT

- cutting board
- chef's knife
- plastic wrap
- meat pounder or mallet

A cutlet is simply a thin piece of meat. In the case of chicken, cutlets are typically made by cutting a chicken breast in half horizontally (although on occasion, like for our Crisp Breaded Chicken Cutlets, we pound a whole breast thin; see page 304). Sure, you can find chicken cutlets ready to go in the supermarket—a tempting option since part of the motivation of cooking cutlets in the first place is the fact that they require so little time. But shortcutting this prep step is one we wouldn't recommend; store-bought cutlets are often ragged and they vary widely in size and thickness. Instead, buy boneless, skinless chicken breasts and make the cutlets yourself. You'll not only guarantee your cutlets are of equal size but also save a little money in the process. Also see How to Sauté Chicken Cutlets (opposite).

1. REMOVE TENDERLOIN

Remove tenderloin from 6- to 8-ounce boneless, skinless chicken breast.

WHY? Sometimes a thin strip of meat, the tenderloin, is attached to the breast. This loose strip is likely to come off during cooking, so we always remove it. Also trim any excess fat, gristle, or pieces of bone that might remain where the wing and ribs were attached.

2. SLICE BREASTS IN HALF CROSSWISE

Lay chicken breast flat on cutting board, smooth side facing up. Rest one hand on top of chicken and, using chef's knife, slice chicken in half horizontally.

WHY? Holding the breast steady as you cut will help ensure you cut on a level plane. If you have time, you can freeze the chicken breasts for 15 minutes first to make the slicing easier. Each cutlet should weigh 3 to 4 ounces each and be about ½ inch thick.

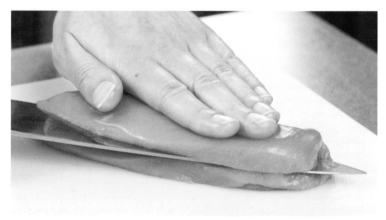

3. POUND CUTLETS TO EVEN THICKNESS

Place cutlets, smooth side down, on large sheet of plastic wrap. Cover with second sheet of plastic and pound gently to even thickness.

WHY? Chicken breasts are always thicker on one end; pounding the meat so that it is even from end to end helps ensure even cooking. Often we pound cutlets thinner, to ¼ inch. Pounding between plastic wrap is an easy way to keep the counter and the meat pounder clean.

How to Sauté Chicken Cutlets

Cutlets are a great choice when you want to get dinner on the table quickly, but their selling point is also a drawback—they are so thin and lean that it's all too easy to turn out overcooked, rubbery cutlets. They're half as thick as chicken breasts, so it makes sense they cook twice as fast. Furthermore, getting browning to develop in such a short amount of time is also a challenge. We found flouring the cutlets and cooking them over moderately high heat for longer on the first side than the second was the answer. This method will also work with turkey cutlets; however, since they are bigger you will need to cook them in batches.

Sautéed chicken cutlets are the perfect canvas for a flavorful pan sauce, so we keep our sautéed cutlets warm in a low oven while we make a sauce in the skillet. Also see How to Make Chicken Cutlets (opposite) and How to Make a Pan Sauce (page 232). Serve with one of our pan sauces on pages 324–325 and 331–332.

1. PAT CUTLETS DRY

Pat 8 chicken cutlets, pounded to even ¼-inch thickness, dry with paper towels.

WHY? To ensure the seasoning and flour in the next step adhere to the cutlets, it's important to pat them dry first.

2. DREDGE IN FLOUR AND SEASONING

Combine ¼ cup all-purpose flour, 1 teaspoon salt, and ½ teaspoon pepper in shallow dish or pie plate. Working with 1 cutlet at a time, dredge in flour mixture, shake off excess, and transfer to large plate.

WHY? Flouring chicken prior to sautéing protects the meat from drying out and helps to keep it from sticking to the skillet. The flour also encourages browning and helps pan sauces cling to the cutlets. Mixing the seasoning into the flouring keeps the process streamlined.

3. SAUTÉ QUICKLY

Heat 1 tablespoon vegetable oil in 12-inch skillet over medium-high heat until just smoking. Place 4 cutlets in skillet and cook until browned on first side, about 2 minutes. Flip cutlets and cook until second side is opaque, 15 to 20 seconds.

WHY? Vegetable oil has a high smoke point and neutral flavor, which make it the best choice here. Cutlets are so thin that to avoid overcooking it's best to deeply brown one side and cook the second side for only a few seconds. This is sufficient to develop flavor, lend visual appeal, and leave some fond in the pan to make a sauce, all without overcooking the chicken.

4. KEEP WARM IN OVEN, COOK SECOND BATCH

Transfer cutlets to ovensafe platter, tent with aluminum foil, and transfer to 200-degree oven. Repeat with 1 tablespoon oil and remaining 4 cutlets.

WHY? Thin cutlets cool off quickly, so tent them with foil and keep them warm in a low oven while making a pan sauce.

How to Pan-Roast Chicken Pieces

ESSENTIAL EQUIPMENT

- chef's knife
- cutting board
- kitchen shears
- 12-inch ovensafe skillet
- paper towels
- tongs
- instant-read thermometer
- whisk
- potholder

Like roasting a whole chicken, pan-roasting chicken pieces allows for the economy of buying a whole bird and delivers crisp skin, tender meat, and flavorful drippings to incorporate into a pan sauce, but on a weeknight time frame. In addition to the obvious fact that smaller pieces of chicken cook more quickly than a whole bird, pan roasting speeds up the cooking time by starting the chicken on the stovetop to brown the exterior, then moves to the oven to finish. White and dark meat cook at different rates, but by cutting each split breast in half, the breasts will be done at the same time as the thinner thighs and slim drumsticks, which require a higher doneness temperature.

While a pan sauce isn't required, the chicken needs to rest regardless, so it makes sense to utilize that time—and the flavorful drippings in the skillet—to make a quick sauce.

Also see How to Cut Up a Whole Chicken (page 290), How to Make a Pan Sauce (page 232), and our brining chart on page 288. Serve with one of our pan sauces on pages 324–325 and 331–332.

1. CUT CHICKEN INTO 8 PIECES

Cut 1 (3½- to 4-pound) chicken into 8 pieces, setting wings aside for another use. Brine pieces if desired.

WHY? Two thighs, two drumsticks, and four portions of breast meat mean that everyone can have both white and dark meat. There isn't enough room in the pan for the wings, so we reserve them for another use. Cutting the large breasts in half ensures they will cook through in about the same amount of time as the thighs and drumsticks. Brining the chicken isn't required, but it makes for juicier meat and also adds some insurance against overcooking the more delicate breast meat. However, note that brined meat won't brown as well.

2. HEAT OIL IN LARGE OVENSAFE SKILLET

Heat 1 tablespoon vegetable oil in 12-inch ovensafe skillet over medium-high heat until just smoking.

WHY? A 12-inch skillet ensures the chicken isn't crowded and will brown rather than steam. You should be able to fit all eight pieces in a 12-inch skillet. Since the chicken will go into the oven, skillet and all, after browning, make sure your skillet is ovensafe. While chicken skin is fatty, we have found chicken browns unevenly in a dry skillet, so we add 1 tablespoon of oil to the pan first. Make sure you wait until the oil is smoking before you add the chicken to the skillet, or else the chicken won't brown properly.

3. BROWN CHICKEN

Pat chicken dry with paper towels and season with salt and pepper. Add chicken, skin side down, to skillet and cook until well browned, 6 to 8 minutes. Flip chicken and brown on second side, about 3 minutes.

WHY? Browning the chicken lends visual appeal, builds flavor, and creates fond that can be used to build a pan sauce. Browning also jump-starts the cooking process.

4. FINISH IN OVEN

Roast chicken, skin side down, in 450-degree oven until thickest parts of breasts register 160 degrees and thighs/drumsticks register 175 degrees, about 10 minutes. Transfer chicken to serving platter and tent with aluminum foil.

WHY? Finishing in the oven ensures even cooking; a 500-degree oven leads to singed drippings, and anything lower than 450 simply takes longer than we want. Keeping the chicken skin side down ensured perfectly crisp, dark russet–colored skin. The dark meat and white meat finished at the same time; the thickness of the breast pieces made them cook more slowly than the flat, thin thighs and slim drumsticks. That said, it's a good idea to check any smaller pieces a few minutes early and remove them from the oven if they are done.

5. MAKE SAUCE

While chicken rests, make pan sauce.

WHY? It takes only about 5 minutes to make a pan sauce, which can be conveniently prepared while the chicken rests. Just make sure you are careful of the hot handle on the skillet during this step; in the test kitchen we usually leave a potholder on the handle as a reminder.

Troubleshooting Pan-Roasting Chicken Pieces

PROBLEM	SOLUTION
I want to cook all thighs/all breasts.	That's not a problem. You can fit six bone-in thighs or four bone-in breasts in the skillet (you don't have to cut the breasts in half since they will all cook at approximately the same rate). Use exactly the same method as above, and cook them to the appropriate temperature before removing the skillet from the oven.
I'm not sure if my skillet is ovensafe.	If you have any doubts, especially if you have a handle made from anything other than metal, double-check your skillet's specs. If you didn't save any of that information or packaging from when you bought it, look it up online. Most manufacturers will note on the product pages if the skillet is ovensafe and, if so, up to what temperature.
I burned the fond.	Burnt fond will make a bitter-tasting pan sauce, so it's best to clean it out of the skillet before making the sauce.

How to Roast a Whole Chicken

ESSENTIAL EQUIPMENT

- large container
- cutting board
- paper towels
- V-rack
- roasting pan
- chef's knife
- carving board

Simple and satisfying, roast whole chicken represents the best of straightforward home cooking, but that doesn't mean it's easy to do well. The biggest challenge is getting the white and dark meat to finish cooking at the same time. The bird is thicker and thinner in spots, and the breast meat dries out at an internal temperature above 160 degrees, while the dark meat isn't even done until it reaches at least 175 degrees. In addition, the skin is often flabby and plucked off before eating.

You'll find all manner of recipes resorting to all sorts of tricks, trussing, and basting of the chicken to produce a perfectly cooked bird. But in the end, it's not all that complicated. All the chicken needs is a little bit of prep, then you pop it in the oven, flipping it twice, and you'll have a beautifully bronzed bird that required minimal hands-on work. We put plain unsalted butter under the skin to baste the meat as it cooks, but feel free to swap in a compound butter. Also see How to Carve a Whole Bird (page 300) and page 288 for more information on brining.

1. BRINE CHICKEN

Stir ½ cup table salt into 2 quarts cold water in large container. Submerge 1 (3½- to 4-pound) chicken, cover, and refrigerate for 1 hour. Remove chicken from brine and pat dry with paper towels.

WHY? Brining seasons the chicken and helps to keep the white meat from drying out. However, don't brine kosher chickens; they will be far too salty if brined.

2. LOOSEN SKIN, SPREAD BUTTER ON MEAT

Use your fingers to gently loosen center portion of skin covering each breast. Place 2 tablespoons softened unsalted butter under skin, directly on meat in center of each breast. Gently press on skin to distribute butter over meat.

WHY? Loosening the skin makes it easier for the fat in the skin to render and drain. Make sure to be gentle so as not to tear it. Applying butter under the skin helps ensure moist meat.

3. RUB SKIN WITH OIL

Tuck wings behind back. Rub skin with 1 tablespoon olive oil and season with pepper.

WHY? Oil helps the skin crisp in the oven. Since the bird has been brined, there's no need to season with salt.

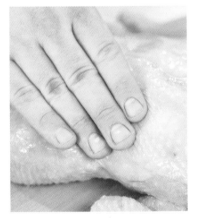

4. ROAST FOR 15 MINUTES ON EACH SIDE

Place chicken, one wing side up, on V-rack sprayed with vegetable oil spray. Place V-rack in roasting pan preheated in 400-degree oven. Roast chicken for 15 minutes. Using paper towels, rotate chicken so opposite wing side is facing up, and roast for another 15 minutes.

WHY? For even cooking, we start by laying the chicken with one wing facing up and roast for 15 minutes. Then we flip it to the other side and roast another 15 minutes. Spraying the rack keeps the skin from sticking, and preheating the pan ensures the thighs and breast cook at the same rate. For a good grip, hold a wad of paper towels in each hand when you flip the chicken.

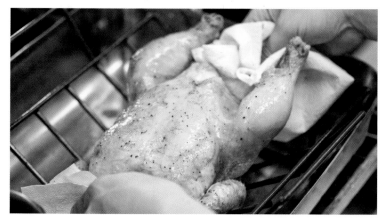

5. FINISH COOKING BREAST SIDE UP

Remove roasting pan from oven and, using 2 large wads of paper towels, flip chicken so that breast side is facing up. Roast until breast registers 160 degrees and thighs register 175 degrees, 20 to 25 minutes longer.

WHY? Cooking the chicken breast side up for the last 20 to 25 minutes ensures evenly cooked meat. If the pan starts smoking, the drippings are probably burning; add 1 cup water to the pan. Use an instant-read thermometer to determine when the chicken is done. Take several readings in the thickest part of both the breast and the thigh to ensure an accurate reading.

6. REST BEFORE CARVING

Transfer chicken to carving board and let rest for 15 to 20 minutes. Carve and serve.

WHY? The heat of the oven forces the juices of the meat toward the center of the bird. Letting the chicken rest for 15 to 20 minutes gives the juices time to redistribute, ensuring moist, flavorful chicken in every bite.

Roasting Times for Whole Chicken

RAW CHICKEN WEIGHT	ROASTING TIME, WING SIDES UP	ROASTING TIME, BREAST SIDE UP
3½ to 4 pounds	15 minutes per side	20 to 25 minutes
4 to 5 pounds	15 minutes per side	25 to 35 minutes
5 to 6 pounds	20 minutes per side	25 to 35 minutes
6 to 8 pounds	25 minutes per side	25 to 45 minutes

Troubleshooting Roasting a Whole Chicken

PROBLEM	SOLUTION
The skin is flabby, not crispy.	Brining is a great way to season a bird and to add moisture, but it wreaks havoc on the skin. You can mitigate these problems by blotting the brined bird really well with paper towels. You should go through several towels. You want that skin to be as dry as possible when it goes into the oven.
Can I roast two chickens at once?	Sure, the only difference is that you'll need to make sure you have a large enough V-rack and roasting pan to accommodate both. Make sure to check the temperature of each to ensure both are done before pulling them from the oven. If one is done before the other, just transfer the finished one to the carving board and let it rest while the second one continues to cook.

How to Carve a Whole Bird

ESSENTIAL EQUIPMENT

• carving board
• chef's knife

After brining and roasting the perfect bird, you still have one task left before bringing it to the table: carving it. And while carving isn't difficult, there is definitely a way to approach it that will yield nicely portioned chicken parts and slices of boneless breast. You want portions that look attractive on the platter and are easy to serve. Before you start, make sure that you've let the chicken rest. The resting time not only allows the juices to redistribute, but it also makes carving easier.

While you might think a carving knife is the proper tool for this task given its name, a chef's knife is, in fact, the better choice because of the maneuvering carving requires—it's something you just can't do with the long blade of a carving knife. (Keep your carving knife handy for boneless roasts instead.) Also see How to Roast a Whole Chicken (page 298) and our tutorial for Classic Holiday Turkey (page 320). The technique for carving a whole turkey is similar, although we recommend slicing meat off of the thigh bone.

1. START WITH LEG QUARTER
Cut chicken where leg meets breast.
WHY? Removing the leg quarters first makes carving the breast much easier since it gets them out of the way.

2. SEPARATE LEG JOINT, REMOVE LEG QUARTER
Pull leg quarter away from carcass. Separate joint by gently pressing leg out to side and pushing up on joint. Cut through joint to remove leg quarter.
WHY? After the initial cut, you'll run into the bone. Rather than hacking through it, use your hands to pop the joint out of the socket. It requires only a little force and makes cutting through the rest of the leg quarter much easier. Then cut through the space created where you popped the joint out of the socket.

3. SEPARATE DRUMSTICK AND THIGH
Cut through joint that connects drumstick to thigh. Repeat steps 1–3 on chicken's other side.
WHY? Leg quarters are rather large; smaller portions of dark meat (and white) means everyone can enjoy some of both.

4. REMOVE BREAST MEAT
Cut down along side of breastbone, pulling breast meat away from breastbone as you cut.
WHY? Many people carve the breast into serving pieces right off the carcass, but the last few pieces usually look ragged. It's tidier to carve the meat off in one piece from either side of the bone first. Follow the curvature of the breastbone as you cut, pulling the meat away from the bone as you go.

5. SLICE BREAST MEAT
Remove wing from breast by cutting through wing joint. Slice breast crosswise into slices. Repeat with other side.
WHY? Slicing the breast crosswise into smaller slices makes for attractive portions.

How to Fry

Whether you want to fry chicken, shrimp, or potatoes, the process is generally the same. Frying causes moisture to flee the food once it lands in hot oil. As the food cooks and more moisture escapes, the food's exterior dries out and you achieve the final goal: a crisp crust.

But fryer beware: If the oil is too hot, you'll burn the food's exterior before it cooks through. If it's not hot enough, the food won't release moisture and thus will fry up limp and soggy. As such, a thermometer that can register high temperatures is essential. One that clips to the side of the pot, like a candy thermometer, saves you from dipping a thermometer in and out of the pot (although an instant-read thermometer will certainly work). If you diligently monitor the oil temperature and keep in mind just a few other points, you'll find frying is as manageable as any other cooking technique. Also see our tutorial on Extra-Crunchy Fried Chicken (page 316) and How to Fry Potatoes (page 106). The equipment needed will depend on what you are frying: Tongs are necessary when cooking larger pieces of food like chicken, while a spider skimmer or slotted spoon is best for French fries.

ESSENTIAL EQUIPMENT

- chef's knife
- cutting board
- large Dutch oven
- candy or deep-fry thermometer
- long-handled tongs
- spider skimmer or large slotted spoon
- wire racks (2)
- rimmed baking sheet
- paper towels

1. CUT FOOD EVENLY

Cut potatoes or other vegetable into evenly sized batons or pieces; cut chicken breasts in half crosswise and separate leg quarters into drumsticks and thighs.

WHY? Cutting food into evenly sized pieces ensures that all the pieces cook through at the same rate. It's also important to cut large pieces of food, like chicken breasts, in half, so that the interior can cook through by the time the exterior is done.

2. COAT IN STARCH

Coat foods in cornstarch or flour, as directed in recipe.

WHY? Starchy foods fry best. As food cooks in oil, its coating of starch dries out, becoming porous and crispy. We coat potatoes lightly in cornstarch for ideally crispy results, and non-starchy foods, like chicken, usually get dredged in flour.

3. USE LARGE POT AND PEANUT OIL

Fill large Dutch oven no more than halfway with peanut oil.

WHY? A large, heavy pot that is at least 6 quarts in capacity ensures even heating and plenty of room for the food to fry. An oil with a high smoke point is a must for frying; we prefer the clean flavor of refined peanut oil, but vegetable oil will also work. Fill the pot no more than halfway with oil. This will minimize any dangerous splattering once the food has been added. And more important, when you add the food, the oil will bubble and rise because of displacement, and an overflowing pot of oil is very dangerous.

4. KEEP OIL AT PROPER TEMPERATURE

Clip candy/deep-fry thermometer onto side of pot and bring oil to 325 to 375 degrees (as directed in recipe) over medium heat, adjusting heat as necessary during cooking to maintain proper frying temperature.

WHY? In the end, successful frying is all about the temperature of the oil. If the oil isn't hot enough, the trademark brown and crispy crust won't form and the food will turn out limp and soggy. If it's too hot, the crust will burn before the food cooks through. When we fry food, the oil typically is brought to between 325 and 375 degrees before the food is added. The temperature will drop a little when you first add the food to the pot, so we usually increase the heat right after adding the food to minimize the temperature change. Monitor the temperature as you proceed and adjust as needed. If oil splatters onto your stovetop, wipe up any big splatters as you go—the less uncontained oil close to a lit burner, the better.

5. FRY IN BATCHES

Add food to hot oil in small portions and fry, stirring with spider skimmer or slotted spoon, until golden brown.

WHY? Putting a large amount of food in the hot oil all at once will make the temperature drop too much and will turn out soggy—rather than crispy—fried food. So we fry food in multiple smaller batches to keep the temperature from dropping too much with each addition. Smaller batches also minimize dangerous and messy splatter. Stirring the food with a spider skimmer or slotted spoon as it fries prevents clumping.

6. DRAIN ON PAPER TOWELS

Using spider skimmer or slotted spoon, transfer fried food to paper towel–lined baking sheet and let drain for 5 minutes.

WHY? To minimize greasiness, we let excess oil drain from the food on paper towels when it comes out of the hot oil.

7. KEEP WARM IN OVEN

Transfer food to wire rack set in baking sheet and keep warm in oven.

WHY? Since we're frying in batches, we don't want the early batch(es) to get cold, so we keep the food warm in a 200-degree oven. Setting the food on a wire rack allows for air circulation, keeping the exterior crisp.

Troubleshooting Frying

PROBLEM	SOLUTION
I don't have peanut oil; can I use canola oil?	We wouldn't recommend it. When we tested frying in various types of oils, our tasters found that canola oil leaves food with a stale, slightly fishy flavor and aroma when used for frying. Don't use olive oil either. Its high cost, low smoke point, and distinctive flavor make it a poor choice for frying. If you don't have peanut oil on hand use vegetable oil.
Is there any way to minimize the messy splattering?	The oil will sputter when frying, but you can minimize the mess it makes on your stovetop by using a splatter screen. These flat mesh disks fit over pots like a lid and catch large splatters while still letting steam escape. We think it's a worthwhile, inexpensive investment since they're good for not only deep frying but also shallow frying and many sautéing recipes.
My fried food always comes out greasy.	If you are crowding the food into the pot, the oil temperature will plummet, resulting in greasy food. Make sure to fry in batches and give the food plenty of room.
My food is pale and soggy.	The temperature of the oil is too low, which means the food retains more moisture than it should, thus you'll have soggy results. Make sure to bring your oil up to the temperature called for in the recipe.
My food is burnt on the outside and underdone on the inside.	Your oil is probably too hot; make sure you are using an accurate thermometer and following the temperature called for in the recipe. If you find the oil is too hot, move the pot off the heat and let the temperature drop before you proceed with adding the food. Also make sure you are cutting the food to the size called for in the recipe.
The oil is smoking; what do I do?	This is a sign that the oil is overheated and starting to break down. Remove the pot from the heat until the oil cools to the correct temperature. It's important to do this at the first sign of smoke, as a significant amount of smoke will impart an off-flavor to foods, in which case the oil should be discarded.
I don't want to throw out all this oil; can I reuse it?	As long as you weren't frying fish, which will impart a distinct flavor to the oil and so should be discarded, frying oil can be reused several times before its smoke point becomes too low and its flavor too degraded (at that point, it should be thrown out). To save oil for another use, let the oil cool to room temperature, strain it to remove any stray bits of food, then store in the freezer to prevent rancidity.
Could I use shortening or lard for the frying oil?	Lard and shortening make great fries, but we assume most home cooks won't want to use these saturated fat–laden products. However, we have found that adding just ¼ cup bacon fat to your pot with the peanut or vegetable oil will lend the food a great mildly meaty flavor that you just can't get when you use oil alone.

Breaded Chicken Cutlets with Parmesan

Recipe Stats

TOTAL TIME **45 minutes**
PREPARATION TIME **15 minutes**
ACTIVE COOKING TIME **30 minutes**
YIELD **4 servings**
MAKE AHEAD **Serve immediately**
DIFFICULTY **Easy**

Tools

- rimmed baking sheet
- 12-inch nonstick skillet
- food processor
- chef's knife
- cutting board
- dry measuring cups
- liquid measuring cup
- measuring spoons
- baking dishes or
  pie plates (3) *
- fork
- large heatproof plate
- meat pounder
- metal spatula
- rasp-style grater
- tongs
- wire rack
- paper towels
- plastic wrap

* The baking dishes or pie plates are for containing each of the breading ingredients: flour, eggs, and bread crumbs with Parmesan. It doesn't matter if the baking dishes or pie plates are of the same size or dimension—what's most important is that the vessels are shallow and wide enough so that it's easy to coat the chicken breasts evenly.

Overview

Basic breaded chicken breasts are one of those preparations that every cook should have in his or her repertoire. They're quick yet tasty, made with just a few ingredients that are probably already in your kitchen, and they go with just about any type of side dish. They also offer a breadth of dinner possibilities: Topped with tomato sauce and served with spaghetti, they become chicken Parmesan. Between two pieces of bread, along with lettuce, tomato, and mayonnaise, they make chicken cutlet sandwiches. Served with steamed short-grain rice and tonkatsu sauce, they're Japanese-style chicken cutlets.

This recipe for chicken cutlets includes Parmesan cheese in the bread crumbs, which adds an extra layer of savoriness to the breading. This Italian angle lends the dish the name "Chicken Milanese." The breaded cutlets are shallow-fried in a large skillet with just enough vegetable oil to submerge the cutlets about halfway, arranged in a single layer in the skillet and cooked in two batches, turned with tongs, and, finally, drained on paper towels to remove excess oil after frying.

Once you master this technique, you can vary the flavorings in a number of different ways: Omit the Parmesan, if you like, and add any number of ingredients to the egg mixture—minced fresh herbs, minced garlic, Dijon mustard, Worcestershire sauce, cayenne pepper, and hot sauce are all worthy additions. For variations on this recipe, see page 326. Before you begin, see How to Make Chicken Cutlets on page 294.

Ingredients

4   (6- to 8-ounce) boneless, skinless chicken breasts, tenderloins removed, trimmed
Salt and pepper
4–6   slices hearty white sandwich bread, crusts removed, torn into 1½-inch pieces *
¼   cup finely grated Parmesan cheese
¾   cup all-purpose flour
2   large eggs
1   tablespoon plus ¾ cup vegetable oil **
Lemon wedges

* Use a good-quality sandwich bread with a sturdy crumb. Avoid soft, squishy-textured sandwich bread such as Wonder bread.
** Peanut oil is another option for this recipe.

What Can Go Wrong

Here's a list of common mistakes cooks make when preparing this recipe.

COMMON MISTAKE	BAD OUTCOMES	WHAT YOU SHOULD DO
Not Pounding Cutlets Thin Enough	• **The cutlets do not cook through.**	Pound the chicken breasts to an even ½-inch thickness. Use a ruler, if you must, to make sure that the cutlets are the correct thickness. If they're too thick, they may not cook through on the inside.
Pounding Cutlets Too Thin	• **The cutlets do not fit into the skillet.** • **The cutlets overcook.**	Pound the chicken breasts to an even ½-inch thickness, but no thinner, so go easy. Use a ruler, if you must, to make sure that the cutlets are of the correct thickness. If the chicken breasts are pounded too thin, you may run into two problems: (1) the cutlets are too large to fit two in the skillet, and (2) the cutlets overcook, turning dry and tough.
Using Store-Bought Bread Crumbs	• **The breading tastes stale.** • **The breading lacks crispness.**	Don't try to take a shortcut by using store-bought bread crumbs instead of making your own fresh bread crumbs. Commercial bread crumbs are so fine that they're dusty, and they have a stale off-flavor that doesn't do any dish any favors. Fresh homemade bread crumbs are quick and easy to make in a food processor, and have a flavor and texture that are superior to store-bought.
Forgetting to Rest Breaded Cutlets	• **The coating peels off.**	To create a stable coating, you must first dry the chicken, flour it, dip it into the egg wash, and then apply the crumbs. But in order for the coating to stay in place, it helps to let the breaded cutlets rest on a wire rack for at least 5 minutes before cooking. During this time the flour and egg wash become gluelike (in a good way), ensuring that the crumbs won't peel off the chicken when it is fried.
Insufficiently Heating Oil	• **The cutlets are greasy.** • **The cutlets are poorly browned.**	If you don't heat the oil sufficiently, the breading will soak up excess oil and won't brown properly. There's not really enough oil in the pan to take its temperature when pan-frying, so you have to rely on other cues. When the oil is ready, it should be shimmering. (Smoking oil is a sign that it has overheated.) Also, test the oil by dipping the tapered end of one cutlet into the pan; if the oil barely sizzles, it's not hot enough.

1. Pound 4 (6- to 8-ounce) boneless, skinless chicken breasts, trimmed and tenderloins removed, to even ½-inch-thick cutlets.

2. Pat cutlets dry with paper towels and season with salt and pepper.

3. Finely grate enough Parmesan cheese to yield ¼ cup.

4. Remove crusts from 4 to 6 slices hearty white sandwich bread.

5. Tear bread into rough 1½-inch pieces.

6. Process bread in food processor until evenly fine-textured, 20 to 30 seconds. You should have about 1½ cups fresh bread crumbs.

7. Transfer crumbs to baking dish or pie plate and mix in Parmesan.

8. Spread ¾ cup all-purpose flour in second baking dish or pie plate.

9. Beat 2 large eggs with 1 tablespoon vegetable oil in third baking dish or pie plate.

10. Adjust oven rack to lower-middle position and set large heatproof plate on rack.

11. Heat oven to 200 degrees.

12. Working with one cutlet at a time, dredge cutlets in flour, shaking off excess.

13. Using tongs, dip both sides of cutlet in egg mixture, allowing excess to drip back into baking dish to ensure very thin coating.

14. Dip both sides of cutlet in bread crumbs, pressing crumbs with fingers to form even, cohesive coating.

15. Place breaded cutlets in single layer on wire rack set over baking sheet.

16. Allow coating to dry for about 5 minutes.

17. Meanwhile, heat ¾ cup vegetable oil in heavy-bottomed 12-inch nonstick skillet over medium-high heat until shimmering but not smoking.

18. Lay 2 cutlets gently in skillet in single layer, leaving space between them.

19. Cook until deep golden brown and crisp on first side, gently pressing on cutlets with metal spatula for even browning, about 3 minutes.

20. Flip cutlets, reduce heat to medium, and cook until meat feels firm and second side is deep golden brown and crisp, 2½ to 3 minutes longer.

21. Remove warmed plate from oven, line with double layer of paper towels, and set cutlets on top. Return plate to oven.

22. Increase heat under skillet to medium-high and reheat oil until shimmering.

23. Repeat from step 18 to cook remaining cutlets.

24. Cut lemon into wedges and serve with cutlets.

Pan-Roasted Chicken Breasts

Recipe Stats

TOTAL TIME **50 minutes**
PREPARATION TIME **10 minutes**
ACTIVE COOKING TIME **20 minutes**
YIELD **4 servings**
MAKE AHEAD **Serve immediately**
DIFFICULTY **Intermediate**

Tools

- 12-inch ovensafe skillet *
- chef's knife
- cutting board
- liquid measuring cup
- measuring spoons
- instant-read thermometer **
- kitchen shears
- large, shallow spoon
- serving platter
- tongs
- wooden spoon
- whisk
- paper towels
- potholder ***

* A heavy-bottomed 12-inch skillet is a must for this recipe.
** Undercooked chicken is dangerous to consume, but over-cooked chicken is dry. You should check the internal tempera-ture of several pieces and remove any that are done, while leaving the rest in the oven for a few more minutes.
*** Pan roasting is easy, but the skillet will emerge from the oven with a very hot handle. Use a potholder to move the skillet. We recommend leaving the handle covered with the potholder; it will remind you (or passersby in the kitchen) that this skillet should not be touched with a bare hand.

Overview

Pan roasting is a great way to cook chicken breasts. In the oven, the skin never seems to crisp up enough. That's because chicken breasts cook much faster than a whole bird. Our solu-tion is simple: Brown chicken breasts in a skillet until the fat has rendered and the skin is really crisp, then transfer the skil-let to the oven so the chicken can finish cooking through.

Once the chicken is done, it can be set aside on a plat-ter and you can prepare a pan sauce based on the flavorful browned bits in the pan. Just be careful—the skillet handle is very, very hot.

Another option is to brown the chicken, take it out of the pan, prepare a quick glaze in the pan, and then return the chicken to the pan and continue with the roasting part of this technique. Either way, there are dozens of sauces you can prepare to vary this basic recipe.

We use four split breasts here, but this method also works with eight thighs or a cut-up chicken (we like to use two thighs, two drumsticks, and two split breasts, each breast cut in half crosswise; see How to Pan-Roast Chicken Pieces on page 296 for more details). Before you begin, see How to Split and Trim Breasts on page 293 and How to Make a Pan Sauce on page 232. In this tutorial, we pair the chicken with the Sage-Vermouth Pan Sauce; for pan sauce variations, see pages 331–332.

Ingredients

4 **(10- to 12-ounce) bone-in split chicken breasts, trimmed, brined if desired ***
Salt and pepper
1 **tablespoon vegetable oil**
1 **large shallot, minced**
¾ **cup chicken broth**
½ **cup dry vermouth**
4 **large fresh sage leaves, each leaf torn in half**
3 **tablespoons unsalted butter, cut into 3 pieces and chilled**

* Make sure to trim off the rib section with kitchen shears. For added flavor and moisture, you can brine the chicken (see page 288 for details about brining). However, do not brine kosher chicken; it's already plenty salty.

What Can Go Wrong

Here's a list of common mistakes cooks make when preparing this recipe.

COMMON MISTAKE	BAD OUTCOMES	WHAT YOU SHOULD DO
Not Trimming Chicken Breasts	• **The chicken doesn't brown well.**	Most bone-in, skin-on split chicken breasts are sold with a portion of the rib still attached. There's nothing to eat here and the rib section just makes it challenging to fit four breasts in a single skillet. Removing the rib section with kitchen shears is easy and the breasts will rest a bit flatter in the pan, so they brown better.
Forgetting to Pat Chicken Dry	• **The chicken doesn't brown well.**	Perfectly crisp skin isn't going to happen if you leave moisture on the exterior of the chicken breasts before you put them in the skillet. It's especially important if you brine the chicken breasts since it adds even more moisture that can impede browning. Whether or not you brine the chicken, make sure to pat each chicken breast with paper towels to guarantee good browning.
Impatient Browning	• **The skin is flabby in spots.**	Make sure to brown the skin side of the chicken really well. You need to render all the fat before the chicken goes into the oven. The skin should almost crackle.
Not Using Instant-Read Thermometer	• **The chicken is overcooked and gray.**	Don't try to guess if the chicken is done. Check its progress with an instant-read thermometer and be prepared to remove any smaller pieces that finish cooking a few minutes before the larger ones. Yes, it's easier to buy four pieces that are the same size, but that can be hard to do, especially if you buy pieces shoved tightly into a shrink-wrapped package that distorts their actual size.
Forgetting Skillet Handle Is Hot	• **You badly burn your hand.**	Pan roasting isn't complicated, but things can get tricky when you use the pan to make a sauce. The technique isn't hard: Just transfer the chicken to a platter and build a quick pan sauce on top of the flavorful fond left in the skillet. The trouble is that most cooks are used to holding the skillet handle when it sits on the stovetop. We suggest leaving a potholder on the handle to remind yourself of the risk. Just make sure the potholder is well away from the burner. You don't need to prevent one problem and cause another.

1. Adjust oven rack to middle position and heat oven to 450 degrees.

2. Using kitchen shears, trim off rib section from 4 (10- to 12-ounce) bone-in split chicken breasts.

3. Pat chicken dry with paper towels and season with salt and pepper.

4. Mince 1 large shallot to yield 4 tablespoons.

5. Tear 4 large fresh sage leaves in half.

6. Cut 3 tablespoons butter into 3 pieces and return to refrigerator to keep cold.

7. Heat 1 tablespoon vegetable oil in 12-inch ovensafe skillet over medium-high heat until just smoking.

8. Carefully lay chicken pieces skin side down in skillet and cook until well browned, 6 to 8 minutes.

9. Flip chicken and brown lightly on second side, about 3 minutes.

10. Flip chicken skin side down and transfer skillet to oven.

11. Roast chicken until thickest part of breasts registers 160 degrees on instant-read thermometer, 15 to 18 minutes.

12. Using potholder or dish towel (skillet handle will be very hot), remove skillet from oven.

13. Transfer chicken to serving platter and let rest while making sauce.

14. Being careful of hot skillet handle, pour off all but 1 teaspoon of fat in pan.

15. Add shallot and cook over medium heat until softened, about 2 minutes.

16. Stir in ¾ cup chicken broth, ½ cup vermouth, and sage, scraping up any browned bits.

17. Bring to simmer and cook until liquid is slightly thickened and measures about ¾ cup, about 5 minutes.

18. Stir in any accumulated chicken juices, return to simmer, and cook for 30 seconds.

19. Off heat, remove sage leaves and whisk in butter, 1 piece at a time.

20. Season sauce with salt and pepper to taste, spoon sauce over chicken, and serve.

HOW TO COOK POULTRY

Chicken Provençal

Tools

- Dutch oven
- chef's knife
- cutting board
- paring knife
- dry measuring cups
- liquid measuring cup
- measuring spoons
- can opener
- dish towels
- fine-mesh strainer
- garlic press
- large plate
- rasp-style grater
- tongs
- wooden spoon
- paper towels

Ingredients

- 12   (5- to 7-ounce) bone-in chicken thighs, trimmed
        Salt and pepper
- 3   tablespoons olive oil *
- 1   pound white mushrooms, trimmed, halved if small or medium, quartered if large
- 2   onions, chopped fine
- 6   garlic cloves, minced (2 tablespoons)
- 1   anchovy fillet, rinsed and minced **
- 1   teaspoon herbes de Provence ***
- ⅛   teaspoon cayenne pepper
- 2   tablespoons all-purpose flour
- 2   tablespoons tomato paste
- ⅓   cup dry white wine
- 2½   cups chicken broth
- 1   (14.5-ounce) can diced tomatoes, drained
- 2   bay leaves
- ½   cup niçoise olives, pitted and chopped
- ¼   cup minced fresh parsley
- ½   teaspoon grated lemon zest

Overview

Chicken stews and chicken braises are prepared with boneless and bone-in parts, respectively. As with meat stews and braises, choosing the right part to use is key to success. The delicate white meat of chicken breasts dries out with long cooking, and drumsticks are awkward to eat. Fortunately, chicken thighs are ideal.

This recipe, Chicken Provençal, is a chicken braise, so you'll be using bone-in, skin-on chicken thighs. The thighs are browned in batches to give them good color and develop fond that will give deep, chicken-y richness to the sauce. Next, aromatic vegetables are sautéed to coax out and concentrate their flavors, then flour for thickening is stirred in, along with tomato paste. Both wine and broth are poured into the pot to create the simmering liquid, but before the browned chicken thighs are added, you'll be removing and discarding the skin. If left on, the skin turns soggy and limp and is no fun to eat. This braise cooks for more than an hour, so simmering takes place in a 300-degree oven.

After you master this technique, you can create chicken braises with any number of flavor profiles—from Italian to Southwestern—simply by altering the seasonings.

* The olive oil called for here is for browning the chicken and sautéing the mushrooms and onions. Save your best-quality extra-virgin olive oil for a recipe where heat won't destroy its flavor compounds. Instead, use less-expensive regular olive oil—it has a higher smoke point, which makes it good for browning.

** Anchovy fillets, a traditional ingredient in chicken Provençal, are a staple in our pantry and a secret ingredient in many of our recipes—they add a big boost of flavor, but not always the fishy flavor that one might expect. Anchovies are sold either packed in salt or in olive oil. Because salt-packed anchovies are whole (they contain bones and heads), they require more work on the cook's part. Oil-packed anchovies are already filleted and so can be used straight from the tin or jar.

*** Herbes de Provence is an aromatic blend of dried Mediterranean herbs such as rosemary, basil, marjoram, bay leaves, thyme, and lavender. It is available in the spice aisle of most supermarkets. Briefly sautéing the herbes de Provence allows the flavors to bloom and become more fragrant.

Recipe Stats

TOTAL TIME **3 hours**
PREPARATION TIME **30 minutes**
ACTIVE COOKING TIME **2½ hours**
YIELD **6 to 8 servings**
MAKE AHEAD **Refrigerate for up to 2 days**
DIFFICULTY **Intermediate**

What Can Go Wrong

Here's a list of common mistakes cooks make when preparing this recipe.

COMMON MISTAKE	BAD OUTCOMES	WHAT YOU SHOULD DO
Not Trimming Chicken	• **The sauce is greasy.**	Take the time to trim the chicken thighs well—don't cook them straight out of the package. Use a sharp paring knife to cut away any skin that extends beyond the meat, as well as any clumps of fat. Chicken thighs are fatty, and trimming off what you can before braising will reduce the amount of grease that ends up in the sauce.
Not Browning Chicken Enough	• **The sauce is bland.** • **The sauce isn't very chicken-y.**	When browning the chicken thighs, heat the oil until it begins to smoke, and don't add the thighs any sooner. Once the thighs are in the pot, leave them alone—don't move or flip them before it's time—so that they brown deeply. The better the browning on the chicken, the more fond that develops on the bottom of the pot and the better the flavor of the braise will be. Don't worry if the thighs are taking longer to brown than the recipe indicates—there's no risk of overcooking them at this point.
Not Browning Mushrooms Enough	• **The sauce tastes weak and washed-out.** • **The mushrooms have an unappealing "canned" texture.**	Vegetables are loaded with water. This is especially true of mushrooms, one of the aromatic vegetables in this braise. The mushrooms will release some of their moisture as they cook; by cooking them until the moisture evaporates and the mushrooms are browned, you are ensuring that no excess water will make its way into the braise and dilute the taste and texture of the sauce. Nicely browned mushrooms will also have a meaty flavor of their own and possess a better texture.
Shortening Simmering Time	• **The chicken is chewy.** • **The chicken doesn't easily come away from the bone.**	For fully tender chicken, there's no rushing the simmering time. When you test the chicken for doneness, test the largest thigh in the pot. If it's done—a paring knife inserted into the thickest part meets very little resistance—you can be certain that the others are ready, too.

1. Adjust oven rack to lower-middle position and heat oven to 300 degrees.

2. Pat chicken dry with paper towels and season with salt and pepper.

3. Heat 1 tablespoon olive oil in Dutch oven over medium-high heat until just smoking.

4. Add 6 trimmed chicken thighs skin side down and cook without moving them until skin is crisp and well browned, about 5 minutes.

5. Using tongs, turn chicken pieces and brown on second side, about 5 minutes longer.

6. Transfer chicken to large plate.

7. Repeat with 1 tablespoon more oil and 6 more chicken thighs, then transfer to plate and set aside. Discard fat from pot.

8. Add 1 tablespoon olive oil to Dutch oven and heat over medium heat until shimmering.

9. Trim 1 pound white mushrooms and halve (quarter if large). Add mushrooms, 2 finely chopped onions, and ¼ teaspoon salt to pot.

10. Cover and cook until mushrooms have released their liquid and onions have softened, about 5 minutes.

11. Uncover and continue to cook until mushrooms are dry and browned, about 10 minutes, stirring occasionally with wooden spoon.

12. Mince 6 garlic cloves. Rinse and mince 1 anchovy fillet.

13. Stir minced garlic and anchovy, 1 teaspoon herbes de Provence, and ⅛ teaspoon cayenne into pot. Cook until fragrant, 30 seconds.

14. Stir in 2 tablespoons all-purpose flour and 2 tablespoons tomato paste and cook for 1 minute.

15. Stir in ⅓ cup dry white wine, scraping up any browned bits.

16. Gradually stir in 2½ cups chicken broth, smoothing out any lumps.

17. Stir in 1 (14.5-ounce) can drained diced tomatoes and 2 bay leaves.

18. Remove and discard skin from chicken thighs.

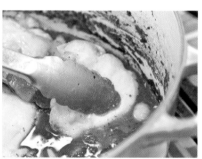

19. Submerge chicken in liquid and add accumulated chicken juices to pot.

20. Increase heat to high, bring to simmer, and cover.

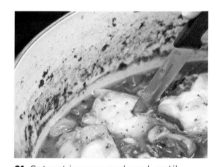

21. Set pot in oven and cook until chicken offers little resistance when poked with tip of paring knife but still clings to bones, about 1¼ hours.

22. Remove pot from oven.

23. Discard bay leaves. Stir in ½ cup pitted and chopped niçoise olives, cover, and let sit for 5 minutes.

24. Stir in ¼ cup minced fresh parsley and ½ teaspoon grated lemon zest. Season with salt and pepper to taste and serve.

Extra-Crunchy Fried Chicken

Recipe Stats

TOTAL TIME **2 hours**
PREPARATION TIME **15 minutes**
ACTIVE COOKING TIME **40 minutes**
MAKE AHEAD **Serve immediately**
YIELD **4 servings**
DIFFICULTY **Intermediate**

Tools

- Dutch oven *
- rimmed baking sheet
- chef's knife
- cutting board
- dry measuring cups
- liquid measuring cup
- measuring spoons
- candy/deep-fry thermometer **
- kitchen shears
- large plate or platter
- large mixing bowls
- tongs
- whisk
- wire rack
- paper towels
- plastic wrap

* A pot that has a capacity of at least 6 quarts (11 inches in diameter) will allow you to fry all the pieces at once. If your pot is smaller, you will need to fry the chicken in two batches.
** We prefer to clip a candy/deep-fry thermometer onto the side of the pot before turning on the heat. However, if you have a digital instant-read thermometer capable of registering temperatures up to 400 degrees, you can spot-check the oil instead.

Overview

There's no arguing the point: Making even the simplest fried chicken is a kitchen production. So when you do go through the trouble, the recipe had better deliver. With a quick buttermilk brine to season the meat, keep it moist, and tenderize it, and with a simple coating of buttermilk-moistened flour that fries up to a deeply bronzed, crisp, and crunchy crust, this recipe will please the cook and diners alike.

Although it's not uncommon for fried chicken to be deep-fried, here we use the shallow-frying technique, but because the chicken is still cooking in a fair amount of fat, we call on a Dutch oven as the cooking vessel rather than a skillet. With the chicken parts only partially submerged in oil, the cooking time is longer than if they were fully submerged, but this suits slow-cooking bone-in chicken pieces just fine. Covering the pot during the first half of cooking helps ensure that the interior meat will be done at the same time as the exterior crust.

If you have leftovers, they crisp up and reheat nicely. Heat them in a 375-degree oven for 10 to 15 minutes. Before you begin, see How to Cut Up a Whole Chicken on page 290 and How to Fry on page 301.

Ingredients

2	**tablespoons salt**
2	**cups plus 6 tablespoons buttermilk**
1	**(3½-pound) whole chicken, cut into 8 pieces (4 breast pieces, 2 drumsticks, 2 thighs), trimmed, wings discarded ***
3	**cups all-purpose flour**
2	**teaspoons baking powder**
¾	**teaspoon dried thyme**
½	**teaspoon pepper**
¼	**teaspoon garlic powder**
4–5	**cups peanut oil ****

* Because the chicken is put into a buttermilk brine, do not use a kosher chicken. If your chicken is larger than 3½ pounds, you may have to fry the chicken in two batches.
** You can also use vegetable shortening or vegetable oil in this recipe. Do not use canola oil.

What Can Go Wrong

Here's a list of common mistakes cooks make when preparing this recipe.

COMMON MISTAKE	BAD OUTCOMES	WHAT YOU SHOULD DO
Soaking Chicken Too Long	• **The chicken is too salty.**	After putting the brining chicken into the refrigerator, note the time or set a timer for 1 hour. Do not let the chicken brine for much longer than that, because the chicken will absorb too much salt and will taste overseasoned.
Frying in Wrong Type of Fat	• **The chicken has a slight off-flavor.**	For the best-tasting fried chicken, use refined peanut oil, vegetable oil, or vegetable shortening. Do not use canola oil, which we dislike for frying because it leaves food with a stale, slightly fishy flavor and aroma. Do not use olive oil, either—its high cost, low smoke point, and distinctive flavor make it a poor choice for frying.
Crowding Chicken in Pot	• **The chicken is greasy.** • **The chicken pieces stick together.**	Rather than overcrowd, cook in batches. It's best to avoid even a "tight squeeze"—not only might the pieces end up sticking together, the oil temperature will plummet, resulting in greasy fried chicken. Before you add any chicken to the pot, assess whether all the pieces will fit comfortably in a single layer. If not, add only four of the pieces; do not place six in the first batch and two in the second because having so few pieces in the pot will throw off the timing of the cooking.
Not Getting Oil Hot Enough	• **The chicken is greasy.** • **The chicken does not crisp properly.** • **The chicken does not brown properly.**	Use a thermometer to monitor the oil's temperature, and don't add the chicken until the oil reaches 375 degrees. If after 10 or 15 minutes the oil refuses to come up to temperature, turn up the burner a bit and keep heating the oil. If the chicken is added before the oil is ready, the chicken will be greasy and won't crisp or brown properly.
Getting Oil Too Hot	• **The chicken's exterior browns faster than the interior cooks through.**	Use a thermometer to monitor the oil's temperature, and if the temperature rises above 375 degrees, remove the pot from the heat and allow the oil to cool to 375 degrees before adding the chicken.
Forgetting to Cover Pot at Outset	• **The chicken doesn't cook through in the time indicated.**	Make sure to cover the pot immediately after adding the chicken to the hot oil. The cover traps heat inside the pot so that the chicken cooks through in a timely fashion. The cover also helps the temperature of the oil to recover faster. After turning the chicken pieces so that the browned side is facing up, continue cooking uncovered so that the crisp crusts won't soften.

1. Cut 1 (3½-pound) whole chicken into 8 pieces (2 thighs, 2 drumsticks, 4 breast pieces).

2. Whisk together 2 cups buttermilk and 2 tablespoons salt in large bowl until salt is dissolved.

3. Add chicken pieces to bowl and stir to coat.

4. Cover bowl with plastic wrap and refrigerate for 1 hour. (Don't let chicken soak much longer or it will become too salty.)

5. Whisk together 3 cups all-purpose flour, 2 teaspoons baking powder, ¾ teaspoon dried thyme, ½ teaspoon pepper, and ¼ teaspoon garlic powder.

6. Add 6 tablespoons buttermilk to flour mixture.

7. With your fingers, rub flour mixture and buttermilk together until buttermilk is evenly incorporated and mixture resembles coarse, wet sand.

8. Working in 2 batches, drop chicken pieces into flour mixture and turn to thoroughly coat, gently pressing flour mixture onto chicken.

9. Shake excess flour from each piece of chicken and transfer to wire rack set over rimmed baking sheet.

10. Clip candy/deep-fry thermometer onto side of heavy-bottomed Dutch oven with at least a 6-quart capacity.

11. Add 4 to 5 cups peanut oil to Dutch oven to measure ¾ inch deep. Heat over medium-high heat until oil reaches 375 degrees.

12. Place chicken pieces skin side down in oil.

13. Cover and fry for 4 minutes.

14. Remove lid and lift chicken pieces to check for even browning; rearrange if some pieces are browning faster than others.

15. Check temperature of oil. Oil should be about 300 degrees. Adjust burner, if necessary, to regulate temperature of oil.

16. Cover and continue frying until deep golden brown, another 4 to 6 minutes.

17. Using tongs, turn chicken pieces over.

18. Check temperature of oil. Adjust burner as needed to maintain oil temperature of about 315 degrees for remainder of cooking time.

19. Continue to fry, uncovered, until chicken pieces are deep golden brown on second side, 6 to 8 minutes longer.

20. Using tongs, transfer chicken to plate lined with triple layer of paper towels.

21. Let sit for 5 minutes to drain before serving.

Classic Holiday Turkey

Overview

Cooking the holiday turkey can strike fear into the most seasoned cook. The challenge is the bird itself. The white meat overcooks easily and can turn out chalky and dry. The dark meat has the opposite problem—it has a lot of connective tissue and fat and benefits from more cooking. In fact, the white meat is best cooked to an internal temperature of 160 degrees, while the dark meat is best cooked to 175 degrees. Plus, you have the challenge of getting the skin crisp at the same time the meat is actually done.

Relax. We have a solution. First, we brine the bird (see chart on page 288). The salt seasons the bird and changes the muscle structure so that the breast is able to hold on to more of its natural juices, even if it is slightly overcooked. Brining requires 6 to 12 hours, so start this process the day before you plan to serve the turkey.

Once the turkey comes out of the brine, it's very wet, and all that moisture will make it tough to get crisp skin. Start by patting the bird dry with paper towels. Then air-dry the bird, uncovered, in the refrigerator for at least 8 hours (or overnight). A similar technique is used to make the skin on Peking duck shatteringly crisp.

As for our roasting technique, we much prefer smaller birds—and we don't stuff them. It's much easier to get a 12- to 14-pound bird evenly cooked if it's not packed with stuffing, which just slows down the process and ensures that the breast meat will be dried out by the time the entire bird is done. Finally, we found it best to roast the turkey in a V-rack, and we start the bird breast side down. This shields the breast meat during the first part of the cooking time and helps ensure that the dark meat is fully cooked by the time the breast meat is done. Serve with Giblet Pan Gravy (page 339). Before you begin, see How to Carve a Whole Bird on page 300.

Recipe Stats

TOTAL TIME **17 hours**
PREPARATION TIME **30 minutes**
ACTIVE COOKING TIME **20 minutes**
YIELD **10 to 12 servings**
MAKE AHEAD **Brine and air-dry up to 1 day ahead**
DIFFICULTY **Intermediate**

Tools

- rimmed baking sheet
- roasting pan *
- small saucepan
- V-rack
- carving board
- chef's knife
- cutting board
- slicing knife
- liquid measuring cup
- instant-read thermometer
- large container or bucket **
- mixing bowl
- pastry brush
- vegetable peeler
- whisk
- wire rack
- aluminum foil
- kitchen twine
- paper towels

* If you don't have a roasting pan, you can use a disposable pan. We recommend that you set a disposable pan on a rimmed baking sheet for extra stability.

** Brining the turkey ensures that the white meat doesn't dry out in the oven. You will need a container or bucket large enough to hold the turkey and 2 gallons of water. If the container won't fit in your refrigerator, you can keep it in a cool spot where the temperature is below 40 degrees. Alternatively, brine the turkey in an insulated cooler, adding some ice to ensure the temperature remains below 40 degrees.

Ingredients

- 1 **cup salt**
- 1 **(12- to 14-pound) turkey, trimmed, neck, giblets, and tailpiece removed and reserved for Giblet Pan Gravy (page 339) ***
- 6 **sprigs fresh thyme**
- 2 **onions, chopped coarse**
- 2 **carrots, peeled and chopped coarse**
- 2 **celery ribs, chopped coarse**
- 3 **tablespoons unsalted butter**
- 1 **cup water, plus extra as needed**

* We use a natural turkey, but a kosher bird or a bird that has been injected with a salty broth solution, such as a Butterball, can be used (skip the brining step). See page 286 for more details about buying a turkey. The gravy relies on making a broth with the reserved turkey parts, then utilizing the caramelized vegetables left in the pan after roasting the turkey. We make the broth for the gravy while the turkey air-dries (it will keep for up to 1 day), but depending on the timing, you can also prepare it while the turkey is brining.

What Can Go Wrong

Here's a list of common mistakes cooks make when preparing this recipe.

COMMON MISTAKE	BAD OUTCOMES	WHAT YOU SHOULD DO
Buying Kosher or Self-Basting Bird	• **The turkey is too salty.**	These birds are processed with salt, so if you brine these birds, they will be too salty. However, you can still use our air-drying and roasting techniques. If you aren't sure if you bought a self-basting bird, check the label. If there are ingredients (like broth) listed, the bird is self-basting. Note that the classic Butterball is self-basting.
Not Brining Bird	• **The turkey is bland.** • **The white meat is dry and chalky.**	Trust us: Brining works. If you skip this step, the turkey will be bland and the white meat will be so dry that it will need to be smothered in gravy to be edible. But don't brine the bird for longer than 12 hours; the bird will continue to absorb salt and become unpleasantly salty.
Not Flipping Turkey During Roasting	• **The white meat is chalky and dry.** • **The dark meat is bloody at the bone.**	Starting the bird breast side down and then flipping it is the key to getting the legs to cook faster. If you skip this step (and simply cook the turkey breast side up, as recommended in most recipes), you will need to overcook the white meat while you wait for the dark meat to come up to temperature, or you will serve bloody dark meat.
Cooking Bird by Time, Not Temperature	• **The turkey is undercooked.** • **The turkey is overcooked.**	When cooking such a big roast, there are a lot of variables. Depending on the size and accuracy of your oven, the cooking time might change. Use an instant-read thermometer to determine when the turkey is done. Check the temperature in both sides of the breast, sliding the probe into the thickest part of the meat, away from the bone. Also check the temperature of the dark meat. The white meat is done when its temperature reaches 160 degrees; the dark meat should be cooked to 175 degrees.
Not Resting Bird for 30 Minutes	• **The bird is hard to carve.** • **The meat is very dry.**	Letting the roasted bird rest for 30 minutes before carving accomplishes several things. First, it's easier to slice the bird when it's not scorchingly hot. The meat will still be plenty hot after resting; there's a lot of residual heat inside the bird. Second, as the bird rests, the muscle fibers relax and reabsorb juices in the meat. If you slice any roast too early, those juices end up on the carving board, not in the meat. If you want a juicy bird, let it rest. Use the half-hour of resting time to finish up side dishes!

Roasting Times for Turkeys

Use the times below as guidelines; gauge doneness according to internal temperatures. Roast the turkey until the legs move freely and the thickest part of the breast registers 160 degrees and the thickest part of the thigh registers 175 degrees on an instant-read thermometer. If cooking an 18- to 22-pound bird, you may choose not to rotate the bird; in that case, roast it breast-side up for the entire cooking time.

	12 TO 15 POUNDS	15 TO 18 POUNDS	18 TO 22 POUNDS
Number of Servings	10 to 12	14 to 16	20 to 22
Oven Temperature	400 degrees	400 degrees	425 degrees, reduce to 325 after 1 hour
Breast Side Down Roasting Time	45 minutes	45 minutes	1 hour
Breast Side Up Roasting Time	50 to 60 minutes	1¼ hours	2 hours
Resting Time	30 minutes	30 minutes	35 to 40 minutes

1. Trim any excess fat from 1 (12- to 14-pound) turkey. Remove neck, giblets, and tailpiece; reserve for pan gravy.

2. Dissolve 1 cup salt in 2 gallons cold water in large container.

3. Submerge turkey in brine, cover, and refrigerate or store in cool spot (40 degrees or less) for 6 to 12 hours.

4. Set wire rack in rimmed baking sheet.

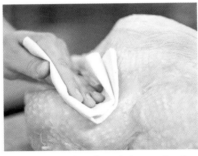

5. Remove turkey from brine and pat dry, inside and out, with paper towels.

6. Place turkey on prepared wire rack. Refrigerate, uncovered, for at least 8 hours or overnight. (Meanwhile, make gravy broth; see recipe page 339).

7. Peel and coarsely chop 2 onions.

8. Peel and coarsely chop 2 carrots.

9. Trim and coarsely chop 2 celery ribs.

10. Melt 3 tablespoons unsalted butter.

11. Adjust oven rack to lowest position and heat oven to 400 degrees.

12. Line V-rack with heavy-duty aluminum foil and poke several holes in foil.

13. Set V-rack in roasting pan and spray foil with vegetable oil spray.

14. Toss 6 sprigs fresh thyme and half of vegetables with 1 tablespoon melted butter in bowl and place inside turkey.

15. Tie turkey legs together with kitchen twine and tuck wings behind back.

16. Scatter remaining vegetables in pan. Pour 1 cup water over vegetable mixture in pan.

17. Brush turkey breast with 1 table-spoon melted butter, then place turkey breast side down on V-rack.

18. Brush back of turkey with 1 tablespoon butter.

19. Roast turkey for 45 minutes, then remove pan from oven. While turkey is roasting, prepare gravy.

20. Using 2 large wads of paper towels, turn turkey breast side up. If liquid in pan has totally evaporated, add another ½ cup water.

21. Return turkey to oven and roast until breast registers 160 degrees and thighs register 175 degrees, 50 to 60 minutes.

22. Remove turkey from oven. Gently tip turkey so that any accumulated juices in cavity run into pan.

23. Transfer turkey to carving board and let rest, uncovered, for 30 minutes.

24. While turkey rests, finish gravy, deglazing pan on stovetop and stirring pan drippings into gravy. Carve turkey and serve with gravy.

HOW TO COOK POULTRY

Recipe Library

Sautéed Chicken Cutlets

✔ **WHY THIS RECIPE WORKS:** Thin, lean chicken cutlets can all too easily overcook. Plus, it's tricky to get good browning (which translates to both flavor and visual appeal, and also leaves behind fond to create a pan sauce). Flouring the cutlets protected the meat from drying out and helped encourage browning and prevent sticking. To avoid overcooking, we cooked long enough on the first side to achieve browning, then flipped the cutlets and cooked them only a few seconds on the second side. Because the cutlets are so thin and would cool off quickly, we kept them warm in a low oven while making our pan sauce.

Sautéed Chicken Cutlets
SERVES 4

To make slicing the chicken easier, freeze it for 15 minutes. Prepare the pan sauce after transferring the cutlets to the oven. Any of the pan sauces on pages 331–332 would also pair well with the cutlets. See Core Techniques on pages 294 and 295 for more details on preparing and cooking cutlets.

- 4 (6- to 8-ounce) boneless, skinless chicken breasts, tenderloins removed, trimmed
- ¼ cup all-purpose flour
- 1 teaspoon salt
- ½ teaspoon pepper
- 2 tablespoons vegetable oil
- 1 recipe pan sauce (recipes follow)

1. Adjust oven rack to middle position and heat oven to 200 degrees. Halve chicken horizontally, then cover chicken halves with plastic wrap and pound to even ¼-inch thickness with meat pounder. Combine flour, salt, and pepper in shallow dish or pie plate. Pat chicken dry with paper towels. Working with 1 cutlet at a time, dredge in flour mixture, shaking off excess, and transfer to large plate.

2. Heat 1 tablespoon oil in 12-inch skillet over medium-high heat until just smoking. Place 4 cutlets in skillet and cook until browned on first side, about 2 minutes. Flip cutlets and continue to cook until second side is opaque, 15 to 20 seconds; transfer to large ovensafe platter. Repeat with remaining 1 tablespoon oil and remaining 4 cutlets. Tent loosely with aluminum foil, and transfer to oven to keep warm. Prepare sauce; pour sauce over chicken and serve immediately,

Lighter Pan Sauces for Chicken

✔ **WHY THIS RECIPE WORKS:** Sautéed chicken cutlets topped with a pan sauce are quick and easy to prepare. But while the chicken is lean, the sauces are not—classic pan sauces typically call for a generous amount of butter. We wanted a lighter, less rich sauce for our chicken that would still take advantage of the fond left in the skillet for flavor. We followed the usual steps for preparing a pan sauce—sautéing aromatics in the empty skillet, adding liquid and scraping up the browned bits from the bottom of the pan, simmering to concentrate flavors, and finally finishing the sauce with cold butter. But adding 1 teaspoon of flour to the aromatics as a thickener was a simple step that allowed us to cut back the butter. Cutting back on the butter also allowed the other flavors to take center stage.

Lemon-Caper Pan Sauce
MAKES ENOUGH FOR 1 RECIPE SAUTÉED CHICKEN CUTLETS
See Core Technique on page 232 for more details on preparing pan sauces.

- 2 teaspoons vegetable oil
- 1 shallot, minced
- 1 teaspoon all-purpose flour
- ¾ cup chicken broth
- 1 tablespoon capers, rinsed and chopped
- 1 tablespoon chopped fresh parsley
- 1 tablespoon unsalted butter, chilled
- 2 teaspoons lemon juice
  Salt and pepper

Heat oil in now-empty skillet over low heat until shimmering. Add shallot and cook, stirring often, until softened, about 2 minutes. Add flour and cook, stirring constantly, for 30 seconds. Slowly whisk in broth, scraping up any browned bits. Bring to simmer and cook until reduced to ½ cup, 2 to 3 minutes. Stir in any accumulated chicken juices; return to simmer and cook for 30 seconds. Off heat, whisk in capers, parsley, butter, and lemon juice. Season with salt and pepper to taste. Pour sauce over chicken and serve immediately.

Vermouth, Leek, and Tarragon Pan Sauce
MAKES ENOUGH FOR 1 RECIPE SAUTÉED CHICKEN CUTLETS
See Core Technique on page 232 for more details on preparing pan sauces.

- 2 teaspoons vegetable oil
- 1 leek, white and light green parts only, halved lengthwise, sliced ¼ inch thick, and washed thoroughly
- 1 teaspoon all-purpose flour
- ¾ cup chicken broth
- ½ cup dry vermouth or dry white wine
- 1 tablespoon unsalted butter, chilled
- 2 teaspoons chopped fresh tarragon
- 1 teaspoon whole-grain mustard
  Salt and pepper

Heat oil in now-empty skillet over medium heat until shimmering. Add leek and cook, stirring often, until softened and lightly browned, about 5 minutes. Add flour and cook, stirring constantly, for 30 seconds. Slowly whisk in broth and vermouth, scraping up any browned bits. Bring to simmer and cook until reduced to ¾ cup, 3 to 5 minutes. Stir in any accumulated chicken juices; return to simmer and cook for 30 seconds. Off heat, whisk in butter, tarragon, and mustard. Season with salt and pepper to taste. Pour sauce over chicken and serve immediately.

Sherry, Red Pepper, and Toasted Garlic Pan Sauce

MAKES ENOUGH FOR 1 RECIPE SAUTÉED CHICKEN CUTLETS
See Core Technique on page 232 for more details on preparing pan sauces.

- 2 teaspoons vegetable oil
- 3 garlic cloves, minced
- 1 teaspoon all-purpose flour
- ¼ teaspoon paprika
- ¾ cup chicken broth
- ½ cup plus 1 teaspoon dry sherry
- ¼ cup jarred roasted red peppers, patted dry and cut into ¼-inch pieces
- 1 tablespoon unsalted butter, chilled
- ½ teaspoon chopped fresh thyme
  Salt and pepper

Heat oil and garlic in now-empty skillet over low heat. Cook, stirring often, until garlic turns golden but not brown, about 1 minute. Add flour and paprika and cook, stirring constantly, for 30 seconds. Slowly whisk in broth and ½ cup sherry, scraping up any browned bits. Bring to simmer and cook until reduced to ¾ cup, 3 to 5 minutes. Stir in any accumulated chicken juices; return to simmer and cook for 30 seconds. Off heat, whisk in peppers, butter, thyme, and remaining 1 teaspoon sherry. Season with salt and pepper to taste. Pour sauce over chicken and serve immediately.

Brandy, Cream, and Chive Pan Sauce

MAKES ENOUGH FOR 1 RECIPE SAUTÉED CHICKEN CUTLETS
Be sure to add the broth to the skillet before adding the brandy. See Core Technique on page 232 for more details on preparing pan sauces.

- 2 teaspoons vegetable oil
- 1 shallot, minced
- 1 teaspoon all-purpose flour
- ¾ cup chicken broth
- ¼ cup plus 1 tablespoon brandy
- 2 tablespoons heavy cream
- 2 tablespoons chopped fresh chives
- 2 teaspoons lemon juice
- 1 teaspoon Dijon mustard
  Salt and pepper

Heat oil in now-empty skillet over low heat until shimmering. Add shallot and cook, stirring often, until softened, about 2 minutes. Add flour and cook, stirring constantly, for 30 seconds. Slowly whisk in broth, then ¼ cup brandy, scraping up any browned bits. Bring to simmer and cook until reduced to ½ cup, 2 to 3 minutes. Stir in cream and any accumulated chicken juices; return to simmer and cook until thickened, about 1 minute. Off heat, whisk in chives, lemon juice, mustard, and remaining 1 tablespoon brandy. Season with salt and pepper to taste. Pour sauce over chicken and serve immediately.

Sautéed Turkey Cutlets

WHY THIS RECIPE WORKS: Turkey cutlets offer a quick, satisfying option for a weeknight dinner. Choosing cutlets of even thickness was the first step in ensuring that they cooked uniformly from end to end. We found it wasn't necessary to flour the cutlets as long as the pan was hot enough, and olive oil was the best medium for sautéing the cutlets, providing pleasant flavor and a relatively high smoke point. Heating the pan properly was essential to a well-browned crust. Finally, we determined it was best to brown the cutlets on one side only; they are simply too thin to brown well on both sides without overcooking.

Sautéed Turkey Cutlets with Honey-Mustard Pan Sauce

SERVES 4

One cutlet per person makes a skimpy serving, so we call for a total of six to serve four people. If you prefer, replace the Honey-Mustard Pan Sauce with Warm-Spiced Pan Sauce with Currants and Almonds (page 326). If not making a pan sauce, let the turkey rest for 5 minutes before serving in step 2.

TURKEY
- 6 (4-ounce) turkey cutlets, trimmed
  Salt and pepper
- 2 tablespoons olive oil

SAUCE
- 1 shallot, minced
- 1 cup dry white wine
- ½ cup chicken broth
- 2 teaspoons honey
- 3 tablespoons unsalted butter, cut into 3 pieces and chilled
- 1 tablespoon Dijon mustard
- 1 tablespoon chopped fresh tarragon
  Salt and pepper

1. FOR THE TURKEY: Adjust oven rack to middle position and heat oven to 200 degrees. Pat turkey dry with paper towels and season with salt and pepper.

2. Heat 1 tablespoon oil in 12-inch skillet over medium-high heat. Place half of cutlets in skillet and cook until light golden brown on first side, 2 to 2½ minutes. Flip cutlets and continue to cook until second side is opaque, about 1 minute; transfer to large ovensafe platter. Repeat with remaining 1 tablespoon oil and remaining cutlets; transfer to platter. Tent loosely with aluminum foil and transfer to oven to keep warm while preparing sauce.

3. FOR THE SAUCE: Add shallot to oil left in skillet and cook over medium-low heat, stirring constantly, until softened, about 1 minute. Stir in wine, broth, and honey, scraping up any browned bits. Bring to boil and cook until liquid is reduced to ⅓ cup, about 10 minutes, adding any accumulated turkey juices after about 8 minutes. Off heat, whisk in butter and mustard until butter is melted and sauce is slightly thickened. Stir in tarragon and season with salt and pepper to taste. Spoon sauce over turkey and serve immediately.

Warm-Spiced Pan Sauce with Currants and Almonds

MAKES ABOUT ⅔ CUP, ENOUGH FOR 1 RECIPE SAUTÉED
TURKEY CUTLETS

We prefer a fruity red wine, such as Zinfandel, in this recipe.

- 2 teaspoons brown sugar
- ⅛ teaspoon cayenne pepper
  Pinch ground cloves
  Pinch ground allspice
- 1 tablespoon olive oil
- 2 cinnamon sticks
- 1 shallot, minced
- 2 garlic cloves, minced
- 2 teaspoons grated fresh ginger
- 1 cup red wine
- ½ cup chicken broth
- 3 tablespoons dried currants
- 3 tablespoons unsalted butter, cut into 3 pieces and chilled
- 2 tablespoons chopped fresh parsley
  Salt and pepper
- ¼ cup sliced almonds, toasted

Mix brown sugar, cayenne, cloves, and allspice in bowl; set aside. Add oil, spice mixture, and cinnamon sticks to now-empty skillet and cook, stirring constantly, until fragrant, about 1 minute. Add shallot and cook, stirring frequently, until softened, about 1 minute. Add garlic and ginger and cook, stirring constantly, until fragrant, about 30 seconds. Stir in wine, broth, and currants, scraping up any browned bits. Bring to boil and cook until liquid is reduced to ⅓ cup, about 10 minutes, adding any accumulated turkey juices after about 8 minutes. Off heat, discard cinnamon sticks, then whisk in butter until melted and sauce is slightly thickened. Stir in parsley and season with salt and pepper to taste. Spoon sauce over turkey, sprinkle with almonds, and serve immediately.

Crisp Breaded Chicken Cutlets

✔ **WHY THIS RECIPE WORKS:** Most chicken cutlets offer a thin, uneven, pale crust; we wanted a thick, crisp, flavorful coating that stayed put. We found that pounding the chicken ensured the cutlets would cook evenly. Homemade bread crumbs were a must, providing a subtly sweet flavor and light, crisp texture, while adding a little oil to our egg wash allowed the crust to brown more deeply. Finally, pan-frying the cutlets two at a time (rather than four) reduced the amount of steam in the skillet, allowing the breading to crisp and brown evenly.

Crisp Breaded Chicken Cutlets

SERVES 4

If you'd rather not prepare fresh bread crumbs, use panko, the extra-crisp Japanese bread crumbs. The chicken is cooked in batches of two because the crust is noticeably more crisp if the pan is not overcrowded.

- 4 (6- to 8-ounce) boneless, skinless chicken breasts, tenderloins removed, trimmed
  Salt and pepper
- 4–6 slices hearty white sandwich bread, crusts removed, torn into 1½-inch pieces
- ¾ cup all-purpose flour
- 2 large eggs
- 1 tablespoon plus ¾ cup vegetable oil
  Lemon wedges

1. Cover chicken breasts with plastic wrap and pound to even ½-inch thickness with meat pounder. Pat chicken dry with paper towels and season chicken with salt and pepper.

2. Adjust oven rack to lower-middle position, set large heatproof plate on rack, and heat oven to 200 degrees. Process bread in food processor until evenly fine-textured, 20 to 30 seconds (you should have 1½ cups bread crumbs). Transfer bread crumbs to shallow baking dish or pie plate. Place flour in second dish. Lightly beat eggs and 1 tablespoon oil together in third dish.

3. Working with 1 cutlet at a time, dredge in flour, shaking off excess, then coat with egg mixture, allowing excess to drip off. Coat all sides of cutlet with bread crumbs, pressing gently so that crumbs adhere; transfer to prepared wire rack and let sit for 5 minutes.

4. Heat ¾ cup oil in 12-inch nonstick skillet over medium-high heat until shimmering. Place 2 cutlets in skillet and cook until deep golden brown and crisp on first side, about 2½ minutes. Flip cutlets, reduce heat to medium, and continue to cook until deep golden brown and crisp on second side and meat feels firm when pressed gently, 2½ to 3 minutes longer. Remove plate from oven, line with double layer of paper towels, and set cutlets on top. Return plate to oven. Repeat with remaining 2 cutlets. Serve with lemon wedges.

Deviled Crisp Breaded Chicken Cutlets

Rub each breast with generous pinch cayenne pepper before dredging in flour. Lightly beat 3 tablespoons Dijon mustard, 1 tablespoon Worcestershire sauce, and 2 teaspoons minced fresh thyme into eggs along with oil.

Crisp Breaded Chicken Cutlets with Garlic and Oregano

Lightly beat 3 tablespoons minced fresh oregano and 8 minced garlic cloves into eggs along with oil.

Crisp Breaded Chicken Cutlets with Parmesan (Chicken Milanese)

Though Parmesan is the traditional cheese to use in this dish, feel free to substitute Pecorino Romano cheese if you prefer a stronger, more tangy flavor. The cheese is quite susceptible to burning, so be sure to keep a very close eye on the cutlets as they cook. See Recipe Tutorial on page 304 for more details on this recipe.

Mix ¼ cup finely grated Parmesan cheese with bread crumbs in pie plate.

Chicken Saltimbocca

✓ **WHY THIS RECIPE WORKS:** Chicken saltimbocca is a new spin on an old Italian classic, veal saltimbocca. It sounds promising, but adaptations typically take this dish too far from its roots. We wanted to avoid overcomplicating things and give each main element—chicken, prosciutto, sage—its due. Flouring the chicken first allowed the chicken to brown evenly and prevented gummy, uncooked spots. Using thinly sliced prosciutto prevented its flavor from overwhelming the dish. A single sage leaf is the usual garnish, but we wanted more sage flavor, so, in addition to a whole leaf garnish, we also sprinkled some chopped fresh sage over the floured chicken before adding the prosciutto.

Chicken Saltimbocca

SERVES 4

Make sure to buy prosciutto that is thinly sliced, not shaved; also avoid slices that are too thick, as they won't stick to the chicken. The prosciutto slices should be large enough to fully cover one side of each cutlet. To make slicing the chicken easier, freeze it for 15 minutes. Although whole sage leaves make a beautiful presentation, they are optional and can be left out of step 3. See Core Technique on page 294 for more details on cutting chicken breasts into cutlets.

- 4 **(6- to 8-ounce) boneless, skinless chicken breasts, tenderloins removed, trimmed**
- ½ **cup all-purpose flour**
   Salt and pepper
- 1 **tablespoon minced fresh sage plus 8 large fresh leaves (optional)**
- 8 **thin slices prosciutto (3 ounces)**
- ¼ **cup olive oil**
- 1¼ **cups dry vermouth or dry white wine**
- 2 **teaspoons lemon juice**
- 4 **tablespoons unsalted butter, cut into 4 pieces and chilled**
- 1 **tablespoon minced fresh parsley**

1. Halve chicken horizontally, then cover chicken halves with plastic wrap and pound to even ¼-inch thickness with meat pounder. Combine flour and 1 teaspoon pepper in shallow dish or pie plate.

2. Pat chicken dry with paper towels. Working with 1 cutlet at a time, dredge in flour mixture, shaking off excess, and transfer to work surface. Sprinkle cutlets evenly with minced sage. Place 1 prosciutto slice on top of each cutlet, covering sage, and press lightly to help it adhere.

3. Heat 2 tablespoons oil in 12-inch skillet over medium-high heat until shimmering. Add sage leaves, if using, and cook until leaves begin to change color and are fragrant, about 15 to 20 seconds. Remove sage with slotted spoon and transfer to paper towel–lined plate; set aside.

4. Place 4 cutlets in now-empty skillet, prosciutto side down, and cook over medium-high heat until golden brown on first side, about 3 minutes. Flip cutlets, reduce heat to medium, and continue to cook until no longer pink and lightly browned on second side, about 2 minutes longer. Transfer cutlets to large platter. Wipe out skillet with paper towels. Repeat with remaining 2 tablespoons oil and remaining 4 cutlets; transfer to platter. Tent loosely with aluminum foil and set aside while preparing sauce.

5. Pour off all fat left in skillet. Add vermouth, scraping up any browned bits. Bring to simmer and cook until reduced to ⅓ cup, 5 to 7 minutes. Stir in lemon juice. Reduce heat to low and whisk in butter, 1 piece at a time. Off heat, stir in parsley and season with salt and pepper to taste. Pour sauce over chicken, place sage leaf on top of each cutlet, if using, and serve immediately.

Chicken Marsala

✓ **WHY THIS RECIPE WORKS:** Chicken Marsala is an Italian restaurant staple that sounds promising, but often disappoints, with watery sauce, dry chicken, and overcooked, slimy mushrooms. To rescue this dish, we began by determining the best way to cook it. Not surprisingly, the classic method of sautéing the meat, then using the browned bits left behind as a flavor base for the sauce, was the way to go. Adding some pancetta to the skillet after cooking the chicken gave our dish a flavor boost, and also provided rendered fat in which to cook the mushrooms; this allowed them to brown and crisp. For the sauce, we found that using sweet Marsala—and no chicken broth—was best; reducing it concentrated its flavor, while a little lemon juice tempered the Marsala's sweetness. We finished our sauce with butter for a silky richness.

Chicken Marsala

SERVES 4

Our wine of choice for this dish is Sweet Marsala Fine, an imported wine that gives the sauce body, soft edges, and a smooth finish. To make slicing the chicken easier, freeze it for 15 minutes. See Core Technique on page 294 for more details on cutting chicken breasts into cutlets.

- 4 **(6- to 8-ounce) boneless, skinless chicken breasts, tenderloins removed, trimmed**
- 1 **cup all-purpose flour**
   Salt and pepper
- ¼ **cup vegetable oil**
- 2½ **ounces pancetta, cut into pieces 1 inch long and ⅛ inch wide**
- 8 **ounces white mushrooms, trimmed and sliced thin**
- 1 **garlic clove, minced**
- 1 **teaspoon tomato paste**
- 1½ **cups sweet Marsala**
- 4½ **teaspoons lemon juice**
- 4 **tablespoons unsalted butter, cut into 4 pieces and chilled**
- 2 **tablespoons chopped fresh parsley**

1. Adjust oven rack to middle position and heat oven to 200 degrees. Halve chicken horizontally, then cover chicken halves with plastic wrap and pound to even ¼-inch thickness with meat pounder. Place flour in shallow dish or pie plate.

2. Pat chicken dry with paper towels and season with salt and pepper. Working with 1 cutlet at a time, dredge in flour mixture, shaking off excess, and transfer to large plate.

3. Heat 2 tablespoons oil in 12-inch skillet over medium-high heat until shimmering. Place 4 cutlets in skillet and cook until golden brown on first side, about 3 minutes. Flip cutlets, reduce heat to medium, and cook until no longer pink and lightly browned on second side, about 2 minutes longer; transfer to large ovensafe platter. Wipe out skillet. Repeat with remaining 2 tablespoons oil and remaining 4 cutlets; transfer to platter. Tent loosely with aluminum foil and transfer to oven to keep warm while making sauce.

4. Cook pancetta in now-empty skillet over low heat, stirring occasionally and scraping up any browned bits, until crisp, about 5 minutes. Remove pancetta with slotted spoon and transfer to paper towel–lined plate. Add mushrooms to now-empty skillet, increase heat to medium-high, and cook, stirring occasionally, until softened and lightly browned, about 8 minutes. Stir in garlic, tomato paste, and crisp pancetta and cook until tomato paste begins to brown, about 1 minute. Off heat, stir in Marsala, scraping up any browned bits. Return to high heat, bring to vigorous simmer, and cook, stirring occasionally, until sauce is thickened and measures 1¼ cups, about 5 minutes. Off heat, stir in lemon juice and any accumulated chicken juices. Whisk in butter, 1 piece at a time. Stir in parsley and season with salt and pepper to taste. Pour sauce over chicken and serve immediately.

Chicken Pot Pie with Savory Crumble Topping

WHY THIS RECIPE WORKS: For a streamlined chicken pot pie recipe, we poached boneless, skinless breasts and thighs in chicken broth, which we then used as the foundation of a full-bodied sauce. We opted for the traditional vegetable combination of onion, carrots, and celery and sautéed them separately to preserve their texture. To add chicken flavor to our chicken pot pie's sauce, we stirred a butter-and-flour roux into milk and the poaching liquid and used sautéed mushrooms, soy sauce, and tomato paste to enhance its savory character. Sweet, bright green frozen peas required no precooking—just a stir into the filling. Every chicken pot pie recipe—even a speedy one—needs a crisp, buttery top, so we settled on a "crumble" crust. It was a snap to prepare, and a quick stay in the oven before topping the pot pie with it made sure the savory crumble crust cooked through and crisped up once baked on top of the pot pie.

Chicken Pot Pie with Savory Crumble Topping
SERVES 6

This recipe relies on two unusual ingredients: soy sauce and tomato paste. Do not omit them. They don't convey their distinctive tastes but greatly deepen the savory flavor of the filling. When making the topping, do not substitute milk or half-and-half for the heavy cream.

FILLING

- 1½ pounds boneless, skinless chicken breasts and/or thighs, trimmed
- 3 cups chicken broth
- 2 tablespoons vegetable oil
- 1 onion, chopped fine
- 3 carrots, peeled and sliced ¼ inch thick
- 2 small celery ribs, minced
  Salt and pepper
- 10 ounces cremini mushrooms, trimmed and sliced thin
- 1 teaspoon soy sauce
- 1 teaspoon tomato paste
- 4 tablespoons unsalted butter
- ½ cup all-purpose flour
- 1 cup whole milk
- 2 teaspoons lemon juice
- 3 tablespoons minced fresh parsley
- ¾ cup frozen peas

CRUMBLE TOPPING

- 2 cups (10 ounces) all-purpose flour
- 2 teaspoons baking powder
- ¾ teaspoon salt
- ½ teaspoon pepper
- ⅛ teaspoon cayenne pepper
- 6 tablespoons unsalted butter, cut into ½-inch pieces and chilled
- 1 ounce Parmesan cheese, grated fine (½ cup)
- ¾ cup plus 2 tablespoons heavy cream

1. FOR THE FILLING: Bring chicken and broth to simmer in covered Dutch oven and cook until chicken is tender and cooked through, 8 to 10 minutes. Transfer chicken to large bowl. Pour broth through fine-mesh strainer into liquid measuring cup and reserve. Do not wash pot. Meanwhile, adjust oven rack to upper-middle position and heat oven to 450 degrees.

2. FOR THE TOPPING: Combine flour, baking powder, salt, pepper, and cayenne in large bowl. Sprinkle butter pieces over top of flour. Using fingers, rub butter into flour mixture until it resembles coarse cornmeal. Stir in Parmesan. Add cream and stir until just combined. Crumble mixture into irregularly shaped pieces ranging from ½ to ¾ inch each onto parchment paper–lined rimmed baking sheet. Bake until fragrant and starting to brown, 10 to 13 minutes. Set aside.

3. Heat 1 tablespoon oil in now-empty pot over medium heat until shimmering. Add onion, carrots, celery, ¼ teaspoon salt, and ¼ teaspoon pepper; cover and cook, stirring occasionally, until just tender, 5 to 7 minutes. While vegetables are cooking, use 2 forks to shred chicken into bite-size pieces. Transfer vegetables to bowl with chicken; set aside.

4. Heat remaining 1 tablespoon oil in again-empty pot over medium heat until shimmering. Add mushrooms; cover and cook, stirring occasionally, until mushrooms have released their liquid, about 5 minutes. Remove cover and stir in soy sauce and tomato paste. Increase heat to medium-high and cook, stirring often, until liquid has evaporated, mushrooms are well browned, and dark fond begins to form on surface of pan, about 5 minutes. Transfer mushrooms to bowl with chicken and vegetables. Set aside.

5. Melt butter in again-empty pot over medium heat. Add flour and cook, stirring constantly, for 1 minute. Slowly whisk in reserved chicken broth and milk. Bring to simmer, scraping up any browned bits, and cook until sauce thickens, about 1 minute. Off heat, stir in lemon juice and 2 tablespoons parsley, then stir chicken mixture and peas into sauce. Season with salt and pepper to taste.

6. Pour chicken mixture into 13 by 9-inch baking dish. Scatter crumble topping evenly over filling. Place pot pie on aluminum foil–lined rimmed baking sheet and bake until filling is bubbling and topping is well browned, 12 to 15 minutes. Sprinkle with remaining 1 tablespoon parsley and serve.

Chicken Stir-Fries

✔ WHY THIS RECIPE WORKS: Tired of dry, stringy meat in our chicken stir-fry recipes, we came up with a solution: We soaked the chicken in a combination brine-marinade to add flavor and moisture, then dipped the marinated pieces of chicken in a cornstarch-oil mixture. The cornstarch coating, a modified version of the Chinese technique called velveting, helped the chicken stay moist even with a high-heat cooking method.

Gingery Stir-Fried Chicken and Bok Choy
SERVES 4

To make slicing the chicken easier, freeze it for 15 minutes. Serve with Chinese-Style Sticky Rice (page 206). See Core Technique on page 234 for more details on making stir-fries.

SAUCE
- ¼ cup chicken broth
- 2 tablespoons dry sherry
- 1 tablespoon soy sauce
- 1 tablespoon oyster sauce
- 2 teaspoons grated fresh ginger
- ½ teaspoon toasted sesame oil
- 1 teaspoon cornstarch
- 1 teaspoon sugar
- ¼ teaspoon red pepper flakes

CHICKEN STIR-FRY
- 2 teaspoons grated fresh ginger
- 1 garlic clove, minced
- 2 tablespoons plus 2 teaspoons vegetable oil
- 1 cup water
- ¼ cup soy sauce
- ¼ cup dry sherry
- 1 pound boneless, skinless chicken breasts, trimmed and sliced thin

- 2 **tablespoons toasted sesame oil**
- 1 **tablespoon cornstarch**
- 1 **tablespoon all-purpose flour**
- 1 **pound bok choy, stalks cut on bias into ¼-inch slices and greens cut into ½-inch strips**
- 1 **small red bell pepper, stemmed, seeded, and cut into ¼-inch strips**

1. FOR THE SAUCE: Whisk all ingredients together in small bowl.

2. FOR THE STIR-FRY: Combine ginger, garlic, and 1 teaspoon vegetable oil in small bowl and set aside. Combine water, soy sauce, and sherry in medium bowl. Add chicken and stir to break up clumps. Cover with plastic wrap and refrigerate for at least 20 minutes or up to 1 hour. Pour off excess liquid from chicken.

3. Mix sesame oil, cornstarch, and flour in medium bowl until smooth. Toss chicken in cornstarch mixture until evenly coated.

4. Heat 2 teaspoons vegetable oil in 12-inch nonstick skillet over high heat until smoking. Add half of chicken to skillet in single layer and cook, without stirring, until golden brown on first side, about 1 minute. Flip chicken pieces over and cook until lightly browned on second side, about 30 seconds. Transfer chicken to clean bowl. Repeat with 2 teaspoons vegetable oil and remaining chicken.

5. Add remaining 1 tablespoon vegetable oil to skillet and heat until just smoking. Add bok choy stalks and bell pepper and cook, stirring, until beginning to brown, about 1 minute. Clear center of skillet, add ginger mixture, and cook, mashing mixture into pan, until fragrant, 15 to 20 seconds. Stir mixture into vegetables and continue to cook until stalks are crisp-tender, about 30 seconds longer. Stir in bok choy greens and cook until beginning to wilt, about 30 seconds.

6. Return chicken to skillet. Whisk sauce to recombine, add to skillet, reduce heat to medium, and cook, stirring constantly, until sauce is thickened and chicken is cooked through, about 30 seconds. Transfer to platter and serve immediately.

Spicy Stir-Fried Sesame Chicken with Green Beans and Shiitake Mushrooms
SERVES 4

To make slicing the chicken easier, freeze it for 15 minutes. Serve with Chinese-Style Sticky Rice (page 206). See Core Technique on page 234 for more details on making stir-fries.

SAUCE
- ½ cup chicken broth
- 3 tablespoons soy sauce
- 2 tablespoons dry sherry
- 1 tablespoon plus 1 teaspoon Asian chili-garlic sauce
- 1 tablespoon plus 1 teaspoon sugar
- 2 teaspoons sesame seeds, toasted
- 1 teaspoon toasted sesame oil
- 1 teaspoon cornstarch
- 1 garlic clove, minced

CHICKEN STIR-FRY

- 2 garlic cloves, minced
- 1 teaspoon grated fresh ginger
- 2 tablespoons plus 2 teaspoons vegetable oil
- ¼ cup soy sauce
- ¼ cup dry sherry
- 1 cup water
- 1 pound boneless, skinless chicken breasts, trimmed and sliced thin
- 2 tablespoons plus 1 teaspoon toasted sesame oil
- 1 tablespoon cornstarch
- 1 tablespoon all-purpose flour
- 1 pound green beans, trimmed and cut on bias into 1-inch pieces
- 8 ounces shiitake mushrooms, stemmed and sliced ⅛ inch thick
- 1 teaspoon sesame seeds, toasted

1. FOR THE SAUCE: Whisk all ingredients together in small bowl.

2. FOR THE STIR-FRY: Combine garlic, ginger, and 1 teaspoon vegetable oil in small bowl and set aside. Combine soy sauce, sherry, and water in medium bowl. Add chicken and stir to break up clumps. Cover with plastic wrap and refrigerate for at least 20 minutes or up to 1 hour. Pour off excess liquid from chicken.

3. Mix 2 tablespoons sesame oil, cornstarch, and flour in medium bowl until smooth. Toss chicken in cornstarch mixture until evenly coated.

4. Heat 2 teaspoons vegetable oil in 12-inch nonstick skillet over high heat until smoking. Add half of chicken to skillet in single layer and cook, without stirring, until golden brown on first side, about 1 minute. Flip chicken pieces over and cook until lightly browned on second side, about 30 seconds. Transfer chicken to clean bowl. Repeat with 2 teaspoons vegetable oil and remaining chicken.

5. Add remaining 1 tablespoon vegetable oil to skillet and heat until just smoking. Add green beans and cook, stirring occasionally, 1 minute. Add mushrooms and cook until mushrooms are lightly browned, about 3 minutes. Clear center of skillet, add garlic mixture, and cook, mashing mixture into pan, until fragrant, 15 to 20 seconds. Stir mixture into beans and mushrooms and continue to cook until beans are crisp-tender, about 30 seconds.

6. Return chicken to skillet. Whisk sauce to recombine, add to skillet, reduce heat to medium, and cook, stirring constantly, until sauce is thickened and chicken is cooked through, about 30 seconds. Transfer to platter, drizzle with remaining 1 teaspoon sesame oil, and sprinkle with sesame seeds. Serve immediately.

Pan-Roasted Chicken Breasts

✔ **WHY THIS RECIPE WORKS:** Bone-in chicken breasts offer more flavor than boneless, skinless breasts, but getting the skin to crisp without overcooking the delicate meat can be a challenge. We turned to pan roasting—browning in a skillet on the stovetop and then sliding the skillet into a hot oven to finish. Brining the chicken ensured the meat stayed moist and flavorful. Cooking the chicken at 450 degrees allowed the skin to crisp while the meat cooked through relatively quickly.

Pan-Roasted Chicken Breasts
SERVES 4

We prefer to split whole chicken breasts ourselves because store-bought split chicken breasts are often sloppily butchered. However, if you prefer to purchase split chicken breasts, try to choose 10- to 12-ounce pieces with the skin intact. If using kosher chicken, do not brine. You will need a 12-inch ovensafe skillet for this recipe. Any of the pan sauces on pages 324–325 would also pair well with the chicken. See Recipe Tutorial on page 308 for more details on this recipe.

- 4 (10- to 12-ounce) bone-in split chicken breasts, trimmed, brined if desired (see page 288)
  Salt and pepper
- 1 tablespoon vegetable oil
- 1 recipe pan sauce (pages 331–332)

1. Adjust oven rack to middle position and heat oven to 450 degrees. Pat chicken dry with paper towels and season with salt and pepper.

2. Heat oil in 12-inch ovensafe skillet over medium-high heat until just smoking. Place chicken breasts skin side down in skillet and cook until well browned, 6 to 8 minutes, reducing heat if pan begins to scorch. Flip chicken skin side up and continue to cook until lightly browned on second side, about 3 minutes.

3. Flip chicken skin side down and transfer skillet to oven. Roast until chicken registers 160 degrees, 15 to 18 minutes.

4. Using potholder (skillet handle will be hot), remove skillet from oven. Transfer chicken to serving platter and let rest while making sauce. Pour sauce over chicken and serve immediately.

Pan-Roasted Chicken Pieces

✔ **WHY THIS RECIPE WORKS:** We wanted a recipe that shortened the preparation and cooking time of a classic roast chicken without sacrificing crisp skin. To do so, we turned to pan roasting. We cut up a whole chicken into eight pieces, which fit comfortably in a 12-inch skillet. Brining took just 30 minutes and added welcome flavor and moisture. Before roasting the chicken pieces, we browned them on both sides in oil on the stovetop, turned the chicken skin side down, then slid the pan into a 450-degree oven to finish cooking. The whole process took only 20 minutes. Once the chicken was removed from the skillet, the fond was crusty and plentiful, so we needed only a handful of ingredients—some minced shallot, chicken broth, vermouth, thyme, and butter—to turn it into a flavorful sauce.

Pan-Roasted Chicken Pieces

SERVES 4

If using kosher chicken, do not brine. You will need a 12-inch ovensafe skillet for this recipe. Any of the pan sauces on pages 324–325 would also pair well with the chicken. See Core Technique on page 296 for more details on this recipe.

- 1 (3½- to 4-pound) chicken, cut into 8 pieces (4 breast pieces, 2 thighs, 2 drumsticks), trimmed, wings discarded, and brined if desired (see page 288)
  Salt and pepper
- 1 tablespoon vegetable oil
- 1 recipe pan sauce (recipes follow)

1. Adjust oven rack to middle position and heat oven to 450 degrees. Pat chicken dry with paper towels and season with salt and pepper.

2. Heat oil in 12-inch ovensafe skillet over medium-high heat until just smoking. Carefully lay chicken pieces skin side down in skillet and cook until well browned, 6 to 8 minutes. Flip chicken and continue to brown lightly on second side, about 3 minutes.

3. Flip chicken skin side down and transfer skillet to oven. Roast chicken until thickest part of breasts registers 160 degrees and thighs register 175 degrees, about 10 minutes.

4. Using potholder (skillet handle will be hot), remove skillet from oven. Transfer chicken to serving platter, tent with foil, and let rest while making sauce. Pour sauce over chicken and serve immediately.

Classic Pan Sauces for Chicken

✔ **WHY THIS RECIPE WORKS:** Pan sauces are the easiest way to dress up pan-roasted chicken, whether boneless or bone-in (as well as steaks and chops). Once the chicken was cooked, we set it aside to rest and built our sauce in the empty pan, utilizing the flavorful browned bits, or fond, left behind by the meat. We built on that flavor, adding aromatics (shallot or garlic) to the pan and cooking them briefly, then loosening and dissolving the fond with broth, vermouth, or another liquid to create a simple sauce. Adding herbs with the liquid lent further depth. We simmered the liquid to reduce it and concentrate the flavors before finishing with butter for just the right amount of richness.

Sage-Vermouth Sauce

MAKES ENOUGH FOR 1 RECIPE PAN-ROASTED CHICKEN BREASTS OR PAN-ROASTED CHICKEN PIECES

Fresh herbs make a big difference in a simple pan sauce; avoid substituting dried herbs. See Core Technique on page 232 for more details on making pan sauces.

- 1 large shallot, minced
- ¾ cup chicken broth
- ½ cup dry vermouth
- 4 fresh sage leaves, each leaf torn in half
- 3 tablespoons unsalted butter, cut into 3 pieces and chilled
  Salt and pepper

Being careful of hot skillet handle, pour off all but 1 teaspoon fat left in skillet, add shallot, and cook over medium heat until softened, about 2 minutes. Stir in chicken broth, vermouth, and sage leaves, scraping up any browned bits. Bring to simmer and cook until thickened and measures ¾ cup, about 5 minutes. Stir in any accumulated chicken juices; return to simmer and cook for 30 seconds. Off heat, discard sage leaves and whisk in butter, 1 piece at a time. Season with salt and pepper to taste.

Garlic-Sherry Sauce

MAKES ENOUGH FOR 1 RECIPE PAN-ROASTED CHICKEN BREASTS OR PAN-ROASTED CHICKEN PIECES

Fresh herbs make a big difference in a simple pan sauce; avoid substituting dried herbs. See Core Technique on page 232 for more details on making pan sauces.

- 7 garlic cloves, peeled and sliced thin
- ¾ cup chicken broth
- ½ cup dry sherry
- 2 sprigs fresh thyme
- 3 tablespoons unsalted butter, cut into 3 pieces and chilled
- ½ teaspoon lemon juice
  Salt and pepper

Being careful of hot skillet handle, pour off all but 1 teaspoon fat left in skillet, add garlic, and cook over medium heat, stirring often, until garlic turns golden but not brown, about 1½ minutes. Stir in broth, sherry, and thyme sprigs, scraping up any browned bits. Bring to simmer and cook until thickened and measures ¾ cup, about 5 minutes. Stir in any accumulated chicken juices; return to simmer and cook for 30 seconds. Off heat, discard thyme sprigs and whisk in butter, 1 piece at a time. Stir in lemon juice and season with salt and pepper to taste.

Sherry-Rosemary Sauce

MAKES ENOUGH FOR 1 RECIPE PAN-ROASTED CHICKEN BREASTS OR PAN-ROASTED CHICKEN PIECES

Fresh herbs make a big difference in a simple pan sauce; avoid substituting dried herbs. See Core Technique on page 232 for more details on making pan sauces.

- 1 large shallot, minced
- ¾ cup chicken broth
- ½ cup dry sherry
- 2 sprigs fresh rosemary
- 3 tablespoons unsalted butter, cut into 3 pieces and chilled
  Salt and pepper

Being careful of hot skillet handle, pour off all but 1 teaspoon fat left in skillet, add shallot, and cook over medium heat until softened, about 2 minutes. Stir in broth, sherry, and rosemary sprigs, scraping up any browned bits. Bring to simmer and cook until thickened and measures ⅔ cup, about 6 minutes Stir in any accumulated chicken juices; return to simmer and cook for 30 seconds. Off heat, discard rosemary sprigs and whisk in butter, 1 piece at a time. Season with salt and pepper to taste.

Shallot-Thyme Sauce

MAKES ENOUGH FOR 1 RECIPE PAN-ROASTED CHICKEN BREASTS OR PAN-ROASTED CHICKEN PIECES

Fresh herbs make a big difference in a simple pan sauce; avoid substituting dried herbs. See Core Technique on page 232 for more details on making pan sauces.

- 1 large shallot, minced
- ¾ cup chicken broth
- ½ cup dry vermouth
- 2 sprigs fresh thyme
- 3 tablespoons unsalted butter, cut into 3 pieces and chilled
  Salt and pepper

Being careful of hot skillet handle, pour off all but 1 teaspoon fat left in skillet, add shallot, and cook over medium-high heat until softened, about 2 minutes. Stir in broth, vermouth, and thyme sprigs, scraping up any browned bits. Bring to simmer and cook until thickened and measures ⅔ cup, about 6 minutes Stir in any accumulated chicken juices; return to simmer and cook for 30 seconds. Off heat, discard thyme sprigs and whisk in butter, 1 piece at a time. Season with salt and pepper to taste.

Mustard-Cognac Sauce

MAKES ENOUGH FOR 1 RECIPE PAN-ROASTED CHICKEN BREASTS OR PAN-ROASTED CHICKEN PIECES

Be sure to add the broth to the skillet before adding the cognac. See Core Technique on page 232 for more details on making pan sauces.

- 1 large shallot, minced
- ¾ cup chicken broth
- ¼ cup dry white wine
- ¼ cup cognac or brandy
- 2 sprigs fresh thyme
- 2 tablespoons unsalted butter, cut into 2 pieces and chilled
- 1 tablespoon Dijon mustard
  Salt and pepper

Being careful of hot skillet handle, pour off all but 1 teaspoon fat left in skillet, add shallot, and cook over medium-high heat until softened, about 2 minutes. Stir in broth, wine, cognac, and thyme sprigs, scraping up any browned bits. Bring to simmer and cook until thickened and measures ⅔ cup, about 6 minutes Stir in any accumulated chicken juices; return to simmer and cook for 30 seconds. Off heat, discard thyme sprigs and whisk in butter, 1 piece at a time. Stir in mustard and season with salt and pepper to taste.

Onion-Ale Sauce

MAKES ENOUGH FOR 1 RECIPE PAN-ROASTED CHICKEN BREASTS OR PAN-ROASTED CHICKEN PIECES

Brown ale gives this sauce a nutty, toasty, bittersweet flavor. Newcastle Brown Ale and Samuel Smith's Nut Brown Ale are good choices. See Core Technique on page 232 for more details on making pan sauces.

- ½ onion, sliced very thin
- ¾ cup chicken broth
- ½ cup brown ale
- 1 tablespoon brown sugar
- 1 sprig fresh thyme
- 1 bay leaf
- 3 tablespoons unsalted butter, cut into 3 pieces and chilled
- ½ teaspoon cider vinegar
  Salt and pepper

Being careful of hot skillet handle, pour off all but 1 teaspoon fat left in skillet, add onion, and cook over medium-high heat until softened, about 5 minutes. Stir in broth, ale, brown sugar, thyme sprig, and bay leaf, scraping up any browned bits. Bring to simmer and cook until thickened and measures ⅔ cup, about 6 minutes Stir in any accumulated chicken juices; return to simmer and cook for 30 seconds. Off heat, discard thyme sprig and bay leaf and whisk in butter, 1 piece at a time. Stir in vinegar and season with salt and pepper to taste.

Sweet-Tart Red Wine Sauce

MAKES ENOUGH FOR 1 RECIPE PAN-ROASTED CHICKEN BREASTS OR PAN-ROASTED CHICKEN PIECES

This sauce is a variation on the Italian sweet-sour flavor combination called *agrodolce*. See Core Technique on page 232 for more details on making pan sauces.

- 1 large shallot, minced
- ¾ cup chicken broth
- ¼ cup dry red wine
- ¼ cup red wine vinegar
- 1 tablespoon sugar
  Salt and pepper
- 1 bay leaf
- 3 tablespoons unsalted butter, cut into 3 pieces and chilled

Being careful of hot skillet handle, pour off all but 1 teaspoon fat left in skillet, add shallot, and cook over medium-high heat until softened, about 2 minutes. Stir in chicken broth, wine, vinegar, sugar, ¼ teaspoon pepper, and bay leaf, scraping up any browned bits. Bring to simmer and cook until thickened and measures ⅔ cup, about 6 minutes. Stir in any accumulated chicken juices; return to simmer and cook for 30 seconds. Off heat, discard bay leaf and whisk in butter, 1 piece at a time. Season with salt and pepper to taste.

Roasted Chicken Breasts

✔ **WHY THIS RECIPE WORKS:** Recipes for roasted chicken breasts often produce bland, dry meat and flabby skin. Attempts to cover up such disappointment with potent ingredients only make matters worse for this simple dish. We discovered that cooking whole (rather than split) breasts helped the meat retain more moisture. Before serving, we simply carved the meat off the bone into thin slices for an attractive presentation. Elevating the meat was also key: we not only perched the chicken on the slotted top of a broiler pan, but also created a natural rack by pulling out the rib cage on each side of the whole breast so that it could stand up on its own, allowing the heat to circulate evenly around the meat. Gently separating the skin from the meat and rubbing butter and salt underneath the skin and oil on top further guaranteed ultracrisp skin and well-seasoned meat.

Roasted Chicken Breasts
SERVES 4

To make sure that the breasts cook at the same rate, purchase 2 similarly sized whole breasts (not split breasts) with skins fully intact. Whole chicken breasts weighing about 1½ pounds work best because they require a cooking time long enough to ensure that the skin will brown and crisp nicely.

- 2 **tablespoons unsalted butter, softened**
  Salt and pepper
- 2 **(1½-pound) bone-in whole chicken breasts, trimmed**
- 1 **tablespoon vegetable oil**

1. Adjust oven rack to middle position and heat oven to 450 degrees. Set wire rack in aluminum foil–lined rimmed baking sheet.

2. Combine butter and ¼ teaspoon salt in bowl. Pat chicken dry with paper towels. Using your hands or handle of wooden spoon, gently loosen center portions of skin covering each breast. Place butter (about 1½ teaspoons per breast) under skin, directly on meat in center of each breast. Gently press on skin to distribute butter evenly over meat. Rub skin with oil and season with pepper. Set chicken breasts on prepared wire rack, propping up breasts on rib bones.

3. Roast until chicken registers 160 degrees, 35 to 40 minutes. Transfer chicken to carving board and let rest for 5 minutes. Carve chicken and serve.

Roasted Chicken Breasts with Herbs and Porcini Mushrooms

Microwave ¼ cup water and 2 tablespoons dried porcini mushrooms in covered bowl until steaming, about 1 minute. Let stand until softened, about 5 minutes. Drain mushrooms through fine-mesh strainer lined with coffee filter, discarding liquid and finely chopping mushrooms. Mix chopped mushrooms, 1 teaspoon minced fresh thyme, and 1 teaspoon minced fresh rosemary into softened butter along with salt.

Roasted Chicken Breasts with Garlic, Rosemary, and Lemon

Mix 2 minced garlic cloves, 2 teaspoons minced fresh rosemary, and 1 teaspoon grated lemon zest into softened butter along with salt.

Roasted Chicken Breasts with Chipotle, Cumin, and Cilantro

Mix 2 teaspoons minced canned chipotle chile in adobo, 1 teaspoon ground cumin, and 2 teaspoons chopped fresh cilantro into softened butter along with salt.

Roasted Chicken Breasts with Olives, Parsley, and Lemon

Mix 1 tablespoon chopped pitted kalamata olives, 1 teaspoon grated lemon zest, and 2 teaspoons chopped fresh parsley into softened butter along with salt.

Chicken Provençal

✔ **WHY THIS RECIPE WORKS:** Chicken Provençal represents the best of rustic peasant food—bone-in chicken simmered all day in a tomatoey, garlicky herb broth flavorful enough to mop up with crusty bread. We started with bone-in chicken thighs and browned them in olive oil to develop rich flavor and create fond. To keep the sauce from becoming greasy, we poured off the fat left behind and then sautéed our garlic and onion in a tablespoon of oil. Diced tomatoes, white wine, and chicken broth also went into the sauce before we braised the browned chicken; minced anchovy made the dish taste richer and fuller. We used fresh parsley in addition to the traditional herbes de Provence, and we finished with grated lemon zest and pitted niçoise olives for a chicken Provençal with authentic, long-simmered flavor.

Chicken Provençal
SERVES 4

This dish is often served with rice or slices of crusty bread, but soft polenta is also a good accompaniment. Be sure to use niçoise olives here; other olives are too potent. See Recipe Tutorial on page 312 for more details on this recipe.

- 12 **(5- to 7-ounce) bone-in chicken thighs, trimmed**
  Salt and pepper
- 3 **tablespoon olive oil**
- 1 **pound white mushrooms, trimmed, halved if small or medium, quartered if large**
- 2 **onions, chopped fine**
- 6 **garlic cloves, minced**
- 1 **anchovy fillet, rinsed and minced**
- 1 **teaspoon herbes de Provence**
- ⅛ **teaspoon cayenne pepper**
- 2 **tablespoons all-purpose flour**
- 2 **tablespoons tomato paste**
- ⅓ **cup dry white wine**
- 2½ **cups chicken broth**
- 1 **(14.5-ounce) can diced tomatoes, drained**
- 2 **bay leaves**
- ½ **cup niçoise olives, pitted and chopped**
- ¼ **cup minced fresh parsley**
- ½ **teaspoon grated lemon zest**

1. Adjust oven rack to lower-middle position and heat oven to 300 degrees. Pat chicken dry with paper towels and season both sides with salt and pepper. Heat 1 tablespoon oil in Dutch oven over medium-high heat until just smoking. Add 6 chicken thighs skin side down and cook without moving until skin is crisp and well browned, about 5 minutes. Using tongs, flip chicken and brown on second side, about 5 minutes longer; transfer to large plate. Repeat with 1 tablespoon more oil and remaining 6 chicken thighs and transfer to plate. Discard fat from pot.

2. Add remaining 1 tablespoon oil to now-empty pot and heat over medium heat until shimmering. Add mushrooms, onions, and ¼ teaspoon salt, cover, and cook, stirring occasionally, until mushrooms have released their liquid and onions have softened, about 5 minutes. Uncover and continue to cook, stirring occasionally, until mushrooms are dry and browned, about 10 minutes.

3. Add garlic, anchovy, herbes de Provence, if using, and cayenne, and cook until fragrant, about 30 seconds. Stir in flour and tomato paste and cook for 1 minute. Add wine, scraping up any browned bits, then gradually stir in broth, smoothing out any lumps. Stir in tomatoes and bay leaves. Remove and discard skin from chicken thighs, then submerge chicken in liquid and add any accumulated chicken juices to pot. Increase heat to high, bring to simmer, cover, and transfer pot to oven; cook until chicken offers little resistance when poked with tip of paring knife but still clings to bones, about 1¼ hours.

4. Remove pot from oven and discard bay leaves. Stir in olives, cover, and let sit for 5 minutes. Stir in parsley and lemon zest, season with salt and pepper to taste, and serve. (Chicken can be refrigerated for up to 2 days.)

Lighter Chicken and Dumplings

✔ **WHY THIS RECIPE WORKS:** The best chicken and dumplings boast airy dumplings in a broth with clean, concentrated chicken flavor. Browning chicken thighs, then adding store-bought chicken broth produced the most flavorful base. To give our broth body, we added chicken wings to the pot; they readily gave up their collagen, giving the stew a velvety texture. For light but sturdy dumplings with good flavor, we came up with a formula that employed buttermilk for flavor and swapped in baking soda for baking powder. Wrapping the lid of the Dutch oven in a kitchen towel to prevent moisture from saturating our light-as-air dumplings was the final step in perfecting our chicken and dumplings.

Lighter Chicken and Dumplings
SERVES 6

We strongly recommend buttermilk for the dumplings, but you can substitute ½ cup plain yogurt thinned with ¼ cup milk. If you want to include white meat (and don't mind losing a bit of flavor), replace 2 chicken thighs with two 8-ounce boneless, skinless chicken breasts; brown the chicken breasts along with the thighs and remove them from the stew once they register 160 degrees, 20 to 30 minutes. The collagen in the wings helps thicken the stew; do not omit or substitute. Since the wings yield only about 1 cup of meat, using their meat is optional.

STEW
- 2½ **pounds bone-in chicken thighs, trimmed**
  Salt and pepper
- 2 **teaspoons vegetable oil**
- 2 **small onions, chopped fine**
- 2 **carrots, peeled and cut into ¾-inch pieces**
- 1 **celery rib, chopped fine**
- ¼ **cup dry sherry**
- 6 **cups chicken broth**
- 1 **teaspoon minced fresh thyme**
- 1 **pound chicken wings**
- ¼ **cup chopped fresh parsley**

DUMPLINGS
- 2 **cups (10 ounces) all-purpose flour**
- 1 **teaspoon sugar**
- 1 **teaspoon salt**
- ½ **teaspoon baking soda**
- ¾ **cup buttermilk, chilled**
- 4 **tablespoons unsalted butter, melted and hot**
- 1 **large egg white**

1. FOR THE STEW: Pat chicken thighs dry with paper towels and season with 1 teaspoon salt and ¼ teaspoon pepper. Heat oil in Dutch oven over medium-high heat until shimmering. Add chicken thighs skin side down and cook until skin is crisp and well browned, 5 to 7 minutes. Using tongs, flip chicken pieces and brown on second side, 5 to 7 minutes longer; transfer to large plate. Discard all but 1 teaspoon fat from pot.

2. Add onions, carrots, and celery to now-empty pot; cook, stirring occasionally, until caramelized, 7 to 9 minutes. Stir in sherry, scraping up any browned bits from bottom of pot. Stir in broth and thyme. Return chicken thighs, with any accumulated juices, to pot and add chicken wings. Bring to simmer, cover, and cook until thigh meat offers no resistance when poked with tip of paring knife but still clings to bones, 45 to 55 minutes.

3. Remove pot from heat and transfer chicken to cutting board. Allow broth to settle 5 minutes, then skim fat from surface. When cool enough to handle, remove and discard skin from chicken. Using fingers or fork, pull meat from chicken thighs (and wings, if desired) and cut into 1-inch pieces. Return meat to pot. (At this point, stew can be cooled to room temperature, then refrigerated for up to 2 days. Bring to simmer over medium-low heat before proceeding.)

4. FOR THE DUMPLINGS: Whisk flour, sugar, salt, and baking soda in large bowl. Combine buttermilk and melted butter in medium bowl, stirring until butter forms small clumps; whisk in egg white. Add buttermilk mixture to dry ingredients and stir with rubber spatula until just incorporated and batter pulls away from sides of bowl.

5. Return stew to simmer, stir in parsley, and season with salt and pepper to taste. Using greased tablespoon measure (or #60 portion scoop), scoop level amount of batter and drop over top of stew, spacing about ¼ inch apart (you should have about 24 dumplings). Wrap lid of Dutch oven with clean kitchen towel (keeping towel away from heat source) and cover pot. Simmer gently until dumplings have doubled in size and toothpick inserted into center comes out clean, 13 to 16 minutes. Serve immediately.

Chicken and Rice

✔ **WHY THIS RECIPE WORKS:** Chicken and rice is a dish with obvious appeal: It's a one-dish supper, it's easy, and it's eminently variable. The solution to overcooked breast meat was simple; we just added it to the pot about 15 minutes after the legs went in. Avoiding heavy, greasy rice was a little more challenging. We finally found the answer in reducing the amount of liquid (a combination of white wine, water, chopped canned tomatoes, and tomato liquid) that we added to the rice. Decreasing the amount of liquid helped, as long as we stirred the rice once to prevent the top layer from drying out. Although we tried (and liked) several varieties of rice, we settled on basic long-grain rice for this all-purpose dish.

Chicken and Rice with Tomatoes, White Wine, and Parsley

SERVES 4

Though we rarely suggest stirring rice while it cooks, in this dish it is necessary, or the top layer might dry out or be under-cooked. If you prefer, substitute 2 pounds of breast meat or boneless thighs for the pieces of a whole chicken. See Core Technique on page 290 for more details on cutting up a whole chicken.

- 1 (3½- to 4-pound) whole chicken, cut into 8 pieces (4 breast pieces, 2 drumsticks, 2 thighs), trimmed, wings discarded
  Salt and pepper
- 2 tablespoons olive oil
- 1 onion, chopped fine
- 3 garlic cloves, minced
- 1½ cups long-grain white rice
- 2 cups water
- 1 (14.5-ounce) can diced tomatoes, drained with ½ cup juice reserved
- ½ cup dry white wine
- ⅓ cup chopped fresh parsley

1. Pat chicken dry with paper towels and season with salt and pepper. Heat oil in Dutch oven over medium-high heat until just smoking. Place chicken skin side down in pot and cook until well browned, 6 to 8 minutes, reducing heat if pan begins to scorch. Flip chicken skin side up and continue to cook until lightly browned on second side, about 3 minutes; transfer to plate.

2. Pour off all but 2 tablespoons fat from pot, add onion, and cook over medium heat, stirring often, until softened, about 5 minutes. Stir in garlic and cook until fragrant, about 30 seconds. Add rice and cook, stirring frequently, until coated and glistening, about 1 minute. Stir in water, tomatoes with reserved juice, wine, and 1 teaspoon salt, scraping up any browned bits. Nestle chicken thighs and legs into pot and bring to boil. Reduce heat to low, cover, and simmer gently for 15 minutes. Nestle chicken breast pieces into pot and stir ingredients gently until rice is thoroughly mixed; cover and simmer until both rice and chicken are tender, 10 to 15 minutes longer. Stir in parsley, cover, and let dish sit for 5 minutes; serve immediately.

Chicken and Rice with Chiles, Cilantro, and Lime

Add 2 minced jalapeño chiles to pot along with onion. Stir 2 teaspoons ground cumin, 2 teaspoons ground coriander, and 1 teaspoon chili powder into pot along with garlic. Substitute ¼ cup chopped fresh cilantro and 3 tablespoons lime juice (2 limes) for parsley.

Chicken and Rice with Indian Spices

Omit parsley. Add 1 cinnamon stick to pot in step 2 and cook, stirring often, until it unfurls, about 15 seconds, before adding onion and 2 green bell peppers, cut into ¼-inch pieces. Stir 1 teaspoon ground turmeric, 1 teaspoon ground coriander, and 1 teaspoon ground cumin into pot with garlic.

Chicken and Rice with Anchovies, Olives, and Lemon

Add 5 rinsed and minced anchovy fillets to pot along with onion. Stir ½ cup pitted Italian black olives, halved, 1 tablespoon lemon juice, and 2 teaspoons grated lemon zest into pot along with parsley.

Extra-Crunchy Fried Chicken

✔ **WHY THIS RECIPE WORKS:** For well-seasoned, extra-crunchy fried chicken we started by brining the chicken in heavily salted buttermilk. For the crunchy coating, we combined flour with a little baking powder, then added buttermilk to make a thick mixture that clung tightly to the meat. Frying the chicken with the lid on the pot for half the cooking time contained the splatter-prone oil and kept it hot.

Extra-Crunchy Fried Chicken

SERVES 4

Don't let the chicken soak in the buttermilk brine much longer than 1 hour or it will be too salty. Keeping the oil at the correct temperature is essential to producing crunchy fried chicken that is neither too brown nor too greasy. You will need at least a 6-quart Dutch oven for this recipe. If you want to produce a slightly lighter version of this recipe, you can remove the skin from the chicken before soaking it in the buttermilk. The chicken will be slightly less crunchy. See Recipe Tutorial on page 316 for more details on this recipe.

- 2 tablespoons salt
- 2 cups plus 6 tablespoons buttermilk
- 1 (3½-pound) whole chicken, cut into 8 pieces (4 breast pieces, 2 drumsticks, 2 thighs), trimmed, wings discarded
- 3 cups all-purpose flour
- 2 teaspoons baking powder
- ¾ teaspoon dried thyme
- ½ teaspoon pepper
- ¼ teaspoon garlic powder
- 4–5 cups peanut or vegetable oil

1. Dissolve salt in 2 cups buttermilk in large container. Submerge chicken in brine, cover, and refrigerate for 1 hour. Remove chicken from brine and pat dry with paper towels.

2. Whisk flour, baking powder, thyme, pepper, and garlic powder together in large bowl. Add remaining 6 tablespoons buttermilk; with your fingers rub flour mixture and buttermilk together until buttermilk is evenly incorporated and flour mixture resembles coarse, wet sand.

3. Set wire rack inside rimmed baking sheet. Dredge chicken pieces in flour mixture and turn to coat thoroughly, gently pressing flour mixture onto chicken to adhere. Shake excess flour from each piece of chicken and transfer to prepared wire rack.

4. Line platter with triple layer of paper towels. Add oil to Dutch oven to measure ¾ inch deep and heat over medium-high heat to 375 degrees. Place chicken pieces skin side down in oil, cover, and fry for 4 minutes. Remove lid and lift chicken pieces to check for even browning; rearrange if browning is uneven. Adjust burner, if necessary, to maintain oil temperature of about 315 degrees. Cover and continue frying until deep golden brown, 4 to 6 minutes. Turn chicken pieces over using tongs. Adjust burner, if necessary, to maintain oil temperature of about 315 degrees. Continue to fry, uncovered, until chicken pieces are deep golden brown on second side, 6 to 8 minutes longer. Using tongs, transfer chicken to prepared platter; let sit for 5 minutes. Serve.

Classic Roast Chicken

✔ **WHY THIS RECIPE WORKS:** Roasting chicken should be a simple affair, but getting the white and dark meat to cook at the same rate while also developing crisp, golden skin is often a challenge. After testing almost every variable we could think of—oven temperature, turning the bird halfway through cooking, basting, and trussing—we found that roasting a chicken is actually quite easy as long as you use the proper technique. Roasting the chicken at 400 degrees for the duration of cooking (rather than adjusting the temperature partway) worked best. Continuous basting didn't improve our roast chicken; we found that applying butter under the skin and rubbing the bird with olive oil before it went into the oven gave it great color and a crisp texture. Trussing also proved unnecessary; the dark meat cooked more quickly when left untrussed. The only extra step we found truly important was turning the bird twice for evenly cooked meat and crisp, browned skin.

Classic Roast Chicken
SERVES 3 TO 4

If using kosher chicken, do not brine in step 1, and season with salt as well as pepper in step 3. We recommend using a V-rack to roast the chicken. If you don't have a V-rack, set the bird on a regular roasting rack and use balls of aluminum foil to keep the chicken propped up on its side. See Core Technique on page 298 for more details on this recipe.

   ½ **cup salt**
   1 **(3½- to 4-pound) whole chicken, giblets discarded**
   2 **tablespoons unsalted butter, softened**
   1 **tablespoon olive oil**
      Pepper

1. Dissolve salt in 2 quarts cold water in large container. Submerge chicken in brine, cover, and refrigerate for 1 hour. Remove chicken from brine and pat dry with paper towels.

2. Adjust oven rack to lower-middle position, place roasting pan on rack, and heat oven to 400 degrees. Coat V-rack with vegetable oil spray and set aside.

3. Use your fingers to gently loosen center portion of skin covering each breast; place butter under skin, directly on meat in center of each breast. Gently press on skin to distribute butter over meat. Tuck wings behind back. Rub skin with oil, season with pepper, and place chicken, wing side up, on prepared V-rack. Place V-rack in preheated roasting pan and roast for 15 minutes.

4. Remove roasting pan from oven and, using 2 large wads of paper towels, rotate chicken so that opposite wing side is facing up. Return roasting pan to oven and roast for another 15 minutes.

5. Using 2 large wads of paper towels, rotate chicken again so that breast side is facing up and continue to roast until breast registers 160 degrees and thighs register 175 degrees, about 20 to 25 minutes longer. Transfer chicken to carving board and let rest for 20 minutes. Carve and serve.

Crisp Roast Chicken

✔ **WHY THIS RECIPE WORKS:** Most roast chicken recipes put juiciness and evenly cooked meat first and simply make do with so-so skin. Our goal was to create a roast chicken with super-crisp skin. First we rubbed the chicken with a mixture of salt and baking powder, then let the chicken air-dry in the refrigerator overnight—this combination of steps dehydrated the skin, leading to a crunchier texture. But for the ultimate crisp skin, we need to provide an escape route for the rendered fat. Making a few incisions along the back of the bird, separating the skin from the meat, and poking holes in the skin of the breast and thighs allowed multiple channels for excess fat and juices to escape. Finally, we roasted the chicken at high heat until the skin was a perfect golden brown.

Crisp Roast Chicken
SERVES 3 TO 4

Do not brine the bird; it will prohibit the skin from becoming crisp. The sheet of foil between the roasting pan and V-rack will keep drippings from burning and smoking.

   1 **(3½- to 4-pound) whole chicken, giblets discarded**
   1½ **teaspoons salt**
   1 **teaspoon baking powder**
   ½ **teaspoon pepper**

1. Place chicken breast side down on cutting board. Insert tip of sharp knife to make four 1-inch incisions along back of chicken. Using your fingers, gently loosen skin covering breast and thighs. Using metal skewer, poke 15 to 20 holes in fat deposits on top of breast and thighs. Tuck wings behind back.

2. Combine salt, baking powder, and pepper in bowl. Pat chicken dry with paper towels and sprinkle all over with salt mixture. Rub in mixture with hands, coating entire surface evenly. Set chicken breast side up in V-rack set on rimmed baking sheet and refrigerate, uncovered, for 12 to 24 hours.

3. Adjust oven rack to lowest position and heat oven to 450 degrees. Using paring knife, poke 20 holes about 1½ inches apart in 16 by 12-inch piece of aluminum foil. Place foil loosely in roasting pan. Flip chicken breast side down and set V-rack in prepared pan on top of foil. Roast chicken for 25 minutes.

4. Remove pan from oven. Using 2 large wads of paper towels, rotate chicken breast side up. Continue to roast until breast registers 135 degrees, 15 to 25 minutes.

5. Increase oven temperature to 500 degrees. Continue to roast chicken until skin is golden brown and crisp, breast registers 160 degrees, and thighs register 175 degrees, 10 to 20 minutes. Transfer chicken to carving board and let rest for 20 minutes. Carve and serve.

Weeknight Roast Chicken

WHY THIS RECIPE WORKS: Roast chicken is often described as simple. When properly made, the rich flavor and juicy meat need little adornment. But the process of making roast chicken is anything but simple; recipes often call for complicated trussing and rotating the bird multiple times, plus time-consuming salting or brining to ensure juicy, well-seasoned meat. We found we could just tie the legs together and tuck the wings underneath. We also discovered we could skip both the V-rack and flipping the chicken by using a preheated skillet and placing the chicken breast side up; this method gave the thighs a jump-start on cooking. Starting the chicken in a 450-degree oven and then turning the oven off while the chicken finished slowed the evaporation of juices, ensuring moist, tender meat.

Weeknight Roast Chicken
SERVES 4
We prefer to use a 3½- to 4-pound chicken for this recipe. If roasting a larger bird, increase the time when the oven is on in step 2 to 35 to 40 minutes. Serve with a pan sauce, if desired (see pages 324–325 and 331–332). If making the sauce, be sure to save 1 tablespoon of the pan drippings.

- 1 **tablespoon kosher salt**
- ½ **teaspoon pepper**
- 1 **(3½- to 4-pound) whole chicken, giblets discarded**
- 1 **tablespoon olive oil**

1. Adjust oven rack to middle position, place 12-inch oven-safe skillet on rack, and heat oven to 450 degrees. Combine salt and pepper in bowl. Pat chicken dry with paper towels. Rub entire surface with oil. Sprinkle salt mixture evenly over surface of chicken, then rub in mixture with hands to coat evenly. Tie legs together with twine and tuck wingtips behind back.

2. Transfer chicken, breast side up, to preheated skillet in oven. Roast chicken until breast registers 120 degrees and thighs register 135 degrees, 25 to 35 minutes. Turn oven off and leave chicken in oven until breast registers 160 degrees and thighs register 175 degrees, 25 to 35 minutes.

3. Transfer chicken to carving board and let rest for 20 minutes. Carve and serve.

Roast Chicken with Root Vegetables

WHY THIS RECIPE WORKS: Roasting some vegetables with a chicken sounds like an easy one-dish meal. But getting both components to cook just right is a challenge. Most recipes focus on the chicken, and the vegetables wind up greasy and mushy. We found the best way to infuse the vegetables with great chicken flavor was to cook them separately. We added broth to the pan partway through roasting the chicken to prevent the fond from burning, then while the chicken rested, we tossed the vegetables with oil and seasoning and roasted them. We then drizzled some reserved broth over the vegetables and broiled them, which reduced the liquid to a flavorful glaze.

Roast Chicken with Root Vegetables
SERVES 4 TO 6
If using kosher chicken, do not brine in step 1, and season with salt as well as pepper in step 2. If using a nonstick roasting pan, refrain from turning up the oven to broil when cooking the vegetables and stir them every 5 to 7 minutes to ensure they don't become too dark. If your broiler does not accommodate a roasting pan, continue to cook the vegetables at 500 degrees until done. We prefer to use small red potatoes in this recipe. Use potatoes that are 1½ to 2 inches in diameter; larger potatoes should be cut into halves or quarters. You can substitute the following seasonal vegetables for any of those in the recipe: beets, celery root, fennel, rutabagas, and turnips; peel these vegetables (except for the fennel) and cut them into 2- to 3-inch pieces.

CHICKEN
- ½ **cup salt**
- ½ **cup sugar**
- 2 **garlic heads, cloves separated, peeled, and lightly crushed**
- 6 **bay leaves, crumbled**
- 1 **(6- to 7-pound) whole chicken, giblets discarded**
  Pepper
- 1 **cup chicken broth, plus extra as needed**

VEGETABLES
- 1 **pound small red potatoes, unpeeled**
- 1 **pound carrots, peeled and cut into 2- to 3-inch lengths, tapered ends left whole, large upper portions halved lengthwise**
- 8 **ounces parsnips, peeled and cut into 2- to 3-inch lengths, tapered ends left whole, large upper portions halved lengthwise**
- 3 **small onions, peeled, root end left intact, and quartered**
- 3 **tablespoons vegetable oil**
- ½ **teaspoon salt**
- ⅛ **teaspoon pepper**

1. FOR THE CHICKEN: Dissolve salt and sugar in 2 quarts cold water in large container; stir in garlic and bay leaves. Submerge chicken in brine, cover, and refrigerate for 1 hour. Remove chicken from brine and pat dry with paper towels.

2. Adjust oven rack to middle position and heat oven to 400 degrees. Set V-rack in roasting pan and lightly spray with vegetable oil spray. Tuck chicken wings behind back and season chicken with pepper. Place chicken wing side up on prepared V-rack and roast for 30 minutes. Remove pan from oven and, using 2 large wads of paper towels, rotate chicken so that other wing side faces up; continue to roast for 30 minutes.

3. Remove pan from oven and, using 2 large wads of paper towels, turn chicken breast side up. Add broth to pan and continue to roast until chicken is golden brown, breast registers 160 degrees, and thighs register 175 degrees, about 40 minutes. (If pan begins to smoke and sizzle, add additional ½ cup broth to pan.) Transfer chicken to carving board and let rest while roasting vegetables. Remove V-rack from pan.

4. FOR THE VEGETABLES: While chicken is resting, adjust oven rack to middle position and increase oven temperature to 500 degrees. Using wooden spoon, scrape browned bits in pan and pour drippings into fat separator. Return now-empty pan to oven and heat until oven reaches 500 degrees, about 5 minutes.

5. Toss potatoes, carrots, parsnips, and onions with oil, salt, and pepper and scatter in single layer in pan, arranging carrots, parsnips, and onions cut side down. Roast, without stirring, for 25 minutes.

6. While vegetables are roasting, measure out and reserve ½ cup liquid from fat separator; discard remaining liquid and fat (if necessary, add additional broth to make ½ cup). Remove pan from oven and heat broiler. Drizzle liquid over vegetables and broil, without stirring, for 5 minutes. Stir vegetables, coating well with juices, and continue to broil until tender and deep golden brown, about 5 minutes. Transfer vegetables to serving platter. While vegetables are broiling, carve chicken. Transfer to platter with vegetables and serve.

Two Roast Chickens with Root Vegetables

Substitute two 3- to 4-pound chickens for one 6- to 7-pound chicken. Reduce wing-side-up roasting time to 20 minutes per side in step 2. Continue to roast chicken as directed, reducing breast-side-up roasting time to 30 to 40 minutes.

Easy Roast Turkey Breast

✔ **WHY THIS RECIPE WORKS:** Achieving crisp skin without drying out the delicate white meat is easier said than done when roasting a whole turkey breast. Brining was a good first step, flavoring the mild breast meat and helping it hold moisture. Loosening the skin and rubbing the meat underneath with softened butter promoted even browning and crispier skin. But the real challenge was determining the best roasting technique. After testing a range of oven temperatures, we determined that a dual-temperature approach was necessary: starting the turkey breast in a 425-degree oven jump-started the browning process, while reducing the heat to 325 degrees for the remainder of the time allowed the meat to gently finish cooking.

Easy Roast Turkey Breast
SERVES 8 TO 10

Many supermarkets are now selling "hotel-cut" turkey breasts (see page 287). Try to avoid these if you can, as they still have the wings and rib cage attached. If this is the only type of breast you can find, you will need to remove the wings and cut away the rib cage with kitchen shears before proceeding with the recipe. If using a self-basting turkey or kosher turkey, do not brine in step 1.

½   **cup salt**
1   **(6- to 7-pound) whole bone-in turkey breast, trimmed**
4   **tablespoons unsalted butter, softened**
¼   **teaspoon pepper**

1. Dissolve salt in 1 gallon cold water in large container. Submerge turkey in brine, cover, and refrigerate for 3 to 6 hours.

2. Adjust oven rack to middle position and heat oven to 425 degrees. Set V-rack inside roasting pan and spray with vegetable oil spray. Combine butter and pepper in bowl.

3. Remove turkey from brine and pat dry with paper towels. Using your fingers, gently loosen center portion of skin covering each side of breast; place butter mixture under skin, directly on meat in center of each side of breast. Gently press on skin to distribute butter mixture over meat. Place turkey skin side up on prepared V-rack and add 1 cup water to pan.

4. Roast turkey for 30 minutes. Reduce oven temperature to 325 degrees and continue to roast until turkey registers 160 degrees, about 1 hour longer. Transfer turkey to carving board and let rest for 20 minutes. Carve turkey and serve.

Easy Roast Turkey Breast with Lemon and Thyme

Add 3 minced garlic cloves, 2 tablespoons minced fresh thyme, and 1 teaspoon grated lemon zest to butter mixture.

Easy Roast Turkey Breast with Orange and Rosemary

Add 3 minced garlic cloves, 1 tablespoon minced fresh rosemary, 1 teaspoon grated orange zest, and ¼ teaspoon red pepper flakes to butter mixture.

Easy Roast Turkey Breast with Southwestern Flavors

Add 3 minced garlic cloves, 1 tablespoon minced fresh oregano, 2 teaspoons ground cumin, 2 teaspoons chili powder, ¾ teaspoon cocoa powder, and ½ teaspoon cayenne pepper to butter mixture.

Classic Holiday Turkey

✓ **WHY THIS RECIPE WORKS:** Cooking the holiday turkey can strike fear into the most seasoned cook, so we set out to determine what makes a difference (and what doesn't) once you bring home the bird. First, we found that a standard brine solution works with most any size bird, but timing is key—at least 6 hours is required to get the full benefits of brining. We chose to skip stuffing the turkey, since cooking the stuffing to a safe internal temperature almost always resulted in an overcooked bird. A V-rack proved essential, not only to hold the turkey in place but also to elevate the meat above the roasting pan, which promoted more even browning and cooking. Turning the bird once during roasting protected the delicate breast meat from overcooking, and brushing the turkey with butter at the outset contributed to browning. Finally, letting the turkey rest after roasting allowed for the redistribution and reabsorption of the juices in the meat.

Classic Holiday Turkey

SERVES 10 TO 12

If using a self-basting or kosher turkey, do not brine in step 1, and season with salt after brushing with melted butter in step 5. Resist the temptation to tent the roast turkey with foil while it rests on the carving board. Covering the bird will make the skin soggy. See Recipe Tutorial on page 320 for more details on this recipe.

- 1 **cup salt**
- 1 **(12- to 14-pound) turkey, trimmed, neck, giblets, and tailpiece removed and reserved for gravy (recipe follows)**
- 6 **sprigs fresh thyme**
- 2 **onions, chopped coarse**
- 2 **carrots, peeled and chopped coarse**
- 2 **celery ribs, chopped coarse**
- 3 **tablespoons unsalted butter, melted**
- 1 **cup water, plus extra as needed**
- 1 **recipe Giblet Pan Gravy (recipe follows)**

1. Dissolve salt in 2 gallons cold water in large container. Submerge turkey in brine, cover, and refrigerate or store in very cool spot (40 degrees or less) for 6 to 12 hours.

2. Set wire rack in rimmed baking sheet. Remove turkey from brine and pat dry, inside and out, with paper towels. Place turkey on prepared wire rack. Refrigerate, uncovered, for at least 8 hours or overnight.

3. Adjust oven rack to lowest position and heat oven to 400 degrees. Line V-rack with heavy-duty aluminum foil and poke several holes in foil. Set V-rack in roasting pan and spray foil with vegetable oil spray.

4. Toss thyme and half of vegetables with 1 tablespoon melted butter in bowl and place inside turkey. Tie legs together with kitchen twine and tuck wings behind back. Scatter remaining vegetables in pan.

5. Pour water over vegetable mixture in pan. Brush turkey breast with 1 tablespoon melted butter, then place turkey breast side down on V-rack. Brush with remaining 1 tablespoon butter.

6. Roast turkey for 45 minutes. Remove pan from oven. Using 2 large wads of paper towels, turn turkey breast side up. If liquid in pan has totally evaporated, add another ½ cup water. Return turkey to oven and roast until breast registers 160 degrees and thighs register 175 degrees, 50 to 60 minutes.

7. Remove turkey from oven. Gently tip turkey so that any accumulated juices in cavity run into pan. Transfer turkey to carving board and let rest, uncovered, for 30 minutes. Carve turkey and serve with gravy.

Giblet Pan Gravy

MAKES ABOUT 6 CUPS

Begin step 3 once the bird has been removed from the oven and is resting on a carving board.

- 1 **tablespoon vegetable oil**
  Reserved turkey neck, giblets, and tailpiece
- 1 **onion, chopped**
- 4 **cups chicken broth**
- 2 **cups water**
- 2 **sprigs fresh thyme**
- 8 **sprigs fresh parsley**
- 3 **tablespoons unsalted butter**
- ¼ **cup all-purpose flour**
- 1 **cup dry white wine**
  Salt and pepper

1. Heat oil in Dutch oven over medium heat until shimmering. Add neck, giblets, and tailpiece and cook until golden and fragrant, about 5 minutes. Stir in onion and cook until softened, about 5 minutes. Reduce heat to low, cover, and cook until turkey parts and onion release their juices, about 15 minutes. Stir in broth, water, thyme, and parsley, bring to boil, and adjust heat to low. Simmer, uncovered, skimming any impurities that may rise to surface, until broth is rich and flavorful, about 30 minutes longer. Strain broth into large container and reserve giblets. When cool enough to handle, chop giblets. Refrigerate giblets and broth until ready to use. (Broth can be stored in refrigerator for up to 1 day.)

2. While turkey is roasting, return reserved turkey broth to simmer in saucepan. Melt butter in separate large saucepan over medium-low heat. Add flour and cook, whisking constantly (mixture will froth and then thin out again), until nutty brown and fragrant, 10 to 15 minutes. Vigorously whisk all but 1 cup of hot broth into flour mixture. Bring to boil, then continue to simmer, stirring occasionally, until gravy is lightly thickened and very flavorful, about 30 minutes longer. Set aside until turkey is done.

3. When turkey has been transferred to carving board to rest, spoon out and discard as much fat as possible from pan, leaving caramelized herbs and vegetables. Place pan over 2 burners set on medium-high heat. Return gravy to simmer. Add wine to pan of caramelized vegetables, scraping up any browned bits. Bring to boil and cook until reduced by half, about 5 minutes. Add remaining 1 cup turkey broth, bring to simmer, and cook for 15 minutes; strain pan juices into gravy, pressing as much juice as possible out of vegetables. Stir reserved giblets into gravy and return to boil. Season with salt and pepper to taste and serve.

Old-Fashioned Stuffed Turkey

✔ **WHY THIS RECIPE WORKS:** Stuffing a turkey generally complicates the matter of properly cooking the bird; still, we couldn't help but wonder if there was a way to have it all—juicy meat, burnished skin, richly flavored stuffing, and drippings suitable for gravy. Focused first on crisp skin, we opted to salt the bird rather than brine it; using a minimal amount of salt ensured the gravy wouldn't be too salty. We also rubbed the skin with a mixture of baking powder and salt and poked holes in the skin to help render the fat. Starting the turkey in a low oven and then cranking up the heat yielded breast meat that was moist and tender. To solve the stuffing dilemma, we removed the stuffing from the turkey when the meat had reached a safe temperature. Because it was saturated with turkey juices, we were able to mix it with the remaining stuffing (the portion that didn't fit in the bird) so that every bite of stuffing was infused with turkey flavor. Finally, we draped salt pork over the turkey during the first part of cooking for an intense flavor boost.

Old-Fashioned Stuffed Turkey

SERVES 10 TO 12

If using a self-basting or kosher turkey, do not salt in step 1. Table salt is not recommended for this recipe because it is too fine. Look for salt pork that is roughly equal parts fat and lean meat. The bread can be toasted up to 1 day in advance. See page 341 for more stuffing recipes and the Core Technique on page 300 for more details on carving.

TURKEY

- 1 (12- to 14-pound) turkey, trimmed, neck, giblets, and tailpiece removed and reserved for gravy
- 3 tablespoons plus 2 teaspoons kosher salt
- 2 teaspoons baking powder
- 1 (36-inch) square cheesecloth, folded in quarters

CLASSIC HERB STUFFING

- 1½ pounds hearty white sandwich bread, cut into ½-inch cubes (12 cups)
- 4 tablespoons unsalted butter
- 1 onion, chopped fine
- 2 celery ribs, minced
- 1 teaspoon table salt
- 1 teaspoon pepper
- 2 tablespoons minced fresh thyme
- 1 tablespoon minced fresh marjoram
- 1 tablespoon minced fresh sage
- 1½ cups chicken broth
- 2 large eggs

- 12 ounces salt pork, cut into ¼-inch-thick slices and rinsed
- 1 recipe Giblet Pan Gravy (page 339) (optional)

1. FOR THE TURKEY: Use your fingers or thin wooden spoon handle to gently loosen skin covering breast, thighs, drumsticks, and back; avoid breaking skin. Rub 1 tablespoon kosher salt evenly inside cavity of turkey, 1½ teaspoons kosher salt under skin of each side of breast, and 1½ teaspoons kosher salt under skin of each leg. Wrap turkey tightly with plastic wrap and refrigerate for at least 24 hours or up to 48 hours.

2. FOR THE STUFFING: Adjust oven rack to lowest position and heat oven to 250 degrees. Spread bread cubes in single layer on rimmed baking sheet; bake until edges have dried but centers are slightly moist (cubes should yield to pressure), about 45 minutes, stirring several times during baking. (Bread can be toasted up to 1 day in advance.) Transfer dried bread to large bowl.

3. While bread dries, melt butter in 12-inch skillet over medium-high heat. Add onion, celery, table salt, and pepper and cook, stirring occasionally, until vegetables are softened and lightly browned, 5 to 7 minutes. Stir in thyme, marjoram, and sage and cook until fragrant, about 1 minute. Add vegetable mixture to bowl with dried bread; add 1 cup broth and toss until evenly moistened (you should have about 12 cups stuffing).

4. Remove turkey from refrigerator and pat dry, inside and out, with paper towels. Using metal skewer, poke 15 to 20 holes in fat deposits on top of breast halves and thighs, 4 to 5 holes in each deposit. Tuck wings behind back.

5. Increase oven temperature to 325 degrees. Combine remaining 2 teaspoons kosher salt and baking powder in bowl. Sprinkle surface of turkey with salt mixture and rub in mixture with hands, coating entire surface evenly. Line turkey cavity with cheesecloth, pack with 4 to 5 cups stuffing, and tie ends of cheesecloth together. Cover remaining stuffing with plastic wrap and refrigerate. Using kitchen twine, loosely tie turkey legs together. Place turkey breast side down in V-rack set in roasting pan and drape salt pork slices over back.

6. Roast turkey until breast registers 130 degrees, 2 to 2½ hours. Remove pan from oven (close oven door to retain oven heat) and increase oven temperature to 450 degrees. Transfer turkey in V-rack to rimmed baking sheet. Remove and discard salt pork. Using 2 large wads of paper towels, rotate turkey breast side up. Cut twine binding legs and remove stuffing bag; empty into reserved stuffing in bowl. Pour drippings from roasting pan into fat separator and reserve for gravy, if making.

7. Once oven has come to temperature, return turkey in V-rack to roasting pan and roast until skin is golden brown and crisp, breast registers 160 degrees, and thighs register 175 degrees, about 45 minutes, rotating pan halfway through roasting. Transfer turkey to carving board and let rest, uncovered, for 30 minutes.

8. While turkey rests, reduce oven temperature to 400 degrees. Whisk eggs and remaining ½ cup broth from stuffing recipe together in bowl. Pour egg mixture over stuffing and toss to combine, breaking up any large chunks; spread stuffing into buttered 13 by 9-inch baking dish. Bake until stuffing registers 165 degrees and top is golden brown, about 15 minutes. Carve turkey and serve with stuffing and gravy.

Dried Fruit and Nut Stuffing

MAKES ABOUT 12 CUPS

Dried cranberries can be substituted for the raisins.

1½ **pounds hearty white sandwich bread, cut into ½-inch cubes (12 cups)**
4 **tablespoons unsalted butter**
1 **onion, chopped fine**
2 **celery ribs, minced**
1 **teaspoon salt**
1 **teaspoon pepper**
2 **tablespoons minced fresh thyme**
1 **tablespoon minced fresh marjoram**
1 **tablespoon minced fresh sage**
1 **cup raisins**
1 **cup dried apples, chopped fine**
1 **cup walnuts, chopped coarse**
1½ **cups chicken broth**
3 **large eggs**

1. Adjust oven rack to lowest position and heat oven to 250 degrees. Spread bread cubes in single layer on rimmed baking sheet; bake until edges have dried but centers are slightly moist (cubes should yield to pressure), about 45 minutes, stirring several times during baking. (Bread can be toasted up to 1 day in advance.) Transfer dried bread to large bowl and increase oven temperature to 325 degrees.

2. While bread dries, melt butter in 12-inch skillet over medium-high heat. Add onion, celery, salt, and pepper and cook, stirring occasionally, until vegetables are softened and lightly browned, 5 to 7 minutes. Stir in thyme, marjoram, and sage and cook until fragrant, about 1 minute. Add vegetable mixture, raisins, dried apples, and walnuts to bowl with dried bread; add 1 cup broth and toss until evenly moistened (you should have about 12 cups stuffing).

3. Use stuffing as directed in Old-Fashioned Stuffed Turkey, adding eggs and remaining ½ cup broth in step 8.

Sausage and Fennel Stuffing

MAKES ABOUT 12 CUPS

See page 100 for information on preparing the fennel.

1½ **pounds hearty white sandwich bread, cut into ½-inch cubes (12 cups)**
1 **teaspoon vegetable oil**
8 **ounces bulk pork sausage**
4 **tablespoons unsalted butter**
1 **onion, chopped fine**
1 **fennel bulb, stalks discarded, bulb halved, cored, and chopped fine**
1 **teaspoon salt**
1 **teaspoon pepper**
2 **tablespoons minced fresh sage**
1 **tablespoon minced fresh thyme**
1 **tablespoon minced fresh marjoram**
1½ **cups chicken broth**
3 **large eggs**

1. Adjust oven rack to lowest position and heat oven to 250 degrees. Spread bread cubes in single layer on rimmed baking sheet; bake until edges have dried but centers are slightly moist (cubes should yield to pressure), about 45 minutes, stirring several times during baking. (Bread can be toasted up to 1 day in advance.) Transfer dried bread to large bowl and increase oven temperature to 325 degrees.

2. While bread dries, heat oil in 12-inch nonstick skillet over medium-high heat until shimmering. Add sausage and cook, breaking it up into small pieces with wooden spoon, until browned, 5 to 7 minutes. Remove sausage with slotted spoon and transfer to paper towel–lined plate.

3. Melt butter in fat left in skillet over medium-high heat. Add onion, fennel, salt, and pepper and cook, stirring occasionally, until vegetables are softened and lightly browned, 5 to 7 minutes. Stir in sage, marjoram, and thyme and cook until fragrant, about 1 minute. Add vegetable mixture and sausage to bowl with dried bread; add 1 cup broth and toss until evenly moistened (you should have about 12 cups stuffing).

4. Use stuffing as directed in Old-Fashioned Stuffed Turkey, adding eggs and remaining ½ cup broth in step 8.

Inside This Chapter

CHAPTER 8

How to Cook Seafood

In this chapter we explain how to select the right fish at the market and show you the best and most foolproof ways to prepare it successfully, from steaming and poaching to pan searing and roasting. Shellfish presents its own challenges, so we set the record straight here on buying and preparing shrimp, mussels, clams, scallops, and lobster. For information on other ways to prepare seafood, see the How to Grill chapter (page 387) and How to Stir-Fry on page 234.

Getting Started

How to Buy Fish

Buying top-quality fish is just as important as employing the proper cooking technique. But before you even head to the market, decide what you are looking for: A thin fillet you can roll and steam or simply pan-sear? A thick fillet for pan roasting? A rich and meaty steak or fillet for oven roasting or grilling? How you plan to cook your fish will drive your decision at the market. The second and equally important factor is making sure the fish you buy is fresh. One good way to do this is to always buy from a trusted source (preferably one with high volume to help ensure freshness). The store, and the fish in it, should smell like the sea, not fishy or sour. And all the fish should be on ice or be properly refrigerated. Fillets and steaks should look bright, shiny, and firm, not dull or mushy. Whole fish should have moist, taut skin, clear eyes, and bright red gills.

It is always better to have your fishmonger slice steaks and fillets to order rather than buying precut pieces that may have been sitting around. Don't be afraid to be picky at the seafood counter; bringing home a ragged piece of cod or a tail-end piece of salmon will just cause cooking problems (see below for more details about buying salmon).

It is important to keep your fish cold. If you have a long ride home, ask your fishmonger for a plastic bag of ice that you can put under the fish.

In our testing of frozen fish, we found that thin fish fillets (like flounder and sole) are the best choice if you have to buy your fish frozen. Thin fillets freeze quickly, minimizing moisture loss, and most tasters couldn't tell the difference between frozen fillets that had been thawed and fresh fillets, with some even preferring frozen. For firm fillets like halibut, snapper, tilapia, and salmon, most tasters couldn't tell the difference if the fish was cooked beyond medium-rare, but lower degrees of doneness revealed a dry, stringy texture.

When buying frozen fish, make sure the fish is frozen solid, with no signs of freezer burn or excessive crystallization around the edges and no blood inside the packaging. Read the ingredients listed on the package, which should include nothing but the name of the fish you are buying.

As for defrosting, we found that doing a "quick thaw" by leaving the vacuum-sealed bags under cool running tap water for 30 minutes produced results identical to an overnight thaw in the refrigerator. To defrost in the refrigerator overnight, remove the fish from its packaging, place it in a single layer on a rimmed plate or dish (to catch released water), and cover it with plastic wrap. Do not use a microwave to defrost fish since it is impossible to do so without altering the texture of the fish or, worse, partially cooking it. Dry the fish thoroughly with paper towels before seasoning and cooking it.

How to Buy Salmon

In season, we've always preferred the more pronounced flavor of wild-caught salmon to farmed Atlantic salmon, traditionally the main farm-raised variety in this country. If you're going to spend the extra money for wild salmon, make sure it looks and smells fresh, and realize that high quality is available only from late spring through the end of summer.

At the market, there are many ways to buy salmon. Our preference is to buy thick, center-cut fillets, which can be poached, steamed, pan-seared, roasted, or grilled. Cut from the head end or center, these fillets are the prime cut of the fish. They are thick enough to sear nicely without overcooking and are easy to skin (if desired). Buy a piece that is the total amount you need and cut the individual fillets yourself.

You will also see thin fillets at the market. Stay away from these. These are cut from the tail end, and they cook so fast that it is impossible to get a nice sear before the fish is overcooked—plus one end is very, very thin while the other is always much thicker. Note that for some recipes you will want to buy the salmon skin-on; for recipes that call for skinless salmon, you can easily remove it yourself (see page 348) or ask your fishmonger to do it for you.

Bone-in steaks are an excellent choice for pan searing, grilling, or roasting, but they should not be poached. You may also see boneless steaks rolled and tied into a circular shape. These are as versatile as the bone-in steaks.

How to Store Fish

Because fish is so perishable, it's best to buy it the day it will be cooked. But if that's not possible, here's what to do.

As soon as you get home with your fish, unwrap it, pat it dry, put it in a zipper-lock bag, press out the air, and seal the bag. Then set the fish on a bed of ice in a bowl or other deep container (that can contain the water once the ice melts), and place the bowl in the back of the fridge, where it is coldest. If the ice melts before you use the fish, replenish it. The fish should keep for one day.

How to Buy Shrimp

Virtually all of the shrimp sold today in supermarkets have been previously frozen, either in large blocks of ice or by a method called "individually quick-frozen," or IQF for short. Supermarkets simply defrost the shrimp before displaying them on ice at the fish counter, where they look as though they have been freshly plucked from the sea. As a general rule, we highly recommend purchasing bags of still-frozen, shell-on IQF shrimp and defrosting them as needed at home, since there is no telling how long "fresh" shrimp may have been kept on ice at the market. IQF shrimp also have a better flavor and texture than shrimp frozen in blocks. IQF shrimp

are available both with and without their shells, but we find the shell-on shrimp to be firmer and sweeter. Also, shrimp should be the only ingredient listed on the bag. Some packagers add sodium-based chemicals as preservatives, but we find shrimp treated in this way to have a strange translucency and an unpleasant, rubbery texture.

Shrimp are sold by size (small, medium, large, and extra-large) as well as by the number needed to make 1 pound, usually given in a range. Choosing shrimp by the numerical rating is more accurate, because the size label varies from store to store. Here's how the two sizing systems generally compare:

SIZE OF SHRIMP	NUMBER PER POUND
Small	51 to 60 per pound
Medium	41 to 50 per pound
Large	31 to 40 per pound
Extra-Large	21 to 25 per pound
Jumbo	16 to 20 per pound

How to Buy Mussels and Clams

Most mussels and clams nowadays are farmed and virtually free of grit. Occasionally, you may come across "wild" mussels or clams that may have some grit at your local fish store. And despite the common folklore, this grit is impossible to purge. Look for tightly closed mussels and clams (some shells may gape slightly but should close when they are tapped) and avoid any that are cracked, broken, or sitting in a puddle of water. They should smell clean, not sour or sulfurous, and

the shells should appear moist. Both clams and mussels need to be scrubbed and rinsed before cooking, and some mussels may also need to be debearded (see page 355). (Note that if you are buying soft-shell clams, they need to be rinsed several times; see page 355.) The best way to store mussels and clams is in the refrigerator in a colander of ice set over a bowl; discard any water that accumulates so that the shellfish are never submerged.

How to Buy Scallops

For the most part, there is really only one type of scallop worth buying: sea scallops. The other scallop varieties, bay and calico, are much smaller and either too rare and expensive or very cheap and rubbery.

Many scallops are also dipped in preservatives to help extend their shelf life. These are called wet scallops. Unfortunately, these watery preservatives (a solution of water and sodium tripolyphosphate, known as STP) dull the flavor significantly and ruin the texture. Unprocessed, or dry, scallops have much more flavor and a creamy, smooth texture, plus they brown very nicely.

If the scallops at your store are not labeled, you can easily find out if they are wet or dry with this quick microwave test: Place one scallop on a paper towel–lined microwave-safe plate and microwave for 15 seconds. A dry scallop will exude very little water, while a wet scallop will leave a sizable ring of moisture on the paper towel. (The microwaved scallop can be cooked as is.)

When you can find only wet scallops, you can hide the off-putting taste of the STP by soaking the scallops in a solution of 1 quart cold water, ¼ cup lemon juice, and 2 tablespoons salt for 30 minutes. Be sure to pat the scallops very dry after soaking them. Even with this treatment, these scallops will be harder to brown than untreated dry scallops.

If you are wondering about the pink scallops that sometimes appear at the market, these are female scallops that have turned pink during spawning as their glands fill with orange roe, giving them an overall rosy hue. To see if there were any differences besides color, we pan-seared and tasted white male scallops alongside peachy female scallops. They cooked in the same amount of time and had identical textures, although tasters did note that the pink scallops—which retained their tint even after cooking—had a somewhat sweeter, richer flavor. Both colors, however, are absolutely normal and do not indicate anything about the freshness, doneness, or edibility of a scallop.

How to Buy Crabs and Crabmeat

Fresh crabs are a truly local product. On the West Coast you are likely to find Dungeness crabs, while blue crabs are the most common offering at markets on the East Coast. Whatever type you're buying, make sure to buy live crabs.

For salads and crab cakes, you will likely be buying fresh or packaged crabmeat. Freshly cooked and picked crabmeat is best, but refrigerated crabmeat is surprisingly good. Because it has been pasteurized and vacuum-sealed, this product has a shelf life of 18 months. Unfortunately, it's just as expensive as fresh crabmeat. Most canned crabmeat is of very poor quality and should be avoided.

How to Buy Lobsters

After some research into the life cycle of the lobster, we discovered that the variations in the texture of lobster meat depended a great deal on what part of the molting cycle a lobster was in. During the late spring, when waters begin to turn warm, lobsters start to form new shell tissue under their hard shells. By late June and into July or August, depending on the location, lobsters start to molt, meaning that the lobsters available during the later summer weeks and into the early fall are generally soft-shell lobsters, which have less meaty claws and are more perishable than hard-shell lobsters.

That said, the meat from soft-shell lobsters is just as flavorful. They should, however, be cooked slightly less than hard-shell lobsters (see chart below). If serving whole soft-shell lobsters, you may consider buying larger ones or, if the price is good, which it usually is in the summer when they are plentiful, buying two small ones per person. If you are using a recipe that calls for a specific amount of lobster meat, the chart will also show you the yield per size and type of lobster so you can buy only what you will need.

Markets don't usually advertise which type of lobster they are selling but you can certainly ask. It is also easy to tell which type of lobster you have. Simply squeeze the side of the lobster's body: A soft-shell lobster will yield to pressure while a hard-shell lobster will be hard, brittle, and tightly packed.

Lobster Steaming Times

	LOBSTER SIZE	COOKING TIME	MEAT YIELD
Soft-Shell	1 pound	8 to 9 minutes	About 3 ounces
	1¼ pounds	11 to 12 minutes	3½ to 4 ounces
	1½ pounds	13 to 14 minutes	5½ to 6 ounces
	1¾ to 2 pounds	17 to 18 minutes	6¼ to 6½ ounces
Hard-Shell	1 pound	10 to 11 minutes	4 to 4½ ounces
	1¼ pounds	13 to 14 minutes	5½ to 6 ounces
	1½ pounds	15 to 16 minutes	7½ to 8 ounces
	1¾ to 2 pounds	About 19 minutes	8½ to 9 ounces

Key Principles of Seafood Cookery

There are a few cooking principles that apply just about anytime you cook fish or shellfish; all are simple and straightforward. Follow these basics and you will be off to a good start with any recipe.

SIZE MATTERS

Follow the recipe with respect to the size of the fillets called for. Timing is everything when it comes to cooking fish and if you buy fillets that are larger or smaller than the recipe specifies, you will need to adjust the cooking time accordingly. Also, if you are cutting the fillets yourself, make sure to cut them into evenly sized portions so all the fish is cooked through properly.

DRY FISH, SHRIMP, AND SCALLOPS THOROUGHLY

To avoid splatter, the source of lots of mess and burns when pan-searing fish, shrimp, or scallops, first pat the seafood dry with paper towels. When the moisture on the surface of the seafood comes in contact with the hot oil, the water erupts out of the pan. Removing excess moisture prevents this, and, most important, drying encourages browning and helps any spice rub adhere better.

BRINE QUICKLY FOR PRETTIER FISH

We often advocate brining meat, and sometimes fish and shellfish, before cooking to ensure moist, tender, flavorful results. But we have also discovered a whole different reason to soak fish in a salt solution: A quick exposure can reduce the unsightly white layer of albumin that coagulates on the surface during cooking. Just 10 minutes in our standard 9 percent solution (1 tablespoon of salt per cup of water) is enough to minimize the effect. The method works in much the same way as a longer soak improves moisture retention. The salt partially dissolves the muscle fibers near the surface of the flesh, so that when cooked they congeal without contracting and squeezing out albumin. We tested the method on white fish (including cod and haddock) as well as on fattier salmon and saw a dramatic improvement in both. The brief soak also seasoned the fish's exterior, making it unnecessary to salt it before cooking.

USE A NONSTICK PAN

Unless you are poaching fish (in which case the type of skillet you use is not that critical), the best way to ensure your fish or shellfish doesn't stick to the pan or break apart when you try to remove it is to use a nonstick skillet. This doesn't mean you cannot use a traditional skillet in some instances, but you are less likely to have issues if you use a nonstick pan, and you will also have less cleanup.

GET YOUR PAN SMOKING HOT

When pan-searing fish or shellfish, the first step is to heat your oil (don't use butter because it will burn) until just smoking. This will both help keep seafood from sticking and encourage browning.

HANDLE FISH GENTLY

Fish is delicate, and whether you are flipping it in the pan or removing it for serving, you need to take care that it does not break apart. Use two thin nonstick spatulas when flipping, and transfer fillets carefully from the pan to the plate.

DON'T OVERCOOK FISH

Overcooking fish is one of the most common cooking mistakes. The trick to perfectly cooked fish—fish that is cooked all the way through, but not dried out and flavorless—is knowing when to remove it from the oven (or skillet) so that it is just slightly underdone, and then allowing the residual heat to finish the cooking. This is easy to do with salmon because the change in color is so obvious. With white fish, the change in color is much more subtle. The most accurate way to make sure thicker fish fillets and steaks are properly cooked is to use an instant-read thermometer. Salmon should register 125 degrees in the thickest part; white fish should register 135 to 140 degrees. A thermometer is not practical if you are cooking very thin fish fillets. In these cases, use a paring knife to peek inside; the fish should separate into neat flakes but still appear moist.

KEEP TRACK OF SHRIMP AND SCALLOPS

To keep track of shrimp or scallops during cooking, position them in the pan in a circular pattern and work your way around. When it's time to flip or remove them, start again at the same place so all the food is in the pan for the same amount of time. Tongs come in handy for this task.

Essential Equipment

When cooking seafood, you don't need any specialty equipment to get started. Two essentials are listed below. It also helps to have a good paring and chef's knife, and a sturdy rimmed baking sheet. Also, if you cook thicker fish fillets or steaks often, having a good instant-read thermometer will come in very handy. You want one that can take a reading quickly since the cooking time for fish is pretty short. For more details on what to look for in an instant-read thermometer, see page 10.

NONSTICK SKILLET

A large (12-inch) nonstick skillet is essential when you are cooking seafood. It minimizes the risk that delicate fish or shellfish will stick to the pan, and it eliminates a big, messy cleanup job. Because nonstick skillets don't last forever (if you use yours a lot, the pan's surface will eventually become scratched and lose its slickness), we don't recommend buying an expensive one. But you should buy one with an ovensafe handle because, for some fish recipes, it is very effective to sear on the stovetop and finish cooking more gently in the oven. For more details on what to look for, see page 22.

SPATULAS

Flipping delicate fish fillets in a skillet, or getting them out of the pan for serving in one piece, can be nerve-racking unless you have the right spatulas. We recommend that you buy two nonstick spatulas if you plan to cook fish, as flipping fish properly is easier using two. A metal fish spatula will also work; just be careful not to scratch the surface of your nonstick pans. Most people don't give much thought to choosing a spatula, but choice really does matter. A good spatula must have a slim front edge that can slide under any food, fish included, with ease, a flexible head with an upward tilt to keep food secure, and slots to help ease friction. For more details on what to look for, see page 31.

How to Prepare Fish

How you prepare your fish for cooking depends on many things: the recipe, the type of fish, and the cooking method. Regardless, evenly cut and properly prepared fish are the first steps to a successful recipe. Before you cook fish you should first assess the thickness of the individual pieces. While we recommend buying thicker center-cut fillets when shopping for meaty fish like salmon, that's not really possible when shopping for thinner fillets like flounder or sole. In that case, you can even out the cooking time by tucking the tails under. Many fish still contain bones, but you can easily check for bones and remove them. Sometimes we like to keep skin on the fish and crisp it to add texture to the final dish, but in other cases we remove the skin prior to cooking. The equipment needed will depend on the task your are performing.

ESSENTIAL EQUIPMENT

- cutting board
- bowl
- needle-nose pliers or tweezers
- boning knife or chef's knife
- paper towel

A. TUCK TAIL UNDER

Fold thinner portion of fish under before cooking. **WHY?** If you end up with a piece of fish with a thinner tail end, it will not cook at the same rate as the other pieces of fish unless you fold the tail end under the thicker part of the fillet.

B–C. REMOVE PINBONES

For large side of salmon, drape fish skin side down over inverted bowl. Grasp protruding pinbones with needle-nose pliers or tweezers and pull to remove. For fillet, run fingers over surface to locate pinbones. Remove and discard.
WHY? Pinbones are small white bones that run through the center of a side of fish or a fish fillet. They should be removed by your fishmonger, but it is important to check before cooking in case any were missed. An inverted bowl forces pinbones from a side of salmon to stick out, making them easier to spot.

D–E. SKIN FILLETS

Using tip of boning knife or sharp chef's knife, cut skin away from fish at corner of fillet. When sufficient skin is exposed, grasp skin firmly with paper towel, hold it taut, and slice remaining skin off flesh.
WHY? It is hard to remove skin from a fish fillet unless you first cut away a small portion of it and use it as a handle to help steady the fish and guide you as you cut the rest away. If you simply try to slice away the skin, you will likely end up with a mangled fish fillet.

How to Oven-Roast Salmon

Steaming and poaching are tried-and-true methods for delivering the silky and moist interior that is the hallmark of salmon, while pan searing delivers a caramelized crust. We found that roasting, with a few tricks, could deliver succulent, moist salmon with an appealing contrast in texture on the exterior. Plus, it is conveniently hands-off, making it a good choice when entertaining. Our hybrid method uses both high and low heat, making the most of what each has to offer, to deliver perfectly cooked salmon that can easily be dressed up with a relish (see recipes on page 377). For evenly sized fillets that cook through at the same rate, we prefer to buy one whole piece and cut it into individual fillets at home. You can cook four to eight fillets at one time; just make sure they aren't touching each other on the baking sheet.

ESSENTIAL EQUIPMENT

- rimmed baking sheet
- sharp boning or paring knife
- paper towels
- tongs
- instant-read thermometer

1. PREHEAT BAKING SHEET

Adjust oven rack to lowest position, place rimmed baking sheet on rack, and heat oven to 500 degrees.

WHY? A super-hot oven to start gives the fish an initial blast of heat that firms its exterior and helps render out some of the excess fat that usually makes slow-roasted salmon mushy. Preheating the baking sheet kept the temperature of the oven from dropping too quickly once we lowered the heat.

2. SCORE FISH

Using sharp knife, remove any whitish fat from belly of 1 (1¾- to 2-pound) skin-on salmon fillet, about 1½ inches thick. Cut salmon into 4 equal pieces, then cut 4 or 5 shallow slashes, about 1 inch apart, through skin of each piece. Be careful not to cut into flesh.

WHY? Keeping the skin on the salmon protects it from the hot baking sheet and also prevents the fish from falling apart and losing moisture as it cooks, but you need to score the skin to keep it from buckling. A boning knife works best, but a paring knife would also work.

3. PLACE SKIN SIDE DOWN ON HOT SHEET

Pat salmon dry with paper towels, rub fillets evenly with 2 teaspoons olive oil, and season with salt and pepper. Place skin side down on preheated baking sheet.

WHY? The preheated baking sheet helps to quickly render out some of the excess fat just below the skin.

4. LOWER HEAT AND ROAST

Reduce oven temperature to 275 degrees and roast fish until it flakes apart when gently prodded with paring knife, 9 to 13 minutes. Salmon should register 125 degrees in thickest part.

WHY? As the oven temperature slowly drops, the fish cooks gently in the ambient heat of the oven, giving the salmon a little firmness on the outside and a lot of moist meat on the inside.

How to Steam Fish

ESSENTIAL
EQUIPMENT

Steaming is a terrific way to cook fish without introducing any extra fat. Many types of fish can be prepared using this method (see fish steaming chart on opposite page for suggestions). The key to perfectly steamed fish is to simmer the water underneath the steamer basket rather than let it boil—the gentle heat helps the fish cook slowly and evenly. Note that only very thin fish fillets (less than ½ inch thick) need to be rolled into bundles before cooking. Limes, oranges, or grapefruits can be substituted for the lemons. Serve the fish simply with lemon wedges and a sprinkling of chopped fresh herbs (chives, tarragon, cilantro, basil, or parsley would all be good here). We also like serving simple steamed fish with a light sauce or relish (see recipes on page 372). See chart on opposite page for cooking times for specific types of fish.

- steamer basket
- Dutch oven
- liquid measuring cup
- cutting board
- chef's knife
- paper towels
- paring knife
- metal spatula

1. SET UP STEAMER

Set steamer basket inside Dutch oven and fill pot with water until it just touches bottom of basket. **WHY?** A large pot with a cover and a simple, inexpensive collapsible steamer basket are all that you need for successfully steaming many types of fish. You need a deep, wide pot in order to open up the steamer basket wide enough to accommodate several pieces of fish and steam them properly.

2. LINE BASKET WITH LEMON

Slice 1 lemon into ¼-inch-thick rounds and arrange slices on steamer basket. Bring water to boil. **WHY?** We start by placing lemon slices on the steamer basket. Not only do they lend flavor, but they also keep the fish from sticking to the steam basket.

3. ROLL FISH, IF NECESSARY

Pat fish dry with paper towels and season with salt and pepper. If fillets are thin, arrange each fillet skinned side up and, starting at tail end, roll into tight bundle. **WHY?** Very thin fish fillets, such as sole or flounder, need to be rolled into a bundle before steaming; otherwise they will break apart and be impossible to remove from the basket in one piece. Fish that are ½ inch thick or thicker do not have to be rolled.

4. ADD FISH AND LEMON

Reduce heat to simmer and arrange fillets on lemon slices, seam side down if rolled. Slice second lemon into ¼-inch-thick rounds and place on top of fish. **WHY?** Rolled fish will stay intact if placed on the steamer basket seam side down. Putting more lemon slices on top of the fish ensures the fillets are infused with a delicate, fragrant flavor.

5. COVER AND STEAM

Cover pot and steam until fish flakes when gently prodded with paring knife.

WHY? The key to perfectly steamed fish is to simmer the water underneath the steamer basket rather than boil it. The gentle heat helps the fish cook evenly and slowly. Since it can be hard to maneuver delicate steamed fish out of the steamer basket while it is still in the pot, it is best to gently lift the basket out of the pot with the fish still in it and rest it on a cutting board. This gives you more room to lift the fish out using a thin spatula.

Cooking Times for Steamed Fish

The chart below provides guidelines for steaming various types of fish, but some fish we particularly like to steam include sole, cod, and salmon. The temperature, thickness, and quality of the fish will all influence the cooking time. Check the fish for doneness a minute or so before the suggested time. If using a fish not listed on the chart, follow the cooking times for a fish similar in texture and thickness. If using a thin fish fillet (less than ½ inch thick), be sure to roll it into a bundle before steaming.

TYPE OF FISH	CUT	STEAMING TIME
Arctic Char	Fillet, 1 inch thick	5 to 7 minutes
Cod and Haddock	Fillet, 1 inch thick	6 to 8 minutes
Flounder, Sole, and Tilapia	Fillet, ¼ to ½ inch thick, rolled into a bundle	4 to 6 minutes
Grouper	Fillet, 1 to 1½ inches thick	10 to 12 minutes
Halibut	Fillet or Steak, 1 inch thick	6 to 8 minutes
Red Snapper	Fillet, 1¼ inches thick	8 to 10 minutes
Salmon	Fillet or Steak, 1¼ to 1½ inches thick	6 to 8 minutes for medium-rare; 7 to 9 minutes for medium
Sea Bass	Fillet, 1 to 1¼ inches thick	8 to 10 minutes
Tilefish	Fillet, ¾ to 1 inch thick	6 to 8 minutes

How to Pan-Roast Fish

ESSENTIAL EQUIPMENT

- paper towels
- 12-inch ovensafe nonstick skillet
- nonstick or metal spatulas (2)
- instant-read thermometer
- potholder

Pan roasting is a great way to cook thicker white fish fillets. Since salmon and tuna are best served rare or medium-rare, they can be pan-seared without a trip into the oven. However, thick white fish, such as halibut, cod, sea bass, or red snapper, must be cooked through, and that can cause quite a mess on the stovetop. Starting these white fish in a hot skillet on the stovetop and then transferring the skillet to the oven ensure that the crust is well browned and the interior is cooked but moist. It also reduces cooking time on the stovetop to just a few minutes, so the mess is minimal. As for serving, you can keep it simple and just offer lemon wedges. Or dollop some compound butter, a potent sauce, or relish (see recipes on page 373) over each fillet.

1. PAT FISH DRY

Thoroughly pat dry 4 skinless white fish fillets, 1 to 1½ inches thick (6 to 8 ounces each), with paper towels and season with salt and pepper.
WHY? For a good sear, the fish must be dry. Damp fish will just steam, not brown. Thick white fish fillets with a meaty texture, like halibut, cod, sea bass, and red snapper, work best with this method.

2. SUGAR FISH

Sprinkle very light dusting of sugar (about ⅛ teaspoon) evenly over 1 side of each fillet.
WHY? Just a small amount of sugar helps caramelize the exterior of the fish, giving it an attractively browned crust after just a few minutes in a smoking hot skillet.

3. SEAR IN HOT PAN

Heat 1 tablespoon vegetable oil in 12-inch ovensafe nonstick skillet over high heat until just smoking. Place fillets in skillet sugar side down and press lightly to ensure even contact with pan.
WHY? This recipe depends on the heat of the stovetop to jump-start the browning process. The oil should be smoking when you add the fish, and you should keep the burner set to high while cooking it. There is no risk of burning the fish, as the cooking time is very short. An ovensafe pan is essential.

4. FLIP CAREFULLY

Cook until browned, 1 to 1½ minutes. Using 2 spatulas, flip fillets.
WHY? Flipping delicate fish fillets is not easy, but using two spatulas makes the process much easier. Slide one spatula under the piece of fish and use the second spatula to guide the fish. Use plastic nonstick spatulas, or you can use thin metal fish spatulas if you take care not to scratch the surface of the pan.

5. TRANSFER TO HOT OVEN

Transfer skillet to middle rack in 425-degree oven. **WHY?** After the fish is seared and turned, a short cooking time in a very hot oven ensures the fillets are properly cooked through. Cooking them through on the stovetop is not as foolproof and creates a splattery mess. There's plenty of residual heat in the pan to brown the second side in the oven.

6. COOK TO PROPER TEMPERATURE

Roast fillets until centers are just opaque and register 135 degrees, 7 to 10 minutes. Use potholder to remove skillet from oven and immediately transfer fish to plates.

WHY? For the most reliable results, it pays to use an instant-read thermometer and check the internal temperature of the fish. White fish doesn't have much fat, so it will be very dry if you overcook it, and mushy and unappealing if you undercook it. Once fish reaches the proper temperature, don't let it sit in the hot pan or it will continue to cook.

Troubleshooting Pan-Roasted Fish

PROBLEM	SOLUTION
My fish is pale, not browned.	This recipe depends on a blast of heat on the stovetop to jump-start the browning process. Get the pan really hot before you add the fish (you should see wisps of smoke from the oil), and don't omit the sugar, which helps the browning process.
My fish broke apart when I tried to turn it.	Turning delicate fish fillets, even thick ones, is tricky. You need to use two spatulas for this task—and they need a thin edge you can easily slide under the fish. Use one spatula to get underneath the fish, while using the other both to hold the fish in place and to "catch" it after it's been flipped over. An extra-wide spatula works well on the catching end.
My fish is dry and overcooked.	Fish can go from tender and perfectly cooked to dry and overcooked very quickly. Since the cooking time in the oven is short, check the temperature of your fish early in the time range. Also, once you remove your skillet from the oven, immediately transfer the fish to plates otherwise they will continue to cook in the hot skillet.

How to Oven-Fry White Fish

ESSENTIAL EQUIPMENT

- food processor
- rimmed baking sheets (2)
- chef's knife
- pie plates (3)
- whisk
- paper towels
- tongs
- wire rack
- instant-read thermometer

The allure of moist, flaky fish surrounded by a golden, crunchy coating is hard to resist, but we wanted all the crunch and flavor without all the mess and the fat. Moving the fish from the fryer to the oven was our starting point, as was making our own bread crumbs and toasting them first. A flavorful batter kept the fish from tasting bland. This technique works best with skinless fillets that are 1 to 1½ inches thick; thinner fillets will overcook by the time the coating is crisp. We especially like to cook cod this way, but haddock works well, too. We like to serve oven-fried fish with a creamy sauce like Sweet and Tangy Tartar Sauce (page 376).

1. MAKE CRUMBS

Pulse 4 slices hearty white sandwich bread, torn into quarters, in food processor with 2 tablespoons melted unsalted butter, ¼ teaspoon salt, and ¼ teaspoon pepper to coarse crumbs. Transfer to rimmed baking sheet and bake in 350-degree oven on middle rack until brown, about 15 minutes. Cool and combine with 2 tablespoons minced fresh parsley and 1 minced shallot in pie plate.

WHY? Homemade bread crumbs taste fresher than store-bought. Toasting them in the oven gives them the crunch that normally comes from frying.

2. MAKE BATTER

Whisk 2 large eggs, 3 tablespoons mayonnaise, 2 teaspoons prepared horseradish (optional), ½ teaspoon paprika, and ¼ teaspoon cayenne pepper (optional) in pie plate until combined. Whisk in ¼ cup plus 1 tablespoon all-purpose flour until smooth.

WHY? Thickened with flour, this egg mixture keeps the fish moist and helps the crumbs stick.

3. FLOUR IT, BATTER IT, BREAD IT

Place ¼ cup all-purpose flour in pie plate. Cut 1¼ pounds skinless cod, haddock, or other thick white fish fillets into 4 pieces, pat dry, then dredge in flour. Dip fish in egg batter, then coat in bread-crumb mixture, pressing gently so that crumbs adhere.

WHY? Coating the fish lightly with flour helps the batter stick to the fish, which in turn gives the crumbs something to cling to.

4. BAKE ON WIRE RACK

Spray wire rack with vegetable oil spray and set over rimmed baking sheet. Place fish on rack and bake on middle rack in 425-degree (note higher temperature) oven for 18 to 25 minutes, or until fish registers 140 degrees.

WHY? The wire rack allows air to circulate around the fish, which keeps the breading crisp.

How to Prepare Scallops, Mussels, and Clams

Shellfish today requires very little in the way of prep before cooking. Scallops require the least amount of attention—simply rinse them, remove any tough side muscles, and pat them dry before cooking. If you are harvesting clams and mussels yourself, they may require a little more attention than those you buy at the market, but with several rinses of cold water and a little scrubbing (and debearding in the case of mussels) they will be ready to cook. The equipment needed will depend on the task you are performing.

ESSENTIAL EQUIPMENT

- paring knife
- vegetable brush
- colander
- bowl

A. REMOVE MUSCLE FROM SCALLOPS

Use fingers to peel crescent-shaped muscle that is often attached to side of scallop.

WHY? This muscle is incredibly tough once cooked and must be removed.

B. DEBEARD MUSSELS

Holding mussel in one hand, tug beard after placing it between flat side of paring knife and thumb.

WHY? Occasionally, mussels will have a harmless weedy piece (known as the beard) protruding from between the shells, and it should be removed before cooking.

C. SCRUB MUSSELS AND HARD-SHELL CLAMS

Place mussels or clams in colander and scrub briefly with vegetable brush under cold running water.

WHY? Most mussels today need little prep because they are rope- or net-grown, but it is a good idea to rinse them and give them a quick scrub before cooking. Discard any mussels that are cracked or open. Hard-shell clams (such as quahogs, cherrystones, and littlenecks) live along sandy beaches and bays, and when harvested they remain tightly closed. In our tests, we found the meat inside to be sand-free. Once scrubbed, these clams can be cooked without further worry about gritty broths.

D. SOAK SOFT-SHELL CLAMS

Submerge clams in large bowl of cold water, then drain; repeat several times before cooking.

WHY? Soft-shell clams (such as razor clams and steamers) open widely in the muddy tidal flats where they live, and they almost always contain a lot of sand. While it's worthwhile to soak them in several batches of cold water to remove some of the sand, you can never get rid of it all. In the end, you must strain the cooking liquid (we have found that a paper coffee filter works best). It's a good idea to rinse the cooked clams, too.

How to Prepare Shrimp

ESSENTIAL EQUIPMENT

• colander
• paper towels
• paring knife

Almost all the shrimp in today's supermarkets have been previously frozen, and they simply defrost the shrimp before displaying them at the fish counter—where they look like they've been just caught. Because of this, we highly recommend buying bags of still-frozen shrimp and thawing as needed. Once shrimp is thawed, it is easy to both peel and devein. And for most recipes, you will want to do this, though there are some reasons to cook shrimp in the shell (a shrimp boil, for instance). Whether or not you take the peel off the tail end of the shrimp depends on the recipe; sometimes the tail is left on for presentation purposes, and other times it needs to be removed when the shrimp is incorporated into a dish that would be awkward to eat with the shrimp tail shells still on. Note that you can freeze the shells for later use—they can be part of a flavorful liquid or sauce that greatly enhances a variety of seafood stew, pasta, or risotto recipes.

1. DEFROST AND DRY

Thaw shrimp either overnight in refrigerator in covered bowl or in colander under cool running water for about 10 minutes until fully thawed. Dry thoroughly before cooking.

WHY? Because we recommend buying individually-quick-frozen shrimp versus shrimp frozen in blocks, they can be thawed quickly, just before you want to use them.

2. PEEL SHELLS

Break shell under swimming legs; legs will come off as shell is removed. Leave tail end intact if desired, or tug tail end to remove shell. If buying shrimp labeled "E-Z" peel (in which the shell has been already split), simply pull shell around and off shrimp, leaving tail end intact if desired.

WHY? It is easiest to start peeling shrimp on the underside, by the swimming legs. If you start here, the shell comes off the body of the shrimp very easily.

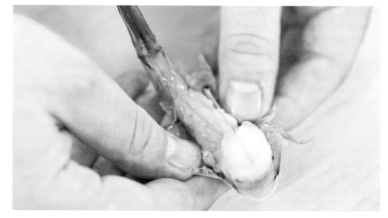

3A–3B. DEVEIN WITH KNIFE

Use paring knife to make shallow cut along back of shrimp to expose vein. Use tip of knife to lift vein out. Discard vein by wiping blade against paper towel.

WHY? Although the vein doesn't affect flavor, we remove it because it affects appearance. Once the vein is exposed, it is very easy to lift out.

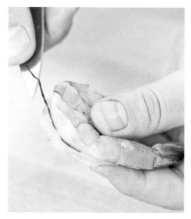

How to Pan-Sear Shrimp

Pan searing is the best way to turn out shrimp that are caramelized on the exterior yet moist, briny, and tender on the inside. Requiring only a few minutes to properly cook 1½ pounds of shrimp, this method isn't hard, but it is precise. First, you must cook the shrimp in batches and cook them only on one side. They are flipped off the heat, where the residual heat from the skillet finishes the job. Once the second batch is cooked, both batches are combined in the skillet and you can then add a sauce if desired. See page 382 for sauce recipes.

ESSENTIAL EQUIPMENT

- large mixing bowl
- 12-inch skillet with lid
- tongs
- large plate or platter

1. SEASON AND SUGAR SHRIMP

Toss 1½ pounds extra-large (21 to 25 per pound) peeled and deveined shrimp with ¼ teaspoon salt, ¼ teaspoon pepper, and ⅛ teaspoon sugar. **WHY?** Seasoning the shrimp with salt and pepper helps bring out their flavor, while the sugar aids in browning and complements the shrimp's natural sweetness.

2. COOK IN BATCHES IN HOT PAN

Heat 1 tablespoon vegetable oil in 12-inch skillet over high heat until smoking. Add half of shrimp to pan and cook until spotty brown and edges turn pink, about 1 minute. Off heat, flip each shrimp using tongs and allow shrimp to continue to cook in skillet until all but very center is opaque, about 30 seconds. Transfer shrimp to large plate or platter. Repeat with 1 tablespoon vegetable oil and remaining shrimp.

WHY? Since shrimp cook so quickly, and since you want to create a caramelized exterior without overcooking, you need to start with a really hot pan. A nonstick pan will minimize cleanup but a traditional skillet works fine too. Cooking the shrimp in batches in a large skillet ensures that the shrimp won't be crowded, which would cause them to steam—a surefire way to prevent caramelization. The residual heat from the skillet is the key to finish cooking both batches gently, off the heat.

3. RETURN FIRST BATCH TO PAN

After second batch has cooked off heat, return first batch to skillet and toss to combine. Cover skillet and let sit until shrimp are cooked through, 1 to 2 minutes. If saucing shrimp, add sauce when adding first batch back to skillet.

WHY? Tossing both batches together and then covering the skillet to finish the cooking ensure that both batches of shrimp are warm and ready to eat.

Classic Fish Meunière

Overview

Fish *meunière* is a classic French restaurant dish that should be easy enough to prepare at home but actually takes some finesse to pull off properly. Fillets of sole or flounder are dredged lightly in flour (no need for eggs or bread crumbs) and cooked on the stovetop just until a golden crust forms, while the inside stays moist and flavorful. A browned butter sauce infused with lemon is the delicious finishing touch.

Attention to detail was the key to perfecting this dish. Since thin fillets cook through (and cool off) in a flash, and because we were cooking the fish in two batches, heating dinner plates in advance made a big difference—we kept the first batch warm in a low oven while we cooked the second batch. Proper, even browning is also important here. We got the best results by seasoning the fish with salt and pepper and letting it sit until it was glistening before we floured it. The salt drew moisture from the fish, creating a thin film on the exterior that ensured an even coating of flour.

For perfect browning high heat is typically best, but the exterior of our fillets burned before the interior cooked through. Instead, we took a two-step approach. We heated the skillet over high but lowered the temperature to cook the fish. When it came to the cooking fat, butter equals flavor but it also burns easily, so we used a combination of vegetable oil and butter. After three minutes on one side and two minutes on the other, we achieved both a flavorful, perfectly browned exterior and a moist, delicate interior. For the browned butter sauce, it was critical to use a traditional skillet rather than a nonstick pan since we could more easily watch the color change and halt the cooking before the butter burned. Lemon juice and a little parsley was all it needed for a finishing touch.

Once you master the technique for classic fish meunière, you can easily swap out ingredients to create variations (see recipes pages 371–372).

Recipe Stats

TOTAL COOKING TIME **25 minutes**
PREPARATION TIME **5 minutes**
ACTIVE COOKING TIME **20 minutes**
YIELD **4 servings**
MAKE AHEAD **Serve immediately**
DIFFICULTY **Intermediate**

Tools

- rimmed baking sheet *
- 10-inch skillet **
- 13 by 9-inch baking dish ***
- 12-inch nonstick skillet ****
- chef's knife
- cutting board
- dry measuring cups
- measuring spoons
- heatproof dinner plates (4)
- metal or nonstick spatulas (2) *****
- soupspoon
- paper towels

* A baking sheet is the best place to hold the fish once it has been floured.
** The light-colored surface of a traditional skillet makes it easy to monitor the color of the butter as it browns. Also, the medium size (10 inches is ideal) ensures that the butter covers the entire pan surface. In a large pan, the butter will be so spread out that it can scorch more easily.
*** A baking dish is ideal for holding the flour.
**** A nonstick skillet ensures that the fillets will release from the pan. Make sure to use a pan that measures 12 inches across; you don't want the fillets to crawl up the sides of a smaller pan.
***** Turning the fish is the hardest part of the recipe, so make sure to have two good spatulas on hand. Slide one spatula under the piece of fish and use the second spatula to guide the fish. Either plastic nonstick or metal spatulas will work; if using metal just be careful not to scratch your pan.

Ingredients

½   **cup all-purpose flour**
4   **(5- to 6-ounce) boneless, skinless sole fillets or flounder fillets, ⅜ inch thick ***
    Salt and pepper
2   **tablespoons vegetable oil**
6   **tablespoons unsalted butter, cut into 6 pieces**
1   **tablespoon chopped fresh parsley**
1½ **tablespoons lemon juice (1 lemon)**
    Lemon wedges

* Try to purchase fillets that are of similar size, and avoid those that weigh less than 5 ounces because they will cook too quickly.

What Can Go Wrong

Here's a list of common mistakes cooks make when preparing this recipe.

COMMON MISTAKE	BAD OUTCOMES	WHAT YOU SHOULD DO
Not Seasoning Fish Before Flouring	• **The fish have blotchy browned crusts.** • **Flour falls off the fish in the skillet and burns.**	The best way to give the fish a delicate coating with flour is to first season them with salt and pepper and let them sit for about 5 minutes before dredging. When they are glistening with moisture you can dredge them in flour and shake off any excess. The moisture the fish release helps the flour stick to the fish evenly.
Using Wrong Skillet Sizes or Types	• **The fish sticks to the pan.** • **The sauce burns.**	Yes, it's a pain to use two pans for this recipe, but you need a large nonstick skillet for cooking the fish to guarantee that it won't stick. Unfortunately, it's nearly impossible to judge the color of the butter in a nonstick pan, so the traditional process of using the empty skillet to prepare a pan sauce won't work. Fish doesn't create much fond, so no flavor is really lost by preparing the sauce in a clean, medium traditional skillet with a light-colored interior.
Not Cooking Over High Enough Heat	• **The fish sticks to the pan.** • **The fish doesn't develop sufficient color and flavor.** • **The fish is soft and undercooked.**	Don't add the fish to the pan until the oil is shimmering and the butter has melted and the foaming has stopped. And let the fish cook for 3 minutes before you flip it—you want each side to develop a nice brown crust.
Not Watching the Sauce	• **The butter burns.**	Once you start preparing the butter sauce, don't do anything else. You must watch the butter like a hawk—the difference between golden brown and burnt can be as little as 15 or 20 seconds. Also, make sure to swirl the skillet constantly to ensure that all the butter is cooking at the same rate.
Serving on Cold Dinner Plates	• **The fish is not hot at serving time.**	Preheating the dinner plates in a warm oven might seem like a fussy step, but it ensures that the fish won't get cold in the few minutes it takes to prepare the butter sauce and get the plates to the table. The fish fillets used in this recipe are so thin that they don't retain heat very well, so don't skip this step.

1. Spread ½ cup all-purpose flour into large baking dish.

2. Cut 2 tablespoons unsalted butter into 2 pieces for cooking fish, and 4 tablespoons unsalted butter into 4 pieces for sauce.

3. Chop parsley to measure 1 tablespoon.

4. Juice 1 lemon to obtain 1½ table-spoons. Cut second lemon into wedges for serving.

5. Adjust oven rack to lower-middle position, set 4 heatproof dinner plates on rack, and heat oven to 200 degrees.

6. Pat 4 (5- to 6-ounce) boneless, skinless sole or flounder fillets, ⅜ inch thick, dry with paper towels.

7. Season both sides of each fillet generously with salt and pepper; let stand until fillets are glistening with moisture, about 5 minutes.

8. Coat both sides of fillets with flour, shake off excess, and place in single layer on baking sheet.

9. Heat 1 tablespoon vegetable oil in 12-inch nonstick skillet over high heat until shimmering.

10. Add 1 piece butter and swirl to coat pan bottom.

11. When foaming subsides, carefully place 2 fillets in skillet, skinned side down.

12. Reduce heat to medium-high and cook, without moving fish, until edges of fillets are opaque and bottom is golden brown, about 3 minutes.

13. Using 2 spatulas, gently flip fillets, using one spatula to gently lift long side of fillet and second spatula to catch fish and lower it back into pan.

14. Cook on second side until thickest part of fillet easily separates into flakes when paring knife is inserted, about 2 minutes longer.

15. Transfer fillets, one to each heated dinner plate with skinned side down, and return plates to oven.

16. Wipe out skillet and repeat with 1 tablespoon each oil and butter and remaining 2 fish fillets.

17. Melt 4 pieces unsalted butter in 10-inch skillet over medium-high heat, 1 to 1½ minutes.

18. Continue to cook, swirling pan constantly, until butter is golden brown and has nutty aroma, 1 to 1½ minutes; remove skillet from heat.

19. Remove plates from oven and sprinkle fillets with parsley.

20. Add lemon juice to browned butter and season with salt to taste.

21. Spoon sauce over fish and serve immediately with lemon wedges.

Cod Baked in Foil with Leeks and Carrots

Recipe Stats

TOTAL TIME **1 hour**
PREPARATION TIME **20 minutes**
ACTIVE COOKING TIME **25 minutes**
YIELD **4 servings**
MAKE AHEAD **Assembled packets can be refrigerated for up to 4 hours**
DIFFICULTY **Intermediate**

Tools

- rimmed baking sheet
- chef's knife
- cutting board
- dry measuring cups
- measuring spoons
- garlic press
- kitchen shears
- metal spatula *
- mixing bowls
- rasp-style grater
- soupspoon
- vegetable peeler
- aluminum foil
- paper towels

* A thin metal spatula comes in handy when transferring the fish and vegetables from the packets to individual dinner plates.

Ingredients

- **4   tablespoons unsalted butter, softened**
- **2   garlic cloves, minced**
- **1¼ teaspoons finely grated lemon zest, plus lemon wedges for serving**
- **1   teaspoon minced fresh thyme**
    Salt and pepper
- **2   tablespoons minced fresh parsley**
- **2   carrots, peeled and cut into 2-inch-long matchsticks**
- **2   leeks, white and light green parts only, halved lengthwise, washed thoroughly, and cut into 2-inch-long matchsticks**
- **¼   cup vermouth or dry white wine**
- **4   (6-ounce) skinless cod fillets, 1 to 1¼ inches thick ***

* Haddock, red snapper, halibut, and sea bass also work well in this recipe as long as the fillets are 1 to 1¼ inches thick.

Overview

Fish cooked *en papillote* is a French preparation that features clean, pure flavors in a very healthful preparation. The food is sealed in packets and steams in its own juices. Parchment paper is the traditional choice for forming the individual papillotes, or packets, but we prefer aluminum foil because it makes creating a tight seal virtually foolproof, and a good seal is key for trapping steam inside the packets.

In this recipe, just a tablespoon of white wine or vermouth drizzled on top of the vegetables in each packet adds not only some acidity that brightens the flavors in the dish, but also some moisture that generates steam to cook both the vegetables and the fish. Garlic, herbs, and lemon zest are accents that perk up the flavor and fragrance of the fish and vegetables.

Without a doubt, our fish en papillote is one of the tastiest ways to prepare steamed fish. In addition, it's a simple one-packet meal: Protein and vegetables cook together, so there's no worrying about preparing a side dish or enlisting a battery of kitchen equipment to get dinner on the table.

The packets can be assembled up to 4 hours in advance and refrigerated until ready to cook. If the packets have been refrigerated for more than 30 minutes, increase the cooking time by 2 minutes. See page 375 for a variation on this recipe with fennel and shallot.

What Can Go Wrong

Here's a list of common mistakes cooks make when preparing this recipe.

COMMON MISTAKE	BAD OUTCOMES	WHAT YOU SHOULD DO
Buying Fish Fillets That Are Too Thick	• **The fish is undercooked.**	Shop for fillets that are 1 to 1¼ inches thick, and no thicker. If the fillets are too thick, they will not cook through in the time indicated in the recipe. If you're stuck with thick fillets, you can try adding a few minutes to the cooking time, but this is really guesswork. Once you open the packets, all the steam is released and it's hard to restart the cooking process.
Buying Fish Fillets That Are Too Thin	• **The fish is overcooked.**	Shop for fillets that are 1 to 1¼ inches thick, and no thinner. If the fillets are too thin, they will end up dry and overdone if cooked for the amount of time indicated in the recipe. If you happen to buy a fillet with a thinner end, fold that end under so the fillet has a uniform thickness.
Cutting Carrots and Leeks Too Large	• **The vegetables are crunchy and underdone.**	Tedious though it may seem, take the time to prep the vegetables according to the recipe specifications. If they're cut too large, they won't cook through properly and will retain a crunchy, underdone texture. This recipe relies on vegetables cut into matchstick pieces that are about ⅛ inch thick. Make sure your chef's knife is sharp before you start.
Not Seasoning Compound Butter Enough	• **The fish tastes dull and bland.**	Don't skimp on the garlic, lemon zest, thyme, and salt and pepper that go into the compound butter. This butter mixture melts onto the fish as it cooks and imparts richness and bright flavor. Without it, this dish will taste dull. Also make sure your butter is properly softened to allow the seasonings to be mixed in evenly.
Not Opening Packets Immediately After Cooking	• **The fish is overcooked.**	As soon as the packets come out of the oven, open them up (use caution to avoid steam burns). This will allow the steam and heat to escape so that the fish does not continue cooking and end up dry and overcooked.

1. Peel 2 carrots and cut into 2-inch segments.

2. Cut thin slice from base of each carrot segment to create flat base.

3. Cut each carrot segment into ⅛-inch-thick planks.

4. Working with 3 planks at a time, stack planks and cut into ⅛-inch-thick matchsticks. You should have about 1½ cups.

5. Trim off and discard dark green parts and root ends from 2 leeks.

6. Halve each segment lengthwise and rinse under running water to remove dirt. Cut leeks into 2-inch segments.

7. Working with 3 to 4 layers at a time, stack layers and then cut into ⅛-inch-thick matchsticks. You should have about 2 cups.

8. Mix 4 tablespoons butter, ¼ teaspoon lemon zest, 1 minced garlic clove, 1 teaspoon minced thyme, ¼ teaspoon salt, and ⅛ teaspoon pepper.

9. Combine 2 tablespoons minced fresh parsley, 1 teaspoon grated lemon zest, and 1 minced garlic clove in separate bowl; set aside.

10. Place carrots and leeks in medium bowl.

11. Season with salt and pepper to taste and toss together.

12. Adjust oven rack to lower-middle position and heat oven to 450 degrees.

13. Cut eight 12-inch-long sheets of aluminum foil.

14. Arrange 4 sheets of foil flat on counter.

15. Divide carrot and leek mixture among foil sheets, mounding in center of each.

16. Pour 1 tablespoon vermouth over each mound of vegetables.

17. Pat 4 (6-ounce) skinless cod fillets dry with paper towels and season with salt and pepper.

18. Place 1 fillet on top of each vegetable mound.

19. Spread one-quarter of butter mixture on top of each fillet.

20. Place second square of foil on top of each fish.

21. Crimp edges together in ½-inch fold, then fold over 3 more times to create packet that is about 7 inches square.

22. Place packets on rimmed baking sheet, overlapping slightly if necessary, and bake for 15 minutes.

23. Carefully open foil with kitchen shears, allowing steam to escape away from you.

24. Using thin metal spatula, slide fish and vegetables onto plate with any accumulated juices, top with parsley mixture, and serve with lemon wedges.

Poached Salmon

Overview

Poaching has a reputation for producing dishes that are healthful and wholesome, but not necessarily big on flavor. Our approach to poaching fish fillets fixes this flavor problem.

The reason that these poached salmon fillets are so rich and flavorful is that, as they cook, only their bottoms make contact with the poaching liquid—the flesh retains its flavor compounds instead of releasing them into surrounding liquid. In addition, a layer of lemon slices lifts the fillets off the bottom of the pan to protect them from overcooking. After the fillets are removed from the pan, the poaching liquid is made into a sauce to accompany the fish.

Note that we cook the salmon to medium-rare in this recipe. If you prefer rare salmon (with a large translucent area in the middle of each fillet), shorten the cooking time by 2 minutes, or remove the salmon when the internal temperature reaches 110 degrees. Before you begin, see How to Prepare Fish on page 348 for details on removing pin bones and skin from salmon before cooking.

Recipe Stats

TOTAL TIME **45 minutes**
PREPARATION TIME **15 minutes**
ACTIVE COOKING TIME **15 minutes**
YIELD **4 servings**
MAKE AHEAD **Serve immediately**
DIFFICULTY **Easy**

Tools

- 12-inch skillet with lid
- chef's knife
- cutting board
- liquid measuring cup
- measuring spoons
- fine-mesh strainer
- instant-read thermometer *
- large plate or platter
- mixing bowls
- metal spatula
- rubber spatula
- soupspoon
- aluminum foil
- paper towels

* An instant-read thermometer is the best means of gauging the doneness of the fish fillets. The alternative to using a thermometer is to simply cut into a fillet to check if it is translucent at the very center of the thickest part.

Ingredients

2   **lemons**
2   **tablespoons chopped fresh parsley, stems reserved ***
2   **tablespoons chopped fresh tarragon, stems reserved ***
1   **large shallot, minced (¼ cup)**
½   **cup dry white wine**
½   **cup water**
1   **(1¾- to 2-pound) skinless salmon fillet, about 1½ inches thick ****
2   **tablespoons capers, rinsed and chopped**
2   **tablespoons extra-virgin olive oil**
1   **tablespoon honey**
   Salt and pepper

* For this recipe, you'll need 2 tablespoons each of chopped parsley and tarragon leaves for the vinaigrette; reserve the stems after plucking off the leaves—you'll need them to flavor the poaching liquid.
** To ensure servings of equal size, we prefer to buy a whole center-cut fillet and cut it into four pieces. If a skinless whole fillet is unavailable, either ask the fishmonger to skin it for you, skin it yourself, or follow the recipe as directed with a skin-on fillet, adding 3 to 4 minutes to the cooking time; remove the skin after cooking. In a side-by-side tasting, we preferred wild salmon to farmed salmon because it had a richer, fresher flavor.

What Can Go Wrong

Here's a list of common mistakes cooks make when preparing this recipe.

COMMON MISTAKE	BAD OUTCOMES	WHAT YOU SHOULD DO
Buying Salmon That Is Too Thin	• **The fillets are overcooked and dry.**	When shopping for salmon, look for a fillet that is about 1½ inches at the thickest part. If the fillet is much thinner than that, you may encounter two problems: (1) the pieces may not fit into the skillet in a single layer, and (2) they will cook faster than the recipe indicates. If necessary, to make the fillets fit, overlap only the thinnest areas, and make adjustments in the cooking time to ensure that the fish does not end up dry and overcooked.
Buying Salmon That Is Too Thick	• **The fillets take longer to cook than indicated.**	When shopping for salmon, look for a fillet that is about 1½ inches at the thickest part. If the fillet is much thicker than that, it will take longer to cook through than the recipe indicates. Extend the cooking time by a minute or two, and be sure to check for doneness in the thickest part of the fillet.
Not Cutting Your Own Salmon Fillets	• **Some fillets are over- or undercooked.**	Sure, it will save you a step to buy four individual salmon fillets, but the likelihood they are all the same size is slim. And that means they will cook through at different rates. We strongly advise that you buy one large piece of salmon and cut it into four individual portions yourself so that you can guarantee they are the same size.
Not Lining Skillet with Lemon Slices	• **The bottoms of fillets are overcooked.**	Don't skip—or forget—the step of lining the pan with lemon slices. The slices shield the bottoms of the fillets from the heat of the skillet so that they do not end up overcooked.
Cooking Over Too High Heat	• **The fillets are overcooked.** • **The fillets fray around the edges.**	Once the poaching liquid reaches a simmer over high heat, turn down the burner to low. If the liquid is allowed to boil or simmer vigorously, the fish will end up overcooked and the edges may eventually fray and fall apart.
Not Reducing the Cooking Liquid Properly	• **The vinaigrette is thin and watery.** • **Th vinaigrette won't properly coat the fish.**	You need to reduce the cooking liquid over high heat until you have just 2 tablespoons left. This will take about 5 minutes. Reducing the cooking liquid concentrates its flavor. If you try to make the flavorful vinaigrette with too much cooking liquid, it will water down the oil and honey and run right off the fish.

1. Chop enough parsley and enough tarragon to yield 2 tablespoons of each; reserve stems.

2. Remove white membrane from 1¾-to 2-pound skinless salmon fillet.

3. Cut salmon fillet into 4 equal pieces.

4. Rinse 2 tablespoons capers and chop.

5. Cut top and bottom off 1 lemon.

6. Cut lemon into eight to ten ¼-inch-thick slices.

7. Cut another lemon into 8 wedges and set aside.

8. Arrange lemon slices in single layer across bottom of 12-inch skillet.

9. Scatter herb stems and 2 tablespoons minced shallots evenly over lemon slices.

10. Add ½ cup dry white wine and ½ cup water.

11. Place salmon fillets in skillet, skinned side down, on top of lemon slices.

12. Set pan over high heat and bring liquid to simmer.

13. Reduce heat to low and cover.

14. Cook until sides are opaque but center of thickest part is still translucent and fish registers 125 degrees, 11 to 16 minutes.

15. Remove pan from heat.

16. Using wide metal spatula, carefully transfer salmon and lemon slices to paper towel–lined plate.

17. Tent loosely with aluminum foil.

18. Return pan to high heat and simmer cooking liquid until slightly thickened and reduced to 2 tablespoons, 4 to 5 minutes.

19. Combine 2 tablespoons minced shallot, chopped herbs, capers, 1 tablespoon honey, and 2 tablespoons extra-virgin olive oil in medium bowl.

20. Strain reduced cooking liquid through fine-mesh strainer into bowl with herb-caper mixture, pressing on solids to extract liquid. to taste.

21. Stir to combine and season with salt and pepper to taste.

22. Season salmon lightly with salt and pepper.

23. Using spatula, carefully lift and tilt salmon fillets to remove lemon slices.

24. Place salmon on serving platter or individual plates and spoon vinaigrette over top. Serve, passing reserved lemon wedges separately.

Recipe Library

Sautéed White Fish Fillets

✔ **WHY THIS RECIPE WORKS:** To have the fish and sauce in our sautéed fish fillet recipe ready to serve at the same time, we used fillets of uniform size, between ¼ and 1 inch thick, small enough so that four fillets could fit in a skillet. We reversed the cooking process specified in most sautéed fish fillet recipes, making the sauce first and keeping it warm in a separate saucepan while cooking the fish.

Sautéed White Fish Fillets

SERVES 4

When it comes to the size of a fish fillet, there are two general categories: thick and thin. Thickness determines in part how long the fillet must be cooked. Do not use fillets thinner than ¼ inch, as they will overcook very quickly. These fillets are good served simply with lemon wedges, or you can prepare them with a sauce (recipes follow).

- ½ **cup all-purpose flour**
- 4 **(6-ounce) boneless, skinless white fish fillets, ½ to 1 inch thick, or 8 (3-ounce) boneless, skinless white fish fillets, ¼ to ½ inch thick**
  Salt and pepper
- 2 **tablespoons vegetable oil**
  Lemon wedges

1. Place flour in baking dish or pie plate. Pat fish dry with paper towels. Season both sides of each fillet with salt and pepper; let stand until fillets are glistening with moisture, about 5 minutes. If using any tail-end fillets, score and tuck tail under. Coat both sides of fillets with flour, shake off excess, and place in single layer on baking sheet.

2. Heat 1 tablespoon oil in 12-inch nonstick skillet over high heat until shimmering. Place half of fillets in skillet in single layer and immediately reduce heat to medium-high. For thick fillets: Cook, without moving fish, until edges of fillets are opaque and bottoms are golden brown, 3 to 4 minutes. For thin fillets: Cook, without moving fish, until edges of fillets are opaque and bottoms are lightly browned, 2 to 3 minutes.

3. Using 2 spatulas, gently flip fillets. For thick fillets: Cook on second side until thickest part of fillets is firm to touch and fish flakes easily, 2 to 3 minutes. For thin fillets: Cook on second side until thickest part of fillets is firm to touch and fish flakes easily, 30 to 60 seconds.

4. Transfer fillets to serving platter and tent with aluminum foil. Repeat steps 2 and 3 with remaining 1 tablespoon oil and remaining 2 fillets.

5. Place second batch of fillets on platter with first batch; tilt platter to discard any accumulated liquid. Serve fish immediately with lemon wedges.

White Wine–Shallot Sauce

MAKES ENOUGH FOR 1 RECIPE SAUTÉED WHITE FISH FILLETS

One tablespoon of lemon juice is cooked into the sauce; an additional tablespoon can be added later, if desired, for a bright, tart flavor. Make sure to prepare the sauce through step 1 before cooking the fish.

- 2 **teaspoons vegetable oil**
- 2 **large shallots, minced**
- ½ **cup dry white wine**
- 1–2 **tablespoons lemon juice, plus lemon wedges for serving**
- 4 **tablespoons unsalted butter, chilled**
- 1 **tablespoon capers, rinsed**
- 1 **tablespoon chopped fresh parsley**
  Salt and pepper

1. Heat oil in medium saucepan over medium heat until shimmering. Add shallots and cook, stirring frequently, until softened and beginning to color, about 1½ minutes. Add wine and 1 tablespoon lemon juice, increase heat to high, and bring to boil. Boil until reduced to ¾ cup, 3 to 5 minutes. Off heat, whisk in butter, capers, parsley, and, if desired, remaining 1 tablespoon lemon juice until combined; season with salt and pepper to taste. Cover to keep warm and set aside, stirring once after about 1 minute, while preparing fish.

2. To serve, stir sauce to recombine and spoon ½ cup over cooked fish fillets. Serve immediately with lemon wedges, passing remaining sauce separately.

Coconut–Red Curry Sauce

MAKES ENOUGH FOR 1 RECIPE SAUTÉED WHITE FISH FILLETS

For those who like assertive flavors, the amount of red curry paste can be doubled; in this case, be conservative when seasoning with salt and pepper. Make sure to prepare the sauce through step 1 before cooking the fish.

- 2 **teaspoons vegetable oil**
- 2 **teaspoons minced fresh ginger**
- 2 **teaspoons red curry paste**
- 1 **small garlic clove, minced**
- ½ **teaspoon brown sugar**
- 1 **cup canned coconut milk**
- 3 **tablespoons water**
- 1½ **tablespoons lime juice**
- 2 **teaspoons fish sauce**
- 1 **tablespoon chopped fresh cilantro**
  Salt and pepper
  Lime wedges

1. Heat oil in medium saucepan over medium heat until shimmering. Off heat, add ginger, curry paste, garlic, and sugar and cook, stirring constantly, until fragrant, about

30 seconds. Add coconut milk, water, lime juice, and fish sauce. Increase heat to high, bring sauce to boil, and boil until sauce is reduced to about 1 cup, about 3 minutes. Off heat, stir in cilantro and season with salt and pepper to taste. Cover to keep warm and set aside, stirring once after about 1 minute, while preparing fish.

2. Stir sauce to recombine and spoon ½ cup over cooked fish fillets. Serve immediately with lime wedges, passing remaining sauce separately.

Orange-Tarragon Cream Sauce
MAKES ENOUGH FOR 1 RECIPE SAUTÉED WHITE FISH FILLETS
We like the delicate, fruit flavor of champagne vinegar in this sauce, but white wine vinegar can also be used. Make sure to prepare the sauce through step 1 before cooking the fish.

- 2 teaspoons vegetable oil
- 1 shallot, minced
- 1 cup orange juice
- 3 tablespoons Champagne vinegar
- ¼ cup heavy cream
- 2 tablespoons unsalted butter, chilled
- 1 tablespoon minced fresh tarragon
  Salt and pepper
  Orange wedges

1. Heat oil in medium saucepan over medium heat until shimmering; add shallot and cook, stirring frequently, until softened and beginning to color, about 1½ minutes. Add orange juice and vinegar, increase heat to high, and bring to boil; boil until reduced to ¾ cup, 4 to 6 minutes. Add heavy cream and continue to cook until slightly reduced, about 1 minute. Off heat, whisk in butter and tarragon, and season with salt and pepper to taste. Cover to keep warm and set aside, stirring once after about 1 minute, while preparing fish.

2. To serve, stir sauce to recombine and spoon ½ cup over cooked fish fillets. Serve immediately with orange wedges, passing remaining sauce separately.

Fish Meunière

✔ **WHY THIS RECIPE WORKS:** The best versions of fish *meunière* feature perfectly cooked fillets that are delicately crisp and golden brown on the outside and moist and flavorful on the inside, napped with a buttery yet light sauce. Whole Dover sole is the most authentic choice, but it's also prohibitively expensive; either sole or flounder fillets proved to be good stand-ins. To prevent the likelihood of overcooking the fish, the fillets needed to be no less than ⅜ inch thick. For the perfect coating, there was no need to use eggs or bread crumbs. We simply dried the fillets, seasoned them with salt and pepper, and allowed them to sit for five minutes, in which time beads of moisture appeared on the fillets' surface. Then we simply dredged the fillets in flour. A nonstick skillet coated with a mixture of oil and butter prevented sticking.

For the sauce, we browned the butter in a traditional skillet (so the changing color was easy to monitor), and brightened it with lemon juice, then poured the mixture over the fish.

Fish Meunière with Browned Butter and Lemon
SERVES 4 TO 6
Try to purchase fillets that are of similar size, and avoid those that weigh less than 5 ounces because they will cook too quickly. A nonstick skillet ensures that the fillets will release from the pan, but for the sauce a traditional skillet is preferable because its light-colored surface will allow you to monitor the color of the butter as it browns. See Recipe Tutorial on page 358 for more details on this recipe.

FISH
- ½ cup all-purpose flour
- 4 (5- to 6-ounce) boneless, skinless sole or flounder fillets, ⅜ inch thick
  Salt and pepper
- 2 tablespoons vegetable oil
- 2 tablespoons unsalted butter, cut into 2 pieces

BROWNED BUTTER
- 4 tablespoons unsalted butter, cut into 4 pieces
- 1 tablespoon chopped fresh parsley
- 1½ tablespoons lemon juice
  Salt
  Lemon wedges

1. FOR THE FISH: Adjust oven rack to lower-middle position, set 4 heatproof dinner plates on rack, and heat oven to 200 degrees. Place flour in baking dish or pie plate. Pat fish dry with paper towels, season both sides generously with salt and pepper, and let stand until fillets are glistening with moisture, about 5 minutes. Coat both sides of fillets with flour, shake off excess, and place in single layer on baking sheet.

2. Heat 1 tablespoon oil in 12-inch nonstick skillet over high heat until shimmering, then add 1 tablespoon butter and swirl to coat pan bottom. Carefully place 2 fillets, skinned side down, in skillet. Immediately reduce heat to medium-high and cook, without moving fish, until edges of fillets are opaque and bottom is golden brown, about 3 minutes. Using 2 spatulas, gently flip fillets and cook on second side until thickest part of fillet easily separates into flakes when paring knife is inserted, about 2 minutes longer. Transfer fillets, one to each heated dinner plate, skinned side down, and return plates to oven. Wipe out skillet and repeat with remaining 1 tablespoon oil, remaining 1 tablespoon butter, and remaining 2 fish fillets.

3. FOR THE BROWNED BUTTER: Heat butter in 10-inch skillet over medium-high heat until butter melts, 1 to 1½ minutes. Continue to cook, swirling pan constantly, until butter is golden brown and has nutty aroma, 1 to 1½ minutes. Remove skillet from heat.

4. Remove plates from oven and sprinkle fillets with parsley. Add lemon juice to browned butter and season with salt to taste. Spoon sauce over fish and serve immediately with lemon wedges.

Fish Meunière with Capers

Add 2 tablespoons rinsed capers along with lemon juice in step 3.

Fish Meunière with Toasted Slivered Almonds

Add ¼ cup toasted slivered almonds to skillet when butter has melted in step 2.

Lemony Steamed Fish

✓ **WHY THIS RECIPE WORKS:** Not only is steaming a quick and easy cooking method for fish fillets, but it also keeps the fish moist and its flavor pure. We found that the key to perfectly steamed fish was to simmer the water underneath the steamer basket rather than let it boil. The gentle heat helped the fish cook slowly and evenly. For very thin fish fillets, such as sole, we found that rolling the fish into bundles before putting them in the basket ensured they stayed moist, didn't overcook, and were easy to remove in one piece once cooked. Surrounding the fish with lemon (or other citrus) slices as it steamed gave the fish a delicate, fresh flavor.

Lemony Steamed Fish

SERVES 4

We use sole here, but many types of fish can be prepared using this method; see the fish steaming chart on page 351. Note that only very thin fish fillets (less than ½ inch thick) need to be rolled into bundles before cooking. Limes, oranges, or grapefruits can be substituted for the lemons. Serve with one of the following sauces, if desired; these sauces also work well when paired with Oven-Roasted Salmon (page 376). See Core Technique on page 350 for more details on this recipe.

- 2 lemons, sliced into ¼-inch-thick rounds, plus lemon wedges for serving
- 4 (6-ounce) boneless, skinless sole fillets
  Salt and pepper
- 1 tablespoon chopped fresh basil or minced fresh chives, tarragon, cilantro, or parsley

1. Set steamer basket inside Dutch oven. Fill pot with water until it just touches bottom of basket. Line basket with half of lemon slices, cover, and bring to boil.

2. Meanwhile, pat fish dry with paper towels, season with salt and pepper, and roll each fillet into bundle.

3. Reduce heat to simmer. Lay fish bundles in steamer basket seam side down and top with remaining lemon slices. Cover pot and steam until fish flakes apart when gently prodded with paring knife, 4 to 6 minutes.

4. Gently transfer fish bundles to individual plates, sprinkle with chives, and serve with lemon wedges.

Grapefruit and Basil Relish

MAKES ABOUT 1 CUP, ENOUGH FOR 1 RECIPE LEMONY STEAMED FISH
Regular grapefruits can be substituted for the red grapefruits.

- 2 red grapefruits
- 2 tablespoons chopped fresh basil
- ½ small shallot, minced
- 2 teaspoons lemon juice
- 2 teaspoons extra-virgin olive oil
  Salt and pepper

1. Peel grapefruits, making sure to remove all pith, and cut into ½-inch pieces. Place pieces in fine-mesh strainer set over medium bowl and drain for 15 minutes.

2. Pour off all but 1 tablespoon grapefruit juice from bowl; whisk in basil, shallot, lemon juice, and oil. Stir in grapefruit pieces and season with salt and pepper to taste.

Sweet Sesame-Soy Vinaigrette

MAKES ABOUT ½ CUP, ENOUGH FOR 1 RECIPE LEMONY STEAMED FISH

- 2 tablespoons rice vinegar
- 2 tablespoons low-sodium soy sauce
- 2 tablespoons honey
- 1 scallion, sliced thin
- 2 teaspoons canola oil
- 1 teaspoon Asian chili-garlic sauce
- 1 teaspoon toasted sesame oil
- 1 teaspoon sesame seeds, toasted
- ½ teaspoon grated fresh ginger

Combine all ingredients in bowl. Let sit for 10 minutes before serving.

Pan-Roasted Fish Fillets

✓ **WHY THIS RECIPE WORKS:** Pan-roasting fish seems like a simple task, but it often results in dry, overbaked fillets. We quickly learned we needed thick fillets; skinnier pieces overcooked by the time they achieved a serious sear. We then turned to a common restaurant method to cook the fish: We seared the fillets in a hot pan, flipped them, then transferred the pan to a hot oven to finish cooking. Sprinkling the fillets with sugar accelerated browning on the stovetop, shortening the cooking time and thus ensuring the fish didn't dry out. After a short stay in the oven to finish cooking through, the fish emerged well browned, tender and moist, and best of all, not one taster detected any out-of-place sweetness.

Pan-Roasted Fish Fillets

SERVES 4

Thick white fish fillets with a meaty texture, like halibut, cod, sea bass, or red snapper, work best in this recipe. Most fish fillets differ in thickness; some pieces may finish cooking before others. Be sure to immediately remove each fillet when it reaches 135 degrees. You will need a 12-inch ovensafe nonstick skillet for this recipe. See Core Technique on page 352 for more details on this recipe.

4 (6- to 8-ounce) skinless white fish fillets,
   1 to 1½ inches thick
   Salt and pepper
½ teaspoon sugar
1 tablespoon vegetable oil
   Lemon wedges or relish (recipes follow)

Adjust oven rack to middle position and heat oven to 425 degrees. Pat fish dry with paper towels and season with salt and pepper. Sprinkle very light dusting of sugar (about ⅛ teaspoon) evenly over 1 side of each fillet. Heat oil in 12-inch oven-safe nonstick skillet over high heat until just smoking. Place fillets in skillet, sugar side down, and press down lightly to ensure even contact with pan. Cook until browned, 1 to 1½ minutes. Using 2 spatulas, flip fillets, then transfer skillet to oven. Roast fillets until centers are just opaque and register 135 degrees, 7 to 10 minutes. Immediately transfer to serving plates and serve with lemon wedges or relish spooned over each fillet.

Green Olive, Almond, and Orange Relish

MAKES ABOUT 1½ CUPS, ENOUGH FOR 1 RECIPE PAN-ROASTED
FISH FILLETS

If the olives are marinated, rinse and drain them before chopping.

½ cup slivered almonds, toasted
½ cup green olives, pitted and chopped coarse
1 garlic clove, minced
1 teaspoon grated orange zest plus ¼ cup juice
¼ cup extra-virgin olive oil
¼ cup minced fresh mint
2 teaspoons white wine vinegar
   Salt and cayenne pepper

Pulse almonds, olives, garlic, and orange zest in food processor until nuts and olives are finely chopped, 10 to 12 pulses. Transfer to bowl and stir in orange juice, oil, mint, and vinegar. Season with salt and cayenne to taste.

Roasted Red Pepper, Hazelnut, and Thyme Relish

MAKES ABOUT 1½ CUPS, ENOUGH FOR 1 RECIPE PAN-ROASTED
FISH FILLETS

Rubbing the toasted hazelnuts in a dish towel is an easy way to remove their skins.

½ cup hazelnuts, toasted and skinned
½ cup jarred roasted red peppers, rinsed, patted dry, and chopped coarse
1 garlic clove, minced
½ teaspoon grated lemon zest plus 4 teaspoons juice
¼ cup extra-virgin olive oil
2 tablespoons chopped fresh parsley
1 teaspoon chopped fresh thyme
¼ teaspoon smoked paprika
   Salt and pepper

Pulse hazelnuts, roasted peppers, garlic, and lemon zest in food processor until finely chopped, 10 to 12 pulses. Transfer to bowl and stir in lemon juice, oil, parsley, thyme, and paprika. Season with salt and pepper to taste.

Pan-Roasted Halibut Steaks

✔ **WHY THIS RECIPE WORKS:** Chefs often choose to braise halibut instead of pan-roasting or sautéing because this moist-heat cooking technique keeps the fish from drying out. The problem is that braising doesn't allow for browning, which adds great flavor to fish. We didn't want to make any compromises on either texture or flavor, so we set out to develop a technique for cooking halibut that would produce perfectly cooked, moist, and tender fish with good browning. A combination of pan searing and oven roasting proved best. To be sure the steaks wouldn't overcook, we seared them on one side in a piping hot skillet, then turned them over before placing them in the oven to finish cooking through. When they were done, the steaks were browned but still moist inside. To complement the lean fish, we developed a couple of flavored butters and a bright vinaigrette.

Pan-Roasted Halibut Steaks

SERVES 4 TO 6

If you plan to serve the fish with a flavored butter or sauce (recipes follow), prepare it before cooking the fish. Even well-dried fish can cause the hot oil in the pan to splatter. You can minimize splattering by laying the halibut steaks in the pan gently and putting the edge closest to you in the pan first so the far edge falls away from you.

2 (1¼-pound) skin-on full halibut steaks, 1¼ inches thick and 10 to 12 inches long
2 tablespoons olive oil
   Salt and pepper
1 recipe flavored butter or vinaigrette (recipes follow)

1. Rinse halibut steaks, dry well with paper towels, and trim cartilage from both ends. Adjust oven rack to middle position and heat oven to 425 degrees. When oven reaches 425 degrees, heat oil in 12-inch skillet over high heat until just smoking.

2. Meanwhile, sprinkle both sides of steaks with salt and pepper. Reduce heat to medium-high and swirl oil in skillet to distribute. Carefully lay steaks in skillet and cook, without moving, until spotty brown, about 4 minutes (if steaks are thinner than 1¼ inches, check browning at 3½ minutes; steaks thicker than 1½ inches may require extra time, so check at 4½ minutes). Off heat, flip steaks using 2 thin-bladed metal spatulas.

3. Transfer skillet to oven and roast until steaks register 140 degrees, flakes loosen, and flesh is opaque when checked with paring knife, about 9 minutes (thicker steaks may take up to 10 minutes). Carefully remove hot skillet from oven and separate skin and bones from fish with spatula. Transfer fish to warm platter and serve immediately dolloped with flavored butter or drizzled with vinaigrette.

Anchovy-Garlic Butter with Lemon and Parsley

MAKES ABOUT ¼ CUP, ENOUGH FOR 1 RECIPE PAN-ROASTED
HALIBUT STEAKS

The anchovy adds great depth to this butter.

- 4 tablespoons unsalted butter, softened
- 2 tablespoons minced fresh parsley
- 1½ teaspoons lemon juice
- 1 garlic clove, minced
- 1 anchovy fillet, rinsed and minced
- ½ teaspoon salt

Beat butter with fork until light and fluffy. Stir in parsley, lemon juice, garlic, anchovy, and salt until thoroughly combined.

Chipotle-Garlic Butter with Lime and Cilantro

MAKES ABOUT ¼ CUP, ENOUGH FOR 1 RECIPE PAN-ROASTED
HALIBUT STEAKS

This flavorful butter is great with halibut as well as swordfish and other meaty fish.

- 4 tablespoons unsalted butter, softened
- 2 teaspoons minced fresh cilantro
- 1½ teaspoons minced canned chipotle chile in adobo sauce, plus 1 teaspoon adobo sauce
- 1 garlic clove, minced
- 1 teaspoon honey
- 1 teaspoon grated lime zest
- ½ teaspoon salt

Beat butter with fork until light and fluffy. Stir in cilantro, chipotle and adobo sauce, garlic, honey, lime zest, and salt until thoroughly combined.

Chunky Cherry Tomato–Basil Vinaigrette

MAKES ABOUT 1½ CUPS, ENOUGH FOR 1 RECIPE PAN-ROASTED
HALIBUT STEAKS

Two scallions can be substituted for the shallots.

- 6 ounces cherry or grape tomatoes, quartered
- ¼ teaspoon salt
- ¼ teaspoon pepper
- 6 tablespoons extra-virgin olive oil
- 3 tablespoons lemon juice
- 2 shallots, minced
- 2 tablespoons chopped fresh basil

Combine tomatoes with salt and pepper in medium bowl and let stand until juicy and seasoned, about 10 minutes. Whisk oil, lemon juice, shallots, and basil in small bowl; add to tomatoes and toss to combine.

Cod Baked in Foil

✔ **WHY THIS RECIPE WORKS:** Cooking mild fish like cod *en papillote*—in a tightly sealed, artfully folded parchment paper package so it can steam in its own juices—is an easy, mess-free way to enhance its delicate flavor. If you throw in vegetables, it should add up to a light but satisfying meal. However, without the right blend of flavorings, the fish can taste lean and bland, and not all vegetables pair well with cod. We found that aluminum foil was easier to work with than parchment. Placing the packets on the oven's lower-middle rack concentrated the exuded liquid and deepened the flavor. Leeks, carrots, and fennel all worked well as the vegetable component. And a compound butter contributed to a full-flavored sauce.

Cod Baked in Foil with Leeks and Carrots

SERVES 4

Haddock, red snapper, halibut, and sea bass also work well in this recipe as long as the fillets are 1 to 1¼ inches thick. The packets may be assembled up to 4 hours ahead of time and refrigerated until ready to cook. If the packets have been refrigerated for more than 30 minutes, increase the cooking time by 2 minutes. Open each packet promptly after baking to prevent overcooking and make sure to open packets away from you to avoid steam burns. See Recipe Tutorial on page 362 for more details on this recipe.

- 4 tablespoons unsalted butter, softened
- 2 garlic cloves, minced
- 1¼ teaspoons finely grated lemon zest, plus lemon wedges for serving
- 1 teaspoon minced fresh thyme
  Salt and pepper
- 2 tablespoons minced fresh parsley
- 2 carrots, peeled and cut into 2-inch-long matchsticks
- 2 leeks, white and light green parts only, halved lengthwise, washed thoroughly, and cut into 2-inch-long matchsticks
- ¼ cup dry vermouth or dry white wine
- 4 (6-ounce) skinless cod fillets, 1 to 1¼ inches thick

1. Combine butter, 1 teaspoon garlic, ¼ teaspoon lemon zest, thyme, ¼ teaspoon salt, and ⅛ teaspoon pepper in small bowl. Combine parsley, remaining 1 teaspoon lemon zest, and remaining garlic in another small bowl and set aside. Place carrots and leeks in medium bowl, season with salt and pepper to taste, and toss to combine.

2. Adjust oven rack to lower-middle position and heat oven to 450 degrees. Cut eight 12-inch-long sheets of aluminum foil; arrange 4 pieces flat on counter. Divide carrot-leek mixture among arranged foil sheets, mounding vegetables in center of each piece. Pour 1 tablespoon vermouth over each mound of vegetables. Pat fish dry with paper towels, season with salt and pepper, and place 1 fillet on top of each vegetable mound. Divide butter mixture among fillets, spreading over top of each piece. Place second square of foil on top of fish, crimp edges together in ½-inch fold, then fold over 3 more times to create a packet about 7 inches square. Place packets on rimmed baking sheet, overlapping slightly if necessary.

3. Bake packets for 15 minutes, then carefully open foil, allowing steam to escape away from you. Using thin metal spatula, gently slide fish and vegetables onto plate, along with any accumulated juices, and sprinkle with parsley mixture. Serve immediately, passing lemon wedges separately.

Cod Baked in Foil with Fennel and Shallots

SERVES 4

Haddock, red snapper, halibut, and sea bass also work well in this recipe as long as the fillets are 1 to 1¼ inches thick. The packets may be assembled up to 4 hours ahead of time and refrigerated until ready to cook. If the packets have been refrigerated for more than 30 minutes, increase the cooking time by 2 minutes. Open each packet promptly after baking to prevent overcooking and make sure to open packets away from you to avoid steam burns.

- 1 **large fennel bulb, stalks discarded, bulb halved, cored, and sliced into ¼-inch strips**
- 2 **large shallots, sliced thin**
- 4 **tablespoons unsalted butter, softened**
- 2 **teaspoons minced fresh tarragon**
- 1 **garlic clove, minced**
- ¼ **teaspoon grated orange zest plus 2 oranges peeled, quartered, and cut crosswise into ¼-inch-thick pieces**
  Salt and pepper
- ¼ **cup dry vermouth or dry white wine**
- 4 **(6-ounce) skinless cod fillets, 1 to 1¼ inches thick**

1. Combine fennel and shallots in large bowl, cover tightly, and microwave until fennel has started to wilt, 3 to 4 minutes, stirring once halfway through cooking. Combine butter, 1 teaspoon tarragon, garlic, orange zest, ¼ teaspoon salt, and ⅛ teaspoon pepper in small bowl. Combine orange pieces and remaining 1 teaspoon tarragon in second small bowl and set aside.

2. Adjust oven rack to lower-middle position and heat oven to 450 degrees. Cut eight 12-inch-long sheets of aluminum foil; arrange 4 pieces flat on counter. Divide fennel-shallot mixture among arranged foil sheets, mounding vegetables in center of each piece. Pour 1 tablespoon vermouth over each mound of vegetables. Pat fish dry with paper towels, season with salt and pepper, and place 1 fillet on top of each vegetable mound. Divide butter mixture among fillets, spreading over top of each piece. Place second square of foil on top of each fish, crimp edges together in ½-inch fold, then fold over 3 more times to create a packet about 7 inches square. Place packets on rimmed baking sheet, overlapping slightly if necessary.

3. Bake packets for 15 minutes, then carefully open foil, allowing steam to escape away from you. Using thin metal spatula, gently slide fish and vegetables onto plate, along with any accumulated juices. Spoon orange and tarragon mixture over fish and serve immediately.

Baked Sole Fillets

✔ **WHY THIS RECIPE WORKS:** We wanted a fuss-free, foolproof sole preparation that was suitable for a weeknight dinner yet impressive and elegant enough to serve to company. We found that rolling the fillets into compact bundles eased the transport from baking dish to plate and covering the baking dish with aluminum foil protected the delicate fish from the drying heat of the oven. To ramp up the fillets' mild flavor, we

brushed them with Dijon mustard; seasoned them with salt, pepper, fresh herbs, and lemon zest; and drizzled them with melted butter and garlic. Then we rolled them up, drizzled them with more butter, and baked them. For texture, we added a mixture of herbs, butter, and panko bread crumbs to the sole at two intervals. We removed the foil before the fish was done cooking, basted the fillets with pan juices, topped them with most of the bread-crumb mixture, and then returned them to the oven uncovered. Just before serving, we sprinkled the remaining crumbs over the fillets.

Baked Sole Fillets with Herbs and Bread Crumbs

SERVES 6

Try to purchase fillets of similar size. If using smaller fillets (about 3 ounces each), serve 2 fillets per person and reduce the baking time in step 3 to 20 minutes. We strongly advise against using frozen fish in this recipe. Freezing can undermine the texture of the fish, making it hard to roll. Fresh basil or dill can be used in place of the tarragon.

- 3 **tablespoons minced fresh parsley**
- 3 **tablespoons minced fresh chives**
- 1 **tablespoon minced fresh tarragon**
- 1 **teaspoon grated lemon zest**
- 5 **tablespoons unsalted butter, cut into 5 pieces**
- 2 **garlic cloves, minced**
- 6 **(6-ounce) boneless, skinless sole or flounder fillets**
  Salt and pepper
- 1 **tablespoon Dijon mustard**
- ⅔ **cup panko bread crumbs**
  Lemon wedges

1. Adjust oven rack to middle position and heat oven to 325 degrees. Combine parsley, chives, and tarragon in small bowl. Reserve 1 tablespoon herb mixture; stir lemon zest into remaining herb mixture.

2. Heat 4 pieces butter in 8-inch skillet over medium heat until just melted. Add half of garlic and cook, stirring frequently, until fragrant, 1 to 2 minutes. Remove from heat and set aside.

3. Pat fillets dry with paper towels and season both sides with salt and pepper. Arrange fillets, skinned side up, with tail end pointing away from you. Spread ½ teaspoon mustard on each fillet, sprinkle each evenly with about 1 tablespoon herb–lemon zest mixture, and drizzle each with about 1½ teaspoons garlic butter. Tightly roll fillets from thick end to form cylinders. Set fillets, seam side down, in 13 by 9-inch baking dish. Drizzle remaining garlic butter over fillets, cover baking dish with aluminum foil, and bake 25 minutes. Wipe out skillet with paper towels but do not wash.

4. While fillets are baking, melt remaining 1 tablespoon butter in now-empty skillet over medium heat. Add panko and cook, stirring frequently, until crumbs are deep golden brown, 5 to 8 minutes. Reduce heat to low, add remaining garlic, and cook, stirring constantly, until garlic is fragrant and evenly distributed in crumbs, about 1 minute. Transfer to small bowl, stir in ¼ teaspoon salt, and season with pepper to taste. Let cool, then stir in reserved 1 tablespoon herb mixture.

5. After fillets have baked 25 minutes, remove baking dish from oven. Baste fillets with melted garlic butter from baking dish, sprinkle with all but 3 tablespoons bread crumbs, and continue to bake, uncovered, until fillets register 135 degrees, 6 to 10 minutes longer. Using thin metal spatula, transfer fillets to plates, sprinkle with remaining bread crumbs, and serve with lemon wedges.

Crunchy Oven-Fried Fish

✔ **WHY THIS RECIPE WORKS:** We wanted a recipe for moist, flavorful oven-baked fillets coated in a crunchy crust that would not merely play second fiddle to batter-fried fish, but stand as a worthy dish on its own. Fresh bread crumbs created the best coating. To avoid soft, undercooked crumbs, we started by adding melted butter while processing the bread crumbs, and then crisped the crumbs in the oven. We dipped the fillets first in flour and then in a thick wash made from eggs and mayonnaise before applying the browned crumbs. Placing the coated fish on a wire rack while baking allowed air to circulate, crisping all sides. We also boosted flavor by adding shallot and parsley to the breading and horseradish, cayenne, and paprika to the egg wash.

Crunchy Oven-Fried Fish
SERVES 4

To prevent overcooking, buy fish fillets at least 1 inch thick. The bread crumbs can be made up to 3 days in advance, cooled, and stored at room temperature in an airtight container. Make sure you buy refrigerated prepared horseradish, not the shelf-stable kind, which contains preservatives and additives. Serve with Sweet and Tangy Tartar Sauce (recipe follows). See Core Technique on page 354 for more details on this recipe.

- 4 hearty slices white sandwich bread, torn into quarters
- 2 tablespoons unsalted butter, melted
  Salt and pepper
- 2 tablespoons minced fresh parsley
- 1 shallot, minced
- ½ cup plus 1 tablespoon all-purpose flour
- 2 large eggs
- 3 tablespoons mayonnaise
- 2 teaspoons prepared horseradish (optional)
- ½ teaspoon paprika
- ¼ teaspoon cayenne pepper (optional)
- 1¼ pounds skinless cod, haddock, or other thick white fish fillets, 1 to 1½ inches thick, cut into 4 pieces
  Lemon wedges

1. Adjust oven rack to middle position and heat oven to 350 degrees. Pulse bread, melted butter, ¼ teaspoon salt, and ¼ teaspoon pepper in food processor to coarse crumbs, about 10 pulses (you should have about 3½ cups crumbs). Transfer to rimmed baking sheet and bake until deep golden brown and dry, about 15 minutes, stirring twice during baking time. Cool crumbs to room temperature, about 10 minutes. Transfer crumbs to pie plate and toss with parsley and shallot. Increase oven temperature to 425 degrees.

2. Place ¼ cup flour in second pie plate. In third pie plate, whisk eggs, mayonnaise, horseradish (if using), paprika, cayenne (if using), and ¼ teaspoon pepper until combined. Whisk in remaining ¼ cup plus 1 tablespoon flour until smooth.

3. Spray wire rack with vegetable oil spray and place in rimmed baking sheet. Dry fish thoroughly with paper towels and season with salt and pepper. Dredge 1 fillet in flour and shake off excess. Coat fillet with egg mixture, then coat with bread-crumb mixture, pressing gently so that thick layer of crumbs adheres to fish. Transfer breaded fish to prepared wire rack. Repeat with remaining 3 fillets.

4. Bake fish until fillets register 140 degrees, 18 to 25 minutes. Using thin spatula, transfer fillets to plates and serve immediately with lemon wedges.

Sweet and Tangy Tartar Sauce
MAKES ABOUT 1 CUP

Making this classic seafood sauce at home is easy and the results are far better than store-bought options.

- ¾ cup mayonnaise
- ½ shallot, minced
- 2 tablespoons capers, rinsed and minced
- 2 tablespoons sweet pickle relish
- 1½ teaspoons distilled white vinegar
- ½ teaspoon Worcestershire sauce
- ½ teaspoon pepper

Mix all ingredients together in small bowl. Cover and let sit to blend flavors, about 15 minutes. Stir again before serving.

Oven-Roasted Salmon

✔ **WHY THIS RECIPE WORKS:** Roasting a salmon fillet can create a brown exterior, but often the price is a dry, overcooked interior. We developed a hybrid roasting method, preheating the oven to 500 degrees, and turning down the heat to 275 just before placing the fish in the oven. The initial blast of heat firmed the exterior and rendered excess fat. Then the fish gently cooked through and at the same time stayed moist as the temperature slowly dropped, while some of the remaining fat was eliminated through several slits made in the skin. Adding an easy relish lent acidity and flavors that balanced the richness of the fish.

Oven-Roasted Salmon
SERVES 4

To ensure uniform pieces of fish that cook at the same rate, buy a whole center-cut fillet and cut it into 4 pieces. If your knife is not sharp enough to easily cut through the skin, try a serrated knife. It is important to keep the skin on during cooking to protect the flesh; remove it afterward if you choose not to serve it. See Core Technique on page 349 for more detail on this recipe.

- 1 (1¾- to 2-pound) skin-on salmon fillet, about 1½ inches thick
- 2 teaspoons olive oil
  Salt and pepper
- 1 recipe relish (recipes follow)

1. Adjust oven rack to lowest position, place rimmed baking sheet on rack, and heat oven to 500 degrees. Use sharp knife to remove any whitish fat from belly of salmon and cut fillet into 4 equal pieces. Make 4 or 5 shallow slashes about 1 inch apart along skin side of each piece of salmon, being careful not to cut into flesh.

2. Pat salmon dry with paper towels. Rub fillets evenly with oil and season with salt and pepper. Reduce oven temperature to 275 degrees and remove baking sheet. Carefully place salmon, skin side down, on baking sheet. Roast until centers of thickest part of fillets are still translucent when cut into with paring knife and thickest part of fillets registers 125 degrees, 9 to 13 minutes. Transfer fillets to serving platter or individual plates, top with relish, and serve.

Fresh Tomato Relish
MAKES ABOUT 1½ CUPS, ENOUGH FOR 1 RECIPE
OVEN-ROASTED SALMON
Use fine summer tomatoes for this relish.

- 12 ounces tomatoes, cored, seeded, and cut into ¼-inch dice
- ½ small shallot, minced
- 1 small garlic clove, minced
- 1 tablespoon extra-virgin olive oil
- 1 teaspoon red wine vinegar
- 2 tablespoons chopped fresh basil
  Salt and pepper

Combine all ingredients in medium bowl. Season with salt and pepper to taste.

Spicy Cucumber Relish
MAKES ABOUT 2 CUPS, ENOUGH FOR 1 RECIPE
OVEN-ROASTED SALMON
Parsley can be substituted for the mint.

- 1 cucumber, peeled, halved lengthwise, seeded, and cut into ¼-inch dice
- 1 serrano chile, stemmed, seeded, and minced
- 2 tablespoons chopped fresh mint
- ½ small shallot, minced
- 1–2 tablespoons lime juice
  Salt

Combine cucumber, chile, mint, shallot, 1 tablespoon lime juice, and ¼ teaspoon salt in medium bowl. Let stand at room temperature to blend flavors, 15 minutes. Adjust seasoning with additional lime juice and salt to taste.

Tangerine and Ginger Relish
MAKES ABOUT 1¼ CUPS, ENOUGH FOR 1 RECIPE
OVEN-ROASTED SALMON
Oranges can be substituted for the tangerines.

- 4 tangerines
- 1 scallion, sliced thin
- 1½ teaspoons grated fresh ginger
- 2 teaspoons lemon juice
- 2 teaspoons extra-virgin olive oil
  Salt and pepper

1. Peel tangerines, making sure to remove all pith, and cut into ½-inch pieces. Place pieces in fine-mesh strainer set over medium bowl and drain for 15 minutes.

2. Pour off all but 1 tablespoon tangerine juice from bowl; whisk in scallion, ginger, lemon juice, and oil. Stir in tangerine pieces and season with salt and pepper to taste.

Poached Salmon

✓ **WHY THIS RECIPE WORKS:** When salmon is poached incorrectly, not only is it dry, but the flavor is so washed out that not even the richest sauce can redeem it. We wanted irresistibly supple salmon accented by the delicate flavor of the poaching liquid, and a simple pan sauce. Poaching the salmon in just enough liquid to come half an inch up the side of the fillets meant all we needed was a large shallot, a few herbs, and some wine to boost the liquid's flavor. However, the part of the salmon that wasn't submerged needed to be steamed for thorough cooking, and the low cooking temperature required to poach the salmon evenly didn't create enough. The solution was to increase the ratio of wine to water. The additional alcohol lowered the liquid's boiling point, producing more vapor even at the lower temperature. To keep the bottom of the fillets from overcooking, we placed them on top of lemon slices for insulation. After removing the salmon, we reduced the liquid and added a few tablespoons of olive oil to create an easy vinaigrette-style sauce.

Poached Salmon with Herb and Caper Vinaigrette
SERVES 4
To ensure uniform pieces of fish that cook at the same rate, buy a whole center-cut fillet and cut it into 4 pieces. If a skinless whole fillet is unavailable, remove the skin yourself or follow the recipe as directed with a skin-on fillet, adding 3 to 4 minutes to the cooking time in step 2. This recipe will yield salmon fillets cooked to medium-rare. See Recipe Tutorial on page 366 for more details on this recipe.

- 2 lemons
- 2 tablespoons chopped fresh parsley, stems reserved
- 2 tablespoons chopped fresh tarragon, stems reserved
- 1 large shallot, minced (¼ cup)
- ½ cup dry white wine
- ½ cup water
- 1 (1¾- to 2-pound) skinless salmon fillet, about 1½ inches thick
- 2 tablespoons capers, rinsed and chopped
- 2 tablespoons extra-virgin olive oil
- 1 tablespoon honey
  Salt and pepper

1. Line plate with paper towels. Cut top and bottom off 1 lemon, then cut into eight to ten ¼-inch-thick slices. Cut remaining lemon into 8 wedges and set aside. Arrange lemon slices in single layer across bottom of 12-inch skillet. Scatter herb stems and 2 tablespoons minced shallot evenly over lemon slices. Add wine and water to skillet.

2. Use sharp knife to remove any whitish fat from belly of salmon and cut fillet into 4 equal pieces. Place salmon fillets in skillet skinned side down on top of lemon slices. Set pan over high heat and bring liquid to simmer. Reduce heat to low, cover, and cook until sides are opaque but center of thickest part of fillet is still translucent when cut into with paring knife, or until fillet registers 125 degrees (for medium-rare), 11 to 16 minutes. Remove pan from heat and, using spatula, carefully transfer salmon and lemon slices to prepared plate and tent loosely with aluminum foil.

3. Return pan to high heat and simmer cooking liquid until slightly thickened and reduced to 2 tablespoons, 4 to 5 minutes. Meanwhile, combine chopped parsley and tarragon, remaining minced shallot, capers, oil, and honey in medium bowl. Strain reduced cooking liquid through fine-mesh strainer into bowl with herb mixture, pressing on solids to extract as much liquid as possible. Whisk to combine and season with salt and pepper to taste.

4. Season salmon with salt and pepper. Using spatula, carefully lift and tilt salmon fillets to remove lemon slices. Place salmon on serving platter or individual plates and spoon vinaigrette over top. Serve, passing lemon wedges separately.

Oven-Poached Side of Salmon

✔ **WHY THIS RECIPE WORKS:** For this alternative to traditionally poached salmon, we got rid of the water altogether and steamed the salmon in its own moisture in a low oven. We wrapped the seasoned fish in heavy-duty aluminum foil and placed it directly on the oven rack, which offered more even cooking between top and bottom than using a baking sheet.

Oven-Poached Side of Salmon
SERVES 8 TO 10

If serving a crowd, you can oven-poach two individually wrapped sides of salmon in the same oven (on the upper-middle and lower-middle racks) without altering the cooking time. The salmon is good with lemon wedges, or you can serve it with Horseradish Cream Sauce with Chives (recipe follows). See Core Technique on page 348 for more details on removing pinbones.

- 1 (4-pound) skin-on side of salmon, pinbones removed
  Salt
- 2 tablespoons cider vinegar
- 6 sprigs fresh tarragon or dill
- 2 lemons, sliced thin
- 2 tablespoons minced fresh tarragon or dill
  Lemon wedges

1. Adjust oven rack to middle position and heat oven to 250 degrees. Cut 2 sheets of heavy-duty aluminum foil about 1 foot longer than fish. Fold up 1 long side of each piece of foil by 3 inches. Lay sheets side by side, folded sides together; overlap edges and fold to create 1-inch seam, then press seam

flat with your fingers. Lay third sheet of foil over seam and spray with vegetable oil spray.

2. Pat salmon dry with paper towels, then season with salt. Lay salmon skin side down on top of foil. Sprinkle with vinegar and lay herb sprigs on top. Arrange lemon slices on top of herbs. Crimp foil down over fish.

3. Lay foil-wrapped fish directly on baking rack (without baking sheet) and cook until flesh has turned from pink to orange and thickest part registers 135 to 140 degrees, 45 to 60 minutes.

4. Remove fish from oven and open foil. Let salmon cool at room temperature for 30 minutes.

5. Pour off any accumulated liquid. Reseal salmon in foil and refrigerate until cold, about 1 hour.

6. To serve, unwrap salmon. Brush away lemon, herbs, and any solidified poaching liquid. Transfer fish to serving platter. Sprinkle salmon with minced tarragon and serve with lemon wedges.

Horseradish Cream Sauce with Chives
MAKES ABOUT 2 CUPS

The cream in this sauce is meant to be thickened, not fully whipped. If you like your sauce less spicy, feel free to use less horseradish. Make sure you buy refrigerated prepared horseradish, not the shelf-stable kind, which contains preservatives and additives.

- 1 cup heavy cream, chilled
- ¼ cup minced fresh chives
- 1 (2-inch) piece fresh horseradish root, grated, or 2 tablespoons prepared horseradish
- 2 teaspoons lemon juice

Beat cream in deep bowl with hand-held mixer at medium speed until thick but not yet able to hold soft peaks, about 1½ minutes. Whisk in chives, horseradish root, and lemon juice until just combined. (Sauce can be covered and refrigerated for up to 2 hours; whisk briefly just before serving.)

Glazed Salmon

✔ **WHY THIS RECIPE WORKS:** We wanted a foolproof method for glazed salmon that was succulent and pink throughout with a slightly crusty, flavorful browned exterior—no fussy broiling required. Gently baking the fish cooked the salmon perfectly, and to rapidly caramelize the fillets before their exteriors had a chance to toughen, we sprinkled them with sugar and quickly pan-seared each side before transferring them to the oven. To ensure the glaze stayed put, we rubbed the fish with a mixture of cornstarch, brown sugar, and salt before searing.

Glazed Salmon
SERVES 4

Prepare the glaze before you cook the salmon. You will need a 12-inch ovensafe nonstick skillet for this recipe. If your nonstick skillet isn't ovensafe, sear the salmon as directed in step 2, then transfer it to a rimmed baking sheet, glaze it, and bake as directed in step 3.

1 teaspoon packed light brown sugar
½ teaspoon kosher salt
¼ teaspoon cornstarch
1 (1½- to 2-pound) skin-on salmon fillet, about 1½ inches thick
Pepper
1 teaspoon vegetable oil
1 recipe glaze (recipes follow)

1. Adjust oven rack to middle position and heat oven to 300 degrees. Combine brown sugar, salt, and cornstarch in small bowl. Use sharp knife to remove any whitish fat from belly of salmon and cut fillet into 4 equal pieces. Pat fillets dry with paper towels and season with pepper. Sprinkle sugar mixture evenly over top of flesh side of salmon, rubbing to distribute.

2. Heat oil in 12-inch ovensafe nonstick skillet over medium-high heat until just smoking. Place salmon, flesh side down, in skillet and cook until well browned, about 1 minute. Using tongs, carefully flip salmon and cook on skin side for 1 minute.

3. Remove skillet from heat and spoon glaze evenly over salmon fillets. Transfer skillet to oven and cook until fillets register 125 degrees (for medium-rare) and are still translucent when cut into with paring knife, 7 to 10 minutes. Transfer fillets to serving platter or individual plates and serve.

Asian Barbecue Glaze
MAKES ABOUT ½ CUP, ENOUGH FOR 1 RECIPE GLAZED SALMON
Toasted sesame oil gives this teriyaki-like glaze rich flavor.

2 tablespoons ketchup
2 tablespoons hoisin sauce
2 tablespoons rice vinegar
2 tablespoons packed light brown sugar
1 tablespoon soy sauce
1 tablespoon toasted sesame oil
2 teaspoons Asian chili-garlic sauce
1 teaspoon grated fresh ginger

Whisk ingredients together in small saucepan. Bring to boil over medium-high heat; simmer until thickened, about 3 minutes. Remove from heat and cover to keep warm.

Pomegranate-Balsamic Glaze
MAKES ABOUT ½ CUP, ENOUGH FOR 1 RECIPE GLAZED SALMON
This fruity, tangy glaze is a perfect match for rich salmon.

3 tablespoons light brown sugar
3 tablespoons pomegranate juice
2 tablespoons balsamic vinegar
1 tablespoon whole-grain mustard
1 teaspoon cornstarch
Pinch cayenne pepper

Whisk ingredients together in small saucepan. Bring to boil over medium-high heat; simmer until thickened, about 1 minute. Remove from heat and cover to keep warm.

Orange-Miso Glaze
MAKES ABOUT ½ CUP, ENOUGH FOR 1 RECIPE GLAZED SALMON
Miso is a fermented soy bean paste that adds deep flavor to foods. We prefer milder, white miso here, rather than the strong-flavored red miso.

1 teaspoon grated orange zest plus ¼ cup juice
2 tablespoons white miso
1 tablespoon packed light brown sugar
1 tablespoon rice vinegar
1 tablespoon whole-grain mustard
¾ teaspoon cornstarch
Pinch cayenne pepper

Whisk ingredients together in small saucepan. Bring to boil over medium-high heat; simmer until thickened, about 1 minute. Remove from heat and cover to keep warm.

Crispy Salmon Cakes

WHY THIS RECIPE WORKS: We wanted to give the classic New England fish cake a new spin by using salmon. We were after pure salmon flavor, combined with a few complementary ingredients and a minimal amount of binder. Fresh salmon easily beat out canned, and we ditched the typical potato binder in favor of mayonnaise and bread crumbs. For cakes that held together but weren't pasty, we pulsed chunks of fresh salmon in the food processor in batches. Coating the cakes in panko bread crumbs ensured the right crisped exterior. A few additions (Dijon mustard, scallion, shallot, lemon juice, and parsley) took our salmon cakes to the next level without adding much more work.

Crispy Salmon Cakes
SERVES 4
When processing the salmon it is okay to have some pieces that are larger than ¼ inch. It is important to avoid over-processing the fish. If buying a skin-on salmon fillet, purchase 1⅓ pounds of fish; this will yield 1¼ pounds of fish after skinning. You can serve these salmon cakes simply with lemon wedges or with Sweet and Tangy Tartar Sauce (page 376).

3 tablespoons plus ¾ cup panko bread crumbs
1 scallion, sliced thin
1 shallot, minced
2 tablespoons minced fresh parsley
2 tablespoons mayonnaise
4 teaspoons lemon juice
1 teaspoon Dijon mustard
¾ teaspoon salt
¼ teaspoon pepper
Pinch cayenne pepper
1 (1¼-pound) skinless salmon fillet, cut into 1-inch pieces
½ cup vegetable oil
Lemon wedges

1. Line plate with paper towels and set aside. Combine 3 tablespoons panko, scallion, shallot, parsley, mayonnaise, lemon juice, mustard, salt, pepper, and cayenne in bowl. Working in 3 batches, pulse salmon in food processor until coarsely chopped into ¼-inch pieces, about 2 pulses, transferring each batch to bowl with panko mixture. Gently mix until uniformly combined.

2. Place remaining ¾ cup panko in shallow baking dish or pie plate. Using ⅓-cup measure, scoop level amount of salmon mixture and transfer to baking sheet; repeat to make 8 cakes. Carefully coat each cake in panko, gently patting cake into disk measuring 2¾ inches in diameter and 1 inch high. Return coated cakes to baking sheet.

3. Heat oil in 12-inch skillet over medium-high heat until shimmering. Place cakes in skillet and cook, without moving, until golden brown, about 2 minutes. Carefully flip cakes and cook until second side is golden brown, 2 to 3 minutes. Transfer cakes to prepared plate to drain for 1 minute. Serve with lemon wedges.

Crab Cakes

✔ **WHY THIS RECIPE WORKS:** We wanted to come up with the best possible crab cakes regardless of whether we were starting with fresh crabmeat. We opted for jumbo lump or lump crabmeat, which we soaked in milk to get rid of its fishiness. Celery, onion, and Old Bay seasoning were classic additions. but the flavor-muting binders were a trickier issue. We decided to call on something used in high-end restaurants: a mousseline. This delicate, savory mousse is mainly composed of pureed meat or seafood and just a little cream. We pureed some shrimp and cream, plus the seasonings to create a binder that allowed the clean crab flavor to shine.

Crab Cakes
SERVES 4
Fresh crabmeat will make these crab cakes taste even better. With packaged crab, if the meat smells clean and fresh when you first open the package, skip steps 1 and 4 and simply blot away any excess liquid.

 1   **pound lump crabmeat, picked over for shells**
 1   **cup milk**
1½   **cups panko bread crumbs**
       Salt and pepper
 2   **celery ribs, chopped**
 ½   **cup chopped onion**
 1   **garlic clove, peeled and smashed**
 1   **tablespoon unsalted butter**
 4   **ounces shrimp, peeled, deveined, and tails removed**
 ¼   **cup heavy cream**
 2   **teaspoons Dijon mustard**
 ½   **teaspoon hot sauce**
 1   **teaspoon lemon juice, plus lemon wedges for serving**
 ½   **teaspoon Old Bay seasoning**
 4   **tablespoons vegetable oil**
       Rémoulade Sauce (recipe follows)

1. Place crabmeat and milk in bowl, making sure crab is totally submerged. Cover and refrigerate for at least 20 minutes.

2. Meanwhile, place ¾ cup panko in small zipper-lock bag and finely crush with rolling pin. Transfer crushed panko to 10-inch nonstick skillet and add remaining ¾ cup panko. Toast over medium-high heat, stirring constantly, until golden brown, about 5 minutes. Transfer panko to shallow dish and stir in ¼ teaspoon salt and pepper to taste. Wipe out skillet.

3. Pulse celery, onion, and garlic in food processor until finely chopped, 5 to 8 pulses, scraping down bowl as needed. Transfer vegetables to large bowl. Rinse processor bowl and blade and set aside. Melt butter in now-empty skillet over medium heat. Add chopped vegetables, ½ teaspoon salt, and ⅛ teaspoon pepper; cook, stirring frequently, until vegetables are softened and all moisture has evaporated, 4 to 6 minutes. Return vegetables to large bowl and let cool to room temperature. Rinse out pan and wipe clean.

4. Strain crabmeat through fine-mesh strainer, pressing firmly to remove milk but being careful not to break up lumps of crabmeat.

5. Pulse shrimp in now-empty food processor until finely ground, 12 to 15 pulses, scraping down bowl as needed. Add cream and pulse to combine, 2 to 4 pulses, scraping down bowl as needed. Transfer shrimp puree to bowl with cooled vegetables. Add mustard, hot sauce, lemon juice, and Old Bay; stir until well combined. Add crabmeat and fold gently with rubber spatula, being careful not to overmix and break up lumps of crabmeat. Divide mixture into 8 balls and firmly press into ½-inch-thick patties. Place cakes on rimmed baking sheet lined with parchment paper, cover tightly with plastic wrap, and refrigerate for 30 minutes.

6. Coat each cake in panko, firmly pressing to adhere crumbs to exterior. Heat 1 tablespoon oil in now-empty skillet over medium heat until shimmering. Place 4 cakes in skillet and cook without moving them until golden brown, 3 to 4 minutes. Using 2 spatulas, carefully flip cakes, add 1 tablespoon oil, reduce heat to medium-low, and continue to cook until second side is golden brown, 4 to 6 minutes. Transfer cakes to platter. Wipe out skillet and repeat with remaining 4 cakes and remaining 2 tablespoons oil. Serve immediately with lemon wedges and Rémoulade Sauce.

Rémoulade Sauce
MAKES ABOUT ½ CUP
The rémoulade can be refrigerated for up to 3 days.

 ½   **cup mayonnaise**
 ½   **teaspoon capers, rinsed**
 ½   **teaspoon Dijon mustard**
 1   **small clove garlic, chopped coarse**
1½   **teaspoons sweet pickle relish**
 1   **teaspoon hot sauce**
 1   **teaspoon lemon juice**
 1   **teaspoon minced fresh parsley**
       Salt and pepper

Pulse all ingredients except salt and pepper in food processor until well combined but not smooth, about 10 pulses. Season with salt and pepper to taste. Transfer to serving bowl.

Pan-Seared Scallops

✓ **WHY THIS RECIPE WORKS:** Producing crisp-crusted restaurant-style scallops means overcoming two obstacles: chemically treated scallops and weak stovetops. We wanted superior pan-seared scallops that had a perfectly brown crust and no hint of off-flavors. We decided to work with wet scallops (those that are chemically treated with STP, a solution of water and sodium tripolyphosphate, to increase shelf life and retain moisture) first. If we could develop a good recipe for finicky wet scallops, it would surely work with premium dry (untreated) scallops. Waiting to add the scallops to the skillet until the oil was beginning to smoke, cooking the scallops in two batches instead of one, and switching to a nonstick skillet were all steps in the right direction. But it wasn't until we tried a common restaurant technique—butter basting—that our scallops really improved. We seared the scallops in oil on one side and added butter to the skillet after flipping them. (Butter contains milk proteins and sugars that brown rapidly when heated.) We then used a large spoon to ladle the foaming butter over the scallops. Waiting to add the butter ensured that it had just enough time to work its browning magic on the scallops, but didn't burn. Next we addressed the lingering flavor of STP. Unable to rinse it away, we masked it by soaking the scallops in a saltwater brine containing lemon juice. For dry scallops, we simply skipped the soaking step and proceeded with the recipe.

Pan-Seared Scallops

SERVES 4

We strongly recommend purchasing "dry" scallops (those without chemical additives). Dry scallops will look ivory or pinkish and feel tacky; wet scallops look bright white and feel slippery (see page 345 for more detail). If using wet scallops, soak them in a solution of 1 quart cold water, ¼ cup lemon juice, and 2 tablespoons salt for 30 minutes before proceeding with step 1, and do not season with salt in step 2. See Core Technique on page 355 for more details on preparing scallops.

- 1½ **pounds large sea scallops, tendons removed**
  Salt and pepper
- 2 **tablespoons vegetable oil**
- 2 **tablespoons unsalted butter**
  Lemon wedges or sauce (recipes follow)

1. Place scallops on rimmed baking sheet lined with clean dish towel. Place second clean dish towel on top of scallops and press gently on towel to blot liquid. Let scallops sit at room temperature 10 minutes while towels absorb moisture.

2. Sprinkle scallops on both sides with salt and pepper. Heat 1 tablespoon oil in 12-inch nonstick skillet over high heat until just smoking. Add half of scallops in single layer, flat side down, and cook, without moving, until well browned, 1½ to 2 minutes.

3. Add 1 tablespoon butter to skillet. Using tongs, flip scallops and continue to cook, using large spoon to baste scallops with melted butter (tilt skillet so butter runs to one side) until sides of scallops are firm and centers are opaque, 30 to 90 seconds longer (remove smaller scallops as they finish cooking). Transfer scallops to large plate and tent loosely with aluminum foil. Wipe out skillet with wad of paper towels and repeat cooking with remaining oil, scallops, and butter. Serve immediately with lemon wedges or sauce.

Lemon Browned Butter

MAKES ABOUT ¼ CUP, ENOUGH FOR 1 RECIPE PAN-SEARED SCALLOPS
Watch the butter carefully, as it can go from brown to burnt quickly.

- 4 **tablespoons unsalted butter, cut into 4 pieces**
- 1 **small shallot, minced**
- 1 **tablespoon minced fresh parsley**
- ½ **teaspoon minced fresh thyme**
- 2 **teaspoons lemon juice**
  Salt and pepper

Heat butter in small saucepan over medium heat and cook, swirling pan constantly, until butter turns dark golden brown and has nutty aroma, 4 to 5 minutes. Add shallot and cook until fragrant, about 30 seconds. Remove pan from heat and stir in parsley, thyme, and lemon juice. Season with salt and pepper to taste. Cover to keep warm.

Tomato-Ginger Sauce

MAKES ABOUT ½ CUP, ENOUGH FOR 1 RECIPE PAN-SEARED SCALLOPS
Watch the butter carefully, as it can go from brown to burnt quickly.

- 6 **tablespoons unsalted butter**
- 1 **plum tomato, cored, seeded, and chopped**
- 1 **tablespoon grated fresh ginger**
- 1 **tablespoon lemon juice**
- ¼ **teaspoon red pepper flakes**
  Salt

Heat butter in small saucepan over medium heat and cook, swirling pan constantly, until butter turns dark golden brown and has nutty aroma, 4 to 5 minutes. Add tomato, ginger, lemon juice, and pepper flakes and cook, stirring constantly, until fragrant, about 1 minute. Season with salt to taste. Cover to keep warm.

Orange-Lime Vinaigrette

MAKES ABOUT ½ CUP, ENOUGH FOR 1 RECIPE PAN-SEARED SCALLOPS
We like the fruity, peppery flavor extra-virgin olive oil adds to this vinaigrette, but it is overpowering on its own so we use half vegetable oil, half extra-virgin olive oil here.

- 2 **tablespoons orange juice**
- 2 **tablespoons lime juice**
- 1 **small shallot, minced**
- 1 **tablespoon minced fresh cilantro**
- ⅛ **teaspoon red pepper flakes**
- 2 **tablespoons vegetable oil**
- 2 **tablespoons extra-virgin olive oil**
  Salt

Combine orange juice, lime juice, shallot, cilantro, and pepper flakes in medium bowl. Slowly whisk in vegetable and olive oils. Season with salt to taste.

Pan-Seared Shrimp

✓ **WHY THIS RECIPE WORKS:** We wanted shrimp that were well caramelized but still moist, briny, and tender. Brining peeled shrimp inhibited browning so instead, we seasoned the shrimp with salt, pepper, and sugar, which brought out their natural sweetness and aided in browning. We cooked the shrimp in batches in a large, piping hot skillet and then paired them with thick, glazelike sauces with assertive ingredients and plenty of acidity as a foil for the shrimp's richness.

Pan-Seared Shrimp

SERVES 4

Either a nonstick or a traditional skillet will work for this recipe, but a nonstick will simplify cleanup. See Core Techniques on pages 356 and 357 for more details on this recipe.

- 2 **tablespoons vegetable oil**
- 1½ **pounds extra-large shrimp (21 to 25 per pound), peeled and deveined**
- ¼ **teaspoon salt**
- ¼ **teaspoon pepper**
- ⅛ **teaspoon sugar**

Heat 1 tablespoon oil in 12-inch skillet over high heat until just smoking. Meanwhile, toss shrimp, salt, pepper, and sugar in medium bowl. Add half of shrimp to pan in single layer and cook until spotty brown and edges turn pink, about 1 minute. Off heat, flip each shrimp using tongs and allow shrimp to continue to cook in skillet until all but very center is opaque, about 30 seconds. Transfer shrimp to large plate or platter. Repeat with remaining 1 tablespoon oil and remaining shrimp. After second batch has cooked off heat, return first batch to skillet and toss to combine. Cover skillet and let sit until shrimp are cooked through, 1 to 2 minutes. Serve immediately.

Pan-Seared Shrimp with Garlic-Lemon Butter

Beat 3 tablespoons softened unsalted butter with fork in small bowl until light and fluffy. Stir in 2 tablespoons chopped fresh parsley, 1 tablespoon lemon juice, 1 minced garlic clove, and ⅛ teaspoon salt until combined. Add butter mixture to skillet when returning first batch of shrimp to skillet. Serve with lemon wedges if desired.

Pan-Seared Shrimp with Chipotle-Lime Glaze

Stir together 2 tablespoons lime juice, 2 tablespoons chopped fresh cilantro, 1½ teaspoons minced canned chipotle chile in adobo sauce and 2 teaspoons adobo sauce, and 4 teaspoons packed brown sugar in small bowl. Add chipotle mixture to skillet when returning first batch of shrimp to skillet.

Stir-Fried Shrimp

✓ **WHY THIS RECIPE WORKS:** Our typical high-heat stir-fry technique, which works well with chicken, beef, and pork, doesn't fly with quick-cooking shrimp. We started out cooking the vegetables over high heat, then removed them and turned the heat down before adding the aromatics and shrimp (which we marinated in oil, salt, and garlic for better flavor and texture). Once the shrimp were cooked through in the sauce, we returned the vegetables to the pan. For our sauce, the heavily soy-based brews we turn to for meat stir-fries were a poor match with the shrimp. Sweeter or spicier sauces flavored with garlic and chiles were better suited, and they reduced to a consistency that tightly adhered to the shellfish.

Stir-Fried Shrimp with Snow Peas and Red Bell Pepper in Hot and Sour Sauce

SERVES 4

Serve with Chinese-Style Sticky Rice (page 206). See Core Technique on page 234 for more details on stir-frying.

SAUCE

- 3 **tablespoons sugar**
- 3 **tablespoons distilled white vinegar**
- 1 **tablespoon Asian chili-garlic sauce**
- 1 **tablespoon dry sherry or Chinese rice wine**
- 1 **tablespoon ketchup**
- 2 **teaspoons toasted sesame oil**
- 2 **teaspoons cornstarch**
- 1 **teaspoon soy sauce**

SHRIMP STIR-FRY

- 1 **pound extra-large shrimp (21 to 25 per pound), peeled, deveined, and tails removed**
- 3 **tablespoons vegetable oil**
- 1 **tablespoon grated fresh ginger**
- 2 **garlic cloves, 1 minced, 1 sliced thin**
- ½ **teaspoon salt**
- 1 **large shallot, sliced thin**
- 8 **ounces snow peas or sugar snap peas, strings removed**
- 1 **red bell pepper, stemmed, seeded, and cut into ¾-inch pieces**

1. FOR THE SAUCE: Whisk all ingredients together in small bowl and set aside.

2. FOR THE STIR-FRY: Combine shrimp with 1 tablespoon vegetable oil, ginger, minced garlic, and salt in medium bowl. Let shrimp marinate at room temperature for 30 minutes.

3. Combine sliced garlic with shallot in small bowl. Heat 1 tablespoon vegetable oil in 12-inch nonstick skillet over high heat until just smoking. Add snow peas and bell pepper and cook, stirring frequently, until vegetables begin to brown, 1½ to 2 minutes. Transfer vegetables to medium bowl.

4. Heat remaining 1 tablespoon vegetable oil over high heat until just smoking. Add shallot mixture and cook, stirring frequently, until just beginning to brown, about 30 seconds. Add shrimp, reduce heat to medium-low, and cook, stirring frequently, until shrimp are light pink on both sides, 1 to 1½ minutes. Stir sauce to recombine and add to skillet. Return to high heat and cook, stirring constantly, until sauce is thickened and shrimp are cooked through, 1 to 2 minutes. Return vegetables to skillet, toss to combine, and serve.

Stir-Fried Shrimp with Garlicky Eggplant, Scallions, and Cashews

SERVES 4

Serve with Chinese-Style Sticky Rice (page 206). See Core Technique on page 234 for more details on stir-frying.

SAUCE

- 2 **tablespoons soy sauce**
- 2 **tablespoons oyster sauce**
- 2 **tablespoons dry sherry or Chinese rice wine**
- 2 **tablespoons sugar**
- 1 **tablespoon toasted sesame oil**
- 1 **tablespoon distilled white vinegar**
- 2 **teaspoons cornstarch**
- ⅛ **teaspoon red pepper flakes**

SHRIMP STIR-FRY

- 1 **pound extra-large shrimp (21 to 25 per pound), peeled, deveined, and tails removed**
- 3 **tablespoons vegetable oil**
- 6 **garlic cloves, 1 minced, 5 sliced thin**
- ½ **teaspoon salt**
- 6 **large scallions, white parts sliced thin and green parts cut into 1-inch pieces**
- ½ **cup cashews**
- 12 **ounces eggplant, cut into ¾-inch pieces**

1. FOR THE SAUCE: Whisk all ingredients together in small bowl and set aside.

2. FOR THE STIR-FRY: Combine shrimp with 1 tablespoon vegetable oil, minced garlic, and salt in medium bowl. Let shrimp marinate at room temperature for 30 minutes.

3. Combine sliced garlic with scallion whites and cashews in small bowl. Heat 1 tablespoon oil in 12-inch nonstick skillet over high heat until just smoking. Add eggplant and cook, stirring frequently, until lightly browned, 3 to 6 minutes. Add scallion greens and continue to cook until scallion greens begin to brown and eggplant is fully tender, 1 to 2 minutes longer. Transfer vegetables to medium bowl.

4. Heat remaining 1 tablespoon vegetable oil over high heat until just smoking. Add scallion whites mixture and cook, stirring frequently, until just beginning to brown, about 30 seconds. Add shrimp, reduce heat to medium-low, and cook, stirring frequently, until shrimp are light pink on both sides, 1 to 1½ minutes. Stir sauce to recombine and add to skillet. Return to high heat and cook, stirring constantly, until sauce is thickened and shrimp are cooked through, 1 to 2 minutes. Return vegetables to skillet, toss to combine, and serve.

Spanish-Style Garlic Shrimp

✓ WHY THIS RECIPE WORKS: *Gambas al ajillo*—a Spanish *tapa* of shrimp sizzling in a pool of olive and garlic—is a popular choice when dining out. But simply scaling up this dish at home causes problems. Traditional recipes call for submerging the shrimp in oil, which allows them to heat evenly and gently at a low temperature, but it requires 2 cups of oil. Arranging the shrimp in a single layer in a 12-inch skillet allowed us to use a more reasonable ½ cup oil. The oil reached halfway up the side of each shrimp. After a brief period, we turned the shrimp to cook the other side. Using less oil meant the shrimp couldn't absorb much garlic flavor. So we added garlic in three ways: We added raw minced garlic to a marinade, we browned smashed cloves in the oil in which the shrimp would be cooked, and we cooked slices of garlic along with the shrimp.

Spanish-Style Garlic Shrimp

SERVES 6

Serve shrimp with crusty bread for dipping in the richly flavored olive oil. The dish can be served directly from the skillet (make sure to use a trivet) or, for a sizzling effect, transferred to an 8-inch cast-iron skillet that's been heated for 2 minutes over medium-high heat. We prefer the slightly sweet flavor of dried chiles in this recipe, but ¼ teaspoon sweet paprika can be substituted. If sherry vinegar is unavailable, use 2 teaspoons dry sherry and 1 teaspoon white vinegar.

- 14 **garlic cloves, peeled**
- 1 **pound large shrimp (26 to 30 per pound), peeled, deveined, and tails removed**
- ½ **cup olive oil**
- ½ **teaspoon salt**
- 1 **bay leaf**
- 1 **(2-inch) piece mild dried chile, such as New Mexican, roughly broken, seeds included**
- 1½ **teaspoons sherry vinegar**
- 1 **tablespoon chopped fresh parsley**

1. Mince 2 garlic cloves and toss with shrimp, 2 tablespoons olive oil, and salt in medium bowl. Let shrimp marinate at room temperature for 30 minutes.

2. Meanwhile, using flat side of chef's knife, smash 4 garlic cloves. Heat smashed garlic with remaining 6 tablespoons olive oil in 12-inch skillet over medium-low heat, stirring occasionally, until garlic is light golden brown, 4 to 7 minutes. Remove pan from heat and allow oil to cool to room temperature. Using slotted spoon, remove smashed garlic from skillet and discard.

3. Thinly slice remaining 8 garlic cloves. Return skillet to low heat and add sliced garlic, bay leaf, and chile. Cook, stirring occasionally, until garlic is tender but not browned, 4 to 7 minutes (if garlic has not begun to sizzle after 3 minutes, increase heat to medium-low). Increase heat to medium-low; add shrimp with marinade to pan in single layer. Cook shrimp, undisturbed, until oil starts to gently bubble, about 2 minutes. Using tongs, flip shrimp and continue to cook until almost cooked through, about 2 minutes longer. Increase heat to high and add sherry vinegar and parsley. Cook, stirring constantly, until shrimp are cooked through and oil is bubbling vigorously, 15 to 20 seconds. Serve immediately.

Mussels Steamed in White Wine

✓ **WHY THIS RECIPE WORKS:** Preparing mussels can be an all-day affair, what with scrubbing, debearding, and rinsing. Yet despite all that work, the broth is often gritty and the mussels sometimes taste funky. For steamed mussels that were quick to prepare, flavorful, and grit-free, we began with rope-cultured Great Eastern bottom mussels (a widely available variety), which we found to be the cleanest. Garlic in the broth balanced and enriched the flavor of the mollusks and simmering the cooking liquid with a few flavorful additions (like shallots, garlic, and parsley) for a few minutes before adding the mussels deepened the flavor. We found that larger mussels needed to cook a few minutes after they opened to firm up. It all evened out if we simply cooked them until all the mussels opened.

Mussels Steamed in White Wine
SERVES 4

Serve with crusty bread or rice. See Core Technique on page 355 for more details on preparing mussels.

- 2 cups white wine
- ½ cup minced shallots
- 4 garlic cloves, minced
- ½ cup chopped fresh parsley
- 1 bay leaf
- 4 pounds mussels, scrubbed and debearded
- 4 tablespoons unsalted butter, cut into 4 pieces
   Salt and pepper

1. Bring wine, shallots, garlic, parsley, and bay leaf to simmer in Dutch oven and simmer to blend flavors, about 3 minutes. Increase heat to high, add mussels, cover, and cook, stirring twice, until mussels open, 4 to 8 minutes. Discard any unopened mussels.

2. Remove mussels from liquid and transfer to serving bowl. Whisk in butter, 1 piece at a time. Pour broth over mussels, season with salt and pepper to taste, and serve immediately.

Steamed Mussels with Asian Flavors
SERVES 4

Serve with crusty bread or rice to soak up the cooking liquid.

- 1 cup chicken broth
- 2 teaspoons rice vinegar
- ⅛ teaspoon cayenne pepper
- 2 tablespoons grated fresh ginger
- 2 garlic cloves, minced
- 4 scallions, minced
- 2 tablespoons grated lime zest (3 limes) (optional), plus lime wedges for serving
- 4 pounds mussels, scrubbed and debearded
- 2 tablespoons minced fresh chives, cilantro, or scallions

1. Bring chicken broth, rice vinegar, cayenne, ginger, garlic, scallions, and lime zest (if using) to simmer in Dutch oven and simmer to blend flavors, about 3 minutes. Increase heat to high, add mussels, cover, and cook, stirring twice, until mussels open, 4 to 8 minutes.

2. Remove mussels from liquid and transfer to serving bowl. Pour broth over mussels, garnish with chives. Serve immediately with lime wedges.

Steamed Mussels with Tomato and Basil

Serve these tomato-bathed mussels over cappellini or angel hair pasta.

Decrease wine to 1 cup and substitute ½ cup chopped fresh basil for parsley. After removing mussels from broth in step 2, add 2 cups canned crushed tomatoes. Substitute ¼ cup olive oil for butter, simmering after adding to pot until reduced to sauce consistency, about 10 minutes. Season with salt and pepper to taste. Return mussels to pot with reduced sauce and gently stir to coat. Serve.

Steamed Mussels with Curry and Basil

Add 1 teaspoon Madras curry powder to wine mixture in step 1 and reduce parsley to 2 tablespoons. Right before swirling in butter, stir in 2 tablespoons chopped fresh cilantro and 2 tablespoons chopped fresh basil.

Steamed Whole Lobsters

✓ **WHY THIS RECIPE WORKS:** The secret to tender lobster is not so much in the preparation and cooking as in the selection of the creature itself. After some research into the life cycle of the lobster, we discovered that the variations in the texture of lobster meat depended a great deal on what part of the molting cycle a lobster is in. You will find both hard-shell and soft-shell lobsters available; lobsters are in their prime when their shells are fully hardened. Soft-shell lobsters have claw meat that is shriveled, scrawny, and spongy in texture and tail meat that is underdeveloped. Steaming is far tidier than boiling, as you avoid dealing with waterlogged crustaceans at the dinner table. Neither beer nor wine improved the flavor. As for dry-heat cooking methods, we found the steady heat of the oven preferable to broiling. And to keep the tail from curling during roasting, we simply ran a skewer through it.

Steamed Whole Lobsters
SERVES 4

While we prefer hard-shell lobsters to soft-shell lobsters, soft-shell lobsters are more available in the summer (late spring and early summer is the best time to find hard-shell lobsters). However, because hard-shell lobsters are more packed with meat than soft-shell ones, you may want to buy 1½- to 1¾-pound soft-shell lobsters per person.

- 4 live lobsters
- 8 tablespoons butter, melted (optional)
   Lemon wedges

Fit stockpot or Dutch oven with steamer basket or pasta insert. Add water, keeping level below basket. Bring water to boil. Add lobsters, cover, and return water to boil. Reduce heat to medium-high and steam until lobsters are done, following cooking times in chart on page 346. Serve immediately with melted butter and lemon wedges.

Paella

✔ **WHY THIS RECIPE WORKS:** The key to our paella was finding equipment and ingredients that stayed true to the dish's heritage. First, we substituted a Dutch oven for the more obscure specialty vessel, the paella pan. Then we pared down our ingredient list, dismissing lobster (too much work), diced pork (sausage would be enough), fish (flakes too easily), and rabbit and snails (too unconventional). Chorizo, chicken, shrimp, and mussels (favored over scallops, clams, and calamari) were all in. Canned diced tomatoes replaced the typical fresh. And when we focused on the rice, we found we preferred short-grain varieties. Valencia was our favorite, with Italian Arborio a close second. Chicken broth, white wine, saffron, and a bay leaf were the perfect choices for liquid and seasoning, adding the right amount of flavor without overcomplicating our recipe.

Paella

SERVES 6

This recipe is for making paella in a Dutch oven (the Dutch oven should be 11 to 12 inches in diameter with at least a 6-quart capacity). With minor modifications, it can also be made in a paella pan. Dry-cured Spanish chorizo is the sausage of choice for paella, but fresh chorizo or linguiça is an acceptable substitute. Socarrat, a layer of crusty browned rice that forms on the bottom of the pan, is a traditional part of paella. In our version, socarrat does not develop because most of the cooking is done in the oven. We have provided instructions to develop socarrat in step 5; if you prefer, skip this step and go directly from step 4 to 6. See Core Technique on page 355 for more details on preparing mussels and page 356 for more details on preparing shrimp.

- 1 **pound extra-large shrimp (21 to 25 per pound), peeled and deveined**
  Salt and pepper
- 2 **tablespoons olive oil, plus extra as needed**
- 8 **garlic cloves, minced**
- 1 **pound boneless, skinless chicken thighs, trimmed and halved crosswise**
- 1 **red bell pepper, stemmed, seeded, and cut into ½-inch-wide strips**
- 8 **ounces Spanish-style chorizo sausage, sliced ½ inch thick on bias**
- 1 **onion, chopped fine**
- 1 **(14.5-ounce) can diced tomatoes, drained, minced, and drained again**
- 2 **cups Valencia or Arborio rice**
- 3 **cups chicken broth**
- ⅓ **cup dry white wine**
- ½ **teaspoon saffron threads, crumbled**
- 1 **bay leaf**
- 12 **mussels, scrubbed and debearded**
- ½ **cup frozen peas, thawed**
- 2 **teaspoons chopped fresh parsley**
  Lemon wedges

1. Adjust oven rack to lower-middle position and heat oven to 350 degrees. Toss shrimp, ¼ teaspoon salt, ¼ teaspoon pepper, 1 tablespoon oil, and 1 teaspoon garlic in medium bowl. Cover and refrigerate until needed. Season chicken thighs with salt and pepper and set aside.

2. Heat 2 teaspoons oil in Dutch oven over medium-high heat until shimmering. Add bell pepper and cook, stirring occasionally, until skin begins to blister and turn spotty black, 3 to 4 minutes. Transfer bell pepper to small plate and set aside.

3. Heat 1 teaspoon oil in now-empty pot until shimmering. Add chicken pieces in single layer and cook, without moving, until browned, about 3 minutes. Turn pieces and cook until browned on second side, about 3 minutes. Transfer chicken to medium bowl. Reduce heat to medium and add chorizo to pot. Cook, stirring frequently, until deeply browned and fat begins to render, 4 to 5 minutes. Transfer chorizo to bowl with chicken and set aside.

4. Add enough oil to fat in pot to equal 2 tablespoons and heat over medium heat until shimmering. Add onion and cook, stirring frequently, until softened, about 3 minutes. Stir in remaining garlic and cook until fragrant, about 1 minute. Stir in tomatoes and cook until mixture begins to darken and thicken slightly, about 3 minutes. Stir in rice and cook until grains are well coated with tomato mixture, 1 to 2 minutes. Stir in chicken broth, wine, saffron, bay leaf, and ½ teaspoon salt. Return chicken and chorizo to pot, increase heat to medium-high and bring to boil, stirring occasionally. Cover pot, transfer to oven, and cook until rice absorbs almost all liquid, about 15 minutes. Remove pot from oven. Uncover pot, scatter shrimp over rice, insert mussels, hinged side down, into rice (so they stand upright), arrange bell pepper strips in pinwheel pattern, and scatter peas over top. Cover, return to oven, and cook until shrimp are opaque and mussels have opened, 10 to 12 minutes.

5. FOR SOCARRAT: If socarrat is desired, set pot, uncovered, over medium-high heat for about 5 minutes, rotating pot 180 degrees after about 2 minutes for even browning.

6. Let paella stand, covered, for 5 minutes. Discard any mussels that have not opened and bay leaf, if it can be easily removed. Sprinkle with parsley and serve, passing lemon wedges separately.

Inside This Chapter

CHAPTER 9

How to Grill

Despite today's fancy grills and gear, grilling remains a basic—primitive, even—cooking technique: Go outside, put food over hot coals or an open flame, and cook until it's done. Grilling is much less precise than stovetop cooking because of the differences among various grills, the vagaries of live flames, and environmental conditions (weather has an impact). Understanding how your grill works, from how to heat it properly to building the right type of fire, will reduce these variables and ensure success.

Getting Started

Types of Outdoor Cooking

The words "grilling" and "barbecuing" are often used interchangeably, but they are actually different cooking techniques. Whereas grilling works best with quick-cooking foods that are smallish in size (such as shrimp and skewered meats) or foods that are individually portioned (such as steaks and chops), barbecuing, and grill roasting, works best with larger, slower-cooking foods. It may help to think of grilling, grill roasting, and barbecuing along a cooking-time continuum.

Grilling is the speediest and simplest cooking method performed on the grill, and typically uses high or moderately high heat. Most of the cooking takes place directly over the fire, and the lid is often not used, especially on a charcoal grill. Grilled foods derive their "grilled" flavor from the dripping juices and fat that hit the heat source and create smoke that subtly seasons the exterior of the food.

Grill roasting involves longer cooking times than grilling simply because the foods are larger, and this method calls for heat that is more moderate. The grill is set up for indirect cooking—that is, part of the grill is left free of coals, or some of the gas burners are turned off. The lid is employed to create an ovenlike cooking environment. As a result, foods can be cooked through without danger of scorching the exterior.

Barbecuing takes even longer than grill roasting—it's not unusual for cooking times to exceed 3 hours—because the beef, pork, or poultry is cooked until proteins break down to a meltingly tender texture. This type of cooking requires low, gentle heat. As with grill roasting, food is not cooked directly over the coals or the lit burner. Barbecued foods derive their "barbecued" flavor from wood chips or chunks. The wood generates a deep, intense smoke that permeates the food.

To make indoor cooking method analogies, grilling is like sautéing on the stovetop in a hot skillet, and grill roasting is like roasting in the oven—both cook foods until just done and no further. Barbecuing is like braising—food is cooked past the point of what's considered well-done, until the collagen breaks down and the meat is fork-tender. The table below summarizes the differences between the three cooking methods.

	GRILLING	GRILL ROASTING	BARBECUING
Best For	Small foods that are naturally tender and cook quickly	Large foods that are naturally tender but require more time to cook through	Foods that are naturally tough and sinewy and require prolonged cooking
Prime Examples	Steaks, chops, vegetables, seafood	Beef tenderloin, pork loin, whole birds	Ribs, brisket, pork shoulder
Grill Setup	Cooked directly over fire, often uncovered	Cooked by indirect heat with cover on; sometimes seared first	Cooked by indirect heat with cover on
Cooking Time	5 to 20 minutes	20 minutes to 2 hours	At least 2 hours
Temperature	400 to 600 degrees	300 to 400 degrees	250 to 300 degrees
Use of Wood Chips or Chunks	Rarely	Optional	Required

Essential Equipment

Outdoor cooking requires some specialized equipment, starting with the grill. In the test kitchen, we use both charcoal and gas grills. Charcoal gives the cook more choices to customize the fire, but it requires more effort. Gas is easy to use but doesn't impart nearly as much smoke flavor to barbecued foods. The choice is yours. If you are using a charcoal grill, in addition to the equipment below it's also helpful to keep water-filled spray bottle handy to squelch any flare-ups from fat dripping on the coals (if using a gas grill, check the drip pan and empty excess fat regularly).

CHARCOAL GRILL

The test kitchen's charcoal grill standard is the 22-inch kettle grill. But any charcoal grill will cook your food—the difference being that some grills have features that make them easier to use. A generous cooking surface is always best; a deep lid can cover large foods like a whole turkey; a built-in thermometer is a handy tool; and a side table is the ultimate convenience. Charcoal grills also come in small portable versions; while they may be fine for cookouts in the park or camping excursions, they are simply too small to use for most grilling applications.

CHARCOAL

Many grill aficionados are fans of hardwood charcoal (aka lump charcoal), but we find that it can be inconsistent in its heat output and that it burns too quickly. For consistently great results, we prefer to use regular charcoal briquettes. We avoid using instant-lighting briquettes because we find that they have a slightly off-odor as they burn and because we simply prefer to use a less-processed product.

CHIMNEY STARTER

For igniting charcoal briquettes, nothing is safer or more effective than a chimney starter (aka flue starter). You place briquettes in the top chamber, then you crumple a sheet of newspaper, place it in the smaller chamber under the coals, and light it. In about 20 minutes, the coals are covered in a fine, gray ash and are ready to be poured into the grill. We prefer large chimney starters—ones that can hold at least 6 quarts of briquettes.

GAS GRILL

A gas grill is convenient and easy to use; all you need to do to start the fire is open the valve and press the igniter. The trade-off is that it doesn't deliver the woodsy, smoky flavor that a charcoal grill does. For some cooks, that's a fair swap. Our gas grill testing revealed that it is not necessary to break the bank to get a good performer, and that even heat distribution and good fat drainage are two important factors. We like our gas grills to have a generous cooking surface area—at least 350 square inches—and three independently operating burners.

GRILL BRUSH

Nothing works better than a good grill brush for getting burnt-on gunk off a cooking grate. Most feature stiff metal bristles, but sticky goo can quickly get stuck in the bristles. We prefer grill brushes with replaceable scouring pads as the scrubbers. Whichever type you opt for, make sure that it has a long handle to keep your hands a safe distance from fire; wood is preferable over plastic (which can easily melt if it's not heat-resistant) and metal (which heats up quickly).

TONGS

Tongs are the most useful tool for turning foods, from slender asparagus spears to racks of ribs, when grilling. But forget tongs made especially for grilling—many are cumbersome to use and are ill suited for picking up smaller or more delicate items. A pair of 16-inch standard kitchen tongs keeps your hands a safe distance from the fire and affords you ample dexterity. For more details on what to look for, see page 31.

BARBECUE MITT

A good mitt is invaluable; if you can't pick up a hot cooking grate or reach over the coals to tend to the food, you might as well stay indoors. It should meet two core requirements: enough heat resistance to keep hands from burning and enough pliability to keep cooks from inadvertently dropping grates or smashing food.

INSTANT-READ THERMOMETER

For a variety of foods, using an instant-read thermometer is the only way to reliably test the doneness. A good digital instant-read thermometer will quickly register the food's temperature and is much easier to read than a dial-face thermometer. For more details on what to look for, see page 10.

BASTING BRUSH

When you're trying to brush sauce on chicken or meat that's on a ripping-hot grill, you want to keep your fingers safe. Look for a basting brush with a long handle made from a heat-resistant material that is dishwasher-safe. An angled brush head facilitates basting. We prefer silicone brush bristles, which won't melt or singe, to nylon or boar bristles.

How to Set Up a Charcoal Grill

ESSENTIAL EQUIPMENT

- charcoal grill
- chimney starter
- newspaper
- charcoal briquettes
- matches
- barbecue mitt
- grill brush
- small bowl
- paper towels
- tongs

A charcoal grill offers some advantages over gas, including more options for creating custom fires and a better ability to impart smoke flavor. That said, using a charcoal grill does require some extra effort. Make sure to position the grill on a flat surface, well away from the house or other structures. Never grill indoors or in the garage. Locate the grill away from the usual foot traffic, especially areas where kids or pets play.

Properly heating and cleaning the grill before cooking are as important to successful grilling as cooking the food just right. Why? Because not only does a too-cool and gunked-up cooking grate cause food to stick, it can also leave food coated with sooty residue and tasting of icky burnt matter. Here's how to heat and clean a charcoal grill. Also see How to Create Custom Grill Fires (pages 392–393).

1. GET COALS HOT

Remove cooking grate from grill and open bottom grill vent halfway or completely, according to recipe. Fill bottom section of chimney starter with crumpled newspaper, set starter on charcoal rack, and fill top of starter with charcoal briquettes according to recipe. Ignite newspaper and allow charcoal to burn until briquettes on top are partly covered with thin layer of gray ash. **WHY?** We strongly recommend using a chimney starter. Lighter fluid imparts an off-flavor to grilled foods. Don't pour out the coals prematurely; you will be left with unlit coals at the bottom of the pile that may never ignite, resulting in a cooler fire than you wanted or needed.

2. GET GRATE HOT

Empty briquettes onto grill and distribute as indicated in recipe. Set cooking grate in place, cover, and heat grate for about 5 minutes. **WHY?** A hot grate jump-starts the cooking process and reduces sticking of food. Also, a blast of heat will make it easier to clean the grate in the next step). But don't let the grate heat longer than 5 minutes, or the fire will start to die.

3. SCRUB GRATE CLEAN

Use grill brush to scrape cooking grate clean. **WHY?** We don't understand why some cooks think a dirty grate "seasons" food. You wouldn't cook in a dirty pan. If you skip this step, food is more likely to stick and to pick up off-flavors.

4. SLICK DOWN GRATE

Using tongs, dip wad of paper towels in vegetable oil and wipe cooking grate several times. **WHY?** The oil offers another layer of protection against sticking. For really delicate foods (such as fish), we recommend slicking down the grate as many as 5 or 10 times, almost like seasoning a cast-iron skillet. But this seasoning burns off and needs to be reapplied every time you grill. Pouring the oil into a small bowl makes it easy to dip the paper towels to apply multiple coats.

How to Set Up a Gas Grill

First and foremost, read all instructions in your owner's manual thoroughly, and follow the directions regarding the order in which the burners must be lit. On most gas grills, an electric igniter lights the burners, though we have found that electric igniters can fail occasionally, especially in windy conditions. For these situations, most models have a hole for lighting the burners with a match. Be sure to wait several minutes (or as directed) between attempts at lighting the grill. This waiting time allows excess gas to dissipate and is an important safety measure.

As with a charcoal grill, make sure to position the grill on a flat surface, well away from the house or other structures. Never grill indoors, or in the garage. Locate the grill away from the usual foot traffic, especially areas where kids or pets play. Also see How to Create Custom Grill Fires (pages 392–393).

ESSENTIAL EQUIPMENT

- gas grill
- teakettle or saucepan
- grill brush
- small bowl
- paper towels
- tongs

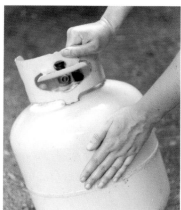

1A–1B. CHECK PROPANE LEVEL

If grill is equipped with gas gauge or tank scale, check to make sure you have enough fuel. If grill doesn't have gauge, bring about 1 cup water to boil in teakettle or saucepan, then pour boiling water over side of tank. Place your hand on tank. Where water succeeds in warming tank, tank is empty; where tank remains cool to touch, there is fuel inside.

WHY? Running out of fuel is an easy way to ruin dinner. If your grill relies on a tank of propane gas, always check the level before you start. Also, we suggest keeping a backup tank on hand. Our method for testing without an indicator relies on the fact that air heats faster than propane gas. It's not the most precise test, but it's better than nothing and can save you from running out of fuel midway through cooking.

2. LIGHT WITH LID UP

With grill cover open, turn all burners to high and ignite.

WHY? Don't attempt to light a gas grill with the lid down; this can trap gas and cause a dangerous explosion of fire.

3. COVER GRILL AND GET GRATE HOT

Cover grill and let it heat for about 15 minutes.

WHY? Once the burners are safely lit, put the lid down to trap heat. Most grills will reach their maximum heat level within 15 minutes, although you might need to heat the grill a few extra minutes on a cold or windy day.

4. SCRAPE GRATE CLEAN, THEN SLICK DOWN GRATE

Once grill is hot, scrape cooking grate clean with grill brush to remove any burnt-on residue. Using tongs, dip wad of paper towels in vegetable oil and wipe grate several times (see photo on opposite page). Adjust burners as directed in recipe to create custom grill fire.

WHY? Once the grill is hot, get it clean and slick down the cooking surface to prevent sticking.

How to Create Custom Grill Fires

ESSENTIAL EQUIPMENT

- charcoal grill and charcoal, or gas grill
- tongs (if using charcoal grill)
- disposable aluminum pan (optional)

Cooks make two basic mistakes when grilling: creating too much fire, and setting up the fire incorrectly. The first problem is easy to avoid—add the amount of charcoal called for in recipes or, if cooking on a gas grill, adjust the burner temperatures as directed. You don't cook everything on high heat on your stovetop, so why would you cook only on high heat on the grill?

The second problem—the wrong setup for the fire—is more complicated. Different types of foods require different types of fires. For example, thin steaks need only single-level high heat to give them a good sear and to cook them through, whereas extra-thick pork chops need a two-level fire—high heat for a deep sear and lower heat over which they can cook through. Depending on the food being cooked, we use one of the five grill setups outlined on these two pages. Keep in mind that you might have to adapt these setups based on the shape, depth, and/or circumference of your grill. See recipes at the end of this chapter for specific amounts of charcoal required.

A. SINGLE-LEVEL FIRE

Charcoal Grill: Distribute lit coals in even layer across bottom of grill.

Gas Grill: After preheating grill, turn all burners to heat setting as directed in recipe.

WHY? A single-level fire delivers a uniform level of heat across the entire cooking surface and is often used for small, quick-cooking pieces of food, such as hamburgers, sausages, fish, shellfish, and some vegetables.

B. TWO-LEVEL FIRE

Charcoal Grill: Evenly distribute two-thirds of lit coals over half of grill, then distribute remainder of coals in even layer over other half of grill.

Gas Grill: After preheating grill, leave primary burner on high and turn other burner(s) to medium.

WHY? This setup creates two cooking zones: a hotter area for searing and a slightly cooler area to cook food more gently. It is often used for big, thick chops and bone-in chicken pieces. A gas grill's primary burner is the one that must be left on; see your owner's manual if in doubt.

C. MODIFIED TWO-LEVEL (HALF-GRILL) FIRE

Charcoal Grill: Distribute lit coals over half of grill, piling them in even layer. Leave other half of grill free of coals.

Gas Grill: After preheating grill, adjust primary burner if directed in recipe, and turn off other burner(s).

WHY? Like a two-level fire, this fire has two cooking zones, but the difference in heat level is much more dramatic. One side is intensely hot, and the other side is very cool. It's great for cooking fatty foods because the heat-free zone provides a place to set food while flare-ups die down. For foods that require long cooking times, you can brown the food on the hot side, then set it on the cool side to finish with indirect heat. It's also good for cooking chicken breasts over the cooler side gently, then giving them a quick sear on the hot side.

D. BANKED FIRE

Charcoal Grill: Bank all lit coals steeply against one side of grill, leaving rest of grill free of coals.

Gas Grill: After preheating grill, adjust primary burner as directed in recipe, and turn off other burner(s).

WHY? A banked fire is similar to a modified two-level fire, except the heat is concentrated in an even smaller part of the grill. The large heat-free area can accommodate a pan of water and large cuts. This setup is often used for large foods that require hours on the grill, such as brisket or pulled pork.

E. DOUBLE-BANKED FIRE

Charcoal Grill: Divide lit coals into two steeply banked piles on opposite sides of grill, leaving center free of coals.

Gas Grill: After preheating grill, leave primary burner and burner at opposite end of grill on medium-high, medium, or as directed in recipe, and turn off center burner(s).

WHY? A double-banked fire sets up a cool area in the middle so that the food cooks evenly without the need for rotating it. Since the flame-free area is quite narrow and the heat output of this type of fire is not steady over an extended time, a double-banked fire is good for relatively small, quick-cooking foods such as a whole chicken. We sometimes place a disposable pan in the empty center area of the grill to catch drips and prevent flare-ups. The pan also keeps the piles of coals banked against the sides of the grill. This type of fire can be created in a gas grill only if the grill has at least three burners—and burners that ideally run from front to back on the grill.

Troubleshooting Custom Grill Fires

PROBLEM	SOLUTION
I never know how to position the vents on a charcoal grill.	We provide instructions in our recipes for how vents should be positioned. Both the bottom vent and lid vent can have an effect on how hot and how fast the charcoal burns. Opening the vents provides more oxygen to the fire so that it burns hotter and faster. In general, we open the bottom vent and don't use the lid when grilling something that takes a short period of time. For longer-cooking items, we use the lid and often adjust vents to maintain a lower-temperature fire for a longer period of time.
When do I use the grill cover?	Depending on the food being cooked and whether you're using a gas or charcoal, you may need to cover the grill; refer to specific recipes. In general, slow-cooking food is cooked covered so that the grill turns into an oven of sorts; we generally don't use the lid when grilling quick-cooking items on a charcoal grill. A gas grill requires lidded cooking more often than charcoal because it tends to run cooler.
I have trouble getting food to cook evenly when I use indirect heat.	Because the part(s) closest to the heat source will cook more quickly than those facing away from the fire, it's important to rotate the food once (at the halfway mark in the projected cooking time). This should ensure that both sides of a turkey or both edges of a rack of ribs are done at the same time. Also, don't open the lid too often.

How to Use Wood

Wood chips or chunks are optional when grill-roasting, but when barbecuing (see page 396) they are essential for providing the deep smoky flavor that is the hallmark of good barbecue. Wood chips will work on either a charcoal or a gas grill, but chunks are suited only to charcoal fires since they must rest in a pile of lit coals to smoke. Soaked wood chunks can be added directly to lit charcoal, but wood chips typically require a little more prep before putting them on the fire (although occasionally we put chips directly on lit coals). Wood chips and chunks are made from hardwoods because they burn more slowly than softer woods. Hickory and mesquite are most common, though some stores may also carry apple, cherry, or oak. Resinous woods like pine are not used for grilling because they give foods an off-flavor.

ESSENTIAL EQUIPMENT

- wood chips or chunks
- bowl
- fine-mesh strainer
- aluminum foil and paring knife, or disposable aluminum pan (if using gas grill)
- charcoal grill and charcoal, or gas grill

1. SOAK THOROUGHLY

Place amount of chips or chunks specified in recipe in bowl and cover with water. Soak chips for 15 minutes; soak chunks for 1 hour. Drain.

WHY? Using wood chips or chunks is the easiest way to add smoke flavor when cooking on a grill. With the exception of mesquite, which we find can overpower the food's flavor, almost any variety will work. Hickory is a solid all-purpose choice. The wood should smolder, releasing smoke over an extended period of time, not burn up as soon as it hits the fire. To that end, soaking the chips or chunks in water adds enough moisture to prevent them from igniting as soon as they're set on the fire. One medium chunk is equivalent to 1 cup of chips. Soaked chunks can go directly on the coals.

2A. WRAP CHIPS IN FOIL

Wrap soaked and drained wood chips in large piece of heavy-duty aluminum foil. Use paring knife to poke about 6 holes in packet. Place packet on primary burner before lighting grill if using gas, or on lit coals if using charcoal grill.

WHY? Wood chips are typically wrapped in a foil packet to protect them from burning too quickly. Holes poked or cut into the packet allow smoke to escape. A single foil packet can hold up to 2 cups of wood chips; if a recipe calls for more wood chips, you'll want to divide the chips between multiple packets.

2B. PLACE CHIPS IN DISPOSABLE PAN

If using gas grill, place soaked and drained chips in disposable aluminum pan as directed in recipe and add water to pan. Set pan on primary burner before lighting grill.

WHY? Sometimes when using gas we put chips in a disposable aluminum pan with water. This will provide more protection than a foil packet, allowing the chips to burn more slowly for long-cooking recipes. You can also add more water to the pan to slow down the rate at which the chips smoke.

How to Grill-Roast

Grill roasting is best for relatively large foods that are already tender and don't require prolonged cooking, like whole birds and tender roasts like loin and tenderloin cuts. Grill-roasting temperatures typically range from 300 to 400 degrees, and cooking times are relatively short, usually less than 1 or 2 hours. (Whole turkeys, which can take up to 3 hours, are an exception.) Grill-roasted meats and poultry can be seasoned a number of ways. You can simply let the smokiness from the grill be the primary flavoring, or add wood chips or chunks during cooking to bump up the smoke factor. Meat and poultry can also be dusted with a spice rub or seasoned with herbs and/or garlic before grill roasting. Or, during the final minutes of cooking, the food can be basted with a glaze. At the table, grill-roasted meats and poultry can be served with a sauce, relish, salsa, or chutney. Also see How to Use Wood (opposite page) and How to Create Custom Grill Fires (pages 392–393).

ESSENTIAL EQUIPMENT

- charcoal grill and charcoal, or gas grill
- chimney starter (if using charcoal grill)
- wood chips
- aluminum foil
- tongs
- instant-read thermometer

1. SET UP FIRE FOR INDIRECT COOKING

Set up modified two-level fire or double-banked fire so that part of grill has no fire.

WHY? Grill roasting relies on indirect cooking; the food isn't placed directly over the coals or lit burner, so the fire must be fashioned accordingly.

2. ADD WOOD CHIPS, IF DESIRED

Place aluminum foil packet filled with soaked chips on lit coals of charcoal grill or over primary burner on gas grill.

WHY? Grill-roasted foods can be given a boost of smoky flavor by adding wood chips to the fire during cooking, but they are not always used.

3. SEAR OVER HOT SIDE

Clean and oil cooking grate. Place food over hot side of grill and cook, turning as infrequently as possible, until well browned.

WHY? In most cases (but not when cooking whole birds), the hot side of the grill is used to sear the exterior of the food to develop color and flavor.

4. COVER AND COOK OVER COOL SIDE

After searing, slide food to cool side of grill, cover, and cook, rotating food once if necessary, until it reaches desired internal temperature. Let meat rest, then slice and serve.

WHY? After searing, the food is moved to the cooler side to finish cooking (in the case of a whole bird, it is set over the cool side from the get-go). The grill is always covered when grill-roasting so that heat stays trapped inside. Most of the foods that are grill-roasted (beef roast, pork roast, whole birds) are cooked to a specific internal temperature. If using a modified two-level fire, make sure to rotate the food at the midway point in the projected cooking time so that the side that had been facing the fire is now turned away from the fire. In some cases, you might need replenish a charcoal fire with additional hot coals (see step 4 on page 397).

How to Barbecue

In barbecuing, the goal is to impart a deep, intense smokiness while transforming chewy, tough, fatty cuts into tender, succulent meats. This means a long cooking time (usually several hours) over low heat—hence the barbecue tagline: "Low and slow is the way to go." Although there is some debate among experts as to the proper heat level for barbecuing, we find a cooking temperature between 250 and 300 degrees to be optimal for most types of meats.

Some barbecue purists would call it heretical to barbecue on a gas grill; we admit that, in comparison with a charcoal grill, a gas grill results in milder, less-pervasive smoky flavor, but it still yields good results. Either way, you will need to use wood—without smoke you're not barbecuing. Remember, you should use wood chunks only with a charcoal grill. Refer to How to Use Wood (page 394). Also see How to Create Custom Grill Fires (pages 392–393).

ESSENTIAL EQUIPMENT

- charcoal grill and charcoal, or gas grill
- chimney starter (if using charcoal grill)
- wood chips and aluminum foil, or wood chunks
- barbecue mitt (if using charcoal grill)
- rimmed baking sheet

1. BUILD VERY SMALL FIRE

Build modified two-level fire or banked fire as directed in recipe so that most of grill has no coals.

WHY? The fire for barbecuing is built in much the same way as it is for grill roasting, with one side of the grill hotter than the other, but often with fewer coals or with the primary burner at a lower setting.

2. ADD WOOD CHIPS OR CHUNKS

Place foil packet filled with soaked chips on lit coals of charcoal grill or over primary burner on gas grill (or nestle soaked chunks into charcoal).

WHY? Wood chips or chunks are added to the hot side of the grill to generate smoke that envelops and flavors the food. It's not uncommon for a small pan of water to sit in the grill under the cooking grate when barbecuing to provide just a little moisture that prevents the surface of the meat from becoming completely desiccated during cooking.

3. COVER AND COOK ON COOL SIDE

Clean and oil cooking grate. Place food on grill as far from fire as possible. Cover and cook, turning as infrequently as possible.

WHY? The grill is always covered when barbecuing so that heat, smoke, and moisture are trapped inside. Barbecued foods are usually not seared or browned before or after cooking—a coating of spice rub and the long cooking time take care of providing color and a nice crust. (Salt and pepper, ground cumin, cinnamon, coriander, or chili powder, and dried herbs such as thyme and bay leaves all work well for a rub. Garlic or onion powder and sugar are also commonly used.) Make sure to rotate the food at the midway point of the projected cooking time so that the side that has been facing the fire is now turned away from the fire. Don't open the grill more than necessary—otherwise the fire might die out before the food is cooked.

4. ADD HOT COALS AS NEEDED

If necessary, light more coals in chimney and add hot coals to fire to keep it going.

WHY? Barbecued foods that cook for more than a couple of hours often require a fuel replenishment to keep the fire sufficiently hot. (The same can be true of grill-roasted foods.) On a charcoal grill, this means adding a few fresh coals to the fire. (On a gas grill, just make sure you have plenty of gas.) If your charcoal grill comes with a hinged cooking grate, you can simply lift part of the cooking grate to add the hot coals. If not, you will have to don fireproof gloves and remove the food and cooking grate to add hot coals.

5. FINISH IN OVEN

Transfer food to rimmed baking sheet (or other pan as directed) and finish in oven until meat is fork-tender. Let meat rest, then slice and serve.

WHY? Depending on the cut of meat, barbecuing can take the better part of a day on the grill and require monitoring and multiple fuel replenishments. For a simpler way that yields equally great results, we cook the food long enough on the grill for it to pick up plenty of smoke. Then we move indoors and finish in a low oven, where cooking can proceed practically unattended. We sometimes wrap the food in foil to trap steam to speed up the cooking process in the oven.

Troubleshooting Barbecue

PROBLEM	SOLUTION
How can I tell when barbecued foods are done?	Connective tissue makes cuts like brisket or pork shoulder tough. But once the internal temperature of the meat exceeds 140 degrees, the collagen in the connective tissue begins to break down into gelatin, and fat in and around the muscles starts melting and moistening the meat. When held at this temperature, or ideally a bit higher (160 to 180 degrees), for an extended period, tough cuts turn incredibly tender and moist. Low-and-slow barbecuing allows this to happen in a relatively cool grill that won't scorch the exterior. For this process to be successful, barbecued meats must be cooked until they are fork-tender. While it's possible to overcook barbecued meats, undercooking is the bigger risk, so err on the side of cooking too much rather than too little.
I tend to burn ribs and such. What am I doing wrong?	Assuming that you're using a small fire in a large enough grill and barbecuing over indirect heat, we suspect that the sauce is the problem. Most types of barbecued meats should not be coated with barbecue sauce during cooking. Rather, sauce is best introduced only after cooking—passed at the table or, in the case of pulled meats, tossed with the meat after shredding. If you would like to apply sauce to barbecued foods as they cook, do so only in the last 5 to 10 minutes of cooking so that the sugars in the sauce will not burn.

Grilled Glazed Bone-In Chicken Breasts

Tools

- charcoal or gas grill
- small saucepan
- chef's knife
- cutting board
- dry measuring cups
- liquid measuring cup
- measuring spoons
- barbecue basting brush
- barbecue mitt *
- charcoal briquettes *
- citrus juicer
- grill brush
- instant-read thermometer
- kitchen shears
- large container or bowl **
- large chimney starter *
- large plate or platter
- mixing bowls
- rasp-style grater
- spray bottle filled with water *
- tongs
- whisk
- aluminum foil
- matches and newspaper *
- paper towels
- plastic wrap

* The mitt, briquettes, chimney starter, spray bottle, matches, and newspaper are needed only if using a charcoal grill.
** For the brining, step, you will need a container large enough to hold 2 quarts of water and the split chicken breasts.

Overview

Grilling bone-in chicken breasts is trickier than it seems. You want well-browned, crisp skin as well as moist meat. The challenge is that the thick part of the breast is quite slow to cook, while the tapered end cooks quickly. Adding a glaze to that equation makes the situation even a little thornier.

First, we brine the chicken breasts to boost their moistness and to season them. Second, we set up the grill with a modified two-level fire; the hot side is used for browning and crisping, and the cooler side for the bulk of the cooking time. To minimize temperature fluctuations, we create a sort of oven within an oven by covering the chicken with a piece of aluminum foil before closing the lid.

To ensure that the skin is really crisp, we return the chicken parts to the hotter part of the grill when they are nearly done. The glaze is applied to the chicken breasts at this point late in the grilling process—adding the sugary glaze any earlier would lead to burning.

Once you master this basic technique for grilling chicken breasts, you can apply any number of glazes or sauces, even barbecue sauce, if you like. We use an orange chipotle-glaze here; for other glaze options see page 420. Before you begin, see the Core Techniques on pages 390–393 for more details on setting up the grill.

Ingredients

ORANGE-CHIPOTLE GLAZE

- 1 teaspoon grated orange zest plus ⅔ cup juice (2 oranges)
- 1–2 tablespoons minced canned chipotle chile in adobo sauce
- 1 small shallot, minced
- 2 teaspoons minced fresh thyme
- 1 tablespoon molasses
- ¾ teaspoon cornstarch
  Salt

CHICKEN

- ⅓ cup salt
- 6 (12-ounce) bone-in split chicken breasts, ribs and excess fat trimmed *
  Pepper

* To help ensure that all the chicken breasts finish cooking at the same time, try to buy pieces of similar size. Don't use boneless, skinless chicken breasts—the bone and skin protect the easily overcooked breast meat from becoming dry and chalky, and the skin gives the glaze a surface to which it can cling. If you purchase kosher chicken, omit the brining step.

Recipe Stats

TOTAL TIME 1½ **hours**
PREPARATION TIME **15 minutes**
ACTIVE COOKING TIME **1 hour**
YIELD **6 servings**
MAKE AHEAD **Serve immediately**
DIFFICULTY **Easy**

What Can Go Wrong

Here's a list of common mistakes cooks make when preparing this recipe.

COMMON MISTAKE	BAD OUTCOMES	WHAT YOU SHOULD DO
Using Chicken Breasts of Different Sizes	• **The chicken breasts are done at different times.**	Try to purchase chicken breasts that are similar in size so that all the pieces cook at about the same rate. If you wind up with chicken breasts that vary in size because the breasts were sold prepackaged or because the butcher wasn't very careful in his or her selections, be prepared for the smaller pieces to be done ahead of the larger ones. Test each piece to determine doneness.
Not Brining Chicken or Cutting Brine Time Short	• **The chicken is not well seasoned.** • **The chicken is dry.**	Don't skip or shortcut the brining step. The white meat of chicken breasts can easily overcook and turn dry and chalky. Brining adds seasoning that penetrates the meat and adds moisture that provides a cushion should you overcook the chicken.
Building Wrong Type of Fire	• **The chicken breasts brown before they cook through.**	Be sure to create a modified two-level fire (see page 392). If using a charcoal grill, arrange the lit coals in half of the grill; if using a gas grill, leave the primary burner on high and turn off the other burner(s). A modified two-level fire provides a hot fire over which to brown the chicken breasts, as well as a cooler area where they can cook through without become overly charred.
Improperly Positioning Chicken on Grill	• **The chicken breasts cook unevenly.**	When moving the chicken breasts to the cool side of the grill, make sure that the thick, wide end of each breast is facing the hot side of the grill. If they are arranged with the narrow ends facing the hot side of the grill, the tips will end up dry and overdone while the thick ends very slowly come up to the proper doneness temperature.
Not Covering Chicken with Foil	• **The chicken breasts take too long to cook through.**	Even though the grill is covered after the chicken breasts have been moved to the cooler side of the grill, don't opt out of covering the breasts with a sheet of aluminum foil. This creates an oven within an oven and keeps heat close to the chicken so that the pieces cook in a timely fashion.
Applying Glaze Too Soon	• **The glaze scorches.** • **The glaze tastes bitter and burnt.**	Don't apply the glaze until the final stage of cooking, when the internal temperature of the chicken breasts registers 150 degrees and the pieces are ready to be moved to the hot side of the grill. If the glaze is brushed on too early, the plentiful sugars will scorch, the flavor will become bitter, and the glaze will blacken.
Not Finishing Chicken Skin Side Down	• **The skin is soggy.**	Over the course of cooking, the chicken breasts require a few flips to brown all sides. Make sure to grill the chicken breasts for the final few minutes with the skin side facing down on the hot side of the grill. This will give the skin a chance to crisp up nicely.

1. PREPARE GLAZE: Grate 1 teaspoon zest from 1 orange. Squeeze ⅔ cup juice from 2 oranges. Combine zest and juice in small saucepan.

2. Add 1 minced small shallot, 1 to 2 tablespoons minced canned chipotle chile in adobo sauce, and 2 teaspoons minced fresh thyme.

3. Whisk in 1 tablespoon molasses and ¾ teaspoon cornstarch.

4. Simmer mixture over medium heat until thickened, about 5 minutes. Season with salt to taste.

5. Reserve half of glaze for serving and use other half for brushing on chicken while grilling.

6. PREPARE AND BRINE CHICKEN: Trim ribs off 6 (12-ounce) bone-in, skin-on split chicken breasts. Trim excess fat from each chicken breast.

7. Dissolve ⅓ cup salt in 2 quarts cold water in large container. Submerge chicken in brine, cover with plastic wrap, and refrigerate 1 hour.

8. Rinse chicken under cold water. Dry thoroughly with paper towels, then season with pepper. (If using gas grill, proceed to step 14.)

9. FOR A CHARCOAL GRILL: Open bottom grill vent completely. Light large chimney starter filled with charcoal briquettes (6 quarts).

10. Allow to burn until coals are fully ignited and partially covered with thin layer of ash, about 20 minutes. Build modified two-level fire (see page 392).

11. Set cooking grate in place, cover, and open lid vent completely. Heat grill until hot, about 5 minutes.

12. Scrape grate clean with grill brush. Dip wad of paper towels in vegetable oil; holding wad with tongs, wipe cooking grate.

13. Grill is ready when coals are medium-hot (you can hold your hand 5 inches above grate for 3 to 4 seconds). (Proceed to step 16.)

14. FOR A GAS GRILL: Turn all burners to high, cover, and heat grill until hot, about 15 minutes.

15. Leave primary burner on high and turn off other burner(s). Clean and oil grate.

16. GRILL CHICKEN: Cook chicken on hot side until lightly browned on both sides, 6 to 8 minutes for charcoal or 10 to 14 minutes for gas, covered.

17. If constant flare-ups occur, slide chicken to cooler side of grill and mist fire with water using spray bottle.

18. Move chicken, skin side down, to cooler side of grill, with thicker side of breast facing hotter side. Cover loosely with aluminum foil.

19. Cover grill and continue to cook until instant-read thermometer inserted into thickest part of breast registers 150 degrees, 15 to 25 minutes longer.

20. Brush bone side of chicken with glaze.

21. Move chicken, bone side down, to hotter side of grill and cook until browned, 4 to 6 minutes.

22. Brush skin side of chicken with glaze.

23. Turn chicken over and continue to cook until browned and thermometer inserted into thickest part registers 160 degrees, 2 to 3 minutes longer.

24. Transfer chicken to plate. Tent chicken with foil. Let rest 5 minutes. Serve, passing remaining glaze separately.

Grilled Steaks with Chimichurri Sauce

Overview

To make a perfect grilled steak, it is crucial to create a deeply caramelized, well-formed crust—it translates to bold, savory flavor. Our technique to achieve this goal is unique in a couple of ways.

First, the steaks are dusted with a mixture of cornstarch and salt. The salt is strictly for seasoning; the cornstarch absorbs excess moisture on the surface of the meat, which promotes dark browning.

Second, the steaks are chilled in the freezer for about 30 minutes before grilling. Extra-cold steaks take longer to cook through, which means that the exteriors have more time to develop a nice, crusty sear.

The steaks are served with a sauce from Argentina called *chimichurri*. This vibrant, potent mixture of parsley, cilantro, garlic, oregano, vinegar, and olive oil is an excellent foil to the richness of the beef. Make the sauce first—the bold flavors need about an hour to mellow. Before you begin, see the Core Techniques on pages 390–393 for more details on setting up the grill.

Recipe Stats

TOTAL TIME **1½ hours**
PREPARATION TIME **15 minutes**
ACTIVE COOKING TIME **45 minutes**
YIELD **6 to 8 servings**
MAKE AHEAD **Chimichurri sauce can be refrigerated for up to 3 days**
DIFFICULTY **Easy**

Tools

- charcoal or gas grill
- rimmed baking sheet
- food processor
- chef's knife
- cutting board
- dry measuring cups
- liquid measuring cup
- measuring spoons
- barbecue mitt *
- charcoal briquettes *
- grill brush
- instant-read thermometer
- large chimney starter *
- large plate or platter
- mixing bowls
- rubber spatula
- tongs
- whisk
- wire rack
- aluminum foil
- matches and newspaper *
- paper towels
- plastic wrap

* The mitt, briquettes, chimney starter, matches, and newspaper are needed only if using a charcoal grill.

Ingredients

CHIMICHURRI SAUCE
- ¼ **cup hot water**
- 2 **teaspoons dried oregano**
- 2 **teaspoons kosher salt ***
- 1⅓ **cups loosely packed flat-leaf parsley leaves**
- ⅔ **cup loosely packed fresh cilantro leaves**
- 6 **garlic cloves, minced**
- ½ **teaspoon red pepper flakes**
- ¼ **cup red wine vinegar**
- ½ **cup extra-virgin olive oil**

STEAK
- 2 **tablespoons kosher salt ***
- 1 **tablespoon cornstarch ****
- 4 **(1-pound) boneless strip steaks, 1½ inches thick ***** **Pepper**

* We find it easier to evenly distribute the large crystals of kosher salt over the steaks, so we use kosher salt in the sauce as well. If you prefer, you can use table salt both in the sauce and for seasoning the steaks, as long as you cut the amounts in half.

** Cornstarch is an unorthodox ingredient for grilled steak, but we found that cornstarch effectively absorbs surface moisture on the steaks. Drier surfaces mean deeper, darker browning, which translates to bigger, bolder flavor.

*** The thickness of the steaks is key. If your steaks are thinner or thicker than 1½ inches, be prepared to make adjustments in the cooking time. Use an instant-read thermometer to monitor the steaks for doneness.

What Can Go Wrong

Here's a list of common mistakes cooks make when preparing this recipe.

COMMON MISTAKE	BAD OUTCOMES	WHAT YOU SHOULD DO
Purchasing Wrong Steaks	• **The steaks are bland.** • **The steaks are tough.**	Strip steak (also called top loin steak or New York strip steak) is among our favorite cuts for grilling. If you use another cut (especially from the sirloin), the dish will be slightly less flavorful and the meat can be chewy. If you can't find strip steaks (they are among the most widely available steaks so this really shouldn't be a problem), consider using rib eyes, which are also well marbled with fat, flavorful, and tender.
Making Sauce at Last Minute	• **The sauce tastes harsh.** • **The flavors in the sauce are underdeveloped.**	Make the chimichurri sauce before you begin grilling. Allow the sauce to stand at room temperature for at least 1 hour before serving; this gives the flavors a chance to meld and mellow out. The sauce can be refrigerated for up to 3 days; just bring it to room temperature before serving.
Not Patting Steaks Dry	• **The steaks do not brown properly.**	Straight out of the wrapper, steaks are often moist with natural juices. Patting the steaks dry with paper towels removes surface moisture, which would otherwise interfere with browning—and with deeper browning comes better flavor.
Not Rubbing Steaks with Cornstarch	• **The steaks do not brown properly.**	As odd as it sounds, don't skip the cornstarch. The cornstarch absorbs additional moisture from the surface of the steaks. Drier exteriors mean even darker, more intense browning, which translates to bigger, more complex flavor.
Not Chilling Steaks in Freezer	• **The steaks are overcooked.**	Put the steaks in the freezer before you fire up the grill, and let them chill for about 30 minutes. This time in the freezer brings down the internal temperature of the steaks so that they take longer to cook—a longer cooking time means that the exteriors of the steaks have even more opportunity to form nice brown crusts. If you don't chill the steaks in the freezer before putting them onto the grill but you still follow the recipe's cooking times, the steaks will wind up overcooked.
Not Testing Steaks with Instant-Read Thermometer	• **The steaks are undercooked.** • **The steaks are overcooked.**	Don't rely on imprecise methods (like nicking the meat with a knife) to judge doneness. Invest in a good instant-read thermometer and you will never ruin another piece of meat. Make sure to slide the probe into the thickest part of the steak. We like to pick up each steak with a pair of tongs and slide the probe in through the side to confirm that each steak is done. If some of the steaks are thicker or seem to be cooking more slowly because they are on a cooler part of the grill, let them grill for an additional minute or so as needed.

1. PREPARE SAUCE: Measure 1⅓ cups loosely packed fresh flat-leaf parsley and ⅔ cup loosely packed fresh cilantro. Set aside.

2. Combine ¼ cup hot water, 2 tea-spoons dried oregano, and 2 teaspoons kosher salt in liquid measuring cup or small bowl. Let sit for 5 minutes.

3. Pulse parsley, cilantro, 6 minced gar-lic cloves, and ½ teaspoon red pepper flakes in food processor until coarsely chopped, about 10 pulses.

4. Scrape down sides of food processor bowl. Add water mixture and ¼ cup red wine vinegar and pulse briefly to combine.

5. Transfer mixture to medium bowl and slowly whisk in ½ cup extra-virgin olive oil until incorporated.

6. Cover with plastic wrap and let sit at room temperature at least 1 hour.

7. PREPARE STEAKS: Combine 2 table-spoons kosher salt and 1 tablespoon cornstarch in bowl.

8. Pat 4 (1-pound) boneless strip steaks, 1½ inch thick, dry with paper towels.

9. Place steaks on wire rack set in rimmed baking sheet. Rub entire surface of steaks with cornstarch mixture.

10. Place steaks, uncovered, in freezer until very firm, about 30 minutes. (If using gas grill, proceed to step 15.)

11. FOR A CHARCOAL GRILL: Open bottom grill vent completely. Light large chimney starter filled with charcoal (6 quarts).

12. Allow to burn until coals are fully ignited and partially covered with thin layer of ash, about 20 minutes. Arrange coals in single layer.

13. Set cooking grate in place, cover, and open lid vent completely. Heat grill until hot, about 5 minutes. Scrape cooking grate clean with grill brush.

14. Dip wad of paper towels in vegetable oil; holding wad with tongs, wipe cooking grate. (Proceed to step 16.)

15. FOR A GAS GRILL: Turn all burners to high, cover, and heat grill until hot, about 15 minutes. Clean and oil cooking grate.

16. GRILL STEAKS: Season steaks with pepper.

17. Place steaks on grill. Cover and grill until steaks begin to char, 2 to 3 minutes.

18. Using tongs, flip steaks. Cook on second side, with grill uncovered, until beginning to char, 2 to 3 minutes.

19. Flip steaks again and cook first side until well charred, 2 to 3 minutes.

20. Flip one last time and continue to cook until second side is well charred, 2 to 4 minutes.

21. Steaks are done when instant-read thermometer inserted into center registers 115 degrees (for rare) or 120 degrees (for medium-rare).

22. Transfer steaks to large plate. Cover steaks loosely with aluminum foil and let rest for 10 minutes.

23. Slice steaks crosswise. Serve, passing chimichurri sauce separately.

Inexpensive Grill-Roasted Beef

Overview

There's no rule that says that the centerpiece of Sunday's roast beef dinner needs to be cooked in the oven. With this recipe, we take the affair outdoors and grill-roast a very affordable beef roast to rosy-hued perfection. We've added a garlic and rosemary rub that gives the roast bold, savory flavor that enhances the meatiness of the beef.

Here, a quick sear over the hot side of the grill kicks off the cooking and helps develop flavor while creating an attractive exterior. After browning, the roast is placed in a disposable aluminum pan and set on the cool side of the grill to cook with indirect heat. The pan protects the meat from cooking too quickly, thereby helping ensure a tender texture.

The longer it takes for the meat to reach its final serving temperature, the longer the enzymes in the meat will remain active and help to break down muscle fibers and act as a natural meat tenderizer. That's why we start this recipe with relatively few coals (or a single gas burner turned to medium) and then keep the meat in the pan once it is has been seared.

Some beef roasts are sold tied with kitchen twine. If the roast you purchase is tied, leave the twine in place and snip off the twine just before carving it; but if the roast isn't tied, there's no need to do so. Before you begin, see How to Grill-Roast on page 395.

Recipe Stats

TOTAL TIME **20 hours**
PREPARATION TIME **15 minutes**
ACTIVE COOKING TIME **40 minutes**
YIELD **6 to 8 servings**
MAKE AHEAD **Serve immediately**
DIFFICULTY **Intermediate**

Tools

- charcoal or gas grill
- rimmed baking sheet
- carving board
- chef's knife
- cutting board
- paring knife *
- slicing knife
- measuring spoons
- barbecue mitt **
- charcoal briquettes **
- garlic press
- grill brush
- instant-read thermometer
- large chimney starter **
- mixing bowls
- tongs
- wire rack
- aluminum foil
- matches and newspaper **
- paper towels
- plastic wrap
- 13 by 9-inch disposable aluminum roasting pan ***

* A paring knife works well for punching the holes in the aluminum pan.
** The mitt, briquettes, chimney starter, matches, and newspaper are needed only if using a charcoal grill.
*** The disposable roasting pan is for holding the roast as it cooks with indirect heat. The bottom and sides of the pan protect the roast against overcooking so that the roast is perfectly cooked from edge to edge.

Ingredients

- **6   garlic cloves, minced**
- **2   tablespoons minced fresh rosemary**
- **4   teaspoons kosher salt**
- **1   tablespoon pepper**
- **1   (3- to 4-pound) top sirloin roast ***

* Top sirloin roast is our first choice for this recipe. If you're unable to find it in the grocery store, other good options are top round and bottom round. Or you can use a chuck roast, but cook it to medium so that some of the abundant intramuscular fat renders out. (Chuck roast often comes tied; leave the twine on for cooking, and remove it as you slice the roast. However, if the roast is held together by elastic netting, remove the netting and tie the roast with regular kitchen twine.) The eye-round roast is our least favorite but still acceptable option; this very lean roast has a subtle flavor.

What Can Go Wrong

Here's a list of common mistakes cooks make when preparing this recipe.

COMMON MISTAKE	BAD OUTCOMES	WHAT YOU SHOULD DO
Using Wrong Cut of Beef	• **The meat is tough.** • **The meat is dry.** • **The meat lacks flavor.**	Even though it may be the most expensive of the inexpensive cuts, opt for a top sirloin roast, which has a good, meaty flavor and enough fat to keep it moist. Top round and bottom round (in that order) are our favorites after top sirloin, followed by chuck roast (this very fatty cut is best cooked to medium). At the bottom of our list is eye-round roast, which has a very mild flavor.
Not Salting Roast Long Enough	• **The meat is underseasoned.** • **The meat is tough.**	Plan ahead, and don't skip or try to shortcut salting the roast. The salting process not only allows the salt (as well as the garlic and rosemary) to penetrate the meat for through-and-through seasoning, it also helps the proteins break down so that the roast becomes more tender.
Letting Grill Get Too Hot	• **The roast cooks too quickly.** • **The meat is tough.**	To get the meat to cook more quickly, it's tempting to fire up more briquettes if you're using a charcoal grill or crank up the primary burner if you're using gas, but the success of this recipe hinges on gentle heat—don't give in to temptation. Very gradual cooking allows the enzymes naturally present in the beef to help tenderize the meat, so don't rush the process.
Not Using Disposable Roasting Pan	• **The roast cooks too quickly.** • **The roast is unevenly cooked.** • **The meat is tough.**	Don't consider the disposable aluminum pan an optional piece of equipment. The bottom and sides of the pan act as a shield that protects the roast from the grill's heat and slows down the rate at which it cooks. As a result, the roast cooks more evenly from edge to center.
Not Resting Roast	• **The juices flow out of meat when sliced.** • **The roast is dry.**	Give the roast its full 20-minute rest after grill-roasting. During this time, the juices that were forced to the center of the roast during cooking will redistribute throughout the meat so that the muscle fibers will be evenly moist from edge to edge. Tented with foil, the meat will remain hot, so don't worry that resting means you'll be serving dinner cold.
Slicing Roast Too Thick	• **The meat is chewy.**	Use a sharp knife to carve the roast into thin slices, ideally no thicker than ¼ inch. Slicing the meat thin cuts the muscle fibers into short lengths, resulting in a texture that's perceived as more tender than if the meat is cut into thick slices with longer sections of muscle fibers.

1. Combine 6 minced garlic cloves, 2 tablespoons minced fresh rosemary, 4 teaspoons kosher salt, and 1 tablespoon pepper in bowl.

2. Sprinkle all sides of 1 (3- to 4-pound) top sirloin roast evenly with salt mixture.

3. Wrap roast with plastic wrap. Refrigerate roast for 18 to 24 hours. (If using gas grill, proceed to step 12.)

4. FOR A CHARCOAL GRILL: Open bottom grill vent halfway.

5. Light large chimney starter half-filled with charcoal briquettes (3 quarts).

6. Allow to burn until coals are fully ignited and partially covered with thin layer of ash, about 15 minutes.

7. Arrange coals over one-third of grill.

8. Set cooking grate in place.

9. Cover, open lid vent halfway, and heat grill until hot, about 5 minutes.

10. Scrape grate clean with grill brush.

11. Dip wad of paper towels in vegetable oil; holding wad with tongs, wipe cooking grate. (Proceed to step 15.)

12. FOR A GAS GRILL: Turn all burners to high, cover, and heat grill until hot, about 15 minutes.

13. Scrape grate clean with grill brush.

14. Dip wad of paper towels in vegetable oil; holding wad with tongs, wipe cooking grate.

15. GRILL ROAST: Place roast over hot part of grill and cook (covered if using gas) until well browned on all sides, about 10 minutes.

16. Meanwhile, punch fifteen ¼-inch holes in center of 13 by 9-inch disposable aluminum roasting pan in area roughly same size as roast.

17. Once beef is browned, place in pan over holes.

18. Set pan on grill over cool side if using charcoal grill; if using gas, reduce primary burner to medium and turn off other burner(s).

19. Cover grill. (Position vent over meat if using charcoal.) Cook roast for 20 minutes, then rotate pan 180 degrees.

20. Continue roasting until center of roast registers 120 to 125 degrees (for medium-rare) or 130 to 135 degrees (for medium), 20 to 40 minutes.

21. Transfer meat to wire rack set in rimmed baking sheet.

22. Tent loosely with aluminum foil and let rest for 20 minutes.

23. Transfer meat to carving board and cut across grain into thin slices. Serve immediately.

HOW TO GRILL

Memphis-Style Barbecued Ribs

Overview

If you think that great barbecued ribs are best left to expert pit masters with highly specialized smokers and super-secret spice rubs, think again. Not only will this recipe turn your standard charcoal or gas grill into your own barbecue pit, but our unique outdoor-indoor technique shaves a lot of time and effort off the traditional barbecue method.

Memphis-style spareribs are dry-rubbed, wet-mopped, sauce-free ribs that are barbecued until tender, but not to the point where the meat falls off the bones. During the low-and-slow cooking, the ribs form a "bark"—a crusty outer layer that's appealing to both the eye and the palate. These ribs are more savory and more serious than the sticky, sugary, saucy ribs that many of us have become accustomed to.

For a charcoal grill, this recipe calls for a rather unconventional method of emptying lit coals onto a pile of unlit coals. The unlit coals are slow to ignite, which is desirable for producing steady, unflagging heat over the 1½-hour cooking time on the grill and obviates the need to add fresh coals midway through cooking. After a smoke-filled stint on the grill, the ribs are moved to the oven to finish cooking. In a couple of hours, the ribs are ready. Before you begin, see How to Use Wood on page 394.

Recipe Stats

TOTAL TIME **5 hours**
PREPARATION TIME **15 minutes**
ACTIVE COOKING TIME **40 minutes**
YIELD **4 to 6 servings**
MAKE AHEAD **Serve immediately**
DIFFICULTY **Intermediate**

Tools

- charcoal or gas grill
- rimmed baking sheet
- chef's knife
- cutting board
- liquid measuring cup
- measuring spoons
- barbecue basting brush
- barbecue mitt *
- charcoal briquettes *
- fine-mesh strainer
- grill/barbecue thermometer *
- grill brush
- instant-read thermometer
- large chimney starter *
- mixing bowls
- soupspoon
- tongs
- wire rack
- aluminum foil
- matches and newspaper *
- 9-inch disposable aluminum pie plates (2) **
- paper towels
- 13 by 9-inch disposable aluminum roasting pan *

* The mitt, briquettes, chimney starter, matches, newspaper, disposable aluminum roasting pan, and grill thermometer are needed only if using a charcoal grill. A disposable aluminum roasting pan is ideal for holding water in a charcoal grill to create a slightly humid environment that protects the ribs from drying out. A grill/barbecue thermometer inserted through a lid vent allows you to monitor the grill's inside temperature, which is especially important here given the long cooking time. You can also periodically insert an instant-read thermometer through the vent (just be careful as they aren't heat-resistant).
** The disposable aluminum pie plates are needed only if using a gas grill. One is for holding water, and the second is for wood chips.

Ingredients

- 2 (2½- to 3-pound) racks St. Louis–style spareribs, trimmed *
- 2 tablespoons paprika
- 2 tablespoons packed light brown sugar
- 1 tablespoon salt
- 2 teaspoons chili powder
- 1½ teaspoons pepper
- 1½ teaspoons garlic powder
- 1½ teaspoons onion powder
- 1½ teaspoons cayenne pepper
- ½ teaspoon dried thyme
- ½ cup apple juice
- 3 tablespoons cider vinegar
- ½–¾ cup wood chips, soaked in water for 15 minutes and drained **

* St. Louis–style spareribs are full racks that have been trimmed of belly meat and cartilage. Don't use untrimmed racks, and avoid substituting baby back ribs, which are smaller and leaner. Don't remove the membrane that covers the bone side of the ribs; it prevents some of the fat from rendering, leading to more tender, flavorful results.
** On a charcoal grill, ½ cup wood chips will produce sufficient smoke; we recommend using ¾ cup wood chips on a gas grill.

What Can Go Wrong

Here's a list of common mistakes cooks make when preparing this recipe.

COMMON MISTAKE	BAD OUTCOMES	WHAT YOU SHOULD DO
Using Wrong Cut of Ribs	• **The ribs must be aggressively trimmed before cooking.** • **The ribs are dry.**	Purchase St. Louis–style spareribs; butcher shops and most well-stocked supermarkets sell this cut. If you bring home untrimmed racks of spareribs, they will require aggressive trimming to get rid of excess fat, and unless you remove the cartilaginous portion at the top of the ribs, the racks may not fit on the grill. Baby back ribs don't require trimming but they are so much smaller and leaner than spareribs that they will end up dry if used in place of St. Louis–style ribs.
Getting Grill Too Hot	• **The exterior of the ribs is dry.** • **The exterior of the ribs is burnt.** • **The ribs are tough.**	To get the ribs to cook more quickly, it's tempting to want to fire up more briquettes if you're using a charcoal grill or crank up the primary burner to high if you're using gas, but the success of this recipe hinges on a 250- to 275-degree grill temperature, so don't give in to temptation. Remember: Low-and-slow is the way to go.
Not Putting Water in Pan	• **The exterior of the ribs is dry.**	The water pan in the grill bottom serves an important purpose, so don't skip this component. Without any water, the grill's heat is unforgivingly dry, and the surface of the ribs will dry out over such a long cooking time. The water also helps stabilize the grill's temperature by absorbing heat.
Opening Grill During Cooking	• **The ribs take longer to cook.**	Do not open the grill except to rotate the ribs after 45 minutes of cooking. Opening the lid allows heat to escape, which means that the cooking time must be extended to compensate for the heat loss.
Using Small Gas Grill	• **The ribs are too close to the primary burner.** • **The ribs burn.**	If using a small two-burner gas grill, you may find it necessary to cut each rack of ribs in half crosswise between the bones and use an aluminum foil shield to protect the ribs from the direct heat of the primary burner. To make a shield, place a 24-inch length of heavy-duty aluminum foil down the center of the grill. Place the halved racks over the cool side of the grill, perpendicular to the cooking grate, so that they cover about half of the foil. Lift up the foil to shield the ribs.

1. Soak ½ cup wood chips if using charcoal grill, or ¾ cup wood chips if using gas grill, with water to cover. Let chips soak for 15 minutes, then drain.

2. Combine 2 tablespoons paprika, 2 tablespoons packed light brown sugar, 1 tablespoon salt, 2 teaspoons chili powder, and 1½ teaspoons pepper.

3. Add 1½ teaspoons garlic powder, 1½ teaspoons onion powder, 1½ teaspoons cayenne pepper, and ½ teaspoon dried thyme and stir to combine.

4. Place 2 (2½- to 3-pound) racks St. Louis-style spareribs on rimmed baking sheet. Sprinkle rub on both sides of each rack and press to adhere.

5. Combine ½ cup apple juice and 3 tablespoons cider vinegar in bowl; set aside. (If using gas grill, proceed to step 11.)

6. FOR A CHARCOAL GRILL: Open bottom grill vent halfway. Arrange 15 unlit charcoal briquettes evenly on one side of grill.

7. Place 13 by 9-inch disposable aluminum roasting pan filled with 1 inch water on other side of grill.

8. Light large chimney starter filled one-third with charcoal (2 quarts). Allow to burn until coals are half-coated with thin layer of ash.

9. Empty coals into grill on top of unlit briquettes to cover half of grill. Sprinkle soaked wood chips over coals.

10. Set cooking grate in place, cover, and open lid vent halfway. Heat grill until hot, about 5 minutes. Clean and oil cooking grate. (Proceed to step 15.)

11. FOR A GAS GRILL: Place soaked wood chips in 9-inch disposable aluminum pie plate with ¼ cup water. Set pie plate on primary burner.

12. Place second 9-inch disposable aluminum pie plate filled with 1 inch water on other burner(s).

13. Set cooking grate in place. Turn all burners to high, cover, and heat grill until hot, about 15 minutes.

14. Turn primary burner to medium-high and turn off other burner(s). Clean and oil cooking grate.

15. GRILL RIBS: Place ribs meat side down on grate over water-filled pan. Cover grill, positioning top vent over ribs if using charcoal.

16. Cook ribs 45 minutes, adjusting vent or primary burner to maintain temperature inside grill between 250 and 275 degrees.

17. Flip ribs meat side up, turn 180 degrees, and switch positions so that rack that was nearer fire is on outside.

18. Brush each rack with 2 tablespoons apple juice mixture. Cover grill and cook another 45 minutes.

19. About 20 minutes before removing ribs from grill, adjust oven rack to middle position and heat oven to 300 degrees.

20. Transfer ribs meat side up to wire rack set in rimmed baking sheet. Brush top of each rack with 2 tablespoons apple juice mixture.

21. Pour 1½ cups water into bottom of baking sheet. Bake 1 hour.

22. Brush ribs with remaining apple juice mixture.

23. Continue to bake until meat is tender but not falling off bone (internal temperature should be 195 to 200 degrees), 1 to 2 hours.

24. Transfer ribs to cutting board. Tent loosely with aluminum foil and let rest 15 minutes. Cut ribs between bones to separate, and serve.

Grilled Salmon with Olive Vinaigrette

Tools

- charcoal or gas grill
- rimmed baking sheet
- chef's knife
- cutting board
- liquid measuring cup
- dry measuring cups
- measuring spoons
- barbecue basting brush
- barbecue mitt *
- charcoal briquettes *
- citrus juicer
- dish towels (2)
- grill brush
- instant-read thermometer
- large chimney starter *
- large plate or platter
- metal spatulas (2) **
- mixing bowls
- spoon
- tongs
- matches and newspaper *
- paper towels

* The mitt, briquettes, chimney starter, matches, and newspaper are needed only if using a charcoal grill.
** It's much easier to flip fish fillets if you have two spatulas—one to lift the fish from the cooking grate and one to "catch" the fish and gently lower it back onto the cooking grate.

Overview

Fish fillets have a bad reputation on the grill. Why? Because you can bet that they'll stick to the cooking grate, and when they do, you can forget about removing them in whole pieces—the delicate texture of cooked fish makes it virtually impossible to remove fillets neatly, so what you bring to the table are inelegant shards of fish.

Enter this recipe. For perfectly grilled, easy-release salmon fillets, we build a modified two-level fire for a charcoal grill (and use only the hot side of the grill), or a single-level fire when using a gas grill. Heating and cleaning the cooking grate and then wiping it with oil-dipped paper towels until it's well seasoned (similar to seasoning a cast-iron pan) are the keys to success.

Some people find salmon skin good eating, some don't. If you do, make sure the fillets that you use are scaled. You can serve the grilled fish skin side up (as in the photo) or skin side down, as you like.

This recipe works best with salmon fillets but can also be used with any thick, firm-fleshed white fish, including red snapper, grouper, halibut, and sea bass. Cook white fish to 140 degrees, up to 2 minutes longer per side. Before you begin, see the Core Techniques on pages 390–393 for more details on setting up the grill.

Recipe Stats

TOTAL TIME **1 hour**
PREPARATION TIME **15 minutes**
ACTIVE COOKING TIME **45 minutes**
YIELD **4 servings**
MAKE AHEAD **Serve immediately**
DIFFICULTY **Easy**

Ingredients

OLIVE VINAIGRETTE
- ½ **cup green or kalamata olives, pitted and chopped coarse ***
- ¼ **cup extra-virgin olive oil**
- 2 **tablespoons chopped fresh parsley**
- 1 **small shallot, minced**
- 2 **teaspoons lemon juice**
   Salt and pepper

SALMON
- 1 **(1½- to 2-pound) skin-on salmon fillet, about 1½ inches thick ***
   Vegetable oil
   Kosher salt and pepper

* Green olives tend to be quite mild and mellow in flavor; large, plump green Cerignola olives from Italy are one of the most commonly available types of green olives. Black kalamata olives have a sharper, brinier flavor than green olives. Use whichever type you prefer to make the vinaigrette.
** To ensure servings of equal size, we prefer to buy a whole center-cut fillet and cut it into four pieces. These days, many supermarkets offer both wild and farmed salmon varieties. We prefer wild salmon because we find its texture to be firmer and its flavor more buttery and fresh than farmed salmon. It is, however, more pricey. If all you can find are skinless salmon fillets, they'll work too; treat the skinned side as if it were the skin side.

What Can Go Wrong

Here's a list of common mistakes cooks make when preparing this recipe.

COMMON MISTAKE	BAD OUTCOMES	WHAT YOU SHOULD DO
Buying Fillets That Are Too Thick/Too Thin	• **The fillets cook too slow/fast.**	Try to purchase salmon fillets that are about 1½ inches thick; the cooking times in the recipe are for fillets of this thickness. If the fillets are thinner, they may wind up overcooked. If the fillets are thicker, increase the cooking time on the second side until the fillets reach the desired internal temperature.
Not Drying Fish Well	• **The fillets stick to the cooking grate.**	Be sure to dry the salmon fillets well before grilling by blotting away surface moisture with dish towels, and keep the fillets wrapped in the towels while the grill heats. Moisture on the fillets will cause the temperature of the grill grate to drop, which can lead to sticking.
Not Properly Cleaning and Oiling Grill	• **The fillets stick to the cooking grate.**	After heating the cooking grate, make sure to scrub it as clean as possible with a grill brush to remove any burnt-on residue. Then, rub it multiple times with a wad of paper towels dipped in vegetable oil, dipping the paper towels in oil between each pass. Cleaning and oiling the grate seasons the metal, which is key for fillets that release easily from the cooking grate.
Not Testing Salmon for Doneness with Thermometer	• **The fillets are overcooked.**	The usual advice for determining doneness of fish is to see if the flesh "flakes" when cut with a knife. But because salmon is best when it is cooked only until medium (the center has only just turned opaque), this test does not work reliably well. Instead, use an instant-read thermometer inserted into the thickest part of the fillet to gauge doneness—when it registers 125 degrees, the fish is perfectly cooked.
Using Low-Quality Olives and Oil	• **The vinaigrette is bland.**	The vinaigrette should be nicely balanced: briny from the olives, fresh with parsley and lemon juice, savory with shallot, and fruity with extra-virgin olive oil. If you use bland California olives or low-quality olive oil, the vinaigrette will be bland. Taste the vinaigrette before serving and add more lemon juice, salt, and pepper to perk up flavors if necessary.

1. PREPARE VINAIGRETTE: Coarsely chop ½ cup pitted green or kalamata olives.

2. Stir together olives, ¼ cup extra-virgin olive oil, 2 tablespoons chopped fresh parsley, 1 minced small shallot, and 2 teaspoons lemon juice.

3. Season vinaigrette with salt and pepper to taste. Set vinaigrette aside.

4. PREPARE SALMON: Place 4 (6- to 8-ounce) salmon fillets skin side up on rimmed baking sheet or large plate lined with dish towel.

5. Place second dish towel on top of fillets and press down to blot liquid.

6. Refrigerate fish, wrapped in towels, while preparing grill, at least 20 minutes. (If using gas grill, proceed to step 14.)

7. FOR A CHARCOAL GRILL: Open bottom grill vent completely. While fish dries, light large chimney starter filled two-thirds with charcoal (4 quarts).

8. Allow to burn until coals are fully ignited and partially covered with thin layer of ash, 15 to 20 minutes.

9. Build modified two-level fire by arranging coals to cover one-half of grill, leaving other half empty.

10. Set cooking grate in place, cover, and open lid vent completely. Heat grill until hot, about 5 minutes.

11. Use grill brush to scrape cooking grate clean.

12. Lightly dip wad of paper towels in vegetable oil; holding wad with tongs, wipe grate.

13. Continue to wipe grate, redipping towels in oil between applications, until grate is black and glossy, 5 to 10 times. (Proceed to step 17.)

14. FOR A GAS GRILL: While fish dries, turn all burners to high, cover, and heat grill until hot, about 15 minutes.

15. Use grill brush to scrape cooking grate clean. Lightly dip wad of paper towels in vegetable oil; holding wad with tongs, wipe grate.

16. Continue to wipe grate with oiled paper towels, redipping towels in oil between applications, until grate is black and glossy, 5 to 10 times.

17. GRILL SALMON: Brush both sides of fish with thin coat of vegetable oil.

18. Season fish with kosher salt and pepper.

19. Place fish skin side down and diagonal to grate slats, over hot side of grill if using charcoal, or turn all burners to medium if using gas.

20. Cover and cook without moving until skin side is brown, well marked, and crisp, 2 to 4 minutes.

21. Try lifting fish gently with spatula after 3 minutes; if it doesn't cleanly lift off grill, continue to cook, checking at 30-second intervals, until it releases.

22. Using 2 spatulas, flip fish to second side.

23. Cover grill and cook until centers of fillets are opaque and register 125 degrees on instant-read thermometer, 3 to 7 minutes longer.

24. Transfer fish to platter. Stir vinaigrette, spoon over fish, and serve.

HOW TO GRILL

Recipe Library

Grilled Boneless Chicken Breasts

✔ **WHY THIS RECIPE WORKS:** Because they have no skin and little fat, plain boneless chicken breasts invariably turn out dry and leathery when grilled. A common solution—marinating them in bottled salad dressings, which are typically laden with sweeteners and stabilizers—often imparts off-flavors. We wanted grilled chicken breasts that would come off the grill juicy and flavorful and we wanted to look beyond bottled salad dressing to get there. To start, we made a simple homemade marinade with olive oil, lemon juice, garlic, parsley, sugar, and Dijon mustard, and we made a separate vinaigrette to serve with the grilled chicken for extra moisture and flavor. We slowly cooked the chicken breasts on the cool side of the grill until they were almost done. We then gave the breasts a quick sear on the hot side of the grill to finishing cooking and add grill flavor. With a drizzle of our simple vinaigrette, these chicken breasts were moist, tender, and full of flavor.

Grilled Lemon-Parsley Chicken Breasts
SERVES 4

The chicken should be marinated for no less than 30 minutes and no more than 1 hour. Serve with a simply prepared vegetable or use in a sandwich or salad.

- 6 tablespoons olive oil
- 2 tablespoons lemon juice
- 1 tablespoon minced fresh parsley
- 1¼ teaspoons sugar
- 1 teaspoon Dijon mustard
  Salt and pepper
- 2 tablespoons water
- 3 garlic cloves, minced
- 4 (6- to 8-ounce) boneless, skinless chicken breasts, trimmed

1. Whisk 3 tablespoons oil, 1 tablespoon lemon juice, parsley, ¼ teaspoon sugar, mustard, ¼ teaspoon salt, and ¼ teaspoon pepper together in bowl and set aside for serving.

2. Whisk remaining 3 tablespoons oil, remaining 1 tablespoon lemon juice, remaining 1 teaspoon sugar, 1½ teaspoons salt, ½ teaspoon pepper, water, and garlic together in bowl. Place marinade and chicken in 1-gallon zipper-lock bag and toss to coat; press out as much air as possible and seal bag. Refrigerate for at least 30 minutes or up to 1 hour, flipping bag every 15 minutes.

3A. FOR A CHARCOAL GRILL: Open bottom vent completely. Light large chimney starter filled with charcoal briquettes (6 quarts). When top coals are partially covered with ash, pour evenly over half of grill. Set cooking grate in place, cover, and open lid vent completely. Heat grill until hot, about 5 minutes.

3B. FOR A GAS GRILL: Turn all burners to high, cover, and heat grill until hot, about 15 minutes. Leave primary burner on high and turn off other burner(s).

4. Clean and oil cooking grate. Remove chicken from bag, allowing excess marinade to drip off. Place chicken on cooler side of grill, smooth side down, with thicker sides facing coals and flames. Cover and cook until bottom of chicken just begins to develop light grill marks and is no longer translucent, 6 to 9 minutes.

5. Flip chicken and rotate so that thinner sides face coals and flames. Cover and continue to cook until chicken is opaque and firm to touch and registers 140 degrees, 6 to 9 minutes longer.

6. Move chicken to hot side of grill and cook until dark grill marks appear on both sides and chicken registers 160 degrees, 2 to 6 minutes longer.

7. Transfer chicken to carving board, tent loosely with aluminum foil, and let rest for 5 to 10 minutes. Slice each breast on bias into ¼-inch-thick slices and transfer to individual plates. Drizzle with reserved sauce and serve.

Grilled Chipotle-Lime Chicken Breasts

Substitute lime juice for lemon juice and use an extra teaspoon juice in reserved sauce. Substitute minced canned chipotle chile in adobo sauce for mustard and cilantro for parsley.

Grilled Orange-Tarragon Chicken Breasts

Substitute orange juice for lemon juice and tarragon for parsley. Add ¼ teaspoon grated orange zest to reserved sauce.

Barbecued Chicken Kebabs

✔ **WHY THIS RECIPE WORKS:** Skewered chicken can often turn dry and chalky on the grill. As for the flavor, that's usually subpar, too, because by the time the barbecue flavor develops, the meat has dried out. We wanted moist chunks of well-seasoned chicken with full-on barbecued flavor. To give us a head start on the flavor we "marinated" the chicken chunks in bacon paste (made by processing bacon in a food processor) instead of oil, aromatics, and herbs. Tasters liked the smoky flavor that the bacon added, but wanted more. Smoked paprika gave the chicken the flavor tasters were after. For more depth, we also coated the chicken with sweet paprika and turbinado sugar. To keep the skewers from drying out, we turned them every two minutes. In the final minutes on the grill, we brushed the chicken with a simple barbecue sauce for a final layer of flavor.

Barbecued Chicken Kebabs
SERVES 6

Use a coarse grater to grate the onion for the sauce. We prefer flavorful dark thigh meat for these kebabs, but white meat can be used. Whichever you choose, don't mix white and dark meat on the same skewer, since they cook at different rates. If you have thin pieces of chicken, cut them larger than 1 inch and roll or fold them into approximate 1-inch cubes. Turbinado sugar is commonly sold as Sugar in the Raw. Demerara sugar can be substituted. You will need four 12-inch metal skewers for this recipe.

SAUCE
- ½ **cup ketchup**
- ¼ **cup molasses**
- 2 **tablespoons grated onion**
- 2 **tablespoons Worcestershire sauce**
- 2 **tablespoons Dijon mustard**
- 2 **tablespoons cider vinegar**
- 1 **tablespoon packed light brown sugar**

CHICKEN
- 2 **tablespoons sweet paprika**
- 4 **teaspoons turbinado sugar**
- 2 **teaspoons kosher salt**
- 2 **teaspoons smoked paprika**
- 2 **slices bacon, cut into ½-inch pieces**
- 2 **pounds boneless, skinless chicken thighs or breasts, trimmed, cut into 1-inch chunks**

1. FOR THE SAUCE: Bring all ingredients to simmer in small saucepan over medium heat and cook, stirring occasionally, until reduced to about 1 cup, 5 to 7 minutes. Transfer ½ cup sauce to small bowl and set remaining sauce aside for serving.

2. FOR THE CHICKEN: Combine sweet paprika, sugar, salt, and smoked paprika in large bowl. Process bacon in food processor until smooth paste forms, 30 to 45 seconds, scraping down bowl as needed. Add bacon paste and chicken to spice mixture and mix with hands or rubber spatula until ingredients are thoroughly blended and chicken is completely coated. Cover with plastic wrap and refrigerate for 1 hour. Thread chicken tightly onto four 12-inch metal skewers.

3A. FOR A CHARCOAL GRILL: Open bottom vent completely. Light large chimney starter three-quarters filled with charcoal briquettes (4½ quarts). When top coals are partially covered with ash, pour evenly over half of grill. Set cooking grate in place, cover, and open lid vent completely. Heat grill until hot, about 5 minutes.

3B. FOR A GAS GRILL: Turn all burners to high, cover, and heat grill until hot, about 15 minutes. Turn all burners to medium-high.

4. Clean and oil cooking grate. Place skewers on hot part of grill (if using charcoal), and cook (covered if using gas), turning kebabs every 2 to 2½ minutes, until well browned and slightly charred, 8 to 10 minutes. Brush top surface of skewers with ¼ cup sauce, flip, and cook until sauce is sizzling and browning in spots, about 1 minute. Brush second side with remaining ¼ cup sauce, flip, and continue to cook until sizzling and browning in spots, about 1 minute longer.

5. Transfer skewers to serving platter, tent loosely with aluminum foil, and let rest for 5 to 10 minutes. Serve, passing reserved sauce separately.

Grilled Glazed Bone-In Chicken Breasts

✔ WHY THIS RECIPE WORKS: We wanted glazed chicken breasts with tender meat and crisp, lacquered skin. Brining the chicken breasts before grilling helped ensure juicy, seasoned meat. For the glazes, we balanced sweet ingredients, like molasses and sugar, with bold flavors, like chipotle chile, ginger, and curry powder. To keep the glazes from burning on the grill, we first seared the breasts over high heat, then moved them to the cool side of the grill, where we brushed them with the glaze in the last few minutes. For extra flavor, we reserved half of the glaze for serving.

Grilled Glazed Bone-In Chicken Breasts
SERVES 6

If using kosher chicken, do not brine in step 1, and season with salt as well as pepper. Remember to reserve half of the glaze for serving. See Recipe Tutorial on page 398 for more details on this recipe.

- ⅓ **cup salt**
- 6 **(12-ounce) bone-in split chicken breasts, ribs trimmed**
  Pepper
- 1 **recipe glaze (recipes follow)**

1. Dissolve salt in 2 quarts cold water in large container. Submerge chicken in brine, cover, and refrigerate for 1 hour. Remove chicken from brine, rinse under cold water, and pat dry with paper towels. Season chicken with pepper.

2A. FOR A CHARCOAL GRILL: Open bottom vent completely. Light large chimney starter filled with charcoal briquettes (6 quarts). When top coals are partially covered with ash, pour evenly over half of grill. Set cooking grate in place, cover, and open lid vent completely. Heat grill until hot, about 5 minutes.

2B. FOR A GAS GRILL: Turn all burners to high, cover, and heat grill until hot, about 15 minutes. Leave primary burner on high and turn off other burner(s). (Adjust primary burner as needed during cooking to maintain grill temperature around 350 degrees.)

3. Clean and oil cooking grate. Place chicken on hot side of grill, skin side up, and cook (covered if using gas) until lightly browned on both sides, 6 to 8 minutes for charcoal grill and 10 to 14 minutes for gas grill, flipping halfway through cooking. Move chicken, skin side down, to cool side of grill, with thicker end of breasts facing coals and flames. Cover loosely with aluminum foil, cover grill, and continue to cook until chicken registers 150 degrees, 15 to 25 minutes longer.

4. Brush bone side of chicken generously with half of glaze, move to hot side of grill, and cook, bone side down, until browned, 4 to 6 minutes. Brush skin side of chicken with remaining glaze, flip chicken, and continue to cook until chicken registers 160 degrees, 2 to 3 minutes longer.

5. Transfer chicken to serving platter, tent loosely with foil, and let rest for 5 minutes before serving, passing reserved glaze separately.

Orange-Chipotle Glaze

MAKES ABOUT ¾ CUP, ENOUGH FOR 1 RECIPE GRILLED GLAZED
BONE-IN CHICKEN BREASTS

For a spicier glaze, use the greater amount of chipotle chiles.

- 1 teaspoon grated orange zest plus ⅔ cup juice (2 oranges)
- 1–2 tablespoons minced canned chipotle chile in adobo sauce
- 1 small shallot, minced
- 2 teaspoons minced fresh thyme
- 1 tablespoon molasses
- ¾ teaspoon cornstarch
  Salt

Combine orange zest and juice, chipotle, shallot, and thyme in small saucepan. Whisk in molasses and cornstarch, bring to simmer, and cook over medium heat until thickened, about 5 minutes. Season with salt to taste. Reserve half of glaze for serving and use remaining glaze to brush on chicken.

Soy-Ginger Glaze

MAKES ABOUT ¾ CUP, ENOUGH FOR 1 RECIPE GRILLED GLAZED
BONE-IN CHICKEN BREASTS

Reduce the amount of salt in the brine to ¼ cup when using this glaze.

- ⅓ cup water
- ¼ cup soy sauce
- 2 tablespoons mirin
- 1 tablespoon grated fresh ginger
- 2 garlic cloves, minced
- 3 tablespoons sugar
- ¾ teaspoon cornstarch
- 2 scallions, minced

Combine water, soy sauce, mirin, ginger, and garlic in small saucepan. Whisk in sugar and cornstarch, bring to simmer over medium heat, and cook until thickened, about 5 minutes; stir in scallions. Reserve half of glaze for serving and use remaining glaze to brush on chicken.

Curry-Yogurt Glaze

MAKES ABOUT ¾ CUP, ENOUGH FOR 1 RECIPE GRILLED GLAZED
BONE-IN CHICKEN BREASTS

- ¾ cup plain whole-milk yogurt
- 2 garlic cloves, minced
- 2 teaspoons grated fresh ginger
- 2 teaspoons minced fresh cilantro
- ½ teaspoon grated lemon zest
- 1½ teaspoons curry powder
- ½ teaspoon sugar
  Salt and pepper

Whisk all ingredients together in bowl and season with salt and pepper to taste. Reserve half of glaze for serving and use remaining glaze to brush on chicken.

Smoked Chicken

✔ **WHY THIS RECIPE WORKS:** Smoked chicken needs to be cooked for a long time to be truly imbued with smoke flavor, but the breast meat dries out easily, and without high heat it's difficult to get the skin to crisp. We wanted a recipe for perfectly cooked meat with a pervasive smoky flavor and crisp mahogany skin. First, a salt and sugar brine guaranteed moist, well-seasoned meat. We found that chicken parts were easier and better than whole chickens; the breasts could cook evenly on the coolest part of the grill and more of the bird was exposed to the smoke and heat, adding flavor and rendering more fat from the skin. To keep the skin moist, we brushed it with oil and added a pan of water to the grill. One wood chip packet burned too quickly to permeate the meat, so we added a second, which produced the ideal amount of smoke for meat subtly flavored all the way through. In the end, we had wonderfully smoky, moist chicken with glossy skin after only 90 minutes on the grill.

Smoked Chicken

SERVES 6 TO 8

If using kosher chicken, do not brine in step 1. Two medium wood chunks, soaked in water for 1 hour, can be substituted for the wood chip packet on a charcoal grill. See Core Technique on page 394 for more details on using wood chips.

- 1 cup salt
- 1 cup sugar
- 6 pounds bone-in chicken parts (breasts, thighs, and/or drumsticks), trimmed
- 3 tablespoons vegetable oil
  Pepper
- 3 cups wood chips, 1½ cups soaked in water for 15 minutes and drained, plus 1½ cups wood chips unsoaked
- 1 (16 by 12-inch) disposable aluminum roasting pan (if using charcoal) or 1 disposable aluminum pie plate (if using gas)

1. Dissolve salt and sugar in 4 quarts cold water in large container. Submerge chicken pieces in brine, cover, and refrigerate for 30 minutes to 1 hour. Remove chicken from brine and pat dry with paper towels. Brush chicken evenly with oil and season with pepper.

2. Using large piece of heavy-duty aluminum foil, wrap soaked chips in foil packet and cut several vent holes in top. Repeat with another sheet of foil and unsoaked wood chips.

3A. FOR A CHARCOAL GRILL: Open bottom vent halfway. Arrange 2 quarts unlit charcoal banked against 1 side of grill and disposable pan filled with 2 cups water on empty side of grill. Light large chimney starter half filled with charcoal briquettes (3 quarts). When top coals are partially covered with ash, pour on top of unlit charcoal, to cover one-third of grill with coals steeply banked against side of grill. Place wood chip packets on top of coals. Set cooking grate in place, cover, and open lid vent halfway. Heat grill until hot and wood chips begin to smoke, about 5 minutes.

3B. FOR A GAS GRILL: Place wood chip packets directly on primary burner. Place disposable pie plate filled with 2 cups water on other burner(s). Turn all burners to high, cover, and heat grill until hot and wood chips begin to smoke, about 15 minutes. Turn primary burner to medium-high and turn off other burner(s). (Adjust primary burner as needed to maintain grill temperature around 325 degrees.)

4. Clean and oil cooking grate. Place chicken on cool side of grill, skin side up, as far away from heat as possible with thighs closest to heat and breasts farthest away. Cover (positioning lid vents over chicken if using charcoal) and cook until breasts register 160 degrees and thighs/drumsticks register 175 degrees, 1¼ to 1½ hours.

5. Transfer chicken to serving platter, tent loosely with foil, and let rest for 5 to 10 minutes before serving.

Italian-Style Grilled Chicken

✔ **WHY THIS RECIPE WORKS:** We wanted an Italian-style grilled chicken with evenly cooked, juicy meat, crackly skin, and bold Mediterranean flavor. We started by butterflying the bird, which helped it cook through evenly. Next, we salted it so it would retain its juices, which had the added advantage of loosening the chicken's skin from the meat, increasing crispness. We briefly sautéed Mediterranean seasonings in olive oil, strained the mixture, and then spread the resulting paste under the skin in our grilled chicken, to infuse the meat with flavor without making the skin soggy. Placing preheated bricks on the chicken while it cooked ensured that the skin browned evenly and was well rendered.

Italian-Style Grilled Chicken

SERVES 4

Use an oven mitt or dish towel to safely maneuver the hot bricks. You will need two standard-size bricks. A cast-iron skillet or other heavy pan can be used in place of the bricks. See Core Technique on page 292 for more details on butterflying a whole chicken.

- ⅓ cup extra-virgin olive oil
- 8 garlic cloves, minced
- 1 teaspoon grated lemon zest plus 2 tablespoons juice
  Pinch red pepper flakes
- 4 teaspoons minced fresh thyme
- 1 tablespoon minced fresh rosemary
  Salt and pepper
- 1 (3½- to 4-pound) whole chicken, giblets discarded

1. Heat oil, garlic, lemon zest, and pepper flakes in small saucepan over medium-low heat until sizzling, about 3 minutes. Stir in 1 tablespoon thyme and 2 teaspoons rosemary and continue to cook for 30 seconds longer. Strain mixture through fine-mesh strainer set over small bowl, pushing on solids to extract oil. Transfer solids to bowl and cool; set oil and solids aside.

2. Use kitchen shears to cut along both sides of backbone to remove it. Flatten breastbone and tuck wings behind back. Use hands or handle of wooden spoon to loosen skin over breast and thighs and remove any excess fat.

3. Combine 1½ teaspoons salt and 1 teaspoon pepper in bowl. Mix 2 teaspoons salt mixture with cooled garlic solids. Spread salt-garlic mixture evenly under skin over chicken breast and thighs. Sprinkle remaining ½ teaspoon salt mixture on exposed meat of bone side. Place chicken skin side up on wire rack set in rimmed baking sheet and refrigerate for 1 to 2 hours.

4A. FOR A CHARCOAL GRILL: Open bottom vent halfway. Light large chimney starter three-quarters filled with charcoal briquettes (4½ quarts). When top coals are partially covered with ash, pour evenly over half of grill. Set cooking grate in place, wrap 2 bricks tightly in aluminum foil, and place on cooking grate. Cover and open lid vent halfway. Heat grill until hot, about 5 minutes.

4B. FOR A GAS GRILL: Wrap 2 bricks tightly in aluminum foil and place on cooking grate. Turn all burners to high, cover, and heat grill until hot, about 15 minutes. Leave primary burner on high and turn off other burner(s). (Adjust primary burner as needed during cooking to maintain grill temperature around 350 degrees.)

5. Clean and oil cooking grate. Place chicken on cooler side of grill, skin side down, with legs facing coals and flames. Place hot bricks lengthwise over each breast half, cover, and cook until skin is lightly browned and faint grill marks appear, 22 to 25 minutes. Remove bricks from chicken. Using tongs, grip legs and flip chicken (chicken should release freely from grill; use thin metal spatula to loosen if stuck), then transfer to hot side of grill, skin side up. Place bricks over breast, cover, and cook until chicken is well browned, 12 to 15 minutes.

6. Remove bricks, flip chicken skin side down, and continue to cook until skin is well browned and breast registers 160 degrees and thighs register 175 degrees, 5 to 10 minutes longer. Transfer chicken to carving board, tent loosely with foil, and let rest for 15 minutes.

7. Whisk lemon juice, remaining 1 teaspoon thyme, and remaining 1 teaspoon rosemary into reserved oil and season with salt and pepper to taste. Carve chicken and serve, passing sauce separately.

Grilled Beef Kebabs

✔ **WHY THIS RECIPE WORKS:** Most beef kebabs are disappointing, with overcooked meat and vegetables that are either raw or mushy. We wanted to develop a foolproof approach to creating meaty kebabs that looked and tasted like the real thing: chunks of beef with a thick, caramelized char on the outside and a juicy, pink interior, all thoroughly seasoned by a marinade and paired with nicely browned, tender-firm vegetables. For the meat, we chose well-marbled steak tips, with their beefy flavor and tender texture. For the marinade, we included salt for moisture, oil for flavor, and sugar for browning. For even more depth, we used tomato paste, a host of seasonings and herbs, and beef broth. We chose three grill favorites for the vegetables: bell pepper, onion, and zucchini. Grilling the beef kebabs and vegetables on separate skewers over a two-level fire, which has hotter and cooler areas, allowed us to cook the vegetables over a lower temperature while the beef seared over the hotter area.

Grilled Beef Kebabs with Lemon and Rosemary Marinade

SERVES 4 TO 6

If you can't find sirloin steak tips, sometimes labeled "flap meat," substitute 2½ pounds blade steak; if using, cut each steak in half to remove the gristle. You will need four 12-inch metal skewers for this recipe. If you have long, thin pieces of meat, roll or fold them into approximate 2-inch cubes before skewering.

MARINADE

- 1 onion, chopped
- ⅓ cup beef broth
- ⅓ cup vegetable oil
- 3 tablespoons tomato paste
- 6 garlic cloves, chopped
- 2 tablespoons chopped fresh rosemary
- 2 teaspoons grated lemon zest
- 2 teaspoons salt
- 1½ teaspoons sugar
- ¾ teaspoon pepper

BEEF AND VEGETABLES

- 2 pounds sirloin steak tips, trimmed and cut into 2-inch chunks
- 1 large zucchini or summer squash, halved lengthwise and sliced 1 inch thick
- 1 large red or green bell pepper, stemmed, seeded, and cut into 1½-inch pieces
- 1 large red or sweet onion, halved lengthwise, each half cut into 4 wedges and each wedge cut crosswise into thirds

1. FOR THE MARINADE: Process all ingredients in blender until smooth, about 45 seconds. Transfer ¾ cup marinade to large bowl and set aside.

2. FOR THE BEEF AND VEGETABLES: Place remaining marinade and beef in 1-gallon zipper-lock bag and toss to coat; press out as much air as possible and seal bag. Refrigerate for at least 1 to 2 hours, flipping bag every 30 minutes.

3. Add zucchini, bell pepper, and onion to bowl with reserved marinade and toss to coat. Cover and let sit at room temperature for at least 30 minutes.

4. Remove beef from bag and pat dry with paper towels. Thread beef tightly onto two 12-inch metal skewers. Thread vegetables onto two 12-inch metal skewers, in alternating pattern of zucchini, bell pepper, and onion.

5A. FOR A CHARCOAL GRILL: Open bottom vent completely. Light large chimney starter mounded with charcoal briquettes (7 quarts). When top coals are partially covered with ash, pour evenly over center of grill, leaving 2-inch gap between grill wall and charcoal. Set cooking grate in place, cover, and open lid vent completely. Heat grill until hot, about 5 minutes.

5B. FOR A GAS GRILL: Turn all burners to high, cover, and heat grill until hot, about 15 minutes. Leave primary burner on high and turn other burner(s) to medium-low.

6. Clean and oil cooking grate. Place beef skewers on grill (directly over coals if using charcoal or over hotter side of grill if using gas). Place vegetable skewers on grill (near edge of coals but still over coals if using charcoal or over cooler side of grill if using gas). Cook (covered if using gas), turning skewers every 3 to 4 minutes, until beef skewers are well browned and register 120 to 125 degrees (for medium-rare) or 130 to 135 degrees (for medium), 12 to 16 minutes. Transfer beef skewers to platter and tent loosely with foil. Continue cooking vegetable skewers until tender and lightly charred, about 5 minutes longer; serve with beef skewers.

Grilled Beef Kebabs with North African Marinade

Substitute 20 cilantro sprigs, 2 teaspoons paprika, 1½ teaspoons ground cumin, and ½ teaspoon cayenne pepper for lemon zest and rosemary.

Grilled Beef Kebabs with Red Curry Marinade

Substitute ½ cup packed fresh basil leaves, 3 tablespoons red curry paste, 2 teaspoons lime zest, and 2 teaspoons grated fresh ginger for lemon zest and rosemary.

Grilled Steak Tips

✔ **WHY THIS RECIPE WORKS:** Steak tips have long been the darling of all-you-can-eat restaurant chains where quantity takes precedence over quality. Sometimes they are mushy, but usually they're tough and dry. We wanted steak tips with deep flavor and tender texture. We chose sirloin steak tips, also known as flap meat, an affordable cut of meat that stayed tender and moist during a brief stint on the grill. To further tenderize and flavor the meat, we use a soy sauce–based marinade. Grilling the tips over a two-level fire helped us to cook this often unevenly shaped cut evenly. Letting the steak tips rest for 5 to 10 minutes after grilling also helped to ensure juicy meat.

Grilled Steak Tips

SERVES 4 TO 6

Sirloin steak tips are sometimes labeled "flap meat." A two-level fire allows you to brown the steak over the hot side of the grill, then move it to the cooler side if it is not yet cooked through. If your steak is thin, however, you may not need to use the cooler side of the grill. Serve lime wedges with the Southwestern-marinated tips, orange wedges with the tips marinated in garlic, ginger, and soy sauce, and lemon wedges with the garlic-herb marinade.

- 1 recipe marinade (recipes follow)
- 2 pounds sirloin steak tips, trimmed
  Lime, orange, or lemon wedges

1. Combine marinade and beef in 1-gallon zipper-lock bag and toss to coat; press out as much air as possible and seal bag. Refrigerate for 1 hour, flipping bag halfway through marinating.

2A. FOR A CHARCOAL GRILL: Open bottom vent completely. Light large chimney starter filled with charcoal briquettes (6 quarts). When top coals are partially covered with ash, pour two-thirds evenly over grill, then pour remaining coals over half of grill. Set cooking grate in place, cover, and open lid vent completely. Heat grill until hot, about 5 minutes.

2B. FOR A GAS GRILL: Turn all burners to high, cover, and heat grill until hot, about 15 minutes.

3. Clean and oil cooking grate. Remove beef from bag and pat dry with paper towels. Place steak tips on grill (on hotter side if using charcoal) and cook (covered if using gas) until well browned on first side, about 4 minutes. Flip steak tips and continue to cook (covered if using gas) until meat registers 120 to 125 degrees (for medium-rare) or 130 to 135 degrees (for medium), 6 to 10 minutes longer. If exterior of meat is browned but beef is not yet cooked through, move to cooler side of grill (if using charcoal) or turn down burners to medium (if using gas) and continue to cook to desired doneness.

4. Transfer steak tips to carving board, tent loosely with aluminum foil, and let rest for 5 to 10 minutes. Slice steak tips very thin on bias and serve with lime wedges.

Southwestern Marinade
MAKES ABOUT ¾ CUP, ENOUGH FOR 1 RECIPE GRILLED STEAK TIPS

- ⅓ **cup soy sauce**
- ⅓ **cup vegetable oil**
- 3 **garlic cloves, minced**
- 1 **tablespoon packed dark brown sugar**
- 1 **tablespoon tomato paste**
- 1 **tablespoon chili powder**
- 2 **teaspoons ground cumin**
- ¼ **teaspoon cayenne pepper**

Combine all ingredients in bowl.

Garlic, Ginger, and Soy Marinade
MAKES ABOUT ⅔ CUP, ENOUGH FOR 1 RECIPE GRILLED STEAK TIPS

- ⅓ **cup soy sauce**
- 3 **tablespoons vegetable oil**
- 3 **tablespoons toasted sesame oil**
- 2 **tablespoons packed dark brown sugar**
- 1 **tablespoon grated fresh ginger**
- 2 **teaspoons grated orange zest**
- 1 **scallion, sliced thin**
- 3 **garlic cloves, minced**
- ½ **teaspoon red pepper flakes**

Combine all ingredients in bowl.

Garlic and Herb Marinade
MAKES ABOUT ¾ CUP, ENOUGH FOR 1 RECIPE GRILLED STEAK TIPS

- ⅓ **cup soy sauce**
- ⅓ **cup olive oil**
- 3 **garlic cloves, minced**
- 1 **tablespoon minced fresh rosemary**
- 1 **tablespoon minced fresh thyme**
- 1 **tablespoon packed dark brown sugar**
- 1 **tablespoon tomato paste**
- 1 **teaspoon pepper**

Combine all ingredients in bowl.

Grilled Steaks with Chimichurri Sauce

WHY THIS RECIPE WORKS: We wanted a grilled steak with a mahogany-hued char that snapped with each bite. We chose well-marbled strip steak for its beefy flavor and moist meat. For the steaks' requisite deep-brown char, we needed to get the exterior bone-dry. To do this, we sprinkled the steaks with salt and cornstarch (which helped dry out the exterior) and then left them uncovered in the freezer. For an accompanying sauce, we settled on a traditional Argentine *chimichurri* sauce. With parsley, cilantro, oregano, garlic, red wine vinegar, red pepper flakes, and salt—emulsified with extra-virgin olive oil—this bright sauce was the perfect foil to the rich flavor of the steaks.

Grilled Steaks with Chimichurri Sauce
SERVES 6 TO 8

If you prefer, you can use table salt both in the sauce and for seasoning the steaks, just make sure to use half of the amounts listed below. See Recipe Tutorial on page 402 for more details on this recipe.

CHIMICHURRI SAUCE
- ¼ **cup hot water**
- 2 **teaspoons dried oregano**
- 2 **teaspoons kosher salt**
- 1⅓ **cups loosely packed parsley leaves**
- ⅔ **cup loosely packed fresh cilantro leaves**
- 6 **garlic cloves, minced**
- ½ **teaspoon red pepper flakes**
- ¼ **cup red wine vinegar**
- ½ **cup extra-virgin olive oil**

STEAKS
- 2 **tablespoons kosher salt**
- 1 **tablespoon cornstarch**
- 4 **(1-pound) boneless strip steaks, 1½ inches thick**
  Pepper

1. FOR THE SAUCE: Combine hot water, oregano, and salt in liquid measuring cup or bowl; let sit for 5 minutes to soften oregano. Pulse parsley, cilantro, garlic, and red pepper flakes in food processor until coarsely chopped, about 10 pulses. Add water mixture and vinegar and pulse briefly to combine. Transfer mixture to medium bowl and slowly whisk in oil until incorporated and mixture is emulsified. Cover with plastic wrap and let sit at room temperature at least 1 hour. (Sauce can be refrigerated for up to 3 days; bring to room temperature before using.)

2. FOR THE STEAKS: Combine salt and cornstarch in bowl. Pat steaks dry with paper towels and place on wire rack set in rimmed baking sheet. Rub entire surface of steaks with cornstarch mixture and place steaks, uncovered, in freezer until very firm, about 30 minutes.

3A. FOR A CHARCOAL GRILL: Open bottom grill vent completely. Light large chimney starter filled with charcoal (6 quarts). When top coals are partially covered with ash, pour coals evenly over grill. Set cooking grate in place, cover, and open lid vent completely. Heat grill until hot, about 5 minutes.

3B. FOR A GAS GRILL: Turn all burners to high, cover, and heat grill until hot, about 15 minutes.

4. Clean and oil cooking grate. Season steaks with pepper. Place steaks on grill, cover, and cook until steaks begin to char, 2 to 3 minutes. Using tongs, flip steaks and cook on second side until beginning to char, 2 to 3 minutes. Flip again and cook on first side until well charred, 2 to 3 minutes. Flip one last time and continue to cook until second side is well charred and steaks register 115 degrees for rare, about 2 minutes, or 120 degrees for medium-rare, about 4 minutes. Transfer to large plate, tent loosely with foil, and let rest for 10 minutes. Slice steaks crosswise and serve, passing chimichurri sauce separately.

Inexpensive Grill-Roasted Beef

✓ **WHY THIS RECIPE WORKS:** To capture perfectly juicy, tender, and inexpensive beef on the grill, we started with the meat. Top sirloin won out over other inexpensive contenders. To keep our grill-roasted beef tender, we seared it on the hot side of the grill, then transferred the roast inside a disposable aluminum pan (in which we poked holes to preserve the sear) and continued cooking it on the cool side of the grill. We also found that cutting the roast into thin slices made the meat taste even more tender.

Inexpensive Grill-Roasted Beef with Garlic and Rosemary
SERVES 6 TO 8

A paring knife or pair of kitchen shears works well for punching the holes in the aluminum pan. We prefer a top sirloin roast, but you can substitute a top round or bottom round roast. Start this recipe the day before you plan to grill so the salt rub has time to flavor and tenderize the meat. See Recipe Tutorial on page 406 for more details on this recipe.

- 6 garlic cloves, minced
- 2 tablespoons minced fresh rosemary
- 4 teaspoons kosher salt
- 1 tablespoon pepper
- 1 (3- to 4-pound) top sirloin roast
- 1 (13 by 9-inch) disposable aluminum roasting pan

1. Combine garlic, rosemary, salt, and pepper in bowl. Sprinkle all sides of roast evenly with salt mixture, wrap with plastic wrap, and refrigerate for 18 to 24 hours.

2A. FOR A CHARCOAL GRILL: Open bottom vent halfway. Light large chimney starter half-filled with charcoal briquettes (3 quarts). When top coals are partially covered with ash, pour evenly over one-third of grill. Set cooking grate in place, cover, and open lid vent halfway. Heat grill until hot, about 5 minutes.

2B. FOR A GAS GRILL: Turn all burners to high, cover, and heat grill until hot, about 15 minutes.

3. Clean and oil cooking grate. Place roast on grill (hot side if using charcoal) and cook (covered if using gas) until well browned on all sides, 10 to 12 minutes, turning as needed. (If flare-ups occur, move roast to cooler side of grill until flames die down.)

4. Meanwhile, punch fifteen ¼-inch holes in center of disposable pan in area roughly same size as roast. Once browned, place beef in pan over holes and set pan over cool side of grill (if using charcoal) or turn primary burner to medium and other burner(s) off (if using gas). (Adjust burners as needed during cooking to maintain grill temperature between 250 and 300 degrees.) Cover grill (positioning vent over meat if using charcoal) and cook until meat registers 120 to 125 degrees (for medium-rare) or 130 to 135 degrees (for medium), 40 minutes to 1 hour, rotating pan halfway through cooking.

5. Transfer meat to wire rack set in rimmed baking sheet, tent loosely with aluminum foil, and let rest for 20 minutes. Transfer meat to carving board, slice thin against grain, and serve.

Inexpensive Grill-Roasted Beef with Shallot and Tarragon
Substitute 1 minced shallot for garlic and 2 tablespoons minced fresh tarragon for rosemary.

Barbecued Beef Brisket

✓ **WHY THIS RECIPE WORKS:** In researching recipes for barbecued brisket, we found cooks could agree on one thing: cooking low and slow (for up to 12 hours) for the purpose of tenderizing. That seemed like a lot of time. We wanted to figure out a way to make cooking this potentially delicious cut of meat less daunting and less time-consuming and we wanted to trade in a specialized smoker for a backyard grill. Brining the brisket seasoned it throughout and allowed the meat to remain juicy even after hours on the grill. To get a good crust, we added a little sugar to the salt and pepper rub. Our "aha!" moment came when we realized that fire can burn down as well as up. We layered unlit briquettes on the bottom of our grill and added 4 quarts of hot coals on top. The result? A fire that burned consistently in the optimal 300-degree range for about three hours. We then transferred the brisket to the oven to finish cooking.

Barbecued Beef Brisket
SERVES 8 TO 10

If your brisket is smaller than 5 pounds or the fat cap has been removed, or if you are using a small charcoal grill, it may be necessary to build an aluminum foil shield in order to keep the brisket from becoming too dark. If using the fattier point cut, omit the step of brining. Two medium wood chunks, soaked in water for 1 hour, can be substituted for the wood chip packet on a charcoal grill. Some of the traditional accompaniments to barbecued brisket include barbecue sauce (recipe follows), sliced white bread or saltines, pickle chips, and thinly sliced onion. See Core Technique on page 394 for more details on using wood chips.

- 1 (5- to 6-pound) beef brisket, flat cut
- ⅔ cup table salt
- ½ cup plus 2 tablespoons sugar
- 2 cups wood chips, soaked in water for 15 minutes and drained
- 3 tablespoons kosher salt

- **2 tablespoons pepper**
- **1 (13 by 9-inch) disposable aluminum roasting pan (if using charcoal) or 1 disposable aluminum pie plate (if using gas)**

1. Using sharp knife, cut slits in fat cap, spaced 1 inch apart, in crosshatch pattern, being careful to not cut into meat. Dissolve table salt and ½ cup sugar in 4 quarts cold water in large container. Submerge brisket in brine, cover, and refrigerate for 2 hours.

2. Using large piece of heavy-duty aluminum foil, wrap soaked chips in foil packet and cut several vent holes in top.

3. Combine remaining 2 tablespoons sugar, kosher salt, and pepper in bowl. Remove brisket from brine and pat dry with paper towels. Transfer to rimmed baking sheet and rub salt mixture over entire brisket and into slits.

4A. FOR A CHARCOAL GRILL: Open bottom vent halfway. Arrange 3 quarts unlit charcoal banked against 1 side of grill and disposable pan filled with 2 cups water on empty side of grill. Light large chimney starter two-thirds filled with charcoal (4 quarts). When top coals are partially covered with ash, pour on top of unlit charcoal to cover one-third of grill with coals steeply banked against side of grill. Place wood chip packet on top of coals. Set cooking grate in place, cover, and open lid vent halfway. Heat grill until hot and wood chips begin to smoke, about 5 minutes.

4B. FOR A GAS GRILL: Place wood chip packet directly on primary burner. Place disposable aluminum pie plate filled with 2 cups water on other burner(s). Turn all burners to high, cover, and heat grill until hot and wood chips begin to smoke, about 15 minutes. Turn primary burner to medium and turn off other burner(s). (Adjust primary burner as needed during cooking to maintain grill temperature between 250 and 300 degrees.)

5. Line rimmed baking sheet with foil and set wire rack inside. Clean and oil cooking grate. Place brisket on cool side of grill, fat side down, as far away from coals and flames as possible with thickest side facing coals and flames. Loosely tent meat with foil. Cover (position lid vent over meat if using charcoal) and cook for 3 hours. Transfer brisket to prepared baking sheet.

6. Adjust oven rack to middle position and heat oven to 325 degrees. Roast brisket until tender and meat registers 195 degrees, about 2 hours.

7. Transfer brisket to carving board, tent loosely with foil, and let rest for 30 minutes. Cut brisket against grain into long, thin slices and serve.

Texas-Style Barbecue Sauce

MAKES ABOUT 1¾ CUPS

This is a simple, vinegary dipping sauce quite unlike the sweet, thick barbecue sauces found in the supermarket. The sauce can be refrigerated in an airtight container for up to 4 days; bring to room temperature before serving.

- **2 tablespoons unsalted butter**
- **¼ cup finely chopped onion**
- **1½ teaspoons chili powder**
- **1 garlic clove, minced**
- **2 cups tomato juice**

- **¾ cup distilled white vinegar**
- **2 tablespoons Worcestershire sauce**
- **2 tablespoons molasses**
- **1 teaspoon minced canned chipotle chile in adobo sauce**
- **½ teaspoon dry mustard mixed with 1 tablespoon water Salt and pepper**

1. Melt butter in small saucepan over medium heat. Add onion and cook, stirring occasionally, until softened, 2 to 3 minutes. Stir in chili powder and garlic and cook until fragrant, about 30 seconds. Add tomato juice, ½ cup vinegar, Worcestershire, molasses, chipotle, mustard mixture, ½ teaspoon salt, and ¼ teaspoon pepper. Bring to simmer and cook over medium heat, stirring occasionally, until slightly thickened and reduced to 1½ cups, 30 to 40 minutes.

2. Off heat, stir in remaining ¼ cup vinegar and season with salt and pepper to taste. Cool to room temperature before serving.

Grill-Smoked Pork Chops

✔ **WHY THIS RECIPE WORKS:** For great grill-smoked pork chops with rosy-pink, ultramoist meat and true smoke flavor throughout, we built a fire on two sides of the grill, leaving the center empty, except for a disposable aluminum roasting pan. We started the chops low and slow on the grill over the roasting pan. Then we applied a few coats of sauce and achieved a beautiful crust by searing them over the hot sides of the grill. We determined that bone-in chops were our best bet. The bones add flavor to the meat as it cooks and contain connective tissues and fat that break down to lend suppleness. What's more, the hollow structure of a bone acts as an insulator, slowing down heat penetration. We used this to our advantage by resting each chop on its bone instead of laying it flat. To keep them from toppling over, we speared them together with skewers, making sure to leave a good inch between each one to allow smoke to circulate, then stood them upright in the center of the grill with bone, not meat, touching the grill.

Grill-Smoked Pork Chops

SERVES 4

Buy chops of the same thickness to ensure they cook uniformly. Use the large holes on a coarse grater to grate the onion. Two medium wood chunks, soaked in water for 1 hour, can be substituted for the wood chip packet on a charcoal grill. You will need two 10-inch metal skewers for this recipe. See Core Technique on page 394 for more details on using wood chips.

SAUCE

- **½ cup ketchup**
- **¼ cup molasses**
- **2 tablespoons grated onion**
- **2 tablespoons Worcestershire sauce**
- **2 tablespoons Dijon mustard**
- **2 tablespoons cider vinegar**
- **1 tablespoon packed light brown sugar**

CHOPS

- **2 cups wood chips, soaked in water for 15 minutes and drained**
- **4 (12-ounce) bone-in pork rib chops, 1½ inches thick, trimmed**
- **2 teaspoons salt**
- **2 teaspoons pepper**
- **1 (13 by 9-inch) disposable aluminum roasting pan (if using charcoal)**

1. FOR THE SAUCE: Bring all ingredients to simmer in small saucepan over medium heat and cook, stirring occasionally, until reduced to about 1 cup, 5 to 7 minutes. Transfer ½ cup sauce to small bowl and set aside remaining sauce for serving.

2. FOR THE CHOPS: Using large piece of heavy-duty aluminum foil, wrap soaked chips in foil packet and cut several vent holes in top. Pat pork chops dry with paper towels. Use sharp knife to cut 2 slits about 1 inch apart through outer layer of fat and connective tissue. Season each chop with ½ teaspoon salt and ½ teaspoon pepper. Place chops side by side, facing in same direction, on cutting board with curved rib bone facing down. Pass 2 skewers through loin muscle of each chop, close to bone, about 1 inch from each end, then pull apart to create 1-inch space between each.

3A. FOR A CHARCOAL GRILL: Open bottom vent halfway and place disposable pan in center of grill. Light large chimney starter filled with charcoal briquettes (6 quarts). When top coals are partially covered with ash, pour into 2 even piles on either side of roasting pan. Place wood chip packet on 1 pile of coals. Set cooking grate in place, cover, and open lid vent halfway. Heat grill until hot and wood chips are smoking, about 5 minutes.

3B. FOR A GAS GRILL: Place wood chip packet over primary burner. Turn all burners to high, cover, and heat grill until hot and wood chips are smoking, about 15 minutes. Turn all burners to medium-high. (Adjust burners as needed during cooking to maintain grill temperature between 300 and 325 degrees.)

4. Clean and oil cooking grate. Place skewered chops bone side down on grill (over disposable pan if using charcoal). Cover and cook until meat registers 120 degrees, 28 to 32 minutes.

5. Remove skewers from chops, tip chops onto flat side and brush surface of each with 1 tablespoon sauce. Transfer chops, sauce side down, to hotter parts of grill (if using charcoal) or turn all burners to high (if using gas) and cook until browned on first side, 2 to 6 minutes. Brush top of each chop with 1 tablespoon sauce, flip, and continue to cook until browned on second side and meat registers 140 degrees, 2 to 6 minutes longer.

6. Transfer chops to serving platter, tent loosely with aluminum foil, and let rest for 5 to 10 minutes. Serve, passing reserved sauce separately.

Grill-Roasted Pork Loin

WHY THIS RECIPE WORKS: A juicy, crisp-crusted pork loin is a great way to dress up an outdoor dinner, but it can be a challenge to keep the lean roast from drying out on the grill. First, we chose the best cut. Our top choice—the blade-end roast—was moist and flavorful and was the hands-down winner over center-cut and sirloin roasts. Brining the meat before grilling ensured that our finished roast met with rave reviews from testers and stayed juicy and moist, and a generous coating of black pepper—or our own spicy rub—provided ample flavoring. We seared the roast for a nice crust and finished it over indirect heat.

Grill-Roasted Pork Loin
SERVES 4 TO 6

If the pork is enhanced (injected with a salt solution; see page 222), do not brine and add 1 tablespoon salt to the pepper or spice rub. Two medium wood chunks, soaked in water for 1 hour, can be substituted for the wood chip packet on a charcoal grill. See Core Technique on page 394 for more details on using wood chips.

- **¼ cup salt**
- **1 (2½- to 3-pound) boneless blade-end pork loin roast, trimmed and tied with kitchen twine at 1½-inch intervals**
- **2 tablespoons olive oil**
- **1 tablespoon pepper or 1 recipe spice rub (recipes follow)**
- **2 cups wood chips, soaked in water for 15 minutes and drained**

1. Dissolve salt in 2 quarts cold water in large container. Submerge pork loin in brine, cover, and refrigerate for 1 to 1½ hours. Remove pork from brine and pat dry with paper towels. Rub pork loin with oil and coat with pepper. Let sit at room temperature for 1 hour.

2. Using large piece of heavy-duty aluminum foil, wrap soaked chips in foil packet and cut several vent holes in top.

3A. FOR A CHARCOAL GRILL: Open bottom vent halfway (and place roasting pan on 1 side of grill). Light large chimney starter three-quarters filled with charcoal briquettes (4½ quarts). When top coals are partially covered with ash, pour evenly over half of grill. Place wood chip packet on coals. Set cooking grate in place, cover, and open lid vent halfway. Heat grill until hot and wood chips are smoking, about 5 minutes.

3B. FOR A GAS GRILL: Place wood chip packet directly on primary burner. Turn all burners to high, cover, and heat grill until hot and wood chips are smoking, about 15 minutes. Leave primary burner on high and turn off other burner(s). (Adjust primary burner as needed during cooking to maintain grill temperature between 300 and 325 degrees.)

4. Clean and oil cooking grate. Place pork loin on hot side of grill, fat side up, and cook (covered if using gas) until well browned on all sides, 10 to 12 minutes, turning as needed. Move to cool side of grill, positioning roast parallel with and as close as possible to heat. Cover (position lid vent over roast if using charcoal) and cook for 20 minutes.

5. Rotate roast 180 degrees, cover, and continue to cook until meat registers 145 degrees, 10 to 30 minutes longer, depending on thickness of roast.

6. Transfer roast to carving board, tent loosely with aluminum foil, and let rest for 15 minutes. Remove twine, cut roast into ½-inch-thick slices, and serve.

Sweet and Savory Spice Rub

MAKES ABOUT 2 TABLESPOONS, ENOUGH FOR 1 RECIPE GRILL-ROASTED PORK LOIN

The warm spices in this rub are a perfect match with pork.

> 1 **tablespoon cumin seeds**
> 1½ **teaspoons coriander seeds**
> 1 **teaspoon fennel seeds**
> ½ **teaspoon ground cinnamon**
> ¼ **teaspoon ground allspice**

Toast cumin, coriander, and fennel seeds in small skillet over medium heat, shaking pan occasionally, until fragrant, about 2 minutes. Transfer to bowl, let cool to room temperature, and grind to powder in spice grinder. Stir in cinnamon and allspice.

Chili-Mustard Spice Rub

MAKES ABOUT 2 TABLESPOONS, ENOUGH FOR 1 RECIPE GRILL-ROASTED PORK LOIN

This rub packs some heat, so use the lesser amount of cayenne if you want a milder rub.

> 2 **teaspoons chili powder**
> 2 **teaspoons dry mustard**
> 1 **teaspoon ground cumin**
> ½–1 **teaspoon cayenne pepper**

Combine all ingredients in bowl.

Barbecued Pulled Pork

✔ **WHY THIS RECIPE WORKS:** Slow-cooked pulled pork is a summertime favorite; however, many barbecue procedures demand the regular attention of the cook for eight hours or more. We wanted to find a way to make moist, fork-tender pulled pork without the marathon cooking time and constant attention to the grill. For the meat, we determined that a shoulder roast (also called Boston butt), which has significant fat, retained the most moisture and flavor during a long, slow cook. We massaged a spicy chili rub into the meat, then wrapped the roast in plastic and refrigerated it for at least three hours to "marinate." We cooked the roast first on the grill to absorb smoky flavor (from wood chips—no smoker required), then finished it in the oven. Finally, we let the pork rest in a paper bag so the meat would steam and any remaining collagen would break down, allowing the flavorful juices to be reabsorbed.

Barbecued Pulled Pork

SERVES 8

Pulled pork can be made with a fresh ham or picnic roast, although our preference is for pork butt, often labeled Boston butt. If using a fresh ham or picnic roast, remove the skin by cutting through it with the tip of a chef's knife; slide the blade just under the skin and work around to loosen it while pulling it off with your other hand. Four medium wood chunks, soaked in water for 1 hour, can be substituted for the wood chip packets on a charcoal grill. Serve on plain white bread or warmed rolls with dill pickle chips and coleslaw. See Core Technique on page 394 for more details on using wood chips.

> 1 **(6- to 8-pound) bone-in pork butt roast**
> ¾ **cup Dry Rub for Barbecue (recipe follows)**
> 4 **cups wood chips, soaked in water for 15 minutes and drained**
> 1 **(13 by 9-inch) disposable aluminum roasting pan**
> 2 **cups barbecue sauce (recipes follow)**

1. Pat pork dry with paper towels, then massage dry rub into meat. Wrap meat in plastic wrap and refrigerate for at least 3 hours or up to 3 days.

2. At least 1 hour prior to cooking, remove roast from refrigerator, unwrap, and let sit at room temperature. Using 2 large pieces of heavy-duty aluminum foil, wrap soaked chips in 2 foil packets and cut several vent holes in tops.

3A. FOR A CHARCOAL GRILL: Open bottom vent halfway. Light large chimney starter three-quarters filled with charcoal briquettes (4½ quarts). When top coals are partially covered with ash, pour evenly over half of grill. Place wood chip packets on coals. Set cooking grate in place, cover, and open lid vent halfway. Heat grill until hot and wood chips are smoking, about 5 minutes.

3B. FOR A GAS GRILL: Place wood chip packets directly on primary burner. Turn all burners to high, cover, and heat grill until hot and wood chips are smoking, about 15 minutes. Turn primary burner to medium-high and turn off other burner(s). (Adjust primary burner as needed to maintain grill temperature around 325 degrees.)

4. Set roast in disposable pan and place on cool side of grill. Cover (position lid vent over roast if using charcoal) and cook for 3 hours. During final 20 minutes of cooking, adjust oven rack to lower-middle position and heat oven to 325 degrees.

5. Wrap disposable pan with heavy-duty foil, transfer to oven, and cook meat until fork-tender, about 2 hours.

6. Carefully slide foil-wrapped pan with roast into brown paper bag. Crimp end shut and let rest for 1 hour.

7. Transfer roast to carving board and unwrap. Separate roast into muscle sections, removing fat, if desired, and tearing meat into shreds with your fingers. Place shredded meat in large bowl and toss with 1 cup barbecue sauce. Serve, passing remaining sauce separately.

Dry Rub for Barbecue

MAKES ABOUT 1 CUP

You can adjust the proportions of spices in this all-purpose rub or add or subtract a spice, as you wish.

- ¼ cup paprika
- 2 tablespoons chili powder
- 2 tablespoons ground cumin
- 2 tablespoons packed dark brown sugar
- 2 tablespoons salt
- 1 tablespoon dried oregano
- 1 tablespoon granulated sugar
- 1 tablespoon black pepper
- 1 tablespoon white pepper
- 1–2 teaspoons cayenne pepper

Combine all ingredients in small bowl.

Eastern North Carolina Barbecue Sauce

MAKES ABOUT 2 CUPS

- 1 cup distilled white vinegar
- 1 cup cider vinegar
- 1 tablespoon sugar
- 1 tablespoon red pepper flakes
- 1 tablespoon hot sauce
  Salt and pepper

Mix all ingredients except salt and pepper together in bowl and season with salt and pepper to taste. (Sauce can be refrigerated for up to 4 days.)

Western South Carolina Barbecue Sauce

MAKES 2 CUPS

- 1 tablespoon vegetable oil
- ½ cup finely chopped onion
- 2 garlic cloves, minced
- ½ cup cider vinegar
- ½ cup Worcestershire sauce
- 1 tablespoon dry mustard
- 1 tablespoon packed dark brown sugar
- 1 tablespoon paprika
- 1 teaspoon salt
- 1 teaspoon cayenne pepper
- 1 cup ketchup

Heat oil in small saucepan over medium heat. Add onion and cook, stirring occasionally, until softened, 5 to 7 minutes. Stir in garlic and cook until fragrant, about 30 seconds. Stir in vinegar, Worcestershire, mustard, sugar, paprika, salt, and cayenne, bring to simmer, and stir in ketchup. Cook over low heat until thickened, about 15 minutes. (Sauce can be refrigerated for up to 4 days.)

Mid–South Carolina Mustard Sauce

MAKES ABOUT 2½ CUPS

- 1 cup cider vinegar
- 1 cup vegetable oil
- 6 tablespoons Dijon mustard
- 2 tablespoons maple syrup or honey
- 4 teaspoons Worcestershire sauce
- 1 teaspoon hot sauce
  Salt and pepper

Mix all ingredients except salt and pepper together in bowl and season with salt and pepper to taste. (Sauce can be refrigerated for up to 4 days.)

Memphis-Style Barbecued Spareribs

✔ **WHY THIS RECIPE WORKS:** In Memphis, ribs get flavor from a spice rub and a thin, vinegary liquid—called a mop—that is basted on the ribs throughout cooking. We started by applying a spice rub to the ribs and let them sit for one hour before grilling. To keep the meat moist on the grill, we stowed a pan of water underneath the cooking grate on the cooler side of the grill, where it would absorb heat and work to keep the temperature stable. For the mop, we combined apple juice and cider vinegar and brushed it on the ribs while they cooked on the grill. Last, as with our other barbecue recipes, we transferred the ribs to the oven to cook through until tender.

Memphis-Style Barbecued Spareribs

SERVES 4 TO 6

Don't remove the membrane that runs along the bone side of the ribs; it prevents some of the fat from rendering out and is authentic to this style of ribs. If using a charcoal grill, ½ cup wood chips is sufficient, but ¾ cup is best for a gas grill. Two medium wood chunks, soaked in water for 1 hour, can be substituted for the wood chip packet on a charcoal grill. See Recipe Tutorial on page 410 for more details on this recipe.

- 2 (2½- to 3-pound) racks St. Louis–style spareribs, trimmed
- 1 recipe Spice Rub (recipe follows)
- ½ cup apple juice
- 3 tablespoons cider vinegar
- ½–¾ cup wood chips, soaked in water for 15 minutes and drained
- 1 (13 by 9-inch) disposable aluminum roasting pan (if using charcoal) or 2 (9-inch) disposable aluminum pie plates (if using gas)

1. Sprinkle rub on both sides of each rack, rubbing and pressing to adhere.

2. Combine apple juice and vinegar in small bowl and set aside.

3A. FOR A CHARCOAL GRILL: Open bottom vent halfway.

Arrange 15 unlit charcoal briquettes on one side of grill. Place disposable pan filled with 1 inch water on other side of grill. Light large chimney starter one-third filled with charcoal briquettes (2 quarts). When top coals are partially covered with ash, pour evenly over unlit coals. Sprinkle soaked wood chips over coals. Set cooking grate in place, cover, and open lid vent halfway. (Adjust vent as needed during cooking to maintain grill temperature between 250 and 275 degrees). Heat grill until hot and wood chips are smoking, about 5 minutes.

3B. FOR A GAS GRILL: Place soaked wood chips in 1 (9-inch) disposable aluminum pie plate with ¼ cup water. Set disposable pie plate on primary burner. Place second disposable 9-inch pie plate filled with 1 inch water on other burner(s). Set cooking grate in place. Turn all burners to high, cover, and heat grill until hot and wood chips are smoking, about 15 minutes. Turn primary burner to medium-high and turn off other burner(s). (Adjust primary burner as needed during cooking to maintain grill temperature between 250 and 275 degrees.)

4. Clean and oil cooking grate. Place ribs meat side down on cool side of grill over water-filled pan. Cover (position lid vent over meat if using charcoal) and cook until ribs are deep red and smoky, about 1½ hours, brushing with 2 tablespoons apple juice mixture and flipping and rotating racks halfway through cooking. During final 20 minutes of cooking, adjust oven rack to middle position and heat oven to 300 degrees.

5. Set wire rack in rimmed baking sheet. Transfer ribs meat side up to prepared rack and brush with 2 tablespoons apple juice mixture. Pour 1½ cups water into bottom of sheet. Bake ribs 1 hour, then brush ribs with remaining apple juice mixture. Continue to bake until meat is tender but not falling off bone (internal temperature should be 195 to 200 degrees), 1 to 2 hours.

6. Transfer ribs to cutting board, tent loosely with aluminum foil, and let rest for 15 minutes. Cut ribs between bones to separate and serve.

Spice Rub

MAKES ABOUT ½ CUP, ENOUGH FOR 1 RECIPE MEMPHIS-STYLE BARBECUED SPARERIBS
For less spiciness, reduce the cayenne to ½ teaspoon.

- 2 **tablespoons paprika**
- 2 **tablespoons packed light brown sugar**
- 1 **tablespoon salt**
- 2 **teaspoons chili powder**
- 1½ **teaspoons pepper**
- 1½ **teaspoons garlic powder**
- 1½ **teaspoons onion powder**
- 1½ **teaspoons cayenne pepper**
- ½ **teaspoon dried thyme**

Combine all ingredients in bowl.

Grilled Salmon Fillets

✔ **WHY THIS RECIPE WORKS:** We wanted grilled salmon with a tender interior and crisp skin, and we wanted each fillet to hold together on the grill. Thicker salmon fillets stood up to the heat of the grill best. To prevent the fish from sticking and falling apart, we dried the fish's exterior by wrapping it in dish towels and "seasoned" our cooking grate by brushing it over and over with multiple layers of oil until it developed a dark, shiny coating. After laying the fillets on the grate, we easily flipped each fillet without even the tiniest bit of sticking. For moist, tender fish we cooked the salmon to a perfect medium-rare—any longer and the fish began to dry out.

Grilled Salmon Fillets

SERVES 4
This recipe can be used with any thick, firm-fleshed white fish, including red snapper, grouper, halibut, and sea bass (cook white fish to 140 degrees, up to 2 minutes longer per side). If you are using skinless fillets, treat the skinned side of each as if it were the skin side. If desired, serve with Olive Vinaigrette (recipe follows) instead of lemon wedges. See Recipe Tutorial on page 414 for more details on this recipe.

- 1 **(1½- to 2-pound) skin-on salmon fillet, about 1½ inches thick**
  Vegetable oil
  Kosher salt and pepper
  Lemon wedges

1. Use sharp knife to remove any whitish fat from belly of salmon and cut fillet into 4 equal pieces. Place salmon fillets skin side up on large plate or rimmed baking sheet lined with dish towel. Place second dish towel on top of fillets and press down to blot liquid. Refrigerate fish, wrapped in towels, while preparing grill, at least 20 minutes.

2A. FOR A CHARCOAL GRILL: Open bottom vent completely. Light large chimney starter two-thirds filled with charcoal briquettes (4 quarts). When top coals are partially covered with ash, pour evenly over half of grill. Set cooking grate in place, cover, and open lid vent completely. Heat grill until hot, about 5 minutes.

2B. FOR A GAS GRILL: Turn all burners to high, cover, and heat grill until hot, about 15 minutes.

3. Clean cooking grate, then repeatedly brush grate with well-oiled paper towels until grate is black and glossy, 5 to 10 times. Lightly brush both sides of fish with oil and season with salt and pepper. Place fish skin side down on hot side of grill (if using charcoal) or turn all burners to medium (if using gas) with fillets diagonal to grate slats. Cover and cook until skin is well browned and crisp, 2 to 4 minutes. (Try lifting fish gently with spatula after 3 minutes; if it doesn't cleanly lift off grill, continue to cook, checking at 30-second intervals, until it releases.)

4. Flip fish and continue to cook, covered, until center registers 125 degrees (for medium-rare) and is still translucent when cut into with paring knife, 3 to 7 minutes longer. Serve immediately with lemon wedges.

Olive Vinaigrette

MAKES ABOUT ½ CUP; ENOUGH FOR 1 RECIPE GRILLED SALMON FILLETS

- ½ cup green or kalamata olives, pitted and chopped coarse
- ¼ cup extra-virgin olive oil
- 2 tablespoons chopped fresh parsley
- 1 small shallot, minced
- 2 teaspoons lemon juice
  Salt and pepper

Combine all ingredients except salt and pepper in bowl, then season with salt and pepper to taste. Whisk to recombine before serving.

Grilled Blackened Red Snapper

🗸 **WHY THIS RECIPE WORKS:** Blackened fish is usually prepared in a cast-iron skillet, but it can lead to a relentlessly smoky kitchen. We thought we'd solve this issue by throwing our fish on the grill, but this introduced a host of new challenges—curled fillets that stuck to the grill and spices that tasted raw and harsh. To prevent curling, we scored the skin. We solved the sticking problem by heavily oiling the grate. Finally, to give the fish its flavorful "blackened, not burned" coating, we bloomed our spice mixture in melted butter, allowed it to cool, and then applied the coating to the fish. Once on the grill, the spice crust acquired the proper depth and richness while the fish cooked through.

Grilled Blackened Red Snapper

SERVES 4

Striped bass, halibut, or grouper can be substituted for the snapper; if the fillets are thicker or thinner, they will have slightly different cooking times. For a gas grill, we superheat the cooking grate by pressing aluminum foil directly onto the surface before cooking; be sure to use heavy-duty foil (thin foil will melt), and skip this step if your grill has ceramic cooking grates (it may damage the ceramic). Serve the fish with lemon wedges, Rémoulade Sauce (page 380), or Pineapple and Cucumber Salsa with Mint (recipe follows).

- 2 tablespoons paprika
- 2 teaspoons onion powder
- 2 teaspoons garlic powder
- ¾ teaspoon ground coriander
- ¾ teaspoon salt
- ¼ teaspoon cayenne pepper
- ¼ teaspoon black pepper
- ¼ teaspoon white pepper
- 3 tablespoons unsalted butter
- 4 (6- to 8-ounce) skin-on red snapper fillets, ¾ inch thick

1. Combine paprika, onion powder, garlic powder, coriander, salt, cayenne, black pepper, and white pepper in bowl. Melt butter in 10-inch skillet over medium heat. Stir in spice mixture and cook, stirring frequently, until fragrant and spices turn dark rust color, 2 to 3 minutes. Transfer mixture to pie plate and let cool to room temperature. Use a fork to break up any large clumps.

2A. FOR A CHARCOAL GRILL: Open bottom vent completely. Light large chimney starter two-thirds filled with charcoal briquettes (4 quarts). When top coals are partially covered with ash, pour evenly over half of grill. Set cooking grate in place, cover, and open lid vent completely. Heat grill until hot, about 5 minutes.

2B. FOR A GAS GRILL: Turn all burners to high, cover, and heat grill until hot, about 15 minutes.

3. Clean cooking grate, then repeatedly brush grate with well-oiled paper towels until black and glossy, 5 to 10 times.

4. Meanwhile, pat fillets dry with paper towels. Using sharp knife, make shallow diagonal slashes every inch along skin side of fish, being careful not to cut into flesh. Place fillets skin side up on large plate. Using your fingers, rub spice mixture in thin, even layer on top and sides of fish. Flip fillets over and repeat on other side (you should use all of spice mixture).

5. Place fish skin side down on grill (hot side if using charcoal) with fillets diagonal to grate. Cook until skin is very dark brown and crisp, 3 to 5 minutes. Carefully flip fish and continue to cook until dark brown and beginning to flake and center is opaque but still moist, about 5 minutes longer. Serve.

Pineapple and Cucumber Salsa with Mint

MAKES ABOUT 3 CUPS, ENOUGH FOR 1 RECIPE GRILLED BLACKENED RED SNAPPER

To make this dish spicier, add the reserved chile seeds.

- ½ large pineapple, peeled, cored, and cut into ¼-inch pieces
- ½ cucumber, peeled, halved lengthwise, seeded, and cut into ¼-inch pieces
- 1 small shallot, minced
- 1 serrano chile, stemmed, seeds reserved, and minced
- 2 tablespoons chopped fresh mint
- 1–2 tablespoons lime juice
- ½ teaspoon grated fresh ginger
  Salt
  Sugar

Combine pineapple, cucumber, shallot, serrano, mint, 1 tablespoon lime juice, ginger, and ½ teaspoon salt in bowl and let sit at room temperature for 15 to 30 minutes. Season with lime juice, salt, and sugar to taste. Transfer to serving bowl.

Grilled Tuna Steaks with Vinaigrette

🗸 **WHY THIS RECIPE WORKS:** Perfectly grilled tuna steaks should combine a hot, smoky, charred exterior with a cool, rare center. For a home cook, this ideal can be an elusive goal. For grilled tuna steaks with an intense smoky char and a tender interior, we started with a hot grill. We moistened the tuna steaks' flesh with a vinaigrette to promote browning and allow the oil to penetrate the meat of the tuna steaks. And instead of using sugar in our vinaigrette, we used honey. Both promote browning, but honey does it faster.

Grilled Tuna Steaks with Vinaigrette

SERVES 6

We prefer our tuna served rare or medium-rare. If you like your fish cooked medium, observe the timing for medium-rare, then tent the steaks loosely with aluminum foil for 5 minutes before serving.

>   3   tablespoons plus 1 teaspoon red wine vinegar
>   2   tablespoons chopped fresh thyme or rosemary
>   2   tablespoons Dijon mustard
>   2   teaspoons honey
>   Salt and pepper
>   ¾   cup olive oil
>   6   (8-ounce) tuna steaks, 1 inch thick

1A. FOR A CHARCOAL GRILL: Open bottom vent completely. Light large chimney starter filled with charcoal briquettes (6 quarts). When top coals are partially covered with ash, pour evenly over half of grill. Set cooking grate in place, cover, and open lid vent completely. Heat grill until hot, about 5 minutes.

1B. FOR A GAS GRILL: Turn all burners to high, cover, and heat grill until hot, about 15 minutes. (Adjust burners as needed to maintain hot fire.)

2. Clean cooking grate, then repeatedly brush grate with well-oiled paper towels until grate is black and glossy, 5 to 10 times.

3. Meanwhile, whisk vinegar, thyme, mustard, honey, ½ teaspoon salt, and pinch pepper together in large bowl. Whisking constantly, slowly drizzle oil into vinegar mixture until lightly thickened and emulsified. Measure out ¾ cup vinaigrette and set aside for cooking fish. Reserve remaining vinaigrette for serving.

4. Pat fish dry with paper towels. Generously brush both sides of fish with vinaigrette and season with salt and pepper. Place fish on grill (hot side if using charcoal) and cook (covered if using gas) until grill marks form and bottom surface is opaque, 1 to 3 minutes.

5. Flip fish and cook until opaque at perimeter and translucent red at center when checked with tip of paring knife and registers 110 degrees (rare), about 1½ minutes, or until opaque at perimeter and reddish pink at center when checked with tip of paring knife and registers 125 degrees (medium-rare), about 3 minutes. Serve, passing reserved vinaigrette.

Grilled Tuna Steaks with Chermoula Vinaigrette

Substitute 2 tablespoons minced fresh parsley for thyme and add ¼ cup minced fresh cilantro, 4 minced garlic cloves, 1 teaspoon paprika, 1 teaspoon ground cumin, and ½ teaspoon ground coriander to vinaigrette.

Grilled Tuna Steaks with Soy-Ginger Vinaigrette

Substitute rice vinegar for red wine vinegar and 2 thinly sliced scallions for thyme. Omit salt and add 3 tablespoons soy sauce, 1 tablespoon toasted sesame oil, 2 teaspoons grated fresh ginger, and ½ teaspoon red pepper flakes to vinaigrette.

Grilled Shrimp Skewers

✔ **WHY THIS RECIPE WORKS:** Shrimp can turn from moist and juicy to rubbery and dry in the blink of an eye—especially when grilled. While grilling shrimp in their shells can shield them from the coals' scorching heat, any seasonings are stripped off along with the shells when it's time to eat. For tender, juicy, boldly seasoned grilled shrimp we decided to go with peeled shrimp and find a way to prevent them from drying out. We seasoned the shrimp with salt, pepper, and sugar (to help browning) and set them over a very hot fire. This worked well with jumbo shrimp, but smaller shrimp overcooked before charring. Because jumbo shrimp cost as much as $25 per pound, we wanted a less expensive solution. We created faux jumbo shrimp by cramming a skewer with several normal-size shrimp pressed tightly together. Our final step was to take the shrimp off the fire before they were completely cooked (but after they had picked up attractive grill marks). We finished cooking them in a heated sauce waiting on the cool side of the grill; this final simmer infused them with bold flavor.

Grilled Shrimp Skewers

SERVES 4

The shrimp and sauce (recipes follow) finish cooking together on the grill, so prepare the sauce ingredients while the grill is heating. To fit all of the shrimp on the cooking grate at once, you will need three 14-inch metal skewers. Serve with grilled bread.

>   1½   pounds extra-large shrimp (21 to 25 per pound),
>   peeled and deveined
>   2–3 tablespoons olive oil
>   Salt and pepper
>   ¼   teaspoon sugar
>   1   recipe sauce (recipes follow)
>   Lemon wedges

1. Pat shrimp dry with paper towels. Thread the shrimp onto 3 skewers, alternating direction of heads and tails. Brush both sides of shrimp with oil and season with salt and pepper. Sprinkle 1 side of each skewer evenly with sugar.

2A. FOR A CHARCOAL GRILL: Open bottom vent completely. Light large chimney starter filled with charcoal briquettes (6 quarts). When top coals are partially covered with ash, pour evenly over half of grill. Set cooking grate in place, cover, and open lid vent completely. Heat grill until hot, about 5 minutes.

2B. FOR A GAS GRILL: Turn all burners to high, cover, and heat grill until hot, about 15 minutes. Leave primary burner on high and turn other burner(s) to medium-low.

3. Clean cooking grate, then repeatedly brush grate with well-oiled paper towels until grate is black and glossy, 5 to 10 times. Place disposable pan with sauce ingredients on hot side of grill and cook, stirring occasionally, until hot, 1 to 3 minutes. Move pan to cool side of grill.

4. Place shrimp skewers sugared side down on hot side of grill and use tongs to push shrimp together on skewers if they have separated. Cook shrimp until lightly charred, 4 to 5 minutes. Using tongs, flip and continue to cook until second side is pink and slightly translucent, 1 to 2 minutes longer.

5. Using potholder, carefully lift each skewer from grill and use tongs to slide shrimp off skewers into pan with sauce. Toss shrimp and sauce to combine. Place pan on hot side of grill and cook, stirring, until shrimp are opaque throughout, about 30 seconds. Remove from the grill, add remaining sauce ingredients, and toss to combine. Transfer to serving platter and serve with lemon wedges.

Spicy Lemon-Garlic Sauce
MAKES ABOUT ½ CUP, ENOUGH FOR 1 RECIPE GRILLED SHRIMP SKEWERS

- 4 tablespoons unsalted butter, cut into 4 pieces
- ¼ cup lemon juice (2 lemons)
- 3 garlic cloves, minced
- ½ teaspoon red pepper flakes
- ⅛ teaspoon salt
- 1 (10-inch) disposable aluminum pie pan
- ⅓ cup minced fresh parsley

Combine butter, lemon juice, garlic, pepper flakes, and salt in aluminum pan. Cook over hot side of grill, stirring occasionally, until butter melts, about 1½ minutes. Move to cool side of grill and proceed to grill shrimp, adding parsley just before serving.

Chermoula Sauce
MAKES ABOUT ½ CUP; ENOUGH FOR 1 RECIPE GRILLED SHRIMP SKEWERS

- ¼ cup extra-virgin olive oil
- 1 small red bell pepper, stemmed, seeded, and finely chopped
- ⅓ cup finely chopped red onion
- 3 garlic cloves, minced
- 1 teaspoon paprika
- ½ teaspoon ground cumin
- ¼ teaspoon cayenne pepper
- ⅛ teaspoon salt
- 1 (10-inch) disposable aluminum pie pan
- ⅓ cup minced fresh cilantro
- 2 tablespoons fresh lemon juice

Combine oil, bell pepper, onion, garlic, paprika, cumin, cayenne, and salt in aluminum pan. Cook over hot side of grill, stirring occasionally, until vegetables soften, 5 to 7 minutes. Move to cool side of grill and proceed to grill shrimp, adding cilantro and lemon juice just before serving.

Fresh Tomato Sauce with Feta and Olives
MAKES ABOUT ½ CUP, ENOUGH FOR 1 RECIPE GRILLED SHRIMP SKEWERS

- ¼ cup extra-virgin olive oil
- 1 large tomato, cored, seeded, and minced
- 1 tablespoon minced fresh oregano
- ⅛ teaspoon salt
- 1 (10-inch) disposable aluminum pie pan
- 4 ounces feta cheese, crumbled (1 cup)
- ⅓ cup kalamata olives, pitted and chopped fine
- 2 tablespoons lemon juice
- 3 scallions, sliced thin

Combine oil, tomato, oregano, and salt in aluminum pan. Cook over hot side of grill, stirring occasionally, until hot, about 1½ minutes. Move to cool side of grill and proceed to grill shrimp, adding feta, olives, lemon juice, and scallions just before serving.

Mexican-Style Grilled Corn

✔ **WHY THIS RECIPE WORKS:** In Mexico, street vendors add kick to grilled corn by slathering it with a creamy, spicy, cheesy sauce. The corn takes on an irresistibly sweet, smoky, charred flavor, which is heightened by the lime juice and chili powder in the sauce. For our own rendition of this south-of-the-border street fare, we ditched the husks, coated the ears with oil to prevent sticking, and grilled them directly on the grate over a hot fire so the corn could develop plenty of char. The traditional base for the sauce is *crema*, a thick, soured Mexican cream. But given its limited availability in supermarkets, we replaced the crema with a combination of mayonnaise (for richness) and sour cream (for tanginess). Most recipes call for *queso fresco* or Cotija, which can be hard to find. Pecorino Romano made a good substitute.

Mexican-Style Grilled Corn
SERVES 6

If you can find queso fresco or Cotija, use either in place of the Pecorino Romano. If you prefer the corn spicy, add the optional cayenne pepper.

- 1½ ounces Pecorino Romano cheese, grated (¾ cup)
- ¼ cup mayonnaise
- 3 tablespoons sour cream
- 3 tablespoons minced fresh cilantro
- 4 teaspoons lime juice
- 1 garlic clove, minced
- ¾ teaspoon chili powder
- ¼ teaspoon pepper
- ¼ teaspoon cayenne pepper (optional)
- 4 teaspoons vegetable oil
- ¼ teaspoon salt
- 6 ears corn, husks and silk removed

1A. FOR A CHARCOAL GRILL: Open bottom vent completely. Light large chimney starter filled with charcoal briquettes (6 quarts). When top coals are partially covered with ash, pour evenly over half of grill. Set cooking grate in place, cover, and open lid vent completely. Heat grill until hot, about 5 minutes.

1B. FOR A GAS GRILL: Turn all burners to high, cover, and heat grill until hot, about 15 minutes.

2. Meanwhile, combine Pecorino, mayonnaise, sour cream, cilantro, lime juice, garlic, ¼ teaspoon chili powder, pepper, and cayenne, if using, in large bowl and set aside. In second large bowl, combine oil, salt, and remaining ½ teaspoon chili powder. Add corn to oil mixture and toss to coat evenly.

3. Clean and oil cooking grate. Place corn on grill (hot side if using charcoal) and cook (covered if using gas) until lightly charred on all sides, 7 to 12 minutes, turning as needed. Place corn in bowl with cheese mixture, toss to coat evenly, and serve.

Grilled Potatoes

✅ **WHY THIS RECIPE WORKS:** Grilled potatoes are a summer classic, but we wanted to put a new spin on this dish by adding rosemary and garlic. Unfortunately, we found it was difficult to add garlic and rosemary flavors to plain grilled potatoes. Coating the potatoes with oil, garlic, and rosemary produced burnt, bitter garlic and charred rosemary. If we tossed the potatoes in garlic oil after cooking, the raw garlic was too harsh. It turned out that we needed to introduce the potatoes to the garlic-oil mixture not once, but three times. Before cooking, we pierced the potatoes, skewered them, seasoned them with salt, brushed on a garlic-rosemary oil, and precooked them in the microwave. Then, before grilling, we brushed them again with the infused oil. After grilling, we tossed them with the garlic and rosemary oil yet again. We finally had it—tender grilled potatoes infused with the smoky flavor of the grill and enlivened with the bold flavors of garlic and rosemary.

Grilled Potatoes with Garlic and Rosemary
SERVES 4

This recipe allows you to grill an entrée while the hot coals burn down in step 4. Once that item is done, start grilling the potatoes. This recipe works best with small potatoes that are about 1½ inches in diameter. If using medium potatoes, 2 to 3 inches in diameter, cut them into quarters. If the potatoes are larger than 3 inches in diameter, cut each potato into eighths. Since the potatoes are first cooked in the microwave, use wooden skewers.

> ¼ **cup olive oil**
> 9 **garlic cloves, minced**
> 1 **teaspoon chopped fresh rosemary**
>   **Salt and pepper**
> 2 **pounds small red potatoes, halved and skewered**
> 2 **tablespoons chopped fresh chives**

1. Heat oil, garlic, rosemary, and ½ teaspoon salt in small skillet over medium heat until sizzling, about 3 minutes. Reduce heat to medium-low and continue to cook until garlic is light blond, about 3 minutes. Pour mixture through fine-mesh strainer into small bowl; press on solids. Measure 1 tablespoon of solids and 1 tablespoon of oil into large bowl and set aside. Discard remaining solids but reserve remaining oil.

2. Place skewered potatoes in single layer on large plate and poke each potato several times with skewer. Brush with 1 tablespoon of strained oil and season with salt. Microwave until the potatoes offer slight resistance when pierced with paring knife, about 8 minutes, turning halfway through cooking. Transfer potatoes to baking sheet coated with 1 tablespoon of strained oil. Brush with remaining 1 tablespoon strained oil and season with salt and pepper to taste.

3A. FOR A CHARCOAL GRILL: Open bottom vent completely. Light large chimney starter filled with charcoal briquettes (6 quarts). When top coals are partially covered with ash, pour two-thirds evenly over grill, then pour remaining coals over half of grill. Set cooking grate in place, cover, and open lid vent completely. Heat grill until hot, about 5 minutes.

3B. FOR A GAS GRILL: Turn all burners to high, cover, and heat grill until hot, about 15 minutes. Turn all burners down to medium-high.

4. Clean and oil cooking grate. Place potatoes on grill (hotter side if using charcoal) and cook (covered if using gas) until grill marks appear, 3 to 5 minutes, flipping halfway through cooking. Move potatoes to cooler side of grill (if using charcoal) or turn all burners to medium-low (if using gas). Cover and continue to cook until paring knife slips in and out of potatoes easily, 5 to 8 minutes longer.

5. Remove potatoes from skewers and transfer to bowl with reserved garlic-oil mixture. Add chives, season with salt and pepper to taste, and toss until thoroughly coated. Serve.

Grilled Potatoes with Oregano and Lemon
Serve this variation with lemon wedges, if desired.

Reduce garlic to 3 cloves, substitute 2 tablespoons chopped fresh oregano for rosemary, and add 2 teaspoons grated lemon zest to oil in skillet. Substitute 2 teaspoons chopped fresh oregano for chives and add an additional 1 teaspoon grated lemon zest to potatoes when they come off grill.

Inside This Chapter

CHAPTER 10

How to Make Stocks and Soups

While it's true that making soup often allows for flexibility in terms of ingredient selection, it does demand solid techniques designed to build flavor. Of course, great soup begins with good stock. Many soups aren't worth making unless you have homemade stock, and we've reinvented this time-consuming process with novel recipes for chicken, beef, and vegetable stock—each delivers superior results in record time. For chilis and stews, refer to the previous chapters on poultry; meat; and rice, grains, and beans.

Getting Started

Six Principles of Soup Making

While the world of soup is diverse, there are some underlying principles that apply to most recipes.

SAUTÉ AROMATICS

The first step in making many soups is sautéing aromatic vegetables such as onion and garlic. Sautéing not only softens their texture so that there is no unwelcome crunch in the soup, it also tames any harsh flavors and develops more complex flavors in the process. Medium heat is usually a good temperature for sautéing.

START WITH GOOD STOCK

Packaged broth is a convenient option for soup making, but most soups benefit from being made with homemade stock. This is especially true of brothy soups in which the flavor of the stock takes center stage. Store-bought broth works better in soups with other liquid ingredients (such as cream or canned tomatoes) as well as in soups with lots of spices or other potent ingredients. But differences among packaged broths are quite significant—some are pretty flavorful, while others taste like salty dishwater. Shop carefully. See page 38 for more information about buying broth.

CUT THE VEGETABLES THE RIGHT SIZE

Most soups call for chunks of vegetables. Haphazardly cut vegetables will cook unevenly—some pieces will be underdone and crunchy while others will be soft and mushy. Cutting the vegetables to the size specified in the recipe ensures that the pieces will all be perfectly cooked.

STAGGER THE ADDITION OF VEGETABLES

When a soup contains a variety of vegetables, their addition to the pot must often be staggered to account for their varying cooking times. Hardy vegetables like potatoes and winter squash can withstand much more cooking than delicate asparagus or spinach.

SIMMER, DON'T BOIL

There is a fine line between simmering and boiling, and it can make a big difference in your soups. A simmer is a restrained version of a boil; fewer bubbles break the surface, and they do so with less vigor. Simmering heats food through more gently and more evenly than boiling; boiling can cause vegetables such as potatoes to break apart or fray at the edges, and it can toughen meat, too.

SEASON JUST BEFORE SERVING

In general, we add salt, pepper, and other seasonings—such as delicate herbs and lemon juice—after cooking, just before serving. The saltiness of the stock and other ingredients, such as canned tomatoes and beans, can vary greatly, so it's always best to taste and adjust the soup once the soup is complete, just before ladling it into bowls for serving.

Storing and Reheating Soup

One reason cooks like to make soup is because it can be made in advance. Here's what to do once you've finished the recipe.

COOLING AND STORING

For safety reasons, the U.S. Food and Drug Administration (FDA) recommends cooling liquids to 70 degrees within the first 2 hours after cooking and 40 degrees within 4 more hours. As tempting as it might seem, don't transfer the hot soup straight to the refrigerator: You may speed up the cooling process, but you'll also raise the internal temperature of the refrigerator to unsafe levels, putting all the other foods in your fridge in danger. We have found that by letting soup cool to 85 degrees on the counter (which takes only an hour) before transferring it to the fridge, we can bring it down to 40 degrees in a total time of 4 hours and 30 minutes (well within the FDA's recommended range).

We find that most soups are fine in the refrigerator for up to two days. The exceptions are soups with starchy ingredients like pasta, rice, or barley, which will continue to absorb liquid. The noodles or other starchy elements become mushy and bloated, and the soup might not have enough broth when you go to reheat it. If you know you're going to have leftovers, reserve them before you add the noodles or other starchy element. Most soups can also be frozen for up to a month. There are two exceptions to this rule. Noodles and dumplings will become very mushy, so soups with these ingredients are not the best candidates for freezing. Also, cream can curdle when frozen, so soups with a lot of dairy are best refrigerated for up to two days instead of being frozen.

Stock can be refrigerated for up to four days or frozen for as long as one month. If you are freezing stock, it makes sense to do so in smaller portions. You can ladle the stock into muffin tins (each slot will hold a scant cup). When the stock is frozen, simply twist the muffin tin as you would an ice cube tray to free them. Transfer the frozen blocks to a zipper-lock bag and return the stock to the freezer. The other option is to pour the stock into a coffee mug lined with a 1-quart zipper-lock bag (the mug keeps the bag open as you pour). Place the sealed bags in a shallow baking dish and freeze. Once the stock is frozen solid, the bags can be removed from the pan and stored flat in the freezer.

THAWING AND REHEATING

If the soup is frozen, it should first be thawed overnight in the refrigerator before being reheated. Yes, you can speed up the process by thawing the soup in the microwave, but the texture of the meat and vegetables will suffer a bit.

We prefer to reheat large amounts of soup in a heavy pot on the stovetop. Bring the soup to a rolling boil and make sure to stir often to ensure that the entire pot reaches the boiling point.

It's fine to microwave individual portions of soup. Transfer the soup to a microwave-safe bowl or dish and cover with a plate to prevent splattering (we don't recommend using plastic wrap). Make sure to stop and stir several times to ensure that the soup reheats evenly.

Essential Equipment

Most stocks and soups rely on only a few pieces of equipment; here are the items you'll put to use most in recipes in this chapter.

MEAT CLEAVER

A cleaver comes in handy when chopping up bones for stock, especially hacking up chicken parts. (Doing this with a chef's knife is a good way to chip the blade edge.) The best meat cleavers feature razor-sharp blades and a perfectly balanced design. Note that vegetable cleavers have thin blades that taper gently to a honed edge. Meat cleavers have much thicker, heavier blades with a blunt edge designed for hacking rather than slicing.

DUTCH OVEN

A Dutch oven is great for making stock and soup. Many stockpots are flimsy and tend to have hot spots that result in scorching and uneven cooking. Since browning is a key step in our stock recipes, we prefer a Dutch oven. A good-quality, heavy-bottomed Dutch oven will conduct heat steadily and evenly and, if properly cared for, will last a lifetime. Use a pot that has a capacity of about 8 quarts when making either stock or soup. For more details on what to look for, see page 21.

FINE-MESH STRAINER

When making stock, no kitchen tool works like a fine-mesh strainer to separate solids from liquid. A diameter of at least 6 inches and a deep, fine-mesh bowl are good qualities to look for in a strainer. Also, sturdy construction and a stable bowl rest allow you to really press down on the solids in the strainer to extract all the liquid. For more details on what to look for, see page 31.

FAT SEPARATOR

Homemade stock often contains a fair amount of fat that must be removed before the stock is used. You can refrigerate the stock overnight, during which time the fat will rise to the surface and harden. But if you want to use the stock right away, a fat separator will quickly remove the fat. Choose a fat separator with a large capacity (ideally 4 cups), an integrated strainer, and a wide mouth that makes for easy filling.

LADLE

A ladle is indispensable for serving soups. We prefer a ladle with a 9- to 10-inch handle; ladles with shorter handles tend to slide into the pot, and a ladle with a longer handle is cumbersome. The handle should also be slightly offset—this allows for clean pouring into a bowl.

BLENDER

A blender is the best appliance for making pureed soups. A blender's design pulls ingredients down to the blade at the bottom of the jar, so it yields a finer, smoother puree than you would get from either a food processor (which tends to get bits caught beneath its blade) or an immersion blender. When you're pureeing hot liquids, remember never to fill the jar more than halfway to prevent an explosion of liquid out of the blender top. For more details on what to look for, see page 28.

Essential Ingredients

Many soups rely on packaged broths. For details on when to use them and when it is acceptable to use homemade stock, see our recommendations on page 39. Also, check out our buying recommendations about packaged chicken, beef, and vegetable broths on pages 38–39.

How to Make Chicken Stock

When it comes to home cooking, chicken stock is one of the most versatile recipes you can make. It's an important component in a wide variety of soups and stews as well as in rice dishes. Sure, you can sometimes get away with store-bought, but in other cases using homemade stock makes all the difference (make risotto with homemade stock and you will find it hard to use packaged broth ever again.)

Most recipes require a very long simmering time to extract flavor from the chicken. Our stock-making method is nontraditional, to say the least—it has been engineered to deliver maximum flavor in minimal time, and employs some cooking techniques that you'd never find in conventional recipes. Note that the process is slightly different when making stock for a soup that requires chicken meat, so read the captions carefully. Refer to the two recipes (one that yields stock, the other that yields stock and white meat for soup) on page 459 for more details. Chicken stock can be refrigerated for up to four days or frozen for up to one month.

ESSENTIAL EQUIPMENT

- meat cleaver
- cutting board
- large Dutch oven
- tongs
- large bowl
- chef's knife
- wooden spoon
- fine-mesh strainer
- large liquid measuring cup
- wide, shallow spoon

1. START WITH FLAVORFUL CUTS, IN SMALL PIECES

Use meat cleaver to hack 3 pounds chicken legs, backs, and/or wings into 2-inch pieces.

WHY? Small pieces of chicken release their flavorful juices quickly, which helps keep the simmering time short, and with the bones cut, the marrow inside readily seeps into the liquid, giving the stock rich flavor and full body. Backs are usually sold at a nominal price specifically for making stock. If backs are not available, legs and wings work just as well but will cost a bit more. If you're making a soup that requires chicken meat, buy a whole chicken, reserve the two breast halves for the soup, and then hack the rest of the chicken to make the stock.

2. SAUTÉ TO BUILD FLAVOR

Heat 1 tablespoon vegetable oil in Dutch oven over medium-high heat until just smoking. Lightly brown chicken pieces on both sides in 2 batches and transfer to large bowl.

WHY? Sautéing the cut-up chicken parts until lightly browned is the first step in building flavor. The browning contributes lightly roasted notes that add complexity to the stock. If you're working with a whole chicken and have reserved the two breast pieces, brown them first to render fat from the skin and then set them aside on a plate before sautéing the cut-up chicken parts. Use a Dutch oven with at least an 8-quart capacity.

3. USE A MINIMUM OF FLAVOR ENHANCERS

Add 1 chopped onion to fat left in pot and cook until softened, about 3 minutes.

WHY? Most recipes try to camouflage the weak chicken flavor with a lot of vegetables and herbs. But if you use the right chicken parts, very little is needed to enhance flavor—just an onion as well as bay leaves and some salt (the latter two get added later, with the water). Sautéing the onion tames its harshness and brings out its natural sweetness.

4. SWEAT TO EXTRACT JUICE

Return chicken pieces (but not breasts, if using) and any accumulated juices to pot, cover, and reduce heat to low. Cook, stirring occasionally, until chicken has released its juices, about 20 minutes.

WHY? The goal of this step is not to attain additional browning, but to gently cook the chicken and draw out its flavorful juices. Sweating—that is, cooking over low heat with the lid on (stirring occasionally)—does this in just 20 minutes.

5. SIMMER GENTLY, COVERED

Add 8 cups water, 2 teaspoons salt, and 2 bay leaves and bring to boil. Cover, reduce heat to gentle simmer, and cook, skimming as needed, until stock tastes rich and flavorful, about 20 minutes longer.

WHY? The stock is covered while it simmers to prevent evaporation, a departure from most traditional recipes that indicate stock should be simmered uncovered. Most chicken stocks must be simmered for at least 2 hours, but our stock needs only 20 minutes of simmering. Keep the stock at a simmer, not a boil. Boiling can cause fat droplets to become suspended in the liquid, resulting in a murky, greasy-tasting stock. If you have reserved and browned the two breast pieces, add them with the water. By the time the stock is done, the breast meat will be perfectly cooked, and you can remove the meat from the bone once the pieces have cooled.

6. STRAIN CAREFULLY

Pour stock through fine-mesh strainer into large liquid measuring cup or other large container.

WHY? Once the chicken has given up its flavor, separate the solids from the liquid. For efficiency, use a large fine-mesh strainer. If your strainer is small, work in batches or remove the large solids by pouring the stock through a colander, then filter the liquid through the fine-mesh strainer. If your strainer has a coarse mesh, line it with damp cheesecloth before use.

7. REMOVE FAT

Let stock settle for 5 to 10 minutes. Use wide, shallow spoon to remove fat that rises to surface.

WHY? During cooking, fat renders out from the chicken into the liquid, so before the stock can be used the fat must be removed. Straining integrates the fat into the stock. Let the stock stand for 5 to 10 minutes after straining to give fat time to rise to the surface. Then the fat can be skimmed off with a spoon or ladle. Or the stock can be refrigerated until the fat solidifies on the surface; the congealed fat layer is easily scraped off with a spoon.

How to Make Beef Stock

ESSENTIAL EQUIPMENT

- chef's knife
- large Dutch oven
- cutting board
- wooden spoon
- fine-mesh strainer
- large liquid measuring cup
- wide, shallow spoon

Beef stock should taste like beef—almost as intense and rich as pot roast jus—and be flavorful enough to need only a few vegetables and a handful of noodles or barley to make a good soup. The traditional method for making beef stock requires at least two pots and a day's worth of prepping and cooking. Beef bones (usually from the shin) and aromatic vegetables are roasted, the pan is deglazed with red wine, and the whole mass is then dumped into a stockpot and covered with cold water. After simmering for many, many hours, the flavor has finally been extracted from the bones.

We shortcut this process by using ground beef, which is ready to release its flavor in minutes, not hours. And while it might seem wasteful to throw out the ground beef once the stock is done, a pound of ground meat costs just $3 or $4, far less than the 4 or 5 pounds of beef shin you'd need to make an equivalent amount of stock. Beef stock can be refrigerated for up to four days or frozen for up to one month.

1. SAUTÉ MUSHROOMS AND ONION TO BUILD FLAVOR

Heat 1 teaspoon vegetable oil in Dutch oven over medium-high heat until just smoking. Add 1 pound white mushrooms, trimmed and quartered, and 1 large chopped onion, and cook until browned, 8 to 12 minutes.

WHY? Cooking the mushrooms and onions until browned bits (fond) form on the bottom of the pot is essential for flavor development. The browning adds a lightly roasted flavor that accentuates the meatiness of the stock. The mushrooms also add meaty notes. Make sure the pot has at least an 8-quart capacity.

2. SWEAT GROUND BEEF TO EXTRACT JUICE

Add 1 pound 85 percent lean ground beef to pot and cook, breaking up meat with wooden spoon, until no longer pink, about 3 minutes.

WHY? Rather than using the usual bone-in cuts from the shin, we found that store-bought ground beef imparted bold, beefy flavor to stock, and in a fraction of the time the bone-in cuts require. Sweating the ground beef to start extracting juices requires just a few minutes.

3. ADD FLAVOR ENHANCERS

Stir in 2 tablespoons tomato paste and cook until fragrant, about 30 seconds. Stir in ½ cup dry red wine, scraping up any browned bits, and cook until nearly evaporated, 1 to 2 minutes. Add 8 cups water along with 1 large peeled and chopped carrot, 1 large chopped celery rib, 2 tablespoons soy sauce, 2 teaspoons salt, and 2 bay leaves, and bring to boil.

WHY? For broth with a full, round flavor, glutamate-rich ingredients are key (glutamate is an amino acid that produces a meaty, savory taste): Mushrooms are a good start, and tomato paste and soy sauce further boost the meaty flavor. Red wine lends complexity and acidity. Onion, carrot, celery, and bay leaves (traditional flavorings for stock) are also worthwhile additions.

4. SIMMER GENTLY, COVERED

Cover, reduce heat to gentle simmer, and cook, skimming as needed, until stock tastes rich and flavorful, about 1½ hours.

WHY? Like our chicken stock, our beef stock is simmered covered to prevent moisture loss. Beef stock made the traditional way usually must simmer for upwards of 4 hours—our beef stock needs only 1½ hours. Keep the stock at a simmer, not a boil. Boiling will not hasten flavor extraction from the ingredients, but it will cause fat droplets to become suspended in the liquid, resulting in a murky, greasy-tasting stock.

5. STRAIN CAREFULLY

Pour stock through fine-mesh strainer into large liquid measuring cup or other large container.

WHY? For efficiency, use a large fine-mesh strainer. If your strainer is small, work in batches or remove the large solids by pouring the stock through a colander, then filter the liquid through the fine-mesh strainer. If your strainer has a coarse-mesh, line it with damp cheesecloth before use.

6. REMOVE FAT

Let stock settle for 5 to 10 minutes and then use wide, shallow spoon to remove fat that rises to surface.

WHY? During cooking, fat renders out from the meat into the liquid. Before the stock can be used, the fat must be removed in a step called "defatting." The action of straining integrates the fat into the stock, so allow the stock to stand for 5 to 10 minutes after straining to give the fat time to rise to the surface. At this point, the fat can be skimmed off with a spoon or ladle. Or, if time permits, the stock can be refrigerated until the fat solidifies on the surface; the congealed fat layer is easily scraped off with a spoon.

Troubleshooting Beef Stock

PROBLEM	SOLUTION
Can I use another type of ground beef?	We find that 85 percent lean ground beef has a lot of flavor with a moderate amount of fat. You can use 93 percent lean ground beef but the stock will be a bit less flavorful.
My stock tastes a bit liver-y.	While it could be that the ground beef wasn't the best quality, it sounds like you might have cooked the stock too long. After 1½ hours of simmering, we find that the stock begins to take on the liver-y flavor we associate with very overcooked meat.

How to Make Vegetable Stock

Packaged vegetable broth is often very sweet and very salty. Our homemade stock has a clean, vegetal flavor that's much more balanced. Unfortunately, there's no way to create good vegetable stock from just a few vegetables. The mix of vegetables (and flavors) is key to making good stock. As with our chicken and beef stocks, we don't rely strictly on simmering—vegetable stock really benefits from sweating the key components prior to simmering. In fact, we sweat the vegetables long enough that they develop a golden fond on the bottom of the pot. This fond is essential not only for flavor but for giving the stock a nice golden hue. Vegetable stock can be refrigerated for up to four days or frozen for up to one month.

- chef's knife
- cutting board
- large Dutch oven
- wooden spoon
- fine-mesh strainer
- large liquid measuring cup

1. SWEAT AROMATICS

Combine 3 chopped onions, 2 chopped celery ribs, 2 peeled and chopped carrots, 8 chopped scallions, 15 peeled and smashed garlic cloves, 1 teaspoon olive oil, and 1 teaspoon salt in Dutch oven. Cover and cook over medium-low heat, stirring often, until golden brown fond has formed on bottom of pot, 20 to 30 minutes.

WHY? In order to use as little oil as possible, we sweat the aromatic vegetables in a covered pot. One teaspoon oil coats the vegetables and helps promote the development of a golden (not dark brown) fond.

2. ADD WATER, CAULIFLOWER, TOMATO, AND HERBS

Stir in 12 cups water, 1 head cauliflower, cored and cut into 1-inch florets, 1 chopped plum tomato, 8 sprigs fresh thyme, 3 bay leaves, and 1 teaspoon black peppercorns.

WHY? Cauliflower adds nutty, earthy notes, but we found no benefit to sweating this vegetable, so we add it with the water. The acidity of the tomato balances the stock's sweetness, while the herbs and peppercorns add complexity.

3. SIMMER GENTLY TO EXTRACT FLAVOR

Bring to simmer, partially cover, reduce heat to gentle simmer, and cook until stock tastes rich and flavorful, about 1½ hours.

WHY? Don't attempt to rush the process by boiling the stock; this will yield a cloudy stock. But after 1½ hours, the vegetables will be spent so there's no gain from further simmering.

4. STRAIN BUT DON'T PRESS

Pour stock through fine-mesh strainer into large liquid measuring cup or other large container. Do not press on solids.

WHY? You might be tempted to press every last drop of liquid from the spent vegetables, but this will only make the stock cloudy. Unlike chicken and beef stock, there's no need to defat vegetable stock.

How to Make a Pureed Soup

A pureed soup should be as smooth and as creamy as possible. We find that a standard blender is the best tool for this task. The blade on the blender pulls ingredients down from the top of the container, so no stray bits go untouched by the blade. And as long as plenty of headroom is left at the top of the blender, there is no leakage. A food processor does a decent job of pureeing, but some small bits of vegetables can get trapped under the blade and remain unchopped. Also, food processors have a tendency to leak hot liquid—fill the workbowl more than halfway and you are likely to see liquid running down the side of the food processor base. An immersion blender has appeal because it can be brought to the pot, eliminating the need to ladle hot ingredients from one vessel to another. However, this kind of blender can leave some bits of food unblended. Also see our tutorial for Silky Butternut Squash Soup (page 456).

ESSENTIAL EQUIPMENT

- chef's knife
- cutting board
- Dutch oven
- wooden spoon
- ladle
- blender
- dish towel
- liquid measuring cup

1. BUILD FLAVOR BASE
Cook minced aromatic vegetables in olive oil or butter until softened.

WHY? As with most soups, you need to start with a few aromatics, such as onions, leeks, carrots, celery, and garlic. Sautéing the aromatics before simmering draws out their flavor, as does chopping them quite fine.

2. COOK VEGETABLES UNTIL TENDER
Add stock or broth and main vegetable and simmer gently until tender but not overcooked.

WHY? Whether making pureed broccoli, potato, asparagus, or pea soup, the process is the same. Once the flavor base has been built, add the main vegetable along with stock or broth (vegetable or chicken) and simmer until tender. (There's no need to cook the vegetables until they're mushy and spent.) Do bulk up on the starring vegetable so that the vegetable—rather than lots of flour or cream—thickens the soup.

3. PUREE SAFELY
Let vegetables and cooking liquid cool for 5 minutes. Working in small batches, fill blender halfway. Hold lid in place with folded dish towel. Pulse several times, then blend continuously. Pour pureed soup into clean pot.

WHY? A blender explosion is messy and dangerous. Letting the soup cool for 5 minutes before pureeing reduces the amount of steam that can cause blender mishaps. Don't overfill the blender, and start with the pulse function to release built-up pressure. Make sure to process each batch thoroughly and add enough cooking liquid so that the vegetables can be pureed easily.

4. REHEAT AND ENRICH
Warm pureed soup in pot, simmering to thicken if necessary. Stir in dairy element, if using, and adjust seasonings.

WHY? Once dairy has been added, the soup should not simmer, so adjust the consistency of the pureed soup before adding it.

Chicken Noodle Soup

Overview

No recipe repertoire is complete without a good recipe for chicken noodle soup. This version is basic and no-frills, but it delivers better chicken flavor than most of us are accustomed to. The key is making a rich homemade chicken stock to use as the soup's base. Instead of using chicken legs, backs, and/or wings (our usual choices for basic stock), we make stock with a whole chicken cut into pieces (although the chicken breast requires special treatment because the meat is shredded and added to the soup).

The simplicity of this soup lends it to variations of all sorts. Once you've mastered it, you can try wild rice, cooked dried beans, or small pasta shapes like orzo or ditalini in place of the egg noodles; season it with herbs of your choice; or change up the vegetables to suit your taste.

Once chicken noodle soup is done, it should be served immediately; those noodles will become soft and mushy very quickly. You can make the stock and chicken up to 2 days in advance; just refrigerate the stock and poached breast meat separately until you're ready to make the soup. For a variation on this recipe with orzo, fennel, and leeks, see page 461.

Recipe Stats

TOTAL TIME **2 hours**
PREPARATION TIME **25 minutes**
ACTIVE COOKING TIME **35 minutes**
YIELD **6 to 8 servings**
MAKE AHEAD **Serve soup immediately; stock and poached chicken breasts can be refrigerated separately for up to 2 days**
DIFFICULTY **Intermediate**

Tools

- Dutch oven
- chef's knife
- cutting board
- meat cleaver *
- dry measuring cups
- large liquid measuring cup or bowl
- measuring spoons
- fine-mesh strainer **
- forks (2) ***
- instant-read thermometer
- large plate or platter
- mixing bowls
- tongs
- vegetable peeler
- wide, shallow spoon or fat separator
- wooden spoon

* A meat cleaver is necessary for hacking the chicken parts into small pieces. A good cleaver has a sharp blade that can cut cleanly through bones, a comfortable handle, and a well-balanced design. Do not use a Chinese vegetable cleaver here—the blade is not made for cutting through bone.

** A fine-mesh strainer is essential for separating the solids from the stock. Coarse mesh will let bone fragments slip through. If a coarse-mesh strainer is what you have on hand, line it with damp cheesecloth before use. If your strainer is smaller than 6 inches in diameter, strain the stock in batches or first pour the stock through a colander to remove most of the solids, then filter just the liquid through the strainer.

*** To shred meat, we use two forks. Holding one fork in each hand, insert the tines into the meat, then gently pull the forks away from each other to break the meat into strands.

Ingredients

STOCK

- 1 (3½- to 4-pound) whole chicken, cut into 7 pieces (2 split breasts, 2 legs, 2 wings, backbone)
- 1 tablespoon vegetable oil
- 1 onion, chopped
- 8 cups water
- 2 teaspoons salt
- 2 bay leaves

SOUP

- 1 tablespoon vegetable oil *
- 1 onion. chopped fine
- 1 carrot, peeled and sliced ¼ inch thick
- 1 celery rib, sliced ¼ inch thick
- 1 teaspoon minced fresh thyme or ¼ teaspoon dried
- 3 ounces (2 cups) wide egg noodles **
- 2 tablespoons minced fresh parsley
  Salt and pepper

* Alternatively, for an extra boost of chicken flavor, you can save some of the fat from skimming the stock and use it in place of the vegetable oil.

** Dried egg noodles are sold in the pasta aisle and are usually packaged in clear cellophane bags. Thin egg noodles can be used in place of wide noodles, if desired.

What Can Go Wrong

Here's a list of common mistakes cooks make when preparing this recipe.

COMMON MISTAKE	BAD OUTCOMES	WHAT YOU SHOULD DO
Leaving Chicken Pieces Too Big	• **The chicken releases only a little juice.** • **The stock tastes weak.**	Left in large pieces, the chicken will be slow to release its juices and may not fully relinquish its flavor in the time indicated, resulting in weak-tasting stock. It's important that the chicken parts be cut into small pieces, which not only increases the surface area for quicker flavor release, but also exposes the bone marrow so that it readily seeps into the water. A meat cleaver is the best tool for hacking up the chicken parts.
Sweating Chicken Breasts	• **The breast meat has no flavor.** • **The breast meat is overcooked.**	The chicken breasts, like the hacked-up chicken parts, are sautéed to develop some flavor, but be sure to set them aside when the hacked pieces are sweated; the breasts are added to the pot with the water and simmered for only 20 minutes until just cooked through. If sweated along with the other pieces, the breast meat would wind up overcooked, dry, and nearly flavorless.
Letting Stock Boil	• **The stock is cloudy.** • **The stock tastes greasy.**	When cooking the stock, keep the liquid at a gentle simmer, not a vigorous boil. If the stock boils, some of the fat will disperse as droplets in the liquid, which not only causes the stock to appear murky, but also gives it a greasy flavor and feel.
Skipping Skimming Step	• **The soup is greasy.**	Skimming off the fat is an essential step after making stock. Allowing the stock to rest for several minutes after straining allows the fat to rise to the surface. The fat can be skimmed off warm or at room temperature with a ladle or a wide, shallow spoon, or the stock can be defatted with a fat separator. If time permits, refrigerating the stock will cause the fat to congeal in a layer on the surface that can easily be scraped or lifted off.
Cutting Carrot Pieces Too Thick	• **The carrots are hard and undercooked.**	Cut the carrots and other vegetables according to the recipe so that they will cook in the time indicated. Before you add the noodles to the pot, it's a good idea to taste a carrot to test for tenderness, because once the noodles are tender (this takes just a few minutes), you will want to serve the soup.
Boiling Noodles Separately	• **The noodles are soft and mushy.** • **The noodles taste bland.**	The dried noodles are added uncooked to the soup and are simmered until tender. If they are boiled in water separately from the soup, they wind up tasting bland, and their texture in the finished dish will be soft and limp.

1. PREPARE STOCK: Cut 1 (3½- to 4-pound) chicken into 7 pieces (2 split breasts, 2 legs, 2 wings, and backbone).

2. Set breasts aside, then hack remaining chicken into 2-inch pieces with cleaver.

3. Heat 1 tablespoon vegetable oil in Dutch oven over medium-high heat until just smoking. Add breasts and brown lightly on both sides, about 5 minutes.

4. Transfer breasts to plate and set aside.

5. Add half of chicken pieces and brown lightly on both sides, about 5 minutes.

6. Transfer chicken pieces to large bowl. Repeat with remaining chicken pieces and transfer to bowl.

7. Add 1 chopped onion to fat left in pot and cook until softened, about 3 minutes.

8. Return chicken pieces (not breasts) and any accumulated juices to pot.

9. Cover and reduce heat to low.

10. Cook, stirring occasionally, until chicken has released its juices, about 20 minutes.

11. Add reserved chicken breasts, 8 cups water, 2 teaspoons salt, and 2 bay leaves and bring to boil.

12. Cover, reduce heat to gentle simmer, and cook, skimming as needed, until chicken breasts register 160 to 165 degrees, about 20 minutes.

13. Remove chicken breasts from pot and let cool slightly.

14. Strain stock through fine-mesh strainer into large liquid measuring cup or bowl.

15. Let stock settle for 5 to 10 minutes. Wash and dry Dutch oven.

16. Defat stock by skimming using wide, shallow spoon or fat separator.

17. PREPARE SOUP: Mince 1 onion. Slice 1 peeled carrot and 1 celery rib ¼ inch thick. Heat 1 tablespoon vegetable oil in Dutch oven over medium heat.

18. Add onion, carrot, and celery and cook until softened, 5 to 7 minutes. Stir in 1 teaspoon minced fresh thyme and cook for 30 seconds.

19. Stir in stock and bring to boil.

20. Reduce heat to simmer and cook until vegetables are nearly tender, 6 to 8 minutes.

21. Stir in 2 cups wide egg noodles and simmer until tender, about 10 to 15 minutes.

22. Remove skin and shred chicken into bite-size pieces using two forks. Discard skin and bones.

23. Stir in shredded chicken and cook until heated through, about 2 minutes.

24. Off heat, stir in 2 tablespoons minced fresh parsley and season with salt and pepper to taste, and serve.

HOW TO MAKE STOCKS AND SOUPS

Tortilla Soup

Tools

- Dutch oven
- rimmed baking sheet
- food processor
- chef's knife
- cutting board
- paring knife
- dry measuring cups
- large liquid measuring cup or bowl
- measuring spoons
- can opener
- fine-mesh strainer *
- forks (2)
- instant-read thermometer
- ladle
- large plates or platters (2)
- mixing bowls
- rubber spatula
- serving bowls
- soupspoon
- tongs
- wide, shallow spoon or fat separator
- wooden spoon
- paper towels

* A fine-mesh strainer is essential for separating the solids from the broth. Coarse mesh will let bits of food slip through. Alternately, line a coarse-mesh strainer with damp cheesecloth. If your strainer is less than 6 inches in diameter, strain in batches or pour stock through a colander first.

Overview

With its spicy, garlicky, tomatoey broth, chunks of chicken, and garnishes galore, tortilla soup aims to please. While traditional Mexican recipes start with homemade stock, there's so much flavor in this soup that we have found you can start with store-bought broth and still create a great soup.

The first step is to poach chicken in chicken broth. At the same time, we infuse the store-bought broth with more character by adding onion, garlic, cilantro, and oregano to the pot. Once the chicken is cooked, the aromatics are strained out and discarded. What's left is broth that has been transformed by their flavor (as well as by the flavor of the chicken pieces).

Once the broth and chicken (which is cooled, then shredded) are ready, the soup comes together fairly easily. Corn tortillas are cut into strips, lightly oiled, and baked until crisp. As for the vegetables, we puree tomatoes, more onion, more garlic, and more chiles in the food processor and then cook this mixture in a pot until fragrant and darkened. The strained broth is added, and after 15 minutes our tortilla soup is ready to serve.

We assemble the soup in individual bowls: tortilla strips, then broth, chicken, and garnishes (we like Cotija, avocado, *crema* or sour cream, cilantro, lime wedges, and minced chile).

Ingredients

- 8 **cups chicken broth**
- 2 **onions, quartered**
- 4 **garlic cloves, peeled**
- 8 **sprigs fresh cilantro**
- 1 **sprig fresh oregano**
  Salt and pepper
- 1½ **pounds bone-in split chicken breasts or 1¼ pounds bone-in chicken thighs, trimmed**
- 8 **(6-inch) corn tortillas, cut into ½-inch-wide strips**
- 3 **tablespoons vegetable oil**
- 2 **tomatoes, cored and quartered**
- 1 **jalapeño chile, stemmed and seeded ***
- 1½ **teaspoons minced canned chipotle chile in adobo sauce, plus up to 2½ teaspoons for seasoning ****
- 8 **ounces Cotija cheese, crumbled (2 cups) *****
- 1 **avocado, halved, pitted, and cut into ½-inch dice**
- ½ **cup Mexican crema or sour cream ******
- ½ **cup fresh cilantro leaves**
- 1 **jalapeño chile, stemmed, seeded, and minced**
  Lime wedges

* For a spicier soup, leave the seeds in the chile and just puree the whole chile (minus the stem) with the other vegetables.
** Canned chipotle chiles vary in spiciness, so we suggest adding 1½ teaspoons to the vegetable puree and then adjusting the heat level of the soup just before serving.
*** Cotija is a sharp, rich Mexican cheese with a crumbly texture. You can substitute an equal amount of crumbled *queso fresco* or shredded Monterey Jack.
**** Mexican *crema* is a cultured cream with a thick but pourable texture. Sour cream, thinned with a little milk if you like, can be used in its place.

Recipe Stats

TOTAL TIME **1 hour, 15 minutes**
PREPARATION TIME **30 minutes**
ACTIVE COOKING TIME **45 minutes**
YIELD **6 to 8 servings**
MAKE AHEAD **Serve soup immediately; stock and poached chicken can be refrigerated separately for up to 2 days**
DIFFICULTY **Easy**

What Can Go Wrong

Here's a list of common mistakes cooks make when preparing this recipe.

COMMON MISTAKE	BAD OUTCOMES	WHAT YOU SHOULD DO
Using Boneless, Skinless Chicken Breasts	• **The soup has weak chicken flavor.**	Although only the meat makes it into the final soup, our recipe calls for using bone-in chicken parts (either breasts or thighs). The bones (and skin) don't make it into the soup, but they do impart a ton of flavor to the broth. Also, make sure to use a good-quality packaged broth (see page 38). Cooking the bone-in parts in packaged broth (rather than water) is economical (you cook only as much chicken as needed for the soup) and delivers excellent chicken flavor to the finished dish.
Overcooking Chicken	• **The chicken is tough and dry.**	Cooking the chicken pieces in the store-bought broth greatly improves the flavor of the broth, especially if you use bone-in, skin-on parts as recommended in the recipe. However, don't overdo it, especially with the breasts; you want to use the meat for the soup, so make sure to check the progress of the chicken pieces with an instant-read thermometer—once the breasts reach a temperature of 160 and the thighs register 175 degrees, pull them out of the pot. If cooked any longer, they will give up too much moisture (and flavor) to the broth, and the chunks of chicken will be dry and bland in the final soup.
Leaving Tortilla Strips in Oven Too Long	• **The tortilla strips burn.**	This one is simple: Set a timer and keep an eye on the oven. Baking the tortilla strips is much easier than the traditional pan-frying process, but it is easy to forget about them, and the tortillas will start to burn rather quickly in the hot oven.
Undercooking Tomato Puree	• **The soup lacks depth.** • **The soup is a bit watery.**	In Mexico, the tomatoes, onions, garlic, and chiles are roasted on a cast-iron griddle (called a *comal*) to enhance their flavor. They are then pureed and sautéed in a pot with some vegetable oil. We skip the roasting step and use canned chipotle chiles to impart a smoky flavor to the mix. But for the best results, the vegetable puree should be cooked quite aggressively. You're really doing two things: browning the vegetable puree so it becomes much more flavorful, and driving off moisture in the vegetables. When you add the puree to the hot pot, it should really sizzle. You will know the puree has cooked enough when it becomes quite thick and brick colored.
Adding Too Much Chipotle	• **The soup is spicy.**	Don't go overboard with the chipotle chile. It's a key ingredient in our soup but a little goes a long way. Also, brands vary in intensity. Our recommendation is to add a modest amount (1½ teaspoons) up front, with the vegetable puree. When the soup is nearly done, taste it and then add more if you like.

1. Bring 8 cups chicken broth, 1 quartered onion, 2 peeled garlic cloves, 8 sprigs cilantro, and 1 sprig oregano to boil in Dutch oven.

2. Add ½ teaspoon salt and 1½ pounds bone-in split chicken breasts or 1¼ pounds bone-in chicken thighs, trimmed of excess fat, and cover pot.

3. Simmer gently until breasts register 160 degrees or thighs register 175 degrees on instant-read thermometer, 15 to 20 minutes.

4. Transfer chicken to plate, let cool slightly, then shred meat into bite-size pieces with 2 forks, discarding skin and bones.

5. Strain broth through fine-mesh strainer into large liquid measuring cup or bowl.

6. Let broth settle for 5 to 10 minutes.

7. Defat broth by skimming with wide, shallow spoon or using fat separator. Wash and dry Dutch oven.

8. Meanwhile, adjust oven rack to middle position and heat oven to 425 degrees.

9. Cut 8 (6-inch) corn tortillas into ½-inch-wide strips. Toss tortilla strips with 2 tablespoons vegetable oil, then spread over rimmed baking sheet.

10. Bake, stirring occasionally, until crisp and dark golden, 10 to 15 minutes. Season with salt to taste and transfer to paper towel–lined plate.

11. Core and quarter 2 tomatoes.

12. Stem and seed 1 jalapeño chile. (Leave seeds in chile for spicier soup.)

13. Mince 1½ teaspoons canned chipotle chile in adobo sauce, or more to taste, up to 4 teaspoons total.

14. Process tomatoes, jalapeño, 1½ teaspoons chipotle, 1 quartered onion, 2 peeled garlic cloves, and ⅛ teaspoon salt in food processor until smooth.

15. Heat 1 tablespoon vegetable oil in Dutch oven over medium-high heat until shimmering.

16. Add pureed tomato mixture and cook, stirring frequently, until fragrant and darkened, about 10 minutes.

17. Stir in strained broth, bring to simmer, and cook until flavors blend, about 15 minutes.

18. Stir in additional minced chipotle chile (up to 2½ teaspoons) to taste.

19. Stir in shredded chicken and simmer until heated through, about 2 minutes. Off heat, season with salt and pepper to taste.

20. While soup cooks, crumble 2 cups Cotija or queso fresco (or shredded Monterey Jack) into serving bowl.

21. Halve 1 avocado. Remove pit. Make ½-inch crosshatch incisions in flesh with knife. Gently scoop avocado cubes into serving bowl.

22. Stem, seed, and mince 1 jalapeño chile and put in serving bowl.

23. Place ½ cup Mexican crema or sour cream, ½ cup cilantro leaves, and lime wedges each in its own serving bowl.

24. Place tortilla strips in individual bowls and ladle soup over top. Serve, passing Cotija, avocado, jalapeño, crema, cilantro, and lime separately.

HOW TO MAKE STOCKS AND SOUPS

Beef and Barley Soup

Overview

Beef and barley soup is a savory, stick-to-your-ribs meal in a bowl. As a base, this recipe uses homemade beef stock that gets deep meaty flavor from the addition of browned beef and sautéed mushrooms. This stock breaks with tradition—forget about simmering bones all day. We take the fast route and sac- rifice a pound of ground beef (less money than shin bones, and it gives up its flavor in minutes, not hours). For more details on making beef stock, see the Core Technique on page 440. For the soup itself, we use quick-cooking, flavorful whole sirloin steak tips (aka flap meat) rather than steak tips cut into small pieces for stir-fries that never fully turn tender. (If sirloin steak tips are unavailable, it's best to substitute flank steak or blade steak that has been well trimmed of gristle and fat.)

As with the noodles in chicken soup, the barley means that this soup doesn't do well in the refrigerator. (The barley con- tinues to soak up liquid and becomes very bloated.) You can prepare the beef stock several days in advance of making the soup. If you'd like to try different twists on this classic comfort food, you can substitute parsnips for the carrots, use chunks of red potatoes instead of barley, or add shredded kale leaves during the last 15 minutes of cooking. For variations on this recipe, see page 462.

Recipe Stats

TOTAL TIME **3 hours, 45 minutes**
PREPARATION TIME **45 minutes**
ACTIVE COOKING TIME **45 minutes**
YIELD **6 to 8 servings**
MAKE AHEAD **Serve soup immediately; stock can be refrigerated for up to 4 days**
DIFFICULTY **Intermediate**

Tools

- Dutch oven
- chef's knife
- cutting board
- paring knife
- dry measuring cups
- large liquid measuring cup or bowl
- measuring spoons
- can opener
- fine-mesh strainer *
- mixing bowl
- vegetable peeler
- whisk
- wide, shallow spoon
- wooden spoon
- paper towels

* Don't use a coarse-mesh strainer for the stock, as ground meat will slip through. If it's is your only option, line it with damp cheesecloth before use. If your strainer is smaller than 6 inches in diameter, strain the stock in batches or pour it through a colander first to remove the solids.

Ingredients

STOCK

- 1   teaspoon vegetable oil
- 1   pound white mushrooms, trimmed and quartered
- 1   large onion, chopped
- 1   pound 85 percent lean ground beef
- 2   tablespoons tomato paste
- ½   cup dry red wine *
- 8   cups water
- 1   large carrot, peeled and chopped
- 1   large celery rib, chopped
- 2   tablespoons soy sauce
- 2   teaspoons salt
- 2   bay leaves

SOUP

- 1   pound sirloin steak tips, trimmed and cut into ½-inch pieces
     Salt and pepper
- 2   tablespoons vegetable oil
- ½   pound cremini mushrooms, trimmed and sliced ½ inch thick
- 1   onion, chopped
- 1   garlic clove, minced
- 1½   teaspoons minced fresh thyme or ½ teaspoon dried
- 2   tablespoons all-purpose flour
- ¼   cup dry red wine *
- 1   (14.5-ounce) can diced tomatoes, drained
- ½   cup pearl barley **
- 3   carrots, peeled and cut into ½-inch pieces
- 2   celery ribs, cut into ½-inch pieces
- 2   bay leaves
- 2   tablespoons minced fresh parsley

* Use a medium-bodied unoaked red wine, such as Côtes du Rhône or Pinot Noir.
** Barley is sold in several forms. Be sure to use pearl barley, which is quick to cook.

What Can Go Wrong

Here's a list of common mistakes cooks make when preparing this recipe.

COMMON MISTAKE	BAD OUTCOMES	WHAT YOU SHOULD DO
Underbrowning Mushrooms and Onion	• **The stock tastes weak.**	Browning the mushrooms and onion is an important step in flavor development for the stock. Not only does the process of browning cook off excess moisture that would otherwise dilute the stock, but the browned bits (or fond) that form on the bottom of the pot contribute depth, complexity, and color to the finished stock.
Simmering Stock Too Long	• **The stock tastes liver-y.**	Our testing showed that simmering the stock for more than 1½ hours does not yield beefier flavor. In fact, longer simmering caused the stock to take on an overcooked, liver-y quality, so resist the urge to extend the simmering time in an effort to coax out more flavor from the ground beef.
Using Wrong Cut of Beef	• **The beef is tough.** • **The beef is bland.**	The best cut for beef soup is one with a loose, open grain—with less than an hour of cooking, the muscle fibers of cuts such as sirloin steak tips, flank steak, and blade steak take on the tender texture of slow-cooked beef. Do not use cuts with a firm, tight grain such as steaks cut from the loin; they will cook up tough and relatively tasteless.
Adding Too Much Barley	• **The soup is too thick.**	Pearl barley expands considerably with cooking, so even though the amount called for—½ cup—may seem like a small quantity for the amount of soup, do not use any more. Too much barley will absorb a lot of the stock and the soup will be too thick, dry, and dense with barley.
Cutting Carrots Too Thick	• **The carrots are hard and undercooked.**	Cut the carrots and other vegetables to spec so that they will cook in the time indicated. As much as possible, cut the carrots into even shapes so that all the pieces will cook at the same rate.
Making Soup Days in Advance	• **The barley is bloated.** • **The soup is too thick.**	Barley will continue to soak up liquid as it sits, so it doesn't keep well over a long period of time. If you want to work ahead, make the beef stock a few days in advance, but it is best to make the soup the day you plan to serve it.

1. PREPARE STOCK: Trim thin slice from stem ends of 1 pound white mushrooms. Quarter mushrooms.

2. Heat 1 teaspoon vegetable oil in Dutch oven over medium-high heat until just smoking. Add mushrooms and 1 large chopped onion.

3. Cook, stirring often, until onion is browned and golden brown fond has formed on bottom of pot, 8 to 12 minutes.

4. Stir in 1 pound 85 percent lean ground beef and cook, breaking up meat with wooden spoon, until no longer pink, about 3 minutes.

5. Stir in 2 tablespoons tomato paste and cook until fragrant, about 30 seconds.

6. Stir in ½ cup red wine, scraping up any browned bits, and cook until nearly evaporated, 1 to 2 minutes.

7. Stir in 8 cups water, 1 large chopped carrot, 1 large chopped celery rib, 2 tablespoons soy sauce, 2 teaspoons salt, and 2 bay leaves and bring to boil.

8. Cover, reduce heat to gentle simmer, and cook, skimming as needed, until stock tastes rich and flavorful, about 1½ hours.

9. Strain stock through fine-mesh strainer.

10. Let stock settle for 5 to 10 minutes. Defat stock by skimming with wide, shallow spoon or using fat separator.

11. PREPARE SOUP: Trim 1 pound sirloin steak tips and cut into ½-inch pieces. Pat steak tips dry with paper towels and season with salt and pepper.

12. Drain 1 (14.5-ounce) can diced tomatoes; set tomatoes aside.

13. Peel 3 carrots and cut into ½-inch pieces. Cut 2 celery ribs into ½-inch pieces.

14. Heat 2 teaspoons vegetable oil in Dutch oven over medium-high heat until just smoking.

15. Add half of meat and cook, stirring occasionally, until well browned, 5 to 7 minutes, reducing heat if pot begins to scorch.

16. Transfer browned beef to medium bowl. Repeat with 2 teaspoons vegetable oil and remaining beef. Transfer second batch of browned beef to bowl.

17. Add 2 teaspoons vegetable oil to now-empty pot and heat over medium heat until shimmering.

18. Add ½ pound trimmed cremini mushrooms, sliced ½ inch thick, and 1 chopped onion and cook until softened, 7 to 10 minutes.

19. Stir in 1 minced garlic clove and 1½ teaspoons minced fresh thyme (or ½ teaspoon dried) and cook until fragrant, about 30 seconds.

20. Stir in 2 tablespoons all-purpose flour and cook for 1 minute.

21. Whisk in ¼ cup dry red wine, scraping up any browned bits, and cook until nearly evaporated, about 1 minute.

22. Stir in reserved beef stock, drained tomatoes, chopped carrots and celery, ½ cup pearl barley, 2 bay leaves, and meat and any accumulated juices.

23. Bring to boil, then cover, reduce heat to gentle simmer, and cook until meat, barley, and vegetables are tender, 30 to 40 minutes.

24. Off heat, remove bay leaves. Stir in 2 tablespoons minced fresh parsley, season with salt and pepper to taste, and serve.

HOW TO MAKE STOCKS AND SOUPS

Silky Butternut Squash Soup

Overview

With a vivid orange-yellow hue, subtle sweetness but under-lying savoriness, spicy, earthy fragrance, and silken texture, this pureed butternut squash soup is a feast for the senses.

To cook the squash, this recipe employs steaming. Steaming produces a soup with a pure squash flavor and bright color. The twist here, though, is that the steaming liquid—which is usually discarded once cooking is complete—is flavored with shallots and the squash seeds and strings and becomes the stock for the soup. For this reason, it's necessary to use a measured amount of water—6 cups—in the bottom of the pot for steaming; don't worry if the bottom of the squash pieces come into contact with the water.

Other than that, the same precepts apply here as they do to steaming in general: Be sure to cut the squash into rela-tively uniform shapes and sizes so that the pieces cook at about the same rate, and keep the pot tightly covered during steaming to prevent excess moisture loss.

In addition to the finishing pinch of nutmeg, this soup can be dressed up with croutons (see recipe for Buttered Cinnamon-Sugar Croutons on page 466), toasted pumpkin seeds, a drizzle of balsamic vinegar, or a dusting of paprika. Before you begin, see How to Make a Pureed Soup on page 443.

Recipe Stats

TOTAL TIME **1 hour**
PREPARATION TIME **15 minutes**
ACTIVE COOKING TIME **15 minutes**
YIELD **4 to 6 servings**
MAKE AHEAD **Refrigerate for up to 2 days**
DIFFICULTY **Easy**

Tools

- Dutch oven *
- rimmed baking sheet
- blender **
- chef's knife
- cutting board
- dish towel ***
- large liquid measuring cup or bowl
- measuring spoons
- fine-mesh strainer
- large spoon
- mixing bowl
- steamer basket *
- tongs
- wooden spoon

* We cook the squash in a steamer basket set in a Dutch oven. If you don't own a steamer basket, you can use a pasta pot with a removable pasta insert.
** A blender is the best appliance for creating a silky smooth pureed soup. Be sure to puree the squash and broth in batches, filling the blender jar only about halfway each time. This will prevent the liquid from exploding out of the jar when the blender is turned on.
*** When pureeing a soup, hold the lid on the blender using a dish towel.

Ingredients

- **4 tablespoons unsalted butter**
- **1 large shallot, minced**
- **1 (3-pound) butternut squash, cut in half lengthwise, seeds and fibers scraped out and reserved ***
- **6 cups water, plus extra if needed**
  Salt
- **½ cup heavy cream**
- **1 teaspoon packed dark brown sugar**
  Pinch ground nutmeg

* Do not purchase already peeled, seeded, and cubed but-ternut squash for this soup—you'll need the seeds and strings to create a flavorful stock that serves as the soup's base. If you would like to try a winter squash other than butternut, delicata also works well in this soup; use it just as you would the butternut squash.

What Can Go Wrong

Here's a list of common mistakes cooks make when preparing this recipe.

COMMON MISTAKE	BAD OUTCOMES	WHAT YOU SHOULD DO
Buying Squash That's Too Large/Too Small	• **The soup is too thick.** • **The soup is too thin.**	This recipe calls for 3 pounds of squash—about the weight of 1 large butternut quash. It will be tempting to use a squash of whatever size that you find. And that will be fine, provided that the variance isn't more than a few ounces and that you're prepared to adjust the amount of liquid in the recipe. If you end up using a slightly too big squash, you will likely need to thin out the pureed soup with a little extra steaming liquid or plain water. (You can instead simmer the pureed soup to drive off excess moisture—but do this before adding the cream.) If you end up using a slightly too small squash, hold back more of the steaming liquid—you can always thin out the finished soup if necessary, but it's hard to thicken the soup once it's done.
Discarding Squash Seeds and Strings	• **The squash flavor is weak.**	When preparing the squash, remember to save the seeds and strings. They're used to create a stock that serves as the soup's base. Without the seeds and strings, the stock would taste of only shallots and water and lack any sweet, earthy, squashy flavor.
Not Covering Pot Tightly	• **The soup is too thick.**	Keep the pot tightly covered as the squash steams to prevent excess moisture loss. If too much steam is allowed to escape, the amount of liquid in the pot that forms the stock will be scant, and with too little stock, the consistency of the pureed soup will be too thick and heavy.
Undercooking Squash	• **The soup is not perfectly smooth.**	Steam the squash until it is fully tender; when gauging doneness, test the largest, thickest pieces. If the squash is not tender throughout, it will not puree to a perfectly smooth, velvety result in the blender. The finished soup will have a coarse texture.
Overfilling Blender	• **The contents of the blender jar explode out the top.**	When pureeing the soup, fill the blender no more than about halfway. If overfilled, the blender jar's contents will explode out the top when the motor is turned on because of the liquid's low viscosity and the steam that's generated by the liquid in motion. Also, whenever you're using a blender you should place a folded dish towel on top of the lid and use your hand to keep the lid in place.

1. Halve 1 large (3-pound) butternut squash lengthwise; do not peel. Using soupspoon, scrape out and reserve seeds and stringy fibers.

2. Cut each piece of squash in half crosswise.

3. Melt 2 tablespoons unsalted butter in Dutch oven over medium-low heat. Add 1 large minced shallot and cook until softened, 2 to 3 minutes.

4. Add squash seeds and fibers and cook, stirring occasionally, until fragrant and butter turns reddish orange, about 4 minutes.

5. Add 6 cups water and 1 teaspoon salt to Dutch oven and bring to boil over high heat.

6. Reduce heat to medium-low, place steamer basket in pot, then add squash cut side down.

7. Cover and steam until squash is completely tender, 30 to 40 minutes. Using tongs, transfer squash to rimmed baking sheet. Reserve steaming liquid.

8. When squash is cool enough to handle, use large spoon to scrape squash flesh from skin into medium bowl. Discard skin.

9. Pour reserved liquid through fine-mesh strainer into liquid measuring cup; discard solids. You should have at least 3 cups; if necessary, add water.

10. In blender, puree squash and 3 cups reserved liquid in batches until smooth. Transfer puree to clean Dutch oven.

11. Stir in ½ cup heavy cream, 1 teaspoon packed dark brown sugar, pinch nutmeg, and 2 tablespoons unsalted butter.

12. Return to simmer, adding additional strained squash broth or water as needed to adjust consistency of soup. Season with salt to taste and serve.

Recipe Library

Chicken Stock

✓ **WHY THIS RECIPE WORKS:** Many recipes for homemade chicken stock simmer a whole chicken in water; we found that cutting the chicken parts into small pieces released the chicken flavor in a shorter amount of time since more surface area of the meat is exposed. This technique also exposed more bone marrow, key for both flavor and a thicker consistency. After testing a variety of vegetables, we found only onion was crucial. Sweating the chicken pieces for 20 minutes before adding the water further sped along the release of flavor, keeping our cooking time short.

Chicken Stock

MAKES ABOUT 8 CUPS

Use a meat cleaver to cut the chicken into smaller pieces. Any chicken meat left over after straining the stock will be very dry and flavorless; it should not be eaten. Chicken thighs can be substituted for the legs, backs, and wings in a pinch. If you'd like to make a chicken stock that also produces edible shredded meat, see Chicken Stock with Shredded Breast Meat (recipe follows). Make sure to use an 8-quart or larger Dutch oven for this recipe. See Core Technique on page 438 for more details on this recipe and page 436 for more information on freezing stock.

- 1 **tablespoon vegetable oil**
- 3 **pounds whole chicken legs, backs, and/or wings, hacked into 2-inch pieces**
- 1 **onion, chopped**
- 8 **cups water**
- 2 **teaspoons salt**
- 2 **bay leaves**

1. Heat oil in large Dutch oven or stockpot over medium-high heat until just smoking. Add half of chicken pieces and cook until lightly browned on both sides, about 5 minutes. Transfer chicken pieces to large bowl. Repeat with remaining chicken pieces.

2. Add onion to fat left in pot and cook until softened, about 3 minutes. Return chicken pieces and any accumulated juices to pot, cover, and reduce heat to low. Cook, stirring occasionally, until chicken has released its juices, about 20 minutes.

3. Add water, salt, and bay leaves and bring to boil. Cover, reduce heat to gentle simmer, and cook, skimming as needed, until stock tastes rich and flavorful, about 20 minutes longer.

4. Strain stock through fine-mesh strainer. Let stock settle for 5 to 10 minutes, then defat using wide, shallow spoon or fat separator. (Stock can be refrigerated for up to 4 days or frozen for up to 1 month.)

Chicken Stock with Shredded Breast Meat

MAKES ABOUT 8 CUPS STOCK WITH 2 CUPS SHREDDED MEAT

Choose this stock when you want to have some breast meat in your soup. See Core Technique on page 438 for more details on this recipe and page 436 for more information on freezing stock.

- 1 **(3½- to 4-pound) whole chicken, cut into 7 pieces (2 split breasts, 2 legs, 2 wings, backbone)**
- 1 **tablespoon vegetable oil**
- 1 **onion, chopped**
- 8 **cups water**
- 2 **teaspoons salt**
- 2 **bay leaves**

1. Hack chicken legs, wings, and backbone into 2-inch pieces (leave split breasts whole). Heat oil in large Dutch oven or stockpot over medium-high heat until just smoking. Add chicken breasts and brown lightly on both sides, about 5 minutes, then transfer to plate and set aside.

2. Add half of chicken pieces and brown lightly on both sides, about 5 minutes. Transfer chicken pieces to large bowl. Repeat with remaining chicken pieces.

3. Add onion to fat left in pot and cook until softened, about 3 minutes. Return chicken pieces (not breasts) and any accumulated juices to pot, cover, and reduce heat to low. Cook, stirring occasionally, until chicken has released its juices, about 20 minutes.

4. Add reserved chicken breasts, water, salt, and bay leaves and bring to boil. Cover, reduce heat to gentle simmer, and cook, skimming as needed, until chicken breasts register 160 to 165 degrees, about 20 minutes.

5. Remove chicken breasts from pot and let cool slightly. Using 2 forks, shred meat into bite-size pieces, discarding skin and bones. Strain stock through fine-mesh strainer. Let stock settle for 5 to 10 minutes, then defat stock using wide, shallow spoon or fat separator. (Stock and chicken breasts can be refrigerated separately for up to 2 days. Stock also can be frozen for up to 1 month.)

Beef Stock

✓ **WHY THIS RECIPE WORKS:** We wanted a flavorful, full-bodied beef stock without the hassle of having to buy and roast pounds of big, heavy, and expensive beef bones. We found that just a pound of ground beef, a few vegetables, water, and wine—plus a few other enhancements—produced a rich, velvety stock in just 1½ hours of simmering. Most recipes sauté onions in the pot before adding the meat. We also added mushrooms along with the onions to create even more-flavorful fond, resulting in stock with a deep, meaty, roasted flavor. Tomato paste and soy sauce enhanced the meaty flavor even more.

Beef Stock

MAKES ABOUT 8 CUPS

We prefer to use 85 percent lean ground beef in this recipe; 93 percent lean ground beef will work, but it will be less flavorful. The fond is important for the flavor and color of the stock, so be sure to let it form on the bottom of the pot in step 1. Make sure to use an 8-quart or larger Dutch oven for this recipe. See Core Technique on page 440 for more details on this recipe and page 436 for more information on freezing stock.

- 1 teaspoon vegetable oil
- 1 pound white mushrooms, trimmed and quartered
- 1 large onion, chopped
- 1 pound 85 percent lean ground beef
- 2 tablespoons tomato paste
- ½ cup dry red wine
- 8 cups water
- 1 large carrot, peeled and chopped
- 1 large celery rib, chopped
- 2 tablespoons soy sauce
- 2 teaspoons salt
- 2 bay leaves

1. Heat oil in large Dutch oven or stockpot over medium-high heat until just smoking. Add mushrooms and onion and cook, stirring often, until onion is browned and golden brown fond has formed on bottom of pot, 8 to 12 minutes.

2. Stir in ground beef and cook, breaking up meat with wooden spoon, until no longer pink, about 3 minutes. Stir in tomato paste and cook until fragrant, about 30 seconds. Stir in red wine, scraping up any browned bits, and cook until nearly evaporated, 1 to 2 minutes.

3. Stir in water, carrot, celery, soy sauce, salt, and bay leaves and bring to boil. Cover, reduce to gentle simmer, and cook, skimming as needed, until stock tastes rich and flavorful, about 1½ hours.

4. Strain stock through fine-mesh strainer. Let stock settle for 5 to 10 minutes, then defat stock using wide, shallow spoon or fat separator. (Stock can be refrigerated for up to 4 days or frozen for up to 1 month.)

Vegetable Stock

✔ **WHY THIS RECIPE WORKS:** We wanted a nicely balanced, robust stock that vegetarians and nonvegetarians alike would consider making. Caramelizing plenty of onions, scallions, and garlic, plus carrots and celery in modest amounts, was a great start to ensuring depth and a sweetness that wasn't one-dimensional. We learned that our nontraditional ingredient—cauliflower—added a nutty complexity that was essential, while a single plum tomato provided the acidity and brightness that balanced the sweetness of our stock, and bay leaves and some thyme contributed the right herbal notes.

Vegetable Stock

MAKES ABOUT 8 CUPS

Be sure to let the fond form on the bottom of the pot in step 1 because it is important for the flavor and color of the stock.

To prevent the stock from looking cloudy, be sure to simmer it gently (don't boil), and don't press on the solids when straining. Make sure to use an 8-quart or larger Dutch oven for this recipe. See Core Technique on page 442 for more details on this recipe and page 436 for more information on freezing stock.

- 3 onions, chopped
- 2 celery ribs, chopped
- 2 carrots, peeled and chopped
- 8 scallions, chopped
- 15 garlic cloves, peeled and smashed
- 1 teaspoon olive oil
- 1 teaspoon salt
- 12 cups water
- 1 head cauliflower (about 2½ pounds), cored and cut into 1-inch florets
- 1 plum tomato, cored and chopped
- 8 sprigs fresh thyme
- 3 bay leaves
- 1 teaspoon black peppercorns

1. Combine onions, celery, carrots, scallions, garlic, oil, and salt in large Dutch oven or stockpot. Cover and cook over medium-low heat, stirring often, until golden brown fond has formed on bottom of pot, 20 to 30 minutes.

2. Stir in water, cauliflower, tomato, thyme, bay leaves, and peppercorns and bring to simmer. Partially cover, reduce to gentle simmer, and cook until stock tastes rich and flavorful, about 1½ hours.

3. Strain stock gently through fine-mesh strainer (do not press on solids). (Stock can be refrigerated for up to 4 days or frozen for up to 1 month.)

Chicken Noodle Soup

✔ **WHY THIS RECIPE WORKS:** For a full-flavored chicken soup recipe, we started with a homemade stock with shredded breast meat. After testing a wide range of vegetables, we decided simple was best for a classic take on chicken noodle soup. We sautéed onion, carrot, and celery to bring out their flavors before adding some thyme and our stock. Cooking the noodles right in the stock was essential to ensuring they melded with the soup and had good flavor—noodles cooked separately were incredibly bland. Egg noodles beat out other varieties since they were a manageable length over longer strands and they added a heft that bulked up the soup. We found that saving the chicken fat skimmed from the homemade stock and using this fat as a cooking medium for the vegetables, while not essential, added another good layer of chicken flavor.

Chicken Noodle Soup

SERVES 6 TO 8

The flavor of this soup depends on homemade stock; do not substitute store-bought broth. If desired, substitute chicken fat (reserved from making the stock) for the vegetable oil. See Recipe Tutorial on page 444 for more details on this recipe.

1 tablespoon vegetable oil
1 onion, chopped fine
1 carrot, peeled and sliced ¼ inch thick
1 celery rib, sliced ¼ inch thick
1 teaspoon minced fresh thyme or ¼ teaspoon dried
8 cups Chicken Stock with Shredded Breast Meat (page 459)
3 ounces (2 cups) wide egg noodles
2 tablespoons minced fresh parsley
   Salt and pepper

1. Heat oil in Dutch oven over medium heat until shimmering. Add onion, carrot, and celery and cook until softened, 5 to 7 minutes. Stir in thyme and cook until fragrant, about 30 seconds. Stir in stock and bring to boil. Reduce to simmer and cook until vegetables are nearly tender, 6 to 8 minutes.

2. Stir in noodles and simmer until tender, 10 to 15 minutes. Stir in shredded chicken and simmer until heated through, about 2 minutes. Off heat, stir in parsley and season with salt and pepper to taste, and serve.

Chicken Soup with Orzo, Fennel, and Leeks

The flavor of this soup depends on homemade stock; do not substitute store-bought broth. If desired, substitute chicken fat (reserved from making the stock) for the vegetable oil.

1 tablespoon vegetable oil
1 leek, white and light green parts only, halved lengthwise, sliced ¼ inch thick, and washed thoroughly
1 fennel bulb, stalks discarded, cored, and chopped fine
1 teaspoon minced fresh thyme or ¼ teaspoon dried
1 teaspoon ground coriander
8 cups Chicken Stock with Shredded Breast Meat (page 459)
¾ cup orzo
1 tablespoon minced fresh tarragon
   Salt and pepper

1. Heat oil in Dutch oven over medium heat until shimmering. Add leek and fennel and cook until softened, 5 to 7 minutes. Stir in thyme and coriander and cook until fragrant, about 30 seconds. Stir in stock and bring to boil. Reduce to simmer and cook until vegetables are nearly tender, 6 to 8 minutes.

2. Stir in orzo and simmer until tender, 10 to 15 minutes. Stir in shredded chicken and simmer until heated through, about 2 minutes. Off heat, stir in tarragon and season with salt and pepper to taste, and serve.

Tortilla Soup

✔ **WHY THIS RECIPE WORKS:** We wanted a recipe that gave us soup with authentic flavor but used easy-to-find ingredients and could be made on a weeknight. After breaking the classic recipe down to its three main components—the flavor base (tomatoes, garlic, onion, and chiles), the chicken stock, and the garnishes (including fried tortilla chips)—we came up with substitute

ingredients and a manageable approach to each. Typically, the vegetables are charred on a *comal* (griddle), then pureed and fried. To simplify, we made a puree from smoky chipotle chiles plus tomatoes, onion, garlic, and jalapeño, then fried the puree over high heat in oil. We poached chicken in store-bought broth infused with onion, garlic, cilantro, and oregano (the latter substituting for the pungent Mexican herb *epazote*), which gave our base plenty of flavor without having to make a from-scratch stock. And turning to the garnish, we oven-toasted tortilla strips instead of frying them and substituted sour cream when we couldn't find Mexican *crema* (a cultured cream), and Monterey Jack for traditional Cotija cheese.

Tortilla Soup
SERVES 6 TO 8
For more heat, include the jalapeño seeds. Look for thin corn tortillas—we found that thicker tortillas baked up chewy rather than crisp. You can also substitute 8 ounces *queso fresco* for the Cotija. See Recipe Tutorial on page 448 for more details on this recipe.

8 cups chicken broth
2 onions, quartered
4 garlic cloves, peeled
8 sprigs fresh cilantro
1 sprig fresh oregano
   Salt and pepper
1½ pounds bone-in split chicken breasts, or 1¼ pounds bone-in chicken thighs, trimmed
8 (6-inch) corn tortillas, cut into ½-inch-wide strips
3 tablespoons vegetable oil
2 tomatoes, cored and quartered
2 jalapeño chiles (1 stemmed and seeded; 1 stemmed, seeded, and minced)
1½ teaspoons minced chipotle chile in adobo sauce, plus up to 2½ teaspoons for seasoning
8 ounces Cotija cheese, crumbled, or Monterey Jack cheese, shredded (2 cups)
1 avocado, halved, pitted, and cut into ½-inch dice
½ cup Mexican crema or sour cream
½ cup fresh cilantro leaves
   Lime wedges

1. Bring broth, 1 onion, 2 garlic cloves, cilantro, oregano, and ½ teaspoon salt to boil in Dutch oven over medium-high heat. Add chicken, cover, and simmer gently until breasts register 160 degrees or thighs register 175 degrees, 15 to 20 minutes.

2. Transfer chicken to plate and let cool slightly. Using 2 forks, shred meat into bite-size pieces, discarding skin and bones. Strain broth through fine-mesh strainer into large liquid measuring cup or bowl, then defat stock using wide, shallow spoon or fat separator. (Stock and chicken can be refrigerated separately for up to 2 days.)

3. Meanwhile, adjust oven rack to middle position and heat oven to 425 degrees. Toss tortilla strips with 2 tablespoons oil, spread strips out over rimmed baking sheet, and bake, stirring occasionally, until crisp and dark golden, 10 to 15 minutes. Season with salt to taste and transfer to paper towel–lined plate.

4. Process tomatoes, remaining 1 onion, 1 jalapeño, remaining 2 garlic cloves, 1½ teaspoons chipotle, and ⅛ teaspoon salt in food processor until smooth. Heat remaining 1 tablespoon oil in Dutch oven over medium-high heat until shimmering. Add pureed tomato mixture and cook, stirring frequently, until fragrant and darkened, about 10 minutes.

5. Stir in strained broth, bring to simmer, and cook until flavors blend, about 15 minutes. Stir in additional chipotle to taste. Stir in shredded chicken and simmer until heated through, about 2 minutes. Off heat, season with salt and pepper to taste. Divide tortilla strips among bottoms of individual bowls, ladle soup over strips, and serve, passing Cotija, avocado, crema, cilantro, lime wedges, and minced jalapeño separately.

Old-Fashioned Beef and Vegetable Soup

✔ **WHY THIS RECIPE WORKS:** For a beef and vegetable soup that we could make in just an hour, we passed over the stew meat at the butcher's counter (these tough scraps wouldn't turn tender enough) and instead turned to quick-cooking, richly flavored sirloin tip steaks. For the vegetables, sticking to the basics kept the meat's flavor at the fore. Mushrooms accentuated the meatiness, and cooking an onion along with the mushrooms created fond in the pot and a caramelized depth. Celery, carrot, and, of course, potatoes also made the cut. Red wine complemented the soup's beefy flavor and added its own complexity. A little flour thickened the soup in lieu of the usual beef bones that normally provide the thickening power of gelatin to long-simmered versions.

Old-Fashioned Beef and Vegetable Soup
SERVES 6 TO 8

Look for whole sirloin steak tips, rather than those that have been cut into small pieces for stir-fries. If sirloin steak tips are unavailable, you can substitute flank steak or blade steak well trimmed of gristle and fat. White mushrooms can be substituted for the cremini mushrooms. If you're tight on time, you can use store-bought broth; substitute 4 cups beef broth and 2 cups chicken broth for the homemade stock.

1 pound sirloin steak tips, trimmed and cut into ½-inch pieces
  Salt and pepper
2 tablespoons vegetable oil
½ pound cremini mushrooms, trimmed and sliced ½ inch thick
1 onion, chopped
1 garlic clove, minced
2 tablespoons all-purpose flour
¼ cup dry red wine
1 recipe Beef Stock (page 459)
3 carrots, peeled and cut into ½-inch pieces
2 celery ribs, cut into ½-inch pieces
2 bay leaves
1 pound red potatoes, peeled and cut into ½-inch pieces
2 tablespoons minced fresh parsley

1. Pat beef dry with paper towels and season with salt and pepper. Heat 2 teaspoons oil in Dutch oven over medium-high heat until just smoking. Add half of meat and cook, stirring occasionally, until well browned, 5 to 7 minutes, reducing heat if pot begins to scorch. Transfer browned beef to medium bowl. Repeat with 2 teaspoons oil and remaining beef.

2. Add remaining 2 teaspoons oil to now-empty pot and heat over medium heat until shimmering. Add mushrooms and onion and cook until softened, 7 to 10 minutes. Stir in garlic and cook until fragrant, about 30 seconds. Stir in flour and cook for 1 minute. Whisk in wine, scraping up any browned bits, and cook until nearly evaporated, about 1 minute.

3. Stir in stock, carrots, celery, bay leaves, and browned meat and any accumulated juices. Bring to boil, then cover, reduce to gentle simmer, and cook for 10 minutes. Stir in potatoes and continue to cook until meat and vegetables are tender, 20 to 30 minutes longer.

4. Off heat, remove bay leaves. Stir in parsley, season with salt and pepper to taste, and serve.

Old-Fashioned Beef and Vegetable Soup with Parsnips and Kale
Omit carrots, celery, and potatoes. In step 3, add 4 parsnips, peeled and cut into ½-inch pieces, with stock, bay leaves, and browned meat and simmer, covered, for 15 minutes. Stir in 8 ounces kale, stemmed and leaves chopped into 1-inch pieces, and continue to simmer until meat and vegetables are tender, 15 to 25 minutes longer. Continue with step 4 as directed.

Old-Fashioned Beef and Barley Soup
See Recipe Tutorial on page 452 for more details on this recipe.

Omit potatoes. Stir in 1½ teaspoons minced fresh thyme or ½ teaspoon dried thyme with garlic in step 2. Add 1 (14.5-ounce) can drained diced tomatoes and ½ cup pearl barley with stock in step 3 and cook as directed.

Old-Fashioned Beef Noodle Soup
Omit potatoes. Before removing soup from heat in step 4, add 2 cups wide egg noodles and continue to simmer until noodles are tender, about 8 minutes longer. Continue with step 4 as directed.

Hot and Sour Soup

✔ **WHY THIS RECIPE WORKS:** Authentic versions of this soup call for ingredients like mustard pickle, pig's-foot tendon, and dried sea cucumber. To get an authentically spicy, rich, and complex version that would use only ingredients from our local supermarket, we created a "hot" side for our soup using two heat sources—a full teaspoon of distinctive, penetrating white pepper and a little chili oil. To create the "sour" side, we preferred Chinese black vinegar but found a combination of balsamic and red wine vinegar to be an acceptable substitute. Cornstarch pulled triple duty, going into our slurry to thicken the soup, into the marinade to keep the meat tender, and getting beaten with the egg to keep the egg light, wispy, and cohesive. We settled on fresh shiitakes in lieu of wood ear mushrooms and canned bamboo shoots instead of lily buds.

Hot and Sour Soup

SERVES 6 TO 8

To make slicing the pork easier, freeze it for 15 minutes. Chinese black vinegar can be found in Asian markets. If you can't find it, a combination of red wine vinegar and balsamic vinegar approximates its flavor. This soup is spicy. For a less spicy soup, omit the chili oil or add only 1 teaspoon.

- 7 ounces extra-firm tofu
- ¼ cup soy sauce
- 1 teaspoon toasted sesame oil
- 3½ tablespoons cornstarch
- 1 (6-ounce) boneless pork chop, ½ inch thick, trimmed and cut into 1 by ⅛-inch matchsticks
- 3 tablespoons plus 1 teaspoon cold water
- 1 large egg
- 6 cups chicken broth
- 1 (5-ounce) can bamboo shoots, sliced lengthwise into ⅛-inch-thick strips
- 4 ounces shiitake mushrooms, stemmed and sliced ¼ inch thick
- 5 tablespoons Chinese black vinegar or 1 tablespoon red wine vinegar plus 1 tablespoon balsamic vinegar
- 2 teaspoons chili oil
- 1 teaspoon white pepper
- 3 scallions, sliced thin

1. Place tofu in paper towel–lined pie plate, top with heavy plate, and weight with 2 heavy cans. Let tofu drain until it has released about ½ cup liquid, about 15 minutes.

2. Whisk 1 tablespoon soy sauce, sesame oil, and 1 teaspoon cornstarch in medium bowl. Add pork to bowl, toss to coat, and let marinate for at least 10 minutes or up to 30 minutes.

3. Combine 3 tablespoons cornstarch with 3 tablespoons water in small bowl. Mix remaining ½ teaspoon cornstarch with remaining 1 teaspoon water in second small bowl. Add egg and beat with fork until combined.

4. Bring broth to boil in large saucepan over medium-high heat. Reduce heat to medium-low, add bamboo shoots and mushrooms, and simmer until mushrooms are just tender, about 5 minutes. While broth simmers, cut tofu into ½-inch cubes. Add tofu and pork with its marinade to pan, stirring to separate any pieces of pork that stick together. Continue to simmer until pork is no longer pink, about 2 minutes.

5. Stir cornstarch mixture to recombine, then add to soup and increase heat to medium-high. Cook, stirring occasionally, until soup thickens and turns translucent, about 1 minute. Stir in vinegar, chili oil, pepper, and remaining 3 tablespoons soy sauce and turn off heat.

6. Without stirring soup, use soupspoon to slowly drizzle very thin streams of egg mixture into saucepan in circular motion. Let soup sit for 1 minute, then return pan to medium-high heat. Bring soup to gentle boil, then immediately remove from heat. Gently stir soup once to evenly distribute egg. Ladle soup into bowls, top with scallions, and serve.

Best French Onion Soup

WHY THIS RECIPE WORKS: We found that the secret to a rich onion soup was caramelizing the onions a full 2½ hours in the oven and then deglazing the pot several times with a combination of water, chicken broth, and beef broth. For the classic crouton topping, we toasted the bread before floating it in the soup to ward off sogginess, and we sprinkled the toasts with just a modest amount of nutty Gruyère to keep its flavor from overwhelming the soup.

Best French Onion Soup

SERVES 6

Use a Dutch oven with at least a 7-quart capacity for this recipe. Sweet onions, such as Vidalia or Walla Walla, will make this recipe overly sweet. Use broiler-safe crocks and keep the rim of the bowls 4 to 5 inches from the heating element to obtain a proper gratinée of melted, bubbly cheese. If using ordinary soup bowls, sprinkle the toasted bread slices with Gruyère and return them to the broiler until the cheese melts, then float them on top of the soup.

SOUP

- 4 pounds onions, halved and sliced through the root end into ¼-inch-thick pieces
- 3 tablespoons unsalted butter, cut into 3 pieces
  Salt and pepper
- 2 cups water, plus extra for deglazing
- ½ cup dry sherry
- 4 cups chicken broth
- 2 cups beef broth
- 6 sprigs fresh thyme, tied with kitchen twine
- 1 bay leaf

CHEESE CROUTONS

- 1 small baguette, cut into ½-inch slices
- 8 ounces shredded Gruyère cheese (2 cups)

1. FOR THE SOUP: Adjust oven rack to lower-middle position and heat oven to 400 degrees. Generously spray inside of Dutch oven with vegetable oil spray. Add onions, butter, and 1 teaspoon salt. Cook, covered, for 1 hour (onions will be moist and slightly reduced in volume). Remove pot from oven and stir onions, scraping bottom and sides of pot. Return pot to oven with lid slightly ajar and continue to cook until onions are very soft and golden brown, 1½ to 1¾ hours longer, stirring onions and scraping bottom and sides of pot after 1 hour.

2. Carefully remove pot from oven (leave oven on) and place over medium-high heat. Cook onions, stirring frequently and scraping bottom and sides of pot, until liquid evaporates and onions brown, 15 to 20 minutes (reduce heat to medium if onions brown too quickly). Continue to cook, stirring frequently, until bottom of pot is coated with dark crust, 6 to 8 minutes, adjusting heat as necessary. (Scrape any browned bits that collect on spoon back into onions.) Stir in ¼ cup water, scraping pot bottom to loosen crust, and cook until water evaporates and pot bottom has formed another dark crust, 6 to 8 minutes. Repeat process of deglazing 2 or 3 more times, until onions are very dark brown. Stir in sherry and cook, stirring frequently, until sherry evaporates, about 5 minutes.

3. Stir in 2 cups water, chicken broth, beef broth, thyme sprigs, bay leaf, and ½ teaspoon salt, scraping up any final bits of browned crust on bottom and sides of pot. Increase heat to high and bring to simmer. Reduce heat to low, cover, and simmer 30 minutes. Remove and discard herbs and season with salt and pepper to taste.

4. FOR THE CHEESE CROUTONS: While soup simmers, arrange baguette slices in single layer on rimmed baking sheet and bake until bread is dry, crisp, and golden at edges, about 10 minutes. Set aside.

5. TO SERVE: Adjust oven rack 7 to 8 inches from broiler element and heat broiler. Set 6 broiler-safe crocks on rimmed baking sheet and fill each with about 1¾ cups soup. Top each bowl with 1 or 2 baguette slices (do not overlap slices) and sprinkle evenly with Gruyère. Broil until cheese is melted and bubbly around edges, 3 to 5 minutes. Let cool 5 minutes before serving.

TO MAKE AHEAD: Onions can be prepared through step 1, cooled in pot, and refrigerated for up to 3 days before proceeding with recipe. Soup can be prepared through step 3 and refrigerated for up to 2 days.

Quicker French Onion Soup

This variation uses a microwave for the initial cooking of the onions, which dramatically reduces the cooking time. The soup's flavor, however, will not be quite as deep as with the stovetop method. If you don't have a microwave-safe bowl large enough to accommodate all of the onions, microwave in a smaller bowl in 2 batches.

Combine onions and 1 teaspoon salt in large bowl and cover with large plate (plate should completely cover bowl and not rest on onions). Microwave for 20 to 25 minutes, until onions are soft and wilted, stirring halfway through cooking. (Use oven mitts to remove bowl from microwave and remove plate away from you to avoid steam.) Drain onions (about ½ cup liquid should drain off) and proceed with step 2, melting butter in Dutch oven before adding wilted onions.

Cream of Broccoli Soup

✔ **WHY THIS RECIPE WORKS:** A good creamy vegetable soup is quintessential comfort food, but most versions fail, using a heavy hand with the cream and/or butter and resulting in a vegetable with diluted flavor and a soup with dull color. We wanted a cream of broccoli soup that was rich but still showcased the flavor and color of our chosen vegetable. Cooking the broccoli stems and florets separately was key. We sautéed the stems with our aromatics, then simmered the florets in the soup toward the end of cooking for deep, well-rounded broccoli flavor and good color. A combination of vegetable and chicken broth helped to highlight the vegetable flavor without tasting too lean. Just ½ cup of half-and-half added the right dairy flavor, body, and richness without overwhelming the broccoli. A little white wine cut the richness just enough.

Cream of Broccoli Soup
SERVES 4 TO 6
Be sure to use fresh broccoli in this soup; do not substitute frozen broccoli. See Core Technique on page 443 for more details on making pureed soups.

  1 tablespoon vegetable oil
  1 onion, chopped
1½ pounds broccoli, florets cut into 1-inch pieces, stalks peeled and sliced thin
  3 garlic cloves, minced
  1 tablespoon all-purpose flour
  ¼ cup dry white wine
  2 cups chicken broth, plus extra as needed
  2 cups vegetable broth
  1 bay leaf
  ½ cup half-and-half
     Salt and pepper
  1 recipe Cheese Toasties (recipe follows)

1. Heat oil in Dutch oven over medium heat until shimmering. Add onion and broccoli stalks and cook until vegetables are softened, 5 to 7 minutes. Stir in garlic and cook until fragrant, about 30 seconds. Stir in flour and cook for 1 minute. Stir in wine, scraping up any browned bits, and cook until almost completely evaporated, about 1 minute.

2. Gradually whisk in chicken broth and vegetable broth, smoothing out any lumps, and bring to simmer. Stir in broccoli florets and bay leaf and simmer until florets are tender, 7 to 10 minutes.

3. Remove bay leaf. Working in batches, process soup in blender until smooth, 1 to 2 minutes. Return soup to clean pot.

4. Stir in half-and-half and additional chicken broth as needed to adjust soup to desired consistency. Heat soup gently over low heat until hot (do not boil). Season with salt and pepper to taste and serve with Cheese Toasties.

Cheese Toasties
MAKES ABOUT 12 SMALL TOASTS
You can use any flavorful shredded, semisoft cheese in place of the cheddar in this recipe, including Gruyère, Swiss, gouda, Colby, Havarti, or Monterey Jack.

  1 small baguette, sliced ½ inch thick on bias
  2 ounces cheddar cheese, shredded (½ cup)

Adjust oven rack to middle position and heat oven to 400 degrees. Lay baguette slices on rimmed baking sheet and sprinkle evenly with cheddar. Bake until bread is crisp and golden at edges and cheddar is melted, 6 to 10 minutes.

Creamless Creamy Tomato Soup

✓ **WHY THIS RECIPE WORKS:** For a velvety smooth tomato soup with bright tomato taste and no cream, we started with canned tomatoes for their year-round availability and consistent quality. When cooking onion and garlic, butter muted the tomato flavor so we opted for olive oil. Brown sugar toned down acidity, and a surprise ingredient—slices of white bread torn into pieces—helped give our soup body without added cream.

Creamless Creamy Tomato Soup

SERVES 6 TO 8

Make sure to purchase canned whole tomatoes in juice, not puree. If half of the soup fills your blender by more than two-thirds, process the soup in three batches. You can also use an immersion blender to process the soup directly in the pot. For an even smoother soup, pass the pureed mixture through a fine-mesh strainer before stirring in the chicken broth in step 2. See Core Technique on page 443 for more details on making pureed soups.

¼ cup extra-virgin olive oil, plus extra for drizzling
1 onion, chopped
3 garlic cloves, minced
  Pinch red pepper flakes (optional)
1 bay leaf
2 (28-ounce) cans whole peeled tomatoes
3 slices hearty white sandwich bread, crusts removed, torn into 1-inch pieces
1 tablespoon packed brown sugar
2 cups chicken broth
2 tablespoons brandy (optional)
  Salt and pepper
¼ cup chopped fresh chives
1 recipe Butter Croutons (recipe follows)

1. Heat 2 tablespoons oil in Dutch oven over medium-high heat until shimmering. Add onion, garlic, pepper flakes, if using, and bay leaf. Cook, stirring frequently, until onion is translucent, 3 to 5 minutes. Stir in tomatoes and their juice. Using potato masher, mash until no pieces bigger than 2 inches remain. Stir in bread and sugar. Bring soup to boil. Reduce heat to medium and cook, stirring occasionally, until bread is completely saturated and starts to break down, about 5 minutes. Remove and discard bay leaf.

2. Transfer half of soup to blender. Add 1 tablespoon oil and process until soup is smooth and creamy, 2 to 3 minutes. Transfer to large bowl and repeat with remaining soup and oil. Rinse out Dutch oven and return soup to pot. Stir in chicken broth and brandy, if using. Return soup to boil and season with salt and pepper to taste. Ladle soup into bowls, sprinkle with chives, and drizzle with olive oil. Serve with croutons.

Butter Croutons

MAKES ABOUT 3 CUPS

Either fresh or stale bread can be used in this recipe, although stale bread is easier to cut and crisps more quickly in the oven. If using stale bread, reduce the baking time by about 2 minutes. Croutons made from stale bread will be more crisp than those made from fresh. Be sure to use regular or thick-sliced bread (do not use thin-sliced bread).

6 slices hearty white sandwich bread, crusts removed, cut into ½-inch cubes (about 3 cups)
  Salt and pepper
3 tablespoons unsalted butter, melted

1. Adjust oven rack to upper-middle position and heat oven to 350 degrees. Combine bread cubes and salt and pepper to taste in medium bowl. Drizzle with butter and toss well with rubber spatula to combine.

2. Spread bread cubes in single layer on rimmed baking sheet or in shallow baking dish. Bake croutons until golden brown and crisp, 8 to 10 minutes, stirring halfway through baking time. Let cool on baking sheet to room temperature. (Croutons can be stored in airtight container for up to 3 days.)

Creamy Gazpacho Andaluz

✓ **WHY THIS RECIPE WORKS:** The gazpacho popular in Andalusia, the southern region of Spain, is creamy and complex, with the bright, fresh flavor of naturally ripened vegetables. The key to fresh tomato flavor was salting the tomatoes and letting them sit to release more flavor. We then followed the same process with the other vegetables—cucumber, bell pepper, and onion—and soaked the bread, which we used to thicken the soup, in the exuded vegetable juices. A final dash of olive oil and sherry vinegar further brightened the flavor of our gazpacho, and a diced-vegetable garnish lent a fresh finish. See Core Technique on page 443 for more details on making pureed soups.

Creamy Gazpacho Andaluz

SERVES 4 TO 6

For ideal flavor, allow the gazpacho to sit in the refrigerator overnight before serving. Red wine vinegar can be substituted for the sherry vinegar. Although we prefer to use kosher salt in this soup, half the amount of table salt can be used. Serve the soup with additional extra-virgin olive oil, sherry vinegar, pepper, and diced vegetables for diners to season and garnish their own bowls as desired. See Core Technique on page 443 for more details on making pureed soups.

3 pounds tomatoes, cored
1 small cucumber, peeled, halved lengthwise, and seeded
1 green bell pepper, halved, stemmed, and seeded
1 small red onion, halved
2 garlic cloves, peeled and quartered
1 small serrano chile, stemmed and halved lengthwise
  Kosher salt and pepper
1 slice hearty white sandwich bread, crust removed, torn into 1-inch pieces
½ cup extra-virgin olive oil, plus extra for serving
2 tablespoons sherry vinegar, plus extra for serving
2 tablespoons minced fresh parsley, chives, or basil

1. Coarsely chop 2 pounds tomatoes, half of cucumber, half of bell pepper, and half of onion and place in large bowl. Add garlic, chile, and 1½ teaspoons salt and toss to combine.

2. Cut remaining tomatoes, cucumber, and bell pepper into ¼-inch dice and place in medium bowl. Mince remaining onion and add to diced vegetables. Toss with ½ teaspoon salt and transfer to fine-mesh strainer set over medium bowl. Drain for 1 hour. Transfer drained diced vegetables to medium bowl and set aside, reserving exuded liquid (there should be about ¼ cup; discard extra liquid).

3. Add bread pieces to exuded liquid and soak 1 minute. Add soaked bread and any remaining liquid to roughly chopped vegetables and toss thoroughly to combine.

4. Transfer half of vegetable-bread mixture to blender and process 30 seconds. With blender running, slowly drizzle in ¼ cup oil and continue to blend until completely smooth, about 2 minutes. Strain soup through fine-mesh strainer into large bowl, using back of ladle or rubber spatula to press soup through strainer. Repeat with remaining vegetable-bread mixture and ¼ cup oil.

5. Stir vinegar, parsley, and half of diced vegetables into soup and season with salt and pepper to taste. Cover and refrigerate overnight or for at least 2 hours to chill completely and develop flavors. Serve, passing remaining diced vegetables, oil, vinegar, and pepper separately.

Silky Butternut Squash Soup

✔ **WHY THIS RECIPE WORKS:** For soup with intense squash flavor, we cooked shallots and butter with the squash seeds and fibers, simmered the mixture in water, and then used the liquid to steam the unpeeled squash. We scooped the squash flesh from the skin once cooled, then pureed it with the reserved strained steaming liquid for a perfectly smooth texture with big butternut squash flavor.

Silky Butternut Squash Soup
SERVES 4 TO 6

Appealing accompaniments to this soup, in addition to the croutons, include lightly toasted pumpkin seeds, a drizzle of balsamic vinegar, or a dusting of paprika. See Recipe Tutorial on page 456 for more details on this recipe.

- 4 tablespoons unsalted butter
- 1 large shallot, minced
- 1 (3-pound) butternut squash, cut in half lengthwise, each half cut in half widthwise; seeds and fibers scraped out and reserved
- 6 cups water, plus extra if needed
  Salt
- ½ cup heavy cream
- 1 teaspoon packed dark brown sugar
  Pinch ground nutmeg
  Buttered Cinnamon-Sugar Croutons (recipe follows)

1. Melt 2 tablespoons butter in Dutch oven over medium-low heat. Add shallot and cook, stirring frequently, until softened, 2 to 3 minutes. Add seeds and fibers from squash and cook, stirring occasionally, until butter turns saffron color, about 4 minutes.

2. Add water and 1 teaspoon salt to pot and bring to boil over high heat. Reduce heat to medium-low, place steamer basket in pot, and place squash cut side down in basket. Cover and steam until squash is completely tender, 30 to 40 minutes.

3. Using tongs, transfer squash to rimmed baking sheet. When cool enough to handle, use large spoon to scrape flesh from skin. Reserve squash flesh in bowl and discard skin.

4. Strain steaming liquid through fine-mesh strainer into large liquid measuring cup; discard solids in strainer. (If you do not have 3 cups of liquid, add water to make 3 cups.) Rinse and dry pot.

5. Working in batches, puree squash in blender with 3 cups reserved liquid until smooth. Transfer puree to rinsed and dried pot. Stir in cream, sugar, nutmeg, and remaining 2 tablespoons butter. Return soup to simmer, adding additional strained liquid or water as needed to adjust consistency. Season with salt to taste and serve. (Soup can be refrigerated for up to 2 days.)

Buttered Cinnamon-Sugar Croutons
MAKES ABOUT 1 CUP

- 2 slices hearty white sandwich bread, crusts removed, cut into ½-inch cubes (about 1 cup)
- 1 tablespoon unsalted butter, melted
- 2 teaspoons sugar
- ½ teaspoon ground cinnamon

1. Adjust oven rack to middle position and heat oven to 350 degrees. Combine bread cubes and melted butter in medium bowl and toss to coat. Combine sugar and cinnamon in separate bowl, then add to bowl with bread cubes and toss to coat.

2. Spread bread cubes in single layer on parchment paper–lined rimmed baking sheet and bake, stirring occasionally, until crisp, 8 to 10 minutes. Let cool on baking sheet to room temperature. (Croutons can be stored for up to 3 days.)

Curried Butternut Squash Soup with Cilantro Yogurt

Sprinkle lightly toasted pumpkin seeds over each bowl of soup for a nice textural contrast.

Stir together ¼ cup plain whole-milk yogurt, 2 tablespoons minced fresh cilantro, 1 teaspoon lime juice, and ⅛ teaspoon salt in bowl while squash steams. Add 1½ teaspoons curry powder to squash while pureeing in blender. Garnish each bowl of soup with dollop of cilantro yogurt.

Garlic-Potato Soup

✔ **WHY THIS RECIPE WORKS:** Choosing the right potato was the first step in developing this soup. Russets broke down and thickened the broth well, while red potatoes ramped up the potato flavor. The key to getting the garlic right proved to be in the cooking technique. We cooked three minced cloves in the pot before adding the broth, and we poached two whole heads in the broth, then squeezed out the softened pods, mashed them, and added them back to the soup. Topping the soup with garlic chips crisped in a skillet made just the right garnish.

Garlic-Potato Soup

SERVES 6

A garnish is essential to add texture to this soup. We like Garlic Chips, but crisp bacon bits are a good option too. A potato masher can be used instead of an immersion blender to mash some of the potatoes right in the pot, though the consistency will not be as creamy. If leeks are not available, substitute an equal amount of yellow onion. The test kitchen prefers the soup made with chicken broth, but vegetable broth can be substituted.

- 3 **tablespoons unsalted butter**
- 1 **leek, white and light green parts only, halved lengthwise, chopped fine, and washed thoroughly**
- 3 **garlic cloves, minced, plus 2 heads garlic, outer papery skins removed and top third of heads cut off and discarded**
- 6-7 **cups chicken broth**
- 2 **bay leaves**
   Salt and pepper
- 1½ **pounds russet potatoes, peeled and cut into ½-inch cubes**
- 1 **pound red potatoes, unpeeled, cut into ½-inch cubes**
- ½ **cup heavy cream**
- 1½ **teaspoons minced fresh thyme**
- ¼ **cup minced fresh chives**
- 1 **recipe Garlic Chips (recipe follows)**

1. Melt butter in Dutch oven over medium heat. Add leek and cook until soft (do not brown), 5 to 8 minutes. Stir in minced garlic and cook until fragrant, about 1 minute. Add garlic heads, 6 cups broth, bay leaves, and ¾ teaspoon salt. Partially cover pot and bring to simmer over medium-high heat. Reduce heat and simmer until garlic is very tender when pierced with tip of knife, 30 to 40 minutes. Add russet potatoes and red potatoes and continue to simmer, partially covered, until potatoes are tender, 15 to 20 minutes.

2. Discard bay leaves. Remove garlic heads from pot and, using tongs or paper towels, squeeze at root end until cloves slip out of their skins into bowl. Using fork, mash garlic to smooth paste.

3. Stir cream, thyme, and half of mashed garlic into soup. Heat soup until hot, about 2 minutes. Taste soup and add remaining garlic paste if desired.

4. Using immersion blender, process soup until creamy, with some potato chunks remaining. Alternatively, transfer 1½ cups potatoes and 1 cup broth to blender or food processor and process until smooth. (Process more potatoes for thicker consistency.) Return puree to pot and stir to combine, adjusting consistency with up to 1 cup more broth if necessary. Season with salt and pepper to taste, sprinkle with chives and Garlic Chips, and serve.

Garlic Chips

MAKES ABOUT ¼ CUP

- 3 **tablespoons olive oil**
- 6 **garlic cloves, sliced thin lengthwise**
   Salt

Heat oil and garlic in 10-inch skillet over medium-high heat. Cook, turning frequently, until light golden brown, about 3 minutes. Using slotted spoon, transfer garlic to paper towel–lined plate. Season with salt to taste.

Modern Corn Chowder

WHY THIS RECIPE WORKS: For this version of corn chowder, we were looking for a recipe that would pack lots of corn flavor in every spoonful while still maintaining a satisfying, yet not too thick, chowder texture. Inspired by a recipe we found that juiced corn kernels, a trick that delivered pronounced corn flavor, we strained the scrapings and pulp from several cobs through a dish towel to get unadulterated corn juice (when we added the unstrained pulp to the pot, the soup curdled). This delivered the intense corn flavor we were after. We lightened things up by using water as our primary liquid, which allowed the pure corn flavor to shine through, then added just 1 cup of half-and-half to give our chowder the right richness. A sprinkling of basil before serving lent a fresh finish.

Modern Corn Chowder

SERVES 6

Make sure to remove only the part of the kernel sticking out of the cob. Cutting deeper will result in too much fibrous material coming off the corn. Yukon Gold potatoes can be substituted for the red potatoes. Minced chives can be used in place of the basil. See Core Technique on page 443 for more details on making pureed soups.

- 8 **ears corn, husks and silk removed**
- 3 **tablespoons unsalted butter**
- 1 **onion, chopped fine**
- 4 **slices bacon, halved lengthwise, then cut into ¼-inch pieces**
- 2 **teaspoons minced fresh thyme**
   Salt and pepper
- ¼ **cup all-purpose flour**
- 5 **cups water**
- 12 **ounces red potatoes, unpeeled, cut into ½-inch cubes**
- 1 **cup half-and-half**
   Sugar
- 3 **tablespoons chopped fresh basil**

1. Using paring knife, cut kernels from corn (you should have 5 to 6 cups). Holding cobs over second bowl, use back of butter knife or vegetable peeler to firmly scrape any pulp remaining on cobs into bowl (you should have 2 to 2½ cups of pulp). Transfer pulp to center of clean dish towel set in medium bowl. Wrap towel tightly around pulp and squeeze tightly until dry. Discard pulp in towel and set corn juice aside (you should have about ⅔ cup of juice).

2. Melt butter in Dutch oven over medium heat. Add onion, bacon, thyme, 2 teaspoons salt, and 1 teaspoon pepper and cook, stirring frequently, until onion is softened and beginning to brown, 8 to 10 minutes. Stir in flour and cook, stirring constantly, for 2 minutes. Whisking constantly, gradually add water and then bring to boil. Add corn kernels and potatoes. Return to simmer, reduce heat to medium-low, and cook until potatoes have softened, 15 to 18 minutes.

3. Transfer 2 cups chowder to blender and process until smooth, 1 to 2 minutes. Return puree to pot, stir in half-and-half, and return to simmer. Remove pot from heat and stir in reserved corn juice. Season with salt, pepper, and up to 1 tablespoon sugar to taste. Sprinkle with basil and serve.

Hearty Minestrone

✔ **WHY THIS RECIPE WORKS:** We wanted a minestrone with fresh, bright flavors that didn't have to rely on market-fresh vegetables like the best Italian versions. First, we needed a manageable list of supermarket vegetables; we settled on onion, celery, carrot, cabbage, zucchini, and tomato. Slowly layering flavors to create complexity was key. We sautéed pancetta, then browned the vegetables in the rendered fat. Salt-soaking dried beans seasoned them throughout, and simmering them vigorously helped them release starch and thicken the soup. A diced supermarket tomato added little, so we turned to V8 juice for consistent flavor. Adding a Parmesan rind to the soup added cheesy flavor. Finally, we took a cue from the minestrone of northern Italy and finished the soup with a deconstructed pesto, adding chopped basil, a swirl of fruity olive oil, and freshly grated Parmesan.

Hearty Minestrone
SERVES 6 TO 8

If you are pressed for time you can "quick-salt-soak" your beans (see page 190). In step 1, combine the salt, water, and beans in a Dutch oven and bring to a boil over high heat. Remove the pot from the heat, cover, and let stand 1 hour. Drain and rinse the beans and proceed with the recipe. We prefer cannellini beans, but navy or great Northern beans can be used. We prefer pancetta, but bacon can be used. To make this soup vegetarian, substitute vegetable broth for chicken broth and 2 teaspoons olive oil for the pancetta. Parmesan rind is added for flavor, but can be replaced with a 2-inch chunk of the cheese. In order for the starch from the beans to thicken the soup, it is important to maintain a vigorous simmer in step 3.

Salt and pepper
8   ounces dried cannellini beans (1¼ cups), picked over and rinsed
3   ounces pancetta, cut into ¼-inch pieces
1   tablespoon extra-virgin olive oil, plus extra for serving
2   celery ribs, cut into ½-inch pieces
1   carrot, peeled and cut into ½-inch pieces
2   small onions, cut into ½-inch pieces
1   zucchini, cut into ½-inch pieces (1 cup)
2   garlic cloves, minced
½   small head green cabbage, halved, cored, and cut into ½-inch pieces (2 cups)
⅛–¼   teaspoon red pepper flakes
8   cups water
2   cups chicken broth
1   Parmesan cheese rind, plus grated Parmesan for serving
1   bay leaf
1½   cups V8 juice
½   cup chopped fresh basil

1. Dissolve 1½ tablespoons salt in 2 quarts cold water in large bowl or container. Add beans and soak for at least 8 hours and up to 24 hours. Drain beans and rinse well.

2. Heat pancetta and oil in Dutch oven over medium-high heat. Cook, stirring occasionally, until pancetta is lightly browned and fat has rendered, 3 to 5 minutes. Add celery, carrot, onions, and zucchini and cook, stirring frequently, until vegetables are softened and lightly browned, 5 to 9 minutes. Stir in garlic, cabbage, ½ teaspoon salt, and pepper flakes and continue to cook until cabbage starts to wilt, 1 to 2 minutes longer. Transfer vegetables to rimmed baking sheet and set aside.

3. Add soaked beans, water, broth, Parmesan rind, and bay leaf to Dutch oven and bring to boil over high heat. Reduce heat and simmer vigorously, stirring occasionally, until beans are fully tender and liquid begins to thicken, 45 to 60 minutes.

4. Add reserved vegetables and V8 juice to pot and cook until vegetables are soft, about 15 minutes. Discard bay leaf and Parmesan rind, stir in chopped basil, and season with salt and pepper to taste. Serve with oil and grated Parmesan. (Soup can be refrigerated for up to 2 days. Reheat it gently and add basil just before serving.)

Split Pea and Ham Soup

✔ **WHY THIS RECIPE WORKS:** We wanted a spoon-coating broth studded with shreds of sweet-smoky meat, without requiring the hambone traditionally used to infuse the soup with flavor. Substituting ham hock made the soup greasy and was skimpy on the meat. Ham steak, however, was plenty meaty and lent a fuller pork flavor. Without the bone, our soup needed richness and smokiness, and adding a few strips of raw bacon to the pot did the job. Unsoaked peas broke down just as well as soaked and were better at absorbing the flavor of the soup.

Split Pea and Ham Soup
SERVES 6 TO 8

Four ounces of regular sliced bacon can be used, but the thinner slices are a little harder to remove from the soup. Depending on the age and brand of split peas, the consistency of the soup may vary slightly. If the soup is too thin at the end of step 3, increase the heat and simmer, uncovered, until the desired consistency is reached. If it is too thick, thin it with a little water. In addition to sprinkling the soup with the Butter Croutons, we also like to garnish it with fresh peas, chopped mint, and a drizzle of aged balsamic vinegar.

2   tablespoons unsalted butter
1   large onion, chopped fine
   Salt and pepper
2   garlic cloves, minced
7   cups water
1   ham steak (about 1 pound), rind removed, cut into quarters
3   slices thick-cut bacon

1 **pound split peas (2½ cups), picked over and rinsed**
2 **sprigs fresh thyme**
2 **bay leaves**
2 **carrots, peeled and cut into ½-inch pieces**
1 **celery rib, cut into ½-inch pieces**
1 **recipe Butter Croutons (page 465)**

1. Heat butter in Dutch oven over medium-high heat. Add onion and ½ teaspoon salt and cook, stirring frequently, until onion is softened, about 3 to 4 minutes. Add garlic and cook until fragrant, about 30 seconds. Add water, ham steak, bacon, peas, thyme sprigs, and bay leaves. Increase heat to high and bring to simmer, stirring frequently to keep peas from sticking to bottom. Reduce heat to low, cover, and simmer until peas are tender but not falling apart, about 45 minutes.

2. Remove ham steak, cover with aluminum foil or plastic wrap to prevent drying out, and set aside. Stir in carrots and celery and continue to simmer, covered, until vegetables are tender and peas have almost completely broken down, about 30 minutes longer.

3. When cool enough to handle, use 2 forks to shred ham into small bite-size pieces. Remove and discard thyme sprigs, bay leaves, and bacon slices. Stir ham back into soup and return to simmer. Season with salt and pepper to taste, top with croutons, and serve. (Soup can be refrigerated for up to 3 days. If necessary, thin it with water when reheating.)

Black Bean Soup

✔ **WHY THIS RECIPE WORKS:** For a black bean soup recipe full of sweet, spicy, smoky flavors, we went with dried beans, which release flavor into the broth as they cook, unlike canned beans. Furthermore, they proved to be a timesaver: We discovered that it was unnecessary to soak them overnight or to use the "quick-salt-soak method" to make them tender. We also found that we didn't need from-scratch stock; we maximized flavor by using a mixture of water and store-bought chicken broth enhanced with ham and seasonings.

Black Bean Soup

SERVES 6

Dried beans tend to cook unevenly, so be sure to taste several beans to determine their doneness in step 1. For efficiency, you can prepare the soup ingredients while the beans simmer and the garnishes while the soup simmers. Though you do not need to offer all of the garnishes listed below, do choose at least a couple; garnishes are essential for this soup as they add not only flavor but texture and color as well.

BEANS
5 **cups water, plus extra as needed**
1 **pound (2½ cups) dried black beans, picked over and rinsed**
4 **ounces ham steak, rind removed**
2 **bay leaves**
⅛ **teaspoon baking soda**
1 **teaspoon salt**

SOUP
3 **tablespoons olive oil**
2 **large onions, chopped fine**
1 **large carrot, peeled and chopped fine**
3 **celery ribs, chopped fine**
½ **teaspoon salt**
5–6 **garlic cloves, minced**
½ **teaspoon red pepper flakes**
1½ **tablespoons ground cumin**
6 **cups chicken broth**
2 **tablespoons cornstarch**
2 **tablespoons water**
2 **tablespoons lime juice**

GARNISHES
Lime wedges
Minced fresh cilantro
Red onion, diced fine
Avocado, halved, pitted, and diced
Sour cream

1. FOR THE BEANS: Place water, beans, ham steak, bay leaves, and baking soda in large saucepan with tight-fitting lid. Bring to boil over medium-high heat. Using large spoon, skim foam from surface as needed. Stir in salt, reduce heat to low, cover, and simmer briskly until beans are tender, 1¼ to 1½ hours (if after 1½ hours the beans are not tender, add 1 cup more water and continue to simmer until tender); do not drain beans. Discard bay leaves. Remove ham steak, cut into ¼-inch cubes, and set aside.

2. FOR THE SOUP: Heat oil in Dutch oven over medium-high heat until shimmering. Add onions, carrot, celery, and salt and cook, stirring occasionally, until vegetables are soft and lightly browned, 12 to 15 minutes. Reduce heat to medium-low, add garlic, pepper flakes, and cumin and cook, stirring constantly, until fragrant, about 3 minutes. Stir in beans, bean cooking liquid, and chicken broth. Increase heat to medium-high and bring to boil, then reduce heat to low and simmer, uncovered, stirring occasionally, to blend flavors, about 30 minutes.

3. Ladle 1½ cups beans and 2 cups liquid into food processor or blender, process until smooth, and return to pot. Stir together cornstarch and water in small bowl until combined, then gradually stir half of cornstarch mixture into soup. Bring to boil over medium-high heat, stirring occasionally, to fully thicken. If soup is still thinner than desired once boiling, stir remaining cornstarch mixture to recombine and gradually stir mixture into soup; return to boil to fully thicken. Off heat, stir in lime juice and reserved ham; ladle soup into bowls and serve immediately, passing garnishes separately. (Soup can be refrigerated for up to 4 days. If necessary, thin it with additional chicken broth when reheating.)

Black Bean Soup with Chipotle Chiles

The addition of chipotle chiles in adobo—smoked jalapeños packed in a seasoned tomato-vinegar sauce—makes this a spicier, smokier variation on Black Bean Soup.

Omit pepper flakes and add 1 tablespoon minced canned chipotle chile in adobo sauce plus 2 teaspoons adobo sauce along with chicken broth in step 2.

Inside This Chapter

CHAPTER 11

How to Make Salad

Whether you're making a composed salad for company or simple mixed greens for a weeknight dinner, paying attention to the details and knowing the right techniques make all the difference. In this chapter we start by showing you how to select greens, how to wash and store them, and how to make a foolproof vinaigrette. We also reveal some inventive tricks for turning out great-tasting basics like tuna and chicken salad. We also show you how to make great center-stage salads, like Caesar and Cobb salad.

Getting Started

How to Buy Salad Greens

Not only is there a dizzying array of greens available at the supermarket now, but in a good market you can buy the same greens more than one way: full heads, prewashed in a bag, in a clamshell, and loose in bulk bins. Which is the right choice for you? Do you need greens that will stay fresh for the duration of the week, or do you plan on using them in the next few days?

A sturdy lettuce like romaine can be washed and stored for up to a week (see chart opposite page), making it a good option for many nights' worth of salads. Prewashed bags of baby spinach, arugula, and mesclun mix offer great convenience, but be sure to turn over the bags and inspect the greens as closely as you can; the sell-by date alone doesn't ensure quality, so if you see moisture in the bag or hints of any blackened leaf edges, move on.

Don't buy bags of already-cut lettuce that you can otherwise buy as whole heads, like romaine or Bibb or red leaf. Precut lettuce will be inferior in quality because the leaves begin to spoil once they are cut (bagged hearts of romaine are fine but stay away from bags of cut romaine). Endive and radicchio are always sold in heads, and because they are sturdy and will last awhile, they are nice to have on hand to complement other greens and to just add more interest to a salad. And for those times when a special salad is planned for company, it's best to buy the greens either the day of the party or the day before for the best results.

Salad Greens A to Z

Here are some of the most common salad greens you'll find at the market. With such a wide array of greens to choose from, it's good to know how to mix and match greens to build interesting salads. Many are great on their own but others are generally best used to add texture or color to other salads. No matter what type of greens you buy, make sure to select the freshest ones possible and avoid any that are wilted, bruised, or discolored.

ARUGULA (ALSO CALLED ROCKET OR ROQUETTE)
Delicate dark green leaves with a peppery bite; sold in bunches, usually with roots attached, or prewashed in cellobags; bruises easily and can be very sandy, so wash thoroughly in several changes of water before using. Serve alone for a full-flavored salad or add to romaine, Bibb, or Boston lettuces to give a spicy punch.

BELGIAN ENDIVE
Small, compact head of firm white or pale yellow leaves; should be completely smooth and blemish-free; slightly bitter flavor and crisp texture. One of the few salad greens we routinely cut rather than tear; remove whole leaves from the head and slice crosswise into bite-size pieces. Add to Bibb, Boston, and looseleaf lettuces and watercress; combine with diced apples, blue cheese, and walnuts for an interesting first-course salad.

BIBB LETTUCE
Small, compact heads; pale to medium green; soft, buttery outer leaves; inner leaves have surprising crunch and a sweet, mild flavor. Combine with Boston or looseleaf lettuces, romaine, watercress, or endive; great tossed with fresh herbs.

BOSTON LETTUCE
Loose, fluffy head, ranging in color from pale green to red-tipped; similar in texture and flavor to Bibb lettuce, but with softer leaves. Combine with Bibb lettuce, baby spinach, watercress, endive, or romaine.

CABBAGE (GREEN OR RED)
Very tight head of smooth, firm leaves; very crisp texture; mild mustard flavor. Shred and use to make coleslaw or toss with romaine or looseleaf lettuces for visual and textural accent.

CHICORY (ALSO CALLED CURLY ENDIVE)
Loose, feathery head of bright green, bitter leaves; texture is somewhat chewy. Add to bitter green salads or use sparingly to add punch to mild mixed greens; toss with warm bacon dressing.

ESCAROLE
Type of chicory with tough, dark green leaves and a mildly bitter flavor; inner leaves are slightly milder. Use as an accent to romaine or serve on its own with a lemony vinaigrette.

FRISÉE

Type of chicory that is milder in flavor than other chicories but with similar feathery leaves; pale green to white in color. Combine with arugula, watercress, or Boston or Bibb lettuces; serve on its own with warm bacon dressing or balsamic vinaigrette.

ICEBERG

Large, round, tightly packed head of pale green leaves; very crisp and crunchy, with minimal flavor. Cut into wedges and slather with blue cheese or other creamy dressing; tear into small chunks and toss with Bibb, Boston, or looseleaf lettuces.

LOOSELEAF LETTUCES (RED LEAF, GREEN LEAF)

Ruffled dark red or deep green leaves that grow in big, loose heads; both are versatile and have a soft, yet crunchy texture; green leaf lettuce is crisp and mild; red leaf has an earthier flavor. Pair red leaf with romaine or watercress; pair green leaf with arugula, radicchio, or watercress.

MÂCHE (ALSO CALLED LAMB'S TONGUE OR LAMB'S LETTUCE)

Small heads of three or four stems of small, sweet, deep green leaves; very delicate and must be handled carefully; usually sold prewashed in bags, but heads can be sandy, so wash thoroughly. Combine with arugula or watercress.

MESCLUN (ALSO CALLED MESCLUNE, SPRING MIX, FIELD GREENS)

Mixture of up to 14 different baby greens, generally including spinach, red leaf, oak leaf, lolla rossa, frisée, radicchio, and green leaf; delicate leaves; does not need washing; flavors range from mild to slightly bitter depending on the blend. Great as a delicate salad.

RADICCHIO

Tight heads of red or deep purple leaves streaked with prominent white ribs; bitter flavor. Cut into ribbons and mix with arugula and endive; red and green leaf, Boston, or Bibb lettuces; or watercress. Adds color to any salad.

ROMAINE

Long, full heads with stiff, deep green leaves; crisp, crunchy leaves with a mild earthy flavor; also sold in bags of three romaine hearts; tough dry outer leaves should be discarded from full heads. A great all-purpose lettuce; mix with Boston, Bibb, or red leaf lettuces, spinach, watercress, arugula, endive, or radicchio.

SPINACH (FLAT-LEAF, BABY)

Vibrant green color and earthy flavor shared by all varieties; use tender, deep green flat-leaf or baby spinach for salads; use tough and fibrous curly-leaf spinach for steaming and sautéing; rinse loose spinach thoroughly in several changes of water to remove dirt; all varieties are generally available prewashed in bags. Delicious mixed with arugula, watercress, romaine, or Bibb, Boston, or leaf lettuces.

WATERCRESS

Delicate, dark green leaves with tough, bitter stems that should be removed; refreshing mustardlike flavor similar to arugula; usually sold in bunches, sometimes available prewashed in bags. If buying watercress in bunches, take care to wash thoroughly. Adds flavorful punch and texture to mildly flavored or tender greens such as Bibb or Boston lettuces.

Storing Salad Greens

Here's the best way to store the most common types of lettuce when you get home from the supermarket.

LETTUCE TYPE	HOW TO STORE
Crisp heads, such as iceberg and romaine	Core lettuce, wrap in moist paper towels, and refrigerate in plastic produce bag or zipper-lock bag left slightly open.
Leafy greens, such as arugula, baby spinach, and mesclun	If prewashed, store in original plastic container or bag. If not prewashed, wash and dry thoroughly in salad spinner and store directly in spinner between layers of paper towels, or lightly roll in paper towels and store in zipper-lock bag left slightly open.
Tender heads, such as Boston, Bibb, and butterhead lettuce	If lettuce comes with root attached, leave lettuce portion attached to root and store in original plastic container, plastic produce bag, or zipper-lock bag left slightly open. If lettuce is without root, wrap in moist paper towels and refrigerate in plastic produce bag or zipper-lock bag left slightly open.

Pairing Leafy Greens with Vinaigrettes

Vinaigrettes are always the best choice for dressing leafy greens; heavier, creamier dressings should be reserved for use on sturdy lettuce such as romaine or iceberg. Most salad greens fall into one of two categories: mellow or assertive. When you're making a green salad, it's important to choose your vinaigrette recipe carefully to complement the greens you are using.

Mellow-flavored: Boston, Bibb, mâche, mesclun, red and green leaf, red oak, and flat-leaf spinach. Their mild flavors are easily overpowered and are best complemented by a simple dressing such as a classic red wine vinaigrette.

Assertive or spicy greens: arugula, escarole, chicory, Belgian endive, radicchio, frisée, and watercress. These greens can easily stand up to strong flavors like mustard, shallots, and balsamic vinegar and can also be paired with a slightly sweet or creamy vinaigrette.

How to Measure Salad Greens

For a side salad we usually call for 2 cups lightly packed greens per person. To lightly pack greens, simply drop them by the handful into a measuring cup, then gently pat down, using your fingertips rather than the palm of your hand. We like to measure greens for a salad using a very large glass measuring cup.

Essential Equipment

You don't need any specialty equipment to make salads, but there are a few things that will make the process decidedly more efficient, and each of these will be useful in other ways in your kitchen.

SALAD SPINNER

This is perhaps one of the most essential items, as nothing ruins a salad faster than gritty lettuce or lettuce that has not been properly dried. A good salad spinner will solve that problem, plus the bowl can be used for rinsing the greens. A salad spinner is also great for washing and drying herbs. Look for one with a hand pump rather than a crank as it will be easier to use and more efficient. You also want to buy one with a decent-size bowl and a solid, nonskid bottom. For more details on what to look for, see page 31.

WHISK

Most dressings and vinaigrettes are whisked together by hand, so a good whisk is essential. An all-purpose whisk, one that is neither too large and bulky nor too small, is ideal. Look for one with at least 10 wires of moderate thickness and a comfortable rubber handle. Stay away from balloon-type whisks—they are just too big for whisking dressings. For more details on what to look for, see page 31.

RASP-STYLE GRATER

When you're incorporating garlic or citrus zest into a dressing, it has to be very finely grated, or you will be left with unattractive hard bits that will mar your salad. The easiest way to accomplish this is to use a rasp-style grater, whose sharp teeth and long, narrow shape make this job almost effortless. For more details on what to look for, see page 30.

TONGS

You do a lot of tossing when making a salad in order to get the ratio of dressing to greens just right. Tongs are perfect for this task and give you a lot of control, as you can hold the bowl with one hand and toss delicate greens with the other. Look for tongs with slightly concave pincers and a length of 12 inches. Tongs with nylon tips are a plus, but not essential, when tossing delicate greens. For more details on what to look for, see page 31.

CITRUS JUICER

Citrus juice adds brightness and balancing acidity to numerous salad dressings. A good juicer will allow you to extract maximum juice from a lemon, lime, or orange with minimum mess. And while there are many styles, including sticklike reamers and squeeze-style juicers, our favorite is an electric model, which is especially helpful if you need to collect a lot of juice. We also like a simple squeeze-style manual juicer with curved handles and a well-shaped plunger.

Essential Ingredients

A well-stocked pantry will allow you to make an array of salads. While nonessential add-ins (such as some dried fruits or nuts) might be interchangeable, even for the simplest of salads, you need to make sure you have a few basics on hand.

OIL AND VINEGAR

A good extra-virgin olive oil is a must when making vinaigrettes or other dressings. But you will also need a pure olive oil and/or canola oil for recipes that call for a lot of oil, like mayonnaise and Caesar salad, where the flavor of extra-virgin olive oil alone is too pungent and overpowering. That said, for vinaigrettes we almost always call for extra-virgin olive oil because it tastes good with all greens and vinegars; it pays to reach for a high-quality extra-virgin olive oil when making vinaigrettes.

You will want to stock several vinegars, including red wine, white wine, balsamic, and rice vinegar. Sherry vinegar is also very nice to have on hand because it adds strong flavor to vinaigrettes. Note that vinegars can vary in acidity—which in effect measures intensity. For example, rice vinegars have a 4 percent acidity level and require less oil to make a smooth-tasting dressing; red wine vinegars can have an acidity level as high as 7 percent and so require much more oil to make a smooth dressing. For more details on oils and vinegars, see pages 37–38.

CHEESE

We often incorporate cheese into our salad recipes and, in the case of blue cheese, also use it to make dressings. High-quality cheeses make a big difference in both salads and dressings, so choose carefully. For more details on shopping for cheese, see pages 40–42.

MAYONNAISE

Although fresh mayonnaise is a snap to prepare (see page 479), it has a short shelf life, which is why just about everyone has a jar of store-bought mayo in their fridge. When making creamy salads like tuna, egg, potato, and chicken salads, not to mention coleslaw, you use a fair amount of mayonnaise, so which one (and which type) you reach for can make a big difference.

While homemade mayo is made with just a handful of ingredients, mass-produced mayonnaise also has stabilizers and preservatives to extend shelf life. And instead of yolks, some manufacturers use whole eggs to cut costs; but egg whites are not as rich and as flavorful, so other ingredients are added to enhance taste. Ultimately, we found that less was more—the best-tasting brands had the fewest ingredients and the simplest flavor profile. In our testing of mayonnaise, we downgraded brands that added other notes and nuances such as cider vinegar instead of neutral-tasting distilled vinegar, or honey for balance instead of sugar, or ingredients such as dried garlic or onion that turned them halfway into salad dressing. Surprisingly, our top-rated brands, Blue Plate Real Mayonnaise and Hellmann's Real Mayonnaise (sold as Best Foods west of the Rockies), didn't even use lemon juice or mustard, though we include both in our own recipe.

If you are looking to cut fat and calories, note that the world of lighter mayonnaise can be confusing. Some are labeled light while others are labeled low fat or reduced fat, and some are not mayonnaise at all but "dressings" that will add a gummy texture if used in any quantity. In our tests, we found Hellmann's Light (with 35 calories and 3.5 grams of fat per tablespoon, about half that of regular mayonnaise) to be almost as good as its full-fat cousin.

DIJON MUSTARD

Whether you're making a vinaigrette or a creamy dressing, a good Dijon mustard can add bright, sharp flavor that cuts through the olive oil; it also has emulsifying qualities that help keep these dressings from separating.

A good Dijon mustard should have a smooth texture, a clean aftertaste without any off-flavors, and nose-tingling heat. It also shouldn't be too acidic, as less acid results in a mustard with more heat-producing chemicals. Heat was the most important factor in our tasting; the spicier mustards quickly rose to the head of the pack. But the other important quality was balance. Mustards that were too acidic, too salty, or muddied with other flavors were downgraded by our tasters. Our winning mustard is Grey Poupon Dijon Mustard. We are also fans of coarser-grain varieties for sandwiches and sauces.

TUNA

Even if you have a good recipe for tuna salad, choose the wrong type or brand and you're likely to wind up with a lackluster salad. In addition to chunk light and solid white, oil- and water-packed, pouched and canned, and regular and low sodium, some brands now offer premium versions with gourmet-sounding names like "select" grade and "prime fillet." We found that premium was the way to go. Our winning brand is a relative industry newcomer, Wild Planet Wild Albacore Tuna. It's a little more expensive than those made by the big tuna companies that dominate the market. The reason it tops our list is that, unlike most other manufacturers—which cook the tuna twice (before and after canning)—Wild Planet packs raw tuna into cans by hand and then cooks it just once, preserving the fresh flavor and meaty texture of the fish. Also, while most brands pack their tuna in water or vegetable broth to add back moisture and cover up bland flavor, Wild Planet does not use any packing liquid, which contributes to the fresh taste of its fish and ensures more meat per can.

How to Make a Vinaigrette

ESSENTIAL EQUIPMENT

- mixing bowl
- whisk
- liquid measuring cup

Vinaigrette may be the most useful sauce in any cook's repertoire. In addition to dressing greens, vinaigrettes can be used to sauce chicken, fish, or vegetables. The ingredient list is short, and the method is simple. So what's the problem? By the time you pour the dressing over greens and get the salad to the table, this emulsified sauce has often broken and you end up with bites of salad that are either vinegary or oily. Our vinaigrette will not break, and it works with nearly any type of greens but is especially well suited to mild, tender greens. For a hint of garlic flavor, rub the inside of your salad bowl with a clove of peeled garlic before adding the greens. Master this technique and you can vary the vinegar, the oil, and the seasonings to create dozens of dressings. This recipe yields enough dressing for 8 to 10 cups of lightly packed greens (enough for four generous portions of salad). It can be refrigerated for up to two weeks. If you plan to store the vinaigrette, it's best to keep it in a nonreactive container (such as glass); otherwise the dressing can pick up a metallic taste. Also see How to Dress a Salad (page 478). For variations on this recipe, see page 493.

1. COMBINE VINEGAR AND MAYONNAISE

Combine 1 tablespoon red, white, or champagne vinegar, 1½ teaspoons minced shallot, ½ teaspoon mayonnaise, ½ teaspoon Dijon mustard, ⅛ teaspoon salt, and pepper to taste in small bowl.

WHY? In order to seamlessly blend ingredients that normally don't blend, you need an emulsifier, and eggs (in the mayonnaise) and mustard both have emulsifying powers. By combining vinegar with mayonnaise, we created a stable base into which we could whisk the oil and create a vinaigrette that would not separate for more than an hour. Because the egg yolk in mayonnaise contains lecithin, a fatty substance that emulsifies brilliantly, you need only a small amount. Dijon, which also acts as an emulsifier, adds sharp flavor, as does minced shallot.

2. WHISK WELL

Whisk until mixture is milky in appearance and no lumps of mayonnaise remain.

WHY? Once the mixture turns milky, you will know you've successfully combined the vinegar with the mayonnaise and the other ingredients.

3. PUT OIL IN MEASURING CUP

Place 3 tablespoons extra-virgin olive oil in small measuring cup.

WHY? Since you want to drizzle the oil into the vinegar-mayonnaise mixture, pouring it from a measuring cup makes this task much easier.

4. DRIZZLE IN OIL

Whisking constantly, very slowly drizzle oil into vinegar mixture. If pools of oil gather on surface as you whisk, stop addition of oil and whisk mixture well to combine, then resume drizzling oil in slow stream while continuing to whisk steadily. Vinaigrette should be glossy and lightly thickened.

WHY? The oil will combine with the vinegar mixture and become emulsified more easily if you add it a little at a time.

How to Wash and Dry Salad Greens

ESSENTIAL EQUIPMENT

• salad spinner
• large bowl
• paper towels
• zipper-lock bags

To make a great salad, the only thing that is more critical than using crisp, fresh greens is using clean, dry greens. Nothing ruins a salad faster than biting into gritty leaves. And trying to dress a salad while the greens are still wet is a losing battle—the dressing will slide off and the water from the greens will dilute the dressing that you so carefully crafted.

While some suggest that the best method for drying greens involves spreading them out on towels and patting them dry, we believe that the only foolproof method for drying them is to use a salad spinner. If you are using a crank-style salad spinner, place it in a corner of your sink, which will stabilize it and make it easier to use.

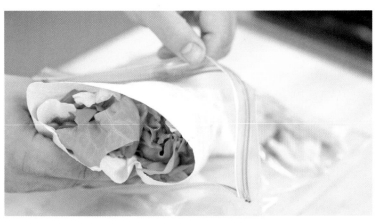

1. WASH GREENS

Fill sink or salad spinner bowl with cool water, add cut greens, and gently swish them around. Let grit settle to bottom of sink or bowl, then lift greens out and drain water. Repeat until greens no longer release any dirt.

WHY? Delicate greens are easily bruised, so instead of subjecting them to the force of running water, gently swish them in a pool of water. Small amounts of greens can be easily rinsed in the bowl of a salad spinner, but use a sink if you need to clean large amounts of greens. Either way, you need ample room to swish the leaves about with your hands to thoroughly rid the leaves of sand and dirt.

2. DRY GREENS

Dry greens in salad spinner, stopping several times to dump out excess moisture from bottom of spinner. Keep spinning greens until no more moisture accumulates in spinner.

WHY? Greens must be dry for the dressing to cling; also, you don't want to store damp greens or they will spoil quickly. A salad spinner is the best route to properly dried greens. After spinning, we like to blot greens dry with paper towels because we have found that even the best salad spinners don't dry greens completely.

3. STORE GREENS

Loosely roll washed leaves in paper towels, place rolled leaves in plastic bag, and put bag, very loosely sealed, in refrigerator.

WHY? Paper towels will protect the greens and absorb any additional moisture; sealing the bag only loosely ensures that no humidity develops (which would cause the greens to wilt). Most greens and lettuces will keep for several days. For shorter-term storage, you can simply line the basket of your salad spinner with paper towels and make layers of greens separated by more paper towels. Stored this way, greens will stay fresh for a day or two.

How to Dress a Salad

We have all encountered delicate greens that are simply flattened and wilted by way too much dressing or, on the other side of the spectrum, salads that are so light on dressing that they are just unappealing.

Once you have made your vinaigrette, the route to a properly dressed salad requires a few simple steps. You never want to dump a set amount of dressing over greens at one time and assume they will be perfectly coated. Once you have overdressed your salad, there is no going back, so drizzling and tossing a couple of times is the best way to go. For the freshest salad, make sure to dress your greens just before serving. Also, for just a hint of garlic flavor, you can rub the inside of the salad bowl with half a clove of peeled garlic before adding the lettuce. Also see How to Make a Vinaigrette (page 476).

ESSENTIAL EQUIPMENT

- wide, shallow salad bowl
- liquid measuring cup
- tongs

1. TEAR GREENS

Tear leaves into bite-size pieces just before serving and place in wide, shallow salad bowl. You will need 2 cups of greens per person.

WHY? Tearing leaves just before serving avoids discoloration. Since you will be tossing the leaves with dressing or simply with oil, vinegar, and salt and pepper, you will need sufficient space to ensure all greens are properly coated when they are tossed. A wide, shallow salad bowl enables the greens to be evenly and quickly coated with dressing. Use a bowl that is roughly 50 percent larger than the amount of greens to make sure there is adequate room for tossing.

2. DRIZZLE LIGHTLY

Rewhisk dressing and drizzle small amount over greens.

WHY? It is hard to know exactly how much dressing you will need to properly coat a bowl of salad greens, so start cautiously by drizzling a small amount of dressing over the greens.

3. TOSS GENTLY

Using tongs, toss greens carefully until dressing is incorporated.

WHY? You won't be able to tell how much dressing is really needed until after you've made the first addition of dressing and tossed the greens well.

4. TASTE AND ADD MORE DRESSING

Taste greens and, if necessary, add more dressing until greens are lightly coated and just glistening.

WHY? Getting a salad dressed properly is an exercise in dressing, tossing, and tasting because achieving the perfect salad is an art, not a science.

How to Make Mayonnaise

- food processor
- liquid measuring cup
- rubber spatula

If you have never made your own mayonnaise, you will be surprised by just how easy it is to do and how much better it tastes than the store-bought versions. Made with just a handful of ingredients—egg yolks, oil, lemon juice, salt, sugar (to balance the sourness of the lemon juice), and pepper (preferably white, since it won't be visible)—it emerges from the food processor silky smooth and creamy, with a rich, lush flavor. Another advantage to homemade mayonnaise is that it is easy to customize by adding garlic, herbs, or spices. It is of course great on sandwiches, but it is also wonderful served alongside cold vegetable salads or seafood, or slathered on sliced fresh tomatoes.

To make mayonnaise, you first process the yolks in a food processor with all the ingredients except the olive oil. Then slowly drizzle the oil while the food processor is running; going slowly ensures that the oil and egg yolks emulsify properly, creating a sturdy mayonnaise that won't break. Homemade mayonnaise can be refrigerated for up to three days. For variations on this recipe, see page 494.

1. PROCESS YOLKS

Process 2 large egg yolks, 4 teaspoons lemon juice, ¼ teaspoon salt, ⅛ teaspoon sugar, and white pepper to taste in food processor until combined, about 10 seconds.

WHY? Egg yolks contain lecithin, an emulsifying ingredient that prevents the oil droplets from sticking together when making mayonnaise. It is this emulsifying power that transforms egg yolks and oil into a creamy sauce. Before the oil is added, the food processor makes quick work of combining the yolks with other seasonings for a stable base to which the oil can be slowly added. Although you could whisk the yolks and oil together vigorously by hand in a bowl, we have found that it is easier and more foolproof to use a food processor.

2. ADD OIL

With processor running, add ¾ cup olive oil in slow, steady stream (process should take about 30 seconds).

WHY? The oil must be added in a steady stream in order to form a more stable, less-breakable emulsion. We prefer using olive oil here because it is milder and less harsh tasting than extra-virgin olive oil and more flavorful than vegetable oils. If you can't find regular olive oil, you can substitute equal parts extra-virgin olive oil and vegetable oil.

3. PROCESS

Scrape down bowl with rubber spatula and process 5 seconds longer, then season with salt and white pepper to taste.

WHY? You need to stop just before finishing to incorporate ingredients clinging to the sides of the bowl. You will know you are done when all the ingredients come together to form a creamy and smooth emulsion.

How to Make Coleslaw

ESSENTIAL EQUIPMENT

- chef's knife
- cutting board
- coarse grater
- colander
- medium mixing bowl
- paper towels
- tongs

Although recipes for coleslaw vary greatly (there are many regional specialties), the same bothersome issues can plague them all: This summertime classic can all too easily turn into a waterlogged bowl of limp cabbage. Follow the method below and you will turn out crisp coleslaw every time. You need to plan ahead when making coleslaw because the salting step, which draws water out of the cabbage and leaves it pickle-crisp, takes at least an hour. Once you've completed this step and have rinsed and dried the cabbage, you can refrigerate it overnight. It is best to dress coleslaw close to serving time. For details on shredding cabbage, see page 99.

This recipe is for classic Deli-Style Coleslaw (see the recipe on page 501), just about the simplest coleslaw you can make. If you like caraway or celery seeds in your coleslaw, you can add ¼ teaspoon of either with the mayonnaise and vinegar.

1. SALT SHREDDED VEGETABLES

Toss ½ head red or green cabbage, cored and shredded or chopped, and 1 large peeled and shredded carrot with 1 teaspoon salt in colander set over medium bowl. Let stand until cabbage wilts, at least 1 hour or up to 4 hours.

WHY? To avoid watery slaw, the cabbage must be salted and drained. When shredded cabbage is salted, the salt outside the cabbage is greater than the salt contained in the cells. The cell water is drawn out by the salt clinging to the exterior of the cabbage leaves. This partially dehydrated cabbage is limp but still crisp, so you end up with coleslaw with crunch that won't get soggy. Also, cabbage that has less water in it as a result of salting will soak up more of the flavors of the dressing.

2. RINSE WELL

Pour draining liquid from bowl; rinse bowl and dry. Dump wilted cabbage and carrots into bowl. Rinse thoroughly in cold water.

WHY? The salting process leaves the cabbage too salty, but a quick rinse is all it needs. If you are eating the coleslaw immediately, rinse it in ice water instead of tap water.

3. DRAIN AND DRY

Pour cabbage mixture back into colander and pat dry with paper towels.

WHY? The cabbage and carrot must be dry, or else the dressing will not cling and will be diluted.

4. DRESS AND SEASON

Return vegetables to bowl. Add ½ small finely chopped onion, ½ cup mayonnaise, and 2 tablespoons rice vinegar and toss to coat. Season with pepper to taste. Cover and refrigerate until ready to serve.

WHY? Once the vegetables are patted dry you can combine them with the mayonnaise and other ingredients and toss well. Rice vinegar adds a mellow tang, so we prefer it here over lemon juice.

How to Make Chicken Salad

Chicken salad can mean just about anything these days, from shredded meat dressed in vinaigrette to grilled strips tossed with leafy greens. But there is no beating the classic version, with tender cubes lightly bound with mayonnaise and freshened up with celery and herbs. The key to making the ideal chicken salad is to cook the chicken to precisely the right doneness. While most recipes poach the chicken, we take a somewhat unorthodox approach that approximates the *sous vide* technique used in many restaurants, in which sealed foods are submerged in a water bath preset to the food's ideal cooked temperature. Here, however, we submerge the chicken directly in cold water, heat the water to just above the ideal temperature for cooked chicken breasts (165 degrees), and then take the pot off the heat until the chicken is perfectly cooked through. While the chicken cools off in the refrigerator, we make a light and fresh dressing, then toss it altogether. The chicken salad can be refrigerated for up to 2 days. For variations on this recipe, see page 504.

ESSENTIAL EQUIPMENT

- Dutch oven
- instant-read thermometer
- tongs
- chef's knife
- paper towels
- rimmed baking sheet
- large mixing bowl
- whisk
- rubber spatula

1. COOK CHICKEN

Dissolve 2 tablespoons salt in 6 cups cold water in Dutch oven. Submerge 4 (6- to 8-ounce) boneless, skinless chicken breasts. Heat pot over medium heat until water registers 170 degrees. Turn off heat, cover pot, and let stand until chicken registers 165 degrees, 15 to 17 minutes.

WHY? Starting with cold water ensures that the chicken cooks through gently as the temperature of the water increases. We have found that if we heat the water to 170 degrees, the chicken will reach 165 degrees in 15 to 17 minutes when the pot is taken off the heat and covered, with no risk of overshooting the mark.

2. REFRIGERATE CHICKEN

Transfer chicken to paper towel–lined rimmed baking sheet. Refrigerate until chicken is cool, about 30 minutes.

WHY? The chicken will be easier to slice when cool (you also want to avoid making chicken salad with warm chicken).

3. CUT UP CHICKEN

Pat chicken dry with paper towels and cut into ½-inch pieces.

WHY? It's important to remove moisture from the chicken so it doesn't dilute the dressing. We prefer to cut the chicken into pieces, rather than shredding it, for a classic and substantial salad.

4. MAKE DRESSING, STIR IN CHICKEN AND HERBS

Whisk ½ cup mayonnaise, 2 tablespoons lemon juice, 1 teaspoon Dijon mustard, and ¼ teaspoon pepper in large bowl. Transfer chicken to bowl. Add 2 minced celery ribs, 1 minced shallot, 1 tablespoon minced fresh parsley, and 1 tablespoon minced fresh tarragon. Toss to combine and season with salt and pepper.

WHY? For brightly flavored chicken salad, we use a minimum of mayonnaise and add a hefty dose of lemon juice. Shallot and celery add crunch, while the herbs add freshness.

How to Make Tuna Salad

ESSENTIAL EQUIPMENT

- fine-mesh strainer
- paper towels
- mixing bowl
- microwave-safe bowl
- microwave

Although tuna salad sounds like a no-brainer, the truth is that there is a big gap between a salad good enough to feed your kids and a really good tuna salad you'd go out of your way to make right.

This recipe turns out the ultimate tuna salad. To avoid a watered-down salad, we found it was key to not just drain the canned tuna, but also to press it dry. To boost its flavor, we then microwave onion and oil (to temper the onion's bite), and then "marinate" the tuna in the onion-oil mixture with a few other flavorful ingredients before dressing it. Often, canned tuna also has a chalky texture, and this marinating step was also key to ensuring tuna salad with a great final texture—no trace of chalkiness.

We found whether using our favorite brand of canned tuna (see page 475), which is packed in nothing but its own juices, or solid white albacore tuna packed in water (our second choice), these few steps turn ordinary tuna salad into a standout. The steps below demonstrate the classic tuna salad; the same technique applies to more adventurous flavor variations (see recipes on page 505).

1. DRY TUNA

Place 3 (5-ounce) cans solid white albacore tuna in fine-mesh strainer and press dry with paper towels. Transfer to medium bowl and mash with fork until finely flaked.

WHY? Because the tuna is packed in water, removing that liquid is one key to making tuna salad that isn't watery. The simple step of pressing the tuna dry in a mesh strainer is a foolproof way to dry the tuna.

2. MICROWAVE ONION AND OIL

Microwave ¼ cup finely chopped onion and 2 tablespoons olive oil in bowl until onion begins to soften, about 2 minutes. Cool slightly, about 5 minutes.

WHY? Raw onion tastes too harsh in tuna salad. To temper it, we simply cook the onion in oil in the microwave rather than drag out a skillet.

3. MARINATE TUNA AND DRESS

Combine onion mixture, 2 teaspoons lemon juice, ½ teaspoon salt, ½ teaspoon pepper, and ½ teaspoon sugar with tuna and let sit 10 minutes. Stir in ½ cup plus 2 tablespoons mayonnaise and 1 finely chopped celery rib.

WHY? Letting the tuna soak up the onion mixture before dressing it allows it to absorb a surprising amount of flavor, and the oil keeps the tuna from tasting dry or chalky.

RECIPE TUTORIAL

GETTING STARTED
CORE TECHNIQUES
SALAD | RECIPE TUTORIALS
RECIPE LIBRARY

483

Caesar Salad

Overview

If you want a great Caesar salad, you'd better make it your-self at home or be sure you are ordering it from a first-rate restaurant. The classic version has been all but eclipsed by shortcuts and poor techniques, not to mention dubious updates like grilled romaine and additions like lackluster grilled chicken or shrimp. With a marriage of crisp romaine hearts, homemade croutons, and a clingy, garlicky dressing, this salad, when made well, is an exercise in coaxing the most from each ingredient.

We start with the croutons, which must be homemade if they are to take center stage. We found that tossing them with a little water before adding them to the skillet delivered croutons with perfectly browned and crisped exteriors and interiors that were tender (not stale). Then, once they were hot, we mixed them with garlic paste, olive oil, and Parmesan, which gave them great flavor.

Opinions abound when it comes to the dressing (and whether to coddle the eggs or not) and how to infuse it with the flavor of anchovy and garlic. We used two egg yolks and a mix of robust extra-virgin olive oil and milder canola oil as its base. To bring out the garlic flavor without overpowering the dressing, we used garlic paste (simply grate the garlic on a rasp-style grater) and tempered it by soaking it in a little lemon juice first.

Recipe Stats

TOTAL TIME **45 minutes**
PREPARATION TIME **15 minutes**
ACTIVE COOKING TIME **30 minutes**
YIELD SERVES **4 to 6**
MAKE AHEAD **Serve immediately**
DIFFICULTY **Easy**

Tools

- 12-inch nonstick skillet
- chef's knife
- cutting board
- serrated knife
- dry measuring cups
- liquid measuring cups
- measuring spoons
- citrus juicer
- garlic press
- mixing bowls *
- rasp-style grater
- rubber spatula
- salad spinner
- soupspoon
- tongs
- whisk

* You will need one large mixing bowl to make the croutons and dress the salad.

Ingredients

CROUTONS

2	garlic cloves, peeled
5	tablespoons extra-virgin olive oil
½–¾	loaf ciabatta, cut into ¾-inch cubes (about 5 cups)
¼	cup water
¼	teaspoon salt
2	tablespoons finely grated Parmesan cheese

SALAD

2–3	tablespoons lemon juice
2	large egg yolks *
6	anchovy fillets, rinsed, patted dry, minced, and mashed to paste with fork (1 tablespoon) **
½	teaspoon Worcestershire sauce
5	tablespoons canola oil
5	teaspoons extra-virgin olive oil
1½	ounces Parmesan cheese, grated fine (¾ cup) Pepper
2	romaine lettuce hearts (12 ounces), cut into ¾-inch pieces (8 cups)

* The eggs in this recipe are not cooked. If you prefer, ¼ cup Egg Beaters may be substituted for the egg yolks.
** The deep flavor of good-quality, oil-packed fillets is a must in this recipe. The fishier, flatter taste of commercial anchovy paste won't do.

What Can Go Wrong

Here's a list of common mistakes cooks make when preparing this recipe.

COMMON MISTAKE	BAD OUTCOMES	WHAT YOU SHOULD DO
Not Making Garlic Paste	• The dressing is too harsh. • The croutons are not as flavorful.	For our Caesar dressing, we grate the garlic on a rasp-style grater. You can also mince or press it, add a little salt, and mash it by drawing the edge of a chef's knife back and forth over it (see page 100 for more details). Garlic paste is easier to incorporate into a dressing and eliminates the risk of mixing in any raw bits of garlic, which taste harsh. In this recipe we also toss some garlic paste with the warm croutons to ensure that all the croutons are flavored with just a little garlic.
Not Cooking Croutons Long Enough	• The croutons are not browned or crunchy.	Properly browned and crisp croutons are an essential element of a Caesar salad. It takes about 10 minutes to cook them properly in a large nonstick skillet. Don't skimp on the timing and be sure to toss them around in the skillet as they cook so that all sides of the croutons get properly coated with the oil and have time to brown.
Not Drying Romaine Thoroughly After Washing	• The dressing is watered down. • The dressing doesn't cling to the lettuce.	After you cut up the romaine, be sure to use a salad spinner to dry it thoroughly. If you don't you'll wind up with naked leaves and a puddle of dressing at the bottom of the bowl.
Using Only Extra-Virgin Olive Oil in Dressing	• The dressing is not balanced.	Our recipe calls for a mix of canola and extra-virgin olive oil for a more balanced dressing. Although we love good extra-virgin olive oil, you need just a small amount here; if you use more, its fruity and bitter flavors will be at odds with the other assertive ingredients. We found that 5 tablespoons canola oil and just 5 teaspoons extra-virgin olive oil provided the right base for our dressing.
Not Whisking Dressing Properly	• The dressing doesn't emulsify. • The dressing breaks.	To create a well-emulsified dressing for this salad, you first need to mix the base ingredients together thoroughly, and then you must whisk constantly as you add the oils in a slow, steady stream until fully emulsified.

1. Grate 2 peeled garlic cloves into paste using rasp-style grater. Measure out ½ teaspoon for croutons and ¾ teaspoon for dressing.

2. PREPARE CROUTONS: Combine 1 tablespoon extra-virgin olive oil and ½ teaspoon garlic paste in small bowl; set aside.

3. Cut half to three-quarters loaf ciabatta into ¾-inch cubes to yield 5 cups. Place in large bowl and sprinkle with ¼ cup water and ¼ teaspoon salt.

4. Toss cubes, squeezing gently so bread absorbs water. Place 4 tablespoons extra-virgin olive oil and soaked bread cubes in 12-inch nonstick skillet.

5. Cook over medium-high heat, stirring frequently, until browned and crisp, 7 to 10 minutes.

6. Remove skillet from heat. Push croutons to sides to clear center. Add garlic mixture to clearing and cook with residual heat of pan, about 10 seconds.

7. Sprinkle with 2 tablespoons finely grated Parmesan; toss until garlic and Parmesan are evenly distributed. Transfer croutons to clean bowl.

8. PREPARE SALAD: Whisk 2 tablespoons lemon juice and reserved ¾ teaspoon garlic paste together in large bowl. Let stand 10 minutes.

9. Whisk in 2 egg yolks, 6 rinsed and dried anchovy fillets, mashed into paste with fork (1 tablespoon), and ½ teaspoon Worcestershire sauce.

10. Whisking constantly, drizzle 5 tablespoons canola oil and 5 teaspoons extra-virgin olive oil into bowl in slow, steady stream until emulsified.

11. Add ½ cup finely grated Parmesan and pepper to taste, and whisk until incorporated. Add 2 romaine hearts, cut into ¾-inch pieces, and toss to coat.

12. Add croutons and mix gently until evenly distributed. Season with up to 1 tablespoon lemon juice. Serve, passing ¼ cup finely grated Parmesan.

HOW TO MAKE SALAD

Cobb Salad

Overview

When it comes to salads with name recognition, Cobb salad is high on the list. It originated in Hollywood in 1926 at the Brown Derby, a local restaurant where the stars of the day were known to dine. Its fame continues, and it is still replicated on restaurant menus all over the country. The classic version of this main course salad features chicken, avocado, tomatoes, blue cheese, bacon, and plenty of salad greens. Versions abound, but all too often this salad arrives in a gigantic bowl with an array of the classic ingredients hastily tossed over greens. If a salad has chicken, bacon, and blue cheese, it seems to earn the moniker Cobb salad regardless of what else might be in it.

A well-made Cobb salad makes a satisfying dinner or the centerpiece of a summer buffet, but it requires a little time and much attention to detail. To make the most of each component and create a beautifully presented salad, our recipe is crafted to be layered onto a platter, with each component carefully dressed. The vinaigrette itself is unusual and lively, as it contains Dijon, lemon juice, and Worcestershire sauce—ingredients that were the hallmark of the original version. When the components are tossed with this piquant dressing, they take on its flavor for a salad that is more than the sum of its parts.

While you cannot assemble this salad in advance, you can cook the chicken and hard-cook the eggs well in advance and refrigerate them. Before you begin, see How to Hard-Cook Eggs on page 52, and page 98 for more detail on how to cut up an avocado.

Recipe Stats

TOTAL TIME **50 minutes**
PREPARATION TIME **20 minutes**
ACTIVE COOKING TIME **15 minutes**
YIELD **6 to 8 servings**
MAKE AHEAD **Serve immediately**
DIFFICULTY **Intermediate**

Tools

- broiler pan with top
- medium saucepan
- 10-inch skillet
- chef's knife
- cutting board
- dry measuring cups
- liquid measuring cup
- measuring spoons
- citrus juicer
- garlic press
- instant-read thermometer
- large plate
- mixing bowls
- rasp-style grater
- rubber spatula
- salad spinner
- serving spoon
- serving platter
- slotted spoon
- tongs
- whisk
- paper towels

Ingredients

VINAIGRETTE
- ½ **cup extra-virgin olive oil**
- 2 **tablespoons red wine vinegar**
- 2 **teaspoons lemon juice**
- 1 **teaspoon Worcestershire sauce**
- 1 **teaspoon Dijon mustard**
- 1 **garlic clove, minced**
- ½ **teaspoon salt**
- ¼ **teaspoon sugar**
- ⅛ **teaspoon pepper**

SALAD
- 3 **(6-ounce) boneless, skinless chicken breasts, trimmed**
   Salt and pepper
- 1 **large head romaine lettuce (14 ounces), torn into bite-size pieces**
- 4 **ounces (4 cups) watercress, torn into bite-size pieces**
- 10 **ounces grape tomatoes, halved**
- 3 **Hard-Cooked Eggs (page 80), peeled and cut into ½-inch cubes**
- 2 **avocados, halved, pitted, and cut into ½-inch pieces**
- 8 **slices bacon, cut into ¼-inch pieces, cooked in 10-inch skillet over medium heat until crisp, 5 to 7 minutes, and drained**
- 2 **ounces blue cheese, crumbled (½ cup)**
- 3 **tablespoons minced fresh chives**

What Can Go Wrong

Here's a list of common mistakes cooks make when preparing this recipe.

COMMON MISTAKE	BAD OUTCOMES	WHAT YOU SHOULD DO
Not Prepping Components in Right Order	• **The salad will not taste fresh.** • **Some of the components get soggy.**	The best way to tackle this salad so it comes together in the freshest way possible is to prep all the ingredients (except chives and avocado) before dressing each one. Once you prep the rest of the raw ingredients, hard-cook the eggs, fry the bacon, and broil the chicken, it is a snap to dress the components and assemble the salad.
Not Dressing Ingredients Separately	• **The salad is lackluster.** • **The salad is not properly dressed.**	The success of this recipe depends on the technique of dressing its components separately and with a particular amount of dressing. Not only does this ensure that the salad is fully dressed without the need to toss it at the end, but the ingredients take on flavor from the dressing. If you tried to arrange this salad on a platter and then dress it, you would have to toss it—after which you will have a mess, not an artfully arranged Cobb salad.
Using Platter That Is Too Small	• **The ingredients can't be arranged as directed.** • **The salad looks messy.**	You need a very large platter to make this salad properly, as the point of this recipe is to spotlight each component by artfully arranging it along the length of the platter, on top of the lettuces.
Not Using Romaine Lettuce	• **The salad has no crunch.** • **The salad has no height on the platter.** • **The other components flatten the substituted lettuce.**	Romaine lettuce (which we pair with watercress to bump up the flavor) is the classic choice for this salad. Not only is romaine sturdy enough to stand up to the chicken and other ingredients, but it will stay fresh and crisp longer, which is an important factor, especially if you are serving this salad for a party and it might sit out on the table for a while.
Assembling Salad Too Far in Advance	• **The salad will not taste fresh.** • **The components get soggy.**	While you can cook the eggs and the chicken well in advance, don't be tempted to start assembling this salad until close to serving time.

1. Cover 3 eggs with 1 inch water in medium saucepan. Bring to boil over high heat. Remove from heat, cover, and let sit for 10 minutes.

2. Fill medium bowl with 1 quart water and 4 cups ice cubes. Transfer eggs to ice water bath with slotted spoon; let sit 5 minutes.

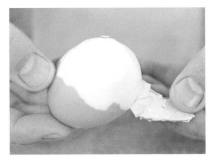

3. Remove and peel eggs, cut into ½-inch pieces, and set aside.

4. Cut 10 ounces grape tomatoes in half and set aside.

5. Crumble 2 ounces blue cheese and set aside.

6. Cut 8 slices bacon into ¼-inch pieces.

7. Cook bacon in 10-inch skillet over medium heat until crisp, 5 to 7 minutes.

8. Drain on paper towels and set aside.

9. Whisk together ½ cup extra-virgin olive oil, 2 tablespoons red wine vinegar, and 1 teaspoon Worcestershire.

10. Whisk in 2 teaspoons lemon juice, 1 teaspoon Dijon mustard, 1 minced garlic clove, ½ teaspoon salt, ¼ teaspoon sugar, and ⅛ teaspoon pepper.

11. Season 3 (6-ounce) trimmed boneless, skinless chicken breasts with salt and pepper.

12. Adjust oven rack to 6 inches from broiler element; heat broiler.

13. Spray broiler pan top with vegetable oil spray; place chicken breasts on top and broil until browned, 4 to 8 minutes.

14. Flip chicken over using tongs and continue to broil until thickest part registers 160 degrees, 6 to 8 minutes.

15. When cool enough to handle, cut chicken into ½-inch cubes and set aside.

16. Toss 1 large head romaine and 4 cups watercress, both torn into bite-size pieces, with 5 tablespoons vinaigrette in large bowl.

17. Arrange romaine mixture on serving platter, then place chicken in now-empty bowl. Add ¼ cup vinaigrette and toss to coat.

18. Arrange chicken in row along one edge of greens.

19. Place halved grape tomatoes in now-empty bowl, add 1 tablespoon vinaigrette, and toss to coat. Arrange on opposite edge of greens.

20. Halve and pit 2 avocados and cut into ½-inch pieces.

21. Mince fresh chives to yield 3 tablespoons.

22. Arrange chopped eggs and avocado in separate rows near center of greens and drizzle with remaining vinaigrette.

23. Sprinkle bacon, blue cheese, and 3 tablespoons minced fresh chives evenly over salad and serve immediately.

French Potato Salad

Recipe Stats

TOTAL TIME **45 minutes**
PREPARATION TIME **15 minutes**
ACTIVE COOKING TIME **20 minutes**
YIELD **6 servings**
MAKE AHEAD **Cooked and dressed potatoes can be refrigerated for up to 2 hours**
DIFFICULTY **Intermediate**

Tools

- large saucepan
- rimmed baking sheet
- chef's knife
- cutting board
- paring knife
- liquid measuring cup
- measuring spoons
- garlic press
- large serving bowl
- mixing bowls
- rubber spatula *
- soupspoon
- skewer **
- whisk

* A rubber spatula is essential for this recipe and will allow you to toss the potatoes gently with the herbs and shallot without breaking them.
** To tame the garlic's raw flavor for the vinaigrette, we skewer it and blanch it in the same pot with the potatoes as they cook.

Overview

Having little in common with its American counterpart, French potato salad is served warm or at room temperature, and is composed of sliced potatoes glistening with olive oil, white wine vinegar, and plenty of fresh herbs. This salad is fresher and more elegant than a mayonnaise-based potato salad, looks beautiful on a platter, and is especially nice served with grilled fish, chicken, and even beef.

The trick to making this salad successfully lies in how you handle the potatoes, which are fragile when sliced so thinly. We found that slicing them before boiling was the first step to avoiding a salad with broken bits of potato pieces (cutting perfect thin slices of potatoes is nearly impossible once they are cooked and still hot). And carefully arranging the drained potatoes on a rimmed baking sheet not only allowed them to cool quickly so they didn't turn mushy, it also gave us a sure-fire way to dress them easily. We simply drizzled the dressing over the potatoes, which absorbed the flavorful vinaigrette as they cooled. Adding a dose of minced fresh herbs and shallot just before serving provided a burst of fresh flavor. And after working so hard to keep the slices beautifully intact, we knew that tossing them with tongs was out of the question.

This recipe is easy to vary and can be dressed up with a variety of bold and colorful ingredients (see page 503). If you want to make this salad ahead, you can refrigerate the potatoes, covered with plastic wrap, for up to 2 hours after drizzling them with the vinaigrette. Before serving, bring the potatoes to room temperature and add the shallot and herbs.

Ingredients

2 **pounds small red potatoes, unpeeled, cut into ¼-inch-thick slices**
2 **tablespoons salt**
1 **garlic clove, peeled and threaded on skewer**
1½ **tablespoons champagne vinegar or white wine vinegar**
2 **teaspoons Dijon mustard**
¼ **cup olive oil**
½ **teaspoon pepper**
1 **small shallot, minced**
1 **tablespoon minced fresh chervil ***
1 **tablespoon minced fresh parsley**
1 **tablespoon minced fresh chives**
1 **teaspoon minced fresh tarragon**

* If fresh chervil isn't available, substitute an additional ½ tablespoon minced fresh parsley and an additional ½ teaspoon minced fresh tarragon.

What Can Go Wrong

Here's a list of common mistakes cooks make when preparing this recipe.

COMMON MISTAKE	BAD OUTCOMES	WHAT YOU SHOULD DO
Using Russet or Yukon Gold Potatoes Instead of Red Potatoes	• **The potatoes are mealy and dry.** • **The potatoes are grainy and soggy.** • **The potatoes don't soak up the dressing.**	Low-starch, high-moisture waxy red potatoes are the only choice for this recipe. They hold together when sliced, look pretty on the platter, and have a sweet, earthy flavor. Russet and all-purpose potatoes will be dry and floury in the final dish and won't soak up much dressing, and Yukon Golds will be too mealy and not firm enough.
Boiling Potatoes Whole	• **The potato slices are mangled and the skins torn.**	It is far better to slice the potatoes before boiling than to boil them whole and then try to slice them. You have much more control over the slicing process if you attempt to do it when the potatoes are raw (and not hot). The red skin will come off when you try to slice a hot potato, not to mention the fact that getting intact slices doing it this way is nearly impossible.
Not Blanching Garlic	• **The garlic flavor is harsh.** • **The dressing's flavor is out of balance.**	Blanching the garlic clove seems fussy, but it's a simple step to do while the potatoes are simmering. Just make sure to avoid leaving it in the simmering water too long or it's flavor will be too muted.
Not Reserving Potato Cooking Water	• **The vinaigrette isn't flavorful.**	You should reserve ¼ cup of the salted potato cooking water for the vinaigrette. The starch in the water adds plenty of salt and potato flavor to the vinaigrette. If you happen to forget to reserve the cooking water, you can use chicken broth instead.
Not Spreading Potatoes on Baking Sheet Right Away	• **The potatoes are mushy.**	Don't be tempted to let the potatoes sit in a colander while you chop the herbs or make the vinaigrette. Spreading them out evenly on a rimmed baking sheet right away helps them cool and eliminates residual cooking, which will turn the potatoes mushy—and make them impossible to remove from the sheet without breaking.
Stirring in Shallot-Herb Mixture Too Aggressively	• **The potato slices are mangled and the skins are torn.**	Letting the potatoes soak up the dressing on the baking sheet helps prevent busting apart the potatoes, but you still need to be very gentle when you are folding in the shallot-herb mixture to avoid breaking the potato slices.

1. Cut 2 pounds small red potatoes into ¼-inch-thick slices. Place potatoes and 2 tablespoons salt in large saucepan and add water to cover by 1 inch.

2. Bring to boil over high heat, then reduce heat to medium.

3. Thread 1 peeled garlic clove on skewer and lower into simmering water and partially blanch, about 45 seconds.

4. Run garlic under cold running water; remove garlic from skewer and set aside.

5. Continue to simmer potatoes until knife can be slipped into and out of center with no resistance, about 5 minutes.

6. Drain potatoes, reserving ¼ cup cooking water.

7. Arrange hot potatoes close together in single layer on rimmed baking sheet.

8. Press garlic through garlic press into mixing bowl or mince by hand. Add reserved potato cooking water.

9. Whisk in 1½ tablespoons champagne vinegar, 2 teaspoons Dijon mustard, ½ teaspoon pepper, and ¼ cup olive oil until combined.

10. Drizzle dressing evenly over warm potatoes and let stand 10 minutes.

11. Combine 1 minced shallot, 1 table-spoon minced chervil, 1 tablespoon minced parsley, 1 tablespoon minced chives, and 1 teaspoon minced tarragon.

12. Transfer potatoes to large serving bowl, add shallot-herb mixture, and mix gently with rubber spatula to combine. Serve.

Recipe Library

Foolproof Vinaigrettes

✓ **WHY THIS RECIPE WORKS:** Vinaigrettes often seem a little slipshod—harsh and bristling in one bite, dull and oily in the next—plus they tend to separate soon after being prepared. We found that top-notch ingredients are crucial for the best, balanced flavor. Fruity extra-virgin olive oil is preferred as an all-purpose option, while walnut oil is best for nuttier vinaigrettes. Wine vinegar (red or white) is a better match for mild greens and balsamic vinegar is pungent enough to stand up to assertive greens. For a well-balanced vinaigrette that wouldn't separate, we whisked the oil and vinegar together with a little mayonnaise, which acts as an emulsifier.

Foolproof Vinaigrette
MAKES ABOUT ¼ CUP

This vinaigrette works with nearly any type of greens. For a hint of garlic flavor, rub the inside of the salad bowl with a clove of garlic before adding the lettuce. You can use red wine, white wine, or champagne vinegar here; however, it is important to use high-quality ingredients. Use about 2 tablespoons of this dressing per 4 cups greens, serving two. See Core Technique on page 476 for more details on this recipe.

  1 **tablespoon wine vinegar**
1½ **teaspoons minced shallot**
  ½ **teaspoon regular or light mayonnaise**
  ½ **teaspoon Dijon mustard**
  ⅛ **teaspoon salt**
       Pepper
  3 **tablespoons extra-virgin olive oil**

  1. Combine vinegar, shallot, mayonnaise, mustard, salt, and pepper to taste in small bowl. Whisk until mixture is milky in appearance and no lumps of mayonnaise remain.

  2. Place oil in small measuring cup so that it is easy to pour. Whisking constantly, very slowly drizzle oil into vinegar mixture. If pools of oil gather on surface as you whisk, stop addition of oil and whisk mixture well to combine, then resume whisking in oil in slow stream. Vinaigrette should be glossy and lightly thickened, with no pools of oil on its surface. (Vinaigrette can be refrigerated for up to 2 weeks.)

Lemon Vinaigrette
This is best for dressing mild greens.

  Substitute fresh lemon juice for vinegar, omit shallot, and add ¼ teaspoon finely grated lemon zest and pinch of sugar along with salt and pepper.

Balsamic-Mustard Vinaigrette
This is best for dressing assertive greens.

  Substitute balsamic vinegar for wine vinegar, increase mustard to 2 teaspoons, and add ½ teaspoon chopped fresh thyme along with salt and pepper.

Walnut Vinaigrette
Substitute 1½ tablespoons roasted walnut oil and 1½ tablespoons regular olive oil for extra-virgin olive oil.

Herb Vinaigrette
Add 1 tablespoon minced fresh parsley or chives and ½ teaspoon minced fresh thyme, tarragon, marjoram, or oregano to vinaigrette just before use.

Blue Cheese Dressing

✓ **WHY THIS RECIPE WORKS:** We found that the secret to good blue cheese dressing lay in the creamy components, which we narrowed down to three: mayonnaise to give the dressing body, sour cream to supply tang, and buttermilk both to thin out the dressing and to support the sour cream. We also added a little white wine vinegar for zing and just a bit of sugar to take off any harsh edge. As for the main ingredient—the cheese—we ruled out really pungent blue cheeses as too overpowering; a mild blue cheese works best. For the right chunky consistency, we mixed the crumbled blue cheese with the buttermilk before adding any other ingredients.

Rich and Creamy Blue Cheese Dressing
MAKES ¾ CUP

In a pinch, whole milk may be used in place of buttermilk. The dressing will be a bit lighter and milder in flavor, but will still taste good. We dressed a variety of different salad greens and found that delicate ones, such as mesclun and butterhead lettuce, became soggy under the weight of the dressing. Sturdy romaine and curly-leaf lettuce were our two favorites. Remember that aggressive seasoning with salt and pepper is necessary because the dressing will be dispersed over the greens. Use 1 to 2 tablespoons of this dressing per 4 cups of greens, serving two.

2½ **ounces blue cheese, crumbled (⅔ cup)**
  3 **tablespoons buttermilk**
  3 **tablespoons sour cream**
  2 **tablespoons mayonnaise**
  2 **teaspoons white wine vinegar**
  ¼ **teaspoon sugar**
  ⅛ **teaspoon garlic powder**
       Salt and pepper

Mash blue cheese and buttermilk in small bowl with fork until mixture resembles cottage cheese with small curds. Stir in sour cream, mayonnaise, vinegar, sugar, and garlic powder. Season with salt and pepper to taste. (Dressing can be refrigerated for up to 1 week.)

Mayonnaise

✓ **WHY THIS RECIPE WORKS:** Beyond serving as a classic sandwich spread, mayonnaise also acts as a creamy binder and adds richness to numerous salads. Three thin liquids—oil, lemon juice, and egg yolk—combine to create a thick, creamy sauce. For the oil, we found that the peppery, fruity flavor of extra-virgin olive oil was too overpowering. Regular olive oil, however, added just the right amount of mild flavor (a blend of equal parts extra-virgin olive oil and vegetable oil works equally well). To keep the mayonnaise from breaking, we found it necessary to process the egg yolks and lemon juice thoroughly before adding the oil. Whisking by hand worked beautifully, but after 4 minutes, our arms grew tired. The food processor, which pulled the sauce together in just 30 seconds, won out.

Mayonnaise

MAKES ABOUT ¾ CUP

If you do not have regular olive oil, use a blend of equal parts extra-virgin olive oil and vegetable oil. Ground white pepper is preferred because it's not as visible as black pepper, but either can be used. See Core Technique on page 479 for more details on this recipe.

  2   **large egg yolks**
  4   **teaspoons lemon juice**
  ⅛   **teaspoon sugar**
      Salt and pepper (preferably white pepper)
  ¾   **cup olive oil**

1. Process egg yolks, lemon juice, sugar, ¼ teaspoon salt, and pepper to taste in food processor until combined, about 10 seconds.

2. With processor running, gradually add oil in slow, steady stream (process should take about 30 seconds); scrape down bowl with rubber spatula and process for 5 seconds longer. Season with salt and pepper to taste. (Mayonnaise can be refrigerated in airtight container for 3 days.)

Lemon Mayonnaise

Add 1½ teaspoons grated lemon zest along with lemon juice.

Dijon Mayonnaise

Whisk 2 tablespoons Dijon mustard into finished mayonnaise.

Tarragon Mayonnaise

Stir 1 tablespoon minced fresh tarragon into finished mayonnaise.

Classic Caesar Salad

✓ **WHY THIS RECIPE WORKS:** For our Caesar salad, we wanted crisp-tender romaine lettuce napped in a creamy, garlicky dressing boasting a pleasing salty undertone, with crunchy, savory croutons strewn throughout. To start, we cut the extra-virgin olive oil in the dressing with canola oil, which made for a less harsh flavor, and we used egg yolks instead of a whole egg to add richness. For a robust, though not aggressive, garlic flavor we grated the garlic into a pulp and then steeped it in lemon juice. Incorporating a portion of the Parmesan into the dressing while saving some to serve over the salad provided a double layer of cheese flavor. We preferred chewy, crisp ciabatta bread for our croutons and tossed them with a little water before frying them in a skillet until crisp. The water ensured the interiors stay moist and chewy while the exterior crisped. For a flavor boost, we tossed the croutons with a mixture of garlic, olive oil, and Parmesan. Tossed with slices of crisp romaine, our Caesar is better than ever.

Classic Caesar Salad

SERVES 4 TO 6

If you can't find ciabatta, a similar crusty, rustic loaf of bread can be substituted. A ¼ cup of Egg Beaters may be substituted for the egg yolks. Since anchovy fillets vary in size, more than 6 fillets may be necessary to yield 1 tablespoon of minced anchovies. The easiest way to turn garlic cloves into a paste is to grate them on a rasp-style grater. See Recipe Tutorial on page 483 for more details on this recipe.

CROUTONS
  2   **garlic cloves, peeled**
  5   **tablespoons extra-virgin olive oil**
½–¾   **loaf ciabatta, cut into ¾-inch cubes (about 5 cups)**
  ¼   **cup water**
  ¼   **teaspoon salt**
  2   **tablespoons finely grated Parmesan cheese**

SALAD
2–3   **tablespoons lemon juice**
  2   **large egg yolks**
  6   **anchovy fillets, rinsed, patted dry, minced, and mashed to paste with fork (1 tablespoon)**
  ½   **teaspoon Worcestershire sauce**
  5   **tablespoons canola oil**
  5   **teaspoons extra-virgin olive oil**
1½   **ounces Parmesan cheese, grated fine (¾ cup)**
      Pepper
  2   **romaine lettuce hearts (12 ounces), cut into ¾-inch pieces (8 cups)**

1. FOR THE CROUTONS: Grate garlic into paste using rasp-style grater. Measure out ½ teaspoon garlic paste for croutons and ¾ teaspoon garlic paste for dressing (discard remaining garlic). Combine 1 tablespoon oil and ½ teaspoon garlic paste in small bowl; set aside. Place bread cubes in large bowl. Sprinkle with water and salt. Toss, squeezing gently so bread absorbs water. Place remaining 4 tablespoons oil and soaked bread cubes in 12-inch nonstick skillet. Cook over medium-high heat, stirring frequently, until browned and crisp, 7 to 10 minutes.

2. Remove skillet from heat, push croutons to sides of skillet to clear center; add garlic mixture to clearing and cook with residual heat of pan, about 10 seconds. Sprinkle with Parmesan; toss until garlic and Parmesan are evenly distributed. Transfer croutons to clean bowl; set aside.

3. FOR THE SALAD: Whisk 2 tablespoons lemon juice and reserved ¾ teaspoon garlic paste together in large bowl. Let stand 10 minutes.

4. Whisk egg yolks, anchovies, and Worcestershire into garlic mixture. While whisking constantly, drizzle canola oil and olive oil into bowl in slow, steady stream until fully emulsified. Add ½ cup Parmesan and pepper to taste; whisk until incorporated.

5. Add romaine to dressing and toss to coat. Add croutons and mix gently until evenly distributed. Taste and season with up to additional 1 tablespoon lemon juice. Serve immediately, passing remaining ¼ cup Parmesan separately.

Greek Salad

✔ **WHY THIS RECIPE WORKS:** Most versions of Greek salad consist of iceberg lettuce, chunks of green pepper, and a few pale wedges of tomato, sparsely dotted with cubes of feta and garnished with one forlorn olive of questionable heritage. For our Greek salad, we aimed a little higher: We wanted a salad with crisp ingredients and bold flavors, highlighted by briny olives and tangy feta, all blended together with a bright-tasting dressing infused with fresh herbs. For a dressing with balanced flavor, we used a combination of lemon juice and red wine vinegar and added fresh oregano, olive oil, and a small amount of garlic. We poured the dressing over fresh vegetables, including romaine lettuce, tomatoes, onion, and cucumber, as well as other ingredients, including fresh mint and parsley, roasted red peppers, and a generous sprinkling of feta cheese and olives. Marinating the onion and cucumber in the vinaigrette tones down the onion's harshness and flavors the cucumber.

Greek Salad

SERVES 6 TO 8

For the sake of efficiency, prepare the other salad ingredients while the onion and cucumber marinate.

VINAIGRETTE
- 6 tablespoons olive oil
- 3 tablespoons red wine vinegar
- 2 teaspoons minced fresh oregano
- 1½ teaspoons lemon juice
- 1 garlic clove, minced
- ½ teaspoon salt
- ⅛ teaspoon pepper

SALAD
- ½ red onion, sliced thin
- 1 cucumber, peeled, halved lengthwise, seeded, and cut into ⅛-inch-thick slices
- 2 romaine lettuce hearts (12 ounces), torn into 1½-inch pieces
- 2 large tomatoes, cored, seeded, and cut into 12 wedges
- ¼ cup chopped fresh parsley
- ¼ cup torn fresh mint
- 1 cup jarred roasted red peppers, rinsed, patted dry, and cut into 2 by ½-inch strips
- ½ cup large pitted kalamata olives, quartered lengthwise
- 5 ounces feta cheese, crumbled (1¼ cup)

1. FOR THE VINAIGRETTE: Whisk all ingredients in large bowl until combined. Add onion and cucumber to vinaigrette and toss; let stand 20 minutes.

2. FOR THE SALAD: Add romaine, tomatoes, parsley, mint, and peppers to bowl with onions and cucumbers; toss to coat with dressing.

3. Transfer salad to wide, shallow serving bowl or platter; sprinkle olives and feta over salad. Serve immediately.

Country-Style Greek Salad

This salad made without lettuce is known as "country" or "peasant" salad and is served throughout Greece. It's excellent with garden-ripe summer tomatoes.

Reduce red wine vinegar to 1½ tablespoons and lemon juice to 1 teaspoon in vinaigrette. Use 2 cucumbers, peeled, halved lengthwise, seeded, and cut into ⅛-inch-thick slices, and 6 large tomatoes, cored, seeded, and cut into 12 wedges; omit romaine.

Fresh Spinach Salad

✔ **WHY THIS RECIPE WORKS:** With such smooth and flat leaves, baby spinach tends to stick together in salad. We knew that we needed a sturdier element to break up the leaves, but we wanted one that wouldn't overwhelm the spinach. The first step was rethinking our knife work. Thinly slicing the vegetables (or at least tearing them into pieces) allowed us to use harder, more crisp produce, such as carrots. In addition to fluffing up the spinach, carrots provided welcome crunch and sweetness. We also reasoned that fresh fruit would add bright, clean flavors and textural appeal. For the dressing, we altered the oil-to-acid ratio of our Foolproof Vinaigrette (page 493) until it was tangy enough to bring out the fruit's natural acidity.

Fresh Spinach Salad with Carrot, Orange, and Sesame

SERVES 6

- 6 ounces (6 cups) baby spinach
- 2 carrots, peeled and shaved with vegetable peeler lengthwise into ribbons
- 2 oranges, ½ teaspoon finely grated zest from 1, both peeled and segmented
- 2 scallions, sliced thin
- 7 teaspoons rice vinegar
- 1 small shallot, minced
- 1 teaspoon Dijon mustard
- ¾ teaspoon mayonnaise
- ¼ teaspoon salt
- 3 tablespoons vegetable oil
- 1½ tablespoons toasted sesame oil
- 1 tablespoon sesame seeds, toasted

1. Place spinach, carrots, orange segments, and scallions in large bowl.

2. Combine orange zest, vinegar, shallot, mustard, mayonnaise, and salt in small bowl. Whisk until mixture appears milky and no lumps remain. Place vegetable oil and sesame oil in liquid measuring cup. Whisking constantly, very slowly drizzle oils into mixture. If pools of oil gather on surface, stop addition of oils and whisk mixture well to combine, then resume whisking in oils in slow stream. Vinaigrette should be glossy and lightly thickened.

3. Pour dressing over spinach mixture and toss to coat. Sprinkle with sesame seeds and serve immediately.

Fresh Spinach Salad with Frisée and Strawberries

SERVES 6

This salad is best when made with in-season strawberries.

6	ounces (6 cups) baby spinach
1	head frisée (6 ounces) torn into 2-inch pieces
10	ounces strawberries, hulled and quartered (2 cups)
2	tablespoons chopped fresh basil
7	teaspoons balsamic vinegar
1	small shallot, minced
1	teaspoon Dijon mustard
¾	teaspoon mayonnaise
¼	teaspoon salt
½	teaspoon pepper
4½	tablespoons extra-virgin olive oil

1. Place spinach, frisée, strawberries, and basil in large bowl.

2. Combine vinegar, shallot, mustard, mayonnaise, salt, and pepper in small bowl. Whisk until mixture appears milky and no lumps remain. Place oil in liquid measuring cup. Whisking constantly, very slowly drizzle oil into mixture. If pools of oil gather on surface, stop addition of oil and whisk mixture well to combine, then resume whisking in oil in slow stream. Vinaigrette should be glossy and lightly thickened.

3. Pour dressing over spinach mixture and toss to coat. Serve immediately.

Fresh Spinach Salad with Radicchio and Mango

SERVES 6

This salad is especially good paired with grilled foods.

6	ounces (6 cups) baby spinach
1	small head radicchio (6 ounces), halved, cored, and sliced very thin
1	mango, peeled, pitted, and cut into ½-inch pieces
¼	cup chopped fresh cilantro
1	teaspoon finely grated lime zest plus 7 teaspoons juice (3 limes)
1	tablespoon honey
1	small shallot, minced
1	teaspoon Dijon mustard
¾	teaspoon mayonnaise
¼	teaspoon salt
4½	tablespoons extra-virgin olive oil

1. Place spinach, radicchio, mango, and cilantro in large bowl.

2. Combine lime zest and juice, honey, shallot, mustard, mayonnaise, and salt in small bowl. Whisk until mixture appears milky and no lumps remain. Place oil in liquid measuring cup. Whisking constantly, very slowly drizzle oil into mixture. If

pools of oil gather on surface, stop addition of oil and whisk mixture well to combine, then resume whisking in oil in slow stream. Vinaigrette should be glossy and lightly thickened.

3. Pour dressing over spinach mixture and toss to coat. Serve immediately.

Arugula Salad

✓ **WHY THIS RECIPE WORKS:** Arugula has a lively, peppery bite and so for salad, it's important to choose accompaniments that can stand up to its assertive character. We found that the sweet and salty notes of fruits and cheeses work well as supporting players to arugula, and crunchy elements like nuts also provide a nice counterpoint. As for the dressing, a vinaigrette made with mustard alone turned out to be too spicy, but a spoonful of honey added sweetness, pulling the flavors of the salad right in line.

Arugula Salad with Figs, Prosciutto, Walnuts, and Parmesan

SERVES 6

Although frying the prosciutto adds crisp texture to the salad, if you prefer, you can simply cut it into ribbons and use it as a garnish.

¼	cup extra-virgin olive oil
2	ounces thinly sliced prosciutto, cut into ¼-inch-wide ribbons
3	tablespoons balsamic vinegar
1	tablespoon honey
½	cup dried figs, stemmed and chopped into ¼-inch pieces
1	small shallot, minced
	Salt and pepper
8	ounces (8 cups) arugula
½	cup walnuts, toasted and chopped
2	ounces Parmesan cheese, shaved into thin strips with vegetable peeler (1 cup)

1. Heat 1 tablespoon oil in 10-inch nonstick skillet over medium heat; add prosciutto and fry until crisp, stirring frequently, about 5 minutes. Using slotted spoon, transfer to paper towel–lined plate and set aside to let cool.

2. Whisk vinegar and honey in microwave-safe bowl; stir in figs. Cover with plastic wrap, cut several steam vents in plastic, and microwave until figs are plump, 30 seconds to 1 minute. Whisk in remaining 3 tablespoons oil, shallot, ¼ teaspoon salt, and ⅛ teaspoon pepper; toss to combine. Let cool to room temperature.

3. Toss arugula and vinaigrette in large bowl; season with salt and pepper to taste. Divide salad among individual plates; top each with portion of prosciutto, walnuts, and Parmesan. Serve immediately.

Arugula Salad with Grapes, Fennel, Gorgonzola, and Pecans

SERVES 6

Honey can be substituted for the apricot jam.

- 3 **tablespoons white wine vinegar**
- 3 **tablespoons extra-virgin olive oil**
- 1 **small shallot, minced**
- 4 **teaspoons apricot jam**
  Salt and pepper
- ½ **small fennel bulb, fronds chopped (¼ cup), stalks discarded, bulb sliced very thin (1 cup)**
- 8 **ounces (8 cups) arugula**
- 6 **ounces seedless red grapes, halved lengthwise (1 cup)**
- 3 **ounces Gorgonzola cheese, crumbled (¾ cup)**
- ½ **cup pecans, toasted and chopped**

Whisk vinegar, oil, shallot, jam, ¼ teaspoon salt, and ¼ teaspoon pepper in large bowl. Toss fennel bulb with vinaigrette; let stand 15 minutes. Add arugula, fennel fronds, and grapes; toss and season with salt and pepper to taste. Divide salad among individual plates; top each with portion of Gorgonzola and pecans. Serve immediately.

Arugula Salad with Pear, Almonds, Goat Cheese, and Apricots

SERVES 6

Honey can be substituted for the apricot jam.

- 3 **tablespoons white wine vinegar**
- 1 **tablespoon apricot jam**
- ½ **cup dried apricots, chopped into ¼-inch pieces**
- 3 **tablespoons extra-virgin olive oil**
- 1 **small shallot, minced**
- ¼ **small red onion, sliced very thin**
  Salt and pepper
- 8 **ounces (8 cups) arugula**
- 1 **pear, halved, cored, and sliced into ¼-inch-thick slices**
- ⅓ **cup sliced almonds, toasted**
- 3 **ounces goat cheese, crumbled (¾ cup)**

1. Whisk vinegar and jam in microwave-safe bowl; stir in apricots. Cover with plastic wrap, cut several steam vents in plastic, and microwave until apricots are plump, 30 seconds to 1 minute. Whisk in oil, shallot, onion, ¼ teaspoon salt, and ⅛ teaspoon pepper; toss to combine. Let cool to room temperature.

2. Toss arugula, pear, and vinaigrette in large bowl; season with salt and pepper to taste. Divide salad among individual plates; top each with portion of almonds and goat cheese. Serve immediately.

Herbed Baked Goat Cheese Salad

✓ **WHY THIS RECIPE WORKS:** Warm goat cheese salad, a French classic, can often misfire, being nothing more than flavorless warm cheese melted onto limp greens. We wanted creamy cheese infused with the flavor of fresh herbs and surrounded by crisp, golden breading, all cradled in lightly dressed greens. For cheese rounds with an exceptionally crisp crust, we found that white Melba toast crumbs beat out other contenders like fresh bread crumbs and other cracker crumbs. Freezing the breaded goat cheese rounds for 30 minutes before baking them in a hot oven ensured a crunchy coating and a smooth, but not melted, interior. Just like in the finest French bistros, we served our warm, breaded goat cheese on hearty greens, lightly dressed with a classic vinaigrette.

Salad with Herbed Baked Goat Cheese and Vinaigrette

SERVES 6

Prepare the salad components while the cheese is in the freezer, then toss the greens and vinaigrette while the cheese cools a bit after baking. Hearty salad greens, such as a mix of arugula and frisée, work best here.

- 2 **tablespoons red wine vinegar**
- 1 **tablespoon Dijon mustard**
- 1 **teaspoon minced shallot**
- ¼ **teaspoon salt**
- 6 **tablespoons extra-virgin olive oil**
  Pepper
- 14 **ounces (14 cups) mixed hearty salad greens**
- 1 **recipe Herbed Baked Goat Cheese (recipe follows)**

1. Combine vinegar, mustard, shallot, and salt in small bowl. Whisking constantly, drizzle in oil; season with pepper to taste.

2. Place greens in large bowl, drizzle vinaigrette over, and toss to coat. Divide greens among individual plates; place 2 rounds warm goat cheese on each salad. Serve immediately.

Herbed Baked Goat Cheese

MAKES 12 ROUNDS

The baked goat cheese should be served warm.

- 3 **ounces white Melba toasts (2 cups)**
- 1 **teaspoon pepper**
- 3 **large eggs**
- 2 **tablespoons Dijon mustard**
- 1 **tablespoon minced fresh thyme**
- 1 **tablespoon minced fresh chives**
- 12 **ounces goat cheese, firm**
  Extra-virgin olive oil

1. Process Melba toasts in a food processor to fine even crumbs, about 1½ minutes; transfer crumbs to medium bowl and stir in pepper. Whisk eggs and mustard in another bowl until combined. Combine thyme and chives in small bowl.

2. Using kitchen twine or dental floss, divide cheese into 12 evenly sized pieces. Roll each piece into a ball; roll each ball in herbs to coat lightly. Transfer 6 pieces to egg mixture, turn each piece to coat; transfer to Melba crumbs and turn each piece to coat, pressing crumbs into cheese. Flatten each ball into disk about 1½ inches wide and 1 inch thick and set on baking sheet. Repeat process with remaining 6 pieces cheese. Freeze cheese until firm, about 30 minutes. (Cheese may be wrapped tightly in plastic wrap and frozen for 1 week.) Adjust oven rack to top position; heat oven to 475 degrees.

3. Remove cheese from freezer and brush tops and sides evenly with olive oil. Bake until crumbs are golden brown and cheese is slightly soft, 7 to 9 minutes (or 9 to 12 minutes if cheese is completely frozen). Using thin metal spatula, transfer cheese to paper towel–lined plate and let cool 3 minutes before serving on top of greens.

Salad with Apples, Walnuts, Dried Cherries, and Herbed Baked Goat Cheese

SERVES 6

Prepare the salad components while the cheese is in the freezer, then toss the greens and vinaigrette while the cheese cools a bit after baking. Hearty salad greens, such as a mix of arugula and frisée, work best here.

    1 cup dried cherries
    2 tablespoons cider vinegar
    1 tablespoon Dijon mustard
    1 teaspoon minced shallot
    ¼ teaspoon salt
    ¼ teaspoon sugar
    6 tablespoons extra-virgin olive oil
       Pepper
   14 ounces (14 cups) mixed hearty salad greens
    2 Granny Smith apples, cored, quartered, and cut
       into ⅛-inch-thick slices
    ½ cup walnuts, toasted and chopped
    1 recipe Herbed Baked Goat Cheese (page 497)

1. Plump cherries in ½ cup hot water in small bowl, about 10 minutes; drain.

2. Combine vinegar, mustard, shallot, salt, and sugar in small bowl. Whisking constantly, drizzle in oil; season with pepper to taste. Place greens in large bowl, drizzle vinaigrette over, and toss to coat. Divide greens among individual plates; divide cherries, apples, and walnuts among plates; and place 2 rounds warm goat cheese on each salad. Serve immediately.

Chopped Salad

✔ **WHY THIS RECIPE WORKS:** Chopped salads should be lively, thoughtfully chosen compositions of lettuce, vegetables, and perhaps fruit, cut into bite-size pieces, with nuts and cheese contributing flavor and texture. Too often, though, the salad is a bland mix of watery vegetables. To avoid a watery salad, we used techniques like seeding cucumbers and quartering tomatoes before salting them to expose more surface area to the salt. Equal parts oil and vinegar or lime juice delivered the bright acidic flavor we were looking for in our dressing. Briefly marinating the other ingredients in the dressing delivered an additional flavor boost.

Fennel and Apple Chopped Salad

SERVES 4

Pecans can be substituted for the walnuts. Good apple choices include Braeburn, Jonagold, and Red Delicious.

    1 cucumber, peeled, halved lengthwise, seeded, and
       cut into ½-inch dice
       Salt and pepper
    3 tablespoons extra-virgin olive oil
    3 tablespoons white wine vinegar
    1 fennel bulb, stalks discarded, bulb halved, cored, and
       cut into ¼-inch dice
    2 apples, cored and cut into ¼-inch dice
    ½ small red onion, chopped fine
    ¼ cup chopped fresh tarragon
    1 romaine lettuce heart (6 ounces), cut into ½-inch
       pieces
    ½ cup walnuts, toasted and chopped
    4 ounces goat cheese, crumbled (1 cup)

1. Combine cucumber and ½ teaspoon salt in colander set over bowl and let stand 15 minutes.

2. Whisk oil and vinegar together in large bowl. Add drained cucumber, fennel, apples, onion, and tarragon; toss and let stand at room temperature to blend flavors, about 5 minutes.

3. Add romaine and walnuts; toss to combine. Season with salt and pepper to taste. Divide salad among plates; top each with some goat cheese and serve.

Mediterranean Chopped Salad

SERVES 4

In-season cherry tomatoes can be substituted for the grape tomatoes.

    1 cucumber, peeled, halved lengthwise, seeded, and
       cut into ½-inch dice
   10 ounces grape tomatoes, quartered
       Salt and pepper
    3 tablespoons extra-virgin olive oil
    3 tablespoons red wine vinegar
    1 garlic clove, minced
    1 (14-ounce) can chickpeas, rinsed
    ½ cup pitted kalamata olives, chopped
    ½ small red onion, chopped fine
    ½ cup chopped fresh parsley
    1 romaine lettuce heart (6 ounces), cut into ½-inch
       pieces
    4 ounces feta cheese, crumbled (1 cup)

1. Combine cucumber, tomatoes, and 1 teaspoon salt in colander set over bowl and let stand 15 minutes.

2. Whisk oil, vinegar, and garlic together in large bowl. Add drained cucumber and tomatoes, chickpeas, olives, onion, and parsley; toss and let stand at room temperature to blend flavors, about 5 minutes.

3. Add romaine and feta; toss to combine. Season with salt and pepper to taste and serve.

Radish and Orange Chopped Salad

SERVES 4

Pepitas, or pumpkin seeds, are available at most supermarkets and natural foods stores.

- 1 **cucumber, peeled, halved lengthwise, seeded, and cut into ½-inch dice**
  Salt and pepper
- 3 **tablespoons extra-virgin olive oil**
- 3 **tablespoons lime juice (2 limes)**
- 1 **garlic clove, minced**
- 2 **oranges**
- 10 **radishes, halved and sliced thin**
- 1 **avocado, halved, pitted, and cut into ½-inch pieces**
- ½ **small red onion, chopped fine**
- ½ **cup fresh cilantro, chopped**
- 1 **romaine lettuce heart (6 ounces), cut into ½-inch pieces**
- 3 **ounces Manchego cheese, shredded (¾ cup)**
- ½ **cup unsalted pepitas, toasted**

1. Combine cucumber and ½ teaspoon salt in colander set over bowl and let stand 15 minutes. Whisk oil, lime juice, and garlic together in large bowl.

2. Peel oranges, making sure to remove all pith, and cut into ½-inch pieces. Add oranges, drained cucumber, radishes, avocado, onion, and cilantro; toss and let stand at room temperature to blend flavors, about 5 minutes.

3. Add romaine, Manchego, and pepitas; toss to combine. Season with salt and pepper to taste and serve.

Salad Niçoise

✔ **WHY THIS RECIPE WORKS:** The ideal salad niçoise should have well-dressed, well-seasoned components that complement rather than crowd one another. We paired fruity extra-virgin olive oil and lemon juice to create the base of the vinaigrette, then added fresh thyme, basil, and oregano, shallot, and Dijon mustard to deepen the flavor. We used only the finest tuna, vine-ripened tomatoes, butterhead lettuce, fresh green beans, freshly cooked eggs, and Red Bliss potatoes—and seasoned and dressed each component of the salad individually for great flavor in every forkful. Niçoise olives are a hallmark of salad niçoise. If they're not available, substitute another small, black, brined olive (do not use canned olives). Anchovies are another classic garnish, but they met with mixed reviews from our tasters, so they are optional. If you cannot find tuna packed in olive oil, substitute water-packed solid white tuna, not tuna packed in vegetable oil. Or use fresh tuna. For a grilled variation on our salad, we marinated tuna steaks in olive oil and then seasoned the tuna with salt and pepper before grilling them until they were medium-rare.

Salad Niçoise

SERVES 6

Prepare all the vegetables before you begin cooking the potatoes and this salad will come together very easily. Try to buy potatoes that are about 2 inches in diameter. Compose the salad on your largest, widest, flattest serving platter. Do not blanket the bed of lettuce with the other ingredients; leave some space between the mounds of potatoes, tomatoes and onions, and beans so that leaves of lettuce peek through.

VINAIGRETTE
- ¾ **cup extra-virgin olive oil**
- ½ **cup lemon juice (2 to 3 lemons)**
- 1 **shallot, minced**
- 2 **tablespoons chopped fresh basil**
- 1 **tablespoon minced fresh thyme**
- 2 **teaspoons minced fresh oregano**
- 1 **teaspoon Dijon mustard**
  Salt and pepper

SALAD
- 1¼ **pounds small red potatoes, quartered**
  Salt and pepper
- 2 **tablespoons dry vermouth**
- 2 **heads Boston or Bibb lettuce (1 pound), torn into bite-size pieces**
- 2 **(6-ounce) cans olive oil–packed tuna, drained**
- 3 **small tomatoes, cored and cut into eighths**
- 1 **small red onion, sliced very thin**
- 8 **ounces green beans, trimmed and halved crosswise**
- 4 **Hard-Cooked Eggs (page 80), peeled and quartered**
- ¼ **cup niçoise olives, pitted**
- 10–12 **anchovy fillets, rinsed (optional)**
- 2 **tablespoons capers, rinsed (optional)**

1. FOR THE VINAIGRETTE: Whisk oil, lemon juice, shallot, basil, thyme, oregano, and mustard in medium bowl; season with salt and pepper to taste and set aside.

2. FOR THE SALAD: Bring potatoes and 4 quarts cold water to boil in large Dutch oven or stockpot over high heat. Add 1 tablespoon salt and cook until potatoes are tender when poked with paring knife, 5 to 8 minutes. With slotted spoon, gently transfer potatoes to medium bowl (do not discard boiling water). Toss warm potatoes with vermouth and salt and pepper to taste; let stand 1 minute. Toss in ¼ cup vinaigrette; set aside.

3. While potatoes cook, toss lettuce with ¼ cup vinaigrette in large bowl until coated. Arrange bed of lettuce on very large, flat serving platter. Place tuna in now-empty bowl and break up with fork. Add ½ cup vinaigrette and stir to combine; mound tuna in center of lettuce. Toss tomatoes, onion, 3 tablespoons vinaigrette, and salt and pepper to taste in now-empty bowl; arrange tomato-onion mixture in mound at edge of lettuce bed. Arrange reserved potatoes in separate mound at edge of lettuce bed.

4. Return water to boil; add 1 tablespoon salt and green beans. Cook until tender but crisp, 3 to 5 minutes. Meanwhile, fill medium bowl with 1 quart water and 1 tray ice cubes. Drain beans, transfer to ice bath, and let stand until just cool, about 30 seconds; dry beans well on triple layer of paper towels. Toss beans, 3 tablespoons vinaigrette, and salt and pepper to taste in now-empty bowl; arrange in separate mound at edge of lettuce bed.

5. Arrange eggs, olives, and anchovies, if using, in separate mounds at edge of lettuce bed. Drizzle eggs with remaining 2 tablespoons dressing, sprinkle entire salad with capers, if using, and serve immediately.

Salad Niçoise with Grilled Fresh Tuna

1. Combine two 8-ounce tuna steaks, each about ¾ inch thick, with 2 tablespoons olive oil in 1-gallon zipper-lock bag; seal bag, place in refrigerator, and marinate, turning several times, for at least 1 hour or up to overnight. Remove tuna from bag, sprinkle with salt and pepper, and set aside.

2A. FOR A CHARCOAL GRILL: Open bottom vent completely. Light large chimney starter filled with charcoal briquettes (6 quarts). When top coals are partially covered with ash, pour evenly over half of grill. Set cooking grate in place, cover grill, and heat grill until hot, about 5 minutes.

2B. FOR A GAS GRILL: Turn all burners to high, cover, and heat grill until hot, about 15 minutes.

3. Clean cooking grate, then repeatedly brush grate with well-oiled paper towels until grate is black and glossy, 5 to 10 times. Grill fish (with lid down for gas grill) without moving until grill marks form and bottom surface is opaque, about 1½ minutes. Carefully flip, cooking until grill marks form on second side, about 1½ minutes longer for rare (opaque at perimeter and translucent red at center when checked with tip of paring knife) or 3 minutes for medium-rare (opaque at perimeter and reddish pink at center). Cut into ½-inch-thick slices. Substitute grilled tuna for canned tuna.

Cobb Salad

✔ **WHY THIS RECIPE WORKS:** Cobb salad's classic vinaigrette dressing is both the tie that binds the dish together and its biggest problem. More often than not, the flavors are dull and muted, with the salad components either drowned in puddles of liquid or sitting high and unhappily dry. Using Dijon mustard instead of dry powder and extra-virgin olive oil instead of the more common vegetable oil and water made a rich, well-seasoned dressing. Romaine lettuce lent crunch and watercress added flavor. For ease, we broiled the chicken breasts, and we used grape tomatoes instead of tasteless beefsteak tomatoes, plus plenty of avocado and blue cheese. Dressing each ingredient separately ensured that each was perfectly seasoned.

Cobb Salad

SERVES 6 TO 8

You'll need a large platter or shallow wide pasta bowl to accommodate this substantial salad. Though watercress is traditional, feel free to substitute an equal amount of arugula, chicory, curly endive, or a mixture of assertive lettuce greens. Grape tomatoes are preferred, but cherry tomatoes can be used. See Recipe Tutorial on page 486 for more details on this recipe.

VINAIGRETTE
- ½ cup extra-virgin olive oil
- 2 tablespoons red wine vinegar
- 2 teaspoons lemon juice
- 1 teaspoon Worcestershire sauce
- 1 teaspoon Dijon mustard
- 1 garlic clove, minced
- ½ teaspoon salt
- ¼ teaspoon sugar
- ⅛ teaspoon pepper

SALAD
- 3 (6-ounce) boneless, skinless chicken breasts, trimmed
  Salt and pepper
- 1 large head romaine lettuce (14 ounces), torn into bite-size pieces
- 4 ounces (4 ounces) watercress, torn into bite-size pieces
- 10 ounces grape tomatoes, halved
- 3 Hard-Cooked Eggs (page 80), peeled and cut into ½-inch cubes
- 2 avocados, halved, pitted, and cut into ½-inch pieces
- 8 slices bacon, cut into ¼-inch pieces, cooked in 10-inch skillet over medium heat until crisp, 5 to 7 minutes, and drained
- 2 ounces blue cheese, crumbled (½ cup)
- 3 tablespoons minced fresh chives

1. FOR THE VINAIGRETTE: Whisk all ingredients in medium bowl until well combined; set aside.

2. FOR THE SALAD: Season chicken with salt and pepper. Adjust oven rack to 6 inches from broiler element; heat broiler. Spray broiler pan top with vegetable oil spray; place chicken breasts on top and broil chicken until lightly browned, 4 to 8 minutes. Using tongs, flip chicken over and continue to broil until thickest part is no longer pink when cut into and registers about 160 degrees, 6 to 8 minutes. When cool enough to handle, cut chicken into ½-inch cubes and set aside.

3. Toss romaine and watercress with 5 tablespoons vinaigrette in large bowl until coated; arrange on very large, flat serving platter. Place chicken in now-empty bowl, add ¼ cup vinaigrette, and toss to coat; arrange in row along one edge of greens. Place tomatoes in now-empty bowl, add 1 tablespoon vinaigrette and toss gently to combine; arrange on opposite edge of greens. Arrange eggs and avocado in separate rows near center of greens and drizzle with remaining vinaigrette. Sprinkle bacon, cheese, and chives evenly over salad and serve.

Creamy Buttermilk Coleslaw

✔ **WHY THIS RECIPE WORKS:** We wanted a buttermilk coleslaw with crisp pieces of cabbage lightly coated with a flavorful buttermilk dressing that would cling to the cabbage instead of collecting in the bottom of the bowl. We found that salting and draining the cabbage removed excess water and wilted it to a pickle-crisp texture. For a dressing that was both hefty and tangy, we combined buttermilk, mayonnaise, and sour cream.

Creamy Buttermilk Coleslaw

SERVES 4

If you are planning to serve the coleslaw immediately, rinse the salted cabbage in a large bowl of ice water, drain it in a colander, pick out any ice cubes, then pat the cabbage dry before dressing.

- ½   **head red or green cabbage, cored and sliced thin (6 cups)**
     Salt and pepper
- 1   **carrot, peeled and shredded**
- ½   **cup buttermilk**
- 2   **tablespoons mayonnaise**
- 2   **tablespoons sour cream**
- 1   **small shallot, minced**
- 2   **tablespoons minced fresh parsley**
- ½   **teaspoon cider vinegar**
- ½   **teaspoon sugar**
- ¼   **teaspoon Dijon mustard**

1. Toss shredded cabbage and 1 teaspoon salt in colander or large-mesh strainer set over medium bowl. Let stand until cabbage wilts, at least 1 hour or up to 4 hours. Rinse cabbage under cold running water. Press, but do not squeeze, to drain; pat dry with paper towels. Place wilted cabbage and carrot in large bowl.

2. Stir buttermilk, mayonnaise, sour cream, shallot, parsley, vinegar, sugar, mustard, ¼ teaspoon salt, and ⅛ teaspoon pepper together in small bowl. Pour dressing over cabbage and toss to combine; refrigerate until chilled, about 30 minutes. (Coleslaw can be refrigerated for up to 3 days.)

Deli-Style Coleslaw

✔ **WHY THIS RECIPE WORKS:** For a deli-style slaw with crisp cabbage and a piquant dressing that wasn't too sharp, we salted the cabbage. Salting helps the cabbage exude its liquid, leaving the cabbage pickle-crisp. After a number of failed experiments with dressings, we decided to give low-acidity rice vinegar a try. We drizzled a bit over the mayonnaise-tossed cabbage and found its mild acidity perfect.

Deli-Style Coleslaw

SERVES 4

You can add ¼ teaspoon of either caraway or celery seeds with the mayonnaise and vinegar. You can shred, salt, rinse, and pat the cabbage dry a day ahead, but dress it close to serving time. See Core Technique on page 480 for more details on this recipe.

- ½   **head red or green cabbage, cored and shredded or chopped (6 cups)**
- 1   **large carrot, peeled and shredded**
     Salt and pepper
- ½   **small onion, chopped fine**
- ½   **cup mayonnaise**
- 2   **tablespoons rice vinegar**

1. Toss cabbage and carrot with 1 teaspoon salt in colander set over medium bowl. Let stand until cabbage wilts, at least 1 hour or up to 4 hours.

2. Pour draining liquid from bowl; rinse bowl and dry. Dump wilted cabbage and carrots into bowl. Rinse thoroughly in cold water (ice water if serving slaw immediately). Pour vegetables back into colander. Pat dry with paper towels. (Vegetables can be stored in zipper-lock bag and refrigerated overnight.)

3. Pour cabbage and carrots back again into bowl. Add onion, mayonnaise, and vinegar; toss to coat. Season with pepper to taste. Cover and refrigerate until ready to serve. (Coleslaw can be refrigerated for up to 1 day.)

Pasta Salad with Pesto

✔ **WHY THIS RECIPE WORKS:** At its best, pesto is fresh, green, and full of herbal flavor, but when incorporated into an American-style pasta salad, it can turn dull and muddy. We found that adding another green element—fresh baby spinach—provided the pesto with long-lasting color without interfering with the basil flavor. Adding mayonnaise to the pesto created the perfect binder, keeping the salad creamy and luscious and preventing it from clumping up and drying out.

Pasta Salad with Pesto

SERVES 8 TO 10

This salad is best served the day it is made; if it's been refrigerated, bring it to room temperature before serving. Garnish with additional shaved or grated Parmesan.

- ¾   **cup pine nuts**
- 2   **garlic cloves, unpeeled**
     Salt
- 1   **pound farfalle**
- 5   **tablespoons extra-virgin olive oil**
- 3   **cups fresh basil leaves**
- 1   **ounce (1 cup) baby spinach**
- ½   **teaspoon pepper**
- 2   **tablespoons lemon juice**
- 1½ **ounces Parmesan cheese, grated fine (¾ cup), plus extra for serving**
- 6   **tablespoons mayonnaise**
- 12 **ounces cherry tomatoes, quartered, or grape tomatoes, halved (optional)**

1. Bring 4 quarts water to boil in large pot. Toast pine nuts in small dry skillet over medium heat, shaking pan occasionally, until just golden and fragrant, 4 to 5 minutes.

2. When water is boiling, add garlic and let cook 1 minute. Remove garlic with slotted spoon and rinse under cold water to stop cooking; set aside and let cool. Add pasta and 1 tablespoon salt to water and cook, stirring often, until tender (just past al dente). Reserve ¼ cup cooking water, drain pasta, toss with 1 tablespoon oil, spread in single layer on rimmed baking sheet, and let cool to room temperature, about 30 minutes.

3. When garlic is cool, peel and mince or press through garlic press. Place ¼ cup nuts, garlic, basil, spinach, pepper, lemon juice, remaining ¼ cup oil, and 1 teaspoon salt in bowl of food processor and process until smooth, scraping sides of bowl as necessary. Add Parmesan and mayonnaise and process until thoroughly combined. Transfer mixture to large serving bowl. Cover and refrigerate until ready to assemble salad.

4. When pasta is cool, toss with pesto, adding reserved pasta water, 1 tablespoon at a time, until pesto evenly coats pasta. Fold in remaining ½ cup nuts and tomatoes, if using; serve with extra Parmesan.

Tabbouleh

✔ **WHY THIS RECIPE WORKS:** In the Middle East, tabbouleh is basically a parsley salad with bulgur rather than the bulgur salad with parsley that is frequently found in the United States. Perfect tabbouleh should be tossed in a penetrating, minty lemon dressing with bits of ripe tomato. For the parsley, we found that either type—flat-leaf "Italian" or curly-leaf—made an acceptable salad. As for processing the bulgur, the all-out winning method simply involved rinsing and then mixing it with fresh lemon juice. The mixture is then set aside to allow the juice to be absorbed. When treated in this way, bulgur acquires a fresh and intense flavor, but without the heaviness that the added olive oil produces. Finally, we liked a ratio of 5 parts parsley to 3 or 4 parts grain. When we tried increasing the parsley, the wholesome goodness of the wheat was lost.

Tabbouleh
SERVES 4 TO 6
Middle Eastern cooks frequently serve this salad with the crisp inner leaves of romaine lettuce, using them as spoons to scoop the salad from the serving dish.

- ½ cup bulgur, fine or medium grind, rinsed and drained
- ⅓ cup lemon juice (2 lemons)
- ⅓ cup olive oil
  Salt
- ⅛ teaspoon cayenne pepper (optional)
- 2 cups minced fresh parsley
- 2 tomatoes, cored, halved, seeded, and cut into very small dice
- 4 scallions, minced
- 2 tablespoons minced fresh mint or 1 teaspoon dried

1. Mix bulgur with ¼ cup lemon juice in medium bowl; set aside until grains are tender and fluffy, 20 to 40 minutes, depending on age and type of bulgur.

2. Mix remaining lemon juice, olive oil, salt to taste, and cayenne, if desired. Mix bulgur, parsley, tomatoes, scallions, and mint; add dressing and toss to combine. Cover and refrigerate to let flavors blend, 1 to 2 hours. Serve.

All-American Potato Salad

✔ **WHY THIS RECIPE WORKS:** Classic potato salad is too often blanketed in a mayonnaise-rich dressing that results in bland flavor. We were looking for flavorful, tender potatoes punctuated by crunchy bits of onion and celery. We found that seasoning the potatoes while they're hot maximizes flavor, so we tossed hot russet potatoes with white vinegar. A conservative hand with the mayonnaise made for a creamy, but not soupy, salad. In the crunch department, celery is a must, and one rib fit the bill. Among scallions, shallots, and red, yellow, white, and Vidalia onions, red onion was the winner for its bright color and taste. For a pickled flavor, we decided on pickle relish, which requires no preparation and gives the potato salad a subtle sweetness. We tested celery seeds, a seasoning that has fallen out of favor; celery seeds didn't merely add strong celery flavor but also provided an underlying complexity and depth.

All-American Potato Salad
SERVES 4 TO 6
Note that this recipe calls for celery seeds, not celery salt; if only celery salt is available, use the same amount but omit the addition of salt in the dressing. When testing the potatoes for doneness, simply taste a piece; do not overcook the potatoes or they will become mealy and will break apart. The potatoes must be just warm, or even fully cooled, when you add the dressing. If the potato salad seems a little dry, add up to 2 tablespoons more mayonnaise.

- 2 pounds russet potatoes, peeled and cut into ¾-inch cubes
  Salt
- 2 tablespoons distilled white vinegar
- 1 celery rib, chopped fine
- ½ cup mayonnaise
- 3 tablespoons sweet pickle relish
- 2 tablespoons finely chopped red onion
- 2 tablespoons minced fresh parsley
- ¾ teaspoon dry mustard
- ¾ teaspoon celery seeds
- ¼ teaspoon pepper
- 2 Hard-Cooked Eggs (page 80), peeled and cut into ¼-inch cubes (optional)

1. Place potatoes in large saucepan and add water to cover by 1 inch. Bring to boil over medium-high heat; add 1 tablespoon salt, reduce heat to medium, and simmer, stirring once or twice, until potatoes are tender, about 8 minutes.

2. Drain potatoes and transfer to large bowl. Add vinegar and, using rubber spatula, toss gently to combine. Let stand until potatoes are just warm, about 20 minutes.

3. Meanwhile, in small bowl, stir together celery, mayonnaise, relish, onion, parsley, mustard, celery seeds, pepper, and ½ teaspoon salt. Using rubber spatula, gently fold dressing and eggs, if using, into potatoes. Cover with plastic wrap and refrigerate until chilled, about 1 hour; serve. (Potato salad can be refrigerated for up to 1 day.)

French Potato Salad

☑ **WHY THIS RECIPE WORKS:** French potato salad should be pleasing not only to the eye but also to the palate. The potatoes (small red potatoes are traditional) should be tender but not mushy, and the flavor of the vinaigrette should penetrate the relatively bland potatoes. To eliminate torn skins and broken slices, a common pitfall in boiling skin-on red potatoes, we sliced the potatoes before boiling them. Then to evenly infuse the potatoes with the garlicky mustard vinaigrette, we spread the warm potatoes out on a baking sheet and poured the vinaigrette over the top. Gently folding in fresh herbs just before serving helped keep the potatoes intact.

French Potato Salad with Dijon Mustard and Fines Herbes

SERVES 6

If fresh chervil isn't available, substitute an additional ½ tablespoon of minced parsley and an additional ½ teaspoon of minced tarragon. For best flavor, serve the salad warm. See Recipe Tutorial on page 490 for more details on this recipe.

- 2 **pounds small red potatoes, unpeeled, cut into ¼-inch-thick slices**
- 2 **tablespoons salt**
- 1 **garlic clove, peeled and threaded on skewer**
- 1½ **tablespoons champagne vinegar or white wine vinegar**
- 2 **teaspoons Dijon mustard**
- ¼ **cup olive oil**
- ½ **teaspoon pepper**
- 1 **small shallot, minced**
- 1 **tablespoon minced fresh chervil**
- 1 **tablespoon minced fresh parsley**
- 1 **tablespoon minced fresh chives**
- 1 **teaspoon minced fresh tarragon**

1. Place potatoes and salt in large saucepan and add water to cover by 1 inch; bring to boil over high heat, then reduce heat to medium. Lower skewered garlic into simmering water and partially blanch, about 45 seconds. Immediately run garlic under cold running water to stop cooking; remove garlic from skewer and set aside. Continue to simmer potatoes, uncovered, until tender but still firm (thin-bladed paring knife can be slipped into and out of center of potato slice with no resistance), about 5 minutes. Drain potatoes, reserving ¼ cup cooking water. Arrange hot potatoes close together in single layer on rimmed baking sheet.

2. Press garlic through garlic press or mince by hand. Whisk garlic, reserved potato cooking water, vinegar, mustard, oil, and pepper in small bowl until combined. Drizzle dressing evenly over warm potatoes; let stand 10 minutes.

3. Toss shallot and herbs in small bowl. Transfer potatoes to large serving bowl; add shallot-herb mixture and mix gently with rubber spatula to combine. Serve immediately.

TO MAKE AHEAD: Follow recipe through step 2, cover with plastic wrap, and refrigerate for up to 2 hours. Before serving, bring salad to room temperature, then add shallots and herbs.

French Potato Salad with Arugula, Roquefort, and Walnuts

Omit herbs and toss dressed potatoes with ½ cup walnuts, toasted and chopped coarse, 4 ounces Roquefort cheese, crumbled, and 3 cups baby arugula, torn into bite-size pieces along with the shallots in step 3.

French Potato Salad with Fennel, Tomato, and Olives

When chopping the fennel fronds, use only the delicate wispy leaves, not the tough, fibrous stems to which they are attached.

Trim stalks and fronds from 1 small fennel bulb; roughly chop and reserve ¼ cup fronds. Halve bulb lengthwise; using paring knife, core 1 half of bulb, reserving second half for another use. Cut half crosswise into very thin slices. Omit chervil, chives, and tarragon, and increase parsley to 3 tablespoons. Toss dressed potatoes with sliced fennel and chopped fennel fronds, 1 tomato, peeled, seeded, and diced medium, and ¼ cup oil-cured black olives, pitted and quartered, with shallots and parsley in step 3.

French Potato Salad with Radishes, Cornichons, and Capers

Omit herbs and substitute 2 tablespoons finely chopped red onion for shallot. Toss dressed potatoes with 2 thinly sliced red radishes, ¼ cup capers, rinsed, and ¼ cup cornichons, thinly sliced, along with red onion in step 3.

Classic Chicken Salad

☑ **WHY THIS RECIPE WORKS:**
Recipes for chicken salad are only as good as the chicken. If the chicken is dry or flavorless, no amount of dressing or add-in will camouflage it. To ensure silky, juicy, and flavorful chicken, we used a method based on *sous vide* cooking (submerging vacuum-sealed foods in a temperature-controlled water bath). Our ideal formula was four chicken breasts and 6 cups of cold water heated to 170 degrees and then removed from the heat, covered, and left to stand for about 15 minutes. Incomparably moist, this chicken was perfect for our salad.

Classic Chicken Salad

SERVES 4 TO 6

To ensure that the chicken cooks through, don't use breasts that weigh more than 8 ounces or are thicker than 1 inch. Make sure to start with cold water in step 1. This salad can be served in a sandwich or spooned over leafy greens. See Core Technique on page 481 for more details on this recipe.

- **Salt and pepper**
- 4 **(6- to 8-ounce) boneless, skinless chicken breasts, no more than 1 inch thick, trimmed**
- ½ **cup mayonnaise**
- 2 **tablespoons lemon juice**
- 1 **teaspoon Dijon mustard**
- 2 **celery ribs, minced**
- 1 **shallot, minced**
- 1 **tablespoon minced fresh parsley**
- 1 **tablespoon minced fresh tarragon**

1. Dissolve 2 tablespoons salt in 6 cups cold water in Dutch oven. Submerge chicken in water. Heat pot over medium heat until water registers 170 degrees. Turn off heat, cover pot, and let stand until chicken registers 165 degrees, 15 to 17 minutes.

2. Transfer chicken to paper towel–lined rimmed baking sheet. Refrigerate until chicken is cool, about 30 minutes. While chicken cools, whisk mayonnaise, lemon juice, mustard, and ¼ teaspoon pepper together in large bowl.

3. Pat chicken dry with paper towels and cut into ½-inch pieces. Transfer chicken to bowl with mayonnaise mixture. Add celery, shallot, parsley, and tarragon; toss to combine. Season with salt and pepper to taste. Serve. (Salad can be refrigerated for up to 2 days.)

Curried Chicken Salad with Cashews

SERVES 4 TO 6

To ensure that the chicken cooks through, start with cold water in step 1 and don't use breasts that weigh more than 8 ounces or are thicker than 1 inch. This salad can be served in a sandwich or spooned over leafy greens.

>   Salt and pepper
> 4 (6- to 8-ounce) boneless, skinless chicken breasts, no more than 1 inch thick, trimmed
> 1 teaspoon vegetable oil
> 1 teaspoon curry powder
> ⅛ teaspoon cayenne pepper
> ½ cup mayonnaise
> 2 tablespoons lime juice
> 1 teaspoon grated fresh ginger
> 2 celery ribs, minced
> 1 shallot, minced
> ½ cup raw cashews, toasted and chopped coarse
> ⅓ cup golden raisins
> 2 tablespoons minced fresh cilantro

1. Dissolve 2 tablespoons salt in 6 cups cold water in Dutch oven. Submerge chicken in water. Heat pot over medium heat until water registers 170 degrees. Turn off heat, cover pot, and let stand until chicken registers 165 degrees, 15 to 17 minutes.

2. Transfer chicken to paper towel–lined rimmed baking sheet. Refrigerate until chicken is cool, about 30 minutes. While chicken cools, microwave vegetable oil, curry powder, and cayenne, uncovered, until oil is hot, about 30 seconds. Whisk mayonnaise, lime juice, ginger, and curry mixture together in large bowl.

3. Pat chicken dry with paper towels and cut into ½-inch pieces. Transfer chicken to bowl with mayonnaise mixture. Add celery, shallot, cashews, raisins, and cilantro; toss to combine. Season with salt and pepper to taste. Serve. (Salad can be refrigerated for up to 2 days.)

Chicken Salad with Red Grapes and Smoked Almonds

SERVES 4 TO 6

To ensure that the chicken cooks through, start with cold water in step 1 and don't use breasts that weigh more than 8 ounces or are thicker than 1 inch. This salad can be served in a sandwich or spooned over leafy greens.

>   Salt and pepper
> 4 (6- to 8-ounce) boneless, skinless chicken breasts, no more than 1 inch thick, trimmed
> ½ cup mayonnaise
> ¼ teaspoon finely grated lemon zest plus 2 tablespoons juice
> 1 teaspoon Dijon mustard
> 2 celery ribs, minced
> 1 shallot, minced
> 6 ounces seedless red grapes, quartered (1 cup)
> ½ cup smoked almonds, chopped coarse
> 1 tablespoon minced fresh parsley
> 1 teaspoon minced fresh rosemary

1. Dissolve 2 tablespoons salt in 6 cups cold water in Dutch oven. Submerge chicken in water. Heat pot over medium heat until water registers 170 degrees. Turn off heat, cover pot, and let stand until chicken registers 165 degrees, 15 to 17 minutes.

2. Transfer chicken to paper towel–lined rimmed baking sheet. Refrigerate until chicken is cool, about 30 minutes. While chicken cools, whisk mayonnaise, lemon zest and juice, mustard, and ¼ teaspoon pepper together in large bowl.

3. Pat chicken dry with paper towels and cut into ½-inch pieces. Transfer chicken to bowl with mayonnaise mixture. Add celery, shallot, grapes, almonds, parsley, and rosemary; toss to combine. Season with salt and pepper to taste. Serve. (Salad can be refrigerated for up to 2 days.)

The Best Tuna Salad

WHY THIS RECIPE WORKS: Even a simple tuna salad has its problems. It can be simultaneously watery and chalky, flavorless, drowning in mayonnaise, or overpowered by raw onion. There are nearly as many tuna choices at the supermarket as there are fish in the sea. Canned solid white tuna can be somewhat chalky and dry, so we pressed the tuna dry, then marinated it in oil for 10 minutes. Adding the seasoning to the oil, rather than stirring it in along with the mayo, really infused the tuna with flavor. To soften the onion's harsh flavor, the easiest solution was microwaving it in the oil for a couple of minutes before adding the seasoning and tuna. To finish, all our tuna salad needed was some celery for crunch.

The Best Tuna Salad

MAKES 2 CUPS, ENOUGH FOR 4 SANDWICHES

Do not use chunk light tuna in this recipe. Our favorite brand of canned tuna is Wild Planet Wild Albacore Tuna. If you can't find it, use canned solid white albacore tuna packed in water. See Core Technique on page 482 for more details on this recipe.

> 3 (5-ounce) cans solid white albacore tuna
> ¼ cup finely chopped onion
> 2 tablespoons olive oil
> 2 teaspoons lemon juice
>   Salt and pepper
> ½ teaspoon sugar
> ½ cup plus 2 tablespoons mayonnaise
> 1 celery rib, chopped fine

1. Place tuna in fine-mesh strainer and press dry with paper towels. Transfer to medium bowl and mash with fork until finely flaked.

2. Microwave onion and oil in separate bowl until onion begins to soften, about 2 minutes. Cool slightly, about 5 minutes. Add onion mixture, lemon juice, ½ teaspoon salt, ½ teaspoon pepper, and sugar to tuna, stir to combine, and let sit 10 minutes.

3. Stir mayonnaise and celery into tuna mixture. Season with salt and pepper to taste and serve. (Salad can be refrigerated for up to 1 day.)

Tuna Salad with Sweet Pickle and Egg

Add ¼ cup sweet pickle relish to tuna with onion mixture. Stir 2 chopped hard-cooked eggs (page 80) into salad with mayonnaise.

Tuna Salad with Lemon and Dill

Increase lemon juice to 1 tablespoon. Add ½ teaspoon grated lemon zest and 1 tablespoon minced fresh dill to tuna with onion mixture.

Tuna Salad with Roasted Red Peppers and Capers

Add ¼ cup finely chopped jarred roasted red peppers, patted dry, and 2 tablespoons rinsed and minced capers to tuna with onion mixture.

Shrimp Salad

◑ **WHY THIS RECIPE WORKS:** Great shrimp salad should possess firm and tender shrimp and a perfect deli-style dressing that complements, but does not mask, the flavor of the shrimp or drown out the other ingredients. We started by cooking the shrimp in cold court bouillon, then heated the shrimp and liquid to just a near simmer. We kept the traditional mayonnaise in our shrimp salad recipe, but limited the amount to ¼ cup per pound of shrimp. We prefer milder minced shallot over onion and minced celery for its subtle flavor and crunch.

Shrimp Salad
SERVES 4

This recipe can also be prepared with large shrimp (26 to 30 per pound); the cooking time will be 1 to 2 minutes less. The shrimp can be cooked up to 24 hours in advance, but hold off on dressing the salad until ready to serve. The recipe can be easily doubled; cook the shrimp in a 7-quart Dutch oven and increase the cooking time to 12 to 14 minutes. Serve the salad over greens or on buttered and grilled buns.

    1 **pound extra-large shrimp (21 to 25 per pound),
       peeled, deveined, and tails removed**
    5 **tablespoons lemon juice (2 lemons), spent halves
       reserved**

    5 **sprigs fresh parsley plus 1 teaspoon minced**
    3 **sprigs fresh tarragon plus 1 teaspoon minced**
    1 **teaspoon black peppercorns**
    1 **tablespoon sugar**
       Salt and pepper
    ¼ **cup mayonnaise**
    1 **small shallot, minced**
    1 **small celery rib, minced**

1. Combine shrimp, ¼ cup lemon juice, reserved lemon halves, parsley sprigs, tarragon sprigs, peppercorns, sugar, and 1 teaspoon salt with 2 cups cold water in medium saucepan. Place saucepan over medium heat and cook shrimp, stirring several times, until pink, firm to touch, and centers are no longer translucent, 8 to 10 minutes (water should be just bubbling around edge of pan and register 165 degrees). Remove pan from heat, cover, and let shrimp sit in broth for 2 minutes.

2. Meanwhile, fill medium bowl with 1 quart water and 4 cups ice cubes. Drain shrimp into colander, discard lemon halves, herbs, and spices. Immediately transfer shrimp to ice bath to stop cooking and chill thoroughly, about 3 minutes. Remove shrimp from ice bath and pat dry with paper towels.

3. Whisk together mayonnaise, shallot, celery, remaining 1 tablespoon lemon juice, minced parsley, and minced tarragon in medium bowl. Cut shrimp in half lengthwise and then cut each half into thirds; add shrimp to mayonnaise mixture and toss to combine. Season with salt and pepper to taste and serve. (Shrimp salad can be refrigerated overnight.)

Shrimp Salad with Roasted Red Pepper and Basil

Omit tarragon sprigs from cooking liquid. Replace celery, minced parsley, and minced tarragon with ⅓ cup thinly sliced jarred roasted red peppers, 2 teaspoons rinsed capers, and 3 tablespoons chopped fresh basil.

Shrimp Salad with Avocado and Orange

Omit tarragon sprigs from cooking liquid. Replace celery, minced parsley, and minced tarragon with 4 halved and thinly sliced radishes; 1 large orange, peeled and cut into ½-inch pieces; ½ avocado, halved, pitted, and cut into ½-inch pieces; and 2 teaspoons minced fresh mint.

Spicy Shrimp Salad with Corn and Chipotle

Substitute lime juice (3 to 4 limes; save spent halves) for lemon juice and omit tarragon sprigs from cooking liquid. Replace celery, minced parsley, and minced tarragon with ½ cup cooked corn kernels, 2 tablespoons minced canned chipotle chile in adobo sauce, and 1 tablespoon minced fresh cilantro.

Shrimp Salad with Wasabi and Pickled Ginger

Omit tarragon sprigs from cooking liquid. Replace shallot, minced parsley, and minced tarragon with 2 thinly sliced scallions, 2 tablespoons chopped pickled ginger, 1 tablespoon toasted sesame seeds, and 2 teaspoons wasabi powder.

Inside This Chapter

How to Make Quick Breads

This chapter includes a broad range of recipes—everything from pancakes and waffles to banana bread and blueberry scones. The term "quick bread" indicates that these recipes are leavened with baking powder and/or baking soda, rather than with the yeast used in the breads and pizzas in chapter 13 (see page 541). And while a muffin might not appear to have much in common with pancakes, there are some underlying principles that unite the recipes in this chapter.

Getting Started

Types of Quick Breads

In terms of appearance, quick breads vary considerably, from items we think of as "breads" that are baked in a loaf pan (banana bread) to individually baked items (muffins and biscuits). We also include pancakes and waffles in this category. Even though their "baking" methods are quite different, waffle and pancake batters are prepared in a similar fashion to other quick breads.

It's helpful to understand the two basic methods used to prepare the baked goods in this chapter. The quick bread method combines liquid ingredients in one bowl, and dry ingredients in a second bowl. The wet ingredients are then folded into the dry ingredients with a rubber spatula. A gentle hand is required, as overmixing will cause excess gluten development and lead to toughness in the final product. This method is used to prepare most muffins, loaf-style quick breads, pancakes, and waffles.

The biscuit method is similar to the process used to make pie dough because small chunks of cold fat (usually butter, but sometimes butter and shortening) are cut into the dry ingredients. As with pie dough, we use the food processor to do this. The dairy element (milk or buttermilk) is folded into the mixture, which is then lightly handled, rolled, and cut. The goal here is to minimize working the dough so that the butter chunks remain intact and lead to a flaky texture in the final product. This method is used to prepare many biscuits and scones.

Essential Equipment

Several key pieces of equipment needed to prepare quick breads is covered extensively in chapter 1. See pages 20–22 for information on rimmed baking sheets, cast-iron skillets, and nonstick skillets, and pages 26–27 for information on loaf pans and muffin tins. In addition to these items, many quick breads rely on additional pieces of equipment.

BISCUIT CUTTER

Makeshift cutters such as juice glasses produce rounds that rise unevenly. Use real biscuit cutters to avoid this problem. Buy a set (so you can make biscuits in various sizes) or pick up a single 2½-inch cutter (the classic size for biscuits).

BENCH SCRAPER

Bread bakers rely on metal bench scrapers—broad, slightly blunt blades with handles that span the length of the metal—to cut through plump rounds of yeast bread or biscuit dough or to scrape sticky dough loose from the counter. Avoid models with uncomfortable metal handles. A good metal blade is essential, and a plastic, rubber, or nylon grip is preferable. Ruler marks on the blade are handy but not essential.

PORTION SCOOP

Portion scoops (basically ice cream scoops that come in varying sizes) are a great way to portion muffin batter or drop biscuits. Scoop numbers (stamped on the handle or spring-loaded trigger) correspond to the number of level scoops it takes to equal 32 fluid ounces. A #16 scoop holds 2 fluid ounces (or ¼ cup). In the test kitchen, we use this size as well as the #12 scoop (about ⅓ cup) and #8 scoop (½ cup). A regular spring-loaded ice cream scoop can be used instead.

PARCHMENT PAPER

Don't try to bake biscuits, scones, or other quick breads on a rimmed baking sheet that hasn't been lined with a piece of parchment. Not only does parchment eliminate the risk of sticking, but it also speeds cleanup. White and brown paper work equally well. If you bake a lot, order flat sheets cut to fit baking sheets so you can avoid having to uncurl the rolls.

ELECTRIC GRIDDLE

If you routinely prepare breakfast for a crowd, an electric griddle can be a timesaver. The broad cooking surface allows you to cook enough pancakes for an army. There's no point buying a small model; look for something that measures at least 20 by 12 inches. A system for draining grease, especially if you want to cook bacon, is important. Consistent heating from edge to edge is essential.

WAFFLE IRON

You can't make waffles without an iron. Whether you like American-style irons that produce thinner waffles with shallow indentations or Belgian-style irons that produce thicker waffles with deeper pockets, look for a model with variable heat control. We prefer models with an audible signal that tells you when the iron is hot and when the waffles are done.

Essential Ingredients

Quick breads rely on the standard baking ingredients—flour, sugar, butter, and eggs. By definition, all quick breads contain baking powder and/or baking soda to ensure a quick rise. For more information on the difference between these two chemical leaveners, see page 44. Also, many quick breads contain buttermilk—it not only adds good flavor, but it reacts with the baking soda to produce an especially light crumb (a big concern in rich loaves that don't contain any yeast). For more information on buttermilk and buttermilk substitutes, see pages 40 and 45.

Tips for Better Quick Breads

These tips will help you produce top-quality biscuits, scones, muffins, loaf-style quick breads, pancakes, and waffles.

JUDGING DONENESS IN QUICK BREADS

There are two ways to judge doneness in quick breads. Fully baked items should feel springy and resilient when the center is gently pressed. If your finger leaves an impression—or if the center jiggles—the item is not done. This works best with biscuits, scones, and loaf-style quick breads. The other option is to insert a skewer or toothpick into the center of the item; it should emerge fairly clean, with perhaps just a few crumbs attached. If you see moist batter, the item needs to bake longer. This test works well with muffins and loaf breads.

MAKING HALF BATCHES OF MUFFINS

It's commonly taught that if you are making a half batch of muffins or cupcakes and thus don't fill all the cups in the pan with batter, you should fill the empty cups with water. Proponents of this practice contend that filling empty cups with water serves two functions: preventing the pan from warping, and acting as a "heat sink" to ensure that muffins next to empty cups heat evenly (avoiding stunted growth or spotty browning). Sounds good, but in our tests we found that it makes no difference whether you fill the empty cups with water. Go ahead and fill six cups, leaving the others empty. The muffins will turn out just fine.

MAKING MINI MUFFINS

A recipe that yields 12 muffins can generally be converted to yield 36 mini muffins. Simply fill each cup in the mini muffin tins with a scant 2 tablespoons of batter and bake as directed, reducing the baking time to 10 to 15 minutes.

MAKING MINIATURE LOAVES

Mini loaf pans come in many forms, from the connected four-loaf pans available in gourmet shops and specialty catalogs to inexpensive decorative pans and the disposable aluminum pans available at just about every supermarket. These pans turn out small loaves that make great gifts for friends and neighbors, especially around the holidays. Most of these pans hold 2 cups of batter. A standard loaf-style quick bread recipe will make four mini loaves. Simply divide the batter evenly among four greased 2-cup loaf pans and bake as directed, reducing the baking time to about 35 minutes.

TURNING LOAF-STYLE QUICK BREADS INTO MUFFINS

Cornbread, banana bread, cranberry-nut bread, and date-nut bread can all be turned into muffins. Prepare the batter as directed and portion it into a greased standard 12-cup muffin tin. Bake on the middle rack at the oven temperature specified in the recipe. The muffins will be done in a little less than half the time it takes to bake the original loaf version. When a toothpick inserted in the center comes out with just a few crumbs attached, the muffins are done. For even baking, rotate the muffin tin halfway through the baking time.

STORING QUICK BREADS AND MUFFINS

Most leftover biscuits, scones, and muffins can be stored in a zipper-lock bag at room temperature for up to three days. If the leftover quick breads include perishable flavorings like bacon, it is best to refrigerate them, but in general the refrigerator causes baked goods to dry out and so is not our first choice for storage. When ready to serve, refresh quick breads by placing them on a baking sheet and warming them in a 300-degree oven for about 10 minutes.

KEEPING PANCAKES AND WAFFLES WARM

If you want to serve pancakes and waffles all at once, start by greasing a wire rack with vegetable oil spray, then fit it inside a rimmed baking sheet. Place the prepared rack and baking sheet in the oven and turn the heat to 200 degrees. Place the pancakes or waffles on the rack as they are done, making sure not to overlap them. To keep waffles from drying out, cover them with a dish towel, removing the towel only when the last waffle goes into the oven. After a few more minutes in the oven, all the waffles (held for about 30 minutes total) will be perfectly recrisped.

FREEZING LEFTOVER PANCAKES AND WAFFLES

To freeze leftover pancakes, cool the pancakes to room temperature, then wrap them individually in plastic wrap and freeze for up to one month. When ready to serve, unwrap and spread them out on a wire rack set on top of a baking sheet, let thaw on the counter for 15 minutes, then reheat in a 350-degree oven until warm, 5 to 8 minutes.

To freeze leftover waffles, cool the waffles to room temperature, then wrap them individually in plastic wrap and freeze for up to one month. When ready to serve, unwrap and toast the frozen waffles (do not thaw) in a toaster until crispy and hot, about 3 minutes.

How to Make Biscuits

Nobody wants to make biscuits that are lumpy, leaden, lopsided, squat, or doughy, but many people do. What's the secret to light and fluffy biscuits that rise high every time? We think a mix of butter and shortening delivers the best combination of flavor and texture. Because shortening is pure fat (butter contains fat and water), it makes biscuits especially light and tender. If you use all butter, you will sacrifice some rise and tenderness. Below we make plain biscuits; you can add ½–¾ cup shredded cheese, 2 thinly sliced scallions (green parts only), 1 teaspoon coarsely ground black pepper, or ½ teaspoon to 2 tablespoons minced fresh herbs (vary according to the intensity of the herb) to the dough just before adding the buttermilk. See some of our preferred flavor combinations on page 530. Biscuits are best served warm. If you want to work ahead, you can refrigerate the cut rounds on the baking sheet, covered with plastic wrap, for up to a day ahead. To bake, just preheat the oven to 450 degrees and proceed with the recipe.

ESSENTIAL EQUIPMENT

- chef's knife
- food processor
- mixing bowl
- liquid measuring cup
- rubber spatula
- rolling pin
- 2½-inch biscuit cutter
- rimmed baking sheet
- parchment paper

1. CHILL THE FAT

Cut 8 tablespoons unsalted butter and 4 tablespoons vegetable shortening into ½-inch pieces and refrigerate until well chilled, about 30 minutes.

WHY? Start by cutting the butter and shortening into small pieces that will be easy to cut into the dry ingredients. The colder the fat, the more likely the final dough will contain small chunks of fat, which create steam in the oven and result in a flakier texture in the finished biscuits.

2. CUT FAT INTO FLOUR

Pulse 3 cups (15 ounces) all-purpose flour, 1 tablespoon sugar, 1 tablespoon baking powder, 1 teaspoon salt, and ½ teaspoon baking soda in food processor until combined, about 5 pulses. Scatter chilled butter and shortening over dry ingredients and pulse until mixture resembles coarse meal, about 15 pulses.

WHY? The blades of a food processor cut the fat into the dry ingredients quickly and without warming the butter (unlike using your fingers). Don't overprocess the mixture or the biscuits will be crumbly.

3. ADD BUTTERMILK BY HAND

Transfer mixture to large bowl and gently stir in 1¼ cups buttermilk until dough forms.

WHY? Stirring the liquid into the flour mixture by hand ensures that the dough is uniformly combined but prevents overmixing (which can happen if you attempt to do this in the food processor). If you don't have buttermilk on hand, combine 1¼ cups whole or low-fat milk and 1 tablespoon plus ¾ teaspoon lemon juice in measuring cup. This mixture will curdle slightly and will offer a decent approximation of buttermilk.

4. KNEAD FOR TALLER BISCUITS

Turn dough out onto lightly floured counter and knead briefly, 8 to 10 times, to form smooth, cohesive ball.

WHY? It is important to knead the dough to develop the gluten, which helps to produce tall biscuits. But don't overdo the kneading—once the dough is cohesive you should stop.

5. ROLL OUT DOUGH

Roll dough into 9-inch circle, about ¾ inch thick.

WHY? A rolling pin ensures that the dough has a uniform height and is a better option than patting the dough by hand.

6. STAMP, DON'T TWIST

Dip 2½-inch round biscuit cutter in flour and cut out biscuits using stamping motion. Dip cutter in flour before each cut. Gather scraps of dough, pat into ¾-inch-thick circle, and stamp out remaining biscuits.

WHY? Do not twist the cutter as you stamp, or the biscuits will bake up lopsided. (The twisting action presses together the layers of fat and flour in the dough.) Flouring the cutter ensures that it won't stick to the dough, which can also cause biscuits to bake up lopsided. Cut biscuits as closely together as possible; the biscuits made from the scraps are never as tender or as pretty as those cut from the smooth round of dough. Don't reroll the scraps—that will make the biscuits very tough.

7. FLIP, THEN BAKE

Place biscuits upside down on parchment-lined rimmed baking sheet. Bake on middle rack in 450-degree oven for 5 minutes, rotate baking sheet, lower oven temperature to 400 degrees, and continue baking until golden brown, 10 to 12 minutes longer. Cool biscuits on wire rack for 5 minutes before serving.

WHY? With the flat underside on top, the biscuits will rise more evenly and to a greater height. The hot oven jump-starts the rising process, while turning the heat down allows the biscuits to cook through without burning.

How to Shape Scones

ESSENTIAL EQUIPMENT

- 9-inch cake pan
- bench scraper or chef's knife
- baking sheet
- parchment paper

Classic scones are similar to biscuits, with two important changes. The dough generally contains more sugar (scones are supposed to be sweet), and the buttermilk used in most biscuits is replaced with something richer (heavy cream, or perhaps milk mixed with sour cream). One more important change—scones are larger than biscuits and easier to cut out, as demonstrated in the steps below. Below we make simple Cream Scones with currants; see page 531 for details on making the dough and some flavor variations. Also see our recipe for Oatmeal Scones on page 531 (this recipe does not use a cake pan since it requires forming the dough into a 7-inch round). Note that our Blueberry Scones rely on a different technique designed to increase flakiness and make sure the berries are evenly incorporated into the dough (see Recipe Tutorial on page 520).

1. PAT DOUGH INTO PAN

After preparing the dough in the food processor according to recipe, turn dough and any floury bits onto floured counter and knead until rough, slightly sticky ball forms, 5 to 10 seconds. Press dough into even layer in 9-inch cake pan.

WHY? While it's possible to pat the dough into a circle directly on a lightly floured counter, the edges of the scones will be slightly uneven. We often like to use a cake pan to help ensure a perfect round.

2. TURN CIRCLE OF DOUGH ONTO COUNTER

Flip dough out of pan and onto counter.

WHY? Using the cake pan as a mold makes it easy to form a perfect circle. Now, just flip the circle onto the counter. There's no need to grease or flour anything—the dough shouldn't be terribly sticky.

3. CUT INTO UNIFORM WEDGES

Using metal bench scraper or chef's knife, cut dough circle into 8 evenly sized wedges. Transfer wedges to parchment-lined baking sheet and bake as directed.

WHY? A bench scraper is perfect for this task because it's sharp but won't damage delicate surfaces. You can use a knife (a chef's knife is best), but be careful not to scratch laminate or other counter surfaces. We find it easiest to cut the dough circle first in half, then into quarters, and then into eighths.

How to Make Muffins

Muffins are one of the first things many cooks learn how to bake—and that's because the batter is so easy to prepare. Just mix dry ingredients together in a large bowl, whisk together the liquid ingredients in a large measuring cup or bowl, then add the liquid ingredients to the bowl with the dry ingredients. But many cooks are overly aggressive when combining the wet and dry ingredients. Getting the batter into the muffin tin also proves to be a challenge for many novice bakers, as does getting the baked muffins out of the tin. These tips will help avoid all these problems, no matter what type of muffins is being prepared. Note that we don't recommend using paper liners—we think the browned exterior on a muffin adds flavor and textural interest, and you end up peeling this off when you remove the paper. Following is the basic technique; see pages 533–535 for specific muffin recipes.

ESSENTIAL EQUIPMENT

- muffin tin
- rubber spatula
- mixing bowls
- portion scoop
- wire rack

1. GREASE WELL

Use vegetable oil spray to grease each cup in muffin tin.

WHY? Muffins can stick, especially if they have sweet toppings or contain fruit. To make sure your muffins slide effortlessly out of the tins, start by using a good nonstick muffin tin and then grease each cup in the tin. To prevent the spray from getting all over the counter or floor, we suggest spraying the muffin tin over the sink, a garbage can, or even an open dishwasher door.

2. MIX GENTLY

Combine wet and dry ingredients in separate bowls. Use rubber spatula to gently fold wet ingredients into dry ingredients. Stop when few streaks of flour remain.

WHY? Muffins almost always rely on the quick bread mixing method outlined at the beginning of this chapter. Overmixing encourages gluten development, which inhibits rise and makes muffins tough and squat. A perfectly mixed batter should still have a few streaks of unmixed flour.

3. PORTION PRECISELY

Use spring-loaded portion scoop to divide batter among greased cups in muffin tin.

WHY? A spring-loaded portion scoop makes it easy to divide the batter evenly and reduces the risk of batter ending up on the pan, rather than in the cups. Coat the scoop with a little vegetable oil spray so the batter slides out easily. A greased dry measuring cup will also work.

4. COOL BRIEFLY IN PAN

Let baked muffins cool in tin for 5 to 10 minutes. Lift each muffin from tin and transfer to wire rack.

WHY? Trying to remove muffins from a hot tin increases the risk that they will break apart. Letting the muffins cool for 5 to 10 minutes helps them set up. Don't wait longer than 5 minutes, or sticky muffin surfaces will fuse to the pan. If any muffins do stick, carefully cut around them with a paring or grapefruit knife.

How to Make Skillet Cornbread

There are many ways to make cornbread, but the classic method—at least, in the South—involves a cast-iron skillet. Unlike sweet and cakey Northern versions that are baked in a square pan and are sometimes better suited to the dessert table, Southern cornbread contains neither sugar nor flour, so it has a much more savory and strong corn flavor, and a hearty but still moist crumb. Southern cornbread also should have a crunchy crust (otherwise, why use the cast-iron pan?). Note that you will be moving the hot skillet in and out of the oven multiple times and will also be maneuvering the hot skillet to flip the cooked cornbread out of the pan. The skillet handle will be hot, so use good-quality potholders. For more information on buying and taking care of your cast-iron pans, see page 22 and page 25.

- 10-inch cast-iron skillet
- rimmed baking sheet
- mixing bowl
- liquid measuring cup
- whisk
- rubber spatula
- potholders
- wire rack

1. GET SKILLET HOT

Heat 10-inch cast-iron skillet on middle rack of 450-degree oven until hot, about 10 minutes.
WHY? If you don't preheat the pan, the crust of the cornbread will be soft and pale rather than brown and crunchy. Cast iron conducts heat better than other metals and produces cornbread with a great crust; it also has nonstick properties. That said, a traditional skillet (with a stainless steel or anodized aluminum surface) can be used instead, as long as the pan is heavy and ovenproof. Because of the high temperatures involved, do not use a nonstick pan, which can give off toxic fumes if used this way.

2. TOAST CORNMEAL

Spread 2¼ cups (11¼ ounces) cornmeal on rimmed baking sheet. Toast cornmeal on lower-middle rack in oven (while skillet is heating up) until fragrant and lightly golden, about 5 minutes.
WHY? Toasting the cornmeal before making the batter deepens its flavor dramatically. You can use fine-ground cornmeal (such as Quaker), or fine- or medium-ground stone-ground cornmeal for more personality, but avoid coarse-ground cornmeal.

3. SOFTEN CORNMEAL WITH BUTTERMILK

Transfer warm toasted cornmeal to large bowl and whisk in 2 cups buttermilk. Let mixture sit for several minutes to soften before making batter.
WHY? If you skip this step, the cornmeal will retain its hard, crunchy texture in the finished bread. Buttermilk gives cornbread much of its flavor and ensures that the crumb is moist.

4. USE OIL AND BUTTER

Add ¼ cup vegetable oil to hot skillet and continue to heat in oven until just smoking, about 5 minutes. Remove hot skillet from oven, carefully add 4 tablespoons unsalted butter, cut into 4 pieces, and gently swirl to melt and incorporate butter.

WHY? The combination of oil and butter is great because the oil can get very hot without burning, while the butter adds good flavor.

5. ADD FAT TO BATTER

Pour all but 1 tablespoon of hot fat in skillet into cornmeal mixture, whisking to incorporate. Whisk in 1 teaspoon baking powder, 1 teaspoon baking soda, and ¾ teaspoon salt, followed by 2 large eggs.

WHY? Most of the hot fat is added to the batter, but some of it is left in the pan to ensure a crisp crust and flawless release of the bread after it's baked. The baking powder and baking soda ensure good rise (without flour, this recipe needs a lot of lift). The eggs add structure and richness, and a healthy dose of salt is essential.

6. ADD BATTER TO HOT SKILLET

Quickly scrape batter into hot skillet. Bake cornbread on middle rack until top begins to crack and sides are golden brown, 12 to 16 minutes, rotating pan halfway through baking.

WHY? The hot skillet is what gives this bread its crunchy crust, so don't let it cool off before adding the batter. Rotate the pan 180 degrees halfway through the baking time to ensure even browning.

7. COOL, THEN FLIP

Let cornbread cool in skillet for 5 minutes, then gently flip out onto wire rack. Serve warm or at room temperature.

WHY? If you try to flip the cornbread out before letting it cool slightly, it will crumble apart, so make sure to give it some time to set up first.

HOW TO MAKE QUICK BREADS

How to Make Soda Bread

Robust, moist, and permeated with a delicious wheaty sweetness, Irish soda bread is easy to like, very easy to make, and—unlike yeast breads—doesn't require much waiting around. The traditional bread adds coarse, whole-wheat flour to all-purpose flour and is often called "brown bread." In contrast, American-style soda breads often are made solely with all-purpose flour and add more sugar as well as eggs. That style of sweet, cakey bread is a fine snack with tea, but we prefer the original brown bread—which has nutty, savory flavor that makes it appropriate to serve with a meal. And since this bread requires just 10 minutes to prepare, it's something you can add to the dinner table often.

ESSENTIAL EQUIPMENT

- mixing bowl
- whisk
- liquid measuring cup
- rubber spatula
- parchment paper
- rimmed baking sheet
- serrated knife
- instant-read thermometer
- pastry brush

1. USE TOASTED WHEAT GERM

Whisk 2 cups (10 ounces) all-purpose flour, 1½ cups (8¼ ounces) whole-wheat flour, ½ cup toasted wheat germ, 3 tablespoons sugar, 1½ teaspoons salt, 1 teaspoon baking powder, and 1 teaspoon baking soda together in large bowl.

WHY? We found that a mix of all-purpose flour and whole-wheat flour created a loaf with a hearty but not dense texture. For the nutty flavor, we turned to toasted wheat germ, sold in jars in the cereal aisle in most supermarkets. While traditional recipes rely solely on baking soda, we found that a combination of baking powder and baking soda delivered a lighter loaf with a better texture.

2. MIX BUTTER INTO BUTTERMILK

Combine 1¾ cups buttermilk and 2 tablespoons melted unsalted butter in 2-cup liquid measuring cup.

WHY? Buttermilk is the classic choice for soda bread. It imparts tangy flavor to the bread, and it ensures that the crumb is especially tender and moist. If you don't have buttermilk, you can make a close approximation by mixing 5 teaspoons lemon juice into 1¾ cups whole or low-fat milk. Some traditional Irish recipes don't contain any butter. We find that a little adds richness to the loaf.

3. ADD WET INGREDIENTS TO DRY

Add wet ingredients to dry ingredients and stir with rubber spatula until dough just comes together.

WHY? Soda bread must have enough structure to slice neatly. Therefore, unlike other quick breads (like pancakes, for instance), you don't have to worry too much about developing excess gluten, especially if you combine the wet and dry ingredients by hand. Keep mixing until the dough comes together.

4. KNEAD BRIEFLY BY HAND

Turn out dough onto lightly floured counter and knead until cohesive mass forms, about 8 turns.
WHY? Once the dough comes together, you should knead it to develop some structure. A "turn" is the process of pressing the dough with the heel of your hand and then folding the top edge back over.

5. SHAPE INTO ROUND

Pat dough into 7-inch round and transfer to parchment-lined rimmed baking sheet.
WHY? Make sure to shape the dough into a neat round. The parchment paper ensures that the bread doesn't stick.

6. CUT CROSS IN DOUGH

Using sharp serrated knife, make ¼-inch-deep cross about 5 inches long on top of loaf.
WHY? These lines are both decorative and functional, allowing the bread to rise without splitting.

7. TAKE THE TEMPERATURE

Place baking sheet on lower-middle rack in 400-degree oven and bake until skewer inserted in center comes out clean and loaf registers 195 degrees, 45 to 50 minutes, rotating sheet halfway through baking.
WHY? We find that a thermometer is the best way to gauge doneness in all breads, whether or not they contain yeast. Don't overbake the loaf or the crumb will be dry.

8. BRUSH WITH BUTTER

Remove bread from oven. Brush with 1 tablespoon melted butter. Transfer loaf to wire rack and let cool for at least 1 hour before serving.
WHY? The final brush with melted butter adds flavor and moistens the exterior of the bread, which can become dry in the oven. As tempting as it may be to slice into a hot loaf of bread, let it cool to ensure the bread finishes cooking through and has time to set up. If you slice it too early, the interior will be gummy.

How to Make Pancakes

Too often pancakes come out tough and rubbery when they should be light and fluffy. We find that buttermilk not only provides flavor, it also creates pancakes with a better texture, especially if you use both baking powder and soda. If you don't have buttermilk on hand, mix 2 cups whole or low-fat milk with 2 tablespoons lemon juice. You can serve pancakes as you make them, but if you want to make all the pancakes and then serve them at once, place a rimmed baking sheet fitted with a greased wire rack in the oven, preheat the oven to 200 degrees, and then transfer each batch of pancakes to the wire rack as it is done. Don't overlap the pancakes on the rack (overlapping will cause them to steam and become gummy). For a heartier style of pancakes, see the Multigrain Pancakes recipe tutorial on page 527.

ESSENTIAL EQUIPMENT

- mixing bowl
- large liquid measuring cup
- rubber spatula
- whisk
- 12-inch nonstick skillet
- heatproof pastry brush or paper towels
- ¼-cup dry measuring cup
- thin, wide nonstick spatula

1. MAKE WELL

Whisk 2 cups (10 ounces) all-purpose flour, 2 tablespoons sugar, 2 teaspoons baking powder, ½ teaspoon baking soda, and ½ teaspoon salt together in large bowl. Whisk 2 cups buttermilk, 3 tablespoons melted and cooled unsalted butter, and 1 large egg together in large liquid measuring cup or bowl. Make well in center of dry ingredients.

WHY? We like using this "well" method when making liquid-y batters, because it helps incorporate the wet ingredients into the dry without overmixing.

2. LEAVE SOME LUMPS

Pour buttermilk mixture into well, and gently whisk together until just incorporated, with few lumps remaining (do not overmix).

WHY? When whisking the batter, be careful not to overmix it—the batter should actually have a few lumps. Overmixed batter makes for dense pancakes.

3. GET SKILLET HOT BUT NOT SCORCHING

Heat 1 teaspoon vegetable oil in 12-inch nonstick skillet over medium heat until shimmering. Use heatproof pastry brush or paper towels to distribute oil evenly over pan bottom and sides.

WHY? If the skillet is not hot enough before cooking the pancakes, they will be pale and dense. Knowing when the skillet is ready can take some practice; if you're not sure, try cooking just one small pancake to check. If you use too much oil, the delicate cakes will taste greasy and dense. There's not much oil in the pan, so once it's hot we use a pastry brush to make sure it's evenly coating the pan. If you don't have a pastry brush with heatproof bristles, just use a small wad of paper towels.

4. USE ¼-CUP MEASURE TO PORTION BATTER

Add batter to skillet in ¼-cup increments (3 pancakes should fit at a time).

WHY? Using a dry measuring cup ensures that the pancakes are the same size and that they cook at the same rate. Don't crowd the pan, or the pancakes will run together and will be difficult to flip.

5. FLIP WHEN YOU SEE BUBBLES

Cook pancakes on first side until large bubbles begin to appear, about 2 minutes. Using thin, wide nonstick spatula, flip pancakes and continue to cook until golden brown on second side, about 1½ minutes longer.

WHY? The bubbles indicate that the pancakes are ready to be flipped over. If the pancakes are not golden brown when flipped, the skillet needs to be hotter; alternatively, if the pancakes are too brown, turn down the heat.

Customizing Pancakes

It's easy to vary our classic pancake recipe. For the blueberry variation, you will need about 1 cup fruit in total; frozen berries can be used, but to prevent excess bleeding, thaw, rinse, and spread them out on paper towels to dry. To make the 1 cup graham cracker crumbs needed for Grahamcakes, process 9 whole graham crackers in a food processor to fine crumbs.

TO MAKE	DO THIS
Blueberry Pancakes	Sprinkle 1 tablespoon berries over each pancake before flipping
Cornmeal Pancakes	Replace 1 cup flour with 1½ cups yellow cornmeal
Grahamcakes	Replace 1 cup flour with 1 cup graham cracker crumbs and 2 tablespoons yellow cornmeal

Blueberry Scones

Recipe Stats

TOTAL TIME **2 hours**
PREPARATION TIME **15 minutes**
ACTIVE COOKING TIME **1 hour**
YIELD **8 scones**
MAKE AHEAD **Refrigerate unbaked scones on baking sheet overnight or freeze for up to 1 month**
DIFFICULTY **Intermediate**

Tools

- rimmed baking sheet
- dry measuring cups
- liquid measuring cup
- measuring spoons
- bench scraper *
- coarse grater **
- large plate ***
- mixing bowls
- pastry brush
- rasp-style grater ****
- rolling pin
- rubber spatula
- whisk
- wire rack
- parchment paper

* A bench scraper is ideal for loosening the dough from the counter if you find that it is sticking, but a thin metal spatula will also work. Do make sure to dust the counter and your hands with flour to minimize the risk of sticking. We also use a bench scraper to cut the dough into scones, but a chef's knife can be used to do this job.
** Grating the frozen butter is a key step in this recipe. We like the large holes on a flat coarse grater or box grater (the same ones you might use to shred a block of cheese).
*** During the rolling and folding process, the dough goes into the freezer. Place the dough on a dinner plate to keep things tidy.
**** We recommend grating lemon zest with a rasp-style grater.

Overview

All too frequently berries weigh down scones and impart little flavor. Starting with the classic recipe, we increase the amount of sugar and butter to add sweetness and richness; a combination of whole milk and sour cream lends still more richness as well as tang.

To lighten our scones, we borrow a technique from puff pastry, where the dough is turned, rolled, and folded multiple times to create layers that are forced apart by steam when baked. To ensure that the butter stays as cold and as solid as possible going into the oven, we freeze whole sticks, then grate the amount we need into the dry ingredients. This guarantees maximum flakiness.

Adding the blueberries to the dry ingredients (as directed in most recipes) means they will get mashed when the dough is mixed. We found the solution is to press the berries into the dough, roll the dough into a log, and then press the log into a rectangle and cut the scones.

If you would like to prepare the scones in advance, they can be refrigerated on the baking sheet overnight (or frozen for one month) and then brushed with melted butter and sprinkled with sugar just before baking. Refrigerated scones can be baked as directed. Do not thaw frozen scones before baking; put them directly into a 375-degree oven and bake for 25 to 30 minutes.

Ingredients

16 tablespoons unsalted butter (2 sticks), each stick frozen *
7½ ounces (1½ cups) blueberries **
½ cup whole milk
½ cup sour cream
2 cups (10 ounces) all-purpose flour
½ cup (3½ ounces) plus 1 tablespoon sugar
2 teaspoons baking powder
¼ teaspoon baking soda
½ teaspoon salt
1 teaspoon grated lemon zest

* Frozen butter is essential for this recipe. We call for 2 sticks, but only 10 tablespoons are used: We grate half of each stick (8 tablespoons total), and we melt another 2 tablespoons.
** An equal amount of frozen blueberries (not thawed) can be used. An equal amount of raspberries, blackberries, or strawberries can be used in place of the blueberries. Cut larger berries into ¼- to ½-inch pieces.

What Can Go Wrong

Here's a list of common mistakes cooks make when preparing this recipe.

COMMON MISTAKE	BAD OUTCOMES	WHAT YOU SHOULD DO
Not Fully Freezing Butter	• **The butter is hard to grate.** • **The scones are not flaky.**	Thin shreds of butter are the key to this recipe. You must freeze the sticks solid before attempting to grate them. This will take at least an hour, if not longer. Of course, you should always store butter in the freezer and then move sticks, one at a time, to the refrigerator as needed. In the refrigerator, butter will pick up off-flavors in just a few weeks; frozen butter will stay fresh for months.
Freezing Only One Stick of Butter	• **The butter is hard to grate.** • **The butter melts during the grating process.**	This recipe uses a total of 10 tablespoons of butter. Eight tablespoons (the equivalent of one stick) are frozen and grated, and the remaining 2 tablespoons are melted and brushed over the scones right before they go into the oven. So why do we call for freezing two sticks of butter? It's much less messy to grate half of two sticks than it is to grate an entire stick. We peel back the wrapper on half of each stick and use the remaining wrapper to hold the butter as we grate it on the large holes of a flat coarse grater or box grater. Once we have grated half the first stick, we switch to the second stick, again holding the butter by the wrapped portion.
Working in Hot, Humid Kitchen	• **The scones are tough.** • **The scones are dense, not flaky.**	If your kitchen is very hot and humid, you run the risk of the butter melting as you work the dough. Keeping the pieces of butter solid in the dough is the key to flaky texture—the butter releases steam that creates flaky layers in the scones. Make sure to work the dough as little as possible to keep the pieces of butter from melting. You might consider placing the flour mixture and mixing bowls in the freezer to keep everything as cold as possible.
Overworking Dough	• **The scones are tough.** • **The scones are dense.**	A light, tender scone depends on distinct pieces of butter that are distributed throughout the dough and that melt during baking and leave behind pockets of air. For this to happen the butter must be as cold and as solid as possible until baking. It is important to work the dough minimally. Work quickly and knead and fold the dough only the number of times called for or else the scones will turn out tough. Extra rolling or extra folds won't make the scones flakier—it just will make them denser because the butter is more likely to soften during these extra steps.
Adding Berries Too Soon	• **The berries are mashed and stain the scones purple.** • **The scones are soggy in spots.**	How you handle the berries has a big effect on the final scones. If you add the fruit too early, it will get mashed during the kneading, rolling, or folding process. Wait until all these steps are complete. Then roll the dough out one more time and press the berries into the dough. (The process is akin to how you make cinnamon rolls or sticky buns—the dough is rolled out and then the filling is spread evenly over the surface.) Once the berries have been pressed into the dough, we roll the dough up into a log, which we then flatten and cut into individual scones. Briefly freezing the berries helps keep them intact during this process.
Not Baking at High Enough Temperature	• **The scones don't rise properly.** • **The scones don't brown properly.**	The hot oven not only helps to brown the scones (and browning equals flavor), it also jump-starts the rising process. In order to convert the water in the butter to steam, you need a hot oven. Make sure the oven is set to 425 degrees and properly preheated.

HOW TO MAKE QUICK BREADS

1. Adjust oven rack to middle position and heat oven to 425 degrees. Line rimmed baking sheet with parchment paper.

2. Unwrap 2 sticks of frozen unsalted butter halfway. Grate unwrapped halves using coarse grater (grate total of 8 tablespoons butter).

3. Place grated butter in freezer until needed.

4. Melt 2 tablespoons of remaining ungrated butter and set aside. Save remaining 6 tablespoons butter for another use.

5. Place 1½ cups blueberries in freezer until needed.

6. Whisk ½ cup whole milk and ½ cup sour cream together in medium bowl; refrigerate until needed.

7. Whisk 2 cups all-purpose flour, ½ cup sugar, 2 teaspoons baking powder, ¼ teaspoon baking soda, ½ teaspoon salt, and 1 teaspoon lemon zest in bowl.

8. Add frozen grated butter to flour mixture and toss with fingers until butter is thoroughly coated.

9. Add milk mixture to flour mixture and fold with rubber spatula until just combined.

10. Using spatula, transfer dough to liberally floured counter. Dust surface of dough with flour, and flour your hands.

11. Knead dough 6 to 8 times, until it just holds together in ragged ball, adding flour as needed to prevent sticking.

12. Roll dough into 12-inch square.

13. Fold dough into thirds (like a business letter), using bench scraper or metal spatula to release dough if it sticks to counter.

14. Lift short ends of dough and fold into thirds again to form 4-inch square.

15. Transfer dough to plate lightly dusted with flour and chill in freezer for 5 minutes.

16. Transfer dough to floured counter and reroll into 12-inch square.

17. Sprinkle chilled blueberries evenly over surface of dough, then press down so they are slightly embedded in dough.

18. Using bench scraper or thin metal spatula, loosen dough from counter. Roll dough into cylinder, pressing to form tight log.

19. Arrange log seam side down and press into 12 by 4-inch rectangle.

20. Using floured bench scraper or sharp, floured knife, cut rectangle crosswise into 4 equal rectangles.

21. Cut each rectangle diagonally to form 2 triangles and transfer to prepared baking sheet.

22. Brush tops with reserved melted butter and sprinkle with 1 tablespoon sugar.

23. Bake until tops and bottoms are golden brown, 18 to 25 minutes.

24. Transfer to wire rack and let cool for at least 10 minutes before serving.

HOW TO MAKE QUICK BREADS

Banana Bread

Overview

Our ideal banana bread is simple enough—a moist, tender loaf that really tastes like bananas. We discovered that doubling the dose of bananas in our favorite test recipe was both a blessing and a curse. The abundance of fruit makes for intense banana flavor, but the weight and moisture makes the loaf very heavy. Looking to add banana flavor without moisture, we place our bananas in a glass bowl and microwave them for a few minutes, then transfer the fruit to a strainer to drain. We simmer the exuded banana liquid in a saucepan until it is reduced, then incorporate it into the batter.

Brown sugar complements the bananas better than granulated sugar, and vanilla works well with the bananas' faintly boozy, rumlike flavor, as does swapping out the oil used in standard recipes for the nutty richness of melted butter. Toasted walnuts lend a pleasing crunch, but you can omit them if you prefer.

As a final embellishment, we slice an additional banana and shingle it on top of the loaf. Then we sprinkle granulated sugar over the top to help the slices caramelize and to give the loaf an enticingly crunchy top. The texture of this quick bread is best when the loaf is eaten fresh, but it can be stored (let cool completely first), covered tightly with plastic wrap, for up to three days.

Recipe Stats

TOTAL TIME **3 hours**
PREPARATION TIME **15 minutes**
ACTIVE COOKING TIME **35 minutes**
YIELD **10 servings**
MAKE AHEAD **Best served day it is baked**
DIFFICULTY **Easy**

Tools

- 8½ by 4½-inch loaf pan *
- medium saucepan
- microwave
- rimmed baking sheet **
- chef's knife
- cutting board
- dry measuring cups
- liquid measuring cup
- measuring spoons
- fine-mesh strainer
- microwave-safe plate
- mixing bowls
- potato masher
- rubber spatula
- whisk
- wire rack
- toothpick

* The test kitchen's preferred loaf pan measures 8½ by 4½ inches; if you use a 9 by 5-inch loaf pan, start checking for doneness 5 minutes earlier than advised in the recipe.
** If you opt to include the walnuts, toast them on a rimmed baking sheet in a 350-degree oven until fragrant, about 5 minutes. Cool the nuts and then chop them coarsely.

Ingredients

1¾ **cups (8¾ ounces) all-purpose flour**
1 **teaspoon baking soda**
½ **teaspoon salt**
6 **very ripe large bananas (2¼ pounds), peeled ***
8 **tablespoons unsalted butter, melted and cooled**
2 **large eggs**
¾ **cup packed (5¼ ounces) light brown sugar**
1 **teaspoon vanilla extract**
½ **cup walnuts, toasted and chopped coarse (optional)**
2 **teaspoons granulated sugar**

* Be sure to use very ripe, heavily speckled (or even black) bananas in this recipe. This recipe can be made using 5 thawed frozen bananas; since they release a lot of liquid naturally, they can bypass the microwaving in step 3 and go directly into the fine-mesh strainer. Do not use a thawed frozen banana in step 9; it will be too soft to slice. Instead, simply sprinkle the top of the loaf with sugar.

What Can Go Wrong

Here's a list of common mistakes cooks make when preparing this recipe.

COMMON MISTAKE	BAD OUTCOMES	WHAT YOU SHOULD DO
Using Lightly Speckled Bananas	• **The banana bread is bland.**	As bananas ripen, their natural starches convert to sugars, and their flavor improves dramatically. In lab tests, we found that heavily speckled bananas have nearly three times as much fructose (the sweetest of the sugars in fruit) as that in lightly speckled but still ripe bananas. If you use underripe bananas in this recipe, the loaf will be lacking in flavor. The best way to ripen bananas is to enclose them in a paper bag for several days. The bag will trap ethylene gas, which hastens ripening, produced by fruit, while still allowing some moisture to escape. Since fully ripe fruit emits the most ethylene, placing a ripe banana or other ripe fruit in the bag will speed the process along by a day or two.
Not Fully Reducing Banana Juice	• **The banana bread is heavy.** • **The banana bread is soggy.**	The bananas are microwaved so that they will shed their liquid. Five large bananas will yield ½ to ¾ cup of juice. This liquid has flavor, so we simmer it in a saucepan until it reduces to ¼ cup. If you shortcut this process, you will be defeating the purpose of the microwave step. Make sure to pour the contents of the saucepan into a liquid measuring cup to check your progress. If the liquid has not reduced to ¼ cup, return it to the saucepan and keep simmering.
Shingling Bananas Over Entire Top	• **The banana bread does not rise properly.**	We love adding a sixth banana by shingling thin slices over the top of the batter right before it goes into the oven. But believe it or not, it matters how you arrange those slices of banana. If the slices cover the entire surface, the loaf will not rise properly. We found it necessary to shingle the banana slices along the long sides of the pan, leaving at least 1½ inches open down the middle of the loaf so that the center of this quick bread can rise above the sides. (Quick breads, such as banana bread, typically have a peaked middle with a split that runs down the center of the loaf.)
Underbaking or Overbaking	• **The banana bread is gummy and soggy.** • **The banana bread is dry and bland.**	There's a lot of moisture in this recipe, and if you underbake the loaf it will turn out very gummy and soggy. Don't remove the banana bread from the oven until a toothpick inserted in the center comes out clean. That said, you can do harm if you overbake the loaf. Eventually the crumb will become dry and the bread will lose flavor if too much moisture evaporates. Test the loaf 5 minutes before the suggested window of 55 to 75 minutes, and then test again based on how the loaf is progressing.
Not Fully Cooling Loaf	• **The banana bread is crumbly and hard to slice.** • **The banana bread seems gummy.**	As tempting as it might be, don't slice the bread while it's still warm. Right out of the oven the loaf will be very hard to slice—the pieces are likely to crumble as you cut. Even worse, the crumb will still be a bit heavy and moist. But as the loaf cools, the texture of the crumb will firm up and become tender but pleasantly chewy.

1. Adjust oven rack to middle position and heat oven to 350 degrees. Spray 8½ by 4½-inch loaf pan with vegetable oil spray.

2. Whisk 1¾ cups (8¾ ounces) all-purpose flour, 1 teaspoon baking soda, and ½ teaspoon salt together in large bowl.

3. Peel 5 large, very ripe bananas and place in separate bowl. Cover and microwave until bananas are soft and have released liquid, about 5 minutes.

4. Transfer bananas to fine-mesh strainer set over bowl and let drain, stirring occasionally, for 15 minutes (you should have ½ to ¾ cup liquid).

5. Transfer drained liquid to medium saucepan and cook over medium-high heat until reduced to ¼ cup, about 5 minutes.

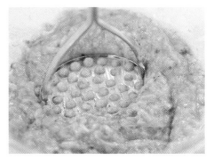

6. Remove pan from heat. Transfer drained bananas to mixing bowl. Add reduced liquid and mash with potato masher until mostly smooth.

7. Whisk in 8 tablespoons melted and cooled unsalted butter, 2 large eggs, ¾ cup packed (5¼ ounces) light brown sugar, and 1 teaspoon vanilla extract.

8. Pour banana mixture into dry ingredients. Stir until just combined; some streaks of flour will remain. Fold in ½ cup toasted, chopped walnuts, if using.

9. Scrape batter into prepared pan. Peel 1 large, very ripe banana and cut on bias into ¼-inch-thick slices.

10. Shingle banana slices on loaf in 2 rows, leaving 1½-inch-wide space down center. Sprinkle 2 teaspoons granulated sugar evenly over loaf.

11. Bake until toothpick inserted in center of loaf comes out clean, 55 to 75 minutes.

12. Let loaf cool in pan for 10 minutes, then turn out onto wire rack and let cool for 1 hour before serving.

Multigrain Pancakes

Overview

Bland, dense, and gummy, most multigrain pancakes are more about appeasing your diet than pleasing your palate. We wanted flavorful, fluffy, and healthful flapjacks. After testing lots of grains, we found that muesli (the cold cereal) had all the ingredients and flavors we wanted in one convenient package; raw rolled oats, wheat germ, rye, barley, toasted nuts, and dried fruit. But pancakes made with whole muesli were too chewy and gummy. Our solution is to process the muesli in the food processor, and then make a muesli "flour," which includes all-purpose flour, whole-wheat flour, and leavening, to achieve just the right lightness. A few tablespoons of unprocessed muesli added just the right amount of whole-grain crunch to the batter.

As with most pancakes, you need melted butter and dairy in the batter. We found the sharp acidity of buttermilk out of place, but pancakes made with plain milk were heavy. We add a balanced acidity and lightness by using a mixture of whole milk whisked with a little lemon juice. Brown sugar works better than the usual granulated sugar with the muesli flour, and a shot of vanilla extract gave our pancakes a more well-rounded flavor. Serve these pancakes with maple syrup or our Apple, Cranberry, and Pecan Topping (see the recipe on page 539).

Recipe Stats

TOTAL TIME **30 minutes**
PREPARATION TIME **15 minutes**
ACTIVE COOKING TIME **15 minutes**
YIELD **4 to 6 servings**
MAKE AHEAD **Serve immediately**
DIFFICULTY **Easy**

Tools

- rimmed baking sheet
- 12-inch nonstick skillet *
- food processor **
- dry measuring cups ***
- large liquid measuring cup
- measuring spoons
- mixing bowl
- thin, wide nonstick spatula
- whisk
- wire rack
- paper towels ****

* If you prefer, the pancakes can be cooked on an electric griddle. Set the griddle temperature to 350 degrees and cook as directed.
** The food processor is essential for turning the packaged muesli cereal into a homemade multigrain flour. It will take the power of a food processor (plus at least 2 minutes) to grind the cereal fine enough.
*** We like to use a ¼-cup dry measuring cup to portion pancake batter into the hot skillet.
**** Once the oil is shimmering, use a small wad of paper towels to ensure it is evenly distributed in the pan. A heatproof pastry brush can also be used.

Ingredients

  2 **cups whole milk**
  4 **teaspoons lemon juice**
1¼ **cups (6 ounces), plus 3 tablespoons no-sugar-added muesli ***
 ¾ **cup (3¾ ounces) all-purpose flour**
 ½ **cup (2¾ ounces) whole-wheat flour**
  2 **tablespoons packed brown sugar**
2¼ **teaspoons baking powder**
 ½ **teaspoon baking soda**
 ½ **teaspoon salt**
  2 **large eggs**
  3 **tablespoons unsalted butter, melted and cooled**
 ¾ **teaspoon vanilla extract**
1-2 **teaspoons vegetable oil**

* Familia brand no-sugar-added muesli is the best choice for this recipe. If you can't find Familia, look for Alpen or any no-sugar-added muesli. (If you can't find muesli without sugar, muesli with sugar added will work; just reduce the brown sugar in the recipe to 1 tablespoon.)

What Can Go Wrong

Here's a list of common mistakes cooks make when preparing this recipe.

COMMON MISTAKE	BAD OUTCOMES	WHAT YOU SHOULD DO
Using Wrong Cereal	• **The pancakes are gritty.**	Be careful when shopping. Most supermarkets sell multigrain hot cereal mixes but they aren't what you want to use here. These cereals must be cooked—we tried soaking and grinding these cereals and they didn't work in our pancake recipe. You must buy muesli, a mix of grains designed to be served as a cold cereal. In addition to delivering great texture to our pancakes (provided that you grind most of the muesli in a food processor as directed), muesli is generally not overly sweet.
Not Processing Cereal	• **The pancakes are gummy.**	If you simply mix the muesli into the pancake batter, the resulting hotcakes will be dense and gummy. You must take the 2 minutes it takes to grind the muesli into a fine powder. But also make sure to reserve 3 tablespoons of the cereal and stir that into the batter, as is. This small amount of unprocessed muesli gives the pancakes a nice crunch without compromising tenderness.
Overmixing Batter	• **The pancakes are tough.** • **The pancakes are dense, not fluffy.**	When you combine the wet and dry ingredients, use a whisk and a light hand. A whisk will combine the wet and dry ingredients while developing a minimum of gluten. Do not use an electric mixer. Even with a whisk, there's a risk of excess gluten development (and therefore toughness in the pancakes) if you overdo it. Once just a few lumps and streaks of flour remain, stop. The goal is not to produce a perfectly homogenous, smooth batter—that is, unless you like tough, dense pancakes.
Not Resting Batter	• **The batter is runny.** • **The pancakes cook up flat.**	Letting the pancake batter sit for 5 minutes while the skillet heats up is crucial. It gives the dry ingredients time to absorb the wet ingredients; the batter will actually become thicker. If you skip this short resting period, the portions of batter will run together in the skillet and the pancakes will be flat and tough.
Not Preheating Pan Properly	• **The pancakes burn.** • **The pancakes are underdone and gummy.**	It's important to get the pan hot enough before you start cooking the pancakes. Use a sturdy nonstick pan that conducts heat well, and make sure to heat the pan until the oil is shimmering. At this point, use a pastry brush or wadded paper towel to distribute the oil in the pan, leaving behind just a light film. If you're not sure if the pan is hot enough, try this test: Add 1 tablespoon of batter and wait for 1 minute. If the pancake is nicely brown, the pan is the right temperature. If the test pancake is scorched or pale after 1 minute, the pan is not the right temperature.

1. Adjust oven rack to middle position and heat oven to 200 degrees. Spray wire rack set in rimmed baking sheet with vegetable oil spray; place in oven.

2. Whisk 2 cups whole milk and 4 teaspoons lemon juice together in large measuring cup; set aside to thicken while preparing other ingredients.

3. Process 1¼ cups (6 ounces) muesli in food processor until finely ground, 2 to 2½ minutes; transfer to large bowl. Add 3 tablespoons unground muesli.

4. Whisk in ¾ cup flour, ½ cup whole-wheat flour, 2 tablespoons brown sugar, 2¼ teaspoons baking powder, ½ teaspoon baking soda, and ½ teaspoon salt.

5. Add 2 large eggs, 3 tablespoons melted and cooled unsalted butter, and ¾ teaspoon vanilla extract to milk mixture and whisk until combined.

6. Make well in center of dry ingredients; pour in milk mixture and whisk gently until just combined (batter should be lumpy with streaks of flour).

7. Allow batter to sit while pan heats, at least 5 minutes. Heat 1 teaspoon vegetable oil in 12-inch nonstick skillet over medium heat until shimmering.

8. Using paper towels, carefully wipe out oil, leaving thin film of oil on bottom and sides of skillet.

9. Using ¼-cup measure, portion batter into skillet in 3 places.

10. Cook until small bubbles begin to appear evenly over surface, 2 to 3 minutes.

11. Using thin, wide spatula, flip pancakes and cook until second side is golden brown, 1½ to 2 minutes longer.

12. Serve pancakes immediately or transfer to wire rack in oven. Repeat with remaining batter, using remaining oil as necessary.

HOW TO MAKE QUICK BREADS

Recipe Library

Light and Fluffy Buttermilk Biscuits

✔ **WHY THIS RECIPE WORKS:** A seemingly simple batch of biscuits can end up with any number of problems. For perfectly shaped biscuits that were also light and fluffy as well as tender and flavorful, we began by chilling a combination of butter and shortening. This ensured the fat melted in the oven, not in the mixing bowl—and thus created pockets of steam that delivered flaky biscuits. Combining the fat and dry ingredients using the food processor rather than our hands, as many recipes prescribe, also helped keep the fats from getting too warm and melting prematurely. Since overprocessing can lead to crumbly biscuits, we stirred in the liquid ingredients by hand and stopped as soon as the dough had a uniform texture. Kneading a few times activated the gluten in the flour and helped the biscuits rise, but to avoid tough biscuits we made sure not to overdo it. After rolling and stamping the dough, we placed our biscuits upside down on the baking sheet. With the flat underside on top, the biscuits rose evenly. A hot oven jump-started the rising process, then we turned the heat down to finish baking without burning the biscuits.

Light and Fluffy Biscuits
MAKES 12 BISCUITS

If you don't have buttermilk, see page 45 for information on buttermilk substitutes. See Core Technique on page 510 for more details on this recipe.

- 3 **cups (15 ounces) all-purpose flour**
- 1 **tablespoon sugar**
- 1 **tablespoon baking powder**
- 1 **teaspoon salt**
- ½ **teaspoon baking soda**
- 8 **tablespoons unsalted butter, cut into ½-inch pieces and chilled**
- 4 **tablespoons vegetable shortening, cut into ½-inch pieces and chilled**
- 1¼ **cups buttermilk**

1. Adjust oven rack to middle position and heat oven to 450 degrees. Line rimmed baking sheet with parchment paper. Pulse flour, sugar, baking powder, salt, and baking soda in food processor until combined, about 5 pulses. Sprinkle chilled butter and shortening pieces over top and pulse until mixture resembles coarse meal, about 15 pulses.

2. Transfer flour mixture to large bowl. Stir in buttermilk until combined. Turn dough out onto lightly floured counter and knead briefly, 8 to 10 times, to form smooth, cohesive ball. Roll dough into 9-inch circle, about ¾ inch thick.

3. Using 2½-inch biscuit cutter dipped in flour, cut out rounds and arrange upside down on prepared baking sheet, dipping cutter in flour before each cut. Gather dough scraps and pat gently into ¾-inch-thick circle. Cut rounds from dough and transfer upside down to prepared baking sheet.

4. Bake until biscuits begin to rise, about 5 minutes, then rotate sheet and reduce oven temperature to 400 degrees. Bake until biscuits are golden brown, 10 to 12 minutes longer. Transfer to wire rack and let cool for 5 minutes. Serve warm.

TO MAKE AHEAD: Cut rounds can be placed on prepared baking sheet and refrigerated, covered with plastic wrap, for up to 1 day. To bake, heat oven to 450 degrees and proceed with step 4.

Cheddar and Scallion Biscuits
Stir ½ cup shredded cheddar cheese and 2 thinly sliced scallions, green parts only, into dry ingredients before adding buttermilk.

Fontina and Rosemary Biscuits
Stir ½ cup shredded fontina cheese and ½ teaspoon minced fresh rosemary into dry ingredients before adding buttermilk.

Swiss and Caraway Biscuits
Stir ½ cup shredded Swiss cheese and 1 tablespoon toasted caraway seeds into dry ingredients before adding buttermilk.

Parmesan and Peppercorn Biscuits
Stir ¾ cup grated Parmesan cheese and 1 teaspoon coarsely ground pepper into dry ingredients before adding buttermilk.

Drop Biscuits

✔ **WHY THIS RECIPE WORKS:** Too many drop biscuits are dense, gummy, and doughy, or lean and dry; we wanted a biscuit that could be easily broken apart and eaten piece by buttery piece. While oil-based biscuits are easy to work with, they lack flavor; butter was a must. Buttermilk instead of milk gave the biscuits a rich, buttery tang and made them crisper on the exterior and fluffier on the interior. In terms of leavener, we needed a substantial amount, but too much baking powder left a metallic taste. Replacing some of the baking powder with baking soda gave the biscuits the rise they needed without the metallic bitterness. Now we were left with only one problem. Properly combining the butter and buttermilk requires that both ingredients be at just the right temperature; if they aren't, the melted butter clumps in the buttermilk. Since this was supposed to be an easy recipe, we tried making a batch with the lumpy buttermilk. The result was a surprisingly better biscuit, slightly higher and with better texture. The water in the lumps of butter turned to steam in the oven, helping create additional height.

Easy Buttermilk Drop Biscuits
MAKES 12 BISCUITS

If you don't have buttermilk, see page 45 for information on substitutions. A ¼-cup portion scoop can be used to portion the batter.

- 2 **cups (10 ounces) all-purpose flour**
- 2 **teaspoons baking powder**
- ½ **teaspoon baking soda**
- 1 **teaspoon sugar**
- ¾ **teaspoon salt**
- 1 **cup buttermilk, chilled**
- 8 **tablespoons unsalted butter, melted and cooled slightly, plus 2 tablespoons melted**

1. Adjust oven rack to middle position and heat oven to 475 degrees. Line rimmed baking sheet with parchment paper. Whisk flour, baking powder, baking soda, sugar, and salt in large bowl. Combine buttermilk and 8 tablespoons melted butter in medium bowl, stirring until butter forms small clumps.

2. Add buttermilk mixture to flour mixture and stir with rubber spatula until just incorporated and batter pulls away from sides of bowl. Using greased ¼-cup dry measure and working quickly, scoop level amount of batter and drop onto prepared baking sheet (biscuits should measure about 2¼ inches in diameter and 1¼ inches high). Repeat with remaining batter, spacing biscuits about 1½ inches apart. Bake until tops are golden brown and crisp, 12 to 14 minutes.

3. Brush biscuit tops with remaining 2 tablespoons melted butter. Transfer to wire rack and let cool for 5 minutes before serving. (Biscuits are best served immediately. However, leftovers can be stored up to 1 day at room temperature; reheat in 300-degree oven for 10 minutes before serving.)

Cream Scones

✓ **WHY THIS RECIPE WORKS:** Traditional British scones are essentially fluffy biscuits. These scones should be sweet, but not too sweet, so that they can be enjoyed with jam and perhaps clotted cream. For a light, tender texture, we tried cake flour, but it made gummy scones. All-purpose flour, on the other hand, gave us light, feathery scones. A modest amount of sugar kept the sweetness level in check and there was no question we would rely on butter over shortening for the best flavor. Heavy cream gave our scones a rich, not-too-dry character. A food processor made quick work of incorporating the butter into the flour; we stirred in the cream by hand and then lightly kneaded the dough before cutting it into wedges. We also found it was important to get the scones into the oven immediately after cutting them out for the best rise. While currants are traditional in British scones, we left them as optional.

Simple Cream Scones

MAKES 8

Resist the urge to eat the scones hot out of the oven, as letting them cool for at least 10 minutes firms them up and improves their texture. See Core Technique on page 512 for more details on shaping scones.

> 2 **cups (10 ounces) all-purpose flour**
> 3 **tablespoons sugar**
> 1 **tablespoon baking powder**
> ½ **teaspoon salt**
> 5 **tablespoons unsalted butter, cut into ¼-inch pieces and chilled**
> ½ **cup dried currants (optional)**
> 1 **cup heavy cream**

1. Adjust oven rack to middle position and heat oven to 450 degrees. Line baking sheet with parchment paper.

2. Pulse flour, sugar, baking powder, and salt together in food processor to combine, about 3 pulses. Scatter butter evenly over top and continue to pulse until mixture resembles

coarse meal with some slightly larger pieces of butter, about 12 more pulses. Transfer mixture to large bowl and stir in currants, if using. Stir in cream until dough begins to form, about 30 seconds.

3. Turn dough and any floury bits out onto counter and knead until rough, slightly sticky ball forms, 5 to 10 seconds. Press dough into 9-inch cake pan. Unmold dough and cut into 8 wedges.

4. Place wedges on prepared baking sheet. Bake until tops of scones are lightly golden brown, 12 to 15 minutes, rotating baking sheet halfway through baking. Transfer baking sheet to wire rack and let cool for at least 10 minutes. Serve warm or at room temperature.

Simple Ginger Cream Scones

Substitute ½ cup coarsely chopped crystallized ginger for currants.

Simple Cranberry-Orange Cream Scones

Add 1 teaspoon grated orange zest with butter and substitute ¾ cup dried cranberries for currants.

Oatmeal Scones

✓ **WHY THIS RECIPE WORKS:** The oatmeal scones served in a typical coffeehouse are so dry and leaden that they seem like a ploy to get people to buy more coffee to wash them down. We wanted rich toasted oat flavor in a tender, flaky, not-too-sweet scone. Whole rolled oats and quick oats performed better than instant and steel-cut oats, and toasting the oats brought out their nutty flavor. We used a minimal amount of sugar and baking powder, but plenty of cold butter. A mixture of milk and heavy cream added richness without making these scones too heavy. An egg proved to be the ultimate touch of richness. Cutting the cold butter into the flour, instead of using melted butter, resulted in a lighter texture. A very hot oven made the scones rise spectacularly, gave them a craggy appearance, and meant less time in the oven and therefore less time to dry out.

Rich and Tender Oatmeal Scones

MAKES 8 SCONES

Rolled oats will give the scones a deeper oat flavor, but the quick-cooking oats will create a softer texture; either type will work here. Half-and-half is a suitable substitute for the milk and cream combination.

> 1½ **cups (4½ ounces) old-fashioned rolled oats or quick oats**
> ¼ **cup whole milk**
> ¼ **cup heavy cream**
> 1 **large egg**
> 1½ **cups (7½ ounces) all-purpose flour**
> ⅓ **cup (2⅓ ounces) plus 1 tablespoon sugar**
> 2 **teaspoons baking powder**
> ½ **teaspoon salt**
> 10 **tablespoons unsalted butter, cut into ½-inch pieces and chilled**

1. Adjust oven rack to middle position and heat oven to 375 degrees. Spread oats evenly on baking sheet and toast in oven until fragrant and lightly browned, 7 to 9 minutes; let cool on wire rack. Increase oven temperature to 450 degrees. When oats are cooled, measure out 2 tablespoons for dusting counter and set aside. Line second baking sheet with parchment paper.

2. Whisk milk, cream, and egg in large measuring cup until incorporated. Reserve 1 tablespoon in small bowl for glazing and set aside.

3. Pulse flour, ⅓ cup sugar, baking powder, and salt in food processor until combined, about 4 pulses. Scatter butter evenly over top and continue to pulse until mixture resembles coarse cornmeal, 12 to 14 pulses. Transfer mixture to medium bowl and stir in cooled oats. Using rubber spatula, fold in liquid ingredients until large clumps form. Mix dough by hand in bowl until dough forms cohesive mass.

4. Dust counter with 1 tablespoon reserved oats, turn dough out onto counter, and dust top with remaining 1 tablespoon reserved oats. Gently pat dough into 7-inch circle about 1 inch thick. Using bench scraper or chef's knife, cut dough into 8 wedges and place on prepared baking sheet, spacing wedges about 2 inches apart. Brush tops with reserved egg mixture and sprinkle with remaining 1 tablespoon sugar. Bake until golden brown, 12 to 14 minutes. Let scones cool on baking sheet on wire rack for 5 minutes, then transfer scones to wire rack and let cool to room temperature, about 30 minutes. Serve.

TO MAKE AHEAD: After placing scones on baking sheet in step 4, either refrigerate them overnight or freeze for up to 1 month. When ready to bake, bake as directed. For frozen scones, do not thaw, heat oven to 375 degrees, increasing baking time to 25 to 30 minutes.

Cinnamon-Raisin Oatmeal Scones

Add ¼ teaspoon cinnamon to food processor with flour and ½ cup raisins to flour-butter mixture with toasted oats.

Apricot-Almond Oatmeal Scones

Reduce oats to 1 cup and toast ½ cup slivered almonds with oats in step 1. Add ½ cup chopped dried apricots to flour-butter mixture with toasted oats and almonds.

Glazed Maple-Pecan Oatmeal Scones

Toast ½ cup chopped pecans with oats in step 1. Omit sugar and whisk ¼ cup maple syrup into milk mixture. When scones are cool, whisk 3 tablespoons maple syrup and ½ cup confectioners' sugar until combined, then drizzle over scones.

Oatmeal Scones with Dried Cherries and Hazelnuts

Reduce oats to 1¼ cups and toast ¼ cup chopped hazelnuts with oats in step 1. Stir ½ cup chopped dried tart cherries into flour-butter mixture with toasted oats.

Blueberry Scones

WHY THIS RECIPE WORKS: More often berries weigh down scones and impart little flavor. Starting with traditional recipes, we increased the amounts of sugar and butter to add sweetness and richness; a combination of whole milk and sour cream lent more richness and tang. For lightness, we borrowed a technique from puff pastry, where the dough is turned, rolled, and folded multiple times to create layers that are forced apart by steam when baked. To ensure that the butter would stay as cold and solid as possible while baking, we froze it and grated it into the dry ingredients using a coarse grater. Adding the blueberries to the dry ingredients meant they got mashed when we mixed the dough, but when we added them to the already-mixed dough, we ruined our pockets of butter. The solution was pressing the berries into the dough, rolling the dough into a log, then pressing the log into a rectangle and cutting the scones.

Blueberry Scones

MAKES 8 SCONES

It is important to work the dough as little as possible—work quickly and knead and fold the dough only the number of times called for or else the scones will turn out tough, rather than tender. The butter should be frozen solid before grating. In hot or humid environments, chill the flour mixture and mixing bowls before use. While this recipe calls for 2 whole sticks of butter, only 10 tablespoons are actually used (see step 1). If fresh berries are unavailable, an equal amount of frozen berries, not thawed, can be substituted. An equal amount of raspberries, blackberries, or strawberries can be used in place of the blueberries. Cut larger berries into ¼- to ½-inch pieces before incorporating. See Recipe Tutorial on page 520 for more details on this recipe.

16	tablespoons unsalted butter (2 sticks), each stick frozen
7½	ounces (1½ cups) blueberries
½	cup whole milk
½	cup sour cream
2	cups (10 ounces) all-purpose flour
½	cup (3½ ounces) plus 1 tablespoon sugar
2	teaspoons baking powder
¼	teaspoon baking soda
½	teaspoon salt
1	teaspoon grated lemon zest

1. Adjust oven rack to middle position and heat oven to 425 degrees. Line baking sheet with parchment paper. Remove half of wrapper from each stick of frozen butter. Grate unwrapped ends (half of each stick) on coarse grater (you should grate total of 8 tablespoons). Place grated butter in freezer until needed. Melt 2 tablespoons of remaining ungrated butter and set aside. Save remaining 6 tablespoons butter for another use. Place blueberries in freezer until needed.

2. Whisk milk and sour cream together in medium bowl; refrigerate until needed. Whisk flour, ½ cup sugar, baking powder, baking soda, salt, and lemon zest in medium bowl. Add frozen grated butter to flour mixture and toss with fingers until butter is thoroughly coated.

3. Add milk mixture to flour mixture and fold with rubber spatula until just combined. Using spatula, transfer dough to liberally floured counter. Dust surface of dough with flour and with floured hands, knead dough 6 to 8 times, until it just holds together in ragged ball, adding flour as needed to prevent sticking.

4. Roll dough into 12-inch square. Fold dough into thirds like a business letter, using bench scraper or metal spatula to release dough if it sticks to counter. Lift short ends of dough and fold into thirds again to form 4-inch square. Transfer dough to plate lightly dusted with flour and chill in freezer 5 minutes.

5. Transfer dough to floured counter and roll into 12-inch square again. Sprinkle chilled blueberries evenly over surface of dough, then press down so they are slightly embedded in dough. Using bench scraper or thin metal spatula, loosen dough from counter. Roll dough into cylinder, pressing to form tight log. Arrange log seam side down and press into 12 by 4-inch rectangle. Using floured bench scraper or sharp, floured knife, cut rectangle crosswise into 4 equal rectangles. Cut each rectangle diagonally to form 2 triangles and transfer to prepared baking sheet.

6. Brush tops with melted butter and sprinkle with remaining 1 tablespoon sugar. Bake until tops and bottoms are golden brown, 18 to 25 minutes. Transfer to wire rack and let cool for at least 10 minutes before serving.

TO MAKE AHEAD: After placing scones on baking sheet in step 5, either refrigerate them overnight or freeze for up to 1 month. When ready to bake, for refrigerated scones, heat oven to 425 degrees and follow directions in step 6. For frozen scones, do not thaw, heat oven to 375 degrees and follow directions in step 6, extending cooking time to 25 to 30 minutes.

Cranberry-Pecan Muffins

✔ **WHY THIS RECIPE WORKS:** To tame the harsh bite of the cranberries found in most cranberry-nut muffins, we chopped the cranberries in a food processor and tossed them with confectioners' sugar and a little salt (which we often use to tame the bitterness in eggplant). As for the nuts, we took a cue from cakes made with nut flour and augmented some of the all-purpose flour with pecan flour (made by grinding pecans in a food processor). These muffins boasted a rich, hearty crumb. But because we were working with less flour, our muffins spread rather than baking up tall and self-contained. We fixed the problem by letting the batter rest for 30 minutes. This allowed what flour there was to become more hydrated, resulting in a properly thickened batter that baked up perfectly domed. To replace the missing crunch of the nuts, we simply topped the muffins with a pecan streusel.

Cranberry-Pecan Muffins
MAKES 12 MUFFINS

If fresh cranberries aren't available, substitute frozen cranberries and microwave until they are partially thawed, 30 to 45 seconds. See Core Technique on page 513 for more details on making muffins.

STREUSEL TOPPING

- **3 tablespoons all-purpose flour**
- **1 tablespoon packed light brown sugar**
- **4 teaspoons granulated sugar**
- **2 tablespoons unsalted butter, cut into ½-inch pieces and softened**
  Pinch salt
- **½ cup pecans**

MUFFINS

- **1⅓ cups (6⅔ ounces) all-purpose flour**
- **1½ teaspoons baking powder**
- **1 teaspoon salt**
- **1¼ cups pecans, toasted and cooled**
- **1 cup (7 ounces) plus 1 tablespoon granulated sugar**
- **2 large eggs**
- **6 tablespoons unsalted butter, melted and cooled**
- **½ cup whole milk**
- **8 ounces (2 cups) fresh cranberries**
- **1 tablespoon confectioners' sugar**

1. Adjust oven rack to upper-middle position and heat oven to 425 degrees. Spray 12-cup muffin tin with vegetable oil spray.

2. FOR THE TOPPING: Process flour, brown sugar, granulated sugar, butter, and salt in food processor until mixture resembles coarse sand, 4 to 5 pulses. Add pecans and process until pecans are coarsely chopped, about 4 pulses. Transfer to small bowl; set aside.

3. FOR THE MUFFINS: Whisk flour, baking powder, and ¾ teaspoon salt together in bowl; set aside.

4. Process toasted pecans and granulated sugar until mixture resembles coarse sand, 10 to 15 seconds. Transfer to large bowl and whisk in eggs, butter, and milk until combined. Whisk flour mixture into egg mixture until just moistened and no streaks of flour remain. Set batter aside for 30 minutes to thicken.

5. Pulse cranberries, remaining ¼ teaspoon salt, and confectioners' sugar in food processor until very coarsely chopped, 4 to 5 pulses. Using rubber spatula, fold cranberries into batter. Using spring-loaded portion scoop or dry measuring cup, divide batter equally among prepared muffin cups (batter should completely fill cups and mound slightly). Evenly sprinkle streusel topping over muffins, gently pressing into batter to adhere.

6. Bake until muffin tops are golden and just firm and toothpick inserted in center of muffin comes out with few crumbs attached, 17 to 18 minutes, rotating muffin tin halfway through baking. Let muffins cool in tin for 10 minutes, then transfer to wire rack and let cool for 10 minutes before serving.

Blueberry Swirl Muffins

WHY THIS RECIPE WORKS: Too often, the blueberry flavor in blueberry muffins is fleeting, thanks to the fact that the berries in the produce aisle have suffered from long-distance shipping. We wanted blueberry muffins that put the berry flavor at the forefront and would taste great even with watery supermarket berries. When we combined blueberry jam with fresh supermarket blueberries, the muffins baked up with a pretty blue filling, but the jam made them too sweet. Instead, we made our own low-sugar jam by simmering fresh blueberries with a bit of sugar. Adding our jam to the batter along with fresh, uncooked berries gave our muffins intense blueberry flavor and the liquid burst that only fresh berries could provide. As for the muffin base, we found that the quick-bread method—whisking together eggs and sugar before adding milk and melted butter, then gently folding in the dry ingredients—produced a hearty, substantial crumb that could support a generous amount of fruit. An equal amount of butter and oil created just the right buttery flavor and moist, tender texture. To make the muffins even richer, we swapped the whole milk for buttermilk. For a nice crunch, we sprinkled lemon-scented sugar over the batter before baking.

Blueberry Swirl Muffins

MAKES 12 MUFFINS

If buttermilk is unavailable, substitute ¾ cup plain whole-milk or low-fat yogurt thinned with ¼ cup milk. See Core Technique on page 513 for more details on making muffins.

LEMON-SUGAR TOPPING
- ⅓ cup (2⅓ ounces) sugar
- 1½ teaspoons grated lemon zest

MUFFINS
- 10 ounces (2 cups) blueberries
- 1⅛ cups (7¾ ounces) plus 1 teaspoon sugar
- 2½ cups (12½ ounces) all-purpose flour
- 2½ teaspoons baking powder
- 1 teaspoon salt
- 2 large eggs
- 4 tablespoons unsalted butter, melted and cooled
- ¼ cup vegetable oil
- 1 cup buttermilk
- 1½ teaspoons vanilla extract

1. FOR THE TOPPING: Stir together sugar and lemon zest in small bowl until combined and set aside.

2. FOR THE MUFFINS: Adjust oven rack to upper-middle position and heat oven to 425 degrees. Spray 12-cup muffin tin with vegetable oil spray. Bring 1 cup blueberries and 1 teaspoon sugar to simmer in small saucepan over medium heat. Cook, mashing berries with spoon several times and stirring frequently, until berries have broken down and mixture is thickened and reduced to ¼ cup, about 6 minutes. Transfer to small bowl and let cool to room temperature, 10 to 15 minutes.

3. Whisk flour, baking powder, and salt together in large bowl. Whisk remaining 1⅛ cups sugar and eggs together in medium bowl until thick and homogeneous, about 45 seconds. Slowly whisk in butter and oil until combined. Whisk in buttermilk and vanilla until combined. Using rubber spatula, fold egg

mixture and remaining 1 cup blueberries into flour mixture until just moistened. (Batter will be very lumpy with few spots of dry flour; do not overmix.)

4. Using spring-loaded portion scoop or dry measuring cup, divide batter evenly among prepared muffin cups (batter should completely fill cups and mound slightly). Spoon 1 teaspoon of cooked berry mixture into center of each mound of batter. Using chopstick or skewer, gently swirl berry filling into batter using figure-eight motion. Sprinkle lemon sugar evenly over muffins.

5. Bake until muffins are golden brown and toothpick inserted in center of muffin comes out with few crumbs attached, 17 to 19 minutes, rotating muffin tin halfway through baking. Let muffins cool in tin for 5 minutes, then transfer to wire rack and let cool for 5 minutes before serving.

Better Bran Muffins

WHY THIS RECIPE WORKS: Classic bran muffins rely on unprocessed wheat bran, but few stores carry this specialized ingredient. We tested bran cereal from the supermarket and found that twig-style cereal worked better than flakes, but soaking the twigs in milk, as most recipes recommend, left our muffins dense and heavy. Instead, we stirred together the wet ingredients, then added the cereal. Grinding half of the twigs in the food processor and leaving the rest whole gave the muffins the right texture. Whole-milk yogurt, plus butter, added needed moisture to the batter. Molasses and brown sugar reinforced the earthy bran flavor. To address the texture of the muffins, we switched to baking soda instead of baking powder and used one egg plus a yolk—two eggs made the muffins too springy. To ensure that they would soften fully, we plumped the raisins in water in the microwave before adding them to the batter.

Better Bran Muffins

MAKES 12 MUFFINS

We prefer Kellogg's All-Bran Original cereal in this recipe. Dried cranberries or dried cherries may be substituted for the raisins. See Core Technique on page 513 for more details on making muffins.

- 1 cup raisins
- 1 teaspoon water
- 2¼ cups (5 ounces) All-Bran Original cereal
- 1¼ cups (6¼ ounces) all-purpose flour
- ½ cup (2¾ ounces) whole-wheat flour
- 2 teaspoons baking soda
- ½ teaspoon salt
- 1 large egg plus 1 large yolk
- ⅔ cup packed (4⅔ ounces) light brown sugar
- 3 tablespoons molasses
- 1 teaspoon vanilla extract
- 6 tablespoons unsalted butter, melted and cooled
- 1¾ cups plain whole-milk yogurt

1. Adjust oven rack to middle position and heat oven to 400 degrees. Spray 12-cup muffin tin with vegetable oil spray. Line plate with paper towel. Combine raisins and water in small bowl, cover, and microwave for 30 seconds. Let stand, covered, until raisins are softened and plump, about 5 minutes. Transfer raisins to prepared plate to cool.

2. Process 1 cup plus 2 tablespoons cereal in food processor until finely ground, about 1 minute. Whisk all-purpose flour, whole-wheat flour, baking soda, and salt in large bowl until combined and set aside. Whisk egg and egg yolk together in medium bowl until well combined and light-colored, about 20 seconds. Add sugar, molasses, and vanilla to bowl with eggs and whisk until mixture is thick, about 30 seconds. Add melted butter and whisk to combine. Add yogurt and whisk to combine. Stir in processed cereal and remaining 1 cup plus 2 tablespoons unprocessed cereal. Let mixture sit until cereal is evenly moistened (there will still be some small lumps), about 5 minutes.

3. Add wet ingredients to dry ingredients and mix gently with rubber spatula until batter is just combined and evenly moistened (do not overmix.) Gently fold raisins into batter. Using spring-loaded portion scoop or dry measuring cup, divide batter evenly among prepared muffin cups, dropping batter to form mounds (do not level or flatten batter).

4. Bake until muffins are dark golden and toothpick inserted in center of muffin comes out with few crumbs attached, 16 to 20 minutes, rotating muffin tin halfway through baking. Let muffins cool in tin for 5 minutes, then transfer to wire rack and let cool for 10 minutes before serving.

Southern-Style Skillet Cornbread

✔ **WHY THIS RECIPE WORKS:** Savory skillet-baked Southern-style cornbread should boast hearty corn flavor, a sturdy, moist crumb, and a dark brown crust. For the right texture, we used fine-ground cornmeal. Toasting it in the oven for a few minutes intensified the corn flavor. Buttermilk added a sharp tang that worked well with the corn, and soaking the cornmeal in the buttermilk helped to soften it so our cornbread was moist and tender. When it came to the fat, a combination of butter (for flavor) and vegetable oil (which can withstand high heat without burning) worked best, and greasing the pan with both delivered the crisp crust we were after.

Southern-Style Skillet Cornbread
SERVES 12

We prefer a cast-iron skillet here, but any ovensafe 10-inch skillet will work fine. Fine-ground cornmeal (such as Quaker) or fine- or medium-ground stone-ground cornmeal will work in this recipe; avoid coarse-ground cornmeal, as it will make the cornbread gritty. If you don't have buttermilk, see page 45 for information on buttermilk substitutes. See Core Technique on page 514 for more details on this recipe.

- 2¼ **cups (11¼ ounces) cornmeal**
- 2 **cups buttermilk**
- ¼ **cup vegetable oil**
- 4 **tablespoons unsalted butter, cut into 4 pieces**
- 1 **teaspoon baking powder**
- 1 **teaspoon baking soda**
- ¾ **teaspoon salt**
- 2 **large eggs**

1. Adjust oven racks to lower-middle and middle positions and heat oven to 450 degrees. Heat 10-inch cast-iron skillet on middle rack for 10 minutes. Spread cornmeal over rimmed baking sheet and bake on lower-middle rack until fragrant and color begins to deepen, about 5 minutes. Transfer hot cornmeal to large bowl and whisk in buttermilk; set aside.

2. Carefully add oil to hot skillet and continue to bake until oil is just smoking, about 5 minutes. Remove skillet from oven and add butter, carefully swirling pan until butter is melted. Pour all but 1 tablespoon oil mixture into cornmeal mixture, leaving remaining oil mixture in pan. Whisk baking powder, baking soda, and salt into cornmeal mixture, until combined, then whisk in eggs.

3. Pour cornmeal mixture into hot skillet and bake on middle rack until top begins to crack and sides are golden brown, 12 to 16 minutes, rotating pan halfway through baking. Let cornbread cool in pan for 5 minutes, then turn out onto wire rack. Serve.

All-Purpose Cornbread

✔ **WHY THIS RECIPE WORKS:** Cornbread can be sweet and cakey (the Northern version) or savory and light (the Southern version). We wanted a combination of the two. And most important, we wanted our cornbread to be bursting with corn flavor. The secret was pretty simple: Use corn, not just cornmeal. While fresh corn was best, frozen was nearly as good and pureeing the kernels in a food processor made them easy to use while eliminating tough, chewy kernels. Buttermilk provided a tangy flavor, while light brown sugar enhanced the naturally sweet flavor of the corn. For a thick crust, we baked the bread at a higher than conventional temperature, producing a crunchy crust full of toasted corn flavor.

All-Purpose Cornbread
SERVES 6

Before preparing the baking dish or any of the other ingredients, measure out the frozen kernels and let them stand at room temperature until needed. When corn is in season, fresh cooked kernels can be substituted for the frozen corn. This recipe was developed with Quaker yellow cornmeal; a stone-ground whole-grain cornmeal will work but will yield a drier and less tender cornbread. We prefer a Pyrex glass baking dish because it yields a nice golden brown crust, but a metal baking pan (nonstick or traditional) will also work. If you don't have buttermilk, see page 45 for information on buttermilk substitutes.

- 1½ **cups (7½ ounces) all-purpose flour**
- 1 **cup (5 ounces) cornmeal**
- 2 **teaspoons baking powder**
- ¼ **teaspoon baking soda**
- ¾ **teaspoon salt**
- ¼ **cup packed (1¾ ounces) light brown sugar**
- ¾ **cup frozen corn, thawed**
- 1 **cup buttermilk**
- 2 **large eggs**
- 8 **tablespoons unsalted butter, melted and cooled**

1. Adjust oven rack to middle position and heat oven to 400 degrees. Spray 8-inch square baking dish with vegetable oil spray. Whisk flour, cornmeal, baking powder, baking soda, and salt in medium bowl until combined; set aside.

2. In food processor or blender, process brown sugar, corn kernels, and buttermilk until combined, about 5 seconds. Add eggs and process until well combined (corn lumps will remain), about 5 seconds longer.

3. Using rubber spatula, make well in center of dry ingredients; pour wet ingredients into well. Begin folding dry ingredients into wet, giving mixture only a few turns to barely combine. Add melted butter and continue folding until dry ingredients are just moistened. Pour batter into prepared baking dish and smooth surface with rubber spatula.

4. Bake until cornbread is deep golden brown and toothpick inserted in center comes out clean, 25 to 35 minutes. Let cool on wire rack for 10 minutes, then invert onto wire rack. Turn right side up and let cool until warm, about 10 minutes longer, and serve. (Leftover cornbread can be wrapped in aluminum foil and reheated in a 350-degree oven for 10 to 15 minutes.)

Brown Soda Bread

WHY THIS RECIPE WORKS: For a brown soda bread with good wheaty flavor but without a gummy, dense texture, we started by finding the right ratio of whole-wheat to all-purpose flour. Toasted wheat germ played up the sweet, nutty flavor of the whole wheat. To keep the texture light, we needed plenty of leavening; baking soda alone gave the bread a soapy taste, so we used a combination of baking soda and baking powder. Just a touch of sugar and a few tablespoons of butter kept our bread wholesome but not "health foody," and brushing a portion of the melted butter on the loaf after baking gave it a rich crust.

Brown Soda Bread
MAKES 1 LOAF

If you don't have buttermilk, see page 45 for information on buttermilk substitutes. See Core Technique on page 516 for more details on this recipe.

- 2 **cups (10 ounces) all-purpose flour**
- 1½ **cups (8¼ ounces) whole-wheat flour**
- ½ **cup toasted wheat germ**
- 3 **tablespoons sugar**
- 1½ **teaspoons salt**
- 1 **teaspoon baking powder**
- 1 **teaspoon baking soda**
- 1¾ **cups buttermilk**
- 3 **tablespoons unsalted butter, melted**

1. Adjust oven rack to lower-middle position and heat oven to 400 degrees. Line rimmed baking sheet with parchment paper. Whisk all-purpose flour, whole-wheat flour, wheat germ, sugar, salt, baking powder, and baking soda together in large bowl. Combine buttermilk and 2 tablespoons melted butter in 2-cup liquid measuring cup.

2. Add wet ingredients to dry ingredients and stir with rubber spatula until dough just comes together. Turn out dough onto lightly floured counter and knead until cohesive mass forms, about 8 turns. Pat dough into 7-inch round and transfer to prepared sheet. Using sharp serrated knife, make ¼-inch-deep cross about 5 inches long on top of loaf. Bake until skewer inserted in center comes out clean and loaf registers 195 degrees, 45 to 50 minutes, rotating sheet halfway through baking.

3. Remove bread from oven. Brush with remaining 1 tablespoon melted butter. Transfer loaf to wire rack and let cool for at least 1 hour. Serve.

Brown Soda Bread with Currants and Caraway
Add 1 cup dried currants and 1 tablespoon caraway seeds to dry ingredients in step 1.

Banana Bread

WHY THIS RECIPE WORKS: Our ideal banana bread is simple enough—a moist, tender loaf that really tastes like bananas. We discovered that doubling the dose of bananas in our favorite test recipe was both a blessing and a curse. The abundance of fruit made for intense banana flavor, but the weight and moisture sank the loaf and gave it a cakelike structure. Looking to add banana flavor without moisture, we placed our bananas in a glass bowl and microwaved them for a few minutes, then transferred the fruit to a strainer to drain. We simmered the exuded banana liquid in a saucepan until it was reduced, then incorporated it into the batter. Brown sugar complemented the bananas better than granulated sugar, and vanilla worked well with the bananas' faintly boozy, rumlike flavor, as did swapping out the oil for the nutty richness of butter. Toasted walnuts lent a pleasing crunch. As a final embellishment, we sliced a sixth banana and shingled it on top of the loaf. A final sprinkle of sugar helped the slices caramelize and gave the loaf an enticingly crunchy top.

Banana Bread
SERVES 10

Be sure to use very ripe, heavily speckled (or even black) bananas in this recipe. This recipe can be made using 5 thawed frozen bananas; since they release a lot of liquid naturally, they can bypass the microwaving in step 2 and go directly into the fine-mesh strainer. Do not use a thawed frozen banana in step 4; it will be too soft to slice. Instead, simply sprinkle the top of the loaf with sugar. We developed this recipe using a loaf pan that measures 8½ by 4½ inches; if you use a 9 by 5-inch loaf pan, start checking for doneness 5 minutes earlier than advised in the recipe. The texture is best when the loaf is eaten fresh, but it can be stored (let cool completely first), covered tightly with plastic wrap, for up to 3 days. See Recipe Tutorial on page 524 for more details on this recipe.

- 1¾ **cups (8¾ ounces) all-purpose flour**
- 1 **teaspoon baking soda**
- ½ **teaspoon salt**
- 6 **very ripe large bananas (2¼ pounds), peeled**
- 8 **tablespoons unsalted butter, melted and cooled**

2 large eggs
¾ cup packed (5¼ ounces) light brown sugar
1 teaspoon vanilla extract
½ cup walnuts, toasted and chopped coarse (optional)
2 teaspoons granulated sugar

1. Adjust oven rack to middle position and heat oven to 350 degrees. Spray 8½ by 4½-inch loaf pan with vegetable oil spray. Whisk flour, baking soda, and salt together in large bowl.

2. Place 5 bananas in separate bowl, cover, and microwave until bananas are soft and have released liquid, about 5 minutes. Transfer bananas to fine-mesh strainer over medium bowl and allow to drain, stirring occasionally, for 15 minutes (you should have ½ to ¾ cup liquid).

3. Transfer liquid to medium saucepan and cook over medium-high heat until reduced to ¼ cup, about 5 minutes. Remove pan from heat, stir reduced liquid into bananas, and mash with potato masher until mostly smooth. Whisk in butter, eggs, brown sugar, and vanilla.

4. Pour banana mixture into dry ingredients and stir until just combined, with some streaks of flour remaining. Gently fold in walnuts, if using. Scrape batter into prepared pan. Slice remaining banana on bias into ¼-inch-thick slices. Shingle banana slices on top of loaf in 2 rows, leaving 1½-inch-wide space down center to ensure even rise. Sprinkle granulated sugar evenly over loaf.

5. Bake until toothpick inserted in center of loaf comes out clean, 55 to 75 minutes. Let loaf cool in pan for 10 minutes, then turn out onto wire rack and let cool for 1 hour before serving.

Zucchini Bread

✓ **WHY THIS RECIPE WORKS:** It can be difficult to muster enthusiasm for a slice of zucchini bread, especially if the bread is your typical bland loaf. We wanted a zucchini bread that boasted a moist, but not wet, crumb and was subtly spiced with great summery zucchini flavor. To start, we discovered the downfall of many zucchini breads—the excess moisture from the zucchini. Shredding the zucchini and then squeezing it in paper towels not only rid the zucchini of excess moisture for a drier loaf, but also intensified the zucchini flavor for a better-tasting bread. Many zucchini bread recipes use oil, but we found butter improved the flavor of the bread. Zucchini is subtle, so cinnamon and allspice, along with lemon juice, perked the flavor up further, as did the tang of yogurt, which we preferred over milk (too lean and bland) and sour cream (too rich). We tried sprinkling the loaves with nuts, but we preferred them the old-fashioned way, stirred into the batter for nutty flavor in every bite.

Zucchini Bread
SERVES 10

Small zucchini have smaller, drier seeds than large zucchini and are preferred in this recipe. If you are using a large zucchini, cut each zucchini in half lengthwise and use a spoon to scrape out and discard the seeds before shredding. The test kitchen's preferred loaf pan measures 8½ by 4½ inches; if you use a 9 by 5-inch loaf pan, start checking for doneness 5 minutes earlier than advised in the recipe.

2 zucchini (1 pound), trimmed
2 cups (10 ounces) all-purpose flour
1 teaspoon baking soda
1 teaspoon baking powder
1 teaspoon ground cinnamon
1 teaspoon ground allspice
½ teaspoon salt
1½ cups (10½ ounces) sugar
6 tablespoons unsalted butter, melted and cooled
2 large eggs
¼ cup plain whole-milk or low-fat yogurt
1 tablespoon lemon juice
½ cup pecans or walnuts, toasted and chopped coarse

1. Adjust oven rack to middle position and heat oven to 350 degrees. Grease 8½ by 4½-inch loaf pan. Shred zucchini using coarse grater. Squeeze shredded zucchini between several layers of paper towels to absorb excess moisture.

2. Whisk flour, baking soda, baking powder, cinnamon, allspice, and salt together in large bowl. In medium bowl, whisk sugar, melted butter, eggs, yogurt, and lemon juice together until smooth. Gently fold shredded zucchini and yogurt mixture into flour mixture with rubber spatula until just combined (do not overmix). Gently fold in pecans.

3. Scrape batter into prepared pan. Bake until golden brown and toothpick inserted in center of loaf comes out with few crumbs attached, about 1 hour, rotating loaf pan halfway through baking.

4. Let loaf cool in pan for 10 minutes, then turn out onto wire rack and let cool for 1 hour before serving.

Zucchini Bread with Golden Raisins or Dried Cranberries

Fold ¾ cup golden raisins or dried cranberries into batter with pecans.

Classic Pancakes

✓ **WHY THIS RECIPE WORKS:** There's nothing like ruining a Saturday morning pancake breakfast with tough, rubbery, bland pancakes. We set out to deliver perfectly light and fluffy pancakes with good flavor. Buttermilk was a must in our recipe—it not only lent flavor but also created pancakes with better texture, especially since we opted to use both baking powder and baking soda. To keep our pancakes as light and fluffy as possible, we made sure to avoid overmixing the batter, which would develop gluten and make the pancakes tough. We stopped stirring when the batter was lumpy and a few streaks of flour were still visible. A hot skillet also proved critical for avoiding dense, pale pancakes. Since using too much oil in the skillet would turn our delicate pancakes greasy and dense, we used a heatproof pastry brush or paper towels to distribute a small amount of oil over the cooking surface. We knew the first side was cooked as soon as bubbles appeared on the surface of the batter; the second side likewise needed just a short stint until the pancakes were perfectly golden brown.

Classic Pancakes

MAKES ABOUT 16 (4-INCH) PANCAKES, SERVING 4 TO 6

Getting the skillet hot enough before making the pancakes is key. If you don't have buttermilk, see page 45 for information on buttermilk substitutes. Serve with maple syrup. See Core Technique on page 518 for more details on this recipe.

- 2 **cups (10 ounces) all-purpose flour**
- 2 **tablespoons sugar**
- 2 **teaspoons baking powder**
- ½ **teaspoon baking soda**
- ½ **teaspoon salt**
- 2 **cups buttermilk**
- 3 **tablespoons unsalted butter, melted and cooled**
- 1 **large egg**
- 1–2 **teaspoons vegetable oil**

1. Adjust oven rack to middle position and heat oven to 200 degrees. Spray wire rack set in rimmed baking sheet with vegetable oil spray; place in oven.

2. Whisk flour, sugar, baking powder, baking soda, and salt together in large bowl. Whisk buttermilk, melted butter, and egg together in large measuring cup. Make well in center of dry ingredients; pour in buttermilk mixture and whisk very gently until just combined (batter should remain lumpy, with few streaks of flour remaining). Do not overmix.

3. Heat 1 teaspoon oil in 12-inch nonstick skillet over medium heat until shimmering. Using heatproof pastry brush or wad of paper towels, carefully spread thin film of oil over bottom and sides of skillet. Using ¼-cup measure, portion batter into pan in 3 places. Cook until large bubbles begin to appear evenly over surface, about 2 minutes. Using thin, wide nonstick spatula, flip pancakes and cook until second side is golden brown, about 1½ minutes. Serve immediately or transfer to wire rack in preheated oven. Repeat with remaining batter, using remaining oil as necessary.

Blueberry Pancakes

Frozen blueberries can be substituted for fresh; thaw and rinse the berries gently to remove excess juice, then spread out on paper towels to dry before using.

After adding batter to skillet in step 3, sprinkle 1 tablespoon fresh blueberries over each pancake; continue to cook as directed. (You will need 1 cup of blueberries.)

Cornmeal Pancakes

Substitute 1½ cups cornmeal for 1 cup flour.

Grahamcakes

To make 1 cup of graham cracker crumbs, process 5 ounces graham crackers (9 crackers) in a food processor to fine crumbs.

Substitute 1 cup graham cracker crumbs mixed with 2 tablespoons cornmeal for flour.

Multigrain Pancakes

✔ **WHY THIS RECIPE WORKS:** Bland, dense, and gummy, most multigrain pancakes are more about your diet than your palate. We wanted flavorful, fluffy, and healthful flapjacks. After testing lots of grains, we found that muesli had all the ingredients and flavor we wanted in one package—raw whole oats, wheat germ, rye, barley, toasted nuts, and dried fruit. But pancakes made with whole muesli were too chewy and gummy. We converted the muesli into a flour in the food processor and then found the perfect combination of muesli "flour," all-purpose flour, whole-wheat flour, and leavening to achieve the lightness we wanted. The pancakes were perfect after we tweaked the flavor with a little butter, vanilla, and brown sugar and cut the acidity by replacing the buttermilk with a blend of milk and lemon juice.

Multigrain Pancakes

MAKES 16 (4-INCH) PANCAKES, SERVING 4 TO 6

The pancakes can be cooked on an electric griddle. Set the griddle temperature to 350 degrees and cook as directed. Familia brand no-sugar-added muesli is the best choice for this recipe. If you can't find Familia, look for Alpen or any no-sugar-added muesli. (If you can't find muesli without sugar, muesli with sugar added will work; reduce the brown sugar in the recipe to 1 tablespoon.) Mix the batter first and then heat the pan. Letting the batter sit while the pan heats will give the dry ingredients time to absorb the wet ingredients; otherwise, the batter will be runny. Serve with maple syrup or Apple, Cranberry, and Pecan Topping (recipe follows). See Recipe Tutorial on page 527 for more details on this recipe.

- 2 **cups whole milk**
- 4 **teaspoons fresh lemon juice**
- 1¼ **cups (6 ounces), plus 3 tablespoons no-sugar-added muesli**
- ¾ **cup (3¾ ounces) all-purpose flour**
- ½ **cup (2¾ ounces) whole-wheat flour**
- 2 **tablespoons packed brown sugar**
- 2¼ **teaspoons baking powder**
- ½ **teaspoon baking soda**
- ½ **teaspoon salt**
- 2 **large eggs**
- 3 **tablespoons unsalted butter, melted and cooled**
- ¾ **teaspoon vanilla extract**
- 1–2 **teaspoons vegetable oil**

1. Adjust oven rack to middle position and heat oven to 200 degrees. Spray wire rack set in rimmed baking sheet with vegetable oil spray; place in oven. Whisk milk and lemon juice together in large measuring cup; set aside to thicken while preparing other ingredients.

2. Process 1¼ cups muesli in food processor until finely ground, 2 to 2½ minutes; transfer to large bowl. Add remaining 3 tablespoons unground muesli, all-purpose flour, whole-wheat flour, brown sugar, baking powder, baking soda, and salt; whisk to combine.

3. Add eggs, melted butter, and vanilla to milk mixture and whisk until combined. Make well in center of dry ingredients; pour in milk mixture and whisk very gently until just combined (batter should remain lumpy, with few streaks of flour remaining). Do not overmix. Allow batter to sit while pan heats, at least 5 minutes.

4. Heat 1 teaspoon oil in 12-inch nonstick skillet over medium heat until shimmering. Using heatproof pastry brush or wad of paper towels, carefully spread thin film of oil over bottom and sides of skillet. Using ¼-cup measure, portion batter into pan in 3 places. Cook until small bubbles begin to appear evenly over surface, 2 to 3 minutes. Using thin, wide nonstick spatula, flip pancakes and cook until second side is golden brown, 1½ to 2 minutes longer. Serve immediately or transfer to wire rack in preheated oven. Repeat with remaining batter, using remaining oil as necessary.

Apple, Cranberry, and Pecan Topping
SERVES 4 TO 6
We prefer semifirm apples, such as Fuji, Gala, or Braeburn, for this topping. Avoid very tart apples, such as Granny Smith, and soft varieties like McIntosh.

3½	tablespoons unsalted butter, chilled
1¼	pounds apples, peeled, cored, and cut into ½-inch pieces
	Pinch salt
1	cup apple cider
½	cup dried cranberries
½	cup maple syrup
1	teaspoon lemon juice
½	teaspoon vanilla extract
¾	cup pecans, toasted and chopped coarse

Melt 1½ tablespoons butter in 12-inch skillet over medium-high heat. Add apples and salt; cook, stirring occasionally, until softened and browned, 7 to 9 minutes. Stir in cider and cranberries; cook until liquid has almost evaporated, 6 to 8 minutes. Stir in maple syrup and cook until thickened, 4 to 5 minutes. Add remaining 2 tablespoons butter, lemon juice, and vanilla; whisk until sauce is smooth. Serve with toasted nuts.

Buttermilk Waffles

✓ **WHY THIS RECIPE WORKS:** Most "waffle" recipes are merely repurposed pancake recipes that rely on butter and maple syrup to mask the mediocre results. Our waffles had to have a crisp, golden brown crust with a moist, fluffy interior. For our starting point, we adapted a buttermilk pancake recipe, but, while the flavor was terrific, the waffles had a gummy, wet interior and not much crust. We needed a drier batter with much more leavening oomph. In tempura batters, seltzer is often used because the tiny bubbles inflate the batter the same way as a chemical leavener. We tried replacing the buttermilk in our recipe with a mixture of seltzer and buttermilk powder, plus baking soda for browning. The resulting waffles were light and perfectly browned, but after only a few moments off the heat, they lost their crispness. After some experimentation, we found that waffles made with oil stayed significantly crispier than those made with melted butter, which is partly water. And best of all, tasters didn't notice the swap, just the excellent flavor.

Buttermilk Waffles
MAKES ABOUT EIGHT 7-INCH ROUND WAFFLES
While the waffles can be eaten as soon as they are removed from the waffle iron, they will have a crispier exterior if rested in a warm oven for 10 minutes. (This method also makes it possible to serve everyone at the same time.) Use a traditional (not Belgian) waffle iron for this recipe. Buttermilk powder is available in most supermarkets and is generally located near the dried-milk products or in the baking aisle. Leftover buttermilk powder, which can be used in a number of baking applications, can be kept in the refrigerator for up to a year. Seltzer or club soda gives these waffles a light texture that would otherwise be provided by whipped egg whites. (Avoid sparkling water such as Perrier: It's not bubbly enough to make a difference in the batter.) Be sure to use a freshly opened bottle for maximum lift. Serve these waffles with butter and warm maple syrup.

2	cups (10 ounces) all-purpose flour
½	cup (2½ ounces) buttermilk powder
1	tablespoon sugar
¾	teaspoon salt
½	teaspoon baking soda
½	cup sour cream
2	large eggs
¼	cup vegetable oil
¼	teaspoon vanilla extract
1¼	cups seltzer

1. Adjust oven rack to middle position and heat oven to 200 degrees. Set wire rack in rimmed baking sheet; place in oven. Whisk flour, buttermilk powder, sugar, salt, and baking soda together in large bowl. Whisk sour cream, eggs, oil, and vanilla together in medium bowl to combine. Gently stir seltzer into wet ingredients. Make well in center of dry ingredients and pour in wet ingredients. Using rubber spatula, gently stir until just combined (batter should remain lumpy with few streaks of flour).

2. Heat waffle iron and bake waffles according to manufacturer's instructions (use about ⅓ cup for 7-inch round iron). Transfer waffles to wire rack in preheated oven; repeat with remaining batter. Serve.

Inside This Chapter

CHAPTER 13

How to Make Yeast Breads and Pizzas

While many novice cooks shy away from bread making, it's both simple and rewarding. Yes, there's a chance that things will go wrong—loaves can turn out misshapen or squat. Bread is never really the same twice. Dough will rise differently depending on the yeast's freshness or the temperature in your kitchen. You must be prepared to observe and react. This chapter covers a range of yeasted breads, from classic loaves to pizza to sticky buns. You will learn how to assess progress and turn out bakery-quality items.

Getting Started

Essential Equipment

Most of the key equipment needed to prepare yeast breads is covered extensively in chapter 1. See pages 20, 27, and 28 for information on stand mixers, rimmed baking sheets, and loaf pans. In addition to these well-used items, yeast breads rely on a few pieces of specialized equipment outlined below.

BENCH SCRAPER

This basic tool—little more than a blunt-edged rectangular metal blade a little larger than an index card—is handy for transferring bread dough from one surface to another and for cutting dough into chunks. It's useful, too, for scraping off dough stuck to the counter. You'll also find other kitchen uses for a bench scraper, such as scooping up chopped vegetables and herbs off the cutting board, cutting biscuit or scone dough into wedges, and "blocking" the edges of pastry dough as it's rolled out.

BOWL SCRAPER

The best way to remove or fold sticky, soft dough or runny batter in a bowl is with a bowl (or dough) scraper. This hand-held spatula fits between your palm and fingers. The ideal scraper is curved, with enough grip to scrape the bowl clean and enough rigidity to move heavy dough easily. We tried scrapers made of plastic, metal, silicone, and combinations of these materials, and our favorite models were made of contoured silicone covering a metal insert.

BAKING STONE

A ceramic baking stone conducts heat and transfers it evenly and steadily to the bottom of the pizza or bread being baked on it and encourages the development of a thick, nicely browned bottom crust. The stone should be placed in the oven before the oven is turned on and should be allowed to heat for a minimum of 30 minutes (and ideally 60 minutes) to ensure that it is thoroughly heated and will maintain its temperature once the pizza or bread is placed in the oven. In a pinch, an inverted rimmed baking sheet is an acceptable substitute.

PIZZA PEEL

A a wide, paddlelike board or metal spatula with a long handle, a peel is useful for sliding pizza and free-form breads into and out of the oven. Dust it well with flour so that pizza or bread can easily slide off. If the dough is exceptionally sticky, we often shape it on parchment paper (and bake the bread on the parchment), which ensures easy transfer. A rimless cookie sheet or an inverted rimmed baking sheet can stand in for a peel.

WATER-FILLED SPRAY BOTTLE

Some breads benefit from being misted with water before and/or during baking. The moisture delays crust formation so that the loaf will attain the proper rise before the surface sets. If the crust forms before the bread is fully risen, the crust is prone to splitting and tearing, and the inside expands outward.

INSTANT-READ THERMOMETER

For those recipes that give an internal temperature to determine the doneness of bread, an instant-read thermometer is key. Most lean, rustic breads are done when they reach 200 to 210 degrees; rich breads are done at about 190 degrees. For more details on what to look for, see page 10.

DIGITAL SCALE

When baking yeast breads, weighing your ingredients, rather than measuring by volume with cups and spoons, is the most accurate method of measurement and will help ensure more consistent results. We prefer digital scales for their easy readability and incredible precision. Look for one that has a large weight range and that can be "zeroed." For more details on what to look for, see page 9.

Essential Ingredients

Flour is the primary ingredient in all yeast breads. For more information on various types of flour, see pages 42–43. Also see page 9 for tips on measuring successfully, as measuring ingredients when baking, especially flour, is key.

Yeast is also essential. When working with yeast, always check the expiration date, as old yeast will rise slowly, or not at all. Salt kills yeast, so when you're adding bread ingredients to a bowl, it's always best not to pour the salt directly on top of the yeast, or vice versa. For information on the types of yeast and how they are best used and how to store them, see page 44.

CORE TECHNIQUE

GETTING STARTED
YEAST BREADS AND PIZZAS | CORE TECHNIQUES
RECIPE TUTORIALS
RECIPE LIBRARY

543

How to Make Bread

Don't let lengthy yeast bread recipes intimidate you. Making yeast bread is easy—even if you're a beginner—and requires just a few minutes of hands-on work. Below is an overview of how most yeast breads are made. Not all breads require all these steps (or all the equipment listed).

A few things to know about yeast: Yeast begins to die at about 130 degrees, so make sure that the water used to make bread dough is not too hot. We find that 100 to 110 degrees works best. Most types of yeasted dough rise best at room temperature (about 70 degrees). While it's possible to hasten rising times by setting the dough in a very warm spot, like a gas oven heated by the pilot light, the flavors generated by an expedited fermentation are not fully developed. But in the winter, this may be a more attractive option than a cold, drafty kitchen counter.

We prefer the convenience of a stand mixer; refer to How to Knead Bread Dough in a Mixer on page 546 for more detail on this part of the process. If you do want to knead by hand, see How to Knead Bread Dough by Hand (page 547).

ESSENTIAL EQUIPMENT

- digital scale
- mixing bowls
- stand mixer
- plastic wrap
- pizza peel or rimmed baking sheet
- parchment paper
- razor blade and/or water-filled spray bottle
- baking stone
- instant-read thermometer

1. MEASURE CAREFULLY

Measure out flour, preferably using a scale, and water.

WHY? Because the ratio of flour to water greatly impacts the end result, we recommend weighing your ingredients before making bread. That said, bread dough is very flexible—you will have plenty of time during kneading to fix a wet or dry dough.

2. MAKE SPONGE

To develop extra flavor in simple loaves, combine some flour, water, and yeast in bowl and set aside for at least 6 hours.

WHY? Many rustic bread recipes begin by creating a sponge (also called starter, pre-ferment, *poolish* in French, or *biga* in Italian). This is not like a sourdough starter, which takes weeks to create and must be regularly tended. A sponge is nothing more than a mixture of flour, water, and yeast, which is allowed to ferment for at least 6 hours to develop mildly sour and nutty flavors. More flour, yeast, and water are added to the sponge to build a bread dough. The resulting bread is much chewier and more complex in flavor than breads made with unfermented commercial yeast. The key to using a sponge is to let it rise for about 2 hours and then wait for it to fall (another 4 hours) before using. The fall indicates that the yeast is active and ready to go. Once the sponge has fallen, it can be held for up to 24 hours at room temperature before using, or it can be refrigerated for several days.

3. FORM SHAGGY DOUGH

Combine ingredients (including sponge, if using) in bowl of stand mixer.

WHY? Making a smooth, soft, malleable ball of dough is not the point here—you just want to incorporate the water into the flour. Mixing takes only a minute or two.

4. LET IT REST

Cover bowl with plastic wrap and set aside for about 20 minutes.

WHY? Many of our recipes let the dough rest after it's mixed—officially, this rest is called an autolyse. The point of this short resting time is to let the flour fully absorb the water before getting pushed around during kneading. This allows an enzymatic reaction to take place that makes kneading quicker and easier. An autolyse is especially important for leaner breads such as rustic loaves. Salt, because it interferes with the flour's ability to absorb water and inhibits the enzymatic activity, is typically withheld from the dough when autolyse is used, and is added only after autolyse is complete.

5. KNEAD GENTLY

Knead dough as directed in recipe using stand mixer fitted with dough hook.

WHY? Kneading takes 8 to 10 minutes in a stand mixer (or up to 25 minutes if kneading by hand). Kneading develops gluten in the dough that will give the bread structure. Note that overkneading can harm flavor, so follow time and visual cues in recipes when kneading.

6. LET DOUGH RISE

Turn dough into large bowl or container that has been lightly coated with vegetable oil spray or olive oil. Cover with plastic wrap and set aside until dough has doubled in size.

WHY? After kneading, the dough needs to rest, relax, and rise for several hours. This first rise is called fermentation. During this stage, the activity of the yeast causes the dough to rise and fosters flavor development. More often than not, fermentation takes place at room temperature over the course of an hour or two, or until the dough has doubled in bulk. At the start of this process, we like to stretch a rubber band around the container at the same height as the dough. We can then use the rubber band to judge when the dough has doubled.

7. SHAPE DOUGH

After dough has doubled in size, gently deflate dough and shape according to recipe directions.

WHY? Don't punch the dough down as some recipes suggest—you don't want to knock all the air out of the dough. Once the dough has been gently deflated, it is ready to be formed into the final shape of the bread, such as a round loaf, a sandwich loaf, small rolls, or a long, skinny baguette.

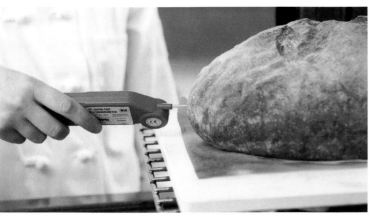

8. LET DOUGH RISE AGAIN

Cover dough with plastic wrap and let rise as directed on pizza peel or inverted baking sheet lined with parchment paper.

WHY? This second rise, also called proofing, is much like the first rise in that the dough needs to rest, relax, and rise. However, since the yeast has already done most of its work, this time the emphasis is on relaxing rather than rising. This step allows both the dough to regain some airiness that was lost during shaping, and the gluten to relax. When properly proofed, the dough will have just the right amount of gas, elasticity, and energy to bake up into a well-risen loaf. To test if dough has been properly proofed, press on it gently with a moistened fingertip or knuckle; it should leave an indentation that slowly fills in.

9. SLASH OR SPRAY BEFORE BAKING

Slash loaf with razor blade and/or spray loaf with water as directed in recipe.

WHY? Spraying loaves with water helps keep the surface of the bread elastic so that the bread can continue to rise nicely as it bakes. Some loaves are also slashed with a sharp knife or razor—the slash acts as a pleat to help the bread rise during baking.

10. TRANSFER TO OVEN QUICKLY

Transfer loaf to oven using parchment paper or pizza peel.

WHY? A bread's rise during baking is called oven spring. The oven's heat causes the alcohol and the carbon dioxide generated by the yeast during the fermentation and proofing stages to expand vigorously. The gluten network swells from the pressure, traps the bubbles as they form, and eventually sets, creating the bread's crumb and crust. For baking pizza, focaccia, ciabatta, and so many other types of breads for which a crisp, well-browned bottom crust is desired, a baking stone is a necessary tool (see page 542 for more details on baking stones).

11. TAKE TEMPERATURE TO JUDGE DONENESS

Bake loaf as directed, using thermometer to determine when loaf is done.

WHY? It's easy to tell when flatbreads like pizza and even focaccia are fully baked, but for loaf breads, judging doneness can be tricky. Color is one indicator, but if the recipe gives an internal temperature, use an instant-read thermometer to tell if the bread is fully baked. To avoid leaving a puncture mark on the surface of the loaf, insert the thermometer through the bottom crust and into the very center of the bread. Lean breads are done when they reach 200 to 210 degrees; rich breads are fully baked at 190 to 195 degrees.

HOW TO MAKE YEAST BREADS AND PIZZAS

How to Knead Bread in a Mixer

ESSENTIAL EQUIPMENT

• stand mixer

The goal of kneading is to build the protein, or gluten, in the dough and create a strong network of cross-linked proteins. When the dough is baked, it expands like a balloon as it releases the carbon dioxide created by the yeast. The elastic network of gluten developed during kneading allows expansion without bursting, resulting in the bubbly, chewy crumb that is the signature of any good loaf. We generally prefer using a stand mixer for this task. Not only does the mixer do all the work, but you're more likely to get good results if you use a mixer. That's because many home bakers add excessive flour when trying to knead dough by hand. The extra flour compromises the texture in the baked loaf.

However, even when using a stand mixer it may be necessary to add more flour during the kneading process. That's because different brands of flour absorb moisture differently. Even the same brand of flour can absorb water differently depending on the humidity in your kitchen. And flour stored in desert kitchens absorbs more liquid than flour kept in pantries in humid climates. When using a stand mixer, look at how the dough sticks to the bowl to determine if the dough needs more flour.

1A. DOUGH HAS ENOUGH FLOUR, BUT KEEP KNEADING

After several minutes, evaluate consistency of dough. It should be starting to pull away from sides of bowl.

WHY? Dough with the right ratio of water to flour will eventually clear the sides of the bowl and form a compact ball that is no longer tacky (see photo 2). The dough in the photo at right requires more kneading, but you can tell that it has enough flour because the dough is starting to pull away from the sides of the bowl.

1B. IF DOUGH IS WET, ADD MORE FLOUR, KEEP KNEADING

If dough is not starting to pull away from sides of bowl after several minutes of kneading, add flour, 1 or 2 tablespoons at a time, with mixer running, allowing 30 to 60 seconds between additions.

WHY? The dough should be pulling away from the sides of the bowl within 5 minutes of starting the kneading process. If this doesn't happen, you'll need to add more flour as directed. It's not unusual to add as much as ¼ cup flour at this stage. If you find that you need to add more than ¼ cup, you might have incorrectly measured the original amount of flour or water.

2. KNEAD UNTIL DOUGH FORMS COMPACT MASS

Continue kneading as directed in recipe until dough has pulled away from sides of bowl and forms compact mass.

WHY? When the dough is no longer tacky, it will pull away from the sides of the bowl and wrap around the dough hook. Note that it's fine if the dough is still sticking to the bottom of the bowl. Once you stop the mixer and remove the dough hook, the dough will release easily.

How to Knead Bread by Hand

Rustic breads are often made from big, wet doughs, which we find easiest to make using a stand mixer. However, if you don't own a mixer, you can still make great loaves of rustic bread using just your hands (our Almost No-Knead Bread is a rustic-style loaf that requires just a few kneads by hand; see page 554). The trick is to use a rhythmic, gentle motion that stretches and massages the dough. Be gentle but firm and try to avoid ripping the dough. As needed, add additional flour by sprinkling it evenly across the counter and gradually kneading this flour into the dough. Just keep in mind to go easy on the flour when mixing and kneading by hand, since the tendency is always to add more than is necessary to avoid sticking. Most dough will require 15 to 25 minutes of hand kneading to form a smooth, round ball. These hand-mixing instructions will work with all but the very wettest doughs, such as ciabatta, which really do require a stand mixer.

1. MIX DOUGH

Whisk liquid ingredients together in medium mixing bowl. Whisk dry ingredients together in large mixing bowl. Stir liquid mixture into dry ingredients with rubber spatula until dough comes together and looks shaggy.

WHY? Before you knead, you must make the dough. A rubber spatula or wooden spoon is the best tool for combining the liquid and dry ingredients.

2. PRESS DOWN AND AWAY

Turn shaggy dough onto lightly floured counter and shape with hands into rough ball. Start each stroke by gently pressing dough down and away from you using heel of your hand.

WHY? The first step is to turn the shaggy mass into a smooth dough that can be kneaded. Add as much flour as is required to get the dough into a smooth mass.

3. LIFT AND FOLD

Lift edge of dough farthest away from you and fold dough in half toward you.

WHY? You are building elasticity in the dough, and folding ensures that you are working all parts of the dough evenly.

4. PRESS DOUGH FORWARD

Press dough forward again using heel of your hand. When dough is finally smooth and elastic (after 15 to 25 minutes of hand kneading), transfer to greased bowl and let rise as directed in recipe.

WHY? This motion works the folded piece of dough back into the center of the dough. Continue this process until dough forms a neat ball.

How to Shape Loaf Breads

ESSENTIAL EQUIPMENT

- mixing bowl
- bowl scraper
- loaf pan

Once dough for sandwich bread and other similar loaf breads has been kneaded and allowed to rise, it should be shaped and placed into the loaf pan. The dough will rise again once in the pan, but you still want to preserve as much of the air as possible from that first rise, so it is important to work the dough gently during the shaping process. Don't use a rolling pin, which will overwork the dough; your hands are a better bet. Make sure to flour them, as well as the counter, to keep the dough from sticking. Note that loaf pan sizes vary, and even small differences in size will affect the rise and appearance of the loaf. Try to use the exact size specified in each recipe.

1. SHAPE DOUGH INTO SQUARE
Scrape dough out of bowl and onto lightly floured counter. Using your hands, press dough into square.
WHY? The goal here is to press the dough into a square that's as long as the loaf pan. For a 9 by 5-inch loaf pan, you want to press the dough into a 9-inch square. If the recipe calls for an 8½ by 4½-inch loaf pan, you should press the dough into an 8½-inch square.

2. ROLL DOUGH INTO CYLINDER
Starting at side closest to you, roll dough into tight cylinder.
WHY? If the cylinder is too loose, the final loaf might be misshapen. Start by folding over the edge of the dough closest to you, then roll the dough, tucking it under as you go. The process is akin to rolling up a jelly roll cake.

3. PINCH SEAM
Once dough has been rolled into cylinder, pinch seam together to secure.
WHY? This will help the dough hold its shape as it proofs in the loaf pan.

4. TRANSFER TO PAN
Place dough seam side down in prepared loaf pan.
WHY? Placing the dough seam side down will help ensure that the seam doesn't split open as the loaf rises. Most recipes will instruct you to prepare the loaf pan by greasing it well with cooking spray. Make sure to grease both the bottom and the sides of the pan.

How to Turn or Fold Rustic Bread Dough

ESSENTIAL EQUIPMENT

- mixing bowl
- bowl scraper or rubber spatula
- plastic wrap

Most doughs are kneaded, left alone to rise, and then shaped. However, when making many rustic breads, we interrupt the process with gentle turning (or folding) of the dough. In some respects, this process is a continuation of kneading, since it is designed to build structure in the dough. Turning is quite simple. We gently fold the dough over itself several times as it rises. Turning stretches the dough, building strength as any wayward sheets of gluten—the protein that gives bread structure once flour and water have been combined—are brought into alignment.

Depending on the recipe, we vary the number of turns in each cycle as well as the number of times we interrupt the rising process to turn the dough. However, here's how the process works in most recipes.

1. LIFT AND FOLD WITH BOWL SCRAPER

Slide bowl scraper or rubber spatula under one side of dough. Gently lift and fold about one-third of dough toward center.

WHY? Many bread recipes call for punching (which is really more like gently pressing) down the dough between the first and second rise to expose the yeast to new food sources. However, this results in a fine crumb, which isn't preferable for a rustic bread. To create a coarser crumb with better chew, we turn rustic bread doughs to reactivate the yeast without pressing out so much air. Turning not only builds structure in the dough, but it also rids the dough of excess carbon dioxide, which otherwise inhibits yeast activity, to ensure maximum flavor and rise. A bowl scraper is a really handy tool for handling dough. (It's flexible, like a credit card, but bigger.) However, a rubber spatula would also work. Many recipes suggest greasing the scraper or spatula with vegetable oil spray since the dough is often sticky.

2. REPEAT LIFTING AND FOLDING

Repeat with opposite side of dough.

WHY? To build structure in the dough as it rises, you want to fold from the outside edges of the dough toward the center.

3. FOLD DOUGH IN HALF

Fold dough in half perpendicular to first series of folds. Dough should be a rough square shape.

WHY? This final fold lifts the dough that was at the bottom of the bowl up to the top. Once you're done folding, make sure to cover the bowl again with plastic wrap. Some recipes call for a second series of turns. Just make sure to replace the plastic wrap each time—the wrap traps moisture and a bit of heat and speeds up the rising process while keeping the dough properly hydrated.

How to Shape Rustic Breads

ESSENTIAL EQUIPMENT

• rimmed baking sheet or pizza peel
• parchment paper

Rustic breads, also known as free-form loaves, can be shaped in numerous ways. The two most common (and easiest) shapes to execute are a torpedo (like a baguette, but wider) and a round (also known as a *boule*). As with shaping breads destined for a loaf pan, you want to handle the dough gently—pressing all the air out of the dough is a big no-no. And because these loaves are not baked in a pan, it is all the more important to close up seams and make sure everything is even. Messy shaping can lead to blown-out loaves, or loaves that are not very attractive. Keep your hands and work surfaces well floured and use parchment paper to help move dough.

Round Shape

1. FOLD LIKE LETTER

Turn risen dough out of bowl and onto floured counter and press into 10-inch square. Fold top and bottom thirds of dough over middle like business letter.

WHY? You might think you can simply shape the blob of risen dough into a round. We find that pressing the dough flat and then folding it back together builds structure in the loaf. Don't use a rolling pin for this task, or you risk deflating the dough, and don't punch down the risen dough. Simply turn the dough out onto the floured counter and press it with your fingertips into a square that measures about 10 inches before folding it.

2. TUCK SIDES UNDER

Gently lift folded dough and tuck sides under.

WHY? At this point the dough should be a square again, with the folds tucked underneath and the smooth side facing up.

3. CUP AND ROUND

Use both hands to round dough into smooth, taut ball.

WHY? The motion here is akin to working clay on a pottery wheel—you're using your entire hand to shape and tuck the dough. Cup both hands around the dough and drag the dough over the counter in a circular motion to build height in the loaf and help secure the seams on the underside. When you're done, transfer the dough to an inverted baking sheet or pizza peel lined with parchment.

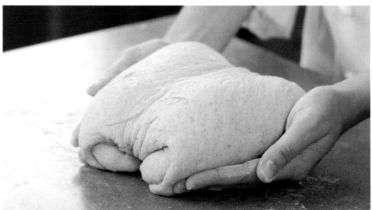

Torpedo Shape

1. FOLD IN TOP CORNERS

Turn risen dough out of bowl and onto floured counter and press into large square. Fold top and bottom corners of dough diagonally into center of square.

WHY? You might think you can simply shape the blob of risen dough into a torpedo. We find that pressing the dough flat and then folding it back together builds structure in the loaf.

2. LIFT AND PULL

Using your fingertips and starting at top of dough, pull underside of dough over top of dough, stretching it considerably as you go. Repeat until dough looks like rough log. With each pull and tuck, press seam firmly to seal.

WHY? This stretching process builds more structure in the dough. Do this motion five to seven more times, or until the dough is taut and has a nice log shape.

3. ROLL OVER

Roll dough onto seam, gently slide your hands underneath each end, and transfer loaf to inverted baking sheet or pizza peel lined with parchment.

WHY? Rolling the log seam side down will help the seam close up as the dough proofs. Since this loaf will bake on a stone, you need to let it proof on a pizza peel or an overturned rimmed baking sheet that you can use like a peel. Make sure to line the peel or baking sheet with parchment (so the loaf can slide right onto the preheated stone at the appropriate time).

4. SHAPE AND TUCK

Finish shaping loaf into taut torpedo shape that is roughly 16 inches long. Tuck edges under with your hands.

WHY? While you should be able to shape a round loaf on the counter and then transfer it to a peel, a long torpedo is likely to stretch a bit in the transfer process. That's why we do the final shaping on the parchment-lined pizza peel or inverted baking sheet.

How to Shape Dinner Rolls

Dinner rolls are surprisingly easy to make and don't require as much attention as rustic loaves—just knead, let rise, and then shape into individual rolls. Of course, turning a mass of dough into neat rolls does require some technique. Don't overhandle the dough—or you risk pressing all the air out. After portioning and shaping the dough into individual rounds, we place the rounds in a baking dish lined with a foil sling; refer to How to Make a Foil Sling (page 595). See the recipe for Fluffy Dinner Rolls on page 576 for details on preparing the dough.

ESSENTIAL EQUIPMENT

- chef's knife or bench scraper
- plastic wrap
- 13 by 9-inch baking dish
- aluminum foil

1. SLICE EVENLY

Turn risen dough onto clean counter and use your hands to stretch dough into even 15-inch-long log. Using chef's knife, cut log into 15 evenly sized pieces.

WHY? Don't try to pinch off pieces from a single mass of dough. Our technique builds structure into the dough and makes it easy to divide the dough into many evenly sized rolls. If you own a bench scraper, use it for this task instead of a chef's knife. To keep pieces of dough from drying out, cover them loosely with plastic wrap.

2. DIMPLE TOP

Working with 1 piece of dough at a time, dimple top of dough with your fingertips.

WHY? This will gently stretch the dough and is a better method than using a rolling pin. Dimpling is also a good technique to use with a rich dough since it's unlikely to cause sticking problems.

3. FOLD ENDS TOGETHER

Pick up dough and gently fold in half, pressing ends together.

WHY? This is the first step toward turning a rectangular piece of dough into a round ball.

4. PRESS SEAMS TOGETHER

Gently press folded dough into thick square shape.

WHY? Make sure to exert a fair amount of pressure so that the dough sticks to itself. You don't want the seams to come apart as you continue to work the dough.

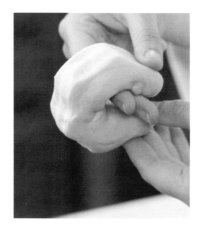

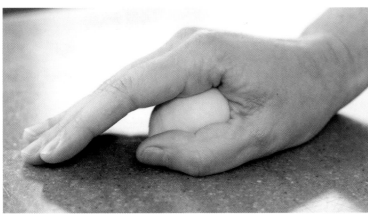

5. STRETCH AND PULL

Stretch dough around your thumbs into smooth, taut ball.

WHY? This technique should pull the dough into a roundish shape and will help hide the seams.

6. DRAG AND CUP

Using cupped hand, drag dough in small circles over clean counter until dough feels firm and round. Transfer round to 13 by 9-inch baking dish that has been lined with foil sling and lightly greased. Repeat with remaining pieces of dough. Let dough rise as directed.

WHY? The friction between the dough and the counter will help the dough take on the characteristic round dinner roll shape. The dough should be spinning underneath your hand, but not turning over. Don't flour the counter—you want the dough to stick a bit as you follow this step. Lining the baking pan with foil ensures easy removal of the rolls once baked.

Troubleshooting Shaping Dinner Rolls

PROBLEM	SOLUTION
The dough is sticky and hard to handle.	Dinner roll dough is supposed to be a bit sticky (usually from all the butter in the dough). If you add more flour, the rolls can be dry. Instead, flour your hands and work the dough lightly.
The dough is becoming a bit tough and hard to handle.	If you work slowly, the individual pieces of dough can start to dry out as they wait for shaping. You can prevent this by covering the sliced pieces of dough with plastic wrap and then taking them out from under the wrap one piece at a time.
I can see seams on my rolls.	Stretching the folded dough down around your thumbs is an important step that you don't want to skip. This will ensure the seams are hidden and your final rolls look nice and smooth.
The rolls aren't perfectly round.	Rolling the dough into symmetrical rounds takes a little practice, but you will quickly get the hang of it. Make sure you don't flour the counter. This may seem wrong at first, but you actually want the dough to stick a little so that it is anchored in place.

How to Make Almost No-Knead Bread

This is the easiest loaf of bread you can make. Kneading is replaced with a very high hydration level and an overnight resting period, which produce gluten slowly but without any work. Just before baking, the dough is kneaded for less than a minute, shaped, and baked in a preheated Dutch oven. Because of the long rising time, very little yeast (just ¼ teaspoon) is required. While this amount of yeast produces sufficient rise, it doesn't build all that much flavor. Our recipe relies on beer (use something mild like Budweiser) and vinegar to amp up the malty, yeasty flavors in the bread. This bread can be stored for up to two days at room temperature wrapped in plastic wrap. Before serving, heat the bread on the middle rack of a 450-degree oven for 6 to 8 minutes. For variations on this recipe, see page 574.

ESSENTIAL EQUIPMENT

- large bowl
- rubber spatula
- plastic wrap
- parchment paper
- 10-inch skillet
- Dutch oven with lid
- serrated knife
- wire rack
- instant-read thermometer

1. MIX BY HAND, THEN REST

Whisk 3 cups (15 ounces) all-purpose flour, 1½ teaspoons salt, and ¼ teaspoon instant yeast together in large bowl. Add ¾ cup plus 2 tablespoons room-temperature water, 6 tablespoons mild-flavored room-temperature beer (lager), and 1 tablespoon distilled white vinegar. Using rubber spatula, fold mixture, scraping up dry flour from bottom of bowl, until shaggy ball forms. Cover bowl with plastic wrap and let sit at room temperature for 8 to 18 hours.

WHY? Letting the dough sit for such a long time actually develops gluten, much like kneading does—this is the trick to making this bread. Don't shortchange the resting time or the bread won't have enough structure and will turn out very flat.

2. KNEAD JUST 10 TO 15 TIMES

Turn dough out onto lightly floured counter and knead by hand just 10 to 15 times.

WHY? These few turns on the counter make a big difference in the texture of the final loaf, and it's very easy to do. When you're done, the dough should be smooth.

3. SHAPE LOAF

Shape dough into ball by pulling edges into middle.

WHY? The dough is very easy to handle and has plenty of structure. You just want to pull up the sides so the ball of dough is taller and narrower, rather than wider and flatter.

4. LET IT RISE IN SKILLET

Lay 18 by 12-inch sheet of parchment paper inside 10-inch skillet and spray paper with vegetable oil spray. Transfer dough, seam side down, to skillet and spray surface of dough with more vegetable oil spray. Cover loosely with plastic wrap and let rise at room temperature until doubled in size, about 2 hours.

WHY? The skillet is the perfect shape to support the round loaf as it rises. (Because the dough has so much liquid it can spread out too much if you let it rise on just a baking sheet.) The parchment will make it easy to transfer the wet dough in the next step. Make sure to grease the parchment so the dough won't stick. Also, make sure to let the dough rise sufficiently. The dough should barely spring back when poked with a knuckle.

5. BAKE IN PREHEATED DUTCH OVEN

Thirty minutes before baking, adjust oven rack to lowest position, place Dutch oven (with lid) on rack, and heat oven to 500 degrees. When dough has risen, lightly flour top of dough and, using serrated knife or razor blade, make two 6-inch-long, ½-inch-deep slashes along top of dough to make X. Carefully transfer pot to wire rack and remove lid. Pick up loaf by lifting parchment overhang and lower into pot, letting any excess parchment hang over pot edge. Cover pot and return to oven. Reduce oven temperature to 425 degrees.

WHY? The pot traps steam and will create a loaf with a thick, hearty crust. The pot must have a tight-fitting lid and a minimum capacity of 6 quarts. Not all knobs are ovensafe to 500 degrees. If your pot has a plastic knob, buy an inexpensive replacement from the manufacturer or try using a metal drawer pull from the hardware store. A heavy enameled cast-iron Dutch oven is best, but any heavy pot can work. Make sure to turn down the temperature when you return the pot with the dough to the oven.

6. BAKE COVERED, THEN UNCOVERED

Bake bread covered for 30 minutes, then remove lid and continue to bake until crust is deep golden brown and center of loaf registers 210 degrees on instant-read thermometer, 20 to 30 minutes longer.

WHY? By baking the bread both covered and uncovered you get a chewy interior and a thick, hearty crust. Once the loaf is done, use the parchment sling to transfer it to a wire rack and let cool for at least 2 hours before serving.

Olive-Rosemary Bread

Recipe Stats

TOTAL TIME **7 hours, 15 minutes**
PREPARATION TIME **10 minutes**
ACTIVE COOKING TIME **1 hour**
YIELD **2 loaves**
MAKE AHEAD **Best served day it is baked**
DIFFICULTY **Intermediate**

Tools

- baking stone *
- pizza peel **
- stand mixer
- chef's knife
- cutting board
- serrated knife ***
- dry measuring cups
- liquid measuring cup
- measuring spoons
- bench scraper
- bowl scraper ****

- digital scale
- instant-read thermometer
- kitchen ruler
- large mixing bowl
- rubber spatula
- spray bottle filled with water
- wire rack
- parchment paper *****
- plastic wrap

Overview

To make really good olive-rosemary bread, you need a great homemade rustic bread—with a coarse crumb, a chewy interior, and a thick, burnished crust—and a way to add olives without ruining the bread. We started with our favorite rustic bread dough and made adjustments.

Because the olives contain a fair amount of moisture, the first thing we did was take down the hydration level of the dough. The olives can make the bread itself seem a bit bland, so we replaced some of the bread flour with whole-wheat flour and added a little honey. For rosemary flavor nothing but fresh will do, and you need a whopping 2 tablespoons.

As for the olives, almost any variety will work. The biggest challenge is keeping the olives in the dough as it is shaped. Many recipes call for adding the olives to the mix, but this just causes the olives to break down and stain the loaf purple or green. The mashed olives also make the loaf heavy and dense.

We found it best to add the olives to the already kneaded dough. To ensure even distribution, we found it best to remove the dough from the mixer, pat it into a rectangle, sprinkle the olives over the dough, then roll up the dough like a jelly roll. As the dough rises, the olives are evenly dispersed and safely embedded in the loaf, so they don't fall out during the shaping process.

There's nothing better than freshly baked bread, but this bread can be wrapped in a double layer of plastic wrap and stored at room temperature for up to 3 days. Or, wrap it with an additional layer of aluminum foil and freeze it for up to 1 month. To recrisp the crust, thaw frozen bread at room temperature and place unwrapped bread in a 450-degree oven for 5 to 10 minutes. Before you begin, see How to Knead Bread in a Mixer on page 546 and How to Turn or Fold Rustic Bread Dough on page 549.

* A baking stone is key for a crisp, well-browned bottom crust. If you don't own one, however, improvise with an inverted rimmed baking sheet on the lowest baking rack, heating it up with the oven just as you would a baking stone. The crust may not be as crisp and as brown as if baked on a stone, but it comes reasonably close.

** We use a pizza peel to help transfer the dough to the baking stone, but you can use an overturned rimmed baking sheet.

*** Although a serrated knife can be used to slash the bread, a single-edged razor or a lame (a specialized bread-baking tool) are also effective tools for this job.

**** A flexible bowl scraper is the best tool to help fold the dough, but a rubber spatula can also be used to do the job.

***** This dough is very, very sticky and must be shaped on parchment paper. Don't try this recipe without it.

Ingredients

1¾ cups water, room temperature
2 tablespoons honey
2 teaspoons instant or rapid-rise yeast
3½ cups (19¼ ounces) bread flour, plus extra as needed
½ cup (2¾ ounces) whole-wheat flour
2 teaspoons salt
2 tablespoons chopped fresh rosemary
1½ cups olives, pitted, rinsed, chopped coarse, and patted dry *

* Almost any variety of brined or oil-cured olive works in this recipe, although we prefer a mix of both green and black olives. Chop the olives fairly rough; if cut too small the olives will bleed into the loaf.

What Can Go Wrong

Here's a list of common mistakes cooks make when preparing this recipe.

COMMON MISTAKE	BAD OUTCOMES	WHAT YOU SHOULD DO
Using Dried Rosemary	• **The bread lacks flavor.**	Fresh rosemary is essential for this recipe. While rosemary is generally used sparingly in most cooking, this recipe requires a whopping 2 tablespoons of chopped rosemary to flavor two loaves.
Adding Olives to Mixer	• **The bread is stained purple and green.** • **The bread is heavy and dense.**	Resist the temptation to add the olives along with the rosemary. If the olives are kneaded in the mixer, they will give up their juices and make the loaves gummy and tough. (They can also stain the bread an unattractive color.) Make sure to remove the dough from the mixer and add the olives as directed. This method ensures even distribution.
Not Folding Dough During Rising Process	• **The bread spreads sideways as it bakes.**	During the rising process, make sure to remove the plastic wrap covering the bowl and fold the dough over itself during the second hour of the rise. This builds structure in the dough and helps the loaves to rise high in the oven. Make sure to complete three folds, turning the bowl 90 degrees after each fold. Perform this three-step folding twice.
Mishandling Dough During Shaping	• **The bread bakes up with a dense crumb.**	When shaping the dough, use a gentle hand and take care not to knock all the air out of it. Because pulling and stretching can cause the dough to deflate, use a liberal amount of flour to prevent the dough from sticking to the counter and your hands, and employ the help of a plastic scraper to manipulate the dough during shaping.
Not Slashing Loaves	• **The bread blows out during baking.**	If the dough is not slashed right before it goes into the oven, carbon dioxide can remain trapped in the dough and can cause the crust to split and tear.
Not Misting Loaves	• **The crust splits as it bakes.** • **The loaves blow out on one side.**	Misting the loaves right before they go into the oven, and twice more during the first 5 minutes of baking time, helps keep the crust from setting too quickly. As a result, the loaves can continue to rise in the oven without causing the crust to split. If you skip this step, the results can be a slightly (or seriously) misshapen loaf (a loaf that blows out to one side is a real disaster). Also, make sure to let the shaped dough rise fully before it goes into the oven. If the loaves are underproofed they are much more likely to blow out in the oven.
Not Lowering Oven Temperature	• **The crust is dark brown and tough.**	The crust should be nicely browned and crisp, thanks to the baking stone. An overbrowned crust can result if your oven runs hot, or if you forget to reduce the oven temperature from 450 degrees to 375 degrees after the first 15 minutes of baking time.

1. Whisk 1¾ cups room-temperature water, 2 tablespoons honey, and 2 teaspoons instant or rapid-rise yeast in bowl of stand mixer.

2. Add 3½ cups (19¼ ounces) bread flour and ½ cup (2¾ ounces) whole-wheat flour.

3. Mix on low speed with dough hook until cohesive dough is formed, about 3 minutes.

4. Cover bowl tightly with plastic wrap and let sit at room temperature for 20 minutes.

5. Remove plastic wrap; make well in center of dough and add 2 teaspoons salt and 2 tablespoons chopped fresh rosemary.

6. Knead dough on low speed for 5 minutes. (If dough creeps up attachment, stop mixer and scrape dough down.)

7. Knead on medium speed until dough is smooth and just tacky, about 1 minute. (If dough is very sticky, add 1 to 2 tablespoons flour; mix for 1 minute.)

8. Transfer dough to lightly floured counter and pat into 12 by 6-inch rectangle.

9. Rinse, roughly chop, and pat dry 1½ cups pitted olives. Press olives evenly into dough, leaving ½ inch border.

10. Starting at long side, roll rectangle into tight log.

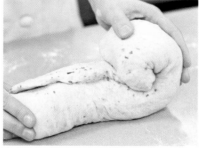

11. With seam side facing up, roll log into coil.

12. Transfer dough, spiral side up, to large (at least 2 quarts) lightly greased bowl and cover tightly with plastic wrap.

13. Let dough rise in warm, draft-free location until it increases in size by 50 percent, about 1 hour.

14. Using greased bowl scraper or rubber spatula, fold partially risen dough over itself.

15. Turn bowl 90 degrees; fold again.

16. Turn bowl again; fold once more.

17. Cover with plastic wrap and let rise 30 minutes.

18. Repeat three-step folding process and replace plastic wrap. Let rise until doubled in volume, about 30 minutes.

19. Transfer dough to lightly floured counter, being careful not to deflate.

20. Divide dough in half.

21. Loosely shape each piece into ball and let rest 15 minutes.

22. Flip each ball over.

23. Starting from top, roll each ball toward you into tight oval shape.

24. Using palms, roll each oval (seam side down) from center outward until 12-inch loaf is formed.

25. Poke any olives that fall off into bottom seam, then pinch seam closed.

26. Transfer each loaf, seam side down, to 12 by 6-inch piece of parchment paper and cover with plastic.

27. Let rise until doubled in size, 1 to 1½ hours. (Dough is ready when it springs back slowly when pressed lightly with finger.)

28. Adjust oven rack to lower-middle position, place baking stone on rack, and heat oven to 450 degrees at least 30 minutes before baking.

29. Slide parchment sheets with loaves onto back of inverted baking sheet or onto pizza peel.

30. Starting and stopping about 1 inch from each end, use serrated knife or razor blade to cut three ½-inch-deep slashes on diagonal on each loaf.

31. Spray loaves lightly with water.

32. Carefully slide parchment with loaves onto baking stone, using jerking motion to transfer from sheet.

33. Bake 15 minutes, spraying loaves with water twice more in first 5 minutes.

34. Reduce oven temperature to 375 degrees.

35. Continue to bake until bread is deep golden brown and center of loaves register 210 degrees, 25 to 30 minutes.

36. Transfer loaves to wire rack, discard parchment, and cool to room temperature, about 2 hours.

Sticky Buns with Pecans

Tools

- baking stone *
- rimmed baking sheets (2) **
- small saucepan
- 13 by 9-inch nonstick baking pan ***
- stand mixer
- chef's knife
- cutting board
- serrated knife
- dry measuring cups
- liquid measuring cup
- measuring spoons
- digital scale
- kitchen ruler
- mixing bowls
- pastry brush
- rolling pin
- rubber spatula
- soupspoon
- whisk
- wire rack
- wooden spoon
- plastic wrap

* If you don't have a baking stone, bake the rolls on an over-turned, preheated rimmed baking sheet on the lowest rack.
** Invert the baked buns onto one baking sheet and use the second baking sheet to toast the nuts while the buns cool.
*** A nonstick metal baking pan is essential to ensure easy release of the buns. A metal pan can be placed directly on a baking stone (a glass baking dish should not be).

Overview

This recipe has four components: the dough, the filling, the caramel glaze that bakes in the bottom of the dish along with the buns, and the pecan topping.

To keep the sticky bun glaze from hardening into a taffy-like shell, we add cream, which keeps the glaze supple. To the dough's basic mix of flour, yeast, and salt, we add buttermilk, which gives the buns a complex flavor and a little acidity that balances the sweetness. Butter and eggs enrich the dough further. After the first rise, we spread the filling—brown sugar, cinnamon, cloves, and butter—over the dough, roll it out, cut the individual buns, and lay them in the pan with the caramel to rise once more before baking. We found that setting the pan on a baking stone in the oven ensures that the bottoms of the buns bake completely. To preserve the crispness of the nuts, we create one more layer: toasted nuts in a lightly sweetened glaze to crown the rolls just before serving.

Leftover sticky buns can be wrapped in aluminum foil or plastic wrap and refrigerated for up to three days. Reheat in the microwave (for two buns, about 2 minutes at 50 percent power works well); they can also be put into a 325-degree oven for about 8 minutes. For overnight and make-ahead versions of this recipe, see page 573.

Ingredients

DOUGH

- **3** large eggs, room temperature
- **¾** cup buttermilk, room temperature
- **¼** cup (1¾ ounces) granulated sugar
- **2¼** teaspoons instant or rapid-rise yeast
- **1¼** teaspoons salt
- **4¼** cups (21¼ ounces) all-purpose flour, plus extra as needed
- **6** tablespoons unsalted butter, melted and cooled

GLAZE

- **6** tablespoons unsalted butter
- **¾** cup packed (5¼ ounces) light brown sugar
- **3** tablespoons corn syrup
- **2** tablespoons heavy cream
- **Pinch salt**

FILLING

- **¾** cup packed (5¼ ounces) light brown sugar
- **2** teaspoons ground cinnamon
- **¼** teaspoon ground cloves
- **Pinch salt**
- **1** tablespoon unsalted butter, melted and cooled

TOPPING

- **¼** cup packed (1¾ ounces) light brown sugar
- **3** tablespoons unsalted butter
- **3** tablespoons corn syrup
- **Pinch salt**
- **1** teaspoon vanilla extract
- **¾** cup pecans, toasted and chopped coarse

Recipe Stats

TOTAL TIME **5 hours**
PREPARATION TIME **15 minutes**
ACTIVE COOKING TIME **1 hour**
YIELD **12 buns**
MAKE AHEAD **Best baked and served warm**
DIFFICULTY **Advanced**

What Can Go Wrong

Here's a list of common mistakes cooks make when preparing this recipe.

COMMON MISTAKE	BAD OUTCOMES	WHAT YOU SHOULD DO
Using Dark Brown Sugar	• **The sticky buns look burnt.**	In most recipes, you can swap dark brown sugar for light with only modest changes to the final dish. In this recipe there's a lot of brown sugar, and it directly affects the appearance of the buns, as well as the flavor of the glaze. The glaze made with dark brown sugar tastes more intense but OK; the real problem is the appearance of the glaze, which makes the buns look very dark, almost burnt. For best results, stick with light brown sugar in the glaze, filling, and pecan topping.
Omitting Cream	• **The glaze is stiff.**	The caramel glaze that coats the baking dish contains just 2 tablespoons of cream, and you might be tempted to omit it. Don't. The cream keeps the glaze pourable and soft. Without the cream, the glaze becomes like taffy. The ideal texture is more gooey and soft than sticky and candylike.
Not Using Baking Stone	• **The buns are doughy and underbaked.** • **The caramel glaze is too light.**	We admit that placing the baking pan on the preheated baking stone does seem a bit odd, but it is necessary. To make sticky buns, you line the pan with the caramel glaze that will be the "top." As a result, you need a lot of heat to cook the glaze to the right color and consistency. Likewise, the bottoms of the buns need a fair amount of heat to cook through. We tried higher oven temperatures, but this caused the tops of the buns to dry out and burn. Since we needed more heat at the bottom of the pan than at the top, we turned to a preheated baking stone. You can use an overturned baking sheet in the same fashion. The goal is to jump-start the heating of the glaze and to make sure that the buns are fully cooked, even the parts sitting in the glaze.
Not Rolling Dough Neatly	• **The buns are misshapen.** • **The buns leak.** • **The buns don't bake evenly.**	Perhaps the most crucial part of this recipe is the assembly. Make sure to roll the dough into a fairly neat rectangle that will then roll up into a neat cylinder. If the rectangle is misshapen, the cylinder and buns will be misshapen, which means a greater likelihood of leaking or of uneven cooking. Make sure the cylinder has an even thickness from end to end so that the two buns cut from the ends aren't smaller than the rest.
Using Glass Baking Dish	• **The glass shatters.**	Never, ever use a glass baking dish with a baking stone. Glass baking dishes can shatter if the glass experiences something called thermal shock. Basically, never move a glass baking dish from a super-hot to a cool environment, or vice versa. It's fine to place a room-temperature glass baking dish in a hot oven. It's the hot stone that's the issue here.
Leaving Buns in Pan Too Long or Not Long Enough	• **The buns fuse to the pan.** • **The glaze is molten and runs off the buns.**	When the sticky buns come out of the oven, the glaze is molten, so if you try to flip the buns out of the pan, the glaze will run off. Wait 10 minutes and the glaze will firm up just enough to stick to the buns. However, don't delay any longer. If you wait too long, the glaze will harden on the pan and it will be very difficult to remove the sticky buns.
Adding Nuts to Filling	• **The nuts are soggy.** • **The nuts are bland.**	Most sticky buns recipes add the nuts with the filling, rolling them up safely inside the buns. Yes, this is a good way to keep the nuts in place, but they will also turn soft and soggy. Our method is a bit unorthodox—we spoon a second glaze with toasted nuts over the finished buns—but it ensures that the nuts are crisp and flavorful. Make sure to toast the nuts to develop their flavor.

1. PREPARE DOUGH: Whisk 3 room-temperature large eggs to combine in stand mixer. Add ¾ cup room-temperature buttermilk. Whisk to combine.

2. Whisk in ¼ cup (1¾ ounces) granulated sugar, 2¼ teaspoons instant or rapid-rise yeast, and 1¼ teaspoons salt.

3. Add 2 cups (10 ounces) all-purpose flour and 6 tablespoons melted and cooled unsalted butter; stir until evenly moistened and combined.

4. Add another 2 cups (10 ounces) all-purpose flour and knead in stand mixer with dough hook at low speed for 5 minutes.

5. Check consistency of dough; it should feel soft and moist but not wet and sticky. (Add up to ¼ cup more flour, if necessary.)

6. Knead 5 minutes longer. Dough should clear sides of bowl but stick to bottom. Turn dough onto lightly floured counter.

7. Knead by hand for 1 minute to ensure dough is uniform. Dough should not stick to counter; if it does, knead in more flour 1 tablespoon at a time.

8. Transfer dough to lightly greased bowl, spray with vegetable oil spray, cover, and set in warm, draft-free spot until doubled in volume, 2 to 2½ hours.

9. PREPARE GLAZE: Combine 6 tablespoons butter, ¾ cup light brown sugar, 3 tablespoons corn syrup, and 2 tablespoons heavy cream in small saucepan.

10. Add pinch salt and cook over medium heat, whisking occasionally, until butter is melted and mixture is thoroughly combined.

11. Pour mixture into 13 by 9-inch nonstick metal baking pan. Using rubber spatula, spread mixture to cover surface of pan; set aside.

12. PREPARE FILLING: Place ¾ cup packed light brown sugar, 2 teaspoons ground cinnamon, ¼ teaspoon ground cloves, and pinch salt in small bowl.

HOW TO MAKE YEAST BREADS AND PIZZAS

13. Mix until thoroughly combined, using fingers to break up sugar lumps; set aside.

14. ASSEMBLE AND BAKE: Turn dough out onto lightly floured counter. Gently shape dough into rough rectangle, with long side nearest you.

15. Lightly flour dough. Use rolling pin to roll dough to 16 by 12-inch rectangle. Lift dough as needed and flour counter to keep dough from sticking.

16. Brush dough with 1 tablespoon melted and cooled unsalted butter, leaving ½-inch border along top edge.

17. Brush sides of baking dish with butter remaining on brush.

18. Sprinkle filling mixture over dough, leaving ¾-inch border along top edge.

19. Smooth filling in even layer with hand, then gently press mixture into dough to adhere.

20. Starting at long side, roll dough, pressing lightly, to form tight cylinder.

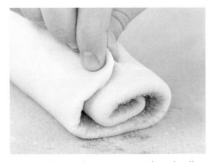

21. Firmly pinch seam to seal and roll cylinder seam side down.

22. Very gently stretch to form cylinder of even diameter and 18-inch length, pushing ends in to create even thickness.

23. Using serrated knife and gentle sawing motion, slice cylinder in half, then slice each half in half again to create evenly sized quarters.

24. Slice each quarter evenly into thirds, yielding 12 buns (end pieces may be slightly smaller).

25. Arrange buns with one cut side down in baking pan, cover, and set in warm, draft-free spot until pressed against one another, about 1½ hours.

26. Meanwhile, adjust oven rack to lowest position, place baking stone on rack, and heat oven to 350 degrees.

27. Place baking pan on baking stone and bake until rolls are golden brown, 25 to 30 minutes.

28. Let cool on wire rack for 10 minutes; invert onto rimmed baking sheet, large rectangular platter, or cutting board.

29. With rubber spatula, scrape any glaze remaining in baking pan onto buns; let cool while making pecan topping.

30. PREPARE TOPPING: Toast ¾ cup pecans on rimmed baking sheet in 350-degree oven until fragrant, about 5 minutes. Cool and coarsely chop.

31. Combine ¼ cup packed light brown sugar, 3 tablespoons unsalted butter, 3 tablespoons corn syrup, and pinch salt in small saucepan.

32. Bring to simmer over medium heat, whisking occasionally to thoroughly combine.

33. Off heat, add 1 teaspoon vanilla extract and toasted and chopped pecans and stir until nuts are evenly coated.

34. Using soupspoon, spoon heaping 1 tablespoon nuts and topping over center of each sticky bun.

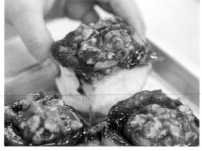

35. Continue to let cool until sticky buns are warm, 15 to 20 minutes. Pull apart or use serrated knife to cut apart buns and serve.

New York–Style Thin-Crust Pizza

Overview

Contending with ovens that reach only 500 degrees and dough that's impossible to stretch thin, even the savviest home cooks struggle to produce parlor-quality pies. By the time most crust recipes crisp, the interior turns dry and tough. If the dough is too wet, it becomes sticky; too dry and it's a stiff, dense wad. And typically the dough either rips or springs back like a rubber band. We opt for high-protein bread flour for a chewy, tanned crust. We knead the flour, water, and yeast in a food processor. The easiest way to build flavor in bread dough is to chill the dough as it proofs. This minimizes the size of the gas bubbles that form in dough, and also makes it more flavorful. We discovered that when the dough was left in the refrigerator for a period of time (up to three days), its flavor improved. Adding vegetable oil and sugar to the dough boosts flavor and helps crisp the dough.

Most recipes call for placing the stone as low in the oven as possible, where it gets maximum exposure to the main heating element. Instead, we move it up close to the top, which results in a pizza with a crust that is crisp and well browned on both top and bottom, and that has a slightly chewy texture. Note that the dough must be refrigerated for at least 24 hours. For a white pizza variation, see page 577.

Recipe Stats

TOTAL TIME **At least 1 day**
PREPARATION TIME **15 minutes**
ACTIVE COOKING TIME **1 hour**
YIELD **Two 13-inch pizzas; serves 4 to 6**
MAKE AHEAD **Serve pizza immediately; refrigerate dough for up to 3 days**
DIFFICULTY **Intermediate**

Tools

- baking stone *
- rimmed baking sheet
- food processor **
- dry measuring cups
- liquid measuring cup
- measuring spoons
- bench scraper
- coarse grater ***
- digital scale
- fine-mesh strainer
- kitchen ruler
- ladle ****
- large mixing bowl
- pizza peel
- rasp-style grater ***
- rubber spatula
- wire rack
- plastic wrap

* A baking stone is key for a crisp, well-browned crust bottom. If you don't own one, use an inverted rimmed baking sheet, heating it up with the oven just as you would a baking stone.
** To make the pizza dough, which calls for 3 cups of bread flour and more than 1 cup of water, it's necessary to use a full-size food processor with at least an 11-cup capacity.
*** We prefer a rasp-style grater to prepare Parmesan and a flat coarse grater to prepare mozzarella. If you prefer, you can use the fine holes of a box grater to grate the Parmesan and the large holes on this same grater to shred the mozzarella.
**** We use the bottom of a ladle to spread the sauce, but the bottom of a soupspoon would also work.

Ingredients

DOUGH
- **3 cups (16½ ounces) bread flour**
- **2 teaspoons sugar**
- **½ teaspoon instant or rapid-rise yeast**
- **1⅓ cups ice water**
- **1 tablespoon vegetable oil**
- **1½ teaspoons salt**

SAUCE
- **1 (28-ounce) can whole peeled tomatoes, drained**
- **1 tablespoon extra-virgin olive oil**
- **1 teaspoon red wine vinegar**
- **2 garlic cloves, minced**
- **1 teaspoon salt**
- **1 teaspoon dried oregano**
- **¼ teaspoon pepper**

CHEESE
- **1 ounce Parmesan cheese, grated fine (½ cup)**
- **8 ounces whole-milk mozzarella cheese, shredded (2 cups) ***

* Although fresh mozzarella—the kind sold floating in liquid—may be more authentically Italian, do not use it in place of the standard whole-milk mozzarella cheese called for here. Given the limitations of baking pizza in a home oven, high-moisture mozzarella cheese can make the crust soggy. Whole-milk mozzarella has richer flavor and creamier texture than its part-skim counterparts.

What Can Go Wrong

Here's a list of common mistakes cooks make when preparing this recipe.

COMMON MISTAKE	BAD OUTCOMES	WHAT YOU SHOULD DO
Using All-Purpose Flour	• **The dough is wet and sticky.** • **The crust lacks chew.**	If you don't already have bread flour in your pantry for this recipe, seek some out; it's widely available in supermarkets. Do not substitute all-purpose flour for bread flour here—because bread flour absorbs more water than all-purpose flour absorbs, using the latter results in a wetter, stickier dough. In addition, for this dough that is minimally kneaded, bread flour's high protein content provides the structure necessary for a pleasantly chewy crust.
Using Wrong Type of Yeast	• **The dough doesn't rise properly.** • **The crust is flat and crackerlike.**	Be sure to use the type of yeast called for in the recipe: instant yeast, which is sometimes marketed as rapid-rise yeast. Teaspoon for teaspoon, instant yeast is more "active" that active dry yeast because it doesn't contain dead cells that are the product of processing. Active dry yeast, if substituted for instant yeast in this recipe, will result in dough that will not rise, as the yeast is added directly to the dry ingredients without first being proofed (active dry yeast requires proofing before use).
Adding Salt Too Soon	• **The crust lacks chew.**	Remember to hold back the salt from the dough until after autolyse (the short resting time that allows the flour to fully absorb the water) is completed. Because salt inhibits the enzymatic action that is the purpose of autolyse (to make kneading quicker and easier), adding it just before kneading begins—rather than at the outset, with the other ingredients—gives the gluten a better chance of forming a strong network, which produces a chewy texture in the baked crust.
Shortening Rising Time	• **The crust lacks flavor.**	Allow the dough its full rising time in the refrigerator, a minimum of 24 hours, or up to three days. This long, slow fermentation is essential for flavor development, and can't be rushed without compromising flavor.
Pizza Peel Not Floured	• **The unbaked pizza won't slide off the peel.**	After you've invested a good amount of time making pizza, there's nothing more maddening than the pie sticking to the peel in the last moments of preparation. Therefore, be generous when flouring the pizza peel so that the pie will easily slide off the peel and onto the baking stone.
Not Preheating Baking Stone	• **The crust does not crisp on the bottom.** • **The crust does not brown on the bottom.**	Before you remove the dough from the refrigerator and allow it to stand at room temperature, position the baking stone in the oven, turn the oven to 500 degrees, and allow the stone to heat as the oven heats. An hour or so later, when the dough is ready for shaping, the pizza stone will be thoroughly heated and ready for baking pizza.

1. PREPARE DOUGH: Process 3 cups (16½ ounces) bread flour, 2 teaspoons sugar, and ½ teaspoon instant yeast in food processor to combine, 2 seconds.

2. With processor running, slowly add 1⅓ cups ice water through feed tube.

3. Process until dough is just combined and no dry flour remains, about 10 seconds. Let dough sit for 10 minutes.

4. Add 1 tablespoon vegetable oil and 1½ teaspoons salt. Process until dough forms satiny, sticky ball that clears sides of workbowl, 30 to 60 seconds.

5. Remove dough from bowl and knead briefly on lightly oiled counter until smooth, about 1 minute.

6. Shape dough into tight ball and place in large, lightly oiled bowl.

7. Cover tightly with plastic wrap and refrigerate for at least 24 hours or up to 3 days.

8. PREPARE SAUCE: Drain 1 (28-ounce) can whole peeled tomatoes and discard juice. Place drained tomatoes in food processor.

9. Mince 2 garlic cloves. Add to food processor with tomatoes, then add 1 tablespoon extra-virgin olive oil and 1 teaspoon red wine vinegar.

10. Add 1 teaspoon dried oregano, 1 teaspoon salt, and ¼ teaspoon pepper to food processor and process until smooth, about 30 seconds.

11. Transfer to medium bowl or container and refrigerate until ready to use.

12. MAKE PIZZA: Adjust oven rack to be 4 to 5 inches from broiler element. Set baking stone on rack and turn oven to 500 degrees. Heat for 1 hour.

13. Remove dough from refrigerator and divide in half.

14. Shape each half into smooth, tight ball. Place on lightly oiled baking sheet, spaced at least 3 inches apart.

15. Cover loosely with plastic wrap coated with vegetable oil spray. Let stand for 1 hour.

16. Coat 1 ball of dough generously with flour and place on well-floured counter (keep other ball covered).

17. Using fingertips, gently flatten into 8-inch disk, leaving 1 inch of outer edge slightly thicker than center.

18. Using hands, gently stretch disk into 12-inch round, working along edges and giving disk quarter turns as you stretch.

19. Transfer dough to well-floured pizza peel and stretch into 13-inch round.

20. Spread ½ cup tomato sauce in thin layer over surface of dough, leaving ¼-inch border around edge (keep leftover sauce for another use).

21. Sprinkle ¼ cup grated Parmesan evenly over sauce, followed by 1 cup shredded mozzarella.

22. Slide pizza onto stone. Bake until crust is well browned and cheese is bubbly and starting to brown, 10 to 12 minutes, rotating pizza halfway through.

23. Remove pizza and place on wire rack for 5 minutes before slicing and serving.

24. Repeat to shape, top, and bake second pizza.

Recipe Library

American Loaf Bread

✓ **WHY THIS RECIPE WORKS:** Many people who might enjoy making terrific sandwich bread at home don't even try it because they think it takes most of a day. We wanted a good, solid sandwich bread recipe that could be prepared in two hours, start to finish, including baking time. We found that sandwich bread improved markedly when kneaded with a stand mixer. This method helped us resist the temptation to add extra flour in an effort to tame the sticky bread dough, which tends to make the dough denser and less flavorful; it also makes it rise less. We were also surprised to find that we preferred rapid-rise yeast to active dry yeast for our sandwich bread recipe. Not only did it greatly reduce rising times, but it also made for better-tasting bread.

American Loaf Bread

MAKES ONE 9-INCH LOAF

All-purpose flour can be used if bread flour is unavailable. If you don't have a stand mixer, you can knead the bread dough by hand; see Core Technique on page 547 for more details. If you don't have a baking stone, bake the bread on an overturned and preheated rimmed baking sheet. See Core Technique on page 548 for more details on shaping loaf breads.

- 1 cup whole milk, heated to 110 degrees
- ⅓ cup water, heated to 110 degrees
- 3 tablespoons honey
- 2 tablespoons unsalted butter, melted
- 3½ cups (19¼ ounces) bread flour
- 2¼ teaspoons instant or rapid-rise yeast
- 2 teaspoons salt

1. Adjust oven rack to lowest position and heat oven to 200 degrees. Once oven temperature reaches 200 degrees, maintain heat for 10 minutes, then turn off oven.

2. Whisk milk, water, honey, and butter together in 4-cup liquid measuring cup. Using stand mixer fitted with dough hook, combine flour, yeast, and salt on low speed. Slowly add milk mixture and let dough come together, about 2 minutes. Increase speed to medium and knead until dough is smooth and satiny, about 10 minutes, scraping down dough from bowl and hook as needed. Transfer dough to lightly floured counter and knead by hand to form smooth, round ball, about 15 seconds. Place dough in large, lightly greased bowl; cover tightly with plastic wrap and let rise in warm oven until doubled in size, 40 to 50 minutes.

3. Grease 9 by 5-inch loaf pan. Transfer dough to lightly floured counter and press into rectangle about 1 inch thick and no longer than 9 inches, with long side facing you. Roll dough toward you into firm cylinder, keeping roll taut by tucking it under itself as you go. Turn loaf seam side up and pinch it closed. Place loaf seam side down in prepared pan, pressing gently into corners. Cover loaf loosely with greased plastic and let rise at room temperature until nearly doubled in size, 20 to 30 minutes. (Dough should barely spring back when poked with knuckle.)

4. One hour before baking, place baking stone on lowest rack, place empty loaf pan or other heatproof pan on baking stone, and heat oven to 350 degrees. Bring 2 cups water to boil on stovetop. Working quickly, pour boiling water into empty loaf pan in oven and set loaf in pan on baking stone. Bake until crust is golden brown and loaf registers 195 degrees, 40 to 50 minutes. Transfer pan to wire rack and let cool for 5 minutes. Remove loaf from pan, return to rack, and let cool to room temperature, about 2 hours, before slicing and serving. (Bread can be wrapped in double layer of plastic wrap and stored at room temperature for up to 3 days. Wrapped with additional layer of aluminum foil, bread can be frozen for up to 1 month.)

Buttermilk Loaf Bread

Substitute buttermilk, heated to 110 degrees, for whole milk. Increase first rise to 50 minutes to 1 hour.

Oatmeal-Raisin Loaf Bread

Do not substitute instant oats in this recipe. To turn this loaf into Oatmeal-Raisin Bread, knead ¾ cup raisins, tossed with 1 tablespoon all-purpose flour, into the dough after it comes out of the mixer.

Omit warm water from wet ingredients. Bring ¾ cup water to boil in small saucepan. Stir in ¾ cup old-fashioned rolled oats or quick oats and cook until softened slightly, about 90 seconds. Decrease flour to 2¾ cups and combine cooked oatmeal with flour and salt in mixer before adding milk mixture.

Cornmeal Loaf Bread

To turn this loaf into Anadama Bread, substitute 3 tablespoons molasses for honey.

Decrease milk to ¾ cup. Bring additional ½ cup water to boil in small saucepan. Slowly whisk in ¼ cup cornmeal and cook, stirring constantly, until mixture thickens, about 1 minute. Decrease flour to 3¼ cups and combine cornmeal mixture with flour and salt in mixer before incorporating milk mixture.

Whole-Wheat Sandwich Bread

✓ **WHY THIS RECIPE WORKS:** Most whole-wheat bread recipes turn out either squat bricks or white bread in disguise. We wanted a nutty, hearty, light-textured sandwich loaf that tasted like wheat. We started with a good white-flour recipe and worked our way backward to "unrefine" it, replacing different amounts of all-purpose flour with whole wheat to find the highest percentage of whole-wheat flour that we could use before the texture suffered. To bump the amount of whole wheat up more, we substituted protein-rich bread flour for the all-purpose flour. We soaked the flour overnight in milk, with some wheat germ for added flavor, to soften the grain's fiber, keep the dough moist, and coax out sweet flavor. For well-developed flavor, we turned to a sponge, a mixture of flour, water, and yeast left to sit overnight. Adding honey for better flavor and complexity and swapping some butter for vegetable oil to cut the richness perfected our whole-wheat sandwich bread.

Whole-Wheat Sandwich Bread

MAKES TWO 8-INCH LOAVES

If you don't have a stand mixer, you can knead the bread dough by hand; see Core Technique on page 547 for more details. If you don't have a baking stone, bake the bread on an overturned and preheated rimmed baking sheet. See Core Technique on page 548 for more details on shaping loaf breads. The test kitchen's preferred loaf pan measures 8½ by 4½ inches; if you use a 9 by 5-inch loaf pan, start checking for doneness 5 minutes earlier than advised in recipe.

SPONGE

- **2 cups (11 ounces) bread flour**
- **1 cup water, heated to 110 degrees**
- **½ teaspoon instant or rapid-rise yeast**

SOAKER

- **3 cups (16½ ounces) whole-wheat flour**
- **½ cup wheat germ**
- **2 cups whole milk**

DOUGH

- **6 tablespoons unsalted butter, softened**
- **¼ cup honey**
- **2 tablespoons instant or rapid-rise yeast**
- **2 tablespoons vegetable oil**
- **4 teaspoons salt**

1. FOR THE SPONGE: Combine flour, water, and yeast in large bowl and stir with wooden spoon until uniform mass forms and no dry flour remains, about 1 minute. Cover bowl tightly with plastic wrap and let sit at room temperature for at least 8 hours or up to 24 hours.

2. FOR THE SOAKER: Combine flour, wheat germ, and milk in separate large bowl and stir with wooden spoon until shaggy mass forms, about 1 minute. Transfer dough to lightly floured counter and knead by hand until smooth, 2 to 3 minutes. Return soaker to bowl, cover tightly with plastic, and refrigerate for at least 8 hours or up to 24 hours.

3. FOR THE DOUGH: Tear soaker apart into 1-inch pieces and place in bowl of stand mixer fitted with dough hook. Add sponge, butter, honey, yeast, oil, and salt and mix on low speed until cohesive mass starts to form, about 2 minutes. Increase speed to medium and knead until dough is smooth and elastic, 8 to 10 minutes. Transfer dough to lightly floured counter and knead by hand to form smooth, round ball, about 1 minute. Place dough in large, lightly greased bowl. Cover tightly with plastic and let rise at room temperature for 45 minutes.

4. Gently press down on center of dough to deflate. Spray rubber spatula or bowl scraper with vegetable oil spray; fold partially risen dough over itself by gently lifting and folding edge of dough toward middle. Turn bowl 90 degrees; fold again. Turn bowl and fold dough 6 more times (total of 8 folds). Cover tightly with plastic and allow to rise at room temperature until doubled in size, about 45 minutes.

5. Grease two 8½ by 4½-inch loaf pans. Transfer dough to well-floured counter and divide in half. Press 1 piece of dough into 17 by 8-inch rectangle, with short side facing you. Roll dough toward you into firm cylinder, keeping roll taut by tucking it under itself as you go. Turn loaf seam side up and pinch it closed. Place loaf seam side down in prepared pan, pressing gently into corners. Repeat with second piece of dough. Cover loaves loosely with greased plastic and let rise at room temperature until nearly doubled in size, 1 to 1½ hours (top of loaves should rise about 1 inch over lip of pan).

6. One hour before baking, adjust oven racks to middle and lowest positions, place baking stone on middle rack, place empty loaf pan or other heatproof pan on bottom rack, and heat oven to 400 degrees. Bring 2 cups water to boil on stovetop. Using sharp serrated knife or single-edge razor blade, make one ¼-inch-deep slash lengthwise down center of each loaf. Working quickly, pour boiling water into empty loaf pan in oven and set loaves in pans on baking stone. Reduce oven temperature to 350 degrees. Bake until crust is dark brown and loaves register 200 degrees, 40 to 50 minutes, rotating loaves front to back and side to side halfway through baking. Transfer pans to wire rack and let cool for 5 minutes. Remove loaves from pans, return to rack, and let cool to room temperature, about 2 hours, before slicing and serving. (Bread can be wrapped in double layer of plastic wrap and stored at room temperature for up to 3 days. Wrapped with additional layer of aluminum foil, bread can be frozen for up to 1 month.)

Multigrain Bread

WHY THIS RECIPE WORKS: Often multigrain bread either has great flavor but is as dense and as heavy as a brick, or it has a nice, light sandwich-style texture but so little grain it might as well be white bread. We wanted a multigrain bread with both great flavor and balanced texture. Early tests showed that the whole grains impede the development of gluten, the protein that gives baked goods structure. Bread flour, with its high protein content, would seem the ideal candidate to combat this problem, but we found that it only made the bread chewier, not less dense. We switched to all-purpose flour and came up with a twofold solution: an autolyse, a resting period that gives the flour time to hydrate, followed by long kneading. The result was a loaf that baked up light yet chewy without being tough. For the whole grains, we hit upon a convenient, one-stop-shopping alternative: packaged seven-grain hot cereal. To soften the grains, we made a thick porridge with the cereal before adding it to the dough. A final step of rolling the shaped loaves in oats yielded a finished, professional look.

Multigrain Bread

MAKES TWO 9-INCH LOAVES

If you don't have a stand mixer, you can prepare the dough by hand; see Core Technique on page 547 for more detail.

Don't confuse seven-grain hot cereal mix with boxed cold break-fast cereals that may also be labeled "seven-grain." Our favorite brands of seven-grain mix are Bob's Red Mill and Arrowhead Mills. Do not substitute instant oats in this recipe. For an accurate measurement of boiling water, bring a full kettle of water to a boil, then measure out the desired amount. See Core Technique on page 548 for more details on shaping loaf breads.

- 1¼ cups (6¼ ounces) seven-grain hot cereal mix
- 2½ cups boiling water
- 3 cups (15 ounces) all-purpose flour, plus extra as needed
- 1½ cups (8¼ ounces) whole-wheat flour
- ¼ cup honey
- 4 tablespoons unsalted butter, melted and cooled
- 2½ teaspoons instant or rapid-rise yeast
- 1 tablespoon salt
- ¾ cup unsalted pumpkin seeds or sunflower seeds
- ½ cup (1½ ounces) old-fashioned rolled oats or quick oats

1. Place cereal mix in bowl of stand mixer fitted with dough hook and pour boiling water over it; let stand, stirring occasionally, until mixture cools to 100 degrees and resembles thick porridge, about 1 hour. Whisk flours together in separate bowl.

2. Once grain mixture has cooled, add honey, butter, and yeast and mix on low speed until combined. Add flour mixture, ½ cup at a time, and knead until cohesive mass starts to form, 1½ to 2 minutes; cover bowl tightly with plastic wrap and let dough rest for 20 minutes. Add salt and knead on medium-low speed until dough clears sides of bowl, 3 to 4 minutes (if it does not clear sides, add 2 to 3 tablespoons additional all-purpose flour and knead until it does); continue to knead dough for 5 more minutes. Add seeds and knead for another 15 seconds. Transfer dough to lightly floured counter and knead by hand until seeds are dispersed evenly and dough forms smooth, round ball. Place dough in large, lightly greased bowl; cover tightly with plastic and let rise at room temperature until nearly doubled in size, 45 minutes to 1 hour.

3. Grease two 9 by 5-inch loaf pans. Transfer dough to lightly floured counter and divide in half. Press 1 piece of dough into 9 by 6-inch rectangle, with short side facing you. Roll dough toward you into firm cylinder, keeping roll taut by tucking it under itself as you go. Turn loaf seam side up and pinch it closed. Repeat with second piece of dough. Spray loaves lightly with water or vegetable oil spray. Roll each loaf in oats to coat evenly and place seam side down in prepared pans, pressing gently into corners. Cover loaves loosely with greased plastic and let rise at room temperature until nearly doubled in size, 30 to 40 minutes. (Dough should barely spring back when poked with knuckle.)

4. Thirty minutes before baking, adjust oven rack to middle position and heat oven to 375 degrees. Bake until loaves register 200 degrees, 35 to 40 minutes. Transfer pans to wire rack and let cool for 5 minutes. Remove loaves from pans, return to rack, and let cool to room temperature, about 2 hours, before slicing and serving. (Bread can be wrapped in double layer of plastic wrap and stored at room temperature for up to 3 days. Wrapped with additional layer of aluminum foil, bread can be frozen for up to 1 month.)

Sticky Buns with Pecans

✔ **WHY THIS RECIPE WORKS:** Sticky buns are often too sweet, too big, too rich, and just too much. We wanted a bun that was neither dense nor bready, with a crumb that was tender and feathery and a gently gooey and chewy glaze. To keep the sticky bun glaze from hardening into a tooth-pulling, taffylike shell, we added cream, which kept the glaze supple. To the dough's basic mix of flour, yeast, and salt we added buttermilk, which gave the buns a complex flavor and a little acidity that balanced the sweetness. Butter and eggs enriched the dough further. After the first rise, we spread the filling—brown sugar, cinnamon, cloves, and butter—over the dough, rolled it, cut the individual buns, and laid them in the pan with the caramel to rise once more before being baked. We found that setting the pan on a baking stone in the oven ensured that the bottoms of the buns (which would end up on top) baked completely. To preserve the crispness of the nuts, we created one more layer: toasted nuts in a lightly sweetened glaze to crown the rolls before serving.

Sticky Buns With Pecans

MAKES 12 BUNS

Although the ingredient list may look long, note that many ingredients are repeated. If you don't have a baking stone, bake the rolls on an overturned and preheated rimmed baking sheet set on the lowest oven rack. See Recipe Tutorial on page 561 for more details on this recipe.

DOUGH

- 3 large eggs, room temperature
- ¾ cup buttermilk, room temperature
- ¼ cup (1¾ ounces) granulated sugar
- 2¼ teaspoons instant or rapid-rise yeast
- 1¼ teaspoons salt
- 4¼ cups (21¼ ounces) all-purpose flour, plus extra as needed
- 6 tablespoons unsalted butter, melted and cooled

GLAZE

- 6 tablespoons unsalted butter
- ¾ cup packed (5¼ ounces) light brown sugar
- 3 tablespoons corn syrup
- 2 tablespoons heavy cream
  Pinch salt

FILLING

- ¾ cup packed (5¼ ounces) light brown sugar
- 2 teaspoons ground cinnamon
- ¼ teaspoon ground cloves
  Pinch salt
- 1 tablespoon unsalted butter, melted and cooled

TOPPING

- ¼ cup packed (1¾ ounces) light brown sugar
- 3 tablespoons unsalted butter
- 3 tablespoons corn syrup
  Pinch salt
- 1 teaspoon vanilla extract
- ¾ cup pecans, toasted and chopped coarse

1. **FOR THE DOUGH:** In bowl of stand mixer, whisk eggs to combine; add buttermilk and whisk to combine. Whisk in sugar, yeast, and salt. Add 2 cups flour and butter; stir with wooden spoon or rubber spatula until evenly moistened and combined. Add all but about ¼ cup remaining flour. Fit stand mixer with dough hook and knead dough on low speed for 5 minutes. Check consistency of dough (dough should feel soft and moist but not wet and sticky; add more flour, if necessary); knead for 5 minutes longer (dough should clear sides of bowl but stick to bottom). Turn dough onto lightly floured counter; knead by hand for about 1 minute to ensure dough is uniform (dough should not stick to counter; if it does stick, knead in additional flour 1 tablespoon at a time).

2. Transfer dough to large, lightly greased bowl, spray dough lightly with vegetable oil spray, cover bowl, and set in warm, draft-free spot until doubled in volume, 2 to 2½ hours.

3. **FOR THE GLAZE:** Combine butter, sugar, corn syrup, cream, and salt in small saucepan and cook over medium heat, whisking occasionally, until butter is melted and mixture is thoroughly combined. Pour mixture into nonstick metal 13 by 9-inch baking pan. Using rubber spatula, spread mixture to cover surface of pan; set aside.

4. **FOR THE FILLING:** Combine sugar, cinnamon, cloves, and salt in small bowl and mix until thoroughly combined, using fingers to break up sugar lumps; set aside.

5. **TO ASSEMBLE AND BAKE:** Turn dough out onto lightly floured counter. Gently shape dough into rough rectangle with long side nearest you. Lightly flour dough and roll to 16 by 12-inch rectangle. Brush dough with 1 tablespoon melted butter, leaving ½-inch border along top edge; brush sides of baking dish with butter remaining on brush. Sprinkle filling mixture over dough, leaving ¾-inch border along top edge; smooth filling in even layer with hand, then gently press mixture into dough to adhere. Starting at long side, roll dough, pressing lightly, to form tight cylinder. Firmly pinch seam to seal. Very gently stretch to form cylinder of even diameter and 18-inch length, pushing ends in to create even thickness. Using serrated knife and gentle sawing motion, slice cylinder in half, then slice each half in half again to create evenly sized quarters. Slice each quarter evenly into thirds, yielding 12 buns (end pieces may be slightly smaller).

6. Arrange buns with one cut side down in prepared baking pan, cover, and set in warm, draft-free spot until puffy and pressed against one another, about 1½ hours. Meanwhile, adjust oven rack to lowest position, place baking stone on rack, and heat oven to 350 degrees.

7. Place baking pan on baking stone and bake until rolls are golden brown, 25 to 30 minutes. Let cool on wire rack for 10 minutes; invert onto rimmed baking sheet, large rectangular platter, or cutting board. With rubber spatula, scrape any glaze remaining in baking pan onto buns; let cool while making pecan topping.

8. **FOR THE TOPPING:** Combine sugar, butter, corn syrup, and salt in small saucepan and bring to simmer over medium heat, whisking occasionally to thoroughly combine. Off heat, add vanilla and pecans and stir until pecans are evenly coated. Using soupspoon, spoon heaping 1 tablespoon nuts and topping over center of each sticky bun. Continue to let cool until sticky buns are warm, 15 to 20 minutes. Pull apart or use serrated knife to cut apart buns and serve.

Overnight Sticky Buns with Pecans

Sticky buns can be prepared and shaped the night before and then refrigerated. Setting the baking dish in a warm-water bath the next morning speeds the dough's rise.

After arranging buns in baking pan in step 6, cover pan and refrigerate for 10 to 14 hours. Place baking pan in warm-water bath (about 120 degrees) in kitchen sink or large roasting pan for 20 minutes. Remove from water bath and let stand at room temperature until buns look slightly puffy and are pressed against one another, about 1½ hours. About an hour before baking, adjust oven rack to lowest position, place baking stone on rack, and heat oven to 350 degrees. Proceed with step 6 as directed.

Make-Ahead Sticky Buns with Pecans

This make-ahead version makes sticky buns possible during hectic times, like the holidays.

After buns have risen 1½ hours in step 6, place baking pan, covered tightly with plastic wrap, in freezer and store for up to 1 month. To bake, adjust oven rack to middle position and heat oven to 350 degrees. Remove buns from freezer, remove plastic wrap, wrap dish tightly with aluminum foil, and set on baking sheet. Bake buns for 30 minutes, then remove foil and continue to bake until golden brown and center of dough registers about 180 degrees, about 20 minutes longer. Proceed with cooling buns and making topping as directed in step 8.

Almost No-Knead Bread

☑ WHY THIS RECIPE WORKS: The no-knead method of bread making replaces kneading, the mechanical process that forms the gluten that gives bread structure, with a very high hydration level (85 percent—for every 10 ounces of flour, there are 8.5 ounces of water) and a 8- to 18-hour autolyse, or resting period, that allows the flour to hydrate and rest before the dough is briefly kneaded. It is baked in a preheated Dutch oven; the humid environment gives the loaf a dramatic open crumb structure and crisp crust. However, as we baked loaf after loaf, we found two big problems: the dough deflated when carried to the pot, causing misshapen loaves, and it lacked flavor. To give the dough more strength, we lowered the hydration and added the bare minimum of kneading time (under a minute) to compensate. Using a parchment paper sling, we were able to transfer the dough without it deflating. For flavor, we introduced two elements that a starter adds to artisan breads: an acidic tang with vinegar and a shot of yeasty flavor with beer.

Almost No-Knead Bread

MAKES 1 LARGE ROUND LOAF

You will need at least a 6-quart Dutch oven for this recipe. An enameled cast-iron Dutch oven with a tight-fitting lid yields the best results, but the recipe also works in a regular cast-iron Dutch oven or heavy stockpot. Take note of the knobs on your Dutch oven lid, as not all are ovensafe at 500 degrees; look for inexpensive replacement knobs from the manufacturer of your Dutch oven (or try using a metal drawer handle from a hardware store). See Core Technique on page 554 for more details on this recipe.

3 cups (15 ounces) all-purpose flour
1½ teaspoons salt
¼ teaspoon instant or rapid-rise yeast
¾ cup plus 2 tablespoons water, room temperature
6 tablespoons mild-flavored lager, such as Budweiser, room temperature
1 tablespoon distilled white vinegar

1. Whisk flour, salt, and yeast together in large bowl. Add water, beer, and vinegar. Using rubber spatula, fold mixture, scraping up dry flour from bottom of bowl, until shaggy ball forms. Cover bowl with plastic wrap and let sit at room temperature for 8 to 18 hours.

2. Lay 18 by 12-inch sheet of parchment paper inside 10-inch skillet and spray with vegetable oil spray. Transfer dough to lightly floured counter and knead by hand 10 to 15 times. Shape dough into ball by pulling edges into middle. Transfer loaf, seam side down, to prepared skillet and spray surface of dough with oil spray. Cover loosely with plastic and let rise at room temperature until doubled in size, about 2 hours. (Dough should barely spring back when poked with knuckle.)

3. Thirty minutes before baking, adjust oven rack to lowest position, place Dutch oven (with lid) on rack, and heat oven to 500 degrees. Lightly flour top of dough and, using sharp serrated knife or single-edge razor blade, make two 6-inch-long, ½-inch-deep slashes along top of dough to make X. Carefully remove pot from oven, transfer to wire rack, and remove lid. Pick up loaf by lifting parchment overhang and lower into pot (let any excess parchment hang over pot edge). Cover pot and place in oven. Reduce oven temperature to 425 degrees and bake, covered, for 30 minutes. Remove lid and continue to bake until crust is deep golden brown and loaf registers 210 degrees, 20 to 30 minutes longer. Carefully remove loaf from pot; transfer to wire rack, discard parchment, and let cool to room temperature, about 2 hours, before slicing and serving. (Bread is best eaten on day it is baked but will keep wrapped in double layer of plastic wrap and stored at room temperature for up to 2 days. To recrisp crust, place unwrapped bread in 450-degree oven for 6 to 8 minutes.)

Almost No-Knead Seeded Rye Bread
Replace 1⅜ cups all-purpose flour with 1⅛ cups rye flour. Add 2 tablespoons caraway seeds to flour mixture in step 1.

Almost No-Knead Whole-Wheat Bread
Replace 1 cup all-purpose flour with 1 cup whole-wheat flour. Stir 2 tablespoons honey into water before adding it to dry ingredients in step 1.

Almost No-Knead Cranberry-Pecan Bread
This bread makes especially good toast.

Add ½ cup dried cranberries and ½ cup toasted pecans to flour mixture in step 1.

Olive-Rosemary Bread

WHY THIS RECIPE WORKS: To make really good olive-rosemary bread, we needed a great homemade rustic bread—with a coarse crumb, chewy interior, and thick, burnished crust—and a way to add olives without ruining the bread. We started by simply adding olives to a plain rustic Italian bread recipe, but the moisture from the olives made the bread gummy, and the assertive olive flavor made the bread itself seem bland. To compensate, we added some whole-wheat flour and reduced the hydration level (the weight of the water divided by the weight of the flour) from 68 to 63 percent. Honey added sweetness and brought out the olives' savory flavor. Rolling the olives up in the dough before the first rise gave us a nicely textured loaf with evenly dispersed olives. Just about any good brined or oil-cured olives worked well (after a quick rinse to control saltiness). Surprisingly, it took a whopping 2 tablespoons of rosemary to achieve the demure background flavor we wanted.

Olive-Rosemary Bread
MAKES 2 LARGE LOAVES

If you don't have a stand mixer, you can mix the dough by hand; see Core Technique on page 547 for more details. If you don't have a baking stone, bake the bread on an overturned and preheated rimmed baking sheet on the lowest oven rack. Almost any variety of brined or oil-cured olives works in this recipe, although we prefer a mix of both green and black olives. See Recipe Tutorial on page 556 for more details on this recipe.

1¾ cups water, room temperature
2 tablespoons honey
2 teaspoons instant or rapid-rise yeast
3½ cups (19¼ ounces) bread flour, plus extra as needed
½ cup (2¾ ounces) whole-wheat flour
2 teaspoons salt
2 tablespoons chopped fresh rosemary
1½ cups olives, pitted, rinsed, chopped coarse, and patted dry

1. Whisk water, honey, and yeast together in bowl of stand mixer fitted with dough hook. Add bread flour and whole-wheat flour to bowl and mix on low speed until cohesive dough is formed, about 3 minutes; cover bowl tightly with plastic wrap and let sit at room temperature for 20 minutes.

2. Make well in center of dough and add salt and rosemary. Knead dough on low speed for 5 minutes, scraping down bowl and dough hook as needed. Increase speed to medium and continue to knead until dough is smooth and slightly tacky, about 1 minute. If dough is very sticky, add 1 to 2 tablespoons bread flour and continue mixing for 1 minute. Transfer dough to lightly floured counter and press into 12 by 6-inch rectangle, with long side facing you. Press olives evenly into dough, then roll dough away from you into firm cylinder, keeping roll taut by tucking it under itself as you go. Turn loaf seam side up and roll cylinder into coil. Transfer dough, spiral side up, to large, lightly greased bowl, cover tightly with plastic, and let rise at room temperature until it increases in size by 50 percent, about 1 hour.

3. Spray rubber spatula or bowl scraper with vegetable oil spray. Fold partially risen dough over itself by gently lifting and folding edge of dough toward middle. Turn bowl 90 degrees; fold again. Turn bowl again; fold once more. Cover with plastic and let rise for 30 minutes. Repeat folding, replace plastic, and let rise until doubled in size, about 30 minutes.

4. Transfer dough to lightly floured counter, being careful not to deflate. Divide dough in half, loosely shape each piece into ball, and let rest for 15 minutes. Flip each ball over and, starting from top, roll dough toward you into firm oval shape. Using palms, roll each oval (seam side down) from center outward until 12-inch loaf is formed. Poke any olives that fall off into bottom seam, then pinch seam closed. Transfer each loaf, seam side down, to 12 by 6-inch piece of parchment paper and cover with plastic. Let rise until doubled in size, 1 to 1½ hours. (Dough should barely spring back when pressed lightly with finger.)

5. One hour before baking, adjust oven rack to lower-middle position, place baking stone on rack, and heat oven to 450 degrees. Slide parchment with loaves onto pizza peel. Using sharp serrated knife or single-edge razor blade, make three 3½-inch-deep slashes on diagonal along top of each fully risen loaf, starting and stopping about 1 inch from ends. Spray loaves with water and slide parchment with loaves onto baking stone. Bake for 15 minutes, spraying loaves with water twice more during first 5 minutes of baking time. Reduce oven temperature to 375 degrees and continue to bake until crust is deep golden brown and loaves register 210 degrees, 25 to 30 minutes. Transfer loaves to wire rack, discard parchment, and let cool to room temperature, about 2 hours, before slicing and serving. (Bread can be wrapped in double layer of plastic wrap and stored at room temperature for up to 3 days. Wrapped with additional layer of aluminum foil, bread can be frozen for up to 1 month. To recrisp the crust, thaw bread at room temperature, if frozen, and place unwrapped bread in 450-degree oven for 5 to 10 minutes.)

Ciabatta

✓ **WHY THIS RECIPE WORKS:** Whether they lack flavor or have holes so big there's hardly any bread, most loaves of ciabatta available just aren't any good. Uninterested in a lackluster loaf from the supermarket, we decided to make our own, aiming for a crisp, flavorful crust, a tangy flavor, and a chewy, open crumb. We started with the flour selection; all-purpose, with less protein than bread flour, produced loaves with a more open, springy texture. We built flavor through the sponge—as it ferments, the yeast produces lactic and acetic acids, which give the bread its characteristic sourness. Kneading on its own produced loaves that spread out instead of rising, so we turned to a combination of kneading, folding, and letting the dough rest. This process gave the dough structure but also oversized holes. Adding a small amount of milk slightly weakened the gluten strands and took down the size of those big bubbles. We baked the loaves at a cooler temperature than most recipes recommend and sprayed them with water in the first minutes of baking for a crispier crust and a bit more rise.

Ciabatta

MAKES 2 LOAVES

If you don't have a baking stone, bake the bread on an overturned and preheated rimmed baking sheet set on the lowest oven rack. As you make this bread, keep in mind that the dough is wet and very sticky. The key to manipulating it is working quickly and gently; rough handling will result in flat, tough loaves. When possible, use a large rubber spatula or bowl scraper to move the dough. If you have to use your hands, make sure they are well floured. Because the dough is so sticky, it must be prepared in a stand mixer; do not attempt to prepare it by hand. See Core Technique on page 549 for more details on folding partially risen dough.

SPONGE

  1 cup (5 ounces) all-purpose flour
 ⅛ teaspoon instant or rapid-rise yeast
 ½ cup water, room temperature

DOUGH

  2 cups (10 ounces) all-purpose flour
1½ teaspoons salt
 ½ teaspoon instant or rapid-rise yeast
 ¾ cup water, room temperature
 ¼ cup milk, room temperature

1. FOR THE SPONGE: Combine flour, yeast, and water in medium bowl and stir with wooden spoon until uniform mass forms, about 1 minute. Cover bowl tightly with plastic wrap and let stand at room temperature for at least 8 hours or up to 24 hours.

2. FOR THE DOUGH: Place sponge and dough ingredients in bowl of stand mixer fitted with paddle attachment. Mix on low speed until roughly combined and shaggy dough forms, about 1 minute, scraping down bowl and paddle as needed. Increase speed to medium-low and continue mixing until dough becomes uniform mass that collects on paddle and pulls away from sides of bowl, 4 to 6 minutes. Change to dough hook and knead bread on medium speed until smooth and shiny (dough will be very sticky), about 10 minutes, scraping down bowl and dough hook as needed. Transfer dough to large bowl, cover tightly with plastic, and let rise at room temperature until doubled in size, about 1 hour. (Dough should barely spring back when poked with knuckle.)

3. Spray rubber spatula or bowl scraper with vegetable oil spray. Fold partially risen dough over itself by gently lifting and folding edge of dough toward middle. Turn bowl 90 degrees; fold again. Turn bowl and fold dough 6 more times (for total of 8 turns). Cover with plastic and let rise for 30 minutes. Repeat folding, replace plastic, and let rise until doubled in size, about 30 minutes longer.

4. One hour before baking, adjust oven rack to lower-middle position, place baking stone on rack, and heat oven to 450 degrees. Cut two 12 by 6-inch pieces of parchment paper and dust liberally with flour. Transfer dough to floured counter, being careful not to deflate it completely. Liberally flour top of dough and divide in half with bench scraper. Turn 1 piece of dough cut side up and dust with flour. With well-floured hands, press dough into rough 12 by 6-inch rectangle. Fold shorter sides of dough toward center, overlapping them like business letter to form 7 by 4-inch loaf. Repeat with second piece of dough. Gently transfer each loaf, seam side down, to parchment sheets, dust with flour, and cover with plastic. Let loaves sit at room temperature for 30 minutes (surface of loaves will develop small bubbles).

5. Slide parchment with loaves onto pizza peel. Using floured fingertips, evenly poke entire surface of each loaf to form 10 by 6-inch rectangle; spray loaves lightly with water. Slide parchment with loaves onto baking stone. Bake, spraying loaves with water twice more during first 5 minutes of baking time, until crust is deep golden brown and loaves register 210 degrees, 22 to 27 minutes. Transfer loaves to wire rack, discard parchment, and let cool to room temperature, about 1 hour, before slicing and serving. (Bread can be wrapped in double layer of plastic wrap and stored at room temperature for up to 3 days. Wrapped with additional layer of aluminum foil, bread can be frozen for up to 1 month. To recrisp crust, thaw bread at room temperature, if frozen, and place unwrapped bread in 450-degree oven for 6 to 8 minutes.)

Fluffy Dinner Rolls

✔ **WHY THIS RECIPE WORKS:** Soft, rich homemade dinner rolls beat store-bought versions any day. The key to rich flavor and tender texture was using butter for richness and shortening to keep them light and tender. To save a step, we melted the butter and shortening in the microwave in a measuring cup with the other liquid ingredients. This heated the milk, softened the honey (making it easier to combine with the other ingredients), and melted the butter and shortening all in one step. We found that lining a baking dish with a foil sling made it especially easy to get these tightly packed rolls out of the pan without flipping the pan over and damaging the tops of the rolls.

Fluffy Dinner Rolls
MAKES 15 ROLLS

It is important to keep the pieces of dough covered while rounding them into rolls or they will quickly dry out and develop a skin. Don't try to make this bread in a food processor as the volume of flour and other ingredients makes it hard to mix the dough properly. See Core Technique on page 552 for more details on shaping dinner rolls. See Core Technique on page 595 for more details on making a foil sling.

- 1½ cups whole milk
- ⅓ cup honey
- ¼ cup vegetable shortening
- 3 tablespoons unsalted butter
- 2 large eggs
- 5–5½ cups (25 to 27½ ounces) all-purpose flour
- 2¼ teaspoons instant or rapid-rise yeast
- 2 teaspoons salt

1. Microwave milk, honey, shortening, and butter together in large liquid measuring cup until butter and shortening are mostly melted, about 2 minutes. Whisk to melt any remaining pieces of butter or shortening, then set aside to cool until just warm (about 110 degrees). Whisk in 1 egg.

2. Combine 5 cups flour, yeast, and salt in bowl of stand mixer. Place bowl on stand mixer fitted with dough hook, add milk mixture, and mix on low speed until dough comes together, about 2 minutes.

3. Increase speed to medium-low and knead until dough is smooth and elastic, about 8 minutes. If after 4 minutes more flour is needed, add remaining ½ cup flour, 2 tablespoons at a time, until dough clears sides of bowl but sticks to bottom.

4. Turn dough out onto lightly floured counter and knead by hand to form smooth, round ball. Place dough in large, lightly oiled bowl and cover tightly with greased plastic wrap. Let rise in warm place until doubled in size, 1 to 1½ hours.

5. Line 13 by 9-inch baking dish with foil sling and grease foil. Turn dough out onto clean counter and stretch it into even 15-inch-long log. Using chef's knife, cut log into 15 equal pieces; cover with lightly greased plastic wrap. Working with one piece of dough at a time, dimple top of dough with your fingertips, then pick up dough and gently fold short ends underneath. Gently press folded dough into thick square shape, then stretch dough around your thumbs into smooth, taut ball. Drage dough in small circles over clean counter using cupped hand until dough feels firm and round (should feel like dough is spinning underneath your hand; not turning over). Arrange in prepared baking dish.

6. Lightly press on rolls so they just touch each other. Mist rolls with vegetable oil spray, cover loosely with plastic wrap, and let rise in warm place until nearly doubled in size and dough barely springs back when poked with knuckle, 45 to 75 minutes.

7. Adjust oven rack to lower-middle position and heat oven to 350 degrees. Beat remaining egg with 1 tablespoon water and brush rolls gently with egg mixture, then spray lightly with water. Bake rolls until deep golden brown, 25 to 30 minutes, rotating pan halfway through baking. Let rolls cool in pan on wire rack for 10 minutes, then remove from pan using foil sling. Serve warm.

TO MAKE AHEAD: In step 4, do not let dough rise; refrigerate it overnight or up to 16 hours. Let dough sit at room temperature for 30 minutes, then continue with step 5. Alternatively, to freeze unbaked rolls, let rolls rise in step 6, then wrap baking dish tightly with plastic wrap then foil and freeze. To bake, let frozen rolls sit at room temperature for 30 minutes, then brush with egg wash and spray with water as directed. Bake in 350-degree oven as directed, increasing the baking time to 30 to 35 minutes.

New York–Style Thin-Crust Pizza

✔ **WHY THIS RECIPE WORKS:** With home ovens that reach only 500 degrees and dough that's impossible to stretch thin, even the savviest cooks can struggle to produce New York–style parlor-quality pizza. We were in pursuit of a New York–style pizza with a perfect crust—thin, crisp, and spottily charred on the exterior; tender yet chewy within. High-protein bread flour gave us a chewy, nicely tanned pizza crust, and the right ratio of flour, water, and yeast gave us dough that would stretch and retain moisture as it baked. We kneaded the dough quickly in a food processor then let it proof in the refrigerator for at least 24 hours to develop its flavors. After we shaped and topped the pizza, it went onto a blazing-hot baking stone to cook. Placing the stone near the top of the oven was a surprising improvement, allowing the top of the pizza to brown as well as the bottom. In minutes we had a pizza with everything in sync: a thoroughly crisp, browned crust with a slightly chewy texture.

New York–Style Thin-Crust Pizza

MAKES TWO 13-INCH PIZZAS; SERVES 4 TO 6

If you don't have a baking stone, bake the pizzas on an overturned and preheated rimmed baking sheet. You can shape the second dough round while the first pizza bakes, but don't add the toppings until just before baking. You will need a pizza peel for this recipe. It is important to use ice water in the dough to prevent it from overheating in the food processor. Semolina flour is ideal for dusting the peel; use it in place of bread flour if you have it. The sauce will yield more than needed in the recipe; extra sauce can be refrigerated for up to one week or frozen for up to one month. See Recipe Tutorial on page 566 for more details on this recipe.

DOUGH
- **3 cups (16½ ounces) bread flour**
- **2 teaspoons sugar**
- **½ teaspoon instant or rapid-rise yeast**
- **1⅓ cups ice water**
- **1 tablespoon vegetable oil**
- **1½ teaspoons salt**

SAUCE
- **1 (28-ounce) can whole peeled tomatoes, drained**
- **1 tablespoon extra-virgin olive oil**
- **1 teaspoon red wine vinegar**
- **2 garlic cloves, minced**
- **1 teaspoon salt**
- **1 teaspoon dried oregano**
- **¼ teaspoon pepper**

- **1 ounce Parmesan cheese, grated fine (½ cup)**
- **8 ounces whole-milk mozzarella cheese, shredded (2 cups)**

1. FOR THE DOUGH: Process flour, sugar, and yeast in food processor until combined, about 2 seconds. With processor running, slowly add water; process until dough is just combined and no dry flour remains, about 10 seconds. Let dough sit for 10 minutes.

2. Add oil and salt to dough and process until dough forms satiny, sticky ball that clears sides of bowl, 30 to 60 seconds. Transfer dough to lightly oiled counter and knead briefly by hand until smooth, about 1 minute. Shape dough into tight ball and place in large, lightly oiled bowl; cover bowl tightly with plastic wrap and refrigerate for at least 24 hours or up to 3 days.

3. FOR THE SAUCE: Process all ingredients in clean bowl of food processor until smooth, about 30 seconds. Transfer to bowl and refrigerate until ready to use.

4. One hour before baking, adjust oven rack 4 to 5 inches from broiler, set baking stone on rack, and heat oven to 500 degrees. Transfer dough to clean counter and divide in half. With cupped palms, form each half into smooth, tight ball.

Place balls of dough on lightly greased baking sheet, spacing them at least 3 inches apart; cover loosely with greased plastic and let sit for 1 hour.

5. Coat 1 ball of dough generously with flour and place on well-floured counter (keep other ball covered). Use fingertips to gently flatten dough into 8-inch disk, leaving 1 inch of outer edge slightly thicker than center. Using hands, gently stretch disk into 12-inch round, working along edges and giving disk quarter turns. Transfer dough to well-floured pizza peel and stretch into 13-inch round. Using back of spoon or ladle, spread ½ cup tomato sauce in thin layer over surface of dough, leaving ¼-inch border around edge. Sprinkle ¼ cup Parmesan evenly over sauce, followed by 1 cup mozzarella. Slide pizza carefully onto baking stone and bake until crust is well browned and cheese is bubbly and beginning to brown, 10 to 12 minutes, rotating pizza halfway through baking. Transfer pizza to wire rack and let cool for 5 minutes before slicing and serving. Repeat step 5 to shape, top, and bake second pizza.

New York–Style Thin-Crust White Pizza

MAKES TWO 13-INCH PIZZAS; SERVES 4 TO 6

If you don't have a baking stone, bake the pizzas on an overturned and preheated rimmed baking sheet. You can shape the second dough round while the first pizza bakes, but don't add the toppings until just before baking. You will need a pizza peel for this recipe. It is important to use ice water in the dough to prevent overheating the dough while in the food processor. Semolina flour is ideal for dusting the peel; using it in place of bread flour if you have it. The sauce will yield more than needed in the recipe; extra sauce can be refrigerated for up to 1 week or frozen for up to 1 month.

DOUGH
- **3 cups (16½ ounces) bread flour**
- **2 teaspoons sugar**
- **½ teaspoon instant or rapid-rise yeast**
- **1⅓ cups ice water**
- **1 tablespoon vegetable oil**
- **1½ teaspoons salt**

WHITE SAUCE
- **1 cup whole-milk ricotta cheese**
- **¼ cup extra-virgin olive oil**
- **¼ cup heavy cream**
- **1 large egg yolk**
- **4 garlic cloves, minced**
- **2 teaspoons minced fresh oregano**
- **1 teaspoon minced fresh thyme**
- **½ teaspoon salt**
- **¼ teaspoon pepper**
- **⅛ teaspoon cayenne pepper**
- **2 scallions, sliced thin, dark green tops reserved for garnish**

- **1 ounce Pecorino Romano cheese, grated fine (½ cup)**
- **8 ounces whole-milk mozzarella cheese, shredded (2 cups)**
- **½ cup (4 ounces) whole-milk ricotta cheese**

1. FOR THE DOUGH: Process flour, sugar, and yeast in food processor until combined, about 2 seconds. With processor running, slowly add water; process until dough is just combined and no dry flour remains, about 10 seconds. Let dough sit for 10 minutes.

2. Add oil and salt to dough and process until dough forms satiny, sticky ball that clears sides of bowl, 30 to 60 seconds. Transfer dough to lightly oiled counter and knead briefly by hand until smooth, about 1 minute. Shape dough into tight ball and place in large, lightly oiled bowl; cover bowl tightly with plastic wrap and refrigerate for at least 24 hours and up to 3 days.

3. FOR THE SAUCE: Whisk all ingredients except scallion greens together in bowl; refrigerate until ready to use.

4. TO TOP AND BAKE THE PIZZA: One hour before baking, adjust oven rack 4 to 5 inches from broiler, set baking stone on rack, and heat oven to 500 degrees. Transfer dough to clean counter and divide in half. With cupped palms, form each half into smooth, tight ball. Place balls of dough on lightly greased baking sheet, spacing them at least 3 inches apart; cover loosely with greased plastic and let sit for 1 hour.

5. Coat 1 ball of dough generously with flour and place on well-floured counter (keep other ball covered). Use fingertips to gently flatten dough into 8-inch disk, leaving 1 inch of outer edge slightly thicker than center. Using hands, gently stretch disk into 12-inch round, working along edges and giving disk quarter turns. Transfer dough to well-floured pizza peel and stretch into 13-inch round. Using back of spoon or ladle, spread ½ cup white sauce in thin layer over surface of dough, leaving ¼-inch border around edge. Sprinkle ¼ cup Pecorino evenly over sauce, followed by 1 cup mozzarella. Dollop ¼ cup ricotta in teaspoon amounts evenly over pizza. Slide pizza carefully onto baking stone and bake until crust is well browned and cheese is bubbly and beginning to brown, 10 to 12 minutes, rotating pizza halfway through baking. Transfer pizza to wire rack and let cool for 5 minutes. Sprinkle with reserved scallion greens, slice, and serve. Repeat step 5 to shape, top, and bake second pizza.

Classic Pan Pizza

✔ **WHY THIS RECIPE WORKS:** Unlike its thin-crust cousin, pan pizza has a soft, chewy, thick crust that can stand up to substantial toppings. We wanted to try our hand at making this pizza without a lot of fuss. Most of the allure of deep-dish pizza is in the crust, so it was important to get it right. After trying numerous ingredients and techniques, we found a surprising solution: adding boiled potato gave the crust exactly the right qualities. It was soft and moist, yet with a bit of chew and good structure. The potato even made the unbaked dough easier to handle. To keep the outside of the crust from toughening during baking, we added a generous amount of olive oil to the pan before putting in the dough. Topping the pizza before it went into the oven weighed down the crust so that it didn't rise enough, so we baked the crust untopped for a few minutes first. Our crust wasn't just a platform for the topping; it had great flavor and texture of its own.

Classic Pan Pizza with Tomatoes, Mozzarella, and Basil

MAKES ONE 14-INCH PIZZA; SERVES 4 TO 6

If you don't have a stand mixer, you can knead the bread dough by hand following the instructions on page 547. If you don't have a baking stone, bake the pizza on an overturned and preheated rimmed baking sheet set on the lowest oven rack. Prepare the topping while the dough is rising so it will be ready at the same time the dough is ready. The amount of oil used to grease the pan may seem excessive, but in addition to preventing sticking, the oil helps the crust brown nicely.

DOUGH

- **9** ounces russet potatoes, peeled and quartered
- **3½** cups (17½ ounces) all-purpose flour
- **1** cup water, heated to 115 degrees
- **1½** teaspoons instant or rapid-rise yeast
- **6** tablespoons extra-virgin olive oil
- **1¾** teaspoons salt

TOPPING

- **4** tomatoes, cored, seeded, and cut into 1-inch pieces
- **2** garlic cloves, minced
   Salt and pepper
- **6** ounces mozzarella cheese, shredded (1½ cups)
- **1** ounce Parmesan cheese, grated (½ cup)
- **3** tablespoons shredded fresh basil

1. FOR THE DOUGH: Bring 1 quart water and potato to boil in medium saucepan and cook until tender, 10 to 15 minutes. Drain potato and process through ricer or food mill onto plate. Measure out and reserve 1⅓ cups potato; discard remaining potato.

2. Adjust oven racks to upper-middle and lowest positions and heat oven to 200 degrees. Once oven temperature reaches 200 degrees, maintain heat for 10 minutes, then turn off oven.

3. Using stand mixer fitted with dough hook, mix ½ cup flour, ½ cup water, and yeast together on low speed until combined; cover bowl tightly with plastic wrap and let sit until bubbly, about 20 minutes.

4. Add 2 tablespoons oil, remaining 3 cups flour, remaining ½ cup water, salt, and potato to flour mixture and mix on low speed until dough comes together. Increase speed to medium and knead until dough comes together and is slightly tacky, about 5 minutes. Transfer dough to large, lightly greased bowl; cover tightly with plastic and let rise on lower rack in warm oven until doubled in size, 30 to 35 minutes.

5. Grease bottom of 14-inch cake pan with remaining 4 tablespoons oil. Remove dough from oven; transfer to clean counter and press into 12-inch round. Transfer round to pan, cover with plastic, and let rest until dough no longer resists shaping, about 10 minutes. Uncover dough and pull up into edges and up sides of pan to form 1-inch-high lip. Cover with plastic; let rise at room temperature until doubled in size, about 30 minutes.

6. FOR THE TOPPING: Mix tomatoes and garlic together in bowl and season with salt and pepper to taste; set aside.

7. TO BAKE THE PIZZA: One hour before baking, set baking stone on lowest rack and heat oven to 425 degrees. Uncover dough and prick generously with fork. Bake on baking stone until dry and lightly browned, about 15 minutes.

8. Remove pizza from oven. Spread partially baked crust with tomato mixture; sprinkle with mozzarella, then Parmesan. Return pizza to baking stone and continue baking until cheese melts, 10 to 15 minutes longer. Move pizza to upper-middle rack and continue to bake until cheese is spotty brown, about 5 minutes longer. Remove pizza from oven, sprinkle with basil, and let rest for 10 minutes before slicing and serving.

Classic Four-Cheese Pan Pizza with Pesto

Omit tomatoes, garlic, salt, pepper, and basil from topping. Spread ½ cup Classic Basil Pesto (page 169) onto partially baked crust in step 8, then sprinkle with mozzarella, followed by 1 cup shredded provolone cheese, ¼ cup crumbled blue cheese, and Parmesan. Continue baking as directed.

Rosemary Focaccia

✔ **WHY THIS RECIPE WORKS:** Focaccia can easily disappoint when it turns out heavy and thick. We wanted a light, airy loaf, crisp-crusted and topped with a smattering of herbs. A sponge gave us the flavor benefits of a long fermentation with minimal effort. But our loaves weren't tender and airy enough. Thinking that kneading was developing too much gluten, we tried a gentler approach. A high proportion of water to flour and a long resting process let the natural enzymes in the wheat replicate the effect of kneading. We shaved an hour off our proofing time by adding the salt later in the process, preventing it from slowing down the activity of the enzymes. To give our loaves a flavorful, crisp crust, we oiled the baking pans and added coarse salt.

Rosemary Focaccia

MAKES TWO 9-INCH ROUND LOAVES

If you don't have a baking stone, bake the bread on an overturned and preheated rimmed baking sheet. For more information on folding and turning the dough in step 3, see page 549.

SPONGE
- ½ **cup (2½ ounces) all-purpose flour**
- ⅓ **cup water, heated to 110 degrees**
- ¼ **teaspoon instant or rapid-rise yeast**

DOUGH
- 2½ **cups (12½ ounces) all-purpose flour, plus extra for shaping**
- 1¼ **cups water, heated to 110 degrees**
- 1 **teaspoon instant or rapid-rise yeast**
  Kosher salt
- 4 **tablespoons extra-virgin olive oil**
- 2 **tablespoons chopped fresh rosemary**

1. FOR THE SPONGE: Combine flour, water, and yeast in large bowl and stir with wooden spoon until uniform mass forms and no dry flour remains, about 1 minute. Cover bowl tightly with plastic wrap and let stand at room temperature at least 8 hours or up to 24 hours. (Use immediately or store in refrigerator for up to 3 days; allow to stand at room temperature 30 minutes before proceeding with recipe).

2. FOR THE DOUGH: Stir flour, water, and yeast into sponge with wooden spoon until uniform mass forms and no dry flour remains, about 1 minute. Cover with plastic and let rise at room temperature for 15 minutes.

3. Sprinkle 2 teaspoons salt over dough; stir into dough until thoroughly incorporated, about 1 minute. Cover with plastic and let rise at room temperature for 30 minutes. Spray rubber spatula or bowl scraper with vegetable oil spray. Fold partially risen dough over itself by gently lifting and folding edge of dough toward middle. Turn bowl 90 degrees; fold again. Turn bowl and fold dough 6 more times (for total of 8 folds). Cover with plastic and let rise for 30 minutes. Repeat folding, turning, and rising 2 more times, for total of three 30-minute rises.

4. One hour before baking, adjust oven rack to upper-middle position, place baking stone on rack, and heat oven to 500 degrees. Gently transfer dough to lightly floured counter. Lightly dust top of dough with flour and divide it in half. Shape each piece of dough into 5-inch round by gently tucking under edges. Coat two 9-inch round cake pans with 2 tablespoons oil each. Sprinkle each pan with ½ teaspoon salt. Place round of dough in 1 pan, top side down; slide dough around pan to coat bottom and sides with oil, then flip dough over. Repeat with second piece of dough. Cover pans with plastic and let rest for 5 minutes.

5. Using fingertips, press dough out toward edges of pan, taking care not to tear it. (If dough resists stretching, let it relax for 5 to 10 minutes before trying to stretch it again.) Using dinner fork, poke entire surface of dough 25 to 30 times, popping any large bubbles. Sprinkle rosemary evenly over top of dough. Let dough rest in pans until slightly bubbly, 5 to 10 minutes.

6. Place pans on baking stone and lower oven temperature to 450 degrees. Bake until tops are golden brown, 25 to 28 minutes, rotating pans halfway through baking. Transfer pans to wire rack and let cool for 5 minutes. Remove loaves from pans and return to rack. Brush tops with any oil remaining in pans. Cool for 30 minutes before serving. (Leftover bread can be wrapped in double layer of plastic wrap and stored at room temperature for 2 days. Wrapped with additional layer of aluminum foil, bread can be frozen for up to 1 month.)

Focaccia with Kalamata Olives and Anchovies

Omit salt from pans in step 4. Substitute 1 cup kalamata olives, pitted, rinsed, and chopped coarse, 4 rinsed and minced anchovy fillets, and 1 teaspoon red pepper flakes for rosemary. Sprinkle each focaccia with ¼ cup finely grated Pecorino Romano as soon as it is removed from oven.

Focaccia with Caramelized Red Onion, Pancetta, and Oregano

Cook 4 ounces finely chopped pancetta in 12-inch skillet over medium heat, stirring occasionally, until most of fat has been rendered, about 10 minutes. Remove pancetta with slotted spoon and transfer to paper towel–lined plate. Add 1 chopped red onion and 2 tablespoons water to fat left in skillet and cook over medium heat, stirring often, until onion is soft and beginning to brown, about 12 minutes. Remove skillet from heat and set aside. Omit rosemary. After poking surface of dough rounds in step 5, sprinkle with pancetta, onion, and 2 teaspoons minced fresh oregano. Continue with recipe as directed.

Inside This Chapter

CHAPTER 14

How to Make Cookies

Despite their humble appearance, most cookies are actually complicated chemical systems. Cookie dough is relatively dry—many recipes contain no liquid ingredients, other than perhaps an egg. For this reason, small changes to a single ingredient can have a big effect on more than just flavor. (Add more sugar, for instance, and the cookies will not only taste sweeter but also will spread more.) In addition to presenting a wide range of cookies, this chapter will also explore brownies and bar cookies.

Getting Started

Types of Cookies

Cookies can be divided into broad categories based on the ways the dough is portioned.

DROP COOKIES
Many bakers learn to make these simple cookies as children. Traditionally, the dough is dropped from a spoon onto the baking sheet; in the test kitchen we generally measure each portion with a tablespoon or portion scoop, then roll the dough into a ball for even sizing. This category includes chocolate chip, oatmeal, and peanut butter cookies.

ICEBOX COOKIES
Fairly thin and with a sandy, shortbreadlike texture, icebox cookies are an old-fashioned favorite. The dough is shaped into a long cylinder, chilled until firm, and then sliced into thin rounds. Pecan sandies are the classic icebox cookie.

ROLL-AND-CUT COOKIES
A favorite for bakers during the holidays, this type of cookie relies on a buttery dough that is rolled thin and then stamped with a cookie cutter into various shapes. These cookies bake up quite thin and crisp, making them the perfect vehicle for glazes, colored sugar, and other decorations.

MOLDED AND SHAPED COOKIES
This broad category includes cookies that are piped through a pastry bag, such as meringue and spritz cookies, as well as cookies that require shaping or molding by hand (everything from nut crescents to rugelach).

BAR COOKIES
The dough for bar cookies is baked in a large pan, then cut into individual portions; they don't really resemble "cookies" until after they are cut. Brownies are the classic bar, but many have distinct layers, with a tender but firm shortbread on the bottom that is topped with an intensely flavored, gooey filling (jam, lemon curd, sugary pecans). Many have a buttery streusel topping as well. Lemon squares, pecan bars, raspberry streusel bars, and turtle brownies are all examples of bar cookies.

Essential Ingredients

Most cookie recipes start with the same ingredients: butter, sugar, flour, eggs, baking powder, and baking soda. See the pantry section of Chapter 1 and pages 48–49 for detailed information on all of these ingredients. Pay special attention to the section on sugar and other sweeteners on page 43; differences among sweeteners can be quite significant, especially in a cookie recipe. Also, vanilla extract is used in almost every cookie recipe; see page 756 for information on vanilla extract (as well as vanilla beans). Brownies as well as many cookies rely on chocolate, and it's critical to use the correct type of chocolate in a recipe to ensure the best results.

UNSWEETENED CHOCOLATE
Often called baking chocolate or chocolate liquor, this is pure chocolate made from roasted cocoa beans. It contains about 50 percent cocoa solids (which lend flavor) and 50 percent cocoa butter (which creates its creamy, melting qualities). With bold chocolate flavor, it is used in many brownie recipes.

BITTERSWEET AND SEMISWEET CHOCOLATES
These are made by grinding unsweetened chocolate with sugar, then kneading for a smooth, creamy texture. They are 30 to 60 percent sugar, so they have less chocolate flavor than unsweetened chocolate, but the flavor is less bitter and more complex. They also have a superior texture (essential in frostings and glazes). We typically prefer bittersweet with about 60 percent cacao.

MILK CHOCOLATE
The classic "candy bar," milk chocolate varies widely from brand to brand. Some have very little chocolate while others are similar to semisweet chocolate, with the only difference being the addition of milk solids. Look for a minimum of 35 percent cacao; those with less chocolate are very sweet.

CHOCOLATE CHIPS
These little morsels are similar to semisweet or bittersweet bars, with one exception. Most chips contain less cocoa butter so that the morsels will hold their shape better when heated. We prefer bittersweet chips to the sweeter semisweet chips.

COCOA POWDER
This potent source of chocolate flavor is nothing more than unsweetened chocolate with much of the fat removed. Dutch-processed cocoa has been treated with an alkaline substance to make it less acidic. We have had good results with both regular (natural) brands as well as Dutched cocoas.

WHITE CHOCOLATE
This product contains the same ingredients as milk chocolate—cocoa butter, milk, and sugar—except for one crucial component: cocoa solids. Many brands are made with palm oil in place of some or all of the cocoa butter, a change that can actually improve texture and has no impact on flavor.

Essential Equipment

Below are the basic pans and specialty tools you will need to make most cookies. In addition, some recipes call for brushing cookies with an egg wash or melted butter. We recommend a pastry brush with silicone bristles for this job, rather than boar bristles, which harbor odors and tend to fall off. Buy a brush that has perforated flaps, which trap liquid, and an angled head, which makes it easy to reach tight spots.

HAND-HELD MIXER

Many cookie recipes can be made without an electric mixer. For those that do require an electric mixer, a hand-held model is just fine (you can certainly use a stand mixer if you have one). We prefer simple, slim wire beaters to traditional beaters with flat metal strips around a center post because this post tends to be a good spot for thick cookie dough to collect. For more details on what to look for, see page 28.

RIMMED BAKING SHEET

We use rimmed baking sheets in our cookie recipes. You should already own rimmed baking sheets for other purposes, so why not use them for cookies? Buy large (18 by 13 inches is ideal), heavy-duty baking sheets. For more details on what to look for, see page 20.

COOKIE SHEETS

Some bakers like the convenience of cookie sheets, which are rimless on two or three sides. Without rims, it's easy to slide cookies and parchment right off the sheet and onto a wire rack. The lack of rims translates to a slightly faster baking time, so pay attention to the clock (our recipes were tested on baking sheets). If you invest in cookie sheets, choose heavy models with handles on the two short sides, and with a light-colored matte finish. (Darker sheets brown too quickly.)

METAL BAKING PANS

We use these versatile pans to bake snack cakes, sheet cakes, brownies, and bar cookies. It's good to own both 8- and 9-inch square metal pans as well as a 13 by 9-inch metal pan. We prefer metal to glass primarily because metal pans are typically coated with non-stick finishes. For more details on what to look for, see page 26.

OFFSET SPATULAS

A thin metal offset spatula can be used to move cookies from the baking sheet to a wire rack. Look for a spatula with a blade that's at least 8 inches long. A smaller model (with a 4-inch blade) is ideal for glazing cookies.

WIRE RACK

A good cooling rack should do more than simply cool off cookies. It should be sturdy, able to withstand a hot broiler, and clean up without warping or getting damaged. It should also fit inside a standard 18 by 13-inch baking sheet so that it can be used for tasks beyond cooling. For more details on what to look for, see page 27.

COOKIE SPATULA

Reaching between cookies on a crowded baking sheet and removing brownies from a pan are tricky with a full-size spatula. A small silicone spatula is the perfect tool for the job. The blade should measure roughly 2 inches by 3 inches and have a flexible edge. An angled handle will help you slide the blade under individual cookies. While not essential, it is handy if you bake a lot of cookies.

ROLLING PIN

An old-fashioned wooden pin does a better job than marble, nonstick, or other high-tech options. We like French-style rolling pins without handles. American-style pins with ball bearings and handles can exert too much pressure on dough. We prefer a long pin (20 inches or so). Tapered ends can help you get a good feel for pie dough but are less important when rolling out large sheets of cookie dough.

COOKIE CUTTERS

We prefer metal cutters to plastic ones because the former are sharper and more likely to make clean cuts. Look at the cutting edges and make sure they are thin and sharp. Ideally, cutters will be at least 1 inch tall (so they can cut through thicker cookie dough as well). A rounded or rubber top offers nice protection for your hands.

PARCHMENT PAPER

Lining your baking sheets with parchment paper is a quick and easy way to make sure your baking sheets stay clean and your cookies release effortlessly. We prefer parchment to reusable pan liners (such as Silpat baking mats), which can transfer flavors and stain over time. We prefer wider rolls that will fit large baking sheets. If you bake a lot of cookies, you might want to order flat sheets cut to fit baking sheets.

How to Brown Butter

ESSENTIAL EQUIPMENT

• heavy-bottomed skillet or saucepan with light-colored interior
• large heatproof bowl

When we want a chewy cookie, we melt the butter rather than cream it. Butter is about 18 percent water, and melting the butter frees that water to bond with the proteins in the flour and form gluten—the elastic matrix that makes not just bread but also cookies chewy. And in some cases, we don't simply melt the butter; instead, we brown it for added flavor. Browned butter, or *beurre noisette* (hazelnut butter) as it is called in French, is a key ingredient in several of our cookie recipes, including our Chocolate Chip Cookies (page 612). The reason the French call it hazelnut butter is because the butter takes on the flavor and aroma of toasted nuts as it browns. Browned butter is used in both baked goods and savory preparations; brightened with lemon juice, it serves as a simple "sauce" for Fish Meunière with Browned Butter and Lemon (page 371) as well as for a variety of vegetables.

1. LET IT FOAM

Cut butter into chunks and place in heavy-bottomed skillet or saucepan with light-colored interior. Turn heat to medium-high and cook, swirling pan occasionally, until butter melts and begins to foam.

WHY? Medium-high heat speeds up the process but demands that the cook pay attention. If you're browning butter for the first time, you can lower the heat to medium to give yourself a bigger cushion. A pan with a light-colored interior is absolutely essential. Don't use a nonstick pan—the dark surface makes it impossible to track the color change. Gently swirl the butter a few times to make sure there are no hot spots.

2. SWIRL AND WATCH

Continue to cook, swirling pan constantly, until butter is dark golden brown and has nutty aroma, 1 to 3 minutes.

WHY? Foaming, which happens when the water in the butter boils off, is your clue that the butter is nearly done. Almost immediately, you'll see tiny specks settling to the bottom of the pan. These are the milk solids that give the browned butter its color and flavor. Once the butter starts to foam, swirl the pan constantly—if you don't, the butter solids on the bottom of the pan will burn. The butter is done when it turns chestnut brown and smells toasty.

3. COOL QUICKLY

Immediately transfer browned butter to large heatproof bowl.

WHY? Because residual heat will continue to cook the butter, as soon as the butter looks and smells right, pour it into a bowl. In some cookie recipes, we add a chunk or two of solid butter to the bowl to help bring down the temperature of the butter quickly. (If making a savory brown butter sauce, you will likely leave the butter in the pan and add lemon juice or vinegar and other sauce ingredients, which stop the cooking process.)

How to Toast and Chop Nuts

Most nuts benefit from toasting before they are added to cookie dough, cake batter, or salads. Toasting brings the natural oils in nuts to the surface and intensifies their flavors. Toasting also makes nuts crunchier—which not only is nice in a salad, but helps counteract the softening process that can occur when nuts are added to batters or doughs. You have two options for toasting nuts—a skillet or a rimmed baking sheet—and each has its pros and cons. We prefer to buy whole nuts (almonds, hazelnuts) or nut halves (walnuts, pecans) and then chop them after toasting. That said, if you've bought chopped nuts they can be used in our recipes—simply toast them but skip the chopping step. Note that if you're storing nuts in the freezer (and you should to prevent rancidity), toasting times might be slightly longer than indicated below. Whichever method you choose, pay close attention. Scorched nuts can ruin a dish. The equipment needed will depend on the method you choose.

ESSENTIAL EQUIPMENT

- skillet
- rimmed baking sheet
- cutting board
- apple cutter
- chef's knife and dish towel

1A. TOAST SMALL BATCHES ON STOVETOP

Place nuts in empty skillet and turn heat to medium. Toast nuts, stirring occasionally, until fragrant and lightly browned, 2 to 5 minutes.

WHY? When toasting less than 1 cup of nuts, or when toasting nuts for a recipe that otherwise doesn't require the use of the oven, we usually opt for this method. Depending on the amount of nuts and the heat output of your stove, this process can take as little as 2 minutes, so this method requires vigilance and stirring. Pine nuts, in particular, can quickly burn. Transfer the toasted nuts to a cutting board to cool.

1B. TOAST LARGE BATCHES IN OVEN

Spread nuts out in single layer over rimmed baking sheet. Toast nuts in 350-degree oven, shaking sheet every few minutes, until nuts are fragrant and lightly browned, 5 to 10 minutes.

WHY? When toasting more than 1 cup of nuts, or when toasting nuts for a recipe that already calls for preheating the oven, we usually opt for the oven. Depending on the type and amount of nuts, this process will take 5 to 10 minutes. Shake the pan at least two or three times to turn the nuts and ensure even browning. Transfer the toasted nuts to a cutting board to cool.

2A. CHOP WITH APPLE CUTTER

Gather nuts into pile and press straight down with apple cutter to chop.

WHY? Edges sharp enough to slice an apple can chop nuts, and the ring keeps the pieces from flying around. This works well for small quantities of soft nuts, like walnuts or pecans.

2B. CHOP WITH KNIFE AND TOWEL

Shape damp dish towel into ring on cutting board, leaving enough room for nuts and knife blade. Chop nuts.

WHY? The towel catches the nuts and keeps them on the board. This method is especially helpful when chopping rounded nuts, such as hazelnuts and almonds.

How to Chop and Melt Chocolate

ESSENTIAL
EQUIPMENT

Most recipes that call for chocolate also call for chopping and melting that chocolate. Why chop chocolate if it's just going to be melted? If left in large chunks, the chocolate will melt unevenly and you increase the risk of scorching it. Small pieces melt faster and more evenly. Chopping thin bars is pretty easy, but we often buy large blocks of chocolate because they are such a good deal—we particularly like Callebaut chocolate, which is sold this way—and chopping these thick blocks requires some finesse. Once the chocolate is chopped, it's ready to be melted. You can use the old-fashioned stovetop method or streamline operations in the microwave. With either method, the key is to go slowly to prevent scorching the chocolate. The equipment needed will depend on the methods you choose.

- chef's knife
- carving fork
- cutting board
- heatproof mixing bowl and saucepan
- microwave-safe mixing bowl and microwave
- rubber spatula

1A. CHOP WITH KNIFE

To chop large block of chocolate, hold chef's knife at 45-degree angle to one corner and bear down evenly. After cutting about 1 inch from corner, repeat with other corners.

WHY? It's easy to chop a thin bar of chocolate, but a thick block requires more care. The corners are the easiest place to start the cutting process. Placing the guiding hand on top of the blade gives you extra leverage and keeps the knife steady.

1B. BREAK UP WITH CARVING FORK

To break up large block of chocolate, use sharp two-tined carving fork or meat fork to split into smaller pieces.

WHY? This low-tech method works surprisingly well and doesn't require as much strength as the knife method. Also, with the knife out of the picture, there's no risk of the blade slipping and cutting your hand.

2A. MELT ON STOVETOP

Place chopped chocolate in heatproof bowl set over saucepan of simmering water (water should not touch bottom of bowl). Adjust heat as necessary to maintain simmer, and stir occasionally until chocolate melts.

WHY? The key here is to use gentle steam. If the bowl is sitting in the simmering water, the chocolate will scorch. It's a good idea to check before turning on the heat: If the bottom of the bowl gets wet after you set it in the pan, you are using too much water. Also, choose a bowl with edges that hang over the pot (for easier removal). Remember to stir occasionally—this facilitates the melting process.

2B. MELT IN MICROWAVE

Place chopped chocolate in microwave-safe bowl and heat in microwave at 50 percent for 1 minute. Stir chocolate and continue heating until melted, stirring once every additional 30 seconds.

WHY? Full power in the microwave is too much—you will scorch the chocolate. Using 50 percent power requires a bit more time but greatly reduces the risk of overheating the chocolate. Make sure to stir frequently to encourage the melting process.

Troubleshooting Chopping and Melting Chocolate

PROBLEM	SOLUTION
Can I melt butter with chocolate?	If using the stovetop method, just add the butter at the outset. If using the microwave method, wait to add the butter until the chocolate is nearly melted. (The fat in the butter can splatter if you put the butter in sooner.) With either method, cut the butter into small chunks to facilitate quick melting.
How should I melt chocolate for dipping?	Dipping cookies in melted chocolate is an easy way to dress them up. To produce a glossy coating, it's important to melt the chocolate properly. That's because when melted chocolate resolidifies, the fat can recrystallize into any one of six different forms, only one of which (called the beta crystal) hardens up shiny. The key to preserving the shiny beta crystal is keeping the temperature of the chocolate below 94 degrees. Many recipes have you temper the chocolate—a painstaking process that involves repeatedly taking the chocolate's temperature. Our method barely melts the chocolate and then rapidly cools it by adding more chopped chocolate: Warm 8 ounces of chopped bittersweet chocolate via the stovetop method until barely melted (about 89 degrees); remove the bowl from the heat and immediately stir in 2 ounces of finely chopped bittersweet chocolate until smooth.
My melted chocolate looks lumpy/grainy.	If your melted chocolate looks lumpy or grainy, it has seized—a nearly instantaneous transformation of chocolate from a fluid state to a stiff, grainy one. When chocolate is melted, its ingredients disperse evenly, creating a fluid mass. But if even a tiny amount of moisture is introduced, the liquid and the sugar will form a syrup that cements the cocoa solids together, creating grainy clumps. But don't worry, reversing the reaction is surprisingly easy. The addition of more liquid can actually bring the chocolate back to its fluid state. To prevent seizing in recipes that contain no liquid, take great care not to let any moisture into the chocolate. In recipes that do contain liquid (such as melted butter, water, or liqueur), always melt the chocolate along with these ingredients. And if your chocolate does happen to seize, add boiling water to it, 1 teaspoon at a time, and stir vigorously after each addition until the chocolate is smooth (note that this chocolate-water mixture can no longer be used reliably for baking; save it for a sauce, hot cocoa, or drizzling on cookies).

How to Make Drop Cookies

ESSENTIAL EQUIPMENT

- rimmed baking sheets
- parchment paper
- large plate (if freezing dough)
- zipper-lock bag (if freezing dough)
- wire rack

Drop cookies are the simplest cookies to make. Once the dough is prepared, it is divided into individual portions and "dropped" onto the prepared baking sheet—no rolling pin or cookie cutters necessary. Over the years, our test kitchen has developed a number of subtle refinements to this process, starting with shaping portions of dough into balls and then carefully placing those balls on the baking sheet. This method also allows for freezing some (or all) of the dough balls to bake later (see step 3). Most drop cookies (oatmeal, peanut butter, chocolate, chocolate chip) are best when they have a chewy texture. Using large balls of dough is key—a big cookie is much more likely to have a chewy middle than a small one. Underbaking the cookies slightly and then allowing them to firm up on the baking sheet also help create a chewy texture. We use large baking sheets that measure 18 by 13 inches. We recommend that you do the same. If using smaller baking sheets, you need to bake fewer cookies on each sheet.

1. LINE BAKING SHEETS

Line each baking sheet with piece of parchment paper.

WHY? You might be tempted to grease the baking sheets or spray them with vegetable oil—don't. The extra fat will cause the cookies to spread and bake unevenly. We prefer parchment paper when baking cookies. Its slick surface prevents sticking and doesn't affect how the cookies spread. If you're out of parchment, use aluminum foil instead. While the cookies might seem to stick, you can easily lift (or peel) them off the foil. Most cookie recipes require 2 sheets.

2. ROLL INTO BALLS

Roll specified amount of dough between palms into round ball.

WHY? Simply dropping the dough onto the baking sheet from a spoon will result in unevenly shaped cookies. This method is also much more likely to produce cookies of varying sizes, and so they won't bake at the same rate. By portioning the dough (2 tablespoons is a standard amount in many of our recipes) and then rolling it into a neat ball, you avoid both problems.

3. FREEZE EXTRA DOUGH BALLS FOR LATER

To save some or all cookie dough for later baking, place dough balls on parchment-lined plate and freeze until completely firm, 2 to 3 hours. Transfer dough balls to zipper-lock bag for long-term storage.

WHY? Dough balls can be frozen for at least one month and then baked as desired. You can even bake one or two cookies at a time. If you have room in your freezer, use a parchment-lined rimmed baking sheet for this step. Whether using a large plate or a baking sheet, make sure the dough balls are not touching each other when they go into the freezer—you don't want them to stick together. Once they are frozen hard, they can be piled into a bag for storage. There's no need to defrost the dough; bake as directed, increasing the time by a few minutes.

4. SPACE EVENLY

Place dough balls on prepared baking sheets, making sure to leave specified space between each ball.

WHY? Many novice bakers don't account for the fact that cookies spread in the oven. They either cram too many balls onto the sheet and/or they don't leave enough space between each ball. Make either mistake and the cookies will fuse together in the oven. Sure, you can cut between the cookies, but they won't look as nice. Some recipes call for placing dough balls in staggered rows (three in first row, two in second row, three in third row, two in final row).

5. UNDERBAKE SLIGHTLY

Bake cookies as directed until edges are set and firm but centers are still soft and puffy.

WHY? When texture is paramount, we bake one sheet of cookies at a time since two can compromise air flow. If you want cookies that are chewy in the middle, take them out of the oven when they are slightly underdone—they will finish baking as they cool. If the edges look firm and golden (in light-colored cookies) and the center looks puffy and soft (but not raw), the cookies are ready. If there are cracks in the top of the cookie, the batter will still look moist inside the cracks.

6. COOL ON BAKING SHEET

Transfer rimmed baking sheet to wire rack and let cookies cool until firm, about 10 minutes.

WHY? Slightly underbaked cookies are very soft. To avoid misshapen cookies, wait until they are firm enough that a spatula doesn't cause damage. Also, this step gives the residual heat in the baking sheet time to finish baking the cookies. However, if the cookies are slightly overbaked, don't let them cool on the sheet. Move cookies to a rack to cool quickly. (If the cookies are slightly burnt, you can try to scrape off burnt spots with a rasp-style grater. This isn't ideal, but it's better than serving cookies with burnt edges.)

Troubleshooting Drop Cookies

PROBLEM	SOLUTION
The dough is really soft and difficult to roll.	Cookies are rich with butter, and if your kitchen is hot or humid, the dough can get very soft and sticky. If this happens, place the bowl of dough in the refrigerator for 10 to 30 minutes. This will firm up the dough so that it can be rolled without sticking.
I never seem to get the correct yield.	To ensure consistent size and proper yield, try using a portion scoop. For recipes that call for 2 tablespoons of dough per cookie, a #30 scoop works well.

How to Make Icebox Cookies

ESSENTIAL
EQUIPMENT

Icebox cookies (also known as slice-and-bake cookies) have a bit more polish than drop cookies but are still very easy to make. The dough is simply rolled into a cylinder, chilled until firm, and then sliced into thin rounds. Vanilla icebox cookies require few ingredients (just seven, in fact), and variations are easy to prepare. You also have the option of rolling the log of dough in a garnish, such as sanding sugar or finely chopped nuts. These buttery cookies belong in every baker's repertoire. In addition to the equipment listed at right, you will want a rubber spatula and whisk on hand. Also see How to Cream Butter (page 630).

- hand-held mixer
  or stand mixer
- mixing bowls
- plastic wrap
- chef's knife
- cutting board
- kitchen ruler
- rimmed baking
  sheets
- parchment paper
- wire rack

1. CREAM BUTTER AND TWO SUGARS

Beat 16 tablespoons softened unsalted butter, ¾ cup granulated sugar, and ½ cup confectioners' sugar with mixer on medium-high speed until light and fluffy, 3 to 6 minutes.

WHY? A classic icebox cookie begins by creaming softened butter (65 to 67 degrees) with sugar. We found that a combination of two sugars delivered good snap and structure (granulated), and tenderness (confectioners').

2. ADD YOLKS, THEN FLOUR

Beat in 2 large egg yolks and 2 teaspoons vanilla extract until combined, about 30 seconds. Scrape down bowl as needed. Whisk together 2¼ cups all-purpose flour and ½ teaspoon salt in medium bowl. With mixer on low, gradually add dry ingredients and mix until just combined, about 30 seconds.

WHY? Two yolks (rather than a whole egg) add richness and reduce rise (icebox cookies should bake up flat and crisp, not puffy). Make sure the mixer is on low when adding the flour; overbeating can develop excess gluten and make the cookies tough.

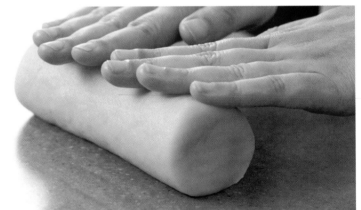

3. DIVIDE AND ROLL

Scrape dough onto counter and divide into 2 equal pieces. Roll each piece into 6-inch-long cylinder, about 2 inches thick.

WHY? It's important to divide the dough evenly and then roll the cylinders to a consistent width so the cookies are all the same size. Don't flour the counter. If the dough is sticky, simply chill it in the refrigerator for several minutes.

4. COAT WITH SUGAR OR NUTS, IF DESIRED

If desired, roll each dough log in colored sugar, finely chopped nuts, or sprinkles.

WHY? This is an easy way to add flavor, crunch, and visual appeal. You will need about 1 cup of garnish for the two dough logs. Coarse sanding sugar (available at baking supply shops) is a particularly nice garnish around the holidays.

5. WRAP AND CHILL

Tightly wrap each log of dough in plastic wrap, twisting wrap to help square off ends of dough. Chill dough in refrigerator until firm, at least 2 hours or up to 2 days.

WHY? The dough must be cold for slicing. The plastic wrap not only protects the dough from drying out in the refrigerator, but it also helps in shaping the dough into a neat cylinder with a smooth surface and squared-off (not tapered) ends.

6. SLICE THIN

Slice chilled dough into ¼-inch-thick rounds, rotating log one-quarter turn every few slices. Work with 1 log at a time, keeping other log in refrigerator.

WHY? If the slices are too thick, the cookies will bake up doughy, not crisp. Use a ruler if in doubt. Rotating the dough log every few slices helps keep the slices round. (If you don't rotate the log, the repeated weight of the knife can distort the shape of the log, especially as the dough warms up.)

7. BAKE A LOT AT ONCE

Divide rounds of dough between 2 parchment paper–lined baking sheets, spacing rounds about ¾ inch apart. Bake on upper-middle and lower-middle racks until edges begin to brown, 12 to 15 minutes, switching and rotating sheets halfway through baking. Cool on sheets for 3 minutes, then transfer to wire racks to cool completely.

WHY? Icebox cookies don't contain any leavening agent, so they don't rise or spread much. You should be able to fit 24 rounds of dough on each rimmed baking sheet. You can bake both sheets at the same time (on the upper-middle and lower-middle racks), but do remember to switch the position of the sheets and rotate each sheet 180 degrees, so the front is now facing the back of the oven.

Customizing Icebox Cookies

It's easy to flavor these basic vanilla icebox cookies.

TO MAKE	DO THIS
Butterscotch Icebox Cookies	Replace granulated sugar with brown sugar
Chocolate Icebox Cookies	Add 2 ounces melted and cooled semisweet chocolate along with egg yolk and vanilla; replace ¼ cup of flour with equal amount of cocoa powder
Nutty Icebox Cookies	Add ½ cup finely chopped nuts to flour mixture

How to Make Cutout Cookies

ESSENTIAL
EQUIPMENT

- plastic wrap
- parchment paper
- rolling pin
- rimmed baking
  sheets (2)
- cookie cutter
- small offset
  spatula
- wire rack

When the holidays come, many bakers want to use their cookie cutters to create cookies with festive shapes. This means rolling the dough thin (almost like pie dough) and then stamping out the cookies. The dough has to taste good, but it must be sturdy enough to roll and decorate. It certainly can't be sticky. And ideally the dough will tolerate being rolled a second time (so you can make cookies from the scraps left behind). We have found that superfine sugar helps achieve a fine, delicate texture, while a little cream cheese assists in making the dough workable without turning the cookies tough. Finally, using the reverse-creaming method (see page 631), in which the butter is beaten into the flour and sugar (rather than the standard creaming method in which the butter and sugar are whipped together), produces flat, crisp cookies without any airy pockets—just what you want for glazing or decorating. See our recipe for Holiday Cookies on page 619 for directions on preparing the dough, then follow the steps below. Also see How to Decorate Cutout Cookies (opposite page).

1. CHILL DOUGH, ROLL, THEN CHILL AGAIN

Divide dough into 2 pieces. Shape each piece into 4-inch disk, wrap in plastic wrap, and refrigerate for at least 30 minutes or up to 2 days. Dough should be firm but malleable. Unwrap 1 disk, place it between 2 pieces of parchment paper, and roll out to even ⅛-inch thickness. Slide parchment and dough onto rimmed baking sheet and refrigerate for 10 minutes. Repeat with second disk.

WHY? Chilling the disks makes them easier to roll out. If they spend more than a few hours chilling, they will be rock hard and should sit on the counter for several minutes. The parchment prevents sticking and means you don't have to flour the counter, which would make the cookies tough. Chilling the rolled-out dough will make it easier to cut out cookies with sharp edges.

2. STAMP OUT COOKIES

Remove top sheet of parchment from 1 piece of dough. Use desired cutter to stamp out cookies, leaving minimal space between each cookie. Peel away scraps, shape into ball, wrap in plastic, and chill. Use thin offset spatula to transfer cutout cookies to parchment-lined rimmed baking sheet, spacing cookies about 1 inch apart.

WHY? Cutting out the cookies on the parchment means no sticking. Don't use your hands to move the cutout pieces of dough—you will mar their shape. Peeling away the scraps makes it easier to lift the cookies up cleanly. You can chill the scraps for one more batch. (But if rolled a third time, the scraps will make tough cookies.)

3. DON'T OVERBAKE

Place one baking sheet in 375-degree oven and bake, rotating sheet halfway through, until cookies are light golden brown, about 10 minutes. (Cookies should show slight resistance to touch and edges should be starting to brown.) Cool on sheet for 3 minutes, then transfer to wire rack.

WHY? These cookies go from perfectly baked to overbaked quickly, so watch for subtle signs. Baking one sheet at a time ensures even baking.

How to Decorate Cutout Cookies

Decorating cutout cookies is the place to express your creativity. We've outlined general tips and techniques on this page and the next, but feel free to go your own way. You will likely want a good glaze—one that is fluid enough to spread or pipe easily. The traditional recipe is just milk and confectioners' sugar, which is fluid when first prepared but then hardens as it dries. We find that the classic glaze requires so much confectioners' sugar that it is awfully sweet. Therefore, we add extra body with softened cream cheese—not more sugar. The tang of the cream cheese also adds some flavor. See the chart on page 594 for the correct proportions and simple ways to vary this glaze. It's important to let glazes dry before packing away or serving decorated cookies. This will take at least 30 minutes, or longer in a hot or humid kitchen. One final note: Always let cookies cool completely before starting the decorating process. The equipment needed will depend on the how you opt to decorate your cookies.

ESSENTIAL EQUIPMENT

- muffin tin
- plastic wrap
- small spoon or offset spatula
- plastic bag
- kitchen shears
- toothpick
- pie plate
- fine-mesh sieve
- rubber spatula
- water mister or pastry brush

A. GET ORGANIZED

Place cookie decorations in muffin tin, using each cup to hold a different decoration.

WHY? During the holidays you may find yourself making cookies several times over a period of several weeks. A muffin tin keeps sprinkles, colored sugars, and other decorations organized and reusable. Just cover the muffin tin with plastic wrap between uses.

B. GLAZE FROM CENTER OUT

Spoon small amount of glaze in center of cookie and use back of small spoon to spread glaze into even layer.

WHY? Spreading the glaze from the center outward is the best way to ensure even coverage. The back of a spoon will work; you can also use a small offset spatula. For the lightest touch, use a very small paintbrush.

C. MAKE PIPING BAG

Place glaze in small zipper-lock bag and snip off tiny piece from one corner with kitchen shears. Pipe glaze through hole in bag onto cookies.

WHY? Glaze can be used to add detail to a cutout cookie, especially if you pipe along the perimeter of the cookie. There's no need to use a pastry bag for this task; a small plastic bag works just fine. Just make sure to snip a very small hole and push the glaze down into that corner of the bag; exert even pressure to ensure even flow of the glaze through the hole.

D. ADD EMBELLISHMENTS

While glaze is still soft, place decorations in glaze and allow them to set.

WHY? Small confections, often shiny silver or gold balls known as dragées, can be used to dress up cookies. Other small candies—red hots, gumdrops, mini chocolate morsels, jelly beans—can be used in a similar fashion. Add these candies immediately after applying the glaze. As the glaze hardens, it will affix the candies in place.

E. TWO GLAZES

Glaze entire cookie (see step B), then pipe small drops of second glaze in decorative pattern. Drag toothpick through glazes to create design. **WHY?** As long as both glazes are still wet, you can create a range of designs, everything from hearts (shown here) to stars, wiggly lines, and swirls. This idea works best with glazes that are two different colors.

F. MAKE YOUR OWN COLORED SUGAR

Sprinkle ½ cup granulated sugar evenly into pie plate. Add 5 drops of food coloring and mix thoroughly. Push sugar through fine-mesh sieve. Spread sugar back into pie plate and let dry.

WHY? The trick to making your own colored sugar is to mix the food coloring into the sugar, then press the sugar through a fine-mesh sieve to ensure that the color is distributed evenly. The sugar should dry thoroughly before you use it; this might take several hours. It's best to apply colored sugar to plain cookies before they are baked. Lightly mist or brush the surface of each cutout piece of dough with a little water, then apply the sugar. To apply to glazed cookies, hold your hand about 12 inches above the cookies, then sprinkle the colored sugar onto the glaze. Once the glaze dries, you can gently brush or shake off any excess colored sugar.

Easy Cookie Glazes

Simply whisk together the ingredients listed below to make any one of these four easy glazes. These glazes each produce about 1 cup, enough for several dozen cookies. For a shock of color, stir a few drops of food coloring into the All-Purpose Glaze. Let glazed cookies dry for at least 30 minutes before serving.

GLAZE	CONFECTIONERS' SUGAR	LIQUID	CREAM CHEESE	FLAVORINGS
All-Purpose Glaze	2 cups (8 ounces)	3 tablespoons whole milk	2 tablespoons, softened	N/A
Citrus Glaze	2 cups (8 ounces)	3 tablespoons lemon, lime, or orange juice	2 tablespoons, softened	N/A
Nutty Glaze	2 cups (8 ounces)	3 tablespoons whole milk	2 tablespoons, softened	½ teaspoon almond or coconut extract
Coffee Glaze	2 cups (8 ounces)	3 tablespoons whole milk	2 tablespoons, softened	1¼ teaspoons instant espresso powder or instant coffee powder

How to Make a Foil Sling

With their gooey fillings and high sugar content, brownies and bar cookies can be nearly impossible to remove from their baking pans, no matter how well the pan is greased. And cutting out individual pieces often becomes a hack job—literally. What's the point of doing all that work and then ruining the baked good at serving time? Lining the baking pan with a foil sling (you can use parchment, if you prefer) prevents any casualties. Once cooled, brownies and bar cookies can be lifted easily from the pan using the overhanging pieces of foil and transferred to a cutting board in one piece. You should be able to slide the foil out from under the block, then cut it into tidy squares or rectangles. Knowing how to make a foil sling is also indispensable when making many quick breads.

ESSENTIAL EQUIPMENT

- baking pan
- aluminum foil

1. FOLD AND LINE

Fold 2 long sheets of aluminum foil to be same width as baking pan. (If dish is rectangular, sheets will be of different widths.) Lay sheets of foil in pan, perpendicular to one another, with extra foil hanging over edges of pan.

WHY? The genius of this method is that two sheets of foil ensure total coverage, not only of the pan bottom but of all four sides. If you make the sling correctly, the pan will require no washing. We prefer heavy-duty foil in general, and it certainly is the best choice for making a sling. You will need to fold in the sides of the foil to get the desired width. It's best to place the sheets of foil in the pan with the folds facing down, away from the batter that will be added later.

2. SMOOTH OUT WRINKLES

Push foil into corners and up sides of pan. Try to iron out wrinkles in foil, smoothing it flush with pan.

WHY? It's important that the foil follow the contours of the pan as closely as possible. Push the foil into the edges of the pan, and make sure the corners are sharp. Tuck the overhanging ends of each piece of foil neatly out of the way. Ideally you will have about 4 inches of overhang—enough to pick up the final baked good, but not so much that the foil becomes a nuisance.

3. GREASE WELL

Coat foil sling with vegetable oil spray, making sure to cover bottom and sides of pan.

WHY? Just because you're using a sling doesn't mean you don't need to grease it. Skip this step and you might have trouble separating the brownies or bar cookies from the foil (although they will come out of the pan). Don't use softened butter or vegetable shortening here—you will mess up the sling if you try to rub either of them over the foil. Vegetable oil spray means you don't have to touch the foil. Make sure to coat the bottom and all four sides.

HOW TO MAKE COOKIES

Chocolate Chip Cookies

Recipe Stats

TOTAL TIME **1 hour**
PREPARATION TIME **10 minutes**
ACTIVE COOKING TIME **15 minutes**
YIELD **16 large cookies**
MAKE AHEAD **Keep at room temperature for up to 2 days**
DIFFICULTY **Intermediate**

Tools

- heavy-bottomed 10-inch skillet *
- rimmed baking sheets (2)
- chef's knife
- cutting board
- dry measuring cups
- measuring spoons
- cookie spatula
- dish towel
- kitchen timer
- large heatproof bowl
- mixing bowls
- rubber spatula
- whisk
- wire racks (2)
- parchment paper

* Use a light-colored skillet, preferably a pan lined with shiny stainless steel, so you can track the color of the butter. A dark skillet, especially one coated with a nonstick surface, makes it impossible to judge the progress of the butter as it browns.

Ingredients

1¾ **cups (8¾ ounces) all-purpose flour**
½ **teaspoon baking soda**
14 **tablespoons unsalted butter**
¾ **cup packed (5¼ ounces) dark brown sugar ***
½ **cup (3½ ounces) granulated sugar**
1 **teaspoon salt**
2 **teaspoons vanilla extract**
1 **large egg plus 1 large yolk**
1¼ **cups (7½ ounces) semisweet or bittersweet chocolate chips or chunks ****
¾ **cup pecans or walnuts, toasted and chopped (optional) *****

* Use fresh, moist brown sugar, as hardened brown sugar will make the cookies too dry. This recipe works with light brown sugar, but the cookies will be less full-flavored.
** Good chocolate makes great cookies. Use good-quality semisweet or bittersweet chocolate chips or chunks.
*** Make sure to toast the nuts before adding them to the dough—otherwise, they will be soft and fairly bland.

Overview

Since Nestlé first began printing the recipe for Toll House cookies on the back of chocolate chip bags in 1939, generations of bakers have packed chocolate chip cookies into lunches and have taken them to potlucks. And while we're not knocking this classic recipe, we wondered if this was really the best that a chocolate chip cookie could be. The Toll House cookie is more cakey than chewy (and we like chewy), and the flavors are a bit one-dimensional. We wanted to refine this recipe to create a moist and chewy chocolate chip cookie with crisp edges and deep notes of toffee and butterscotch to balance its sweetness—in short, a more sophisticated cookie than the standard bake-sale offering.

Melting a generous amount of butter before combining it with the other ingredients delivers the right chewy texture. That's because butter is about 18 percent water, and melting the butter frees up the water to bond with the proteins in the flour and form gluten—the elastic network that gives baked goods their chew. Browning a portion of the butter adds nutty flavor. Using a bit more brown sugar than white sugar enhanced chewiness, while a combination of one egg and one egg yolk makes the cookies supremely moist. For crisp edges and deep toffee flavor, we allow the sugar to dissolve and rest in the melted butter.

Finally, we bake the cookies until golden brown and just set, but still soft in the center. (They continue to firm up as they cool.) The resulting cookies are crisp and chewy with gooey chocolate, and they boast a complex medley of sweet, buttery, caramel, and toffee flavors. We think they might just be the perfect chocolate chip cookies. Before you begin, see How to Brown Butter on page 584 and How to Toast and Chop Nuts on page 585 (if you are adding the nuts).

What Can Go Wrong

Here's a list of common mistakes cooks make when preparing this recipe.

COMMON MISTAKE	BAD OUTCOMES	WHAT YOU SHOULD DO
Burning Butter	• **The cookies taste burnt.** • **The cookies taste bitter.**	Browning the butter develops a range of flavorful notes in the butter, but there's a fine line between brown butter (good) and black butter (bad). If the butter burns, start the recipe over. As soon as the butter is the correct color (dark golden brown), pour the browned butter into a large heatproof bowl and immediately add the remaining butter, which will quickly lower the temperature of the browned butter and prevent further browning. Don't leave the browned butter in the hot pan—even with the pan off the heat the butter can continue to cook.
Not Resting and Stirring Batter	• **The edges are not crisp.** • **The cookies seem too sweet.** • **The toffee and butterscotch notes are muted.**	Once the sugars are added to the melted butter, the recipe instructs you to rest the batter and whisk it several times over a period of 10 minutes. As you complete this step, you will notice that the consistency of the dough is changing, becoming thicker, smoother, and shinier. The sugar is dissolving, and the more sugar that dissolves, the more caramelization that can occur in the oven. Caramelizing as much sugar as possible is the key to a more complex flavor as well as crisp edges.
Incorrectly Portioning Dough	• **The cookies are crisp, not chewy.** • **The cookies are small, not large.**	This recipe should produce large, chewy cookies. In order to make this happen, we use 3 tablespoons of dough for each cookie. Yes, that's a lot of dough. But if you use less, you end up with smaller cookies. While there's nothing wrong with small cookies, it's much harder to produce one with a chewy center. Large cookies, such as this one, can easily have a contrast between the edges (which should be crisp) and the center (which should be soft and chewy). If you're in doubt, double-check by counting the number of cookies—you should have 16 balls of dough divided among two parchment paper–lined rimmed baking sheets.
Baking Batches Together	• **The cookies bake unevenly.**	When texture is paramount, we generally bake cookies one batch at a time. If you put two baking sheets in the oven, the airflow is compromised and you end up overbaking a few cookies on each sheet. The risk of this happening is greatly reduced if you place a single baking sheet in the middle of the oven. Also, make sure to rotate the baking sheet 180 degrees (the front of the sheet should be turned so it's facing the back of the oven) at the halfway mark. This will ensure that all the cookies on the sheet are baked to the same degree of doneness.
Baking Cookies Too Long	• **The cookies are crisp rather than chewy.** • **The edges are very browned and very brittle.**	Many bakers overbake their cookies. They don't account for residual heat that will continue to firm up cookies as they cool. If you like chewy cookies, always take them out of the oven just before you think they are done. Once the edges are golden brown and set, take the cookies out. The puffy, soft centers will continue to firm up. If you wait until the centers look done, you have overbaked these cookies.
Not Cooling Cookies on Baking Sheets	• **The spatula makes a mess of the cookies.** • **The cookies are underdone in the middle.**	The timing in this recipe calls for taking the cookies out of the oven before they are fully baked and then cooling the cookies on the hot baking sheet. The residual heat in the baking sheet finishes the job slowly, and ensures chewy results. By the time the baking sheet has cooled off, the cookies will have firmed up enough that you can transfer them to a wire rack for further cooling. If you attempt to move the cookies too early, they will likely fall apart because they are so soft. Also, they might be slightly underbaked in the dead center.

1. Adjust oven rack to middle position and heat oven to 375 degrees.

2. Measure ¾ cup packed (5¼ ounces) dark brown sugar.

3. Line 2 baking sheets with parchment paper.

4. Toast ¾ cup pecans in 10-inch skillet over medium heat, stirring occasionally, until fragrant and lightly browned, 2 to 5 minutes. Let cool, then chop.

5. Whisk 1¾ cups (8¾ ounces) all-purpose flour and ½ teaspoon baking soda together in medium bowl; set aside.

6. Melt 10 tablespoons unsalted butter in heavy-bottomed 10-inch skillet over medium-high heat.

7. Continue cooking, swirling pan constantly, until butter is dark golden brown and has nutty aroma, 1 to 3 minutes.

8. Transfer browned butter to large heatproof bowl.

9. Add 4 tablespoons unsalted butter. Stir until completely melted.

10. Add brown sugar, ½ cup (3½ ounces) granulated sugar, 1 teaspoon salt, and 2 teaspoons vanilla extract; whisk until fully incorporated.

11. Add 1 large egg and 1 large egg yolk; whisk until mixture is smooth with no sugar lumps remaining, about 30 seconds.

12. Let mixture stand for 3 minutes, then whisk for 30 seconds.

13. Repeat process of resting and whisking 2 more times until mixture is thick, smooth, and shiny.

14. Using rubber spatula, stir in flour mixture until just combined, about 1 minute.

15. Stir in 1¼ cups (7½ ounces) semi-sweet or bittersweet chocolate chips. Add pecans or walnuts, if using.

16. Give dough final stir to ensure that no flour pockets remain and ingredients are evenly distributed.

17. Working with 3 tablespoons of dough at a time, roll into balls and place 2 inches apart on prepared baking sheets.

18. Place 1 baking sheet on middle rack in preheated oven.

19. Bake until cookies are golden brown and puffy, and edges have begun to set but centers are still soft, 10 to 14 minutes, rotating halfway through.

20. Transfer baking sheet to wire rack; let cookies cool to room temperature. Place second baking sheet in oven; bake and cool as directed.

Glazed Lemon Cookies

Recipe Stats

TOTAL TIME **3 hours**
PREPARATION TIME **15 minutes**
ACTIVE COOKING TIME **30 minutes**
YIELD **30 cookies**
MAKE AHEAD **Dough log can be refrigerated for up to 3 days or frozen for up to 2 weeks; baked cookies are best the day they are glazed**
DIFFICULTY **Easy**

Tools

- rimmed baking sheets (2)
- food processor *
- chef's knife
- cutting board
- dry measuring cups
- liquid measuring cup
- measuring spoons
- citrus juicer
- fork
- kitchen ruler **
- large plate
- mixing bowls
- rasp-style grater ***
- rubber spatula
- small spoon ****
- whisk
- wire racks (2)
- parchment paper

* A food processor is used to break down the lemon zest with the sugar and release the most flavor from the zest. Since the food processor is already being used, we make the cookie dough in it as well.
** We use a ruler to measure the first few slices of dough to ensure the cookies are of even thickness.
*** A rasp-style grater is our preferred tool for grating zest from citrus fruits, including lemon. Remember that the colored skin has the best flavor; the white pith is fairly bitter, and you shouldn't be grating it.
**** We use a small spoon to spread the glaze; a small offset spatula will also work.

Overview

Glazed lemon cookies are dressier than your average drop cookie, but they are simple to prepare. Most recipes spike icebox cookie dough with lemon zest or lemon juice. The dough is chilled, sliced, and baked into thin, crisp rounds that are then coated with a simple glaze. Unfortunately, despite such a simple recipe, it's easy to go wrong. Many versions are often saccharine-sweet, with a thin veneer of frosting and a barely detectable lemon flavor. We wanted a lemon cookie with the perfect balance of lemony zing and rich, buttery sweetness. And we wanted a glaze that wasn't too sweet or too harsh.

The cookies were fairly easy to fix. Grinding the lemon zest with the sugar in the food processor releases the natural oils in the zest and produces a cookie with much more flavor. Grinding the zest and sugar also breaks down the zest so there are no stringy bits in the cookies. Just an egg yolk instead of a whole egg adds more tenderness and richness. The removal of the white from the recipe also allows us to add lemon juice without making the dough too soft or sticky.

Most glazes are simply lemon juice and confectioners' sugar. Unfortunately, you need to add a lot of sugar in order to make a thick glaze, but in thinner glazes the lemon juice can be overly tart. We found that a tablespoon of softened cream cheese helps create a thick glaze with just the right amounts of sugar and lemon juice, and the tang of the cream cheese balances the sweetness of the glaze.

The cookies are best the day they are glazed. The log of dough can be refrigerated for up to three days, then sliced, baked, and glazed. If you plan on refrigerating it for more than a few hours, add a layer of plastic wrap around the parchment to keep the dough from drying out. You can freeze the dough log (wrapped in parchment, then plastic) for up to two weeks.

Before you begin, see How to Make Icebox Cookies on page 590. For variations on this recipe, see page 617.

Ingredients

COOKIES
- ¾ cup (5¼ ounces) granulated sugar
- 2 tablespoons grated lemon zest plus 2 tablespoons juice (2 lemons)
- 1¾ cups (8¾ ounces) all-purpose flour
- ¼ teaspoon salt
- ¼ teaspoon baking powder
- 12 tablespoons unsalted butter, cut into ½-inch cubes and chilled
- 1 large egg yolk
- ½ teaspoon vanilla extract

GLAZE
- 1 tablespoon cream cheese, softened
- 2 tablespoons lemon juice
- 1½ cups (6 ounces) confectioners' sugar

What Can Go Wrong

Here's a list of common mistakes cooks make when preparing this recipe.

COMMON MISTAKE	BAD OUTCOMES	WHAT YOU SHOULD DO
Not Using Food Processor to Make Dough	• **The lemon flavor is weak.** • **The cookie dough is crumbly and hard to handle.** • **The cookies are marred by stringy bits of zest.**	The food processor is absolutely essential for this recipe—it breaks down the grated zest, releasing its full range of flavors. The food processor also ensures that the texture of the cookies is not marred by the zest. The rest of the recipe has been engineered to work in a food processor. Rather than creaming softened butter with the sugar, we chill the butter and make the cookie dough as we would pie dough—pulsing cubes of cold butter into the dry ingredients and then adding the liquid ingredients (in this case, egg yolk, lemon juice, and vanilla).
Not Chilling Butter	• **The dough is sticky.** • **The dough is hard to shape into a log.**	The second step in this recipe is to cut the butter into small cubes and then place those cubes on a plate in the refrigerator. The food processor blade can heat up the butter rather quickly; if the butter isn't chilled the result is a soft, sticky dough. Let the butter chill for 30 minutes or so. If you want to speed up the process, pop the plate into the freezer for 10 minutes.
Not Chilling Dough Before Slicing	• **The dough is sticky and hard to slice.** • **The cookies are misshapen.**	Don't attempt to slice the dough log until it has been chilled for at least 45 minutes in the freezer or 2 hours in the refrigerator. If you try to slice the dough too early, the weight of the knife will squish the log and the cookies will be ovals, not circles.
Not Rotating Dough Log During Slicing	• **The dough sticks to the cutting board.** • **The cookies are misshapen.**	Even with chilling, the dough log can become misshapen as you slice it. But this is easy to prevent—simply give the dough a quarter turn after every few slices. If the dough does soften as you slice, rotating the log will ensure that it stretches equally in every direction, rather than in a single direction. Also, make sure not to exert excess pressure on the dough log as you slice it.
Slicing Cookies Too Thick	• **The baking time is off.** • **The cookies are thick and chewy, not crisp and airy.**	It's important to slice the dough log evenly, and thinly, into 3/8-inch-thick rounds. It helps to have a ruler on hand to check the first few slices. Once you're sure that you're cutting the dough correctly, you can use those first few slices to keep you on track.
Omitting Cream Cheese from Glaze	• **The glaze is too thin.** • **The glaze is both too sweet and too tart.**	It might be tempting to leave out the cream cheese in the glaze. It's just a tablespoon, so it can't be that important, right? Wrong. The cream cheese does two things. It thickens up the glaze so that it spreads beautifully. It also balances the sweetness and the acidity, ensuring that the glaze is lemony but not sour.
Not Giving Glaze Time to Set	• **The glaze is too soft.** • **The cookies are very messy to eat.**	It will be tempting to eat the cookies as soon as they are glazed, but you will be rewarded with patience. The glaze needs about an hour (maybe a bit longer in a hot, humid kitchen) to set and dry. Don't shortcut the process—a soft glaze makes the cookies very messy to eat. Also, make sure to wait until the cookies have cooled completely before glazing them. The glaze will run off warm cookies.

1. PREPARE COOKIES: Adjust oven racks to upper-middle and lower-middle positions and heat oven to 375 degrees.

2. Cut 12 tablespoons unsalted butter into ½-inch cubes, place butter on plate, and chill in refrigerator or freezer.

3. Grate zest from 2 lemons to yield 2 tablespoons.

4. Juice lemons to yield ¼ cup (enough for cookies and glaze).

5. In food processor, process ¾ cup granulated sugar and zest until sugar looks damp and zest is thoroughly incorporated, about 30 seconds.

6. Add 1¾ cups (8¾ ounces) all-purpose flour, ¼ teaspoon salt, and ¼ teaspoon baking powder; pulse to combine, about 10 pulses.

7. Scatter chilled butter over flour mixture.

8. Pulse until mixture resembles fine cornmeal, about 15 pulses.

9. In liquid measuring cup, beat 2 tablespoons lemon juice, 1 large egg yolk, and ½ teaspoon vanilla extract with fork to combine.

10. With processor running, add juice mixture in slow, steady stream (process should take about 10 seconds).

11. Continue processing until dough begins to form ball, 10 to 15 seconds longer.

12. Turn dough and any dry bits onto counter; working quickly, gently knead together to ensure that no dry bits remain and dough is homogeneous.

13. Shape dough into log about 10 inches long and 2 inches in diameter.

14. Wrap log in parchment paper and twist ends to seal.

15. Chill dough until firm, about 45 minutes in freezer or 2 hours in refrigerator.

16. Line 2 rimmed baking sheets with parchment.

17. Remove dough log from parchment. Using chef's knife, slice dough into ⅜-inch-thick rounds, rotating log so that it won't become misshapen.

18. Place rounds 1 inch apart on prepared baking sheets.

19. Bake until centers of cookies just begin to color and edges are golden brown, 14 to 16 minutes, switching and rotating sheets halfway through baking.

20. Let cookies cool on baking sheets for 5 minutes. Transfer cookies to wire rack and let cool to room temperature before glazing.

21. PREPARE GLAZE: Whisk 1 tablespoon softened cream cheese and remaining 2 tablespoons lemon juice in medium bowl until no lumps remain.

22. Add 1½ cups (6 ounces) confectioners' sugar and whisk until smooth.

23. When cookies have cooled, working with one at a time, spread glaze evenly over each cookie with back of small spoon.

24. Let cookies stand on wire rack until glaze is set and dry, about 1 hour.

HOW TO MAKE COOKIES

Almond Biscotti

Recipe Stats

TOTAL TIME **2½ hours**
PREPARATION TIME **15 minutes**
ACTIVE COOKING TIME **20 minutes**
YIELD **30 cookies**
MAKE AHEAD **Store at room temperature for up to 1 month**
DIFFICULTY **Easy**

Tools

- rimmed baking sheets (2)
- food processor *
- cutting board
- serrated knife **
- digital scale ***
- dry measuring cups
- liquid measuring cup ****
- measuring spoons
- kitchen ruler
- mixing bowls
- pastry brush
- rubber spatula
- wire rack
- parchment paper
- pencil *****

* One of the secrets to this recipe is grinding some of the toasted almonds into a fine meal to keep the biscotti from baking up too crunchy or hard; a food processor is essential for this step. We also use the food processor to chop the remaining nuts and then combine the rest of the ingredients for the cookie dough.

** Biscotti are baked twice. The first time they are shaped into wide loaves and baked. The cookies are then sliced on the bias and baked again until crisp. A serrated knife is the best tool for slicing through the baked loaves.

*** When halving the dough, we like to use a scale to ensure each loaf is of equal size.

**** Use a liquid measuring cup to make pouring the sugar through the processor feed tube neat and tidy.

***** We like to draw neat rectangles onto the parchment paper and then use the lines as a guide when we shape the dough into logs.

Overview

Italians like biscotti dry and hard—after all, they dunk them in cappuccino or dessert wine before eating them. American versions are buttery and more tender so they can be eaten without dunking. This recipe delivers something in between.

The cookies' crunch, or lack thereof, corresponds in part with the amount of butter in the recipe. With this in mind, we experimented with quantities until we found that 4 tablespoons gives us a dough that is neither too hard and lean nor too soft and rich. But this amount is too small to work with the traditional creaming method—the butter will simply soften instead of aerating. We needed to find other elements of the dough that could be aerated in the mixer. The answer was eggs. We whip the eggs until they are light in color, then add the sugar and continue to beat the mixture. Finally, we fold in the butter (melted for easy incorporation), followed by the dry ingredients.

The whipped eggs give the dough the lightness and lift. Swapping out some of the flour for nuts that we grind in the food processor makes our cookies crumbly and crunchy, but easy to bite. Since we are using the food processor to grind the nuts, we use the food processor for the whole operation.

In terms of flavor, we add more nuttiness along with the dry ingredients in the form of coarsely chopped nuts. Since almond extract's flavor dissipates after the biscotti's second stint in the oven, we start with a higher-than-average dose. Similarly, we load up on other ingredients with volatile compounds in our anise, hazelnut-orange, hazelnut-lavender, and pistachio-spice variations (see recipes on page 621).

Ingredients

1¼ **cups (6¼ ounces) whole almonds, lightly toasted** *
1¾ **cups (8¾ ounces) all-purpose flour**
2 **teaspoons baking powder**
¼ **teaspoon salt**
2 **large eggs, plus 1 large white beaten with pinch salt**
1 **cup (7 ounces) sugar**
4 **tablespoons unsalted butter, melted and cooled**
1½ **teaspoons almond extract**
½ **teaspoon vanilla extract**
  Vegetable oil spray

* The almonds will continue to toast while the biscotti bake, so toast the nuts only until they are fragrant.

What Can Go Wrong

Here's a list of common mistakes cooks make when preparing this recipe.

COMMON MISTAKE	BAD OUTCOMES	WHAT YOU SHOULD DO
Omitting Almond Meal	• **The dough is too sticky.** • **The biscotti bake up too hard.**	Grinding a portion of the almonds into a fine meal turns this portion of the nuts into a dry ingredient. If you simply chop these nuts, there won't be as much of the dry ingredients to absorb the liquid ingredients (the egg, melted butter, and vanilla and almond extracts) and the dough might be sticky and hard to handle. More important, the nut meal helps break up the gluten network created by the flour and keeps the cookies from being overly hard once baked.
Not Fully Whipping Eggs	• **The biscotti are squat.** • **The biscotti are dense.**	The baking powder in the recipe provides most of the lift, but the eggs do play a supporting role—that is, if you whip them for a full 3 minutes in the food processor. The whirring blade creates air bubbles that the baking powder then expands in the oven. You should process the eggs long enough so that they double in volume. If you shortcut this step, the baking powder can't do its job as effectively, and the resulting biscotti will be dense, heavy, and misshapen.
Not Cooling Melted Butter	• **The dough is sticky.** • **The dough is marred by bits of scrambled egg.**	Once the eggs have been whipped in the food processor, it's time to add the sugar and the melted and cooled butter. If the butter is not allowed to cool, it can melt some of the sugar and make the dough sticky. There's even a chance that the hot butter can cook some of the egg. Make sure to let the melted butter cool so that it's just a bit warm, not actually hot.
Shaping Loaves Incorrectly	• **The cookies vary in size.** • **The cookies vary in crunch.**	It might seem a bit compulsive, but we trace two rectangles onto the parchment paper used to line the baking sheet and then use those tracings to ensure that each of the two loaves of dough are the same size, with neat edges.
Not Cooling Loaves Before Slicing	• **The cookies don't have neat edges.** • **The cookies crumble as you slice them.**	The word *biscotti* translates as "twice baked," a reference to the traditional method for making these crunchy cookies. The dough is shaped into wide, flat loaves and baked until firm. The loaves are then cooled, sliced, and baked again. If you don't let the loaves cool for 30 minutes, the knife will rip and pull the loaves. The resulting cookies will look pretty ragged, and you're going to lose lots of little bits to the cutting board. Wait until the loaves have cooled, and you can slice through them neatly. (We like a serrated knife for this job.) Also, letting the loaves cool on the baking sheet ensures that the loaves don't break when you transfer them to the cutting board.
Not Baking Cookies on Wire Rack	• **The cookies don't bake evenly.** • **The cookies don't become truly crisp.**	Once the loaves have been sliced into individual cookies, the cookies go back into the oven. Most recipes simply put the cookies back on the baking sheet used for baking the loaves. We set a wire rack inside the baking sheet and place the cookies on the rack to ensure even air circulation. This also helps the cookies dry out properly and become nice and crunchy.

1. Adjust oven rack to middle position and heat oven to 325 degrees.

2. Draw two 8 by 3-inch rectangles, spaced 4 inches apart, on piece of parchment paper.

3. Grease baking sheet and place parchment on it, drawing side down.

4. Place 1¼ cups almonds on second rimmed baking sheet and toast in oven until fragrant, 5 to 8 minutes. Let cool completely.

5. Pulse 1 cup (5 ounces) toasted and cooled almonds in food processor until coarsely chopped, 8 to 10 pulses; transfer to bowl.

6. Process remaining ¼ cup (1¼ ounces) almonds until finely ground, about 45 seconds.

7. Add 1¾ cups (8¾ ounces) all-purpose flour, 2 teaspoons baking powder, and ¼ teaspoon salt; process to combine, about 15 seconds.

8. Transfer flour mixture to second bowl.

9. Process 2 eggs in now-empty food processor until lightened in color and almost doubled in volume, about 3 minutes.

10. With processor running, slowly add 1 cup (7 ounces) sugar until thoroughly combined, about 15 seconds.

11. Add 4 tablespoons melted, cooled butter, 1½ teaspoons almond extract, and ½ teaspoon vanilla extract. Process until combined, about 10 seconds.

12. Transfer egg mixture to medium bowl.

13. Sprinkle half of flour mixture over egg mixture and, using rubber spatula, gently fold until just combined.

14. Add remaining flour mixture and chopped almonds and gently fold until just combined.

15. Divide batter in half.

16. Using floured hands, form each half into 8 by 3-inch rectangle, using lines on parchment as guide.

17. Spray each loaf lightly with vegetable oil spray.

18. Using rubber spatula lightly coated with vegetable oil spray, smooth tops and sides of rectangles.

19. Gently brush tops of loaves with 1 large egg white beaten with pinch salt.

20. Bake until loaves are golden and just beginning to crack on top, 25 to 30 minutes, rotating sheet halfway through baking.

21. Let loaves cool on baking sheet on wire rack for 30 minutes.

22. Transfer loaves to cutting board. Using serrated knife, slice each loaf on slight bias into ½-inch-thick slices.

23. Lay slices with one cut side down about ¼ inch apart on wire rack set in rimmed baking sheet.

24. Bake until crisp and golden brown on both sides, about 35 minutes, flipping slices halfway through baking. Let cool completely before serving.

HOW TO MAKE COOKIES

Turtle Brownies

Overview

Dark chocolate brownies, rich and chewy caramel, and sweet pecans—it's hard to go wrong with turtle brownies. But it's even harder to make them right. Most homemade turtle brownie recipes call for boxed brownie mixes and jarred caramel sauce, yielding lackluster results. You'll find our recipe hits the sweet spot. Reminiscent of candy turtles, these brownies are rich, chewy, and chocolaty, with bittersweet caramel and an abundance of pecans.

Using two types of chocolate is key: 4 ounces of bittersweet lends complexity and 2 ounces of unsweetened provides assertiveness. Two eggs, ¾ cup flour, and ½ teaspoon baking powder gives these brownies a texture between cakey and fudgy. Chopped pecans and a handful of chocolate chips adds further dimension.

The real challenge is getting the right texture for the caramel sauce and the application process. Classic caramel sauce is much too fluid for this recipe. For a sauce that is stiffer and more candylike, we found a mere 6 tablespoons of cream produces a caramel that is pleasantly chewy and gooey, 2 tablespoons of corn syrup keeps the caramel from crystallizing or turning gritty, and 2 tablespoons of butter makes it smooth and silky. We add half the brownie batter to the pan, drizzle some of the caramel on top, add the rest of the brownie batter, and then drizzle and swirl more caramel on top. After baking the brownies, we pour on even more caramel, completely covering the surface before setting it in the refrigerator.

Yes, these brownies are a bit of a project, but they are absolutely worth the time. Plus, they keep well. The brownies can be wrapped in plastic and refrigerated for up to 3 days; serve chilled or at room temperature. Before you begin, see How to Toast and Chop Nuts on page 585, How to Make a Foil Sling on page 595, and How to Chop and Melt Chocolate on page 586.

Recipe Stats

TOTAL TIME **5 hours**
PREPARATION TIME **15 minutes**
ACTIVE COOKING TIME **45 minutes**
YIELD **25 brownies**
MAKE AHEAD **Refrigerate for up to 3 days**
DIFFICULTY **Intermediate**

Tools

- heavy-bottomed 3-quart saucepan with lid
- 9-inch square baking pan
- rimmed baking sheet *
- butter knife **
- chef's knife
- cutting board
- paring knife
- dry measuring cups
- measuring spoons
- liquid measuring cup
- medium heatproof bowl
- instant-read thermometer
- mixing bowls
- rubber spatula
- soupspoon
- whisk
- wire rack
- aluminum foil
- toothpick

* Each brownie is garnished with a toasted pecan half. While the brownies cool, toast the nuts on a rimmed baking sheet.
** The brownie batter and some of the caramel sauce are layered into the prepared baking pan and then swirled together; we use the tip of a butter knife to perform this task.

Ingredients

CARAMEL
- **6 tablespoons heavy cream**
- **¼ teaspoon salt**
- **¼ cup water**
- **2 tablespoons light corn syrup**
- **1¼ cups (8¾ ounces) sugar**
- **2 tablespoons unsalted butter**
- **1 teaspoon vanilla extract**

BROWNIES
- **8 tablespoons unsalted butter, cut into 8 pieces**
- **4 ounces bittersweet chocolate, chopped**
- **2 ounces unsweetened chocolate, chopped**
- **¾ cup (3¾ ounces) all-purpose flour**
- **½ teaspoon baking powder**
- **2 large eggs, room temperature**
- **1 cup (7 ounces) sugar**
- **¼ teaspoon salt**
- **2 teaspoons vanilla extract**
- **⅔ cup chopped pecans**
- **⅓ cup (2 ounces) chocolate chips (optional)**

GARNISH
- **25 pecan halves, toasted**

What Can Go Wrong

Here's a list of common mistakes cooks make when preparing this recipe.

COMMON MISTAKE	BAD OUTCOMES	WHAT YOU SHOULD DO
Not Lining Pan with Foil Sling	• **The brownies and caramel fuse to the pan.** • **The brownies can't be cut into neat squares.**	When making brownies and bar cookies, we always line the baking pan with a foil sling (see page 595 for details on this technique). The sling prevents sticking and makes it easy to remove the baked good from the pan in a single block, and then to cut it into neat pieces on the cutting board. In some recipes, the sling makes this process easier, but it's not essential. In this recipe, the sling is absolutely essential: All that caramel can fuse to the pan, making it impossible to cut the brownies in the pan. Make sure to grease the foil too.
Burning Caramel	• **The caramel tastes bitter.** • **The caramel is very stiff and hard to drizzle.**	Caramel is burnt sugar, but there's a difference between "burnt a little" and "too burnt." You can rely on color (once the mixture is the color of honey, or a tad darker, it's done), but an instant-read thermometer is the better option. At 350 degrees, the sauce will have a nice balance of sweet and bitter notes. If you want more bitter notes, cook the caramel to a temperature of 360 degrees. However, if the caramel goes beyond this point it will taste scorched and its consistency will be very thick. Also, make sure to add the cream as soon as the caramel reaches the right temperature—the cream will immediately cool down the sugar and prevent further cooking.
Letting Caramel Cool Too Much	• **The caramel is not evenly distributed inside the brownies.** • **The caramel topcoat is too thick in some spots, too thin in others.**	Once the caramel is done, it should be transferred to a microwave-safe liquid measuring cup. (Pyrex is ideal.) The caramel will cool off as you prepare the brownie batter. It should be fluid but no longer hot when it comes time to drizzle the caramel over the brownie batter. However, if you work slowly, the caramel sauce might cool down so much that it no longer pours. Simply microwave the sauce for a few seconds so that it can be drizzled evenly over the brownie batter.
Not Greasing Dry Measuring Cup for Caramel	• **The caramel sticks to the cup.** • **The caramel doesn't drizzle evenly.**	For even distribution of the caramel within the brownies, we place half the brownie batter in the pan, drizzle with ¼ cup caramel, add the remaining batter, then drizzle with another ¼ cup caramel. A ¼-cup dry measuring cup is the best tool for the job. Make sure to coat the inside of the cup with vegetable oil spray so that the caramel won't stick to the cup and will pour easily and evenly.
Not Chilling Finished Brownies	• **The caramel is soft and squishy.** • **The brownies are hard to cut neatly.**	Once the baked brownies have cooled, the remaining caramel sauce (about ¾ cup) is heated in the microwave until it is warm and pourable. The sauce is then poured over the cooled brownies and spread into an even layer. This top layer of caramel will set up into a firm but chewy, candylike topping after a few hours in the refrigerator. Don't shortcut this process—if you attempt to cut the brownies before the caramel sets up, the caramel will run off the brownies and you won't be able to cut neat squares. Depending on how much you heat the caramel, it might take a bit longer to firm up in the fridge.

1. PREPARE CARAMEL: Combine
6 tablespoons heavy cream and ¼ teaspoon salt in small bowl; stir well to
dissolve salt.

2. Combine ¼ cup water and
2 tablespoons light corn syrup in
heavy-bottomed 3-quart saucepan.

3. Pour 1¼ cups sugar into center of
saucepan, taking care not to let granules hit sides of pan. Gently stir with
spatula to moisten sugar thoroughly.

4. Cover and bring to boil over
medium-high heat. Cook, covered,
until sugar is completely dissolved and
liquid is clear, 3 to 5 minutes.

5. Uncover and continue to cook,
without stirring, until bubbles show
faint golden color, 3 to 5 minutes more.
Reduce heat to medium-low.

6. Continue to cook, swirling occasionally, until caramel is light amber
and registers 350 to 360 degrees, 1 to
3 minutes longer.

7. Remove saucepan from heat and
add cream to center of pan (mixture
will bubble vigorously); stir until cream
is incorporated and bubbling subsides.

8. Stir in 2 tablespoons unsalted
butter and 1 teaspoon vanilla extract
until combined; transfer caramel to
microwave-safe measuring cup.

9. PREPARE BROWNIES: Adjust oven
rack to lower-middle position and
heat oven to 325 degrees. Line 9-inch
square pan with foil sling. Grease foil.

10. Combine 8 tablespoons butter, cut in
pieces, 4 ounces chopped bittersweet
chocolate, and 2 ounces chopped unsweetened chocolate in heatproof bowl.

11. Set bowl over saucepan of almost-
simmering water, stirring occasionally,
until smooth and combined; set aside
to cool slightly.

12. Meanwhile, whisk ¾ cup
(3¾ ounces) all-purpose flour and
½ teaspoon baking powder together in
small bowl.

13. Whisk 2 large room-temperature eggs in large bowl to combine. Whisk in 1 cup sugar, ¼ teaspoon salt, and 2 teaspoons vanilla extract.

14. Add chocolate mixture to egg mixture; whisk until combined. Using rubber spatula, stir in flour mixture until almost combined.

15. Mix in ⅔ cup chopped pecans and ⅓ cup semisweet chocolate chips, if using, until incorporated and no flour streaks remain.

16. Spread half of brownie batter in even layer in prepared pan. Transfer ¼ cup caramel to greased ¼-cup dry measuring cup; drizzle over batter.

17. Drop remaining batter in large mounds over caramel layer; spread evenly and into corners of pan with rubber spatula.

18. Drizzle ¼ cup caramel over top. Using tip of butter knife, swirl caramel and batter.

19. Bake until toothpick inserted in center of brownies comes out with few moist crumbs attached, 35 to 40 minutes, rotating pan halfway through.

20. Let brownies cool in pan on wire rack to room temperature, about 1½ hours.

21. Microwave remaining caramel until warm and pourable but still thick (do not boil), 45 to 60 seconds, stirring once or twice.

22. Pour caramel over brownies. Spread caramel to cover surface. Refrigerate brownies, uncovered, at least 2 hours.

23. Remove brownies from pan using foil sling, loosening sides with paring knife, if needed. Using chef's knife, cut brownies into 25 evenly sized squares.

24. Press 1 toasted pecan half (25 in total) onto surface of each brownie. Serve chilled or at room temperature.

Recipe Library

Chocolate Chip Cookies

✓ **WHY THIS RECIPE WORKS:** Since Nestlé first began printing the recipe for Toll House cookies on the back of chocolate chip bags in 1939, generations of bakers have packed chocolate chip cookies into lunches and taken them to potlucks. But after a few samples, we wondered if this was really the best that a chocolate chip cookie could be. We wanted to refine this recipe to create a moist and chewy chocolate chip cookie with crisp edges and deep notes of toffee and butterscotch to balance its sweetness—in short, a more sophisticated cookie than the standard bake-sale offering. Melting a generous amount of butter before combining it with other ingredients gave us the chewy texture we wanted. Since we were melting butter, we browned a portion of it to add nutty flavor. Using a bit more brown sugar than white sugar enhanced chewiness, while a combination of one egg and one egg yolk gave us supremely moist cookies. For the crisp edges and deep toffee flavor, we allowed the sugar to dissolve and rest in the melted butter. We baked the cookies until golden brown and just set, but still soft in the center. The resulting cookies were crisp and chewy and gooey with chocolate, and boasted a complex medley of sweet, buttery, caramel, and toffee flavors.

Chocolate Chip Cookies
MAKES ABOUT 16 LARGE COOKIES

Avoid using a nonstick skillet to brown the butter; the dark color of the nonstick coating makes it difficult to gauge when the butter is sufficiently browned. Use fresh, moist brown sugar, as hardened brown sugar will make the cookies too dry. This recipe works with light brown sugar, but the cookies will be less full-flavored. See Recipe Tutorial on page 596 for more details on this recipe.

- 1¾ cups (8¾ ounces) all-purpose flour
- ½ teaspoon baking soda
- 14 tablespoons unsalted butter
- ¾ cup packed (5¼ ounces) dark brown sugar
- ½ cup (3½ ounces) granulated sugar
- 1 teaspoon salt
- 2 teaspoons vanilla extract
- 1 large egg plus 1 large yolk
- 1¼ cups (7½ ounces) semisweet or bittersweet chocolate chips or chunks
- ¾ cup pecans or walnuts, toasted and chopped (optional)

1. Adjust oven rack to middle position and heat oven to 375 degrees. Line 2 baking sheets with parchment paper. Whisk flour and baking soda together in medium bowl; set aside.

2. Melt 10 tablespoons butter in 10-inch skillet over medium-high heat. Continue cooking, swirling pan constantly, until butter is dark golden brown and has nutty aroma, 1 to 3 minutes. Transfer browned butter to large heatproof bowl. Add remaining 4 tablespoons butter and stir until completely melted.

3. Add brown sugar, granulated sugar, salt, and vanilla to melted butter; whisk until fully incorporated. Add egg and yolk; whisk until mixture is smooth with no sugar lumps remaining, about 30 seconds. Let mixture stand for 3 minutes, then whisk for 30 seconds. Repeat process of resting and whisking 2 more times until mixture is thick, smooth, and shiny. Using rubber spatula, stir in flour mixture until just combined, about 1 minute. Stir in chocolate chips and pecans, if using. Give dough final stir to ensure that no flour pockets remain and ingredients are evenly distributed.

4. Working with 3 tablespoons of dough at a time, roll into balls and place 2 inches apart on prepared baking sheets.

5. Bake 1 sheet at a time until cookies are golden brown and still puffy and edges have begun to set but centers are still soft, 10 to 14 minutes, rotating baking sheet halfway through baking. Transfer baking sheet to wire rack; let cookies cool to room temperature. (Cookies can be stored at room temperature for up to 2 days.)

Chewy Sugar Cookies

✓ **WHY THIS RECIPE WORKS:** Traditional recipes for sugar cookies require obsessive attention to detail. The butter must be at precisely the right temperature and it must be creamed to the proper degree of airiness. Slight variations in measures can result in cookies that spread or become brittle and hard. We didn't want a cookie that depended on such a finicky process; we wanted an approachable recipe for great sugar cookies that anyone could make anytime. We melted the butter so our sugar cookie dough could easily be mixed together with a spoon—no more fussy creaming. Replacing a portion of the melted butter with vegetable oil ensured a chewy cookie without affecting flavor. And incorporating an unusual addition, cream cheese, into the cookie dough kept our cookies tender, while the slight tang of the cream cheese made for a rich, not-too-sweet flavor.

Chewy Sugar Cookies
MAKES ABOUT 24 COOKIES

The final dough will be slightly softer than most cookie dough. For best results, handle the dough as briefly and gently as possible when shaping the cookies. Overworking the dough will result in flatter cookies.

- 2¼ cups (11¼ ounces) all-purpose flour
- 1 teaspoon baking powder
- ½ teaspoon baking soda
- ½ teaspoon salt
- 1½ cups (10½ ounces) plus ⅓ cup (2⅓ ounces) sugar
- 2 ounces cream cheese, cut into 8 pieces
- 6 tablespoons unsalted butter, melted
- ⅓ cup vegetable oil
- 1 large egg
- 1 tablespoon whole milk
- 2 teaspoons vanilla extract

1. Adjust oven rack to middle position and heat oven to 350 degrees. Line 2 baking sheets with parchment paper. Whisk flour, baking powder, baking soda, and salt together in medium bowl; set aside.

2. Place 1½ cups sugar and cream cheese in large bowl. Place remaining ⅓ cup sugar in shallow baking dish or pie plate and set aside. Pour warm melted butter over sugar and cream cheese and whisk to combine (some small lumps of cream cheese will remain but will smooth out later). Whisk in oil until incorporated. Add egg, milk, and vanilla; continue to whisk until smooth. Add flour mixture and mix with rubber spatula until soft, homogeneous dough forms.

3. Working with 2 tablespoons of dough at a time, roll into balls. Roll half of dough balls in sugar to coat. Place dough balls on prepared baking sheet; repeat with remaining dough. Using bottom of greased measuring cup, flatten dough balls until 2 inches in diameter. Sprinkle tops of cookies evenly with remaining sugar in dish, using 2 teaspoons for each baking sheet. (Discard remaining sugar.)

4. Bake 1 sheet at a time until edges of cookies are set and beginning to brown, 11 to 13 minutes, rotating baking sheet halfway through baking. Let cookies cool on baking sheet for 5 minutes; transfer cookies to wire rack and let cool to room temperature.

Chewy Chai-Spice Sugar Cookies

Add ¼ teaspoon ground cinnamon, ¼ teaspoon ground ginger, ¼ teaspoon ground cardamom, ¼ teaspoon ground cloves, and pinch pepper to sugar and cream cheese mixture and reduce vanilla to 1 teaspoon.

Chewy Coconut-Lime Sugar Cookies

Whisk ½ cup sweetened shredded coconut, chopped fine, into flour mixture in step 1. Add 1 teaspoon finely grated lime zest to sugar and cream cheese mixture and substitute 1 tablespoon lime juice for vanilla.

Chewy Hazelnut–Browned Butter Sugar Cookies

Add ¼ cup finely chopped toasted and skinned hazelnuts to sugar and cream cheese mixture. Heat butter in 10-inch skillet over medium-high heat until melted, about 2 minutes. Continue to cook, swirling pan constantly until butter is dark golden brown and has nutty aroma, 1 to 3 minutes. Immediately pour butter over sugar and cream cheese mixture and proceed with recipe as directed, increasing milk to 2 tablespoons and omitting vanilla.

Chewy Chocolate Cookies

✓ **WHY THIS RECIPE WORKS:** Cookie recipes that trumpet their extreme chocolate flavor always leave us a bit suspicious. While they provide plenty of intensity, these over-the-top confections also tend to be delicate and crumbly, more like cakey brownies than cookies. We set out to make an exceptionally rich chocolate cookie that we could sink our teeth into without having it fall apart. Our first batch, which used modest amounts of cocoa powder and melted chocolate, baked up too cakey and tender.

The chocolate was the culprit—its fat was softening the dough. We scaled back the chocolate until we eliminated it entirely, which made the cookies less cakey and tender, and thus, more cookielike. To restore chocolate flavor without adding too much fat, we increased the cocoa powder and reduced the flour. Using an egg white rather than a whole egg (or yolk) gave us the structure we wanted. Adding dark corn syrup gave the cookies a nice chewiness and lent a hint of caramel flavor. For more richness, we folded in chopped bittersweet chocolate; the chunks stayed intact and added intense flavor. After rolling the dough into balls, we dipped them in granulated sugar to give the cookies a sweet crunch and an attractive crackled appearance.

Chewy Chocolate Cookies

MAKES ABOUT 16 COOKIES

Use a high-quality bittersweet or semisweet chocolate here. Light brown sugar can be substituted for the dark, as can light corn syrup for the dark, but with some sacrifice in flavor.

- ½ cup (3½ ounces) plus ⅓ cup (2⅓ ounces) granulated sugar
- 1½ cups (7½ ounces) all-purpose flour
- ¾ cup (2¼ ounces) Dutch-processed cocoa powder
- ½ teaspoon baking soda
- ⅜ teaspoon salt
- ½ cup dark corn syrup
- 1 large egg white
- 1 teaspoon vanilla extract
- 12 tablespoons unsalted butter, softened
- ⅓ cup packed (2⅓ ounces) dark brown sugar
- 4 ounces bittersweet or semisweet chocolate, chopped into ½-inch pieces

1. Adjust oven racks to upper-middle and lower-middle positions and heat oven to 375 degrees. Line 2 baking sheets with parchment paper. Place ½ cup granulated sugar in shallow baking dish or pie plate. Whisk flour, cocoa, baking soda, and salt together in medium bowl. Whisk corn syrup, egg white, and vanilla together in small bowl.

2. Using stand mixer fitted with paddle, beat butter, brown sugar, and remaining ⅓ cup granulated sugar at medium-high speed until light and fluffy, about 2 minutes. Reduce speed to medium-low, add corn syrup mixture, and beat until fully incorporated, about 20 seconds, scraping down bowl as needed. Reduce speed to low, add flour mixture and chopped chocolate, and mix until just incorporated, about 30 seconds, scraping down bowl as needed. Give dough final stir to ensure that no flour pockets remain and ingredients are evenly distributed. Refrigerate dough for 30 minutes to firm slightly.

3. Working with 2 tablespoons of dough at a time, roll into balls. Roll half of dough balls in sugar to coat. Place dough balls 2 inches apart on prepared baking sheet; repeat with remaining dough. Bake until cookies are puffed and cracked and edges have begun to set but centers are still soft (cookies will look raw between cracks and seem underdone), 10 to 11 minutes, switching and rotating baking sheets halfway through baking. Do not overbake.

4. Let cookies cool on baking sheets for 5 minutes; transfer cookies to wire rack and let cool to room temperature.

Peanut Butter Cookies

✓ **WHY THIS RECIPE WORKS:** Recipes for peanut butter cookies tend to fall into one of two categories: sweet and chewy with a mild peanut flavor, or sandy and crumbly with a strong peanut flavor. We, of course, wanted the best of both worlds—cookies that were crisp on the edges and chewy in the center, with lots of peanut flavor. First off, we had to determine the amount and type of sugar. Granulated sugar was necessary for crisp edges and chewy centers, while dark brown sugar enriched the peanut flavor. As for flour, too little resulted in an oily cookie, whereas too much made for dry cookies. Baking soda contributed to browning and amplified the peanut flavor and baking powder provided lift, making both leaveners necessary. Extra-crunchy peanut butter also helped the cookies rise and achieve a crispier edge and a softer center. But the best way to get the true peanut flavor we sought was to use peanuts and salt. Adding some roasted salted peanuts, ground in a food processor, and then adding still more salt (directly to the batter as well as in the form of salted rather than unsalted butter) produced a strong roasted nut flavor without sacrificing anything in terms of texture.

Peanut Butter Cookies
MAKES ABOUT 36 COOKIES

These cookies have a strong peanut flavor that comes from extra-crunchy peanut butter as well as from roasted salted peanuts that are ground in a food processor and worked into the dough. In our testing, we found that salted butter brings out the flavor of the nuts. If using unsalted butter, increase the salt to 1 teaspoon.

- 2½   cups (12½ ounces) all-purpose flour
- ½   teaspoon baking soda
- ½   teaspoon baking powder
- ½   teaspoon salt
- 16   tablespoons salted butter, softened
- 1   cup packed (7 ounces) dark brown sugar
- 1   cup (7 ounces) granulated sugar
- 1   cup extra-crunchy peanut butter, room temperature
- 2   large eggs
- 2   teaspoons vanilla extract
- 1   cup dry-roasted salted peanuts, pulsed in food processor to resemble bread crumbs, about 14 pulses

1. Adjust oven racks to upper-middle and lower-middle positions and heat oven to 350 degrees. Line 2 baking sheets with parchment paper.

2. Whisk flour, baking soda, baking powder, and salt together in medium bowl; set aside.

3. Using stand mixer fitted with paddle, beat butter, brown sugar, and granulated sugar at medium speed until light and fluffy, about 2 minutes, scraping down bowl as needed. Add peanut butter and mix until fully incorporated, about 30 seconds; add eggs, one at a time, and vanilla and mix until combined, about 30 seconds. Reduce speed to low and add dry ingredients; mix until combined, about 30 seconds. Mix in ground peanuts until just incorporated. Give dough final stir to ensure that no flour pockets remain and ingredients are evenly distributed.

4. Working with 2 tablespoons of dough at a time, roll into balls and place 2½ inches apart on prepared baking sheets. Press each dough ball twice, at right angles, with dinner fork dipped in cold water to make crisscross design.

5. Bake until cookies are puffy and slightly brown around edges but not on top, 10 to 12 minutes (cookies will not look fully baked), switching and rotating baking sheets halfway through baking. Let cookies cool on baking sheets for 5 minutes; transfer cookies to wire rack and let cool to room temperature .

Chocolate-Chunk Oatmeal Cookies

✓ **WHY THIS RECIPE WORKS:** It's easy to get carried away and overload cookie dough with a crazy jumble of ingredients, resulting in a poorly textured cookie monster. Our ultimate oatmeal cookie would have just the right amount of added ingredients and an ideal texture—crisp around the edges and chewy in the middle. We wanted to add four flavor components—sweet, tangy, nutty, and chocolaty—to the underlying oat flavor. Bittersweet chocolate, dried sour cherries, and toasted pecans gave the right balance of flavors. We also analyzed the cookie dough ingredients and discovered that cookies made with brown sugar were moister and chewier than cookies made with granulated sugar. A combination of baking powder and baking soda (we doubled the usual amount) produced cookies that were light and crisp on the outside, but chewy, dense, and soft in the center. Finally, we focused on appearance to decide when to remove the cookies from the oven—they should be set but still look wet between the fissures; if they look matte rather than shiny, they've been overbaked.

Chocolate-Chunk Oatmeal Cookies with Pecans and Dried Cherries
MAKES ABOUT 16 LARGE COOKIES

We like these cookies made with pecans and dried sour cherries, but walnuts or toasted and skinned hazelnuts can be substituted for the pecans and dried cranberries for the cherries. Quick oats used in place of the old-fashioned oats will yield a cookie with slightly less chewiness.

- 1¼   cups (6¼ ounces) all-purpose flour
- ¾   teaspoon baking powder
- ½   teaspoon baking soda
- ½   teaspoon salt
- 1¼   cups (3¾ ounces) old-fashioned rolled oats
- 1   cup pecans, toasted and chopped
- 1   cup (4 ounces) dried sour cherries, chopped coarse
- 4   ounces bittersweet chocolate, chopped into chunks about size of chocolate chips
- 12   tablespoons unsalted butter, softened
- 1½   cups packed (10½ ounces) dark brown sugar
- 1   large egg
- 1   teaspoon vanilla extract

1. Adjust oven racks to upper-middle and lower-middle positions and heat oven to 350 degrees. Line 2 baking sheets with parchment paper.

2. Whisk flour, baking powder, baking soda, and salt together in medium bowl. In second medium bowl, stir oats, pecans, cherries, and chocolate together.

3. Using stand mixer fitted with paddle, beat butter and sugar at medium speed until no sugar lumps remain, about 1 minute, scraping down bowl as needed. Add egg and vanilla and beat on medium-low until fully incorporated, about 30 seconds, scraping down bowl as needed. Reduce speed to low, add flour mixture, and mix until just combined, about 30 seconds. Gradually add oat-pecan mixture; mix until just incorporated. Give dough final stir to ensure that no flour pockets remain and ingredients are evenly distributed.

4. Working with ¼ cup of dough at a time, roll into balls and place 2½ inches apart on prepared baking sheets. Press dough to 1-inch thickness using bottom of greased measuring cup. Bake until cookies are medium brown and edges have begun to set but centers are still soft, 20 to 22 minutes (cookies will seem underdone and will appear raw, wet, and shiny in cracks), switching and rotating baking sheets halfway through baking.

5. Let cookies cool on baking sheets for 5 minutes; transfer cookies to wire rack and let cool to room temperature.

Thin and Crispy Oatmeal Cookies

✔ **WHY THIS RECIPE WORKS:** Thin and crispy oatmeal cookies can be irresistible—crunchy and delicate, these cookies really let the flavor of the oats take center stage. But the usual ingredients that give thick, chewy oatmeal cookies great texture—generous amounts of sugar and butter, a high ratio of oats to flour, a modest amount of leavener, eggs, raisins, and nuts—won't all fit in a thin, crispy cookie. We wanted to adjust the standard ingredients to create a crispy, delicate cookie in which the simple flavor of buttery oats really stands out. Given this cookie's simplicity, creating a rich butter flavor was critical, so we kept almost the same amount of butter as in our standard big, chewy oatmeal cookie, but we scaled back the amount of sugar. Fine-tuning the amount and type of leavener led to a surprising result that solved our texture and shape problems. During baking, large carbon dioxide bubbles created by the baking soda and baking powder (upped from our traditional recipe) caused the cookies to puff up, collapse, and spread out, producing the thin, flat cookies we were looking for. Baking the cookies until they were fully set and evenly browned made them crisp throughout but not tough.

Thin and Crispy Oatmeal Cookies
MAKES ABOUT 24 COOKIES
Do not use instant or quick oats.

1	cup (5 ounces) all-purpose flour
¾	teaspoon baking powder
½	teaspoon baking soda
½	teaspoon salt
14	tablespoons unsalted butter, softened but still cool
1	cup (7 ounces) granulated sugar
¼	cup packed (1¾ ounces) light brown sugar
1	large egg
1	teaspoon vanilla extract
2½	cups (7½ ounces) old-fashioned rolled oats

1. Adjust oven rack to middle position and heat oven to 350 degrees. Line 3 baking sheets with parchment paper. Whisk flour, baking powder, baking soda, and salt in medium bowl; set aside.

2. Using stand mixer fitted with paddle, beat butter, granulated sugar, and brown sugar at medium-low speed until just combined, about 20 seconds. Increase speed to medium and continue to beat until light and fluffy, about 1 minute longer, scraping down bowl as needed. Add egg and vanilla and beat on medium-low until fully incorporated, about 30 seconds, scraping down bowl as needed. Reduce speed to low, add flour mixture, and mix until just incorporated and smooth, about 10 seconds. With mixer still running on low, gradually add oats and mix until well incorporated, about 20 seconds. Give dough final stir to ensure that no flour pockets remain and ingredients are evenly distributed.

3. Working with 2 tablespoons of dough at a time, roll into balls and place 2½ inches apart on prepared baking sheets. Using fingertips, gently press each dough ball to ¾-inch thickness.

4. Bake 1 sheet at a time until cookies are deep golden brown, edges are crisp, and centers yield to slight pressure when pressed, 13 to 16 minutes, rotating baking sheet halfway through baking. Transfer baking sheet to wire rack and let cookies cool completely.

Thin and Crispy Coconut-Oatmeal Cookies
Decrease oats to 2 cups and add 1½ cups sweetened flaked coconut to batter with oats in step 2.

Thin and Crispy Orange-Almond Oatmeal Cookies
Beat 2 teaspoons grated orange zest with butter and sugars in step 2. Decrease oats to 2 cups and add 1 cup coarsely chopped toasted almonds to batter with oats in step 2.

Salty Thin and Crispy Oatmeal Cookies
We prefer the texture and flavor of a coarse-grained sea salt, like Maldon or fleur de sel, but kosher salt can be used. If using kosher salt, reduce the amount sprinkled over the cookies to ¼ teaspoon.

Reduce amount of salt in dough to ¼ teaspoon. Lightly sprinkle ½ teaspoon coarse sea salt evenly over flattened dough balls before baking.

Molasses Spice Cookies

✔ **WHY THIS RECIPE WORKS:** Molasses spice cookies are often miserable specimens, no more than flat, tasteless cardboard rounds of gingerbread. They can be dry and cakey without the requisite chew; others are timidly flavored with molasses and scantily spiced. We wanted to create the ultimate molasses spice cookie—soft, chewy, and gently spiced with deep, dark molasses flavor. We also wanted it to have the traditional cracks and crinkles so characteristic of these charming cookies. We started with all-purpose flour and butter for full, rich flavor. Using just the right amount of molasses and brown sugar and flavoring the cookies with a combination of vanilla, ginger, cinnamon, cloves, black pepper, and allspice gave these spiced cookies the warm tingle that we were after. We found that to keep the cookies mild, using a light or mild molasses is imperative; but if it's a stronger flavor you want, dark molasses is in order. We pulled the cookies from the oven when they still looked a bit underdone; residual heat finished the baking and kept the cookies chewy and moist.

Molasses Spice Cookies

MAKES ABOUT 22 COOKIES

For best flavor, make sure that your spices are fresh. Light or mild molasses gives the cookies a milder flavor; for a stronger flavor, use dark molasses.

- ½ cup (3½ ounces) plus ⅓ cup (2⅓ ounces) granulated sugar
- 2¼ cups (11¼ ounces) all-purpose flour
- 1 teaspoon baking soda
- 1½ teaspoons ground cinnamon
- 1½ teaspoons ground ginger
- ½ teaspoon ground cloves
- ¼ teaspoon ground allspice
- ¼ teaspoon pepper
- ¼ teaspoon salt
- 12 tablespoons unsalted butter, softened
- ⅓ cup packed (2⅓ ounces) dark brown sugar
- 1 large egg yolk
- 1 teaspoon vanilla extract
- ½ cup light or dark molasses

1. Adjust oven rack to middle position and heat oven to 375 degrees. Line 2 baking sheets with parchment paper. Place ½ cup granulated sugar in shallow baking dish or pie plate; set aside.

2. Whisk flour, baking soda, cinnamon, ginger, cloves, allspice, pepper, and salt together in medium bowl; set aside.

3. Using stand mixer fitted with paddle, beat butter, brown sugar, and remaining ⅓ cup granulated sugar on medium-high speed until light and fluffy, about 3 minutes. Reduce speed to medium-low and add egg yolk and vanilla; increase speed to medium and beat until incorporated, about 20 seconds. Reduce speed to medium-low and add molasses; beat until fully incorporated, about 20 seconds, scraping down bowl as needed. Reduce speed to low and add flour mixture; beat until just incorporated, about 30 seconds, scraping down bowl as needed. Give dough final stir to ensure that no flour pockets remain and ingredients are evenly distributed. Dough will be soft.

4. Working with 1 tablespoon of dough at a time, roll into balls. Roll half of dough balls in sugar and toss to coat. Place dough balls 2 inches apart on prepared baking sheet. Repeat with remaining dough.

5. Bake 1 sheet at a time until cookies are browned, still puffy, and edges have begun to set but centers are still soft (cookies will look raw between cracks and seem underdone), about 11 minutes, rotating baking sheet halfway through baking. Do not overbake.

6. Let cookies cool on baking sheet for 5 minutes; transfer cookies to wire rack and let cool to room temperature.

Molasses Spice Cookies with Dark Rum Glaze

If the glaze is too thick to drizzle, whisk in up to an additional ½ tablespoon rum.

Whisk 1 cup confectioners' sugar and 2½ tablespoons dark rum together in medium bowl until smooth. Drizzle or spread glaze using back of spoon on cooled cookies. Allow glazed cookies to dry at least 15 minutes.

Molasses Spice Cookies with Orange Essence

The orange zest in the sugar coating causes the sugar to become sticky and take on a light orange hue, giving the baked cookies a unique frosty look.

Process ⅔ cup granulated sugar and 2 teaspoons grated orange zest in food processor until pale orange, about 10 seconds; transfer sugar to shallow baking dish or pie plate and set aside. Add 1 teaspoon grated orange zest to dough along with molasses and substitute orange sugar for granulated sugar when coating dough balls in step 4.

Icebox Cookies

✔ **WHY THIS RECIPE WORKS:** Also known as slice-and-bake and refrigerator cookies, icebox cookies are a classic thin, crisp American cookie. The trick is making them tender and "snappy" without making them hard. We found the key to a tender texture was to use two types of sugar: granulated and confectioners'. The granulated sugar gave the cookie some structure and a good snap, while the confectioners' sugar ensured tenderness. Some recipes call for baking powder, but we found it made the cookies either too soft or too cakey. For a rich cookie that stayed thin, we added two yolks rather than whole eggs. Once the dough was fully chilled, we sliced it thin, making sure to rotate the dough log every few slices to avoid creating a flat side.

Vanilla Icebox Cookies

MAKES ABOUT 4 DOZEN COOKIES

If the dough becomes soft while slicing the cookies, return it to the refrigerator until firm. We use a hand-held mixer for this simple recipe, but a stand mixer will work fine as well. See Core Technique on page 590 for more details and flavor variations on this recipe.

- 2¼ cups (11¼ ounces) all-purpose flour
- ½ teaspoon salt
- 16 tablespoons unsalted butter, softened
- ¾ cup (5¼ ounces) granulated sugar
- ½ cup (2 ounces) confectioners' sugar
- 2 large egg yolks
- 2 teaspoons vanilla extract

1. Whisk flour and salt together in medium bowl. Using hand-held mixer set at medium-high speed, beat butter, granulated sugar, and confectioners' sugar together in large bowl until light and fluffy, 3 to 6 minutes. Beat in egg yolks and vanilla until combined, about 30 seconds, scraping down bowl as needed. Reduce speed to low, slowly add flour mixture, and beat until combined, about 30 seconds.

2. Transfer dough to clean counter and divide into 2 equal pieces. Roll each piece of dough into log that is 6 inches long and 2 inches thick. Wrap dough tightly in plastic wrap and refrigerate until firm, about 2 hours.

3. Adjust oven racks to upper-middle and lower-middle positions and heat oven to 325 degrees. Line 2 baking sheets with parchment paper.

4. Working with 1 log of dough at a time, remove dough log from plastic and, using chef's knife, slice into ¼-inch-thick rounds, rotating dough so that it won't become misshapen from weight of knife. Place rounds on prepared sheets, spaced about ¾ inch apart. Bake until edges begin to brown, 12 to 15 minutes, switching and rotating sheets halfway through baking.

5. Let cookies cool on sheets for 3 minutes; transfer to wire rack to cool to room temperature.

Glazed Lemon Cookies

WHY THIS RECIPE WORKS: Store-bought lemon cookies are often saccharine-sweet and artificial tasting, with a thin veneer of frosting and a barely detectable lemon flavor. For a lemon cookie recipe with the perfect balance of lemony zing and rich, buttery sweetness, we started with all-purpose flour, which made our cookies tender. Just an egg yolk instead of a whole egg added even more tenderness, and a touch of baking powder gave our cookies just the right amount of airy crispness. Grinding some lemon zest with the sugar before adding it to the dough contributed bold lemon flavor without harshness. A simple glaze of cream cheese, lemon juice, and confectioners' sugar perfected these lemony treats.

Glazed Lemon Cookies
MAKES ABOUT 30 COOKIES
The cookies are best eaten the day they are glazed. See Recipe Tutorial on page 600 for more details on this recipe.

COOKIES
- ¾ cup (5¼ ounces) granulated sugar
- 2 tablespoons grated lemon zest plus 2 tablespoons juice (2 lemons)
- 1¾ cup (8¾ ounces) all-purpose flour
- ¼ teaspoon salt
- ¼ teaspoon baking powder
- 12 tablespoons unsalted butter, cut into ½-inch cubes and chilled
- 1 large egg yolk
- ½ teaspoon vanilla extract

GLAZE
- 1 tablespoon cream cheese, softened
- 2 tablespoons lemon juice
- 1½ cups (6 ounces) confectioners' sugar

1. FOR THE COOKIES: Adjust oven racks to upper-middle and lower-middle positions and heat oven to 375 degrees.

2. In food processor, process granulated sugar and lemon zest until sugar looks damp and zest is thoroughly incorporated, about 30 seconds. Add flour, salt, and baking powder;

pulse to combine, about 10 pulses. Scatter butter over flour mixture; pulse until mixture resembles fine cornmeal, about 15 pulses. In liquid measuring cup, beat lemon juice, egg yolk, and vanilla with fork to combine. With processor running, add juice mixture in slow, steady stream (process should take about 10 seconds); continue processing until dough begins to form ball, 10 to 15 seconds longer.

3. Turn dough and any dry bits onto counter; working quickly, gently knead together to ensure that no dry bits remain and dough is homogeneous. Shape dough into log about 10 inches long and 2 inches thick. Wrap log in parchment paper and twist ends to seal. Chill dough until firm, about 45 minutes in freezer or 2 hours in refrigerator. (Parchment-wrapped dough can be wrapped in plastic and refrigerated for up to 3 days or frozen for up to 2 weeks.)

4. Line 2 baking sheets with parchment. Remove dough log from parchment and, using chef's knife, slice dough into ⅜-inch-thick rounds, rotating dough so that it won't become misshapen from weight of knife. Place rounds 1 inch apart on prepared sheets. Bake until centers of cookies just begin to color and edges are golden brown, 14 to 16 minutes, switching and rotating sheets halfway through baking. Let cookies cool on sheets for 5 minutes; transfer cookies to wire rack and let cool to room temperature before glazing.

5. FOR THE GLAZE: Whisk cream cheese and lemon juice in medium bowl until no lumps remain. Add confectioners' sugar and whisk until smooth.

6. TO GLAZE THE COOKIES: When cookies have cooled, working with one at a time, spread glaze evenly over each cookie with back of small spoon. Let cookies stand on wire rack until glaze is set and dry, about 1 hour.

Glazed Lemon-Orange Cornmeal Cookies
Substitute 1 tablespoon grated orange zest for equal amount of lemon zest and ¼ cup cornmeal for equal amount of flour.

Glazed Lemon and Crystallized Ginger Cookies
Process 3 tablespoons finely chopped crystallized ginger along with sugar and lemon zest.

Pecan Sandies

WHY THIS RECIPE WORKS: Pecan sandies run the gamut from greasy and bland to dry and crumbly. We wanted a pecan sandie with a tender but crisp texture and sandy melt-in-the-mouth character. Some recipes use oil in place of butter for a sandy texture. We found that while oil did yield the desired texture, the flavor was abysmal, so we stuck with butter. We tried both light and dark brown sugars, settling on light, and to tenderize our cookies, we swapped out some of the brown sugar for confectioners' sugar. A whole egg made the dough too sticky, so we settled on a yolk. A rich pecan flavor was obtained by toasting the nuts and then grinding them in a food processor. While we were grinding the nuts, it occurred to us that we might as well use the food processor to mix the dough as well. After briefly kneading the dough together out of the food processor, we shaped it into dough logs to chill, so that we could slice and bake the dough for pecan sandies with clean, crisp edges.

Pecan Sandies

MAKES ABOUT 32 COOKIES

Don't substitute another type of sugar for the confectioners' sugar—it is important for a tender, sandy texture.

- 2 cups (8 ounces) pecans, toasted
- ½ cup packed (3½ ounces) light brown sugar
- ¼ cup (1 ounce) confectioners' sugar
- 1½ cups (7½ ounces) all-purpose flour
- ¼ teaspoon salt
- 12 tablespoons unsalted butter, cut into ½-inch pieces and chilled
- 1 large egg yolk

1. Reserve 32 of prettiest pecan halves for garnishing. Process remaining pecans with brown sugar and confectioners' sugar in food processor until nuts are finely ground, about 20 seconds. Add flour and salt and process to combine, about 10 seconds.

2. Add butter pieces and process until mixture resembles damp sand and rides up sides of bowl, about 20 seconds. With processor running, add egg yolk and process until dough comes together into rough ball, about 20 seconds.

3. Transfer dough to clean counter, knead briefly, and divide into 2 equal pieces. Roll each piece of dough into log that is 6 inches long and 2 inches thick. Wrap dough tightly in plastic wrap and refrigerate until firm, about 2 hours.

4. Adjust oven racks to upper-middle and lower-middle positions and heat oven to 325 degrees. Line 2 baking sheets with parchment paper.

5. Working with 1 dough log at a time, remove dough log from plastic and, using chef's knife, slice into ⅜-inch-thick rounds, rotating dough so that it won't become misshapen from weight of knife. Place rounds 1 inch apart on prepared baking sheets. Gently press pecan half in center of each cookie. Bake until edges of cookies are golden brown, 20 to 25 minutes, switching and rotating baking sheets halfway through baking. Let cookies cool on baking sheets for 3 minutes, then transfer to wire rack and let cool to room temperature.

Best Shortbread

✔ WHY THIS RECIPE WORKS: Often shortbread turns out bland and chalky. We wanted superlative shortbread with an alluring tawny brown crumb and pure, buttery richness. In initial tests, we tinkered with various mixing methods and found that reverse creaming—mixing the flour and sugar before adding the butter, creating less aeration—yielded the most reliable results. To smooth out an objectionable granular texture, we swapped the white sugar for confectioners' sugar. Still, our shortbread was unpleasantly tough. The problems were gluten and moisture. Gluten, the protein matrix that lends baked goods structure and chew, forms naturally when liquid and all-purpose flour are combined, even without kneading. The liquid in our recipe was coming from butter, which contains 18 percent water. To curb gluten development, we replaced some of our flour with powdered old-fashioned oats. We ground some oats to a powder and supplemented it with a modest amount of cornstarch (using all oat powder muted the buttery flavor). The cookies were now perfectly crisp and flavorful, with an appealing hint of oat flavor. As for the moisture problem, we baked the dough briefly, then shut off the heat and let it sit in the still-warm oven. The batch was dry through and through, with an even golden brown exterior. Crisp and buttery, our shortbread was anything but bland.

Best Shortbread

MAKES 16 WEDGES

Use the collar of a springform pan to form the shortbread into an even round. Mold the shortbread with the collar in the closed position, then open the collar, but leave it in place. This allows the shortbread to expand slightly but keeps it from spreading too far. The extracted round of dough in step 2 is baked alongside the rest of the shortbread.

- ½ cup (1½ ounces) old-fashioned rolled oats
- 1½ cups (7½ ounces) all-purpose flour
- ¼ cup cornstarch
- ⅔ cup (2⅔ ounces) confectioners' sugar
- ½ teaspoon salt
- 14 tablespoons unsalted butter, cut into ⅛-inch-thick slices and chilled

1. Adjust oven rack to middle position and heat oven to 450 degrees. Pulse oats in spice grinder or blender until reduced to fine powder, about 10 pulses (you should have ¼ to ⅓ cup oat flour). Using stand mixer fitted with paddle, mix oat flour, all-purpose flour, cornstarch, sugar, and salt on low speed until combined, about 5 seconds. Add butter to dry ingredients and continue to mix until dough just forms and pulls away from sides of bowl, 5 to 10 minutes.

2. Place upside-down (grooved edge should be at top) collar of 9- or 9½-inch springform pan on parchment paper–lined baking sheet (do not use springform pan bottom). Press dough into collar in even ½-inch-thick layer, smoothing top of dough with back of spoon. Place 2-inch biscuit cutter in center of dough and cut out center. Place extracted round alongside springform collar on baking sheet and replace cutter in center of dough. Open springform collar, but leave it in place.

3. Bake shortbread 5 minutes, then reduce oven temperature to 250 degrees. Continue to bake until edges turn pale golden, 10 to 15 minutes longer. Remove baking sheet from oven; turn off oven. Remove springform pan collar; use chef's knife to score surface of shortbread into 16 even wedges, cutting halfway through shortbread. Using wooden skewer, poke 8 to 10 holes in each wedge. Return shortbread to oven and prop door open with handle of wooden spoon, leaving 1-inch gap at top. Allow shortbread to dry in turned-off oven until pale golden in center (shortbread should be firm but giving to touch), about 1 hour.

4. Transfer baking sheet to wire rack; let shortbread cool to room temperature. Cut shortbread at scored marks to separate and serve. (Shortbread can be stored at room temperature for up to 1 week.)

Chocolate-Dipped Pistachio Shortbread

Add ½ cup finely chopped toasted pistachios to dry ingredients in step 1. Bake and cool shortbread as directed. Once shortbread is cool, melt 8 ounces finely chopped bittersweet chocolate in microwave at 50 percent power for 2 minutes. Stir chocolate and continue heating until melted, stirring once every additional minute. Stir in additional 2 ounces finely chopped bittersweet chocolate until smooth. Carefully dip base of each wedge in chocolate, allowing chocolate to come halfway up cookie. Scrape off excess with finger and place on parchment paper–lined rimmed baking sheet. Refrigerate until chocolate sets, about 15 minutes.

Ginger Shortbread

Turbinado sugar is commonly sold as Sugar in the Raw. Demerara sugar, sanding sugar, or another coarse sugar can be substituted.

Add ½ cup chopped crystallized ginger to dry ingredients in step 1. Sprinkle shortbread with 1 tablespoon turbinado sugar after poking holes in shortbread in step 3.

Toasted Oat Shortbread

To toast the oats, heat them in an 8-inch skillet over medium-high heat until light golden brown, 5 to 8 minutes. We prefer the texture and flavor of a coarse-grained sea salt like Maldon or fleur de sel, but kosher salt can be used.

Add ½ cup toasted oats to dry ingredients in step 1. Sprinkle ½ teaspoon coarse salt evenly over surface of dough before baking.

Nut Crescent Cookies

✔ **WHY THIS RECIPE WORKS:** When nut crescent cookies are well made, they can be delicious: buttery, nutty, slightly crisp, slightly crumbly, with a melt-in-your mouth quality. Too often, however, they turn out bland and dry. We wanted to develop a recipe that would put them back in their proper place. The ratio of 1 cup butter to 2 cups flour in almost all the recipes we looked at is what worked for us. We tried three kinds of sugar in the dough: granulated, confectioners', and superfine. The last resulted in just what we wanted: cookies that melted in our mouths. In determining the amount, we had to remember that the cookies would be sweetened once more by their traditional coating of confectioners' sugar. Before rolling them, we let the cookies cool to room temperature; coating them with sugar while still warm results in a pasty outer layer we wanted to avoid.

Pecan or Walnut Crescent Cookies

MAKES ABOUT 48 SMALL COOKIES

If you cannot find superfine sugar, process granulated sugar in a food processor for 30 seconds. If you make these cookies ahead, roll them again in confectioners' sugar, shaking off the excess, before serving.

2 cups (8 ounces) pecans or walnuts, chopped fine
2 cups (10 ounces) all-purpose flour
½ teaspoon salt
16 tablespoons unsalted butter, softened
⅓ cup (2½ ounces) superfine sugar
1½ teaspoons vanilla extract
1½ cups (6 ounces) confectioners' sugar

1. Adjust oven racks to upper-middle and lower-middle positions and heat oven to 325 degrees. Line 2 baking sheets with parchment paper.

2. Whisk 1 cup chopped pecans, flour, and salt together in medium bowl; set aside. Process remaining 1 cup chopped pecans in food processor until they are texture of coarse cornmeal, 10 to 15 seconds (do not overprocess). Stir pecans into flour mixture and set aside.

3. Using stand mixer fitted with paddle, beat butter and superfine sugar at medium-low speed until light and fluffy, about 2 minutes; add vanilla, scraping down bowl as needed. Add flour mixture and beat on low speed until dough just begins to come together but still looks scrappy, about 15 seconds. Scrape down bowl as needed; continue beating until dough is cohesive, 6 to 9 seconds longer. Do not overbeat.

4. Working with 1 tablespoon of dough at a time, roll into balls. Roll each dough ball between your palms into rope that measures 3 inches long. Place ropes on prepared baking sheets and turn up ends to form crescent shape. Bake until tops of cookies are pale golden and bottoms are just beginning to brown, 17 to 19 minutes, switching and rotating baking sheets halfway through baking.

5. Let cookies cool on baking sheets for 2 minutes; transfer cookies to wire rack and let cool to room temperature. Place confectioners' sugar in shallow baking dish or pie plate. Working with 3 or 4 cookies at a time, roll cookies in sugar to coat thoroughly; gently shake off excess.

Almond or Hazelnut Crescent Cookies

Almonds can be used raw for cookies that are light in both color and flavor or toasted to enhance the almond flavor and darken the crescents.

Substitute 1¾ cups whole blanched almonds (toasted, if desired) or 2 cups skinned toasted hazelnuts for pecans or walnuts. If using almonds, add ½ teaspoon almond extract along with vanilla extract.

Holiday Cookies

✔ **WHY THIS RECIPE WORKS:** We wanted a simple recipe that would produce cookies sturdy enough to decorate yet tender enough to be worth eating. Superfine sugar helped to achieve a fine, delicate texture, while a little cream cheese assisted in making the dough workable without turning the cookies tough. Finally, using the reverse-creaming method of beating the butter into the flour-sugar mixture made for flat cookies, without any air pockets, that were easy to decorate. Baking them one sheet at a time ensured that they all baked evenly.

Holiday Cookies

MAKES ABOUT 3 DOZEN COOKIES

If you can't find superfine sugar in the supermarket, simply process 1 cup granulated sugar in a food processor for about 30 seconds, then measure out ¾ cup for the recipe. The dough scraps can be patted together, chilled, and rerolled one time only. For best results, be sure to bake the cookies one sheet at a time. See Core Technique on page 592 for more details on this recipe. This recipe can easily be doubled; simply double all the ingredients and prepare the dough as directed. If decorating, see Core Technique on page 593 for tips and glaze recipes; make sure to let the cookies cool completely before decorating.

- 2½ **cups (12½ ounces) all-purpose flour**
- ¾ **cup (5¼ ounces) superfine sugar**
- ¼ **teaspoon salt**
- 16 **tablespoons unsalted butter, cut into ½-inch pieces and softened**
- 2 **tablespoons cream cheese, softened**
- 2 **teaspoons vanilla extract**

1. Whisk flour, sugar, and salt together in bowl of stand mixer. Using stand mixer fitted with paddle, beat butter into flour mixture, 1 piece at a time, on medium-low speed. Continue to beat until dough looks crumbly and slightly wet, 1 to 2 minutes.

2. Beat in cream cheese and vanilla until dough just begins to form large clumps, about 30 seconds. Knead dough in bowl by hand a few times until it forms a large cohesive mass.

3. Transfer dough to clean counter and divide into 2 equal pieces. Press each piece into 4-inch disk, wrap tightly in plastic wrap, and refrigerate until dough is firm yet malleable, at least 30 minutes. (Wrapped dough can be refrigerated up to 2 days or frozen up to 2 weeks; defrost frozen dough in refrigerator. Let dough that has been refrigerated for more than 2 hours soften on counter for several minutes before rolling out.)

4. Working with 1 piece of dough at a time, roll dough out between 2 large sheets of parchment paper to even ⅛-inch thickness. Slide dough, still between the parchment, onto baking sheet and refrigerate until firm, about 10 minutes.

5. Adjust oven rack to middle position and heat oven to 375 degrees. Line 2 baking sheets with parchment paper.

6. Working with 1 sheet of dough at a time, remove top piece of parchment and stamp out cookies using cookie cutters. Using thin offset spatula, transfer cookies to prepared baking sheet, spaced about 1 inch apart.

7. Bake cookies, 1 sheet at a time, until light golden brown, about 10 minutes, rotating baking sheet halfway through baking. Let cookies cool on baking sheet for 3 minutes, then transfer to wire rack to cool to room temperature. Repeat with remaining dough using freshly lined baking sheets.

Chocolate Butter Cookies

✔ **WHY THIS RECIPE WORKS:** Chocolate butter cookies usually taste bland or surrender their crisp, delicate appeal to a chewy, brownielike texture. We wanted to cram big chocolate flavor into a tender, crisp cookie. Cocoa powder—with a much higher percentage of cocoa solids than other forms of chocolate—was clearly the best candidate to maximize chocolate flavor, so we first doubled the amount of cocoa in our working recipe. The cocoa did indeed boost the flavor, but the texture of our cookie was now dry and pasty. Reducing the flour and adding egg yolks for more structure was the answer. Extra vanilla extract enhanced the aromatics in the chocolate for even more chocolate flavor. Then we discovered that "blooming" the cocoa powder in melted butter (along with a teaspoon of instant espresso) before adding it to the dough really maximized the chocolate flavor. The only remaining challenge was to take the cookies out of the oven at just the right moment, as overcooking robbed the cookies of the chocolate flavor we had worked so hard to establish.

Chocolate Butter Cookies

MAKES ABOUT 48 COOKIES

Natural cocoa powder will work in this recipe, but we found that Dutch-processed yields the best chocolate flavor. Espresso powder provides complexity, but instant coffee can be substituted in a pinch. The cookies are refined enough to serve plain, although a dusting of sifted confectioners' sugar or chocolate glaze is a nice touch.

COOKIES
- 20 **tablespoons (2½ sticks) unsalted butter, softened**
- ½ **cup (1½ ounces) Dutch-processed cocoa powder**
- 1 **teaspoon instant espresso powder**
- 1 **cup (7 ounces) sugar**
- ¼ **teaspoon salt**
- 2 **large egg yolks**
- 1 **tablespoon vanilla extract**
- 2¼ **cups (11¼ ounces) all-purpose flour**

BITTERSWEET CHOCOLATE GLAZE (OPTIONAL)
- 4 **ounces bittersweet chocolate, chopped**
- 4 **tablespoons unsalted butter**
- 2 **tablespoons corn syrup**
- 1 **teaspoon vanilla extract**

1. FOR THE COOKIES: Melt 4 tablespoons butter in medium saucepan over medium heat. Add cocoa and espresso; stir until mixture forms smooth paste. Set aside to cool, 15 to 20 minutes.

2. Using stand mixer fitted with paddle, mix remaining 16 tablespoons butter, sugar, salt, and cooled cocoa mixture on high speed until well combined and fluffy, about 1 minute, scraping down bowl once or twice. Add egg yolks and vanilla and mix on medium speed until thoroughly combined, about 30 seconds. Scrape down bowl. With mixer running on low, add flour in 3 additions, waiting until each addition is incorporated before adding next and scraping down bowl after each addition. Continue to mix until dough forms cohesive ball, about 5 seconds. Turn dough onto counter; divide into three 4-inch disks. Wrap each disk in plastic wrap and refrigerate until dough is firm yet malleable, 45 minutes to 1 hour. (Alternatively, shape dough into log that is 12 inches long and 2 inches thick; use parchment paper to roll into neat cylinder and twist ends to seal. Chill until very firm and cold, at least 1 hour.)

3. Adjust oven rack to middle position and heat oven to 375 degrees. Line 2 baking sheets with parchment paper. Working with 1 piece of dough at a time, roll ³⁄₁₆ inch thick between 2 large sheets of parchment paper. If dough becomes soft and sticky, slide rolled dough on parchment onto baking sheet and refrigerate until firm, about 10 minutes.

4. Peel parchment from 1 side of dough and cut into desired shapes using cookie cutters; place shapes 1 inch apart on prepared baking sheets. (For cylinder-shaped dough, simply slice cookies ¼ inch thick and place on prepared baking sheets.) Bake 1 sheet at a time until cookies show slight resistance to touch, 10 to 12 minutes, rotating baking sheet halfway through baking; if cookies begin to darken on edges, they have over-baked. (Dough scraps can be patted together, chilled, and rerolled once.) Let cookies cool on baking sheet for 5 minutes; transfer cookies to wire rack and let cool to room temperature. Decorate as desired.

5. FOR THE GLAZE (OPTIONAL): Melt bittersweet chocolate with butter in heatproof bowl set over saucepan of barely simmering water; whisk until smooth. Add corn syrup and vanilla extract and mix until smooth and shiny. Use back of spoon to spread scant 1 teaspoon glaze almost to edge of each cookie. (If necessary, reheat to prolong fluidity of glaze.) Allow glazed cookies to dry at least 20 minutes.

Glazed Chocolate-Mint Cookies

Replace vanilla extract with 2 teaspoons mint extract. Glaze cookies with Bittersweet Chocolate Glaze and dry as directed. Melt 1 cup white chocolate chips and drizzle over glazed cookies. Let dry at least 20 minutes before serving.

Mexican Chocolate Butter Cookies

In medium skillet over medium heat, toast ½ cup sliced almonds, 1 teaspoon ground cinnamon, and ⅛ teaspoon cayenne until fragrant, about 3 minutes; set aside to cool. In food processor fitted with metal blade, process cooled mixture until very fine, about 15 seconds. Whisk nut-spice mixture into flour before adding flour to dough in step 2. Proceed with recipe, rolling dough into log. Roll chilled log in ½ cup raw or sanding sugar before slicing.

Almond Biscotti

✔ **WHY THIS RECIPE WORKS:** We wanted biscotti that were hard and crunchy, but not hard to eat, and bold in flavor. To keep the crumb hard, we used just a small amount of butter (4 tablespoons), and to keep the biscotti from being too hard, we ground some of the nuts to a fine meal, which helped minimize gluten development in the crumb. To ensure bold flavor in a biscuit that gets baked twice, we increased the quantities of aromatic ingredients.

Almond Biscotti

MAKES 30 COOKIES

The almonds will continue to toast while the biscotti bake, so toast the nuts only until they are just fragrant. See Recipe Tutorial on page 604 for more details on this recipe.

1¼ cups (6¼ ounces) whole almonds, lightly toasted
1¾ cups (8¾ ounces) all-purpose flour
  2 teaspoons baking powder
  ¼ teaspoon salt
  2 large eggs, plus 1 large white beaten with pinch salt
  1 cup (7 ounces) sugar
  4 tablespoons unsalted butter, melted and cooled
1½ teaspoons almond extract
  ½ teaspoon vanilla extract
    Vegetable oil spray

1. Adjust oven rack to middle position and heat oven to 325 degrees. Using ruler and pencil, draw two 8 by 3-inch rectangles, spaced 4 inches apart, on piece of parchment paper. Grease baking sheet and place parchment on it, drawing side down.

2. Pulse 1 cup almonds in food processor until coarsely chopped, 8 to 10 pulses; transfer to bowl and set aside. Process remaining ¼ cup almonds in food processor until finely ground, about 45 seconds. Add flour, baking powder, and salt; process to combine, about 15 seconds. Transfer flour mixture to second bowl. Process 2 eggs in now-empty food processor until lightened in color and almost doubled in volume, about 3 minutes. With processor running, slowly add sugar until thoroughly combined, about 15 seconds. Add melted butter, almond extract, and vanilla and process until combined, about 10 seconds. Transfer egg mixture to medium bowl. Sprinkle half of flour mixture over egg mixture and, using spatula, gently fold until just combined. Add remaining flour mixture and chopped almonds and gently fold until just combined.

3. Divide batter in half. Using floured hands, form each half into 8 by 3-inch rectangle, using lines on parchment as guide. Spray each loaf lightly with oil spray. Using rubber spatula lightly coated with oil spray, smooth tops and sides of rectangles. Gently brush tops of loaves with egg white wash. Bake until loaves are golden and just beginning to crack on top, 25 to 30 minutes, rotating pan halfway through baking.

4. Let loaves cool on baking sheet for 30 minutes. Transfer loaves to cutting board. Using serrated knife, slice each loaf on slight bias into ½-inch-thick slices. Lay slices with one cut side down about ¼ inch apart on wire rack set in rimmed baking sheet. Bake until crisp and golden brown on both sides, about 35 minutes, flipping slices halfway through baking. Let cool to room temperature. (Biscotti can be stored in airtight container for up to 1 month.)

Anise Biscotti

Add 1½ teaspoons anise seeds to flour mixture in step 2. Substitute anise-flavored liqueur for almond extract.

Hazelnut-Orange Biscotti

Substitute lightly toasted and skinned hazelnuts for almonds. Add 2 tablespoons minced fresh rosemary to flour mixture in step 2. Substitute orange-flavored liqueur for almond extract and add 1 tablespoon grated orange zest to egg mixture with melted butter.

Pistachio-Spice Biscotti

Substitute shelled pistachios for almonds. Add 1 teaspoon ground cardamom, ½ teaspoon ground cloves, ½ teaspoon pepper, ¼ teaspoon ground cinnamon, and ¼ teaspoon ground ginger to flour mixture in step 2. Substitute 1 teaspoon water for almond extract and increase vanilla extract to 1 teaspoon.

Hazelnut-Lavender Biscotti

Substitute lightly toasted and skinned hazelnuts for almonds. Add 2 teaspoons dried lavender flowers to flour mixture in step 2. Substitute 1½ teaspoons water for almond extract and add 2 tablespoons grated lemon zest to egg mixture with butter.

Classic Brownies

WHY THIS RECIPE WORKS: Brownies should be a simple and utterly satisfying affair. But too often, they are heavy, dense, and remarkably low on chocolate flavor. For tender texture and delicate chew, we shelved the all-purpose flour in favor of cake flour; baking powder further lightened the crumb. Getting the number of eggs just right prevented our brownies from being cakey or dry. Plenty of unsweetened chocolate provided maximum chocolate flavor—not too sweet, with profound chocolate notes. Nailing the baking time was essential—too little time in the oven and the brownies were gummy and underbaked, too much time and they were dry. Finally, for nut-lovers, we toasted pecans and topped the brownies with them just before baking; baked inside the brownies, they steam and get soft.

Classic Brownies

MAKES 24 BROWNIES

Be sure to test for doneness before removing the brownies from the oven. If underbaked (the toothpick has batter, not just crumbs, clinging to it), the texture of the brownies will be dense and gummy; if overbaked (the toothpick comes out completely clean), the brownies will be dry and cakey. To melt the chocolate in a microwave, heat it at 50 percent power for 2 minutes. Stir the chocolate, add the butter, and continue heating until melted, stirring once every additional minute. See Core Technique on page 595 for more details on preparing a foil sling.

- 1¼ cups (5 ounces) cake flour
- ¾ teaspoon baking powder
- ½ teaspoon salt
- 6 ounces unsweetened chocolate, chopped fine
- 12 tablespoons unsalted butter, cut into 6 pieces
- 2¼ cups (15¾ ounces) sugar
- 4 large eggs
- 1 tablespoon vanilla extract
- 1 cup pecans or walnuts, toasted and chopped coarse (optional)

1. Adjust oven rack to middle position and heat oven to 325 degrees. Make foil sling by folding 2 long sheets of aluminum foil so that they are as wide as 13 by 9-inch baking pan (one 13-inch sheet and one 9-inch sheet). Lay sheets of foil in pan perpendicular to one another, with extra foil hanging over edges of pan. Push foil into corners and up sides of pan, smoothing foil flush to pan. Grease foil and set aside.

2. Whisk flour, baking powder, and salt in medium bowl until combined; set aside.

3. Melt chocolate and butter in medium heatproof bowl set over saucepan of barely simmering water, stirring occasionally, until smooth. Off heat, gradually whisk in sugar. Add eggs, one at a time, whisking after each addition, until thoroughly combined. Whisk in vanilla. Add flour mixture in 3 additions, folding with rubber spatula until batter is completely smooth and homogeneous.

4. Transfer batter to prepared pan; spread batter into corners of pan and smooth surface. Sprinkle toasted nuts, if using, evenly over batter. Bake until toothpick inserted in center of brownies comes out with few moist crumbs attached, 30 to 35 minutes, rotating pan halfway through baking. Let brownies cool in pan on wire rack to room temperature, about 2 hours. Remove brownies from pan using foil. Cut brownies into 2-inch squares and serve. (Brownies can be stored at room temperature for up to 3 days.)

Turtle Brownies

WHY THIS RECIPE WORKS: Dark chocolate brownies, rich and chewy caramel, and pecans—it's hard to go wrong with turtle brownies. But recipes that call for brownie mixes and jarred caramel yield lackluster results. We wanted a brownie reminiscent of a candy turtle: rich, chewy, and chocolaty, with bittersweet caramel and pecans. We landed on using bittersweet chocolate for complexity and unsweetened for assertiveness. For the caramel, a little cream made the caramel pleasantly chewy and gooey, corn syrup kept it from crystallizing or turning gritty, and a little butter made it smooth and silky. We added half the brownie batter to the pan, drizzled some caramel on top, added the rest of the batter, and then drizzled and swirled more caramel on this layer. We poured even more caramel over the baked brownies to perfect our ultimate turtle brownies.

Turtle Brownies

MAKES 25 BROWNIES

To drizzle the caramel in step 4, use a ¼-cup dry measuring cup that has been sprayed with vegetable oil spray. If the caramel is too cool to be fluid, reheat it in the microwave. See Recipe Tutorial on page 608 for more details on this recipe.

CARAMEL

- 6 tablespoons heavy cream
- ¼ teaspoon salt
- ¼ cup water
- 2 tablespoons light corn syrup
- 1¼ cups (8¾ ounces) sugar
- 2 tablespoons unsalted butter
- 1 teaspoon vanilla extract

BROWNIES

- 8 **tablespoons unsalted butter, cut into 8 pieces**
- 4 **ounces bittersweet chocolate, chopped**
- 2 **ounces unsweetened chocolate, chopped**
- ¾ **cup (3¾ ounces) all-purpose flour**
- ½ **teaspoon baking powder**
- 2 **large eggs, room temperature**
- 1 **cup (7 ounces) sugar**
- ¼ **teaspoon salt**
- 2 **teaspoons vanilla extract**
- ⅔ **cup chopped pecans**
- ⅓ **cup semisweet chocolate chips (optional)**

GARNISH

- 25 **pecan halves, toasted**

1. FOR THE CARAMEL: Combine cream and salt in small bowl; stir well to dissolve salt. Combine water and corn syrup in heavy-bottomed 3-quart saucepan; pour sugar into center of saucepan, taking care not to let sugar granules touch sides of pan. Gently stir with clean spatula to moisten sugar thoroughly. Cover and bring to boil over medium-high heat; cook, covered and without stirring, until sugar is completely dissolved and liquid is clear, 3 to 5 minutes. Uncover and continue to cook, without stirring, until bubbles show faint golden color, 3 to 5 minutes more. Reduce heat to medium-low. Continue to cook (swirling occasionally) until caramel is light amber and registers 350 to 360 degrees, 1 to 3 minutes longer. Remove saucepan from heat and carefully add cream to center of pan; stir with whisk or spatula (mixture will bubble and steam vigorously) until cream is fully incorporated and bubbling subsides. Stir in butter and vanilla until combined; transfer caramel to microwave-safe measuring cup and set aside.

2. FOR THE BROWNIES: Adjust oven rack to lower-middle position and heat oven to 325 degrees. Make foil sling by folding 2 long sheets of aluminum foil so that they are as wide as 9-inch square baking pan. Lay sheets of foil in pan perpendicular to one another, with extra foil hanging over edges of pan. Push foil into corners and up sides of pan, smoothing foil flush to pan. Grease foil and set aside.

3. Melt butter, bittersweet chocolate, and unsweetened chocolate in medium heatproof bowl set over saucepan of almost-simmering water, stirring occasionally, until smooth and combined; set aside to cool slightly. Meanwhile, whisk flour and baking powder together in small bowl; set aside. When chocolate has cooled slightly, whisk eggs in large bowl to combine; add sugar, salt, and vanilla and whisk until incorporated. Add melted chocolate mixture to egg mixture; whisk until combined. Add flour mixture; stir with rubber spatula until almost combined. Add chopped pecans and chocolate chips, if using; mix until incorporated and no flour streaks remain.

4. Transfer half of brownie batter into prepared baking pan, spreading in even layer. Drizzle ¼ cup caramel over batter. Drop remaining batter in large mounds over caramel layer; spread evenly and into corners of pan with rubber spatula. Drizzle ¼ cup caramel over top. Using tip of butter knife, swirl caramel and batter. Bake until toothpick inserted in center of brownies comes out with few moist crumbs attached, 35 to 40 minutes,

rotating pan halfway through baking. Let brownies cool in pan on wire rack to room temperature, about 1½ hours.

5. Heat remaining caramel (you should have about ¾ cup) in microwave until warm and pourable but still thick (do not boil), 45 to 60 seconds, stirring once or twice; pour caramel over brownies. Spread caramel to cover surface. Refrigerate brownies, uncovered, at least 2 hours.

6. Remove brownies from pan using foil, loosening sides with paring knife, if needed. Using chef's knife, cut brownies into 25 evenly sized squares. Press 1 pecan half onto surface of each brownie. Serve chilled or at room temperature. (Brownies can be wrapped in plastic wrap and refrigerated for up to 3 days.)

Blondies

✓ **WHY THIS RECIPE WORKS:** Blondies are first cousins to both brownies and chocolate chip cookies. Although blondies are baked in a pan like brownies, the flavorings are similar to those in chocolate chip cookies—vanilla, butter, and brown sugar. They're sometimes laced with nuts and chocolate chips or butterscotch chips. But blondies can be pretty bland, floury, and dry. We set out to fix the blondie so it would be chewy but not dense, sweet but not cloying, and loaded with nuts and chocolate. We found that the key to chewy blondies was using melted, not creamed, butter because the creaming process incorporates too much air into the batter. For sweetening, light brown sugar lent the right amount of earthy molasses flavor. And combined with a substantial amount of vanilla extract and salt (to sharpen the sweetness), the light brown sugar developed a rich butterscotch flavor. To add both texture and flavor to the cookies, we included chocolate chips and pecans. We also tried butterscotch chips, but we found that they did little for this recipe. On a whim, we included white chocolate chips with the semisweet chips, and we were surprised that they produced the best blondies yet.

Blondies

MAKES 36 BARS

Walnuts can be substituted for the pecans. See Core Technique on page 595 for more details on preparing a foil sling.

- 1½ **cups (7½ ounces) all-purpose flour**
- 1 **teaspoon baking powder**
- ½ **teaspoon salt**
- 1½ **cups packed (10½ ounces) light brown sugar**
- 12 **tablespoons unsalted butter, melted and cooled**
- 2 **large eggs**
- 1½ **teaspoons vanilla extract**
- 1 **cup pecans, toasted and chopped coarse**
- ½ **cup (3 ounces) semisweet chocolate chips**
- ½ **cup (3 ounces) white chocolate chips**

1. Adjust oven rack to middle position and heat oven to 350 degrees. Make foil sling by folding 2 long sheets of aluminum foil so that they are as wide as 13 by 9-inch baking pan (one 13-inch sheet and one 9-inch sheet). Lay sheets of foil in pan perpendicular to one another, with extra foil hanging over edges of pan. Push foil into corners and up sides of pan, smoothing foil flush to pan. Grease foil and set aside.

2. Whisk flour, baking powder, and salt together in medium bowl; set aside.

3. Whisk sugar and melted butter together in medium bowl until combined. Add eggs and vanilla and mix well. Using rubber spatula, fold dry ingredients into egg mixture until just combined. Do not overmix. Fold in pecans and semisweet and white chocolate chips and turn batter into prepared pan, smoothing top with rubber spatula.

4. Bake until top is shiny and cracked and feels firm to touch, 22 to 25 minutes. Transfer pan to wire rack and let cool completely. Loosen edges with paring knife and remove bars from pan using foil. Cut into 2 by 1½-inch bars.

Congo Bars

Keep a close eye on the coconut as it toasts because it can burn easily.

Adjust oven rack to middle position and heat oven to 350 degrees. Toast 1½ cups unsweetened shredded coconut on a rimmed baking sheet, stirring 2 or 3 times, until light golden, 4 to 5 minutes. Let cool. Add toasted coconut with chocolate chips and nuts in step 3.

Lemon Squares

✔ **WHY THIS RECIPE WORKS:** For our perfect lemon bar recipe, we tackled the crust first. Granulated sugar is often the first option bakers turn to for the sort of crust we were after, but we discovered that confectioners' sugar gave us the most tender texture. The addition of a little cornstarch also helped move the crust in the melt-in-your-mouth direction. To make the filling lemony enough, we ended up using the juice from four lemons, plus some zest. Arriving at a smooth and pleasant texture involved eggs, a little flour for thickening, and, somewhat unexpectedly, milk, which seemed to balance the flavor with the texture.

Lemon Squares

MAKES 24 BARS

The lemon filling must be added to a warm crust, so be sure to prepare the filling while the crust chills and bakes. Alternatively, you can prepare the filling ahead of time and stir to blend just before pouring it into the crust. Any leftover bars can be sealed in plastic wrap and refrigerated for up to 2 days. See Core Technique on page 595 for more details on preparing a foil sling.

CRUST
- 1¾ **cups (8¾ ounces) all-purpose flour**
- ⅔ **cup (2⅔ ounces) confectioners' sugar, plus extra for garnish**
- ¼ **cup cornstarch**
- ¾ **teaspoon salt**
- 12 **tablespoons unsalted butter, chilled and cut into 1-inch pieces**

LEMON FILLING
- 4 **large eggs, lightly beaten**
- 1⅓ **cups (9⅓ ounces) granulated sugar**
- 3 **tablespoons all-purpose flour**

- 2 **teaspoons grated lemon zest plus ⅔ cup juice (4 lemons)**
- ⅓ **cup whole milk**
- ⅛ **teaspoon salt**

1. FOR THE CRUST: Adjust oven rack to middle position and heat oven to 350 degrees. Make foil sling by folding 2 long sheets of aluminum foil so that they are as wide as 13 by 9-inch baking pan (one 13-inch sheet and one 9-inch sheet). Lay sheets of foil in pan perpendicular to one another, with extra foil hanging over edges of pan. Push foil into corners and up sides of pan, smoothing foil flush to pan. Grease foil and set aside.

2. Process flour, confectioners' sugar, cornstarch, and salt in food processor until combined, 15 seconds. Add butter and process to blend, 8 to 10 seconds, then pulse until mixture is pale yellow and resembles coarse meal, about 3 pulses. (To do this by hand, mix flour, confectioners' sugar, cornstarch, and salt in medium bowl. Freeze butter and grate it on large holes of box grater into flour mixture. Toss butter pieces to coat. Rub pieces between fingers for a minute, until flour turns pale yellow and coarse.) Sprinkle mixture into prepared pan and press firmly with fingers into even ¼-inch layer over entire pan bottom and about ½ inch up sides. Refrigerate for 30 minutes, then bake until golden brown, about 20 minutes.

3. FOR THE FILLING: Whisk eggs, granulated sugar, and flour in medium bowl, then stir in lemon zest and juice, milk, and salt to blend well.

4. Reduce oven temperature to 325 degrees. Stir filling mixture to reblend; pour into warm crust. Bake until filling feels firm when touched lightly, about 20 minutes. Transfer pan to wire rack; let cool to near room temperature, at least 30 minutes. Remove lemon bars from pan using foil. Cut into squares and sieve confectioners' sugar over squares, if desired. (Bars can be refrigerated for up to 2 days; crust will soften slightly.

Raspberry Streusel Bars

✔ **WHY THIS RECIPE WORKS:** We realized early in developing our raspberry streusel bar recipe that the bottom crust needs to be firm and sturdy, while the topping should be light as well as sandy and dry so it can adhere to the filling. Since we didn't want to make two separate mixtures for the top and bottom layers, we used a butter-rich shortbread for the bottom, then rubbed more butter into the same dough to produce a great streusel topping. The filling for our raspberry streusel bar recipe also needed complementary textures: Good raspberry preserves made the filling sweet and viscous, while fresh raspberries—lightly mashed for easier spreading—combined with the preserves to produce a bright, well-rounded flavor and perfectly moist consistency.

Raspberry Streusel Bars

MAKES 20 BARS

This recipe can be made in a stand mixer or a food processor. Frozen raspberries can be substituted for fresh; be sure to defrost them before combining with the raspberry preserves. If your fresh raspberries are very tart, add only 1 or 2 teaspoons of lemon juice to the filling. See Core Technique on page 595 for more details on preparing a foil sling.

2½   cups (12½ ounces) all-purpose flour
⅔   cup (4⅔ ounces) granulated sugar
½   teaspoon salt
18   tablespoons unsalted butter, cut into ½-inch pieces and softened
¼   cup packed (1¾ ounces) brown sugar
½   cup (1½ ounces) old-fashioned rolled oats
½   cup pecans, chopped fine
¾   cup raspberry jam
3½   ounces (¾ cup) fresh raspberries
1   tablespoon lemon juice

1. Adjust oven rack to middle position and heat oven to 375 degrees. Make foil sling by folding 2 long sheets of aluminum foil so that they are as wide as 13 by 9-inch baking pan (one 13-inch sheet and one 9-inch sheet). Lay sheets of foil in pan perpendicular to one another, with extra foil hanging over edges of pan. Push foil into corners and up sides of pan, smoothing foil flush to pan. Grease foil and set aside.

2. Using stand mixer fitted with paddle, mix flour, granulated sugar, and salt at low speed until combined, about 10 seconds. Add 16 tablespoons butter, 1 piece at a time; then continue mixing until mixture resembles damp sand, 1 to 1½ minutes. (If using food processor, process flour, granulated sugar, and salt until combined, about 5 seconds. Scatter 16 tablespoons butter pieces over flour mixture and pulse until mixture resembles damp sand, about 20 pulses.)

3. Measure 1¼ cups flour mixture into medium bowl and set aside; distribute remaining flour mixture evenly in bottom of prepared baking pan. Using bottom of measuring cup, firmly press mixture into even layer to form bottom crust. Bake until edges begin to brown, 14 to 18 minutes.

4. While crust is baking, add brown sugar, oats, and pecans to reserved flour mixture; toss to combine. Work in remaining 2 tablespoons butter by rubbing mixture between fingers until butter is fully incorporated. Pinch mixture with fingers to create hazelnut-size clumps; set streusel aside.

5. Combine jam, raspberries, and lemon juice in small bowl; mash with fork until combined but some berry pieces remain.

6. Spread filling evenly over hot crust; sprinkle streusel topping evenly over filling (do not press streusel into filling). Return pan to oven and bake until topping is deep golden brown and filling is bubbling, 22 to 25 minutes, rotating pan halfway through baking. Transfer to wire rack and let cool to room temperature, 1 to 2 hours; remove bars from pan using foil. Cut into squares and serve. (Bars are best eaten the day they are baked but can stored at room temperature for up to 3 days; crust and streusel will soften slightly.)

Strawberry Streusel Bars
Thawed frozen strawberries will also work here.

Substitute strawberry jam and chopped fresh strawberries for raspberry jam and raspberries.

Blueberry Streusel Bars
Thawed frozen blueberries will also work here.

Substitute blueberry jam and fresh blueberries for raspberry jam and raspberries.

Pecan Bars

✔ **WHY THIS RECIPE WORKS:** Pecan bars often suffer the same problems as their pie counterpart. To avoid an overly sweet filling, we added a hefty amount of vanilla as well as a hit of bourbon (rum works, too) and plenty of salt. For a shortbread-like crust, the food processor not only made the mixing easy but also ensured we didn't overheat the butter. Adding nuts to the crust gave it appealing texture that was a good contrast to the filling. Partially baking the crust before adding the filling (as well as the requisite pecans) and returning the pan to the oven gave us a crust with the best texture and a deeper flavor.

Pecan Bars
MAKES 16 BARS
You can substitute dark rum for the bourbon if desired. See Core Technique on page 595 for more details on preparing a foil sling.

CRUST
1   cup (5 ounces) all-purpose flour
⅓   cup packed (2⅓ ounces) light brown sugar
¼   cup pecans, toasted and chopped coarse
1   teaspoon salt
¼   teaspoon baking powder
6   tablespoons unsalted butter, cut into ½-inch pieces and chilled

FILLING
½   cup packed (3½ ounces) light brown sugar
⅓   cup light corn syrup
4   tablespoons unsalted butter, melted and cooled
1   tablespoon bourbon
2   teaspoons vanilla extract
½   teaspoon salt
1   large egg
1¾   cups pecans, chopped coarse

1. FOR THE CRUST: Adjust oven rack to middle position and heat oven to 350 degrees. Make foil sling by folding 2 long sheets of aluminum foil so that they are as wide as 8-inch square baking pan. Lay sheets of foil in pan perpendicular to one another, with extra foil hanging over edges of pan. Push foil into corners and up sides of pan, smoothing foil flush to pan. Grease foil and set aside.

2. Process flour, sugar, pecans, salt, and baking powder together in food processor until combined, about 5 pulses. Sprinkle butter over top and pulse until mixture is pale yellow and resembles coarse cornmeal, about 8 pulses.

3. Sprinkle mixture into prepared pan and press into even layer with bottom of measuring cup. Bake crust until fragrant and beginning to brown, 20 to 24 minutes.

4. FOR THE FILLING: Meanwhile, whisk sugar, corn syrup, melted butter, bourbon, vanilla, and salt together in large bowl until sugar dissolves. Whisk in egg until combined.

5. Spread filling evenly over crust and sprinkle with pecans. Bake bars until top is brown and cracks start to form across surface, 25 to 30 minutes, rotating pan halfway through baking.

6. Set pan on wire rack and let bars cool completely, about 2 hours. Remove bars from pan using foil, cut into squares, and serve.

Inside This Chapter

CHAPTER 15

How to Make Cakes

Making a cake is a celebratory act, whether you are making a simple snack cake for after school or assembling a multitiered cake for a special occasion. Cakes generally rely on chemical leaveners to create rise in a rich, sweet batter. (A few cakes, such as angel food, rely solely on the power of egg whites for leavening.) In this chapter we cover making simple cakes like pound cake, coffee cake, sheet cake, and cheesecake, as well as more involved layer cakes, including assembly and decorating.

Getting Started

Types of Cakes

There are three basic ways to classify the world of cakes. The first way is to start with the pan. Bundt cakes wouldn't be Bundt cakes without their special pan. A second way to classify cakes is by construction. Is it a single-layer cake, a two-layer cake, or a four-layer cake? Finally, there is the divide between frosted and unfrosted. Layer cakes are always frosted, as are sheet cakes. However, rich cakes, especially those with fruit, might receive nothing more than a dusting of confectioners' sugar.

No matter how you classify cakes, it's helpful to understand the basic features of the following cakes that are especially popular among American home bakers.

POUND CAKE

These old-fashioned cakes were typically made with a pound each of butter, sugar, flour, and eggs. Modern formulas have been tweaked to produce a richer, more tender cake. Many recipes also rely on a little baking powder to lighten the load—traditional pound cakes are quite dense and heavy. Flavorings remain simple; perhaps a little vanilla and salt, or maybe a dash of citrus zest and juice. Pound cakes can be glazed but they are rarely frosted.

SNACK CAKE

Many simple cakes are baked in metal pans—either square or rectangular. Although many snack cakes are quite plain and demand some frosting, just as many are rich affairs made moist with fruits (such as apples) or molasses (think gingerbread) and don't require frosting.

COFFEE CAKE

This variant on the snack cake is topped with streusel. The tender crumbs (typically made with brown sugar, flour, and butter) offer a nice contrast to the tender yellow cake.

SHEET CAKE

A sheet cake is generally a simple cake (yellow, white, or chocolate) that is baked in a large rectangular pan and then frosted. A sheet cake serves a crowd, is relatively easy to prepare, and is easy to decorate—making it the classic choice for casual parties.

LAYER CAKE

A layer cake is made from simple cake layers (usually yellow cake, white cake, or chocolate cake) that are stacked, with frosting between each layer as well as on the top and sides of the construction. Fancier layer cakes might use jam, curd, or another type of filling between the layers as well as a separate frosting to coat the top and sides. Some layer cakes are made with relatively thick cake layers—each baked in its own pan. Others are made with thin layers, generally fashioned by sawing thicker cake layers in half horizontally.

BUNDT CAKE

The Bundt pan came to prominence in America after World War II. This pan is modeled on a classic German pan, called the *kugelhopf*, which is used to bake a yeasted bread. The Bundt pan ushered in a revolution in home baking. The height and fluted edges produce a cake that looks impressive. A dusting of confectioners' sugar or a drizzling with a simple glaze and the cake is ready to serve.

TUBE PAN CAKES

Like Bundt cakes, tube pan cakes are large cakes made in pans with a central tube that conducts heat, baking the batter from the outside and the inside. Chiffon cakes as well as angel food cakes are made in tube pans. Many tube pan cakes rely on egg foam (whole eggs for chiffon cakes, and just whites in the case of angel food) for height and volume.

Essential Equipment

Below are the basic pans and tools you will need to make most cakes.

HAND-HELD MIXER

The hand-held mixer's light weight and ease of use make it an essential tool for anyone who wants to bake, even if only occasionally. It's great for whipping cream or egg whites, creaming butter and sugar, or mixing a cake batter. We prefer simple, slim wire beaters to traditional beaters with flat metal strips around a center post since this post tends to be a good spot for batter to collect. For more details on what to look for, see page 28.

STAND MIXER

If you are a serious baker, dealing with a hand-held mixer for mixing cake batters will get tiresome. A stand mixer allows for hands-free mixing, which means multitasking—such as making additions to a batter or frosting as it's mixing—is far simpler. And with a motor more powerful than any you will find in a hand-held mixer, a stand mixer can handle bigger jobs. For more details on what to look for, see page 28.

METAL BAKING PANS

We use these versatile pans to bake snack cakes, sheet cakes, brownies, and bar cookies. It's good to own both 8- and 9-inch square metal pans as well as a 13 by 9-inch metal pan. We prefer metal to glass primarily because metal pans are typically coated with non-stick finishes For more details on what to look for, see page 26.

ROUND CAKE PANS

These pans come in two sizes, 8 and 9 inches, and are the classic choice for baking cake layers. Look for pans with straight rather than flared sides, and make sure those sides measure at least 2 inches tall. A nonstick surface is a must. For more details on what to look for, see page 26.

LOAF PANS

These pans are used for a variety of baking recipes, everything from simple pound cakes to quick breads and yeasted sandwich breads. An 8½ by 4½-inch pan with a nonstick surface is the most useful choice. For more details on what to look for, see page 27.

BUNDT PAN

The nooks and crannies mean that sticking is a threat with this pan. A heavy, cast-aluminum nonstick pan is a must. Clearly defined ridges produce a cake that has neat lines and that is less likely to stick. Handles are helpful. Standard recipes call for a 12-cup pan, although we have found that most recipes will work fine when baked in a 15-cup model. For more details on what to look for, see page 27.

TUBE PAN

The tube in this pan (aka an angel food cake pan) helps cakes bake faster and more evenly by providing more surface area in which to heat the batter. Heavier pans retain heat better and produce more even browning. Most tube pans are two pieces. We have found that pans with lighter bottoms tend to leak. Feet on the top rim are handy for elevating the upturned pan for cooling. For more details on what to look for, see page 26.

SPRINGFORM PAN

This two-piece pan allows the baker to make sticky cakes and skip inverting these cakes to remove them from the pan. A good springform pan will have a tight seal that minimizes leaking. A nonstick surface is a must, and handles make it easy to move this pan in and out of a water bath. We prefer models that don't leave an unsightly seam in the cheesecake where the buckle is fastened, and can be cleaned in the dishwasher. For more details on what to look for, see page 27.

MUFFIN TIN

This pan is used to make its namesake as well as cupcakes; standard models have ½-cup wells. A nonstick surface is essential, and extended rims allow you to easily remove the tin from the oven. A heavy tin will be less likely to buckle. For more details on what to look for, see page 27.

OFFSET SPATULA

A narrow, flexible, offset metal spatula is ideal for spreading fillings and frostings on horizontal surfaces. If you make cakes, you should have two: one with a blade about 8 inches long for frosting, and a smaller model with a 4-inch blade for small jobs like frosting cupcakes.

WIRE RACK

With rare exceptions, all cakes need to be cooled before icing and/or serving. A rack ensures even air circulation and quicker cooling. These racks are lightweight and easy to maneuver, making them useful when inverting a cake onto a platter. For more details on what to look for, see page 27.

PARCHMENT PAPER

A roll of parchment paper (or, better yet, flat sheets that fit baking sheets that you order online) is absolutely essential for lining pans and protecting platters. Don't bake a cake without it.

Essential Ingredients

A cake requires many ingredients—including butter, sugar, flour, milk, eggs, baking powder, and baking soda—that are used in many, many recipes. See chapter 1 (pages 39–44) and chapter 2 (pages 48–49) for detailed information on all these ingredients. Pay special attention to the section on flours on pages 42–43. Many cake recipes call for cake flour, a low-protein flour that is specially formulated to produce tender cakes. We strongly suggest using cake flour—and not all-purpose flour—when so instructed.

How to Cream Butter

ESSENTIAL EQUIPMENT

• stand mixer
• rubber spatula

Many cake recipes require that you beat butter and sugar together until pale and fluffy. This process, known as creaming, accomplishes two things. First, it makes the butter malleable, allowing other ingredients to be easily incorporated into the batter. Second, the sugar crystals act like tiny beaters, helping to incorporate air into the batter. These pockets of air expand in the oven, giving the cake lift. We cream butter in recipes like Classic Yellow Sheet Cake (page 668), Classic Yellow Bundt Cake (page 671), and many muffin recipes.

Starting this process with softened butter is a must. If the butter is too cold, it will be difficult to beat in sufficient air. At the same time, don't let the butter get too warm; if the butter is soft and greasy it won't hold air when creamed. We prefer to use a stand mixer, but a hand-held mixer will also work.

1. SOFTEN BUTTER

Remove unsalted butter from refrigerator and let warm on counter until its temperature reaches 65 to 67 degrees. Softened butter should give slightly when pressed but still hold its shape.
WHY? Chilled butter won't mix easily with the sugar or other ingredients in a cake batter, yielding a squat cake with a poor rise. The first step in many cake recipes is to let the butter soften on the counter until its temperature rises to 65 to 67 degrees. This will take 30 to 60 minutes, depending on the temperature in your kitchen. Don't attempt to soften butter in the microwave; you will end up overheating the butter, and as a result it won't cream properly.

2. BEAT BUTTER WITH SUGAR

Using stand mixer fitted with paddle, beat softened butter with sugar until incorporated.
WHY? The first step is to combine the butter and sugar. At this point, the mixture will be yellow, dense, and grainy. Start with the mixer at medium-low and gradually increase the speed to medium-high. Stop the mixer and scrape down the sides of the bowl as necessary with a rubber spatula.

3. CONTINUE BEATING UNTIL FLUFFY

Continue to beat butter and sugar until mixture is pale in color and fluffy in texture, about 3 minutes.
WHY? The goal when creaming is to produce a mixture that is pale and fluffy. This should take about 3 minutes if using a stand mixer set at medium-high speed. A hand-held mixer will work just fine, but might take an extra minute or two. Don't overbeat the butter; if the mixture begins to appear greasy, stop the mixer immediately.

How to Reverse Cream

In standard creaming, butter and sugar are beaten together, then the eggs are added, and finally the dry ingredients and liquid ingredients are added alternately. This process beats a fair amount of air into the butter, which yields a crumb that is fairly coarse. For many cakes, like our Classic White Sheet Cake (page 668) and Classic White Layer Cake (page 674), we prefer a method known as "reverse creaming." The softened butter is beaten into the dry ingredients, coating the proteins in the flour with fat and thus minimizing gluten development once the liquid ingredients are added. The result is a particularly tender cake with a delicate crumb. And because no air is beaten into the butter (as with standard creaming), the crumb is finer. We prefer to use a stand mixer for this process, but a hand-held mixer will also work.

ESSENTIAL EQUIPMENT

- chef's knife
- whisk
- stand mixer
- liquid measuring cup
- rubber spatula

1. SOFTEN BUTTER
Cut butter into 1-inch pieces and let soften on counter.
WHY? The butter must be softened (65 degrees or so) before it can be mixed into the dry ingredients. If the butter is too cold, the batter will be lumpy and unevenly mixed.

2. WHISK TOGETHER DRY INGREDIENTS
Whisk flour, sugar, baking powder, and salt together in bowl of stand mixer.
WHY? There's no need to sift flour for most cakes. A whisk aerates the flour and ensures that the leavening and salt are evenly distributed.

3. COMBINE LIQUIDS
Combine eggs, milk, and vanilla in large liquid measuring cup.
WHY? Once combined, the wet ingredients are easier to incorporate. Use the liquid measuring cup to measure out the milk first, then add the eggs and vanilla. Since the liquid will be added in two batches, keep the mixture in the measuring cup for easy pouring and measuring.

4. BEAT IN BUTTER
Fit stand mixer with paddle and with mixer on low speed, add softened butter, one piece at a time. Mix until only pea-size pieces remain, about 1 minute.
WHY? Adding the butter gradually ensures that the proteins in the flour are evenly coated with fat, which will inhibit gluten development once the liquid ingredients are added.

5. ADD LIQUID IN STAGES
Add half of milk mixture, increase speed to medium-high, and beat until fluffy. Reduce speed to medium-low, add remaining milk mixture, and beat until incorporated, about 30 seconds. Give batter final stir with rubber spatula.
WHY? The liquid will be absorbed more efficiently in two batches. The end result is an even batter with no streaks of flour.

How to Make a Pound Cake

ESSENTIAL EQUIPMENT

- 8½ by 4½-inch loaf pan
- measuring spoons
- liquid measuring cup
- food processor
- mixing bowls
- whisk
- fine-mesh strainer
- rubber spatula
- toothpick
- wire rack

Most classic pound cake recipes require ingredients at a precise temperature and a mixing method that is finicky. Why? Because there's no milk in a pound cake, you have to get the butter and eggs to form a proper emulsion. If the eggs are too cold or the butter is too warm, you end up with a curdled batter and a dense, heavy cake. We reimagined pound cake to make it utterly foolproof. We use melted butter and the food processor to ensure perfect emulsification. Unlike old-fashioned pound cakes that rely solely on eggs for leavening, we have found that a little baking powder provides just the right amount of lift—and does so reliably. We also use cake flour, which has less protein than all-purpose flour and ensures a tender crumb. Here we make a pound cake flavored with simply vanilla extract; for flavor variations on this recipe, see page 663.

1. GREASE AND FLOUR LOAF PAN

Coat 8½ by 4½-inch loaf pan with vegetable oil spray. Dust pan with several tablespoons of flour, making sure to thoroughly coat both bottom and sides of pan. Dump out excess flour.
WHY? A dusting of flour helps the pound cake climb the sides of the pan and prevents the edges from forming a hard, crusty lip. Make sure to grease the pan well to avoid any sticking. If you prefer, use baking spray with flour to grease and flour the pan in one step.

2. START BATTER IN FOOD PROCESSOR

Process 1¼ cups sugar, 4 large room-temperature eggs, and 1½ teaspoons vanilla extract in food processor until combined, about 10 seconds.
WHY? The food processor ensures that the liquid ingredients (the sugar dissolves, so it's considered a liquid) are evenly combined. Let the eggs come to room temperature on the counter (this will take about an hour) or warm them in a bowl of warm tap water for 5 minutes.

3. ADD HOT, MELTED BUTTER

Melt 16 tablespoons unsalted butter. With food processor running, pour hot butter through feed tube in steady stream until incorporated. Pour mixture into large bowl.
WHY? Using a food processor ensures perfect emulsification of the eggs and butter.

4. SIFT IN DRY INGREDIENTS

Whisk 1½ cups cake flour, 1 teaspoon baking powder, and ½ teaspoon salt together in separate bowl. Sift one-third flour mixture over egg mixture. Whisk to combine until only few streaks of flour remain. Repeat twice more with remaining flour mixture, then continue to whisk batter gently until most lumps are gone (do not overmix).
WHY? Because the batter is quite heavy and overmixing will lead to a heavy, dense cake, it's best to sift the dry ingredients with a fine-mesh strainer over the batter. This breaks them into small particles that will mix in more quickly.

5. TAP PAN ON COUNTER

Scrape batter into prepared pan and smooth top. Wipe any batter from sides of pan and gently tap pan on counter to release air bubbles.

WHY? Tapping the loaf pan on the counter releases large air bubbles from the batter that could cause tunneling (large holes) in the crumb of the finished cake.

6. BAKE, THEN COOL BRIEFLY IN PAN

Bake on middle rack in 350-degree oven until toothpick inserted in center comes out with few moist crumbs attached, 50 to 60 minutes, rotating pan halfway through baking. Cool cake in pan for 10 minutes on wire rack. Run paring knife around edge of cake to loosen, then flip cake onto wire rack. Turn cake right side up and cool completely, about 2 hours.

WHY? Rotating the cake as it bakes ensures even heating, even if your oven has hot spots. Cooling the cake briefly in the loaf pan allows it to firm up a little so that it won't break apart when you remove it from the pan. But don't let the cake cool too long in the pan, or it might be very hard to remove.

Troubleshooting Pound Cake

PROBLEM	SOLUTION
My loaf pan measures 9 by 5 inches. Can I use it?	Not unless you want a squat cake. Unfortunately, small differences in loaf pan sizes make significant differences in baked cakes. The interior dimensions of the pan should be 8½ inches long and 4½ inches across. If you use a wider, longer pan, the cake won't rise properly and won't have that attractive split down the center of the top.
I don't have cake flour. Can I use all-purpose?	If you bake cakes, you should keep cake flour on hand. That said, you can lower the protein of regular all-purpose flour by combining it with a little cornstarch. For this recipe, replace the cake flour with 1⅓ cups all-purpose flour mixed with 3 tablespoons cornstarch.

How to Make a Coffee Cake

ESSENTIAL EQUIPMENT

- mixing bowls
- whisk
- rubber spatula
- 9-inch round cake pans (2)
- toothpick
- wire rack

Everybody should have a basic coffee cake like this one in their repertoire. Our recipe serves 12—enough for a crowd at brunch. This heavy batter bakes up best in two small pans (when we tried a large pan the edges became overcooked and dry as we waited for the center to cook through). You can cut the recipe in half and make one cake (use one large egg plus one yolk). However, because the batter and topping can be made in advance, we suggest making two cakes and freezing one for later use. Simply portion batter and topping into pans as directed and wrap tightly in plastic wrap. Cake pans can be refrigerated for 24 hours (so you can pop the pans into the oven in the morning, just before guests arrive) or frozen for one month. Bake cakes straight from the refrigerator or freezer (do not thaw before baking); increase the baking time to 30 to 35 minutes if refrigerated, or 40 to 45 minutes if frozen. This simple coffee cake can be jazzed up by making some ingredient additions; see the chart on opposite page.

1. MAKE STREUSEL BY HAND

Place ⅓ cup packed light brown sugar, ⅓ cup granulated sugar, and ⅓ cup all-purpose flour in bowl. Add 4 tablespoons softened unsalted butter and 1 tablespoon ground cinnamon. Using your fingers, work ingredients until they have texture of wet sand. Stir in 1 cup chopped pecans or walnuts. Set streusel mixture aside.

WHY? No need to drag out a mixer or processor here—using your fingers does the job quickly and produces a topping with bigger, crunchier crumbs. Make sure the butter is soft enough to work into the dry ingredients.

2. COMBINE DRY INGREDIENTS

Whisk 3 cups all-purpose flour, 1 tablespoon baking powder, 1 teaspoon baking soda, 1 teaspoon ground cinnamon, and ¼ teaspoon salt together in large bowl.

WHY? No need to sift ingredients; a whisk does a fine job. Make sure to use a bowl that is large enough to hold the finished batter.

3. COMBINE WET INGREDIENTS THEN FOLD INTO DRY

Whisk 1¾ cups sour cream, 1 cup packed light brown sugar, 1 cup granulated sugar, 3 large eggs, and 7 tablespoons melted and cooled unsalted butter together in bowl until smooth. Gently fold wet ingredients into dry ingredients until just combined; do not overmix.

WHY? It's important not to overmix the batter, or the cakes will turn out tough and dense. Use a rubber spatula to do the mixing; it's OK to leave a few streaks of flour.

4. DIVIDE BATTER

Scrape batter into 2 greased 9-inch round cake pans.

WHY? If you tried to bake all this batter in one large pan, the cake would bake unevenly. That's because the batter is quite thick and the streusel topping so generous. We find that two smaller pans yield perfectly baked coffee cake.

5. SMOOTH TOPS, SPRINKLE WITH STREUSEL
Sprinkle streusel evenly over top of smoothed batter in both pans.

WHY? Because the batter is so thick, you will need to smooth it out with a rubber spatula before covering the batter the streusel.

6. DON'T OVERBAKE
Place both pans on middle rack in 350-degree oven and bake until topping looks crisp and toasted and toothpick inserted into center comes out with few moist crumbs attached, 25 to 30 minutes, switching and rotating pans halfway through baking. Let cakes cool on wire rack for at least 15 minutes before serving.

WHY? Baking both cakes on the same rack keeps heat circulating evenly in the oven. Do switch the position of the pans to guarantee even baking, and don't overbake the cake or it will be very dry.

Customizing Coffee Cake

It's easy to flavor this basic coffee cake recipe by adding grated citrus zest to the dry ingredients in step 2, or folding fruit (fresh or dried) into the batter once step 3 is nearly complete.

TO MAKE	ADD TO DRY INGREDIENTS	FOLD INTO BATTER
Lemon-Blueberry Coffee Cake	1 teaspoon grated lemon zest	2 cups fresh or frozen (not thawed) blueberries tossed with 1 tablespoon flour
Apricot-Orange Coffee Cake	1 teaspoon grated orange zest	1 cup chopped dried apricots
Cranberry-Orange Coffee Cake	1 teaspoon grated orange zest	1 cup dried cranberries
Cherry-Orange Coffee Cake	1 teaspoon grated orange zest	1 cup dried cherries

How to Make a Sheet Cake

A basic sheet cake will feed a small crowd, is quite simple to execute, and is easy to decorate; here we make a yellow sheet cake. It's a classic choice for casual parties. You can also convert a sheet cake recipe into a layer cake. Simply divide the batter between two 9-inch round cake pans and bake both pans on the middle oven rack for 20 to 25 minutes (see How to Prepare Cake Pans, page 638, and How to Bake Cake Layers, page 639). Or bake the sheet cake as directed and then make a squared-off layer cake. Cut the cooled sheet cake in half crosswise to yield two layers, each measuring 6½ by 9 inches. Note that this batter can also be used to make 24 yellow cupcakes (see page 668 for instructions). Also see How to Cream Butter (page 630) and How to Make Buttercream Frosting (page 640).

- 13 by 9-inch metal baking pan
- parchment paper
- whisk
- mixing bowls
- stand mixer
- rubber spatula
- toothpick
- paring knife
- wire rack
- serving platter

1. PREPARE PAN

Grease 13 by 9-inch metal baking pan and line bottom of pan with parchment paper. Grease parchment, then flour pan.

WHY? The greased-and-floured parchment serves two purposes—it prevents sticking and it also helps keep the cake from cracking when it's removed from the pan.

2. CREAM BUTTER AND SUGAR, ADD EGGS

Whisk 2¾ cups (11 ounces) cake flour, 2 teaspoons baking powder, and ¾ teaspoon salt together in bowl and set aside. Using stand mixer fitted with paddle, beat 16 tablespoons softened unsalted butter and 1¾ cups (12¼ ounces) sugar on medium-high speed until pale and fluffy, about 3 minutes. Beat in 4 large room-temperature eggs, one at a time, then 1 tablespoon vanilla extract, until combined.

WHY? Creaming the softened butter with the sugar lightens the butter so that the other ingredients will be easy to incorporate into the batter. Creaming also aerates the butter and helps the cake rise. Adding the eggs one a time ensures that the batter remains emulsified and does not curdle.

3. ALTERNATE DRY INGREDIENTS AND MILK

Reduce mixer speed to low and beat in one-third of flour mixture, followed by ¾ cup room-temperature whole milk. Repeat with half of remaining flour mixture and another ¾ cup milk. Beat in remaining flour mixture until just incorporated. Scrape down bowl as needed.

WHY? Using room-temperature milk and adding it in two batches ensures a smooth, emulsified batter. When adding the last batch of flour, stop once the batter is smooth. Overbeating can cause the cake to bake up tough and dry.

4. SCRAPE INTO PAN

Give batter final stir with rubber spatula to make sure it is thoroughly combined. Scrape batter into prepared pan, smooth top, then gently tap pan on counter to release air bubbles.

WHY? Rather than using the stand mixer to find every last trace of flour, use your rubber spatula—it's far gentler and helps prevent excess gluten from developing. Smooth the batter in the pan so that the cake bakes up flat, and tap the pan on the counter to release air bubbles that could cause tunnels in the crumb.

5. TEST FOR DONENESS

Bake on middle rack in 350-degree oven until toothpick inserted in center comes out with few moist crumbs attached, 25 to 30 minutes, rotating pan halfway through baking.

WHY? Don't overbake this large cake. Because of its size, the edges already have a tendency to dry out. Rotate the pan to counteract the effect of any hot spots in your oven.

6. LET CAKE COOL, THEN FLIP ONTO RACK

Let cake cool completely in pan, about 2 hours. Run paring knife around edge of cake and flip cake out onto wire rack.

WHY? If you attempt to remove the cake from the pan too early, it is much more likely to crack and break in the process. Make sure to loosen the edges of the cake from the pan with a paring knife before attempting to invert the cake onto a rack. If you notice your cake looks sunken in the middle once cooled, this means you've underbaked the cake. But don't worry, you can usually camouflage it with a little extra frosting. (However, if it's severely sunken, we suggest saving the cake for making a trifle.)

7. PEEL OFF PARCHMENT

Peel parchment off bottom of cake. Place large inverted platter over cake.

WHY? The parchment has done its job and can be peeled off. Don't worry if the parchment takes some crumbs with it—this will be the bottom of the cake. Make sure to choose a flat platter that is large enough to accommodate the cake.

8. INVERT ONTO PLATTER

Holding both rack and platter firmly, gently flip cake right side up onto platter. Spread frosting evenly over top and sides of cake and serve.

WHY? This "sandwich and flip" method ensures that the large cake doesn't crack as you turn it right side up on the platter. Let the cake cool completely before frosting.

How to Prepare Cake Pans

To ensure a dependable release every time, cake pans should be greased and floured and lined with parchment paper. The steps below show how to prepare a round cake pan; however, the same method can be used to prepare square or 13 by 9-inch cake pans. Don't skip this crucial step. If the pan is improperly prepared, the cake will stick and break into pieces as you attempt to remove it.

ESSENTIAL EQUIPMENT

- cake pan(s)
- parchment paper
- pencil or pen
- scissors

1. TRACE CIRCLE
Place cake pan on sheet of parchment paper and trace around bottom of pan with pencil or pen.
WHY? The trick to getting a piece of parchment that fits perfectly into a round cake pan is to trace the outline of the bottom of the pan onto a piece of parchment paper. When cutting out the outline, cut on the inside of the line so that the round fits snugly inside the pan.

2. GREASE PAN
Evenly spray bottom and sides of cake pan with vegetable oil spray.
WHY? It's imperative to grease the pan—otherwise the cake is sure to stick. Since we also grease the parchment (see step 4), we have found it's easiest to use vegetable oil spray. However, softened butter or vegetable shortening will also work (greasing the parchment will just be a bit more difficult). Make sure to coat both the bottom and sides of the pan evenly. If you a miss a spot, the cake will stick.

3. LINE PAN WITH PAPER
Fit trimmed piece of parchment into pan.
WHY? The paper prevents the formation of a tough outer crust and helps the cake hold together when it is removed from the pan.

4. GREASE PARCHMENT AND FLOUR PAN
Spray parchment with vegetable oil spray, then sprinkle several tablespoons of flour into pan. Shake and rotate pan to coat evenly with flour. Once pan is coated, shake out excess flour.
WHY? Greasing and flouring the parchment ensure it can be peeled off the baked cake cleanly. The dusting of flour also prevents the cake batter from rising too quickly up the sides of the pan and forming a hard, crusty lip.

How to Bake Cake Layers

Whether you're using the creaming or reverse-creaming method (see pages 630 and 631), at some point the cake batter will be scraped into prepared pans and baked. The steps that follow show how to portion, bake, and cool cake layers. Portioning with a scale may seem fussy, but it's all too easy to pour more batter into one pan, and the difference in layer thickness is noticeable once the assembled cake is sliced. Weighing the pans is simple and guarantees you'll have a picture-perfect cake. Note that while a sheet cake cools in the pan for several hours, these cakes should only cool in the pan for 10 minutes. Also see How to Prepare Cake Pans (opposite) and How to Frost a Layer Cake (page 642).

ESSENTIAL EQUIPMENT

- round cake pans (2)
- rubber spatula
- digital scale
- toothpick
- wire racks (2)

1. DIVIDE EVENLY, THEN TAP ON COUNTER

Divide batter evenly between prepared pans. Gently tap pans on counter to release air bubbles.
WHY? If you want even layers, you need to portion the batter evenly. Rather than eyeballing it, weigh the filled pans and make sure each pan contains the same amount of batter. Make sure the pans are greased, floured, and lined with parchment paper before starting. Tapping releases air bubbles that may have formed during mixing; if left in the batter these bubbles can cause tunnels in the baked crumb.

2. BAKE, SWITCH, AND TEST

Bake cake layers side by side on middle oven rack until toothpick inserted in center comes out clean, switching and rotating position of cake pans at halfway mark in baking time.
WHY? If you stack the cake pans on different racks in the oven, you interrupt the airflow and the cakes will bake at different rates. Switch the position of the pans once half the baking time has elapsed to mitigate any side-to-side heating differences. Use a toothpick to test for doneness. If still in doubt, press the top of the cake lightly with your finger. It should spring back.

3. COOL BRIEFLY IN PAN, THEN TURN OUT

Transfer pans to wire racks and cool for 10 minutes. Working with one pan at a time, set wire rack on top of pan. Flip cake out of pan onto wire rack. Flip cake onto second wire rack so that cake layer is right side up.
WHY? Cooling on a wire rack allows air to circulate so that the cakes cool more quickly, preventing further cooking. Don't attempt to remove the cakes from the pans too soon. They need to firm slightly to ensure they won't break apart. That said, don't let cakes stay in pans for more than 10 minutes; as they continue to cool they are also more likely to fuse to the metal surface and become increasingly difficult to remove in one piece. Always cool cake layers completely before wrapping in plastic or frosting them.

How to Make Buttercream Frosting

ESSENTIAL EQUIPMENT

• stand mixer
• small saucepan
• heatproof rubber spatula

Classic American frosting is often nothing more than softened butter beaten with confectioners' sugar and some vanilla extract or other flavorings. While adequate, this "quick" frosting is very sweet and can have a slightly gritty texture. We think it's worth the time investment to make a buttercream frosting. It's less sweet, and the texture is silky and rich because the frosting contains eggs. Because you need to pour hot sugar syrup into the bowl with the eggs while the mixer is running, we find this operation is much, much simpler in a stand mixer. If you don't have a stand mixer, you will need to stabilize the mixing bowl with a towel so that one hand can operate the hand-held mixer while the other pours in the hot syrup.

This frosting can be colored; just beat a little food coloring in at the end. Use the frosting right away or refrigerate it for up to three days. If refrigerated, let it soften on the counter for 2 hours, then beat it with the mixer on medium speed until smooth, 2 to 5 minutes. Below is the general process; see chart opposite for ingredient amounts for various cake sizes. For flavor variations, see page 670.

1. WHIP EGG YOLKS

Using stand mixer fitted with whisk, whip egg yolks on medium speed until slightly thickened and pale yellow, 4 to 6 minutes.

WHY? You want to make sure that the egg yolks are thick and pale before you pour the sugar mixture into the mixing bowl or else the mixture won't come together properly. While some recipes call for whole eggs, we prefer the richer texture achieved by using just the yolks. Whipping egg yolks is not as fussy as whipping egg whites, but it is still important that the bowl and beaters are clean before adding the yolks.

2. MEANWHILE, COOK SUGAR AND CORN SYRUP

While egg yolks are whipping, bring sugar and corn syrup to boil in small saucepan over medium heat, stirring occasionally to dissolve sugar, about 3 minutes.

WHY? It's important to heat the sugar syrup at the same time the yolks are whipping so that the hot syrup will be ready once the yolks are done. Don't let the syrup cool off. It should be just off the boil when used in the next step. While classic French recipes rely on just sugar, we find that the corn syrup gives the finished buttercream a fluid but stable consistency. The corn syrup also makes it easy to melt the sugar.

3. SLOWLY ADD HOT SYRUP

With mixer turned to low, pour hot sugar syrup into whipped egg yolks without hitting side of bowl or beaters.

WHY? Pouring the hot syrup into the egg yolks gently raises their temperature to a safe level. However, if you dump the syrup into the bowl all at once you can scramble the eggs. For this reason, make sure the mixer is on and the pouring goes slowly. Because the mixer is running, the syrup can make a mess if it hits the whisk attachment. Aim to pour the syrup into the bowl so that it avoids both the whisk and the sides of the bowl (where it can seize up).

4. WHIP UNTIL COOL

Increase mixer speed to medium-high and whip egg yolk and syrup mixture until light and fluffy and bowl is no longer warm, 5 to 10 minutes.

WHY? Whipping aerates the yolk mixture and makes it easier to add the butter. Whipping also causes heat to dissipate. If you add soft butter to a warm mixture it will break and create pools of grease. If the bowl feels warm, keeping whipping.

5. BEAT IN SOFTENED BUTTER

Reduce mixer speed to medium-low and add vanilla and salt. Gradually add softened butter, one piece at a time, until completely incorporated, about 2 minutes.

WHY? It's imperative to use softened butter here. Cold butter will clump up and you will have to overbeat the frosting to smooth it back out. Softened butter incorporates quickly and smoothly. Cut each stick of butter into quarters to speed softening, which will take about 30 minutes on the counter.

6. WHIP UNTIL SILKY SMOOTH

Increase mixer speed to medium-high and whip buttercream until smooth and silky, about 2 minutes.

WHY? Once the last of the butter has been added, you want to continue whipping the frosting until the texture is lightened. You can go overboard here, so stop the mixer once the texture is right. If the finished frosting looks curdled, the butter was probably too cold. Wrap a wet, hot towel around the mixing bowl and continue to whip until smooth, another minute or two.

Formula for Buttercream Frosting

TO FROST	EGG YOLKS	SUGAR	LIGHT CORN SYRUP	VANILLA EXTRACT	SALT	BUTTER
24 cupcakes (3 cups frosting)	4 large	⅔ cup	⅓ cup	2 teaspoons	⅛ teaspoon	3½ sticks
2-layer cake or sheet cake (4 cups frosting)	6 large	¾ cup	½ cup	2½ teaspoons	¼ teaspoon	4 sticks
3-layer cake (5 cups frosting)	8 large	1 cup	¾ cup	1 tablespoon	¼ teaspoon	5 sticks

How to Frost a Layer Cake

ESSENTIAL EQUIPMENT

- serrated knife
- cake stand or large, flat platter
- parchment paper
- large offset spatula
- glass filled with warm water

Most home cooks think a bakery-smooth frosted cake is well beyond their ability, so they make do with a cake that "looks homemade." The truth is that a polished appearance is easy if you have the right tools and use the right technique. Starting with flat layers is absolutely essential. If the layers aren't flat, you will end up using too much frosting in places and the end results might still be uneven. Regularly dipping the spatula into a glass of warm water will keep extra frosting from piling up on the spatula and will make sure the frosting is smooth. It's essential to start with cool cake layers. If the layers are still warm, the frosting will start to melt and you will have a mess on your hands. While not essential, a turntable-style cake stand elevates the cake, giving the baker a better view and making it possible to hold the spatula steady while rotating the stand. It improves the likelihood of seamless frosting and makes the process easier. However, if you don't own one, a fixed cake stand or even a large flat platter will work fine. Also see How to Bake Cake Layers (page 639), How to Make Buttercream Frosting (page 640), and How to Decorate a Layer Cake (page 644).

1. REMOVE THE DOME
Using serrated knife, gently slice back and forth with sawing motion to remove domed portion from each cake layer.

WHY? Cake layers with a domed top are difficult to stack and frost. If your layers dome, trim enough of the top to ensure a flat surface. Brush crumbs off the cake since they can mar the frosting.

2. KEEP PLATTER CLEAN
Cover edges of cake stand or platter with strips of parchment paper.

WHY? The strips of parchment paper ensure that extra frosting doesn't end up on the platter. Once the cake is frosted, you can slide out and discard the parchment. While a footed cake stand elevates the cake and will make frosting easier, any large, flat platter (preferably one without a rim) can be used.

3. ANCHOR THE CAKE
Dollop small amount of frosting in center of cake stand or platter.

WHY? The frosting will glue the bottom layer to the cake stand or platter and prevent it from sliding around as you frost it.

4. FROST FIRST LAYER
Dollop large portion of frosting in center of cake layer. Spread frosting into even layer right to edge of cake.

WHY? An offset spatula makes it easy to push the frosting out from the center of the cake layer to the edges. The thin blade is flexible so it won't tear the cake, and the offset handle keeps your hand out of the way.

5. ALIGN SECOND LAYER
Place second layer on top, making sure it is aligned with first layer.

WHY? As you place the top layer, you don't want to push down on it or you risk squeezing the frosting out the sides of the cake.

6. FROST TOP, THEN SIDES

Spread more frosting over top layer, push-ing frosting slightly over edge of cake. Gather several tablespoons of frosting with tip of off-set spatula and gently smear onto side of cake. Repeat until side is covered with frosting.

WHY? You need a more gentle approach to frosting the side of the cake. If you spread a large amount of frosting you risk getting crumbs in the frosting or, worse, causing the layers to shift. Use a gentle motion and don't press too hard. Clean off the spatula in a glass filled with warm water as needed.

7. SMOOTH OUT ROUGH SPOTS

Gently run edge of spatula around sides to smooth out bumps and tidy area where frosting on top and sides merge.

WHY? The super-thin edge of an offset spatula will pick up excess blobs of frosting and fill any holes. You can run the edge of the spatula over the top of the cake to give it a smooth look, too. Remove the strips of parchment and the cake is ready to serve. (If decorating the frosted cake, leave the parchment in place.)

Troubleshooting Frosting a Layer Cake

PROBLEM	SOLUTION
I'm getting crumbs into the frosting. How should I remove them?	Make sure to brush excess crumbs from the cake layers before you start. A small pastry brush is ideal for this. If you see crumbs marring the frosting, consider a two-stage approach. First, cover the entire cake with a thin base layer of frosting, then refrigerate the cake for 15 to 30 minutes, just long enough for the frosting (with the crumbs) to firm up. Now, use the remaining frosting to cover the top and sides of the cake with a finish coat. Because the base layer will be firm, the crumbs should stay in place and not mar the final coat.
What's the best way to store a cake if I don't have a domed cake stand?	Once the cake is frosted it should be served within a few hours, or refrigerated for up to one day. If your cake is on a platter, the bowl from your salad spinner will probably be large enough to invert over the cake and protect it until serving time. If the cake has been refrigerated, make sure to remove it at least one hour before serving time—cakes are best served at room temperature.
I always put too much or too little frosting between layers.	Slicing into a layer cake only to realize you put too much or too little frosting between layers (and thus too much or too little on the exterior) is always disappointing after all that effort. Our cake recipes that make two 9-inch layers require 4 cups of frosting. We specify to spread about 1½ cups frosting between the layers and 1½ cups on top of the cake, and the remainder of the frosting (about 1 cup) goes around the sides. For a three-layer cake, you'll need 5 cups of frosting (1¼ cups between layers and on top and 1¼ cups for the perimeter). If you aren't sure, you can always measure. It's a small amount of effort that ensures a perfect-looking layer cake.

How to Decorate a Layer Cake

ESSENTIAL EQUIPMENT

- soupspoon
- cake comb or fork
- vegetable peeler

Even simple decorations can give a frosted layer cake a professional look. The ideas on this page are very basic; if you want to try piping decorations with a pastry bag, see pages 646–647. Note that for all but the first technique below, it's imperative to create a smooth finish on the frosted cake. To do this, use the edge of an offset spatula to create a level surface for decorating (see the last step on page 643). When decorating a cake, leave the strips of parchment used to protect the platter during the frosting process in place. Any excess decoration will fall onto the parchment rather than the platter. Once you're finished decorating, carefully remove and discard the parchment. The equipment needed will depend on the option you choose.

A. GIVE FROSTING TEXTURE

Press back of soupspoon into frosting, then twirl spoon as you lift it away.

WHY? One of the simplest ways to decorate a cake is to give the frosting some texture. To make wavy lines or a stripe pattern, simply drag a cake comb (or fork) around the cake's sides.

B. ADORN JUST THE BOTTOM EDGE

Use fingers to gently press toasted sliced nuts, one at a time, around bottom edge of cake.

WHY? This simple trick makes the cake look elegant and also camouflages any messiness at the base of the cake. Instead of nuts, you can also use fruit, sprinkles, candies, or even cookies.

C. COVER SIDES COMPLETELY

Press small handful of crushed candies into sides of frosted cake.

WHY? This is a great way to hide a messy or uneven frosting job. It also looks great. Instead of crushed candies, you can also use sprinkles, toasted nuts, shredded coconut (toasted or plain), chocolate shavings (made with a vegetable peeler), or crushed cookies (choose something fairly plain like chocolate wafer cookies).

D. MARK EACH SLICE

Mark each slice of cake with small garnish, such as two raspberries and tiny sprig of fresh mint.

WHY? Marking each slice helps guide your knife as you slice the cake. Cut between the garnishes so that each slice has a garnish in the center. The garnish can represent the flavors inside the cake (such as fruit or nuts) or simply be decorative.

E. COVER TOP COMPLETELY

Cover top of cake completely with shavings made by running sharp vegetable peeler over block of chocolate.

WHY? Covering the top can hide imperfections in the frosting and will make a short cake look taller and more impressive. Instead of chocolate shavings, also try fruit or shaved coconut.

How to Cut Cake Layers

Some recipes call for cutting a baked cake layer into two thinner layers before frosting. For instance, most four-layer cakes actually require baking two cake layers, which are each halved. As you can imagine, absolute precision is necessary when cutting a single cake into two layers. If the layers are cut unevenly, the thinner portion will be extremely delicate and can fall apart as you attempt to fill and frost the cake. Even if the layers do remain intact, a cake with layers of varying thicknesses will look odd. Here's how to get perfectly even layers. Also see How to Frost a Layer Cake (page 642).

ESSENTIAL EQUIPMENT

- cutting board
- kitchen ruler
- paring knife
- serrated knife

1. MEASURE AND MARK

Measure height of cake. Use paring knife to mark midpoint at several places around sides of cake. **WHY?** In order to ensure that each cake layer is the same height, you must use a ruler. If the cake is slightly domed, account for this and measure from the top of the dome. If the cake is seriously domed, trim the domed top first. Marking the sides of the cake provides you with handy guides you will use in the next step to ensure that the layers have an even thickness.

2. SCORE SIDES

Using marks as guide, score entire circumference of cake with long serrated knife.
WHY? Scoring the side of the cake provides a clear entry point for the knife in the next step. Make sure to hold the knife parallel to your work surface. A knife with a 10-inch blade is ideal because the blade is long enough to cut across the entire cake with each stroke.

3. SAW SLOWLY

Following score lines, run knife around cake several times, slowly cutting inward. Once knife is inside cake, use back-and-forth motion. Keep your hand on top of cake and make sure knife remains aligned with scoring around sides.
WHY? The top hand keeps the cake from moving. Working slowly lets you check often to see that the knife is staying aligned with the scoring around the edge.

4. LIFT AND SEPARATE

Once knife cuts through cake, separate layers, gently inserting your fingers between them. Lift top layer and place it on counter.
WHY? Once the knife work is done, it's best to separate the layers. If there are a lot of crumbs, use your hands or a pastry brush to get them off the cake layers; those crumbs will otherwise mar the appearance of the frosting. Each layer can be wrapped in plastic wrap if frosting later.

How to Use a Pastry Bag

ESSENTIAL EQUIPMENT

A pastry bag has a variety of uses, from decorating cakes and cookies to filling pastries. A large bag (roughly 18 inches long) will give you enough length to grip and twist the top. While canvas is traditional, we like materials such as plastic and coated canvas that are easier to clean.

While there are many different tips, most bags come with only a few basic ones. We find the following tips are most helpful: a small line tip for writing a message on a frosted cake, a star tip for decorating, and a large tip for piping cookies. If you plan on decorating cakes often, you will want to invest in a more extensive set of tips, capable of producing everything from flowers to a basket weave design. Most tip sets also include a handy two-piece item called a coupler, which allows you to switch out tips on a single pastry bag.

- pastry bag and tips
- rubber spatula
- parchment paper

1. FIT TIP INSIDE BAG

Holding bag in one hand, fold top down about halfway. Insert selected tip into point of bag and press it securely in place.

WHY? Folding down the top of the bag will make it easier to fill the bag (and it will be less messy). Ideally, about ½ inch of the tip should be peeking through the hole in the bag. You might need to trim the end of the bag to make the hole larger. Be careful, though; if the hole is too big the force of the frosting will pop the tip through the hole and you will have a mess on your hands—and probably on your cake.

2. FILL BAG

Scrape frosting into bag until bag is half full.

WHY? Don't overfill the bag or you will end up squeezing frosting out the top and onto your hands.

3. SQUEEZE OUT AIR

Pull up sides of bag, push down frosting, and twist tightly. Push down on bag to squeeze air out and move frosting into tip.

WHY? The twisted top serves two functions: It helps keep the frosting away from your hands, and it also gives you a place to exert pressure that will start the flow of frosting through and out the tip. Make sure to squeeze out air bubbles in the frosting; if you don't, the frosting will come out of the tip in spurts. Ideally, the frosting should flow through the tip at a steady, even pace.

4. PRACTICE FIRST

Grab base of bag, twist, and squeeze to pipe out frosting. Practice briefly on sheet of parchment paper before decorating cake.

WHY? Steady pressure with both hands will keep the frosting flowing. Make sure the top hand is keeping the top of the bag twisted. Practicing on parchment lets you confirm that the right tip has been installed and gives you a chance to remove air bubbles that often form in the initial flow of frosting.

How to Make Professional-Style Cake Decorations

With a few specialty tips and a good pastry bag, you can create a wide range of professional-looking decorations. The four decorations shown here are classic. We strongly suggest practicing (on parchment paper or a "practice" cake) before attempting these decorations on a cake you plan to serve at a special occasion. If you want to switch tips on the icing bag, owning a coupler (which is used in the photos below) is worthwhile. If you buy a set of tips, a coupler is typically included; you can also purchase one separately at most kitchen supply stores. The tip required will depend on the option you choose.

ESSENTIAL EQUIPMENT

- pastry bag
- rubber spatula
- round tip
- closed star tip
- star or leaf tip
- petal tip

A. MAKE DOT PATTERN

Use round tip and hold bag perpendicular to surface of cake. Pipe out small amount of frosting, then stop piping and pull bag straight away from cake.

WHY? Dots are easy to make and can look elegant when piped into a pattern. Space individual dots evenly across the top and sides of the cake, or group several dots as shown here. The most important thing is to pull the tip away from the cake after forming each dot. This will ensure neat dots that hold their shape.

B. MAKE ROSETTES

Use closed star tip and hold bag perpendicular to surface of cake. Slowly pipe out frosting while directing tip in tight, circular motion, then stop piping and pull bag straight away from cake.

WHY? A rosette is a classic design that looks attractive on its own, or it can be garnished with a small piece of fruit or chocolate shavings. A rosette can also finish off a swag (see D).

C. MAKE SHELL BORDER

Use star or leaf tip and hold bag at angle to surface of cake. Pipe out small amount of frosting, then lightly draw tip forward while reducing flow of frosting to make tail. Pipe next ruffle on tail of previous one.

WHY? A shell (or ruffled) border along the bottom and top edge is a festive finish, and it's also ideal for covering the awkward space between the cake and the platter.

D. MAKE A SWAG

Use petal tip and hold bag at slight angle to surface of cake. With tip very close to cake, pipe out frosting while directing tip to make drooping motion. For even swags around cake, divide cake into quarters and determine number of swags within each quarter.

WHY? A swag is a pretty design often used to adorn the sides of a cake. You can pipe a single swag or multiple swags with different lengths.

Chocolate Cupcakes

Overview

A chocolate cupcake catch-22 befalls bakery and homemade confections alike: If the cupcakes have decent chocolate flavor, their structure is too crumbly, but if the cakes balance moisture and tenderness without crumbling, the cake and frosting are barely palatable. We wanted a moist, tender cupcake capped with just enough creamy, not-too-sweet frosting.

We started by making cupcakes using our favorite chocolate cake recipe, but their crumbly texture made them impossible to eat. To strengthen the batter we cut back on both kinds of chocolate, then we enhanced the chocolate flavor without disrupting the structure two ways: We mixed the cocoa powder with hot coffee, and we replaced the butter with neutral-flavored vegetable oil. Still, we wanted more. Could we enhance the structure so that we could add back extra chocolate without overtenderizing? Bread flour (rather than all-purpose) turned out a cupcake that was markedly less crumble-prone, but not tough.

For a final chocolate burst, we spooned a dollop of ganache onto each portion of cupcake batter before baking, which turned into a trufflelike center once baked. (We highly recommend the filling, you can omit it for a more traditional cupcake.) A velvety Swiss meringue buttercream, which gets its satiny-smooth texture from whisking the egg whites and sugar in a double boiler, then whipping the mixture with softened butter, was the perfect way to crown these cupcakes. Cupcake liners made it easy to remove cupcakes from the tin and also provided support during the frosting process.

To prepare in advance, store the cooled cupcakes in an airtight container at room temperature and refrigerate the frosting. When ready to frost, warm the frosting briefly in the microwave until slightly softened, 5 to 10 seconds. Once warmed, stir until creamy. Before you begin, see How to Chop and Melt Chocolate on page 586. For frosting variations, see page 673.

Key Stats

TOTAL TIME **2 hours, 15 minutes**
PREPARATION TIME **20 minutes**
ACTIVE COOKING TIME **30 minutes**
YIELD **12 cupcakes**
MAKE AHEAD **Keep cupcakes, unfrosted, at room temperature and refrigerate frosting for up to 1 day**
DIFFICULTY **Intermediate**

Tools

- medium saucepan
- 12-cup muffin tin
- stand mixer
- microwave
- chef's knife
- cutting board
- paring knife
- dry measuring cups
- liquid measuring cup
- measuring spoons
- ice cream scoop or soupspoon
- instant-read thermometer
- microwave-safe bowls (2)
- medium heatproof bowl
- mixing bowls
- small offset spatula
- rubber spatula
- whisk
- wire rack
- paper or foil cupcake liners

Ingredients

GANACHE FILLING
- 2   ounces bittersweet chocolate, chopped fine
- ¼   cup heavy cream
- 1   tablespoon confectioners' sugar

CHOCOLATE CUPCAKES
- 3   ounces bittersweet chocolate, chopped fine
- ⅓   cup (1 ounce) Dutch-processed cocoa powder
- ¾   cup brewed coffee, hot
- ¾   cup (4⅛ ounces) bread flour
- ¾   cup (5¼ ounces) granulated sugar
- ½   teaspoon salt
- ½   teaspoon baking soda
- 6   tablespoons vegetable oil
- 2   large eggs
- 2   teaspoons distilled white vinegar
- 1   teaspoon vanilla extract

CREAMY CHOCOLATE FROSTING
- ⅓   cup (2⅓ ounces) granulated sugar
- 2   large egg whites
   Pinch salt
- 12   tablespoons unsalted butter, cut into 12 pieces and softened
- 6   ounces bittersweet chocolate, melted and cooled *
- ½   teaspoon vanilla extract

* Use a high-quality bittersweet chocolate for this recipe.

What Can Go Wrong

Here's a list of common mistakes cooks make when preparing this recipe.

COMMON MISTAKE	BAD OUTCOMES	WHAT YOU SHOULD DO
Using Wrong or Poor-Quality Chocolate	• **The cupcakes are too sweet.** • **The frosting and ganache filling are gritty.**	The sweetness level of bittersweet chocolate varies significantly. Choose a brand that is labeled 60 percent cacao. (Sugar makes up the balance of the ingredients, or roughly 40 percent.) If you choose an overly sweet chocolate (with just 50 percent cacao), the cupcakes will be very sweet. Likewise, low-quality chocolate can be gritty, and while this won't affect the cake portion of this recipe, the frosting and ganache filling won't be perfectly smooth.
Using Wrong Type of Flour	• **The cupcakes are crumbly.**	Bread flour might seem like an odd choice in a cake recipe, but it's essential when making these cupcakes. The bread flour has enough protein to create a cupcake that is sturdy enough to hold its shape when eaten. If you use cake or all-purpose flour, the cupcakes might fall apart during the frosting process and will end up crumbling as you eat them.
Not Cooling Chocolate	• **The ganache filling melts into the cake portion.** • **The eggs in the cake batter curdle.** • **The frosting is too soft.**	The three components in this recipe—the cake, the ganache filling, and the frosting—each require that you melt and then cool chocolate. If you rush the cooling steps, bad things will happen. The ganache should be cool enough to scoop into firm balls. If the ganache is too soft it won't hold its shape during the baking process. Likewise, the melted chocolate for the cake should be chilled briefly so that it won't overheat the other ingredients in the cake, especially the eggs. Finally, melted chocolate is added to the frosting. It's imperative to cool this chocolate to a temperature below 100 degrees or you risk melting the butter in the frosting.
Overbaking Cupcakes	• **The cupcakes are dry.** • **The chocolate flavor is wan.**	The volatile oils in chocolate dissipate during the baking process, so if you overbake the cupcakes, not only will they be dry, but their flavor will be compromised. Because of the ganache filling, you can't test these cupcakes for doneness with a toothpick. Instead, gently touch the tops of the cupcakes. They should be firm to the touch. Also, watch the sides of the cupcakes. They should be starting to pull away from the muffin tin.
Frosting Cupcakes When Warm	• **The frosting becomes soft.** • **The frosting becomes greasy.**	Never frost any cake—including these little cupcakes—until cooled to room temperature. If you jump-start this process, the frosting won't hold its shape and the butter can even start to melt, giving the frosting a greasy feeling when you bite into it. This recipe calls for cooling the cupcakes in the tin for 10 minutes—just long enough to ensure that they will hold together—and then on a wire rack for another hour.
Improperly Heating Meringue	• **The meringue is too cool and the frosting turns out a bit thin.** • **The meringue is too cool and the egg whites pose a danger.** • **The meringue is too hot and the butter melts when added.**	The classic cupcake frosting made with confectioners' sugar, butter, and milk is very sweet, and very gritty. In this recipe, a Swiss meringue (made with egg whites and a modest amount of granulated sugar) provides minimal sweetness and a light, silky texture. The meringue mixture must be heated to 150 degrees in order to unleash the thickening power of the raw egg whites and to kill bacteria. The most likely danger is overheating the egg whites—a sure bet if the bowl of the stand mixer is touching the simmering water. Fill a tall, narrow saucepan with a little water and then set the bowl in the saucepan to check that the bowl will be suspended above the water. At this point, go ahead and turn on the heat and bring the water to a simmer. Use an instant-read thermometer to determine when the meringue mixture is done.

1. PREPARE FILLING: Place 2 ounces finely chopped bittersweet chocolate, ¼ cup heavy cream, and 1 tablespoon confectioners' sugar in medium bowl.

2. Microwave chocolate mixture until warm to touch, about 30 seconds.

3. Whisk until smooth, then transfer bowl to refrigerator and let sit until just chilled, no longer than 30 minutes.

4. PREPARE CUPCAKES: Adjust oven rack to middle position and heat oven to 350 degrees. Line 12-cup muffin tin with paper or foil liners.

5. Place 3 ounces finely chopped bittersweet chocolate and ⅓ cup Dutch-processed cocoa powder in medium heatproof bowl.

6. Pour ¾ cup hot brewed coffee over chocolate mixture and let sit, covered, for 5 minutes.

7. Whisk mixture gently until smooth, then transfer to refrigerator to cool completely, about 20 minutes.

8. Whisk ¾ cup (4⅛ ounces) bread flour, ¾ cup (5¼ ounces) granulated sugar, ½ teaspoon salt, and ½ teaspoon baking soda together in bowl.

9. Whisk 6 tablespoons vegetable oil, 2 large eggs, 2 teaspoons distilled white vinegar, and 1 teaspoon vanilla extract into cooled cocoa mixture.

10. Add flour mixture and whisk until smooth.

11. Using ice cream scoop or soupspoon, divide batter evenly among prepared muffin cups.

12. Place 1 slightly rounded teaspoon ganache filling on top of each portion of batter.

13. Bake cupcakes until set and just firm to touch, 17 to 19 minutes.

14. Let cupcakes cool in muffin tin on wire rack until cool enough to handle, about 10 minutes.

15. Lift each cupcake from tin, set on wire rack, and let cool completely before frosting, about 1 hour.

16. PREPARE FROSTING: Cut 12 tablespoons unsalted butter into 12 even pieces and let soften on counter.

17. Melt 6 ounces bittersweet chocolate and let cool.

18. Combine ⅓ cup granulated sugar, 2 large egg whites, and pinch salt in stand mixer bowl. Set over saucepan with 1 inch of just simmering water.

19. Whisking gently but constantly, heat mixture until slightly thickened, foamy, and registers 150 degrees, 2 to 3 minutes.

20. Fit stand mixer with whisk and beat mixture on medium speed until consistency of shaving cream and slightly cooled, 1 to 2 minutes.

21. Add softened butter, 1 piece at a time, until smooth and creamy. (Frosting may look curdled at first; it will smooth with additional butter.)

22. Mix in melted chocolate (cooled to 85 to 100 degrees) and ½ teaspoon vanilla extract. (If frosting is soft, chill briefly, then rewhip until creamy.)

23. Increase speed to medium-high and beat until light and fluffy, about 30 seconds, scraping down beater and sides of bowl with rubber spatula.

24. Spread 2 to 3 tablespoons frosting over each cooled cupcake and serve.

Fluffy Yellow Layer Cake

Overview

It's easy to create a supremely fluffy layer cake with additives. Box mixes are engineered to produce a cake with an ultralight texture. But most homemade cakes are either dense or too fragile to support frosting. We set out to change that.

Chiffon cakes are weightless, springy, and moist. But unlike butter cakes, they are too light to stand up to a serious slathering of frosting. So we adapted a chiffon technique (using a large quantity of whipped egg whites to get a high volume and light texture) to combine the ingredients from our butter cake recipe. It worked beautifully, creating a light, porous cake that was hefty enough to hold the frosting's weight. But the cake lacked moistness and some tenderness. Using a combination of butter and vegetable oil kept the butter flavor intact while improving the moistness of the cake. For extra tenderness, we increased the sugar and substituted buttermilk for milk. The buttermilk not only introduced a new flavor dimension, but also allowed us to replace some of the baking powder with a little baking soda to ensure an even rise.

For the frosting, we used both milk chocolate and cocoa powder for big flavor and combined softened butter and confectioners' sugar for a classic, easy frosting. Using a food processor made it billowy and avoided the usual gritty texture.

This cake can be assembled and refrigerated for up to one day. Bring to room temperature before serving. If you prefer, the cooled cakes can be wrapped tightly in plastic wrap prior to frosting and kept at room temperature for up to one day. Cakes can also be wrapped tightly in plastic, then aluminum foil, and frozen for up to one month. Defrost cakes at room temperature before unwrapping and frosting. The frosting can be kept at room temperature for up to 3 hours before frosting the cake or refrigerated for up to three days. If refrigerated, let stand at room temperature for 1 hour before using.

Key Stats

TOTAL TIME **2½ hours**
PREPARATION TIME **15 minutes**
ACTIVE COOKING TIME **30 minutes**
YIELD **10 to 12 servings**
MAKE AHEAD **Refrigerate frosted cake for up to 1 day**
DIFFICULTY **Intermediate**

Tools

- 9-inch round cake pans (2) *
- food processor
- stand mixer
- dry measuring cups
- liquid measuring cup
- measuring spoons
- cake platter
- large offset spatula
- mixing bowls
- rubber spatula
- scissors
- soupspoon
- whisk
- wire rack
- parchment paper
- toothpick

* Be sure to use cake pans with at least 2-inch-tall sides. This recipe won't work in flimsy pans with 1½ inch sides.

Ingredients

CAKE
- 2½   **cups (10 ounces) cake flour ***
- 1¼   **teaspoons baking powder**
- ¼   **teaspoon baking soda**
- ¾   **teaspoon salt**
- 1¾   **cups (12¼ ounces) granulated sugar**
- 10   **tablespoons unsalted butter, melted and cooled**
- 1   **cup buttermilk, room temperature**
- 3   **tablespoons vegetable oil**
- 2   **teaspoons vanilla extract**
- 3   **large eggs, separated, plus 3 large yolks, room temperature**
  Pinch cream of tartar

FROSTING
- 20   **tablespoons (2½ sticks) unsalted butter, softened**
- 1   **cup (4 ounces) confectioners' sugar**
- ¾   **cup (2¼ ounces) Dutch-processed cocoa powder**
  Pinch salt
- ¾   **cup light corn syrup**
- 1   **teaspoon vanilla extract**
- 8   **ounces chocolate, melted and cooled ****

* Do not substitute all-purpose flour or the cake will be tough, dry, and dense.

** We prefer milk chocolate, but you can use semisweet or bittersweet chocolate; cool the chocolate to between 85 and 100 degrees before adding it to the butter mixture.

What Can Go Wrong

Here's a list of common mistakes cooks make when preparing this recipe.

COMMON MISTAKE	BAD OUTCOMES	WHAT YOU SHOULD DO
Using Buttermilk, Eggs, and Butter Straight from Refrigerator	• **The batter is curdled.** • **The cake layers don't rise sufficiently.**	In order for all the ingredients in this recipe to blend properly and produce maximum rise, they have to be at room temperature. Separate the eggs straight from the refrigerator (cold eggs are easier to separate because the yolks are firmer) but then let the whites and yolks warm in bowls on the counter. Likewise, let the buttermilk warm on the counter. As for the butter, it's important to melt and then cool it.
Not Fully Whipping Egg Whites	• **The cake layers don't rise sufficiently.** • **The cake layers are dense.**	For maximum height, it's important to whip the egg whites to stiff peaks. Adding the cream of tartar at the outset will help produce a stable, voluminous foam. Don't add the granulated sugar until the whites are foamy. Adding the sugar gradually at this stage ensures maximum volume. Make sure to whip egg whites to stiff peaks. When the whisk attachment is removed from the bowl the whites should hold their shape.
Folding in Egg Whites Improperly	• **The cake layers don't rise sufficiently.** • **The cake layers are dense.**	The batter is fairly thick, and if you attempt to fold the stiff whites into it you will end up using a lot of strokes and knock all the air out of the whites. Instead, use one-third of the whites to lighten the batter. Make sure to incorporate this first portion of the beaten whites well. Then add the rest of the whites, making sure to use a light touch to fold them. Stop folding as soon as you no longer see streaks of white. Make sure to use a rubber spatula—not an electric mixer—for this step.
Baking Cake Layers Too Long	• **The cake is dry.** • **The cake is crumbly.**	Many novice bakers overbake cake layers, and the end result is a dry, crumbly cake. Use a toothpick inserted into the center to judge doneness—when it comes out clean the layers are done. If in doubt, lightly press the top of the cake layers—they should spring back. Also, if the cake is pulling away from the sides of the pan it is likely done.
Not Cooling Cakes Before Frosting	• **The frosting becomes too soft to decorate.** • **The frosting melts.**	It might be tempting, but never, ever frost a cake until it has cooled completely. Even a little residual heat is enough to soften the butter in the frosting and cause a real mess.
Not Cooling Chocolate for Frosting	• **The frosting is too soft.** • **The frosting turns greasy.**	If the melted chocolate is still hot when added to the frosting, it will ruin the texture of the frosting. As you might imagine, warm chocolate can make the frosting too soft to spread. But it can also cause some of the butter in the frosting to melt, which will give the frosting an unappealing greasy sheen and feel. Let the melted chocolate cool to between 85 and 100 degrees. (If your kitchen is warm, err on the side of caution and let it cool to the lower temperature.)

1. PREPARE CAKE: Heat oven to 350 degrees. Grease two 9-inch round cake pans, line with parchment paper, grease parchment, and flour pans.

2. Whisk 2½ cups cake flour, 1¼ teaspoons baking powder, ¼ teaspoon baking soda, ¾ teaspoon salt, and 1½ cups granulated sugar in large bowl.

3. Melt 10 tablespoons unsalted butter and cool to room temperature.

4. Separate 3 eggs into 2 bowls. Separate 3 more eggs, discarding whites and adding yolks to bowl with other yolks. Bring to room temperature.

5. In medium bowl, whisk melted butter, 1 cup room-temperature buttermilk, 3 tablespoons vegetable oil, 2 teaspoons vanilla extract, and egg yolks.

6. Using stand mixer fitted with whisk, whip egg whites and pinch cream of tartar on medium-low speed until foamy, about 1 minute.

7. Increase speed to medium-high and whip whites to soft, billowy mounds, about 1 minute.

8. Gradually add remaining ¼ cup granulated sugar and whip until glossy, stiff peaks form, 2 to 3 minutes. Transfer to bowl and set aside.

9. Add flour mixture to now-empty bowl.

10. With mixer on low speed, gradually add butter mixture and mix until almost incorporated (a few streaks of flour will remain), about 15 seconds.

11. Scrape down bowl, then beat on medium-low speed until smooth and fully incorporated, 10 to 15 seconds.

12. Using rubber spatula, stir one-third of whites into batter, then add remaining two-thirds and gently fold into batter until no white streaks remain.

13. Divide batter evenly between prepared pans, smooth tops with rubber spatula, and gently tap pans on counter to release air bubbles.

14. Bake cakes on middle rack until toothpick inserted in centers comes out clean, 20 to 22 minutes, switching and rotating pans halfway through.

15. Let cakes cool in pans on wire rack for 10 minutes. Remove from pans, discard parchment, and let cool completely, about 2 hours, before frosting.

16. PREPARE FROSTING: Soften 2½ sticks unsalted butter on counter. Melt 8 ounces milk chocolate and cool to between 85 and 100 degrees.

17. Process butter, 1 cup confectioners' sugar, ¾ cup cocoa, and pinch salt in food processor until smooth, about 30 seconds, scraping down bowl.

18. Add ¾ cup light corn syrup and 1 teaspoon vanilla extract and process until just combined, 5 to 10 seconds.

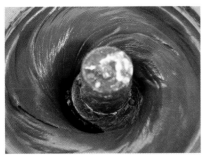

19. Scrape down bowl, then add melted and cooled chocolate and process until smooth and creamy, 10 to 15 seconds.

20. ASSEMBLE CAKE: Line edges of cake platter with 4 strips of parchment paper to keep platter clean. Place 1 cake layer on prepared platter.

21. Place about 1½ cups frosting in center of cake layer and, using large spatula, spread in even layer right to edge of cake.

22. Place second cake layer on top, making sure layers are aligned. Frost top, this time spreading frosting until slightly over edge.

23. Gather more frosting on tip of spatula and gently spread icing onto side of cake.

24. Create billows by pressing back of soupspoon into frosting and twirling spoon as you lift away. Pull out pieces of parchment from beneath cake.

New York–Style Cheesecake

Overview

The ideal New York cheesecake should be tall, bronze-skinned, and dense. At the core, it should be cool, thick, smooth, satiny, and creamy. The flavor should be pure and minimalist, sweet and tangy, and rich. But many recipes fall short—going wrong in a number of ways—with textures that range from fluffy to rubbery and leaden, and flavors that are starchy or overly citrusy. We wanted to find the secret to perfect New York cheesecake.

After trying a variety of crusts, we settled on the classic graham cracker crust: a simple combination of graham crackers, butter, and sugar. For the filling, we found that cream cheese, boosted by the extra tang of a little sour cream, delivers the best flavor. A little lemon juice and vanilla adds just the right sweet, bright accents without calling attention to themselves. A combination of eggs and egg yolks yields a texture that is dense but not heavy.

We found that the New York method works better for this cheesecake than the typical water bath—baking the cake in a hot oven for 10 minutes, then in a low oven for a full hour and a half, yields the perfect satiny texture.

The flavor and texture of the chilled cheesecake are best if the cake is allowed to sit at room temperature for 30 minutes before serving. The cake can be refrigerated for up to three days, but the crust will begin to lose its crispness after only a day. When cutting the cake, have a pitcher of hot tap water nearby; dipping the blade of the knife into the water and wiping it clean with a dish towel after each cut helps make neat slices. Serve with Fresh Strawberry Topping (page 677) if desired.

Key Stats

TOTAL TIME **9 hours**
PREPARATION TIME **10 minutes**
ACTIVE COOKING TIME **30 minutes**
YIELD **12 to 16 servings**
MAKE AHEAD **Refrigerate for up to 3 days**
DIFFICULTY **Easy**

Tools

- 9-inch springform pan
- rimmed baking sheet *
- food processor
- stand mixer
- chef's knife
- cutting board
- paring knife **
- slicing knife
- dry measuring cups
- measuring spoons
- dish towel
- fork
- instant-read thermometer ***
- mixing bowls
- large offset spatula
- pastry brush
- rubber spatula
- serving platter
- wire rack
- plastic wrap

* Placing the springform pan on a rimmed baking sheet will catch any drips.

** As the cheesecake cools, the surface tension can increase, especially if the sides of the cake are stuck to the pan. Running a paring knife around the inside of the pan 5 minutes after it comes out the oven frees the cake from the pan and allows it to contract as it cools.

*** If you overcook any cheesecake, the eggs will curdle and cracks will develop. Using an instant-read thermometer is the only reliable way to gauge doneness.

Ingredients

CRUST

- 8 **whole graham crackers, broken into rough pieces ***
- 1 **tablespoon sugar**
- 5 **tablespoons unsalted butter, melted**

FILLING

- 2½ **pounds cream cheese, cut into 1-inch chunks and softened ****
- 1½ **cups (10½ ounces) sugar**
- ⅛ **teaspoon salt**
- ⅓ **cup sour cream**
- 2 **teaspoons lemon juice**
- 2 **teaspoons vanilla extract**
- 6 **large eggs plus 2 large yolks**
- 1 **tablespoon unsalted butter, melted**

* Don't use store-bought graham cracker crumbs. You can substitute 14 chocolate wafers for graham crackers if desired.
** Use regular—not light or whipped—cream cheese.

What Can Go Wrong

Here's a list of common mistakes cooks make when preparing this recipe.

COMMON MISTAKE	BAD OUTCOMES	WHAT YOU SHOULD DO
Using Cold Cream Cheese	• **The batter is lumpy, not smooth.** • **The cheesecake is dense.**	The first step in making this recipe is cutting the cream cheese into small chunks and letting it soften on the counter. If you try to beat the sugar and eggs into cold cream cheese, the batter will appear lumpy and curdled. In addition, you won't be able to aerate cold cream cheese, and the cheesecake will bake up heavy and dense.
Not Prebaking Crust	• **The crust is soggy.** • **The crust is crumbly.**	Many cheesecake recipes don't bother prebaking the crumb crust. If you skip this step, the moisture in the filling will cause the crust to become soggy very quickly. Likewise, the crust won't be very cohesive. Baking makes the crust stronger and firmer. In addition, make sure to press the crumbs firmly in place—we use the bottom of a dry measuring cup for this step. Compacting the crumbs is the first step to a firm, cohesive crust.
Not Scraping Down Mixer Bowl	• **The batter is lumpy.** • **The cheesecake has pockets of cream cheese.**	The instructions for this recipe suggest scraping down the bowl at every step. That's because there's so much cream cheese in this recipe. The tendency of heavy cream cheese is to clump up around the beater or at the bottom of the bowl. Scraping the bowl often ensures that all the little bits of cream cheese get fully incorporated. Skip this step and you will end up with chalky bits of cream cheese in the finished cake.
Overbaking Cheesecake	• **The top burns.** • **The top cracks.** • **The cheesecake is watery and grainy.**	This recipe relies on a dual-temperature method that produces a bronzed cheesecake that is smooth and evenly baked. It's imperative to watch the clock carefully and lower the oven temperature from 500 degrees to 200 degrees after 10 minutes of baking. If you forget this step, the cheesecake will burn on top. Don't open the oven door—the recipe is designed for the temperature to lower gradually. When the cheesecake has been in the oven for 90 minutes total, you should start checking for doneness with an instant-read thermometer. If the eggs heat past 150 degrees they can curdle, and the result is a grainy, watery, cracked mess.
Not Loosening Edges Before Cooling Completely	• **The cheesecake sticks to the pan.** • **The top cracks as it cools.**	Once the cheesecake has cooled for 5 minutes, you must run a paring knife around the interior of the springform pan. This will loosen the cake and make it easier to remove the side piece of the pan at serving time. Perhaps more important, this step frees the sides of the cake so that the top can contract as it cools. Skip this step and surface tension will cause a fissure to develop in the top as the cheesecake cools and attempts to contract.
Not Fully Chilling Cheesecake Before Slicing It	• **The cheesecake is difficult to slice.** • **The cheesecake is not fully set.**	You must cool the cheesecake until barely warm, then chill it for at least 3 hours before attempting to slice it. If you rush these two steps, the cheesecake will not set up properly. Keep the cheesecake in the springform pan until you're ready to serve it.

1. Cut 2½ pounds cream cheese into 1-inch chunks and let soften on counter.

2. Adjust oven rack to lower-middle position and heat oven to 325 degrees.

3. PREPARE CRUST: Break 8 whole graham crackers into rough pieces. Process in food processor to fine crumbs, about 30 seconds.

4. Combine crumbs and 1 tablespoon sugar in bowl, add 5 tablespoons melted unsalted butter, and toss with fork until evenly moistened.

5. Empty crumbs into 9-inch springform pan.

6. Using bottom of ramekin or dry measuring cup, press crumbs firmly and evenly into pan bottom, keeping sides as clean as possible.

7. Bake crust until fragrant and beginning to brown around edges, about 13 minutes.

8. Let crust cool in pan on wire rack while making filling.

9. PREPARE FILLING: Increase oven temperature to 500 degrees.

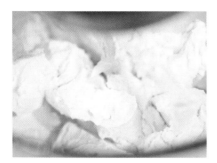

10. Using stand mixer fitted with paddle, beat cream cheese on medium-low until broken up and slightly softened, about 1 minute. Scrape down bowl.

11. Add ¾ cup sugar and ⅛ teaspoon salt and beat on medium-low speed until combined, about 1 minute.

12. Scrape down bowl, then beat in ¾ cup sugar until combined, about 1 minute.

13. Scrape down bowl, add ⅓ cup sour cream, 2 teaspoons lemon juice, and 2 teaspoons vanilla. Beat on low speed until combined, about 1 minute.

14. Scrape down bowl, add 2 large egg yolks, and beat on medium-low speed until thoroughly combined, about 1 minute.

15. Scrape down bowl, add 6 whole eggs, 2 at a time, beating until thoroughly combined, about 1 minute, and scraping bowl between additions.

16. Being careful not to disturb baked crust, brush inside of pan with 1 tablespoon melted unsalted butter. Set pan on rimmed baking sheet.

17. Pour filling into cooled crust. Slide baking sheet into oven and bake for 10 minutes.

18. Without opening oven door, reduce temperature to 200 degrees.

19. Continue to bake until cheesecake registers about 150 degrees, about 1½ hours.

20. Let cake cool on wire rack for 5 minutes, then run paring knife around cake to loosen from pan.

21. Let cake cool until barely warm, 2½ to 3 hours. Wrap cake tightly in plastic wrap and refrigerate until cold, at least 3 hours or up to 4 days.

22. To unmold cheesecake, wrap hot dish towel around pan and let stand for 1 minute.

23. Remove sides of pan. Slide large offset spatula between crust and pan bottom to loosen.

24. Slide cake onto serving platter. Let cheesecake sit at room temperature for about 30 minutes before serving.

French Apple Cake

Overview

This French classic is neither a cake, nor a custard, nor a cla-fouti. With a bit of culinary magic, it is all three: a dessert with a custardy, apple-rich base beneath a light, cakelike topping.

We started with choosing the best type of apple. We opt for Granny Smith since it holds its shape well and it has a tart-ness that can stand out clearly against the sweet, dense back-ground of the cake. Tossing the apples with some Calvados (a French apple brandy) and some lemon juice adds complexity. To ensure that the apple slices soften fully by the end of bak-ing, we microwave them briefly before folding them into the batter for the custard layer.

For distinct cake and custard layers, we make the batter in two stages. We make a base batter, then we add two extra egg yolks to one portion to create the custard layer, and we add extra flour to the rest to make the cakey top layer. The custard layer goes in first, then is topped with the cakey bat-ter. The result is a creamy, custardy base and a light cakey top. The simplicity of this cake required an equally simple garnish: a dusting of confectioners' sugar.

Key Stats

TOTAL TIME **4 hours**
PREPARATION TIME **15 minutes**
ACTIVE COOKING TIME **30 minutes**
YIELD **8 to 10 servings**
MAKE AHEAD **Best served the day it is baked**
DIFFICULTY **Easy**

Tools

- 9-inch springform pan
- rimmed baking sheet
- microwave
- chef's knife
- cutting board
- paring knife
- dry measuring cups
- liquid measuring cup
- measuring spoons
- citrus juicer
- fine-mesh strainer *
- ladle
- microwave-safe pie plate
- mixing bowls
- large offset spatula **
- rubber spatula
- vegetable peeler
- whisk
- wire rack
- aluminum foil
- plastic wrap
- toothpick

* We like to use a fine-mesh strainer to dust the cake with confectioners' sugar since it will break up any lumps in the sugar and ensure even coverage.

** This recipe depends upon careful layering of two batters, and it's important to smooth out the top of the first layer in the pan. An offset spatula is the best tool for the job because you can push the batter into the edges of the pan and also press down on the apples to create an even, compact layer.

Ingredients

1½   **pounds Granny Smith apples, peeled, cored, cut into 8 wedges, and sliced ⅛ inch thick crosswise**
1   **tablespoon Calvados ***
1   **teaspoon lemon juice**
1   **cup (5 ounces) plus 2 tablespoons all-purpose flour**
1   **cup (7 ounces) plus 1 tablespoon granulated sugar**
2   **teaspoons baking powder**
½   **teaspoon salt**
1   **large egg plus 2 large yolks**
1   **cup vegetable oil**
1   **cup whole milk**
1   **teaspoon vanilla extract**
    Confectioners' sugar

* If Calvados is unavailable, 1 tablespoon of any apple brandy or white rum can be substituted.

What Can Go Wrong

Here's a list of common mistakes cooks make when preparing this recipe.

COMMON MISTAKE	BAD OUTCOMES	WHAT YOU SHOULD DO
Using Wrong Apple Variety	• **The apples are mushy.** • **The cake is too sweet.**	We chose Granny Smith apples for two reasons. First, they hold their shape when baked, providing just enough textural contrast to the tender cake and creamy custard layers. Second, their tart flavor is a nice contrast to the sweet cake and custard. If you use a sweet apple that tends to fall apart when cooked, such as McIntosh, both the texture and the flavor of the cake will suffer.
Not Microwaving Apples	• **The apples are leathery and tough.**	Precooking the apples jump-starts the softening process so that the apples bake up tender. Cooking the apples in the microwave also sets their pectin, which prevents excessive softness. Make sure the microwaved apples are pliable. To test for doneness, take one slice and try to bend it. If it snaps in half, it's too firm; microwave the apples for an additional 30 seconds and test again. But the apples shouldn't be completely soft. If they are, you've either used the wrong kind of apple or microwaved them for too long.
Not Neatly Layering Batters	• **The custard layer is too dry.** • **The cake layer is too moist.**	This recipe requires that you make a single batter, divide it, and then tweak each portion to create the two layers of the cake. Egg yolks make the bottom layer custardy, while some extra flour makes the top layer cakey. Of course, all of this is for naught if you don't layer the first batter into the pan neatly. The first layer should be perfectly flat and spread all the way to the edges of the pan.
Overbaking Cake	• **The cake layer is dry.** • **The custard layer is too stiff.**	This cake bakes for a long time in a relatively cool 325-degree oven. Make sure that your oven is set to the proper temperature—at slightly higher temperatures we had trouble getting this heavy batter to set up properly. It can be a bit tricky to judge doneness in this cake. The center should be set (if the center jiggles, the cake is not done) and golden brown. Insert a toothpick into the center; it should come out clean. You might want to perform the toothpick test in multiple spots—just in case you're hitting apple slices when you test.
Not Loosening Edges Before Cooling	• **The cake sticks to the pan.** • **The top cracks as it cools.**	Once the cake has cooled for 5 minutes, you must run a paring knife around the interior of the springform pan. This will loosen the cake and make it easier to remove the side piece of the pan at serving time. But perhaps more important, this step also frees the sides of the cake so that the top can contract as it cools. Skip this step and surface tension will cause a fissure to develop in the top as the cake cools and attempts to contract.

1. Adjust oven rack to lower-middle position and heat oven to 325 degrees. Grease 9-inch springform pan and place on foil-lined rimmed baking sheet.

2. Cut 1½ pounds peeled, cored Granny Smith apples into 8 wedges, then slice wedges ⅛ inch thick crosswise. Place in microwave-safe pie plate and cover.

3. Microwave until pliable and slightly translucent, about 3 minutes. Toss with 1 tablespoon Calvados and 1 teaspoon lemon juice. Let cool for 15 minutes.

4. Whisk 1 cup all-purpose flour, 1 cup granulated sugar, 2 teaspoons baking powder, and ½ teaspoon salt together in bowl.

5. Whisk 1 large egg, 1 cup vegetable oil, 1 cup whole milk, and 1 teaspoon vanilla extract together in second large bowl until smooth.

6. Add dry ingredients to wet ingredients and whisk until just combined.

7. Transfer 1 cup batter to liquid measuring cup and set aside.

8. Add 2 large egg yolks to remaining batter and whisk to combine. Using rubber spatula, gently fold in cooled apples.

9. Transfer batter to prepared pan. Using large offset spatula, spread batter to pan edges, gently pressing on apples to create even, compact layer.

10. Whisk 2 tablespoons all-purpose flour into reserved batter. Pour over batter in pan. Spread batter evenly to pan edges and smooth surface.

11. Sprinkle cake with 1 tablespoon granulated sugar. Bake until toothpick inserted in center comes out clean and top is golden brown, about 1¼ hours.

12. Transfer pan to wire rack; cool for 5 minutes. Run paring knife around sides of pan and cool completely, 2 to 3 hours. Dust with confectioners' sugar.

Recipe Library

Easy Pound Cake

✔ **WHY THIS RECIPE WORKS:** Classic pound cake recipes tend to be very particular, requiring ingredients at certain temperatures and finicky mixing methods to ensure a proper emulsion of the eggs and batter. (If you're off, you end up with a curdled batter and a dense, heavy cake.) For a simpler, foolproof pound cake, we discovered that hot melted butter (rather than softened) and the food processor were key. The fast-moving blade of the processor plus the hot melted butter emulsified the liquid ingredients quickly before they had a chance to curdle. Sifting the dry ingredients over our emulsified egg mixture in three additions, and whisking it in after each addition, allowed us to incorporate the dry ingredients easily and ensured no pockets of flour marred our final cake.

Easy Pound Cake

SERVES 8

This recipe will also make four miniature pound cakes; use four 2-cup mini loaf pans and reduce the baking time to 40 minutes. See Core Technique on page 632 for more details on this recipe.

- 1½ **cups (6 ounces) cake flour**
- 1 **teaspoon baking powder**
- ½ **teaspoon salt**
- 1¼ **cups (8¾ ounces) sugar**
- 4 **large eggs, room temperature**
- 1½ **teaspoons vanilla extract**
- 16 **tablespoons unsalted butter, melted and hot**

1. Adjust oven rack to middle position and heat oven to 350 degrees. Grease and flour 8½ by 4½-inch loaf pan. Whisk flour, baking powder, and salt together in bowl.

2. Process sugar, eggs, and vanilla together in food processor until combined, about 10 seconds. With processor running, add hot melted butter in steady stream until incorporated. Pour mixture into large bowl.

3. Sift flour mixture over egg mixture in 3 additions, whisking to combine after each addition until few streaks of flour remain. Continue to whisk batter gently until almost no lumps remain (do not overmix).

4. Scrape batter into prepared pan and smooth top. Wipe any drops of batter off sides of pan and gently tap pan on counter to release air bubbles. Bake cake until toothpick inserted in center comes out with few moist crumbs attached, 50 to 60 minutes, rotating pan halfway through baking.

5. Let cake cool in pan on wire rack for 10 minutes. Run small knife around edge of cake to loosen, then flip it out onto wire rack. Turn cake right side up and let cool completely, about 2 hours, before serving.

Easy Ginger Pound Cake

Add 3 tablespoons minced crystallized ginger, 1½ teaspoons ground ginger, and ½ teaspoon ground mace to food processor with sugar, eggs, and vanilla.

Easy Lemon Pound Cake

Add 2 tablespoons grated lemon zest and 2 teaspoons lemon juice to food processor with sugar, eggs, and vanilla.

Easy Orange Pound Cake

Add 1 tablespoon grated orange zest and 1 tablespoon orange juice to food processor with sugar, eggs, and vanilla.

Easy Almond Pound Cake

Add 1 teaspoon almond extract and ¼ cup slivered almonds to food processor with sugar, eggs, and vanilla. Sprinkle 2 tablespoons slivered almonds over cake before baking.

Quick Coffee Cake

✔ **WHY THIS RECIPE WORKS:** We wanted a simple coffee cake that wasn't a chore to make for a crowd or brunch, and that could be easily put together ahead of time and then baked straight from the freezer when we needed it. We found there was no need to drag out our stand mixer or food processor for this recipe; mixing the batter by hand actually helped guard against overmixing, which produces a dense, tough cake. We simply mixed our dry ingredients together in one bowl, the wet ingredients in another, and then combined the two. Sour cream kept the cake moist and delivered just the right amount of richness. For the streusel topping, working the butter into our dry ingredients not only was easy but also delivered bigger, crunchier crumbs than what we would get from a mixer or food processor. Sticking with just cinnamon and some pecans or walnuts was all the streusel needed to complement the cake beneath perfectly. Because the batter was fairly dense, we found it was best to divide it between two cake pans to ensure even cooking.

Quick Coffee Cake

MAKES TWO 9-INCH CAKES; SERVES 12

Do not try to put all the batter into one large cake pan because it will bake very unevenly. See Core Technique on page 634 for more details on this recipe.

TOPPING
- ⅓ **cup packed (2⅓ ounces) light brown sugar**
- ⅓ **cup (2⅓ ounces) granulated sugar**
- ⅓ **cup (1⅔ ounces) all-purpose flour**
- 4 **tablespoons unsalted butter, softened**
- 1 **tablespoon ground cinnamon**
- 1 **cup pecans or walnuts, chopped coarse**

CAKE

- **3 cups (15 ounces) all-purpose flour**
- **1 tablespoon baking powder**
- **1 teaspoon baking soda**
- **1 teaspoon ground cinnamon**
- **¼ teaspoon salt**
- **1¾ cups sour cream**
- **1 cup packed (7 ounces) light brown sugar**
- **1 cup (7 ounces) granulated sugar**
- **3 large eggs**
- **7 tablespoons unsalted butter, melted and cooled**

1. Adjust oven rack to middle position and heat oven to 350 degrees. Grease two 9-inch round cake pans.

2. FOR THE TOPPING: Using your fingers, mix brown sugar, granulated sugar, flour, butter, and cinnamon together in medium bowl until mixture resembles wet sand. Stir in pecans.

3. FOR THE CAKE: Whisk flour, baking powder, baking soda, cinnamon, and salt together in large bowl. In medium bowl, whisk sour cream, brown sugar, granulated sugar, eggs, and melted butter together until smooth. Gently fold sour cream mixture into flour mixture until smooth (do not overmix; some streaks of flour might remain).

4. Scrape batter into prepared pans and smooth tops. Sprinkle topping evenly over both cakes.

5. Bake until topping looks crisp and toasted, and toothpick inserted into centers comes out with few crumbs attached, 25 to 30 minutes, switching and rotating pans halfway through baking. Let cakes cool on wire rack for 15 minutes before serving.

TO MAKE AHEAD: Portion batter and topping into cake pans but do not bake. Cover pans tightly with plastic wrap and refrigerate for up to 24 hours, or freeze for up to 1 month. Bake cakes as directed, increasing baking time to 30 to 35 minutes if refrigerated, or 40 to 45 minutes if frozen (do not thaw before baking).

Quick Lemon-Blueberry Coffee Cake

Add 1 teaspoon grated lemon zest to flour mixture. Toss 2 cups fresh or frozen berries (do not thaw if frozen) with 1 tablespoon flour, then gently fold into batter.

Quick Apricot-Orange Coffee Cake

Add 1 teaspoon grated orange zest to flour mixture, and gently fold 1 cup chopped dried apricots into batter.

Quick Cranberry-Orange Coffee Cake

Dried cherries can be substituted for the cranberries.

Add 1 teaspoon grated orange zest to flour mixture, and gently fold 1 cup dried cranberries into batter.

Pecan Sour Cream Coffee Cake

✔ **WHY THIS RECIPE WORKS:** We set out to make a Bundt-style coffee cake that not only tasted rich and decadent but was also elegant enough for a nice brunch or festive holiday morning. And for a cake beyond ordinary, we wanted a swirl of pecan streusel. A half-dozen eggs, plus plenty of sour cream and butter, achieved the richness we were after, while ample baking powder plus baking soda ensured it was statuesque. For plenty of pecan flavor, we put pecans in both the cake and the streusel. Toasting the nuts deepened their flavor, then we ground them very fine in the food processor since larger pieces would be distracting in the batter and the thin line of streusel. Adding a little maple syrup to the batter complemented the nuts perfectly. We poured half of the prepared batter into the pan, sprinkled it with the streusel, and then topped it with the remaining batter. An orange and cinnamon glaze, drizzled over the cake before serving, was the perfect finish.

Pecan Sour Cream Coffee Cake

SERVES 12 TO 16

Use real maple syrup here. For maximum efficiency, toast and grind all of the pecans together, then split between the streusel and the cake. Be careful not to overprocess the nuts or you will end up making nut butter.

STREUSEL

- **½ cup pecans, toasted and cooled**
- **3 tablespoons dark brown sugar**
- **1 tablespoon all-purpose flour**
- **1 teaspoon ground cinnamon**

CAKE

- **6 large eggs**
- **1¾ cups sour cream**
- **¼ cup maple syrup**
- **1½ tablespoons vanilla extract**
- **3 cups (15 ounces) all-purpose flour**
- **½ cup pecans, toasted and cooled**
- **1¼ cups (8¾ ounces) granulated sugar**
- **4½ teaspoons baking powder**
- **1¼ teaspoons baking soda**
- **1 teaspoon salt**
- **16 tablespoons unsalted butter, cut into ½-inch pieces and softened**

GLAZE

- **1 cup (4 ounces) confectioners' sugar**
- **2 tablespoons orange juice**
- **½ teaspoon ground cinnamon**
- **1 teaspoon grated orange zest**

1. FOR THE STREUSEL: Using food processor, process pecans until finely ground (do not overprocess). Mix half of ground pecans with brown sugar, flour, and cinnamon in bowl.

2. FOR THE CAKE: Adjust oven rack to lowest position and heat oven to 350 degrees. Grease 12-cup nonstick Bundt pan. Whisk eggs, sour cream, maple syrup, and vanilla together in bowl.

3. Whisk flour, remaining ground pecans, granulated sugar, baking powder, baking soda, and salt together in bowl of stand mixer. Using stand mixer fitted with paddle, beat butter and half of egg mixture into flour mixture on low speed until mixture starts to come together, about 15 seconds. Scrape down bowl, add remaining egg mixture, and beat on medium speed until batter is light and fluffy, 2 to 3 minutes, scraping down bowl as needed.

4. Add 5 cups batter to Bundt pan and smooth top with rubber spatula. Sprinkle streusel evenly over batter, then evenly cover with remaining batter and smooth top.

5. Bake until skewer inserted into middle of cake comes out with few crumbs attached, 50 to 60 minutes, rotating pan halfway through baking. Cool cake in pan on wire rack for 30 minutes, then invert onto wire rack to cool completely before glazing, about 1 hour. (Unglazed cake can be stored in large zipper-lock bag at room temperature for up to 3 days or wrapped tightly in plastic wrap, then aluminum foil, and frozen for up to 1 month; let thaw completely at room temperature, 6 to 8 hours, then glaze and serve.)

6. FOR THE GLAZE: Whisk all ingredients together in bowl, then drizzle over cake before serving.

Applesauce Snack Cake

✔ **WHY THIS RECIPE WORKS:** Applesauce cakes run the gamut from dense, chunky fruitcakes to gummy "health" cakes without much flavor. We wanted a moist and tender cake that actually tasted like its namesake. It was easy to achieve the looser, more casual crumb that is best suited to a rustic snack cake. Since this texture is similar to that of quick breads and muffins, we used the same technique, mixing the wet ingredients separately and then gently adding the dry ingredients by hand. The harder challenge was to develop more apple flavor; simply adding more applesauce made for a gummy cake and fresh apples added too much moisture. But two other sources worked well. Apple cider, reduced to a syrup, contributed a pleasing sweetness and a slight tang without excess moisture. And plumping dried apples in the cider while it was reducing added even more apple taste without making the cake chunky. With such great apple flavor, we didn't want the cake to be too sweet or rich, so we rejected the idea of topping the cake with a glaze or frosting. But we found we liked the modicum of textural contrast provided by a simple sprinkling of spiced granulated sugar.

Applesauce Snack Cake
SERVES 8

The cake is very moist, so it is best to err on the side of overdone when testing its doneness. The test kitchen prefers the rich flavor of cider, but apple juice can be substituted.

- ¾ **cup dried apples, cut into ½-inch pieces**
- 1 **cup apple cider**
- 1½ **cups (7½ ounces) all-purpose flour**
- 1 **teaspoon baking soda**
- ⅔ **cup (4⅔ ounces) sugar**
- ½ **teaspoon ground cinnamon**
- ¼ **teaspoon ground nutmeg**
- ⅛ **teaspoon ground cloves**
- 1 **cup unsweetened applesauce, room temperature**
- 1 **large egg, room temperature, lightly beaten**
- ½ **teaspoon salt**
- 8 **tablespoons unsalted butter, melted and cooled**
- 1 **teaspoon vanilla extract**

1. Adjust oven rack to middle position and heat oven to 325 degrees. Make foil sling by folding 2 long sheets of aluminum foil so that they are as wide as 8-inch square baking pan. Lay sheets of foil in pan perpendicular to one another, with extra foil hanging over edges of pan. Push foil into corners and up sides of pan, smoothing foil flush to pan. Spray foil with vegetable oil spray.

2. Bring dried apples and cider to simmer in small saucepan over medium heat and cook until liquid evaporates and mixture appears dry, about 15 minutes. Let cool to room temperature.

3. Whisk flour and baking soda in medium bowl to combine. In second medium bowl, whisk sugar, cinnamon, nutmeg, and cloves. Measure 2 tablespoons sugar mixture into small bowl and reserve for topping.

4. Process cooled apple mixture and applesauce in food processor until smooth, 20 to 30 seconds, scraping down sides of bowl as needed, and set aside. Whisk egg and salt in large bowl to combine. Add sugar mixture and whisk until well combined and light colored, about 20 seconds. Add butter in 3 additions, whisking after each addition. Add applesauce mixture and vanilla and whisk to combine. Add flour mixture to wet ingredients and fold gently using rubber spatula until just combined and evenly moistened.

5. Scrape batter into prepared pan and smooth top with rubber spatula. Sprinkle reserved sugar mixture evenly over batter. Bake cake until toothpick inserted in center comes out clean, 35 to 40 minutes. Let cake cool completely on wire rack, about 2 hours. Remove cake from pan using foil and transfer to platter. Gently push side of cake with knife and remove foil, 1 piece at a time. Serve. (Cake can be stored at room temperature for up to 2 days.)

Ginger-Cardamom Applesauce Snack Cake
Omit cinnamon, nutmeg, and cloves. Whisk ½ teaspoon ground ginger and ¼ teaspoon ground cardamom into sugar in step 3. Reserve 2 tablespoons sugar mixture and add 1 tablespoon finely chopped crystallized ginger to topping.

Applesauce Snack Cake with Oat-Nut Streusel
In step 3, measure 2 tablespoons sugar mixture into medium bowl. Add 2 tablespoons brown sugar, ⅓ cup chopped pecans or walnuts, and ⅓ cup old-fashioned rolled oats or quick oats. Work in 2 tablespoons softened unsalted butter until fully incorporated by rubbing mixture between fingers. Pinch mixture into hazelnut-size clumps and sprinkle evenly over batter before baking.

Gingerbread

✓ **WHY THIS RECIPE WORKS:** Most gingerbread recipes that are moist also suffer from a dense, sunken center, and flavors range from barely gingery to addled with enough spices to make a curry fan cry for mercy. Our ideal gingerbread was moist through and through and utterly simple. Focusing on flavor first, we bumped up the ginger flavor by using a hefty dose of ground ginger and folded in grated fresh ginger. Cinnamon and fresh-ground pepper helped produce a warm, complex, lingering heat. As for the liquid components, dark stout, gently heated to minimize its booziness, had a bittersweet flavor that brought out the caramel undertones of the molasses. Finally, swapping out the butter for vegetable oil and replacing some of the brown sugar with granulated let the spice flavors come through. To prevent a sunken center, we looked at our leaveners first. Baking powder isn't as effective at leavening if too many other acidic ingredients are present in the batter. In this case, we had three: molasses, brown sugar, and stout. Bucking the usual protocol for cakes and incorporating the baking soda with the wet ingredients instead of the other dry ones helped to neutralize those acidic ingredients before they get incorporated into the batter and allowed the baking powder to do a better job. And while stirring develops flour's gluten, which is typically the enemy of tenderness, our batter was so loose that vigorous stirring actually gave our cake the structure necessary to further ensure the center didn't collapse.

Gingerbread
SERVES 8

This cake packs potent, yet well-balanced, fragrant, spicy heat. If you are particularly sensitive to spice, you can decrease the amount of ground ginger to 1 tablespoon. Avoid opening the oven door until the minimum baking time has elapsed. Serve the gingerbread plain or with whipped cream.

- ¾ **cup stout, such as Guinness**
- ½ **teaspoon baking soda**
- ⅔ **cup molasses**
- ¾ **cup packed (5¼ ounces) light brown sugar**
- ¼ **cup (1¾ ounces) granulated sugar**
- 1½ **cups (7½ ounces) all-purpose flour**
- 2 **tablespoons ground ginger**
- ½ **teaspoon baking powder**
- ½ **teaspoon salt**
- ¼ **teaspoon ground cinnamon**
- ¼ **teaspoon pepper**
- 2 **large eggs, room temperature**
- ⅓ **cup vegetable oil**
- 1 **tablespoon grated fresh ginger**

1. Adjust oven rack to middle position and heat oven to 350 degrees. Grease 8-inch square baking pan, line with parchment paper, grease parchment, and flour pan.

2. Bring stout to boil in medium saucepan over medium heat, stirring occasionally. Remove from heat and stir in baking soda (mixture will foam vigorously). When foaming subsides, stir in molasses, brown sugar, and granulated sugar until dissolved; set aside. Whisk flour, ground ginger, baking powder, salt, cinnamon, and pepper together in large bowl.

3. Transfer stout mixture to second large bowl. Whisk in eggs, oil, and grated ginger until combined. Whisk wet mixture into flour mixture in thirds, stirring vigorously until completely smooth after each addition.

4. Scrape batter into prepared pan, smooth top with rubber spatula, and gently tap pan on counter to release air bubbles. Bake cake until top is just firm to touch and toothpick inserted in center comes out clean, 35 to 45 minutes. Let cake cool in pan on wire rack, about 1½ hours. Serve warm or at room temperature. (Cake can be stored at room temperature for up to 2 days.)

French Apple Cake

✓ **WHY THIS RECIPE WORKS:** For our own version of this classic French cake, we wanted the best of both worlds: a dessert with a custardy, apple-rich base, and a light, cakelike topping. For the apple, Granny Smiths stood out since they held their shape and lent a tart flavor that played well against the dense, sweet cake. We microwaved them briefly to ensure that the apple slices cooked up tender and retained their structure, then we tossed them with some Calvados (apple brandy) and lemon juice to add complexity. For the distinct cake and custard layers, we prepared a single base batter, then added egg yolks to one part to make the custardy base, and flour to the rest to form the cake layer above it. Baked in a moderate oven, our cake baked up creamy and custardy below and airy above.

French Apple Cake
SERVES 8 TO 10

The microwaved apples should be pliable but not completely soft. To test for doneness, take one apple slice and try to bend it. If it snaps in half, it's too firm; microwave it for an additional 30 seconds and test again. If Calvados is unavailable, 1 tablespoon of apple brandy or white rum can be substituted. See Recipe Tutorial on page 660 for more details on this recipe.

- 1½ **pounds Granny Smith apples, peeled, cored, cut into 8 wedges, and sliced ⅛ inch thick crosswise**
- 1 **tablespoon Calvados**
- 1 **teaspoon lemon juice**
- 1 **cup (5 ounces) plus 2 tablespoons all-purpose flour**
- 1 **cup (7 ounces) plus 1 tablespoon granulated sugar**
- 2 **teaspoons baking powder**
- ½ **teaspoon salt**
- 1 **large egg plus 2 large yolks**
- 1 **cup vegetable oil**
- 1 **cup whole milk**
- 1 **teaspoon vanilla extract**
   Confectioners' sugar

1. Adjust oven rack to lower-middle position and heat oven to 325 degrees. Spray 9-inch springform pan with vegetable oil spray. Place prepared pan on rimmed baking sheet lined with aluminum foil. Place apple slices into microwave-safe pie plate, cover, and microwave until apples are pliable and slightly translucent, about 3 minutes. Toss apple slices with Calvados and lemon juice and let cool for 15 minutes.

2. Whisk 1 cup flour, 1 cup granulated sugar, baking powder, and salt together in bowl. Whisk egg, oil, milk, and vanilla together in second bowl until smooth. Add dry ingredients to wet ingredients and whisk until just combined. Transfer 1 cup batter to liquid measuring cup and set aside.

3. Add egg yolks to remaining batter and whisk to combine. Using rubber spatula, gently fold in cooled apples. Transfer batter to prepared pan; using large offset spatula, spread batter evenly to pan edges, gently pressing on apples to create even, compact layer and smooth surface.

4. Whisk remaining 2 tablespoons flour into reserved batter. Pour over batter in pan and spread batter evenly to pan edges and smooth surface. Sprinkle remaining 1 tablespoon granulated sugar evenly over cake.

5. Bake until center of cake is set, toothpick inserted in center comes out clean, and top is golden brown, about 1¼ hours. Transfer pan to wire rack; let cool for 5 minutes. Run paring knife around sides of pan and let cool completely, 2 to 3 hours. Dust lightly with confectioners' sugar, cut into wedges, and serve.

Simple Carrot Cake with Cream Cheese Frosting

✔ **WHY THIS RECIPE WORKS:** Carrot cake was once heralded for its use of vegetable oil in place of butter and carrots as a natural sweetener. Sure, the carrots add sweetness, but they also add a lot of moisture. And oil? It makes this cake dense and, well, oily. We wanted a moist, not soggy, cake that was rich, with a tender crumb and balanced spice.

Cake flour proved too delicate to support the grated carrots, so we started with all-purpose. Some carrot cakes use a heavy hand with the spices; we took a conservative approach and used modest amounts of cinnamon, nutmeg, and cloves. We settled on 1 pound grated carrots for a pleasantly moist texture, and 1½ cups vegetable oil for a rich, but not greasy, cake. For a simple mixing method, we used a food processor fitted with the shredding disk to shred the carrots, then swapped out the blade and made the batter (if you don't own a food processor a coarse grater and mixer will suffice). Cream cheese frosting is the perfect partner to carrot cake—we enriched our version with sour cream for extra tang and vanilla for depth of flavor. It was easy to prepare the frosting in the food processor so that start to finish, we only had to dirty one piece of equipment.

Simple Carrot Cake
SERVES 15

If you like nuts in your cake, stir 1½ cups toasted chopped pecans or walnuts into the batter along with the carrots. Raisins are also a good addition; 1 cup can be added along with the carrots. If you add both nuts and raisins, the cake will need an additional 10 to 12 minutes in the oven.

2½ **cups (12½ ounces) all-purpose flour**
1¼ **teaspoons baking powder**
1 **teaspoon baking soda**
1¼ **teaspoons ground cinnamon**
½ **teaspoon ground nutmeg**
⅛ **teaspoon ground cloves**
½ **teaspoon salt**
1 **pound carrots, peeled**
1½ **cups (10½ ounces) granulated sugar**
½ **cup packed (3½ ounces) light brown sugar**
4 **large eggs, room temperature**
1½ **cups vegetable oil**
1 **recipe Cream Cheese Frosting (recipe follows)**

1. Adjust oven rack to middle position and heat oven to 350 degrees. Grease 13 by 9-inch baking pan, line with parchment paper, grease parchment, and flour pan.

2. Whisk flour, baking powder, baking soda, cinnamon, nutmeg, cloves, and salt together in large bowl and set aside.

3A. FOOD PROCESSOR METHOD: Using food processor fitted with large shredding disk, shred carrots (you should have about 3 cups); transfer to bowl. Wipe out processor bowl and fit processor with metal blade. Process granulated sugar, brown sugar, and eggs in food processor until frothy and thoroughly combined, about 20 seconds. With processor running, add oil in steady stream and process until mixture is light in color and well emulsified, about 20 seconds. Transfer mixture to medium bowl and stir in carrots and flour mixture until incorporated and no streaks of flour remain.

3B. STAND MIXER METHOD: Shred carrots on large holes of coarse grater (you should have about 3 cups); transfer carrots to bowl and set aside. Using stand mixer fitted with paddle, beat granulated sugar, brown sugar, and eggs on medium-high speed until thoroughly combined, about 45 seconds. Reduce speed to medium; with mixer running, add oil in slow, steady stream, being careful to pour oil against inside of bowl (if oil begins to splatter, reduce speed to low until oil is incorporated, then resume adding oil). Increase speed to high and mix until mixture is light in color and well emulsified, about 45 seconds to 1 minute longer. Turn off mixer and stir in carrots and dry ingredients by hand until incorporated and no streaks of flour remain.

4. Scrape batter into prepared pan, smooth top with rubber spatula, and gently tap pan on counter to release air bubbles. Bake cake until toothpick inserted in center comes out clean, 35 to 40 minutes, rotating pan halfway through baking. Let cake cool completely in pan on wire rack, about 2 hours.

5. Run paring knife around edge of cake to loosen from pan. Invert cake onto wire rack, discard parchment, then turn cake right side up onto serving platter. Spread frosting evenly over cake and serve. (Cake can be refrigerated for up to 3 days.)

Cream Cheese Frosting
MAKES 3 CUPS

Do not use low-fat or nonfat cream cheese or the frosting will turn out too soupy to work with.

12 **ounces cream cheese, softened**
6 **tablespoons unsalted butter, softened**
4 **teaspoons sour cream**
1 **teaspoon vanilla extract**
¼ **teaspoon salt**
1¾ **cups (7 ounces) confectioners' sugar**

1A. FOOD PROCESSOR METHOD: Process cream cheese, butter, sour cream, vanilla, and salt in food processor until combined, about 5 seconds, scraping down bowl as needed. Add confectioners' sugar and process until smooth, about 10 seconds.

1B. STAND MIXER METHOD: Using stand mixer fitted with whisk, whip cream cheese, butter, sour cream, vanilla, and salt at medium-high speed until well combined, about 30 seconds, scraping down bowl with rubber spatula as needed. Add confectioners' sugar and mix until very fluffy, about 1 minute.

Spiced Carrot Cake with Vanilla Bean–Cream Cheese Frosting

The Indian tea called chai inspired this variation.

For the cake, substitute ½ teaspoon pepper for nutmeg, increase cloves to ¼ teaspoon, and add 1 tablespoon ground cardamom along with spices. For the frosting, halve and scrape seeds from 2 vanilla beans and add seeds to food processor along with vanilla extract.

Classic Yellow Sheet Cake

✔ **WHY THIS RECIPE WORKS:** Perfect for everything from birthday parties to potlucks and cookouts, sheet cake is easy to make, doesn't require a lot of ingredients, and is a crowd-pleaser because of its simplicity. We started by using lower-protein cake flour instead of all-purpose flour because it would give the cake an ultralight texture. Creaming the butter incorporated some air and thus gave our cake lift, and it also ensured the other ingredients would easily incorporate into the batter. To keep our batter from curdling, we mixed in the eggs one at a time. Then we added our dry ingredients and milk, alternating between the two in a few increments to ensure our batter stayed smooth, and we stopped the mixer as soon as we incorporated the last addition of the dry ingredients to avoid overbeating and creating a dry, tough cake. Taking the baked and cooled cake out of the pan was as easy as flipping it onto a rack, peeling off the parchment, and inverting it onto a platter. All it needed was our buttercream of choice to make our sheet cake ready to go.

Classic Yellow Sheet Cake

SERVES 15

You can serve the cake right out of the pan, in which case you'll need only 3 cups of frosting for the top of the cake. See Core Technique on page 636 for more details on this recipe.

2¾	cups (11 ounces) cake flour
2	teaspoons baking powder
¾	teaspoon salt
16	tablespoons unsalted butter, softened
1¾	cups (12¼ ounces) sugar
4	large eggs, room temperature
1	tablespoon vanilla extract
1½	cups whole milk, room temperature
4	cups buttercream frosting (pages 669–670)

1. Adjust oven rack to middle position and heat oven to 350 degrees. Grease 13 by 9-inch metal baking pan, line with parchment paper, grease parchment, then flour pan.

2. Whisk flour, baking powder, and salt together in bowl; set aside. Using stand mixer fitted with paddle, beat butter and sugar on medium-high speed until light and fluffy, about 3 minutes. Add eggs, one at a time, then vanilla, and beat until combined.

3. Reduce speed to low and add flour mixture in 3 additions, alternating with milk in 2 additions, scraping down bowl as needed. Give batter final stir by hand.

4. Scrape batter into prepared pan, smooth top, and gently tap pan on counter to release air bubbles. Bake until toothpick inserted in center comes out with few moist crumbs attached, 25 to 30 minutes, rotating pan halfway through baking.

5. Let cake cool completely in pan, about 2 hours. Run paring knife around edge of cake and flip cake out onto wire rack. Peel off parchment, then flip cake right side up onto serving platter. Spread frosting evenly over top and sides of cake and serve.

Classic Yellow Cupcakes

This recipe yields 24 cupcakes; you will need only 3 cups of frosting.

Line two 12-cup muffin tins with paper or foil liners. Prepare batter as directed through step 3. Use greased ¼-cup measure to portion batter into each cup. Bake cupcakes on upper-middle and lower-middle racks until toothpick inserted in center comes out with few moist crumbs attached, 15 to 20 minutes, switching and rotating muffin tins halfway through baking. Let cupcakes cool in muffin tins for 10 minutes, then lift each cupcake from muffin tin, transfer to wire rack, and let cool completely. Spread frosting evenly over cupcakes and serve.

Classic White Sheet Cake

✔ **WHY THIS RECIPE WORKS:** White cake is an old-fashioned classic, but while straightforward in appearance it comes with its own unique set of challenges. White cake is simply a basic butter cake made with egg whites rather than whole eggs (as you would find in yellow cake). Theoretically, the whites should make the cake soft and fine-grained. But most white cakes come out dry and chewy (or cottony) and usually riddled with tunnels and small holes. Reverse creaming—beating the butter into the dry ingredients and then adding the liquid ingredients—delivered a fine crumb and tender texture. And while most white cake recipes call for folding stiffly beaten whites into the batter at the end, we found that combining the whites with the milk before adding them to the batter actually produced a cake that was lighter and had a greater rise. Plus, the method was dead simple.

Classic White Sheet Cake

SERVES 15

You can serve the cake right out of the pan, in which case you'll need only 3 cups of frosting for the top of the cake.

1 cup whole milk, room temperature

6 large egg whites, room temperature

2 teaspoons almond extract (optional)

1 teaspoon vanilla extract

2¼ cups (9 ounces) cake flour

1¾ cups (12¼ ounces) sugar

4 teaspoons baking powder

1 teaspoon salt

12 tablespoons unsalted butter, cut into 12 pieces and softened

4 cups buttercream frosting (at right)

1. Adjust oven rack to middle position and heat oven to 350 degrees. Grease 13 by 9-inch baking pan, line with parchment paper, grease parchment, then flour pan. Whisk milk, egg whites, almond extract, if using, and vanilla together in bowl.

2. Whisk flour, sugar, baking powder, and salt together in bowl of stand mixer. Fit mixer with paddle and beat in butter, one piece at a time, on low speed until only pea-size pieces remain, about 1 minute.

3. Add half of milk mixture, increase speed to medium-high and beat until light and fluffy, about 1 minute. Reduce speed to medium-low add remaining milk mixture, and beat until incorporated, about 30 seconds (batter will look slightly curdled). Give batter final stir by hand.

4. Scrape batter into prepared pan, smooth top, and gently tap pan on counter to release air bubbles. Bake until toothpick inserted in center comes out with few moist crumbs attached, 25 to 30 minutes, rotating pan halfway through baking.

5. Let cake cool completely in pan, about 2 hours. Run paring knife around edge of cake and flip cake out onto wire rack. Peel off parchment, then flip cake right side up onto serving platter. Spread frosting evenly over top and sides of cake and serve.

Classic White Cupcakes

This recipe yields 24 cupcakes; you will need only 3 cups of frosting.

Line two 12-cup muffin tins with paper or foil liners, and prepare batter as directed through step 3. Use greased ¼-cup measure to portion batter into each cup. Bake cupcakes on upper-middle and lower-middle racks until toothpick inserted in center comes out with few moist crumbs attached, 15 to 20 minutes, switching and rotating muffin tins halfway through baking. Let cupcakes cool in muffin tins for 10 minutes, then lift each cupcake from muffin tin, transfer to wire rack, and let cool completely. Spread frosting evenly over cupcakes and serve.

Vanilla Buttercream

WHY THIS RECIPE WORKS: The familiar quick and easy frostings, made by beating confectioners' sugar and flavorings into softened butter, get the job done but can have a gritty texture and taste overly sweet. Buttercream, however, is rich and silky, with a more balanced sweetness, achieved by adding a hot sugar syrup to egg yolks. Classic French recipes rely on sugar alone, but we discovered substituting some corn syrup gave our buttercream a fluid but stable consistency and also made it easy to melt the sugar. Some recipes also call for whole eggs, but we preferred the richer texture from using only the yolks. It was key to heat the sugar syrup at the same time the yolks were whipping so that the hot syrup was ready once the yolks were done. Pouring the hot syrup into the egg yolks was essential to raise their temperature to a safe level; making sure to pour the syrup into the eggs slowly avoided scrambling the eggs. We whipped the yolk-syrup mixture to both aerate it and cool it off before adding the softened butter, which ensured the butter wouldn't melt into pools of grease. A couple of minutes of whipping and we had the smooth and silky buttercream we were after.

Vanilla Buttercream

MAKES ABOUT 4 CUPS, ENOUGH FOR A SHEET CAKE OR 2-LAYER CAKE

Make sure that the sugar mixture is poured into the egg yolks while still hot. Because you need to pour hot sugar syrup into the bowl with the eggs with the mixer on, we find this operation is much, much simpler in a stand mixer. If you don't have a stand mixer, you will need to stabilize the mixing bowl with a towel so that one hand can operate the hand-held mixer while the other pours in the hot syrup. For a colored frosting, stir in drops of food coloring at the end; this buttercream has a natural pale yellow color; if storing buttercream in the refrigerator, it will become yellower over time. See Core Technique on page 640 for more details on this recipe.

6 large egg yolks

¾ cup (5¼ ounces) sugar

½ cup light corn syrup

2½ teaspoons vanilla extract

¼ teaspoon salt

1 pound (4 sticks) unsalted butter, each stick cut into quarters and softened

1. Using stand mixer fitted with whisk, whip egg yolks on medium speed until slightly thickened and pale yellow, 4 to 6 minutes.

2. Meanwhile, bring sugar and corn syrup to boil in small saucepan over medium heat, stirring occasionally to dissolve sugar, about 3 minutes.

3. Without letting hot sugar mixture cool off, turn mixer to low and slowly pour hot sugar syrup into whipped egg yolks without hitting side of bowl or beaters. Increase speed to medium-high and whip until mixture is light and fluffy and bowl is no longer warm, 5 to 10 minutes.

4. Reduce speed to medium-low and add vanilla and salt. Gradually add butter, one piece at a time, and whip until completely incorporated, about 2 minutes. Increase speed to medium-high and whip until buttercream is smooth and silky, about 2 minutes. (If mixture looks curdled, wrap hot, wet towel around bowl and continue to whip until smooth, 1 to 2 minutes.) (Buttercream can be refrigerated in airtight container for up to 3 days. Let buttercream sit at room temperature until softened, about 2 hours, then, using stand mixer fitted with whisk, whip on medium speed until smooth, 2 to 5 minutes.)

Chocolate Buttercream

After buttercream has become smooth and silky in step 4, add 8 ounces melted and cooled bittersweet or semisweet chocolate and continue to mix on medium-low speed until completely incorporated, about 1 minute.

Coffee Buttercream

Add 2 tablespoons instant espresso powder or instant coffee powder to saucepan with sugar and corn syrup in step 2.

Peppermint Buttercream

Add 2 teaspoons peppermint extract with vanilla.

Almond Buttercream

Add 2 teaspoons almond extract with vanilla.

Coconut Buttercream

Add 1 tablespoon coconut extract with vanilla.

Simple Chocolate Sheet Cake

✔ **WHY THIS RECIPE WORKS:** Sheet cakes, for all their simplicity, can still turn out dry, sticky, or flavorless and, on occasion, can even sink in the middle. We wanted a simple, dependable recipe, one that was moist yet also light and chocolaty. We started with the mixing method, testing everything from creaming butter to beating egg yolks, whipping egg whites, and gently folding together everything in the end. The best of the lot was the most complicated to make, so we took a step back. The simplest technique we tried was simply whisking all the ingredients together without beating, creaming, or whipping. The recipe needed work, but the approach was clearly what we were after. We added buttermilk and baking soda to lighten the batter, and we reduced the sugar, flour, and butter to increase the chocolate flavor. To further deepen the chocolate taste, we used semisweet chocolate in addition to the cocoa. We baked the cake at a low temperature for a long time—40 minutes—to produce a perfectly baked cake with a lovely flat top. Though this cake can be frosted with almost anything, we like a classic American milk chocolate frosting, which pairs well with the darker flavor of the cake.

Simple Chocolate Sheet Cake

SERVES 15

We prefer Dutch-processed cocoa powder for the deeper chocolate flavor it gives the cake. The baked and cooled cake can also be served with lightly sweetened whipped cream or topped with any frosting you like in lieu of the milk chocolate frosting. This frosting needs about an hour to cool before it can be used, so begin making it when the cake comes out of the oven.

CAKE
- 1¼ cups (6¼ ounces) all-purpose flour
- ¾ cup (2¼ ounces) Dutch-processed cocoa powder
- ¼ teaspoon salt
- 8 ounces semisweet chocolate, chopped
- 12 tablespoons unsalted butter
- 4 large eggs, room temperature
- 1½ cups (10½ ounces) granulated sugar
- 1 teaspoon vanilla extract
- 1 cup buttermilk
- ½ teaspoon baking soda

FROSTING
- ½ cup heavy cream
- 1 tablespoon corn syrup
  Pinch salt
- 10 ounces milk chocolate, chopped
- ½ cup (2 ounces) confectioners' sugar
- 8 tablespoons unsalted butter, cut into 8 pieces and chilled

1. FOR THE CAKE: Adjust oven rack to middle position and heat oven to 325 degrees. Grease 13 by 9-inch baking pan, line with parchment paper, grease parchment, and flour pan.

2. Sift flour, cocoa, and salt together into medium bowl; set aside. Microwave chocolate at 50 percent power for 2 minutes; stir, add butter, and continue heating until melted, stirring once every additional minute. Whisk eggs, sugar, and vanilla together in medium bowl.

3. Whisk chocolate into egg mixture until combined. Combine buttermilk and baking soda; whisk into chocolate mixture, then whisk in dry ingredients until batter is smooth and glossy. Scrape batter into prepared pan and smooth top. Bake cake until firm in center when lightly pressed and toothpick inserted in center comes out clean, about 40 minutes. Let cool on wire rack until room temperature, at least 1 hour.

4. FOR THE FROSTING: Microwave cream, corn syrup, and salt in bowl until simmering, about 1 minute, or bring to simmer in small saucepan over medium heat. Place chocolate in food processor. With processor running, gradually add hot cream mixture, then process for 1 minute. Stop processor, add confectioners' sugar, and process to combine, about 30 seconds. With processor running, add butter, 1 piece at a time, then process until incorporated and smooth, about 20 seconds longer. Transfer frosting to medium bowl and let cool at room temperature, stirring frequently, until thick and spreadable, about 1 hour. Spread frosting evenly over top and sides of cake and serve.

Classic Yellow Bundt Cake

✓ **WHY THIS RECIPE WORKS:** With its decorative shape, a Bundt cake doesn't need frosting or fussy finishing techniques to look good. But most Bundt cakes have a dry, uninspired texture that is too crumbly and coarse. Creaming the butter was critical for a light, even crumb, and while most recipes call for 1 cup, we found that upping the amount of butter by a couple of tablespoons gave us a richer, more tender crumb. Likewise using buttermilk instead of the usual milk gave our cake a lighter, more tender crumb as well as a nice, mild tang. Adding lemon juice and baking soda ensured the heavy batter would rise properly. And last, we found that brushing the interior of the pan with a paste made with flour and melted butter was the best way to get every crevice of the pan greased, ensuring we could get our cake out in one attractive piece.

Classic Yellow Bundt Cake
SERVES 12

Serve this cake as is or dress it up with a dusting of confectioners' sugar or lightly sweetened berries.

  3 **cups (15 ounces) plus 1 tablespoon all-purpose flour**
  1 **tablespoon unsalted butter, melted, plus
     18 tablespoons (2¼ sticks), softened**
  1 **teaspoon salt**
  1 **teaspoon baking powder**
  ½ **teaspoon baking soda**
  ¾ **cup buttermilk, room temperature**
  1 **tablespoon vanilla extract**
  1 **tablespoon lemon juice**
  2 **cups (14 ounces) sugar**
  3 **large eggs plus 1 large yolk, room temperature**

1. Adjust oven rack to lower-middle position and heat oven to 350 degrees. Mix 1 tablespoon flour and melted butter into paste. Using pastry brush, thoroughly coat interior of 12-cup nonstick Bundt pan. Whisk remaining 3 cups flour, salt, baking powder, and baking soda together in bowl. In separate bowl, whisk buttermilk, vanilla, and lemon juice together.

2. Using stand mixer fitted with paddle, beat softened butter and sugar together on medium-high speed until pale and fluffy, about 3 minutes. Beat in eggs and egg yolk, one at a time, until combined.

3. Reduce speed to low and add flour mixture in 3 additions, alternating with buttermilk mixture in 2 additions, scraping down bowl as needed. Give batter final stir by hand.

4. Scrape batter into prepared pan and smooth top. Wipe any drops of batter off sides of pan and gently tap pan on counter to release air bubbles. Bake until wooden skewer inserted in middle of cake comes out with few moist crumbs attached, 50 to 60 minutes, rotating pan halfway through baking.

5. Let cake cool in pan on wire rack set over baking sheet for 10 minutes, then invert cake onto rack. Let cake cool completely, about 2 hours, before serving.

Lemon Bundt Cake

Increase amount of lemon juice to 3 tablespoons and add 3 tablespoons grated lemon zest to buttermilk with vanilla and juice.

Orange Bundt Cake

Add 2 tablespoons grated orange zest and 2 tablespoons orange juice to buttermilk with vanilla and lemon juice.

Marble Bundt Cake

Microwave 3 ounces bittersweet chocolate, 2 tablespoons unsalted butter, and 2 tablespoons Dutch-processed cocoa powder together in microwave-safe bowl, stirring often, until melted and smooth, 1 to 3 minutes. Prepare cake batter as directed through step 3, then pour half of batter into separate bowl. Add chocolate mixture to one bowl of batter and stir until combined. Scrape plain batter into prepared Bundt pan, then top with chocolate batter. Using butter knife, swirl batters together. Bake as directed.

Best Angel Food Cake

✓ **WHY THIS RECIPE WORKS:** Angel food cake should be tall and perfectly shaped, have a snowy-white, tender crumb, and be encased in a thin, delicate golden crust. The difficulty with making a great angel food cake is that it requires a delicate balance of ingredients and proper technique. First, we found it key to create a stable egg-white base, starting the whites at medium-low speed just to break them up into a froth and increasing the speed to medium-high speed to form soft, billowy mounds. Next, the sugar should be added a tablespoon at a time. Once all the sugar is added, the whites become shiny and form soft peaks when the beater is lifted. A delicate touch is required when incorporating the remaining ingredients, such as the flour, which should be sifted over the batter and gently folded in. Angel food cakes are baked in a tube pan. We like to use a tube pan with a removable bottom but a pan without one can be lined with parchment paper. We avoid greasing the sides of the pan so that the cake can climb up and cling to the sides as it bakes—a greased pan will produce a disappointingly short cake.

Best Angel Food Cake
SERVES 12

If your tube pan has a removable bottom, you do not need to line it with parchment.

  ¾ **cup (3 ounces) cake flour**
  1½ **cups (10½ ounces) sugar**
  12 **large egg whites, room temperature**
  1 **teaspoon cream of tartar**
  ¼ **teaspoon salt**
  1½ **teaspoons vanilla extract**
  1½ **teaspoons lemon juice**
  ½ **teaspoon almond extract**

1. Adjust an oven rack to the lower-middle position and heat oven to 325 degrees. Line 16-cup tube pan with parchment paper but do not grease. Whisk flour and ¾ cup sugar together in small bowl. Place remaining ¾ cup sugar in second small bowl.

2. Using stand mixer fitted with whisk, whip egg whites, cream of tartar, and salt on medium-low speed until foamy, about 1 minute. Increase speed to medium-high and whip to soft, billowy mounds, about 1 minute. Gradually add ¾ cup sugar and whip until soft, glossy peaks form, 1 to 2 minutes. Add vanilla, lemon juice, and almond extract and beat until just blended.

3. Sift flour mixture over egg whites, about 3 tablespoons at a time, gently folding mixture into whites using large rubber spatula after each addition.

4. Gently scrape batter into prepared pan, smooth top with rubber spatula, and gently tap pan on counter to release air bubbles. Bake cake until golden brown and top springs back when pressed firmly, 50 to 60 minutes. If cake has prongs around rim for elevating cake, invert pan on them. If not, invert pan over neck of bottle or funnel so that air can circulate all around it. Let cake cool completely, 2 to 3 hours.

5. Run paring knife around edge of cake to loosen, then gently tap pan upside down on counter to release cake. Peel off parchment, turn cake right side up onto serving platter, and serve.

Ultimate Chocolate Cupcakes with Ganache Filling

✓ **WHY THIS RECIPE WORKS:** A chocolate cupcake catch-22 befalls bakery and homemade confections alike: If the cupcakes have decent chocolate flavor, their structure is too crumbly for out-of-hand consumption. Conversely, if the cakes balance moisture and tenderness without crumbling, the cake and frosting are barely palatable. We wanted a moist, tender (but not crumbly) cupcake capped with just enough creamy, not-too-sweet frosting. We started by making cupcakes using our favorite chocolate cake recipe. Tasters liked the real chocolate flavor, but their crumbly texture made them impossible to eat without a fork. To strengthen the batter we cut back on both kinds of chocolate, then we found two ways to enhance the chocolate flavor without disrupting the batter's structure: We mixed the cocoa powder with hot coffee, and we replaced the butter with more neutral-flavored vegetable oil. Still, we wanted more chocolate flavor. Could we enhance the structure of the cupcake so that we could then add back extra chocolate without overtenderizing? Substituting bread flour for all-purpose flour did the trick. Specifically engineered for gluten development, bread flour turned out a cupcake that was markedly less crumble-prone, but not tough. For a final chocolate burst, we spooned a dollop of ganache onto each portion of cupcake batter before baking, which turned into a truffle-like center once baked. A velvety Swiss meringue buttercream, which gets its satiny-smooth texture from whisking the egg whites and sugar in a double boiler, then whipping the mixture with softened butter, was the perfect way to crown these cupcakes.

Ultimate Chocolate Cupcakes with Ganache Filling

MAKES 12 CUPCAKES

Use a high-quality bittersweet chocolate for this recipe. Though we highly recommend the ganache filling, you can omit it for a more traditional cupcake. See Recipe Tutorial on page 648 for more details on this recipe.

FILLING

- **2** ounces bittersweet chocolate, chopped fine
- ¼ cup heavy cream
- **1** tablespoon confectioners' sugar

CUPCAKES

- **3** ounces bittersweet chocolate, chopped fine
- ⅓ cup (1 ounce) Dutch-processed cocoa powder
- ¾ cup brewed coffee, hot
- ¾ cup (4⅛ ounces) bread flour
- ¾ cup (5¼ ounces) granulated sugar
- ½ teaspoon salt
- ½ teaspoon baking soda
- **6** tablespoons vegetable oil
- **2** large eggs
- **2** teaspoons distilled white vinegar
- **1** teaspoon vanilla extract

- **1** recipe frosting (recipes follow)

1. FOR THE FILLING: Microwave chocolate, cream, and sugar in medium bowl until mixture is warm to touch, about 30 seconds. Whisk until smooth, then transfer bowl to refrigerator and let sit until just chilled, no longer than 30 minutes.

2. FOR THE CUPCAKES: Adjust oven rack to middle position and heat oven to 350 degrees. Line 12-cup muffin tin with paper or foil liners. Place chocolate and cocoa in medium heatproof bowl. Pour hot coffee over mixture and let sit, covered, for 5 minutes. Whisk mixture gently until smooth, then transfer to refrigerator to cool completely, about 20 minutes.

3. Whisk flour, sugar, salt, and baking soda together in medium bowl. Whisk oil, eggs, vinegar, and vanilla into cooled chocolate mixture until smooth. Add flour mixture and whisk until smooth.

4. Using ice cream scoop or large spoon, divide batter evenly among prepared muffin cups. Place 1 slightly rounded teaspoon ganache filling on top of each portion of batter. Bake cupcakes until set and just firm to touch, 17 to 19 minutes. Let cupcakes cool in muffin tin on wire rack until cool enough to handle, about 10 minutes. Lift each cupcake from tin, set on wire rack, and let cool completely before frosting, about 1 hour. (Unfrosted cupcakes can be stored at room temperature for up to 1 day.)

5. TO FROST: Spread 2 to 3 tablespoons frosting over each cooled cupcake and serve.

Creamy Chocolate Frosting

MAKES ABOUT 2¼ CUPS

The melted chocolate should be cooled to between 85 and 100 degrees before being added to the frosting. If the frosting seems too soft after adding the chocolate, chill it briefly in the refrigerator and then rewhip it until creamy.

⅓ cup (2⅓ ounces) granulated sugar
2 large egg whites
Pinch salt
12 tablespoons unsalted butter, cut into 12 pieces and softened
6 ounces bittersweet chocolate, melted and cooled
½ teaspoon vanilla extract

1. Combine sugar, egg whites, and salt in bowl of stand mixer and set bowl over saucepan filled with 1 inch of barely simmering water. Whisking gently but constantly, heat mixture until slightly thickened, foamy, and registers 150 degrees, 2 to 3 minutes.

2. Fit stand mixer with whisk and beat mixture on medium speed until consistency of shaving cream and slightly cooled, 1 to 2 minutes. Add butter, 1 piece at a time, until smooth and creamy. (Frosting may look curdled after half of butter has been added; it will smooth with additional butter.) Once all butter is added, add cooled melted chocolate and vanilla; mix until combined. Increase speed to medium-high and beat until light, fluffy, and thoroughly combined, about 30 seconds, scraping down beater and sides of bowl with rubber spatula as necessary.

TO MAKE AHEAD: Frosting can be made up to 1 day in advance and refrigerated in an airtight container. When ready to frost, warm frosting briefly in microwave until just slightly softened, 5 to 10 seconds. Once warmed, stir until creamy.

Creamy Malted Milk Frosting

Reduce sugar to ¼ cup, substitute milk chocolate for bittersweet chocolate, and add ¼ cup malted milk powder to frosting with vanilla in step 2.

Creamy Vanilla Frosting

Omit bittersweet chocolate and increase sugar to ½ cup. (If final frosting seems too thick, warm mixer bowl briefly over pan filled with 1 inch of simmering water and beat a second time until creamy).

Creamy Peanut Butter Frosting

Omit bittersweet chocolate, increase sugar to ½ cup, and increase salt to ⅛ teaspoon. Add ⅔ cup creamy peanut butter to frosting with vanilla in step 2. Garnish cupcakes with ½ cup chopped peanuts.

Creamy Butterscotch Frosting

Substitute dark brown sugar for granulated sugar and increase salt to ½ teaspoon.

Fluffy Yellow Layer Cake with Chocolate Frosting

✔ **WHY THIS RECIPE WORKS:** Box mixes are famous for engineering cakes with ultralight texture. We set out to make an even fluffier cake without chemicals and additives. Chiffon cakes are especially weightless, springy, and moist. But unlike butter cakes, they are too light to stand up to a serious slathering of frosting. So we adapted a chiffon technique (using a large quantity of whipped egg whites to get a high volume and light texture) to combine the ingredients from our butter cake recipe. This gave us a light, porous cake that was sturdy enough to hold the frosting's weight. We used both butter and vegetable oil, which kept the butter flavor intact while improving the moistness of the cake. For extra tenderness, we increased the sugar and substituted buttermilk for milk. The buttermilk also allowed us to replace some of the baking powder with a little baking soda to ensure an even rise. As for the frosting, a fluffy chocolate frosting is the perfect partner to this cake. A hefty amount of cocoa powder combined with melted chocolate gave the frosting a deep chocolate flavor. A combination of confectioners' sugar and corn syrup made it smooth and glossy. To keep the frosting from separating and turning greasy, we moved it out of the stand mixer and into the food processor. The faster machine minimized any risk of overbeating, as it blended the ingredients quickly without melting the butter or incorporating too much air. The result was a thick, fluffy chocolate frosting that spread like a dream.

Fluffy Yellow Layer Cake with Chocolate Frosting

SERVES 10 TO 12

Bring all the ingredients to room temperature before beginning this recipe. Be sure to use cake pans with at least 2-inch-tall sides. This frosting may be made with milk, semisweet, or bittersweet chocolate; we prefer a frosting made with milk chocolate for this recipe. Cool the chocolate to between 85 and 100 degrees before adding it to the butter mixture. See Recipe Tutorial on page 652 for more details on this recipe.

CAKE
2½ cups (10 ounces) cake flour
1¼ teaspoons baking powder
¼ teaspoon baking soda
¾ teaspoon salt
1¾ cups (12¼ ounces) granulated sugar
10 tablespoons unsalted butter, melted and cooled
1 cup buttermilk, room temperature
3 tablespoons vegetable oil
2 teaspoons vanilla extract
3 large eggs, separated, plus 3 large yolks, room temperature
Pinch cream of tartar

FROSTING
20 tablespoons (2½ sticks) unsalted butter, softened
1 cup (4 ounces) confectioners' sugar
¾ cup (2¼ ounces) Dutch-processed cocoa powder
Pinch salt
¾ cup light corn syrup
1 teaspoon vanilla extract
8 ounces chocolate, melted and cooled

1. FOR THE CAKE: Adjust oven rack to middle position and heat oven to 350 degrees. Grease two 9-inch round cake pans, line with parchment paper, grease parchment, and flour pans. Whisk flour, baking powder, baking soda, salt, and 1½ cups sugar together in large bowl. In medium bowl, whisk together melted butter, buttermilk, oil, vanilla, and egg yolks.

2. Using stand mixer fitted with whisk, whip egg whites and cream of tartar on medium-low speed until foamy, about 1 minute. Increase speed to medium-high and whip whites to soft billowy mounds, about 1 minute. Gradually add remaining ¼ cup sugar and whip until glossy, stiff peaks form, 2 to 3 minutes. Transfer to bowl and set aside.

3. Add flour mixture to now-empty bowl. With mixer on low speed, gradually pour in butter mixture and mix until almost incorporated (a few streaks of dry flour will remain), about 15 seconds. Scrape down bowl, then beat on medium-low speed until smooth and fully incorporated, 10 to 15 seconds.

4. Using rubber spatula, stir one-third of whites into batter, then add remaining two-thirds whites and gently fold into batter until no white streaks remain. Divide batter evenly between prepared pans, smooth tops with rubber spatula, and gently tap pans on counter to release air bubbles.

5. Bake cakes until toothpick inserted in centers comes out clean, 20 to 22 minutes, switching and rotating pans halfway through baking. Let cakes cool in pans on wire rack for 10 minutes. Remove cakes from pans, discard parchment, and let cool completely, about 2 hours, before frosting. (Cooled cakes can be wrapped tightly in plastic wrap and kept at room temperature for up to 1 day. Cakes can also be wrapped tightly in plastic, then aluminum foil, and frozen for up to 1 month; defrost cakes at room temperature before unwrapping and frosting.)

6. FOR THE FROSTING: Process butter, sugar, cocoa, and salt in food processor until smooth, about 30 seconds, scraping down bowl as needed. Add corn syrup and vanilla and process until just combined, 5 to 10 seconds. Scrape down bowl, then add chocolate and process until smooth and creamy, 10 to 15 seconds. (Frosting can be kept at room temperature for up to 3 hours before frosting cake or refrigerated for up to 3 days. If refrigerated, let stand at room temperature for 1 hour before using.)

7. TO ASSEMBLE THE CAKE: Line edges of cake platter with 4 strips of parchment paper to keep platter clean. Place 1 cake layer on prepared platter. Place about 1½ cups frosting in center of cake layer and, using large spatula, spread in even layer right to edge of cake. Place second cake layer on top, making sure layers are aligned, then frost top in same manner as first layer, this time spreading frosting until slightly over edge. Gather more frosting on tip of spatula and gently spread frosting onto side of cake. Smooth frosting by gently running edge of spatula around cake and leveling ridge that forms around top edge, or create billows by pressing back of spoon into frosting and twirling spoon as you lift away. Carefully pull out pieces of parchment from beneath cake before serving. (Assembled cake can be refrigerated for up to 1 day. Bring to room temperature before serving.)

Old-Fashioned Birthday Cake

✔ **WHY THIS RECIPE WORKS:** White layer cakes have been the classic birthday cake for more than 100 years. White cake is simply a butter cake made with egg whites instead of whole eggs (using the latter would make it a yellow cake). The whites are supposed to make the cake soft and fine-grained. Unfortunately, most white cakes fall short, coming out dry and cottony and riddled with tunnels and small holes. Traditional recipes call for folding stiffly beaten egg whites into the batter at the end. We suspected that it was the beaten whites that were forming the large air pockets and holes in the baked cakes. We solved the problem by mixing the whites with the milk before beating them into the flour-butter mixture. This cake was not only fine-grained and free from holes but it was also larger and lighter than the ones made with beaten whites. And the method couldn't be simpler, quicker, or more foolproof. To make this cake birthday-special, we iced it with an easy butter frosting and added a layer of raspberry jam and chopped toasted almonds.

Classic White Layer Cake with Raspberry-Almond Filling
SERVES 10 TO 12

There is enough frosting to pipe a border around the base and top of the cake. If you want to decorate the cake more elaborately, you should make 1½ times the frosting recipe. If desired, finish the sides of the cake with 1 cup of sliced almonds.

CAKE

- 1 cup whole milk, room temperature
- 6 large egg whites, room temperature
- 2 teaspoons almond extract
- 1 teaspoon vanilla extract
- 2¼ cups (9 ounces) cake flour
- 1¾ cups (12¼ ounces) granulated sugar
- 4 teaspoons baking powder
- 1 teaspoon salt
- 12 tablespoons unsalted butter, cut into 12 pieces and softened

FROSTING AND FILLING

- 16 tablespoons unsalted butter, softened
- 4 cups (16 ounces) confectioners' sugar
- 1 tablespoon vanilla extract
- 1 tablespoon whole milk
  Pinch salt
- ½ cup slivered almonds, toasted and chopped coarse
- ⅓ cup seedless raspberry jam

1. FOR THE CAKE: Adjust oven rack to middle position and heat oven to 350 degrees. Grease two 9-inch round cake pans, line with parchment paper, grease parchment, and flour pans.

2. Whisk milk, egg whites, almond extract, and vanilla together in small bowl. Whisk cake flour, sugar, baking powder, and salt together in bowl of stand mixer. Fit mixer with paddle and beat in butter, 1 piece at a time, until only pea-size pieces remain, about 1 minute.

3. Add all but ½ cup milk mixture, increase speed to medium-high, and beat until light and fluffy, about 1 minute. Reduce speed to medium-low, add remaining ½ cup milk mixture, and beat until incorporated, about 30 seconds (batter may look slightly curdled). Give batter final stir by hand.

4. Divide batter evenly between prepared pans and smooth tops with rubber spatula. Bake cake until toothpick inserted in centers comes out clean, 23 to 25 minutes, switching and rotating pans halfway through baking. Let cakes cool in pans on wire rack for 10 minutes. Remove cakes from pans, discard parchment, and let cool completely, about 2 hours, before frosting. (Cooled cakes can be wrapped tightly in plastic wrap and kept at room temperature for up to 1 day. Wrapped tightly in plastic, then aluminum foil, cakes can be frozen for up to 1 month. Defrost cakes at room temperature before unwrapping and frosting.)

5. FOR THE FROSTING AND FILLING: Using stand mixer fitted with paddle, beat butter, confectioners' sugar, vanilla, milk, and salt on low speed until sugar is moistened. Increase speed to medium-high and beat until creamy and fluffy, about 1½ minutes, stopping twice to scrape down bowl. (Avoid overbeating, or frosting will be too soft to pipe.)

6. TO ASSEMBLE THE CAKE: In small bowl, combine ½ cup frosting with almonds. Line edges of cake platter with 4 strips of parchment paper to keep platter clean. Place 1 cake layer on prepared platter. Place almond frosting in center of cake layer and, using large spatula, spread in even layer right to edge of cake. Carefully spread jam on top. Place second cake layer on top, making sure layers are aligned. Spread about 1½ cups plain frosting over top, spreading frosting until slightly over edge. Gather more frosting on tip of spatula and gently spread frosting onto side of cake. Smooth frosting by gently running edge of spatula around cake and leveling ridge that forms around top edge, or create billows by pressing back of spoon into frosting and twirling spoon as you lift away. Carefully pull out pieces of parchment from beneath cake before serving. (Assembled cake can be refrigerated for up to 1 day. Bring to room temperature before serving.)

Old-Fashioned Chocolate Layer Cake

✔ **WHY THIS RECIPE WORKS:** Over the years, chocolate cakes have become denser, richer, and squatter. We wanted an old-style, mile-high chocolate layer cake with a tender, airy, open crumb and a soft, billowy frosting. The mixing method was the key to getting the right texture. After trying a variety of techniques, we turned to a popular old-fashioned method, ribboning. Ribboning involves whipping eggs with sugar until they double in volume, then adding the butter, dry ingredients, and milk. The egg foam aerated the cake, giving it both structure and tenderness. To achieve a moist cake with rich chocolate flavor, we once again looked to historical sources, which suggested using buttermilk and making a "pudding" with a mixture of chocolate, water, and sugar. We simply melted unsweetened chocolate and cocoa powder in hot water over a double boiler, then stirred in sugar until it dissolved. Turning to the frosting, we wanted the intense chocolate flavor of a ganache and the volume of a meringue or buttercream. The solution turned out to be a simple reversal of the conventional ganache procedure: We poured cold (rather than heated) cream into warm (rather than room-temperature) chocolate, waited for it to cool to room temperature, then whipped until fluffy.

Old-Fashioned Chocolate Layer Cake
SERVES 10 TO 12

For a smooth, spreadable frosting, use chopped semisweet chocolate, not chocolate chips—chocolate chips contain less cocoa butter than bar chocolate and will not melt as readily. As for other bar chocolate, bittersweet chocolate that is 60 percent cacao can be substituted but it will produce a stiffer, although still spreadable, frosting. Bittersweet chocolate with 70 percent cacao, however, should be avoided—it will produce a frosting that is crumbly and will not spread. For best results, do not make the frosting until the cakes are cooled, and use the frosting as soon as it is ready. If the frosting gets too cold and stiff to spread easily, wrap the mixer bowl with a kitchen towel soaked in hot water and mix on low speed until the frosting appears creamy and smooth. Be sure to use cake pans with at least 2-inch-tall sides.

CAKE
- **4** ounces unsweetened chocolate, chopped coarse
- **¼** cup (¾ ounce) Dutch-processed cocoa powder
- **½** cup hot water
- **1¾** cups (12¼ ounces) sugar
- **1¾** cups (8¾ ounces) all-purpose flour
- **1½** teaspoons baking soda
- **1** teaspoon salt
- **1** cup buttermilk
- **2** teaspoons vanilla extract
- **4** large eggs plus 2 large yolks, room temperature
- **12** tablespoons unsalted butter, cut into 12 pieces and softened

FROSTING
- **1** pound semisweet chocolate, chopped fine
- **8** tablespoons unsalted butter
- **⅓** cup (2⅓ ounces) sugar
- **2** tablespoons corn syrup
- **2** teaspoons vanilla extract
- **¼** teaspoon salt
- **1¼** cups heavy cream, chilled

1. FOR THE CAKE: Adjust oven rack to middle position and heat oven to 350 degrees. Grease two 9-inch round cake pans, line with parchment paper, grease parchment, and flour pans. Combine chocolate, cocoa, and hot water in medium heatproof bowl set over saucepan filled with 1 inch of barely simmering water and stir with heat-resistant rubber spatula until chocolate is melted, about 2 minutes. Add ½ cup sugar to chocolate mixture and stir until thick and glossy, 1 to 2 minutes. Remove bowl from heat; set aside to cool.

2. Whisk flour, baking soda, and salt together in medium bowl. Combine buttermilk and vanilla in small bowl. Using stand mixer fitted with whisk, whip eggs and egg yolks on medium-low speed until combined, about 10 seconds. Add remaining 1¼ cups sugar, increase speed to high, and whip until light and fluffy, 2 to 3 minutes. Fit stand mixer with paddle. Add cooled chocolate mixture to egg mixture and mix on medium speed until thoroughly combined, 30 to 45 seconds, scraping down bowl as needed. Add butter, 1 piece at a time, mixing about 10 seconds after each addition. Add flour in 3 additions, alternating with 2 additions of buttermilk mixture, mixing until incorporated after each addition (about 15 seconds), scraping down bowl as needed (batter may appear curdled). Mix at medium-low speed until batter is thoroughly combined, about 15 seconds. Remove bowl from mixer and give batter final stir by hand.

3. Divide batter evenly between prepared pans and smooth tops with rubber spatula. Bake cake until toothpick inserted in centers comes out with few crumbs attached, 25 to 30 minutes, switching and rotating pans halfway through baking. Let cakes cool in pans on wire rack for 10 minutes. Remove cakes from pans, discard parchment, and let cool completely, about 2 hours, before frosting. (Cooled cakes can be wrapped tightly in plastic wrap and kept at room temperature for up to 1 day. Cakes can be wrapped tightly in plastic, then aluminum foil, and frozen for up to 1 month; defrost cakes at room temperature before unwrapping and frosting.)

4. FOR THE FROSTING: Melt chocolate in heatproof bowl set over saucepan containing 1 inch of barely simmering water, stirring occasionally until smooth. Remove from heat and set aside. Meanwhile, melt butter in small saucepan over medium-low heat. Increase heat to medium, add sugar, corn syrup, vanilla, and salt and stir with heat-resistant rubber spatula until sugar is dissolved, 4 to 5 minutes. In bowl of stand mixer, combine melted chocolate, butter mixture, and cream and stir until thoroughly combined.

5. Place mixer bowl over ice bath and stir mixture constantly with rubber spatula until frosting is thick and just beginning to harden against sides of bowl, 1 to 2 minutes (frosting should be 70 degrees). Fit stand mixer with paddle and beat frosting on medium-high speed until frosting is light and fluffy, 1 to 2 minutes. Using rubber spatula, stir until completely smooth.

6. TO ASSEMBLE THE CAKE: Line edges of cake platter with 4 strips of parchment paper to keep platter clean. Place 1 cake layer on prepared platter. Place about 1½ cups frosting in center of cake layer and, using large spatula, spread in even layer right to edge of cake. Place second cake layer on top, making sure layers are aligned, then frost top in same manner as first layer, this time spreading frosting until slightly over edge. Gather more frosting on tip of spatula and gently spread frosting onto side of cake. Smooth frosting by gently running edge of spatula around cake and leveling ridge that forms around top edge, or create billows by pressing back of spoon into frosting and twirling spoon as you lift away. Carefully pull out pieces of parchment from beneath cake before serving. (Assembled cake can be refrigerated for up to 1 day. Bring to room temperature before serving.)

New York–Style Cheesecake

WHY THIS RECIPE WORKS: The ideal New York cheesecake should be tall and bronze-skinned, and at the core, it should be cool, thick, smooth, satiny, and creamy. The flavor should be pure and minimalist, sweet and tangy, and rich. But many recipes fall short—going wrong in a number of ways—with textures that range from fluffy to rubbery and leaden, and flavors that are starchy or overly citrusy. We wanted to find the secret to perfect New York cheesecake. After trying a variety of crusts, we settled on the classic graham cracker crust: a simple combination of graham crackers, butter, and sugar. For the filling, cream cheese, boosted by the extra tang of a little sour cream, delivered the best flavor. A little lemon juice and vanilla added just the right sweet, bright accents without calling attention to themselves. A combination of eggs and egg yolks yielded a texture that was dense but not heavy. We found that the New York method worked better for this cheesecake than the typical water bath—baking the cake in a hot oven for 10 minutes then in a low oven for a full hour and a half yielded the satiny texture we were after.

New York–Style Cheesecake

SERVES 12 TO 16

For the crust, chocolate wafers can be substituted for graham crackers; you will need about 14 wafers. The flavor and texture of the cheesecake is best if the cake is allowed to sit at room temperature for 30 minutes before serving. When cutting the cake, have a pitcher of hot tap water nearby; dipping the blade of the knife into the water and wiping it clean with a dish towel after each cut helps make neat slices. Serve with Fresh Strawberry Topping (recipe follows) if desired. See Recipe Tutorial on page 656 for more details on this recipe.

CRUST

- 8 whole graham crackers, broken into rough pieces
- 1 tablespoon sugar
- 5 tablespoons unsalted butter, melted

FILLING

- 2½ pounds cream cheese, cut into 1-inch chunks and softened
- 1½ cups (10½ ounces) sugar
- ⅛ teaspoon salt
- ⅓ cup sour cream
- 2 teaspoons lemon juice
- 2 teaspoons vanilla extract
- 6 large eggs plus 2 large yolks
- 1 tablespoon unsalted butter, melted

1. FOR THE CRUST: Adjust oven rack to lower-middle position and heat oven to 325 degrees. Process graham cracker pieces in food processor to fine crumbs, about 30 seconds. Combine graham cracker crumbs and sugar in medium bowl, add melted butter, and toss with fork until evenly moistened. Empty crumbs into 9-inch springform pan and, using bottom of ramekin or dry measuring cup, press crumbs firmly and evenly into pan bottom, keeping sides as clean as possible.

Bake crust until fragrant and beginning to brown around edges, about 13 minutes. Let crust cool in pan on wire rack while making filling.

2. FOR THE FILLING: Increase oven temperature to 500 degrees. Using stand mixer fitted with paddle, beat cream cheese on medium-low speed until broken up and slightly softened, about 1 minute. Scrape down bowl. Add ¾ cup sugar and salt and beat on medium-low speed until combined, about 1 minute. Scrape down bowl, then beat in remaining ¾ cup sugar until combined, about 1 minute. Scrape down bowl, add sour cream, lemon juice, and vanilla, and beat on low speed until combined, about 1 minute. Scrape down bowl, add egg yolks, and beat on medium-low speed until thoroughly combined, about 1 minute. Scrape down bowl, add whole eggs, 2 at a time, beating until thoroughly combined, about 1 minute, and scraping bowl between additions.

3. Being careful not to disturb baked crust, brush inside of pan with melted butter and set pan on rimmed baking sheet to catch any spills in case pan leaks. Pour filling into cooled crust and bake 10 minutes; without opening oven door, reduce temperature to 200 degrees and continue to bake until cheesecake registers about 150 degrees, about 1½ hours. Let cake cool on wire rack for 5 minutes, then run paring knife around cake to loosen from pan. Let cake continue to cool until barely warm, 2½ to 3 hours. Wrap tightly in plastic wrap and refrigerate until cold, at least 3 hours. (Cake can be refrigerated for up to 4 days.)

4. To unmold cheesecake, wrap hot dish towel around pan and let stand for 1 minute. Remove sides of pan. Slide large offset spatula between crust and pan bottom to loosen, then slide cake onto serving platter. Let cheesecake sit at room temperature for about 30 minutes before serving. (Cheesecake can be made up to 3 days in advance; however, crust will begin to lose its crispness after only 1 day.)

Fresh Strawberry Topping

MAKES ABOUT 1½ QUARTS

This accompaniment to cheesecake is best served the same day it is made.

- 2 **pounds strawberries, hulled and sliced lengthwise ¼ to ⅛ inch thick (3 cups)**
- ½ **cup (3½ ounces) sugar**
  Pinch salt
- 1 **cup strawberry jam**
- 2 **tablespoons lemon juice**

1. Toss strawberries, sugar, and salt in medium bowl and let sit until strawberries have released juice and sugar has dissolved, about 30 minutes, tossing occasionally to combine.

2. Process jam in food processor until smooth, about 8 seconds, then transfer to small saucepan. Bring jam to simmer over medium-high heat and simmer, stirring frequently, until dark and no longer frothy, about 3 minutes. Stir in lemon juice, then pour warm liquid over strawberries and stir to combine. Let cool, then cover with plastic wrap and refrigerate until cold, at least 2 hours or up to 12 hours.

The Ultimate Flourless Chocolate Cake

✔ **WHY THIS RECIPE WORKS:** While all flourless chocolate cake recipes share common ingredients (chocolate, butter, and eggs), the techniques used to make them vary, as do the results. You can end up with anything from a fudge brownie to a chocolate soufflé. We wanted something dense, moist, and ultra-chocolaty, but with some textural finesse. A cake made with unsweetened chocolate was neither smooth nor silky enough, but both bittersweet and semisweet chocolate delivered deep chocolate flavor and a smooth texture. Comparing cakes made with room-temperature whole eggs and whole eggs taken straight from the fridge, the batter made with chilled eggs produced a denser foam and the resulting cake boasted a smooth, velvety texture. And the gentle, moist heat of a water bath further preserved the cake's lush texture.

The Ultimate Flourless Chocolate Cake

SERVES 12 TO 16

Even though the cake may not look done, pull it from the oven when it registers 140 degrees. It will continue to firm up as it cools. If you use a 9-inch springform pan instead of the preferred 8-inch, reduce the baking time to 18 to 20 minutes.

- 8 **large eggs, chilled**
- 1 **pound bittersweet or semisweet chocolate, chopped coarse**
- 16 **tablespoons unsalted butter, cut into ½-inch pieces**
- ¼ **cup strong brewed coffee, room temperature**
  Confectioners' sugar or unsweetened cocoa powder

1. Adjust oven rack to lower-middle position and heat oven to 325 degrees. Grease 8-inch springform pan, line with parchment paper, then grease sides. Wrap outside of pan with two 18-inch-square pieces of aluminum foil; set in roasting pan. Bring kettle of water to boil.

2. Using stand mixer fitted with whisk, whip eggs on medium speed until doubled in volume, about 5 minutes.

3. Meanwhile, melt chocolate with butter and coffee in large heatproof bowl set over saucepan filled with 1 inch of barely simmering water, stirring once or twice until smooth and very warm (should register about 115 degrees). Using large rubber spatula, fold one-third of egg foam into chocolate mixture until few streaks of egg are visible. Fold in remaining foam in 2 additions until mixture is totally homogeneous.

4. Scrape batter into prepared pan and smooth top with rubber spatula. Set roasting pan on oven rack and pour enough boiling water into roasting pan to come about halfway up sides of springform pan. Bake until cake has risen slightly, edges are just beginning to set, thin glazed crust (like a brownie crust) has formed on surface, and cake registers 140 degrees, 22 to 25 minutes. Remove cake pan from water bath and set on wire rack; let cool to room temperature. Cover and refrigerate overnight. (Cake can be refrigerated for up to 4 days).

5. About 30 minutes before serving, run paring knife between cake and sides of pan; remove sides of pan. Invert cake onto sheet of waxed paper, discard parchment, and turn cake right side up onto serving platter. Dust with confectioners' sugar or cocoa, if using, and serve.

Inside This Chapter

CHAPTER 16

How to Make Fruit Desserts

The world of fruit desserts includes an array of seemingly humble recipes that make the fruit the star, often marrying sweetened fruit or fruit fillings with buttery or biscuit toppings. As with many simple desserts, success depends on both technique and the best ingredients, so in this chapter we explain how to buy, store, and prep fresh fruit and how to make classics like shortcakes, cobblers, crisps, and parfaits. Also see the next chapter on pies and tarts.

Getting Started

Fruit 101

When the star of a recipe is the fruit, it pays to use the right variety and to take care when buying it. Storage and handling are also important because many fruits are delicate and highly perishable. Here are some general guidelines about fruit and some information about particular fruits and their varieties.

BUYING IN SEASON

This sounds obvious, but when it comes to fresh fruit, buying at the height of its growing season will make a huge difference in the quality of your fruit dessert. Sure, you can buy blueberries or raspberries year-round, but they are not nearly as good as those you will find in your market in the summer months. The rock-hard peaches you can find in the supermarket in April will likely be mealy and may or may not ripen after you bring them home; they are absolutely no match for the fresh and fragrant summer peaches you can buy in July. If you want to make a peach cobbler before peach season, it is probably better to use a recipe designed to work with frozen peaches. Stick to locally grown varieties or wait for in-season fruit shipped in from other parts of the country.

WASHING FRUIT

There is no need to buy expensive fruit and vegetable washes. A spray bottle filled with 3 parts water and 1 part distilled white vinegar works just as well to clean smooth-surfaced produce like apples and pears. Just spray and rinse under tap water. In our tests, this method removed 98 percent of surface bacteria.

For delicate fruits like berries, fill a bowl with 3 parts water and 1 part vinegar and add berries. Drain, rinse with tap water, and pat dry with paper towels.

It is also good practice to wash produce that has inedible rinds and peels, such as melons, because cutting into a contaminated peel can drag pathogens inside.

RIPENING

Fruits fall into two categories: climacteric fruits, which can ripen off the parent plant, and nonclimacteric fruits, which cannot, meaning that they must be purchased at the peak of sweetness because ripening stops completely once picked. Note that you can speed up the ripening of climacteric fruits by placing them in a paper bag with a piece of ripe fruit. The ethylene gas released by the ripe fruit triggers the release of ethylene in the unripe fruit, causing it to soften, ripen, and become sweeter.

WILL RIPEN ON THE COUNTER	WON'T RIPEN ON THE COUNTER
• apples	• cherries
• apricots	• citrus fruits
• bananas	• honeydew melon
• cantaloupe	• lemons
• kiwis	• pineapples
• mangos	• raspberries
• papayas	• strawberries
• peaches	
• pears	
• plums	

Fruit A to Z

Although we don't cover every fruit, this section is designed to provide helpful information about the fruits, or categories of fruits, we use most often in the test kitchen when making fruit desserts.

APPLES

• Choosing apple varieties for fruit desserts is critical. Apart from flavor differences, some turn mushy in the oven while others hold their shape. In general, more acidic, or tart, apples—Cortland, Empire, Granny Smith—hold their shape. McIntosh apples, although tart and great eaten fresh, fall apart and become very watery when baked. Meanwhile, Golden Delicious, Braeburn, and Jonagold varieties fall into the sweet apple category and will break down in the oven.
• Because it is impossible to know how long or under what conditions supermarket apples have been stored, your best bet is to use fresh, local apples whenever possible.
• Since apples are not prone to chill-injury, they can be stored anywhere in the fridge.

BANANAS

• Bananas continue to ripen after you buy them, so if you are not going to use them for a few days it is fine to buy green bananas and store them at room temperature. Do not store them in a plastic produce bag because the moisture that collects in the bag could cause them to rot.
• Bananas that have developed a smattering of black speckles on the skin are the sweetest (more than three times sweeter than unspeckled) but will soon turn overripe, so use them soon or refrigerate them to slow down the ripening.
• Ripe bananas can be frozen in a zipper-lock bag.
• If you need to ripen bananas in a hurry, enclose them in a paper bag for a couple of days. The bag will trap the ethylene gas produced by the fruit and hasten ripening.

BERRIES

- Fresh berries of any kind require special handling to preserve their delicate texture and flavor. Don't wash berries until you are going to use them.
- To store berries, it is best to take them out of the containers in which they were purchased, especially if they've been packed in cardboard containers found at most farm stands; place berries in a zipper-lock bag or other container between layers of paper towels.

Blueberries

- There are two types of fresh blueberries: tiny field-grown berries such as the wild Maine blueberries available for a few weeks in the summer, and the larger berries. Buy fresh local berries for the best flavor. When not in season, you can buy berries from South America, but they do not have the flavor of fresh-picked berries.
- Frozen blueberries, which are picked when fully ripe and immediately individually quick-frozen, make a good stand-in for fresh in many recipes, and they cost far less than fresh. In fact, a blueberry pie made out of season will taste better (and be much cheaper) if you use frozen berries. That said, be sure to use a recipe that has been tested using frozen blueberries and that includes instructions on how they should be handled.

Raspberries

- Raspberries are in season in the late spring and summer months. They are delicate and highly perishable, so you should use them soon after you buy them.
- Look for berries that are bright red, plump, and juicy and free of signs of mold. Inspect the packaging for dark stains, which indicate that some of the berries have been crushed.
- Raspberries are usually sold in small, flat containers that keep the berries separate, but if you are buying them in a larger container at a farm stand, lay them out on a plate lined with paper towels for storage in the refrigerator.

Strawberries

- Buy strawberries at the peak of season if possible; small height-of-season strawberries have an intense sweetness but make only a fleeting appearance at summer farm stands and are highly perishable.
- Look for strawberries that have a bright sheen and that are fragrant, red through to the center, and firm. Larger strawberries are less flavorful and sometimes hollow in the middle, so look for medium strawberries. If buying packaged berries, inspect the packaging to be sure that the berries are free of mold and that those on the bottom are not crushed.
- Strawberries will not continue to ripen after you bring them home, so don't buy them if they are yellow around the stem.
- Frozen strawberries (usually individually quick-frozen) are widely available. In our testing we found that brand does make a difference and that some had off-flavors. Our favorite brand is Cascadian Farm Frozen Premium Organic Strawberries.

CITRUS FRUITS

- Citrus fruits are at their best in the winter months, although most varieties are available year-round.
- Look for fruit that feels heavy, with brightly colored skin that is free of blemishes. The fruit should not be overly firm and should yield when the skin is pressed (these will yield the most juice).
- With the exception of lemons and limes (see below), citrus fruits are sensitive to chill-injury and should be placed in the front of the fridge, where the temperatures tend to be higher.
- Citrus zest can be frozen in a zipper-lock bag for up to three weeks. It will lose its color but will work fine for baking.
- We do not recommend buying shelf-stable lemon or lime juice. We find bottled juice to be bitter at best and rancid in some cases. And since you need zest as well in most recipes calling for juice, you are better off buying fresh fruit.

Lemons

- Generally, the only lemon you'll find is the common Eureka variety, whose juice has a mouth-puckering tartness. However, between January and April you may also find Meyer lemons, which are a cross between a lemon and an orange. A Meyer lemon's skin is a deep yellowish-orange, and its juice is sweeter than that of other lemons. Meyer lemons are great for making marmalade, chutney, and a variety of desserts.
- Lemons are best stored in a sealed zipper-lock bag in the crisper.

Limes

- There are two types of limes: common Persian limes, and golf ball–size, slightly yellow Key limes. Named for the Florida Keys, where they are used in the region's famous Key lime pies, Key limes are actually native to Southeast Asia. They have a complex flavor and are slightly less tart and bracing than Persian limes. That said, in a side-by-side tasting of Key lime bars made using both Key limes and Persian limes, those made with Key limes tasted a bit more tart, but we did not think they made a better bar and juicing the smaller Key limes required much more work.
- Like lemons, limes are best stored in a sealed zipper-lock bag in the crisper.

Oranges

You have many choices when using oranges. Here are some of the most common varieties.

- **Blood Oranges** These thin-skinned oranges have a red blush on their skin and beautiful magenta flesh. Their color and complex flavor make them a great addition to winter salads. You usually see these oranges only in the winter months.
- **Navel Oranges** The most common supermarket variety and a basic all-purpose orange, navel oranges go by several other names as well, including Valencia and Cara Cara (which have salmon-colored flesh, a sweet taste, and low acidity).

- **Seville Oranges** These sour oranges have tart flesh and a high pectin content, making them ideal for use in marmalades.
- **Tangelo Oranges** A cross between a tangerine and a pomelo (a giant citrus thought to be an ancestor of grapefruit), the tangelo is slightly larger than a navel orange and has a tapered neck. Its flesh has a silky quality and bright acidity.

Grapefruit

- In general you have a choice between white grapefruit, which is bracingly sharp in flavor, and ruby red grapefruit, which has a less sour flavor and beautiful blushing pink–colored flesh.
- Grapefruit can be stored at room temperature for about a week but will keep in the refrigerator for about two weeks.

KIWI

- Though native to China, this brown, egg-shaped fruit is so named because it was first commercially grown in New Zealand. Beneath its furry skin lies brilliant green or gold flesh studded with tiny crunchy black seeds. Its flavor is sweet-tart and berrylike, and it has a firm but juicy texture.
- Kiwis will ripen at room temperature and can be refrigerated for up to three weeks.

MELONS

- Melons of many kinds are widely available in the late spring and summer. Because they have hard rinds, it can be difficult to judge ripeness; there is nothing worse that bringing home a melon, like cantaloupe, cutting into it, and seeing a green ring around the edge of tough, unripe fruit. In general look for a melon that is heavy and firm and that has no indentations or soft spots. Smell the stem end—a ripe melon will have a slightly sweet fragrance.
- Melons can be stored at room temperature but will last a few weeks if refrigerated.

Cantaloupe

- This melon should have corky veins that are visible over the rind, but the rind should not be green. It will continue to ripen at room temperature; once it's ripe, the rind will be golden yellow.

Honeydew

- Honeydew should be creamy white with a smooth surface. Once harvested, it will not ripen further.

Watermelon

- A ripe watermelon will sound hollow when tapped. Look for a watermelon that is firm and symmetrical.

PEARS

- Since pears will continue to ripen after they have been harvested, purchase firm pears and let them ripen at room temperature for a few days to ensure the best quality. Ripening can be accelerated by putting them in a paper bag with a banana. But check them frequently; they go from just right to mush in a matter of hours. Here are common varieties.

Anjou

- With their light yellow-green hue, Anjou pears are creamy, tender, and incredibly juicy when ripe. They can be eaten out of hand and are also great for roasting; the hot oven concentrates their mild flavor (though we do not recommend them for our pear crisp).

Bartletts

- Bartletts are our favorite. Yellow when underripe, these pears turn a beautiful greenish-yellow when ready to eat. Their sweet, flowery flavor becomes more powerful when they are roasted or baked.

Bosc

- Easily recognized for their dull, brownish skin, Bosc pears are very sweet when ripe and have a hearty (some would say mealy) texture. We have found that Boscs are best poached. The moist heat softens their texture and makes them more appealing.

PINEAPPLE

- We prefer Costa Rican–grown pineapples, also labeled "extra-sweet" or "gold." They are consistently honey-sweet in comparison with the acidic Hawaiian pineapples, which have greenish (not yellow) skin.
- Pineapple will not ripen further once picked, so purchase golden, fragrant fruit that gives slightly when pressed. You can also tell if a pineapple is ripe by tugging at a leaf in the center of the fruit. If the leaf releases with little effort, the pineapple is ripe. Avoid pineapple with dried-out leaves and a fermented aroma, as these indicate that the fruit is overripe.
- Peeled strips of pineapple sold at supermarkets make a fine stand-in for buying and peeling a whole pineapple yourself, especially if you don't need a lot. We do not recommend buying cut-up pineapple.
- Store unpeeled pineapple at room temperature.

RHUBARB

- In season in the spring, rhubarb will have either green or deep red stalks. Red rhubarb is tarter than the green variety, which is mellower in flavor.
- Look for rhubarb that is crisp, with shiny, firm skin.
- Rhubarb should be stored loosely wrapped in plastic in the crisper drawer.

STONE FRUITS

- At their best in the summer months, stone fruits are used to make an array of fruit desserts, including pies, rustic tarts, cobblers, and crisps. In addition to those listed below, apricots and plums fall into this category of fruit.

Cherries

- Ruby-hued sour cherries are the best choice for pies and cobblers because their soft, juicy flesh and bright flavor hold up in the oven, but they're rarely available in supermarkets.
- Bing (or Rainier) cherries are more available in the supermarket, but their sweet, dense flesh is challenging when baking; they are best eaten out of hand.
- Sour Morello cherries in a jar are the best bet for making cherry pie or cobbler, because the season for fresh sour cherries is so fleeting.
- Buy cherries with firm, plump, unwrinkled, and unblemished flesh.
- Store cherries in the refrigerator in a zipper-lock bag, and do not wash them until you are ready to use them.

Mangos

- Native to Southeast Asia, mangos have sweet, floral, and silky-smooth flesh that clings to a large, flat pit. Mangos are very fragrant when ripe and should yield to gentle pressure.
- Store mangos on the counter; they will ripen at room temperature.

Nectarines

- Nectarines resemble peaches but are smoother skinned and taste sweeter. Nectarines have dense flesh that is either white or yellow.
- You can use nectarines in any recipe that calls for peaches.

Peaches

- Peaches are generally classified as clingstone, freestone, or semifreestone, all of which refer to how firmly the pit attaches to the flesh of the peach. In most grocery stores, you will find freestone peaches, which are obviously easier to deal with.
- The usual choices among varieties are yellow or white, distinguished by the hue of the skin and the flavor and color of the flesh. Yellow peaches are more acidic but they tend to mellow as they soften, while white peaches are prized for their very sweet taste.
- Store peaches at room temperature unless they are fully ripe and you are trying to extend their shelf life—refrigerating peaches can make them mealy.

Essential Equipment

There is little specialty equipment needed to make simple fruit desserts, but there are a few things that will make your job easier since prepping the fruit will demand the bulk of your time. In addition to the items below, a rasp-style grater is handy for making quick work of zesting lemons and other citrus fruit, while a good, sharp vegetable peeler with a comfortable handle is good for peeling apples; see page 30 for more details on these two items.

PARING KNIFE

A good paring knife is key for nearly every fruit dessert recipe. It will enable you to maneuver around fruits of all shapes and sizes and cut out stems and cores, among other jobs. For more details on what to look for, see page 18.

CITRUS JUICER

A juicer should allow you to extract maximum juice from a lemon, lime, or orange with minimal mess. And while there are many styles, including sticklike reamers and squeeze-style juice presses, our favorite is an electric model, which is especially helpful if you need to collect a lot of juice. We also like a simple squeeze-style manual juicer with curved handles and a well-shaped plunger.

APPLE CORER

Rather than slicing an apple into quarters and then removing the core and seeds from each piece, we'd rather reach for an apple corer, which does the job in one fell swoop. We found those with either narrow blade diameters or stubby metal tubes to be clumsy and ineffective. We reach for one with a wide mouth, extremely sharp teeth, and an easy-to-grip plastic handle.

FRUIT PEELER

At first glance, a serrated fruit peeler looks just like a vegetable peeler. But these blades have tiny serrations that lift away tomato and peach skins without damaging the delicate flesh. If you hate to blanch and shock these fruits in order to peel them by hand, a good serrated peeler is worth the investment. A razor-sharp blade is essential, especially when handling ripe fruit.

How to Prepare Fruit A to Z

Whether you are cutting up fruit for a simple fruit salad or making a more involved recipe with a lot of prep work, it helps to know the most efficient way to peel, pit, core, stem, juice, or zest the fruit involved. After years of making fruit desserts in the test kitchen, we've found the following methods to be the easiest.

APPLE: CORING WITH A CORER
1A. Cut small slice from top and bottom of apple.
1B. Holding apple steady on bottom side, push corer through, then cut apple according to recipe.

APPLE: CORING WITHOUT A CORER
1A. Cut sides of apple squarely away from core.
1B. Cut each piece of apple into slices according to recipe.

BERRIES: WASHING
1. Place berries in large bowl of clean water and bob them about gently with hands.
2. Line salad spinner with layers of paper towels and carefully disperse berries. Spin gently until berries are dry, about 20 seconds.

CHERRIES: PITTING
Using cherry pitter, punch stone from flesh of cherries.

CITRUS: SECTIONING
1. Cut thin slice from top and bottom of fruit, then use sharp knife to slice off rind, including white pith.
2. Insert blade of paring knife between membrane and section, and slice to center of fruit. Turn blade so that it faces outward, then slice along membrane on other side until section falls out.

CITRUS: ZESTING
Rub fruit against holes of rasp-style grater, grating over same area of fruit only once or twice to avoid grating bitter white pith beneath skin.

CITRUS: JUICING
1. Roll fruit vigorously on hard surface to tear juice sacs, for maximum extraction of juice.
2. Slice fruit in half, then use reamer or citrus juicer to extract juice. It is best to squeeze the juice at the last minute, as its flavor mellows and turns bland in a short time.

KIWI: PEELING
1. Trim ends of kiwi, then insert small spoon between skin and flesh. Gently slide spoon around fruit, separating flesh from skin.
2. Pull loosened skin away from flesh, then chop or slice according to recipe.

MANGO: CUTTING UP
1. Cut thin slice from one end of mango so it sits flat on counter.
2. Resting mango on trimmed end, cut off skin in thin strips from top to bottom.
3. Cut down along each side of flat pit to remove flesh.
4. Trim around pit to remove any remaining flesh. Chop or slice according to recipe.

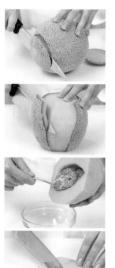

MELON: CUTTING UP

1. Cut small slice off each end of melon so it sits flat on counter.

2. Resting melon on one trimmed end, carefully cut off rind in sections from top to bottom.

3. Once rind is removed, cut melon in half and scoop out seeds with large spoon.

4. Slice each melon half into ¾-inch-thick wedges, then cut each wedge into pieces according to recipe.

PEACH: PEELING

1. Using paring knife, score small X at base of each peach.

2. Lower peaches into boiling water with slotted skimmer. Cover and blanch until skins loosen, about 2 minutes.

3. Use slotted skimmer to remove peaches to ice water and let stand to stop cooking, about 1 minute.

4. Use paring knife to remove strips of loosened peel, starting at X on base of each peach.

PEACH, FREESTONE: HALVING AND PITTING

1. Cut peach in half, pole to pole around pit, using crease in peach skin as guide.

2. Grasp both halves of fruit and twist apart. Remove pit.

PEAR: CORING

1. Use melon baller to cut around central core of halved peeled pear with circular motion and remove core.

2. Draw melon baller from central core to top of pear, removing interior stem. Then remove blossom end.

PINEAPPLE: CUTTING UP

1. Trim off bottom and top of pineapple so it sits flat on counter.

2. Rest pineapple on trimmed bottom and cut off skin in thin strips from top to bottom, using sharp paring, chef's, or serrated knife.

3. Quarter pineapple lengthwise, then cut tough core from each quarter. Slice pineapple according to recipe.

RHUBARB: PEELING

1. Trim both ends of stalk. Partially slice thin disk from bottom end, being careful not to cut through stalk entirely. Gently pull partially attached disk away from stalk to remove outer peel.

2. Make second cut partway through bottom of stalk in reverse direction. Pull back peel on other side and discard. Slice or chop according to recipe.

STRAWBERRIES: HULLING

A. Use serrated tip of grapefruit spoon to cut around leafy stem and remove white core and stem.

B. Alternately, push plastic straw through bottom of berry and up through leafy steam end to remove core as well as leafy top.

How to Make a Crumble

ESSENTIAL EQUIPMENT

- food processor
- parchment paper
- rimmed baking sheet
- 8-inch square baking dish
- aluminum foil
- wire rack

A crumble is one of the simplest ways to make a dessert with fresh fruit. When baked until browned and crunchy, the topping is the perfect counterpoint to a sweet and juicy fruit filling. The key to a well-made crumble, regardless of the type of fruit you're using, is to parbake the crumble topping first. The fruit needs less time in the oven, so this approach delivers the best results: tender fruit and an ultracrunchy topping. We prepare the filling, parbake the topping, then assemble and bake for about 30 minutes. Note that not all fillings are made the same way—it depends on the fruit. While you must macerate the fruit for a peach filling to remove excess juice, this step isn't necessary for an apple crumble (see the recipes on pages 700–701 for directions on preparing these two fillings). Note that you can store the parbaked topping, once cooled, in an airtight container for up to two days before making the crumble.

1. PROCESS, THEN CRUMBLE

Pulse 1 cup all-purpose flour, ¼ cup granulated sugar, ¼ cup packed brown sugar, ⅛ teaspoon salt, and 2 teaspoons vanilla extract in food processor to combine, about 5 pulses. Add 6 tablespoons softened butter, cut into 6 pieces, and ¼ cup sliced almonds; process until mixture clumps into large, crumbly balls, about 30 seconds. Sprinkle with ¼ cup sliced almonds and pulse 2 times. Break mixture into roughly ½-inch chunks with some smaller bits over rimmed baking sheet lined with parchment.

WHY? Softened butter instead of melted butter creates a tender-crisp topping. Adding nuts in stages creates the right texture, and breaking it up into chunks ensures a crunchy (not sandy) topping.

2. BAKE TOPPING

Bake on middle rack in 350-degree oven until chunks are lightly browned and firm, 18 to 22 minutes, rotating baking sheet halfway through baking.

WHY? The crumble topping needs to be properly browned and crunchy so that it serves as a foil to the sweet baked fruit. If the crumble and fruit are baked together from the outset, the fruit filling will be mushy and overcooked by the time the crumble is properly browned.

3. MAKE FILLING, ASSEMBLE, AND BAKE

Prepare filling and transfer to 8-inch square baking dish set on aluminum foil–lined rimmed baking sheet. Spread topping over filling, packing down lightly. Sprinkle with 1 tablespoon granulated sugar. Bake on lowest oven rack in 375-degree oven until well browned and filling is bubbling around edges, 25 to 35 minutes, rotating baking sheet halfway through baking. Transfer to wire rack and let cool 15 minutes.

WHY? About 30 minutes of baking is enough time to fully brown the topping and make the fruit tender, and to allow thickened juice to bubble up and around the crumble topping.

How to Make Shortcakes

While shortcakes seem like the simplest of fruit desserts given that they have just three components (fruit, biscuits, and whipped cream), the truth is that they rarely live up to their promise unless care is taken with each part. First, the fruit. It is essential to macerate and crush a portion of the fruit for both peach and strawberry shortcakes. This ensures that the fruit releases its juices and gives the filling just the right texture. Rich-tasting homemade biscuits are also key, and our recipes incorporate both a stick of butter for richness and an egg for tenderness. Sprinkled with sugar before baking, these biscuits emerge from the oven browned, tender, and ready to serve as a bed for the juicy fruit. Properly whipped cream is the crowning glory for this summertime dessert. Here we demonstrate the general procedure that applies to making either peach or strawberry shortcakes. However, both the fruit filling and biscuits are made slightly differently for each; see the recipes on pages 701–702 for specific ingredient amounts and directions.

ESSENTIAL EQUIPMENT

- potato masher
- mixing bowl
- food processor
- rimmed baking sheet
- parchment paper
- stand mixer
- 2¾-inch biscuit cutter or ⅓ cup dry measure
- soupspoon
- serving plates

1. MACERATE AND MASH FRUIT

Combine fruit with sugar according to recipe, mashing portion as directed, and let macerate for 30 minutes.

WHY? Macerating fruit with sugar draws out the sweet juices and softens the fruit. We crush a portion of the strawberries and add the rest sliced before macerating. For the peach short-cakes, we combine some slices with sugar and microwave the rest with peach schnapps and sugar and then mash the mixture, ensuring a filling with both moisture and flavor.

2. BAKE RICH BISCUITS TOPPED WITH SUGAR

Make biscuit dough enriched with egg. Sprinkle biscuits with sugar before baking in hot oven.

WHY? Whether you're making stamped biscuits (strawberry shortcakes) or drop (peach shortcakes), an egg, which is not in traditional biscuits, gives them a tender, fork-friendly texture. The sprinkling of sugar adds the sweetness these dessert biscuits need.

3. WHIP CREAM

Using stand mixer fitted with whisk, whip cold heavy cream, sugar, and vanilla extract on medium-low speed until foamy, about 1 minute. Then whip on high speed until soft peaks form, 1 to 3 minutes.

WHY? The secret to billowy whipped cream is to start with cold cream. If your kitchen is warm, chill the mixer bowl and whisk too. We add the sugar at the outset to ensure it dissolves; if added later, the whipped cream will have a grainy texture.

4. LAYER BISCUIT, FRUIT, CREAM, BISCUIT

Split each biscuit in half and place bottoms on individual plates. Spoon portion of fruit over each bottom, dollop with whipped cream, and cap with biscuit top.

WHY? We layer the fruit on the biscuit bottoms so that the biscuits can soak up some of the flavorful juices. If desired, you can add some of the fruit on top of the whipped cream too.

How to Make a Cobbler

ESSENTIAL EQUIPMENT

- whisk
- mixing bowls
- rubber spatula
- ¼-cup dry measure, greased with vegetable oil spray
- parchment paper
- rimmed baking sheets (2)
- 9-inch deep-dish glass pie plate
- aluminum foil

The appeal of a cobbler is hard to deny, especially when made with fresh, height-of-the-season fruit. Plus, it is easy to make: drop biscuits and a simple fruit filling take little time. Paired with ice cream, it makes a great ending to any meal. We prefer to make cobblers using juicy fruit and berries for a filling with the best texture; blueberries, blackberries, peaches, nectarines, strawberries, and sour cherries all work well.

Since one problem that plagues cobblers is gummy biscuits, we parbake our simple drop biscuits as well as the filling. Once they are combined, the cobbler needs only about 15 minutes in the oven to fully brown the biscuits and thicken the filling. This approach puts an end to biscuits that are gummy on the underside. Be sure to cool the cobbler for at least 10 minutes before serving so the fruit juices can thicken a little more. See chart on opposite page for details about preparing fillings for various types of fruit.

1. MAKE DROP BISCUITS

Whisk 1½ cups (7½ ounces) all-purpose flour, ¼ cup sugar, 1½ teaspoons baking powder, ¼ teaspoon baking soda, and ¼ teaspoon salt in large bowl. In medium bowl, combine ¾ cup chilled buttermilk and 6 tablespoons melted and slightly cooled unsalted butter together until butter forms clumps. Stir buttermilk mixture into flour mixture until just incorporated and dough pulls away from sides of bowl. Using greased ¼-cup measure, scoop out and drop 8 mounds of dough 1½ inches apart onto parchment paper–lined rimmed baking sheet.

WHY? The key to great drop biscuits is to mix cold buttermilk with melted butter until it clumps—this clumpy butter gives the biscuits a flaky texture.

2. PARBAKE BISCUITS

Toss 2 teaspoons sugar with ⅛ teaspoon ground cinnamon in bowl and sprinkle over biscuit tops. Bake in 400-degree oven until puffed and lightly browned on bottom, about 10 minutes.

WHY? Parbaking the biscuits prevents them from becoming soggy on the bottom when they're placed on top of the fruit filling.

3. MAKE AND PARBAKE FRUIT FILLING

Prepare fruit filling using desired fruit and transfer to 9-inch deep-dish glass pie plate or round baking dish. Cover dish tightly with aluminum foil and place on foil-lined rimmed baking sheet. Bake in 400-degree oven until fruit is hot and has released its juices, 20 to 25 minutes.

WHY? Giving the fruit a head start in the oven ensures that when the cobbler is assembled, the biscuits and filling will be perfectly done at the same time.

4. ADD BISCUITS AND BAKE

When fruit is finished baking, remove foil, stir gently, and lay parbaked biscuits on top. Return to 400-degree oven and bake cobbler, uncovered, until biscuits are browned and filling is bubbly, about 15 minutes, rotating dish halfway through baking.

WHY? Marrying biscuits and filling for just 15 minutes ensures a cobbler that will have browned biscuits that are tender throughout and a filling that is thickened but not overcooked.

Customizing Fruit Cobblers

The chart below provides guidelines for making a cobbler filling that will fit in a 9-inch deep-dish glass pie plate or round baking dish of similar size. Before preparing your filling, taste the fruit. Add the smaller amount of sugar if the fruit is on the sweet side, or more sugar if the fruit is tart. To prepare any of the fruit fillings below, whisk the specified amounts of sugar and cornstarch together in a large bowl, add the prepared fruit and flavorings, and toss gently to combine.

FRUIT	QUANTITY	PREPARATION	CORNSTARCH	SUGAR	FLAVORINGS
Blackberries	6 cups (30 ounces)	Rinse	1 tablespoon	⅓ to ½ cup	1 teaspoon lemon juice and 1 teaspoon vanilla extract
Blueberries	6 cups (30 ounces)	Rinse	4 teaspoons	⅓ to ⅔ cup	1 tablespoon lemon juice and ½ teaspoon ground cinnamon
Peaches/ Nectarines	3 pounds (6 to 9 peaches)	Peel, halve, pit, and cut into ½-inch-thick wedges	1 tablespoon	⅓ to ⅔ cup	1 teaspoon lemon juice and 1 teaspoon vanilla extract
Sour Cherries	3 pounds fresh or 72 ounces jarred/canned	Pit if fresh, thoroughly drain if jarred/canned	4½ teaspoons	⅔ to ¾ cup	2 tablespoons red wine and ¼ teaspoon almond extract
Strawberries	8 cups (40 ounces)	Hull and rinse, halve large berries	5 teaspoons	⅓ to ⅔ cup	2 teaspoons lemon juice and 1 teaspoon vanilla extract

Baked Apples

Recipe Stats

TOTAL TIME **1 hour**
PREPARATION TIME **25 minutes**
ACTIVE COOKING TIME **35 minutes**
YIELD **6 servings**
MAKE AHEAD **Serve immediately**
DIFFICULTY **Intermediate**

Tools

- rimmed baking sheet
- 12-inch ovensafe nonstick skillet *
- chef's knife
- cutting board
- dry measuring cups
- liquid measuring cup
- measuring spoons
- apple corer
- melon baller **
- mixing bowls
- rasp-style grater
- skewer
- slotted spoon
- soupspoon
- tongs
- vegetable peeler

* Because the skillet goes into the oven for this recipe, it must be ovensafe. If you don't have an ovensafe skillet, transfer the browned apples to a 13 by 9-inch baking dish before transferring to the oven.

** A melon baller makes it easy to hollow out a cavity for the filling, but you can also use a spoon.

Overview

The charm of a sweet-tart stuffed baked apple surrounded by a rich, buttery sauce is hard to deny, but the truth is that this ideal is seldom realized. All too often this dessert is weak in flavor and mushy in texture, leaving us grateful for the ice cream so often served on the side. Attempting to rescue this humble dessert and give it a place on the table once again, we discovered a few easy tricks that take it from a dowdy also-ran to star contender, able to hold its own against even a chocolate soufflé.

Choosing the right apples—Granny Smiths—is the first step in developing a version with good texture and flavor. They hold up well in the heat of the oven, and their acerbic bite balances nicely with the sweetness of the filling and sauce. Peeling the apples solves a persistent problem—apples that "blow out" and collapse in the oven—and starting the cooking on the stovetop in a skillet and transferring it to the oven allows us to add rich flavor and browning to the apples. Capping the apples with sliced-off tops makes for a nice presentation and also prevents the filling from burning in the oven. Before you begin, see How to Prepare Fruit A to Z on page 684. For variations on this recipe, see page 707.

Ingredients

7 large Granny Smith apples (8 ounces each) *
6 tablespoons unsalted butter, softened
⅓ cup dried cranberries, chopped coarse
⅓ cup pecans, toasted and chopped coarse **
¼ cup packed (1¾ ounces) brown sugar
3 tablespoons old-fashioned rolled oats
1 teaspoon finely grated orange zest
½ teaspoon ground cinnamon
    Pinch salt
⅓ cup maple syrup
⅓ cup plus 2 tablespoons apple cider

* Do not substitute any other apple variety here or the apples may not hold their shape when baked.

** You can substitute an equal amount of walnuts for the pecans if desired.

What Can Go Wrong

Here's a list of common mistakes cooks make when preparing this recipe.

COMMON MISTAKE	BAD OUTCOMES	WHAT YOU SHOULD DO
Using Wrong Apple Variety	• **The apples turn mushy when baked.**	Just because you like the flavor of an apple variety when eaten out of hand doesn't mean that it will work in this recipe. Granny Smiths are the best choice here, as they will hold their shape under the oven's heat. Even the flesh of a McIntosh, a variety often prized for both snacking and baking, turned to mush here.
Not Peeling Apples	• **The apples collapse.** • **The apples turn mushy.**	Although you might think unpeeled apples will be prettier when baked, the reverse is true. It is important to peel the apples (except for the top piece, which you slice off). Skin-off apples will hold their shape perfectly. If the apples are not peeled, the peel traps moisture that is transformed into steam. As the steam attempts to escape, its outward pressure ruptures cells and bursts through the skin, causing "blowouts."
Not Shaving Thin Slice Off Bottoms of Apples	• **The apples fall over in the skillet.** • **The filling falls out of the apples.**	Shaving a thin slice off the bottom (blossom end) of the apples will allow them to sit flat in the skillet. Don't skip this step if you want attractive baked stuffed apples.
Not Making Large Enough Cavity for Filling	• **The apples hold only a paltry amount of filling.** • **You have leftover filling.**	We found that you should use a melon baller or spoon to remove a 1½-inch-diameter core, which provides room for just the right amount of filling. Any smaller and you won't have enough space for a proper amount of filling. That said, when making the cavity, be careful not to cut through the bottom of the apple.
Not Basting Apples While Baking	• **The apples are dry.** • **The apples are less flavorful.**	The flavorful buttery sauce in the skillet, which is a mix of melted butter, maple syrup, and apple cider, keeps the apples moist as it infuses them with flavor. You should baste the apples with this mixture every 10 minutes while they are cooking.

1. Adjust oven rack to middle position and heat oven to 375 degrees. Peel, core, and cut 1 Granny Smith apple into ¼-inch dice.

2. Spread ⅓ cup pecans over rimmed baking sheet and toast until fragrant, about 5 minutes. Cool and chop coarsely. (Don't turn off oven.)

3. Combine diced apple, 5 tablespoons softened unsalted butter, and ⅓ cup chopped dried cranberries in bowl.

4. Add pecans, ¼ cup packed brown sugar, 3 tablespoons rolled oats, 1 teaspoon grated orange zest, ½ teaspoon cinnamon, and pinch salt; mix well.

5. Cut thin slice off bottom of 6 Granny Smith apples; cut off top ½-inch of stem end and reserve.

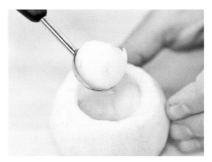

6. Peel apples and use melon baller or small measuring spoon to remove 1½-inch-diameter core, being careful not to cut through bottom of apples.

7. Melt 1 tablespoon butter in 12-inch ovensafe nonstick skillet over medium heat.

8. Add apples, stem end down, and cook until cut surface is golden brown, about 3 minutes.

9. Flip apples, reduce heat to low, and spoon filling inside, mounding excess over cavities; top with reserved apple caps.

10. Add ⅓ cup maple syrup and ⅓ cup apple cider to skillet; transfer skillet to oven.

11. Bake until skewer inserted into apples meets little resistance, 35 to 40 minutes, basting every 10 minutes with maple syrup mixture in pan.

12. Using tongs and slotted spoon, transfer apples to plates. Stir up to 2 tablespoons cider into sauce to adjust consistency. Pour over apples.

Berry Fool

Overview

The British seem to have a talent for creating luscious fruit desserts, and the berry trifle and the berry fool, both of which date back to the 16th century, are two prime examples. There are many modern takes on the berry fool, which is usually made by folding pureed stewed fruit into a sweet custard, then alternating layers of this fruited custard with sweet, macerated berries. All too often, however, recipes just swap plain whipped cream for the custard. The result is a soupy, loose, and boring parfait.

To capture the essence of this dish, we start by pureeing berries in the food processor, then we strain this puree. Next, we soften gelatin in some of the puree—a must to ensure the proper thickened consistency since these berries are relatively low in pectin—then stir the mixture into the rest of the puree, which we heat on the stovetop first to help melt and evenly distribute the gelatin. This delivers a smooth puree with intense fruit flavor that we can combine with the custard.

As for the custard, we don't fuss with making a traditional egg-based custard. Instead, we combine heavy cream with sour cream (and vanilla and sugar) for the right substantive, silky texture as well as tangy flavor—the perfect foil for the berry puree and the macerated berries. Layering uncooked berries and the creamy fruit filling in a parfait glass makes for a beautiful presentation and ensures intense berry flavor in every bite. Topped with a little of the whipped cream mixture (which we reserve before adding the puree) and crushed sweet wheat crackers, these fools are a great finish for a special-occasion dinner.

Note that the thickened fruit puree can be made up to 4 hours in advance and refrigerated; just make sure to whisk it well to break up any clumps before combining it with the whipped cream. Before you begin, see How to Prepare Fruits A to Z on page 684.

Recipe Stats

TOTAL TIME **2½ hours**
PREPARATION TIME **15 minutes**
ACTIVE COOKING TIME **15 minutes**
YIELD **6 servings**
MAKE AHEAD **Serve assembled fools immediately; fruit puree can be refrigerated for up to 4 hours**
DIFFICULTY **Intermediate**

Tools

- small saucepan
- food processor
- stand mixer *
- chef's knife
- cutting board
- dry measuring cups
- large liquid measuring cup
- measuring spoons
- fine-mesh strainer
- grapefruit spoon **
- mixing bowls
- rubber spatula
- 6 tall parfait or sundae glasses ***
- soupspoon
- whisk
- plastic wrap

* You can use a hand-held mixer to make this recipe, but the timing will be longer than indicated in the recipe.
** We use a grapefruit spoon to hull the strawberries, but you can also use a plastic straw or paring knife.
*** Make sure you use glasses with about a 2-cup capacity.

Ingredients

30 **ounces strawberries, hulled (6 cups) ***
12 **ounces (2⅓ cups) raspberries ***
¾ **cup (5¼ ounces) sugar**
2 **teaspoons unflavored gelatin**
1 **cup heavy cream, chilled**
¼ **cup sour cream, chilled**
½ **teaspoon vanilla extract**
4 **Carr's Whole Wheat Crackers, crushed fine (¼ cup) ****
6 **sprigs fresh mint (optional)**

* Blackberries or blueberries can be substituted for the raspberries. You may also substitute frozen fruit for fresh, but it will slightly compromise the final texture. If using frozen fruit, reduce the amount of sugar in the puree by 1 tablespoon.
** We like the granular texture and nutty flavor of Carr's Whole Wheat Crackers, but graham crackers or gingersnaps will also work.

What Can Go Wrong

Here's a list of common mistakes cooks make when preparing this recipe.

COMMON MISTAKE	BAD OUTCOMES	WHAT YOU SHOULD DO
Not Straining Fruit Puree	• **The puree is not smooth.** • **The filling is gritty.**	A portion of the berries is processed until smooth and then strained through a fine-mesh strainer. As you push the puree through the strainer, small seeds will be left behind. This ensures a supremely smooth puree, which will ultimately be combined with the whipped cream to make the creamy, flavorful filling.
Mishandling Gelatin	• **The gelatin clumps up when added to the hot puree.**	Gelatin must be hydrated before it is melted, which is why it is important to add the gelatin to a small amount of unheated berry puree and let it sit for 5 minutes before mixing it into the puree that has been heated. Also, the gelatin should be added to the heated puree after the pan has been taken off the heat. If you skip the first step and add the unhydrated gelatin directly to the heated puree, it will likely clump up and not dissolve.
Not Macerating Fruit Long Enough	• **The fruit remains too firm.**	After adding sugar to the berries, you need to let them sit for a full hour at room temperature. If you shortchange this time, the sugar won't have enough time to soften (and sweeten) the berries, and they won't meld well with the other ingredients.
Not Draining Macerated Fruit Well	• **The parfaits are watery and loose.**	Be sure to drain the berries. If you do not drain them well, they will be too wet and will make the parfaits too loose.
Not Whipping Cream Properly	• **The whipped cream does not hold its shape.** • **The layers in the parfaits are messy.**	You need to beat the cream mixture (heavy cream, sour cream, vanilla, and sugar) until the mixture is doubled in volume and holds stiff peaks. If you shortchange this process, the whipped cream will be too soft and will make sloppy-looking layers in the parfait glasses. The key is to follow the instructions exactly, starting on low speed first, then increasing to medium and, finally, high speed. When you think the cream is nearly done whipping, go slowly; you don't want to overbeat the cream and give it a curdled, clumpy texture. Working with cold ingredients makes whipping cream easier; for best results, also chill the bowl and whisk attachment.
Assembling Recipe Ahead of Time	• **The parfaits are watery and loose.**	Although it takes some time to make this recipe from start to finish, do not be tempted to assemble the layers in the glasses until just before serving. If you do, the fruit will release liquid and make the parfaits loose. You can, however, make the fruit puree up to 4 hours in advance, and this represents the bulk of the work. You can also crush the crackers in advance.
Not Reserving Portion of Whipped Cream	• **The parfaits look unfinished.**	It's easy to miss the instructions to reserve a little of the whipped cream mixture, but you need ⅓ cup as the crowning glory of these parfaits, which are then sprinkled with crushed sweet wheat crackers.

1. Hull 30 ounces strawberries.

2. Process half of hulled strawberries, 6 ounces raspberries, and ½ cup sugar in food processor until mixture is smooth, about 1 minute.

3. Strain puree through fine-mesh strainer into large liquid measuring cup (you should have about 2½ cups puree; reserve excess for another use).

4. Transfer ½ cup of puree to small bowl and sprinkle 2 teaspoons unflavored gelatin over top; let sit until gelatin softens, about 5 minutes, and stir.

5. Heat remaining 2 cups puree in small saucepan over medium heat until beginning to bubble, 4 to 6 minutes.

6. Off heat, stir in gelatin mixture until dissolved.

7. Transfer puree mixture to medium bowl, cover with plastic wrap, and refrigerate until well chilled, about 2 hours.

8. Meanwhile, chop remaining hulled strawberries into rough ¼-inch pieces.

9. Toss chopped strawberries, 6 ounces raspberries, and 2 tablespoons sugar together in medium bowl. Set aside for 1 hour.

10. Using stand mixer fitted with whisk, whip 1 cup chilled heavy cream, ¼ cup chilled sour cream, ½ teaspoon vanilla, and 2 tablespoons sugar on low speed.

11. When bubbles form (about 30 seconds), increase speed to medium and whip until whisk leaves trail, about 30 seconds.

12. Increase speed to high and whip until mixture has nearly doubled in volume and stiff peaks form, about 30 seconds.

13. Transfer ⅓ cup whipped cream mixture to small bowl; set aside.

14. Remove puree from refrigerator; whisk until smooth. With mixer on medium speed, slowly add two-thirds of puree to cream mixture in bowl.

15. Mix until incorporated, about 15 seconds.

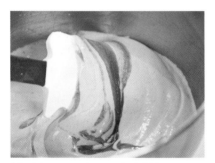

16. Using spatula, gently fold in remaining puree, leaving streaks of puree.

17. Transfer uncooked berries to fine-mesh strainer; shake gently to remove excess juice.

18. Process 4 Carr's Whole Wheat Crackers in clean food processor until finely crushed, about 15 seconds; set aside.

19. Divide two-thirds of uncooked berries evenly among 6 tall parfait or sundae glasses.

20. Divide creamy berry mixture evenly among glasses, followed by remaining uncooked berries.

21. Top each serving with reserved plain whipped cream mixture.

22. Sprinkle with crushed crackers and garnish with sprigs of mint, if using. Serve immediately.

Individual Pavlovas with Tropical Fruit

Recipe Stats

TOTAL TIME **4 hours**
PREPARATION TIME **15 minutes**
ACTIVE COOKING TIME **30 minutes**
YIELD **6 servings**
MAKE AHEAD **Meringue shells can be stored at room temperature for up to 2 weeks; whipped topping can be refrigerated for up to 8 hours**
DIFFICULTY **Intermediate**

Tools

- rimmed baking sheet
- stand mixer
- chef's knife
- cutting board
- paring knife
- dry measuring cups
- liquid measuring cup
- measuring spoons
- individual serving plates
- mixing bowl
- rubber spatula
- soupspoon
- parchment paper

Overview

Pavlovas are delicate meringue shells filled with fresh fruit and topped with whipped cream. Created in Australia as the culinary expression of the ethereal dancing of legendary Russian prima ballerina Anna Pavlova, the dish has become a national treasure for Australians and New Zealanders and a hit on restaurant menus stateside. A study in textural contrasts, with its thin, crisp meringue, rich whipped cream, and fresh fruit, pavlovas are simple to prepare and great for entertaining because you can make the meringue weeks in advance. Just as restaurants tend to do, our recipe makes individual meringues because a large one is almost impossible to slice neatly and elegantly.

The key to this recipe lies in successfully making the meringues. Individual meringues are easy to shape; we portion out the mixture into small mounds on a baking sheet and use the back of a spoon to create a concave center for holding the whipped cream and fruit. Baking the meringues at 200 degrees for an hour and a half yields perfectly dry, crisp, white shells, but they require gradual cooling off in a turned-off oven to ensure crispness.

We especially like the flavors of tropical fruit on the pavlovas, but fresh berries and peaches make fine options too (see the recipe variations on page 709).

Note that you can make the meringue shells up to two weeks in advance and store them in an airtight container at room temperature. You can also make and refrigerate the whipped topping in a fine-mesh strainer set over a bowl and covered with plastic wrap for up to 8 hours. Before you begin, see How to Whip Egg Whites on page 51 and How to Prepare Fruit A to Z on page 684.

Ingredients

MERINGUES AND FRUIT

- 4 **large egg whites, room temperature**
- ¾ **teaspoon vanilla extract**
- ¼ **teaspoon cream of tartar ***
- 1 **cup (7 ounces) plus 1 tablespoon sugar**
- 1 **mango, peeled, pitted, and cut into ¼-inch pieces**
- 2 **kiwis, peeled, quartered, and sliced thin**
- 1½ **cups ½-inch pineapple pieces ****

TOPPING

- 1 **cup heavy cream, chilled**
- ½ **cup sour cream, chilled**
- 1 **tablespoon sugar**
- 1 **teaspoon vanilla extract**

* Cream of tartar helps stiffly beaten egg whites keep their shape.

** It is fine to buy ready-to-use fresh pineapple that has been peeled and cut into strips (we do not recommend buying the cut-up pieces); if you buy a whole pineapple you will have at least half of it leftover for another use.

What Can Go Wrong

Here's a list of common mistakes cooks make when preparing this recipe.

COMMON MISTAKE	BAD OUTCOMES	WHAT YOU SHOULD DO
Not Using Room-Temperature Egg Whites	• **The whites don't achieve the right volume or consistency.** • **The individual meringues are difficult to form.**	After separating your eggs, make sure to let the whites sit out until they come to room temperature, and be sure to follow the instructions carefully for whipping them in stages (adding the sugar gradually). When you're done, you will have glossy, stiff peaks almost the texture of shaving cream. If your whites aren't at room temperature, they will likely fall short of reaching the proper stiffness, and the resulting meringue won't hold its shape.
Not Shaping Meringues Properly	• **The meringues don't look attractive.** • **The meringues don't hold the fruit properly.**	Make sure to evenly portion the meringue onto the baking sheet—use a ½-cup dry measure rather than eyeballing it. And don't forget to use the back of a spoon to make a shallow indentation in each one. This well will hold the fruit in place on the baked meringues. If you skip this step, the fruit will topple off.
Oven Is Too Hot	• **The meringues dry out and crack.**	Making meringue shells is not hard, but the process is exacting and this means that you need an oven that is properly calibrated and doesn't run too hot. Use an oven thermometer if you are uncertain.
Not Letting Meringues Cool in Oven	• **The meringues are soft and sticky.**	To keep the meringues bright white but also ensure their exteriors are properly dry and crisp, we bake them in a low oven for 1½ hours, then turn off the oven and let them completely cool and continue to dry about 2 hours more. Baking them any longer would lead to browning, and removing them from the oven before the time is up will result in unappealingly soft, sticky meringues.
Not Cutting Fruit Evenly	• **The final presentation is not elegant.** • **The fruit topples off the meringue shells.**	Whether you are making the tropical-fruit topping shown here or a topping in one of our recipe variations, it is very important to follow the instructions for preparing the fruit. Presentation is an important aspect of this dessert, and unevenly cut fruit will look sloppy. Furthermore, if you cut the fruit into large or uneven pieces, the pavlovas will not be as easy to eat.
Using Unripe Fruit	• **The meringues and fruit topping seem unfinished.** • **The fruit doesn't soften when macerated.**	For the best results, start with ripe fruit and don't skip the macerating step. You want sweet, softened fruit and a little bit of fruit juice to drizzle over the whipped cream and meringue and to marry the two components together.

1. Adjust oven rack to middle position and heat oven to 200 degrees. Line rimmed baking sheet with parchment paper.

2. Using stand mixer fitted with whisk, whip 4 large room-temperature egg whites, ¾ teaspoon vanilla, and ¼ teaspoon cream of tartar on medium-low.

3. When foamy (about 1 minute), increase speed to medium-high and whip whites to soft, billowy mounds, about 1 minute.

4. Gradually add 1 cup (7 ounces) sugar and whip until glossy, stiff peaks form, 1 to 2 minutes.

5. Scoop six ½-cup mounds meringue onto sheet, spacing them about 1 inch apart. Make small bowl-like indentation in each meringue using back of spoon.

6. Bake until exteriors are smooth, firm, and dry, about 1½ hours. Turn off oven and leave meringues in oven until completely dry and hard, about 2 hours.

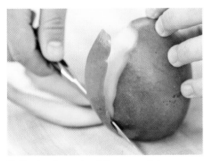

7. Peel, pit, and cut 1 mango into ¼-inch pieces.

8. Peel 2 kiwis, then quarter and slice thin. Cut pineapple into ½-inch pieces to yield 1½ cups.

9. Toss fruit gently in large bowl with 1 tablespoon sugar and let sit at room temperature until sugar has dissolved and fruit is juicy, about 30 minutes.

10. Using stand mixer fitted with whisk, whip 1 cup heavy cream, ½ cup sour cream, 1 tablespoon sugar, and 1 teaspoon vanilla on medium-low speed.

11. Whip mixture until foamy, about 1 minute, then increase speed to high and whip until soft peaks form, 1 to 3 minutes.

12. Place meringue shells on plates. Spoon about ⅓ cup cream mixture into each shell. Top each with about ½ cup fruit and serve immediately.

HOW TO MAKE FRUIT DESSERTS

Recipe Library

Peach Crumble

✔ **WHY THIS RECIPE WORKS:** A soggy topping and watery, flavorless filling are the norm for the simple, humble peach crumble. The problem is the peaches—you never know just how juicy or how flavorful they will be until you cut them open. We wanted a peach crumble that consisted of fresh-tasting, lightly sweetened peaches topped with a buttery, crisp, and nutty-tasting crumble—no matter how sweet the peaches were (or weren't). Solving the peach problem involved letting peeled, sliced peaches macerate in sugar before draining them and measuring out the amount of peach juice that would be added back to the filling: always ¼ cup. The sweetness of the filling was adjusted by adding more or less lemon juice as needed. One challenge remained: getting a crisp, well-browned topping required too much oven time for the peaches, which turned to mush. Instead, we baked the topping separately and then married it to the filling, baking the combination just until the fruit bubbled around the edges.

Peach Crumble

SERVES 6

Add the lemon juice to taste in step 2 according to the sweetness of your peaches. If ripe peaches are unavailable, you can substitute 3 pounds frozen peaches, thawed overnight in the refrigerator. If your peaches are firm, you should be able to peel them with a vegetable peeler. If they are too soft and ripe to withstand the pressure of a peeler, you'll need to blanch them in a pot of simmering water for 15 seconds and then shock them in a bowl of ice water before peeling. Serve with vanilla ice cream. See Core Technique on page 686 for more details on this recipe.

FILLING

- 3½ pounds peaches, peeled, halved, pitted, and cut into ¾-inch wedges
- ⅓ cup (2⅓ ounces) granulated sugar
- 1¼ teaspoons cornstarch
- 3–5 teaspoons lemon juice
  - Pinch salt
  - Pinch ground cinnamon
  - Pinch ground nutmeg

CRUMBLE TOPPING

- 1 cup (5 ounces) all-purpose flour
- ¼ cup (1¾ ounces) plus 1 tablespoon granulated sugar
- ¼ cup packed (1¾ ounces) brown sugar
- ⅛ teaspoon salt
- 2 teaspoons vanilla extract
- 6 tablespoons unsalted butter, cut into 6 pieces and softened
- ½ cup sliced almonds

1. Adjust oven racks to lowest and middle positions and heat oven to 350 degrees. Line rimmed baking sheet with parchment paper.

2. FOR THE FILLING: Gently toss peaches and sugar together in large bowl and let sit for 30 minutes, gently stirring several times. Drain peaches in colander set over large bowl and reserve ¼ cup juice (discard remaining juice). Whisk reserved juice, cornstarch, lemon juice to taste, salt, cinnamon, and nutmeg together in small bowl. Combine peaches and juice mixture in bowl and transfer to 8-inch square baking dish.

3. FOR THE CRUMBLE TOPPING: While peaches are macerating, combine flour, ¼ cup granulated sugar, brown sugar, and salt in food processor and drizzle vanilla over top. Pulse to combine, about 5 pulses. Scatter butter pieces and ¼ cup almonds over top and process until mixture clumps together into large, crumbly balls, about 30 seconds, scraping down bowl halfway through. Sprinkle remaining ¼ cup almonds over mixture and pulse 2 times to combine. Transfer mixture to prepared baking sheet and spread into even layer (mixture should break up into roughly ½-inch chunks with some smaller, loose bits). Bake on middle rack until chunks are lightly browned and firm, 18 to 22 minutes, rotating baking sheet halfway through baking. (Cooled topping can be stored in an airtight container for up to 2 days.)

4. TO ASSEMBLE AND BAKE: Grasp edges of parchment paper, slide topping off paper over peaches, and spread into even layer with spatula, packing down lightly and breaking up any very large pieces. Sprinkle remaining 1 tablespoon granulated sugar evenly over top and place dish on aluminum foil–lined rimmed baking sheet; place on lowest rack. Increase oven temperature to 375 degrees and bake until well browned and filling is bubbling around edges, 25 to 35 minutes, rotating baking sheet halfway through baking. Transfer baking dish to wire rack and let cool for 15 minutes; serve warm.

Apple Crumble

SERVES 6

In this variation, the apples do not need to macerate with the sugar. You can substitute Empire or Cortland apples for the Granny Smith apples if desired. Serve with vanilla ice cream. See Core Technique on page 686 for more details on this recipe.

- ½ teaspoon cornstarch
- 4 teaspoons lemon juice
- 1½ pounds Granny Smith apples, peeled, cored, and cut into ½-inch cubes
- 1½ pounds Golden Delicious apples, peeled, cored, and cut into ½-inch cubes
- ⅔ cup (4⅔ ounces) sugar
  - Pinch salt
  - Pinch ground cinnamon
  - Pinch ground nutmeg
- 1 recipe Crumble Topping (at left)

1. Adjust oven racks to lowest and middle positions and heat oven to 350 degrees. Line rimmed baking sheet with parchment paper.

2. Stir cornstarch and lemon juice together in large bowl until cornstarch is dissolved. Add apples, sugar, salt, cinnamon, and nutmeg; toss to combine. Transfer mixture to 8-inch square baking dish. Cover tightly with aluminum foil; set aside.

3. Place topping mixture on middle rack in oven and apple filling mixture on lowest rack. Bake topping until chunks are lightly browned and firm, about 20 minutes. Remove topping and apples from oven.

4. TO ASSEMBLE AND BAKE: Uncover apple filling and gently stir. Grasp edges of parchment paper, slide topping off paper over apples, and spread into even layer with spatula, packing down lightly and breaking up any very large pieces. Sprinkle remaining 1 tablespoon sugar evenly over top and place dish on aluminum foil–lined rimmed baking sheet; place on lowest rack. Increase oven temperature to 375 degrees and bake until well browned and filling is bubbling around edges, about 25 minutes, rotating baking sheet halfway through baking. Transfer baking dish to wire rack and let cool for 15 minutes; serve warm.

Strawberry Shortcakes

✔ **WHY THIS RECIPE WORKS:** While some folks like to spoon strawberries over pound cake, sponge cake, and even angel food cake, our idea of strawberry shortcake definitely involves a biscuit. We wanted a juicy strawberry filling and mounds of freshly whipped cream sandwiched in between a lightly sweetened, tender biscuit. While eggs are not traditional, we found that a single egg gave our biscuits a light, tender texture. And we used just enough dairy (half-and-half or milk) to bind the dough together. A modest amount of sugar yielded slightly sweet biscuits. For the strawberries, we wanted to avoid both a mushy puree and dry chunks of fruit. We found our solution in a compromise—mashing a portion of the berries and slicing the rest for a chunky, juicy mixture that didn't slide off the biscuits. And freshly whipped cream provided a cool, creamy contrast to the berries and biscuits.

Strawberry Shortcakes

SERVES 6

Preparing the fruit first gives it time to release its juices. See Core Technique on page 687 for more details on this recipe.

FRUIT
- 2½ **pounds strawberries, hulled (8 cups)**
- 6 **tablespoons sugar**

BISCUITS
- 2 **cups (10 ounces) all-purpose flour**
- 5 **tablespoons (2¼ ounces) sugar**
- 1 **tablespoon baking powder**
- ½ **teaspoon salt**
- 8 **tablespoons unsalted butter, cut into ½-inch pieces and chilled**
- ½ **cup plus 1 tablespoon half-and-half or milk**
- 1 **large egg, lightly beaten, plus 1 large white, lightly beaten**

WHIPPED CREAM
- 1 **cup heavy cream, chilled**
- 1 **tablespoon sugar**
- 1 **teaspoon vanilla extract**

1. FOR THE FRUIT: Crush 3 cups strawberries in large bowl with potato masher. Slice remaining 5 cups berries. Stir sliced berries and sugar into crushed berries. Set aside until sugar has dissolved and berries are juicy, at least 30 minutes or up to 2 hours.

2. FOR THE BISCUITS: Adjust oven rack to lower-middle position and heat oven to 425 degrees. Line baking sheet with parchment paper. Pulse flour, 3 tablespoons sugar, baking powder, and salt in food processor until combined. Scatter butter pieces over top and pulse until mixture resembles coarse meal, about 15 pulses. Transfer mixture to large bowl.

3. Whisk half-and-half and whole egg together in bowl, then stir into flour mixture until large clumps form. Turn out onto lightly floured counter and knead lightly until dough comes together (do not overwork dough).

4. Pat dough into 9 by 6-inch rectangle, about ¾ inch thick. Using floured 2¾-inch biscuit cutter, cut out 6 dough rounds. Arrange biscuits on prepared sheet, spaced about 1½ inches apart. Brush tops with egg white and sprinkle evenly with remaining 2 tablespoons sugar. (Unbaked biscuits can be refrigerated, covered with plastic wrap, for up to 2 hours.)

5. Bake until biscuits are golden brown, 12 to 14 minutes, rotating baking sheet halfway through baking. Transfer baking sheet to wire rack and let biscuits cool, about 10 minutes. (Cooled biscuits can be stored at room temperature for up to 1 day. Before assembling, reheat in 350-degree oven for 3 to 5 minutes.)

6. FOR THE WHIPPED CREAM: Using stand mixer fitted with whisk, whip cream, sugar, and vanilla on medium-low speed until foamy, about 1 minute. Increase speed to high and whip until soft peaks form, 1 to 3 minutes.

7. To assemble, split each biscuit in half and place bottoms on individual plates. Spoon portion of berries over each bottom, dollop with whipped cream, and cap with biscuit tops. Serve immediately.

Peach Shortcakes

✔ **WHY THIS RECIPE WORKS:** Making peach shortcake with supermarket peaches often produces a flavorless filling over a crumbly biscuit. We wanted to develop a recipe for peach shortcake that would work with farm stand or supermarket peaches. Macerating fruit in sugar is the traditional method used to pull out the fruit's juices when it comes to strawberry shortcake, but for peaches, this step alone isn't enough. We sliced the peaches very thin to maximize the surface that would come in contact with the sugar, then we microwaved a few of the peaches with peach schnapps until they were tender, mashing these cooked peaches to create a peach jam. This gave our shortcakes the right moisture and sweetness. For the shortcakes, we added an egg and mechanically developed more gluten by vigorously stirring to make a cake that would hold up under the weight of the fruit. Freshly whipped cream topped off this summer classic.

Peach Shortcakes

SERVES 6

This recipe works well with any peaches, regardless of quality. If your peaches are firm, you should be able to peel them with a sharp vegetable peeler. If they are too soft to withstand the pressure of a peeler, you'll need to blanch them in a pot of simmering water for 15 seconds and then shock them in a bowl of ice water before peeling. You can substitute ½ cup low-fat yogurt mixed with 3 tablespoons of milk for the buttermilk, if desired. Orange juice or orange liqueur can be used in place of the peach schnapps. See Core Technique on page 687 for more details on this recipe.

FRUIT

- 2 **pounds peaches, peeled, halved, pitted, and cut into ¼-inch wedges**
- 6 **tablespoons sugar**
- 2 **tablespoons peach schnapps**

BISCUITS

- 2 **cups (10 ounces) all-purpose flour**
- 2 **tablespoons sugar**
- 2 **teaspoons baking powder**
- ¾ **teaspoon salt**
- ⅔ **cup buttermilk, chilled**
- 1 **large egg**
- 8 **tablespoons unsalted butter, melted and cooled**

WHIPPED CREAM

- ½ **cup heavy cream, chilled**
- 1 **tablespoon sugar**
- ½ **teaspoon vanilla extract**

1. FOR THE FRUIT: Gently toss three-quarters of peaches with 4 tablespoons sugar in large bowl. Let sit 30 minutes. Toss remaining peaches with remaining 2 tablespoons sugar and schnapps in medium bowl. Microwave until peaches are bubbling, about 1 to 1½ minutes, stirring twice. Using potato masher, crush peaches into coarse pulp. Let sit 30 minutes.

2. FOR THE BISCUITS: Adjust oven rack to middle position and heat oven to 475 degrees. Line baking sheet with parchment paper. Whisk flour, 1 tablespoon sugar, baking powder, and salt together in large bowl. Whisk buttermilk and egg together in bowl; add melted butter and stir until butter forms small clumps.

3. Add buttermilk mixture to dry ingredients and stir with wooden spoon until dough comes together and no dry flour remains. Continue to stir vigorously for 30 seconds. Using greased ⅓-cup measure, portion dough onto prepared baking sheet to create 6 biscuits, spaced about 1½ inches apart. Sprinkle remaining 1 tablespoon sugar evenly over top of biscuits. Bake until tops are golden brown and crisp, about 15 minutes, rotating baking sheet halfway through baking. Transfer baking sheet to wire rack and let cool, about 15 minutes. (Cooled biscuits can be stored at room temperature for up to 1 day. Before assembling, reheat in 350-degree oven for 3 to 5 minutes.)

4. FOR THE WHIPPED CREAM: Using stand mixer fitted with whisk, whip cream, sugar, and vanilla on medium-low speed until foamy, about 1 minute. Increase speed to high and whip until soft peaks form, 1 to 3 minutes.

5. To assemble, split each biscuit in half and place bottoms on individual plates. Spoon portion of crushed peach mixture over each bottom, followed by peach slices and juices. Dollop each shortcake with 2 tablespoons whipped cream, cap with biscuit tops, and dollop with remaining whipped cream. Serve immediately.

Blueberry Cobbler with Biscuit Topping

✓ **WHY THIS RECIPE WORKS:** Too often, blueberry cobbler means a filling that is too sweet, overspiced, and unappealingly thick. We wanted a not-too-thin, not-too-thick filling where the blueberry flavor would be front and center. And over the fruit we wanted a light, tender biscuit topping that could hold its own against the fruit filling, with an ingredient list simple enough to allow the blueberries to play the starring role. We started by preparing a filling using 6 cups of fresh berries and just enough sugar to sweeten them. Cornstarch worked well to thicken the fruit's juices. A little lemon and cinnamon were all that we needed to enhance the filling without masking the blueberry flavor. Parbaking our biscuit topping ensured the biscuits wouldn't become soggy once placed on top of the fruit, and precooking the fruit filling meant all we had to do was marry the parbaked biscuits and precooked filling and heat together for 15 minutes until bubbly.

Blueberry Cobbler with Biscuit Topping

SERVES 8

This recipe works best with very juicy fruit. Before preparing the filling, taste the fruit, adding the smaller amount of sugar if the fruit is on the sweet side and more if the fruit is tart. Do not let the biscuit batter sit for longer than 5 minutes or so before baking. If you don't have a deep-dish glass pie plate, use a round baking dish of similar size; the round shape of the dish makes it easy to fit the biscuits on top. See Core Technique on page 688 for more details on this recipe.

FRUIT FILLING

- ⅓–⅔ **cup sugar**
- 4 **teaspoons cornstarch**
- 30 **ounces (6 cups) blueberries**
- 1 **tablespoon lemon juice**
- ½ **teaspoon ground cinnamon**

BISCUIT TOPPING

- 1½ **cups (7½ ounces) all-purpose flour**
- ¼ **cup (1¾ ounces) plus 2 teaspoons sugar**
- 1½ **teaspoons baking powder**
- ¼ **teaspoon baking soda**
- ¼ **teaspoon salt**
- ¾ **cup buttermilk, chilled**
- 6 **tablespoons unsalted butter, melted and cooled**
- ⅛ **teaspoon ground cinnamon**

1. FOR THE FILLING: Line rimmed baking sheet with aluminum foil. Adjust oven rack to middle position and heat oven to 400 degrees. Whisk sugar and cornstarch together in large bowl. Add blueberries, lemon juice, and cinnamon and toss gently to combine. Transfer fruit mixture to 9-inch deep-dish glass pie plate, cover with foil, and set on prepared sheet. (Fruit filling can be assembled in baking dish and held at room temperature for up to 4 hours.)

2. FOR THE BISCUIT TOPPING: Line rimmed baking sheet with parchment paper. Whisk flour, ¼ cup sugar, baking powder, baking soda, and salt together in large bowl. In medium bowl, stir buttermilk and melted butter together until butter forms small clumps. Using rubber spatula, stir buttermilk mixture into flour mixture until just incorporated and dough pulls away from sides of bowl.

3. Using greased ¼-cup measure, scoop out and drop 8 mounds of dough onto prepared baking sheet, spaced about 1½ inches apart. Toss remaining 2 teaspoons sugar with cinnamon in bowl and sprinkle cinnamon-sugar mixture over biscuit tops. Bake biscuits until puffed and lightly browned on bottom, about 10 minutes. Remove biscuits from oven and set aside. (Parbaked biscuits can be held at room temperature for up to 4 hours.)

4. TO ASSEMBLE AND BAKE: Place fruit in oven and bake until fruit is hot and has released its juices, 20 to 25 minutes. Remove fruit from oven, uncover, and stir gently. Arrange biscuits over top, squeezing them slightly as needed to fit into dish. Bake cobbler until biscuits are golden brown and fruit is bubbling, about 15 minutes, rotating dish halfway through baking. Let cobbler cool for 10 minutes; serve warm.

Blackberry Cobbler with Biscuit Topping

Substitute 6 cups blackberries for blueberries and omit cinnamon. Reduce cornstarch to 1 tablespoon, sugar to ⅓ to ½ cup, and lemon juice to 1 teaspoon. Add 1 teaspoon vanilla extract to bowl with blackberries.

Peach or Nectarine Cobbler with Biscuit Topping

Substitute 3 pounds peaches or nectarines, peeled, halved, pitted, and cut into ½-inch-thick wedges, for blueberries. Omit cinnamon. Reduce cornstarch to 1 tablespoon and lemon juice to 1 teaspoon. Add 1 teaspoon vanilla extract to bowl with fruit.

Sour Cherry Cobbler with Biscuit Topping

Substitute 3 pounds pitted fresh sour cherries or 72 ounces drained jarred or canned sour cherries for blueberries. Omit lemon juice and cinnamon. Increase cornstarch to 4½ teaspoons and sugar to ⅔–¾ cup. Add 2 tablespoons red wine and ¼ teaspoon almond extract to bowl with cherries.

Strawberry Cobbler with Biscuit Topping

Substitute 8 cups hulled strawberries for blueberries (halve large strawberries) and omit cinnamon. Increase cornstarch to 5 teaspoons and lemon juice to 2 teaspoons. Add 1 teaspoon vanilla extract to bowl with strawberries.

Skillet Apple Pie

✓ **WHY THIS RECIPE WORKS:** Apple pandowdy harks back to Colonial-era New England—the dessert takes a more rustic approach to apple pie in that it features just one pastry crust, placed on top of a lightly sweetened apple filling. During or after baking, the pastry is broken and pushed into the filling—a technique known as "dowdying." We found the idea of an easier approach to apple pie very appealing—no fussy crimping and only one piece of pastry dough to roll out—so we set out to make our own version. For a juicy apple filling with bright fruit flavor, we added cider to the apples and sweetened them with maple syrup, both of which made for a pleasantly saucy filling. Parcooking the apples in a skillet until caramelized before adding the other ingredients helped to deepen their flavor. For the crust, we cut a standard pie crust into squares after rolling it over the fruit right in the skillet—this encouraged a multitude of crisp edges that contrasted nicely with the tender fruit and recalled (in a less dowdy way) the broken-up crusts of a traditional pandowdy.

Skillet Apple Pie

SERVES 6 TO 8

If your skillet is not ovensafe, precook the apples and stir in the cider mixture as instructed, then transfer the apples to a 13 by 9-inch baking dish. Roll out the dough to a 13 by 9-inch rectangle and cut the crust and bake as instructed. If you do not have apple cider, reduced apple juice may be used as a substitute; simmer 1 cup apple juice in a small saucepan over medium heat until reduced to ½ cup, about 10 minutes. Serve warm or at room temperature with vanilla ice cream or Whipped Cream (page 709). Use a combination of sweet, crisp apples such as Golden Delicious and firm, tart apples such as Cortland or Empire.

CRUST
- 1 cup (5 ounces) all-purpose flour
- 1 tablespoon sugar
- ½ teaspoon salt
- 2 tablespoons vegetable shortening, chilled
- 6 tablespoons unsalted butter, cut into ¼-inch pieces and chilled
- 3–4 tablespoons ice water

FILLING
- ½ cup apple cider
- ⅓ cup maple syrup
- 2 tablespoons lemon juice
- 2 teaspoons cornstarch
- ⅛ teaspoon ground cinnamon (optional)
- 2 tablespoons unsalted butter
- 2½ pounds apples, peeled, cored, and cut into ½-inch-thick wedges
- 1 large egg white, lightly beaten
- 2 teaspoons sugar

1. FOR THE CRUST: Pulse flour, sugar, and salt in food processor until combined, about 4 pulses. Add shortening and pulse until mixture resembles coarse sand, about 10 pulses. Sprinkle butter pieces over top and pulse until mixture is pale yellow and resembles coarse crumbs, with butter bits no larger than small peas, about 10 pulses. Transfer mixture to medium bowl.

2. Sprinkle 3 tablespoons ice water over mixture. With rubber spatula, use folding motion to mix, pressing down on dough until dough is slightly tacky and sticks together, adding up to 1 tablespoon more ice water if dough does not come together. Flatten dough into 4-inch disk, wrap in plastic wrap, and refrigerate for at least 1 hour or up to 2 days. Let sit at room temperature for 15 minutes before rolling.

3. FOR THE FILLING: Adjust oven rack to upper-middle position and heat oven to 500 degrees. Whisk cider, maple syrup, lemon juice, cornstarch, and cinnamon, if using, together in bowl until smooth. Melt butter in 12-inch ovensafe skillet over medium-high heat. Add apples and cook, stirring 2 or 3 times, until apples begin to caramelize, about 5 minutes. (Do not fully cook apples.) Off heat, add cider mixture and gently stir until apples are well coated. Set aside to cool slightly.

4. TO ASSEMBLE AND BAKE: Roll dough out on lightly floured counter to 11-inch round. Roll dough loosely around rolling pin and unroll over apple filling. Brush dough with egg white and sprinkle with sugar. With sharp knife, gently cut dough into 6 pieces by making one vertical cut followed by 2 evenly spaced horizontal cuts (perpendicular to first cut). Bake until apples are tender and crust is deep golden brown, about 20 minutes, rotating skillet halfway through baking. Let cool about 15 minutes; serve warm.

Skillet Apple Crisp

✔ **WHY THIS RECIPE WORKS:** Most recipes for apple crisp recipes yield unevenly cooked fruit and an unremarkable topping. We wanted an exemplary apple crisp—a lush (but not mushy) sweet-tart apple filling covered with truly crisp morsels of buttery, sugary topping. Our first few crisps contained unevenly cooked apples lacking any fruity punch. Stirring the fruit helped solve the texture problem, but reaching into a hot oven to do so was a hassle. Instead, we softened the apples on the stovetop—in a skillet. The shallow, flared pan also encouraged evaporation, browning, and better flavor overall. To improve the flavor further, we turned to apple cider, reducing it to a syrupy consistency. As for the topping, we added brown sugar to white to play up the apples' caramel notes, and swapped out some flour for rolled oats to give the topping character and chew. Chopped pecans not only improved the crunch factor, but added rich flavor as well. After a few minutes in the oven, our crisp was just that.

Skillet Apple Crisp

SERVES 6 TO 8

If your skillet is not ovensafe, prepare the recipe through step 3 and then transfer the filling to a 13 by 9-inch baking dish; top the filling as directed and bake for an additional 5 minutes. We like Golden Delicious apples in this recipe, but Honeycrisp or Braeburn apples can be substituted; do not use Granny Smith apples. While old-fashioned rolled oats are preferable in this recipe, quick oats can be substituted. Serve with vanilla ice cream.

TOPPING
- ¾ **cup (3¾ ounces) all-purpose flour**
- ¾ **cup pecans, chopped fine**
- ¾ **cup (2¼ ounces) old-fashioned rolled oats**
- ½ **cup packed (3½ ounces) light brown sugar**
- ¼ **cup (1¾ ounces) granulated sugar**
- ½ **teaspoon ground cinnamon**
- ½ **teaspoon salt**
- 8 **tablespoons unsalted butter, melted**

FILLING
- 3 **pounds Golden Delicious apples, peeled, cored, halved, and cut into ½-inch wedges**
- ¼ **cup (1¾ ounces) granulated sugar**
- ¼ **teaspoon ground cinnamon (optional)**
- 1 **cup apple cider**
- 2 **teaspoons lemon juice**
- 2 **tablespoons unsalted butter**

1. FOR THE TOPPING: Adjust oven rack to middle position and heat oven to 450 degrees. Line rimmed baking sheet with aluminum foil. Combine flour, pecans, oats, brown sugar, granulated sugar, cinnamon, and salt in bowl. Stir in melted butter until mixture is thoroughly moistened and crumbly. Set aside.

2. FOR THE FILLING: Toss apples, sugar, and cinnamon, if using, together in large bowl; set aside. Bring cider to simmer in 12-inch ovensafe skillet over medium heat; cook until reduced to ½ cup, about 5 minutes. Transfer reduced cider to bowl or liquid measuring cup; stir in lemon juice and set aside.

3. Melt butter in now-empty skillet over medium heat. Add apple mixture and cook, stirring frequently, until apples are beginning to soften and become translucent, 12 to 14 minutes. (Do not fully cook apples.) Off heat, gently stir in cider mixture until apples are coated.

4. Sprinkle topping evenly over fruit, breaking up any large chunks. Place skillet on prepared baking sheet and bake until fruit is tender and topping is deep golden brown, 15 to 20 minutes, rotating baking sheet halfway through baking. Transfer to wire rack and let cool for 15 minutes; serve warm.

Skillet Apple Crisp with Raspberries and Almonds

Substitute slivered almonds for pecans. Add ⅛ teaspoon almond extract to reduced cider with lemon juice in step 2. Stir 1 cup raspberries into apple mixture along with reduced cider in step 3.

Skillet Apple Crisp with Vanilla, Cardamom, and Pistachios

Substitute ½ cup shelled pistachios and ¼ cup walnuts for pecans. Substitute ½ teaspoon ground cardamom for cinnamon in filling and add seeds from 1 vanilla bean to apple, sugar, and cardamom mixture.

Pear Crisp

WHY THIS RECIPE WORKS: Simply substituting pears for apples in a classic crisp is a recipe for disaster; pears exude so much moisture that a traditional crisp topping will sink into the filling and won't get crunchy. We wanted to create a classic crisp with tender fruit and a crunchy, sweet topping using pears. Ripe yet firm Bartlett pears worked best. To compensate for the liquid they released in the oven, we added a slurry of cornstarch mixed with lemon juice. Even with the thickened juices, our standard fruit crisp topping washed down into the filling. A streusel-type topping proved sturdier and kept its crunchiness. Adding nuts to the topping provided crunch. Keeping the topping to a modest amount prevented it from sinking into the fruit.

Pear Crisp

SERVES 6

The test kitchen prefers a crisp made with Bartlett pears, but Bosc pears can also be used. The pears should be ripe but firm, which means the flesh at the base of the stem should give slightly when gently pressed with a finger. Bartlett pears will turn from green to greenish-yellow when ripe. Although almost any unsalted nut may be used in the topping, we prefer almonds or pecans. Serve with vanilla ice cream.

TOPPING

- ¾ **cup nuts, chopped coarse**
- ½ **cup (2½ ounces) all-purpose flour**
- ¼ **cup packed (1¾ ounces) light brown sugar**
- 2 **tablespoons granulated sugar**
- ¼ **teaspoon ground cinnamon**
- ⅛ **teaspoon ground nutmeg**
- ⅛ **teaspoon salt**
- 5 **tablespoons unsalted butter, melted and cooled**

FILLING

- 2 **tablespoons granulated sugar**
- 2 **teaspoons lemon juice**
- 1 **teaspoon cornstarch**
  Pinch salt
- 3 **pounds pears, peeled, halved, cored, and cut into 1½-inch pieces**

1. Adjust oven rack to lower-middle position and heat oven to 425 degrees. Line rimmed baking sheet with aluminum foil.

2. FOR THE TOPPING: Pulse nuts, flour, brown sugar, granulated sugar, cinnamon, nutmeg, and salt in food processor until nuts are finely chopped, about 9 pulses. Drizzle melted butter over flour mixture and pulse until mixture resembles crumbly wet sand, about 5 pulses, scraping down bowl halfway through. Set aside.

3. FOR THE FILLING: Whisk sugar, lemon juice, cornstarch, and salt together in large bowl. Gently toss pears with sugar mixture and transfer to 8-inch square baking dish.

4. Sprinkle topping evenly over fruit, breaking up any large chunks. Place baking dish on prepared baking sheet and bake until fruit is bubbling around edges and topping is deep golden brown, about 30 minutes, rotating baking sheet halfway through baking. Transfer to wire rack and let cool for 15 minutes; serve warm.

Pear Crisp with Oat Topping

Reduce nuts to ½ cup and increase melted butter to 6 tablespoons. After incorporating butter into flour mixture in step 2, add ½ cup old-fashioned rolled oats to food processor and process until evenly incorporated, about 3 pulses.

Triple-Ginger Pear Crisp

Use almonds for nuts and replace cinnamon and nutmeg with ¾ teaspoon ground ginger. Process 2 tablespoons coarsely chopped crystallized ginger with nuts and flour in step 2. Reduce lemon juice to 1 teaspoon and add 1 teaspoon grated fresh ginger to sugar-cornstarch mixture in step 3.

Blueberry Buckle

WHY THIS RECIPE WORKS: The classic blueberry buckle can be regarded as a streusel-topped blueberry coffee cake, but that sells it short—the substance of blueberry buckle should be the blueberries. We wanted to keep the emphasis on the berries yet also keep the berry-to-cake ratio in balance so the moisture released from the fruit during baking wouldn't create a soggy cake. We used an ample amount of blueberries—4 cups—to keep them as the headliner, then built more structure into the batter to support them. In the end, the batter resembled a cookie dough more than a cake batter. We used all-purpose flour, eliminated milk and sour cream, and added baking powder to supplement the natural leavening provided by creamed butter and sugar. For a flavorful, crisp yet crumbly streusel, we turned to a combination of light brown and granulated sugars, softened butter, and cinnamon.

Blueberry Buckle

SERVES 8

The batter will be extremely thick and heavy, and some effort will be required to spread it into the prepared pan. Be sure to use a cake pan with at least 2-inch-high sides. This buckle is best made with fresh blueberries, not frozen ones, which are too moist. Serve with vanilla ice cream.

STREUSEL

- ½ **cup (2½ ounces) all-purpose flour**
- ½ **cup packed (3½ ounces) light brown sugar**
- 2 **tablespoons granulated sugar**
- ¼ **teaspoon ground cinnamon**
  Pinch salt
- 4 **tablespoons unsalted butter, cut into 8 pieces and softened**

CAKE

- 1½ **cups (7½ ounces) all-purpose flour**
- 1½ **teaspoons baking powder**
- 10 **tablespoons unsalted butter, softened**
- ⅔ **cup (4⅔ ounces) granulated sugar**
- ½ **teaspoon salt**
- ½ **teaspoon grated lemon zest**
- 1½ **teaspoons vanilla extract**
- 2 **large eggs, room temperature**
- 1¼ **pounds (4 cups) blueberries**

1. FOR THE STREUSEL: Using stand mixer fitted with paddle, beat flour, brown sugar, granulated sugar, cinnamon, and salt on low speed until well combined and no large brown sugar lumps remain, about 45 seconds. Add butter; beat on low speed until mixture resembles wet sand and no large butter pieces remain, about 2½ minutes. Transfer to bowl; set aside.

2. FOR THE CAKE: Adjust oven rack to lower-middle position and heat oven to 350 degrees. Grease 9-inch round cake pan, line bottom with parchment paper, grease parchment, then flour pan.

3. Whisk flour and baking powder together in bowl; set aside. Using stand mixer fitted with paddle, beat butter, sugar, salt, and zest on medium-high speed until light and fluffy, about 3 minutes, scraping down bowl as necessary. Beat in vanilla until combined, about 30 seconds. With mixer on medium speed, add eggs 1 at a time; beat until partially incorporated, scrape down bowl, and continue to beat until fully incorporated (mixture will appear broken). With mixer on low speed, gradually add flour mixture; beat until flour is almost fully incorporated, about 20 seconds. Stir batter with rubber spatula, scraping bowl, until no flour pockets remain and batter is homogeneous; batter will be very heavy and thick. Gently fold in blueberries until evenly distributed.

4. Transfer batter to prepared pan. Spread batter evenly to pan edges and smooth surface. Squeeze portion of streusel in hand to form large cohesive clump; break up clump with fingers and sprinkle streusel evenly over batter. Repeat with remaining streusel. Bake until cake is deep golden brown and toothpick inserted in center comes out clean, about 55 minutes, rotating pan halfway through baking. Transfer pan to wire rack and let cool, 15 to 20 minutes (cake will fall slightly as it cools).

5. Run paring knife around edges to loosen. Invert cake, then peel off and discard parchment. Invert cake onto serving platter. Let cool for at least 1 hour. Cut into wedges and serve warm or at room temperature. (Buckle can be stored at room temperature, wrapped in plastic wrap, for up to 2 days.)

Individual Blueberry Buckles
Line 12-cup muffin tin with paper or foil liners. In step 4, transfer batter to prepared tin; spread batter evenly to cup edges and smooth surface. (Batter will reach top of liners.) Reduce baking time to 35 minutes. Let buckles cool in pan on wire rack for 10 minutes. Remove from tin and let cool, at least 30 minutes. Serve warm or at room temperature.

Easy Raspberry Gratin

✓ **WHY THIS RECIPE WORKS:** Fragrant, sweet-tart raspberries dressed up with bread crumbs and baked, make a perfect gratin. The topping browns and the fruit is warmed just enough to release a bit of juice. We wanted to find the quickest, easiest route to this pleasing simple summer dessert. We started with perfect raspberries: ripe, dry, and unbruised. Tossing the berries with just a bit of sugar and kirsch (a clear cherry brandy) provided enough additional flavor and sweetness. For the topping,

we combined soft white bread, brown sugar, cinnamon, and butter in the food processor and topped the berries with the fluffy crumbs. As for baking the gratin, we found that a moderately hot oven gave the berries more time to soften and browned the crust more evenly.

Easy Raspberry Gratin
SERVES 4 TO 6
If you prefer, you can substitute blueberries, blackberries, or strawberries for part or all of the raspberries. If using strawberries, hull them and slice them in half lengthwise if small or into quarters if large. Later in the summer, ripe, peeled peaches or nectarines, sliced, can be used in combination with the blueberries or raspberries. If using frozen raspberries, do not thaw them before baking.

- 1¼ **pounds (4 cups) fresh or frozen raspberries**
- 1 **tablespoon granulated sugar**
- 1 **tablespoon kirsch or vanilla extract (optional)**
  Pinch salt
- 3 **slices hearty white sandwich bread, torn into quarters**
- ¼ **cup packed (1¾ ounces) brown sugar**
- 2 **tablespoons unsalted butter, softened**
  Pinch ground cinnamon

1. Adjust oven rack to lower-middle position and heat oven to 400 degrees. Gently toss raspberries, granulated sugar, kirsch, if using, and salt in medium bowl. Transfer mixture to 9-inch pie plate.

2. Pulse bread, brown sugar, butter, and cinnamon in food processor until mixture resembles coarse crumbs, about 10 pulses. Sprinkle crumbs evenly over fruit and bake until crumbs are deep golden brown, 15 to 20 minutes. Transfer pie plate to wire rack, let cool for 5 minutes; serve warm.

Baked Apples

✓ **WHY THIS RECIPE WORKS:** This homey (and typically dowdy) dessert is often plagued with a mushy texture and one-dimensional, cloyingly sweet flavor. We wanted baked apples that were tender and firm with a filling that perfectly complemented their sweet, tart flavor. Granny Smith, with its firm flesh and tart, fruity flavor, was the best apple for the job. To ensure that our fruit avoided even the occasional collapse, we peeled the apples after cutting off the top; this allowed steam to escape and the apples to retain their tender-firm texture. Our filling base of tangy dried cranberries, brown sugar, and pecans benefited from some finessing by way of cinnamon, orange zest, and butter. To punch up the flavor even more, we intensified the nuttiness with chewy rolled oats, and diced apple added substance. A melon baller helped us scoop out a spacious cavity for the filling. We then capped the filled apples with the tops we had lopped off. Once in the oven, the apples were basted with an apple cider and maple syrup sauce and emerged full of flavor that's far from frumpy.

Best Baked Apples

SERVES 6

If you don't have an ovensafe skillet, transfer the browned apples to a 13 by 9-inch baking dish and bake as directed. The recipe calls for seven apples; six are left whole and one is diced and added to the filling. Serve with vanilla ice cream, if desired. See Recipe Tutorial on page 690 for more details on this recipe.

   7 large Granny Smith apples (8 ounces each)
   6 tablespoons unsalted butter, softened
   ⅓ cup dried cranberries, chopped coarse
   ⅓ cup pecans, toasted and chopped coarse
   ¼ cup packed (1¾ ounces) brown sugar
   3 tablespoons old-fashioned rolled oats
   1 teaspoon finely grated orange zest
   ½ teaspoon ground cinnamon
       Pinch salt
   ⅓ cup maple syrup
   ⅓ cup plus 2 tablespoons apple cider

1. Adjust oven rack to middle position and heat oven to 375 degrees. Peel, core, and cut 1 apple into ¼-inch dice. Combine diced apple, 5 tablespoons butter, cranberries, pecans, sugar, oats, zest, cinnamon, and salt in bowl; set aside.

2. Shave thin slice off bottom (blossom end) of remaining 6 apples to allow them to sit flat. Cut top ½ inch off stem end of apples and reserve. Peel apples and use melon baller or small measuring spoon to remove 1½-inch-diameter core, being careful not to cut through bottom of apples.

3. Melt remaining 1 tablespoon butter in 12-inch ovensafe nonstick skillet over medium heat. Add apples, stem side down, and cook until cut surface is golden brown, about 3 minutes. Flip apples, reduce heat to low, and spoon filling inside, mounding excess filling over cavities; top with reserved apple caps. Add maple syrup and ⅓ cup cider to skillet. Transfer skillet to oven and bake until skewer inserted into apples meets little resistance, 35 to 40 minutes, basting every 10 minutes with maple syrup mixture in pan.

4. Transfer apples to individual plates or serving platter. Stir up to 2 tablespoons of remaining cider into sauce in skillet to adjust consistency. Pour sauce over apples and serve.

Best Baked Apples with Dried Cherries and Hazelnuts

Substitute coarsely chopped dried cherries for cranberries, coarsely chopped toasted hazelnuts for pecans, and pepper for cinnamon.

Best Baked Apples with Dried Figs and Macadamia Nuts

Substitute coarsely chopped dried figs for cranberries, coarsely chopped toasted macadamia nuts for pecans, lemon zest for orange zest, and ¼ teaspoon ground ginger for cinnamon.

Best Baked Apples with Raisins and Walnuts

Substitute coarsely chopped raisins for cranberries, coarsely chopped toasted walnuts for pecans, lemon zest for orange zest, and ¼ teaspoon ground nutmeg for cinnamon.

Best Baked Apples with Dried Apricots and Almonds

Substitute coarsely chopped dried apricots for cranberries, coarsely chopped toasted almonds for pecans, and 1 teaspoon vanilla extract for cinnamon.

Poached Pears with Vanilla

✓ WHY THIS RECIPE WORKS: Poaching is one of the simplest ways of preparing ripe, seasonal fruit. But the timing can be tricky: How long do you cook the fruit so that it is tender but not mushy? We experimented with a variety of methods and learned that the trick was not to cook the fruit at all. Submerging the raw fruit in simmering syrup and allowing it to steep off the heat for 30 minutes worked perfectly. The fruit was tender, sweet, and permeated with the syrup's flavor, but never mushy.

Poached Pears with Vanilla

SERVES 4 TO 6

This recipe works best with just-ripened pears that are neither too soft nor too hard. Although these poached pears taste great on their own, you can serve them with ice cream, Crème Anglaise (page 776), lightly sweetened and whipped crème fraîche, or cheese, such as a blue.

   1½ cups water
   ½   cup sugar
   ½   vanilla bean, split lengthwise, seeds removed and reserved
   4   pears (8 ounces each), peeled, halved, and cored

1. Bring water, sugar, and vanilla bean and seeds to boil in medium saucepan, stirring occasionally, until sugar dissolves, about 5 minutes. Add pears, turn off heat, cover, and let sit off heat until mixture cools to room temperature, about 30 minutes.

2. Remove vanilla bean. Refrigerate pears and poaching liquid, in saucepan, until well chilled, at least 2 hours. Spoon fruit and poaching liquid into individual bowls and serve. (Poached pears can be refrigerated in poaching liquid, covered tightly with plastic wrap, for up to 3 days.)

Berry Fool

✓ WHY THIS RECIPE WORKS: This traditional British fruit dessert is typically made by folding pureed stewed fruit (usually gooseberries) into sweet custard. Modern fool recipes skip the custard and use whipped cream. But whipped cream blunts the fruit flavor and is too light and insubstantial. We wanted a dessert with intense fruitiness and rich body—and we wanted to use strawberries and raspberries rather than gooseberries. Our first challenge was to thicken the fruit properly; unlike gooseberries, raspberries and strawberries are low in pectin. We turned to gelatin to thicken our berries. We softened the gelatin in some uncooked berry puree, then combined the softened mixture with some heated puree to help melt and distribute the gelatin.

Now we had a smooth, thickened puree with intense fruit flavor. When it came to the custard, we liked the ease of using whipped cream; when we combined it with sour cream, we had a mixture that was airy yet substantial, with a rich and slightly tangy flavor. For even more fruit flavor, we layered the fruit puree and cream base with fresh berries that had been macerated in sugar. Finally, topping the dessert with crumbled sweet wheat crackers added a pleasant, nutty contrast.

Berry Fool

SERVES 6

Blueberries or blackberries can be substituted for the raspberries in this recipe. You may also substitute frozen fruit for fresh, but it will slightly compromise the texture. If using frozen fruit, reduce the amount of sugar in the puree by 1 tablespoon. The thickened fruit puree can be made up to 4 hours in advance; just make sure to whisk it well in step 4 to break up any clumps before combining it with the whipped cream. For the best results, chill your whisk attachment and stand mixer bowl before whipping the cream. We like the granular texture and nutty flavor of Carr's Whole Wheat Crackers, but graham crackers or gingersnaps will also work. You will need six tall parfait or sundae glasses. See Recipe Tutorial on page 693 for more details on this recipe.

- 30 ounces strawberries, hulled (6 cups)
- 12 ounces (2⅓ cups) raspberries
- ¾ cup (5¼ ounces) sugar
- 2 teaspoons unflavored gelatin
- 1 cup heavy cream, chilled
- ¼ cup sour cream, chilled
- ½ teaspoon vanilla extract
- 4 Carr's Whole Wheat Crackers, crushed fine (¼ cup)
- 6 sprigs fresh mint (optional)

1. Process half of strawberries, half of raspberries, and ½ cup sugar in food processor until mixture is completely smooth, about 1 minute. Strain berry puree through fine-mesh strainer into large liquid measuring cup (you should have about 2½ cups puree; reserve excess for another use). Transfer ½ cup puree to small bowl. Sprinkle gelatin over top of puree; let sit until gelatin softens, about 5 minutes, and stir. Heat remaining 2 cups puree in small saucepan over medium heat until it begins to bubble, 4 to 6 minutes. Off heat, stir in gelatin mixture until dissolved. Transfer to medium bowl, cover with plastic wrap, and refrigerate until well chilled, about 2 hours.

2. Meanwhile, chop remaining strawberries into rough ¼-inch pieces. Toss strawberries, remaining raspberries, and 2 tablespoons sugar together in medium bowl. Set aside for 1 hour.

3. Using stand mixer fitted with whisk, whip heavy cream, sour cream, vanilla, and remaining 2 tablespoons sugar on low speed until bubbles form, about 30 seconds. Increase speed to medium and whip until whisk leaves trail, about 30 seconds. Increase speed to high; whip until mixture has nearly doubled in volume and holds stiff peaks, about 30 seconds. Transfer ⅓ cup whipped cream mixture to small bowl; set aside.

4. Remove berry puree from refrigerator and whisk until smooth. With mixer on medium speed, slowly add two-thirds of puree to whipped cream mixture; mix until incorporated, about 15 seconds. Using spatula, gently fold in remaining puree, leaving streaks of puree.

5. Transfer uncooked berries to fine-mesh strainer; shake gently to remove any excess juice. Divide two-thirds of uncooked berries evenly among 6 tall parfait or sundae glasses. Divide creamy berry mixture evenly among glasses, followed by remaining uncooked berries. Top each glass with reserved plain whipped cream mixture. Sprinkle with crushed crackers and garnish with mint sprigs, if using. Serve immediately.

Pavlovas

✓ **WHY THIS RECIPE WORKS:** Pavlova is simple to prepare, yet it's often plagued by soggy, sickly sweet meringue and unripe fruit—and cutting it for serving is a messy proposition. We were seeking a pavlova made of pure white, perfectly crisped meringue, its texture softened by whipped cream and its sweetness balanced by a fresh fruit topping. First, we opted to take a restaurant approach and make individual pavlovas for tidier presentation. Then we focused on making and baking the meringue. Whipping room-temperature egg whites with a small amount of cream of tartar and vanilla before slowly adding the sugar gave us a voluminous, billowy, stable meringue. To shape the meringues, we portioned ½ cup of the mixture into small mounds on a baking sheet, then used the back of a spoon to create indentations for holding the whipped cream and fruit. Baking the meringues at 200 degrees for an hour and a half yielded perfectly dry, crisp, white shells. Gradually cooling them in the turned-off oven ensured their crispness. While we especially liked the flavors of tropical fruit on the pavlovas, fresh berries and peaches made fine options too. For the whipped cream topping, we added sour cream for a slight tang that provided a cool, refreshing counterpoint to the sweet fruit and meringues.

Individual Pavlovas with Tropical Fruit

SERVES 6

Be mindful that the fruit is the garnish here, so it's worth taking the time to cut it into tidy pieces. Sour cream gives the whipped cream a slight tang; omit it if you prefer simple whipped cream. Avoid making pavlovas on humid days or the meringue shells will turn out sticky. See Recipe Tutorial on page 697 for more details on this recipe.

MERINGUES AND FRUIT
- 4 large egg whites, room temperature
- ¾ teaspoon vanilla extract
- ¼ teaspoon cream of tartar
- 1 cup (7 ounces) plus 1 tablespoon sugar
- 1 mango, peeled, pitted, and cut into ¼-inch pieces
- 2 kiwis, peeled, quartered, and sliced thin
- 1½ cups ½-inch pineapple pieces

TOPPING
- 1 cup heavy cream, chilled
- ½ cup sour cream, chilled
- 1 tablespoon sugar
- 1 teaspoon vanilla extract

1. FOR THE MERINGUES AND FRUIT: Adjust oven rack to middle position and heat oven to 200 degrees. Line baking sheet with parchment paper.

2. Using stand mixer fitted with whisk, whip egg whites, vanilla, and cream of tartar on medium-low speed until foamy, about 1 minute. Increase speed to medium-high and whip whites to soft, billowy mounds, about 1 minute. Gradually add 1 cup sugar and whip until glossy, stiff peaks form, 1 to 2 minutes.

3. Scoop six ½-cup mounds of meringue onto prepared sheet, spacing them about 1 inch apart. Gently make small, bowl-like indentation in each meringue using back of spoon. Bake until meringues have smooth, dry, and firm exteriors, about 1½ hours. Turn oven off and leave meringues in oven until completely dry and hard, about 2 hours. (Meringue shells can be stored at room temperature in an airtight container for up to 2 weeks.)

4. Gently toss mango, kiwis, and pineapple with remaining 1 tablespoon sugar in large bowl. Let sit at room temperature until sugar has dissolved and fruit is juicy, about 30 minutes.

5. FOR THE TOPPING: Using stand mixer fitted with whisk, whip heavy cream, sour cream, sugar, and vanilla on medium-low speed until foamy, about 1 minute. Increase speed to high and whip until soft peaks form, 1 to 3 minutes. (Whipped cream can be refrigerated in fine-mesh strainer set over small bowl and covered with plastic wrap for up to 8 hours.)

6. To assemble, place meringue shells on individual plates and spoon about ⅓ cup whipped cream mixture into each shell. Top each with about ½ cup fruit (some fruit and juice will fall onto plate). Serve immediately.

Individual Pavlovas with Mixed Berries

Substitute 1½ cups each raspberries and blueberries and 1 cup blackberries for mango, kiwi, and pineapple.

Individual Pavlovas with Strawberries, Blueberries, and Peaches

If your peaches are firm, you should be able to peel them with a vegetable peeler. If they are too soft and ripe to withstand the pressure of a peeler, you'll need to blanch them in a pot of simmering water for 15 seconds and then shock them in a bowl of ice water before peeling.

Substitute 1 cup strawberries, hulled and sliced thin, 1 cup blueberries, and 2 peaches, peeled, halved, pitted, and sliced ¼ inch thick, for mango, kiwi, and pineapple.

Whipped Cream

✔ **WHY THIS RECIPE WORKS:** The lightly sweetened flavor and creamy texture of whipped cream make the perfect partner to numerous desserts, especially pies. But perfect whipped cream can be hard to accomplish—the cream can go from properly whipped to overwhipped and stiff in a matter of seconds. For puffy, cloudlike mounds, we reached for our stand mixer and began whipping the cream and sugar on medium-low speed, then increased the speed and whipped just until the mixture was thick and billowy. For flavor, we added a dash of vanilla.

Whipped Cream
MAKES ABOUT 2 CUPS

For lightly sweetened whipped cream, reduce the sugar to 1½ teaspoons. For the best results, chill the mixer bowl and whisk in the freezer for 20 minutes before whipping the cream.

  1 **cup heavy cream, chilled**
  1 **tablespoon sugar**
  1 **teaspoon vanilla extract**

Using stand mixer fitted with whisk, whip cream, sugar, and vanilla on medium-low speed until foamy, about 1 minute. Increase speed to high and whip until soft peaks form, 1 to 3 minutes. (Whipped cream can be refrigerated in fine-mesh strainer set over small bowl and covered with plastic wrap for up to 8 hours.)

Brown Sugar Whipped Cream
MAKES ABOUT 2½ CUPS

Refrigerating the mixture in step 1 gives the brown sugar time to dissolve. This whipped cream pairs well with any dessert that has lots of nuts, warm spices, or molasses, like gingerbread, pecan pie, or pumpkin pie.

  1 **cup heavy cream, chilled**
  ½ **cup sour cream**
  ½ **cup packed (3½ ounces) light brown sugar**
  ⅛ **teaspoon salt**

1. Using stand mixer fitted with whisk, whip heavy cream, sour cream, sugar, and salt until combined. Cover with plastic wrap and refrigerate until ready to serve, at least 4 hours or up to 1 day, stirring once or twice during chilling to ensure that sugar dissolves.

2. Before serving, using stand mixer fitted with whisk, whip mixture on medium-low speed until foamy, about 1 minute. Increase speed to high and whip until soft peaks form, 1 to 3 minutes.

Brown Sugar and Bourbon Whipped Cream

Add 2 teaspoons bourbon to cream mixture before whipping.

Tangy Whipped Cream
MAKES 1½ CUPS

Sour cream adds a pleasing tang to this whipped cream, which makes a nice accompaniment to richer desserts.

  1 **cup heavy cream, chilled**
  ¼ **cup sour cream**
  ¼ **cup packed (1¾ ounces) light brown sugar**
  ⅛ **teaspoon vanilla extract**

Using stand mixer fitted with whisk, whip heavy cream, sour cream, brown sugar, and vanilla on medium-low speed until foamy, about 1 minute. Increase speed to high and whip until soft peaks form, 1 to 3 minutes.

Inside This Chapter

CHAPTER 17

How to Make Pies and Tarts

At their simplest, pies and tarts are baked pastry shells filled with a sweet or savory filling. In America, the focus is generally on sweet fillings made with fruit, cream, or custard. Pie dough is generally a bit less sweet and rich than tart dough. Likewise, pie fillings are generally a bit less rich (and more voluminous) than intense tart fillings (which must fit into a shallow tart shell). Whether you're making a pie or a tart, the key to success begins with a superb crust.

Getting Started

Types of Pies

You can divide the world of pies in two ways: by type of filling or by type of crust. In terms of filling, there are fruit pies, cream pies, and custard pies. Fruit pies can be made with raw or precooked fruit. Cream pies rely on whipped cream for volume. Custard pies (which includes pumpkin, pecan, and old-fashioned buttermilk pies) contain eggs and often, but not always, some sort of dairy. If you divide pies by crust styles there are two main categories: single crust and double crust.

SINGLE-CRUST PIES

This type of pie contains a bottom crust—a pie shell—that is filled. The pie shell is almost always prebaked until golden brown and crisp; the filling is then added to the prebaked pie shell. If the filling requires no baking (such as a cream pie), the pie shell is fully baked so the filled pie can be refrigerated (to help set the filling and facilitate neat slicing) and then served.

In cases when the filling requires baking, the pie shell is generally partially baked, filled, and then returned to the oven. This is how most custard pies are made, as the oven heat causes the eggs to thicken the filling.

Single-crust pies can be made with pie dough or cookie crumbs. Graham crackers are the classic choice for crumb crusts, but shortbread and chocolate and peanut butter sandwich cookies are also options. Depending on the cookie, the crumbs are generally sweetened with additional sugar, moistened with melted butter, and then pressed into place and prebaked before filling.

DOUBLE-CRUST PIES

Double-crust pies generally require a bit more effort to prepare than single-crust pies, in part because they always rely on pie dough (a cookie-crumb crust isn't an option). The filling is placed between two pieces of raw pie dough, and the pie is then baked. The filling can be raw fruit that has been sliced and sugared, or it can be cooked.

A lattice-top pie is simply a double-crust pie with woven strips of pie dough rather than a solid sheet. Beyond aesthetics, a lattice top allows for greater evaporation of fruit juices, a benefit when working with particularly juicy fruits like peaches or cherries. For drier fruits, like apples, a regular top crust is generally preferred.

The process for making most double-crust pies is quite similar. The pie plate is lined with a piece of pie dough and chilled, the filling is added, the top piece of dough is draped over the filling, the edges of the top and bottom pieces of dough are crimped together, and the pie is baked.

Types of Tarts

There are two basic types of tarts. A classic tart is baked in a shallow metal pan with fluted edges. As with pies, the tart shell can be fully baked, cooled, and filled, or it can be partially baked, filled, and returned to the oven to finish. A free-form tart starts with a single piece of dough rolled into a circle. The filling is piled in the middle of the dough, and the edges of the dough are folded over the filling. Each type of tart requires a different kind of dough.

FREE-FORM TART

A free-form tart generally starts with dough that is very similar to pie dough. It must be easy to roll out and should be pliable enough to fold over the filling without tearing. For our Free-Form Tart Dough (page 750), we use nothing more than flour, butter, salt, and ice water. While pie dough contains a mix of shortening and butter, the dough in a free-form tart is so front and center that we think it's worth sacrificing some flakiness for better flavor. Pie dough also contains sugar. Since we like to sprinkle the tart with sugar before it goes into the oven, we don't add any to the dough itself.

Free-form tarts are almost always filled with fresh fruit. Because the fruit is exposed to direct oven heat, there's usually no need to thicken the fruit—excess juices will simply evaporate. The most important thing to remember when making any free-form tart is to pile the filling in the center of the dough, leaving a wide area around the perimeter free of any fruit. This allows the baker to fold the dough over part of the filling and gives the tart its shape and structure.

CLASSIC TART

A classic French-style tart is made with a dough that is richer and sweeter than pie dough. While pie dough (and free-form tart dough) is tender and flaky, a classic tart crust should be fine textured, buttery-rich, crisp, and crumbly. The dough is often referred to as "short" and has a texture similar to shortbread. Our Classic Tart Dough (page 751) relies on butter as well as an egg yolk and heavy cream to create a flavorful, rich crust. We find that confectioners' sugar, rather than granulated sugar, helps create the right sandy but crisp texture.

A classic tart shell is always prebaked before filling. (Skip this step and the crust will be soggy, not crisp.) If the filling is already cooked (as with pastry cream), the tart shell should be blind-baked with pie weights until the dough has set, then the weights are removed and the shell is baked further until crisp and golden brown. If the filling requires significant oven time, the partially baked tart shell is removed from the oven so that the pie weights can be removed and the filling added, and then the whole tart is returned to the oven to finish.

Essential Equipment

Here are the basic tools you will need to make most pies and tarts.

FOOD PROCESSOR

Sure, you can make pie or tart dough by hand, but the food processor is much more consistent in terms of cutting fat evenly into flour. More important, the food processor works so quickly that there's no time for the fat to soften. Even the standard two-fork (or pastry blender) method heats up the dough and yields less consistent results. You will want a large food processor (with a capacity of at least 11 cups) when making pie dough. For more details on what to look for, see page 28.

ROLLING PIN

Forget about the fancy rolling pins now on the market. An old-fashioned wooden pin does a better job than marble, nonstick, or other high-tech options. We like French-style rolling pins without handles. (We find that pins with ball bearings and handles can exert too much pressure on the dough.) We like a long pin (20 inches or so) with tapered ends that help produce dough that rolls out to an even thickness.

PIE PLATE

We recommend using glass (Pyrex) pie plates so that you can judge the progress of the bottom crust. The glass also browns the crust better than metal does. Also, metal pie plates can react with acidic fillings, while glass is nonreactive. Look for a pan with a ½-inch rim, which makes it easier to create decorative fluting. Shallow, angled sides prevent prebaked crusts from slumping. For more details on what to look for, see page 27.

PIE WEIGHTS

When an empty pie shell or tart shell is prebaked, the dough must be weighted so that the dough doesn't bubble up. Old-fashioned recipes suggest lining the shell with foil and filling the foil with rice or dried beans. While these pantry items will work, we find that ceramic or metal pie weights are better because they conduct heat well and help the crust to brown. If you don't own pie weights, you can use pennies instead (store them in an oven bag to get them in and out of the pie shell).

TART PAN

A classic tart pan is quite shallow, and the edges are deeply scalloped to give the sides an attractive finish. We find that the dark finishes can cause overbrowning. We prefer a light-colored tinned steel pan. The removable bottom is essential—without it you can't cut neat slices. At serving time, simply hold the underside of the bottom and lift up the scalloped ring to separate it. Slide a thin spatula between the tart and the pan bottom and transfer the tart to a serving plate.

PIE SERVER

Without a sharp and sturdy pie server, dessert can go from flawless to fractured in moments. Look for a pie server with a thin, serrated blade, which will slice pie nimbly, rather than thicker blades that will only mar your custard pies with their blunt teeth. Gimmicks like an extra-long neck, swordlike blade, or finger-pushing mechanism are best avoided. Also look for a handle with a comfortable grip.

Essential Ingredients

Here are the basic ingredients you will need to make most pies and tarts. Since so many pies call for fruit, you should also review the Getting Started section of How to Make Fruit Desserts, pages 680–683.

FLOUR

While professionals rely on low-protein pastry flour for many pies and tarts, we find that all-purpose flour is just fine. Given the simplicity of pie and tart dough, we recommend using unbleached all-purpose flour; the bleaching process can impart a chemical flavor. For maximum accuracy, it's best to weigh flour, although the dip-and-sweep method will work.

SHORTENING

Vegetable shortening makes an especially flaky pie dough. Many older recipes use shortening and no butter. The resulting crusts are flaky but bland. For maximum flavor and flakiness, our pie dough recipe combines both butter and shortening.

BUTTER

Pie dough and tart dough are basically fat and flour. Among the various choices (butter, shortening, oil, and lard), butter has the best flavor and we think it is a must. Our recipes rely on unsalted butter. Salted butter often contains a bit more water than unsalted butter, and that can cause problems in pie and tart dough. While we strongly recommend using unsalted butter for all your baking and cooking, if you're using salted butter to make a pie or tart, you should omit the salt in the dough. We have found that regular supermarket butter performs well in pie dough and tart dough, and so there's no reason to spend the money on premium, European-style butter with more fat.

How to Make a Crumb Crust

A crumb crust is a classic choice in many single-crust pies. It's more durable than classic pie dough, making it the right choice for the moist custard-based fillings in recipes like Key Lime Pie (page 742) and Chocolate Cream Pie (page 743). Graham crackers are the classic choice. For chocolate cookie crusts, we prefer Oreos. While buying a store-bought ready-to-go crust is a tempting shortcut, these are always stale and bland. Making your own is incredibly easy and well worth it for a fresh-tasting crust with a crisp texture and balanced sweetness to do your homemade pie filling justice. See chart on opposite page for specific ingredient amounts for the type of crust you want to make.

ESSENTIAL EQUIPMENT

- food processor
- 9-inch pie plate, preferably glass
- dry measuring cup

1. GRIND CRUMBS

Break 8 whole graham crackers or 16 sandwich cookies (such as chocolate or peanut butter sandwich cookies) into rough pieces and place in food processor. If using graham crackers, process to fine crumbs, about 30 seconds. For sandwich cookies, pulse until coarsely ground, then process to fine crumbs. Sprinkle sugar (if using) and melted, cooled butter over crumbs and pulse to incorporate, about 5 pulses.

WHY? The metal blade of a food processor turns hard crackers or cookies into even crumbs in seconds. It's also the best way to incorporate the sugar (a must with graham crackers, but unnecessary with sweeter cookies) and melted butter. Since sandwich cookies are heftier than graham crackers, it's best to break them up before processing.

2. SHAPE INTO CRUST

Sprinkle crumb mixture into 9-inch pie plate. Use bottom of dry measuring cup to press crumb mixture firmly and evenly across bottom of pie plate. Then tightly pack crumbs against side of pie plate using side of measuring cup.

WHY? The butter moistens the crumbs, but a little elbow grease is required to create a cohesive crust. Make sure to build the crust up the sides of the pie plate. A dry measuring cup (the ⅓ or ½ cup measure in most sets works best) keeps your hands clean and allows you to create an even, firmly packed surface.

3. BAKE UNTIL FRAGRANT AND JUST BROWNING

Adjust oven rack to middle position and heat oven to 325 degrees. Bake until crust is fragrant and beginning to brown, 13 to 18 minutes. Use crust immediately or cool as directed in pie recipe.

WHY? Many recipes skip the prebaking step, but this is a big mistake. Baking the crumbs makes the crust cohesive and gives mild graham crackers a nice toasty flavor.

Formula for Crumb Crusts

The method for all crumb crusts is quite similar. Make sure to use granulated sugar and unsalted butter that has been melted and cooled slightly. Avoid using "double-filled" sandwich cookies, and note that sweeter cookies don't require any sugar.

CRACKERS/COOKIES	NUMBER	PREPARATION	SUGAR	BUTTER
Graham Crackers	8 whole	broken into rough pieces	3 tablespoons	5 tablespoons
Chocolate Sandwich Cookies (Oreos)	16	broken into rough pieces	N/A	4 tablespoons
Mint Chocolate Sandwich Cookies (Cool Mint Creme Oreos)	16	broken into rough pieces	N/A	4 tablespoons
Peanut Butter Sandwich Cookies (Nutter Butters)	16	broken into rough pieces	N/A	4 tablespoons

Troubleshooting Crumb Crusts

PROBLEM	SOLUTION
I want to use store-bought graham cracker crumbs.	In theory, these crumbs would work in our recipe, but we have found that they are often quite stale. And they don't save you much time, since you still need to add sugar and melted butter. We strongly recommend you take 30 seconds to grind your own crumbs.
Can I just use a store-bought graham cracker crust?	Please don't! We tasted three leading brands and were shocked at their bland, artificial flavor and sandy, crumbly texture. Commercial crusts are made with shortening, not butter, and you can taste the difference. Also, these crusts aren't sufficiently baked. The 5 minutes of hands-on work needed to make your own crumb crust is time well spent.
I can't tell if the crust is done baking.	While you can easily use color change to judge when pie dough is baked, it's pretty difficult to tell when a crumb crust is done, at least with just your eyes. The crust should be fragrant (but not burned) and firm to the touch. If the crust feels soft or not quite set, give it a few more minutes in the oven.
Can I use chocolate wafer cookies instead of Oreos for a chocolate crust?	We wouldn't recommend it. Chocolate wafer cookies are the more conventional choice for this type of crust, but we have found that they taste bland and tough. Because of the richness of the Oreo filling, the crust is guaranteed to be tender.

How to Make Pie Dough

Pie dough seems easy enough to prepare. Mix flour, salt, and sugar together, cut in some fat, add water just until the dough sticks together, roll it out, and bake it. A study in simplicity. Yet it can all go wrong so easily. The dough is almost always too dry and crumbly to roll out successfully. The crust is either flaky but leathery, or tender but with no flakes. We use a novel approach to combine the fat with the flour to ensure a consistent amount of uncoated flour in the dough. As a result, our dough requires the same amount of liquid every time. And because we replace some of the water with vodka, we can use a generous amount of liquid and not worry about excess gluten development. (The alcohol in vodka doesn't activate the gluten proteins in flour, so it moistens the dough without making it tough.) The result is a dough that has enough moisture to roll out easily but still bakes up flaky and tender. The steps below make enough for one double-crust pie or two single-crust pies. See chart on page 718 for ingredient amounts if you want to make dough for one single-crust pie.

1-2. CUT AND CHILL BUTTER AND SHORTENING

Cut 12 tablespoons unsalted butter into ¼-inch pieces. Cut 8 tablespoons vegetable shortening into 2-tablespoon pieces. Place butter and shortening on plates and chill in freezer.

WHY? A combination of butter and shortening works best in a crust—the shortening makes the crust tender and flaky, while the butter provides flavor. Cutting both into pieces minimizes the time it will take to cut the fat into the flour and reduces the risk of overworking the dough. Because the food processor generates heat that can melt the fat, chill the fat to keep it from melting.

3-4. CHILL TWO LIQUIDS

Fill measuring cup with ice and cold water. Chill ¼ cup vodka.

WHY? Too much water makes pie dough tough, and that's why most recipes are stingy with the water (and thus really hard to roll out). While gluten (the protein that makes crust tough) forms readily in water, it doesn't form in ethanol, and vodka is 60 percent water and 40 percent ethanol. We use equal parts water and vodka to produce a moist, easy-to-roll dough that stays tender (the alcohol vaporizes in the oven).

5. PROCESS SOME FLOUR WITH FAT

Process 1½ cups (7½ ounces) all-purpose flour, 2 tablespoons sugar, and 1 teaspoon salt in food processor until combined, about 5 seconds. Scatter chilled butter and shortening pieces over top of flour mixture. Process until incorporated and mixture begins to form uneven clumps with no remaining floury bits, about 15 seconds.

WHY? The traditional method of pulsing the flour and fat together yields a mix of flour coated with fat and flour that remains uncoated. Depending on the ratio of coated to uncoated flour, the dough will absorb less or more water. With this method there's no way to know how much water will be needed, which is why traditional recipes offer a wide range of water amounts. Our method

fully blends part of the flour with the fat so that the amount of coated flour is fixed. We then pulse in the remaining flour, which ensures a consistent amount of uncoated flour. As a result, we know that our dough needs exactly ½ cup of chilled liquid to form a coherent dough.

6. ADD REST OF FLOUR

Scrape down workbowl and redistribute dough evenly around processor blade. Sprinkle 1 cup (5 ounces) all-purpose flour over dough. Pulse until mixture has broken up into pieces and is evenly distributed around bowl, 4 to 6 pulses.

WHY? Adding the flour in two steps creates a consistent amount of uncoated flour and allows better control over how much liquid to add to make a malleable dough.

7. ADD LIQUID

Transfer mixture to large bowl. Sprinkle vodka and ¼ cup water over mixture. Stir and press dough together, using stiff rubber spatula, until dough sticks together.

WHY? It's easier to incorporate the liquid if the mixture is in a bowl; if this step is done in a food processor, there's a tendency to overwork the dough.

8. CHILL DOUGH

Divide dough into 2 even pieces. Turn each piece of dough onto sheet of plastic and flatten each into 4-inch disk. Wrap each piece tightly and refrigerate for at least 1 hour or up to 2 days. (The dough can also be frozen for up to 1 month.)

WHY? The fat has warmed up during the mixing process. Since cold fat is essential to creating a flaky texture, the dough must go into the fridge to chill before rolling. Also, the gluten in the flour will relax a bit as the dough chills, ensuring that the dough isn't tough.

9. LET DOUGH SOFTEN BEFORE ROLLING

Let dough sit on counter until slightly softened, about 10 minutes, before rolling out.

WHY? Chilled dough is quite stiff and will be hard to roll out. Letting it warm up for 10 minutes means less work for you and less risk of overworking the dough. If you are using frozen dough, make sure to thaw it fully on the counter before attempting to roll it out.

Formula for Single Crust and Double Crust

The process for making a single piece of dough for a single-crust pie is the same as the process for making two pieces of dough for a double-crust pie. The only differences (other than ingredient amounts) are that you will need to process the flour-fat mixture for about 10 seconds for a single crust rather than 15 seconds for a double crust, and the dough is divided into two pieces before chilling when making a double-crust pie.

INGREDIENT	SINGLE CRUST	DOUBLE CRUST
Unsalted Butter	6 tablespoons	12 tablespoons
Vegetable Shortening	4 tablespoons	8 tablespoons
All-Purpose Flour	1¼ cups (6¼ ounces)	2½ cups (12½ ounces)
Sugar	1 tablespoon	2 tablespoons
Salt	½ teaspoon	1 teaspoon
Ice Water	2 tablespoons	¼ cup
Vodka	2 tablespoons	¼ cup

Troubleshooting Making and Rolling Out Pie Dough

PROBLEM	SOLUTION
I don't have vodka on hand.	The alcohol is key to our recipe. You can use another liquor (tequila or white rum work well). Don't worry about adding any flavor—the alcohol bakes off in the oven, so you can't taste it in the finished pie.
I don't have a large food processor.	Our recipe depends on a food processor. Without it, you are back to the traditional mixing method that relies on two forks or a pastry blender. These methods are fairly imprecise and not well suited to our recipe since we call for more liquid than is typical. If you really want to make pie dough but don't have a food processor, you can adapt our recipe accordingly: Mix the flour with the sugar and salt, then use two knives to cut small chunks of chilled butter and shortening into the flour until the mixture resembles coarse crumbs. Add enough chilled liquid until the dough comes together, but make sure to use as little liquid as possible (at least 1 or 2 tablespoons less than the amounts listed in our recipe) to minimize gluten development.
The dough sticks to the counter a bit.	It's fine to flour the counter generously when working with our dough. Many recipes skimp on flour at this stage because more flour can make a tough crust. Our dough is more forgiving, so feel free to dust your rolling pin and counter with flour. If you're having trouble loosening the dough from the counter, slide a bench scraper under the dough to free it.
The dough sticks to the counter a lot.	The dough may have become too warm. Slide it onto a parchment paper–lined baking sheet and return it to the refrigerator for at least 15 minutes before proceeding with the rolling process.
The dough is too small for the pie plate.	Don't forget to use a kitchen ruler to measure the dough side to side and top to bottom to make sure it really is a 12-inch circle. If you forgot and the dough is too small, don't try to stretch it to fit. Instead, roll the dough back around the rolling pin, return it to the floured counter, and continue rolling until it forms a 12-inch circle.

How to Roll Out and Fit Pie Dough

ESSENTIAL EQUIPMENT

- rolling pin
- kitchen ruler
- 9-inch pie plate, preferably glass

Unlike traditional pie dough, where adding too much flour is a no-no, the dough used in our recipe can be rolled out on a generously floured counter. The key is to use even pressure and rotate the dough as you work. We recommend using a dowel-style rolling pin without handles, sometimes called a French-style rolling pin. We find that handles on American-style rolling pins encourage the baker to exert excess pressure on the dough. Simple dowels, with or without tapered ends, apply less pressure and give you a better sense of the dough as you roll.

As for the pie plate, we highly recommend using a tempered glass pie plate, such as Pyrex. The glass conducts heat well and allows you to monitor the browning of the underside of the crust. Also, glass won't react with acidic fruit fillings. Also see How to Make Pie Dough (page 716), How to Bake a Single-Crust Pie Shell (page 720). and How to Make a Double-Crust Pie (page 722).

1. ROLL AND TURN

Lay disk of dough on floured counter and roll dough outward from center into 12-inch circle, giving dough quarter turn after every few rolls.
WHY? Many bakers simply roll back-and-forth. The result is an oval that is thinner in the middle and thicker at the edges. By picking up the dough and rotating it as you work, you can easily produce a round shape. Also, this method ensures uniform thickness. Keep rolling until the dough measures 12 inches (use a kitchen ruler). If you are making a double-crust pie, leave the second piece of dough in the refrigerator while you roll out and fit the bottom crust.

2. FLOUR GENEROUSLY

Toss additional flour underneath dough as needed to keep dough from sticking to counter.
WHY? If the dough sticks, it can tear. Keeping the counter well floured enables you to roll out the dough thinner and thinner without it sticking.

3. ROLL DOUGH AROUND PIN

Starting at edge of dough, loosely roll dough around rolling pin.
WHY? Lifting the dough round with your hands can cause the dough to stretch. You also increase the risk of tearing the dough. Rolling the dough around the rolling pin and then unrolling the dough into the pie plate minimizes the risk of stretching or tearing.

4. FIT DOUGH INTO PIE PLATE

Gently unroll dough over 9-inch pie plate, then lift dough and gently press into pie plate, letting excess hang over pie plate's edge.
WHY? You want to gently fit the dough snugly into the pie plate so that there are no gaps between the pie plate and the dough. From here, proceed with making a single-crust pie or, for a double-crust pie, cover the crust fitted in the pie plate lightly with plastic wrap and refrigerate for at least 30 minutes before filling and topping with the second crust.

How to Bake a Single-Crust Pie Shell

ESSENTIAL EQUIPMENT

- kitchen shears
- 9-inch pie plate, preferably glass
- fork
- plastic wrap
- aluminum foil
- ceramic or metal pie weights
- wire rack

There's nothing worse than putting the work into making homemade pie dough only to end up with a soggy crust on your finished pie. Although on rare occasions we might fill a single-crust pie shell raw, we typically partially or fully bake the crust before adding the filling. This ensures the pie crust is perfectly brown, crisp, and flaky—not soggy—once the filling has been added and the pie has been finished in the oven (unless it's a no-bake filling of course). Many recipes that call for partially baking the crust also suggest filling the pie shell when it's still warm and then quickly returning it to the oven. Read each recipe carefully and have the filling ready when the pie shell comes out of the oven if so directed. Also see How to Make Pie Dough (page 716) and How to Roll Out and Fit Pie Dough (page 719).

1. MAKE THICK EDGE

Using kitchen shears, trim pie dough to hang ½ inch over lip of pie plate, then tuck overhang underneath itself to form tidy, even edge that sits on lip of pie plate.

WHY? For a traditional single-crust pie, you need to make an evenly thick edge before crimping. That thick edge will help keep the filling in place and provide visual appeal to the baked pie. From here, you now have two options for finishing the edge of the dough.

2A. FINISH WITH FLUTED EDGE

Using index finger of one hand and thumb and index finger of other hand, create fluted ridges perpendicular to edge of pie plate.

WHY? Beyond looking nice, the flutes ensure that the dough isn't overly thick and that it bakes through properly.

2B. FINISH WITH RIDGED EDGE

Press tines of fork into dough to flatten it against rim of pie plate.

WHY? This method is a very simple way to flatten the edge to a consistent thickness so that it bakes through properly.

3. CHILL PIE CRUST

Wrap dough-lined pie plate loosely in plastic wrap. Place in freezer until dough is fully chilled and firm, about 30 minutes.

WHY? The biggest risk when prebaking a pie shell is that the shell can shrink in the oven. If this happens, the pie won't look as nice. More important, the shell won't be able to hold all the filling. A cold pie shell will hold its shape better in the oven, in part because the chilling gives the gluten in the dough time to relax.

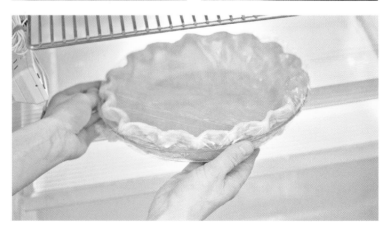

4. LINE CRUST WITH FOIL

Line chilled pie crust with double layer of aluminum foil, covering edges to prevent burning.

WHY? The foil serves two purposes. It will hold the pie weights that keep the dough from bubbling up as it bakes. The foil also gives the crust time to set without coloring too much, and it prevents the edges of the crust from overbrowning.

5. WEIGHT AND BAKE

Fill foil-lined crust with pie weights or pennies. Bake in 375-degree oven until set and very lightly colored, 25 to 30 minutes.

WHY? Forget about using rice or beans to weight the dough; they don't conduct heat nearly as well as ceramic or metal pie weights (or pennies, in a pinch).

6. REMOVE FOIL AND WEIGHTS

Carefully remove foil and weights. For partially baked crust, transfer to wire rack. For fully baked crust, return crust (without weights) to oven and bake 10 to 12 minutes longer, then transfer to wire rack.

WHY? The foil makes it easy to remove the pie weights. Depending on the recipe, after the weights are removed the crust will be filled and baked again, or it will need more time in the oven to become fully crisp and brown.

Troubleshooting a Single-Crust Pie Shell

PROBLEM	SOLUTION
I don't own pie weights.	If you don't have pie weights, pennies make a good substitute. The metal conducts heat much better than the usual dried beans or rice called for in traditional recipes.
I can't tell if the crust is done.	For a partially baked crust, the dough should be firm but only slightly colored. For a fully baked crust, the dough should be golden brown and crisp. Make sure to lift up the pie plate and check the underside when fully baking the pie shell; the bottom as well as the edges of the crust should be golden brown.
The edges of my pie shell are burning.	The foil sling should be lightly crimped over the edges of the pie shell to protect the fluting or ridged edge from burning. If you forget to do this and notice that the edges are starting to burn, simply fold the excess foil over the edges of the crust.
The sides of my pie shell slumped in the oven.	This can happen on occasion, even to experienced bakers. The pie will be fine. You might need to hold back some of the filling, which is a shame, but that's certainly preferable to letting the filling overflow the pie shell and spill into the oven and burn, causing a real mess.

How to Make a Double-Crust Pie

ESSENTIAL EQUIPMENT

- rolling pin
- rimmed baking sheet
- parchment paper
- plastic wrap
- 9-inch pie plate, preferably glass
- kitchen shears
- paring knife
- aluminum foil

Double-crust pies, like our Deep-Dish Apple Pie (page 747) and Blueberry Pie (page 748), do not require prebaking the crust. Instead the raw bottom crust is filled and the top crust is rolled out and used to seal the pie prior to baking. Once the bottom crust has been fit into the pie plate and chilled for 30 minutes (see How to Make Pie Dough, page 716, and How to Roll Out and Fit Pie Dough, page 719), you can fill the pie and add the second crust. Start the steps below after the bottom crust has been fitted into the pie plate. Note that some recipes at the end of this chapter, like our Cherry Pie (page 749) and Peach Pie (page 749), call for our Foolproof Double-Crust Pie Dough (page 745) but go on to make a lattice top. For those recipes, you'll want to review How to Make a Lattice Top Pie (page 724).

1. ROLL AND CHILL TOP CRUST

Remove second piece of dough from refrigerator and roll into 12-inch circle on generously floured counter. Transfer dough to parchment-lined baking sheet, cover with plastic wrap, and refrigerate 30 minutes.

WHY? We recommend rolling out the second crust as soon as you're done with the first crust and then placing it on a parchment-lined baking sheet in the refrigerator. It will be easier to work with the top crust if it's well chilled.

2. UNROLL TOP CRUST OVER FILLING

Once chilled bottom crust has been filled, loosely roll chilled top crust around rolling pin, then gently unroll over filled pie crust bottom.

WHY? Wrapping the dough around a rolling pin limits the risk of stretching or tearing the dough. Make sure to center the dough over the pie plate.

3. TRIM EXCESS DOUGH

Using kitchen shears, trim all but ½ inch of dough overhanging edge of pie plate.

WHY? Too much dough will make an overly thick edge that won't bake through. About ½ inch of dough provides just the right amount for nice fluting.

4. CREATE A STURDY EDGE

Press top and bottom crusts together, then tuck edges underneath.

WHY? Tucking the sealed edges of the top and bottom crusts down into the pie plate ensures that the seam won't split open in the oven.

5. CRIMP EDGES

Use index finger of one hand and thumb and index finger of other hand to create fluted ridges perpendicular to edge of pie plate.

WHY? A crimped edge is not only decorative but also functional because the fluting process seals the two pieces of dough together.

6. CUT STEAM VENTS

Use paring knife to cut at least 4 slits in top crust. (Very juicy pies might need more.)

WHY? Fruit is juicy and produces a lot of steam as it bakes. If you don't cut vents in the top crust, steam will tear holes in the crust. Apples aren't terribly juicy, so four vents will suffice. Juicy berries might need more vents (or even a lattice top; see page 724).

7. BAKE ON FOIL-LINED BAKING SHEET

Place pie on rimmed baking sheet that has been lined with foil and bake on lowest oven rack.

WHY? The baking sheet catches any splatters (the foil makes cleanup easy) and reduces the risk of a smoky mess in your oven. The baking sheet conducts heat well and thus promotes better browning of the bottom crust, which is often undercooked and doughy in traditional recipes. The bottom of the oven is generally quite hot, so placing the baking sheet on the lowest rack ensures that it gets nice and hot. Many double-crust pies start in a hot oven to get the crust browning and then reduce the oven temperature to give the filling time to heat through without running the risk of burning the crust.

Troubleshooting a Double-Crust Pie

PROBLEM	SOLUTION
I tore a hole in the top crust while trying to stretch it over the filling.	You shouldn't have to stretch the dough to cover the filling. Make sure the filling has been lightly compacted into the pie plate, and tuck in any stray pieces of fruit (especially apples, which can tear the dough). If you do tear the top crust, use the dough trimmings to patch up the hole. Remember that you need to cut vents in the top crust, so any tears might be natural places to situate the vents.
The edges of the pie are getting too brown.	Loosely wrap a piece of foil around the rim of the pie and crimp lightly. The foil will help deflect the heat and prevent the crust from burning.
I can't tell if the pie is done.	Many cooks underbake double-crust pies, and the result is a doughy, soupy mess. As long as the crust is not burning, you can keep baking the pie. More browning equals more flavor and better texture in the crust. Remember to lift up the pie (carefully) and check the underside. If the crust isn't golden brown on the bottom, the pie could use more time in the oven.

How to Make a Lattice Top

ESSENTIAL EQUIPMENT

- rimmed baking sheet
- parchment paper
- kitchen ruler
- paring knife
- plastic wrap
- 9-inch pie plate, preferably glass
- kitchen shears

A lattice top is an especially attractive way to finish a double-crust pie. Although making a lattice top does require a bit more work than a regular double-crust pie, a lattice top serves a vital function in pies made with juicy summer fruits. The lattice top allows for maximum evaporation while the fruit cooks—more than can be provided by the usual vents cut in the top crust. A lattice top is traditional with peach, cherry, and berry pies. A lattice top is not recommended with drier fruits, such as apples, because all that evaporation can cause the fruit to become leathery. Note that our Blueberry Pie (page 748) uses an alternate approach that accomplishes the same goal. In that recipe, a small biscuit cutter is used to cut holes in the top piece of dough. See How to Make Pie Dough (page 716) and How to Roll Out and Fit Pie Dough (page 719); start these steps after the bottom crust has been fitted into the pie plate.

1. CUT AND FREEZE DOUGH

Remove second piece of dough from refrigerator. Roll dough into 13½ by 10½-inch rectangle and transfer to parchment paper–lined baking sheet. Trim dough with paring knife to 13 by 10-inch rectangle. Slice rectangle lengthwise into eight 13-inch-long strips, each 1¼ inches wide. Separate strips slightly, cover with plastic wrap, and place baking sheet in freezer until dough strips are very firm, about 30 minutes.

WHY? If you roll the dough into the usual 12-inch round and then cut strips, you end up with short and long pieces. Avoid the problem by rolling the second piece of dough into a rectangle and then cutting the rectangle into strips of identical length. Freezing the dough strips makes it much easier to weave them together because the stiff strips won't tear or break. Frozen dough strips also help the lattice maintain its shape during baking.

2. START WEAVING

Once chilled bottom crust has been filled, lay 4 strips of chilled dough parallel and evenly over filling. Weave fifth strip in opposite direction, lifting every other strip to facilitate weaving.

WHY? Most recipes create the lattice top on the counter and then suggest lifting the lattice onto the pie. The logic here is that the dough is quite soft and will stick to the filling if you try to make the lattice right in the pie plate. However, freezing the dough makes the strips resistant to sticking so that you can build the lattice right on top of the filling, which is much easier.

3. FINISH WEAVING

Continue to weave remaining 3 strips of dough, one at a time, to create evenly spaced lattice, rotating pie as needed.

WHY? For the nicest appearance, weave each strip under every other strip of dough. And adjacent strips should follow the opposite pattern.

4. TRIM STRIPS

Let dough thaw and soften for 5 to 10 minutes, then use kitchen shears to trim overhanging edges of each strip to leave about ½ inch hanging over edge of pie.

WHY? Letting the dough soften for a few minutes before trimming makes it more malleable and prevents it from cracking as you trim. Make sure to leave enough dough to form a nice fluted edge.

5. TUCK ENDS UNDER

Press edges of bottom crust and ends of lattice strips together, then fold pressed edge under, tucking it inside pie plate.

WHY? Tucking the trimmed dough under helps to seal the ends of the strips to the bottom dough and ensures that the lattice top won't come apart in the oven. Also, this process makes an even, tidy edge that is easy to crimp.

6. CRIMP EDGE

Crimp dough evenly around edge of pie plate, using index finger of one hand and thumb and index finger of other hand.

WHY? Crimping the dough gives the pie a decorative edge and a finished look. Crimping also ensures that the lattice top and bottom piece of dough are firmly attached to each other.

Troubleshooting a Lattice Top

PROBLEM	SOLUTION
I'm having trouble rolling the dough into a neat rectangle.	Rolling dough into a rectangle requires a different motion than rolling dough into a round. It helps to flatten the dough into a rectangle rather than disk shape before chilling. And rather than rotating the dough as you roll, you will need to roll the dough in two directions. Don't worry if the edges aren't perfectly neat. That's where trimming comes in. The dough is rolled into a rectangle that is slightly larger than needed to account for the dough that will be lost to the trimming process.
Do I really need a kitchen ruler?	In a word: yes. It's important to use the ruler at two steps in this process—to determine if the dough has been rolled into a 13½ by 10½-inch rectangle and to ensure that the eight lattice strips are each 1¼ inches wide. Precision is especially important for this last step because uneven strips will make for a rather unattractive pie.
My dough is becoming very soft and hard to weave.	On warm days, the frozen dough strips can soften up fairly quickly. Make sure to keep the dough strips in the freezer until you need them. If you find that you're working slowly and/or the dough is becoming too soft, refrigerate the filled pie shell and the remaining dough strips until everything cools down and firms up again. Once the dough is chilled, continue with the weaving process.

How to Make a Free-Form Tart

ESSENTIAL EQUIPMENT

- food processor
- plastic wrap
- parchment paper
- rolling pin
- rimmed baking sheet
- pastry brush
- wire rack
- large offset or metal spatula

Most free-form tarts involve simply taking a piece of pie dough, adding fruit, folding, and baking. The problem is that when the small chunks of butter in traditional pie dough melt in the oven, tiny holes are left behind and the fruit juices can leak out of the dough. Making the dough less rich is an option, but not a good one. Instead, we devised a method for making the buttery dough stronger.

We begin by making the dough in a food processor. The butter is cut into the fat and ice water is added as usual. But before the dough is chilled and rolled, we use a technique called *fraisage* to make the dough especially flaky and strong. The shaggy dough is turned out on the counter and smeared by hand. This smearing process turns the chunks of butter into long streaks that are far less prone to leaking when they melt in the oven. After preparing the dough in the food processor following the recipe on page 750, continue with the steps below. See the recipes for Free-Form Summer Fruit Tart (page 750) and Free-Form Apple Tart (page 751) for instructions on preparing a filling.

1. SMEAR DOUGH AGAINST COUNTER
After preparing dough in food processor, turn shaggy dough out onto lightly floured counter. Gather crumbs into rectangular pile. Starting at farthest end of pile, smear small amount of dough against counter, away from you, with palm of hand. Repeat smearing process until all buttery crumbs have been worked.
WHY? Smearing the dough (a technique called *fraisage*) pushes the butter chunks into long, thin sheets that make the dough flaky and sturdy.

2. REPEAT SMEARING
Gather smeared bits back into rectangular pile and repeat smearing process until all crumbs have been worked second time. Press dough into 6-inch disk, wrap tightly in plastic wrap, and refrigerate for 1 hour.
WHY? This second round of smearing won't take as long and will result in large flakes of dough that stick to your palms.

3. ROLL DOUGH IN PARCHMENT
Unwrap chilled dough and place between two sheets of floured parchment paper. Roll into 12-inch circle. Slide dough, still between parchment, onto rimmed baking sheet. Refrigerate until firm, 15 to 30 minutes.
WHY? Rolling this fragile dough between parchment prevents tearing, and it doesn't matter if the dough sticks to the parchment because the tart is baked right on the paper.

4. ARRANGE FRUIT
After preparing fruit topping, remove baking sheet from refrigerator and discard top sheet of parchment. Arrange fruit in center of dough, leaving 2½-inch border.
WHY? It's important to leave the outer edge of the dough free of fruit. If using apples, stack some slices in a circular wall, then fill in the center with remaining slices. This approach makes a prettier, full-looking tart. Stone fruits and berries should just be piled evenly into the center.

5. FOLD AND PLEAT

Fold outermost 2 inches of dough up over fruit, leaving ½-inch border between fruit and edge of tart shell. As you fold, make pleats in dough every 2 or 3 inches.

WHY? The ½-inch space helps prevent the tart juices from leaking through the folds in the tart shell. If necessary, gently pinch the pleats to secure them, but don't press the dough into the fruit.

6. SUGAR AND BAKE

Lightly brush top and sides of dough with water using pastry brush and sprinkle dough with 1 tablespoon sugar. Place baking sheet in 375-degree oven and bake until crust is deep golden brown and fruit is bubbling, about 1 hour, rotating baking sheet halfway through baking.

WHY? The sugar is optional but provides a nice finish to the tart dough. Baking the tart on a rimmed baking sheet (rather than on a rimless cookie sheet) ensures that any fruit juices that do leak don't cause a mess in the oven.

7. COOL TART DIRECTLY ON RACK

Cool tart on baking sheet on wire rack for 10 minutes. Use parchment to slide tart to wire rack. Loosen tart from parchment using large offset metal spatula, then gently pull parchment out from under tart. Let tart cool on rack until filling thickens, about 25 minutes.

WHY? The tart shell can become soggy if cooled to room temperature on the baking sheet. After 10 minutes of cooling, lift up the paper with the tart and move it to a wire rack. Use a large offset or metal spatula to loosen the paper, then remove and discard the paper and let the tart cool directly on the rack to ensure that the crust stays crisp and can't adhere to the paper.

Troubleshooting a Free-Form Tart

PROBLEM	SOLUTION
The dough is sticking to the counter as I smear it.	A little sticking is to be expected. Dust the counter with flour and use a bench scraper to loosen any bits that stick.
Can I bake the tart in advance?	The tart is best eaten warm, or at least within 3 or 4 hours of baking. Reheat it on a parchment-lined baking sheet in a 350-degree for 10 minutes. Don't make it a day in advance; the crust will become soft. The disk of dough can be refrigerated, wrapped in plastic wrap, for two days. Or roll out the dough a day ahead and refrigerate as directed. Let very cold dough warm up for a few minutes before rolling or folding it.

How to Make a Classic Tart Shell

ESSENTIAL EQUIPMENT

- rolling pin
- rimmed baking sheet
- plastic wrap
- 9-inch tart pan with removable bottom
- large plate
- aluminum foil
- ceramic or metal pie weights
- wire rack

Rolling out tart dough is pretty much the same as rolling out pie dough. However, because the dough can be sticky due to the heavy cream and egg yolk in the dough, it's best to roll out tart dough between two pieces of parchment paper. Otherwise, the rolling out process is quite similar (see How to Roll Out and Fit Pie Dough, page 719). However, fitting tart dough into its pan is a bit different from fitting pie dough into a pie plate. The steps are outlined below, as well as the key step of blind-baking the tart shell. No matter what kind of tart you are making, the tart shell must be prebaked, either partially or completely. If the tart requires further baking once filled (like our Classic Lemon Tart, page 753), you will want to blind-bake the dough for 30 minutes in a 375-degree oven, then fill the tart and continue baking as directed. For tarts that are filled and served with no additional baking (like our Classic Fresh Fruit Tart, page 752), the foil and pie weights should be removed after 30 minutes and the blind-baking process should continue until the crust is fully baked and golden, another 5 to 10 minutes. See the recipe on page 751 for details on preparing the dough.

1. GENTLY UNROLL DOUGH

Roll dough into 11-inch circle on lightly floured counter. Refrigerate dough, on baking sheet and covered with plastic wrap for 30 minutes. Roll dough loosely around rolling pin, then unroll over 9-inch tart pan with removable bottom.
WHY? Don't lift the dough off the counter and try to place it into the tart pan; you run the risk of tearing or stretching it. It's best to drape one end of the dough circle over the far end of the tart pan and then unroll the dough toward you.

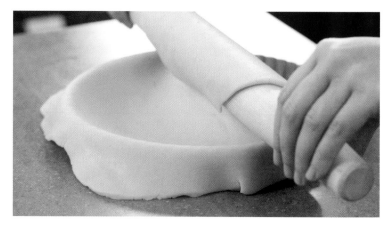

2. FIT DOUGH

Lifting edge of dough, ease it into pan. Press dough into fluted sides of pan and into corners.
WHY? Don't try to place and fit the dough simultaneously. It's best to unroll the dough, then start fitting the dough in the pan. (If the dough is not centered over the pan, you can reposition the dough at this time.) To fit the dough into the pan, lift up the edge of the dough with one hand and use the other hand to press the dough into the corner and sides of the pan while working your way around the circumference of the pan.

3. TRIM EXCESS DOUGH

Run rolling pin over top of tart pan to remove any excess dough and make clean edge.
WHY? Don't bother trimming the dough with kitchen shears or a knife. The sharp edges of the tart pan can do the job, provided you use the rolling pin to apply even pressure to the dough. Save the trimmed dough for the next step.

4. PATCH AS NEEDED

If parts of edge are too thin, reinforce using excess dough.
WHY? With all the butter, plus cream and an egg yolk, tart dough is very forgiving. If the dough tears, it is easily patched. Any thin spots around the edges are best reinforced since strong edges are key to an attractive tart that holds the filling. If the dough is too thick in places, press some dough up over the edge and trim it.

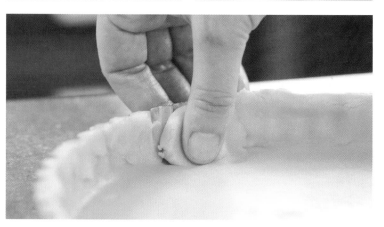

5. FREEZE BEFORE BAKING

Set dough-lined tart pan on large plate and freeze until dough is fully chilled and firm, about 30 minutes. (Dough-lined tart pan can be wrapped tightly in plastic wrap and frozen for up to 1 month.)

WHY? Freezing the dough gives the gluten in the flour time to relax, thus reducing the risk of shrinkage during prebaking. Chilled dough will also hold neat edges better.

6. WEIGHT

Set frozen dough–lined tart pan on rimmed baking sheet. Press double layer of aluminum foil over frozen dough and up over edges of pan. Fill with pie weights.

WHY? Pie weights prevent the dough from melting out of shape as the shell bakes, and they prevent bubbles from forming in the bottom. We always use ceramic or metal pie weights because they conduct heat very well and guarantee even browning.

7. BAKE

Bake on middle rack in 375-degree oven until tart shell is golden brown and set, about 30 minutes, rotating sheet halfway through baking. Some tarts require longer baking times once filled; for these recipes transfer sheet to wire rack and carefully remove foil and weights; add filling and proceed as directed. For tarts that require little or no baking once filled, remove foil and pie weights and continue baking until tart shell is golden brown, 5 to 10 minutes longer. Transfer baking sheet to wire rack, cool, and fill as directed.

WHY? The baking sheet conducts heat and helps ensure a crisp bottom crust. Rotating the baking sheet ensures even browning. For recipes that require little or no baking once the tart shell is filled, make sure the shell is fully baked, crisp, and golden brown all over before removing it from the oven.

Troubleshooting a Classic Tart Shell

PROBLEM	SOLUTION
Can I prepare the tart in advance?	We don't recommend assembling the tart more than a few hours ahead since the crust will become soggy, but you can freeze the unbaked dough–lined tart pan, wrapped in plastic wrap, for up to 1 month. Or bake and cool the tart shell, wrap it in plastic wrap, and store it at room temperature for up to 2 days. Fillings can often be made in advance; refer to particular recipes.

Pecan Pie

Overview

Pecan pies can be overwhelmingly sweet and lack any real pecan flavor, and too often they turn out curdled and separated. Plus, the weepy filling makes the crust soggy and leathery.

We fix the sweetness and flavor problems by using dark brown sugar for rich, deep flavor—but not too much, so that the pecan flavor takes center stage. Toasting the nuts also boosts the nut flavor. Simulating a double boiler when melting the butter and making the filling is an easy way to maintain gentle heat, which helps to keep the filling from curdling. Baking the pie at a low oven temperature (275 degrees) is also key. As for the crust, prebaking the empty pie shell is essential. Adding the hot filling to a warm prebaked pie crust also helps keep the crust from getting soggy.

To serve the pie warm, let it first cool so that it sets, then warm it in a 250-degree oven for about 15 minutes and slice. If you make the pie dough ahead and freeze it, let it thaw completely on counter before rolling it out. Serve with Vanilla Ice Cream (page 780) or Whipped Cream (page 709). Before you begin, see How to Make Pie Dough on page 716, How to Roll Out and Fit Pie Dough on page 719, and How to Bake a Single-Crust Pie Shell on page 720.

Recipe Stats

TOTAL TIME **5½ hours**
PREPARATION TIME **30 minutes**
ACTIVE COOKING TIME **1½ hours**
YIELD **8 servings**
MAKE AHEAD **Best served the day it is baked; dough can be wrapped tightly in plastic wrap and refrigerated for up to 2 days or frozen for up to 1 month**
DIFFICULTY **Intermediate**

Tools

- 9-inch pie plate
- rimmed baking sheet
- 12-inch skillet
- food processor *
- chef's knife
- cutting board
- dry measuring cups
- liquid measuring cup
- measuring spoons
- heatproof bowl **
- instant-read thermometer
- kitchen shears
- mixing bowls
- pie server
- pie weights ***
- plate
- rolling pin
- soupspoon ****
- stiff rubber spatula
- whisk
- wire rack
- aluminum foil
- plastic wrap

* The unique mixing method for this dough requires a food processor to create a uniform fat and flour paste.
** The filling is prepared in a heatproof bowl set inside a skillet of simmering water to ensure that the eggs don't overheat.
*** It's important to use weights when blind-baking the crust to ensure bubbles don't form on top of the pie dough. Metal and ceramic weights conduct heat better than raw rice or dried beans and thus promote better browning. If you don't own pie weights, pennies are the best alternative. Store them in an oven bag to get them in and out of the pie shell easily.
**** The pie is done when it yields like Jello-O; pressing gently on the filling with a soupspoon is a best way to test for doneness.

Ingredients

FOOLPROOF SINGLE-CRUST PIE DOUGH
1¼ cups (6¼ ounces) all-purpose flour, plus extra for counter
1 tablespoon granulated sugar
½ teaspoon salt
6 tablespoons unsalted butter, cut into ¼-inch pieces and chilled
4 tablespoons vegetable shortening, cut into 2 pieces and chilled
2 tablespoons vodka, chilled *
2 tablespoons ice water

FILLING
6 tablespoons unsalted butter, cut into 6 pieces
1 cup packed (7 ounces) dark brown sugar
½ teaspoon salt
3 large eggs
¾ cup light corn syrup
1 tablespoon vanilla extract
2 cups (8 ounces) pecans, toasted and chopped fine

* Vodka is essential to the tender texture of this crust and imparts no flavor—do not substitute extra water.

What Can Go Wrong

Here's a list of common mistakes cooks make when preparing this recipe.

COMMON MISTAKE	BAD OUTCOMES	WHAT YOU SHOULD DO
Not Prebaking Pie Shell	• **The bottom crust is doughy and raw tasting.**	In this recipe, the crust must be partially baked before adding the filling and baking the pie. If you skip prebaking, the filling will be done but the crust will lag behind and remain doughy and soft.
Not Weighting Pie Shell When Prebaking	• **The crust bubbles up and can't hold enough filling.** • **The crust cracks and the filling seeps below the crust, making it very hard to remove slices of pie.**	To keep the unfilled crust from ballooning in the oven during prebaking, it's imperative to weight the dough down. If the pie shell is baked without weights, the dough will bubble and crack. Placing a piece of aluminum foil on top of the dough before adding the weights makes it easy to get the weights in and out of the pie shell and also keeps the crust from overbrowning.
Not Toasting Pecans	• **The pecan flavor is diminished.** • **The pie tastes overly sweet.**	Take 10 minutes to toast the pecans in the oven before adding them to the filling. The heat brings out their flavor, which not only makes the pie taste better but also helps keep the sweetness in check.
Letting Pie Shell Cool Before Filling	• **The crust softens and becomes soggy.** • **The filling takes longer to set up and curdles.**	Adding warm filling to a warm pie shell accomplishes two things. First, the liquid-y filling does less damage to a warm crust than to a cool crust because it sets up more quickly in a warm pie shell. Second, the filling cooks more quickly, which reduces the risk of curdling. Start the filling just before the pie shell comes out of the oven. When the pie shell is done prebaking, remove the foil and weights and finish up the filling while you wait for the oven temperature to drop from 375 degrees (the temperature at which the crust is prebaked) to 275 degrees (the temperature at which the pie is baked).
Overheating Filling	• **The filling curdles and becomes watery.** • **The filling has a gritty texture.**	Pecan pie is actually a variation on custard pie. There's no dairy in the filling but there are three eggs (and lots of sugar). If the eggs are overheated they will curdle and make the filling watery. Also, all that sugar can turn gritty if the filling overheats. In order to achieve a soft, smooth texture in the baked pie, you must heat the filling gently in a makeshift double boiler (a heatproof glass or metal bowl set inside a pan of simmering water). Baking the pie at a very low oven temperature (just 275 degrees) protects the eggs from overheating. Do not overbake this pie. The crust should already be crisp when you add the filling, so once the filling is lightly set, remove the pie from the oven. The filling will continue to firm up as the pie cools.

1. PREPARE DOUGH: Freeze 6 tablespoons butter, cut into ¼-inch pieces, and ¼ cup vegetable shortening, cut into 2 pieces. Chill 2 tablespoons vodka.

2. Process ¾ cup all-purpose flour, 1 tablespoon granulated sugar, and ½ teaspoon salt together in food processor until combined.

3. Scatter chilled butter and shortening over top. Process until incorporated and mixture begins to form uneven clumps with no floury bits, about 10 seconds.

4. Evenly redistribute dough and sprinkle ½ cup flour on top. Pulse until mixture has broken into pieces and is distributed around bowl, 4 to 6 pulses.

5. Transfer mixture to large bowl. Sprinkle with 2 tablespoons each vodka and ice water.

6. Stir and press dough together, using stiff rubber spatula, until dough sticks together.

7. Turn dough onto sheet of plastic wrap, flatten into 4-inch disk, wrap tightly, and refrigerate for 1 hour.

8. Let dough sit on counter to soften slightly, about 10 minutes, then roll out on lightly floured counter to 12-inch circle.

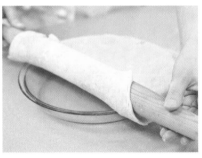

9. Fit dough into 9-inch pie plate, trim all but ½ inch dough overhanging edge. Tuck overhanging dough underneath itself and flute edge.

10. Wrap shell in plastic wrap and place pie plate in freezer until dough is fully chilled and firm, about 30 minutes.

11. PREPARE PIE: Adjust oven rack to middle position and heat oven to 375 degrees.

12. Spread 2 cups pecans over rimmed baking sheet and toast, stirring once, until fragrant, 5 to 10 minutes. Set aside to cool. Do not turn off oven.

13. Finely chop cooled pecans.

14. Line chilled crust with double layer of aluminum foil, covering edges to prevent burning. Fill foil-lined pie plate with pie weights or pennies.

15. Bake on middle rack until pie dough looks dry and is light in color, 25 to 30 minutes.

16. Transfer pie plate to wire rack and remove weights and foil.

17. Reduce oven temperature to 275 degrees. Adjust oven rack to lowest position and place foil-lined rimmed baking sheet on rack.

18. Melt 6 tablespoons butter, cut into 6 pieces, in heatproof bowl set in 12-inch skillet of water maintained at just below simmer.

19. Remove bowl from skillet and stir in 1 cup packed dark brown sugar and ½ teaspoon salt until butter is absorbed.

20. Whisk in 3 eggs, then ¾ cup light corn syrup and 1 tablespoon vanilla until smooth.

21. Return bowl to hot water and stir until mixture is shiny, hot to touch, and registers 130 degrees.

22. Off heat, stir in toasted and chopped pecans, then pour pecan mixture into warm prebaked pie crust.

23. Bake pie on baking sheet until filling looks set but yields like Jell-O when gently pressed with back of spoon, 50 minutes to 1 hour.

24. Let pie cool on wire rack until filling has set, about 2 hours; serve slightly warm or at room temperature.

Deep-Dish Apple Pie

Overview

This apple pie starts with cooked (rather than raw) apples. When raw apples are used in a pie, they shrink to almost nothing, leaving a huge gap between the top crust and filling. Precooking the apples eliminates this problem and actually helps the apples hold their shape once baked in the pie.

This may seem counterintuitive, but when the apples are gently heated, their pectin is converted to a heat-stable form that prevents the apples from becoming mushy when cooked further in the oven. The key is to keep the temperature of the apples below 140 degrees during this precooking stage. Rather than cooking the apples in a skillet (where they are likely to become too hot), it's best to heat the apples and seasonings gently in a large, covered Dutch oven. Cooling the apples before putting them in the pie crust is essential so that the butter in the crust doesn't melt immediately. Finally, we drain almost all of the juice from the apples (reserving just ¼ cup) to ensure a perfectly juicy and moist, but not soupy, apple pie. If you freeze the pie dough, let it thaw on the counter completely before rolling it out. Before you begin, see How to Make Pie Dough on page 716, How to Roll Out and Fit Pie Dough on page 719, and How to Make a Double-Crust Pie on page 722.

Recipe Stats

TOTAL TIME **6 hours**
PREPARATION TIME **30 minutes**
ACTIVE COOKING TIME **2 hours**
YIELD **8 servings**
MAKE AHEAD **Best served the day it is baked; dough can be wrapped tightly in plastic wrap and refrigerated for up to 2 days or frozen for up to 1 month**
DIFFICULTY **Intermediate**

Tools

- Dutch oven
- 9-inch pie plate
- rimmed baking sheets (2)
- food processor *
- chef's knife
- cutting board
- paring knife
- dry measuring cups
- liquid measuring cup
- measuring spoons
- citrus juicer
- colander
- fork
- kitchen shears
- mixing bowls
- pastry brush
- pie server
- rasp-style grater
- rolling pin
- rubber spatula
- vegetable peeler
- wire rack
- aluminum foil
- parchment paper
- plastic wrap

* The unique mixing method for this dough requires a food processor to create a uniform fat and flour paste.

Ingredients

FOOLPROOF DOUBLE-CRUST PIE DOUGH

- 2½ **cups (12½ ounces) all-purpose flour, plus extra for counter**
- 2 **tablespoons granulated sugar**
- 1 **teaspoon salt**
- 12 **tablespoons unsalted butter, cut into ¼-inch pieces and chilled**
- 8 **tablespoons vegetable shortening, cut into 4 pieces and chilled**
- ¼ **cup vodka, chilled ***
- ¼ **cup ice water**

APPLE FILLING

- 2½ **pounds Granny Smith apples, peeled, cored, and sliced ¼ inch thick ****
- 2½ **pounds Golden Delicious apples, peeled, cored, and sliced ¼ inch thick *****
- ½ **cup (3½ ounces) plus 1 tablespoon granulated sugar**
- ¼ **cup packed (1¾ ounces) light brown sugar**
- ½ **teaspoon grated lemon zest plus 1 tablespoon juice**
- ¼ **teaspoon salt**
- ⅛ **teaspoon ground cinnamon**
- 1 **large egg white, lightly beaten**

* Vodka is essential to the tender texture of this crust and imparts no flavor—do not substitute extra water.
** We prefer Granny Smith, Empire, and Cortland when tart baking apples are required.
*** We prefer Golden Delicious, Jonagold, Fuji, and Braeburn when sweet baking apples are required.

What Can Go Wrong

Here's a list of common mistakes cooks make when preparing this recipe.

COMMON MISTAKE	BAD OUTCOMES	WHAT YOU SHOULD DO
Using Wrong Type of Apples	• **The filling is too soft.** • **The filling is too tart.** • **The filling is too sweet.**	Firm apples are much better than soft apples, like McIntosh, when it comes to making pie, especially if you're going to precook the apple filling. Soft apples will produce a mushy, saucy filling. Also, a mix of tart and sweet apples is essential for the right balance of flavors. If you find yourself with only one kind of apple, adjust the amount of sweetener accordingly, but we really do recommend starting out with two types of apples for this recipe.
Undercooking Apple Filling	• **The apples tear the top crust during the assembly process.** • **The apples shed a lot of liquid in the oven and make the bottom crust soggy.**	Precooking the apples shrinks their volume, so you can fit 5 pounds of sliced apples in one 9-inch pie plate. If you don't precook the apples, there's no way to stretch the top piece of dough over the mound of apples. Also, precooking drives off moisture from the apples, which otherwise would come out in the oven and make the crust soggy.
Overcooking Apple Filling	• **The apples are soft and mealy.**	Don't go overboard and let the apples overcook in the Dutch oven. They should be tender when poked with a fork but still hold their shape. Also, make sure to start with firm apples.
Not Cooling and Draining Apple Filling	• **The pie crust is dense rather than flaky.** • **The crust is soggy.**	If you pour the hot apples into a pie plate with the cold dough, the heat of the apples will melt the fat in the dough and the resulting crust will be dense rather than flaky. Also, as the apples cool on the baking sheet, they will shed more juices that should be drained away. A measured amount of the juices (¼ cup) is added back to the filling, thus controlling for variations among various types of apples. If all of the apple juices are added to the pie plate, the bottom crust will be soggy.
Forgetting to Reduce Oven Temperature	• **The crust bakes unevenly, with raw and scorched spots.** • **The apples bake unevenly.**	We bake almost all pies on a baking sheet in a relatively hot oven. In this case, the oven is set to 425 degrees. The baking sheet conducts heat better than the oven's wire rack and thus promotes browning of the bottom crust (always the last part of the pie to get done). It also catches any drips so they can't fall onto the oven floor and make a smoky mess. However, if the temperature were to remain at 425 degrees, the crust would start to burn, especially around the edges. After 25 minutes at 425 degrees, we reduce the oven temperature to 375 degrees to ensure that the crust won't scorch before the bottom is fully browned. This reduction in baking temperature also gives the apples more time in the oven and ensures that they are completely tender.

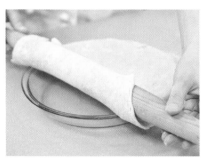

1. PREPARE DOUGH: Make dough for double-crust pie, roll out and fit bottom crust, cover with plastic wrap, and refrigerate (see pages 716–719).

2. Roll out dough for top crust and transfer to parchment-lined sheet. Cover with plastic and refrigerate (see step 1 on page 722).

3. PREPARE FILLING: Peel 2½ pounds tart apples and 2½ pounds sweet apples. Cut away 4 sides of apples, leaving behind core. Discard cores.

4. Turn each piece of apple on flat side and cut into ¼-inch-thick slices. Transfer to Dutch oven.

5. Add ½ cup granulated sugar, ¼ cup light brown sugar, ½ teaspoon lemon zest, ¼ teaspoon salt, and ⅛ teaspoon cinnamon and toss to combine.

6. Cover and cook over medium heat, stirring frequently, until apples are tender when poked with fork but still hold their shape, 15 to 20 minutes.

7. Transfer apples and their juice to rimmed baking sheet. Let cool to room temperature, about 30 minutes.

8. ASSEMBLE PIE: Adjust oven rack to lowest position and heat oven to 425 degrees.

9. Drain cooled apples thoroughly through colander set in large bowl, reserving ¼ cup of juice.

10. Stir 1 tablespoon lemon juice into reserved ¼ cup apple juice.

11. Spread apples into dough-lined pie plate, mounding them slightly in middle. Drizzle apples with lemon juice mixture.

12. Loosely roll second piece of dough around rolling pin and gently unroll it over pie.

13. Using kitchen shears, trim all but ½ inch of dough overhanging edge of pie plate.

14. Press top and bottom crusts together.

15. Tuck edges of dough underneath.

16. Crimp dough evenly around edge of pie, using your fingers.

17. Cut four 2-inch-long vent holes in center of top crust with paring knife.

18. Lightly beat 1 large egg white in small bowl. Brush crust with egg white.

19. Sprinkle with remaining 1 tablespoon granulated sugar.

20. BAKE PIE: Place pie on foil-lined rimmed baking sheet. Bake until crust is golden, about 25 minutes.

21. Reduce oven temperature to 375 degrees.

22. Rotate baking sheet.

23. Continue to bake until juices are bubbling and crust is deep golden brown, 25 to 30 minutes longer.

24. Cool pie on wire rack until filling has set, at least 2 hours. Cut into wedges and serve.

Classic Fresh Fruit Tart

Overview

A classic fruit tart—a tart shell filled with pastry cream and artfully topped with fresh fruit—is a staple in French patisseries and American bakeries. Yet, while these fancy tarts almost always look great, they rarely taste great. The crust is soggy, the pastry cream is starchy or rubbery, and the fruit is tasteless.

To develop the crust's flavor and ensure a crisp texture, we prebake the tart shell. For a pastry cream that has enough body to hold its shape when sliced without being rubbery (an issue caused by adding too much cornstarch), we swap in half-and-half for the usual milk. The half-and-half has more body, so we can use less cornstarch. To ensure the egg yolks in the pastry cream don't scramble, we gently raise their temperature by tempering them (see page 759 for details on tempering). Stirring in cold butter stops the pastry cream's cooking and thickens it. It's essential to chill the pastry cream thoroughly; it will continue to thicken. And wait to fill the tart shell until you're ready to serve it; over time the pastry cream will make the shell soggy.

The fruit is fairly simple to get right if you follow a few rules. Only use ripe, good-quality fruit (this is a good recipe for organic berries). Don't wash delicate berries, as they will turn to mush. And dab warmed jelly over the fruit to make it glisten (we use a pastry brush to apply it evenly over the tart, but we found drizzling it over with a soupspoon worked too).

You can prepare both the tart dough and the pastry cream up to 2 days ahead and refrigerate them separately. You can also freeze the tart dough for 1 month. Or, freeze the dough-lined tart pan, wrapped tightly in plastic wrap, for up to 1 month. Before you begin, see How to Prepare Fruit A to Z on page 684 for details on peeling kiwi and How to Make a Classic Tart Shell on page 728.

Recipe Stats

TOTAL TIME **5 hours**
PREPARATION TIME **20 minutes**
ACTIVE COOKING TIME **40 minutes**
YIELD **8 to 10 servings**
MAKE AHEAD **Serve assembled tart within 30 minutes; tart dough and pastry cream can be refrigerated separately for up to 2 days**
DIFFICULTY **Advanced**

Tools

- medium saucepan
- 9-inch tart pan with removable bottom
- small saucepan
- rimmed baking sheets (2)
- food processor
- chef's knife
- cutting board
- paring knife
- dry measuring cups
- liquid measuring cup
- measuring spoons
- large offset spatula
- large plate
- mixing bowls
- pastry brush
- pie weights
- rolling pin
- rubber spatula
- serving platter
- whisk
- wire rack
- wooden spoon
- aluminum foil
- plastic wrap

Ingredients

CLASSIC TART DOUGH
- **1 large egg yolk**
- **1 tablespoon heavy cream**
- **½ teaspoon vanilla extract**
- **1¼ cups (6¼ ounces) all-purpose flour**
- **⅔ cup (2⅔ ounces) confectioners' sugar**
- **¼ teaspoon salt**
- **8 tablespoons unsalted butter, cut into ¼-inch pieces and chilled**

PASTRY CREAM
- **2 cups half-and-half**
- **½ cup (3½ ounces) granulated sugar**
- **Pinch salt**
- **5 large egg yolks**
- **3 tablespoons cornstarch**
- **4 tablespoons unsalted butter, cut into 4 pieces**
- **1½ teaspoons vanilla extract**

FRUIT
- **2 large kiwis, peeled, halved lengthwise, and sliced ⅜ inch thick**
- **10 ounces (2 cups) raspberries**
- **5 ounces (1 cup) blueberries**
- **½ cup red currant or apple jelly**

What Can Go Wrong

Here's a list of common mistakes cooks make when preparing this recipe.

COMMON MISTAKE	BAD OUTCOMES	WHAT YOU SHOULD DO
Not Chilling Tart Shell Before Baking	• **The sides of the tart slump in the oven.** • **The scalloped edges lose their crisp definition.**	The tart dough must be kept cold at every stage in the process, and not just because cold dough is less sticky and easier to handle. Once the dough is fit into the pan, you might think you could bake it right away. But doing so increases the risk that the sides of the tart will collapse in the oven. As you handle the dough, you activate the gluten in the flour. Letting the dough rest gives the gluten time to relax and reduces the risk that it will act like a rubber band in the oven and contract the dough. Also, a well-chilled tart shell is much more likely to hold on to the neat scalloped edges.
Not Weighting Tart Shell During Baking	• **The bottom of the tart shell bubbles up and cracks.**	The foil and pie weights keep the dough in place so that it sets without bubbling. Skip the pie weights and the dough will balloon and then crack. Yes, you could tamp the dough down, but those cracks will make it very tricky to cut neat slices once the tart shell is filled.
Not Fully Baking Tart Shell	• **The crust is doughy.** • **The crust is a bit bland.**	Once the crust is set, it's important to remove the foil and pie weights and allow the tart shell to continue baking for at least 5 or 10 minutes. Remember that this tart isn't going to see any more oven time, so make sure the crust is golden all over before removing the tart shell from the oven. Fully baking the shell makes the crust crisper and also makes the pastry more flavorful. (All pastry tastes better when well browned.)
Overcooking Pastry Cream	• **The cream is marred by bits of scrambled egg.**	If you temper the eggs as directed and whisk the cornstarch directly into the yolks, you shouldn't have a problem. Both steps should keep the yolks from scrambling. Once the eggs have been added to the saucepan, make sure to reduce the heat and whisk vigorously. Whisking ensures that there aren't hot spots in the bottom of the pan where the eggs could overcook. Once a few bubbles burst on the surface, the pastry cream is ready to come off the heat. If you do notice a few stray bits of coagulated egg in the finished pastry cream, don't panic. Pour the pastry cream through a fine-mesh strainer.
Not Fully Chilling Pastry Cream	• **The pastry cream is runny.** • **The tart is messy to slice.**	It can seem like you're waiting and waiting for the pastry cream in this recipe. Does it really need to chill for 3 hours? Yes! The pastry cream will be cold well before the 3-hour mark, but as the chilling process continues the pastry cream will thicken. Don't shortchange this step. We designed our pastry cream to use as little starch as possible—and to rely on the thickening power of chilling. We suggest that you make the tart dough, put it in the fridge, and then make the pastry cream and get it into the fridge. While you wait for the pastry cream to chill, you can roll out the tart dough, chill it again, fit the dough into the tart pan, chill it again, bake the tart shell, and then allow the tart shell to cool. By the time all these steps are completed, the pastry cream will be ready.
Washing Fruit	• **The fruit is waterlogged and mushy.** • **The fruit bleeds into the pastry cream.**	It's certainly natural to want to wash the berries when making a tart. But don't. First off, you can't get rid of all that water. It will hide in crevices in the berries. While this might not matter in a cobbler or pie that will be baked, that water can ruin this recipe if the fruit bleeds watery juices into the pastry cream. In addition, washing makes delicate berries mushy and often mars their appearance. Buy good fruit (preferably organic). Don't use blemished or mushy fruit either, as it can cause similar problems in this recipe.

1. PREPARE DOUGH: Make tart dough (see recipe on page 751), wrap in plastic wrap, and refrigerate for 1 hour, then let sit on counter for 10 minutes.

2. Roll dough into 11-inch circle on lightly floured counter. Place dough round on baking sheet, cover with plastic, and refrigerate for 30 minutes.

3. Loosely roll dough around rolling pin and gently unroll it onto 9-inch tart pan with removable bottom, letting excess dough hang over edge.

4. Ease dough into pan, press dough into sides, and run rolling pin over top of tart pan to remove excess dough.

5. Wrap pan loosely in plastic, place on large plate, and freeze until dough is fully chilled and firm, about 30 minutes. Preheat oven to 375 degrees.

6. Set pan on rimmed baking sheet. Press double-layer of foil into frozen tart shell, covering edges. Fill with pie weights.

7. Bake tart until tart shell is golden brown and set, about 30 minutes, rotating sheet halfway through baking. Carefully remove weights and foil.

8. Continue to bake until fully baked and golden, 5 to 10 minutes. Transfer tart shell on baking sheet to wire rack. Let cool completely, about 1 hour.

9. PREPARE PASTRY CREAM: Bring 2 cups half-and-half, 6 tablespoons granulated sugar, and pinch salt to simmer in saucepan, stirring occasionally.

10. Whisk 5 large egg yolks, 3 tablespoons cornstarch, and 2 tablespoons granulated sugar together in medium bowl until smooth.

11. Slowly whisk 1 cup simmering half-and-half mixture into yolk mixture to temper.

12. Slowly whisk tempered yolk mixture back into remaining half-and-half mixture.

13. Reduce heat to medium and cook, whisking vigorously, until mixture is thickened and few bubbles burst on surface, about 30 seconds.

14. Off heat, whisk in 4 tablespoons unsalted butter, cut into 4 pieces, and 1½ teaspoons vanilla.

15. Transfer mixture to clean bowl, lay sheet of plastic directly on surface, and refrigerate until pastry cream is chilled and firm, about 3 hours.

16. ASSEMBLE TART: Spread chilled pastry cream evenly over bottom of cooled, baked tart shell.

17. Slice 2 peeled kiwi in half lengthwise and then crosswise into ⅜-inch-thick slices.

18. Shingle kiwi slices around edge of tart.

19. Inside kiwi, arrange 2 cups raspberries in 3 rows.

20. Mound 1 cup blueberries in center of tart.

21. Melt ½ cup red currant jelly in small saucepan over medium-high heat, stirring occasionally to smooth out any lumps.

22. Using pastry brush, dab fruit with melted jelly.

23. Remove outer ring of tart pan.

24. Slide large offset metal spatula between tart and tart pan bottom and carefully slide tart onto serving platter or cutting board.

HOW TO MAKE PIES AND TARTS

Recipe Library

Graham Cracker Crust

✓ WHY THIS RECIPE WORKS: Saving time is always a good idea—just as long as you're not sacrificing quality. But while store-bought graham cracker pie crusts are tempting (all you have to do is fill, chill, then serve), they taste stale and bland. We wanted a fresh-tasting homemade crust that wasn't too sweet, with a crisp texture. Turns out, a classic graham cracker crust couldn't be easier to make: combine crushed crumbs with a little melted butter and sugar to bind them, then use a measuring cup to pack the crumbs into the pie plate. And producing a perfect graham cracker crust has a lot to do with the type of graham crackers used. After experimenting with the three leading brands, we discovered subtle but distinct differences among them and found that these differences carried over into crumb crusts made with each kind of cracker. In the end, we preferred Keebler Grahams Crackers Original in our crust.

Graham Cracker Crust

MAKES ENOUGH FOR ONE 9-INCH PIE

We don't recommend using store-bought graham cracker crumbs here as they can often be stale. Be sure to note whether the crust needs to be warm or cool before filling (the pie recipes will specify) and plan accordingly. See Core Technique on page 714 for more details on this recipe.

- **8 whole graham crackers, broken into 1-inch pieces**
- **5 tablespoons unsalted butter, melted and cooled**
- **3 tablespoons sugar**

1. Adjust oven rack to middle position and heat oven to 325 degrees. Process graham cracker pieces in food processor to fine, even crumbs, about 30 seconds. Sprinkle melted butter and sugar over crumbs and pulse to incorporate, about 5 pulses.

2. Sprinkle mixture into 9-inch pie plate. Using bottom of dry measuring cup, press crumbs into even layer on bottom and sides of pie plate. Bake until crust is fragrant and beginning to brown, 13 to 18 minutes; transfer to wire rack. Following particular pie recipe, use crust while it is still warm or let it cool completely.

Key Lime Pie

✓ WHY THIS RECIPE WORKS: Key lime pie often disappoints us with a harsh and artificial flavor. We wanted a recipe for classic Key lime pie with a fresh flavor and silky filling. Traditional Key lime pie is usually not baked; instead, the combination of egg yolks, lime juice, and sweetened condensed milk firms up when chilled because the juice's acidity causes the proteins in the eggs and milk to bind. We found that just one simple swap—from bottled, reconstituted lime juice to juice and zest from fresh limes—gave us a pie that was pungent and refreshing, cool yet creamy, and very satisfying. We also discovered that while the pie filling will set without baking (most recipes call only for mixing and then chilling), it set much more nicely after being baked for only 15 minutes. We tried more dramatic departures from the "classic" recipe—folding in egg whites, substituting heavy cream for condensed milk—but they didn't work. Just two seemingly minor adjustments to the classic recipe made all the difference.

Key Lime Pie

SERVES 8

Despite this pie's name, we found that most tasters could not tell the difference between pies made with regular supermarket limes (called Persian limes) and true Key limes. Since Persian limes are easier to find and juice, we recommend them. The timing here is different from other pies; you need to make the filling first, then prepare the crust.

PIE
- **4 large egg yolks**
- **4 teaspoons grated lime zest plus ½ cup juice (5 limes)**
- **1 (14-ounce) can sweetened condensed milk**
- **1 recipe Graham Cracker Crust, baked and still warm**

TOPPING (OPTIONAL)
- **1 cup heavy cream, chilled**
- **¼ cup (1 ounce) confectioners' sugar**

1. FOR THE PIE: Whisk egg yolks and lime zest together in medium bowl until mixture has light green tint, about 2 minutes. Whisk in condensed milk until smooth, then whisk in lime juice. Cover mixture and set aside at room temperature until thickened, about 30 minutes.

2. Meanwhile, prepare and bake crust. Transfer pie plate to wire rack and leave oven at 325 degrees. (Crust must still be warm when filling is added.)

3. Pour thickened filling into warm prebaked pie crust. Bake pie until center is firm but jiggles slightly when shaken, 15 to 20 minutes. Let pie cool slightly on wire rack, about 1 hour, then cover loosely with plastic wrap and refrigerate until filling is chilled and set, about 3 hours.

4. FOR THE TOPPING, IF USING: Once pie is chilled, use stand mixer fitted with whisk to whip cream and sugar on medium-low speed until foamy, about 1 minute. Increase speed to high and whip until soft peaks form, 1 to 3 minutes. Spread whipped cream attractively over top of pie. Serve.

Summer Berry Pie

✓ WHY THIS RECIPE WORKS: A fresh berry pie might seem like an easy-to-pull-off summer dessert, but most of the recipes we tried buried the berries in gluey thickeners or embedded them in bouncy gelatin. Our goal was to make a pie with great texture and flavor—and still keep it simple. We started with the test kitchen's quick and easy homemade graham cracker crust, which relies on crushed graham crackers (store-bought graham cracker crumbs often taste stale). For the filling, we used a combination of raspberries, blackberries, and blueberries. After trying a few different methods, we found a solution that both bound the berries in the graham cracker crust and intensified their bright flavor. We processed a portion of berries in a food processor until they made a smooth puree, then we thickened the puree with cornstarch. Next, we tossed the remaining berries with warm jelly for a glossy coat and a shot of sweetness. Pressed gently into the puree, the berries stayed put and tasted great.

Summer Berry Pie

SERVES 8

Feel free to vary the amount of each berry as desired as long as you have 6 cups of berries total; do not substitute frozen berries here. Serve with Whipped Cream (page 709).

- 10 ounces (2 cups) raspberries
- 10 ounces (2 cups) blackberries
- 10 ounces (2 cups) blueberries
- ½ cup (3½ ounces) sugar
- 3 tablespoons cornstarch
- ⅛ teaspoon salt
- 1 tablespoon lemon juice
- 1 recipe Graham Cracker Crust (opposite page), baked and cooled
- 2 tablespoons red currant or apple jelly

1. Gently toss berries together in large bowl. Process 2½ cups of berries in food processor until very smooth, about 1 minute (do not underprocess). Strain puree through fine-mesh strainer into small saucepan, pressing on solids to extract as much puree as possible (you should have about 1½ cups); discard solids.

2. Whisk sugar, cornstarch, and salt together in bowl, then whisk into strained puree. Bring puree mixture to boil, stirring constantly, and cook until it is as thick as pudding, about 7 minutes. Off heat, stir in lemon juice; set aside to cool slightly.

3. Pour warm berry puree into baked and cooled prebaked pie crust. Melt jelly in clean small saucepan over low heat, then pour over remaining 3½ cups berries and toss to coat. Spread berries evenly over puree and lightly press them into puree. Cover pie loosely with plastic wrap and refrigerate until filling is chilled and has set, about 3 hours; serve chilled or at room temperature.

Chocolate Cookie Crust

✔ **WHY THIS RECIPE WORKS:** For a quick and easy chocolate cookie crust, we found that cream-filled Oreo cookies gave us a rich and tender crust. Chocolate wafer cookies are the more conventional choice for this type of crust, but we found that they tasted bland and tough. Because of the richness of the filling, swapping in Oreos gave us a supremely tender crust. All it needed was a bit of melted butter to help the crumbs stick

together. We simply processed the cookies in a food processor until finely ground, pulsed in the melted butter, and pressed the mixture into an even layer in the pie plate.

Chocolate Cookie Crust

MAKES ENOUGH FOR ONE 9-INCH PIE

Other brands of chocolate sandwich cookies may be substituted, but avoid "double-filled" cookies because the proportion of cookie to filling won't be correct. Be sure to note whether the crust needs to be warm or cool before filling (the pie recipes will specify) and plan accordingly. See Core Technique on page 714 for more details on this recipe.

- 16 Oreo cookies, broken into rough pieces
- 4 tablespoons unsalted butter, melted and cooled

1. Adjust oven rack to middle position and heat oven to 325 degrees. Pulse cookies in food processor until coarsely ground, about 15 pulses, then process to fine, even crumbs, about 15 seconds. Sprinkle melted butter over crumbs and pulse to incorporate.

2. Sprinkle mixture into 9-inch pie plate. Using bottom of measuring cup, press crumbs into even layer on bottom and sides of pie plate. Bake until crust is fragrant and looks set, 13 to 18 minutes; transfer to wire rack. Following particular pie recipe, use crust while it is still warm or let it cool completely.

Mint Chocolate Cookie Crust

Substitute 16 Cool Mint Creme Oreo cookies for the Oreo cookies.

Nutter Butter Cookie Crust

Substitute 16 Nutter Butter cookies for the Oreo cookies.

Chocolate Cream Pie

✔ **WHY THIS RECIPE WORKS:** Chocolate cream pies can look superb but they're often gluey, overly sweet, and impossible to slice. We wanted a creamy pie with a well-balanced chocolate flavor and a delicious, easy-to-slice crust. After testing every type of cookie on the market, we hit on pulverized Oreos and a bit of melted butter for the tastiest, most tender, sliceable crumb crust. We found that the secret to perfect chocolate cream pie filling was to combine two different types of chocolate for a deeper, more complex flavor. Bittersweet or semisweet chocolate provides the main thrust of flavor and intensely flavored unsweetened chocolate lends depth. One ounce of unsweetened chocolate may not seem like much, but it gives this pie great flavor. We also discovered that the custard's texture depended upon carefully pouring the egg yolk mixture into simmering half-and-half, then whisking in butter

Chocolate Cream Pie

SERVES 8

Do not combine the egg yolks and sugar in advance of making the filling—the sugar will begin to break down the yolks, and the finished cream will be pitted.

FILLING

2½ **cups half-and-half**
⅓   **cup (2⅓ ounces) sugar**
    Pinch salt
6   **large egg yolks**
2   **tablespoons cornstarch**
6   **tablespoons unsalted butter, cut into 6 pieces**
6   **ounces semisweet or bittersweet chocolate, chopped fine**
1   **ounce unsweetened chocolate, chopped fine**
1   **teaspoon vanilla extract**

1   **recipe Chocolate Cookie Crust (page 743), baked and cooled**

TOPPING

1½ **cups heavy cream, chilled**
2   **tablespoons sugar**
½   **teaspoon vanilla extract**

1. FOR THE FILLING: Bring half-and-half, 3 tablespoons sugar, and salt to simmer in medium saucepan, stirring occasionally.

2. As half-and-half mixture begins to simmer, whisk egg yolks, cornstarch, and remaining sugar together in medium bowl until smooth. Slowly whisk 1 cup of simmering half-and-half mixture into yolk mixture to temper, then slowly whisk tempered yolk mixture back into remaining half-and-half mixture. Reduce heat to medium and cook, whisking vigorously, until mixture is thickened and few bubbles burst on surface, about 30 seconds. Off heat, whisk in butter, semisweet chocolate, and unsweetened chocolate until completely smooth and melted, then stir in vanilla.

3. Pour warm filling into cooled prebaked pie crust. Lay sheet of plastic wrap directly on surface of filling and refrigerate pie until filling is chilled and set, about 4 hours.

4. FOR THE TOPPING: Once pie is chilled, use stand mixer fitted with whisk to whip cream, sugar, and vanilla on medium-low speed until foamy, about 1 minute. Increase speed to high and whip until soft peaks form, 1 to 3 minutes. Spread whipped cream attractively over top of pie. Serve.

Foolproof Pie Dough

✔ **WHY THIS RECIPE WORKS:** Pie dough can go wrong so easily: dry dough that is too crumbly to roll out; a flaky but leathery crust; or a tender crust without flakes. We wanted a recipe for pie dough that would roll out easily every time and produce a tender, flaky crust. A combination of butter and shortening provided the best balance of flavor and tenderness, and the food processor was the best tool to cut the fat into the flour. To ensure pieces of butter that were the same size each time, we processed a portion of the flour with the fat until we had a unified paste. Then we added the reserved flour and pulsed until it was just evenly distributed. In order to roll easily, dough needs a generous amount of water, but too much water makes crusts tough. We found the answer in the liquor cabinet: vodka.

While gluten (the protein that makes crust tough) forms readily in water, it doesn't form in ethanol, and vodka is 60 percent water and 40 percent ethanol. Replacing some of the water with vodka produced a moist, easy-to-roll dough that stayed tender. (The alcohol vaporizes in the oven, so you won't taste it in the baked crust.)

Foolproof Single-Crust Pie Dough

MAKES ENOUGH FOR ONE 9-INCH PIE

Vodka is essential to the tender texture of this crust and imparts no flavor—do not substitute water. This dough is moister than most standard pie doughs and will require lots of flour to roll out (up to ¼ cup). A food processor is essential to making this dough—we don't recommend making it by hand. Many recipes that call for partially baking the crust also suggest filling the pie shell when it's still warm and then quickly returning it to the oven. Read recipes carefully and have the filling ready when the pie shell comes out of the oven if so directed. See Core Techniques on pages 716–721 for more details on this recipe.

1¼ **cups (6¼ ounces) all-purpose flour, plus extra for counter**
1   **tablespoon sugar**
½   **teaspoon salt**
6   **tablespoons unsalted butter, cut into ¼-inch pieces and chilled**
4   **tablespoons vegetable shortening, cut into 2 pieces and chilled**
2   **tablespoons vodka, chilled**
2   **tablespoons ice water**

1. Process ¾ cup flour, sugar, and salt together in food processor until combined, about 5 seconds. Scatter butter and shortening pieces over top and continue to process until incorporated and mixture begins to form uneven clumps with no remaining floury bits, about 10 seconds.

2. Scrape down workbowl and redistribute dough evenly around processor blade. Sprinkle remaining ½ cup flour over dough and pulse until mixture has broken up into pieces and is evenly distributed around bowl, 4 to 6 pulses.

3. Transfer mixture to large bowl. Sprinkle vodka and ice water over mixture. Stir and press dough together, using stiff rubber spatula, until dough sticks together.

4. Turn dough onto sheet of plastic wrap and flatten into 4-inch disk. Wrap tightly and refrigerate for 1 hour. Before rolling dough out, let it sit on counter to soften slightly, about 10 minutes. (Dough can be wrapped tightly in plastic and refrigerated for up to 2 days or frozen for up to 1 month. If frozen, let dough thaw completely on counter before rolling it out.)

5. Adjust oven rack to middle position and heat oven to 375 degrees. Lay dough on generously floured counter and roll dough outward from its center into 12-inch circle. Loosely roll dough around rolling pin and gently unroll it over 9-inch pie plate. Lift dough and gently press it into pie plate, letting excess hang over plate's edge.

6. Using kitchen shears, trim all but ½ inch of dough overhanging edge of pie plate. Tuck dough underneath itself to form tidy, even edge that sits on lip of pie plate. Use index finger of one hand and thumb and index finger of other hand to create fluted ridges perpendicular to edge of pie plate. Wrap dough-lined pie plate loosely in plastic and freeze until dough is firm, about 30 minutes.

7. Line chilled pie crust with double layer of aluminum foil, covering edges to prevent burning, and fill with pie weights or pennies.

8A. FOR A PARTIALLY BAKED CRUST: Bake until pie dough looks dry and is pale in color, 25 to 30 minutes. Transfer pie plate to wire rack and remove weights and foil.

8B. FOR A FULLY BAKED CRUST: Bake until pie dough looks dry and is pale in color, 25 to 30 minutes. Transfer pie plate to wire rack and remove weights and foil. Return crust to oven and continue to bake until deep golden brown, 10 to 12 minutes longer. Transfer pie plate to wire rack and let crust cool completely, about 1 hour.

Foolproof Double-Crust Pie Dough

MAKES ENOUGH FOR ONE 9-INCH PIE

Vodka is essential to the tender texture of this crust and imparts no flavor—do not substitute water. This dough is moister than most standard pie doughs and will require lots of flour to roll out (up to ¼ cup). A food processor is essential to making this dough—we don't recommend making it by hand. See Core Techniques on pages 716–719 and 722–723 for more details on this recipe.

2½ cups (12½ ounces) all-purpose flour, plus extra for counter

2 tablespoons sugar

1 teaspoon salt

12 tablespoons unsalted butter, cut into ¼-inch pieces and chilled

8 tablespoons vegetable shortening, cut into 4 pieces and chilled

¼ cup vodka, chilled

¼ cup ice water

1. Process 1½ cups flour, sugar, and salt together in food processor until combined, about 5 seconds. Scatter butter and shortening pieces over top and continue to process until incorporated and mixture begins to form uneven clumps with no remaining floury bits, about 15 seconds.

2. Scrape down workbowl and redistribute dough evenly around processor blade. Sprinkle remaining 1 cup flour over dough and pulse until mixture has broken up into pieces and is evenly distributed around bowl, 4 to 6 pulses.

3. Transfer mixture to large bowl. Sprinkle vodka and ice water over mixture. Stir and press dough together, using stiff rubber spatula, until dough sticks together.

4. Divide dough into 2 even pieces. Turn each piece of dough onto sheet of plastic wrap and flatten each into 4-inch disk. Wrap each piece tightly and refrigerate for 1 hour. Before rolling dough out, let it sit on counter to soften slightly, about 10 minutes. (Dough can be wrapped tightly in plastic and refrigerated for up to 2 days or frozen for up to 1 month. If frozen, let dough thaw completely on counter before rolling it out.)

Pecan Pie

✔ **WHY THIS RECIPE WORKS:** Pecan pies can be overwhelmingly sweet, with no real pecan flavor. And they too often turn out curdled and separated. What's more, the weepy filling makes the bottom crust soggy and leathery. The fact that the crust usually seems underbaked to begin with doesn't help matters. We wanted to create a recipe for a not-too-sweet pie with a smooth-textured filling and a properly baked bottom crust. We tackled this pie's problems by using brown sugar, for rich, deep flavor, and reducing the amount, so the pecan flavor could take center stage. We also partially baked the crust, which kept it crisp. We found that it's important to add the hot filling to a warm pie crust as this helps keep the crust from getting soggy. In addition, we discovered that simulating a double boiler when you're melting the butter and making the filling is an easy way to maintain gentle heat, which helps ensure that the filling doesn't curdle.

Classic Pecan Pie

SERVES 8

The crust must still be warm when the filling is added. To serve the pie warm, let it cool thoroughly so that it sets completely, then warm it in a 250-degree oven for about 15 minutes and slice. Serve with Vanilla Ice Cream (page 780) or Whipped Cream (page 709). See Recipe Tutorial on page 730 for more details on this recipe.

6 tablespoons unsalted butter, cut into 6 pieces

1 cup packed (7 ounces) dark brown sugar

½ teaspoon salt

3 large eggs

¾ cup light corn syrup

1 tablespoon vanilla extract

2 cups (8 ounces) pecans, toasted and chopped fine

1 recipe Foolproof Single-Crust Pie Dough (opposite page), partially baked and still warm

1. Adjust oven rack to lower-middle position, place aluminum foil-lined rimmed baking sheet on rack, and heat oven to 275 degrees. Melt butter in heatproof bowl set in skillet of water maintained at just below simmer. Remove bowl from skillet and stir in sugar and salt until butter is absorbed. Whisk in eggs, then corn syrup and vanilla until smooth. Return bowl to hot water and stir until mixture is shiny, hot to touch, and registers 130 degrees. Off heat, stir in pecans.

2. Pour pecan mixture into warm prebaked pie crust. Bake pie on heated sheet until filling looks set but yields like Jell-O when gently pressed with back of spoon, 50 minutes to 1 hour. Let pie cool on wire rack until filling has set, about 2 hours; serve slightly warm or at room temperature.

Buttermilk Pecan Pie with Raisins

Substitute 1½ cups (10½ ounces) granulated sugar for brown sugar and ⅔ cup buttermilk for corn syrup and vanilla. Reduce pecans to ½ cup and stir into pie filling along with ½ cup raisins, chopped fine.

Maple Pecan Pie

More liquid than corn syrup, maple syrup yields a softer, more custardlike pie. Toasted walnuts can be substituted for pecans. We prefer to use grade B or grade A dark amber maple syrup for this recipe.

Reduce butter to 4 tablespoons and pecans to 1½ cups. Substitute ½ cup granulated sugar for brown sugar and 1 cup maple syrup for corn syrup and vanilla.

Triple-Chocolate-Chunk Pecan Pie

SERVES 8

Use either just one type of chocolate listed or a combination of two or three types. The crust must still be warm when the filling is added. To serve the pie warm, let it cool thoroughly so that it sets completely, then warm it in a 250-degree oven for about 15 minutes and slice. Serve with Vanilla Ice Cream (page 780) or Whipped Cream (page 709).

- 3 tablespoons unsalted butter, cut into 3 pieces
- ¾ cup packed (5¼ ounces) dark brown sugar
- ½ teaspoon salt
- 2 large eggs
- ½ cup light corn syrup
- 1 teaspoon vanilla extract
- 1 cup pecans, toasted and chopped coarse
- 6 ounces semisweet, milk, and/or white chocolate, chopped coarse
- 1 recipe Foolproof Single-Crust Pie Dough (page 744), partially baked and still warm

1. Adjust oven rack to lower-middle position, place aluminum foil–lined rimmed baking sheet on rack, and heat oven to 275 degrees. Melt butter in heatproof bowl set in skillet of water maintained at just below simmer. Remove bowl from skillet and stir in sugar and salt until butter is absorbed. Whisk in eggs, then corn syrup and vanilla until smooth. Return bowl to hot water and stir until mixture is shiny, hot to touch, and registers 130 degrees. Off heat, stir in pecans.

2. Pour pecan mixture into warm prebaked pie crust. Scatter chocolate over top and lightly press it into filling with back of spoon. Bake pie on heated sheet until filling looks set but yields like Jell-O when gently pressed with back of spoon, 50 minutes to 1 hour. Let pie cool on wire rack until filling has set, about 2 hours; serve slightly warm or at room temperature.

Pumpkin Pie

✔ **WHY THIS RECIPE WORKS:** Too often, pumpkin pie appears at the end of a Thanksgiving meal as a grainy, over-spiced, canned-pumpkin custard encased in a soggy crust. We wanted to create a pumpkin pie destined to be a new classic: velvety smooth, packed with pumpkin flavor, and redolent of just enough fragrant spices. To concentrate its flavor, we cooked the canned pumpkin with sugar and spices, then whisked in heavy cream, milk, and eggs. This improved the flavor and the hot filling helped the custard firm up quickly in the oven, preventing it from soaking into the crust. For spices, we chose nutmeg, cinnamon, and, surprisingly, freshly grated ginger. Sugar and maple syrup sweetened things, but for more complex flavor, we added mashed roasted yams to the filling (switching to canned candied yams streamlined the procedure). To keep the custard from curdling, we started the pie at a high temperature for 10 minutes, followed by a reduced temperature for the remainder of the baking time. This cut the baking time to less than an hour and the dual temperatures produced a creamy pie fully and evenly cooked from edge to center.

Pumpkin Pie

SERVES 8

Make sure to buy unsweetened canned pumpkin; avoid pumpkin pie mix. If candied yams are unavailable, regular canned yams can be substituted. The crust must still be warm when the filling is added. When the pie is properly baked, the center 2 inches of the pie should look firm but jiggle slightly. The pie finishes cooking with residual heat; to ensure that the filling sets, let it cool at room temperature and not in the refrigerator. Serve with Whipped Cream (page 709).

- 1 cup heavy cream
- 1 cup whole milk
- 3 large eggs plus 2 large yolks
- 1 teaspoon vanilla extract
- 1 (15-ounce) can unsweetened pumpkin puree
- 1 cup canned candied yams, drained
- ¾ cup (5¼ ounces) sugar
- ¼ cup maple syrup
- 2 teaspoons grated fresh ginger
- 1 teaspoon salt
- ½ teaspoon ground cinnamon
- ¼ teaspoon ground nutmeg
- 1 recipe Foolproof Single-Crust Pie Dough (page 744), fully baked and still warm

1. Adjust oven rack to lowest position and heat oven to 400 degrees. Line rimmed baking sheet with aluminum foil. Whisk cream, milk, eggs and yolks, and vanilla together in bowl. Bring pumpkin, yams, sugar, maple syrup, ginger, salt, cinnamon, and nutmeg to simmer in large saucepan and cook, stirring constantly and mashing yams against sides of pot, until thick and shiny, 15 to 20 minutes.

2. Remove saucepan from heat and whisk in cream mixture until fully incorporated. Strain mixture through fine-mesh strainer into bowl, using back of ladle or spatula to press solids through strainer. Whisk mixture, then pour into warm prebaked pie crust.

3. Place pie on prepared sheet and bake for 10 minutes. Reduce oven temperature to 300 degrees and continue to bake until edges of pie are set and center registers 175 degrees, 20 to 35 minutes longer. Let pie cool on wire rack to room temperature, 2 to 3 hours. Serve.

Lemon Meringue Pie

✓ **WHY THIS RECIPE WORKS:** The most controversial part of lemon meringue pie is the meringue. It can shrink, bead, puddle, deflate, burn, sweat, break down, or turn rubbery. We wanted a pie with a flaky crust and a rich filling that was soft but not runny, firm but not gelatinous, and that balanced the airy meringue. Most important, we wanted a meringue that didn't break down and puddle on the bottom or "tear" on top. We learned that the puddling underneath the meringue is from undercooking, the beading on top from overcooking. We discovered that if the filling is piping hot when the meringue is applied, the underside of the meringue will not undercook; if the oven temperature is relatively low, the top of the meringue won't overcook. Baking the pie in a relatively cool oven also produces the best-looking, most evenly baked meringue. To further stabilize the meringue and keep it from weeping, we beat in a small amount of cornstarch.

The Ultimate Lemon Meringue Pie

SERVES 8

Make the pie crust, let it cool, and then begin work on the filling. As soon as the filling is made, cover it with plastic wrap to keep it hot and then start working on the meringue topping. You want to add hot filling to the cooled pie crust, apply the meringue topping, and then quickly get the pie into the oven.

FILLING

1½ cups water
 1 cup (7 ounces) sugar
 ¼ cup cornstarch
 ⅛ teaspoon salt
 6 large egg yolks
 1 tablespoon grated lemon zest plus ½ cup juice (3 lemons)
 2 tablespoons unsalted butter, cut into 2 pieces

MERINGUE

 ⅓ cup water
 1 tablespoon cornstarch
 4 large egg whites
 ½ teaspoon vanilla extract
 ¼ teaspoon cream of tartar
 ½ cup (3½ ounces) sugar

 1 recipe Foolproof Single-Crust Pie Dough (page 744), fully baked and cooled

1. FOR THE FILLING: Adjust oven rack to middle position and heat oven to 325 degrees. Bring water, sugar, cornstarch, and salt to simmer in large saucepan, whisking constantly. When mixture starts to turn translucent, whisk in egg yolks, two at a time. Whisk in lemon zest and juice and butter. Return mixture to brief simmer, then remove from heat. Lay sheet of plastic wrap directly on surface of filling to keep warm and prevent skin from forming.

2. FOR THE MERINGUE: Bring water and cornstarch to simmer in small saucepan and cook, whisking occasionally, until thickened and translucent, 1 to 2 minutes. Remove from heat and let cool slightly.

3. Using stand mixer fitted with whisk, whip egg whites, vanilla, and cream of tartar on medium-low speed until foamy, about 1 minute. Increase speed to medium-high and beat in sugar, 1 tablespoon at a time, until incorporated and mixture forms soft, billowy mounds. Add cornstarch mixture, 1 tablespoon at a time; continue to beat to glossy, stiff peaks, 2 to 3 minutes.

4. Meanwhile, remove plastic from filling and return to very low heat during last minute or so of beating meringue (to ensure filling is hot).

5. Pour warm filling into cooled prebaked pie crust. Using rubber spatula, immediately distribute meringue evenly around edge and then center of pie, attaching meringue to pie crust to prevent shrinking. Using back of spoon, create attractive swirls and peaks in meringue. Bake until meringue is light golden brown, about 20 minutes. Let pie cool on wire rack until filling has set, about 2 hours. Serve.

Deep-Dish Apple Pie

✓ **WHY THIS RECIPE WORKS:** The problem with deep-dish apple pie is that the apples are often unevenly cooked and the exuded juice leaves the apples swimming in liquid, producing a bottom crust that is pale and soggy. Then there is the gaping hole left between the shrunken apples and the top crust, making it impossible to slice and serve a neat piece of pie. We wanted our piece of deep-dish pie to be a towering wedge of tender, juicy apples, fully framed by a buttery, flaky crust. Precooking the apples solved the shrinking problem, helped the apples hold their shape, and prevented a flood of juices from collecting in the bottom of the pie plate, thereby producing a nicely browned bottom crust. Why didn't cooking the apples twice (once on the stovetop and once in the oven) cause them to become insipid and mushy? We learned that when the apples are gently heated, their pectin is converted to a heat-stable form that keeps them from becoming mushy when cooked further in the oven. This allowed us to boost the quantity of apples to 5 pounds. A little brown sugar, salt, lemon, and cinnamon contributed flavor and sweetness.

Deep-Dish Apple Pie

SERVES 8

You can substitute Empire or Cortland apples for the Granny Smith apples and Jonagold, Fuji, or Braeburn for the Golden Delicious apples. See Recipe Tutorial on page 734 for more details on this recipe.

 1 recipe Foolproof Double-Crust Pie Dough (page 745)
2½ pounds Granny Smith apples, peeled, cored, and sliced ¼ inch thick
2½ pounds Golden Delicious apples, peeled, cored, and sliced ¼ inch thick
 ½ cup (3½ ounces) plus 1 tablespoon granulated sugar
 ¼ cup packed (1¾ ounces) light brown sugar
 ½ teaspoon grated lemon zest plus 1 tablespoon juice
 ¼ teaspoon salt
 ⅛ teaspoon ground cinnamon
 1 large egg white, lightly beaten

1. Roll 1 disk of dough into 12-inch circle on lightly floured counter. Loosely roll dough around rolling pin and gently unroll it over 9-inch pie plate. Lift dough and gently press it into pie plate, letting excess hang over edge. Wrap dough-lined pie plate loosely in plastic wrap and refrigerate until dough is firm, about 30 minutes. Roll other disk of dough into 12-inch circle on lightly floured counter, then transfer to parchment paper–lined baking sheet; cover with plastic and refrigerate for 30 minutes.

2. Toss apples, ½ cup granulated sugar, brown sugar, lemon zest, salt, and cinnamon together in Dutch oven. Cover and cook over medium heat, stirring often, until apples are tender when poked with fork but still hold their shape, 15 to 20 minutes. Transfer apples and their juices to rimmed baking sheet and let cool to room temperature, about 30 minutes.

3. Adjust oven rack to lowest position and heat oven to 425 degrees. Line rimmed baking sheet with aluminum foil. Drain cooled apples thoroughly in colander, reserving ¼ cup of juice. Stir lemon juice into reserved apple juice.

4. Spread apples into dough-lined pie plate, mounding them slightly in middle, and drizzle with lemon juice mixture. Loosely roll remaining dough round around rolling pin and gently unroll it onto filling. Trim overhang to ½ inch beyond lip of pie plate. Pinch edges of top and bottom dough crusts firmly together. Tuck overhang under itself; folded edge should be flush with edge of pie plate. Crimp dough evenly around edge of pie using your fingers. Cut four 2-inch slits in top of dough. Brush surface with beaten egg white and sprinkle evenly with remaining 1 tablespoon granulated sugar.

5. Place pie on prepared sheet and bake until crust is light golden brown, about 25 minutes. Reduce oven temperature to 375 degrees, rotate baking sheet, and continue to bake until juices are bubbling and crust is deep golden brown, 30 to 40 minutes longer. Let pie cool on wire rack until filling has set, about 2 hours; serve slightly warm or at room temperature.

Blueberry Pie

✔ **WHY THIS RECIPE WORKS:** If the filling in blueberry pie doesn't gel, a wedge can collapse into a soupy puddle topped by a sodden crust. But use too much thickener and the filling can be so dense that cutting into it is a challenge. We wanted a pie that had a firm, glistening filling full of fresh, bright flavor and still-plump berries. To thicken the pie, we favored tapioca, which allowed the fresh yet subtle blueberry flavor to shine through. Too much of it, though, and we had a congealed mess. Cooking and reducing half of the berries helped us cut down on the tapioca required, but not enough. A second inspiration came from a peeled and shredded Granny Smith apple. Apples are high in pectin, a type of carbohydrate that acts as a thickener when cooked. Combined with a modest 2 tablespoons of tapioca, the apple thickened the filling to a soft, even consistency that was neither gelatinous nor slippery. Baking the pie on a baking sheet on the bottom oven rack produced a crisp, golden bottom crust. To vent the steam from the berries, we found a faster, easier alternative to a lattice top in a biscuit cutter, which we used to cut out circles in the top crust.

Blueberry Pie
SERVES 8

This recipe was developed using fresh blueberries, but unthawed frozen blueberries will work as well. In step 3, cook half the frozen berries over medium-high heat, without mashing, until reduced to 1¼ cups, 12 to 15 minutes. Use a coarse grater to shred the apple. Grind the tapioca to a powder in a spice grinder or mini food processor.

- 1 recipe Foolproof Double-Crust Pie Dough (page 745)
- 30 ounces (6 cups) blueberries
- 1 Granny Smith apple, peeled, cored, and shredded
- ¾ cup (5¼ ounces) sugar
- 2 tablespoons instant tapioca, ground
- 2 teaspoons grated lemon zest plus 2 teaspoons juice
  Pinch salt
- 2 tablespoons unsalted butter, cut into ¼-inch pieces
- 1 large egg white, lightly beaten

1. Roll 1 disk of dough into 12-inch circle on lightly floured counter. Loosely roll dough around rolling pin and gently unroll it over 9-inch pie plate. Lift dough and gently press it into pie plate, letting excess hang over edge. Wrap dough-lined pie plate loosely in plastic wrap and refrigerate until dough is firm, about 30 minutes.

2. Line rimmed baking sheet with parchment paper. Roll other disk of dough into 12-inch circle on lightly floured counter. Using 1¼-inch round cookie cutter, cut round from center of dough. Cut 6 more rounds from dough, 1½ inches from edge of center hole and equally spaced around center hole. Transfer dough to prepared baking sheet; cover with plastic and refrigerate for 30 minutes.

3. Place 3 cups berries in medium saucepan and set over medium heat. Using potato masher, mash berries several times to release juices. Continue to cook, stirring often and mashing occasionally, until about half of berries have broken down and mixture is thickened and reduced to 1½ cups, about 8 minutes; let cool slightly.

4. Adjust oven rack to lowest position and heat oven to 400 degrees. Line rimmed baking sheet with aluminum foil.

5. Place shredded apple in dish towel and wring dry. Transfer apple to large bowl and stir in cooked berries, remaining 3 cups uncooked berries, sugar, tapioca, lemon zest and juice, and salt until combined. Spread mixture into dough-lined pie plate and scatter butter over top.

6. Loosely roll remaining dough around rolling pin and gently unroll it onto filling. Trim overhang to ½ inch beyond lip of pie plate. Pinch edges of top and bottom crusts firmly together. Tuck overhang under itself; folded edge should be flush with edge of pie plate. Crimp dough evenly around edge of pie using your fingers. Brush surface with beaten egg white.

7. Place pie on prepared sheet and bake until crust is light golden brown, about 25 minutes. Reduce oven temperature to 350 degrees, rotate baking sheet, and continue to bake until juices are bubbling and crust is deep golden brown, 35 to 50 minutes longer. Let pie cool on wire rack to room temperature, about 4 hours. Serve.

Cherry Pie

✔ **WHY THIS RECIPE WORKS:** For a cherry pie with plenty of fresh cherry flavor, we found tracking down sour cherries was a must, as sweet cherries lost their flavor once cooked. Among the varieties of light and dark cherries, Morellos were our favorite. For flavorings, almond extract complemented the flavor of the cherries while a little cinnamon added a hint of warmth. Making a lattice top for the pie ensured maximum evaporation from the filling as the fruit released its juices.

Lattice-Top Cherry Pie

SERVES 8

Do not use canned cherry pie filling because it has added sugars and thickeners. See Core Technique on page 724 for more details on making a lattice-top pie.

> 1 recipe Foolproof Double-Crust Pie Dough (page 745)
> 2½ pounds fresh sour cherries, pitted
> 1–1¼ cups (7–8¾ ounces) plus 1 tablespoon sugar
> ¼ cup cornstarch
> ¼ teaspoon ground cinnamon
> ¼ teaspoon almond extract
>   Pinch salt
> 1 large egg white, lightly beaten

1. Roll 1 disk of dough into 12-inch circle on lightly floured counter. Loosely roll dough around rolling pin and gently unroll it over 9-inch pie plate. Lift dough and gently press into pie plate, letting excess dough hang over edge. Wrap dough-lined pie plate loosely in plastic wrap and refrigerate until dough is firm, about 30 minutes.

2. Roll other disk of dough into 13½ by 10½-inch rectangle on lightly floured counter, then transfer to parchment paper–lined baking sheet. Trim dough to 13 by 10-inch rectangle and slice lengthwise into eight 13-inch-long strips each 1¼ inches wide. Separate strips slightly, cover with plastic, and freeze until very firm, about 30 minutes.

3. Toss cherries and 1 cup sugar together in large bowl and let sit, tossing occasionally, until cherries release their juice, about 1 hour. Adjust oven rack to lowest position and heat oven to 425 degrees. Line rimmed baking sheet with aluminum foil.

4. Drain cherries thoroughly in colander, reserving ¼ cup juice. In large bowl, toss drained cherries, ¼ cup reserved juice, cornstarch, cinnamon, almond extract, and salt together until well combined. (If cherries taste too tart, add up to ¼ cup more sugar.)

5. Spread cherries into dough-lined pie plate. Lay 4 parallel strips of chilled dough evenly over filling. Weave remaining strips in opposite direction, one at a time, to create lattice (if dough becomes too soft to work with, refrigerate pie and dough strips until dough firms up). Let strips soften for 5 to 10 minutes, then trim overhang to ½ inch beyond lip of pie plate. Pinch edges of crust and lattice strips together, then tuck overhang under itself; folded edge should be flush with edge of pie plate. Crimp dough evenly around edge of pie using fingers. Brush lattice with beaten egg white and sprinkle evenly with remaining 1 tablespoon sugar.

6. Bake pie on prepared sheet until top crust is light golden brown, about 25 minutes. Reduce oven temperature to 375 degrees, rotate sheet, and continue to bake until juices are bubbling and crust is deep golden brown, 30 to 45 minutes longer. Let pie cool on wire rack until the filling has set, about 2 hours; serve slightly warm or at room temperature.

Peach Pie

✔ **WHY THIS RECIPE WORKS:** Fresh peach pies are often soupy or overly sweet, with a bottom crust that is soggy or undercooked. We wanted to create a filling that was juicy but not swimming in liquid, its flavors neither muscled out by spices nor overwhelmed by thickeners, and the crust had to be well browned on the bottom. We peeled and sliced the peaches and found that all they needed in the way of flavor was sugar, lemon juice, cinnamon, nutmeg, and a dash of salt. To thicken the juices, we used a little cornstarch, but it didn't solve the problem. A lattice-top pie crust was our solution—while it requires a bit more work than making a regular double-crust pie, we found that it's worth the effort. Not only is it pretty and very traditional on peach pies, but it serves an important purpose: The structure of a lattice top allows for maximum evaporation while the pie cooks—the juices released by the fruit cook down slowly while baking so the filling isn't soupy. For easy assembly, we rolled and cut the dough, then froze it so the strips were firm and easy to handle.

Lattice-Top Peach Pie

SERVES 8

If your peaches are firm, you should be able to peel them with a sharp vegetable peeler. If they are too soft to withstand the pressure of a peeler, you'll need to blanch them in a pot of simmering water for 15 seconds and then shock them in a bowl of ice water before peeling; see Core Technique on page 685 for more details. See Core Technique on page 724 for more details on making a lattice-top pie.

> 1 recipe Foolproof Double-Crust Pie Dough (page 745)
> 2½ pounds peaches, peeled, halved, pitted, and sliced ⅓ inch thick
> 1 cup (7 ounces) plus 1 tablespoon sugar
> 1 tablespoon cornstarch
> 1 tablespoon lemon juice
>   Pinch ground cinnamon
>   Pinch ground nutmeg
>   Pinch salt
> 1 large egg white, lightly beaten

1. Roll 1 disk of dough into 12-inch circle on lightly floured counter. Loosely roll dough around rolling pin and gently unroll it over 9-inch pie plate. Lift dough and gently press it into pie plate, letting excess hang over plate's edge. Wrap dough-lined pie plate loosely in plastic wrap and refrigerate until dough is firm, about 30 minutes.

2. Roll other disk of dough into 13½ by 10½-inch rectangle on lightly floured counter, then transfer to parchment paper–lined baking sheet. Trim dough to 13 by 10-inch rectangle and slice lengthwise into eight 13-inch-long strips. Separate strips slightly, cover with plastic, and freeze until very firm, about 30 minutes.

3. Toss peaches and 1 cup sugar together in large bowl and let sit, tossing occasionally, until peaches release their juice, about 1 hour. Adjust oven rack to lowest position and heat oven to 425 degrees. Line rimmed baking sheet with aluminum foil.

4. Drain peaches thoroughly in colander, reserving ¼ cup of juice. In large bowl, toss drained peaches, reserved juice, cornstarch, lemon juice, cinnamon, nutmeg, and salt together until well combined.

5. Spread peaches into dough-lined pie plate. Lay 4 parallel strips of chilled dough evenly over filling. Weave remaining strips in opposite direction, one at a time, to create lattice (if dough becomes too soft to work with, refrigerate pie and dough strips until dough firms up). Let strips soften for 5 to 10 minutes, then trim overhang to ½ inch beyond lip of pie plate. Pinch edges of crust and lattice strips together, then tuck overhang under itself; folded edge should be flush with edge of pie plate. Crimp dough evenly around edge of pie using fingers. Brush lattice with beaten egg white and sprinkle evenly with remaining 1 tablespoon sugar.

6. Place pie on prepared sheet and bake until top crust is light golden brown, about 25 minutes. Reduce oven temperature to 375 degrees, rotate sheet, and continue to bake until juices are bubbling and crust is deep golden brown, 30 to 40 minutes longer. Let pie cool on wire rack until filling has set, about 2 hours; serve slightly warm or at room temperature.

Free-Form Tart Dough

✔ **WHY THIS RECIPE WORKS:** A free-form tart—a single layer of buttery pie dough folded up around fresh fruit—is a simpler take on pie. But without the support of a pie plate, tender crusts are prone to leaking juice, and this can result in a soggy bottom. For our crust, we used a high proportion of butter to flour, which provided the most buttery flavor and tender texture without compromising the structure. We then turned to the French *fraisage* method to make the pastry: Chunks of butter are pressed into long, thin sheets that create lots of flaky layers when the dough is baked.

Free-Form Tart Dough
MAKES ENOUGH FOR ONE 9-INCH TART
See Core Technique on page 726 for more details on this recipe.

- 1½ **cups (7½ ounces) all-purpose flour**
- ½ **teaspoon salt**
- 10 **tablespoons unsalted butter, cut into ½-inch pieces and chilled**
- 4–6 **tablespoons ice water**

1. Process flour and salt in food processor until combined, about 5 seconds. Scatter butter pieces over top and pulse until mixture resembles coarse sand and butter pieces are about size of small peas, about 10 pulses. Continue to pulse, adding water 1 tablespoon at a time, until dough begins to form small curds that hold together when pinched with fingers, about 10 pulses.

2. Turn dough crumbs onto lightly floured counter and gather into rectangular-shaped pile. Starting at farthest end, use heel of hand to smear small amount of dough against counter. Continue to smear dough until all crumbs have been worked. Gather smeared crumbs together in another rectangular-shaped pile and repeat process. Press dough into 6-inch disk, wrap tightly in plastic wrap, and refrigerate for 1 hour. Before rolling dough out, let it sit on counter to soften slightly, about 10 minutes. (Dough can be wrapped tightly in plastic and refrigerated for up to 2 days or frozen for up to 1 month. If frozen, let dough thaw completely on counter before rolling it out.)

Free-Form Summer Fruit Tart

✔ **WHY THIS RECIPE WORKS:** For a simple summer fruit tart that's every bit as good as harder-to-prepare pie, we started with a foolproof recipe for free-form tart dough. To keep the delicate dough from breaking, we rolled it out between two sheets of parchment paper, transferred it to a baking sheet, and chilled it until firm. A mix of stone fruits and berries produced an especially nice contrast in flavors and textures. We rolled the dough into a 12-inch circle, which produced a crust that was thick enough to contain a lot of fruit but thin enough to bake evenly. We placed the fruit in the middle, then lifted the dough over the fruit (leaving the center exposed) and pleated it loosely. The bright summer fruit needed only a bit of sugar for enhancement.

Free-Form Summer Fruit Tart
SERVES 6
Taste the fruit before adding sugar; use the lesser amount if the fruit is very sweet, more if it is tart. Do not add the sugar to the fruit until you are ready to fill and form the tart. Serve with Vanilla Ice Cream (page 780) or Whipped Cream (page 709).

- 1 **recipe Free-Form Tart Dough**
- 1 **pound peaches, nectarines, apricots, or plums, halved, pitted, and cut into ½-inch wedges**
- 5 **ounces (1 cup) blackberries, blueberries, or raspberries**
- 5 **tablespoons (2¼ ounces) sugar**

1. Roll dough into 12-inch circle between 2 large sheets of floured parchment paper. (If dough sticks to parchment, gently loosen dough with bench scraper and dust parchment with additional flour.) Slide dough, still between parchment sheets, onto rimmed baking sheet and refrigerate until firm, 15 to 30 minutes.

2. Adjust oven rack to middle position and heat oven to 375 degrees. Gently toss fruit and ¼ cup sugar together in bowl.

3. Remove top sheet of parchment paper from dough. Mound fruit in center of dough, leaving 2½-inch border around edge of fruit. Fold outermost 2 inches of dough over fruit, pleating it every 2 to 3 inches as needed; gently pinch pleated dough to secure, but do not press dough into fruit. Working quickly, brush top and sides of dough with water and sprinkle evenly with remaining 1 tablespoon sugar.

4. Bake until crust is golden brown and fruit is bubbling, about 1 hour, rotating baking sheet halfway through baking. Transfer baking sheet to wire rack and let tart cool for 10 minutes, then use parchment to transfer tart to wire rack. Use large offset or metal spatula to remove tart from parchment. Let tart cool on rack until filling thickens, about 25 minutes; serve slightly warm or at room temperature.

Free-Form Summer Fruit Tartlets

MAKES 4 TARTLETS

Divide dough into 4 equal portions before rolling out in step 1. Roll each portion into 7-inch circle on parchment paper; stack rounds and refrigerate until firm. Continue with step 2, mounding one-quarter of fruit in center of dough round, leaving 1½-inch border around edge. Being careful to leave ¼-inch border of dough around edge of fruit, fold outermost 1 to 1¼ inches of dough over fruit. Transfer parchment with tart to rimmed baking sheet. Repeat with remaining fruit and dough. Brush dough with water and sprinkle each tartlet with portion of remaining 1 tablespoon sugar. Bake until crust is deep golden brown and fruit is bubbling, 40 to 45 minutes, rotating baking sheet halfway through baking.

Free-Form Apple Tart

✔ **WHY THIS RECIPE WORKS:** Four our foolproof free-form tart dough, we rolled it out between two sheets of parchment paper to keep the delicate dough from breaking, transferred everything to a baking sheet, and chilled the dough until firm. A mix of Granny Smith and McIntosh apples gave us a more complex flavor, and just ½ cup of sugar, a squeeze of lemon juice, and a pinch of cinnamon perfected the filling. We stacked the apples in a ring, then filled the ring in with more apples to give the finished tart a neater, fuller appearance. Finally, we just folded and pleated the edge of the dough around the apples before baking the tart until golden brown.

Free-Form Apple Tart

SERVES 6

To prevent the tart from leaking, it is crucial to leave a ½-inch-wide border of dough around the fruit. For more information on arranging the fruit on the dough, see Core Technique on page 726. Serve the tart with Vanilla Ice Cream (page 780) or Whipped Cream (page 709).

1 recipe Free-Form Tart Dough (page 750)
1 pound (2 to 3) Granny Smith apples, peeled, cored, and sliced ¼ inch thick
1 pound (2 to 3) McIntosh apples, peeled, cored, and sliced ¼ inch thick
½ cup (3½ ounces) plus 1 tablespoon sugar
1 tablespoon lemon juice
⅛ teaspoon ground cinnamon

1. Roll dough into 12-inch circle between 2 large sheets of floured parchment paper. (If dough sticks to parchment, gently loosen dough with bench scraper and dust parchment with additional flour.) Slide dough, still between parchment sheets, onto rimmed baking sheet and refrigerate until firm, 15 to 30 minutes.

2. Adjust oven rack to middle position and heat oven to 375 degrees. Toss apples, ½ cup sugar, lemon juice, and cinnamon together in large bowl.

3. Remove top sheet of parchment from dough. Stack some apple slices into circular wall around dough, leaving 2½-inch border of dough around edge of apples. Fill in middle of tart with remaining apples. Fold outermost 2 inches of dough over fruit, pleating it every 2 to 3 inches as needed; gently pinch pleated dough to secure, but do not press dough into fruit. Working quickly, brush top and sides of dough with water and sprinkle dough evenly with remaining 1 tablespoon sugar.

4. Bake until crust is deep golden brown and apples are tender, about 1 hour, rotating baking sheet halfway through baking. Transfer baking sheet to wire rack and let tart cool for 10 minutes, then use parchment to transfer tart to wire rack. Use large offset or metal spatula to remove tart from parchment. Let tart cool on rack until apple juices have thickened, about 25 minutes; serve slightly warm or at room temperature.

Classic Tart Dough

✔ **WHY THIS RECIPE WORKS:** While regular pie crust is tender and flaky, classic tart crust should be fine textured, buttery rich, crisp, and crumbly—it is often described as being shortbread-like. We set out to achieve the perfect tart dough, one that we could use in a number of tart recipes. We found that using a stick of butter made tart dough that tasted great and was easy to handle, yet still had a delicate crumb. Instead of using the hard-to-find superfine sugar and pastry flour that many other recipes call for, we used confectioners' sugar and all-purpose flour to achieve a crisp texture. Rolling the dough and fitting it into the tart pan was easy, and we had ample dough to patch any holes.

Classic Tart Dough

MAKES ENOUGH FOR ONE 9-INCH TART

Tart crust is sweeter, crispier, and less flaky than pie crust—it is more similar in texture to a cookie. See Core Technique on page 728 for more details on this recipe.

1 **large egg yolk**
1 **tablespoon heavy cream**
½ **teaspoon vanilla extract**
1¼ **cups (6¼ ounces) all-purpose flour**
⅔ **cup (2⅔ ounces) confectioners' sugar**
¼ **teaspoon salt**
8 **tablespoons unsalted butter, cut into ¼-inch pieces and chilled**

1. Whisk egg yolk, cream, and vanilla together in small bowl. Process flour, sugar, and salt together in food processor until combined, about 5 seconds. Scatter butter over top and pulse until mixture resembles coarse cornmeal, about 15 pulses. With machine running, add egg mixture and continue to process until dough just comes together around processor blade, about 12 seconds.

2. Turn dough onto sheet of plastic wrap and flatten into 6-inch disk. Wrap tightly and refrigerate for 1 hour. Before rolling dough out, let it sit on counter to soften slightly, about 10 minutes. (Dough can be wrapped tightly in plastic and refrigerated for up to 2 days or frozen for up to 1 month. If frozen, let dough thaw completely on counter before rolling it out.)

3. Roll dough into 11-inch circle on lightly floured counter (if at any point dough becomes too soft and sticky to work with, slip dough onto baking sheet and freeze or refrigerate until workable). Place dough round on baking sheet, cover with plastic, and refrigerate for about 30 minutes.

4. Remove dough from refrigerator; discard plastic but keep dough on baking sheet. Loosely roll dough around rolling pin and gently unroll it onto 9-inch tart pan with removable bottom, letting excess dough hang over edge. Ease dough into pan by gently lifting edge of dough with 1 hand while pressing into corners with other hand. Leave any dough that overhangs pan in place.

5. Press dough into fluted sides of pan, forming distinct seam around pan's circumference. (If some sections of edge are too thin, reinforce them by folding excess dough back on itself.) Run rolling pin over top of tart pan to remove any excess dough. Wrap dough-lined tart pan loosely in plastic, place on large plate, and freeze until dough is fully chilled and firm, about 30 minutes. (Dough-lined tart pan can be wrapped tightly in plastic and frozen for up to 1 month.)

6. Adjust oven rack to middle position and heat oven to 375 degrees. Set dough-lined tart pan on rimmed baking sheet. Press double layer of aluminum foil over frozen dough, covering edges to prevent burning, and fill with pie weights.

7A. FOR A PARTIALLY BAKED SHELL: Bake until tart shell is golden and set, about 30 minutes, rotating baking sheet halfway through baking. Transfer tart shell with baking sheet to wire rack and carefully remove weights and foil. Use crust while it is still warm or let it cool completely (see individual tart recipe instructions).

7B. FOR A FULLY BAKED SHELL: Bake until tart shell is golden and set, about 30 minutes, rotating baking sheet halfway through baking. Carefully remove weights and foil and continue to bake tart shell until it is fully baked and golden brown, 5 to 10 minutes longer. Transfer tart shell with baking sheet to wire rack and let it cool completely, about 1 hour.

Classic Chocolate Tart Dough

Substitute ¼ cup Dutch-processed cocoa for ¼ cup flour.

Classic Fresh Fruit Tart

✔ **WHY THIS RECIPE WORKS:** Fresh fruit tarts usually offer little substance beyond their dazzling beauty: rubbery or puddinglike fillings, soggy crusts, and underripe, flavorless fruit. We set out to create a buttery, crisp crust filled with rich, lightly sweetened pastry cream and topped with fresh fruit. We started with our Classic Tart Dough and baked it until it was golden brown. We then filled the tart with pastry cream made with half-and-half that was enriched with butter and thickened with just enough cornstarch to keep its shape without becoming gummy. For the fruit, we chose a combination of sliced kiwis, raspberries, and blueberries. We found that it was important not to wash the berries, as washing causes them to bruise and bleed and makes for a less than attractive tart. (Buy organic if you're worried about pesticide residues.) The finishing touch: a drizzle of jelly glaze for a glistening presentation.

Classic Fresh Fruit Tart

SERVES 8 TO 10

Do not fill the prebaked tart shell until just before serving. Once filled, the tart should be topped with fruit, glazed, and served within 30 minutes or so. Don't wash the berries or they will lose their flavor and shape. See Recipe Tutorial on page 738 for more details on this recipe.

PASTRY CREAM
2 **cups half-and-half**
½ **cup (3½ ounces) sugar**
Pinch salt
5 **large egg yolks**
3 **tablespoons cornstarch**
4 **tablespoons unsalted butter, cut into 4 pieces**
1½ **teaspoons vanilla extract**

1 **recipe Classic Tart Dough (page 751), fully baked and cooled**

FRUIT
2 **large kiwis, peeled, halved lengthwise, and sliced ⅜ inch thick**
10 **ounces (2 cups) raspberries**
5 **ounces (1 cup) blueberries**
½ **cup red currant or apple jelly**

1. FOR THE PASTRY CREAM: Bring half-and-half, 6 tablespoons sugar, and salt to simmer in medium saucepan, stirring occasionally.

2. As half-and-half mixture begins to simmer, whisk egg yolks, cornstarch, and remaining 2 tablespoons sugar together in medium bowl until smooth. Slowly whisk 1 cup simmering half-and-half mixture into yolk mixture to temper, then slowly whisk tempered yolk mixture back into remaining half-and-half mixture. Reduce heat to medium and cook, whisking vigorously, until mixture is thickened and few bubbles burst on surface, about 30 seconds. Off heat, whisk in butter and vanilla. Transfer mixture to clean bowl, lay sheet of plastic wrap directly on surface, and refrigerate pastry cream until chilled and firm, about 3 hours. (Pastry cream can be refrigerated for up to 2 days.)

3. TO ASSEMBLE: Spread chilled pastry cream evenly over bottom of cooled prebaked tart shell. Shingle kiwi slices around edge of tart, then arrange 3 rows of raspberries inside kiwi. Finally, arrange mound of blueberries in center.

4. Melt jelly in small saucepan over medium-high heat, stirring occasionally to smooth out any lumps. Using pastry brush, dab melted jelly over fruit. To serve, remove outer metal ring of tart pan, slide large offset spatula between tart and tart pan bottom, and carefully slide tart onto serving platter or cutting board.

Mixed Berry Tart with Pastry Cream

Omit kiwi and add 10 ounces extra berries (including blackberries or hulled and quartered strawberries). Combine berries in large plastic bag and toss them gently to mix. Carefully spread berries in even layer over tart. Glaze and serve as directed.

Lemon Tart

✓ **WHY THIS RECIPE WORKS:** Despite its apparent simplicity, there is much that can go wrong with a lemon tart. It can slip over the edge of sweet into cloying; its tartness can grab at your throat; it can be gluey or eggy or, even worse, metallic tasting. Its crust can be too hard, too soft, too thick, or too sweet. We wanted a proper tart, one in which the filling is baked with the shell. For us, that meant only one thing: lemon curd. For just enough sugar to offset the acid in the lemons, we used 3 parts sugar to 2 parts lemon juice, plus a whopping ¼ cup of lemon zest. To achieve a curd that was creamy and dense with a vibrant lemony yellow color, we used a combination of whole eggs and egg yolks. We cooked the curd over direct heat and then whisked in the butter. And for a smooth, light texture, we strained the curd and then stirred in heavy cream just before baking.

Classic Lemon Tart
SERVES 8 TO 10

Once the lemon curd ingredients have been combined, cook the curd immediately; otherwise it will have a grainy finished texture. The shell should still be warm when the filling is added. We dust the tart with confectioners' sugar before serving; you can also serve it with Whipped Cream (page 709).

2   **large eggs plus 7 large yolks**
1   **cup (7 ounces) sugar**
¼   **cup grated lemon zest plus ⅔ cup juice (4 lemons)**
    Pinch salt
4   **tablespoons unsalted butter, cut into 4 pieces**
3   **tablespoons heavy cream**
1   **recipe Classic Tart Dough (page 751), partially baked and still warm**
    Confectioners' sugar

1. Adjust oven rack to middle position and heat oven to 375 degrees. Whisk eggs and yolks together in medium saucepan. Whisk in sugar until combined, then whisk in lemon zest and juice and salt. Add butter and cook over medium-low heat, stirring constantly, until mixture thickens slightly and registers 170 degrees, about 5 minutes. Immediately pour mixture through fine-mesh strainer into bowl and stir in cream.

2. Pour warm lemon filling into tart shell. Bake tart on baking sheet until filling is shiny and opaque and center jiggles slightly when shaken, 10 to 15 minutes, rotating baking sheet halfway through baking. Transfer tart with baking sheet to wire rack and let cool to room temperature, about 2 hours. To serve, remove outer metal ring of tart pan, slide large offset spatula between tart and tart pan bottom, and carefully slide tart onto serving platter or cutting board and dust with confectioners' sugar.

Chocolate Truffle Tart

✓ **WHY THIS RECIPE WORKS:** For an easy-to-make chocolate tart with a silky texture and a dense, slightly bitter flavor, we discovered that a simple ganache—dense to a fault and creamy—made a great start. Adding butter gave it an optimally smooth texture. We opted not to add vanilla since it undercut the robust chocolate flavor—but we found that cognac emphasized the chocolate flavor. Incorporating cocoa into our Classic Tart Dough (page 751), gave us a rich foundation for the filling.

Chocolate Truffle Tart
SERVES 8 TO 10

Brandy or Grand Marnier may be substituted for the cognac. This tart is extremely rich and is best served with fresh berries and unsweetened whipped cream.

1   **cup heavy cream**
12   **ounces bittersweet chocolate, chopped fine**
6   **tablespoons unsalted butter, softened**
1   **tablespoon cognac**
1   **recipe Classic Chocolate Tart Dough (page 752), fully baked and cooled**

1. Bring cream to brief simmer in small saucepan over medium-high heat. Off heat, stir in chocolate and butter, cover pan, and let stand until chocolate is mostly melted, about 2 minutes. Gently stir mixture until smooth, then stir in cognac.

2. Pour filling into tart shell and refrigerate tart, uncovered, until filling is firm, about 2 hours. To serve, remove outer metal ring of tart pan, slide large offset spatula between tart and tart pan bottom, and carefully slide tart onto serving platter or cutting board.

Espresso Truffle Tart

Omit cognac and add 2 teaspoons instant espresso powder or instant coffee powder to hot cream with chocolate.

Peanut Butter Truffle Tart

Spread ½ cup smooth peanut butter over bottom of tart shell and refrigerate while preparing chocolate filling. Smooth chocolate filling over peanut butter and chill as directed.

Inside This Chapter

CHAPTER 18

How to Make Custards, Puddings, and Frozen Desserts

Although puddings, custards, and frozen desserts usually require only a few basic ingredients, they often cause an undeserved amount of anxiety. Perhaps because many of these recipes (think crème brûlée, panna cotta) are restaurant classics, with an aura of mystery attached. In this chapter we demystify such recipes. You'll learn how to make a water bath, prepare a basic custard, then walk through several classic custard-based recipes. Also see our fruit tart tutorial (page 738), where we prepare pastry cream. In addition, see chapter 2 for details on separating eggs as well as sweet soufflé recipes.

Getting Started

Tips for Successful Puddings, Custards, and Frozen Desserts

For most of the recipes in this chapter, the difference between success and failure is largely a matter of paying attention to simple details such as cooking, cooling, chilling times, and the temperature of the custard. Here are a few tips.

PREVENT DAIRY BOILOVERS

Of all liquids, milk has the greatest tendency to boil over, so this is a particular hazard when making custard-based desserts that require scalding or boiling milk or cream. Milk and cream contain casein proteins, which gather near the surface as they heat. Once the milk or cream comes to a boil, steam bubbles rising from the bottom are forced through the protein-rich layer at the top. The proteins stabilize the bubbles, keeping them from bursting, so they rapidly increase in number. The simple solution is to heat dairy in a big, wide pan.

FOLLOW VISUAL CUES AND USE A THERMOMETER

For many custards and sauces, we provide both a visual cue—like "the custard will coat the back of a wooden spoon"—and a temperature; these should eliminate any anxiety about when to take the custard off the heat and will help you avoid overcooking. Also, we provide a doneness temperature for some recipes, which is a clearer signal than deciding how to interpret visual cues like "until centers are barely set."

TILT THE PAN TO CHECK THE TEMPERATURE OF SHALLOW CUSTARDS OR SAUCES

Need to check the temperature of a custard or caramel sauce but there isn't much volume in the pan? Simply tilt the pan to use your instant-read thermometer properly and to avoid having the stem touch the bottom of the hot pan.

FIX BROKEN CUSTARDS

Lumps can form if a custard becomes overheated. You may think it's a lost cause, but there is a simple fix. If you notice lumps beginning to form, immediately pour the custard out of the pot and into a bowl. Pulse it with a hand-held immersion blender in 5-second intervals until it's nearly smooth. Be careful not to overprocess or you will end up with irreparably thin, watery custard. Pour the blended liquid through a fine-mesh strainer to remove any remaining lumps and continue with the recipe. Don't use a blender or food processor; they incorporate too much air and will leave the mixture frothy.

AVOID WATER BATH DISASTERS

Many custard recipes require a water bath, which allows the custards to cook more evenly and slowly, delivering creamy not overcooked, results. Don't add boiling water to a panful of custard-filled ramekins and then attempt to place that pan in the oven. Instead, place the roasting pan on an oven rack, and then pull it out to give you just enough room to maneuver a teakettle of boiling water around the ramekins without splashing water into the custards.

Once the custards are baked, there are a couple of ways to remove the ramekins from the water bath. For fairly small ramekins, tongs will suffice, especially if they are rubber tipped for a sure grip (if not, you can improvise by wrapping a rubber band around each tip). Canning tongs, which are designed to curve around jars, will also do the trick. Alternately, use both tongs (to lift) and a wide spatula (to transfer) the ramekins out of the water bath.

KNOW WHEN CUSTARD IS DONE

Egg-based puddings and custards can curdle if cooked beyond 185 degrees. We take crème anglaise off the heat when the mixture registers 175 degrees, but when making the base for ice cream we push the temperature to 180 for maximum thickness. When done, baked custards such as flan and crème brûlée should jiggle (but not slosh) when gently shaken. This will occur between 170 and 175 degrees. For some custard desserts, such as crème caramel, you will know they are done when a paring knife slipped in halfway between the center and edge comes out clean.

Essential Ingredients

Custards are by definition dairy- and egg-based. See page 40 for details about dairy products, and pages 48–49 for extensive information about buying and storing eggs.

Vanilla, in either bean or extract form, is used in numerous custards, puddings, and frozen desserts. For recipes such as crème brûlée, where the flavor of vanilla is key, we opt to use beans, as they provide a fuller aroma and more complex flavor than extract. Using both the pod and its seeds is key to maximizing the vanilla flavor; typically we steep the pod (along with the seeds) in warm dairy, then remove it before continuing with the recipe. Be sure to use fresh, plump pods for the best results. The beans should be moist and have a bit of sheen to them; avoid those that look like dried, shriveled twigs.

Extract is available in two styles: pure (natural) and imitation. Both are flavored with the compound vanillin, but natural vanillin is derived from vanilla beans whereas imitation vanillin is chemically extracted from wood pulp or cloves. For baked goods, like muffins and cakes, it's actually hard to tell a difference between real and imitation, but for custards you should use only pure vanilla extract. Vanilla extract will last indefinitely as long as you store it in a sealed container away from heat and light.

Essential Equipment

There are several pieces of equipment that you will use time and again when making custards, puddings, and frozen desserts.

HEAVY-BOTTOMED SAUCEPAN

Investing in a high-quality, heavy-bottomed saucepan with a tight-fitting lid is key if you are going to make puddings, sauces like caramel, or custards (including custard-style ice creams). Ideally, keep both a 3- and a 4-quart saucepan. For more details on what to look for, see page 20.

FINE-MESH STRAINER

A fine-mesh strainer that is at least 6 inches in diameter is a must when it comes to removing any lumps to ensure a smooth custard. For more details on what to look for, see page 31.

INSTANT-READ THERMOMETER

Since timing is critical to many of these recipes, and judging doneness is not always easy, an instant-read thermometer provides peace of mind that you are taking the custard off the stovetop or out of the oven at just the right time. A digital display and the capability of giving a reading in less than 10 seconds are key. For more details on what to look for, see page 10.

WHISK

A good all-purpose whisk that will reach into the corners of a saucepan is key; you will need it to beat eggs and to keep sauces, custards, and puddings smooth during cooking. For more details on what to look for, see page 31.

RUBBER SPATULA

A rubber spatula will allow you to delicately fold beaten egg whites into a base of chocolate to make a light and airy chocolate mousse and to scrape every bit of custard out of a saucepan—make sure to buy a sturdy, heat-resistant spatula as it will be far more versatile. For more details on what to look for, see page 31.

WOODEN SPOON

When making a custard, the best visual cue that it's done is when the custard has thickened enough that it coats the back of a wooden spoon. Look for a spoon that has a slim but broad bowl and a comfortable handle. While stain resistance is not critical when making a custard, it's an asset when you use the spoon to stir tomato sauce.

MINI BUTANE KITCHEN TORCH

While not an essential tool for making most custards, a kitchen torch is a must when making crème brûlée. We have found using one is the best way to effectively caramelize the sugar topping (running the custards under the broiler doesn't work very well). You can find them at specialty kitchen stores and sometimes at hardware stores.

RAMEKINS

Many puddings and custards are prepared as individual portions and require ramekins of different sizes, ranging from 4 to 6 ounces. For an all-purpose set, look for ramekins with a capacity of 6 ounces and a diameter of 3 inches, though for some of the recipes in this chapter you will want smaller ramekins. Also, it is best to look for ramekins made of high-fired porcelain (chip resistant) and those that are safe for use in the oven, broiler, microwave, and dishwasher. Small, shallow, fluted ramekins are the best choice when making crème brûlée (because they provide more surface area for the caramelized topping), though you can also use round ramekins. Note that these ramekins come in various sizes. If you use the larger, 6- to 9-ounce ramekins, you will not be able to fit eight of them in a roasting pan (see below) at one time and will instead have to cook your custards in batches.

ROASTING PAN

Roasting pans aren't just for roasts. We find a large, sturdy roasting pan is the perfect vessel for water baths, which are essential for gently cooking custards. For more details on what to look for, see page 21.

ICE CREAM MACHINE

Home ice cream machines fall into two types: pricey self-refrigerating models that let you make batch after batch, or less-expensive models with removable coolant-lined canisters that must be refrozen (usually overnight) each time. Both work well, but the canister-style models take longer to make denser (as opposed to airy) ice cream. Self-refrigerating models, on the other hand, immediately produce firmer, ready-to-serve frozen treats.

How to Make Crème Anglaise

ESSENTIAL EQUIPMENT

- paring knife
- medium heavy-bottomed saucepan
- mixing bowls
- whisk
- liquid measuring cup
- instant-read thermometer
- wooden spoon
- fine-mesh strainer

Crème anglaise is a luxurious, pourable custard that enhances fresh fruit, cakes, and many other desserts. Once you learn to make this, you will be on your way to mastering techniques involved in making the base of creamy desserts like *pots de crème*, crème brûlée, crème caramel, and ice cream.

Crème anglaise relies on the thickening power of egg yolks when they are heated. But warming yolks is tricky business—go too far and they coagulate and form clumps that can mar the texture of creamy custards. The eggs are basically being scrambled when they are overheated. To prevent this, you must first temper the yolks by adding a portion of the heated milk mixture to them. Tempering gradually warms the yolks so that they will be able to withstand the cooking process. Once the tempered yolks are poured into the pan, constant whisking helps eliminate the chance of curdling, while straining the cooked mixture provides insurance that this sauce will be silky smooth when drizzled over cake, fruit, or anything else. Also see How to Crack and Separate Eggs (page 50). You can refrigerate crème anglaise in an airtight container for up to two days.

1–2. REMOVE SEEDS FROM HALF OF VANILLA BEAN

Using paring knife, cut vanilla bean in half crosswise, then slice one half in half lengthwise (save other half for another use). Carefully scrape seeds from pod using tip of paring knife.

WHY? For recipes where the flavor of vanilla is important, we've found that beans impart deeper flavor than extract. Using both the seeds (there are thousands inside the average vanilla bean) and the pod delivers the most vanilla flavor, along with warm caramel notes. Be sure to use a fresh, plump vanilla pod for the best results.

3. STEEP VANILLA IN MILK

Combine scraped vanilla pod and seeds, 1½ cups whole milk, and pinch salt in medium heavy-bottomed saucepan. Bring to simmer over medium-high heat, stirring occasionally.

WHY? Steeping a scraped vanilla pod along with the seeds in hot milk releases additional flavor compounds that give subtle but noticeable vanilla flavor to the custard. Vanilla extract does not deliver the same flavor.

4. COMBINE EGG YOLKS AND SUGAR

In bowl, whisk 5 large egg yolks and ¼ cup sugar together until smooth.

WHY? You need to whisk the egg yolks and sugar vigorously to ensure that the sugar is fully dissolved. Whisk until the yolks are a pale shade of yellow. You can do this step while the milk mixture is coming to a simmer.

5. TEMPER EGG YOLK MIXTURE

Whisk 1 cup simmering milk mixture into egg yolk mixture to temper.

WHY? We heat the eggs very gently with a portion of the hot milk mixture to slow the rate of cooking; this is known as tempering and ensures that when the egg yolk mixture is then added to the rest of the hot milk mixture, the eggs will not curdle. It is absolutely essential to whisk constantly when tempering the egg yolk mixture, so that the hot milk mixture does not scramble the egg yolks. Specks of egg yolk in this otherwise cream-colored sauce are not only visually unappealing, but they also prevent the sauce from thickening properly. Since pouring the liquid straight from the saucepan could get messy, we use a liquid measuring cup to remove a portion and pour it into the egg yolk mixture.

6. ADD TEMPERED EGGS TO SAUCEPAN

Slowly whisk yolk mixture into heated milk mixture.

WHY? Slowly whisking the tempered egg yolk mixture into the hot milk mixture helps ensure a smooth, silky custard sauce. Here, and throughout the cooking process, it is essential to whisk constantly so that the hot liquid does not scramble the eggs.

7A–7B. JUDGE DONENESS BY TEMPERATURE AND CONSISTENCY

Continue to cook sauce, whisking constantly, until it thickens slightly and coats back of wooden spoon, about 6 minutes; sauce should register 175 degrees on instant-read thermometer.

WHY? To determine when to take the sauce off the heat, it is helpful to be able to judge doneness visually and also by temperature (which is foolproof). When done, the sauce should coat the back of the spoon. When using an instant-read thermometer, make sure the probe doesn't touch the sides or bottom of the pan, which will throw off the reading.

8. STRAIN SAUCE

Immediately strain sauce through fine-mesh strainer into medium bowl; discard vanilla bean. Cover and refrigerate until cool, about 30 minutes. Serve chilled.

WHY? Straining ensures that there are no lumps and that the final sauce is silky smooth.

HOW TO MAKE CUSTARDS, PUDDINGS, AND FROZEN DESSERTS

How to Make Crème Brûlée

ESSENTIAL EQUIPMENT

- medium heavy-bottomed saucepan
- large mixing bowl
- whisk
- fine-mesh strainer
- large glass measuring cup
- dish towel
- large roasting pan
- eight (4- or 5-ounce) ramekins
- teakettle
- rimmed baking sheet
- paper towels
- small butane kitchen torch

With its paper-thin film of burnt sugar atop creamy custard, crème brûlée reigns as perhaps the ultimate baked custard. And while making it is not particularly hard, it does demand attention to details. Making the base follows the same process used to make crème anglaise, where the trick is to avoid curdling the eggs by tempering them. Then the custards are baked at a low temperature, which further combats the risk of curdling. And perhaps most important, they require a water bath, or bain-marie (typical of many baked custards). We bake the custard-filled ramekins in a roasting pan with enough water added to come two-thirds of the way up the sides. Since the water never reaches more than 212 degrees, it moderates the temperature around the perimeter of the custards and prevents overcooking. For variations on this recipe, see page 778. Also see How to Crack and Separate Eggs (page 50) and How to Make Crème Anglaise (page 758).

1. STEEP VANILLA IN CREAM

Scrape seeds from 1 halved vanilla bean. Bring 2 cups heavy cream, ⅔ cup granulated sugar, vanilla bean and seeds, and pinch salt to boil in medium heavy-bottomed saucepan, stirring occasionally to dissolve sugar. Remove pan from heat, cover, and let steep for 15 minutes.

WHY? Heavy cream makes a custard that is thick and luxurious, while half-and-half and whipping cream do not. Steeping is important in order to extract the full flavor from the vanilla bean.

2. MAKE CUSTARD AND STRAIN

Stir 2 cups heavy cream into warm cream mixture. Place 10 large egg yolks in large bowl and whisk until uniform. Slowly whisk in 1 cup warm cream mixture until smooth. Repeat with 1 more cup cream mixture. Whisk in remaining cream mixture, then strain custard through fine-mesh strainer into large liquid measuring cup.

WHY? Using egg yolks alone delivers the right creamy texture; whole eggs would yield a much firmer custard, like crème caramel. Whisking the warm cream mixture into the eggs 1 cup at a time at first tempers the yolks, ensuring that they do not curdle. Straining the custard prevents bits of undissolved egg from winding up in the finished custard and marring its smooth, silky texture.

3. SET UP AND FILL RAMEKINS

Place dish towel in bottom of large roasting pan and arrange eight 4- or 5-ounce ramekins on towel (they should not touch). Bring kettle of water to boil. Divide custard evenly among ramekins.

WHY? Lining the roasting pan with a towel protects the bottom of the ramekins from the heat of the pan and also helps keep them in place. (You can set this up while the cream is steeping.) Filling the ramekins after they are in the pan is much easier than moving them after they are filled. Note that if you use larger ramekins, you may need to cook the custards in two batches.

4. BAKE CUSTARDS IN WATER BATH

Place roasting pan on lower-middle rack of oven preheated to 300 degrees. Carefully pour enough boiling water into pan to reach two-thirds up sides of ramekins. Bake custards until centers are just barely set and register 170 to 175 degrees, 30 to 35 minutes (25 to 30 minutes for shallow fluted dishes).

WHY? A water bath ensures even cooking and prevents overcooking at the edges. Pouring the boiling water into the pan while the pan is on the oven rack helps eliminate the risk of accidentally splashing water into the custards. A low oven slows the rate of cooking, which means the window of time when the dessert is perfectly cooked is larger. Start checking the custards about 5 minutes before the recommended minimum time to ensure they don't overcook.

5. COOL, CHILL, THEN BLOT DRY

Remove custards from water bath and place on wire rack. Let cool to room temperature, about 2 hours. Set ramekins on baking sheet, cover tightly with plastic wrap, and refrigerate until cold, at least 4 hours. Gently blot tops dry with paper towels.

WHY? Don't leave the custards in the water bath—they will continue to cook and can curdle. As soon as the custards are done they must be transferred to a wire rack. Using tongs and a spatula makes the transfer secure; canning tongs can also work with round ramekins. Don't worry if the custards seem loose; they continue to set as they cool. After they reach room temperature, refrigerate them to chill them thoroughly before caramelizing the tops. Some water droplets will form on the tops of the custards during refrigeration. It's essential to blot them dry or else the sugar will dissolve and not caramelize properly.

6. BRÛLÉE CUSTARDS

Sprinkle each ramekin with 1 to 1½ teaspoons turbinado sugar, then tap ramekin to spread sugar in even layer. Ignite torch and sweep flame from perimeter of custard toward middle, keeping flame about 2 inches above ramekin. Refrigerate custards, uncovered, for 30 to 45 minutes.

WHY? To achieve a crackly crust, we use turbinado or Demerara sugar. They are better than brown sugar, which is moist and lumpy, and granulated sugar, which can be hard to distribute evenly. If you use wide, shallow ramekins, you will need more sugar to cover the surface area of the custards than if you use narrower, deeper ramekins. We like to refrigerate the custards to rechill them before serving. But keep in mind that after 45 minutes the topping will start to break down—don't caramelize the sugar too far in advance.

How to Make Caramel Sauce

ESSENTIAL EQUIPMENT

• liquid measuring cup
• medium heavy-bottomed saucepan with lid
• rubber spatula
• pastry brush
• instant-read thermometer
• whisk

Caramel sauce is a great partner for many custard-based desserts. It is also a component in recipes like flan, crème caramel, and toffee pudding cake. Depending on the application, caramel recipes might add more or less water, or finish with butter or extra ingredients (like rum), but the basic technique is generally the same.

Note that you are in fact burning the sugar, so there's little room for error in this recipe. Make sure to use a fairly large saucepan (with a capacity of at least 3 quarts) and remember that hot caramel sauce will cause nasty burns, so keep your hands and face at a safe distance, particularly when adding the cream, at which point the caramel will sputter quite a bit. A light-colored saucepan makes it easier to track the color of the caramel. When the sauce has a medium amber color similar to honey, or a tad darker, it is done. Of course, an instant-read thermometer is essential for true precision. Note that caramel cooked to 360 degrees will have more bitter notes than caramel cooked to 350 degrees. Also see the tutorial for Individual Sticky Toffee Pudding Cakes (page 766).

1. MELT SUGAR CAREFULLY

Pour ½ cup water into heavy-bottomed 3-quart saucepan. Pour 1 cup sugar into center of pan; do not let granules touch sides of pan. Gently stir with clean spatula to moisten sugar thoroughly.
WHY? If the sugar sticks to the sides of the pan it will eventually cause the caramel to crystallize and ruin the sauce. If you see any crystals sticking to the sides of the pan, brush them back into the water with a wet pastry brush.

2. DON'T STIR, AT FIRST

Cover pan and bring to boil over medium-high heat. Cook, without stirring, until sugar is dissolved and liquid is clear, 3 to 5 minutes. Uncover and cook, without stirring, until liquid has faint golden color, another 3 to 5 minutes.
WHY? The sugar is most likely to crystallize during this first part of the process. These crystals can be caused by a combination of undissolved sugar granules and other foreign bits that have fallen into the syrup, as well as agitation. By not stirring, you reduce agitation. The lid keeps foreign matter out and helps dissolve the sugar.

3. GO SLOWLY

As soon as liquid starts to change color, reduce heat to medium-low. Continue to cook, swirling contents occasionally, until caramel is medium amber color and registers 350 to 360 degrees on instant-read thermometer, 1 to 2 minutes.
WHY? Caramel cooks quickly; it's imperative to lower the heat once the caramel starts to color. Swirling the pot distributes the heat and ensures that the caramel on the bottom isn't burning.

4. TAKE POT OFF HEAT, ADD CREAM SLOWLY

Remove pan from heat and whisk in 1 cup cream. Stir in ½ teaspoon vanilla and ⅛ teaspoon salt. For richer sauce, add 2 tablespoons butter.
WHY? The cold cream halts the caramelization process. Adding the cream slowly minimizes the sputtering. The vanilla and salt add complexity. For a glossier sauce, add the butter as well.

RECIPE TUTORIAL

GETTING STARTED
CORE TECHNIQUES
CUSTARDS, PUDDINGS, AND FROZEN DESSERTS | RECIPE TUTORIALS
RECIPE LIBRARY

763

Dark Chocolate Mousse

Overview

Chocolate mousse makes a decadent ending to a special meal—but only when all the ingredients are working in harmony. It doesn't help that this dish can suffer from a bit of an identity crisis, as the name seems to get assigned to just about any creamy chocolate dessert served up in a ramekin or glass bowl. A true chocolate mousse should not be sweet like ganache but rather light and airy with a deep chocolate flavor. Working our way through the gamut of chocolate mousse recipes, we learned that the same few ingredients (chocolate, eggs, sugar, and fat) could produce a wide range of results. Proportion and handling were all that separated thick ganache from fluffy pudding. Our ideal mousse falls somewhere in between these two extremes.

We use bittersweet chocolate—a full 8 ounces—because its higher percentage of cocoa solids provides the most complex flavor. And to ramp up the chocolate flavor without destroying the texture of the mousse, we add 2 tablespoons cocoa powder and a little instant espresso powder. To avoid an overly heavy mousse, we omit the butter that most recipes call for. Whipped egg whites folded into the melted chocolate mixture provide the requisite lightness, but we found cutting back on the eggs—both whites and yolks—also helps to keep our recipe light. Whipping heavy cream and folding it in at the end adds richness and airy volume at the same time.

For variations on this recipe, see page 775. Note that you can make the mousse in advance; simply refrigerate it, covered, for up to 24 hours. Let the mousse sit out at room temperature for 10 minutes before serving. Before you begin, see How to Crack and Separate Eggs on page 50, How to Chop and Melt Chocolate on page 586, and How to Whip Egg Whites on page 51.

Recipe Stats

TOTAL TIME **2½ hours**
PREPARATION TIME **30 minutes**
ACTIVE COOKING TIME **5 minutes**
YIELD **6 to 8 servings**
MAKE AHEAD **Refrigerate for up to 1 day**
DIFFICULTY **Easy**

Tools

- tall, narrow saucepan
- stand mixer *
- chef's knife
- cutting board
- liquid measuring cups
- measuring spoons
- medium heatproof bowl
- mixing bowls
- individual serving dishes (6 to 8)
- rubber spatula
- wooden spoon
- whisk
- plastic wrap

* You can use a hand-held mixer in this recipe, but mixing times may vary slightly.

Ingredients

- 8 **ounces bittersweet chocolate, chopped fine** *
- 5 **tablespoons water**
- 2 **tablespoons Dutch-processed cocoa powder**
- 1 **tablespoon brandy**
- 1 **teaspoon instant espresso powder**
- 2 **large eggs, separated**
- 1 **tablespoon sugar**
- ⅛ **teaspoon salt**
- 1 **cup plus 2 tablespoons heavy cream, chilled**

* When developing this recipe, we used Callebaut Intense Dark Chocolate and Ghirardelli Bittersweet Chocolate Baking Bar, which each contain about 60 percent cacao. If you want to use a chocolate with a higher percentage of cacao, see our recipe for Premium Dark Chocolate Mousse on page 775.

What Can Go Wrong

Here's a list of common mistakes cooks make when preparing this recipe.

COMMON MISTAKE	BAD OUTCOMES	WHAT YOU SHOULD DO
Using Semisweet Chocolate	• The mousse has weak chocolate flavor. • The mousse is overly sweet.	We found that mousse made with semisweet chocolate was overly sweet and one-dimensional. Bittersweet chocolate, because it has a higher percentage of cocoa solids, provides the more complex flavor this dish demands.
Using "Extra-Bitter" or Unsweetened Chocolate	• The mousse is grainy and starchy.	Different brands of bittersweet chocolate have different levels of cacao. The brands we used to develop this recipe, Ghirardelli Bittersweet and Callebaut Intense Dark Chocolate, contain about 60 percent cacao. Some high-end brands have 62 to 70 percent cacao, and substituting these inherently starchier, less sweet chocolates will result in a stiffer mousse.
Not Melting Chocolate Properly	• The chocolate burns. • The chocolate seizes, turning grainy and lumpy.	The first step in this recipe is melting the chocolate along with water, brandy, cocoa, and instant espresso. Heating chocolate is tricky and requires your full attention because it can go from velvety smooth to scorched or grainy and lumpy very quickly. That is why heating it in a heatproof bowl over just simmering water is the most foolproof and gentle way to melt it. Don't try melting it directly in a saucepan, as the chocolate will be far more likely to scorch. Heating chocolate with liquids help to prevent seizing, so don't be tempted to put the chocolate over the heat before you've added the brandy and water to the bowl too.
Beating Egg Whites to Stiff Peaks	• The mousse does not have the right texture. • Folding the egg whites into the chocolate mixture is very difficult.	You want a soft and creamy mousse with just the right amount of lightness. If you beat the egg whites too long they will give the mousse a fluffy, rather than a light and creamy, texture. To ensure you don't overbeat the egg whites, beat them just until soft peaks form and then detach the whisk and bowl from the mixer and whisk the last few strokes by hand, making sure to scrape any unbeaten whites from the bottom of the bowl.
Improperly Folding Egg Whites into Chocolate Mixture	• The mousse is not light and airy.	After you have whipped the egg whites, you need to stir a small portion of them into the chocolate mixture to lighten it. Then you must fold in the remaining egg whites—very gently—using a rubber spatula. If you fold too much, or if you stir at this point rather than fold, you will beat the air out of the whites and they won't provide the right amount of lift to the mousse.

1. Using chef's knife, finely chop 8 ounces bittersweet chocolate. Transfer to medium heatproof bowl.

2. Add 5 tablespoons water, 2 tablespoons Dutch-processed cocoa powder, 1 tablespoon brandy, and 1 teaspoon instant espresso powder.

3. Place bowl over saucepan filled with 1 inch barely simmering water, stirring frequently until smooth. Remove from heat.

4. Whisk 2 large egg yolks, 1½ teaspoons sugar, and ⅛ teaspoon salt in bowl until mixture lightens in color and thickens slightly, about 30 seconds.

5. Pour melted chocolate mixture into egg yolk mixture and whisk until combined; let cool until just warmer than room temperature, 3 to 5 minutes.

6. Using stand mixer fitted with whisk, whip 2 large egg whites at medium-low speed until foamy, about 1 minute.

7. Add 1½ teaspoons sugar, increase speed to medium-high, and whip until soft peaks form, about 1 minute.

8. Using whisk, stir one-quarter of egg whites into chocolate mixture. Using rubber spatula, fold in remaining egg whites until few white streaks remain.

9. In now-empty mixer bowl, whip 1 cup plus 2 tablespoons chilled heavy cream on medium speed until it begins to thicken, about 30 seconds.

10. Increase speed to high and whip until soft peaks form, about 15 seconds more.

11. Using rubber spatula, fold whipped cream into mousse until no white streaks remain; spoon mousse into 6 to 8 individual serving dishes.

12. Cover with plastic wrap and refrigerate until set and firm, at least 2 hours or up to 24 hours. Serve.

HOW TO MAKE CUSTARDS, PUDDINGS, AND FROZEN DESSERTS

Individual Sticky Toffee Pudding Cakes

Overview

Sticky toffee pudding is a sophisticated, richly flavored, grown-up dessert with roots in the Anglo culinary past. It has come into favor stateside in recent years, and no wonder. These moist, rich, buttery cakes are studded with dates and drizzled with a warm toffee sauce made with brown sugar, cream, butter, and rum. Sure, there are a few steps involved but none of them are hard. You can make a large sticky toffee pudding cake, but there is something special and more elegant about these individual cakes.

Our recipe showcases the fruity flavor of the dates while keeping the overall sweetness of the cakes in check. For ultimate fruit flavor, we start by soaking half of the sliced dates in water, adding baking soda to the water to help soften them. Then we process the remaining dates with brown sugar until finely ground so that they lend flavor to the batter but don't interfere with its texture. Adding the soaking liquid to the batter instead of water boosts the flavor even more. Stirring the soaked pieces of dates into the batter just before baking the cakes ensures noticeable bites of fruit throughout.

Note that you can make portions of this recipe in advance. Prepare the batter and divide it among individual ramekins, cover, and refrigerate, unbaked, for up to one day, then bake as directed. The sauce can be made up to two days in advance and refrigerated; microwave on 50 percent power, stirring often, until hot, about 3 minutes.

Recipe Stats

TOTAL TIME **2 hours**
PREPARATION TIME **15 minutes**
ACTIVE COOKING TIME **45 minutes**
YIELD **Serves 8**
MAKE AHEAD **Cake batter can be refrigerated for up to 1 day; sauce can be refrigerated for up to 2 days**
DIFFICULTY **Intermediate**

Tools

- 4-ounce ramekins (8)
- large roasting pan
- medium heavy-bottomed saucepan
- food processor
- chef's knife
- cutting board
- dry measuring cups
- liquid measuring cup
- measuring spoons
- citrus juicer
- dish towel
- fine-mesh strainer
- ladle
- metal spatula
- mixing bowls
- rubber spatula
- serving plates or shallow bowls
- soupspoon
- teakettle
- tongs
- whisk
- wire rack
- aluminum foil
- toothpick *

* Poking holes in the cakes with toothpicks allows the toffee sauce to be absorbed.

Ingredients

CAKES
- 8 **ounces pitted dates, cut crosswise into ¼-inch slices (1⅓ cups)**
- ¾ **cup warm tap water**
- ½ **teaspoon baking soda**
- 1¼ **cups (6¼ ounces) all-purpose flour**
- ½ **teaspoon baking powder**
- ½ **teaspoon salt**
- ¾ **cup packed (5¼ ounces) brown sugar**
- 2 **large eggs**
- 4 **tablespoons unsalted butter, melted**
- 1½ **teaspoons vanilla extract**

SAUCE
- 4 **tablespoons unsalted butter**
- 1 **cup packed (7 ounces) brown sugar**
- ¼ **teaspoon salt**
- 1 **cup heavy cream**
- 1 **tablespoon rum**
- ½ **teaspoon lemon juice**

What Can Go Wrong

Here's a list of common mistakes cooks make when preparing this recipe.

COMMON MISTAKE	BAD OUTCOMES	WHAT YOU SHOULD DO
Not Using Baking Soda When Soaking Dates	• **The skins of the dates are leathery.**	We soak a portion of the dates in water with ½ teaspoon baking soda added to weaken and soften the dried dates' tough, papery skin. This ensures that the sliced dates that get scattered over the cake batter are more tender. Don't skip this step; if you do, you'll end up with unappealing dates in your puddings.
Not Saving Date Soaking Liquid	• **The cakes have less fruity date flavor.**	For maximum fruity flavor, we incorporate dates three ways. In addition to the ground dates and the dates that are sliced, soaked, and folded into the batter, we also utilize the soaking liquid by mixing it into the batter instead of water. Make sure not to throw it down the drain after the dates have finished soaking!
Overmixing Batter	• **The cakes are tough.**	In our testing, we compared two mixing methods, a standard creaming method (sugar and butter whipped until light and fluffy, eggs beaten in, and, finally, the dry ingredients incorporated) or a basic quick-bread method (dry and wet ingredients mixed separately and then combined). We settled on the easier quick-bread method, which produced the right dense, springy crumb. But it is important to mix the batter gently. Overmixing encourages gluten development, which makes for a tough cake.
Splashing Water into Ramekins	• **The cakes don't cook properly.**	These puddings are baked in a water bath to ensure gentle, even cooking. Adding the water to the pan using a teakettle helps to minimize the risk of splashing water into the ramekins. But you still must be careful when pouring the water into the pan; pour the water slowly as you maneuver the teakettle around the batter-filled ramekins.
Not Covering Roasting Pan Tightly	• **The cakes are not properly cooked.** • **The cakes are not moist and tender.**	It is important to cover the roasting pan with aluminum foil and crimp the edges tightly to ensure a tight seal. The cakes are cooked in a water bath and covering the pan traps the steam, creating a super-moist environment for steam-cooking the pudding cakes. The result is a cake that falls somewhere between a pudding and a conventional cake. If baked without steam, or with less steam because some is escaping, the puddings will end up with an unappealing, dry consistency, rather than a moist, springy crumb.
Not Removing Cakes from Water Bath When Done	• **The cakes are overcooked.**	As soon as the cakes are done you should immediately transfer the ramekins from the water bath to a wire rack. If you leave them in the water bath, they will continue to cook. To transfer the ramekins, you can use tongs to grip them and a spatula to support the ramekin's bottom, or if you have canning tongs, they are also good for this job.
Not Poking Holes in Cakes	• **The cakes do not absorb the sauce.** • **The cakes are not as flavorful.**	To live up to their name, these cakes need to soak up the toffee sauce. If you simply pour sauce over the cakes, they won't absorb enough. It's essential to use a toothpick to poke 25 holes into each cake before spooning the sauce over. Then let the cakes rest for 5 minutes to allow them to absorb the sauce.

1. PREPARE CAKES: Adjust oven rack to middle position and heat oven to 350 degrees. Grease and flour eight 4-ounce ramekins.

2. Set prepared ramekins in large roasting pan lined with clean dish towel. Bring kettle of water to boil.

3. Cut 8 ounces pitted dates crosswise into ¼-inch-thick slices.

4. Combine half of dates, ¾ cup warm tap water, and ½ teaspoon baking soda in 2-cup liquid measuring cup (dates should be submerged).

5. Soak dates for 5 minutes.

6. Whisk 1¼ cups (6¼ ounces) all-purpose flour, ½ teaspoon baking powder, and ½ teaspoon salt together in medium bowl.

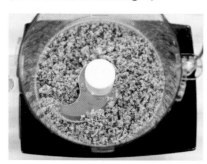

7. Process remaining dates and ¾ cup packed brown sugar in food processor until mixture has texture of coarse sand, about 45 seconds.

8. Drain soaked dates and add soaking liquid to food processor.

9. Add 2 large eggs, 4 tablespoons melted unsalted butter, and 1½ teaspoons vanilla extract and process until smooth, about 15 seconds.

10. Transfer mixture to bowl with dry ingredients and sprinkle drained dates on top.

11. Using rubber spatula, gently fold wet mixture into dry until just combined and date pieces are evenly dispersed.

12. Divide batter among prepared ramekins (should be two-thirds full).

13. Quickly pour enough boiling water into roasting pan to come ¼ inch up sides of ramekins.

14. Cover pan tightly with aluminum foil, crimping edges to seal.

15. Bake cakes until puffed and surfaces are spongy and firm, about 40 minutes.

16. Using tongs and metal spatula, transfer ramekins immediately to wire rack and let cool for 10 minutes.

17. PREPARE SAUCE: Melt 4 tablespoons butter in saucepan over medium-high heat. Whisk in 1 cup brown sugar and ¼ teaspoon salt until smooth.

18. Continue to cook, stirring occasionally, until sugar is dissolved and mixture is slightly darkened, 3 to 4 minutes.

19. Add ⅓ cup heavy cream and stir until smooth. Slowly pour in ⅔ cup more cream and 1 tablespoon rum, whisking constantly until smooth.

20. Reduce heat to low and simmer until frothy, about 3 minutes. Remove from heat and stir in ½ teaspoon lemon juice.

21. Using toothpick, poke 25 holes in top of each cake.

22. Spoon 1 tablespoon sauce over each cake and let cakes sit until sauce is absorbed, about 5 minutes.

23. Invert ramekins onto serving plates or shallow bowls and remove ramekin.

24. Divide remaining toffee sauce among cakes and serve immediately.

HOW TO MAKE CUSTARDS, PUDDINGS, AND FROZEN DESSERTS

Vanilla Ice Cream

Recipe Stats

TOTAL TIME **8½ hours**
PREPARATION TIME **5 minutes**
ACTIVE COOKING TIME **1¼ hours**
YIELD **1 quart**
MAKE AHEAD **Freeze for up to 5 days**
DIFFICULTY **Easy**

Tools

- 8- or 9-inch square metal baking pan
- medium heavy-bottomed saucepan
- ice cream machine *
- cutting board
- paring knife
- liquid measuring cup
- measuring spoons

- fine-mesh strainer
- instant-read thermometer
- mixing bowls
- quart-size airtight container
- rubber spatula
- whisk
- wooden spoon
- plastic wrap

* If using a canister-style ice cream machine, be sure to freeze the empty canister at least 24 hours, and preferably 48 hours, before churning. For self-refrigerating ice cream machines, prechill the canister by running the machine for 5 to 10 minutes before pouring in the custard.

Ingredients

  1 **vanilla bean ***
1¾ **cups heavy cream**
1¼ **cups whole milk**
  ½ **cup (3½ ounces) plus 2 tablespoons sugar**
  ⅓ **cup light corn syrup**
  ¼ **teaspoon salt**
  6 **large egg yolks**

* You can substitute 2 teaspoons vanilla extract for the vanilla bean; stir the vanilla extract into the cold custard in step 9.

Overview

Ice cream requires very little other than preparing a simple custard base made up of milk, heavy cream, eggs, sugar, vanilla, and salt, and then churning and freezing it until firm. At least that is what most home cooks think until they turn out ice cream that is marred by ice crystals or doesn't have the super-rich and creamy texture of artisanal store-bought (or parlor-made) ice cream. It turns out that commercial ice cream makers spend thousands of dollars on churners and fast and powerful freezers that eliminate the problems faced by home cooks, namely ice crystals—the enemy of smooth ice cream.

In our recipe, we replace some of the sugar with corn syrup, which interferes with crystal formation, getting us closer to a super-smooth texture. And since faster freezing also cuts down on crystal formation, we freeze a small portion of the custard and chill the rest in the refrigerator before combining and churning them. Then we take yet one more step to freeze the ice cream faster: Instead of placing the churned ice cream in a tall container, we spread it into a chilled metal pan. Once firm around the edges, it is ready to be transferred to a tall container to be fully frozen. Just these simple, indeed humble, steps—all of which allowed us to freeze the custard quickly—delivers super-premium smoothness in a homemade ice cream. For variations on this recipe, see page 781. Before you begin, see How to Crack and Separate Eggs on page 50, and page 758 for more detail on scraping seeds from a vanilla bean.

What Can Go Wrong

Here's a list of common mistakes cooks make when preparing this recipe.

COMMON MISTAKE	BAD OUTCOMES	WHAT YOU SHOULD DO
Forgetting to Freeze Baking Pan	• **The ice cream takes longer to harden.** • **The ice cream is not as smooth.**	The minute you decide to make this recipe you should place the metal baking pan in the freezer. After you have churned the ice cream you need to transfer it to the frozen metal baking pan and press plastic wrap on the surface. You will then need to return the pan to the freezer until the custard is firm around the edges, about 1 hour. Metal conducts heat faster than glass or plastic, and a larger, flatter surface area (as opposed to a tall container) expedites freezing. Speed of freezing is the most critical factor in ice cream making, and this simple trick makes a big difference in the quality of the ice cream.
Changing Ratio of Heavy Cream to Milk	• **The ice cream is not as creamy.** • **The ice cream is too rich and heavy.**	You might be tempted to adjust the ratio of milk to cream. Don't. After thorough testing, we found 1¾ cups heavy cream to 1¼ cups whole milk delivers the best results: a creamy, high-quality ice cream that is just rich enough.
Substituting Sugar for Corn Syrup	• **The ice cream isn't smooth.** • **The ice cream crystallizes.** • **The ice cream takes longer to freeze.**	We learned in our testing that the key to our ice cream's smoothness was to replace some of the sugar with corn syrup. Just ⅓ cup of corn syrup really does make a difference, so don't be tempted to skip it. Corn syrup is made up of glucose molecules and chains of starch that interrupt the flow of water molecules in a custard base, and this acts to keep these molecules from combining and forming large crystals as the ice cream freezes. Corn syrup also has a higher freezing point than sugar, thereby making the ice cream less susceptible to the temperature shifts that are common in a home refrigerator (freezing and refreezing cause ice crystals to form).
Not Tempering Egg Yolks Properly	• **The custard ice cream base curdles.**	You must slowly whisk 1 cup of the heated cream mixture into the egg yolk mixture before returning this mixture to the saucepan and cooking it until it thickens properly. If you simply dump the egg yolk mixture into the hot cream mixture it will curdle and you will have to start over.

1. Place 8- or 9-inch square metal baking pan in freezer. Halve 1 vanilla bean lengthwise and scrape out seeds; transfer bean and seeds to saucepan.

2. Add 1¾ cups heavy cream, 1¼ cups whole milk, 6 tablespoons sugar, ⅓ cup light corn syrup, and ¼ teaspoon salt.

3. Heat over medium-high heat, stirring occasionally, until mixture is steaming steadily and registers 175 degrees, 5 to 10 minutes. Remove saucepan from heat.

4. While cream heats, whisk 6 large egg yolks and ¼ cup sugar in bowl until smooth. Slowly whisk 1 cup warm cream mixture into yolk mixture.

5. Return mixture to saucepan and cook over medium-low heat, stirring constantly, until mixture thickens and registers 180 degrees, 7 to 14 minutes.

6. Pour custard into large bowl and cool until no longer steaming, 10 to 20 minutes. Transfer 1 cup custard to small bowl; cover with plastic wrap.

7. Place small bowl of custard in freezer. Cover large bowl of custard with plastic wrap and place in refrigerator.

8. After 4 hours (or up to 24 hours), remove custards from refrigerator and freezer. Scrape frozen custard from small bowl into large bowl of custard.

9. Stir occasionally until frozen custard has fully dissolved. Strain custard through fine-mesh strainer.

10. Transfer custard to ice cream machine and churn until mixture resembles thick soft-serve and registers 21 degrees, 15 to 25 minutes.

11. Transfer ice cream to frozen baking pan and press plastic wrap on surface. Return to freezer until firm around edges, about 1 hour.

12. Transfer ice cream to airtight quart-size container, press firmly to remove air pockets, and freeze until firm, at least 2 hours.

Recipe Library

Stovetop Rice Pudding

✔ **WHY THIS RECIPE WORKS:** At its best, rice pudding is lightly sweet and tastes of its primary component, rice. At its worst, the rice flavor is lost to cloying sweetness, overcooked milk, and a pasty, leaden consistency. We wanted a rice pudding with intact, tender grains bound loosely in a subtly sweet, creamy pudding. For simple, straightforward rice flavor, we avoided aromatic rices like basmati and jasmine. Arborio rice, used for risotto, was stiff and gritty. Overall, medium-grain rice produced the best texture (with long-grain rice a close second). We found that cooking the rice in water rather than milk left its flavor intact. After the rice absorbed the water, we added sugar and equal amounts of milk and half-and-half, which delivered the proper degree of richness; the eggs and butter found in other recipes were just too overpowering. When we cooked the rice in water with the lid on the pan, then removed the lid while the rice simmered in the milk mixture, we got the results we wanted: distinct, tender grains of rice in a milky, subtly sweet sauce.

Simple Stovetop Rice Pudding
SERVES 6 TO 8
We prefer pudding made from medium-grain rice, but long-grain rice works, too.

- 2 cups water
- 1 cup medium-grain rice
- ¼ teaspoon salt
- 2½ cups whole milk
- 2½ cups half-and-half
- ⅔ cup (4⅔ ounces) sugar
- 1¼ teaspoons vanilla extract

1. Bring water to boil in large saucepan. Stir in rice and salt, cover, and simmer over low heat, stirring once or twice, until water is almost fully absorbed, 15 to 20 minutes.

2. Stir in milk, half-and-half, and sugar. Increase heat to medium-high and bring to simmer, then reduce heat to maintain simmer. Cook, uncovered and stirring frequently, until mixture starts to thicken, about 30 minutes. Reduce heat to low and continue to cook, stirring every couple of minutes to prevent sticking and scorching, until spoon is just able to stand up in pudding, about 15 minutes longer.

3. Off heat, stir in vanilla. Let cool and serve at room temperature or chilled. (Pudding can be refrigerated, with plastic wrap pressed directly on surface, for up to 2 days.)

Rice Pudding with Cinnamon and Dried Fruit
Add ½ cup dried fruit (raisins, cranberries, cherries, or chopped prunes or apricots) and 1 teaspoon ground cinnamon along with vanilla.

Rice Pudding with Orange and Toasted Almonds
Add ⅓ cup toasted slivered almonds and 2 teaspoons grated orange zest along with vanilla.

Coconut Rice Pudding
SERVES 6 TO 8
We prefer medium-grain rice here for its higher starch content, but long-grain rice works, too, in a pinch. In addition to constant stirring, using a heavy-bottomed saucepan is key to preventing the bottom from burning.

- 2 cups water
- 1 cup medium-grain rice
- ¼ teaspoon salt
- 2½ cups coconut milk
- 2½ cups half-and-half
- ⅔ cup (4⅔ ounces) sugar
- ½ cup raisins
- 1½ teaspoons vanilla extract
- 1 teaspoon ground cinnamon
- 1 cup (3 ounces) sweetened shredded coconut, toasted

1. Bring water to boil in large saucepan. Stir in rice and salt, cover, and simmer over low heat, stirring once or twice, until water is almost fully absorbed, 15 to 20 minutes.

2. Stir in coconut milk, half-and-half, and sugar. Increase heat to medium-high and bring to simmer, then reduce heat to maintain simmer. Cook, uncovered and stirring frequently, until mixture starts to thicken, about 30 minutes. Reduce heat to low and continue to cook, stirring every couple of minutes to prevent sticking and scorching, until spoon is just able to stand up in pudding, about 15 minutes longer.

3. Off heat, stir in raisins, vanilla, and cinnamon. Serve warm, at room temperature, or chilled. Sprinkle with toasted coconut before serving. (To store, press plastic wrap directly on surface of pudding and refrigerate for up to 2 days. Stir in up to 1 cup warm milk, 2 tablespoons at a time, as needed to loosen consistency before serving.)

Creamy Chocolate Pudding

✔ **WHY THIS RECIPE WORKS:** Homemade chocolate pudding often suffers either from lackluster chocolate flavor, caused by a dearth of chocolate, or a grainy texture, caused by too much cocoa butter. We were after chocolate pudding that tasted deeply of chocolate, and was thickened to a perfectly silky, creamy texture. We found that using a moderate amount of bittersweet chocolate in combination with unsweetened cocoa powder and espresso powder helped us achieve maximum chocolate flavor. Cornstarch proved the right thickener for our pudding; using mostly milk and just half a cup of heavy cream, along with three egg yolks, ensured that our pudding had a silky-smooth texture. Salt and vanilla enhanced the chocolate flavor even more.

Creamy Chocolate Pudding

SERVES 6

We prefer this recipe made with 60 percent bittersweet chocolate (our favorite brands are Ghirardelli Bittersweet Chocolate Baking Bar and Callebaut Intense Dark Chocolate). Using a chocolate with a higher cacao percentage will result in a thicker pudding. Low-fat milk (1 percent or 2 percent) may be substituted for the whole milk with a small sacrifice in richness. Do not use skim milk as a substitute.

2	teaspoons vanilla extract
½	teaspoon instant espresso powder
½	cup (3½ ounces) sugar
3	tablespoons Dutch-processed cocoa powder
2	tablespoons cornstarch
¼	teaspoon salt
3	large egg yolks
½	cup heavy cream
2½	cups whole milk
5	tablespoons unsalted butter, cut into 8 pieces
4	ounces bittersweet chocolate, chopped fine

1. Stir together vanilla and espresso powder in bowl; set aside. Whisk sugar, cocoa, cornstarch, and salt together in large saucepan. Whisk in egg yolks and cream until fully incorporated, making sure to scrape corners of saucepan. Whisk in milk until incorporated.

2. Place saucepan over medium heat; cook, whisking constantly, until mixture is thickened and bubbling over entire surface, 5 to 8 minutes. Cook for 30 seconds longer, remove from heat, add butter and chocolate and whisk until melted and fully incorporated. Whisk in vanilla mixture.

3. Strain pudding through fine-mesh strainer into bowl. Place lightly greased parchment paper against surface of pudding and place in refrigerator to cool, at least 4 hours. Serve. (Pudding can be refrigerated for up to 2 days.)

Creamy Mexican Chocolate Pudding

Add ½ teaspoon ground cinnamon, ¼ teaspoon chipotle chile powder, and pinch cayenne pepper to saucepan along with cocoa.

Creamy Mocha Pudding

Increase instant espresso powder to 1 teaspoon. Add 1 tablespoon Kahlúa to vanilla mixture. Substitute ¼ cup brewed coffee for ¼ cup milk.

Butterscotch Pudding

✔ **WHY THIS RECIPE WORKS:** For butterscotch pudding with rich, bittersweet flavor, we made butterscotch sauce by cooking butter, brown and white sugar, corn syrup, lemon juice, and salt together into a dark caramel. We made the process more foolproof by first boiling the caramel to jump-start it and then reducing the heat to a low simmer to provide a large window to take the temperature and stop the cooking at the right moment. To turn our butterscotch into pudding, we ditched the classical (yet time-consuming) tempering method in favor of a revolutionary technique that calls for pouring the boiling caramel sauce directly over the thickening agents (egg yolks and cornstarch thinned with a little milk). The result is the sophisticated bittersweet flavor of traditional butterscotch with less mess and fuss.

Best Butterscotch Pudding

SERVES 8

When taking the temperature of the caramel in step 1, tilt the pan and move the thermometer back and forth to equalize hot and cool spots. Work quickly when pouring the caramel mixture over the egg mixture in step 4 to ensure proper thickening. Serve the pudding with lightly sweetened whipped cream.

12	tablespoons unsalted butter, cut into ½-inch pieces
½	cup (3½ ounces) granulated sugar
½	cup packed (3½ ounces) dark brown sugar
¼	cup water
2	tablespoons light corn syrup
1	teaspoon lemon juice
¾	teaspoon salt
1	cup heavy cream
2¼	cups whole milk
4	large egg yolks
¼	cup cornstarch
2	teaspoons vanilla extract
1	teaspoon dark rum

1. Bring butter, granulated sugar, brown sugar, water, corn syrup, lemon juice, and salt to boil in large saucepan over medium heat, stirring occasionally to dissolve sugar and melt butter. Once mixture is at full rolling boil, cook, stirring occasionally, for 5 minutes (caramel will register about 240 degrees). Immediately reduce heat to medium-low and gently simmer (caramel should maintain steady stream of lazy bubbles—if not, adjust heat accordingly), stirring frequently, until mixture is color of dark peanut butter, 12 to 16 minutes longer (caramel will register about 300 degrees and should have slight burnt smell).

2. Remove pan from heat; carefully pour ¼ cup cream into caramel mixture and swirl to incorporate (mixture will bubble and steam); let bubbling subside. Whisk vigorously and scrape corners of pan until mixture is completely smooth, at least 30 seconds. Return pan to medium heat and gradually whisk in remaining ¾ cup cream until smooth. Whisk in 2 cups milk until mixture is smooth, making sure to scrape corners and edges of pan to remove any remaining bits of caramel.

3. Meanwhile, microwave remaining ¼ cup milk until simmering, 30 to 45 seconds. Whisk egg yolks and cornstarch together in large bowl until smooth. Gradually whisk in hot milk until smooth; set aside (do not refrigerate).

4. Return saucepan to medium-high heat and bring mixture to full rolling boil, whisking frequently. Once mixture is boiling rapidly and beginning to climb toward top of pan, immediately pour into bowl with yolk mixture in one motion (do not add gradually). Whisk thoroughly for 10 to 15 seconds (mixture will thicken after a few seconds). Whisk in vanilla and rum. Place lightly greased parchment paper against surface of pudding. Refrigerate until cold and set, at least 3 hours. Whisk pudding until smooth before serving.

Chocolate Mousse

✔ **WHY THIS RECIPE WORKS:** Rich, creamy, and dense, chocolate mousse can be delicious but too filling after a few mouthfuls. On the other hand, light and airy mousse usually lacks deep chocolate flavor. We wanted chocolate mousse that had both a light, meltingly smooth texture and a substantial chocolate flavor. To start, we addressed the mousse's dense, heavy texture. Most recipes for chocolate mousse contain butter. Could we do without it? We eliminated the butter and found that our mousse tasted less heavy. We further lightened the mousse's texture by reducing the number of egg whites and yolks. To make up for the lost volume of the eggs, we whipped the heavy cream to soft peaks before adding it to the chocolate. Next we tackled the mousse's flavor. We maximized the chocolate flavor with a combination of bittersweet chocolate and cocoa powder. And to further deepen the chocolate flavor, we found that a small amount of instant espresso powder, salt, and brandy did the trick.

Dark Chocolate Mousse

SERVES 6 TO 8

When developing this recipe, we used Callebaut Intense Dark Chocolate and Ghirardelli Bittersweet Chocolate Baking Bar, which each contain about 60 percent cacao. If you want to use a chocolate with a higher percentage of cacao, see our variation, Premium Dark Chocolate Mousse (recipe follows). If you choose to make the mousse a day in advance, let it sit at room temperature for 10 minutes before serving. Serve with Whipped Cream (page 709) and chocolate shavings, if desired. See Recipe Tutorial on page 763 for more details on this recipe.

- **8 ounces bittersweet chocolate, chopped fine**
- **5 tablespoons water**
- **2 tablespoons Dutch-processed cocoa powder**
- **1 tablespoon brandy**
- **1 teaspoon instant espresso powder**
- **2 large eggs, separated**
- **1 tablespoon sugar**
- **⅛ teaspoon salt**
- **1 cup plus 2 tablespoons heavy cream, chilled**

1. Melt chocolate, water, cocoa, brandy, and espresso powder in medium heatproof bowl set over saucepan filled with 1 inch barely simmering water, stirring frequently until smooth. Remove from heat.

2. Whisk egg yolks, 1½ teaspoons sugar, and salt in medium bowl until mixture lightens in color and thickens slightly, about 30 seconds. Pour melted chocolate into egg yolk mixture and whisk until combined. Let cool until just warmer than room temperature, 3 to 5 minutes.

3. Using stand mixer fitted with whisk, whip egg whites at medium-low speed until foamy, about 1 minute. Add remaining 1½ teaspoons sugar, increase speed to medium-high, and whip until soft peaks form, about 1 minute. Using whisk, stir about one-quarter of whipped egg whites into chocolate mixture to lighten it; gently fold in remaining egg whites with rubber spatula until few white streaks remain.

4. In now-empty mixer bowl, whip cream on medium speed until it begins to thicken, about 30 seconds. Increase speed to high and whip until soft peaks form, about 15 seconds more. Using rubber spatula, fold whipped cream into mousse until no white streaks remain. Spoon mousse into 6 to 8 individual serving dishes. Cover with plastic wrap and refrigerate until set and firm, at least 2 hours or up to 24 hours. Serve.

Premium Dark Chocolate Mousse

This recipe is designed to work with a boutique chocolate that contains a higher percentage of cacao than our master recipe.

Replace bittersweet chocolate (containing about 60 percent cacao) with equal amount of bittersweet chocolate containing 62 to 70 percent cacao. Increase water to 7 tablespoons, increase eggs to 3, and increase sugar to 3 tablespoons, adding extra 2 tablespoons to chocolate mixture in step 1.

Chocolate-Orange Mousse

For best flavor, the orange zest needs to steep in the heavy cream overnight, so plan accordingly. Garnish each serving of mousse with a thin strip of orange zest, if desired.

Bring cream to simmer in medium saucepan. Off heat, transfer to 2-cup liquid measuring cup and add three 2-inch strips orange zest. Let cool until just warm, cover, and refrigerate overnight. Remove and discard zest; add more cream, if necessary, to equal 1 cup plus 2 tablespoons. Proceed with step 1, reducing water to 4 tablespoons and omitting brandy. Once chocolate is melted, stir in 2 tablespoons Grand Marnier and proceed as directed.

Chocolate-Raspberry Mousse

Chambord is our preferred brand of raspberry-flavored liqueur for this recipe. Serve the mousse with fresh raspberries, if desired.

Reduce water to 4 tablespoons, omit brandy, and add 2 tablespoons raspberry-flavored liqueur to melted chocolate mixture in step 1.

Chocolate Pots de Crème

✔ **WHY THIS RECIPE WORKS:** Classic *pots de crème* can be finicky and laborious, requiring a hot water bath that threatens to splash the custards every time the pan is moved. We wanted a user-friendly recipe that delivered a decadent dessert with a satiny texture and intense chocolate flavor. First we moved the dish out of the oven, concentrating on an unconventional approach in which the custard is cooked on the stovetop in a saucepan, then poured into ramekins. Our next challenge was developing the right amount of richness and body, which we did by choosing a combination of heavy cream and half-and-half, along with egg yolks only, for maximum richness. For intense chocolate flavor, we focused on bittersweet chocolate—and a lot of it. Our chocolate content was at least 50 percent more than in any other recipe we had encountered.

Chocolate Pots de Crème

SERVES 8

We prefer pots de crème made with 60 percent bittersweet chocolate (our favorite brands are Ghirardelli Bittersweet Chocolate Baking Bar and Callebaut Intense Dark Chocolate), but 70 percent bittersweet chocolate can also be used. If using a 70 percent bittersweet chocolate, reduce the amount of chocolate to 8 ounces.

POTS DE CRÈME

- 10 ounces bittersweet chocolate, chopped fine
- 5 large egg yolks
- 5 tablespoons (2¼ ounces) sugar
- ¼ teaspoon salt
- 1½ cups heavy cream
- ¾ cup half-and-half
- 1 tablespoon water
- ½ teaspoon instant espresso powder
- 1 tablespoon vanilla extract

WHIPPED CREAM AND GARNISH

- ½ cup heavy cream, chilled
- 2 teaspoons sugar
- ½ teaspoon vanilla extract
  Cocoa powder (optional)
  Chocolate shavings (optional)

1. FOR THE POTS DE CRÈME: Place chocolate in medium bowl; set fine-mesh strainer over bowl and set aside.

2. Whisk egg yolks, sugar, and salt together in bowl until combined. Whisk in cream and half-and-half. Transfer mixture to medium saucepan and cook over medium-low heat, stirring constantly and scraping bottom of pot with wooden spoon, until thickened and silky and registers 175 to 180 degrees, 8 to 12 minutes. (Do not let custard overcook or simmer.)

3. Immediately pour custard through fine-mesh strainer over chocolate. Let mixture stand to melt chocolate, about 5 minutes; whisk gently until smooth. Combine water and espresso powder and stir to dissolve, then whisk dissolved espresso and vanilla into chocolate mixture. Divide mixture evenly among eight 5-ounce ramekins. Gently tap ramekins against counter to remove air bubbles.

4. Let pots de crème cool to room temperature, then cover with plastic wrap and refrigerate until chilled, at least 4 hours. Before serving, let pots de crème stand at room temperature for 20 to 30 minutes. (Pots de crème can be refrigerated for up to 3 days.)

5. FOR THE WHIPPED CREAM AND GARNISH: Using stand mixer fitted with whisk, whip cream, sugar, and vanilla on medium-low speed until foamy, about 1 minute. Increase speed to high and whip until stiff peaks form, 1 to 3 minutes. Dollop each pot de crème with about 2 tablespoons whipped cream and garnish with cocoa and/or chocolate shavings, if using. Serve.

Milk Chocolate Pots de Crème

Milk chocolate behaves differently in this recipe than bittersweet chocolate, and more of it must be used to ensure that the custard sets. And because of the increased amount of chocolate, it's necessary to cut back on the amount of sugar so that the custard is not overly sweet.

Substitute 12 ounces milk chocolate, chopped fine, for bittersweet chocolate and reduce sugar in pots de crème to 2 tablespoons.

Crème Anglaise

✔ **WHY THIS RECIPE WORKS:** Crème anglaise is a velvety and versatile custard sauce—it tastes great over fresh or baked fruit and with many different cakes and other desserts. In pursuit of a rich, creamy, perfectly smooth crème anglaise, we learned that properly tempering (raising the temperature of an egg yolk–enriched mixture gradually) the custard was crucial; this prevents the eggs from curdling as they are incorporated into the milk. To do this, we slowly added a cup of the hot milk to the yolk mixture to warm the yolks, then poured the mixture back into the saucepan with the rest of the hot milk. (The initial addition of the hot milk does the tempering, so that the yolks are able to stand the heat of the remaining hot milk.) When adding the hot liquid to the egg yolk mixture, it was essential to whisk constantly so that the milk didn't scramble the egg yolks. Once the yolks were added to the pan, more stirring ensured our crème anglaise had the smoothest texture possible. Straining the sauce before chilling it provided further insurance that it would be silky smooth when drizzled over cake, fruit, or anything else.

Crème Anglaise

MAKES ABOUT 2 CUPS

You can substitute 1½ teaspoons vanilla extract for the vanilla bean; stir the extract into the sauce after straining it in step 4. See Core Technique on page 758 for more details on this recipe.

- ½ vanilla bean
- 1½ cups whole milk
  Pinch salt
- 5 large egg yolks
- ¼ cup (1¾ ounces) sugar

1. Cut vanilla bean in half lengthwise. Using tip of paring knife, scrape out seeds. Combine vanilla bean and seeds, milk, and salt in medium saucepan and bring to simmer over medium-high heat, stirring occasionally.

2. Meanwhile, in separate bowl, whisk egg yolks and sugar together until smooth.

3. Whisk about 1 cup of simmering milk mixture into egg yolks to temper. Slowly whisk egg yolk mixture into simmering milk mixture. Continue to cook sauce, whisking constantly, until it thickens slightly and coats back of spoon and registers about 175 degrees, about 6 minutes.

4. Immediately strain sauce through fine-mesh strainer into medium bowl; remove and discard vanilla bean. Cover and refrigerate until cool, about 30 minutes. Serve chilled. (Crème Anglaise can be refrigerated for up to 2 days.)

Crème Caramel

✔ **WHY THIS RECIPE WORKS:** What many people love about crème caramel is the caramel. While we can't deny its appeal, what most concerned us when we set out to make a really great crème caramel was the custard. We wanted custard that was creamy and tender enough to melt in our mouths, yet firm enough to unmold without collapsing. We also wanted a mellow flavor that was neither too rich nor too eggy. We discovered that the proportion of egg whites to yolks in the custard was critical for the right texture. Too many whites caused the custard to solidify too much, and too few left it almost runny. We settled on three whole eggs and two yolks. Light cream and milk for the dairy provided the proper amount of richness. For contrast with the sweet caramel, we kept the amount of sugar in the custard to a minimum. Baking the ramekins in a water bath was essential for even cooking and ensured a delicate custard; a dish towel on the bottom of the pan stabilized the ramekins and prevented the bottoms of the custards from overcooking. When we unmolded our crème caramel on serving plates, the sweet caramel sauce bathed the rounds of perfectly cooked custard.

Classic Crème Caramel

SERVES 8

You can vary the amount of sugar in the custard to suit your taste. Most tasters preferred the full ⅔ cup, but you can reduce that amount to as little as ½ cup to create a greater contrast between the custard and the caramel. Cook the caramel in a pan with a light-colored interior, since a dark surface makes it difficult to judge the color of the syrup. Caramel can leave a real mess in a pan, but it is easy to clean; simply boil water in the pan for 5 to 10 minutes to loosen the hardened caramel.

CARAMEL
- ⅓ **cup water**
- 2 **tablespoons light corn syrup**
- ¼ **teaspoon lemon juice**
- 1 **cup (7 ounces) sugar**

CUSTARD
- 1½ **cups whole milk**
- 1½ **cups light cream**
- 3 **large eggs plus 2 large yolks**
- ⅔ **cup (4⅔ ounces) sugar**
- 1½ **teaspoons vanilla extract**
  Pinch salt

1. FOR THE CARAMEL: Combine water, corn syrup, and lemon juice in medium saucepan. Pour sugar into center of pan, taking care not to let sugar crystals touch pan sides. Gently stir with spatula to moisten sugar thoroughly. Bring to boil over medium-high heat and cook, without stirring, until sugar is completely dissolved and liquid is clear, 6 to 10 minutes. Reduce heat to medium-low and continue to cook, swirling occasionally, until mixture darkens to honey color, 4 to 5 minutes longer. Working quickly, carefully divide caramel among eight 6-ounce ramekins. Let caramel cool and harden, about 15 minutes. (Caramel-coated ramekins can be refrigerated for up to 2 days; bring to room temperature before adding custard.)

2. FOR THE CUSTARD: Adjust oven rack to middle position and heat oven to 350 degrees. Combine milk and cream in medium saucepan and heat over medium heat, stirring occasionally, until steam appears and mixture registers 160 degrees, 6 to 8 minutes; remove from heat. Meanwhile, gently whisk eggs, yolks, and sugar in large bowl until just combined. Off heat, gently whisk warm milk mixture, vanilla, and salt into eggs until just combined but not foamy. Strain mixture through fine-mesh strainer into 4-cup liquid measuring cup or bowl; set aside.

3. Bring kettle of water to boil. Meanwhile, place dish towel in bottom of large baking dish or roasting pan and set ramekins on towel (they should not touch). Divide custard evenly among ramekins and set dish on oven rack. Taking care not to splash water into ramekins, pour enough boiling water into dish to reach halfway up sides of ramekins; cover dish loosely with aluminum foil. Bake until paring knife inserted halfway between center and edge of custards comes out clean, 35 to 40 minutes. Transfer ramekins to wire rack and let cool to room temperature. (Custards can be refrigerated for up to 2 days.)

4. To unmold, run paring knife around perimeter of each ramekin. Hold serving plate over top of ramekin and invert; set plate on counter and gently shake ramekin to release custard. Repeat with remaining ramekins and serve.

Espresso Crème Caramel

Espresso beans ground in a coffee grinder would be too fine and impart too strong a coffee flavor to the custard. Instead, crush the beans lightly with the bottom of a skillet.

Heat ½ cup lightly crushed espresso beans with milk and cream mixture until steam appears and mixture registers 160 degrees, 6 to 8 minutes. Off heat, cover and let steep until coffee has infused milk and cream, about 15 minutes. Strain mixture through fine-mesh strainer and proceed as directed, discarding crushed espresso beans. Reduce vanilla extract to 1 teaspoon.

Crème Brûlée

✔ **WHY THIS RECIPE WORKS:** Crème brûlée is all about the contrast between the crisp sugar crust and the silky custard underneath. But too often the crust is either stingy or rock-hard, and the custard is heavy and tasteless. We found that the secret to a soft, supple custard was using egg yolks rather than whole eggs. Heavy cream gave the custard a luxurious richness. Sugar, a vanilla bean, and a pinch of salt were the only other additions. Many recipes use scalded cream, but we found that this resulted in overcooked custard, so we left the ingredients cold. However, we needed heat to extract flavor from the vanilla bean and dissolve the sugar. Our compromise was to heat only half of the cream with the sugar and vanilla bean and add the remaining cream cold, which worked perfectly. For the crust, we used crunchy turbinado sugar and a butane or propane torch worked better than the broiler for caramelizing the sugar, and because the blast of heat inevitably warms the custard beneath the crust, we chilled our crèmes brûlées once more before serving.

Classic Crème Brûlée

SERVES 8

Separate the eggs and whisk the yolks after the cream has finished steeping; if left to sit, the surface of the yolks will dry and form a film. A vanilla bean gives the custard the deepest flavor, but 2 teaspoons of vanilla extract, whisked into the yolks in step 4, can be used instead. While we prefer turbinado or Demerara sugar for the caramelized sugar crust, regular granulated sugar will work, too, but use only 1 scant teaspoon on each ramekin or 1 teaspoon on each shallow fluted dish. See Core Technique on page 760 for more details on this recipe.

- 1 vanilla bean
- 4 cups heavy cream
- ⅔ cup (4⅔ ounces) granulated sugar
  Pinch salt
- 10 large egg yolks
- 8–12 teaspoons turbinado or Demerara sugar

1. Adjust oven rack to lower-middle position and heat oven to 300 degrees.

2. Cut vanilla bean in half lengthwise. Using tip of paring knife, scrape out seeds. Combine vanilla bean and seeds, 2 cups cream, granulated sugar, and salt in medium saucepan. Bring mixture to boil over medium heat, stirring occasionally to dissolve sugar. Off heat, cover and let steep for 15 minutes.

3. Meanwhile, place dish towel in bottom of large baking dish or roasting pan; set eight 4- or 5-ounce ramekins (or shallow fluted dishes) on towel (they should not touch). Bring kettle of water to boil.

4. After cream has steeped, stir in remaining 2 cups cream. Whisk egg yolks in large bowl until uniform. Whisk about 1 cup cream mixture into yolks until combined; repeat with 1 cup more cream mixture. Add remaining cream mixture and whisk until evenly colored and thoroughly combined. Strain mixture through fine-mesh strainer into large liquid measuring cup or bowl; discard solids in strainer. Divide mixture evenly among ramekins.

5. Set baking dish on oven rack. Taking care not to splash water into ramekins, pour enough boiling water into dish to reach two-thirds up sides of ramekins. Bake until centers of custards are just barely set and register 170 to 175 degrees, 30 to 35 minutes (25 to 30 minutes for shallow fluted dishes), checking temperature about 5 minutes before recommended minimum time.

6. Transfer ramekins to wire rack and let cool to room temperature, about 2 hours. Set ramekins on baking sheet, cover tightly with plastic wrap, and refrigerate until cold, at least 4 hours.

7. Uncover ramekins; if condensation has collected on custards, blot moisture with paper towel. Sprinkle each with about 1 teaspoon turbinado sugar (1½ teaspoons for shallow fluted dishes); tilt and tap each ramekin to distribute sugar evenly, dumping out excess sugar. Ignite torch and caramelize sugar. Refrigerate ramekins, uncovered, to rechill, 30 to 45 minutes; serve.

Espresso Crème Brûlée

Crush the espresso beans lightly with the bottom of a skillet. Substitute ¼ cup lightly crushed espresso beans for vanilla bean. Whisk 1 teaspoon vanilla extract into yolks in step 4 before adding cream.

Tea-Infused Crème Brûlée

Substitute 10 Irish Breakfast tea bags, tied together, for vanilla bean; after steeping, squeeze bags with tongs or press into fine-mesh strainer to extract all liquid. Whisk 1 teaspoon vanilla extract into yolks in step 4 before adding cream.

Family-Style Crème Brûlée

Substitute 11 by 7-inch baking dish for ramekins and bake for 40 to 50 minutes. Let cool to room temperature, 2½ to 3 hours.

Panna Cotta

WHY THIS RECIPE WORKS: Though its name is lyrical, the literal translation of panna cotta, "cooked cream," does nothing to suggest its ethereal qualities. In fact, panna cotta is not cooked at all. It is a simple, refined dessert where sugar and gelatin are melted in cream and milk, and the mixture is turned into individual ramekins and chilled. While panna cotta is usually found on restaurant menus, we wanted a version for the home cook—one that would guarantee a pudding with the rich flavor of cream and vanilla and a delicate texture. After trying several different recipes, we concluded that we needed a higher proportion of cream to milk to achieve the creamiest flavor and texture. The amount of gelatin proved critical; too much turned the panna cotta rubbery. We used a light hand, adding just enough to make the dessert firm enough to unmold. And because gelatin sets more quickly at cold temperatures, we minimized the amount of heat by softening the gelatin in cold milk, then heating it very briefly until it was melted. To avoid premature hardening, we gradually added cold vanilla-infused cream to the gelatin mixture and stirred everything over an ice bath to incorporate the gelatin.

Classic Panna Cotta

SERVES 8

A vanilla bean gives the panna cotta the deepest flavor, but 2 teaspoons of vanilla extract can be used instead. Serve the panna cotta with lightly sweetened berries or a pureed berry coulis. Though traditionally unmolded, panna cotta may be chilled and served in wineglasses with the sauce on top. If you would like to make the panna cotta a day ahead, reduce the amount of gelatin by ½ teaspoon and chill the filled wineglasses or ramekins for 18 to 24 hours.

1　cup whole milk
2¾　teaspoons unflavored gelatin
3　cups heavy cream
1　vanilla bean
6　tablespoons (2⅔ ounces) sugar
　　Pinch salt

1. Pour milk into medium saucepan; sprinkle surface evenly with gelatin and let stand for 10 minutes. Meanwhile, turn contents of 2 ice cube trays (about 32 cubes) into large bowl; add 4 cups cold water. Place cream in large measuring cup. Cut vanilla bean in half lengthwise. Using tip of paring knife, scrape out seeds. Add vanilla bean and seeds to cream; set aside. Set eight 4-ounce ramekins on rimmed baking sheet.

2. Heat milk and gelatin mixture over high heat, stirring constantly, until gelatin is dissolved and mixture registers 135 degrees, about 1½ minutes. Off heat, add sugar and salt; stir until dissolved, about 1 minute.

3. Stirring constantly, slowly pour cream into milk mixture, then transfer to medium bowl and set over bowl of ice water. Stir frequently until slightly thickened and mixture registers 50 degrees, about 10 minutes. Strain mixture through fine-mesh strainer into large liquid measuring cup, then distribute evenly among ramekins. Cover baking sheet with plastic wrap, making sure plastic does touch surface; refrigerate until just set (mixture should wobble when shaken gently), at least 4 or up to 12 hours.

4. To unmold, run paring knife around perimeter of each ramekin. (If shape of ramekin makes this difficult, quickly dip ramekin into hot water bath to loosen custard.) Hold serving plate over top of ramekin and invert. Shake ramekins gently to unmold panna cotta; lift ramekins from plate and serve.

Lemon Panna Cotta

Cut four 2-inch strips lemon zest into thin strips and add to cream along with vanilla bean. Add ¼ cup lemon juice (2 lemons) to strained cream mixture before dividing among ramekins.

Individual Sticky Toffee Pudding Cakes

✔ **WHY THIS RECIPE WORKS:** Studded with dates and coated in toffee sauce, this moist, rich cake is a British favorite that we hoped to translate for the American kitchen. We wanted a cake packed full of date flavor, with tolerable sweetness and a moist, tender crumb. We cut down the conventional amount of butter but kept the sauce rich and flavorful—eggs and all-purpose flour gave our cake body and stability. We maximized the fruit flavor by first soaking the dates, then processing a portion of them with sugar while leaving the remainder coarsely chopped. Brown sugar stood in for traditional, but hard-to-find treacle. A splash of rum and lemon juice cut through the sticky richness of the sauce. And for the cooking method, we placed the batter-filled ramekins in a roasting pan, adding boiling water, and then covered the pan with foil before baking. Poking the cakes with a toothpick allowed the sauce to be thoroughly absorbed.

Individual Sticky Toffee Pudding Cakes
SERVES 8

We place a dish towel on the bottom of the roasting pan to stabilize the ramekins. It is important to form a tight seal with the aluminum foil to trap the steam inside the roasting pan before baking the cakes. See Recipe Tutorial on page 766 for more details on this recipe.

CAKES

8　ounces pitted dates, cut crosswise into ¼-inch slices (1⅓ cups)
¾　cup warm tap water
½　teaspoon baking soda
1¼　cups (6¼ ounces) all-purpose flour
½　teaspoon baking powder
½　teaspoon salt
¾　cup packed (5¼ ounces) brown sugar
2　large eggs
4　tablespoons unsalted butter, melted
1½　teaspoons vanilla extract

SAUCE

4　tablespoons unsalted butter
1　cup packed (7 ounces) brown sugar
¼　teaspoon salt
1　cup heavy cream
1　tablespoon rum
½　teaspoon lemon juice

1. FOR THE CAKES: Adjust oven rack to middle position and heat oven to 350 degrees. Grease and flour eight 4-ounce ramekins. Set prepared ramekins in large roasting pan lined with clean dish towel. Bring kettle of water to boil.

2. Combine half of dates, water, and baking soda in 2-cup liquid measuring cup (dates should be submerged beneath water) and soak dates for 5 minutes. Whisk flour, baking powder, and salt together in medium bowl.

3. Process remaining dates and sugar in food processor until no large date chunks remain and mixture has texture of damp, coarse sand, about 45 seconds, scraping down bowl as needed. Drain soaked dates and add soaking liquid to processor. Add eggs, melted butter, and vanilla and process until smooth, about 15 seconds. Transfer mixture to bowl with dry ingredients and sprinkle drained soaked dates on top.

4. With rubber spatula or wooden spoon, gently fold wet mixture into dry mixture until just combined and date pieces are evenly dispersed. Divide batter evenly among prepared ramekins (should be two-thirds full). Quickly pour enough boiling water into roasting pan to come ¼ inch up sides of ramekins. Cover pan tightly with aluminum foil, crimping edges to seal. Bake cakes until puffed and surfaces are spongy, firm, and moist to touch, about 40 minutes. Immediately transfer ramekins from water bath to wire rack and let cool for 10 minutes.

5. FOR THE SAUCE: While cakes cool, melt butter in medium saucepan over medium-high heat. Whisk in sugar and salt until smooth. Continue to cook, stirring occasionally, until sugar is dissolved and slightly darkened, 3 to 4 minutes. Add ⅓ cup cream and stir until smooth, about 30 seconds. Slowly pour in remaining ⅔ cup cream and rum, whisking constantly until smooth.

Reduce heat to low and simmer until frothy, about 3 minutes. Remove from heat and stir in lemon juice.

6. Using toothpick, poke 25 holes in top of each cake and spoon 1 tablespoon toffee sauce over each cake. Let cakes sit until sauce is absorbed, about 5 minutes. Invert each ramekin onto plate or shallow bowl and remove ramekin. Divide remaining toffee sauce evenly among cakes and serve immediately.

TO MAKE AHEAD: Prepare batter and divide among individual ramekins as directed, then cover and refrigerate, unbaked, for up to 1 day. Bake as directed in step 4. Sauce can refrigerated for up to 2 days; microwave on 50 percent power, stirring often, until hot, about 3 minutes.

Bread Pudding

✅ **WHY THIS RECIPE WORKS:** Bread pudding started out as a frugal way to transform stale, old loaves of bread into an appetizing dish. But contemporary versions of this humble dish vary from mushy, sweetened porridge to chewy, desiccated cousins of holiday stuffing. We wanted a refined bread pudding, with a moist, creamy (but not eggy) interior and a crisp top crust. The first step was choosing the best bread for the job. We chose challah for its rich flavor. We cut the bread into cubes, toasted them until lightly browned, and soaked the cubes with a batch of basic custard. Once the cubes were saturated, we transferred them to a baking dish and slid our pudding into a low-temperature oven to prevent curdling. The custard turned out creamy and smooth, but not as set as we'd have liked. Adding another egg or two helped firm it up, but tasters complained that the pudding tasted somewhat eggy. It turns out that eggy flavor comes from the sulfur compounds in egg whites. So we got rid of the whites and just used the yolks. We now had a luscious, silky custard. Brushing the surface with melted butter and sprinkling the dish with a mix of white and brown sugar prior to baking gave the pudding a crunchy, buttery, sugary crust.

Classic Bread Pudding

SERVES 8 TO 10

Challah is an egg-enriched bread that can be found in most bakeries and supermarkets. If you cannot find challah, a firm high-quality sandwich bread such as Arnold Country Classics White or Pepperidge Farm Farmhouse Hearty White may be substituted. If desired, serve this pudding with Whipped Cream (page 709). To retain a crisp top crust when reheating leftovers, cut the bread pudding into squares and heat, uncovered, in a 450-degree oven until warmed through, 6 to 8 minutes.

- ¾ **cup (5¼ ounces) plus 1 tablespoon granulated sugar**
- 2 **tablespoons light brown sugar**
- 14 **ounces challah, cut into ¾-inch cubes**
- 9 **large egg yolks**
- 4 **teaspoons vanilla extract**
- ¾ **teaspoon salt**
- 2½ **cups heavy cream**
- 2½ **cups milk**
- 2 **tablespoons unsalted butter, melted**

1. Adjust oven racks to middle and lower-middle positions and heat oven to 325 degrees. Combine 1 tablespoon granulated sugar and brown sugar in small bowl; set aside.

2. Spread challah cubes in single layer on 2 rimmed baking sheets. Bake, tossing occasionally, until just dry, about 15 minutes, switching and rotating baking sheets halfway through baking. Let challah cubes cool for about 15 minutes; set aside 2 cups.

3. Whisk egg yolks, remaining ¾ cup granulated sugar, vanilla, and salt together in large bowl. Whisk in cream and milk until combined. Add remaining cooled challah cubes and toss to coat. Transfer mixture to 13 by 9-inch baking dish and let stand, occasionally pressing challah cubes into custard, until cubes are thoroughly saturated, about 30 minutes.

4. Spread reserved challah cubes evenly over top of soaked bread mixture; gently press into custard. Brush melted butter over top of unsoaked challah cubes. Sprinkle brown sugar mixture evenly over top. Place bread pudding on baking sheet and bake on middle rack until custard has just set, pressing center of pudding with finger reveals no runny liquid, and center of pudding registers 170 degrees, 45 to 50 minutes. Transfer to wire rack and let cool until pudding is set and just warm, about 45 minutes. Serve.

Pecan Bread Pudding with Bourbon and Orange

Add ⅔ cup chopped toasted pecans, 1 tablespoon all-purpose flour, and 1 tablespoon softened butter to brown sugar mixture in step 1 and mix until crumbly. Add 1 tablespoon bourbon and 2 teaspoons finely grated orange zest to egg yolk mixture in step 3.

Rum Raisin Bread Pudding with Cinnamon

Combine ⅔ cup golden raisins and 5 teaspoons dark rum in small bowl. Microwave until hot, about 20 seconds; set aside to cool, about 15 minutes. Add ⅛ teaspoon ground cinnamon to brown sugar mixture in step 1 and stir cooled raisin mixture into custard in step 3.

Vanilla Ice Cream

✅ **WHY THIS RECIPE WORKS:** Homemade vanilla ice cream is never as creamy, smooth, or dense as the "super-premium" ice creams. We wanted an incredibly creamy, dense, custard-based vanilla ice cream that would rival any pricey artisanal batch. A vanilla bean delivered the best vanilla flavor. And a combination of heavy cream and whole milk, along with egg yolks, yielded ice cream with the right richness. Creating smooth ice cream means reducing the size of the ice crystals; the smaller they are, the less perceptible they are. Our first move was to replace some of the sugar in our custard base with corn syrup, which interferes with crystal formation, making for a super-smooth texture. To speed up the freezing process, thereby ensuring small ice crystals, we froze a portion of the custard prior to churning, then mixed it with the remaining refrigerated custard. Spreading the churned ice cream into a thin layer in a cold metal baking pan and chilling it allowed the ice cream to firm up more quickly, helping to deliver the smooth texture we were after.

Ultimate Vanilla Ice Cream

MAKES ABOUT 1 QUART

Two teaspoons of vanilla extract can be substituted for the vanilla bean; stir the extract into the cold custard in step 3. An instant-read thermometer is critical for the best results. Using a prechilled metal baking pan and working quickly in step 4 will help prevent melting and refreezing of the ice cream and will speed the hardening process. If using a canister-style ice cream machine, be sure to freeze the empty canister at least 24 hours and preferably 48 hours before churning. For self-refrigerating ice-cream machines, prechill the canister by running the machine for 5 to 10 minutes before pouring in the custard. See Recipe Tutorial on page 770 for more details on this recipe.

- 1 vanilla bean
- 1¾ cups heavy cream
- 1¼ cups whole milk
- ½ cup (3½ ounces) plus 2 tablespoons sugar
- ⅓ cup light corn syrup
- ¼ teaspoon salt
- 6 large egg yolks

1. Place 8- or 9-inch square metal baking pan in freezer. Cut vanilla bean in half lengthwise. Using tip of paring knife, scrape out vanilla seeds. Combine vanilla bean and seeds, cream, milk, 6 tablespoons sugar, corn syrup, and salt in medium saucepan. Heat over medium-high heat, stirring occasionally, until mixture is steaming steadily and registers 175 degrees, 5 to 10 minutes. Remove saucepan from heat.

2. While cream mixture heats, whisk egg yolks and remaining ¼ cup sugar in bowl until smooth, about 30 seconds. Slowly whisk 1 cup heated cream mixture into egg yolk mixture. Return mixture to saucepan and cook over medium-low heat, stirring constantly, until mixture thickens and registers 180 degrees, 7 to 14 minutes. Immediately pour custard into large bowl and let cool until no longer steaming, 10 to 20 minutes. Transfer 1 cup custard to small bowl. Cover both bowls with plastic wrap. Place large bowl in refrigerator and small bowl in freezer and let cool completely, at least 4 hours or up to 24 hours. (Small bowl of custard will freeze solid.)

3. Remove custards from refrigerator and freezer. Scrape frozen custard from small bowl into large bowl of custard. Stir occasionally until frozen custard has fully dissolved. Strain custard through fine-mesh strainer and transfer to ice-cream machine. Churn until mixture resembles thick soft-serve ice cream and registers about 21 degrees, 15 to 25 minutes. Transfer ice cream to frozen baking pan and press plastic wrap on surface. Return to freezer until firm around edges, about 1 hour.

4. Transfer ice cream to airtight container, press firmly to remove any air pockets, and freeze until firm, at least 2 hours. Serve. (Ice cream can be frozen for up to 5 days.)

Triple Ginger Ice Cream

Freeze the crystallized ginger for at least 15 minutes before adding it to the churning ice cream.

Omit vanilla bean. Add one 3-inch piece fresh ginger, peeled and sliced into thin rounds, and 2 teaspoons ground ginger to cream and milk mixture in step 1 and heat as directed. Add ½ cup chopped crystallized ginger to ice cream during last minute of churning.

Coffee Crunch Ice Cream

Look for chocolate-covered cocoa nibs (roasted pieces of the cocoa bean) in chocolate shops or well-stocked supermarkets. Freeze the cocoa nibs for at least 15 minutes before adding them to the churning ice cream.

Omit vanilla bean. Add ½ cup coarsely ground coffee to cream and milk mixture in step 1 and heat as directed. Add ¾ cup chocolate-covered cocoa nibs to ice cream during last minute of churning.

Raspberry Sorbet

✔ **WHY THIS RECIPE WORKS:** For our raspberry sorbet, we super-chilled the base and used just the right ratio of sweeteners to water to ensure the finest-textured ice crystals possible. We also bumped up the berries' natural amount of pectin to give the sorbet stability both in the freezer and out.

Raspberry Sorbet

MAKES 1 QUART

Super-chilling part of the sorbet base before transferring it to the ice cream machine will keep ice crystals to a minimum. If using a canister-style ice cream machine, be sure to freeze the empty canister for at least 24 hours and preferably 48 hours before churning. For self-refrigerating machines, prechill the canister by running the machine for 5 to 10 minutes before pouring in the sorbet mixture. Allow the sorbet to sit at room temperature for 5 minutes to soften before serving. Fresh or frozen berries may be used. If using frozen berries, thaw them before proceeding. For fruit pectin, we recommend Sure-Jell engineered for low- or no-sugar recipes (packaged in a pink box) and not regular Sure-Jell (in a yellow box).

- 1 cup water
- 1 teaspoon low- or no-sugar-needed fruit pectin
- ⅛ teaspoon salt
- 1¼ pounds (4 cups) raspberries
- ½ cup (3½ ounces) plus 2 tablespoons sugar
- ¼ cup light corn syrup

1. Combine water, pectin, and salt in medium saucepan. Heat over medium-high heat, stirring occasionally, until pectin is fully dissolved, about 5 minutes. Remove saucepan from heat and allow mixture to cool slightly, about 10 minutes.

2. Process raspberries, sugar, corn syrup, and water mixture in blender or food processor until smooth, about 30 seconds. Strain mixture through fine-mesh strainer, pressing on solids to extract as much liquid as possible. Transfer 1 cup mixture to small bowl and place remaining mixture in large bowl. Cover both bowls with plastic wrap. Place large bowl in refrigerator and small bowl in freezer and cool completely, at least 4 hours or up to 24 hours. (Small bowl of base will freeze solid.)

3. Remove mixtures from refrigerator and freezer. Scrape frozen base from small bowl into large bowl of base. Stir occasionally until frozen base has fully dissolved. Transfer mixture to ice cream machine and churn until mixture has consistency of thick milkshake and color lightens, 15 to 25 minutes.

4. Transfer sorbet to airtight container, pressing firmly to remove any air pockets, and freeze until firm, at least 2 hours. Serve. (Sorbet can be frozen for up to 5 days.)

Raspberry-Port Sorbet

Substitute ruby port for water in step 1.

Raspberry–Lime Rickey Sorbet

Reduce water to ¾ cup. Add 2 teaspoons grated lime zest and ¼ cup lime juice to blender with raspberries.

Hot Fudge Sauce

WHY THIS RECIPE WORKS: Commercial hot fudge sauces, while readily available, are often overly sweet and lack chocolate flavor. High-end chocolate makers have their own sauces, which can be quite good, but their cost can often be prohibitive. Homemade hot fudge sauces pose their own problems, as they often turn out grainy and overcooked. We wanted to develop a recipe for hot fudge that was lush and complex, intensely chocolaty, smooth and satiny, and mildly sweet. To produce the intense chocolate flavor we were after, we used not one but two types of chocolate: Dutch-processed cocoa powder (for its deep flavor and rich color) and semisweet chocolate. To make sure the sugar was completely dissolved, thereby avoiding any graininess, we melted the chocolate separately and added it to the other ingredients only after the sugar had dissolved. Separating out the chocolate also minimized the time that it was exposed to heat, which served to keep it from tasting "overcooked." Our hot fudge sauce was now smooth and silky, with deep chocolate flavor.

Hot Fudge Sauce

MAKES ABOUT 2 CUPS

Sifting the cocoa powder prevents lumps from forming in the sauce.

- 10 ounces semisweet chocolate, chopped
- ⅓ cup (1 ounce) Dutch-processed cocoa powder, sifted
- ¾ cup light corn syrup
- ⅓ cup (2⅓ ounces) sugar
- ⅓ cup heavy cream
- ⅓ cup water
  Pinch salt
- 3 tablespoons unsalted butter, cut into ¼-inch pieces
- 1 teaspoon vanilla extract

1. Microwave chocolate in bowl at 50 percent power, stirring occasionally, until melted, 2 to 4 minutes. Whisk in cocoa until dissolved; set aside.

2. Heat corn syrup, sugar, cream, water, and salt in medium saucepan over low heat without stirring until sugar dissolves. Increase heat to medium-high; simmer mixture, stirring frequently, about 4 minutes.

3. Off heat, whisk in butter and vanilla. Let cool slightly, about 2 minutes; whisk in melted chocolate mixture. Serve warm. (Sauce can be refrigerated for up to 2 weeks.)

Caramel Sauce

WHY THIS RECIPE WORKS: Caramel is at home in many settings, whether drizzled over a slice of pound cake, pooled at the base of a flan, or wrapped around a crisp apple. Part of what fascinates about caramel is its alchemy—the transformation of white, odorless sugar into aromatic gold. But this is why many cooks tend to shy away from making caramel; while the transformation that takes place is simple, homemade caramel sauce has a tendency to burn and recrystallize. To reduce the guesswork and anxiety that seem inseparably linked to making caramel sauce at home, we developed a recipe in which the sugar is added after the water, making stirring unnecessary. Increasing the proportion of water in our caramel sauce prevented the sugar from traveling up the sides of the pot, and keeping the pot covered allowed condensation to dissolve any stray crystals.

Caramel Sauce

MAKES ABOUT 1½ CUPS

Be careful when stirring in the cream because the hot mixture may splatter. Use a heavy-bottomed saucepan with a capacity of at least 3 quarts. An instant-read thermometer is especially helpful in this recipe. See Core Technique on page 762 for more details on this recipe.

- ½ cup water
- 1 cup (7 ounces) sugar
- 1 cup heavy cream
- ½ teaspoon vanilla extract
- ⅛ teaspoon salt
- 2 tablespoons unsalted butter (optional)

1. Pour water into 3-quart saucepan. Pour sugar into center of saucepan, taking care not to let sugar granules touch sides of pan. Gently stir with clean spatula to moisten sugar thoroughly.

2. Cover pan and bring to boil over medium-high heat. Cook until sugar is completely dissolved and liquid is clear, 3 to 5 minutes. Do not stir. Uncover and continue to cook, without stirring, until liquid has faint golden color, 3 to 5 minutes longer. Reduce heat to medium-low. Continue to cook (swirling contents occasionally) until caramel is medium amber color and registers 350 to 360 degrees, 1 to 2 minutes.

3. Remove pan from heat and slowly whisk in cream until combined. (Mixture will bubble and steam, so keep hands and face away from pan.) Stir in vanilla and salt. For richer sauce, add butter and stir until smooth. Serve warm. (Sauce can be refrigerated for up to 2 weeks. Reheat in small saucepan over low heat or in microwave, stirring often, until warm and smooth.)

Coconut-Ginger Caramel Sauce

Stir one 3-inch piece ginger, peeled and sliced into thin rounds, and ¼ teaspoon coconut extract into finished sauce. Let sit 10 minutes to infuse flavors; strain through fine-mesh strainer.

Orange-Espresso Caramel Sauce

Whisk 3 tablespoons Kahlúa, 1 tablespoon instant espresso powder, and 2 teaspoons finely grated orange zest into finished sauce.

Appendix

Doneness Temperatures for Meat, Poultry, and Fish

Since the temperature of meat will continue to rise as it rests, an effect called carryover cooking, meat should be removed from the oven, grill, or pan when it's 5 to 10 degrees below the desired serving temperature. Carryover cooking doesn't apply to poultry and fish (they don't retain heat as well as the dense muscle structure in meat), so they should be cooked to the desired serving temperatures. The following temperatures should be used to determine when to stop the cooking process.

FOR THIS INGREDIENT...	COOK TO THIS TEMPERATURE
Beef/Lamb	
Rare	115 to 120 degrees (120 to 125 degrees after resting)
Medium-Rare	120 to 125 degrees (125 to 130 degrees after resting)
Medium	130 to 135 degrees (135 to 140 degrees after resting)
Medium-Well	140 to 145 degrees (145 to 150 degrees after resting)
Well-Done	150 to 155 degrees (155 to 160 degrees after resting)
Pork	
Medium	140 to 145 degrees (145 to 150 degrees after resting)
Well-Done	150 to 155 degrees (155 to 160 degrees after resting)
Chicken	
White Meat	160 degrees
Dark Meat	175 degrees
Fish	
Rare	110 degrees (for tuna only)
Medium-Rare	125 degrees (for tuna or salmon)
Medium	135 to 140 degrees (for white-fleshed fish)

Doneness Temperatures for Various Foods

We rely on the measurement of temperature to tell when many other foods are done cooking, not just meat, poultry, and seafood. Here's a partial list, including temperatures for frying oil and water for bread baking.

FOOD	DONENESS TEMPERATURE
Oil, for frying	325 to 375 degrees
Sugar, for caramel	350 degrees
Yeast bread, rustic and lean	200 to 210 degrees
Yeast bread, sweet and rich	190 to 200 degrees
Custard, for ice cream	180 degrees
Custard, for crème anglaise or lemon curd	170 to 175 degrees
Custard, baked (such as crème brûlée or crème caramel)	170 to 175 degrees
Cheesecake	150 degrees
Water, for bread baking	105 to 115 degrees (sometimes)

Conversions and Equivalencies

The recipes in this book were developed using standard U.S. measures following U.S. government guidelines. The charts below offer equivalents for U.S., metric, and imperial (U.K.) measures. All conversions are approximate and have been rounded to the nearest whole number.

VOLUME CONVERSIONS

U.S.	METRIC
1 teaspoon	5 milliliters
2 teaspoons	10 milliliters
1 tablespoon	15 milliliters
2 tablespoons	30 milliliters
¼ cup	59 milliliters
⅓ cup	79 milliliters
½ cup	118 milliliters
¾ cup	177 milliliters
1 cup	237 milliliters
1¼ cups	296 milliliters
1½ cups	355 milliliters
2 cups (1 pint)	473 milliliters
2½ cups	591 milliliters
3 cups	710 milliliters
4 cups (1 quart)	0.946 liter
1.06 quarts	1 liter
4 quarts (1 gallon)	3.8 liters

CONVERSIONS FOR INGREDIENTS USED IN BAKING

INGREDIENT	OUNCES	GRAMS
1 cup all-purpose flour*	5	142
1 cup cake flour	4	113
1 cup whole-wheat flour	5½	156
1 cup granulated (white) sugar	7	198
1 cup packed brown sugar (light or dark)	7	198
1 cup confectioners' sugar	4	113
1 cup cocoa powder	3	85
4 tablespoons butter† (½ stick, or ¼ cup)	2	57
8 tablespoons butter† (1 stick, or ½ cup)	4	113
16 tablespoons butter† (2 sticks, or 1 cup)	8	227

* U.S. all-purpose flour does not contain leaveners. If you are using leavened (self-rising) flour, take this into consideration before adding leavening to a recipe.

† We generally recommend using unsalted butter; if you use salted, take this into consideration before adding salt to a recipe.

WEIGHT CONVERSIONS

OUNCES	GRAMS
½	14
¾	21
1	28
1½	43
2	57
2½	71
3	85
3½	99
4	113
4½	128
5	142
6	170
7	198
8	227
9	255
10	283
12	340
16 (1 pound)	454

CONVERTING OVEN AND INSTANT-READ THERMOMETER TEMPERATURES

FAHRENHEIT	CELSIUS	GAS MARK (IMPERIAL)
225	105	¼
250	120	½
275	135	1
300	150	2
325	165	3
350	180	4
375	190	5
400	200	6
425	220	7
450	230	8
475	245	9

For temperatures not represented in the chart: Subtract 32 degrees from the Fahrenheit reading, then divide the result by 1.8 to find the Celsius reading.

EXAMPLE:

"Roast chicken until thighs register 175 degrees." To convert:

175°F – 32 = 143°

143° ÷ 1.8 = 79.44°C, rounded down to 79°C

Troubleshooting Baking Recipes at High Altitudes

When you're baking at high altitude, recipes often function differently: Cakes can balloon up only to collapse, cookies turn out thin and crisp instead of chewy, and breads overproof and taste dry or gummy. Generally, it is accepted that these changes begin to emerge at around 3,500 feet and amplify as the elevation increases. Also, the typical mountain climate tends to be dry, thus further affecting the moisture content of baked goods. After much testing, we have come up with the following general guidelines for dealing with the problems associated with baking at high altitude.

WHEN YOU ARE BAKING...	POSSIBLE PROBLEMS	POSSIBLE SOLUTIONS
Quick Breads, Muffins, Biscuits, and Scones	Biscuit or scone dough is dry and hard to knead	Add an extra tablespoon or two of liquid
	Quick breads or muffins collapse and the texture is dense	Use less baking powder and/or baking soda
	Quick breads or muffins are sweet and dry	Reduce the sugar by a tablespoon or two and/or add an extra tablespoon or two of liquid
Yeast Breads and Pastries	Dough is dry	Hold back a small portion of the flour and add only as needed
	Top of loaf blows out and the crumb is dense or gummy	Use less yeast or shorten the rising time
Pie Doughs, Tart Doughs, and Non-Yeasted Pastries	Dough is dry and hard to roll out	Add an extra tablespoon or two of ice water
Cakes	Chemically leavened cakes sink in the center	• Use less baking powder and/or baking soda • Increase the oven temperature and decrease the baking time
	Egg-leavened cakes sink in the center	• Underwhip the egg whites and/or whole eggs • Increase the oven temperature and decrease the baking time
	Cakes are dry and cottony	Use less sugar and/or add an extra egg
	Cakes are greasy	Add an extra tablespoon or two of flour
Cookies	Cookies spread too much in the oven	• Use less sugar • Increase the oven temperature and decrease the baking time
	Cookies are dry	Add an extra egg or egg yolk

Index

Note: Page references in *italics* indicate photographs.

M

U

V

Y

Z